Collins

CONTEMPORARY FRENCH DICTIONARY

Companion Volumes

Collins Contemporary German Dictionary
Collins Contemporary Spanish Dictionary
Collins Contemporary Italian Dictionary

Collins
Contemporary
French Dictionary

French - English
Anglais - Français

Gustave Rudler,
Agr. des Let., Doct. ès Let., M.A.,
formerly Professor of French Literature,
University of Oxford

and

Norman C. Anderson,
L-ès-L., M.A.,
formerly Senior Lecturer in French,
University of Glasgow

Revised by
Anthony C. Brench, M.A.,
Christopher D. Bettinson, B.A.,
W. Mary Billington, M.A.
Françoise Salgues, L.-ès-L.,
Lecturers in French, University of Glasgow

Collins : London and Glasgow

General Editor; J. B. Foreman, M.A.
Executive Editor; Iseabail C. Macleod, M.A.
First publishea in this edition 1969
Latest reprint 1979

© *1969 William Collins Sons & Co. Ltd.*

ISBN 0 00 433421 3

PRINTED IN GREAT BRITAIN
COLLINS CLEAR-TYPE PRESS

Contents

Table des Matières

Introduction

In order to economize space we have not given the feminine form of those French adjectives which regularly form their feminine by adding *e* to the masculine form, e.g., *crue, grivoise, guindée,* will be found under the masculine form only, *cru, grivois, guindé.* The feminine form has been indicated in the case of all other adjectives, e.g., *audacieux, -euse, bon, bonne, décisif, -ive; moyen, -enne, premier, -ière, rêveur, -euse.* We have also on occasion omitted the adverb (often formed by adding *-ment* to the feminine singular of the adjective) and the verbal nouns in *-ment* and *-age,* where the presence of the adjective and the verb should enable the reader to recognize a family of words from one main entry.

Some American words have been included on both sides of the dictionary especially where the variation from British English is likely to cause confusion.

Similarly a few French words for West Africa have been added.

Abbreviations used in the Dictionary

ABRÉVIATIONS		ABBREVIATIONS
adjectif	a	adjective
adverbe	ad	adverb
adjectif et nom	an	adjective and noun
architecture	archit	architecture
automobile	aut	automobile
aviation	av	aviation
botanique	bot	botany
chimie	chem	chemistry
conjonction	cj	conjunction
colonial	col	colonial
commerce	com	commerce
comparatif	comp	comparative
cuisine	cook	cooking
datif	dat	dative
article défini	def art	definite article
disjonctif	disj	disjunctive
ecclésiastique	eccl	ecclesiastical
électricité	el	electricity
exclamation	excl	exclamation
féminin	f	feminine
familier	fam	familiar
figuré	fig	figuratively
finances	fin	finance
gouvernement	govt	government
article indéfini	indef art	indefinite article
interrogatif	inter	interrogative
invariable	inv	invariable
juridique	jur	juridica
masculin	m	masculine
médecine	med	medicine

militaire	mil	military
mines	min	mining
musique	mus	music
nom	n	noun
nautique, marine	naut	nautical
nom féminin	nf	noun feminine
nom masculin	nm	noun masculine
numéral	num	numeral
	o.s.	oneself
péjoratif	pej	pejorative
personne	pers	person
pluriel	pl	plural
pronom	pn	pronoun
politique	pol	politics
participe passé	pp	past participle
préposition	prep	preposition
passé	pt	past tense
quelque chose	qch	
quelqu'un	qn	
marque déposée	®	registered trademark
relatif	rel	relative
chemins de fer	rl	railway
singulier	s	singular
écossais	Scot	Scottish
argot, populaire	sl	slang
	s.o.	someone
	sth	something
superlatif	sup	superlative
technique	tec	technical
télévision	TV	television
États-Unis	US	United States
généralement	usu	usually
verbe	v	verb
verbe intransitif	vi	verb intransitive
verbe impersonnel	v imp	verb impersonal
verbe intransitif, réfléchi	vir	verb intransitive, reflexive
verbe réfléchi	vr	verb reflexive
verbe transitif	vt	verb transitive
verbe transitif, intransitif	vti	verb transitive, intransitive
verbe transitif, intransitif, réfléchi	vtir	verb transitive, intransitive, reflexive
verbe transitif, réfléchi	vtr	verb transitive, reflexive
vulgaire	vul	vulgar

English and French Numerals

CARDINAL NUMBERS—NOMBRES CARDINAUX

1	one—un, une	11	eleven—onze
2	two—deux	12	twelve—douze
3	three—trois	13	thirteen—treize
4	four—quatre	14	fourteen—quatorze
5	five—cinq	15	fifteen—quinze
6	six—six	16	sixteen—seize
7	seven—sept	17	seventeen—dix-sept
8	eight—huit	18	eighteen—dix-huit
9	nine—neuf	19	nineteen—dix-neuf
10	ten—dix	20	twenty—vingt

21 twenty-one—vingt et un	90 ninety—quatre-vingt-dix
22 twenty-two—vingt-deux	91 ninety-one—quatre-
30 thirty—trente	vingt-onze
40 forty—quarante	100 a hundred—cent
50 fifty—cinquante	101 one hundred and one—
60 sixty—soixante	cent un
70 seventy—soixante-dix	300 three hundred—trois
71 seventy-one—soixante-	cents
et-onze	301 three hundred and one—
72 seventy-two—soixante-	trois cent un
douze	1000 a thousand—mille
80 eighty—quatre-vingts	5000 five thousand—cinq mille
81 eighty-one—quatre-	1,000,000 a million—un million
vingt-un	

ORDINAL NUMBERS—NOMBRES ORDINAUX

First—premier, -ère	Fiftieth—cinquantième
Second—deuxième;	Sixtieth—soixantième
second, -e	Seventieth—soixante-dixième
Third—troisième	Seventy-first—soixante-et-
Fourth—quatrième	onzième
Fifth—cinquième	Seventy-second—soixante-
Sixth—sixième	douzième
Seventh—septième	Eightieth—quatre-vingtième
Eighth—huitième	Eighty-first—quatre-vingt-
Ninth—neuvième	unième
Tenth—dixième	Ninetieth—quatre-vingt-
Eleventh—onzième	dixième
Twelfth—douzième	Ninety-first—quatre-vingt-
Thirteenth—treizième	onzième
Fourteenth—quatorzième	Hundredth—centième
Fifteenth—quinzième	Hundred-and-first—cent-
Sixteenth—seizième	unième
Seventeenth—dix-septième	Two hundredth—deux-
Eighteenth—dix-huitième	centième
Nineteenth—dix-neuvième	Two hundred-and-first—
Twentieth—vingtième	deux-cent-unième
Twenty-first—vingt-et-	Thousandth—millième
unième	Thousand-and-first—
Twenty-second—vingt-	mille-et-unième
deuxième	Thousand-and-second—
Thirtieth—trentième	mille-deuxième
Fortieth—quarantième	Millionth—millionième

Pronunciation

A simple and accurate transcription of pronunciation is given by the phonetic system of the International Phonetic Association. Although it is not as widely used in Great Britain as it is in other countries, we thought that its use in this dictionary would help readers to feel at ease with the spoken language. The phonetic transcription of English words is that of Received Pronunciation. It does not mention regional variations. The same convention has been applied to the transcription of French words, Standard French being roughly the pronunciation of educated people from the north of France. The readers will find below a comparative presentation of phonetic symbols (IPA) both French and English.

Length of vowels is noted thus: short—no symbol
    long—(:) after the vowel
In English, stress is shown by the symbol (') before the stressed syllable and also secondary stress by the symbol (ˌ).

Pour la transcription phonétique nous avons employé le système de l'Association internationale de phonétique, système qui, nous semble-t-il, permettra aux lecteurs de ce dictionnaire de se sentir à l'aise avec la langue parlée. La transcription des mots anglais est celle de la prononciation reçue, et ne tient pas compte des variations régionales. Pour le français, la même convention a été suivie. La prononciation donnée ne tient également pas compte des différences locales.

Les lecteurs trouveront en bas une présentation comparative de symboles phonétiques pour les deux langues.

La longueur des voyelles est indiquée de la façon suivante:
    courte—pas de symbole
    longue—(:) après la voyelle
En anglais l'accentuation d'une voyelle est donnée par le symbole (') placé devant le syllabe accentué, et l'accentuation secondaire par le symbole (ˌ).

CONSONNES   CONSONANTS

p	poupée	p	puppy	(in French [p,t,k] are not aspirated)
t	tente	t	tent	(en français [p,t,k] ne sont pas aspirés)
k	coq	k	cork	
b	bombe	b	bobbin	

d	dinde	d	daddy	
g	gringalet	g	gag	
f	ferme	f	farm	
v	vite	v	very	
s	souci	s	so	
z	cousin	z	cousin	
		θ	thorn	
		ð	that	
ʃ	chose	ʃ	sheep	
		tʃ	church	
ʒ	juge	ʒ	pleasure	
		dʒ	judge	
w	oui	w	wall	
ɥ	huit			
j	hier	j	yet	
		h	hat	
		x	loch (*Scots*)	
r	rentrer	r	rat	(English *r* is produced with the tip of the tongue against the front of the palate, French *r* with the back of the tongue against the back of the palate, not unlike, though softer, than the Scots [x] of loch)
				(le *r* anglais se prononce avec le bout de la langue contre le palais)
m	maman	m	mummy	
n	non	n	no	
ɲ	campagne			
		ŋ	singing	
l	lait	l	little	(in English the pronunciation of the two [l] of little is not the same. There is no such difference in French [l] as in lot)
				(en anglais la prononciation des deux [l] de little n'est pas semblable)

VOYELLES   VOWELS

i	ici	iː	heel	(these equivalents are obviously only approximate because French vowels and English vowels are produced differently)
		i	hit	
e	est, été	e	said	
ɛ	mère	ɛə	there	(ces équivalents ne sont pas absolument semblables, les voyelles françaises et anglaises se prononcent différemment)
a	patte	æ	bat	
ɑː	pâte	ɑː	car	
ɔ	donne	ɔ	lot	
o	côte	ɔː	all	
u	cou	u	put	
uː	cour	uː	shoe	
		ʌ	but	
œː	beurre	əː	bird	
ə	le	ə	rodent	
ø	feu	(mouth set as for [əː] of bird, lips rounded as for [uː] of shoe)		
y	rue	(mouth set as for [iː], lips rounded as for [uː])		

nasales (nasals); these French vowels are produced by pronouncing the corresponding oral vowel through the nose

ɑ̃ sang . ɛ̃ vin   œ̃ lundi   ɔ̃ long

diphthongs (diphthongs)

iə beer   ei date   ai life   au fowl   ɔi boil   ou low   uə poor

French – English

A

à [ɑ] *prep* to, at, in, on, according to, by, of, with *etc.*

abaissement [abɛsmɑ̃] *nm* lowering, falling, degradation, derogation, humiliation.

abaisser [abɛse] *vt* to lower, bring down; *vr* to fall away, stoop, droop, demean oneself.

abandon [abɑ̃dɔ̃] *nm* surrender, relinquishing, withdrawal, desertion, neglect, abandon; à l'— neglected, at random.

abandonné [abɑ̃dɔne] *a* forsaken, forlorn, stray, desolate, derelict, shameless.

abandonnement [abɑ̃dɔnmɑ̃] *nm* surrender, desertion, abandon, degradation, profligacy.

abandonner [abɑ̃dɔne] *vt* to surrender, give up, relinquish, make over (to à), desert; *vr* to give oneself up (to), indulge (in).

abasourdir [abazurdiːr] *vt* to astound, take aback, bewilder, stun.

abat-jour [abaʒuːr] *nm* lampshade, awning.

abattage [abataːʒ] *nm* felling, slaughtering.

abats [aba] *nm pl* offal.

abattement [abatmɑ̃] *nm* dejection, prostration.

abattoir [abatwaːr] *nm* slaughterhouse, shambles.

abattre [abatr] *vt* to knock down, overthrow, bring (pull, blow) down, fell, slaughter, depress, lower, lay; *vr* to fall (swoop) down, crash, abate, become downhearted.

abattu [abaty] *a* depressed, despondent, downcast.

abbaye [abe(j)i] *nf* abbey.

abbé [abe] *nm* abbot, priest.

abbesse [abɛs] *nf* abbess.

abcès [apsɛ] *nm* abscess, gathering, fester.

abdiquer [abdike] *vt* to abdicate, (*post*) resign.

abeille [abɛːj] *nf* bee.

aberration [abɛr(r)asjɔ̃] *nf* aberration, derangement, (*mental*) lapse.

abhorrer [abɔr(r)e] *vt* to abhor, detest, loathe.

abîme [abiːm] *nm* abyss, chasm, deep.

abîmer [abime] *vt* to injure, damage, spoil; *vr* to be swallowed up, be sunk, get damaged.

abject [abʒɛkt] *a* despicable, vile.

abjurer [abʒyre] *vt* to abjure, recant.

ablation [ablasjɔ̃] *nf* ablation, removal, excision.

ablution [ablysjɔ̃] *nf* ablution.

abnégation [abnegasjɔ̃] *nf* sacrifice, selflessness.

aboiement [abwamɑ̃] *nm* bark(ing), baying.

abois [abwɑ] *nm pl* aux — at bay, hard pressed.

abolir [abɔliːr] *vt* to abolish.

abolition [abɔlisjɔ̃] *nf* abolition.

abominable [abɔminabl] *a* abominable, loathsome, wretched.

abomination [abɔminasjɔ̃] *nf* abomination; avoir en — to detest.

abondamment [abɔ̃damɑ̃] *ad* abundantly.

abondance [abɔ̃dɑːs] *nf* abundance, plenty; en — galore.

abondant [abɔ̃dɑ̃] *a* abundant, plentiful, copious.

abonder [abɔ̃de] *vi* to abound, be plentiful.

abonnement [abɔnmɑ̃] *nm* subscription, (*hire purchase*) instalment; carte d'— season-ticket.

abonné [abɔne] *n* subscriber, season-ticket holder.

s'abonner [sabɔne] *vr* to subscribe (to à), take a season-ticket.

abord [abɔːr] *nm* access, approach, landing; d'— first, to begin with; de prime —, au premier — at first sight; dès l'— from the start.

abordable [abɔrdabl] *a* approachable, accessible.

abordage [abɔrdaːʒ] *nm* landing, boarding, collision.

aborder [abɔrde] *vi* to land; *vt* to approach, accost, board, tackle, collide.

aboutir [abutiːr] *vi* to lead (to à), end (in), result (in), succeed, come off.

aboyer [abwaje] *vi* to bark, bay.

abrasif [abrazif] *a* abrasive.

abrégé [abreʒe] *nm* abridgment, epitome.

abréger [abreʒe] *vt* to shorten, abbreviate, abridge; *vr* to grow shorter.

abreuver [abrœve] *vt* to water, soak; *vr* to drink, quench one's thirst.

abreuvoir [abrœvwaːr] *nm* watering-place, drinking-trough.

abréviation [abrevjasjɔ̃] *nf* abbreviation, contraction.

abri [abri] *nm* shelter, cover; à l' – sheltered, immune.

abricot [abriko] *nm* apricot.

abricotier [abrikɔtje] *nm* apricot-tree.

abriter [abrite] *vt* to shelter, protect, house, shade; *vr* to take shelter.

abroger [abrɔʒe] *vt* to abrogate, repeal; *vr* to lapse.

abrupt [abrypt] *a* abrupt, sheer.

abruti [abryti] *a* besotted, sodden, stupefied, dazed; *nm* sot, idiot.

abrutir [abrytiːr] *vt* to stupefy, besot.

abrutissant [abrytisɑ̃] *a* stupefying, degrading, killing.

absence [apsɑ̃ːs] *nf* non-appearance.

absent [apsɑ̃] *a* not at home, vacant.

s'absenter [sapsɑ̃te] *vr* to absent oneself, stay away.

absinthe [apsɛ̃ːt] *nf* absinth, worm-wood.

absolu [apsɔly] *a* absolute, utter, unqualified.

absolument [apsɔlymɑ̃] *ad* absolutely, utterly; —I quite so, just so!

absolution [apsɔlysjɔ̃] *nf* absolution.

absorber [apsɔrbe] *vt* to absorb, engross; *vr* to become absorbed (in), pore (over **dans**).

absoudre [apsudr] *vt* to absolve, condone, exonerate.

s'abstenir [sapstəniːr] *vr* to abstain, eschew, refrain.

abstinence [apstinɑ̃ːs] *nf* abstinence.

abstinent [apstinɑ̃] *a* abstinent; *n* teetotaller.

abstraction [apstraksjɔ̃] *nf* abstraction; — **faite de** apart from, disregarding, setting aside

abstraire [apstrɛːr] *vt* to abstract.

abstrait [apstrɛ] *a nm* abstract, absent-minded.

abstrus [apstry] *a* abstruse.

absurde [apsyrd] *a* ludicrous; *nm* absurd.

absurdité [apsyrdite] *nf* absurdity, nonsense.

abus [aby] *nm* abuse, misuse, error; — **de confiance** breach of faith.

abuser [abyze] *vi* to misuse, take advantage of; *vt* to delude; *vr* to delude oneself.

abusif, -ive [abysif, iːv] *a* contrary to usage, wrong, excessive.

acabit [akabi] *nm* (*of people*) nature, stamp.

académicien [akademisjɛ̃] *nm* academician, member of the French Academy.

académie [akademi] *nf* academy, school, regional education unit, learned society, riding-school.

académique [akademik] *a* academic (al), choice, distinguished.

acajou [akaʒu] *nm* mahogany.

acariâtre [akarjɑːtr] *a* shrewish, bad-tempered, cantankerous.

accablant [akablɑ̃] *a* overwhelming, crushing, oppressive.

accablé [akable] *a* overwhelmed, overcome, prostrate.

accablement [akabləmɑ̃] *nm* dejec-

tion, despondency, prostration.

accabler [akable] *vt* to overwhelm, overload, weigh down, snow under.

accalmie [akalmi] *nf* lull, respite.

accaparement [akaparmɑ̃] *nm* cornering, securing, monopoly.

accaparer [akapare] *vt* to corner, monopolize, hoard.

accéder [aksede] *vi* to accede, agree, have access.

accélération [akselerasjɔ̃] *nf* acceleration.

accélérateur [akseleratœːr] *nm* accelerator.

accélérer [akselere] *vtr* to accelerate, quicken.

accent [aksɑ̃] *nm* accent, emphasis, stress; *pl* strains.

accentuation [aksɑ̃tɥasjɔ̃] *nf* accentuation.

accentuer [aksɑ̃tɥe] *vt* to accentuate, stress, emphasize, intensify; *vr* to become more marked.

acceptable [akseptabl] *a* reasonable.

acceptation [akseptasjɔ̃] *nf* acceptance.

accepter [aksepte] *vt* to accept.

acception [aksepsjɔ̃] *nf* acceptation, meaning.

accès [aksɛ] *nm* access, approach, attack, fit, bout.

accessible [aksesibl] *a* available, open (to **à**).

accession [aksesjɔ̃] *nf* accession.

accessoire [akseswaːr] *a* adjunct, accessory, incidental; *nm* accessory; *pl* theatrical properties.

accident [aksidɑ̃] *nm* accident, mishap; (*of ground*) fold; **par** — accidentally, casually.

accidenté [aksidɑ̃te] *a* uneven, eventful; *n* victim (of accident).

accidentel, -elle [aksidɑ̃tɛl] *a* accidental.

acclamation [aklamasjɔ̃] *nf* acclamation; *pl* cheers.

acclamer [aklame] *vt* to acclaim, cheer.

acclimatation [aklimatasjɔ̃] *nf* acclimatization.

acclimater [aklimate] *vt* to acclimatize.

s'accointer [sakwɛ̃te] *vr* to take up (with **avec**).

accolade [akɔlad] *nf* embrace, accolade, bracket.

accoler [akɔle] *vt* to couple, bracket.

accommodant [akɔmɔdɑ̃] *a* accommodating, easy-going.

accommodation [akɔmɔdasjɔ̃] *nf* adaptation.

accommodement [akɔmɔdmɑ̃] *nm* compromise.

accommoder [akɔmɔde] *vt* to suit, adapt, settle, prepare, cook; *vr* to settle down, make the best (of), adapt oneself (to **de**), come to an agreement (with **avec**).

accompagnateur, -trice [akɔ̃paɲatœːr, tris] *n* accompanist.

accompagnement [akɔ̃paɲmɑ̃] *nm* accompaniment.

accompagner [akɔ̃paɲe] *vt* to accompany, escort.

accompli [akɔ̃pli] *a* accomplished, finished, perfect.

accomplir [akɔ̃pliːr] *vt* to accomplish, achieve fulfil complete; *vr* to be fulfilled.

accomplissement [akɔ̃plismɑ̃] *nm* accomplishment, fulfilment, completion.

accord [akɔːr] *nm* agreement, harmony, tune, chord; **d'—** agreed, (all) right; **être d'—** to concur, be at one (with **avec**), be in tune.

accorder [akɔrde] *vt* to reconcile, square, grant, award, concede, extend, tune, key; *vr* to agree, accord, harmonize.

accordeur [akɔrdœːr] *nm* tuner.

accort [akɔːr] *a* trim, pleasing.

accoster [akɔste] *vt* to accost, come alongside.

accoter [akɔte] *vt* to shore up; *vr* to lean (against **contre**).

accouchement [akuʃmɑ̃] *nm* confinement, labour, delivery.

accoucher [akuʃe] *vi* to be confined, give birth (to **de**).

s'accouder [sakude] *vr* to lean on one's elbow.

accoupler [akuple] *vt* to couple, mate, connect.

accourcir [akursiːr] *vt* to shorten.

accourir [akuriːr] *vi* to hasten, come running, rush.

accoutrement [akutrəmɑ̃] *nm* rig (-out), kit.

accoutrer [akutre] *vt* to rig out; *vr* to get oneself up.

accoutumé [akutyme] *a* accustomed, used, customary.

accoutumer [akutyme] *vt* to accustom; *vr* to get used (to **à**).

accréditer [akredite] *vt* to accredit.

accroc [akro] *nm* hitch rip, infraction.

accrochage [akrɔʃaːʒ] *nm* grazing, hanging up, picking up, altercation, set-to, (*aut*) accident.

accroche-cœur [akrɔʃkœːr] *nm* kiss-curl.

accrocher [akrɔʃe] *vt* to hook, catch, collide with, hang up, pick up, tune in; *vr* to cling, hang on, get caught, clinch, have a set-to.

accroire [akrwaːr] *vt* **en faire — à qn** to delude s.o.

accroissement [akrwasmɑ̃] *nm* growth, increase.

accroître [akrwaːtr] *vt* to increase, enlarge, enhance.

s'accroupir [akrupiːr] *vr* to squat, crouch (down), cower.

accueil [akœːj] *nm* welcome, reception.

accueillir [akœjiːr] *vt* to welcome, greet, receive.

acculer [akyle] *vt* to drive back, corner.

accumulateur, -trice [akymylatœːr tris] *n* hoarder; *nm* accumulator, storage battery.

accumulation [akymylasjɔ̃] *nf* accumulation.

accumuler [akymyle] *vt* to accumulate, amass, heap up.

accusateur, -trice [akyzatœːr, tris] *a* accusatory, incriminating; *n* accuser, indicter, plaintiff.

accusation [akyzasjɔ̃] *nf* charge, indictment; **mettre en —** to impeach, arraign.

accusé [akyze] *a* prominent; *n* accused; *nm* acknowledgement.

accuser [akyze] *vt* to accuse, indict, tax (with **de**), accentuate; **— réception de** to acknowledge receipt of.

acerbe [asɛrb] *a* bitter, harsh, sharp, sour.

acerbité [asɛrbite] *nf* bitterness, harshness, sharpness.

acéré [asere] *a* sharp-pointed, cutting.

acharné [aʃarne] *a* eager, keen, desperate, inveterate, fierce, relentless, strenuous.

acharnement [aʃarnəmɑ̃] *nm* eagerness, keenness, desperation, relentlessness.

s'acharner [saʃarne] *vr* to be dead set (against **à**), persist (in), be bent (on).

achat [aʃa] *nm* purchase; **faire des —s** to go shopping.

acheminer [aʃmine] *vt* to direct, dispatch, convey; *vr* to make one's way, proceed.

acheter [aʃte] *vt* to buy, purchase, bribe.

acheteur, -euse [aʃtœːr, øːz] *n* buyer, purchaser.

achevé [aʃve] *a* accomplished, perfect, thorough.

achèvement [aʃɛvmɑ̃] *nm* completion.

achever [aʃve] *vt* to complete, end, finish off; *vr* to draw to a close, end, culminate.

achoppement [aʃɔpmɑ̃] *nm* obstacle; **pierre d'—** stumbling-block.

acide [asid] *a* acid, tart; *nm* acid.

acidité [asidite] *nf* acidity.

acier [asje] *nm* steel.

aciérie [asjeri] *nf* steelworks.

acompte [akɔ̃t] *nm* instalment.

acoquiner [akɔkine] *vr* to be thick with

à-côté [akote] *nm* aside; *pl* side-issues, extras.

à-coup [aku] *nm* jerk, sudden stop, snatch; **par —s** by fits and starts, in spasms.

acoustique [akustik] *nf* acoustics.

acquérir [akeriːr] *vt* to acquire, get.

acquiescer [akjese] *vt* to acquiesce, assent.

acquis [aki] *a* acquired, established, vested; **mal —** ill-got(ten); **— d'avance** foregone; *nm* attainments, acquired knowledge.

acquisition [akizisjɔ̃] *nf* acquisition.

acquit [aki] *nm* acquittance, receipt; **pour —** received, paid (with thanks); **par — de conscience** for conscience' sake.

acquittement [akitmɑ̃] *nm* discharge, acquittal.

acquitter [akite] *vt* to discharge, acquit, clear, fulfil, receipt; *vr* to acquit o.s.; **— de** carry out, discharge.

âcre [ɑːkr] *a* acrid, pungent.

âcreté [akrəte] *nf* acridity, pungency.

acrimonie [akrimɔni] *nf* acrimony.

acrimonieux, -euse [akrimɔnjø, jøːz] *a* acrimonious.

acrobate [akrɔbat] *n* acrobat.

acrobatie [akrɔbasi] *nf* acrobatics.

acte [akt] *nm* act, deed, record; **— de naissance, de décès, de mariage** birth, death, marriage certificate.

acteur, -trice [aktœːr, tris] *n* actor, actress.

actif, -ive [aktif, iːv] *a* active, busy, brisk, live, industrious; *nm* credit, assets.

action [aksjɔ̃] *nf* action, effect, shares, lawsuit.

actionnaire [aksjɔnɛːr] *n* shareholder.

actionner [aksjɔne] *vt* to sue, set in motion, drive.

activer [aktive] *vt* to push on, stir up, whip up.

activité [aktivite] *nf* activity, industry.

actuaire [aktɥɛːr -tyɛːr] *nm* actuary.

actualité [aktɥalite -tya-] *nf* reality, topical question; *pl* current events, newsreel.

actuel, -elle [aktɥɛl -tyɛl] *a* real, current, topical, of the present.

actuellement [aktɥɛlmɑ̃ -tyɛl] *ad* at present.

acuité [akɥite] *nf* keenness, sharpness.

adage [adaːʒ] *nm* adage.

adaptable [adaptabl] *a* adaptable.

adaptation [adaptasjɔ̃] *nf* adaptation.

adapter [adapte] *vt* to adapt, adjust, accommodate.

addition [adisjɔ̃] *nf* addition, appendage, bill.

additionner [ad(d)isjɔne] *vt* to add (up).

adepte [adɛpt] *a* adept.

adhérence [aderɑ̃ːs] *nf* adhesion.

adhérent [aderɑ̃] *a* adherent, adhesive; *n* adherent, member, follower.

adhérer [adere] *vi* to adhere, stick, hold, join.

adhésif, -ive [adezif, iːv] *a nm* adhesive.

adhésion [adezjɔ̃] *nf* adhesion.

adieu [adjø] *ad* good-bye; *nm* farewell, leave-taking; **faire ses —x à** to say farewell to, take leave of.

adjacent [adʒasɑ̃] *a* adjacent.

adjectif, -ive [adʒektif, iːv] *a* adjectival; *nm* adjective.

adjoindre [adʒwɛ̃ːdr] *vt* to unite, associate, add; *vr* to join in (with à).

adjoint [adʒwɛ̃] *an* assistant; **— au maire** deputy mayor, alderman.

adjudant [adʒydɑ̃] *nm* company sergeant-major, adjutant, warrant-officer.

adjudication [adʒydikasjɔ̃] *nf* adjudication; **mettre en —** to invite tenders for, put up for sale by auction.

adjuger [adʒyʒe] *vt* to adjudge, award, knock down; *vr* to appropriate.

adjurer [adʒyre] *vt* to adjure, beseech, conjure.

admettre [admɛtr] *vt* to admit, assume, allow, concede, pass.

administrateur, -trice [administratœːr, tris] *n* administrator, director, trustee.

administration [administrasjɔ̃] *nf* administration, government, civil service, trusteeship.

administrer [administre] *vt* to administer, govern, manage, dispense.

admirable [admirabl] *a* admirable, wonderful.

admirateur, -trice [admiratœːr, tris] *n* admirer, fan.

admiratif, -ive [admiratif, iːv] *a* admiring.

admiration [admirasjɔ̃] *nf* admiration, wonderment.

admirer [admire] *vt* to admire, wonder at, marvel at.

admissible [admisibl] *a* admissible, eligible, qualified for oral examination.

admission [admisjɔ̃] *nf* admission.

admonestation [admɔnɛstasjɔ̃] *nf* reprimand.

admonester [admɔnɛste] *vt* to admonish.

adolescence [adɔlɛssɑ̃ːs] *nf* adolescence, youth.

adolescent [adɔlɛssɑ̃] *n* adolescent, youth, girl.

s'adonner [sadɔne] *vr* to give oneself up (to à), take (to).

adopter [adɔpte] *vt* to adopt.

adoptif, -ive [adɔptif, iːv] *a* adopted, adoptive.

adoption [adɔpsjɔ̃] *nf* adoption.

adorable [adɔrabl] *a* adorable, charming, lovely.

adorateur, -trice [adɔratœːr, tris] *n* adorer, worshipper; *a* adoring.

adorer [adɔre] *vt* to adore, worship.

adosser [adɔse] *vt* to place back to back, lean back (against à); *vr* to lean one's back (against à).

adoucir [adusiːr] *vt* to soften, subdue, alleviate, mitigate, mollify; *vr* to grow softer, milder.

adoucissement [adusismɑ̃] *nm* softening, toning down, alleviation, mitigation.

adresse [adrɛs] nf address, destination, skill, deftness, sleight, adroitness, craftiness.

adresser [adrese] vt to address, direct; vr to address, apply, ask.

adroit [adrwa] a skilful, deft, clever, handy, shrewd

adulation [adylasjɔ̃] nf adulation.

adulte [adylt] an adult, grown-up, full-grown.

adultère [adyltɛːr] a adulterous; n adulterer, adulteress; nm adultery.

advenir [advəniːr] v imp to happen, occur, come to pass, become of; **advienne que pourra** come what may.

adverbe [advɛrb] nm adverb.

adversaire [advɛrsɛːr] nm adversary, opponent.

adverse [advɛrs] a adverse.

adversité [advɛrsite] nf adversity, misfortune.

aération [aɛrasjɔ̃] nf aeration, airing, ventilation.

aérer [aere] vt to air, aerate, ventilate.

aérien, -ienne [aerjɛ̃, jɛn] a airy, aerial, ethereal; **raid —** long-distance flight, air-raid; **forces —nes** air-force.

aéro-club [aerɔklyb, -klœb] nm flying-club.

aérodrome [aerɔdroːm] nm aerodrome.

aérodynamique [aerɔdinamik] a stream-lined.

aéronaute [aerɔnoːt] nm aeronaut.

aéronautique [aerɔnotik] a aeronautical; nf aeronautics.

aéroport [aerɔpɔːr] nm airport.

aéroporté [aerɔpɔrte] a airborne.

aérostat [aerɔsta] nm airship, balloon.

aérostatique [aerɔstatik] a **barrage —** balloon barrage; nf aerostatics.

affabilité [afabilite] nf affability, graciousness.

affable [afaːbl] a affable.

affadir [afadiːr] vt to make insipid; vr to become insipid.

affaiblir [afɛbliːr] vt to weaken, enfeeble, impair, lower, water down; vr to become weaker, flag, abate.

affaiblissement [afɛblismɑ̃] nm weakening, enfeeblement, impairment.

affaire [afɛːr] nf affair, thing, matter, concern, case; pl business, dealings, belongings; **— de cœur** love affair; **son — est faite** it's all up with him; **la belle —!** is that all!; **avoir — à, avec** to deal with; **le Ministère des — étrangères** Foreign Office.

affairé [afere] a busy.

affaissement [afɛsmɑ̃] nm subsidence, collapse.

s'affaisser [safɛse] vr to subside, collapse.

affamé [afame] a hungry, starving, famished.

affectation [afɛktasjɔ̃] nf affectation, primness, assignment, (mil) posting.

affecté [afɛkte] a affected, conceited, prim, (mil) posted.

affecter [afɛkte] vt to affect, assign (to à), post (to).

affection [afɛksjɔ̃] nf affection, liking, trouble.

affectionner [afɛksjɔne] vt to have a liking for.

affectueux, -euse [afɛktɥø, øːz] a affectionate, fond.

affermir [afɛrmiːr] vt to strengthen; vr to grow stronger, harden.

afféterie [afetri] nf affectation, primness, gewgaws.

affichage [afiʃaːʒ] nm bill-posting.

affiche [afiʃ] nf bill, poster, placard; **panneau à —s** hoarding; **tenir l'—** (of a play) to run.

afficher [afiʃe] vt to stick up, post up, make a display of; **défense d'—** no bills; vr to show off.

afficheur [afiʃœːr] nm bill-poster.

affilée [afile] nf d'— at a stretch.

affiler [afile] vt to sharpen, grind, whet, strop.

affiliation [afiljasjɔ̃] nf affiliation, branch.

affilier [afilje] vt to affiliate.

affinité [afinite] nf affinity, connection.

affirmatif, -ive [afirmatif, iːv] a affirmative.

affirmation [afirmasjɔ̃] nf affirmation, assertion.

affirmative [afirmatiːv] nf affirmative.

affirmer [afirme] vt to affirm, assert, aver, avouch.

affleurer [aflœre] vt to make flush; vi to be level.

affliction [afliksjɔ̃] nf affliction, grief.

affligé [afliʒe] a afflicted, aggrieved, sorrowful.

affligeant [afliʒɑ̃] a distressing, sad, grievous.

affliger [afliʒe] vt to afflict, distress; vr to grieve.

affluence [aflyɑ̃ːs] nf flow, influx, affluence, concourse, crowd; **heures d'—** rush hours.

affluent [aflyɑ̃] nm tributary.

affluer [aflye] vi to flow, flock, abound, throng.

affolé [afɔle] a crazy, distracted, panicky.

affolement [afɔlmɑ̃] nm distraction, panic.

affoler [afɔle] vt to distract, drive crazy; vr to become panicky, become infatuated (with de).

affranchi [afrɑ̃ʃi] freed, a stamped, unscrupulous; **colis —** prepaid parcel; n emancipated man, woman.

affranchir [afrɑ̃ʃiːr] vt to set free, emancipate, stamp, enfranchise; vr to become free, shake off (de).

affranchissement [afrɑ̃ʃismɑ̃] nm freeing, setting free, stamping, postage.

affréter [afrete] vt to charter, freight.

affreux, -euse [afrø, øːz] a horrible, awful, dreadful.

affront [afrɔ̃] nm affront, insult, disgrace, public shame.

affronter [afrɔ̃te] vt to affront, face.

affût [afy] nm hiding-place, gun-carriage; à l'— on the watch.

affûter [afyte] vt to sharpen, whet.

afin [afɛ̃] ad — de in order to; cj — que so that.

africain [afrikɛ̃] an African.

Afrique [afrik] nf Africa.

agaçant [agasɑ̃] a annoying, irritating, grating.

agacer [agase] vt to annoy, irritate, set teeth on edge.

âge [ɑːʒ] nm age, period; **d'un certain** —, elderly; **prendre de l'**— to be getting on in years; **quel** — **avez-vous?** how old are you?

âgé [ɑʒe] a old, aged.

agence [aʒɑ̃ːs] nf agency, office.

agencer [aʒɑ̃se] vt to arrange, fit together, set.

agenda [aʒɛ̃da] nm agenda, diary.

agenouillé [aʒnuje] a kneeling.

s'agenouiller [saʒnuje] vr to kneel (down).

agent [aʒɑ̃] nm agent; — **de police** policeman; — **de change** stock-broker; — **voyer** road surveyor.

agglomération [aglɔmerasjɔ̃] nf agglomeration, built-up area.

aggloméré [aglɔmere] nm conglomerate, compressed fuel, coal-dust, briquette.

agglomérer [aglɔmere] vt to agglomerate, cluster, bind.

aggraver [agrave] vt to aggravate, worsen, increase.

agile [aʒil] a agile, nimble.

agilité [aʒilite] nf agility, nimbleness.

agioteur [aʒjɔtœːr] nm speculator, stock-jobber.

agir [aʒiːr] vi to act; v imp s'— to be in question, concern; **il s'agit de** it is a question of; **de quoi s'agit-il?** what is the matter?

agissements [aʒismɑ̃] nm pl dealings, doings.

agitateur. -trice [aʒitatœːr, tris] n agitator.

agitation [aʒitasjɔ̃] nf agitation, restlessness, bustle; **faire de l'**— to agitate.

agité [aʒite] a agitated, restless, excited, agog, rough.

agiter [aʒite] vt to agitate, stir up, wave, flap, dangle; vr to become agitated, bustle, fidget, toss.

agneau [aɲo] nm lamb.

agonie [agɔni] nf death agony; à l'— dying.

agonisant [agɔnizɑ̃] a dying; n dying person.

agoniser [agɔnize] vi to be dying.

agouti [aguti] nm cane-rat.

agrafe [agraf] nf hook, clasp, clip, fastener; —s et portes hooks and eyes.

agrafer [agrafe] vt to fasten, clip.

agrandir [agrɑ̃diːr] vt to enlarge, magnify; vr to grow larger, become more powerful.

agrandissement [agrɑ̃dismɑ̃] nm aggrandizement, enlargement.

agréable [agreabl] a pleasant, congenial, acceptable.

agréer [agree] vt to accept; **veuillez** — **l'expression de mes sentiments distingués** yours faithfully, yours truly.

agrégation [agregasjɔ̃] nf aggregation, aggregate, State competitive examination for recruitment of secondary school teachers.

agrégé [agreʒe] an teacher who has passed the aggregation.

s'agréger [sagreʒe] vr to aggregate, join together.

agrément [agremɑ̃] nm pleasure, charm, approbation.

agrès [agrɛ] nm pl rigging, tackle.

agresseur [agresœːr] nm aggressor.

agressif, -ive [agresif, iːv] a aggressive.

agression [agresjɔ̃] nf aggression, assault.

agreste [agrɛst] a rustic, rural, uncouth.

agricole [agrikɔl] a agricultural.

agriculteur [agrikyltœːr] nm farmer.

agriculture [agrikyltyːr] nf agriculture.

agripper [agripe] vt to clutch, grip; vr to cling, come to grips (with à).

aguerri [ageri] a seasoned.

aguerrir [ageriːr] vt to harden, train, season.

aguets [agɛ] nm pl être aux — to lie in wait, be on the look-out, or the lurk.

aguicher [agiʃe] vt to allure, inflame.

ahuri [ayri] a bewildered, dumbfounded, dazed.

ahurir [ayriːr] vt to bewilder, flabbergast, daze.

ahurissement [ayrismɑ̃] nm bewilderment.

aide [ɛ(ː)d] nf aid, help, assistance; à l'—! help!, **venir en** — à to help, benefit; n assistant, helper, mate.

aide-mémoire [ɛdmemwaːr] nm memorandum.

aider [ɛde] vt to aid, help, assist, avail.

aïeul [ajœl] n ancestor, ancestress, grandfather, grandmother.

aigle [ɛgl] nm eagle, lectern.

aiglefin [ɛglafɛ̃] nm haddock.

aiglon [ɛglɔ̃] nm eaglet.

aigre [ɛːgr] a sour, tart, bitter, crabbed, shrill, sharp.

aigre-doux, -douce [ɛgrədu, dus] a bittersweet.

aigrefin [ɛgrəfɛ̃] nm sharper, swindler, haddock.

aigrette [ɛgrɛt] nf aigrette, tuft, plume.

aigreur [ɛgrœːr] nf sourness, tartness, embitterment, crabbedness; pl heartburn.

aigrir [ɛgriːr] vt to sour, turn sour, embitter.

aigu, -uë [egy] a pointed, sharp, shrill, high-pitched.

aiguière [egjɛːr] nf ewer.

aiguille [egɥiːj] nf needle, hand, pointer, spire, cock, switch; pl points.

aiguiller [egɥije] vt to switch, shunt, divert.

aiguilleur [egɥijœːr] nm pointsman.

aiguillon [egɥijɔ̃] nm goad, spur, prickle, sting.

aiguillonner [egɥijɔne] vt to goad, spur on, stimulate.

aiguisé [eg(ɥ)ize] a sharp.

aiguiser [eg(ɥ)ize] vt to sharpen point, stimulate; pierre à — hone, whetstone.

ail [aːj] nm garlic.

aile [ɛl] nf wing, mudguard, aisle.

ailé [ɛle] a winged.

aileron [ɛlrɔ̃] nm pinion, fin, aileron, wing-flap.

ailette [ɛlɛt] nf fin, blade.

ailier [ɛlje] nm wing-player, winger.

ailleurs [ajœːr] ad elsewhere; d'— moreover, besides; par — in other respects, from another source.

aimable [ɛmabl] a amiable, pleasant, bland, kind.

aimablement [ɛmabləmɑ̃] ad amiably, agreeably.

aimant [ɛmɑ̃] a affectionate; nm magnet, loadstone.

aimanter [ɛmɑ̃te] vt to magnetize.

aimer [ɛme] vt to love, like, be fond of, care for, enjoy.

aine [ɛn] nf groin.

aîné [ɛne] a elder, eldest, senior.

ainsi [ɛ̃si] ad thus, so; et — de suite and so on; — soit-il amen, so be it; pour — dire so to speak; — que as, like, as well as.

air [ɛːr] nm air, wind, appearance, look, tune, melody; avoir l'— to look, seem; en plein — in the open air; qui tient l'— airworthy.

airain [ɛrɛ̃] nm bronze, brass.

aire [ɛːr] nf threshing-floor, area, surface, eyrie, point of the compass.

aisance [ɛzɑ̃ːs] nf ease, comfort, affluence.

aise [ɛːz] nf ease, comfort; à l'— comfortable, well-off; à votre — just as you like; mal à l'— uncomfortable, uneasy; bien — very glad.

aisé [ɛze] a easy, well-to-do.

aisément [ɛzemɑ̃] ad easily.

aisselle [ɛsɛl] nf armpit.

ajonc [aʒɔ̃] nm furze, gorse.

ajournement [aʒurnəmɑ̃] nm postponement.

ajourner [aʒurne] vt to postpone; vr to adjourn.

ajouter [aʒute] vt to add, supplement.

ajustage [aʒystaːʒ] nm adjustment, fitting.

ajustement [aʒystəmɑ̃] nm adjusting, settlement, fit.

ajuster [aʒyste] vt to adjust, fit, settle.

ajusteur [aʒystœːr] nm fitter.

alacrité [alakrite] nf alacrity.

alanguir [alɑ̃giːr] vt to enfeeble; vr to grow languid.

alanguissement [alɑ̃gismɑ̃] nm languor.

alarmant [alarmɑ̃] a alarming.

alarme [alarm] nf alarm.

alarmer [alarme] vt to alarm; vr to take fright.

alarmiste [alarmist] a alarmist, panicky; n scaremonger.

album [albɔm] nm album.

alchimie [alʃimi] nf alchemy.

alchimiste [alʃimist] nm alchemist.

alcool [alkɔl] nm alcohol, spirit(s); — à brûler methylated spirit.

alcoolique [alkɔlik] a alcoholic.

alcoolisme [alkɔlism] nm alcoholism.

alcôve [alkoːv] nf alcove, recess.

aléatoire [aleatwaːr] a risky, chancy.

alène [alɛn] nf awl.

alentour [alɑ̃tuːr] ad around; nm pl surroundings.

alerte [alɛrt] a alert, quick; nf alarm, alert, air-raid warning; fin d'— all clear.

alerter [alɛrte] vt to give the alarm to, warn.

alésage [alezaːʒ] nm (tec) boring, bore.

alèse [alɛːz] nf draw-sheet, rubber sheet.

algèbre [alʒɛbr] nf algebra.

Algérie [alʒeri] nf Algeria.

algérien, -ienne [alʒerjɛ̃, jɛn] an Algerian.

algue [alg] nf alga, seaweed.

alibi [alibi] nm alibi.

aliénation [aljenasjɔ̃] nf alienation, estrangement.

aliéné [aljene] a insane; n lunatic.

aliéner [aljene] vt to alienate, estrange.

aliéniste [aljenist] nm mental specialist.

alignement [aliɲmɑ̃] nm alignment, line, row, putting in lines.

aligner [aliɲe] vt to align, line up, draw up; vr to fall into line.

aliment [alimɑ̃] nm aliment, food.

alimentation [alimɑ̃tasjɔ̃] nf alimentation, feeding, nourishment.

alimenter [alimɑ̃te] vt to feed, nourish.

alinéa [alinea] nm paragraph, break.

s'aliter [salite] vr to take to one's bed.

allaiter [alɛte] vt to suckle.

allant [alɑ̃] nm dash, go.

allécher [al(l)eʃe] vt to entice, allure.

allée [ale] nf avenue, drive, path, lane, passage.

allégation [al(l)egasjɔ̃] nf allegation.

alléger [al(l)eʒe] vt to lighten, alleviate.

allégorie [allegɔri] nf allegory.

allègre [allɛːgr] a lively.

alléguer [al(l)ege] vt to allege, urge, plead.

Allemagne [almaɲ] nf Germany.

allemand [almɑ̃] an German.

aller [ale] vi to go, suit, fit; — **chercher** to fetch; **comment allez-vous?** how do you do?; **allez-y!** fire away!; **cela va de soi** that is a matter of course; y — **de qch.** to be at stake; **allons donc!** come along! nonsense!; vr **s'en** — to go away, clear off, depart; nm single ticket, outward journey; **billet d'**— **et retour** return ticket; **au pis** — if the worst comes to the worst.

alliage [aljaːʒ] nm alloy.

alliance [aljɑ̃ːs] nf alliance, blending, wedding ring.

allier [alje] vt to ally.

allocation [allɔkasjɔ̃] nf allocation, allowance, grant.

allonger [alɔ̃ʒe] vt to lengthen, stretch out, strike, eke out; vr to lengthen, stretch.

allumage [alymaːʒ] nm lighting, putting on, ignition.

allumer [alyme] vt to light, put on, set alight, arouse.

allumette [alymɛt] nf match.

allure [alyːr] nf carriage, gait, walk, speed, turn, style.

aloi [alwa] nm quality, standard; **de bon** — genuine.

alors [alɔːr] ad then, at that time, so, in that case.

alouette [alwɛt] nf lark.

alpinisme [alpinism] nm mountaineering.

altercation [altɛrkasjɔ̃] nf altercation, dispute.

altérer [altere] vt to change, spoil, impair, falsify, make thirsty; vr to change, be spoiled, become thirsty.

alternatif, -ive [altɛrnatif, iːv] a alternative, alternate, alternating.

alterner [altɛrne] vt to alternate, take turn about.

altier [altje] a haughty, lofty.

amabilité [amabilite] nf amiability, civility.

amadouer [amadwe] vt to wheedle, coax, win over.

amaigrir [amegriːr] vt to make thin, reduce.

amande [amɑ̃ːd] nf almond.

amant [amɑ̃] n lover.

amarre [amaːr] nf hawser; pl moorings.

amarrer [amare] vtr to moor, tie up.

amas [amɑ] nm pile, heap.

amasser [amase] vt to amass, pile up; vr to mass.

amateur, -trice [amatœːr, tris] n amateur, lover.

ambages [ɑ̃baːʒ] nf pl **sans** — bluntly, plainly.

ambassade [ɑ̃basad] nf embassy.

ambiance [ɑ̃bjɑ̃ːs] nf surroundings, atmosphere.

ambigu, -uë [ɑ̃bigy] a ambiguous.

ambition [ɑ̃bisjɔ̃] nf ambition.

ambre [ɑ̃ːbr] nm amber.

ambulant [ɑ̃bylɑ̃] a travelling, itinerant, strolling.

âme [ɑːm] nf soul, spirit, core, heart, life; (of gun) bore.

améliorer [ameljɔre] vtr to improve, mend.

aménager [amɛnaʒe] vt to fit up (out), lay out.

amende [amɑ̃ːd] nf fine.

amender [amɑ̃de] vtr to improve.

amener [amne] vt to lead, bring, induce.

amer, -ère [amɛːr] a bitter.

américain [amerikɛ̃] an American.

Amérique [amerik] nf America.

amertume [amɛrtym] nf bitterness.

ameublement [amœbləmɑ̃] n furnishing, furniture.

ameuter [amøte] vt to rouse; vr to mutiny.

ami [ami] n friend, boy-, girl-friend.

amical [amikal] a friendly.

amidon [amidɔ̃] nm starch.

amincir [amɛ̃siːr] vt to make thinner, thin down; vr to grow thinner.

amiral [amiral] nm admiral.

amirauté [amirote] nf admiralty.

amitié [amitje] nf friendship, favour; pl kind regards.

amoindrir [amwɛ̃driːr] vtr to lessen, decrease.

amollir [amɔliːr] vt to soften; vr to grow weak.

amonceler [amɔ̃sle] vtr to pile up; vr to gather.

amont [amɔ̃] nm upper reaches; **en** — upstream.

amorce [amɔrs] nf bait, beginning, detonator.

amortir [amɔrtiːr] vt to deaden, allay, muffle, slacken, pay off, sink, redeem.

amortissement [amɔrtismɑ̃] nm deadening, redemption; **fonds d'**— sinking-fund.

amortisseur [amɔrtisœːr] nm shock-absorber.

amour [amuːr] nm (pl usually f) love; **pour l'**— **de** for love of, for the sake of.

s'amouracher [samuraʃe] vr to fall head over heels in love (with de).

amourette [amurɛt] *nf* passing love affair.

amoureux, -euse [amurø, øːz] *a* loving, amorous; **être — de** to be in love with, enamoured of; *n* lover.

amour-propre [amurprɔpr] *nm* self-esteem, -respect, vanity, egotism.

amovible [amɔvibl] *a* removable, detachable.

amphibie [ɑ̃fibi] *a* amphibious; *nm* amphibian.

ample [ɑ̃ːpl] *a* ample, roomy; **plus — further, fuller.

ampleur [ɑ̃plœːr] *nf* fullness, copiousness, magnitude.

amplificateur, -trice [ɑ̃plifikatœːr, tris] *a* amplifying; *nm* amplifier.

amplification [ɑ̃plifikasjɔ̃] *nf* amplification.

amplifier [ɑ̃plifje] *vt* to amplify.

ampoule [ɑ̃pul] *nf* blister, phial, (electric light) bulb.

ampoulé [ɑ̃pule] *a* bombastic, high-flown, stilted.

amputation [ɑ̃pytasjɔ̃] *nf* amputation.

amputer [ɑ̃pyte] *vt* to amputate, reduce.

amusant [amyzɑ̃] *a* amusing, entertaining.

amusement [amyzmɑ̃] *nm* amusement, entertainment, fun.

amuser [amyze] *vt* to amuse, entertain, interest; *vr* to enjoy oneself, take pleasure (in à), have fun.

amusette [amyzɛt] *nf* toy.

amygdale [ami(g)dal] *nf* tonsil.

amygdalite [ami(g)dalit] *nf* tonsillitis.

an [ɑ̃] *nm* year; **le jour de l'— New Year's Day.

analogie [analɔʒi] *nf* analogy.

analogue [analɔg] *a* analogous, kindred.

analyse [analiːz] *nf* analysis, abstract.

analyser [analize] *vt* to analyse, parse.

analyste [analist] *nm* analyst.

analytique [analitik] *a* analytical.

ananas [ananɑ(ː)s] *nm* pineapple.

anarchie [anarʃi] *nf* anarchy.

anarchiste [anarʃist] *an* anarchist.

anathème [anatɛm] *nm* anathema, curse.

anatomie [anatɔmi] *nf* anatomy.

anatomiste [anatɔmist] *nm* anatomist.

ancestral [ɑ̃sɛstral] *a* ancestral.

ancêtre [ɑ̃sɛːtr] *n* ancestor, ancestress, forefather.

anchois [ɑ̃ʃwa] *nm* anchovy.

ancien, -ienne [ɑ̃sjɛ̃, jɛn] *a* ancient, old, long-standing, former, past, senior; **— combattant** ex-service-man.

anciennement [ɑ̃sjɛnmɑ̃] *ad* formerly.

ancienneté [ɑ̃sjɛnte] *nf* antiquity, seniority.

ancre [ɑ̃ːkr] *nf* anchor; **lever l'— to weigh anchor.

andouille [ɑ̃duːj] *nf* (*chitterling*) sausage, duffer, mug.

âne [ɑːn] *nm* ass, donkey, fool; **en dos d'— hog-backed.

anéantir [aneɑ̃tiːr] *vt* to destroy, wipe out; *vr* to come to nothing.

anéantissement [aneɑ̃tismɑ̃] *nm* destruction, annihilation.

anecdote [anekdɔt] *nf* anecdote.

anémie [anemi] *nf* anaemia.

anémique [anemik] *a* anaemic.

anesthésie [anɛstezi] *nf* anaesthesia.

anesthésier [anɛstezje] *vt* to anaesthetize.

anesthésique [anɛstezik] *a nm* anaesthetic.

anesthésiste [anɛstezist] *nm* anaesthetist.

ange [ɑ̃ːʒ] *nm* angel.

angélique [ɑ̃ʒelik] *a* angelic.

angélus [ɑ̃ʒelyːs] *nm* angelus.

angine [ɑ̃ʒin] *nf* sore throat, quinsy, tonsillitis; **— de poitrine** angina (pectoris).

anglais [ɑ̃glɛ] *a nm* English; *n* Englishman, -woman.

angle [ɑ̃ːgl] *nm* angle.

Angleterre [ɑ̃glətɛːr] *nf* England.

anglican [ɑ̃glikɑ̃] *an* anglican.

angoissant [ɑ̃gwasɑ̃] *a* distressing.

angoisse [ɑ̃gwas] *nf* anguish, anxiety, distress.

anguille [ɑ̃giːj] *nf* eel; **— sous roche** something in the wind, something brewing; **— de mer** conger-eel.

angulaire [ɑ̃gylɛːr] *a* angular; **pierre — corner-stone.

anguleux [ɑ̃gylø] *a* angular, gaunt.

animal [animal] *a nm* animal.

animateur, -trice [animatœːr, tris] *n* animator, moving spirit, organizer.

animation [animasjɔ̃] *nf* animation.

animé [anime] *a* animated, lively, spirited, heated.

animer [anime] *vt* to animate, enliven, vivify, brighten, actuate; *vr* to become animated, brighten up.

animosité [animɔzite] *nf* animosity.

anis [ani] *nm* aniseed.

annales [annal] *nf pl* annals.

anneau [ano] *nm* ring, link, ringlet, quoit.

année [ane] *nf* year, vintage; **bonne—! a Happy New Year!

annexe [an(n)ɛks] *nm* annex.

annexer [an(n)ɛkse] *vt* to annex.

annexion [an(n)ɛksjɔ̃] *nf* annexation.

annihiler [an(n)iile] *vt* to annihilate.

anniversaire [anivɛrsɛːr] *a* anniversary; *nm* anniversary, birthday.

annonce [anɔ̃ːs] *nf* announcement, advertisement.

annoncer [anɔ̃se] *vt* to announce, herald, usher in, advertise, betoken, denote.

annonciation [anɔ̃sjasjɔ̃] *nf* Annunciation, Lady Day.

annotation [an(n)ɔtasjɔ̃] nf annotation.

annoter [an(n)ɔte] vt to annotate, note.

annuaire [an(n)ɥɛːr] nm annual, telephone directory.

annuel [an(n)ɥɛl] a annual.

annuité [an(n)ɥite] nf annuity.

annulaire [an(n)ylɛːr] a annular; nm third finger.

annulation [an(n)ylasjɔ̃] nf annulment, nullification, revocation, cancellation.

annuler [an(n)yle] vt to annul.

anoblir [anɔbliːr] vt to ennoble.

anoblissement [anɔblismɑ̃] nm ennoblement.

anodin [anɔdɛ̃] a anodyne, harmless; nm palliative.

anomalie [anɔmali] nf anomaly.

ânonner [anɔne] vt to mumble, stammer through.

anonymat [anɔnima] nm anonymity.

anonyme [anɔnim] a anonymous; société — limited company; nm anonymity.

anormal [anɔrmal] a abnormal, anomalous.

anse [ɑ̃ːs] nf handle, cove.

antagonisme [ɑ̃tagɔnism] nm antagonism.

antécédent [ɑ̃tesedɑ̃] a nm antecedent.

antenne [ɑ̃tɛn] nf antenna, feeler, aerial.

antérieur [ɑ̃terjœːr] a anterior, former, prior.

antériorité [ɑ̃terjɔrite] nf anteriority.

anthrax [ɑ̃traks] nm carbuncle.

anthropophage [ɑ̃trɔpɔfaːʒ] a nm cannibal.

antiaérien, -ienne [ɑ̃tiaerjɛ̃, jɛn] a anti-aircraft.

antibiotique [ɑ̃tibiɔtik] nm antibiotic.

antichambre [ɑ̃tiʃɑ̃ːbr] nf anteroom, hall, waiting-room.

antichar [ɑ̃tiʃar] a anti-tank.

anticipation [ɑ̃tisipasjɔ̃] nf anticipation.

anticiper [ɑ̃tisipe] vt to anticipate, forestall; vi to anticipate, encroach (upon sur).

anticorps [ɑ̃tikɔr] nm antibody.

antidater [ɑ̃tidate] vt to antedate.

antidérapant [ɑ̃tiderapɑ̃] a nonskid.

antidote [ɑ̃tidɔt] nm antidote.

antipathie [ɑ̃tipati] nf antipathy, repugnance.

antipathique [ɑ̃tipatik] a antipathetic, uncongenial.

antipodes [ɑ̃tipɔd] nm pl antipodes.

antiquaille [ɑ̃tikaːj] nf lumber, junk.

antiquaire [ɑ̃tikɛːr] nm antiquarian.

antique [ɑ̃tik] a antique, ancient, old-fashioned.

antiquité [ɑ̃tikite] nf antiquity.

antiseptique [ɑ̃tisɛptik] a nm antiseptic.

antithèse [ɑ̃titɛːz] nf antithesis.

antithétique [ɑ̃titetik] a antithetical.

antre [ɑ̃ːtr] nm den, lair, sinus.

anxiété [ɑ̃ksjete] nf anxiety, solicitude.

anxieux, -euse [ɑ̃ksjø, øːz] a anxious, solicitous.

aorte [aɔrt] nf aorta.

août [u] nm August.

apache [apaʃ] nm hooligan.

apaiser [apɛze] vt to appease, alleviate, mollify, mitigate; vr to calm down.

aparté [aparte] nm aside, stage whisper.

apathie [apati] nf apathy, listlessness.

apathique [apatik] a apathetic, listless.

apercevoir [apersəvwaːr] vt to perceive, catch sight of; vr to notice, realize.

aperçu [apersy] nm glimpse, sidelight, outline, summary.

apéritif [aperitif] nm appetizer.

aphone [afɔn] a voiceless.

aphteux, -euse [aftø, øz] a aphthou ; la fièvre aphteuse foot-and-mouth disease.

apiculteur [apikyltœːr] nm beekeeper.

apitoyer [apitwaje] vt to move to pity; vr to commiserate (with sur).

aplanir [aplaniːr] vt to smooth (away), plane, level.

aplanissement [aplanismɑ̃] nm smoothing, levelling.

aplatir [aplatiːr] vt to flatten, iron out; vr to grovel, collapse, fall flat.

aplatissement [aplatismɑ̃] nm flattening.

aplomb [aplɔ̃] nm perpendicularity, level, self-possession, nerve; d'— upright, firm on one's feet, foursquare.

apogée [apɔʒe] nm apogee, acme, zenith, peak.

apologie [apɔlɔʒi] nf vindication, justification.

apologiste [apɔlɔʒist] nm apologist.

apoplectique [apɔplɛktik] a apoplectic.

apoplexie [apɔplɛksi] nf apoplexy.

apostat [apɔsta] nm apostate.

apostolat [apɔstɔla] nm apostleship.

apostolique [apɔstɔlik] a apostolic.

apothicaire [apɔtikɛːr] nm apothecary.

apôtre [apoːtr] nm apostle.

apparaître [aparɛːtr] vi to appear, become apparent.

apparat [apara] nm pomp, show, state.

appareil [aparɛːj] nm apparatus, mechanism, plant, set, aeroplane; — photographique camera.

appareillage [aparɛjaːʒ] nm fitting

up, getting under way, equipment.
appareiller [aparɛje] *vt* to fit up;
vi get under way.

apparemment [aparamã] *ad*
apparently, evidently, seemingly.

apparence [aparã:s] *nf* appearance,
look, show, guise.

apparent [aparã] *a* apparent, seeming, obvious.

apparenté [aparãte] *a* related.

apparier [aparje] *vt* to match, pair,
mate.

apparition [aparisjɔ̃] *nf* appearance,
apparition.

appartement [apartəmã] *nm* flat,
(*US*) apartment, suite, rooms.

appartenir [apartəni:r] *vi* to belong;
v imp to appertain (to à), rest
(with à).

appas [apɑ] *nm pl* charms.

appât [apɑ] *nm* bait, lure.

appâter [apɑte] *vt* to lure, bait.

appauvrir [apovri:r] *vt* to impoverish; *vr* to become poor(er).

appeau [apo] *nm* bird-call, decoy.

appel [apɛl] *nm* appeal, call, cry,
call-up, roll-call, muster; **aller,
renvoyer en —** to appeal; **—
d'incendie** fire-alarm.

appeler [aple] *vt* to call (for, in, to,
up); **en — à** to appeal to; **faire —**
to send for; *vr* to be called, named.

appendice [ap(p)ɛdis] *nm* appendix.

appendicite [ap(p)ɛdisit] *nf* appendicitis.

appentis [apãti] *nm* outhouse,
lean-to shed.

appesantir [apəzãti:r] *vt* to make
heavy, dull; *vr* to become heavy,
dwell (upon **sur**).

appétissant [apetisã] *a* appetizing.

appétit [apeti] *nm* appetite; **de bon
—** hearty appetite.

applaudir [aplodi:r] *vt* to applaud.

applaudissements [aplodismã] *nm
pl* applause.

applicable [aplikabl] *a* applicable.

application [aplikasjɔ̃] *nf* application, enforcement, diligence, concentration.

applique [aplik] *nf* bracket.

appliqué [aplike] *a* diligent, assiduous, applied.

appliquer [aplike] *vt* to apply, carry
out; *vr* to apply oneself (to à).

appoint [apwɛ̃] *nm* balance, odd
money, contribution; **faire l'—** to
tender exact amount, ' no change
given '.

appointements [apwɛtmã] *nm pl*
salary.

appontement [apɔ̃tmã] *nm* landing-
stage.

apport [apɔ:r] *nm* contribution,
share.

apporter [apɔrte] *vt* to bring (in,
forward, forth).

apposer [apoze] *vt* to affix.

apposition [apozisjɔ̃] *nf* apposition,
affixing.

appréciation [apresjasjɔ̃] *nf* appreciation, estimate, valuation.

apprécier [apresje] *vt* to appreciate,
estimate, value.

appréhender [apreãde] *vt* to apprehend.

appréhension [apreãsjɔ̃] *nf* apprehension.

apprendre [aprã:dr] *vt* to learn,
teach, inform, tell.

apprenti [aprãti] *n* apprentice.

apprentissage [aprãtisa:ʒ] *nm*
apprenticeship.

apprêté [aprɛte] *a* affected.

apprêter [aprɛte] *vt* to prepare,
dress; *vr* to get ready.

apprivoiser [aprivwaze] *vt* to tame,
domesticate.

approbateur, -trice [aprɔbatœ:r,
tris] *a* approving; *n* approver.

approbatif, -ive [aprɔbatif, i:v] *a*
approving.

approbation [aprɔbasjɔ̃] *nf* approbation, approval, sanction.

approche [aprɔʃ] *nf* approach.

approcher [aprɔʃe] *vt* to approach,
draw near; *vi* to approach, draw
near, border (on); *vr* to come near.

approfondi [aprɔfɔ̃di] *a* deep,
thorough, exhaustive.

approfondir [aprɔfɔ̃di:r] *vt* to
deepen, go deeply into, fathom.

approfondissement [aprɔfɔ̃dismã]
nm deepening, investigation.

approprié [aprɔprie] *a* appropriate,
suitable, proper.

approprier [aprɔprie] *vt* to appropriate, adapt.

approuver [apruve] *vt* to approve
of, favour, consent to.

approvisionnement [aprɔvizjɔnmã]
nm provisioning, victualling, supply,
stores, provisions.

approvisionner [aprɔvizjɔne] *vt* to
stock, supply; *vr* to lay in supplies,
get supplies.

approximatif, -ive [aprɔksimatif,
i:v] *a* approximate, rough.

approximation [aprɔksimasjɔ̃] *nf*
approximation.

appui [apɥi] *nm* support, prop,
stress, rest; **point d'—** strong point,
defended locality.

appuyer [apɥije] *vt* to support, prop,
favour, further; *vi* — **sur** dwell on,
stress, emphasize, press; *vr* to lean,
rest (on, against **sur**, **contre**),
depend, rely (on).

âpre [ɑ:pr] *a* rough, harsh, bitter,
stern, grim, keen.

après [aprɛ] *prep* after; **d'—** according to, from; *ad* afterwards; *cj*
— que after.

après-demain [aprɛdmɛ̃] *ad* the day
after tomorrow.

après-guerre [aprɛgɛ:r] *nm* post-
war period.

après-midi [aprɛmidi] *nm or f*
afternoon.

âpreté [ɑprɛte] *nf* roughness, harshness, bitterness, sternness, keenness, greed.

à-propos [aprɔpo] *nm* aptness, opportuneness.

apte [apt] *a* apt, qualified.

aptitude [aptityd] *nf* aptitude, proficiency.

apurement [apyrmɑ̃] *nm* — de comptes audit(ing).

apurer [apyre] *vt* to audit.

aquarelle [akwarel] *nf* water-colour.

aqueduc [ak(ə)dyk] *nm* aqueduct.

aqueux, -euse [akø, øːz] *a* aqueous, watery.

aquilin [akilɛ̃] *a* aquiline.

arabe [arab] *a* Arab, Arabian, Arabic; *n* Arab, Arabic.

arable [arabl] *a* arable.

arachide [araʃid] *nf* peanut.

araignée [arɛɲe] *nf* spider; — dans le plafond bee in the bonnet.

arbitrage [arbitraːʒ] *nm* arbitration, umpiring, refereeing.

arbitraire [arbitrɛːr] *a* arbitrary, high-handed.

arbitre [arbiːtr] *nm* arbitrator, umpire, referee; libre — freewill.

arbitrer [arbitre] *vt* to arbitrate, umpire, referee.

arborer [arbɔre] *vt* to hoist, raise, sport.

arbre [arbr] *nm* tree, shaft.

arbrisseau [arbriso] *nm* shrub.

arbuste [arbyst] *nm* bush.

arc [ark] *nm* bow, arch, arc; tir à l'— archery.

arcade [arkad] *nf* arcade.

arc-boutant [ar(k)butɑ̃] *nm* flying-buttress, stay.

arceau [arso] *nm* arch, hoop.

arc-en-ciel [arkɑ̃sjɛl] *nm* rainbow.

archaïsme [arkaism] *nm* archaism.

archange [arkɑ̃ːʒ] *nm* archangel.

arche [arʃ] *nf* ark, arch, span.

archéologie [arkeɔlɔʒi] *nf* archaeology.

archéologue [arkeɔlɔg] *nm* archaeologist.

archer [arʃe] *nm* archer.

archet [arʃe] *nm* bow.

archevêché [arʃəveʃe] *nm* archbishopric, archbishop's palace.

archevêque [arʃəveːk] *nm* archbishop.

archicomble [arʃikɔ̃bl] *a* packed.

archipel [arʃipɛl] *nm* archipelago.

architecte [arʃitɛkt] *nm* architect.

architecture [arʃitɛktyːr] *nf* architecture.

archives [arʃiːv] *nf pl* archives, records, Record Office.

arctique [arktik] *a* arctic.

ardemment [ardamɑ̃] *ad* ardently, eagerly.

ardent [ardɑ̃] *a* ardent, glowing, keen, eager, live.

ardeur [ardœːr] *nf* ardour, heat, glow, eagerness, zeal, enthusiasm, spirit.

ardoise [ardwaːz] *nf* slate.

ardu [ardy] *a* arduous, tough.

arène [arɛn] *nf* arena.

arête [arɛt] *nf* fishbone, ridge, edge.

argent [arʒɑ̃] *nm* silver, money; — comptant ready money, cash down.

argenté [arʒɑ̃te] *a* silver, silver-plated.

argenterie [arʒɑ̃tri] *nf* silver-plate.

argentin [arʒɑ̃tɛ̃] *a* silvery, silver-toned.

argile [arʒil] *nf* clay.

argot [argo] *nm* slang.

argument [argymɑ̃] *nm* argument, plea, summary.

argumentation [argymɑ̃tasjɔ̃] *nf* argumentation.

argumenter [argymɑ̃te] *vi* to argue.

argutie [argysi] *nf* quibble.

aride [arid] *a* arid, dry, barren.

aridité [aridite] *nf* aridity.

aristocrate [aristɔkrat] *n* aristocrat.

aristocratie [aristɔkrasi] *nf* aristocracy.

arithmétique [aritmetik] *a* arithmetical; *nf* arithmetic.

armateur [armatœːr] *nm* shipwright, shipowner.

armature [armatyːr] *nf* framework, mainstay, reinforcement, armature.

arme [arm] *nf* arm, weapon, branch of the army; maître d'—s fencing master; prise d'—s parade.

armée [arme] *nf* army, host; — de métier professional army; — de l'air Air Force; aux —s on active service.

armement [armamɑ̃] *nm* arming, fitting out, loading, equipment, crew; *pl* armaments.

armer [arme] *vt* to arm, strengthen, fit out, equip, load, commission, man.

armistice [armistis] *nm* armistice.

armoire [armwaːr] *nf* wardrobe, cupboard, press, closet.

armoiries [armwari] *nf pl* coat of arms, crest.

armure [armyːr] *nf* armour.

armurerie [armyr(ə)ri] *nf* armoury, arms factory.

armurier [armyrje] *nm* armourer, gunsmith.

arôme [aroːm] *nm* aroma.

arpenter [arpɑ̃te] *vt* to measure, survey, pace.

arqué [arke] *a* arched, curved, bow.

arquer [arke] *vt* to arch, bend.

arrache-pied [araʃpje] *ad* d'— steadily.

arracher [araʃe] *vt* to tear away (off, out, up), pull away (out, up), snatch.

arraisonner [arɛzɔne] *vt* to hail, stop and examine a ship.

arrangement [arɑ̃ʒmɑ̃] *nm* arrangement, order.

arranger [arɑ̃ʒe] *vt* to arrange, compose, settle; *vr* to manage, come to terms.

arrérages [arɛraːʒ] *nm pl* arrears.

arrestation [arɛstasjɔ̃] *nf* arrest, detention.

arrêt [arɛ] *nm* stop(ping), stoppage, detention, arrest, seizure, decree, judgment; — **facultatif** ' stop here if required '; **mandat d'—** warrant; **maison d'—** gaol.

arrêté [arɛte] *a* fixed; *nm* decision, decree, by(e)-law.

arrêter [arɛte] *vt* to stop, stem, check, clog, detain, arrest, decide; *vi* to halt, stop, draw up; *vr* to dwell (on **sur**), stop.

arrière [arjɛːr] *a* back, rear; *ad* backwards; **en — behind, in** arrears, back; **en — de behind;** **faire marche — to reverse;** *nm* rear, back part, full back; **à l'— in the rear, at the back,** behind, astern.

arrière-boutique [arjɛrbutik] *nf* back-shop.

arrière-bras [arjɛrbra] *nm* upper arm.

arrière-cour [arjɛrkuːr] *nf* backyard.

arrière-garde [arjɛrgard] *nf* rearguard.

arrière-goût [arjɛrgu] *nm* aftertaste, smack.

arrière-grand-père, -grand'mère [arjɛrgrɑ̃pɛːr, grɑ̃mɛːr] *n* great-grandfather, -grandmother.

arrière-pensée [arjɛrpɑ̃se] *nf* ulterior motive, mental reservation.

arrière-plan [arjɛrplɑ̃] *nm* background.

arrière-saison [arjɛrsɛzɔ̃] *nf* late autumn, (US) fall.

arrière-train [arjɛrtrɛ̃] *nm* hindquarters, hind-carriage.

arriéré [arjere] *a* in arrears, backward, old-fashioned.

arrimer [arime] *vt* to stow, trim.

arrivage [arivaːʒ] *nm* arrival, consignment.

arrivée [arive] *nf* arrival, coming, winning-post.

arriver [arive] *vi* to arrive, reach, get, succeed, happen, occur, come about.

arriviste [arivist] *n* careerist, go-getter.

arrogance [arɔgɑ̃ːs] *nf* arrogance, bumptiousness.

arrogant [arɔgɑ̃] *a* arrogant, bumptious, assuming.

s'arroger [sarɔʒe] *vr* to arrogate, assume as a right.

arrondir [arɔ̃diːr] *vt* to round (off), make round.

arrondissement [arɔ̃dismɑ̃] *nm* rounding (off), subdivision of a French department, municipal ward.

arrosage [arozaːʒ] *nm* watering, spraying.

arroser [aroze] *vt* to water, spray, sprinkle, baste.

arrosoir [arozwaːr] *nm* watering-can, -cart, sprinkler.

arsenal [arsənal] *nm* arsenal, naval dockyard.

arsenic [arsənik] *nm* arsenic

art [aːr] *nm* art, skill.

artère [artɛːr] *nf* artery, thoroughfare.

artériel, -elle [arterjɛl] *a* arterial.

artichaut [artiʃo] *nm* globe artichoke.

article [artikl] *nm* article, implement, paper; *pl* wares; —**s de Paris** fancy goods; **à l'— de la mort** at the point of death.

articulation [artikylasjɔ̃] *nf* articulation, joint.

articuler [artikyle] *vt* to articulate.

artifice [artifis] *nm* artifice, art, expedient, scheming; **feu d'— fireworks.**

artificiel, -elle [artifisjɛl] *a* artificial, imitation.

artillerie [artijri] *nf* artillery.

artimon [artimɔ̃] *nm* **mât d'—** mizzen-mast.

artisan [artizɑ̃] *nm* artisan, workman, maker.

artisanat [artizana] *nm* working classes.

artiste [artist] *a* artistic; *n* artist, performer.

artistique [artistik] *a* artistic.

aryen, -yenne [arjɛ̃, jɛn] *an* aryan.

as [ɑːs] *nm* ace, crack, swell.

asbeste [azbɛst] *nm* asbestos.

ascendance [as(s)ɑ̃dɑ̃s] *nf* ancestry.

ascendant [as(s)ɑ̃dɑ̃] *a* ascending, climbing; *nm* ascendancy; *pl* ancestry.

ascenseur [asɑ̃sœːr] *nm* lift.

ascension [asɑ̃sjɔ̃] *nf* ascent, ascension.

ascète [asɛt] *n* ascetic.

ascétique [asetik] *a* ascetic(al).

ascétisme [asetism] *nm* asceticism.

asepsie [asɛpsi] *nf* asepsis.

aseptique [asɛptik] *a* aseptic.

asiatique [azjatik] *a* asiatic, oriental.

Asie [azi] *nf* Asia.

asile [azil] *nm* shelter, refuge, sanctuary, home, almshouse; — **des** **pauvres** workhouse; — **d'aliénés** lunatic asylum.

aspect [aspɛ] *nm* aspect, appearance, look, sight.

asperge [aspɛrʒ] *nf* asparagus.

asperger [aspɛrʒe] *vt* to sprinkle, splash, spray.

aspérité [asperite] *nf* asperity, roughness, harshness.

asphalte [asfalt] *nm* asphalt, bitumen, pitch.

asphyxiant [asfiksjɑ̃] *a* asphyxiating, poison.

asphyxie [asfiksi] *nf* asphyxia.

asphyxier [asfiksje] *vt* to asphyxiate.

aspirant [aspirɑ̃] *a* sucking; *n* candidate, aspirant; *nm* midshipman.

aspirateur, -trice [aspiratœːr, tris]

a aspiratory; *nm* aspirator, vacuum cleaner.

aspiration [aspirasjɔ̃] *nf* aspiration, longing (for à), inhaling, suction, gasp.

aspirer [aspire] *vt* to aspire, long (for à), hanker (after à), inhale, suck up, aspirate.

aspirine [aspirin] *nf* aspirin.

assaillant [as(s)ajɑ̃] *nm* assailant.

assaillir [as(s)ajiːr] *vt* to assail.

assainir [aseniːr] *vt* to make healthier, cleanse.

assaisonnement [asεzɔnmɑ̃] *nm* seasoning, flavouring, dressing, relish, sauce.

assaisonner [asεzɔne] *vt* to season, flavour, dress.

assassin [asasɛ̃] *n* assassin, murderer.

assassinat [asasina] *nm* assassination, murder.

assassiner [asasine] *vt* to assassinate, murder.

assaut [aso] *nm* assault, onslaught, attack, bout; **emporter d'— to** storm; **troupes d'— shock troops.**

assécher [aseʃe] *vt* to drain, dry; *vir* to dry up.

assemblage [asɑ̃blaːʒ] *nm* collating, gathering, assembly, joining up.

assemblée [asɑ̃ble] *nf* assembly, meeting, gathering, convocation; **Assemblée Nationale** Lower Chamber of French Parliament.

assembler [asɑ̃ble] *vt* to assemble, gather, connect; *vr* to meet, assemble, flock.

assener [asəne] *vt* to deliver, deal, land (a blow).

assentiment [asɑ̃timɑ̃] *nm* assent.

asseoir [aswaːr] *vt* to set, lay, found; *vr* to sit down.

assermenter [asεrmɑ̃te] *vt* to swear in.

asservir [asεrviːr] *vt* to enslave.

asservissement [asεrvismɑ̃] *nm* enslavement.

assesseur [asεsœːr] *nm* assessor.

assez [ase] *ad* enough, rather, fairly.

assidu [asidy] *a* assiduous, sedulous, constant, regular.

assiduité [asidɥite] *nf* assiduity, application, regularity.

assiégeant [asjeʒɑ̃] *a* besieging; *nm* besieger.

assiéger [asjeʒe] *vt* to besiege, beleaguer.

assiette [asjεt] *nf* position, situation, set, foundation, plate; **n'être pas dans son —** to be out of sorts.

assignation [asiɲasjɔ̃] *nf* assignment, writ, subpoena.

assigner [asiɲe] *vt* to assign, allot, allocate, summon, serve a writ on.

assimiler [as(s)imile] *vt* to assimilate, digest.

assimilation [as(s)imilasjɔ̃] *nf* assimilation.

assis [asi] *a* seated, sitting, established, situated.

assise [asiːz] *nf* foundation, base, seating, course; *pl* assizes, sittings, sessions.

assistance [asistɑːs] *nf* assistance, relief, presence, audience.

assistant [asistɑ̃] *n* assistant, onlooker; **—e sociale** welfare worker; *pl* audience, those present.

assister [asiste] *vt* to assist, help; *vi* to be present, witness, attend.

association [asɔsjasjɔ̃] *nf* association, society, partnership.

associé [asɔsje] *n* partner, associate.

associer [asɔsje] *vt* to associate, band, club, connect; *vr* to participate (in à), enter into a partnership (with à).

assoiffé [aswafe] *a* thirsty.

assombrir [asɔ̃briːr] *vt* to darken, dim, cast a gloom over; *vr* to become dark, cloud (over), become sad.

assommant [asɔmɑ̃] *a* overwhelming, tiresome, deadly dull, humdrum, boring.

assommer [asɔme] *vt* to knock senseless, bludgeon, tire out, wear out, bore.

assommeur [asɔmœːr] *nm* slaughterer.

assommoir [asɔmwaːr] *nm* pole-axe, bludgeon, low tavern.

assomption [asɔ̃psjɔ̃] *nf* assumption.

assortiment [asɔrtimɑ̃] *nm* matching, sorting, assortment, set.

assortir [asɔrtiːr] *vt* to match, sort, assort, stock.

assoupi [asupi] *a* dozing.

assoupir [asupiːr] *vt* to send to sleep, allay; *vr* to doze (off), die away.

assoupissement [asupismɑ̃] *nm* drowsiness, allaying.

assourdir [asurdiːr] *vt* to deafen, stun, muffle, subdue, mute; *vr* to die away.

assourdissant [asurdisɑ̃] *a* deafening, stunning.

assouvir [asuviːr] *vt* to satisfy, slake, wreak; *vr* to become sated.

assujetti [asyʒeti] *a* subject (to), tied (to).

assujettir [asyʒetiːr] *vt* to subdue, govern.

assujettissant [asyʒetisɑ̃] *a* tying.

assumer [asyme] *vt* to assume.

assurance [asyrɑːs] *nf* assurance, confidence, insurance.

assurément [asyremɑ̃] *ad* certainly.

assuré [asyre] *a* sure, confident, certain, safe, steady; *n* policyholder.

assurer [asyre] *vt* to assure, ensure, make secure, insure; *vr* to make sure.

assureur [asyrœːr] *nm* underwriter.

astérisque [asterisk] *nm* asterisk.

asthmatique [asmatik] *a* asthmatic, wheezy.

asthme [asm] *nm* asthma.

asticot [astiko] *nm* maggot.

astiquer [astike] *vt* to polish.

astral [astral] *a* astral.

astre [astr] *nm* star.

astreindre [astrɛ̃:dr] *vt* to compel; *vr* to keep (to à).

astrologie [astrɔlɔʒi] *nf* astrology.

astrologue [astrɔlɔg] *nm* astrologer.

astronaute [astrɔnot] *nm* astronaut.

astronef [astrɔnɛf] *nm* space-ship.

astronome [astrɔnɔm] *nm* astronomer.

astronomie [astrɔnɔmi] *nf* astronomy.

astuce [astys] *nf* wile, astuteness, guile, gimmick.

astucieux, -euse [astysjø, ø:z] *a* wily, astute.

atelier [atəlje] *nm* workshop, studio.

atermoyer [atɛrmwaje] *vti* to put off, delay.

athée [ate] *a* atheistic, godless; *n* atheist.

athéisme [ateism] *nm* atheism.

athlète [atlɛt] *nm* athlete.

athlétique [atletik] *a* athletic.

athlétisme [atletism] *nm* athleticism, athletics.

atmosphère [atmɔsfɛ:r] *nf* atmosphere, environment.

atmosphérique [atmɔsferik] *a* atmospheric.

atome [ato:m] *nm* atom.

atomique [atɔmik] *a* atomic.

atomiser [atɔmize] *vt* to atomize, spray.

atomiseur [atɔmizœ:r] *nm* atomizer, spray.

atours [atu:r] *nm pl* finery, attire.

atout [atu] *nm* trump.

être [a:tr] *nm* hearth.

atroce [atrɔs] *a* atrocious, outrageous, heinous, terrible, excruciating, woeful.

atrocité [atrɔsite] *nf* atrocity.

s'attabler [satable] *vr* to sit down to table.

attachant [ataʃɑ̃] *a* interesting, attractive, winning.

attache [ataʃ] *nf* tie, fastening, connection, brace, leash, fastener, paper-clip, joint; **port d'—** home port.

attaché [ataʃe] *nm* attaché.

attachement [ataʃmɑ̃] *nm* attachment, adherence, fondness.

attacher [ataʃe] *vt* to attach, fasten, tie (up), connect, lash, strap, brace; *vr* to cling, stick become attached, apply oneself.

attaquable [atakabl] *a* assailable.

attaque [atak] *nf* attack, thrust, fit, stroke, seizure.

attaquer [atake] *vt* to attack, assault, tackle, attempt, (*cards*) lead; *vr* to attack, grapple (with à).

s'attarder [satarde] *vr* to linger, tarry.

atteindre [atɛ̃:dr] *vt* to reach, attain, hit, affect.

atteint [atɛ̃] *a* affected, attacked, hit.

atteinte [atɛ̃:t] *nf* reach, blow, attack; **porter —** à to hurt, damage.

attelage [atla:ʒ] *nm* harnessing, team, yoke, coupling.

atteler [atle] *vt* to harness, yoke, couple, team; *vr* to buckle to.

attelle [atɛl] *nf* splint.

attenant [atnɑ̃] *a* adjacent, adjoining.

attendant [atɑ̃dɑ̃] *ad* **en —** meanwhile, pending; *cj* **en — que** until.

attendre [atɑ̃:dr] *vt* to await, wait for, expect, look for; *vr* to expect.

attendri [atɑ̃dri] *a* fond, compassionate.

attendrir [atɑ̃dri:r] *vt* to soften, move, touch; *vr* to become tender, be moved.

attendrissant [atɑ̃drisɑ̃] *a* touching, affecting.

attendrissement [atɑ̃drismɑ̃] *nm* tender emotion, pity.

attendu [atɑ̃dy] *prep* considering, owing to, on account of; **— que** seeing that, whereas.

attentat [atɑ̃ta] *nm* attempt, outrage, murder bid.

attente [atɑ̃:t] *nf* wait, expectation, hope; **salle d'—** waiting-room; **être dans l'— de** to be awaiting.

attenter [atɑ̃te] *vt* make an attempt (on, against à).

attentif, -ive [atɑ̃tif, i:v] *a* attentive, careful, heedful, considerate.

attention [atɑ̃sjɔ̃] *nf* attention, care, regard mindfulness; **—! look out!** **faire — à** to pay attention to, heed.

attentionné [atɑ̃sjɔne] *a* thoughtful.

atténuant [atenɥɑ̃] *a* extenuating.

atténuation [atenɥasjɔ̃] *nf* extenuation, qualification, understatement.

atténuer [atenɥe] *vt* to attenuate, extenuate, mitigate, qualify, understate, subdue, dim; *vr* to lessen, diminish.

atterrer [atere] *vt* to overwhelm, fell, stun.

atterrir [atɛri:r] *vi* to ground, alight, land; *vt* to run ashore, beach.

atterrissage [atɛrisa:ʒ] *nm* grounding, landing.

attestation [atɛstasjɔ̃] *nf* attestation, voucher.

attester [atɛste] *vt* to attest, testify, vouch.

attiédir [atjedi:r] *vt* to make tepid, lukewarm.

attifer [atife] *vtr* to dress up.

attirail [atira:j] *nm* outfit, tackle, gear, show.

attirance [atirɑ̃:s] *nf* attraction, lure.

attirant [atirɑ̃] *a* attractive, engaging.

attirer [atire] *vt* to attract, draw, entice, inveigle.

attiser [atize] *vt* to stir (up), poke (up).

attitude [atityd] *nf* attitude.

attouchement [atuʃmɑ̃] *nm* touch(ing), contact.

attraction [atraksjɔ̃] *nf* attraction, attractiveness; *pl* variety show.

attrait [atrɛ] *nm* attraction, allurement, enticement, charm.

attrape [atrap] *nf* trap, snare, trick, catch.

attrape-mouches [atrapmuʃ] *nm* fly-paper.

attrape-nigaud [atrapnigo] *nm* booby-trap.

attraper [atrape] *vt* to catch, trick, get, seize, scold.

attrayant [atrejɑ̃] *a* attractive.

attribuer [atribɥe] *vt* to attribute, ascribe, assign, put down (to à); *vr* to assume.

attribut [atriby] *nm* attribute.

attribution [atribysjɔ̃] *nf* attribution, allocation, award, conferment; *pl* powers, functions.

attristé [atriste] *a* saddened, sorrowful.

attrister [atriste] *vt* to sadden; *vr* to grow sad.

attrition [atrisjɔ̃] *nf* attrition.

attroupement [atrupmɑ̃] *nm* mob.

attrouper [atrupe] *vt* to gather, collect; *vr* to flock, form into a mob, crowd.

au [o] = à + le.

aubaine [obɛn] *nf* windfall, godsend.

aube [oːb] *nf* early dawn, paddle, blade.

aubépine [obepin] *nf* hawthorn, may.

auberge [oberʒ] *nf* inn; — de la jeunesse youth hostel.

aubergine [oberʒin] *nf* egg-plant, aubergine.

aubergiste [oberʒist] *n* innkeeper.

aucun [okœ̃] *pn* anyone, no one, nobody; *pl* some people; *a* any, not any.

aucunement [okynmɑ̃] *ad* not at all, in no way.

audace [odas] *nf* audacity, boldness, daring, hardihood.

audacieux, -euse [odasjø, øːz] *a* audacious, bold, daring, dashing, impudent.

au-delà [od(ə)la] *ad* beyond; *nm* the after-life.

au-dessous [odsu] *ad* underneath, below; *prep* — de below, under.

au-dessus [odsy] *ad* above, over (head); *prep* — de above, over, beyond.

au-devant [odvɑ̃] *ad* aller — de to go to meet.

audience [odjɑ̃ːs] *nf* audience, hearing; lever l'— to close the session, sitting.

auditeur, -trice [oditœːr, tris] *n* listener.

audition [odisjɔ̃] *nf* audition, hearing.

auditoire [oditwaːr] *nm* audience.

auge [oːʒ] *nf* trough.

augmentation [ɔgmɑ̃tasjɔ̃] *nf* increase, rise.

augmenter [ɔgmɑ̃te] *vt* to augment, increase, add, raise; *vr* to increase, rise.

augure [ɔgyːr] *nm* augury, omen; de mauvais — unpropitious, inauspicious.

augurer [ɔgyre] *vt* to augur, promise.

auguste [ɔgyst] *a* august, majestic.

aujourd'hui [oʒurdɥi] *ad* today; d'— en huit today week.

aumône [omoːn] *nf* alms, charity.

aumônier [omonje] *nm* almoner, chaplain.

aune [oːn] *nf* alder.

auparavant [oparavɑ̃] *ad* before, first.

auprès [oprɛ] *ad* hard by, close at hand; *prep* — de close (to, by), near, beside, at, with, in comparison with.

auquel [okɛl] = à + lequel.

auréole [ɔreɔl] *nf* halo.

auriculaire [ɔrikylɛːr] *nm* little finger.

aurore [ɔrɔːr] *nf* dawn.

ausculter [ɔskylte] *vt* to sound.

auspice [ɔspis] *nm* auspice, omen.

aussi [osi] *ad* as, so, also, too; *cj* therefore, so.

aussitôt [osito] *ad* at once, immediately; *cj* — que as soon as; — dit, — fait no sooner said than done.

austère [ɔstɛːr] *a* austere, severe, stern.

austérité [ɔsterite] *nf* austerity, severity, sternness.

Australie [ɔstrali] *nf* Australia.

australien, -ienne [ɔstraljɛ̃, jɛn] *an* Australian.

autant [otɑ̃] *ad* as much, so much, as many, so many; — que as much as, as many as, as far as; d'— que, d'— plus que more especially as, all the more . . . as.

autel [otɛl] *nm* altar.

auteur [otœːr] *nm* author, writer, promoter, originator, perpetrator; femme — authoress; droits d'— royalties.

authenticité [otɑ̃tisite] *nf* authenticity.

authentique [otɑ̃tik] *a* authentic, genuine.

auto [oto] *nf* motor car.

autobiographie [otɔbjɔgrafi] *nf* autobiography.

autobus [otɔbyːs] *nm* motor (omni)bus.

autocar [otɔkaːr] *nm* motor coach, motor charabanc.

autochtone [otɔktoːn, -tɔn] *a* native, indigenous.

autocrate [otɔkrat] *n* autocrat; *a* autocratic.

autocratie [otɔkrasi] *nf* autocracy.

autocratique [otɔkratik] *a* autocratic.

autodémarreur [otodemarœːr] *nm* self-starter.

autodétermination [otodeterminasjɔ̃] *nf* (*govt*) self-determination.

autodidacte [otodidakt] *a* self-taught, -educated; *nm* autodidact.

autodrome [otodrom, -droːm] *nm* motor-racing track.

autographe [otograf] *nm* autograph.

autographier [otografje] *vt* to autograph.

automate [otomat] *nm* automaton, robot.

automatique [otomatik] *a* automatic, automaton-like.

automnal [otomnal] *a* autumnal.

automne [oton] *nm* autumn, (US) fall; *a* d'—autumnal.

automobile [otomobil] *a* motor; *nf* automobile, motor car; **salon de l'**— motor show.

automobilisme [otomobilism] *nm* motoring.

automobiliste [otomobilist] *n* motorist.

automoteur [otomotœːr] *a* self-propelling.

autonome [otonom] *a* autonomous, self-governing.

autonomie [otonomi] *nf* autonomy, home-rule.

autopsie [otopsi] *nf* autopsy, post-mortem examination.

autorail [otoraːj] *nm* rail-car.

autorisation [otorizasjɔ̃, ot-] *nf* authorization, permit, licence.

autorisé [otorize, ot-] *a* authorized, authoritative.

autoriser [otorize, ot-] to authorize, empower, warrant, sanction, license.

autoritaire [otoriteːr, ot-] *a* authoritative, domineering.

autorité [otorite, ot-] *nf* authority, warrant; **faire** — to be an authority; **qui fait** — authoritative.

autoroute [otorut] *nf* motorway.

auto-stop [otostop] *nm* hitch-hiking.

autour [otuːr] *ad* round, about; *prep* — **de** round.

autre [oːtr] *a pn* other; *a* further, different; **d'un moment à l'**— any moment; **de temps à** — now and again; **nous** —s **Francais** we French; **l'un et l'**— both; **les uns . . . les** —s some . . . others; — **chose** something else; **quelqu'un d'**— someone else; **j'en ai vu bien d'**—s that's nothing;— **part** elsewhere.

autrefois [otrəfwa] *ad* formerly, in the past.

autrement [otrəmã] *ad* otherwise, else, in a different way.

Autriche [otriʃ] *nf* Austria.

autrichien, -ienne [otriʃjɛ̃, jɛn] *a n* Austrian.

autruche [otryʃ] *nf* ostrich.

autrui [otrɥi] *pn indef* others, other people.

aux [o] = à + les.

auxiliaire [oksiljeːr, o-] *a* auxiliary, sub-; *nm* auxiliary.

auxquels [okel] = à + lesquels.

aval [aval] *nm* lower part of river; *ad* **en** — downstream; *prep* **en** — **de** below.

avalanche [avalɑ̃ːʃ] *nf* avalanche.

avaler [avale] *vt* to swallow, drink up, gulp down, stomach; — **une insulte** to pocket an insult, affront.

avance [avɑ̃ːs] *nf* advance, start, lead, drive, dash; loan; **à l', d', par** — beforehand, in advance; **être en** — to be fast, before time, ahead.

avancé [avɑ̃se] *a* advanced, forward, onward, well on, high; **vous voilà bien** — much good that has done you.

avancement [avɑ̃smã] *nm* advancing, putting forward, furtherance, rise, promotion, advancement.

avancer [avɑ̃se] *vt* to advance, put (forward, on), carry on, promote; *vi* to move forward, advance, get on, be fast, be ahead of time; *vr* to advance, make one's way, progress, jut out.

avant [avɑ̃] *prep* before; — **peu** presently; *ad* before, far (into), deep, further (in, back); **en** — before, forward, in front, ahead, onward; *cj* — **que** before; *a* fore-; *nm* bow, forward, front.

avantage [avɑ̃taːʒ] *nm* advantage; **tirer** — **de** to turn to account.

avantager [avɑ̃taʒe] *vt* to favour, improve.

avantageux, -euse [avɑ̃taʒø, øːz] *a* advantageous, beneficial, favourable, becoming, self-satisfied.

avant-bras [avɑ̃bra] *nm* forearm.

avant-corps [avɑ̃koːr] *nm* fore-part.

avant-cour [avɑ̃kuːr] *nf* forecourt.

avant-coureur [avɑ̃kurœːr] *a* precursory; *nm* forerunner.

avant-dernier, -ière [avɑ̃dɛrnje, jɛːr] *a* last but one.

avant-garde [avɑ̃gard] *nf* van (guard), advanced guard, avant-garde.

avant-goût [avɑ̃gu] *nm* foretaste, earnest.

avant-guerre [avɑ̃gɛːr] *nm* pre-war period.

avant-hier [avɑ̃tjɛːr] *ad* day before yesterday.

avant-plan [avɑ̃plɑ̃] *nm* foreground.

avant-port [avɑ̃poːr] *nm* outer harbour.

avant-poste [avɑ̃post] *nm* outpost.

avant-première [avɑ̃prəmjeːr] *nf* dress rehearsal.

avant-propos [avɑ̃propo] *nm* preface.

avare [avaːr] *a* miserly, tight-fisted, chary; *nm* miser.

avarice [avaris] *nf* avarice, miserliness, closeness.

avaricieux, -euse [avarisjø, jøːz] *a* avaricious, mean.

avarie [avari] *nf* damage.

avarier [avarje] *vt* to damage; *vr* to deteriorate.

avatar [avataːr] *nm* avatar; *pl* ups and downs.

avec [avɛk] *prep* with; — **ça!** nonsense; **et — ça Monsieur?** do you require anything else? **d'—** from; *ad* with it, with them.

avenant [avnã] *a* comely, prepossessing, buxom; **à l'—** in keeping, to match.

avènement [avɛnmã] *nm* advent, accession.

avenir [avniːr] *nm* future; **à l'—** henceforth, hereafter.

aventure [avãtyːr] *nf* adventure, luck, love-affair; **à l'—** at random, aimlessly; **d'—** by chance; **dire, tirer la bonne —** to tell fortunes.

aventurer [avãtyre] *vtr* to venture, risk.

aventureux, -euse [avãtyrø, øːz] *a* adventurous, venturesome, reckless, risky.

aventurier, -ière [avãtyrje, jɛːr] *n* adventurer, adventuress.

avenu [avny] *a* **non —** cancelled, void.

avenue [avny] *nf* avenue, drive, walk.

avéré [avere] *a* established, proved, authenticated.

averse [avɛrs] *nf* shower of rain, downpour.

aversion [avɛrsjɔ̃] *nf* aversion, dislike, repulsion.

averti [avɛrti] *a* experienced, well-informed, knowing.

avertir [avɛrtiːr] *vt* to warn, caution, give notice (of).

avertissement [avɛrtismã] *nm* warning, notice, caution; **sans — préalable** at a moment's notice.

avertisseur [avɛrtisœːr] *nm* alarm, warning, motor horn, call-boy.

aveu [avø] *nm* confession, avowal, admission, consent.

aveugle [avœgl] *a* blind, sightless; **à l'—** blindly, wildly; *nm* blind person.

aveuglement [avœgləmã] *nm* blindness.

aveuglément [avœglemã] *ad* blindly.

aveugler [avœgle] *vt* to blind, dazzle, hoodwink, plug.

aveuglette [avœglɛt] *ad* **à l'—** blind(ly).

aviateur, -trice [avjatœr, tris] *n* aviator, flyer.

aviation [avjasjɔ̃] *nf* aviation, air force.

avide [avid] *a* avid, greedy, grasping, eager (for de).

avidité [avidite] *nf* avidity, greed, eagerness.

avilir [aviliːr] *vt* to debase, depreciate; *vr* to lower oneself, stoop, lose value.

avilissement [avilismã] *nm* abase-

ment, degradation, depreciation.

avion [avjɔ̃] *nm* aeroplane, aircraft; **— de bombardment** bomber; **— de chasse, de combat** fighter; **— de ligne** airliner; **— en remorque** glider; **— à réaction** jet plane; **par — by** airmail.

aviron [avirɔ̃] *nm* oar, rowing.

avis [avi] *nm* opinion, advice, judgment, notice, warning; **à mon — to** my mind; **changer d'— to** change one's mind.

avisé [avize] *a* far-seeing, wary, canny, shrewd, advised.

aviser [avize] *vt* to warn, perceive; *vi* to see about (à); *vr* to take it into one's head.

avocat [avɔka] *nm* barrister, counsel, advocate.

avoine [avwan] *nf* oats; **folle — wild** oats.

avoir [avwaːr] *vt* to have, possess, get, obtain; **— vingt ans** to be twenty years old; **qu'avez-vous?** what is the matter with you? **en — à, contre** qn. to bear s.o. a grudge; **y — v** *imp* to be; **qu'est-ce qu'il y a?** what's up, what's the matter?; **il y a sept ans** seven years ago; *nm* property, possessions, balance in hand; **doit et —** debit and credit.

avoisinant [avwazinã] *a* neighbouring.

avoisiner [avwazine] *vt* to be near, border on.

avorter [avɔrte] *vi* to abort, miscarry.

avortement [avɔrtmã] *nm* abortion, miscarriage.

avorton [avɔrtɔ̃] *nm* undersized, stunted creature.

avoué [avwe] *a* professed; *nm* solicitor, (US) attorney.

avouer [avwe] *vt* to avow, confess, acknowledge.

avril [avril] *nm* April; **un poisson d'—** an April fool.

axe [aks] *nm* axis, spindle.

axiome [aksjoːm] *nm* axiom.

azimut [azimyt] *nm* azimuth, bearing, (sl) direction.

azote [azɔt] *nm* nitrogen.

azotique [azɔtik] *a* nitric.

azur [azyːr] *nm* azure, blue.

azyme [azim] *a* unleavened; *nm* unleavened bread.

B

baba [baba] *nm* sponge-cake; *a* dumbfounded.

babeurre [babœːr] *nm* buttermilk.

babil [babi(l)] *nm* prattling, twittering.

babillard [babijaːr] *a* talkative, babbling; *n* chatterbox.

babiller [babije] *vi* to chatter, babble, prattle.

babines [babin] *nf pl* chops, drooping lips.

babiole [babjɔl] *nf* bauble, curio, trinket, frippery.

bâbord [babɔːr] *nm* port (side).

babouin [babwɛ̃] *nm* baboon.

bac [bak] *nm* ferryboat, tub.

bâche [baːʃ] *nf* tarpaulin, awning, cistern; **— de campement** ground-sheet.

bachelier, -ière [baʃəlje, jɛːr] *n* pre-university student.

bâcher [baʃe] *vt* to cover with a tarpaulin.

bachot [baʃo] *nm* baccalauréat, punt.

bacille [basil] *nm* bacillus, germ.

bâcler [bakle] *vt* to bolt, bar, block, scamp, dash off.

bactériologie [bakterjɔlɔʒi] *nf* bacteriology.

badaud [bado] *a* idle; *n* stroller, idler.

badauder [badode] *vi* to saunter, idle about.

badigeon [badiʒɔ̃] *nm* distemper, whitewash brush.

badigeonner [badiʒɔne] *vt* to distemper, colour-wash, paint.

badin [badɛ̃] *a* playful, jocular, waggish; *n* joker, wag.

badinage [badinaːʒ] *nm* bantering, joking.

badine [badin] *nf* switch, cane.

badiner [badine] *vt* to tease, banter; *vi* to joke, trifle, banter.

bafoué [bafwe] *a* scorned, discomfited.

bafouer [bafwe] *vt* to scoff, jeer at, sneer at.

bafouiller [bafuje] *vti* to stammer, splutter, gabble.

bâfrer [bafre] *vt* to gobble, guzzle; *vi* to gormandize; *vr* to stuff.

bagage [bagaːʒ] *nm* baggage; *pl* luggage; **plier —** to pack up, clear out.

bagarre [bagaːr] *nf* brawl, disturbance, affray, scrap.

bagatelle [bagatɛl] *nf* trifle.

bagnard [baɲaːr] *n* convict.

bagne [baɲ] *nm* prison.

bagnole [baɲɔl] *nf* worn-out car, car.

bagout [bagu] *nm* **avoir du —** to have the gift of the gab.

bague [bag] *nf* ring, cigar-band.

baguenauder [bagnode] *vi* to waste time, trifle.

baguette [bagɛt] *nf* wand, rod, stick, pointer, beading, long loaf.

bahut [bay] *nm* (*fam*) cupboard, trunk, chest; school.

bai [bɛ] *a* (*colour*) bay.

baie [bɛ] *nf* bay bight. berry, bay-window.

baignade [bɛɲad] *nf* bathe, bathing-place.

baigner [bɛɲe] *vt* to bathe, bath, wash; *vi* to soak, steep; *vr* to take a bath, bathe welter.

baigneur, -euse [bɛɲœːr, øːz] *n* bather. bathing attendant.

baignoire [bɛɲwaːr] *nf* bath, (*theatre*) pit-box.

bail [baːj] *nm* lease.

bâillement [bajmɑ̃] *nm* yawn(ing), gaping.

bâiller [baje] *vi* to yawn, gape, be ajar.

bailleur [bajœːr] *nm* lessor; **— de fonds** money-lender, sleeping-partner.

bâillon [bajɔ̃] *nm* gag.

bâillonner [bajɔne] *vt* to gag, muzzle.

bain [bɛ̃] *nm* bath, bathe, dip; **—s de mer** sea-bathing.; **—(s) de soleil** sunbath(ing).

bain-marie [bɛ̃mari] *nm* double saucepan water-bottle.

baïonnette [bajɔnɛt] *nf* bayonet.

baiser [bɛze] *vt* to kiss; *nm* kiss.

baisse [bɛs] *nf* fall, drop. ebb, abatement.

baisser [bɛse] *vt* to lower, let down, turn down; *vi* to fall, go down, sink, droop, slump; *vr* to stoop.

baissier [bɛsje] *nm* (*Stock Exchange*) bear.

bajoue [baʒu] *nf* cheek, chap, chop.

bal [bal] *nm* ball, dance.

balade [balad] *nf* amble, drive, stroll.

balader [balade] *vir* to go for a stroll, a drive.

baladeuse [baladøːz] *nf* handcart, trailer, inspection-lamp.

baladin [baladɛ̃] *nm* buffoon.

balafre [balafr] *nf* gash, cut, scar.

balafrer [balafre] *vt* to gash, scar, slash.

balai [balɛ] *nm* brush, broom.

balance [balɑ̃ːs] *nf* balance, scale(s), suspense; **faire la —** to strike the balance.

balancer [balɑ̃se] *vt* to balance, swing, rock; *vi* to swing, dangle, waver, hesitate; *vr* to sway. swing, rock.

balancier [balɑ̃sje] *nm* pendulum, balance-wheel, beam, balancing-pole.

balançoire [balɑ̃swaːr] *nf* swing, seesaw.

balayage [balɛjaːʒ] *nm* sweeping, (*radar*) scanning.

balayer [balɛje] *vt* to sweep (out, away, up), scour, throw out.

balayeur, -euse [balɛjœːr, øːz] *nmf* sweeper, cleaner, scavenger; *nf* carpet-sweeper.

balayures [balɛjyːr] *nf pl* sweepings.

balbutier [balbysje] *vti* to stammer, stutter, falter.

balcon [balkɔ̃] *nm* balcony, dress-circle.

baldaquin [baldakɛ̃] *nm* canopy.

baleine [balɛn] *nf* whale, whalebone, rib.

baleinière [balɛnjɛːr] *nf* whaleboat.

balise [baliːz] *nf* beacon, seamark, groundlight. radiosignal.

balistique [balistik] *a* ballistic; *nf* ballistics.

baliverne [balivɛrn] *nf* idle story; *pl* balderdash, rubbish.

ballade [balad] *nf* ballad.

ballant [balɑ̃] *a* dangling.

ballast [balast] *nm* ballast, bottom.

balle [bal] *nf* ball, bullet, franc, bale, pack, chaff, husk; **avoir la — belle** to have the ball at one's feet; **c'est un enfant de la —** he has been brought up in the trade.

ballet [balɛ] *nm* ballet (dancing).

ballon [balɔ̃] *nm* balloon, football; **lancer un — d'essai** to fly a kite.

balloner [balɔne] *vir* to swell, balloon out, distend, bulge.

ballot [balo] *nm* bundle, bale, kitbag.

ballotage [balɔtaːʒ] *nm* shaking, tossing, second ballot.

balloter [balɔte] *vt* to shake, toss about, buffet; *vi* to toss, shake, rattle, swing.

balnéaire [balneɛːr] *a* **station —** seaside resort.

balourd [baluːr] *a* uncouth, clumsy, awkward; *n* awkward person, yokel, dullard.

balourdise [balurdiːz] *nf* clumsiness, stupid mistake.

baluchon [balyʃɔ̃] *nm* bundle, kit.

balustrade [balystrad] *nf* balustrade, rail.

balustre [balystr] *nm* baluster; *pl* banisters.

bambin [bɑ̃bɛ̃] *n* little child, urchin, baby.

bamboche [bɑ̃bɔʃ] *nf* puppet, under-sized person, carousal, spree.

bambou [bɑ̃bu] *nm* bamboo.

ban [bɑ̃] *nm* ban, proclamation, round of cheers, banishment; *pl* banns; **mettre au — to banish, ostracize.

banal [banal] *a* commonplace, hackneyed, trite, casual.

banalité [banalite] *nf* triteness, commonplace remark.

banane [banan] *nf* banana.

bananier [bananje] *nm* banana-tree.

banc [bɑ̃] *nm* bench, form, seat, bed, pew, layer, shoal; **— des accusés** dock; **— de sable** sandbank.

bancal [bɑ̃kal] *a* bow-legged, rickety.

banco [bɑ̃ko] *nm* swish, baked mud, (*for building*) clay.

bandage [bɑ̃daːʒ] *nm* bandaging, bandage, binder, truss, binding.

bande [bɑ̃ːd] *nf* band, group, gang, flock, shoal, stripe, belt, shaft, wrapper, cushion, reel, film; **donner de la —** (*of ship*) to list.

bandeau [bɑ̃do] *nm* headband, bandeau, bandage.

bander [bɑ̃de] *vt* to bind up, bandage, stretch, bend; *vr* to band together; **— les yeux à** to blindfold.

banderole [bɑ̃drɔl] *nf* streamer, shoulder-belt, sling.

bandit [bɑ̃di] *nm* bandit, gangster, rascal.

bandoulière [bɑ̃duljɛːr] *nf* bandolier, shoulder-belt.

banlieue [bɑ̃ljø] *nf* suburb.

banne [ban] *nf* hamper, awning, coal-cart.

banneau [bano] *nm* fruit-basket, hamper.

bannière [banjɛːr] *nf* banner.

banni [bani] *a* outlawed, exiled; *n* outlaw, exile.

bannir [baniːr] *vt* to outlaw, banish.

bannissement [banismɑ̃] *nm* exile, banishment.

banque [bɑ̃ːk] *nf* bank, banking.

banqueroute [bɑ̃krut] *nf* bankruptcy; **faire —** to go bankrupt.

banquet [bɑ̃kɛ] *nm* banquet, feast.

banquette [bɑ̃kɛt] *nf* seat, bench.

banquier, -ière [bɑ̃kje, jɛːr] *a* banking; *n* banker.

banquise [bɑ̃kiːz] *nf* ice-field, -pack, -flow.

baptême [batɛːm] *nm* baptism, christening; *a* **de —** baptismal, maiden.

baptiser [batize] *vt* to baptize, christen.

baquet [bakɛ] *nm* tub, bucket.

bar [baːr] *nm* bar, pub; sea-dace.

baragouiner [baragwine] *vti* to jabber, gibber.

baraque [barak] *nf* hut, booth, stall.

baraquement [barakmɑ̃] *nm* hut, lodging in huts; *pl* hutments.

baratte [barat] *nf* churn.

baratter [barate] *vt* to churn.

barbare [barbaːr] *a* barbarous, cruel, barbaric; *n* barbarian.

barbarie [barbari] *nf* barbarity, barbarousness, barbarism.

barbe [barb] *nf* beard, whiskers; **se faire la —** to shave; **rire dans sa —** to laugh up one's sleeve.

barbelé [barbəle] *a* barbed.

barbiche [barbiʃ] *nf* goatee beard.

barboter [barbɔte] *vt* to splash up and down; *vi* to paddle, flounder, splash about.

barbouillage [barbujaːʒ] *nm* smearing, scrawl, daubing, scribble, scribbling.

barbouiller [barbuje] *vt* to smear, smudge, dirty.

barbu [barby] *a* bearded.

barbue [barby] *nf* brill.

bard [baːr] *nm* hand-trolley.

barde [bard] *nf* pack-saddle, slice of bacon.

barder [barde] *vt* to carry on a hand-barrow, bard; *vi* to rage; **ça va —** there will be ructions.

barème [barɛːm] *nm* ready-reckoner, scale.

baril [bari] *nm* barrel, cask.

barillet [barijɛ] *nm* keg, drum, cylinder.

bariolé [barjɔle] *a* multi-coloured, motley, gaudy.

baromètre [barɔmɛtr] *nm* weather glass.

baroque [barɔk] *a* odd, quaint; *nm* baroque style.

barque [bark] *nf* boat, fishing-smack.

barrage [bɑraːʒ] *nm* road-block, barrier, dam, weir, (*sport*) replay.

barre [baːr] *nf* iron bar, wooden batten, rod, tiller, helm, stroke, (*law courts*) bar, rail, rung, surf, undertow; — **des témoins** witness-box; **homme de** — coxswain, helmsman.

barreau [baro] *nm* (*law courts*) bar, rail, rung; *pl* (*prison*) bars.

barrer [bare] *vt* to bar, block, dam, obstruct, cross out, steer; — **un chèque** to cross a cheque; **rue barrée** no thoroughfare.

barrette [barɛt] *nf* biretta, hairslide.

barreur [barœːr] *nm* helmsman, coxswain.

barricade [barikad] *nf* barricade.

barricader [barikade] *vt* to barricade.

barrière [barjɛːr] *nf* gate, toll-gate, bar, rail.

barrique [barik] *nf* large barrel, cask, hogshead.

baryton [baritɔ̃] *nm* baritone.

bas, -se [bɑ, bɑːs] *a* low, base, deep, mean, lower; *ad* low, quietly; *nm* lower part, end; bottom, stocking; *pl* hose; **en** — downstairs, below; **en** — **de** at the foot of; **à** — down (with); **mettre** — to lay down, bring forth.

basalte [bazalt] *nm* basalt.

basaner [bazane] *vt* to tan; *vr* to become tanned.

bas-bout [babu] *nm* bottom, lower end.

bas-côté [bakote] *nm* aisle, lay-by.

bascule [baskyl] *nf* seesaw, weigh-bridge, rocker; **chaise à** — rocking-chair; **wagon à** — tip-wagon.

basculer [baskyle] *vt* to rock, swing; *vti* to dip, tip.

base [bɑːz] *nf* foundation, basis, foot, root; **de** — basic; **sans** — unfounded.

baser [baze] *vt* to base, found; *vr* to be founded.

bas-fond [bafɔ̃] *nm* low ground, swamp, shoal, deep pool; *pl* riffraff, dregs.

basilique [bazilik] *nf* basilica.

basque [bask] *nf* tail.

basse [bɑːs] *nf* bass.

basse-cour [baskuːr] *nf* farmyard.

bassesse [basɛs] *nf* lowness, vileness, baseness.

basse-fosse [basfoːs] *nf* dungeon.

bassin [basɛ̃] *nm* basin, pond, ornamental lake, dock; — **houiller** coalfield.

bassine [basin] *nf* pan.

bât [bɑ] *nm* pack-saddle; **cheval de** — pack-horse.

bataille [batɑːj] *nf* battle, contest.

batailleur, -euse [batajœːr, øːz] *a* pugnacious, cantankerous, quarrelsome.

bataillon [batajɔ̃] *nm* battalion.

bâtard [bɑtaːr] *an* bastard, mongrel.

bateau [bato] *nm* boat, vessel; — **-école** training ship; — **-feu** light ship; — **pétrolier** tanker.

bateleur, -euse [batlœːr, øːz] *n* juggler, mountebank.

batelier, -ière [batəlje, jɛːr] *n* boatman, -woman, ferryman, -woman, bargee.

bâter [bate] *vt* to put a pack-saddle on.

bath [bat] *a* (*fam*) ripping, topping.

batifoler [batifole] *vi* to frolic, lark.

bâtiment [bɑtimɑ̃] *nm* building (trade), edifice, ship.

bâtir [bɑtiːr] *vt* to build, erect.

bâtisse [bɑtis] *nf* ramshackle building, masonry.

batiste [batist] *nf* cambric.

bâton [bɑtɔ̃] *nm* stick staff, baton, pole, truncheon; **à** — **s rompus** desultory, by fits and starts.

bâtonner [bɑtɔne] *v* to beat, whip, cane.

battage [batɑːʒ] *nm* beating, threshing, churning, boosting.

battant [batɑ̃] *a* beating, driving, pelting, banging; **porte** — **e** swing-door; *nm* bell-clapper, table, counter top.

batte [bat] *nf* beetle, mallet.

battement [batmɑ̃] *nm* beating, stamping, flapping, banging, fluttering, tapping, throbbing, margin (of time), interval.

batterie [batri] *nf* beat of drums, roll of drums, artillery battery; set; — **de cuisine** set of kitchen utensils.

batteur, -euse [batœːr, øːz] *nf* threshing machine, egg whisk; *nm* beater, thresher.

battre [batr] *vt* to beat, thrash, thresh batter, defeat, churn, whisk, (*flag*) fly, shuffle; *vi* to beat, throb, belt, flap, bang; — **la campagne** to scour the countryside, to be delirious; — **des mains** to clap one's hands; *vr* to fight.

battu [baty] *a* beaten, wrought; **avoir les yeux** — **s** to have circles round one's eyes.

battue [baty] *nf* beat, round-up.

baudet [bodɛ] *nm* donkey.

baudrier [bodrije] *nm* shoulder-belt, cross-belt.

bauge [boːʒ] *nf* lair, hole, squirrel's nest, pigsty.

baume [boːm] *nm* balm, balsam.

bauxite [boksit] *nf* bauxite.

bavard [bavaːr] *a* talkative, garrulous; *n* chatterbox, gossip.

bavardage [bavardaːʒ] *nm* chattering, gossip.

bavarder [bavarde] *vi* to gossip, chatter.

bave [ba:v] *nf* froth, foam, slaver, slime.

baver [bave] *vi* to slaver, dribble, foam, run.

bavette [bavɛt] *nf* bib.

baveur, -euse [bavœːr, øːz] *a* slavering, drivelling; *nm* slobberer.

baveux, -euse [bavø, øːz] *a* slobbery, juicy.

bavure [bavyːr] *nf* burr, blot, smudge.

bayer [baje] *vi* — aux corneilles to gape at the moon.

bazar [bazaːr] *nm* bazaar, cheap stores; **tout le** — the whole caboodle.

béant [beɑ̃] *a* gaping, yawning.

béat [bea] *a* smug, complacent.

béatitude [beatityd] *nf* bliss, complacency.

beau, belle [bo, bɛl] *a* lovely, beautiful, fair, fine, handsome, noble; **il en a fait de belles** he has been up to some nice things; **bel et bien** well and truly, fairly; **bel et bon** all very well; **l'échapper belle** to have a narrow escape; **il avait beau faire** in spite of all he did.

beaucoup [boku] *ad* (very) much, a lot, a good deal, (very) many, lots.

beau-fils [bofis] *nm* son-in-law, stepson.

beau-frère [bofrɛːr] *nm* brother-in-law, stepbrother.

beau-père [bopɛːr] *nm* father-in-law, stepfather.

beaupré [bopre] *nm* bowsprit.

beauté [bote] *nf* beauty, loveliness, handsomeness, belle, beautiful woman; **salon de** — beauty parlour; **soins de** — beauty treatment; **se faire une** — to do oneself up; **finir en** — to finish in grand style.

beaux-arts [bozaːr] *nm pl* fine arts.

bébé [bebe] *nm* baby.

bébête [bebɛːt] *a* silly.

bec [bɛk] *nm* beak, bill, spout, mouthpiece, nose, nozzle; — **de gaz** gas burner, jet, lamp-post; — **de plume** pen-nib; **coup de** — peck; **fin** — gourmet; **prise de** — row, altercation; **clouer le** — **à qn.** to shut someone up.

bécane [bekan] *nf* bike.

bécasse [bekas] *nf* woodcock.

bécassine [bekasin] *nf* snipe.

bec-de-cane [bɛkdəkan] *nm* lever, (*of door*) handle, pliers.

bec-de-lièvre [bɛkdəljɛːvr] *nm* harelip.

bêche [bɛʃ] *nf* spade.

bêcher [beʃe] *vt* to dig, run down.

bécot [beko] *nm* kiss, peck.

becquée [beke] *nf* beakful; **donner la** — **à** to feed.

becqueter [bɛkte] *vt* to peck at, pick up, kiss.

bedaine [bədɛn] *nf* paunch.

bedeau [bədo] *nm* verger.

bedon [bədɔ̃] *nm* paunch.

bedonner [bədɔne] *vi* to get stout.

bée [be] *af* gaping; **regarder qn bouche** — to gape at someone.

beffroi [befrwa] *nm* belfry.

bégaiement [begɛmɑ̃] *nm* stammering, stuttering.

bégayer [begeje] *vt* to stammer out, through; *vi* to stutter, splutter, stammer.

bègue [bɛg] *a* stammering; *n* stammerer.

bégueule [begœl] *a* priggish, prudish; *n*, prude.

béguin [begɛ̃] *nm* hood, bonnet; **avoir le** — **pour qn.** to fall for s.o.

beige [bɛː3] *nm* beige.

beignet [bɛɲɛ] *nm* fritter.

béjaune [beʒoːn] *nm* nestling, freshman, greenhorn.

bêler [bele] *vi* to bleat.

bel-esprit [bɛlɛspri] *nm* wit.

belette [bəlɛt] *nf* weasel.

belge [bɛlʒ] *an* Belgian.

Belgique [bɛlʒik] *nf* Belgium.

bélier [belje] *nm* ram, battering-ram.

bellâtre [bɛlɑːtr] *a* foppish; *nm* fop.

belle [bɛl] *nf* beauty; **jouer la** — to play the deciding game.

belle-fille [bɛlfiːj] *nf* daughter-in-law, stepdaughter.

belle-mère [bɛlmɛːr] *nf* mother-in-law, stepmother.

belles-lettres [bɛllɛtr] *nf* humanities.

belle-sœur [bɛlsœːr] *nf* sister-in-law, stepsister.

belligérance [bɛliʒerɑ̃ːs] *nf* belligerance.

belligérant [bɛliʒerɑ̃] *a* belligerant.

belliqueux, -euse [bɛlikø, øːz] *a* bellicose, warlike.

belvédère [bɛlvedeːr] *nm* viewpoint, summer-house.

bémol [bemɔl] *nm* (*music*) flat.

bénédicité [benedisite] *nm* grace, blessing.

bénédictin [benediktɛ̃] *an* Benedictine.

bénédiction [benediksjɔ̃] *nf* blessing.

bénéfice [benefis] *nm* profit, benefit, (eccl) living; *pl* profits, drawings.

bénéficiaire [benefisjɛːr] *an* beneficiary.

bénéficier [benefisje] *vi* to benefit, (make a) profit.

benêt [bənɛ] *a* stupid, silly; *nm* ninny, simpleton.

bénévole [benevɔl] *a* benevolent, gentle, voluntary.

bénin. -igne [benɛ̃, iɲ] *a* benign, mild, kindly.

bénir [beniːr] *vt* to bless, consecrate.

bénit [beni] *a* blessed, holy, consecrated; **eau** — holy water.

bénitier [benitje] *nm* holy-water font.

benne [bɛn] *nf* hamper, basket, hutch, bucket; **camion à** — **basculante** tip-lorry.

benzine [bɛ̃zin] *nf* benzine.

benzol [bɛ̃zɔl] *nm* benzol.

béquille [bekiːj] *nf* crutch, prop, stand.

bercail [bɛrkaːj] *nm* sheep fold.

berceau [bɛrso] *nm* cradle, cot, arbour.

bercer [bɛrse] *vt* to rock, lull, beguile, soothe; *vr* to rock, sway.

berceuse [bɛrsøːz] *nf* swing-cot, lullaby.

bergamote [bɛrgamɔt] *nf* bergamot.

berge [bɛrʒ] *nf* bank, parapet.

berger [bɛrʒe] *nm* shepherd.

bergère [bɛrʒɛːr] *nf* shepherdess, easy-chair, wagtail.

bergerie [bɛrʒəri] *nf* sheepfold, pen.

bergeronnette [bɛrʒərɔnɛt] *nf* wagtail.

berline [bɛrlin] *nf* berline, limousine, truck.

berlingot [bɛrlɛ̃go] *nm* caramel, toffee.

berlue [bɛrly] *nf* **avoir la —** to have a wrong view of things.

berne [bɛrn] *nf* **en —** at half-mast.

berner [bɛrne] *vt* to toss in a blanket, take in, deceive.

bernique [bɛrnik] *int* nothing doing.

besicles [bəzikl] *nf* spectacles, goggles.

besogne [bəzɔɲ] *nf* work, job, task, bit of work.

besogneux -euse [bəzoɲø, øːz] *a* needy, poor.

besoin [bəzwɛ̃] *nm* need, want, necessity, poverty, urge, craving, addiction; **au —** if need be, at a pinch; **avoir — de** to need, require.

bestial [bɛstjal] *a* brutish, beastly.

bestialité [bɛstjalite] *nf* bestiality, beastliness.

bestiaux [bɛstjo] *nm pl* livestock, cattle.

bestiole [bɛstjɔl] *nf* little beast, insect.

bêta [bɛta] *nm* nincompoop, wiseacre, nitwit.

bétail [betaːj] *nm* livestock, cattle.

bête [bɛːt] *nf* animal, beast, blockhead, fool; **faire la —** to act the goat; **— à bon Dieu** ladybird, harmless creature; **— noire** pet aversion; **chercher la petite —** to quibble, be overcritical.

bêtise [betiːz] *nf* stupidity, foolishness, silly thing.

béton [betɔ̃] *nm* concrete; **— armé** reinforced concrete, ferro-concrete.

bétonner [betɔne] *vt* to concrete.

bétonnière [betɔnjɛːr] *nf* concrete mixer.

bette [bɛt] *nf* beet.

betterave [bɛtraːv] *nf* beetroot, mangel'; **— sucrière** sugar-beet.

beuglement [bøgləmɑ̃] *nm* bellowing, lowing.

beugler [bøgle] *vt* to bellow, bawl out; *vi* to bellow, low.

beurre [bœːr] *nm* butter; **cuit au — noir** cooked in brown butter; **œil au — noir** black eye.

beurrer [bœre] *vt* to butter.

bévue [bevy] *nf* blunder.

biais [bjɛ] *a* sloping, slanting, oblique, askew; *nm* slant, slope, bias, expedient; **de —** sideways; **en — on** the slant.

bibelot [biblo] *nm* trinket, curio, knick-knack.

biberon [bibrɔ̃] *nm* feeding-bottle, feeder, tippler.

bible [bibl] *nf* Bible.

bibliographe [bibliɔgraf] *nm* bibliographer.

bibliographie [bibliɔgrafi] *nf* bibliography.

bibliomane [bibliɔman] *nm* book collector.

bibliophile [bibliɔfil] *nm* booklover.

bibliothécaire [bibliɔtekeːr] *nm* librarian.

bibliothèque [bibliɔtɛk] *nf* library, bookcase.

biblique [biblik] *a* biblical.

bicarbonate [bikarbɔnat] *nm* bicarbonate.

biche [biʃ] *nf* hind, doe, darling.

bichon [biʃɔ̃] *n* lapdog, darling.

bicoque [bikɔk] *nf* jerry-built house, shanty.

bicyclette [bisiklɛt] *nf* bicycle; **aller à —** to cycle to; **faire de la — to** cycle.

bidet [bidɛ] *nm* nag, bidet, trestle.

bidon [bidɔ̃] *nm* can, tin, drum, water-bottle; **du —** rubbishy; **bidonville —** shanty town.

bief [bjɛf] *nm* mill-race, -course, -lade, (*of river*) reach.

bielle [bjɛl] *nf* rod, crank-arm.

bien [bjɛ̃] *ad* well, good, right, proper, really, very, quite, indeed, much, many; *nm* property, wealth, blessing; *pl* belongings, chattels, assets; **elle est —** she is nice-looking; **être — avec** to be on good terms with; **— que** *cj* although.

bien-aimé [bjɛ̃nɛme] *an* beloved.

bien-être [bjɛ̃nɛːtr] *nm* comfort, well-being, welfare.

bienfaisance [bjɛ̃fəzɑ̃ːs] *nf* beneficence, generosity, charity; **œuvre de —** charitable society, work.

bienfaisant [bjɛ̃fəzɑ̃] *a* charitable, kind beneficial.

bienfait [bjɛ̃fɛ] *nm* benefit, favour, boon, kindness.

bienfaiteur, -trice [bjɛ̃fɛtœːr, tris] *n* benefactor, -tress.

bien-fondé [bjɛ̃fɔ̃de] *nm* merits, justice, soundness.

bien-fonds [bjɛ̃fɔ̃] *nm* real estate.

bienheureux, -euse [bjɛ̃nœrø, øːz] *a* happy, blessed.

biennal [biɛnnal] *a* biennial.

bienséance [bjɛ̃seɑ̃s] *nf* decorum, propriety.

bienséant [bjɛ̃seɑ̃] *a* decorous, seemly, proper.

bientôt [bjɛ̃to] *ad* soon, before long; **à —** good-bye.

bienveillance [bjɛ̃vɛjɑ̃:s] *nf* benevolence, goodwill, kindness.

bienveillant [bjɛ̃vɛjɑ̃] *a* benevolent, kindly.

bienvenu [bjɛ̃vny] *an* welcome.

bienvenue [bjɛ̃vny] *nf* welcome.

bière [bjɛ:r] *nf* beer, ale; bier, coffin.

biffer [bife] *vt* to delete.

biffin [bifɛ̃] *nm* ragman, foot-soldier, footslogger.

bifteck [biftek] *nm* beefsteak.

bifurcation [bifyrkasjɔ̃] *nf* fork, branch line.

bifurquer [bifyrke] *vi* to fork, branch off.

bigame [bigam] *a* bigamous; *n* bigamist.

bigamie [bigami] *nf* bigamy.

bigarré [bigare] *a* variegated, mottled, motley.

bigorneau [bigɔrno] *nm* periwinkle, whelk.

bigot [bigo] *a* sanctimonious, overdevout; *n* bigot.

bigoudi [bigudi] *nm* hair-curler.

bijou [biʒu] *nm* jewel.

bijouterie [biʒutri] *nf* jewellery, jeweller's shop, jeweller's trade.

bijoutier -ière [biʒutje, jɛ:r] *n* jeweller.

bilan [bilɑ̃] *nm* balance-sheet, schedule; **dresser le —** to strike the balance.

bile [bil] *nf* spleen, anger; **se faire de la —** to worry, fret.

bilieux, -euse [biljø, ø:z] *a* bilious, liverish.

billard [bija:r] *nm* billiards, billiard-table, billiard saloon; **— japonais** bagatelle table.

bille [bi:j] *nf* billiard ball, marble, log; (*rl*) sleeper; rolling pin; **roulement à —s** ball-bearing.

billet [bijɛ] *nm* (*bank-*)note, letter, ticket, bill, permit; **— simple** single ticket; **— d'aller et retour** return ticket; **— à ordre** promissory note.

billot [bijo] *nm* (*of wood*) block.

bimensuel, -elle [bimɑ̃sɥel] *a* fortnightly.

bimestriel [bimɛstriɛl] *a* two-monthly.

binaire [binɛ:r] *a* binary.

bine [bin] *nf* hoe.

biner [bine] *vt* to hoe.

binette [binɛt] *nf* hoe.

binocle [binɔkl] *nm* eye-glasses, pince-nez.

binoculaire [binɔkylɛ:r] *a* two-eyed, binocular.

biographe [biɔgraf] *nm* biographer.

biographie [biɔgrafi] *nf* biography.

biographique [biɔgrafik] *a* biographical.

biologie [biɔlɔʒi] *nf* biology.

biplan [biplɑ̃] *nm* biplane.

birman [birmɑ̃] *an* Burmese.

Birmanie [birmani] *nf* Burma.

bis [bis, bi] *a* greyish-brown; *ad* twice, encore, repeat; **pain —** wholemeal bread.

bisannuel, -elle [bizanɥel] *a* biennial.

bisbille [bisbi:j] *nf* bickering, squabble.

biscornu [biskɔrny] *a* distorted, misshapen, irregular, weird, inconsistent.

biscotte [biskɔt] *nf* rusk.

biscuit [biskɥi] *nm* biscuit, plain cake.

bise [bi:z] *nf* north wind, cold blast; kiss.

biseau [bizo] *nm* bevel, chamfer.

biseauter [bizote] *vt* to bevel, chamfer.

bison [bizɔ̃] *nm* bison.

bisque [bisk] *nf* shellfish soup; ill humour; **donner une —** to give odds.

bissecter [bisɛkte] *vt* to bisect.

bisser [bise] *vt* to encore.

bissextile [bisɛkstil] *a* **année —** leap year.

bistouri [bisturi] *nm* lancet.

bistré [bistre] *a* darkened, swarthy, browned.

bistro(t) [bistro] *nm* café, pub, tavern.

bitte [bit] *nf* bollard.

bitume [bitym] *nm* bitumen, asphalt, pitch.

bivouaquer [bivwake] *vi* to bivouac.

bizarre [biza:r] *a* odd, peculiar, queer, weird, strange.

blackbouler [blakbule] *vt* to blackball, reject.

blafard [blafa:r] *a* wan, pale, livid, pallid.

blague [blag] *nf* tobacco-pouch; joke, banter; **sans —** you don't say! really!

blaguer [blage] *vt* to chaff, pull someone's leg; *vi* to joke.

blagueur, -euse [blagœ:r] *a* scoffing, ironical; *n* cynical scoffer, cynic.

blaireau [blɛro] *nm* badger, shaving-brush.

blâmable [blɑmabl] *a* blameworthy.

blâme [blɑ:m] *nm* blame, reproof

blâmer [blame] *vt* to blame, reprove, rebuke

blanc, -che [blɑ̃, blɑ̃:ʃ] *a* white, pale, pure, clean, blank; *nm* white, blank; **nuit blanche** sleepless night.

blanc-bec [blɑ̃bɛk] *nm* tyro, green-horn, raw youth.

blanchâtre [blɑ̃ʃɑ:tr] *a* whitish.

blanche [blɑ̃:ʃ] *nf* minim, white ball.

blancheur [blɑ̃ʃœ:r] *nf* whiteness, purity, paleness.

blanchir [blɑ̃ʃi:r] *vt* to whiten, bleach, wash, limewash; *vi* to turn white, pale.

blanchissage [blɑ̃ʃisa:ʒ] *nm* laundering, whitewashing, sugar refining.

blanchisserie [blɑ̃ʃisri] *nf* laundry, wash-house.

blanchisseur, -euse [blãʃisœːr, øːz] n laundryman, laundress, bleacher, washer-woman.

blanc-seing [blãsɛ̃] nm (signature to a) blank document; **donner — à** to give a free hand to.

blandices [blãdis] nf pl blandishment.

blanquette [blãkɛt] nf veal stew.

blaser [blaze] vt to blunt, satiate, cloy; vr to become blasé, tired (of de).

blason [blazɔ̃] nm coat of arms, escutcheon, heraldry.

blasphémateur, -trice [blasfɛmatœːr, tris] a blasphemous; n blasphemer.

blasphématoire [blasfɛmatwaːr] a blasphemous.

blasphème [blasfɛm] nm blasphemy, curse.

blasphémer [blasfeme] vti to blaspheme, curse.

blatte [blat] nf cockroach.

blé [ble] nm corn, wheat; **— noir** buckwheat; **— d'Inde** maize, (US) corn.

bled [blɛd] nm (pej) wilds, countryside.

blême [blɛm] a pale, wan.

blêmir [blemiːr] vi to turn pale, blanch, grow dim.

blessé [blɛse] a wounded, hurt; n wounded man, casualty.

blesser [blɛse] vt to wound, hurt, offend, injure; vr to be wounded, be hurt, hurt oneself.

blessure [blɛsyːr] nf wound, injury, hurt, sore.

blet, -te [blɛ, blɛt] a over-ripe, soft.

bleu [blø] a blue; nm recruit, rookie, greenhorn, blue; pl dungarees; **avoir des —s** to be black and blue; **n'y voir que du —** to be all at sea.

bleuâtre [bløaːtr] a bluish.

bleuir [bløiːr] vt to make blue; vi to turn blue.

blindé [blɛ̃de] a armour-plated, timbered; nm pl les **—s** the armour.

blinder [blɛ̃de] vt to armourplate, line with timber.

bloc [blɔk] nm block, mass, lump, pad, coalition, clink, prison; **en —** all together, in one piece; **à —** thoroughly.

blocage [blɔkaːʒ] nm blocking up, clamping, seizing.

bloc-notes [blɔknɔt] nm writing, scribbling pad, (US) scratch pad.

blocus [blɔkyːs] nm blockade; **braver le —** to run the blockade.

blond [blɔ̃] a fair-haired, light, blonde.

blondir [blɔ̃diːr] vt to dye blond, bleach; vi to turn yellow.

bloquer [blɔke] vt to block up, obstruct, blockade, jam, dam; vr to seize up, jam.

se blottir [səblɔtiːr] vr to crouch, cower, huddle, nestle, snuggle.

blouse [bluːz] nf smock, overall.

blouson [bluzɔ̃] nm battle-dress jacket, skiing jacket; **—s noirs** n pl young ruffians.

bluet [blye] nm cornflower, blue-bottle.

bluffer [blœfe] vti to bluff.

bobard [bɔbaːr] nm tall tale, fib.

bobèche [bɔbɛʃ] nf socket, sconce.

bobine [bɔbin] nf bobbin, reel, spool, coil, dial.

bocage [bɔkaːʒ] nm copse.

bocal [bɔkal] nm jar, bottle.

bock [bɔk] nm glass of beer, beer-glass.

bœuf [bœf] nm ox, bullock, beef; **— de conserve** corned beef; **— à la mode** stewed beef.

bohème [bɔɛm] a unconventional, Bohemian; n Bohemian; nf Bohemia, art-world.

bohémien, -ienne [bɔemjɛ̃, jɛn] an gipsy, Bohemian.

boire [bwaːr] vt to drink (in, up), imbibe, absorb, soak in, up; nm drink(ing); **— un coup en vitesse** to have a quick one.

bois [bwa] nm wood, forest, timber; pl antlers, woodwind instruments.

boisage [bwazaːʒ] nm timbering, scaffold(ing), woodwork, afforestation.

boisé [bwaze] a wooded, woody, wainscoted.

boiser [bwaze] vt to timber, put under timber, wainscot.

boiserie [bwazri] nf woodwork, wainscoting, joinery.

boisseau [bwaso] nm bushel, drain, flue-tile.

boisselier [bwasəlje] nm cooper.

boisson [bwasɔ̃] nf drink, beverage; **pris de —** under the influence.

boîte [bwat] nf box, case, tin, casket, jail; **— aux lettres** letter-box; **— à ordures** bin; **— à thé** tea-caddy; **— de nuit** night-club; **— de vitesses** gear-box.

boiter [bwate] vi to limp, hobble, be lame.

boiteux, -euse [bwatø, øːz] a lame, shaky, lop-sided.

boîtier [bwatje] nm case.

bol [bɔl] nm bowl, basin.

bolchevisme [bɔlʃevism] nm Bolshevism.

bolchevique [bɔlʃevik] an bolshevik.

bolide [bɔlid] nm meteor, fast car.

bombance [bɔ̃bãːs] nf feast(ing); **faire —** to carouse, have a blow-out.

bombardement [bɔ̃bardəmã] nm bombardment, bombing, shelling; **— en piqué** dive-bombing.

bombarder [bɔ̃barde] vt to bombard, bomb, shell.

bombardier [bɔ̃bardje] nm bombardier, bomb-aimer, bomber plane.

bombe [bɔ̃b] nf bomb, spree; **— à retardement** time-bomb; **faire la — to** go on the binge.

bombé [bɔ̃be] *a* bulging, convex, cambered.

bomber [bɔ̃be] *vt* to stick out, arch, bend, camber; *vi* bulge, belly.

bon, -ne [bɔ̃, bɔn] *a* good, nice, right, correct, sound, righteous, kind, fitting, profitable; *nm* voucher, warrant, bond, draft, bill; **pour de — for** good, in earnest; **bon! right!**; **— à rien** good-for-nothing.

bonasse [bɔnas] *a* simple, silly.

bonbon [bɔ̃bɔ̃] *nm* sweet(meat), drop; *pl* confections.

bonbonne [bɔ̃bɔn] *nf* carboy.

bonbonnière [bɔ̃bɔnjɛ:r] *nf* sweet-box, well-furnished little house.

bond [bɔ̃] *nm* jump, leap, spring, bounce; **faire faux —** to break.

bonde [bɔ̃:d] *nf* bung, plug, bung-hole.

bondé [bɔ̃de] *a* packed, crowded, crammed.

bondir [bɔ̃di:r] *vi* to jump, leap, spring, bound, bounce, skip about.

bonheur [bɔnœ:r] *nm* happiness, bliss, welfare, success; **par —** fortunately; **au petit —** indiscriminately, haphazardly.

bonhomie [bɔnɔmi] *nf* good nature, humour.

bonhomme [bɔnɔm] *a* good-natured; *nm* (good-natured) man, figure.

boni [bɔni] *nm* surplus, premium, bonus.

bonification [bɔnifikasjɔ̃] *nf* bonus, rebate, improvement.

bonifier [bɔnifje] *vti* to improve.

boniment [bɔnimã] *nm* patter, moonshine.

bonjour [bɔ̃ʒu:r] *nm* good-day, -morning, -afternoon.

bonne [bɔn] *nf* maid servant; **— d'enfants** nursemaid.

bonnet [bɔnɛ] *nm* cap, bonnet; **gros — bigwig; avoir la tête près du —** to be hot tempered; **opiner du —** to agree, have no opinion of one's own.

bonneterie [bɔntri] *nf* hosiery, knitted ware.

bonneteur [bɔntœ:r] *nm* card-sharper, confidence man.

bonnetier, -ière [bɔntje, jɛ:r] *n* hosier.

bon(n)iche [bɔniʃ] *nf* maidservant, skivvy.

bon-papa [bɔ̃papa] *nm* grandpa, grand-dad.

bonsoir [bɔ̃swa:r] *nm* good-evening, -night.

bonté [bɔ̃te] *nf* kindness, goodness, good nature.

bonze [bɔ̃:z] *nm* bonze, buddhist priest, **vieux —** old fossil.

bord [bɔ:r] *nm* edge, brink, brim, rim, bank, verge, side, flap, tack; **livre de —** log book; **à — de aboard; à pleins —s** brim-full.

bordage [bɔrda:ʒ] *nm* border(ing), kerb, edging, planking.

bordeaux [bɔrdo] *nm* Bordeaux wine; **— rouge** claret.

bordée [bɔrde] *nf* broadside, watch, tack, volley; **tirer des —s** to tack; **être en —** to be on the spree.

bordel [bɔrdɛl] *nm* brothel.

border [bɔrde] *vt* to border, edge, run along, fringe, braid, plank; **— qn. dans son lit** to tuck s.o. in.

bordereau [bɔrdəro] *nm* statement, account, memorandum, docket, file.

bordure [bɔrdy:r] *nf* edge, fringe, binding, kerb, rim.

borgne [bɔrɲ] *a* one-eyed, blind in one eye, shady.

borne [bɔrn] *nf* limit, boundary mark, guard-stone, terminal; **— kilométrique** milestone; **cela passe les —s** that is going too far.

borné [bɔrne] *a* limited, narrow, restricted.

borner [bɔrne] *vt* to bound, limit, restrict, stake, mark out the limits of; *vr* to confine, restrict oneself.

bosquet [bɔskɛ] *nm* thicket, grove, arbour.

bosse [bɔs] *nf* hump, lump, bump, dent, bruise; **rouler sa —** to knock about.

bosseler [bɔsle] *vt* to emboss, dent, bash.

bosselure [bɔsly:r] *nf* dent, bruise.

bossoir [bɔswa:r] *nm* davit, cathead, (of ship) bow.

bossu [bɔsy] *a* hunch-backed, humped; *n* hunchback.

bot [bo] *a* **pied —** club-foot, club-footed person.

botanique [bɔtanik] *a* botanical; *nf* botany.

botaniste [bɔtanist] *n* botanist.

botte [bɔt] *nf* boot, field-boot, bunch, truss, bundle, lunge, thrust, slip; **—s retroussées** top boots; **—s à l'écuyère** riding-boots.

botteler [bɔtle] *vt* to truss, bundle, bunch, tie up.

botter [bɔte] *vt* to put boots on, kick.

bottier [bɔtje] *nm* bootmaker.

bottin [bɔtɛ̃] *nm* directory.

bottine [bɔtin] *nf* ankle-boot.

bouc [buk] *nm* he-, billy-goat; **— émissaire,** scapegoat.

boucan [bukã] *nm* din, shindy, row, smoked meat.

boucaner [bukane] *vt* (meat) to cure, to stink.

boucanier [bukanje] *nm* buccaneer, pirate.

bouche [buʃ] *nf* mouth, muzzle, slot, opening; **— d'eau** hydrant; **garder qch. pour la bonne —** to keep something as a titbit; **fine — gourmet; être porté sur la —** to think of nothing but one's belly; **faire la petite —** to pick at one's food, be difficult.

bouché [buʃe] *a* plugged, stopped up, dense.

bouchée [buʃe] nf mouthful, bite, morsel; — à la reine vol-au-vent of chicken; **mettre les —s doubles** to gobble one's food, put a spurt on.

boucher [buʃe] nm butcher; vt to plug, stop (up), cork, bung, obstruct.

boucherie [buʃri] nf butcher's shop, -trade; slaughter, shambles.

bouchon [buʃɔ̃] nm cork, stopper, plug, fishing float.

boucle [bukl] nf buckle, coop, bow, ringlet, curl; — **d'oreille** earring.

bouclé [bukle] a curly.

boucler [bukle] vt to buckle on, knot, fasten, settle, clinch, curl, lock up; vi to buckle, be curly.

bouclier [bukli(j)e] nm shield, buckler.

bouder [bude] vt to be in the sulks with; vi to sulk.

bouderie [budri] nf sulkiness.

boudeur, -euse [budœːr, øːz] a sulky; nf double settee.

boudin [budɛ̃] nm black-pudding, inner tube, twist, roll, flange, beading.

boudoir [budwaːr] nm boudoir.

boue [bu] nf mud, dirt, deposit.

bouée [bwe, bue] nf buoy; — **de sauvetage** lifebuoy.

boueux, -euse [buø, øːz] a muddy, miry, dirty; nm scavenger, dustman.

bouffant [bufã] a puffed, baggy.

bouffe [buf] a **opéra** — comic opera.

bouffée [bufe] nf whiff, puff, waft, gust, breath; **tirer des —s de sa pipe** to puff at one's pipe.

bouffer [bufe] vt to puff out, gobble; vi to balloon out, bag, swell.

bouffi [bufi] a puffed up, puffy, bloated, swollen, turgid.

bouffir [bufiːr] vt to bloat, inflate; vi to become swollen, puffed up.

bouffon, -onne [bufɔ̃, ɔn] a farcical; nm clown, jester.

bouge [buːʒ] nm hovel, slum, den, pigsty, (of ship) bilge.

bougeoir [buʒwaːr] nm candlestick.

bougeotte [buʒɔt] nf **avoir la —** to be fidgety.

bouger [buʒe] vt to move; vi to budge, stir.

bougie [buʒi] nf candle, sparking-plug, (US) spark plug.

bougon, -onne [bugɔ̃, ɔn] a testy, grumpy; n grumbler.

bougonner [bugɔne] vi to grumble, grouse.

bougran [bugrã] nm buckram.

bouillabaisse [bujabɛs] nf fish-soup.

bouillant [bujã] a boiling, ebullient, impetuous.

bouillie [buji] nf gruel, pap.

bouilloire [bujwaːr] nf kettle.

bouillon [bujɔ̃] nm bubble, soup, stock, beeftea, cheap restaurant, unsold copies.

bouillonnement [bujɔnmã] nm boiling, seething.

bouillonner [bujɔne] vt to gather material into puffs; vi to boil up, seethe, bubble.

bouillotte [bujɔt] nf hot-water bottle.

boulanger, -ère [bulãʒe, ɛːr] n baker, baker's wife; vti to bake.

boulangerie [bulãʒri] nf bread-baking, baker's shop.

boule [bul] nf bowl, ball, globe, bulb, lump, head, face; **joueur de —s** bowler; **jeu de —s** bowls, bowling-green.

bouleau [bulo] nm birch-tree.

bouledogue [buldɔg] nm bulldog.

boulet [bule] nm cannonball, fetlock-joint.

boulette [bulɛt] nf pellet, meatball.

boulevard [bulvaːr] nm avenue, boulevard.

boulevardier, -ière [bulvardje, ɛːr] a of the boulevards; nm man-about-town.

bouleversement [bulvɛrsəmã] nm upheaval, overthrow, disturbance, confusion.

bouleverser [bulvɛrse] vt to upset, overturn, perturb, bowl over, astound, stagger.

boulon [bulɔ̃] nm bolt, pin.

boulot, -otte [bulo, ɔt] a chubby, plump, dumpy; nm work, food.

boulotter [bulɔte] vt to eat; vi to jog along, on.

bouquet [bukɛ] nm bunch, posy, bouquet, nosegay, clump, cluster, aroma, crowning-piece, highlight; **c'est le —** that crowns it; **pour le —** . . . last but not least. . .

bouquetier [buktje] nm flower vase.

bouquetière [buktjɛːr] nf flower-girl.

bouquin [bukɛ̃] nm old book, book, buck-rabbit, hare.

bouquiner [bukine] vi to collect old books, read.

bouquiniste [bukinist] nm second-hand bookseller.

bourbe [burb] nf mud, mire.

bourbeux, -euse [burbø, øːz] a muddy, miry.

bourbier [burbje] nm bog, mire.

bourde [burd] nf bloomer, fib.

bourdon [burdɔ̃] nm drone, great bell, bumble-bee.

bourdonnement [burdɔnmã] nm buzzing humming, drumming, whir.

bourdonner [burdɔne] vt to hum; vi to buzz, hum, drone, whirr.

bourg [buːr] nm market town.

bourgeois [burʒwa] a middle-class, plain, common; n citizen, townsman, commoner.

bourgeoisie [burʒwazi] nf middle class; **la haute (petite) —** the upper (lower) middle class.

bourgeon [burʒɔ̃] nm bud, pimple.

bourgeonner [burʒɔne] vi to bud, break out in pimples.

bourgeron [burʒərɔ̃] *nm* workman's overall.

Bourgogne [burgɔɲ] *nf* Burgundy; *m* burgundy wine.

bourguignon [burgiɲɔ̃] *a nmf* Burgundian, of Burgundy.

bourlinguer [burlɛ̃ge] *vi* to labour, make heavy weather, knock about.

bourrade [burad] *nf* blow, thrust, thump, rough word.

bourrage [bura:ʒ] *nm* stuffing, padding, cramming; — de crâne bunkum, eyewash, dope.

bourrasque [burask] *nf* squall.

bourre [bu:r] *nf* flock, floss, wad, waste.

bourreau [buro] *nm* hangman, executioner, tormentor.

bourrée [bure] *nf* bundle of firewood, faggot.

bourreler [burle] *vt* to torment, rack, goad.

bourrelet [burlɛ] *nm* pad, cushion, fold, roll, rim, bead.

bourrelier [burəlje] *nm* saddler.

bourrer [bure] *vt* to pad, stuff, pack, cram, fill, thrash, trounce; — le crâne à qn. to fill someone's head with stuff and nonsense.

bourriche [buriʃ] *nf* basket, hamper.

bourrique [burik] *nf* she-ass, donkey, duffer.

bourru [bury] *a* churlish, surly, rude, gruff.

bourse [burs] *nf* purse, pouch, bag, grant, bursary, scholarship, stock exchange; jouer à la — to speculate.

boursier, -ière [bursje, jɛ:r] *n* scholar, paymaster, speculator.

boursouflé [bursufle] *a* swollen, bloated, turgid.

boursouflement [bursufləmɑ̃] *nm* swelling, blistering.

boursoufler [bursufle] *vt* to swell, blister, bloat; *vi* to swell, blister.

boursouflure [bursufly:r] *nf* swelling, blister, turgidity.

bousculade [buskylad] *nf* scuffle, scurry, hustle, rush.

bousculer [buskyle] *vt* to jostle, hustle, upset.

bouse [bu:z] *nf* dung.

bousiller [buzije] *vt* to bungle, scamp, crash (plane).

boussole [busɔl] *nf* compass.

boustifaille [bustifɑ:j] *nf* grub, food.

bout [bu] *nm* end, extremity, tip, bit, tag, scrap; bas (haut) bout foot (head); à — de forces exhausted, worn out, spent; au — de at the end of, after; jusqu'au — right to the end, to the bitter end, through; de — en — through and through; venir à — de to overcome, manage, cope with; à — portant point-blank.

boutade [butad] *nf* whim, outburst, sally, quip.

boute-en-train [butɑ̃trɛ̃] *nm* bright and cheery companion, life and soul.

boutefeu [butfø] *nm* firebrand.

bouteille [bute:j] *nf* bottle.

bouteroue [butru] *nf* guard-stone, fender.

boutique [butik] *nf* shop, caboodle.

boutiquier, -ière [butikje, jɛ:r] *n* shopkeeper.

bouton [butɔ̃] *nm* button, bud, pimple, handle, knot; — de col stud; — de manchettes cuff-link; — d'or buttercup; tourner le — to switch on, off.

boutonner [butɔne] *vt* to button up; *vi* to bud.

boutonneux, -euse [butɔnø, ø:z] *a* pimply.

boutonnière [butɔnjɛ:r] *nf* buttonhole, rosette.

bouture [buty:r] *nf* cutting.

bouvier [buvje] *nm* cowherd, drover.

bouvreuil [buvrœ:j] *nm* bullfinch.

bovin [bɔvɛ̃] *a* bovine.

box [bɔks] *nm* loose box, lock-up garage cubicle, dock.

boxe [bɔks] *nf* boxing.

boxer [bɔkse] *vt* to box with; *vi* to box, spar.

boxeur [bɔksœ:r] *nm* boxer.

boy [bɔj] *nmf* steward.

boyau [bwajo] *nm* bowel, gut, inner tube, hosepipe, communication trench.

boycotter [bɔjkɔte] *vt* to boycott.

bracelet [braslɛ] *nm* bracelet, bangle, armband.

braconnage [brakɔna:ʒ] *nm* poaching.

braconner [brakɔne] *vti* to poach.

braconnier, -ière [brakɔnje, jɛ:r] *a* poaching; *nm* poacher.

braguette [bragɛt] *nf* (of trousers) fly.

braillard [braja:r] *a* noisy, bawling, rowdy; *n* brawler.

brailler [braje] *vti* to bawl out, shout.

braire [brɛ:r] *vi* to bray.

braise [brɛ:z] *nf* embers.

braiser [brɛze] *vt* to braise.

bramer [brame] *vi* (of stag) to bell.

brancard [brɑ̃ka:r] *nm* shaft, stretcher.

brancardier [brɑ̃kardje] *nm* stretcher-bearer.

branche [brɑ̃:ʃ] *nf* branch, bough, prong, leg, (of family) line.

branchement [brɑ̃ʃmɑ̃] *nm* branching, forking, junction, lead.

brancher [brɑ̃ʃe] *vt* to connect, branch, plug in; on m'a mal branché I was given the wrong number.

brandir [brɑ̃di:r] *vt* to brandish, flourish, wave.

brandon [brɑ̃dɔ̃] *nm* firebrand.

branlant [brɑ̃lɑ̃] *a* shaky, loose, ramshackle.

branle [brɑ̃:l] *nm* swing, impetus, oscillation, motion; mettre qch. en — to set something going.

branle-bas [brɑ̃ləba] *nm* stir, bustle,

commotion; **faire le —** to clear decks for action.

branler [brɑ̃le] *vt* to swing, wag, shake; *vi* to shake, rock, be loose.

braquage [brakaːʒ] *nm* levelling, aiming, pointing; **angle de —** lock (of car).

braquer [brake] *vt* to aim, level, point, fix, direct.

bras [bra, brɑ] *nm* arm, limb, bracket; **— droit** right-hand man, *pl* workmen, hands, henchmen; **— dessus — dessous** arm in arm; **— de mer** arm of the sea, (*Scot*) sea loch; **en — de chemise** in one's shirt sleeves; **à — le corps** round the waist; **— de rivière** backwater; **manquer de —** to be short-handed.

brasero [brazero] *nm* brazier.

brasier [brazje] *nm* fire, inferno, furnace.

brasiller [brazije] *vt* to grill, broil; *vi* to sizzle.

brassard [brasaːr] *nm* armlet, armband.

brasse [brɑːs] *nf* arm-span, fathom, stroke; **nager à la —** to swim the breast stroke.

brassée [brase] *nf* armful.

brasser [brase] *vt* to mix, stir, brew, brace; **— de grosses affaires** to do big business.

brasserie [brasri] *nf* brewery, alehouse, restaurant.

brasseur, -euse [brasœːr, øːz] *n* brewer, puddler, mixer; **— d'affaires** big businessman.

brassière [brasjɛːr] *nf* baby's vest; *pl* slings, leading strings; **— de sauvetage** life-jacket.

bravache [bravaʃ] *a* blustering, swaggering; *nm* braggadocio, bully.

bravade [bravad] *nf* bluster.

brave [braːv] *a* brave, gallant, decent, worthy, good.

braver [brave] *vt* to brave, dare, defy, face, run (blockade).

bravoure [bravuːr] *nf* bravery, valour.

brebis [brəbi] *nf* ewe, sheep; **— galeuse** black sheep.

brèche [brɛʃ] *nf* breach, hole, gap; **battre en —** to breach.

bréchet [breʃɛ] *nm* breastbone.

bredouille [brəduːj] *a inv* empty-handed.

bredouiller [brəduje] *vt* to stammer out, mumble; *vi* to stutter, splutter, gabble.

bref, brève [brɛf, brɛːv] *a* brief, short, curt; *ad* curtly, in short.

breloque [brəlɔk] *nf* trinket, charm.

Brésil [brezil] *nm* Brazil.

brésilien, -ienne [breziljɛ̃, jɛn] *a* Brazilian.

Bretagne [brətaɲ] *nf* Brittany.

bretelle [brətɛl] *nf* strap, sling; *pl* braces.

breton, -onne [brətɔ̃, ɔn] *an* Breton.

bretteur [brɛtœːr] *nm* duellist, swashbuckler.

breuvage [brœvaːʒ] *nm* drink, beverage, draught.

brevet [brəvɛ] *nm* patent, certificate.

breveté [brəvte] *a* certificated, by special appointment; *n* patentee.

breveter [brəvte] *vt* to grant a patent to, patent.

bréviaire [brevjɛːr] *nm* breviary.

brévité [brevite] *nf* shortness.

bribe [brib] *nf* scrap, fragment.

bric-à-brac [brikabrak] *nm* curios, bits and pieces.

bricole [brikɔl] *nf* strap, breast harness strap, ricochet; *pl* trifles, odd jobs.

bricoler [brikɔle] *vt* to arrange; *vi* to do odd jobs, potter about.

bricoleur [brikɔlœːr] *nm* handyman, jobber, jack of all trades.

bride [brid] *nf* bridle, string, flange, strap; **à — abattue** full tilt, at full speed; **lâcher la — à** to give free rein to, full scope to.

brider [bride] *vt* to bridle, curb, restrain, truss, flange, fasten.

bridge [bridʒ] *nm* (*game*) bridge.

bridgeur, -euse [bridʒœːr, øːz] *n* bridge player.

brièvement [brievmɑ̃] *ad* briefly, curtly, succinctly.

brièveté [brievte] *nf* brevity, shortness, conciseness.

brigade [brigad] *nf* brigade, squad, shift, gang.

brigadier [brigadje] *nm* corporal, bombardier, sergeant (*police*).

brigand [brigɑ̃] *nm* robber, brigand, highwayman.

brigandage [brigɑ̃daːʒ] *nm* brigandage, highway robbery.

brigue [brig] *nf* canvassing, intrigue, plot.

briguer [brige] *vt* to canvass for, solicit.

brillament [brijamɑ̃] *ad* brilliantly.

brillant [brijɑ̃] *a* brilliant, shining, glossy; *nm* brilliancy, gloss(iness), shine, polish.

briller [brije] *vi* to shine, sparkle, glitter.

brimade [brimad] *nf* rough joke, rag.

brimbaler [brɛ̃bale] *vt* to lug about; *vi* to swing, wobble.

brimborion [brɛ̃bɔrjɔ̃] *nm* bauble, trifle.

brimer [brime] *vt* to rag, persecute.

brin [brɛ̃] *nm* blade, sprig, stalk, shoot, strand, bit, crumb, jɔː, touch, shred, chit.

brindille [brɛ̃diːj] *nf* twig, tiny branch.

bringue [brɛ̃ːg] *nf* bit, piece; **faire la —** to go on the spree.

brio [bri(j)o] *nm* vigour, dash, gusto, brilliance.

brioche [briɔʃ] *nf* bun.

brique [brik] *nf* brick.

briquet [brikɛ] *nm* flint, tinderbox, cigarette lighter.

brisant [brizã] *a* shattering; *nm* breaker, reef.

brise [bri:z] *nf* breeze.

brise-bise [brizbi:z] *nm* draught-tube, short window curtain.

brisées [brize] *nf pl* tracks; **aller sur les — de qn.** to compete with someone; **suivre les — de qn.** to follow in someone's footsteps.

brise-lames [brizlam] *nm* break-water, mole.

briser [brize] *vt* to break (up, down, off), shatter, smash; *vr* to break.

brisure [brizy:r] *nf* break, flaw, crack.

britannique [britanik] *an* British; *n* Briton.

broc [bro] *nm* jug, pitcher.

brocanter [brokãte] *vt* to sell, barter; *vi* to deal in second-hand goods.

brocanteur, -euse [brokãtœ:r, ø:z] *n* second-hand dealer.

brocard [broka:r] *nm* taunt, lampoon.

brocart [broka:r] *nm* brocade.

broche [broʃ] *nf* spit, skewer, peg, brooch, spindle, pin, spigot.

brocher [broʃe] *vt* to stitch, sew, brocade; **livre broché** paper-bound book.

brochet [broʃɛ] *nm* pike.

brochette [broʃɛt] *nf* skewer, stick; **élevé à la — fed** by hand, brought up with tender care.

brochure [broʃy:r] *nf* booklet, pamphlet.

brodequin [brodkɛ̃] *nm* sock, ankle-boot; *pl* marching boots.

broder [brode] *vt* to embroider, embellish, amplify.

broderie [brodri] *nf* (piece of) embroidery, embellishment.

bromure [bromy:r] *nm* bromide.

broncher [brõʃe] *vi* to stumble, falter, flinch shy.

bronches [brõ:ʃ] *nf pl* bronchial tubes.

bronchite [brõʃit] *nf* bronchitis.

bronze [brõ:z] *nm* bronze statue).

bronzer [brõze] *vt* to bronze, brown, tan.

brosse [brɔs] *nf* brush; **cheveux en — crewcut.**

brosser [brɔse] *vt* to brush, thrash.

brouet [brue] *nm* gruel, skilly.

brouette [bruet] *nf* wheelbarrow.

brouhaha [bruaa] *nm* uproar din, clatter, hubbub.

brouillage [bruja:ʒ] *nm* interference, jamming, mixing.

brouillard [bruja:r] *nm* fog mist, daybook; **fait du — it is** foggy.

brouille [bru:j] *nf* quarrel dispute wrangle, broil; **être en — avec qn.** to have fallen out with s.o.

brouiller [bruje] *vt* to confuse, mix (up), fuddle, scramble, perplex, jam; *vr* to get confused, mixed, blurred, quarrel, fall out.

brouillon, -onne [brujõ, ɔn] *a* muddleheaded; *nm* rough copy, draft.

broussailles [brusa:j] *nf pl* under-wood, brushwood, scrub.

broussailleux, -euse [brusajø, ø:z] *a* bushy, shaggy.

brousse [brus] *nf* bush, scrub, wilds.

brouter [brute] *vt* to graze, crop, browse.

broyer [brwaje] *vt* to crush, grind, pound; **— du noir** to have the blues.

bru [bry] *nf* daughter-in-law.

brugnon [brynõ] *nm* nectarine.

bruine [brɥin] *nf* drizzle.

bruiner [brɥine] *vi* to drizzle, spit.

bruire [brɥi:r] *vi* to rustle, murmur, hum.

bruissement [brɥismã] *nm* rustling, whisper humming.

bruit [brɥi] *nm* noise, clatter, din, rumour, sound, fuss, ado.

brûlant [brylã] *a* burning, blazing, scorching, fervent.

brûlé [bryle] *a* burnt, scorched; **odeur de — smell** of burning.

brûle-gueule [brylgœl] *nm* clay pipe, nose warmer.

brûle-pourpoint [brylpurpwɛ̃] *ad* **à — point-blank.**

brûler [bryle] *vt* to burn (up, down, out, away), singe, nip, scorch; *vi* to burn, be on fire, be aflame, singe, scorch, be eager (to); **— une gare** to run through a station without stopping; **— les feux** to jump the lights; **— la cervelle à qn.** to blow s.o.'s brains out.

brûleur, -euse [brylœ:r, ø:z] *n* burner, distiller; *nm* gas jet, bunsen burner.

brûlot [brylo] *nm* fireship.

brûlure [bryly:r] *nf* burn, scald, blight; *pl* heartburn.

brume [brym] *nf* fog, mist, haze.

brumeux, -euse [brymø, ø:z] *a* foggy misty, hazy.

brun [brœ̃] *a* brown, dark, dusky; *nm* brown; *n* dark person.

brunâtre [bryna:tr] *a* brownish.

brunir [bryni:r] *vt* to brown, darken, tan, burnish; *vi* to become dark, tan.

brusque [brysk] *a* abrupt, hasty, sudden.

brusquer [bryske] *vt* to hurry, rush, be sharp with.

brusquerie [brysk(ə)ri] *nf* blunt-ness, abruptness bluffness, rough-ness.

brut [bryt] *a* rough, crude, un-refined raw, unpolished uncut, gross, extra dry.

brutal [brytal] *a* coarse, callous, rough, blunt.

brutaliser [brytalize] *vt* to bully, ill-treat.

brutalité [brytalite] *nf* (act of) brutality brutishness, callousness.

brute [bryt] *nf* beast, bully.
bruyant [bryjã] *a* noisy, boisterous, loud blatant.
bruyère [bryjɛːr] *nf* heather, heath (land), briar: **coq de —** grouse.
buanderie [bɥãdri] *nf* wash-house.
bucarde [bykard] *nf* cockle.
bûche [by(ː)ʃ] *nf* log, fall spill, duffer.
bûcher [byʃe] *vt* to work at, swot up; *vi* to work, swot; *nm* woodshed, woodpile, pyre, stake.
bûcheron [byʃrɔ̃] *nm* woodcutter, woodman lumberjack.
bûcheur, -euse [byʃœːr, øːz] *n* hard worker, plodder.
bucolique [bykɔʔik] *a* bucolic, pastoral.
budget [bydʒe] *nm* estimates; **boucler le —** to balance the budget.
budgétaire [bydʒetɛːr] *a* fiscal, financial.
buée [bye] *nf* vapour, steam.
buffet [byfɛ] *nm* sideboard, refreshment room.
buffle [byfl] *nm* buffalo, hide.
buffleterie [byflətri] *nf* leather equipment.
buis [bɥi] *nm* boxwood.
buisson [bɥisɔ̃] *nm* bush, thicket, brake.
buissonn er, -ière [bɥisɔnje, jɛːr] *a* which lives in th woods; **faire l'école buissonnière** co play truant.
bulgare [bylgaːr] *an* Bulgarian.
Bulgarie [bylgari] *nf* Bulgaria.
bulbe [bylb] *nm* bulb.
bulle [byl] *nf* bubble, (eccl) bull.
bulletin [byltɛ̃] *nm* report, ticket, receipt ballot; **— de vote** voting paper.
buraliste [byralist] *n* clerk, collector of taxes, tobacconist.
bure [byːr] *nf* rieze homespun.
bureau [byro] *nm* desk, office, board committee, orderly room; **— de placement** Labour Exchange, registry; **— de poste** post office; **— de tabac** tobacconist's shop.
bureaucrate [byrokrat] *nm* bureaucrat.
bureaucratie [byrokrasi] *nf* bureaucracy, officialdom, red tape.
burette [byrɛt] *nf* buret, oilcan, flagon.
burin [byrɛ̃] *nm* graving tool, etcher's pen.
buriner [byrine] *vt* to engrave.
burlesque [byrlɛsk] *a* comical.
busc [by:z] *nm* buzzard, tube, nozzle.
busqué [byske] *a* aquiline, hooked.
buste [byst] *nm* bust; **en —** half-length.
but [by(t)] *nm* aim goal, purpose, object(ive), target, mark; **sans —** aimless(ly); **marquer un —** to score a goal; **de — en blanc** point blank.
buté [byte] *a* obstinate, set.
butée [byte] *nf* buttress, stop.

buter [byte] *vi* to knock, stumble, strike, abut; *vr* to knock, prop oneself up.
butin [bytɛ̃] *nm* booty, loot, spoils, plunder.
butoir [bytwaːr] *nm* buffer, check.
butor [bytɔːr] *nm* bittern, lout, bul'y
butte [byt] *nf* hillock, mound, butts; **être en — à** to be exposed to.
buvable [byvabl] *a* drinkable.
buvard [byvaːr] *a* **papier —** blotting paper *nm* blotter, blotting pad.
buvette [byvɛt] *nf* refreshment room, pump room.
buveur, -euse [byvœːr, øːz] *n* drinker, toper.

C

c' see **ce**
ça [sa] see **cela**.
çà [sa] *ad* here, hither; **— et là** here and there; **ah —!** now then! I say!
caban [kabã] *nm* pea-jacket, pilot-coat.
cabane [kaban] *nf* hut, shanty, hutch.
cabanon [kabanɔ̃] *nm* padded cell, small hut.
cabaret [kabarɛ] *nm* tavern, public house, restaurant.
cabaretier, -ière [kabartje, jɛːr] *n* publican, tavern-keeper.
cabas [kabɑ] *nm* shopping basket, satchel, tool-bag.
cabestan [kabɛstã] *nm* capstan, windlass, winch.
cabillaud [kabijo] *nm* cod.
cabine [kabin] *nf* cabin, saloon, box, call-box, hut.
cabinet [kabinɛ] *nm* closet, small room, office, consulting room, cabinet, government, collection; *pl* water closet, lavatory; **— de travail** study; **— de toilette** dressing room.
câble [kɑːbl] *nm* cable, rope, line, wire.
câbler [kɑble] *vt* to cable.
caboche [kabɔʃ] *nf* pate, head.
cabosse [kabɔs] *nm* pod.
cabot [kabo] *nm* mongrel.
cabotage [kabɔtaːʒ] *nm* coasting-trade.
caboteur [kabɔtœːr] *nm* coaster.
cabotin [kabɔtɛ̃] *n* ham actor.
cabrer [kabre] *vt* (plane) to elevate; *vr* to rear, buck, jib (at).
cabriole [kabrijɔl] *nf* leap, caper, somersault.
cabriolet [kabrijɔlɛ] *nm* gig, cabriolet, coupé.
cacahuète [kakawɛt] *nf* peanut.
cacao [kakao] *nm* cacao, cocoa.
cacaotière [kakaotjɛːr] *nf* cocoa plantation.
cacaoyer [kakaɔje] *nm* cocoa-tree.
cacatoès [kakatɔɛːs] *nm* cockatoo.
cache [kaʃ] *nf* hiding-place.

cache-cache [kaʃkaʃ] nm hide-and-seek.

cache-col [kaʃkɔl] nm man's scarf.

cachemire [kaʃmiːr] nm cashmere.

cache-nez [kaʃne] nm muffler.

cacher [kaʃe] vt to hide, conceal, keep secret; vr to lie in hiding, hide (from à).

cachet [kaʃɛ] nm seal, mark, stamp, fee, cachet.

cacheter [kaʃte] vt to seal (up).

cachette [kaʃɛt] nf hiding-place; en — on the quiet.

cachot [kaʃo] nm dungeon.

cachotterie [kaʃɔtri] nf mystery.

cachottier, -ière [kaʃɔtje, jɛːr] a secretive, reticent.

cadastre [kadastr] nm cadastral survey.

cadavéreux, -euse [kadaverø, øːz] a cadaverous.

cadavre [kadɑːvr] nm corpse, dead body, carcase.

cadeau [kado] nm present, gift.

cadenas [kadnɑ] nm padlock, clasp.

cadenasser [kadnase] vt to padlock, clasp.

cadence [kadɑ̃ːs] nf cadence, rhythm, time, tune.

cadencé [kadɑ̃se] a · measured, rhythmical.

cadet, -ette [kadɛ, ɛt] a younger, junior; n youngest; nm caddie.

cadran [kadrɑ̃] nm dial, face.

cadre [kɑːdr] nm frame(work), limits, bounds, outline, plan, cadre, list, strength, management staff.

cadrer [kɑdre] vi to agree, square, tally, fit in.

caduc, -uque [kadyk] a declining, decrepit, weak, lapsed, null and void.

cafard [kafɑːr] a sanctimonious; nm cockroach, telltale; avoir le — to have the blues.

cafarder [kafarde] vi to tell tales, sneak.

café [kafe] nm coffee, café; — nature black coffee; — crème white coffee; — complet white coffee, roll and butter.

caféier(e) [kafeje] n coffee plant, plantation.

cafetier, -ière [kaftje, jɛːr] n owner of a café.

cafetière [kaftjɛːr] nf coffee-pot.

cafouiller [kafuje] vi to splutter, (car) misfire.

cage [kaːʒ] nf cage, coop, casing, well, shaft, stairway.

cagneux, -euse [kaɲø, øːz] a knock-kneed, crooked.

cagnotte [kaɲɔt] nf pool, kitty.

cagot [kago] a hypocritical; n hypocrite.

cagoule [kagul] nf cowl, hood.

cahier [kaje] nm exercise book, copy-book.

cahin-caha [kaɛ̃kaa] ad middling, so-so, limping.

cahot [kao] nm jolt, bump.

cahoter [kaɔte] vti to jolt, bump, shake, toss about.

cahoteux, -euse [kaɔtø, øːz] a bumpy, rough.

caille [kɑːj] nf quail.

caillebotte [kajbɔt] nf curds.

cailler [kɑje] vtir to clot, curdle; lait caillé curds.

caillot [kajo] nm clot.

caillou [kaju] nm pebble.

caillouter [kajute] vt to metal, pave with pebbles.

caillouteux, -euse [kajutø, øːz] a stony, pebbly.

caïman [kaimɑ̃] nm crocodile.

caisse [kɛs] nf case, chest, casing, tub, body, cashbox, till, pay-desk, counting-house, fund, bank, drum; tenir la — to be in charge of the money; — d'épargne savings bank.

caissier, ière [kɛsje, jɛːr] n cashier.

caisson [kɛsɔ̃] nm box, boot, ammunition wagon, locker, caisson.

cajoler [kaʒɔle] vt to cajole, coax.

cajolerie [kaʒɔlri] nf cajolery, coaxing.

calamité [kalamite] nf calamity.

calamiteux, -euse [kalamitø, øːz] a calamitous, broken-down, seedy.

calao [kalao] nm hornbill.

calcaire [kalkɛːr] a calcareous, chalky; nm limestone.

calcul [kalkyl] nm calculation, reckoning, arithmetic, calculus, (in bladder) stone.

calculé [kalkyle] a calculated, studied, deliberate.

calculer [kalkyle] vt to calculate, reckon.

cale [kal] nf hold, slipway, stocks, wedge, chock, prop; — sèche dry dock; — de radoub graving dock; mettre sur — to lay down.

calé [kale] a wedged, jammed, good (at en).

calebasse [kalbɑːs] nf calabash, gourd.

caleçon [kalsɔ̃] nm drawers, pants.

calembour [kalɑ̃buːr] nm pun.

calendrier [kalɑ̃dri(j)e] nm calendar.

calepin [kalpɛ̃] nm notebook.

caler [kale] vt to wedge, chock (up), prop up, adjust, stall; vi to stall, draw water, funk.

calfat [kalfa] nm caulker.

calfater [kalfate] vt to caulk.

calfeutrer [kalføtre] vt to stop (up), block (up), make draught-proof; vr to shut oneself up, make oneself cosy, comfortable.

calibre [kalibr] nm calibre, bore, gauge, pattern.

calice [kalis] nm calyx, chalice, cup.

calicot [kaliko] nm calico, draper's shop assistant.

califourchon [kalifurʃɔ̃] ad à — astride.

câlin [kalɛ̃] a caressing, winning, wheedling.

câliner [kɑline] *vt* to caress, fondle, pet, wheedle.

câlinerie [kɑlinri] *nf* caress(ing), petting, wheedling.

calleux, -euse [kalø, øːz] *a* horny, callous.

calligraphie [kalligrafi] *nf* penmanship, handwriting.

callosité [kallɔzite] *nf* callosity.

calme [kalm] *a* calm, still, quiet, composed, collected; *nm* calm(ness), stillness.

calmer [kalme] *vt* to calm, quiet, soothe; *vr* to calm down, abate.

calomniateur, -trice [kalɔmnjatœːr, tris] *n* slanderer.

calomnie [kalɔmni] *nf* calumny, slander, libel.

calomnier [kalɔmnje] *vt* to slander.

calomnieux, -euse [kalɔmnjø, øːz] *a* slanderous.

calorie [kalɔri] *nf* calory.

calorifère [kalɔrifɛːr] *nm* central-heating apparatus, hot-air stove.

calorifuge [kalɔrifyːʒ] *a* heat-insulating, heat-proof.

calorique [kalɔrik] *a* caloric, heat.

calot [kalo] *nm* forage cap, rough slate, stone.

calotte [kalɔt] *nf* skull cap, box on the ears.

calotter [kalɔte] *vt* to cuff.

calque [kalk] *nm* tracing, traced copy.

calquer [kalke] *vt* to trace.

calvitie [kalvisi] *nf* baldness.

camarade [kamarad] *n* comrade, chum, friend, mate.

camaraderie [kamaradri] *nf* comradeship, fellowship.

camard [kamaːr] *a* flat-, snub-, pug-nosed.

Cambodge [kɑ̃bodʒ] *nm* Cambodia.

cambouis [kɑ̃bwi] *nm* dirty oil, grease.

cambré [kɑ̃bre] *a* cambered, arched, curved, bent.

cambrer [kɑ̃bre] *vt* to arch, bend, camber, curve; *vr* to brace oneself.

cambriolage [kɑ̃briɔlaːʒ] *nm* burglary.

cambrioler [kɑ̃briɔle] *vt* to burgle, break into.

cambrioleur, -euse [kɑ̃briɔlœːr, øːz] *n* burglar.

cambrure [kɑ̃bryːr] *nf* camber, curve, arch, instep.

cambuse [kɑ̃byːz] *nf* steward's room, glory hole, hovel.

came [kam] *nf* cam.

camée [kame] *nm* cameo.

caméléon [kamelẽ] *nm* chameleon.

camélia [kamelja] *nm* camelia.

camelot [kamlo] *nm* street hawker, newsvendor.

camelote [kamlɔt] *nf* rubbish, trash, shoddy goods.

caméra [kamɛra] *nf* cine-camera.

camion [kamjɔ̃] *nm* wagon, dray, lorry, truck.

camionnage [kamjɔnaːʒ] *nm* cartage, haulage.

camionnette [kamjɔnɛt] *nf* light motor lorry, van.

camionneur [kamjɔnœːr] *nm* carrier.

camisole [kamizɔl] *nf* woman's vest, dressing-jacket; — de force straitjacket.

camouflage [kamuflaːʒ] *n* camouflage.

camoufler [kamufle] *vt* to disguise, fake, camouflage.

camouflet [kamuflɛ] *nm* insult, snub.

camp [kɑ̃] *nm* camp, side.

campagnard [kɑ̃paɲaːr] *a* country, rustic; *n* countryman, -woman.

campagne [kɑ̃paɲ] *nf* country(side), field, campaign; **partie de** — picnic.

campé [kɑ̃pe] *a* **bien** — well set-up, strapping.

campement [kɑ̃pmɑ̃] *nm* encampment, camping.

camper [kɑ̃pe] *vi* to (en)camp; *vt* to put under canvas, place, put, stick; — **là** to leave in the lurch; *vr* to pitch one's camp, plant oneself.

camphre [kɑ̃ːfr] *nm* camphor.

camphrer [kɑ̃fre] *vt* to camphorate.

camus [kamy] *a* snub-, flat-, pug-nosed.

canaille [kanɑːj] *nf* rabble, mob, blackguard, rascal.

canal [kanal] *nm* canal, channel, pipe, duct.

canalisation [kanalizasjɔ̃] *nf* canalization, draining, piping, pipes, wiring, mains.

canaliser [kanalize] *vt* to canalize, pipe, lay down pipes in, wire.

canapé [kanape] *nm* sofa; canapé.

canard [kanaːr] *nm* duck, drake, false report, hoax, lump of sugar dipped in coffee.

canari [kanari] *nm* canary, earthenware pot.

cancan [kɑ̃kɑ̃] *nm* cancan dance, scandal.

cancanier, -ière [kɑ̃kanje, jɛːr] *a* addicted to tittle-tattle; *n* scandalmonger.

cancer [kɑ̃sɛːr] *nm* cancer.

cancéreux, -euse [kɑ̃serø, øːz] *a* cancerous.

cancrelat [kɑ̃krəla] *nm* cockroach.

candélabre [kɑ̃dɛlaːbr] *nm* candelabrum, branched lamp-post.

candeur [kɑ̃dœːr] *nf* ingenuousness, artlessness.

candidat [kɑ̃dida] *nm* candidate.

candide [kɑ̃did] *a* ingenuous, artless, guileless.

cane [kan] *nf* duck.

caneton [kantɔ̃] *nm* duckling.

canette [kanɛt] *nf* beer-bottle, spool.

canevas [kanvɑ] *nm* canvas, outline, sketch.

caniche [kaniʃ] *n* poodle.

canicule [kanikyl] *nf* dog-days.

canif [kanif] *nm* penknife.

caniveau [kanivo] *nm* gutter, conduit.

canne [kan] *nf* cane, walking-stick, fishing-rod; — **à sucre** sugar cane.

cannelle [kanɛl] *nf* cinnamon, spigot, tap.

cannelure [kanlyːr] *nf* groove, fluting.

canner [kane] *vt* to cane-bottom.

cannibale [kanibal] *nm* cannibal, man-eater.

cannibalisme [kanibalism] *nm* cannibalism.

canon [kanɔ̃] *nm* cannon, gun, barrel, pipe, tube, canon.

cañon [kaɲɔ̃] *nm* canyon.

canonique [kanɔnik] *a* canonical.

canoniser [kanɔnize] *vt* to canonize.

canonnade [kanɔnad] *nf* cannonade.

canonnier [kanɔnje] *nm* gunner.

canonnière [kanɔnjɛːr] *nf* gunboat.

canot [kano] *nm* boat, dinghy, cutter.

canotage [kanɔtaːʒ] *nm* boating, rowing.

canoter [kanɔte] *vi* to go rowing, boating.

canotier [kanɔtje] *nm* rower, oarsman, boatman, straw hat, boater.

cantatrice [kɑ̃tatris] *nf* singer, vocalist.

cantine [kɑ̃tin] *nf* canteen.

cantinier, -ière [kɑ̃tinje] *n* canteen-keeper.

cantique [kɑ̃tik] *nm* canticle, hymn.

canton [kɑ̃tɔ̃] *nm* canton, district.

cantonade [kɑ̃tɔnad] *nf* **à la —** in the wings, ' off '.

cantonal [kɑ̃tɔnal] *a* cantonal, district.

cantonner [kɑ̃tɔne] *vt* to divide into cantons, quarter, billet, confine, limit.

cantonnement [kɑ̃tɔnmɑ̃] *nm* cantonment, quarters, billet.

cantonnier [kɑ̃tɔnje] *nm* roadman, road-mender.

canulant [kanylɑ̃] *a* boring.

canule [kanyl] *nf* nozzle.

caoutchouc [kautʃu] *nm* (india) rubber, waterproof coat; *pl* galoshes, overshoes, rubbers.

caoutchouter [kautʃute] *vt* to rubberize, treat with rubber.

cap [kap] *nm* cape, headland.

capable [kapabl] *a* capable, fit, able.

capacité [kapasite] *nf* capacity, ability, capability.

cape [kap] *nf* cape, cloak; **rire sous** — to laugh up one's sleeve.

capillaire [kapilɛːr] *a* capillary.

capitaine [kapitɛn] *nm* captain, master, head; — **de vaisseau** captain (R.N.); — **de frégate** commander; — **de corvette** lieutenant-commander; — **de port** harbour-master.

capital [kapital] *a* capital, chief, principal; *nm* capital, assets, principal.

capitale [kapital] *nf* capital, chief town.

capitaliser [kapitalize] *vt* to capitalize.

capitalisme [kapitalism] *nm* capitalism.

capitaliste [kapitalist] *n* capitalist.

capiteux, -euse [kapitø, øːz] *a* heady, strong.

capitonner [kapitɔne] *vt* to upholster, quilt.

capituler [kapityle] *vi* to capitulate.

caporal [kapɔral] *nm* corporal, (ordinary quality) tobacco.

capot [kapo] *nm* cover, hood, bonnet, cowl.

capotage [kapɔtaːʒ] *nm* capsizing, overturning.

capote [kapɔt] *nf* greatcoat, bonnet, hood, cowl, contraceptive.

capoter [kapɔte] *vt* to capsize, overturn.

câpre [kɑːpr] *nm* caper.

caprice [kapris] *nm* caprice, whim, impulse.

capricieux, -euse [kaprisjø, jøːz] *a* capricious, wayward.

capsule [kapsyl] *nf* capsule, seal, firing-cap.

captage [kaptaːʒ] *nm* catching, collecting.

captation [kaptasjɔ̃] *nf* catching, tapping, picking up.

capter [kapte] *vt* to catch, collect, obtain, pick up.

captieux, -euse [kapsjø, øːz] *a* captious, specious.

captif, -ive [kaptif, iːv] *an* captive.

captiver [kaptive] *vt* to captivate, charm.

captivité [kaptivite] *nf* captivity.

capture [kaptyːr] *nf* capture, seizure, booty.

capturer [kaptyre] *vt* to capture, catch, collect.

capuchon [kapyʃɔ̃] *nm* hood, cowl, cap.

capucine [kapysin] *nf* nasturtium.

caque [kak] *nf* keg, herring barrel.

caquet [kakɛ] *nm* cackle, chattering.

caqueter [kakte] *vi* to cackle, chatter.

car [kaːr] *cj* for, because; *nm* motor coach.

carabin [karabɛ̃] *nm* medical student.

carabine [karabin] *nf* carbine, rifle.

carabiné [karabine] *a* stiff, violent, strong.

carabinier [karabinje] *nm* rifleman.

caractère [karaktɛːr] *nm* character, temper, personality, characteristic, nature.

caractériser [karakterize] *vt* to characterize; *vr* to assume the character (of **par**), be distinguished (by **par**).

caractéristique [karakteristik] *a* characteristic, typical; *nf* trait, feature.

carafe [karaf] *nf* decanter, carafe.
caravane [karavan] *nf* desert caravan, caravan.
carbone [karbɔn] *nm* carbon.
carbonisé [karbɔnize] *a* carbonized, charred, burnt to death.
carburant [karbyrã] *nm* motor fuel.
carburateur [karbyratœːr] *nm* carburettor.
carbure [karbyːr] *nf* carbide.
carcasse [karkas] *nf* carcase, frame.
cardiaque [kardiak] *a* cardiac; **crise** — heart attack.
cardinal [kardinal] *anm* cardinal.
carême [karɛm] *nm* Lent.
carence [karãːs] *nf* insolvency, default, deficiency.
carène [karɛn] *nf* hull, bottom.
caresse [karɛs] *nf* caress.
caresser [karɛse] *vt* to caress, stroke, fondle, cherish.
cargaison [kargɛzɔ̃] *nf* cargo.
cargo [kargo] *nm* cargo boat, tramp steamer.
caricature [karikatyːr] *nf* caricature.
carie [kari] *nf* caries, decay.
carié [karje] *a* decayed.
carillon [karijɔ̃] *nm* chime, peal of bells.
carillonner [karijɔne] *vi* to chime, ring a peal of bells.
carillonneur [karijɔnœːr] *nm* bell-ringer.
carlingue [karlɛ̃ːg] *nf* fuselage, cockpit.
carnage [karnaːʒ] *nm* slaughter, bloodshed.
carnassier, -ière [karnasje, jɛːr] *a* carnivorous.
carnassière [karnasjɛːr] *nf* game-bag.
carnaval [karnaval] *nm* carnival.
carnet [karnɛ] *nm* notebook; — **de banque** pass-book; — **de chèques** cheque-book; — **de bal** dance programme.
carnier [karnje] *nm* game-bag.
carnivore [karnivɔːr] *a* carnivorous.
carotte [karɔt] *nf* carrot; (*of tobacco*) plug; fraud, trick, catch.
carpe [karp] *nf* carp.
carpette [karpɛt] *nf* rug.
carquois [karkwa] *nm* quiver.
carré [kare] *a* square (-shouldered), straightforward; *nm* square, lodgings.
carreau [karo] *nm* tile, floor, small square, window-pane, diamonds.
carrefour [karfuːr] *nm* crossroads, square.
carrelage [karlaːʒ] *nm* tiling, tile-flooring.
carreler [karle] *vt* to pave, lay with tiles.
carrelet [karlɛ] *nm* plaice.
carrément [karemã] *ad* squarely, firmly, bluntly.
carrer [kare] *vt* to square; *vr* to swagger, settle oneself.

carrier [karje] *nm* quarryman.
carrière [karjɛːr] *nf* career, quarry; **donner libre** — **à** to give free play, scope, vent to.
carriole [karjɔl] *nf* light cart.
carrossable [karɔsabl] *a* **route** — carriageway.
carrosse [karɔs] *nm* coach.
carrosserie [karɔsri] *nf* coach-building, body(work).
carrousel [karuzɛl] *nm* tournament, merry-go-round.
carrure [karyːr] *nf* build, stature.
cartable [kartabl] *nm* satchel, portfolio.
carte [kart] *nf* map, chart, card, bill, list, menu; — **blanche** free hand, carte blanche.
cartel [kartɛl] *nm* trust, combine, coalition.
carter [kartɛːr] *nm* gearcase, sump, spool-box.
cartographe [kartɔgraf] *nm* map-maker, cartographer.
cartographie [kartɔgrafi] *nf* map-making.
cartomancie [kartɔmɑ̃si] *nf* fortune-telling by cards.
cartomancien, -ienne [kartɔmɑ̃sjɛ̃, jɛn] *n* fortune-teller by cards.
carton [kartɔ̃] *nm* cardboard box, carton, cartoon.
cartonné [kartɔne] *a* (*books*) bound in boards.
cartouche [kartuʃ] *nf* cartridge.
cartouchière [kartuʃjɛːr] *nf* cartridge-pouch.
cas [kɑ] *nm* case, matter, affair, instance, circumstance; **le** — **échéant** should the occasion arise; **au, dans le** — **où** in the event of; **en tout** — in any case; **faire (grand)** — **de** to value highly.
casanier, -ière [kazanje, jɛːr] *a* stay-at-home, sedentary.
cascade [kaskad] *nf* waterfall, cascade.
case [kɑːz] *nf* hut, cabin, pigeon-hole, compartment, space, division, square.
casemate [kazmat] *nf* casemate.
caser [kaze] *vt* to put away, stow, file, find a place for, settle; *vr* to settle down.
caserne [kazɛrn] *nf* barracks.
casier [kazje] *nm* set of pigeonholes, rack, cabinet; — **judiciaire** police record.
casque [kask] *nm* helmet.
casquette [kaskɛt] *nf* cap.
cassant [kasɑ̃] *a* brittle, crisp, short, blunt, abrupt.
cassation [kasasjɔ̃] *nf* cassation, quashing, reduction to the ranks.
casse [kɑːs] *nf* breakage, ructions, damage.
casse-cou [kasku] *nm* dare-devil, death-trap.
casse-croûte [kaskrut] *nm* snack, quick lunch.

casse-noisettes [kɑsnwazɛt] *nm* nut-crackers.

casser [kɑse] *vt* to break, crack, cashier, degrade, annul, quash; *vr* to break, give way, snap; se — la tête to puzzle, rack one's brains.

casserole [kɑsrɔl] *nf* saucepan, stewpan, casserole.

casse-tête [kɑstɛt] *nm* club, loaded stick, teaser, din.

cassette [kɑsɛt] *nf* casket, money-box.

cassis [kɑsi(s)] *nm* blackcurrant (liqueur); open gutter across road.

cassonade [kɑsɔnad] *nf* brown sugar.

cassure [kɑsyːr] *nf* break, fracture, crack.

castor [kɑstɔːr] *nm* beaver.

casuel [kɑzɥɛl] *nm* perquisites, casual profits, fees.

cataclysme [kataklism] *nm* cataclysm.

catacombes [katakɔ:b] *nf pl* catacombs.

catalepsie [katalɛpsi] *nf* catalepsy.

catalogue [katalɔg] *nm* catalogue.

cataloguer [katalɔge] *vt* to catalogue, list.

catalyseur [katalizœːr] *nm* catalyst.

cataplasme [kataplasm] *nm* poultice; — sinapisé mustard poultice.

cataracte [katarakt] *nf* cataract.

catarrhe [kataːr] *nm* catarrh.

catastrophe [katastrɔf] *nf* catastrophe, disaster.

catch [katʃ] *nm* all-in wrestling.

catéchiser [kateʃize] *vt* to catechize, lecture, reason with, try to persuade.

catéchisme [kateʃism] *nm* catechism.

catégorie [kategɔri] *nf* category.

catégorique [kategɔrik] *a* categorical, positive.

cathédrale [katedral] *nf* cathedral.

catholicisme [katɔlisism] *nm* catholicism.

catholique [katɔlik] *a* catholic, orthodox; universal; *an* Roman Catholic; ce n'est pas — that is fishy.

catimini [katimini] *ad* en — on the sly, stealthily.

cauchemar [kɔʃmaːr, ko-] *nm* nightmare.

cauri [kɔri] *nm* cowrie shell.

cause [koːz] *nf* cause, grounds, suit, action, brief; et pour — for a very good reason, very properly; pour — de for reasons of; à — de on account of, owing to, through; — célèbre famous case, trial; mettre en — to implicate, bring into question; en connaissance de — with full knowledge of the case.

causer [koze] *vt* to cause; *vi* to talk, converse, chat.

causerie [kozri] *nf* talk, chat.

causeur, -euse [kozœːr, øːz] *a* talkative, chatty; *n* talker.

caustique [kostik] *a* caustic, burning, cutting, biting.

cauteleux, -euse [kotlø, øːz] *a* cunning, sly, wary.

cautériser [koterize] *vt* to cauterize.

caution [kosjɔ̃] *nf* security, surety, bail, guarantee; sujet à — unconfirmed.

cautionnement [kosjɔnmɑ̃] *nm* surety deposit, security, guarantee.

cavalerie [kavalri] *nf* cavalry.

cavalier, -ière [kavalje, jeːr] *a* offhand, free and easy, jaunty, riding; *n* horseman, horsewoman, rider; *nm* trooper, escort, cavalier, partner, knight.

cave [kaːv] *a* hollow, sunken, deepset; *nf* cellar, stake.

caveau [kavo] *nm* vault.

caverne [kavɛrn] *nf* cave, cavern, den, cavity.

caverneux, -euse [kavɛrnø, øːz] *a* cavernous, hollow, sepulchral.

caviarder [kavjarde] *vt* to suppress, block-out.

cavité [kavite] *nf* cavity, hollow, pit.

ce [s(ə)] *pn* it, he, she; — qui, — que what, which; sur — thereupon; pour — qui est de as regards; *a* ce, cet, cette, ces this, that, such; *pl* these, those, such; — soir this evening, tonight; cette nuit last night.

ceci [səsi] *pn* this.

cécité [sesite] *nf* blindness.

céder [sede] *vt* to give up, surrender, assign; *vi* to yield, give way, sag; le — à qn. to be inferior to s.o.

cèdre [sɛːdr] *nm* cedar.

ceindre [sɛ̃ːdr] *vt* to gird (on), encircle, encompass.

ceinture [sɛ̃tyːr] *nf* girdle, belt, sash, waist, circle.

ceinturon [sɛ̃tyrɔ̃] *nm* waistbelt, sword-belt.

cela [səla, sla] *pn* that, it, so; comme ci, comme ça so so; c'est ça that's right, that's it.

célèbre [selɛbr] *a* famous.

célébrer [selebre] *vt* to celebrate, observe, hold, solemnize, sing the praises of.

célébrité [selebrite] *nf* celebrity.

céleri [selri] *nm* celery

célérité [selerite] *nf* celerity, speed, swiftness.

céleste [selɛst] *a* celestial, heavenly.

célibat [seliba] *nm* celibacy.

célibataire [selibatɛːr] *a* celibate, unmarried, single; *n* bachelor, spinster.

celle see **celui**.

cellulaire [selylɛːr] *a* cellular; voiture — police van.

cellule [selyl] *nf* cell.

celluloïd [selylɔid] *nm* celluloid.

cellulose [selyloːz] *nf* cellulose.

celte [sɛlt] *n* Celt.

celtique [sɛltik] *a* Celtic.

celui, celle, ceux, celles [səlɥi] *pn* he,

she, the one, those; —ci the latter, this one; —là the former, that one.
cendre [sã:dr] nf ash(es), cinders, embers.
cendré [sãdre] a ashy, ash-grey.
cendrier [sãdrie] nm ashbin, -pan, -pit, -tray.
cène [sɛn] nf the Last Supper.
censé [sãse] a supposed.
censeur [sãsœ:r] nm censor, critic, disciplinary head of French school.
censure [sãsy:r] nf censorship, blame.
censurer [sãsyre] vt to censor, criticize.
cent [sã] a one hundred; nm a hundred; faire les — pas to walk up and down.
centaine [sãtɛn] nf (about) a hundred.
centenaire [sãtnɛ:r] an centenarian; nm centenary.
centième [sãtjɛm] anm hundredth.
centigrade [sãtigrad] a centigrade.
centigramme [sãtigram] nm centi-gramme.
centilitre [sãtilitr] nm centilitre.
centime [sãtim] nm centime.
centimètre [sãtimɛtr] nm centi-metre, tape-measure.
central [sãtral] a central, middle; nm telephone exchange.
centrale [sãtral] nf power-house, electricity works.
centraliser [sãtralize] vt to centralize.
centre [sã:tr] nm centre, middle.
centrifuge [sãtrify:ʒ] a centrifugal.
centuple [sãtypl] a centuple, hundredfold.
cep [sɛ(p)] nm vine-plant.
cependant [s(ə)pãdã] ad meanwhile, meantime; cj still, yet, nevertheless.
cerceau [sɛrso] nm hoop.
cercle [sɛrkl] nm circle, set, club, hoop, ring, dial.
cercler [sɛrkle] vt to encircle, ring, hoop.
cercueil [sɛrkœ:j] nm coffin.
céréale [sereal] anf cereal.
cérébral [serebral] a cerebral, of the brain.
cérémonie [seremɔni] nf ceremony; tenue de — full dress; sans — informally.
cérémonieux, -euse [seremɔnjø, ø:z] ceremonious, formal.
cerf [sɛ:r, sɛrf] nm stag.
cerfeuil [sɛrfœ:j] nm chervil.
cerf-volant [sɛrvɔlã] nm kite.
cerise [s(ə)ri:z] nf cherry.
cerisier [s(ə)rizje] nm cherry-tree.
cerné [sɛrne] a les yeux —s with rings under the eyes.
cerner [sɛrne] vt to encircle, sur-round, hem in.
certain [sɛrtɛ̃] a certain, sure, fixed, stated; pn pl some, certain.
certainement [sɛrtɛnmã] ad certain-ly, by all means.
certes [sɛrt] ad yes indeed, most certainly, to be sure.

certificat [sɛrtifika] nm certificate, script.
certifier [sɛrtifje] vt to attest, authenticate.
certitude [sɛrtityd] nf certainty.
cerveau [sɛrvo] nm brain, mind; — brûlé hot-head.
cervelas [sɛrvəla] nm saveloy.
cervelle [sɛrvɛl] nf brain(s), mind; se creuser la — to rack one's brains.
ces see ce.
cessation [sɛsasjɔ̃] nf cessation, suspension.
cesse [sɛs] nf cease, ceasing.
cesser [sɛse] vit to cease, leave off, stop.
cet see ce.
cette see ce.
ceux see celui.
chacal [ʃakal] nm jackal.
chacun [ʃakœ̃] pn each, each one, every one, everybody, everyone.
chagrin [ʃagrɛ̃] a sad, glum, peevish, fretful; nm grief, annoyance, worry.
chagriner [ʃagrine] vt to grieve, afflict, vex, annoy.
chahut [ʃay] nm noise, uproar, rowdyism.
chahuter [ʃayte] vi to kick up a shindy, boo; vt to rag.
chahuteur, -euse [ʃaytœ:r, ø:z] an rowdy.
chaîne [ʃɛn] nf chain, cable, range, warp; pl bonds, fetters; travail à la — moving-belt production.
chaînon [ʃɛnɔ̃] nm link.
chair [ʃɛ:r] nf flesh, meat, pulp; en — et en os in the flesh; — de poule gooseflesh, creeps; — à canon cannon fodder.
chaire [ʃɛ:r] nf pulpit, desk, rostrum, chair, professorship.
chaise [ʃɛ:z] nf chair, seat.
chaise-longue [ʃɛzlɔ̃:g] nf couch.
chaland [ʃalã] nm customer, lighter, barge.
châle [ʃa:l] nm shawl, wrap.
chalet [ʃalɛ, ʃa-] nm chalet.
chaleur [ʃalœ:r] nf warmth, heat, ardour, zeal; craint la — keep in a cool place.
chaleureux, -euse [ʃalœrø, ø:z] a warm, cordial.
chaloupe [ʃalup] nf launch.
chalumeau [ʃalymo] nm straw, pipe, blowpipe.
chalutier [ʃalytje] nm drifter, trawler.
se chamailler [səʃamaje] vr to quarrel, squabble, row.
chambarder [ʃãbarde] vt to smash up, upset, sack.
chambellan [ʃãbɛlã] nm chamber-lain.
chambranle [ʃãbrã:l] nm frame, mantelpiece.
chambre [ʃã:br] nf (bed)room, chamber, House (parliament); — à air inner tube; — d'ami spare room.

chambrée [ʃɑ̃bre] *nf* roomful, barrack room.

chambrer [ʃɑ̃bre] *vt* to lock up in a room; (wine) take the chill off.

chameau [ʃamo] *nm* camel, scoundrel, beast, swine.

chamois [ʃamwa] *nm* chamois.

champ [ʃɑ̃] *nm* field, ground, course, range, scope; **à tout bout de —** at every turn.

champagne [ʃɑ̃paɲ] *nm* champagne; **fine —** liqueur brandy.

champêtre [ʃɑ̃pɛ:tr] *a* rustic, rural.

champignon [ʃɑ̃piɲɔ̃] *nm* mushroom.

champion, -ionne [ʃɑ̃pjɔ̃, jɔn] *n* champion.

championnat [ʃɑ̃pjɔna] *nm* championship.

chance [ʃɑ̃:s] *nf* chance, luck.

chancelant [ʃɑ̃slɑ̃] *a* staggering, shaky, delicate.

chanceler [ʃɑ̃sle] *vi* to stagger, totter.

chancelier [ʃɑ̃səlje] *nm* chancellor.

chancellerie [ʃɑ̃selri] *nf* chancellery, secretaryship.

chanceux, -euse [ʃɑ̃sø, ø:z] *a* hazardous, lucky.

chancre [ʃɑ̃:kr] *nm* canker, ulcer.

chandail [ʃɑ̃da:j] *nm* sweater, pullover.

Chandeleur [ʃɑ̃dlœ:r] *nf* Candlemas.

chandelier [ʃɑ̃dəlje] *nm* candlestick.

chandelle [ʃɑ̃dɛl] *nf* candle, prop, shore; **voir trente-six —s** to see stars; **économies de bouts de —** cheese-paring.

change [ʃɑ̃:ʒ] *nm* exchange; **lettre de —** bill of exchange.

changeable [ʃɑ̃ʒabl] *a* changeable, exchangeable.

changeant [ʃɑ̃ʒɑ̃] *a* changing, changeable, fickle.

changement [ʃɑ̃ʒmɑ̃] *nm* change, alteration, variation, variety; **— de vitesse** gear, change of gear; **— de voie** points.

changer [ʃɑ̃ʒe] *vt* to change, exchange, alter; *vi* to change; *vr* to alter, change one's clothes.

changeur [ʃɑ̃ʒœ:r] *nm* money-changer.

chanoine [ʃanwan] *nm* canon.

chanson [ʃɑ̃sɔ̃] *nf* song; **—s!** nonsense!

chansonnier, -ière [ʃɑ̃sɔnje, jɛ:r] *n* songwriter; *nm* songbook.

chant [ʃɑ̃] *nm* song, singing, crow(ing), chant, canto.

chantage [ʃɑ̃ta:ʒ] *nm* blackmail.

chantant [ʃɑ̃tɑ̃] *a* singing, musical, sing-song.

chanter [ʃɑ̃te] *vt* to sing, crow, chirp, suit; **faire —** to blackmail.

chanteur, -euse [ʃɑ̃tœ:r, ø:z] *n* singer, vocalist; **maître —** master-singer, blackmailer.

chantier [ʃɑ̃tje] *nm* stand, ship (building) yard, dockyard; **sur le —** in hand.

chantonner [ʃɑ̃tɔne] *vt* to hum.

chanvre [ʃɑ̃:vr] *nm* hemp.

chaos [kao] *nm* chaos.

chaotique [kaotik] *a* chaotic.

chape [ʃap] *nf* cope, coping.

chapeau [ʃapo] *nm* hat, cover, cap, cowl, heading; **donner un coup de — à** to raise one's hat to; **— melon** bowler; **— haut-de-forme, à, de haute forme** top hat.

chapelet [ʃaplɛ] *nm* rosary, string.

chapelier [ʃapəlje] *nm* hatter.

chapelle [ʃapɛl] *nf* chapel, coterie, clique.

chapelure [ʃaply:r] *nf* breadcrumbs.

chaperon [ʃaprɔ̃] *nm* hood, chaperon.

chapitre [ʃapitr] *nm* chapter, heading, item, point; **avoir voix au —** to have a say in the matter.

chapitrer [ʃapitre] *vt* to lecture, reprimand.

chaque [ʃak] *a* each, every.

char [ʃa:r] *nm* chariot, car, wagon; **— d'assaut** tank.

charbon [ʃarbɔ̃] *nm* coal, carbon; **— de bois** charcoal.

charbonnage [ʃarbɔna:ʒ] *nm pl* collieries, coal-mining; (*naut*) bunkering.

charbonner [ʃarbɔne] *vt* to carbonize, blacken with charcoal.

charbonnier [ʃarbɔnje, jɛ:r] *nm* collier, charcoal-burner, coal merchant, coalman.

charcuterie [ʃarkytri] *nf* pork-butcher's shop, pork-butcher's meat, pork.

charcutier, -ière [ʃarkytje, jɛ:r] *n* pork-butcher.

chardon [ʃardɔ̃] *nm* thistle.

chardonneret [ʃardɔnrɛ] *nm* goldfinch.

charge [ʃarʒ] *nf* load, burden, charge, onus, care, trust, expense, office, duty, exaggeration, skit, indictment; **à la —** de chargeable to, dependent on, assigned to; **en — (el)** live; **à — de** on condition that, provided that; **témoin à —** witness for the prosecution.

chargé [ʃarʒe] *a* loaded, live, furred, coated, full, busy, overcast; **lettre —e** registered letter; *nm* **— de cours** lecturer, reader.

chargement [ʃarʒəmɑ̃] *nm* lading, loading (up), charging, registration, freight.

charger [ʃarʒe] *vt* to load, charge, fill, instruct, caricature, exaggerate, saddle; *vr* to undertake, shoulder.

chariot [ʃarjo] *nm* wagon, go-cart, truck, trolley.

charité [ʃarite] *nf* charity, alms.

charme [ʃarm] *nm* charm, spell.

charmer [ʃarme] *vt* to charm, bewitch, delight, please.

charnel, -elle [ʃarnɛl] *a* carnal, sensual.

charnier [ʃarnje] *nm* charnel-house, ossuary.

charnière [ʃarnjɛːr] nf hinge.

charnu [ʃarny] a fleshy, plump.

charognard [ʃarɔɲar] nm vulture.

charogne [ʃarɔɲ] nf carrion, decaying carcase.

charpente [ʃarpɑ̃:t] nf frame(work).

charpenter [ʃarpɑ̃te] vt to frame, build, construct.

charpenterie [ʃarpɑ̃tri] nf carpentry, carpenter's shop.

charpentier [ʃarpɑ̃tje] nm carpenter.

charpie [ʃarpi] nf lint; **en —** in shreds.

charretier [ʃartje] nm carter, carrier.

charrette [ʃarɛt] nf cart; **— à bras** barrow; **— anglaise** trap, dogcart.

charrier [ʃarje] vt to cart, carry.

charron [ʃarɔ̃] nm cartwright, wheelwright.

charrue [ʃary] nf plough.

charte [ʃart] nf charter.

chartreux [ʃartrø] nm Carthusian monk.

chasse [ʃas] nf chase, hunting, shooting, shoot; **— à courre** riding to hounds; **— à l'affût** stalking; **— d'eau** flush.

châsse [ʃaːs] nf reliquary, shrine, frame.

chasser [ʃase] vt to chase, hunt, shoot, drive (away, out), dismiss, expel; vi to hunt, go hunting, shooting, drive.

chasseur, -euse [ʃasœːr, øːz] n huntsman, sportsman, shooter; nm pageboy, messenger, rifleman, fighter-plane; **— de fauves** big-game hunter.

chassieux, -euse [ʃasjø, øːz] a blear-eyed.

chassis [ʃasi] nm frame, sash, chassis, under carriage.

chaste [ʃast] a chaste, pure.

chasteté [ʃastəte] nf chastity, purity.

chat, -atte [ʃa, -at] n cat; **— de gouttières** stray cat.

châtaigne [ʃatɛɲ] nf chestnut.

châtaignier [ʃatɛɲje] nm chestnut tree.

châtain [ʃatɛ̃] a chestnut-brown, auburn.

château [ʃato] nm castle, country-residence, manor, palace; **—x en Espagne** castles in the air; **— d'eau** water tower.

châteaubriant [ʃatobriɑ̃] nm grilled steak.

chat-huant [ʃayɑ̃] nm tawny, brown owl.

châtier [ʃatje] vt to punish, chastise, (style) polish.

châtiment [ʃatimɑ̃] nm punishment, chastisement.

chatoiement [ʃatwamɑ̃] nm shimmer, sheen.

chaton [ʃatɔ̃] nm kitten, catkin, stone in its setting.

chatouiller [ʃatuje] vt to tickle.

chatouilleux, -euse [ʃatujø, øːz] a ticklish, touchy, sensitive, delicate.

chatoyer [ʃatwaje] vi to shimmer, sparkle.

châtrer [ʃatre] vt to castrate, geld.

chatterton [ʃatɛrtɔ̃] nm insulating tape.

chaud [ʃo] a warm, hot; **pleurer à —es larmes** to weep bitterly; **il fait —** it is warm; **tenir au —** to keep in a warm place; **avoir —** to be warm.

chaudière [ʃodjɛːr] nf boiler.

chaudron [ʃodrɔ̃] nm cauldron.

chaudronnerie [ʃodrɔnri] nf coppersmith's work; boiler-making, boiler-works.

chaudronnier [ʃodrɔnje] nm coppersmith, brazier, boiler-smith, boiler-maker.

chauffage [ʃofaːʒ] nm heating, firing, stoking; **— central** central heating.

chauffard [ʃofaːr] nm roadhog.

chauffe [ʃoːf] nf heating, stoking, firing.

chauffer [ʃofe] vt to warm, heat, stoke up, fire up, nurse, cram; vi to get hot, warm (up), get up steam.

chauffeur, -euse [ʃofœːr, øːz] n stoker, fireman, driver.

chaume [ʃoːm] nm thatch, stubble (-field).

chaumière [ʃomjɛːr] nf (thatched) cottage.

chaussée [ʃose] nf causeway, road-way, carriageway.

chausse-pied [ʃospje] nm shoehorn.

chausser [ʃose] vt to put on (shoes, stockings), make footwear for, supply with footwear; vr to put on one's shoes, stockings.

chausse-trape [ʃostrap] nf trap, ruse.

chaussette [ʃosɛt] nf sock.

chausson [ʃosɔ̃] nm slipper, dancing sandal, gymnasium shoe, bootee, bed-sock, footlet; **— aux pommes** apple turnover.

chaussure [ʃosyːr] nf footwear, boot, shoe.

chauve [ʃoːv] a bald.

chauve-souris [ʃovsuri] nf bat.

chauvin [ʃovɛ̃] an chauvinist(ic).

chaux [ʃo] nf lime; **— vive** quick-lime; **blanchir à la —** to whitewash.

chavirer [ʃavire] vi to capsize; vt to upset, tip (up).

chéchia [ʃeʃja] nm fez.

chef [ʃɛf] nm head, chief, leader, principal, foreman, master, authority, right; **— de cuisine** head cook, chef; **— d'orchestre** conductor; **— de train** guard.

chef-d'œuvre [ʃedœːvr] nm master-piece.

chef-lieu [ʃefljø] nm county town.

chelem [ʃlɛm] nm (cards) slam.

chemin [ʃmɛ̃] nm way, road, track, path, headway; **— de fer** railway; **— des écoliers** roundabout road; **— faisant** on the way; **se mettre en —** to set out; **— de traverse**

crossroad; **ne pas y aller par quatre —s** to go straight to the point.

chemineau [ʃmino] *nm* tramp.

cheminée [ʃmine] *nf* fireplace, mantelpiece, chimney, funnel.

cheminer [ʃmine] *vi* to tramp, proceed, walk, trudge.

chemise [ʃmiːz] *nf* shirt, chemise, jacket, folder, casing, dust jacket; **— de nuit** nightshirt (man), nightdress, nightgown (woman); **en bras de —** in one's shirt sleeves.

chenal [ʃ(ə)nal] *nm* channel.

chenapan [ʃnapɑ̃] *nm* rogue, rascal.

chêne [ʃɛn] *nm* oak (tree).

chenet [ʃ(ə)nɛ] *nm* fire-dog, andiron.

chenil [ʃ(ə)ni] *nm* kennel.

chenille [ʃ(ə)niːj] *nf* caterpillar, chenille, caterpillar tracks.

cheptel [ʃtəl, ʃɛptɛl] *nm* livestock.

chèque [ʃɛk] *nm* cheque.

chéquier [ʃekje] *nm* cheque-book.

cher, -ère [ʃɛːr] *a* dear, beloved, expensive, costly, precious; *ad* dearly, at a high price; **cela ne vaut pas —** it is not worth much.

chercher [ʃɛrʃe] *vt* to look (for, up), seek, search for, endeavour, try (to); **envoyer —** to send for.

chère [ʃɛːr] *nf* countenance, food.

chéri [ʃeri] *a* dear, beloved; *n* darling.

chérir [ʃeriːr] *vt* to love dearly, cherish.

cherté [ʃɛrte] *nf* dearness, high price.

chérubin [ʃerybɛ̃] *nm* cherub.

chétif, -ive [ʃetif, iːv] *a* puny, weak, sickly, poor.

cheval [ʃəval, ʃfal] *nm* horse, horse-power; **— à bascule** rocking-horse; **— de bois** wooden horse; *pl* merry-go-round, roundabout; **— de trait** draught horse; **à —** on horseback; **être à — sur** to be astride, straddle, be a stickler for; **remède de —** drastic remedy.

chevaleresque [ʃ(ə)valrɛsk, ʃfal-] *a* chivalrous, knightly.

chevalerie [ʃ(ə)valri, ʃfal-] *nf* chivalry, knighthood.

chevalet [ʃ(ə)valɛ, ʃfalɛ] *nm* support, trestle, stand, easel, clothes-horse.

chevalier [ʃ(ə)valje, ʃfal-] *nm* knight; **— d'industrie** swindler, adventurer.

chevalière [ʃ(ə)valjɛːr, ʃfal-] *nf* signet-, seal-ring.

chevalin [ʃəvalɛ̃, ʃfalɛ̃] *a* equine; **boucherie —e** horse-meat butcher's shop.

cheval-vapeur [ʃəvalvapœːr] *nm* horsepower.

chevaucher [ʃ(ə)voʃe] *vti* to ride; *vt* to span, overlap.

chevelu [ʃəvly] *a* hairy.

chevelure [ʃəvlyːr] *nf* (head) of hair, locks.

chevet [ʃ(ə)vɛ] *nm* bed's head, bedside, bolster.

cheveu [ʃ(ə)vø] *nm* hair; **couper un — en quatre** to split hairs; **argu-**

ment tiré par les —x a far-fetched argument.

cheville [ʃ(ə)viːj] *nf* pin, peg, bolt, expletive, padding, ankle; **— ouvrière** king-pin.

chèvre [ʃɛːvr] *nf* goat.

chevreau [ʃəvro] *nm* kid.

chèvrefeuille [ʃɛvrəfœːj] *nm* honeysuckle.

chevreuil [ʃəvrœːj] *nm* roe-deer, roebuck.

chevron [ʃəvrɔ̃] *nm* rafter, chevron, stripe.

chevrotant [ʃəvrotɑ̃] *a* quavering.

chez [ʃe] *prep* at, in the house of, care of, with, among, in; **— lui** at his home; **— mon frère** at my brother's.

chic [ʃik] *a* stylish, smart, posh, swell, decent.

chicane [ʃikan] *nf* quibbling, wrangling, pettifoggery.

chicaner [ʃikane] *vt* to wrangle with; *vi* to quibble, haggle over, cavil (at **sur**).

chiche [ʃiʃ] *a* scanty, poor, stingy, sparing of; *excl* go on!, I dare you!; **pois —** chick pea.

chichis [ʃiʃi] *nm pl* affected manners, airs.

chicorée [ʃikɔre] *nf* chicory; **— (frisée)** endive.

chien, chienne [ʃjɛ̃, ʃjɛn] *n* dog, bitch; *nm (of gun)* hammer; **faire le — couchant** to cringe, toady; **un temps de —** filthy weather; **entre — et loup** at dusk, in the gloaming; **— loup** Alsatian dog.

chiffon [ʃifɔ̃] *nm* rag, duster, piece of lace, ribbon, material, scrap, chiffon; **parler —s** to talk dress.

chiffonner [ʃifɔne] *vt* to crumple, rumple, annoy.

chiffonnier, -ière [ʃifɔnje, jɛːr] *n* ragman, rag-picker; *nm* small chest of drawers.

chiffre [ʃifr] *nm* figure, number, cipher, account, monogram; **— d'affaires** turnover.

chiffrer [ʃifre] *vt* to number, work out, cipher, mark; *vi* to calculate, reckon.

chignole [ʃiɲɔl] *nf* (hand-)drill.

chimère [ʃimɛːr] *nf* chimera, illusion.

chimérique [ʃimerik] *a* fanciful, unpractical.

chimie [ʃimi] *nf* chemistry.

chimique [ʃimik] *a* chemical.

chimiste [ʃimist] *nm* chemist (scientist).

Chine [ʃin] *nf* China.

chinois [ʃinwa] *an* Chinese, Chinaman, Chinese woman.

chinoiserie [ʃinwazri] *nf* Chinese curio; *pl* red tape, irksome complications.

chiper [ʃipe] *vt* to pinch, pilfer, sneak, scrounge, bag.

chipie [ʃipi] *nf* shrew, ill-natured woman.

chique [ʃik] *nf* quid (tobacco), roundworm.

chiqué [ʃike] *nm* sham, pretense, make-believe.

chiquenaude [ʃiknoːd] *nf* fillip, flick (of fingers).

chiquer [ʃike] *vt* to chew tobacco.

chiromancie [kirɔmɑ̃si] *nf* palmistry.

chiromancien, -ienne [kirɔmɑ̃sjɛ̃, jɛn] *n* palmist.

chirurgical [ʃiryrʒikal] *a* surgical.

chirurgie [ʃiryrʒi] *nf* surgery; — esthétique du visage face-lifting.

chirurgien, -ienne [ʃiryrʒjɛ̃, jɛn] *n* surgeon.

chloroforme [klɔrɔfɔrm] *nm* chloroform.

choc [ʃɔk] *nm* shock, clash, impact, knock.

chocolat [ʃɔkɔla] *nm* chocolate.

chœur [kœːr] *nm* chorus, choir, chancel.

choisi [ʃwazi] *a* choice, select, picked.

choisir [ʃwaziːr] *vt* to choose, select, pick.

choix [ʃwa] *nm* choice, choosing, selection, pick; de — choice, best, first-class; au — all at the same price.

choléra [kɔlera] *nm* cholera.

chômage [ʃomaːʒ] *nm* unemployment, idleness, closing down.

chômer [ʃome] *vi* to stop work, close, shut down, be idle, be unemployed.

chômeur [ʃomœːr] *nm* unemployed person.

chope [ʃɔp] *nf* tankard.

chopine [ʃɔpin] *nf* pint mug.

choquer [ʃɔke] *vt* to shock, offend, strike, bump, clink; *vr* to come into collision, be shocked.

chose [ʃoːz] *nf* thing, case, matter; bien des —s de ma part à remember me to; monsieur — Mr. Thingummy, Mr. What's-his-name; être tout — to feel queer, look queer.

chou [ʃu] *nm* cabbage, rosette, cream-cake; — de Bruxelles Brussels sprouts; feuille de — rag (newspaper); mon — my darling, pet.

choucas [ʃuka] *nm* jackdaw.

choucroute [ʃukrut] *nf* sauerkraut.

chouette [ʃwɛt] *nf* owl; *a* great, posh, swell.

chou-fleur [ʃuflœːr] *nm* cauliflower.

choyer [ʃwaje] *vt* to pet, pamper, cherish.

chrétien, -ienne [kretjɛ̃, jɛn] *an* Christian.

chretienté [kretjɛ̃te] *nf* Christendom.

Christ [krist] *nm* le — Christ.

christianisme [kristjanism] *nm* Christianity.

chromatique [krɔmatik] *a* chromatic.

chrome [kroːm] *nm* chromium, chrome.

chromo [krɔmo] *nm* color-print.

chronique [krɔnik] *a* chronic; *nf* chronicle, news, notes, reports.

chroniqueur [krɔnikœːr] *nm* chronicler, reporter.

chronologie [krɔnɔlɔʒi] *nf* chronology.

chronologique [krɔnɔlɔʒik] *a* chronological.

chronomètre [krɔnɔmɛtr] *nm* chronometer.

chronométrer [krɔnɔmetre] *vt* to time.

chronométreur [krɔnɔmetrœːr] *nm* time-keeper.

chrysalide [krizalid] *nf* chrysalis.

chrysanthème [krizɑ̃tɛ(ː)m] *nm* chrysanthemum.

chuchotement [ʃyʃɔtmɑ̃] *nm* whispering.

chuchoter [ʃyʃɔte] *vti* to whisper.

chuchoterie [ʃyʃɔtri] *nf* whispered conversation.

chut [ʃyt, ʃt] *excl* hush!

chute [ʃyt] *nf* fall, drop, downfall, collapse, chute; la — des reins small of the back.

Chypre [ʃipr] *nf* Cyprus.

ci [si] *ad* par-ci, par-là here and there; de-ci de-là on all sides; dem ɔn *neuter* comme ci, comme ça so-so.

ci-après [siaprɛ] *ad* hereafter, farther on, below.

cible [sibl] *nf* target.

ciboire [sibwaːr] *nm* ciborium, pyx.

ciboulette [sibulɛt] *nf* chives.

cicatrice [sikatris] *nf* scar.

ci-contre [sikɔ̃tr] *ad* opposite, annexed, on the other side, per contra.

ci-dessous [sidsu] *ad* undermentioned, below.

ci-dessus [sidsy] *ad* above (mentioned).

ci-devant [sidvɑ̃] *ad* previously, formerly, late.

cidre [si(ː)dr] *nm* cider.

ciel [sjɛl] *pl* cieux [sjø] *nm* sky, heaven, air, climate, canopy.

cierge [sjɛrʒ] *nm* wax candle, taper.

cigale [sigal] *nf* cicada.

cigare [sigaːr] *nm* cigar.

cigarette [sigarɛt] *nf* cigarette.

ci-gît [siʒi] here lies.

cigogne [sigɔɲ] *nf* stork.

ci-inclus [siɛ̃kly] *a* herewith, enclosed.

ci-joint [siʒwɛ̃] *a* herewith, attached, subjoined.

cil [sil] *nm* eyelash.

cime [sim] *nf* summit, top.

ciment [simɑ̃] *nm* cement; — armé reinforced concrete.

cimenter [simɑ̃te] *vt* to cement, consolidate.

cimetière [simtjɛːr] *nm* cemetery, graveyard.

cinéaste [sineast] *nm* film technician, producer.

cinéma [sinɛma] nm cinema, picture-house.

cinématographier [sinɛmatɔgrafje] vt to cinematograph, film.

cinématographique [sinɛmatɔgrafik] a cinematographic, film.

cinéprojecteur [sineprɔʒɛktœːr] nm cine(matographic) projector.

cinglant [sɛ̃glɑ̃] a biting, cutting, scathing.

cingler [sɛ̃gle] vt to lash, cut with a lash, whip, sting; vi to sail, scud along.

cinq [sɛ̃(ː)k] num a five; moins — a near thing.

cinquantaine [sɛ̃kɑ̃tɛn] nf (about) fifty.

cinquante [sɛ̃kɑ̃ːt] num a fifty.

cinquantenaire [sɛ̃kɑ̃tnɛːr] nm fiftieth anniversary, jubilee; n a man, woman of fifty.

cinquantième [sɛ̃kɑ̃tjɛm] num an fiftieth.

cintre [sɛ̃ːtr] nm curve, bend, arch.

cintrer [sɛ̃tre] vt to curve, arch, take in at the waist.

cirage [siraːʒ] nm polishing, wax (ing) polish.

circoncire [sirkɔ̃siːr] vt to circumcise.

circonférence [sirkɔ̃ferɑ̃ːs] nf circumference perimeter, girth.

circonflexe [sirkɔ̃fleks] a circumflex.

circonscription [sirkɔ̃skripsjɔ̃] nf circumscription, division, constituency.

circonscrire [sirkɔ̃skriːr] vt to circumscribe. encircle, limit.

circonspect [sirkɔ̃spɛ, -spɛk, -spɛkt] a circumspect cautious.

circonspection [sirkɔ̃speksjɔ̃] n circumspection prudence, caution.

circonstance [sirkɔ̃stɑ̃ːs] n circumstance, occasion, event.

circuit [sirkɥi] nm circuit, round; établir le — to switch on; couper le — to switch off, cut out.

circulaire [sirkylɛːr] anf circular.

circulation [sirkylasjɔ̃] nf circulation, traffic; — interdite no thoroughfare.

circuler [sirkyle] vi to circulate, move (on, about).

cire [siːr] nf wax.

ciré [sire] a waxed, polished; toile —e oilcloth; nm oilskins.

cirer [sire] vt to wax, polish.

cireur, -euse [sirœːr øːz] n polisher, shoeblack.

cirque [sirk] nm circus.

cisaille(s) [sizaːj] nf shears, clippers.

ciseau [sizo] nm chisel; pl scissors, shears.

ciseler [sizle] vt to chisel, carve, chase, cut.

citadelle [sitadɛl] nf citadel, stronghold.

citadin [sitadɛ̃] nm townsman.

citation [sitasjɔ̃] nf quotation, summons, (in despatches) mention.

cité [site] nf town. (old) city,

citer [site] vt to quote, cite, summon, mention.

citerne [sitɛrn] nf cistern, tank.

citoyen. -enne [sitwajɛ̃, jɛn] n citizen.

citron [sitrɔ̃] nm lemon, lime; a inv lemon-coloured; — pressé lemon squash.

citronnade [sitrɔnad] nf lemon squash, lime-juice cordial.

citronnier [sitrɔnje] nm lemon tree, lime-tree.

citrouille [sitruːj] nf pumpkin.

civil [sivil] a civil, civic, lay, civilian, polite; en — in mufti, in plain clothes.

civilisation [sivilisasjɔ̃] nf civilization, culture.

civiliser [sivilize] v to civilize.

civilité [sivilite] nf civility, courtesy; pl regards.

clabauder [klabode] vi to babble, chatter; — contre to run down.

claie [klɛ] nf wattle, hurdle, screen, fence.

clair [klɛːr] a clear, obvious, plain, bright, light, pale; ad clearly, plainly; nm ight, clearing; tirer au — to clear up.

claire-voie [klɛrvwa] nf lattice, openwork, grating.

clairière [klɛrjɛːr] nf clearing, glade.

clairon [klɛrɔ̃] nm bugle, bugler.

clairsemé [klɛrsəme] a scattered, thin.

clairvoyance [klɛrvwajɑ̃ːs] nf perspicacity.

clairvoyant [klɛrvwajɑ̃] a perspicacious. shrewd; n clairvoyant.

clameur [klamœːr] nf outcry, clamour, howl.

clandestin [klɑ̃dɛstɛ̃] a clandestine, secret, surreptitious, underground.

clapier [klapje] nm rabbit-hutch.

claque [klak] n, smack, slap, hired applauders; nm opera hat.

claqué [klake] a dog-tired.

claquer [klake] vi to clap, bang, clatter, slap, snap, die; v to smack.

claquettes [klakɛt] nf pl tap-dance.

clarifier [klarifje] vt to clarify.

clarinette [klarinɛt] nf clarinet.

clarté [klarte] nf clearness, brightness ght. perspicacity.

classe [klaːs] nf class, order, form, standard, classroom, contingent, school.

classement [klasmɑ̃] nm classification, grading, filing.

classer [klase] vt to class, classify, sort out grade, file.

classeur [klasœːr] nm file, filing-cabinet sorter.

clas ification [klasifikasjɔ̃] nf classification.

classifier [klasifje] vt to classify.

classique [klasik] a classic, classical, standard; nm pl classics, classicists.

clavicule [klavikyl] nf collarbone.

clavier [klavje] *nm* keyboard.

clé, clef [kle] *nf* key, clue, clef; — **anglaise** screw-spanner; — **de voûte** keystone; **sous** — under lock and key.

clémence [klemɑ̃:s] *nf* clemency, mercy, mildness.

clément [klemɑ̃] *a* clement, merciful, lenient, mild.

clerc [klɛːr] *nm* clerk, cleric, scholar, learned man.

clergé [klɛrʒe] *nm* clergy.

clérical [klerikal] *a* clerical.

cliché [kliʃe] *nm* stereotype, block, negative, hackneyed expression, tag.

client [kliɑ̃] *n* client, customer, patient.

clientèle [kliɑ̃tɛl] *nf* clientele, practice, custom, customers, public, connection.

clignement [kliɲmɑ̃] *nm* blink(ing), wink(ing).

cligner [kliɲe] *vti* to blink, wink, flicker the eyelids.

clignoter [kliɲɔte] *vi* to blink, twinkle, twitch, flicker.

climat [klima, -mɑ] *nm* climate.

climatique [klimatik] *a* climatic.

climatisé [klimatize] *a* air-conditioned.

clin d'œil [klɛ̃dœ:j] *nm* wink, twinkling of an eye.

clinique [klinik] *a* clinical; *nf* nursing home, surgery, clinic.

clinquant [klɛ̃kɑ̃] *nm* foil, tinsel, tawdriness.

clique [klik] *nf* gang, set, clique, bugle-band.

cliqueter [klikte] *vi* to rattle, click, clink, (*of car*) pink.

cliquetis [klikti] *nm* rattling, click, clink(ing), jingle.

cloaque [klɔak] *nf* cesspool.

clochard [klɔʃaːr] *nm* tramp; (*US*) hobo.

cloche [klɔʃ] *nf* bell, blister.

cloche-pied [klɔʃpje] *ad* à — on one foot.

clocher [klɔʃe] *nm* belfry, steeple; *vi* to limp, go wrong.

cloison [klwazɔ̃] *nf* partition, bulk-head.

cloître [klwaːtr] *nm* cloister(s), monastery, convent.

clopin-clopant [klɔpɛ̃klɔpɑ̃] *ad* hobbling about, limping along.

cloque [klɔk] *nf* lump, blister.

clos [klo] *a* closed, shut up; **maison —e** brothel; *nm* enclosure.

clôture [kloty:r] *nf* enclosure, fence, closing, closure, end.

clou [klu] *nm* nail, staple, (*pedestrian crossing*) stud, boil, star turn.

clouer [klue] *vt* to nail (up, down), pin, tie to, root to.

clouté [klute] *a* studded; **passage —** pedestrian crossing.

coaguler [koagyle] *vt* to coagulate, congeal, curdle.

coasser [koase] *vi* to croak.

coassement [koasmɑ̃] *nm* croaking.

cobaye [kɔbaːj] *nm* guinea-pig.

cobra [kɔbra] *nm* cobra.

cocaïne [kɔkain] *nf* cocaine.

cocaïnomane [kɔkainɔman] *n* cocaine addict.

cocarde [kɔkard] *nf* cockade, rosette.

cocasse [kɔkas] *a* comical.

coccinelle [kɔksinɛl] *nf* ladybird.

coche [kɔʃ] *nf* notch, nick; *nm* stage-coach.

cocher [kɔʃe] *nm* coachman, cab-man, driver.

cochon -onne [kɔʃɔ̃, ɔn] *a* beastly, obscene, swinish; *nm* pig; — **d'Inde** guinea-pig.

cochonnerie [kɔʃɔnri] *nf* beastliness, rubbish, trash, obscenity, dirty trick.

coco [kɔko] *nm* **noix de —** coconut.

cocoteraie [kɔkɔtrɛ] *nf* coconut plantation.

cocotier [kɔkɔtje] *nm* coconut tree.

cocotte [kɔkɔt] *nf* darling, pet, woman of easy virtue, stew-pan.

code [kɔd] *nm* code, law, statute-book; **mettre en —** to dim, dip motor lights.

codicille [kɔdisil] *nm* codicil.

coefficient [kɔefisjɑ̃] *nm* coefficient.

coercition [kɔɛrsisjɔ̃] *nf* coercion.

cœur [kœːr] *nm* heart, soul, mind, courage, core depth, height, hearts; **avoir mal au —** to feel sick; **avoir le — gros** to be sad at heart; **de bon —** heartily, ungrudgingly; **de mauvais —** reluctantly.

coffre [kɔfr] *nm* box, chest, bin, trunk.

coffre-fort [kɔfrfɔːr] *nm* safe.

cognac [kɔɲak] *nm* brandy.

cognée [kɔɲe] *nf* axe, hatchet.

cogner [kɔɲe] *vt* to drive in, hit; *vti* to knock hit, bump.

cohérent [kɔerɑ̃] *a* coherent.

cohésion [kɔezjɔ̃] *nf* cohesion.

cohue [kɔy] *nf* crowd, mob, crush.

coiffe [kwaf] *nf* head-dress, cap, lining.

coiffer [kwafe] *vt* to cap, cover, put on hat, dress the hair; *vr* to put on one's hat, do one's hair, take a fancy (to de); **du combien coiffez-vous?** what is your size in hats?

coiffeur, -euse [kwafœːr, øːz] *n* hairdresser; *nf* dressing-table.

coiffure [kwafyːr] *nf* head-dress, style of hairdressing.

coin [kwɛ̃] *nm* corner, spot, plot, patch, wedge, hallmark.

coincer [kwɛ̃se] *vt* to wedge (up); *vr* to jam, stick.

coïncidence [kɔɛ̃sidɑ̃:s] *nf* coincidence.

coïncider [kɔɛ̃side] *vi* to coincide.

coing [kwɛ̃] *nm* quince.

col [kɔl] *nm* collar, neck, mountain pass; **faux —** detachable collar, (*beer*) froth.

coléoptère [kɔleɔptɛːr] *nm* beetle.

colère [kɔlɛːr] *a* angry, irascible; *nf* anger, rage, temper.

colérique [kɔlerik] *a* quick-tempered, choleric, fiery.

colifichet [kɔlifiʃɛ] *nm* trinket, knick-knack.

colimaçon [kɔlimasɔ̃] *nm* snail; **en — ** spiral.

colin-maillard [kɔlɛ̃majaːr] *nm* blindman's buff.

colique [kɔlik] *a* colic; *nf* colic, gripes.

colis [kɔli] *nm* parcel, package, packet, piece of luggage; **par — ** postal by parcel post.

collaborateur, -trice [kɔlaboratœːr, tris] *n* collaborator, contributor.

collaboration [kɔlaborasjɔ̃] *nf* collaboration.

collaborer [kɔlabore] *vi* to collaborate, contribute (to à).

collant [kɔlɑ̃] *a* sticky, clinging, close-fitting; *nm* tights.

collatéral [kɔlateral] *a* collateral, side.

collation [kɔl(l)asjɔ̃] *nf* collation, conferment, snack.

collationner [kɔl(l)asjɔne] *vt* to collate, read over, repeat; *vi* to have a snack.

colle [kɔl] *nf* paste, glue, size, oral test, poser.

collecte [kɔlɛkt] *nf* collection, collect.

collecteur, -trice [kɔlɛktœːr, tris] *n* collector.

collectif, -ive [kɔlɛktif, iːv] *a* collective, joint.

collection [kɔlɛksjɔ̃] *nf* collecting, collection, file.

collectionner [kɔlɛksjɔne] *vt* to collect.

collectionneur, -euse [kɔlɛksjɔnœːr, øːz] *n* collector.

collectivité [kɔlɛktivite] *nf* collectivity.

collège [kɔlɛːʒ] *nm* college, secondary school, electoral body.

collégien, ienne [kɔleʒjɛ̃, jɛn] *n* schoolboy, -girl.

collègue [kɔlɛg] *n* colleague.

coller [kɔle] *vt* to paste, stick, glue, plough, stump; *vi* to adhere, plough, stump; *vi* to adhere, cling, stick (to); *vr* to stick, cling close (to).

collet [kɔlɛ] *nm* collar, scruff of the neck, snare; **— monté** strait-laced, prim.

colleter [kɔlte] *vt* to collar, grapple with.

collier [kɔlje] *nm* necklace, necklet, collar, band; **un coup de — ** tug, great effort.

colline [kɔlin] *nf* hill.

collision [kɔllizjɔ̃] *nf* collision, clash.

colloque [kɔlɔk] *nf* colloquy, conversation.

colombe [kɔlɔ̃b] *nf* dove.

colombier [kɔlɔ̃bje] *nm* dovecot, pigeon-house.

colon [kɔlɔ̃] *nm* colonist, settler.

colonel [kɔlɔnɛl] *nm* colonel.

colonial [kɔlɔnjal] *a nm* colonial.

colonie [kɔlɔni] *nf* colony, settlement; **— de vacances** holiday camp.

colonisation [kɔlɔnizasjɔ̃] *nf* colonization.

coloniser [kɔlɔnize] *vt* to colonize, settle.

colonne [kɔlɔn] *nf* column, pillar; **— vertébrale** spine.

colorer [kɔlɔre] *vt* to colour, stain, tint; *vr* to take on a colour, grow ruddy.

coloris [kɔlɔri] *nm* colour(ing).

colossal [kɔlɔsal] *a* colossal, huge, gigantic.

colporter [kɔlpɔrte] *vt* to hawk, peddle.

colporteur, -euse [kɔlpɔrtœːr, øːz] *n* pedlar.

combat [kɔ̃ba] *nm* combat, fight, battle, action, conflict, struggle, match.

combatif, -ive [kɔ̃batif, iːv] *a* combative, pugnacious.

combattant [kɔ̃batɑ̃] *nm* combatant, fighting-man; **anciens —s** ex-servicemen.

combattre [kɔ̃batr] *vt* to combat, fight, battle with; *vi* to strive, struggle, fight.

combien [kɔ̃bjɛ̃] *ad* how much, how many, how far; **le — sommes-nous?** what day of the month is this?

combinaison [kɔ̃binɛzɔ̃] *nf* arrangement, combine, plan, underslip overalls, flying suit.

combine [kɔ̃bin] *nf* scheme, racket.

combiner [kɔ̃bine] *vt* to combine arrange, contrive.

comble [kɔ̃ːbl] *nm* heap, summit top, acme, roof(ing); **pour — ** malheur as a crowning misfortune ca, **c'est le — ** that's the limit; *d* heaped up, crowded; **faire salle — ** to play to a full house.

combler [kɔ̃ble] *vt* to fill (up, in) make good, crowd, fill to overflowing, gratify.

combustible [kɔ̃bystibl] *a* combustible; *nm* fuel.

combustion [kɔ̃bystjɔ̃] *nf* combustion.

comédie [kɔmedi] *nf* comedy, play drama; **jouer la — ** to act a part.

comédien, -ienne [kɔmedjɛ̃, jɛn] * actor, actress.

comestible [kɔmɛstibl] *a* edible eatable; *nm pl* food, provisions.

comète [kɔmɛt] *nf* comet.

comique [kɔmik] *a* comic, funny *nm* comedy, comedian, humorist joke.

comité [kɔmite] *nm* committee board.

commandant [kɔmɑ̃dɑ̃] *nm* commanding officer, major (army) squadron leader.

commande [kɔmɑ̃ːd] *nf* order

control, lever, driving-gear; de — essential, forced, feigned; sur — made to order, bespoke.

commandement [kɔmɑ̃dmɑ̃] nm command, order, commandment.

commander [kɔmɑ̃de] vt to order, govern, be in command of, compel, control.

commanditaire [kɔmɑ̃ditɛːr] nm (associé) — sleeping partner (in business).

comme [kɔm] ad as, like, such as, in the way of, how; c'est tout — it amounts to the same thing; cj as, since.

commémorer [kɔmmemɔre] vt to commemorate.

commençant [kɔmɑ̃sɑ̃] nm beginner, learner; a budding, beginning, early.

commencement [kɔmɑ̃smɑ̃] nm beginning.

commencer [kɔmɑ̃se] vti to commence, begin, start.

comment [kɔmɑ̃] ad how? what? excl why! what!

commentaire [kɔmɑ̃tɛːr] nm commentary, comment.

commentateur, -trice [kɔmɑ̃tatœːr, tris] n commentator.

commenter [kɔmɑ̃te] vti to comment (on), annotate.

commérage [kɔmeraːʒ] nm gossip, tittle-tattle.

commerçant [kɔmɛrsɑ̃] nm merchant, tradesman; a commercial, mercantile.

commerce [kɔmɛrs] nm commerce, trade, business, intercourse, dealings.

commercial [kɔmɛrsjal] a commercial, trading.

commettre [kɔmɛtr] vt to commit, perpetrate, entrust.

commis [kɔmi] nm clerk, book-keeper, shop-assistant; — voyageur commercial traveller.

commissaire [kɔmisɛːr] nm commissioner, steward, purser, police superintendent, commissar.

commissaire-priseur [kɔmisɛrprizœːr] nm auctioneer.

commissariat [kɔmisarja] nm commissionership, police station.

commission [kɔmisjɔ̃] nf commission, message, errand, board, committee.

commissionnaire [kɔmisjɔnɛːr] nm (commission) agent, porter, messenger.

commode [kɔmɔd] a convenient, handy, commodious, easy-going; nf chest of drawers.

commodité [kɔmɔdite] nf convenience, comfort, commodiousness.

commotion [kɔm(m)osjɔ̃] nf commotion, shock, upheaval, concussion.

commun [kɔmœ̃] a common, usual, ordinary, vulgar; d'un — accord

with one accord; peu — out-of-the-way, uncommon; nm common run, generality, common fund; pl offices, outhouses.

communauté [kɔmynote] nf community, commonwealth, society, religious order.

commune [kɔmyn] nf commune, parish.

communément [kɔmynemɑ̃] ad commonly.

communicatif, -ive [kɔmynikatif, iːv] a communicative, talkative, infectious.

communication [kɔmynikasjɔ̃] nf communication, connection, telephone call, message.

communion [kɔmynjɔ̃] nf communion.

communiqué [kɔmynike] nm communiqué, official statement, bulletin.

communiquer [kɔmynike] vt to communicate, transmit, convey, connect; vr to be communicated.

communisant [kɔmynizɑ̃] n fellow-traveller.

communisme [kɔmynism] nm communism.

communiste [kɔmynist] n communist.

commutateur [kɔmytatœːr] nm commutator, switch.

compagne [kɔ̃paɲ] nf companion, partner, wife.

compagnie [kɔ̃paɲi] nf company, party, firm; de bonne, de mauvaise — well-, ill-bred.

compagnon [kɔ̃paɲɔ̃] nm companion, fellow, mate.

comparable [kɔ̃parabl] a comparable.

comparaison [kɔ̃parezɔ̃] nf comparison, simile.

comparatif, -ive [kɔ̃paratif, iːv] a nm comparative.

comparé [kɔ̃pare] a comparative.

comparer [kɔ̃pare] vt to compare.

compartiment [kɔ̃partimɑ̃] nm compartment.

compas [kɔ̃pɑ] nm compass(es), scale, standard.

compassé [kɔ̃pɑse] a stiff, formal, set, prim.

compassion [kɔ̃pasjɔ̃] nf compassion, pity.

compatible [kɔ̃patibl] a compatible.

compatir [kɔ̃patiːr] vi to sympathize (with à), feel (for).

compatissant [kɔ̃patisɑ̃] a compassionate.

compatriote [kɔ̃patriɔt] nm compatriot.

compensation [kɔ̃pɑ̃sasjɔ̃] nf compensation, offset, balancing, adjustment.

compensé [kɔ̃pɑ̃se] a semelles —es wedge heels.

compenser [kɔ̃pɑ̃se] vt to compensate, make good, set off, balance, adjust.

compétence [kɔ̃petɑ̃ːs] nf jurisdiction, competence, proficiency, skill.

complaisance [kɔ̃plezɑ̃ːs] nf complaisance obligingness, kindness, complacency accommodation.

complaisant [kɔ̃plezɑ̃] a complaisant, obliging, kind, complacent.

complémentaire [kɔ̃plemɑ̃tɛːr] a complementary, fuller.

complet, -ète [kɔ̃plɛ, ɛt] a complete, total, entire, full; nm suit of clothes; **au — complete**, at full strength.

compléter [kɔ̃plete] vt to complete, finish off.

complexe [kɔ̃plɛks] a complex, complicated, compound; nm complex.

complexion [kɔ̃plɛksjɔ̃] nf constitution, temperament.

complexité [kɔ̃plɛksite] nf complexity.

complication [kɔ̃plikasjɔ̃] nf complication, intricacy.

complice [kɔ̃plis] a nm accessory, accomplice.

complicité [kɔ̃plisite] nf complicity, aiding and abetting.

compliment [kɔ̃plimɑ̃] nm compliment; pl greetings, regards, congratulations.

complimenter [kɔ̃plimɑ̃te] vt to compliment, congratulate.

compliqué [kɔ̃plike] a complicated, intricate, difficult.

complot [kɔ̃plo] nm plot.

comploter [kɔ̃plɔte] vt to plot, scheme.

componction [kɔ̃pɔ̃ksjɔ̃] nf compunction.

comporter [kɔ̃pɔrte] vt to admit of, require, comprise, involve; vr to behave.

composé [kɔ̃poze] a composed, impassive, composite; a nm compound.

composer [kɔ̃poze] vt to compose, form. make up, set, arrange; vi to come to terms; vr to consist.

compositeur, -trice [kɔ̃pozitœːr, tris] n composer, compositor.

composition [kɔ̃pozisjɔ̃] nf composing, composition, making-up, setting, essay, rest, arrangement.

compote [kɔ̃pɔt] nf compote. stewed fruit.

compréhensible [kɔ̃preɑ̃sibl] a comprehensible.

compréhensif, -ive [kɔ̃preɑ̃sif, iːv] a comprehensive, inclusive, understanding.

compréhension [kɔ̃preɑ̃sjɔ̃] nf understanding.

comprendre [kɔ̃prɑ̃ːdr] vt to include, comprise, understand, comprehend.

compression [kɔ̃presjɔ̃] nf compression, crushing, repression.

comprimé [kɔ̃prime] nm tablet.

comprimer [kɔ̃prime] vt to compress, repress, restrain.

compris [kɔ̃pri] a y — including; **non —** exclusive of.

compromettre [kɔ̃prɔmɛtr] vt to compromise. implicate endanger.

compromis [kɔ̃prɔmi] nm compromise.

comptabilité [kɔ̃tabilite] nf book-keeping, accountancy accounting dept.

comptable [kɔ̃tabl] a accounting, book-keeping. accountable, responsible; nm accountant. book-keeper; **expert** chartered accountant.

comptant [kɔ̃tɑ̃] a **argent —** ready money; ad (in) cash; **au —** cash down.

compte [kɔ̃ːt] nm account, reckoning, calculation, count; **à bon —** cheap; **out — fait** all things considered; **versement à —** payment on account; **pour mon —** for my part; **— rendu** report, review; **se rendre — de** to realize.

compte-gouttes [kɔ̃tgut] nm dropping-tube. dropper.

compter [kɔ̃te] vt to count, reckon, charge, expect; vi rely, reckon, depend. count.

compteur [kɔ̃tœːr] nm (taxi)meter, counting-machine.

comptoir [kɔ̃twaːr] nm counter; **— d'escompte**, discount bank.

compulser [kɔ̃pylse] vt to go through, examine.

comte [kɔ̃ːt] nm count.

comté [kɔ̃te] nm county.

comtesse [kɔ̃tɛs] nf countess.

concéder [kɔ̃sede] vt to concede, grant allow.

concentrer [kɔ̃sɑ̃tre] vt to concentrate. focus repress; vr to concentrate. centre (in, on round).

concentrique [kɔ̃sɑ̃trik] a concentric.

conception [kɔ̃sɛpsjɔ̃] nf conception.

concerner [kɔ̃sɛrne] vt to concern, affect.

concert [kɔ̃sɛːr] nm concert agreement.

concerter kɔ̃sɛrte] vt to concert, plan; vr to act in concert.

concession [kɔ̃sɛsjɔ̃] nf concession, grant, compound.

concessionnaire [kɔ̃sɛsjɔnɛːr] nm concessionary, grantee, licence-holder.

concevable [kɔ̃s(ə)vabl] a conceivable.

concevoir [kɔ̃səvwaːr] vt to conceive, imagine, understand, word.

concierge [kɔ̃sjɛrʒ] n hall porter, doorkeeper, caretaker.

concilier [kɔ̃silje] vt to conciliate, reconcile, win over.

concis [kɔ̃si] a concise, terse, brief, crisp.

concision [kɔ̃sizjɔ̃] nf concision terseness.

concluant [kɔ̃klyɑ̃] a conclusive, decisive.

conclure [kɔ̃klyːr] vt to conclude, end, clinch, infer.

conclusion

conclusion [kɔklyzjɔ] nf conclusion, end, settlement, inference, decision.
concombre [kɔkɔ:br] nm cucumber.
concorde [kɔkɔrd] nf concord.
concourir [kɔkuri:r] vi to coincide, combine, compete.
concours [kɔku:r] nm concourse, concurrence, coincidence, co-operation, assistance, competition, contest, show.
concret, -ète [kɔkrɛ, -ɛt] a nm concrete.
concurrence [kɔkyrɑ:s] nf concurrence.
condamnable [kɔdanabl] a blameworthy.
condamnation [kɔdanasjɔ] nf condemnation, judgment, sentence, censure.
condamné [kɔdane] n convict, condemned person.
condamner [kɔdane] vt to condemn, sentence, convict, censure, block up.
condensateur [kɔdɑsatœːr] nm condenser.
condensation [kɔdɑsasjɔ] nf condensation.
condenser [kɔdɑse] vt to condense.
condenseur [kɔdɑsœːr] nm condenser.
condescendance [kɔdɛsɑdɑ:s] nf condescension.
condescendre [kɔdɛsɑ:dr] vt to condescend.
condition [kɔdisjɔ] nf condition, state, position, rank; pl conditions, circumstances, terms; à — on approval; à — que on condition that; être en — to be in domestic service.
conditionnel, -elle [kɔdisjɔnɛl, ɛl] a nm conditional.
conditionner [kɔdisjɔne] vt to condition.
condoléance [kɔdɔleɑ:s] nf condolence; pl sympathy.
conducteur, -trice [kɔdyktœːr, tris] a conducting, guiding; n leader, guide, driver; nm conductor, main.
conduire [kɔdɥi:r] vt to conduct, lead, guide, conduce (to), drive, convey, manage; vr to behave, conduct oneself.
conduit [kɔdɥi] nm passage, pipe, conduit, duct.
conduite [kɔdɥit] nf behaviour, driving, pipe, management, conducting, leading.
cône [ko:n] nm cone.
confection [kɔfɛksjɔ] nf confection, putting together, manufacture, making up, ready-made clothes.
confectionner [kɔfɛksjɔne] vt to make up, manufacture.
confectionneur, -euse [kɔfɛksjɔnœːr, øːz] n ready-made outfitter, clothier.

confédération [kɔfedɛrasjɔ] nf federation, confederacy.
confédérer [kɔfedere] vtr to confederate, unite.
conférence [kɔferɑ:s] nf conference, lecture.
conférencier, -ière [kɔferɑsje, jɛːr] n lecturer.
conférer [kɔfere] vt to confer, award, bestow, compare; vi to confer (with avec).
confesser [kɔfese] vt to confess, own; vr to confess.
confesseur [kɔfesœːr] nm confessor.
confession [kɔfesjɔ] nf confession, religion, denomination.
confessional [kɔfesjɔnal] nm confessional (-box).
confiance [kɔfjɑ:s] nf confidence, trust, reliance; de — on trust, reliable.
confiant [kɔfiɑ] a confiding, (self-), confident, assured.
confidence [kɔfidɑ:s] nf confidence, secret; en — in confidence, confidentially.
confidentiel, -elle [kɔfidɑsjɛl, ɛl] a confidential.
confier [kɔfje] vt to confide, disclose, entrust, commit; vr to rely (on à), take into one's confidence.
confiner [kɔfine] vt to confine, shut up; vi to be contiguous, border upon.
confins [kɔfɛ] nm pl confines, borders.
confirmatif, -ive [kɔfirmatif, iːv] a confirmative, corroborative.
confirmation [kɔ. irmasjɔ] nf confirmation, corroboration.
confirmer [kɔfirme] vt to confirm, corroborate.
confiscation [kɔtiskasjɔ] nf confiscation.
confiserie [kɔfizri] nf confectionery, confectioner's shop.
confiseur, -euse [kɔfizœːr, øːz] n confectioner.
confisquer [kɔfiske] vt to confiscate.
confit [kɔfi] a preserved, steeped in; un air — sanctimonious air; nm pl confections, comfits, sweets.
confiture [kɔfityːr] nf preserves, jam; — d'orange marmalade.
conflagration [kɔflagrasjɔ] nf conflagration, blaze, fire.
conflit [kɔfli] nm conflict, clash, strife; être en — to conflict, clash.
confluent [kɔflyɑ] nm confluence, junction, meeting.
confondre [kɔfɔ:dr] vt to confound, mingle blend, mistake, disconcert, put to confusion; vr to blend, intermingle, be identical; se — en excuses to apologize profusely.
confondu [kɔfɔdy] a overwhelmed, disconcerted.
conforme [kɔfɔrm] a conformable, according (to à), in keeping (with à).
conformément [kɔfɔrmemɑ] ad

according (to à), in keeping (with à).
conformer [kɔ̃fɔrme] vt to form,
conform; vr to conform (to),
comply (with à).
conformité [kɔ̃fɔrmite] nf conformity, agreement.
confort [kɔ̃fɔːr] nm comfort.
confortable [kɔ̃fɔrtabl] a comfortable.
confrère [kɔ̃frɛːr] nm colleague,
fellow-member, brother.
confrérie [kɔ̃freri] nf brotherhood,
confraternity.
confrontation [kɔ̃frɔ̃tasjɔ̃] nf confrontation, comparison.
confronter [kɔ̃frɔ̃te] vt to confront,
compare.
confus [kɔ̃fy] a confused, jumbled,
indistinct, embarrassed, abashed,
ashamed.
confusion [kɔ̃fyzjɔ̃] nf confusion,
welter, mistake, embarrassment.
congé [kɔ̃ʒe] nm leave, holiday,
furlough, dismissal, discharge, notice
to quit.
congédier [kɔ̃ʒedje] vt to dismiss,
discharge.
congélation [kɔ̃ʒelasjɔ̃] nf congela-
tion, freezing.
congeler [kɔ̃ʒle] vtr to congeal,
freeze (up).
congénital [kɔ̃ʒenital] a congenital.
congestion [kɔ̃ʒɛstjɔ̃] nf congestion;
— cérébrale stroke; — pulmonaire
pneumonia.
congestionné [kɔ̃ʒɛstjɔne] a congested, apoplectic, red in the face.
congestionner [kɔ̃ʒɛstjɔne] vt to
congest; vr to become congested.
congrégation [kɔ̃gregasjɔ̃] nf congregation.
congrès [kɔ̃grɛ] nm congress.
conique [kɔnik] a conic(al), cone-
shaped, tapering.
conjecture [kɔ̃ʒɛktyːr] nf conjecture,
surmise, guess.
conjecturer [kɔ̃ʒɛktyre] vt to conjecture, surmise.
conjoint [kɔ̃ʒwɛ̃] a conjoined, united,
married; nm pl husband and wife.
conjonction [kɔ̃ʒɔ̃ksjɔ̃] nf union,
conjunction.
conjoncture [kɔ̃ʒɔ̃ktyːr] nf conjuncture.
conjugaison [kɔ̃ʒygɛzɔ̃] nf conjugation.
conjugal [kɔ̃ʒygal] a conjugal,
married, wedded.
conjugué [kɔ̃ʒyge] a conjugated,
interconnected, coupled, twin.
conjuration [kɔ̃ʒyrasjɔ̃] nf plot,
conspiracy; incantation.
conjuré [kɔ̃ʒyre] nm conspirator.
connaissance [kɔnɛsɑ̃ːs] nf knowledge, understanding, acquaintance,
consciousness, senses; pl learning,
attainments; en pays de — on
familiar ground, among familiar
faces; sans — unconscious,
insensible.

connaisseur, -euse [kɔnɛsœːr, øːz]
n expert, connoisseur, judge.
connaître [kɔnɛːtr] vt to know, be
acquainted with, take cognizance,
distinguish, have a thorough knowledge of; vr to be a good judge
(of en), know all (about en).
connexe [kɔnɛks] a connected,
allied, like.
connexion [kɔn(n)ɛksjɔ̃] nf connection, connector.
connivence [kɔnivɑ̃ːs] nf connivance,
collusion.
conquérant [kɔ̃kerɑ̃] a conquering,
n conqueror.
conquérir [kɔ̃keriːr] vt to conquer.
ed, accepted, stock.
consacrer [kɔ̃sakre] vt to devote,
ordain, consecrate.
conscience [kɔ̃sjɑ̃ːs] nf conscience,
consciousness.
consciencieux, -euse [kɔ̃sjɑ̃sjø, jøːz]
a conscientious.
conscient [kɔ̃sjɑ̃] a conscious, aware,
sentient.
conscription [kɔ̃skripsjɔ̃] nf conscription.
conscrit [kɔ̃skri] nm conscript.
consécration [kɔ̃sekrasjɔ̃] nf consecration, dedication.
consécutif, -ive [kɔ̃sekytif, iːv] a
consecutive.
conseil [kɔ̃sɛːj] nm advice, decision,
council, counsel, board, court; —
des ministres cabinet; — de guerre
council of war, court martial.
conseiller, -ère [kɔ̃sɛje, ɛːr] n
adviser, councillor, judge.
conseiller [kɔ̃sɛje] vt to advise,
counsel.
consentement [kɔ̃sɑ̃tmɑ̃] nm consent, assent.
consentir [kɔ̃sɑ̃tiːr] vi to consent,
agree.
conséquemment [kɔ̃sekamɑ̃] ad
consequently.
conséquence [kɔ̃sekɑ̃ːs] nf consequence, outcome, sequel, inference,
importance.
conséquent [kɔ̃sekɑ̃] a consistent,
following, important; par —
accordingly.
conservateur, -trice [kɔ̃sɛrvatœːr,
tris] a preserving, conservative; n
keeper, guardian, curator, conservative.
conservation [kɔ̃sɛrvasjɔ̃] nf preservation, keeping, care.
conservatoire [kɔ̃sɛrvatwaːr] nm
school, academy (of music).
conserve [kɔ̃sɛrv] nf preserved
food, tinned food; pl dark spectacles;
— au vinaigre pickles; de —
together.
conserver [kɔ̃sɛrve] vt to preserve,
keep.
considérable [kɔ̃siderabl] a con-

siderable, large, eminent, important.

considération [kɔ̃siderasjɔ̃] nf consideration, regard, respect.

considérer [kɔ̃sidere] vt to consider, contemplate, regard, respect, esteem.

consigne [kɔ̃siɲ] nf order(s), duty, countersign, detention, cloakroom, left-luggage office, (US) checkroom.

consigner [kɔ̃siɲe] vt to deposit, consign, confine to barracks, keep in, put out of bounds, hold up.

consistance [kɔ̃sistɑ̃:s] nf consistence, consistency, firmness, standing.

consistant [kɔ̃sistɑ̃] a firm, set, solid.

consister [kɔ̃siste] vi to consist, be composed (of en).

consolateur, -trice [kɔ̃solatœːr, tris] a consoling; n consoler, comforter.

consolation [kɔ̃sɔlasjɔ̃] nf consolation, comfort.

console [kɔ̃sɔl] nf bracket, console (table).

consoler [kɔ̃sɔle] vt to console, solace, comfort, cheer.

consolider [kɔ̃sɔlide] vt to consolidate, fund (debt).

consommateur, -trice [kɔ̃sɔmatœːr, tris] n consumer, customer.

consommation [kɔ̃sɔmasjɔ̃] nf consummation, consumption, drink.

consommé [kɔ̃sɔme] a consummate; nm stock, clear soup.

consommer [kɔ̃sɔme] vt to consummate, consume.

consomption [kɔ̃sɔ̃psjɔ̃] nf consuming, consumption.

consonne [kɔ̃sɔn] nf consonant.

conspirateur, -trice [kɔ̃spiratœːr, tris] n conspirer, conspirator, plotter.

conspiration [kɔ̃spirasjɔ̃] nf conspiracy, plot.

conspirer [kɔ̃spire] vti to conspire, plot.

conspuer [kɔ̃spɥe] vt to decry, boo, hoot, barrack.

constamment [kɔ̃stamɑ̃] ad constantly.

constance [kɔ̃stɑ̃:s] nf constancy, steadfastness, perseverance, stability.

constant [kɔ̃stɑ̃] a constant, steadfast, firm.

constatation [kɔ̃statasjɔ̃] nf ascertainment, verification, record, statement.

constater [kɔ̃state] vt to establish, ascertain, state, record.

constellation [kɔ̃stɛllasjɔ̃] nf constellation, galaxy.

consternation [kɔ̃stɛrnasjɔ̃] nf consternation, dismay.

consterner [kɔ̃stɛrne] vt to dismay, stagger.

constipation [kɔ̃stipasjɔ̃] nf constipation.

constipé [kɔ̃stipe] a constipated, costive.

constituer [kɔ̃stitɥe] vt to constitute, form, set up, incorporate, settle (on); se — prisonnier to give oneself up.

constitution [kɔ̃stitysjɔ̃] nf constitution, composition, settlement.

constitutionnel, -elle [kɔ̃stitysjɔnɛl, ɛl] a constitutional.

constructeur [kɔ̃stryktœːr] nm constructor, builder, maker.

construction [kɔ̃stryksjɔ̃] nf construction, making, building, structure.

construire [kɔ̃strɥiːr] vt to construct, build, make.

consul [kɔ̃syl] nm consul.

consulaire [kɔ̃sylɛːr] a consular.

consulat [kɔ̃syla] nm consulate.

consultant [kɔ̃syltɑ̃] a consulting; nm consultant.

consultation [kɔ̃syltasjɔ̃] nf consultation, opinion, advice; cabinet de — consulting-room, surgery.

consulter [kɔ̃sylte] vt to consult.

consumer [kɔ̃syme] vt to consume, destroy, wear away, use up; vr to waste away, burn away.

contact [kɔ̃takt] nm contact, touch, connection, switch.

contagieux, -euse [kɔ̃taʒjø, jøːz] a contagious, infectious, catching.

contagion [kɔ̃taʒjɔ̃] nf contagion, contagiousness.

contamination [kɔ̃taminasjɔ̃] n, contamination, infection.

contaminer [kɔ̃tamine] vt to contaminate, infect.

conte [kɔ̃:t] nm story, tale, yarn, short story; — bleu fairy tale; — à dormir debout cock-and-bull story.

contemplation [kɔ̃tɑ̃plasjɔ̃] nf contemplation, meditation, gazing.

contempler [kɔ̃tɑ̃ple] vt to contemplate, meditate upon, gaze at, upon.

contemporain [kɔ̃tɑ̃pɔrɛ̃] n contemporary; a contemporaneous.

contenance [kɔ̃tnɑ̃:s] nf capacity, content, countenance, bearing.

contenir [kɔ̃tniːr] vt to contain, hold, restrain; vr to contain oneself, keep one's temper.

content [kɔ̃tɑ̃] a content, satisfied, pleased, glad; nm manger tout son— to eat one's fill.

contentement [kɔ̃tɑ̃tmɑ̃] nm satisfaction.

contenter [kɔ̃tɑ̃te] vt to content, satisfy, gratify; vr to be satisfied (with de).

contenu [kɔ̃tny] a restrained, reserved; nm contents.

conter [kɔ̃te] vt to tell.

contestable [kɔ̃tɛstabl] a questionable, debatable.

contestation [kɔ̃tɛstasjɔ̃] nf contestation, dispute.

conteste [kɔ̃tɛst] nf sans — unquestionably.

contester [kɔ̃tɛste] vt to contest, dispute, challenge.

conteur, -euse [kɔ̃tœːr, øːz] *n* narrator, story-teller.

contexte [kɔ̃tɛkst] *nm* context.

contigu, -uë [kɔ̃tigy] *a* contiguous, adjoining.

continent [kɔ̃tinɑ̃] *a* continent, chaste; *nm* continent, mainland.

contingent [kɔ̃tɛ̃ʒɑ̃] *a* contingent; *nm* contingent, quota, share.

continu [kɔ̃tiny] *a* continuous, sustained.

continuation [kɔ̃tinɥasjɔ̃] *nf* continuation.

continuel, -elle [kɔ̃tinɥɛl, el] *a* continual.

continuer [kɔ̃tinɥe] *vt* to continue, proceed with, go on with; *vi* to carry on, continue, go on.

continuité [kɔ̃tinɥite] *nf* continuity.

contour [kɔ̃tuːr] *nm* outline, contour.

contournement [kɔ̃turnəmɑ̃] *nm* route de — by-pass.

contourner [kɔ̃turne] *vt* to shape, get round, by-pass, twist, distort.

contracter [kɔ̃trakte] *vt* to contract, incur, draw together; *vr* to shrink, contract.

contraction [kɔ̃traksjɔ̃] *nf* contraction, shrinking.

contradiction [kɔ̃tradiksjɔ̃] *nf* contradiction, discrepancy, inconsistency.

contradictoire [kɔ̃tradiktwaːr] *a* contradictory.

contraindre [kɔ̃trɛ̃ːdr] *vt* to constrain, compel, force, restrain.

contraint [kɔ̃trɛ̃] *a* constrained, cramped, forced.

contrainte [kɔ̃trɛ̃ːt] *nf* constraint, compulsion, restraint.

contraire [kɔ̃trɛːr] *a* contrary, opposite, opposed, adverse, bad; **jusqu'à avis** — until further notice; *nm* contrary, opposite.

contrarier [kɔ̃trarje] *vt* to thwart, oppose, annoy, vex, provoke, interfere with.

contrariété [kɔ̃trarjete] *nf* contrariety, annoyance, nuisance.

contraste [kɔ̃trast] *nm* contrast.

contraster [kɔ̃traste] *vti* to contrast.

contrat [kɔ̃tra] *nm* contract, agreement, deed, policy.

contravention [kɔ̃travɑ̃sjɔ̃] *nf* contravention, breach, infringement, offence; **dresser une** — **à** to take the name and address of, prosecute.

contre [kɔ̃tr] *prep* against, contrary to, for, to, versus; *ad* against, hard by; **le pour et le** — pros and cons.

contre-amiral [kɔ̃tramiral] *nm* rear-admiral.

contre-attaque [kɔ̃tratak] *nf* counter-attack.

contre-avion(s) [kɔ̃travjɔ̃] *a* anti-aircraft.

contre-avis [kɔ̃travi] *nm* contrary opinion.

contre-balancer [kɔ̃trəbalɑ̃se] *vt* to counterbalance, offset.

contrebande [kɔ̃trəbɑ̃ːd] *nf* contraband, smuggling.

contrebandier [kɔ̃trəbɑ̃dje] *nm* smuggler.

contrecarrer [kɔ̃trəkare] *vt* to thwart cross.

contrecœur [kɔ̃trəkœːr] *ad* à — reluctantly.

contre-coup [kɔ̃trəku] *nm* rebound, recoil, reaction, repercussion.

contredire [kɔ̃trədiːr] *vt* to contradict, gainsay; *vr* to contradict oneself, be inconsistent.

contredit [kɔ̃trədi] *ad* sans — unquestionably.

contrée [kɔ̃tre] *nf* region, district, country.

contre-espionnage [kɔ̃trɛspjɔnaːʒ] *nm* counter-espionage.

contrefaçon [kɔ̃trəfasɔ̃] *nf* counterfeit forgery.

contrefaire [kɔ̃trəfɛːr] *vt* to imitate, feign, forge.

contrefait [kɔ̃trəfɛ] *a* disguised feigned, sham, counterfeit, forged.

contrefort [kɔ̃trəfɔːr] *nm* buttress, spur.

contre-jour [kɔ̃trəʒuːr] *nm* unfavourable light; à — against the light in one's own light.

contremaître, -tresse [kɔ̃trəmɛːtr, trɛs] *n* foreman -woman, overseer.

contremander [kɔ̃trəmɑ̃de] *vt* to countermand, cancel, call off.

contre-ordre [kɔ̃trɔrdr] *nm* counter-order countermand; **sauf** — unless we hear to the contrary.

contre-partie [kɔ̃trəparti] *nf* opposite view, other side counterpart, contra.

contre-pied [kɔ̃trəpje] *nm* opposite, contrary view.

contrepoids [kɔ̃trəpwa] *nm* counterweight, counterbalance, counterpoise.

contre-poil [kɔ̃trəpwal] *ad* à — the wrong way.

contrer [kɔ̃tre] *vt* to counter; *vi* to double.

contre-sens [kɔ̃trəsɑ̃ːs] *nm* misconstruction, mistranslation, wrong way; à — in the wrong direction.

contresigner [kɔ̃trəsiɲe] *vt* to countersign.

contretemps [kɔ̃trətɑ̃] *nm* mishap, hitch, inconvenience; à — inopportunely.

contre-torpilleur [kɔ̃trətɔrpijœːr] *nm* destroyer.

contrevent [kɔ̃trəvɑ̃] *nm* outside shutter.

contre-voie [kɔ̃trəvwa] *ad* à — in the wrong direction, on the wrong side.

contribuable [kɔ̃tribɥabl] *a* tax-paying; *nm* taxpayer.

contribuer [kɔ̃tribɥe] *vi* to contribute.

contribution [kɔ̃tribysjɔ̃] *nf* contribution, share, tax, rate.

contrit [kɔ̃tri] *a* contrite, penitent.

contrition [kɔ̃trisjɔ̃] *nf* contrition, penitence.

contrôle [kɔ̃troːl] *nm* checking, inspection, roll, roster, hallmark, ticket office.

contrôler [kɔ̃trole] *vt* inspect, control, verify.

contrôleur, -euse [kɔ̃trolœːr, øːz] *n* inspector, inspectress, assessor, controller, ticket-collector, time-keeper.

controuvé [kɔ̃truve] *a* fabricated, invented.

controverse [kɔ̃trɔvɛrs] *nf* controversy, dispute.

contumace [kɔ̃tymas] *nf* contumacy.

contusion [kɔ̃tyzjɔ̃] *nf* bruise.

contusionner [kɔ̃tyzjone] *vt* to contuse, bruise.

conurbation [kɔnyrbasjɔ̃] *nf* conurbation.

convaincre [kɔ̃vɛ̃ːkr] *vt* to convince, convict.

convalescence [kɔ̃valɛssɑ̃ːs] *nf* convalescence.

convalescent [kɔ̃valɛssɑ̃] *an* convalescent.

convenable [kɔ̃vnabl] *a* suitable, proper, fit(ting), decent, decorous, well-behaved.

convenance [kɔ̃vnɑ̃ːs] *nf* agreement, suitability, convenience, propriety, decorum; *pl* convention.

convenir [kɔ̃vniːr] *vi* to suit, fit, agree, own, admit, be advisable, befitting.

convention [kɔ̃vɑ̃sjɔ̃] *nf* covenant, agreement, convention.

conventionnel, -elle [kɔ̃vɑ̃sjɔnɛl, ɛl] *a* conventional.

convenu [kɔ̃vny] *a* agreed, stipulated, settled.

conversation [kɔ̃vɛrsasjɔ̃] *nf* conversation, talk.

converser [kɔ̃vɛrse] *vi* to converse, talk.

conversion [kɔ̃vɛrsjɔ̃] *nf* conversion, change.

converti [kɔ̃vɛrti] *n* convert.

convertir [kɔ̃vɛrtiːr] *vt* to convert, change, win over; *vr* to become converted, turn.

convertisseur [kɔ̃vɛrtisœːr] *nm* converter, transformer.

convexe [kɔ̃vɛks] *a* convex.

conviction [kɔ̃viksjɔ̃] *nf* conviction.

convier [kɔ̃vje] *vt* to invite, urge.

convive [kɔ̃viːv] *n* table-companion, guest.

convocation [kɔ̃vɔkasjɔ̃] *nf* convocation, summons, convening, calling-up.

convoi [kɔ̃vwa] *nm* convoy, column, procession.

convoiter [kɔ̃vwate] *vt* to covet, desire.

convoitise [kɔ̃vwatiːz] *nf* covetousness, desire, lust.

convoquer [kɔ̃vɔke] *vt* to convoke, summon, convene, call up.

convulsif, -ive [kɔ̃vylsif, iːv] *a* convulsive.

convulsion [kɔ̃vylsjɔ̃] *nf* convulsion, upheaval.

coopérative [kɔɔperativ] *nf* co-operative stores.

coopérer [kɔɔpere] *vi* to co-operate.

coordination [kɔɔrdinasjɔ̃] *nf* coordination.

coordonner [kɔɔrdɔne] *vt* to coordinate, arrange.

copain [kɔpɛ̃] *nm* chum, pal.

copeau [kɔpo] *nm* shaving, chip.

copie [kɔpi] *nf* copy, (examination-) paper, reproduction, imitation.

copier [kɔpje] *vt* to copy, reproduce, imitate.

copieux, -euse [kɔpjø, jøːz] *a* copious, full, hearty.

copiste [kɔpist] *nm* transcriber, imitator.

coq [kɔk] *nm* cock, weathercock, ship's cook; **poids — bantam weight; vivre comme un — en pâte** to live like a fighting cock.

coq-à-l'âne [kɔkalɑn] *nm* cock-and-bull story.

coque [kɔk] *nf* shell, husk, hull, bottom, loop; **œuf à la — boiled egg.**

coquelicot [kɔkliko] *nm* poppy.

coqueluche [kɔklyʃ] *nf* whooping-cough; darling.

coquerico [kɔkriko] *nm* cock-a-doodle-doo.

coquet, -ette [kɔkɛ, ɛt] *a* coquettish, smart, stylish, trim, interested in dress.

coquetier [kɔktje] *nm* egg-cup, egg merchant.

coquette [kɔkɛt] *nf* flirt.

coquetterie [kɔkɛtri] *nf* coquetry, affectation, love of finery, smartness.

coquillage [kɔkijaːʒ] *nm* shellfish, shell.

coquille [kɔkiːj] *nf* shell, case; misprint, printer's error.

coquin, -e [kɔkɛ̃, in] *nm* rogue, rascal, scamp; *nf* hussy, minx.

cor [kɔːr] *nm* horn, (*of stag*) tine, corn; **réclamer à — et à cri** to clamour for.

corail [kɔraːj] *nm* coral.

coran [kɔrɑ̃] *nm* Koran.

corbeau [kɔrbo] *nm* crow, raven; corbel, bracket.

corbeille [kɔrbɛːj] *nf* basket, round flowerbed; **— de noces** bridegroom's wedding present(s) to bride.

corbillard [kɔrbijaːr] *nm* hearse.

cordage [kɔrdaːʒ] *nm* rope, cordage.

corde [kɔrd] *nf* rope, cord, line, string, wire, thread.

cordeau [kɔrdo] *nm* tracing-line, string, fuse.

cordelière [kɔrdəljɛr] *nf* girdle, cord.

corder [kɔrde] *vt* to twist, cord, rope, string.

cordial [kɔrdjal] *a* hearty, cordial; *nm* cordial.

cordialité [kɔrdjalite] *nf* cordiality, heartiness.

cordon [kɔrdɔ̃] *nm* cordon, row, cord, ribbon, rope, string.

cordonnerie [kɔrdonri] *nf* shoemaking, boot and shoe trade, shoemaker's shop.

cordonnier [kɔrdɔnje] *nm* shoemaker, bootmaker.

coriace [kɔrjas] *a* tough, leathery; hard, grasping.

corne [kɔrn] *nf* (*animal*) horn; coup de — butt, gore; — du sabot horse hoof; — d'un livre (*book*) dog's ear; — à souliers shoehorn; — de brume foghorn.

cornée [kɔrne] *nf* cornea.

corneille [kɔrnɛːj] *nf* crow, rook.

cornemuse [kɔrnəmyːz] *nf* bagpipes.

corner [kɔrne] *vt* to trumpet, din, dog's ear, turn down; *vi* to sound the horn, ring.

cornet [kɔrnɛ] *nm* horn, trumpet, cornet; — à dés dice-box.

corniche [kɔrniʃ] *nf* cornice, ledge,

cornichon [kɔrniʃɔ̃] *nm* gherkin, simpleton.

cornu [kɔrny] *a* horned.

cornue [kɔrny] *nf* retort.

corollaire [kɔrollɛːr] *nm* corollary.

corporation [kɔrpɔrasjɔ̃] *nf* corporation, guild.

corporel, -elle [kɔrpɔrɛl, ɛl] *a* corporeal, corporal, bodily.

corps [kɔːr] *nm* body substance, corpse, corps, frame, main part; — à — hand to hand, clinch; prendre— to take shape; perdu — et biens lost with all hands; à — perdu recklessly.

corpulence [kɔrpylãːs] *nf* stoutness, corpulence.

corpulent [kɔrpylã] *a* stout, corpulent, fat.

corpuscule [kɔrpyskyl] *nm* corpuscle.

correct [kɔr(r)ɛkt] *a* correct, proper, accurate, polite, well-behaved.

correcteur, -trice [kɔr(r)ɛktœːr, tris] *n* corrector, proof-reader.

correction [kɔr(r)ɛksjɔ̃] *nf* correcting, proof-reading, correctness, accuracy, propriety, punishment.

correctionnel, -elle [kɔr(r)ɛksjɔnɛl, ɛl] *a* tribunal de police —le police court; délit — minor offence.

correspondance [kɔrɛspɔ̃dãːs] *nf* correspondence, letters, communication, connection, intercourse.

correspondant [kɔrɛspɔ̃dã] *a* corresponding, connecting; *nm* correspondent, friend acting for parent.

correspondre [kɔrɛspɔ̃ːdr] *vi* to correspond, tally, agree, comunicate.

corridor [kɔridɔːr] *nm* corridor, passage.

corrigé [kɔriʒe] *nm* fair copy, correct version.

corriger [kɔriʒe] *vt* to correct, rectify, (*proofs*) read, cure, chastize.

corroboration [kɔrrɔbɔrasjɔ̃] *nf* corroboration, confirmation.

corroborer [kɔrrɔbɔre] *vt* to corroborate.

corroder [kɔrrɔde] *vt* to corrode, eat away.

corrompre [kɔr(r)ɔ̃ːpr] *vt* to corrupt, spoil, bribe, taint.

corrompu [kɔr(r)ɔ̃py] *a* corrupt, depraved, tainted.

corrosif, -ive [kɔrrozif, iːv] *a nm* corrosive.

corrosion [kɔrrozjɔ̃] *nf* corrosion.

corroyer [kɔrwaje] *vt* to curry, weld, trim, puddle.

corrupteur, -trice [kɔr(r)yptœːr, tris] *a* corrupt(ing); *n* corrupter.

corruptible [kɔr(r)yptibl] *a* corruptible, bribable.

corruption [kɔr(r)ypsjɔ̃] *nf* corruption, bribery, bribing.

corsage [kɔrsaːʒ] *nm* bodice, blouse.

Corse [kɔrs] *nf* Corsica.

corse [kɔrs] *an* Corsican.

corsé [kɔrse] *a* full-bodied, strong, broad meaty.

corser [kɔrse] *vt* to give body to, fortify, intensify; *vr* to get serious, thicken.

corset [kɔrsɛ] *nm* corset; — de sauvetage life-jacket.

corsetier, -ière [kɔrsətje, jɛːr] *n* corset-maker.

cortège [kɔrtɛːʒ] *nm* procession, train, retinue.

corvée [kɔrve] *nf* fatigue duty, task, (piece of) drudgery.

cosmétique [kɔsmetik] *a nm* cosmetic.

cosmopolite [kɔsmɔpolit] *an* cosmopolitan.

cosse [kɔs] *nf* pod, husk.

cossu [kɔsy] *a* wealthy.

costaud [kɔsto] *a nm* strong, burly, brawny (man).

costume [kɔstym] *nm* costume, dress, suit.

costumé [kɔstyme] *a* bal — fancy-dress ball.

cote [kɔt] *nf* share, proportion, assessment, mark, number, classification, quotation, list of prices, odds.

côte [koːt] *nf* rib, hill, slope, coast, shore; — à — side by side.

côté [kote] *nm* side, way, direction, aspect, broadside, beam-ends; à — near, to one side; à — de beside, by the side of, next to; de — on one side, sideways, aside, by; de mon — for my part.

coteau [kɔto] *nm* hill, hillside, slope.

côtelé [kotle] *a* ribbed, corded, corduroy (velvet).

côtelette [kotlɛt] *nf* cutlet, chop.

coter [kɔte] *vt* to assess, quote, classify, number, award marks for, back.

coterie [kɔtri] nf set, clique, circle.

côtier, -ière [kotje, jɛːr] a coast, coastal, inshore; nm coaster.

cotisation [kɔtizasjɔ̃] nf share, contribution, subscription, fee.

se cotiser [səkɔtize] vr to club together, get up a subscription.

coton [kɔtɔ̃] nm cotton; **filer un mauvais —** to be in a poor way, go to the dogs.

cotonnerie [kɔtɔnri] nf cotton plantation.

cotonnier [kɔtɔnje] nm cotton plant.

côtoyer [kotwaje] vt to keep close to, hug, run along, skirt.

cou [ku] nm neck.

couardise [kwardiːz] nf cowardice, cowardliness.

couchage [kuʃaːʒ] nm bedding, bedclothes; **sac de —** sleeping-bag.

couchant [kuʃɑ̃] a setting; nm west, setting sun; **chien —** setter.

couche [kuʃ] nf bed, couch, layer, stratum, coat(ing), baby's napkin; pl confinement.

couché [kuʃe] a lying, recumbent, in bed.

coucher [kuʃe] vt to put to bed, lay down, set down; **— en joue** to aim (at); vi to sleep, spend the night; vr to go to bed, lie down, set, go down; nm night's lodging, setting.

couchette [kuʃɛt] nf crib, cot, berth, bunk, sleeper.

coucou [kuku] nm cuckoo.

coude [kud] nm elbow, bend, crank; **jouer des —s** to elbow one's way.

coudée [kude] nf pl elbow room, scope.

cou-de-pied [kudpje] nm instep.

coudoyer [kudwaje] vt to elbow, jostle, rub shoulders with.

coudre [kudr] vt to sew (up), stitch (on).

coudrier [kudrie] nm hazel tree.

couenne [kwan] nf thick skin, rind, membrane.

coulage [kulaːʒ] nm pouring, casting, running, sinking.

coulant [kulɑ̃] a running, flowing, easy, accommodating; **nœud —** slip-knot, noose.

coulé [kule] a cast, sunk, done for; nm slide, slur.

coulée [kule] nf running, flow, streak, casting.

couler [kule] vt to run, pour, cast, sink, slip, slur; vi to flow, run, leak, sink, slip, slur; vr to slip, glide, slide; **se la —douce** to take it easy, sit back.

couleur [kulœːr] nf colour, complexion, colouring, paint, suit, flag.

couleuvre [kulœːvr] nf grass snake; **avaler une —** to pocket an insult.

coulisse [kulis] nf groove, slot, slide, unofficial stock-market; pl wings, slips; **à —** sliding; **en —** sidelong.

couloir [kulwaːr] nm corridor, passage, lobby, channel, gully, lane.

coup [ku] nm blow, stroke, knock, hit, attempt, deed, attack, poke, stab, shot, blast, gust, move, ring, peal, influence, threat; **manquer son —** to miss the mark; **— de froid** cold snap, chill; **boire à petits —s** to sip; **— d'envoi** kick-off; **tout d'un —** all at once; **du —** now at last, this time; **sur le —** on the spot; **tout à —** suddenly.

coupable [kupabl] a guilty, culpable, sinful; n culprit.

coupe [kup] nf cup, glass, bowl, cut(ting), section, stroke.

coupé [kupe] a cut (up), sliced, broken, jerky, diluted; nm brougham, coupé.

coupe-coupe [kupkup] nm cutlass, matchet.

coupe-jarret [kupʒarɛ] nm cutthroat, ruffian.

coupe-papier [kuppapje] nm paper knife.

couper [kupe] vt to cut (out, up, down, off, in), intersect, cross, turn off, switch off, interrupt, stump, dilute; vr to cut oneself, cut, intersect, contradict oneself.

couperet [kuprɛ] nm chopper, cleaver, knife, blade (of guillotine).

couperosé [kuproze] a blotchy.

couple [kupl] nm couple, pair; nf two, brace, yoke, couple.

coupler [kuple] vt to couple, connect, join up.

couplet [kuplɛ] nm verse.

coupole [kupɔl] nf cupola, dome.

coupon [kupɔ̃] nm coupon, warrant, ticket, cut(ting), remnant, (short) length.

coupure [kupyːr] nf cut, gash, cutting, note.

cour [kuːr] nf court, courtship, courtyard, square, playground; **faire la — à** to make love to.

courage [kuraːʒ] nm courage, fortitude, spirit, heart.

courageux, -euse [kuraʒø, øːz] a brave, courageous.

couramment [kuramɑ̃] ad fluently, easily, generally.

courant [kurɑ̃] a running, current, present, standard, rife; nm current, stream, course; **— d'air** draught.

courbature [kurbatyr] nf stiffness, tiredness, ache.

courbaturé [kurbatyre] a aching, stiff.

courbe [kurb] nf curve, bend, sweep.

courber [kurbe] vtir to curve, bend; vr to stoop.

coureur, -euse [kurœːr, øːz] n runner, racer, sprinter, gadabout, adventurer, rake; **— de dots** fortune-hunter.

courge [kurʒ] nf pumpkin.

courgette [kurʒɛt] nf courgette, small marrow.

courir [kuriːr] vi to run, race, go,

be current, circulate; *vt* run (after), pursue, roam gadabout, haunt, frequent; **le bruit court** it is rumoured; **par le temps qui court** nowadays, as things are.

courlis [kurli] *nm* curlew.

couronne [kurɔn] *nf* crown, coronet, wreath, corona, ring, rim.

couronnement [kurɔnmɑ̃] *nm* crowning, coronation coping.

couronner [kurɔne] *vt* to crown, cap, reward, award a prize to cope.

courrier [kurje] *nm* courier, messenger mail, letters, post, newspaper paragraph.

courroie [kurwa] *nf* strap, transmission, belt, band.

courroux [kuru] *nm* anger, wrath.

cours [kuːr] *nm* course, flow run, path circulation, currency, quotation, price, course of lectures; *pl* classes; **en —** in progress, on hand, present, current.

course [kurs] *nf* run, race, excursion, outing, errand, course, path, flight.

court [kuːr] *a* short, brief limited; *ad* short; **à — de** short of; **tout —** simply, merely; *nm* tennis court.

courtage [kurtaːʒ] *nm* broking, brokerage.

courtaud [kurto] *a* thickset, dumpy.

court-circuit [kursirkɥi] *nm* short-circuit.

courtier [kurtje] *nm* broker.

courtisan [kurtizɑ̃] *nm* courtier.

courtisane [kurtizan] *nf* courtesan prostitute.

courtiser [kurtize] *vt* to court, curry favour with.

courtois [kurtwa] *a* courteous, polite, courtly.

courtoisie [kurtwazi] *nf* courtesy, courteousness.

couru [kury] *a* run after, sought aft r popular.

cousin [kuzɛ̃] *n* cousin; *nm* gnat, midge; **— germain** first cousin; **— à la mode de Bretagne** distant relation.

coussin [kusɛ̃] *nm* cushion.

coussinet [kusinɛ] *nm* pads, small cushion, bearing; **—s à billes** ball-bearings.

cousu [kuzy] *a* sewn, stitched; **— d'or** rolling in money.

coût [ku] *nm* cost; **— de la vie** cost of living.

couteau [kuto] *nm* knife, blade; **à —x tirés** at daggers-drawn.

coutelas [kutla] *nm* cutlass, large knife.

coutelier [kutəlje] *nm* cutler.

coutellerie [kutɛlri] *nf* cutlery, cutler's shop or trade.

coûter [kute] *vi* to cost, pain, cause an effort; **coûte que coûte** at all costs.

coûteux, -euse [kutø, øːz] *a* costly, expensive.

coutil [kuti] *nm* drill, twill, ticking

coutume [kutym] *nf* custom, habit; **de —** usual.

couture [kutyːr] *nf* needlework, seam, scar; **battre à plate(s) —(s)** to trounce.

couturier, -ière [kutyrje, jɛːr] *n* dressmaker.

couvée [kuve] *nf* brood, hatch, clutch.

couvent [kuvɑ̃] *nm* convent, monastery.

couver [kuve] *vt* to sit (on eggs), hatch (out), brood (over); *vi* to smoulder, brew hatch; **— des yeux** to look fondly or longingly at.

couvercle [kuvɛrkl] *nm* lid, cover, cap.

couvert [kuveːr] *a* covered, clad wearing one's hat, shady, wooded, overcast, covert overgrown; *nm* cover(ing), shelter place, knife and fork and spoon, cover charge.

couverture [kuvɛrtyːr] *nf* cover(ing), rug, blanket cloth, bedspread, wrapper, roofing.

couvre-feu [kuvrfø] *nm* curfew, lights out.

couvre-lit [kuvrli] *nm* bedspread.

couvre-pied [kuvrpje] *nm* quilt.

couvreur [kuvrœːr] *nm* roofer, slater, tiler.

couvrir [kuvriːr] *vt* to cover (with, up), clothe conceal, roof, drown (sound); *vr* to clothe oneself, put on one's hat become overcast.

crabe [kraːb] *nm* crab.

crachat [kraʃa] *nm* spittle, spit.

craché [kraʃe] *a* **tout —** the dead spit of, to a tee.

cracher [kraʃe] *vt* to spit (out), splutter; *vi* to spit.

crachoir [kraʃwaːr] *nm* spittoon.

craie [krɛ] *nf* chalk.

craindre [krɛ̃ːdr] *vi* to fear, dread, be afraid of; **il n'y a rien à —** there's no need to worry, nothing to worry about.

crainte [krɛ̃ːt] *nf* fear, dread.

craintif, -ive [krɛ̃tif, iːv] *a* timid, afraid, fearful.

cramoisi [kramwazi] *a* crimson.

crampe [krɑ̃ːp] *nf* cramp.

crampon [krɑ̃pɔ̃] *nm* clamp, fastener, crampon stud, limpet, pest.

cramponner [krɑ̃pɔne] *vt* to cramp, clamp together fasten, pester, stick to; *vr* to hold on, hang on (to à).

cran [krɑ̃] *nm* safety catch, notch, hole, pluck, spirit.

crâne [krɑːn] *nm* skull; *a* plucky, jaunty swaggering.

crâner [krɑne] *vi* to swagger, assume a jaunty air, brazen it out.

crâneur [krɑnœːr] *n* braggart, swaggerer.

crapaud [krapo] *nm* toad.

crapule [krapyl] *nf* debauchery, blackguard.

crapuleux, -euse [krapylø, øːz] *a* debauched dissolute lewd, filthy.

craquelure [kraklyːr] *nf* crack.
craquer [krake] *vi* to crack, crackle, crunch, creak.
crasse [kras] *af* gross; *nf* dirt, squalor, dross, slag, meanness, dirty trick.
crasseux, -euse [krasø, øːz] *a* dirty, grimy, squalid.
cratère [krateːr] *nm* crater.
cravache [kravaʃ] *nf* riding-whip, horsewhip.
cravate [kravat] *nf* (neck)tie.
crayeux, -euse [krɛjø, øːz] *a* chalky.
crayon [krɛjɔ̃] *nm* pencil, pencil-drawing, crayon.
crayonner [krɛjɔne] *vt* to pencil, sketch, jot down.
créance [kreɑ̃ːs] *nf* credence, belief, credit, trust, debt, claim; lettre(s) de — letter of credit, credentials.
créancier, -ière [kreɑ̃sje, jɛːr] *n* creditor.
créateur, -trice [kreatœːr, tris] *a* creative; *n* creator, maker, inventor, founder.
création [kreasjɔ̃] *nf* creation, creating, founding.
créature [kreatyːr] *nf* creature, person.
crèche [krɛʃ] *nf* crib, manger, day-nursery.
crédence [kredɑ̃ːs] *nf* sideboard.
crédibilité [kredibilite] *nf* credibility.
crédit [kredi] *nm* credit, loan, bank, repute, influence.
créditeur, -trice [kreditœːr, tris] *a* credit; *n* creditor.
credo [kredo] *nm* creed.
crédule [kredyl] *a* credulous.
crédulité [kredylite] *nf* credulity, credulousness.
créer [kree] *vt* to create, make, found, build up.
crémaillère [kremajɛːr] *nf* pot hook; pendre la — to give a house-warming.
crématoire [krematwaːr] *a* four — crematorium.
crème [krɛm] *nf* cream, custard.
crémerie [krɛmri] *nf* creamery, dairy, milk-shop, small restaurant.
crémeux, -euse [kremø, øːz] *a* creamy.
crémier, -ière [kremje, jɛːr] *n* dairyman, dairywoman.
crémière [kremjɛːr] *nf* cream-jug.
créneau [kreno] *nm* loophole; *pl* battlements.
crénelé [krenle] *a* crenellated, loop-holed, notched, toothed.
créosote [kreɔzot] *nf* creosote.
crêpe [krɛːp] *nf* pancake; *nm* crape, crêpe.
crêper [krɛpe] *vt* to crimp, crisp, frizz, backcomb.
crépi [krepi] *nm* rough-cast.
crépir [krepiːr] *vt* to rough-cast, grain.
crépiter [krepite] *vi* to crackle, sputter, patter.

crépu [krepy] *a* crimped, crisp frizzy, fuzzy.
crépuscule [krepyskyl] *nm* dusk, twilight, gloaming.
cresson [krəsɔ̃] *nm* cress.
crête [krɛːt] *nf* comb, crest, ridge.
crétin [kretɛ̃] *nm* cretin, idiot, half-wit.
cretonne [krətɔn] *nf* cretonne.
creuser [krøze] *vt* to hollow (out), excavate, dig (out), go deeply into.
creuset [krøzɛ] *nm* crucible, melting-pot.
creux, -euse [krø, øːz] *a* hollow, sunk(en), empty, slack, futile; *nm* hollow, hole, pit, cavity.
crevaison [krəvɛzɔ̃] *nf* puncture, bursting, death.
crevant [krəvɑ̃] *a* funny, killing, exhausting.
crevasse [krəvas] *nf* crevice, crevasse, crack, split.
crève-cœur [krɛvkœːr] *nm* heart-break, disappointment.
crever [krəve] *vi* to burst, split, die; *vt* to puncture, burst, put out.
crevette [krəvɛt] *nf* shrimp, prawn.
cri [kri] *nm* cry, shout, call, squeal; le dernier — the latest fashion, the last word.
criailler [kriɑje] *vi* to shout, bawl, whine, squeal.
criant [kriɑ̃] *a* crying, flagrant, glaring.
criard [kriaːr] *a* crying, squealing, shrill, garish.
crible [kribl] *nm* sieve, riddle, screen.
cribler [krible] *vt* to sift, riddle, screen.
cric [krik] *nm* jack.
cricri [krikri] *nm* chirping, cricket.
criée [krie] *nf* auction.
crier [krie] *vti* to cry, shout; *vi* scream, squeak.
crime [krim] *nm* crime.
criminel, -elle [kriminɛl] *an* criminal.
crin [krɛ̃] *nm* horsehair.
crinière [krinjɛːr] *nf* mane.
crique [krik] *nf* creek, cove.
crise [kriːz] *nf* crisis, problem, shortage, slump, attack.
crispation [krispasjɔ̃] *nf* twitching, clenching, wincing, shrivelling up.
crisper [krispe] *vt* to clench, contract, contort, screw up; *vr* to contract, shrivel up.
crisser [krise] *vi* to grate.
cristal [kristal] *nm* crystal.
cristallin [kristalɛ̃] *a* crystalline, crystal-clear.
cristalliser [kristalize] *vti* to crystal-lize.
critère [kriteːr] *nm* criterion.
critiquable [kritikabl] *a* open to criticism.
critique [kritik] *a* critical, crucial, ticklish, decisive; *nf* criticism, censure; *nm* critic.

critiquer [kritike] vt to criticize, censure.

croasser [krɔase] vi to caw. croak.

croc [kro] nm hook, fang, tusk.

croc-en-jambe [krɔkãʒãːb] nm faire donner un — à qn to trip.

croche [krɔʃ] nf quaver.

crochet [krɔʃe] nm hook, crochet, skeleton key, swerve, sudden turn; pl square brackets.

crochu [krɔʃy] a hooked, crooked.

crocodile [krɔkɔdil] nm crocodile.

croire [krwaːr] vt to believe, think; vi believe (in à, en).

croisade [krwazad] nf crusade.

croisé [krwaze] a crossed, cross, double-breasted; nm crusader.

croisée [krwaze] nf crossing, cross-roads, casement window.

croisement [krwazmã] nm crossing, meeting, intersection, interbreeding.

croiser [krwaze] vt to cross, fold, pass, meet; vi to fold over, cruise; vr to intersect, cross, meet and pass.

croiseur [krwazœːr] nm cruiser.

croisière [krwazjeːr] nf cruise.

croissance [krwasãːs] nf growth.

croissant [krwasã] nm crescent, crescent roll.

croître [krwaːtr] vi to grow, increase, rise, wax, lengthen

croix [krwa] nf cross.

croque-mitaine [krɔkmitɛn] nm bogy(man).

croquer [krɔke] vt to crunch, munch, sketch.

croquis [krɔki] nm sketch.

crosse [krɔs] nf crook, crosier, stick, club, butt.

crotte [krɔtˀ] nf mud, dirt, dung, chocolate sweet.

crotté [krɔte] a dirty, muddy, bespattered.

crottin [krɔtɛ̃] nm dung, droppings.

croulant [krulã] a crumbling, totter-ing.

croulement [krulmã] nm collapse, crumbling, falling in.

crouler [krule] vi to collapse, totter, crumble.

croupe krup] nf croup, crupper, rump.

croupion [krupjɔ̃] nm rump, parson's nose.

croupir [krupiːr] vi to wallow, stagnate.

croustillant [krustijã] a crisp, crusty. spicy, smutty.

croûte [krut] nf crust, rind, scab, daub; casser la — to have a snack.

croûton [krutɔ̃] nm crust, crusty end, croûton.

croyable [krwajabl] a credible, believable, trustworthy.

croyance [krwajãːs] nf belief.

croyant [krwajã] a believing; n believer; pl the faithful.

cru [kry] a raw, crude, broad, coarse, blunt, garish; nm vintage, growth, vineyard, invention; vin du

— local wine; les meilleurs —s the best vineyards; un bon — a good vintage.

cruauté [kryote] nf cruelty.

cruche [kryʃ] nf pitcher, jug, block-head, dolt.

crucifier [krysifie] vt to crucify.

crucifix [krysifi] nm crucifix.

crucifixion [krysifiksjɔ̃] nf crucifi-xion.

crudité [krydite] nf crudity, rawness, coarseness; pl raw fruit or vegetables.

crue [kry] nf rising, flood spate.

cruel, -elle [kryɛl] a cruel.

crûment [krymã] ad crudely, blunt-ly, roughly.

crustacés [krystase] nm pl crust-aceans.

crypte [kript] nf crypt.

cube [kyb] a cubic; nm cube.

cubique [kybik] a cubic(al), cube.

cubisme [kybism] nm cubism.

cueillaison [kœjezɔ̃] nf gathering, picking, gathering season.

cueillette [kœjet] nf gathering, picking, crop.

cueillir [kœjiːr] vt to gather, pick, pluck.

cuiller, -ère [kyjeːr, kɥijeːr] nf spoon.

cuillerée [kyjre, kɥijre] nf spoonful.

cuir [kɥiːr] nm leather, hide, skin, strop; — chevelu scalp.

cuirasse [kɥiras] nf breastplate, armour.

cuirassé [kɥirase] a armour-plated, armoured; nm ironclad, battleship.

cuire [kɥiːr] vt to cook, roast, bake, fire, burn; vi to cook, stew, burn, smart.

cuisant [kɥizã] a burning, smarting, biting, bitter.

cuisine [kɥizin] nf kitchen, cooking, cookery food.

cuisiner [kɥizine] vt to cook; — les comptes cook the books, pull strings, (a suspect) interrogate.

cuisinier, -ière [kɥizinje, jeːr] n cook.

cuisinière [kɥizinjeːr] nf stove, cooker.

cuisse [kɥis] nf thigh, leg.

cuisson [kɥisɔ̃] nf cooking, baking, firing, burning, smarting.

cuistre [kɥistr] nm pedant, ill-mannered man.

cuit [kɥi] a cooked, baked, drunk; — à point done to a turn; trop — overdone; pas assez — underdone.

cuite [kɥit] nf baking, firing, burning, batch; prendre une — to get tight (drunk).

cuivre [kɥiːvr] nm copper, copper-plate; — jaune brass; les —s the brass(es).

cuivré [kɥivre] a coppered, copper-coloured, bronzed, metallic, brassy.

cul [ky] nm (fam) bottom, behind, rump, tail, stern.

culasse [kylas] nf breech.

culbute [kylbyt] *n* somersault, tumble, fall.

culbuter [kylbyte] *vi* to turn a somersault, tumble; *vt* to knock over, dump, trip.

cul-de-sac [kydsak] *nm* blind alley, dead end.

culinaire [kylinɛːr] *a* culinary.

culminant [kylminɑ̃] *a* culminating, highest.

culot [kylo] *nm* bottom, base, dottle, cheek, sauce.

culotte [kylɔt] *nf* breeches, knicker-bockers, shorts.

culotter [kylɔte] *vt* to breech, colour, season.

culpabilité [kylpabilite] *nf* culpability, guilt.

culte [kylt] *nm* worship, cult.

cultivateur [kyltivatœːr] *nm* farmer, cultivator, grower.

cultivé [kyltive] *a* cultivated, cultured.

cultiver [kyltive] *vt* to farm, till, cultivate.

culture [kyltyːr] *nf* cultivation, farming, culture; *pl* fields, land under cultivation.

cumul [kymyl] *nm* plurality of offices.

cumuler [kymyle] *vt* to occupy several posts.

cupide [kypid] *a* covetous, greedy, grasping.

cupidité [kypidite] *nf* covetousness, greed.

Cupidon [kypidɔ̃] *nm* Cupid.

curatif, -ive [kyratif, iːv] *a* curative.

cure [kyːr] *nf* care, heed, presbytery, vicarage, rectory, cure.

curé [kyre] *nm* parish priest.

cure-dents [kyrdɑ̃] *nm* toothpick.

curer [kyre] *vt* to pick, clean (out), cleanse, clear.

curieux, -euse [kyrjø, øːz] *a* interested, curious, odd, quaint.

curiosité [kyrjozite] *nf* interested-ness, inquisitiveness, curiosity, odd-ness, peculiarity, curio; *pl* sights.

curviligne [kyrviliɲ] *a* curvilinear, rounded.

cuticule [kytikyl] *nf* cuticle.

cuve [kyːv] *nf* vat, tun, tank.

cuver [kyve] *vti* to ferment; — son vin to sleep off one's drink.

cuvette [kyvɛt] *nf* wash-basin, dish, pan, basin.

cyanure [sjanyːr] *nm* cyanide.

cycle [sikl] *nm* cycle.

cyclisme [siklism] *nm* cycling.

cyclone [siklon] *nm* cyclone.

cygne [siɲ] *nm* swan.

cylindre [silɛ̃ːdr] *nm* cylinder, drum, roller.

cylindrer [silɛ̃dre] *vt* to roll, calender, mangle.

cylindrique [silɛ̃drik] *a* cylindrical.

cymbale [sɛ̃bal] *nf* cymbal.

cynique [sinik] *a* cynic(al), brazen, barefaced; *nm* cynic.

cynisme [sinism] *nm* cynicism, effrontery.

cynocéphale [sinɔsefal] *nm* baboon.

cyprès [siprɛ] *nm* cypress-tree.

cytise [sitiːz] *nm* laburnum.

D

daba [daba] *nf* hoe.

dactylo(graphe) [daktilɔgraf] *n* typist.

dactylographier [daktilɔgrafje] *vt* to type.

dada [dada] *nm* hobby (-horse).

dadais [dadɛ] *nm* ninny.

dague [dag] *nf* dagger.

daigner [dɛɲe] *vi* to condescend, deign.

daim [dɛ̃] *nm* deer, buck.

dais [dɛ] *nm* canopy, dais.

dallage [dalaːʒ] *nm* paving, tiled floor.

dalle [dal] *nf* flagstone, slice, slab.

daller [dale] *vt* to pave, tile.

daltonisme [daltɔnism] *nm* colour-blindness.

damas [damɑ(ːs)] *nm* damask, damson.

dame [dam] *nf* lady, queen, king (draughts), beetle; *pl* draughts.

damer [dame] *vt* to crown a piece (at draughts).

damier [damje] *nm* draught-board.

damner [dane] *vt* to damn, condemn.

dancing [dɑ̃sɛ̃ːg] *nm* dance hall.

dandiner [dɑ̃dine] *vt* to dandle, dance; *vr* to waddle.

Danemark [danmark] *nm* Denmark.

danger [dɑ̃ʒe] *nm* danger, peril, jeopardy, risk.

dangereux, -euse [dɑ̃ʒrø, øːz] *a* dangerous, perilous, risky.

danois [danwa, waːz] *a* Danish; *n* Dane.

dans [dɑ̃] *prep* in, into, within, out of, from.

danse [dɑ̃ːs] *nf* dance, dancing.

danser [dɑ̃se] *vti* to dance; *vi* to prance, bob.

danseur, -euse [dɑ̃sœːr, øːz] *n* dancer, partner.

dard [daːr] *nm* dart, javelin, harpoon, sting, tongue.

darder [darde] *vt* to dart, hurl, shoot out.

darse [dars] *nf* floating dock.

date [dat] *nf* date.

dater [date] *vti* to date; à — de as from.

datte [dat] *nf* date.

dattier [datje] *nm* date palm.

dauphin [dofɛ̃] *nm* dolphin, dauphin.

davantage [davɑ̃taːʒ] *ad* more, any more, any further.

de [də] *prep* from, of, by, with, in.

dé [de] *nm* thimble, dice, die, tee.

débâcle [debaːkl] *nf* collapse, break-up, downfall, rout.

déballer [debale] *vt* to unpack.

débandade [debɑ̃dad] *nf* rout, stampede; **à la —** in disorder, helter-skelter.

débander [debɑ̃de] *vt* to loosen, relax, unbend.

débarbouiller [debarbuje] *vt* to clean, wash; *vr* wash one's face.

débarcadère [debarkadɛːr] *nm* landing-stage.

débarder [debarde] *vt* to unload, discharge.

débardeur [debardœːr] *nm* stevedore, docker.

débarquement [debarkəmɑ̃] *nm* disembarking, landing, unloading, detraining.

débarquer [debarke] *vti* to land, disembark, detrain; *vt* to unload, set down.

débarras [debarɑ] *nm* lumber-room; **bon —!** good riddance!

débarrasser [debarase] *vt* to rid, free, relieve; *vr* to get rid (of **de**).

débarrer [debare] *vt* to unbar.

débat [deba] *nm* debate, argument, discussion.

débattre [debatr] *vt* to discuss, debate; *vr* to struggle.

débauche [deboːʃ] *nf* debauchery, dissipation.

débaucher [deboʃe] *vt* to corrupt, lead astray; *vr* go to the bad.

débile [debil] *a* feeble, weak, sickly.

débilité [debilite] *nf* feebleness, debility.

débit [debi] *nm* sale, shop, flow, delivery, debit.

débiter [debite] *vt* to sell, retail, deliver, spin, debit.

débiteur, -trice [debitœːr, tris] *n* debtor.

déblai [deblɛ] *nm* clearing, excavation; **voie en —** railway cutting.

déblatérer [deblatere] *vi* to rail (against **contre**).

déblayage [deblɛjaʒ] *nm* clearance, clearing.

déblayer [deblɛje] *vt* to clear away.

déboire [debwaːr] *nm* nasty after-taste, disappointment.

déboisement [debwazmɑ̃] *nm* deforestation.

déboîter [debwate] *vt* to dislocate, disjoint, disconnect.

débonder [debɔ̃de] *vt* to unbung.

débonnaire [debɔnɛːr] *a* good-natured, easy-tempered.

débordement [debɔrdəmɑ̃] *nm* overflowing, depravation, dissoluteness.

déborder [debɔrde] *vti* to overflow, boil over, brim over; *vt* to overlap, extend beyond, to outflank.

débouché [debuʃe] *nm* outlet, opening, market.

déboucher [debuʃe] *vt* to uncork, open, clear; *vi* to emerge, debouch.

déboucler [debukle] *vt* to unbuckle; *vr* (*hair*) to lose its curl.

déboulonner [debulɔne] *vt* to unbolt, unrivet.

débourber [deburbe] *vt* to clean out, sluice, dredge.

débours [deburr] *nm pl* out of pocket expenses.

débourser [deburse] *vt* to spend, disburse.

debout [dəbu] *ad* erect, upright, standing, on end, up.

déboutonner [debutɔne] *vt* to unbutton.

débraillé [debraje] *a* untidy, dishevelled, improper.

débrayer [debrɛje] *vt* to disconnect, throw out of gear, declutch.

débrider [debride] *vt* to unbridle; **sans —** without a stop.

débris [debri] *nm pl* fragments, bits, remains, ruins.

débrouillard [debrujaːr] *a* ingenious, resourceful, smart.

débrouiller [debruje] *vt* to unravel, disentangle. *vr* to find a way out, not to be stuck.

débrousser [debruse] *vt* to clear forest, bush.

débusquer [debyske] *vt* to dislodge, ferret out.

début [deby] *nm* beginning, start, first appearance.

débutant [debytɑ̃] *n* beginner.

débuter [debyte] *vi* to lead, begin, come out.

deçà [dəsa] *ad* on this side.

décacheter [dekaʃte] *vt* to unseal, break open.

décadence [dekadɑ̃ːs] *nf* decay, decline, downfall.

décaler [dekale] *vt* to remove wedge from, alter.

décamper [dekɑ̃pe] *vi* to decamp, scuttle off.

décapiter [dekapite] *vt* to behead.

décati [dekati] *a* worn out, senile.

décatir [dekatiːr] *vt* to sponge, steam, finish.

décéder [desede] *vt* to die, decease.

déceler [desle] *vt* to reveal, disclose, divulge.

décembre [desɑ̃ːbr] *nm* December.

décence [desɑ̃ːs] *nf* decency, propriety, decorum.

décent [desɑ̃] *a* decent, proper, modest.

décentraliser [desɑ̃tralize] *vt* to decentralize.

déception [desɛpsjɔ̃] *nf* deception, disappointment.

décerner [deserne] *vt* to confer, award, decree.

décès [desɛ] *nm* decease.

décevant [des(ə)vɑ̃] *a* deceptive, disappointing.

décevoir [desəvwaːr] *vt* to disappoint, deceive, dash.

déchaîner [deʃɛne] *vt* to unchain, let loose, unfetter; *vr* to break loose, break (out).

décharge [deʃarʒ] *nf* unloading, volley, discharge, acquittal, rebate; **témoin à —** witness for defence.

déchargement [deʃarʒəmɑ̃] nm unloading, discharging.

décharger [deʃarʒe] vt to dump, exonerate, unload, discharge, let off; vr to go off, run down, get rid (of de).

décharné [deʃarne] a gaunt, emaciated, skinny.

déchausser [deʃose] vt to take off s.o.'s shoes; vr take off one's shoes.

déchéance [deʃeɑ̃:s] nf fall, downfall, forfeiture.

déchet [deʃɛ] nm loss, decrease; pl refuse, scraps, failures.

déchiffrer [deʃifre] vt to decipher, decode, read.

déchiqueté [deʃikte] a torn, slashed, jagged.

déchirant [deʃirɑ̃] a heart-rending, ear-splitting, excruciating, harrowing.

déchirer [deʃire] vtr to tear, rend.

déchirure [deʃiry:r] nf tear, slit, rent.

déchoir [deʃwa:r] vi to fall.

décidément [desidemɑ̃] ad decidedly, resolutely.

décider [deside] vt to decide, settle, induce; vir to make up one's mind, decide.

décimale [desimal] nf decimal.

décimer [desime] vt to decimate.

décisif, -ive [desizif, i:v] a decisive, crucial, conclusive.

décision [desizjɔ̃] nf decision, resolution.

déclamation [deklamasjɔ̃] nf declamation, oratory, elocution.

déclamatoire [deklamatwa:r] a declamatory.

déclamer [deklame] vti to declaim, spout.

déclarable [deklarabl] a liable to custom's duty.

déclaration [deklarasjɔ̃] nf announcement, declaration; — assermentée affidavit.

déclarer [deklare] vt to declare, state; vr declare oneself, break out, avow one's love, own up.

déclassé [deklɑse] a degraded, ostracized; n. outcast, pariah.

déclasser [deklɑse] vt to transfer from one class to another, degrade.

déclencher [deklɑ̃ʃe] vt to loosen, release, launch.

déclic [deklik] nm latch, trigger, click, snap.

déclin [deklɛ̃] nm decline, close, end, deterioration.

déclinaison [deklinɛzɔ̃] nf declension, variation.

décliner [dekline] vt to decline, refuse; vi to decline, deteriorate, decay, fall; — son nom to give one's name.

déclivité [deklivite] nf declivity, slope, incline.

décocher [dekɔʃe] vt to shoot, discharge, let fly, fire.

décoiffer [dekwafe] vt to remove s.o.'s hat, undo s.o.'s hair; vr take one's hat off.

décollage [dekɔla:ʒ] nm unsticking, removal of gum, take-off (plane); piste de — runway.

décoller [dekɔle] vt to unstick, loosen, remove gum from; vi to take off; vr to come unstuck, work loose.

décolleté [dekɔlte] a low-necked.

décolorant [dekɔlɔrɑ̃] anm bleaching (agent).

décolorer [dekɔlɔre] vt to discolour, take colour out of.

décombres [dekɔ̃:br] nm pl rubbish, debris.

décommander [dekɔmɑ̃de] vt to cancel, countermand, call off.

décomposer [dekɔ̃poze] vt to decompose, alter, distort; vr to decompose, become distorted.

décompte [dekɔ̃:t] nm discount, deduction.

déconcerter [dekɔ̃sɛrte] vt to confound, take aback.

déconfiture [dekɔ̃fity:r] nf defeat, discomfiture.

déconseiller [dekɔ̃sɛje] vt to dissuade, advise against.

déconsidération [dekɔ̃siderasjɔ̃] nf discredit, disrepute.

déconsidéré [dekɔ̃sidere] a disreputable.

déconsidérer [dekɔ̃sidere] vt to bring into disrepute.

décontenancer [dekɔ̃tnɑ̃se] vt to abash.

déconvenue [dekɔ̃vny] nf mishap, misfortune.

décor [dekɔr] nm decoration, scenery, set(ting).

décorateur, -trice [dekɔratœ:r, tris] n decorator, scene-painter.

décoration [dekɔrasjɔ̃] nf decoration, scene-painting.

décorer [dekɔre] vt to decorate.

décortiquer [dekɔrtike] vt to remove bark from, shell, peel, husk.

découcher [dekuʃe] vi to sleep out.

découdre [dekudr] vt to unstitch, unpick; vr to come unstitched.

découler [dekule] vi to flow, run down, fall.

découpage [dekupa:ʒ] nm cutting out, fretwork.

découper [dekupe] vt to cut out, cut up, carve; vr to stand out.

découplé [dekuple] a bien — well-built.

découpure [dekupy:r] nf cutting out, cutting.

découragé [dekuraʒe] a downhearted, despondent.

décourageant [dekuraʒɑ̃] a disheartening.

découragement [dekuraʒmɑ̃] nm despondency, discouragement.

décousu [dekuzy] a disconnected, incoherent, rambling; nm incoherency.

découvert [dekuvɛːr] a uncovered, open, exposed; à — openly.

découverte [dekuvɛrt] nf discovery.

découvrir [dekuvriːr] vt to uncover, discover, reveal, detect, expose; vr to doff one's hat, be discovered.

décrasser [dekrase] vt to scour, clean.

décrépitude [dekrepityd] nf decay, senility.

décret [dekrɛ] nm decree.

décréter [dekrete] vt to decree, enact.

décrier [dekrie] vt to decry, run down, disparage.

décrire [dekriːr] vt to describe.

décrocher [dekrɔʃe] vt to unhook, take down, undo.

décroissance [dekrwasãːs] nf decrease, decline.

décroître [dekrwaːtr] vi to decrease, grow shorter.

décrotter [dekrɔte] vt to clean, brush, scrape.

décrottoir [dekrɔtwaːr] nm scraper.

déçu [desy] a disappointed.

dédaigner [dedɛɲe] vt to disdain, scorn.

dédaigneux, -euse [dedɛɲø, øːz] a disdainful, supercilious.

dédain [dedɛ̃] nm disdain.

dédale [dedal] nm maze.

dedans [dədã] ad inside, within, in it; nm interior, inside.

dédicace [dedikas] nf dedication.

dédier [dedje] vt to dedicate, inscribe.

se dédire [sədediːr] vr to retract, take back one's words.

dédommagement [dedɔmaʒmã] nm compensation, damages, amends.

dédommager [dedɔmaʒe] vt to compensate, make amends to; vr to make up one's loss.

déduction [dedyksjɔ̃] nf deduction, inference.

déduire [deduiːr] vt to deduce, deduct.

déesse [deɛs] nf goddess.

défaillance [defajãːs] nf weakness, lapse, falling-off, swoon; tomber en — to faint.

défaillant [defajã] a failing, sinking; n defaulter.

défaillir [defajiːr] vi to grow weak, fail, faint.

défaire [defɛːr] vt to undo, untie, defeat; vr to come undone, rid oneself, get rid (of).

défait [defɛ] a haggard, drawn, worn, undone.

défaite [defɛt] nf defeat.

défaitiste [defɛtist] an defeatist.

défalquer [defalke] vt to deduct, write off.

défaut [defo] nm defect, fault, lack, blemish, flaw; à — de for lack of; prendre qn en — to catch someone ou:.

défaveur [defavœːr] nf disgrace, disfavour.

défavorable [defavɔrabl] a unfavourable, disadvantageous.

défection [defɛksjɔ̃] nf disloyalty, defection.

défectueux, -euse [defɛktɥø, øːz] a faulty, defective.

défendable [defɑ̃dabl] a defensible.

défendeur, -eresse [defɑ̃dœːr, ərɛs] n defendant.

défendre [defɑ̃ːdr] vt to defend, uphold, protect, forbid.

défense [defɑ̃ːs] nf defence, support, interdiction; pl tusks; —de fumer no smoking; — passive Anti-Aircraft Defence, Civil Defence.

défenseur [defɑ̃sœːr] nm defender, protector, upholder, counsel for defence.

défensif, -ive [defɑ̃sif, iːv] a defensive.

défensive [defɑ̃siːv] nf defensive.

déférence [deferɑ̃ːs] nf respect, deference, compliance.

déférer [defere] vt to refer, hand over, administer; vi to assent, defer, comply.

déferler [defɛrle] vt to unfurl; vi to break.

déferrer [defere] vt to unshoe, remove the iron from; vr to cast a shoe.

défi [defi] nm defiance, challenge.

défiance [defjãːs] nf distrust, suspicion, diffidence.

défiant [defjã] a distrustful, suspicious, wary.

déficeler [defisle] vt to untie.

déficit [defisit] nm deficit.

déficitaire [defisitɛːr] a deficient, unbalanced.

défier [defje] vt to defy, dare, challenge, beggar; vr to distrust.

défigurer [defigyre] vt to disfigure, distort, deface.

défilade [defilad] nf filing past.

défilé [defile] nm pass, defile, parade, march past.

défiler [defile] vi to march past, parade, flash past.

définir [definiːr] vt to determine, define.

définitif, -ive [definitif, iːv] a final, definitive.

définition [definisjɔ̃] nf definition.

déflation [deflasjɔ̃] nf deflation.

déflorer [deflɔre] vt to take the bloom off, take the novelty off, deflower.

défoncer [defɔ̃se] vt to break in, burst in, knock the bottom out of.

déformer [defɔrme] vt to disfigure, distort, put out of shape; vr to lose its shape.

défraîchi [defrɛʃi] a faded, soiled.

défrayer [defrɛje] vt to defray, pay s.o.'s expenses.

défricher [defriʃe] vt to clear, prepare, break.

défroncer [defrɔ̃se] vt to unplait, smooth.

défroque [defrɔk] nf pl cast-off clothing, wardrobe.

défroquer [defrɔke] vt to unfrock.

défunt [defœ̃] a deceased, dead, defunct.

dégagé [degaʒe] a free, easy, off-hand, airy.

dégagement [degaʒmɑ̃] nm disengagement, release, slackening, redemption.

dégager [degaʒe] vt to disengage, release, to redeem.

dégainer [degɛne] vt to unsheathe, draw.

dégarnir [degarniːr] vt to strip, deplete, dismantle; vr to be stripped, grow bare, empty.

dégâts [degɑ] nm pl damage, havoc.

dégauchir [degoʃiːr] vt to smooth, straighten, take the rough edges off.

dégel [deʒɛl] nm thaw.

dégeler [deʒle] vti to melt, thaw.

dégénération [deʒenɛrasjɔ̃] nf degeneration, degeneracy.

dégénérer [deʒenere] vi to degenerate.

dégingandé [deʒɛ̃gɑ̃de] a ungainly, gawky.

dégivreur [deʒivrœr] nm de-icer.

dégoiser [degwaze] vt to say hurriedly, race through; vi to chatter.

dégonfler [degɔ̃fle] vt to deflate, reduce, debunk, explode; vr to go flat, subside, climb down.

dégorger [degɔrʒe] vt to disgorge, clear; vi to flow out, overflow.

dégouliner [deguline] vi to drip, trickle.

dégourdi [degurdi] a smart, knowing, wide-awake.

dégourdir [degurdiːr] vt to revive, restore circulation to; vr to loosen one's muscles, stretch one's limbs.

dégoût [degu] nm disgust, aversion, distaste, annoyance.

dégoûtant [degutɑ̃] a disgusting, sickening.

dégoûté [degute] a disgusted, sick, fastidious, fed up.

dégoûter [degute] vt to disgust, sicken.

dégoutter [degute] vi to trickle, drip, drop.

dégradation [degradasjɔ̃] nf abasement, degeneracy, reduction to the ranks, shading off.

dégrader [degrade] vt to degrade, reduce to ranks, shade off, graduate.

dégrafer [degrafe] vt to unclasp, unhook, undo.

dégraisser [degrɛse] vt to scour, clean.

degré [dəgre] nm degree, stage, grade, step.

dégringolade [degrɛ̃gɔlad] nf fall, tumble, collapse, slump, bathos.

dégringoler [degrɛ̃gɔle] vti to rush, tumble down.

dégriser [degrize] vt to sober, bring

s.o. to his senses; vr to come back to earth.

dégrossir [degrosiːr] vt to rough plane, rough hew, take the rough edges off.

déguenillé [degnije] a ragged, tattered.

déguisement [degizmɑ̃] nm disguise, fancy dress.

déguiser [degize] vt to disguise; vr to dress in fancy costume, disguise oneself.

déguster [degyste] vt to taste, sample, sip.

dehors [dəɔːr] ad out(side); nm exterior, outside.

déjà [deʒa] ad already, before, by this time, as it is.

déjeuner [deʒœne] vi to breakfast, have lunch; nm lunch; petit — breakfast.

déjouer [deʒwe] vt to baffle, outwit, foil, thwart.

délabrement [delabrəmɑ̃] nm dilapidation, disrepair, ruin, decay.

délabrer [delabre] vt to pull to pieces, wreck; vr to fall into ruins, disrepair.

délacer [delase] vt to unlace; vr to come unlaced.

délai [delɛ] nm delay, notice, extension.

délaissement [delɛsmɑ̃] nm desertion, neglect, relinquishment.

délaisser [delɛse] vt to desert, forsake, relinquish.

délassement [delasmɑ̃] nm pastime, relaxation.

délasser [delase] vt to refresh; vr to take some relaxation.

délateur, -trice [dɛlatœːr, tris] n informer.

délayer [deleje] vt to dilute, water down, spin out.

délégation [delegasjɔ̃] nf delegation, assignment.

déléguer [delege] vt to depute, assign, delegate.

délester [delɛste] vt to unballast, relieve.

délibération [deliberasjɔ̃] nf deliberation, discussion, thought, resolution.

délibéré [delibere] a deliberate, purposeful.

délibérer [delibere] vt to discuss, think over; vi to deliberate, ponder.

délicat [delika] a delicate, dainty, fastidious, ticklish.

délicatesse [delikatɛs] nf delicacy, frailty, daintiness.

délice [delis] nm (Usu pl f) delight, pleasure.

délicieux, -euse [delisjø, øːz] a delightful, delicious.

délié [delje] a slender, slim, shrewd.

délier [delje] vt to untie, unbind; vr to come loose.

délimiter [delimite] vt to mark the limits of, define.

délinquant [delɛ̃kɑ̃] n offender, delinquent.

délirant [delirɑ̃] a raving, frenzied, delirious.

délire [deliːr] nm frenzy, delirium.

délirer [delire] vi to rave, be delirious.

délit [deli] nm offence, misdemeanour.

délivrance [delivrɑ̃ːs] nf deliverance.

délivrer [delivre] vt free release; vr to rid oneself (of **de**).

déloger [delɔʒe] vt to dislodge, eject; vi to remove.

déloyal [delwajal] a unfaithful, false, unfair, unequal.

déloyauté [delwajote] nf unfaithfulness, treachery, dishonesty. disloyalty.

déluge [delyːʒ] nm flood, deluge, downpour.

déluré [delyre] a wide-awake, cute, sly.

demain [dəmɛ̃] ad tomorrow; — **en huit** tomorrow week.

démailler [demaje] vr to ladder (stocking).

demande [d(ə)mɑ̃ːd] nf request, question, inquiry. application, indent.

demander [d(ə)mɑ̃de] vt to ask, ask for, apply for, request, sue; vr to wonder.

demandeur, -eresse [d(ə)mɑ̃dœːr, ərɛs] n claimant, petitioner.

démanger [demɑ̃ʒe] vi to itch.

démanteler [demɑ̃tle] vt to dismantle.

démarcation [demarkasjɔ̃] nf demarcation.

démarche [demarʃ] nf walk, bearing, step, approach.

démarrage [demaraːʒ] nm unmooring, start-off.

démarrer [demare] vt to unmoor; vi to leave moorings, start off.

démarreur [demarœːr] nm self-starter.

démasquer [demaske] vt to unmask, expose; vr to show one's true colours.

démêlé [demele] nm quarrel, tussle.

démêler [demele] vt to unravel, disentangle.

démembrer [demɑ̃bre] vt to dismember, partition.

déménagement [demenaʒmɑ̃] nm removal.

déménager [demenaʒe] vi to remove.

démence [demɑ̃ːs] nf madness, insanity.

démener [demne] vr to struggle, make violent efforts.

démenti [demɑ̃ti] nm contradiction, denial, lie.

démentir [demɑ̃tiːr] vt to contradict, belie; vr to go back on one's word.

démesuré [demzyre] a huge, immoderate.

démettre [demɛtr] vt to dislocate; vr to resign.

demeurant [dəmœrɑ̃] ad **au** — after all, moreover.

demeure [dəmœːr] nf abode, dwelling.

demeurer [dəmœre] vi to dwell, live, remain, stay

demi [dəmi] a ad half; nm half, half-back.

demi-finale [dəmifinal] nf semi-final.

demi-pensionnaire [dəmipɑ̃sjɔnɛːr] n day-boarder.

demi-place [dəmiplas] nf half-fare, half-price.

demi-saison [dəmisɛzɔ̃] nf between-season.

démission [demisjɔ̃] nf resignation.

démissionner [demisjɔne] vi to resign.

demi-tour [dəmituːr] nm **faire** — to turn back.

démobilisation [demɔbilizasjɔ̃] nf demobilization.

démobiliser [demɔbilize] vt to demobilize.

démocrate [demɔkrat] a democratic; n democrat.

démocratie [demɔkrasi] nf democracy.

démocratique [demɔkratik] a democratic.

démodé [demɔde] a old-fashioned, out-of-date.

démographie [demɔgrafi] nf demography.

demoiselle [dəmwazɛl] nf young lady, maiden, spinster; dragonfly, beetle; — **d'honneur** bridesmaid; — **de compagnie** lady companion.

démolir [demɔliːr] vt to pull down, demolish.

démon [demɔ̃] nm demon, fiend, devil, imp.

démonstration [demɔ̃strasjɔ̃] nf demonstration, proof.

démonté [demɔ̃te] a dismounted, stormy, flustered.

démonter [demɔ̃te] vt to unseat, take to pieces.

démontrer [demɔ̃tre] vt to demonstrate, prove.

démoralisateur, -trice [demɔralizatœːr, tris] a demoralizing.

démoraliser [demɔralize] vt to demoralize dishearten; vr to lose heart, be demoralized.

démordre [demɔrdr] vi to let go, give up; **en** — to climb down.

démuni [demyni] a short (of), without. out (of **de**).

dénaturé [denatyre] a unnatural, perverted.

dénaturer [denatyre] vt to falsify, pervert.

dénégation [denɛgasjɔ̃] nf denial.

dénicher [deniʃe] vt to remove from the nest, find, unearth; vi to forsake the nest.

dénigrement [denigrəmɑ̃] nm disparagement

dénigrer [denigre] *vt* to run down, disparage.

dénombrement [denɔ̃brəmɑ̃] *nm* enumeration, numbering, census.

dénommer [denɔme] *vt* to name.

dénoncer [denɔ̃se] *vt* to denounce, declare, inform against, squeal on.

dénonciateur, -trice [denɔ̃sjatœːr, tris] *a* tell-tale; *n* informer.

dénonciation [denɔ̃sjasjɔ̃] *nf* denunciation.

dénoter [denɔte] *vt* to denote, betoken.

dénouement [denumɑ̃] *nm* issue, end(ing), outcome.

dénouer [denwe] *vt* to untie, undo, unravel; *vr* to come loose, be unravelled.

denrée [dɑ̃re] *nf* commodity, foodstuff.

dense [dɑ̃ːs] *a* dense, thick.

densité [dɑ̃site] *nf* density, denseness.

dent [dɑ̃] *nf* tooth, prong, cog; **avoir une — contre qn** to bear s.o. a grudge; **à belles —s** with relish.

dentaire [dɑ̃tɛːr] *a* dental.

denté [dɑ̃te] *a* cogged.

denteler [dɑ̃tle] *vt* to indent, notch, serrate.

dentelle [dɑ̃tɛl] *nf* lace.

dentellerie [dɑ̃tɛlri] *nf* lace manufacture.

dentelure [dɑ̃tlyːr] *nf* indentation, serration.

dentier [dɑ̃tje] *nm* denture, set of false teeth.

dentifrice [dɑ̃tifris] *nm* toothpaste, -powder; **pâte —** toothpaste.

dentiste [dɑ̃tist] *nm* dentist.

dentition [dɑ̃tisjɔ̃] *nf* dentition, teething.

denture [dɑ̃tyːr] *nf* (set of) teeth (natural).

dénudation [denydasjɔ̃] *nf* laying bare, stripping.

dénudé [denyde] *a* bare, bleak.

dénuder [denyde] *vt* to lay bare, denude.

dénué [denɥe] *a* devoid (of **de**).

dénuement [denymɑ̃] *nm* destitution, distress, want.

dénuer [denɥe] *vt* to strip, divest; *vr* to part (with).

dépannage [depanaːʒ] *nm* running or emergency repairs; **équipe de —** breakdown gang.

dépanner [depane] *vt* to repair, help out.

dépaqueter [depakte] *vt* to unpack.

dépareillé [deparɛje] *a* odd, unmatched.

déparer [depare] *vt* to mar, spoil, disfigure.

départ [depaːr] *nm* departure, start (ing), difference.

départager [departaʒe] *vt* to decide between; **— les suffrages** to give the casting vote.

département [departəmɑ̃] *nm* department, administrative subdivision.

départir [departiːr] *vt* to share out, divide, dispense; *vr* to depart (from **de**), part (with **de**).

dépasser [depase] *vt* to pass, surpass, exceed.

dépaysé [depe(j)ize] *a* out of one's element, strange.

dépayser [depe(j)ize] *vt* to bewilder, disconcert.

dépecer [depəse] *vt* to cut up, carve.

dépêche [depɛ(ː)ʃ] *nf* despatch, telegram, wire.

dépêcher [depɛʃe] *vt* to dispatch; *vr* to hurry, hasten.

dépeigner [depɛɲe] *vt* to disarrange, ruffle s.o.'s hair.

dépeindre [depɛ̃ːdr] *vt* to depict, describe.

dépendance [depɑ̃dɑ̃ːs] *nf* dependence appurtenance; *pl* outbuildings.

dépendant [depɑ̃dɑ̃] *a* dependent.

dépendre [depɑ̃ːdr] *vt* to take down; *vi* to depend, be answerable, hinge.

dépens [depɑ̃] *nm pl* cost, expense.

dépense [depɑ̃ːs] *nf* expenditure, outlay, expense, consumption, pantry.

dépenser [depɑ̃se] *vt* to spend, expend, consume, use up; *vr* to expend one's energies.

dépensier, -ière [depɑ̃sje, jɛːr] *a* extravagant.

dépérir [deperiːr] *vi* to pine away, decline, wilt.

dépérissement [deperismɑ̃] *nm* decline, decay.

dépêtrer [depɛtre] *vt* to extricate; *vr* to extricate oneself.

dépeupler [depœple] *vt* to depopulate, thin, empty.

dépiécer [depjese] *vt* to cut up, carve.

dépiècement [depjɛsmɑ̃] *nm* carving, dismemberment.

dépister [depiste] *vt* to run to earth, throw off the scent.

dépit [depi] *nm* spite, annoyance, vexation; **en — de** in spite of.

dépiter [depite] *vt* to annoy, spite.

déplacé [deplase] *a* out of place, incongruous, misplaced, uncalled for.

déplacement [deplasmɑ̃] *nm* displacing, moving, transfer; *pl* movements, journey.

déplacer [deplase] *vt* to displace, move, shift, transfer; *vr* to remove, move about, travel, shift.

déplaire [deplɛːr] *vt* to displease, offend; **ne vous en déplaise** with all due respect.

déplaisant [deplɛzɑ̃] *a* disagreeable, unpleasant.

déplaisir [deplɛziːr] *nm* displeasure, vexation, sorrow.

déplanter [deplɑ̃te] *vt* to lift (plant), transplant.

déplantoir [deplɑ̃twaːr] *nm* trowel.

déplier [deplie] *vtr* to unfold, open.

déplisser [deplise] *vt* to take out of its folds.

déploiement [deplwamɑ̃] *nm* unfolding, display, deployment.

déplorable [deplɔrabl] *a* lamentable.

déplorer [deplɔre] *vt* to deplore, bewail, mourn.

déployer [deplwaje] *vt* to unfold, spread out, display, deploy; *vr* to spread, deploy.

déplumer [deplyme] *vt* to pluck; *vr* to moult.

dépolir [depɔliːr] *vt* to take gloss off, frost (glass).

dépopulation [depɔpylasjɔ̃] *nf* depopulation.

déportements [depɔrtəmɑ̃] *nm pl* misconduct, excesses.

déporter [depɔrte] *vt* to deport.

déposant [depozɑ̃] *n* witness, depositor.

déposer [depoze] *vt* to lay down, deposit, lodge, drop; *vi* to testify, attest.

dépositaire [depozitɛːr] *n* trustee, sole agent.

déposition [depozisjɔ̃] *nf* testimony, evidence, attestation.

déposséder [deposede] *vt* to dispossess, strip.

dépossession [deposɛsjɔ̃] *nf* dispossessing.

dépôt [depo] *nm* deposit(ing), store, depot, warehouse, dump, coating.

dépouille [depuːj] *nf* skin, (earthly) remains, spoils, relics.

dépouiller [depuje] *vt* to skin, strip, plunder, rob; *vr* to cast its skin, rid oneself, shed; **— son courrier** to go through one's mail.

dépourvu [depurvy] *a* devoid, bereft; **pris au —** caught unawares.

dépravation [depravasjɔ̃] *nf* depravity.

dépraver [deprave] *vt* to deprave.

dépréciation [depresjasjɔ̃] *nf* depreciation, wear and tear, disparagement.

déprécier [depresje] *vt* to underrate, depreciate, disparage, cheapen.

déprédation [depredasjɔ̃] *nf* depredation, embezzlement.

dépression [depresjɔ̃] *nf* depression, fall, hollow, gloom, dejection.

déprimer [deprime] *vt* to depress; *vr* to become depressed.

depuis [dəpɥi] *prep* since, for, from; *ad* afterwards, since then.

députation [depytasjɔ̃] *nf* deputation, deputing, membership of Parliament; **se présenter à la —** to stand for Parliament.

député [depyte] *n* deputy, Member of Parliament; **chambre des —s** parliament house.

députer [depyte] *vt* to depute, appoint as deputy.

déraciner [derasine] *vt* to uproot, root out, extirpate.

dérailler [deraje] *vi* to be derailed, run off rails; *vt* **faire —** to derail.

déraison [derɛzɔ̃] *nf* unreasonableness, folly.

déraisonnable [derɛzɔnabl] *a* unreasonable.

déraisonner [derɛzɔne] *vi* to talk nonsense.

dérangement [derɑ̃ʒmɑ̃] *nm* disarrangement, disorder, derangement.

déranger [derɑ̃ʒe] *vt* to disarrange, disturb, upset, derange; *vr* to move, inconvenience oneself, trouble.

dérapage [derapaːʒ] *nm* dragging anchor, skid.

déraper [derape] *vi* to drag its anchor, to skid.

dératé [derate] *a* spleened; **courir comme un —** to run like a hare.

derechef [dərəʃef] *ad* once again.

déréglé [deregle] *a* out of order, dissolute, inordinate.

dérèglement [derɛgləmɑ̃] *nm* disorder, irregularity, profligacy.

dérégler [deregle] *vt* to upset, disarrange, put out of order, unsettle; *vr* to get out of order, go wrong.

dérider [deride] *vt* to smoothe, remove wrinkles from, brighten up; *vr* to unbend.

dérision [derizjɔ̃] *nf* mockery, derision.

dérisoire [derizwaːr] *a* absurd, derisive, ridiculous.

dérivation [derivasjɔ̃] *nf* derivation, diversion, deflection, drift.

dérive [deriːv] *nf* drift, leeway; **à la —** adrift.

dériver [derive] *vt* to divert; *vi* to drift, be derived.

dernier, -ière [dɛrnje, jɛːr] *a* last, latter, latest, hindmost, utmost, extreme.

dernièrement [dɛrnjɛrmɑ̃] *ad* recently, lately.

dérobé [derɔbe] *a* secret; **à la —e** secretly, stealthily.

dérober [derɔbe] *vt* to steal, hide; *vr* to escape, hide, avoid, give way.

dérogatoire [derɔgatwaːr] *a* derogatory.

déroger [derɔʒe] *vi* to derogate, depart (from **à**), lose dignity.

dérouiller [deruje] *vt* to remove rust from, polish, brush up.

dérouler [derule] *vt* to unroll, uncoil, unfold; *vr* to unfold, stretch, spread, happen.

déroute [derut] *nf* rout, flight, downfall.

dérouter [derute] *vt* to lead astray, baffle, put off.

derrière [dɛrjɛːr] *prep* behind, beyond; *ad* behind, astern, at the back, in the rear; *nm* back, rear, bottom.

des [de, dɛ] = **de + les**.

dès [dɛ] *prep* since, from; **— lors** from then; **— que** as soon as.

désabuser [dezabyze] *vt* to disillusion, undeceive.

désaccord [dezakɔːr] *nm* disagreement, variance, clash.

désaccoutumer [dezakutyme] *vt* to break (s.o.) of a habit; *vr* to get out of the habit.

désaffecter [dezafɛkte] *vt* to put to another use, convert.

désaffection [dezafɛksjɔ̃] *nf* disaffection.

désagréable [dezagreabl] *a* unpleasant, offensive.

désagrégation [dezagregasjɔ̃] *nf* disintegration, breaking-up.

désagrément [dezagremɑ̃] *nm* source of irritation, vexatious incident.

désaltérer [dezaltere] *vt* to quench s.o.'s thirst; *vr* to quench one's thirst.

désappointer [dezapwɛ̃te] *vt* to disappoint.

désapprendre [dezaprɑ̃ːdr] *vt* to unlearn.

désapprobateur, -trice [dezaprɔbatœːr, tris] *a* disapproving.

désapprobation [dezaprɔbasjɔ̃] *nf* disapprobation, disapproval.

désapprouver [dezapruve] *vt* to disapprove, frown upon.

désarçonner [dezarsɔne] *vt* to unseat, unsaddle.

désarmement [dezarməmɑ̃] *nm* disarming, disarmament, laying up.

désarmer [dezarme] *vt* to disarm, dismantle, lay up; *vi* to disarm, be disbanded.

désarroi [dezarwa] *nm* confusion, disorder.

désassocier [dezasɔsje] *vt* to dissociate; *vr* to dissociate o.s. (from de).

désassorti [dezasɔrti] *a* made up of odd bits.

désastre [dezastr] *nm* disaster, calamity, catastrophe.

désastreux, -euse [dezastrø, øːz] *a* disastrous.

désavantage [dezavɑ̃taːʒ] *nm* handicap.

désavantager [dezavɑ̃taʒe] *vt* to mar, handicap, put at a disadvantage.

désavantageux, -euse [dezavɑ̃taʒø, øːz] *a* detrimental, disadvantageous.

désaveu [dezavø] *nm* denial, disavowal.

désavouer [dezavwe] *vt* to repudiate, disown, disclaim.

desceller [desɛle] *vt* to unseal, open, loosen.

descendant [dɛsɑ̃dɑ̃] *a* descending, downward; *n* descendant, offspring.

descendre [dɛsɑ̃ːdr] *vt* to go down, carry down, bring down; *vi* to descend, go down, alight, dismount; — **en panne** to come down with engine trouble; — **à un hôtel** to put up at an hotel.

descente [dɛsɑ̃ːt] *nf* descent, declivity, swoop, raid; — **de lit** rug.

descriptible [deskriptibl] *a* describable.

descriptif, -ive [deskriptif, iːv] *a* descriptive.

description [deskripsjɔ̃] *nf* description.

désemballer [dezɑ̃bale] *vt* to unpack.

désemparé [dezɑ̃pare] *a* helpless, crippled, in distress.

désemparer [dezɑ̃pare] *vt* to disable, disjoint; **sans** — without stopping.

désencombrer [dezɑ̃kɔ̃bre] *vt* to clear, free.

désenfler [dezɑ̃fle] *vt* to reduce the swelling of; *vi* to become less swollen, go down.

désengager [dezɑ̃gaʒe] *vt* to release, free, take out of pawn.

désengrener [dezɑ̃grəne] *vt* to put out of gear, disengage.

désenivrer [dezɑ̃nivre] *vt* to sober; *vr* to come to one's senses.

désenterrer [dezɑ̃tɛre] *vt* to disinter, dig up.

déséquilibrer [dezekilibre] *vt* to throw off balance, unbalance.

désert [dezeːr] *a* lonely, empty, deserted, bleak; *nm* desert, wilderness

déserter [dezɛrte] *vt* to desert, abandon; *vi* to desert.

déserteur [dezɛrtœːr] *nm* deserter.

désertion [dezɛrsjɔ̃] *nf* desertion, running away.

désespérance [dezɛsperɑ̃ːs] *nf* despair.

désespérant [dezɛsperɑ̃] *a* hopeless, heartbreaking.

désespéré [dezɛspere] *a* desperate, hopeless.

désespérer [dezɛspere] *vt* to drive to despair; *vi* to despair; *vr* to be in despair.

désespoir [dezɛspwaːr] *nm* despair, despondency.

déshabillé [dezabije] *nm* négligé.

déshabiller [dezabije] *vtr* to undress.

déshabituer [dezabitɥe] *vt* to break s.o. of the habit; *vr* to get out of the habit.

déshériter [dezerite] *vt* to disinherit.

déshonnête [dezɔnɛːt] *a* immodest, improper, indecent.

déshonnêteté [dezɔnɛtəte] *nf* impropriety.

déshonneur [dezɔnœːr] *nm* dishonour, disgrace.

déshonorer [dezɔnɔre] *vt* to dishonour, disgrace.

déshydrater [dezidrate] *vt* dehydrate.

désignation [deziɲasjɔ̃] *nf* designation, appointment, choice, description.

désigner [deziɲe] *vt* to appoint, designate, show, fix, detail, post, draft.

désillusion [dezillyzjɔ̃] *nf* disillusion.

désillusionner [dezillyzjɔne] *vt* to disillusion.

désinfectant [dezɛ̃fɛktɑ̃] *nm* disinfectant.

désinfection [dezɛ̃fɛksjɔ̃] *nf* disinfection, decontamination.

désinfecter [dezɛ̃fɛkte] *vt* to disinfect, decontaminate.

désintégrer [dezɛ̃tegre] *vt* to disintegrate, split.

désintéressé [dezɛ̃terese] *a* disinterested, unselfish, selfless.

désintéressement [dezɛ̃teresmɑ̃] *nm* disinterestedness, unselfishness.

désintéresser [dezɛ̃terese] *vr* to lose interest, take no interest (de in).

désinvolte [dezɛ̃vɔlt] *a* free, off-hand, flippant.

désinvolture [dezɛ̃vɔltyːr] *nf* unselfconsciousness, ease, airy manner, flippancy; **avec —** airily, flippantly.

désir [deziːr] *nm* desire, wish, longing.

désirable [dezirabl] *a* desirable.

désirer [dezire] *vt* to desire, want, long for.

désireux, -euse [dezirø, øːz] *a* desirous, anxious.

désobéir [dezɔbeiːr] *vti* to disobey.

désobéissance [dezɔbeisɑ̃s] *nf* disobedience.

désobligeance [dezɔbliʒɑ̃s] *nf* ungraciousness, disagreeableness.

désobliger [dezɔbliʒe] *vt* to disoblige, offend.

désobstruer [dezɔpstrye] *vt* to clear, free.

désœuvré [dezœvre] *a* idle, at a loose end.

désœuvrement [dezœvrəmɑ̃] *nm* idleness; **par —** for want of something to do.

désolant [dezɔlɑ̃] *a* distressing, grievous.

désolation [dezɔlasjɔ̃] *nf* desolation, grief.

désolé [dezɔle] *a* desolate, dreary, grieved; **je suis —** I am very sorry.

désoler [dezɔle] *vt* to ravage, grieve, distress.

désopilant [dezɔpilɑ̃] *a* screamingly funny.

désordonné [dezɔrdɔne] *a* disordered, untidy, dissolute.

désordre [dezɔrdr] *nm* confusion, disorder, untidiness, disturbance.

désorganisation [dezɔrganizasjɔ̃] *nf* disorganization, disarrangement.

désorganiser [dezɔrganize] *vt* to disorganize.

désorienter [dezɔrjɑ̃te] *vt* to put s.o. off his bearings, bewilder; *vr* to lose one's bearings, get lost.

désormais [dezɔrmɛ] *ad* henceforward, from now on.

désosser [dezose] *vt* to bone.

despote [dɛspɔt] *nm* despot.

despotisme [dɛspɔtism] *nm* despotism.

dessaisir [desɛziːr] *vt* to dispossess;

se **— de** to give up, relinquish.

dessaler [desale] *vt* to remove salt from, teach s.o. a thing or two.

se **dessécher** [sədeseʃe] *vr* to dry, wither; *vt* parch.

dessein [desɛ̃] *nm* plan, design, purpose, intention; **à —** intentionally.

desseller [desɛle] *vt* to unsaddle.

desserrer [desɛre] *vt* to loosen, slacken, release; *vr* to come loose, slacken, relax.

dessert [desɛːr] *nm* dessert.

desservant [desɛrvɑ̃] *nm* officiating priest.

desservir [desɛrviːr] *vt* to clear (away), serve, connect.

dessin [desɛ̃] *nm* drawing, sketch, cartoon, design.

dessinateur, -trice [desinatœːr, tris] *n* designer, draughtsman, black and white artist.

dessiner [desine] *vt* to draw, design, plan, outline; *vr* to stand out, be outlined.

dessouler [desule] *vt* to sober; *vi* to become sober.

dessous [dəsu] *ad* below, underneath, under it, them; **regarder qn en —** to look furtively at s.o. ; **avoir le —** to get the worst of it; *nm* bottom, underside; *pl* seamy side.

dessus [dəsy] *ad* above, over, on it, them, above it, them; *nm* top, upper side, advantage; **avoir le —** to have the best of it; **— d'assiette** doily; **— de lit** bedspread; **— du panier** the pick of the basket.

destin [dɛstɛ̃] *nm* destiny, fate.

destinataire [dɛstinatɛːr] *n* addressee, payee.

destination [dɛstinasjɔ̃] *nf* destination; **à —** de bound for.

destinée [dɛstine] *nf* fate, destiny, fortune.

destiner [dɛstine] *vt* to destine, intend, mean; *vr* to aim, intend to be; **être destiné à** to be fated to.

destituer [dɛstitɥe] *vt* to dismiss, remove.

destitution [dɛstitysjɔ̃] *nf* dismissal.

destructeur, -trice [dɛstryktœːr, tris] *a* destructive; *n* destroyer.

destructif, -ive [dɛstryktif, iːv] *a* destructive.

destruction [dɛstryksjɔ̃] *nf* destruction.

désuet, -uète [desɥɛ, ɛt] *a* obsolete, out-of-date.

désuétude [desɥetyd] *nf* disuse, abeyance.

désunion [dezynjɔ̃] *nf* disunion, separation, breach.

désunir [dezyniːr] *vtr* to disunite.

détaché [detaʃe] *a* loose, detached, unconcerned.

détachement [detaʃmɑ̃] *nm* detaching, detachment, indifference, contingent, draft.

détacher [detaʃe] vt to detach, unfasten, untie, disaffect, detail, draft, remove stains from; vr to come loose, come off, stand out.

détail [deta:j] nm detail, retail; vente au — retail selling.

détailler [detaje] vt to retail, detail, divide up, look over, appraise.

détaler [detale] vi to clear out, scamper off, bolt.

détartrer [detartre] vt to scale, fur.

détection [deteksjɔ̃] nf detection.

détective [detekti:v] nm detective.

déteindre [detɛ̃:dr] vt to take the colour out of; vir to fade, run; vi to influence.

dételer [detle]vt to unyoke, unharness.

détendre [detɑ̃:dr] vtr to slacken loosen, relax.

détenir [detni:r] vt to hold, detain, withhold.

détente [detɑ̃:t] nf slackening, relaxation, trigger.

détenteur, -trice [detɑ̃tœ:r, tris] n holder.

détention [detɑ̃sjɔ̃] nf detention.

détérioration [deterjɔrasjɔ̃] nf damage, wear and tear.

détériorer [deterjɔre] vt to damage, spoil; vr to deteriorate.

détermination [detɛrminasjɔ̃] nf determination.

déterminé [detɛrmine] a determined, definite.

déterminer [detɛrmine] vt to determine, fix, bring about, decide; vr to make up one's mind.

déterrer [detɛre] vt to dig up, unearth, find out.

détestable [detestabl] a wretched, hateful.

détester [detɛste] vt to hate, loathe, dislike.

détonateur [detɔnatœ:r] nm detonator, fog-signal.

détonation [detɔnasjɔ̃] nf detonation, report.

détoner [detɔne] vi to detonate, bang.

détonner [detɔne] vi to be out of tune, jar.

détour [detu:r] nm turning, winding, curve, bend, roundabout way.

détourné [deturne] a circuitous, devious.

détournement [deturnəmɑ̃] nm diversion, embezzlement, abduction.

détourner [deturne] vt to divert, avert, ward off, abduct, alienate, embezzle; vr to turn aside.

détracteur, -trice [detraktœ:r, tris] n detractor.

détraquement [detrakmɑ̃] nm breakdown.

détraquer [detrake] vt to put out of order; vr to break down.

détrempe [detrɑ̃:p] nf distemper, wash.

détremper [detrɑ̃pe] vt to soak, soften.

détresse [detrɛs] nf distress, misery,

détriment [detrimɑ̃] nm detriment, prejudice, loss.

détritus [detrity:s] nm detritus, refuse.

détroit [detrwa] nm strait(s), channel, pass.

détromper [detrɔ̃pe] vt put right; enlighten, vr détrompez-vous! get that out of your head!

détrôner [detrone] vt to dethrone.

détrousser [detruse] vt to let down, rob.

détruire [detrɥi:r] vt to destroy, overthrow, demolish.

dette [dɛt] nf debt, indebtedness, duty.

deuil [dœ:j] nm mourning, grief, bereavement.

deux [dø] a two, second; nm two, deuce.

deuxième [døzjɛm] an second.

dévaler [devale] vti to rush down; vi to slope, descend, rush down.

dévaliser [devalize] vt to rob, rifle, plunder.

dévaluer [devalɥe] vt to devaluate.

devancer [d(ə)vɑ̃se] vt to go before, precede, forestall.

devancier, -ière [d(ə)vɑ̃sje, jɛ:r] n predecessor.

devant [d(ə)vɑ̃] prep before, in front of, in face of; ad ahead, in front; nm front; prendre les —s sur to steal a march on.

devanture [d(ə)vɑ̃ty:r] nf front, shop window.

dévastateur, -trice [devastatœ:r, tris] a damaging, devastating; n ravager.

dévastation [devastasjɔ̃] nf devastation, havoc.

dévaster [devaste] vt to lay waste, devastate, gut.

déveine [devɛn] nf bad luck.

développement [devlɔpmɑ̃] nm development, growth, expansion.

développer [devlɔpe] vt to develop, expand, enlarge (upon); vr to develop, expand.

devenir [dəvni:r] vi to become, get, grow; qu'est-il devenu? what has become of him?

dévergondage [devɛrgɔ̃da:ʒ] nm shamelessness.

dévergondé [devɛrgɔ̃de] a shameless, profligate.

déverrouiller [devɛruje] vt to unbolt.

dévers [devɛr] a leaning, warped, out of plumb; nm slope, warp, banking.

déversement [devɛrs(ə)mɑ̃] nm overflow, tipping.

déverser [devɛrse] vt to slant, incline, pour, dump; vi to lean, get out of true line.

dévêtir [deveti:r] vt to strip, undress, take off; vr to undress, divest oneself.

déviation [devjasjɔ̃] nf deviation,

deflexion, departure, (*road*) detour.
dévider [devide] *vt* to unwind, reel, pay out.
dévidoir [devidwa:r] *nm* reel, drum, winder.
dévier [devje] *vt* to turn aside, deflect; *vi* to swerve, deviate.
deviner [dəvinɛ] *vt* to guess, foretell, make out.
devinette [dəvinɛt] *nf* conundrum, riddle.
devis [dəvi] *nm* estimate.
dévisager [devisaʒe] *vt* to stare at.
devise [dəvi:z] *nf* device, slogan, currency, bill.
dévisser [devise] *vt* to unscrew.
dévoiler [devwale] *vt* to unveil, disclose, reveal.
devoir [dəvwa:r] *vt* to owe, be indebted, have to, be obliged to, must, ought, should; *nm* duty, task, exercise.
dévolu [devɔly] *a* devolving, devolved; *nm* jeter son — sur to choose.
dévorer [devɔre] *vt* to devour, eat up, consume.
dévot [devo] *an* devout, religious (person).
dévotion [devosjɔ̃] *nf* piety, devotion.
dévoué [devwe] *a* devoted, sincere, loyal.
dévouement [devumɑ̃] *nm* devotion, devotedness, self-sacrifice.
dévouer [devwe] *vt* to devote, dedicate; *vr* to devote oneself, sacrifice oneself.
dévoyer [devwaje] *vtr* to lead astray, go off the rails.
dextérité [dɛksterite] *nf* dexterity, skill.
diabète [djabɛt] *nm* diabetes.
diabétique [djabetik] *an* diabetic.
diable [dja:bl] *nm* devil; **allez au —!** go to hell!
diablerie [djabləri] *nf* devilry, witchcraft, mischievousness, turbulence.
diablotin [djablɔtɛ̃] *nm* imp, cracker.
diabolique [djabɔlik] *a* diabolical, fiendish.
diaconesse [djakɔnɛs] *nf* deaconess.
diacre [djakr] *nm* deacon.
diadème [djadɛm] *nm* diadem.
diagnostic [djagnɔstik] *nm* diagnosis.
diagnostiquer [djagnɔstike] *vt* to diagnose.
diagonal [djagɔnal] *a* diagonal.
dialecte [djalɛkt] *nm* dialect.
dialogue [djalɔg] *nm* dialogue.
diamant [djamɑ̃] *nm* diamond.
diamètre [djamɛtr] *nm* diameter.
diane [djan] *nf* reveille.
diantre [djɑ̃:tr] *excl* the deuce!
diapason [djapazɔ̃] *nm* tuning fork, diapason, range.
diaphane [djafan] *a* diaphanous, transparent.
diaphragme [djafragm] *nm* diaphragm, sound-box.

diapré [djapre] *a* mottled, speckled, variegated.
dictateur [diktatœ:r] *nm* dictator.
dictature [diktaty:r] *nf* dictatorship.
dictée [dikte] *nf* dictation.
dicter [dikte] *vt* to dictate.
diction [diksjɔ̃] *nf* diction, elocution.
dictionnaire [diksjɔnɛ:r] *nm* dictionary.
dicton [diktɔ̃] *nm* saying, proverb, maxim.
dièse [djɛ:z] *nm* (*mus*) sharp.
diète [djɛt] *nf* diet, regimen.
dieu [djø] *nm* god; *excl* goodness!
diffamation [diffamasjɔ̃] *nf* slander, libel.
diffamatoire [diffamatwa:r] *a* slanderous, defamatory, libellous.
diffamer [diffame] *vt* to defame, slander.
différence [diferɑ̃:s] *nf* difference, distinction, discrepancy, gap.
différend [diferɑ̃] *nm* difference, dispute.
différent [diferɑ̃] *a* different, unlike, various.
différentiel, -ielle [diferɑ̃sjɛl] *a nm* differential.
différer [difere] *vt* to put off, postpone; *vi* to differ, put off.
difficile [difisil] *a* difficult, hard, hard to please.
difficilement [difisilmɑ̃] *ad* with difficulty.
difficulté [difikylte] *nf* difficulty; **faire des —s** to be fussy, raise difficulties.
difforme [difɔrm] *a* deformed, shapeless.
difformité [difɔrmite] *nf* deformity.
diffus [dify] *a* diffuse, wordy, diffused.
diffuser [difyze] *vt* to diffuse.
diffusion [difyzjɔ̃] *nf* spreading, broadcasting.
digérer [diʒere] *vt* to digest, assimilate.
digestible [diʒɛstibl] *a* digestible.
digestif, -ive [diʒɛstif] *a* digestive.
digestion [diʒɛstjɔ̃] *nf* digestion, assimilation.
digital, -ale, -aux [diʒital, al, o] *a* **empreinte —** fingerprint; *nf* foxglove, digitalis.
digne [diɲ] *a* worthy, stately, dignified, deserving.
dignitaire [diɲitɛ:r] *nm* dignitary.
dignité [diɲite] *nf* dignity, nobility, greatness.
digression [digrɛsjɔ̃] *nf* digression.
digue [dig] *nf* dike, sea-wall, embankment, dam.
dilapider [dilapide] *vt* to waste, squander, embezzle.
dilater [dilate] *vtr* to dilate, expand, distend.
dilemme [dilɛm] *nm* dilemma.
diligence [diliʒɑ̃:s] *nf* application, industry, haste; stage-coach.
diligent [diliʒɑ̃] *a* busy.

diluer [dilɥe] vt to dilute, water down.

dimanche [dimãːʃ] nm Sunday.

dimension [dimãsjɔ̃] nf size; pl measurements.

diminuer [diminɥe] vt to diminish, lessen, reduce; vi to decrease, abate.

diminution [diminysjɔ̃] nf decrease, reduction.

dinde [dɛ̃ːd] nf turkey-hen.

dindon [dɛ̃dɔ̃] nm turkey-cock.

dîner [dine] vi to dine; nm dinner (party).

dîneur, -euse [dinœːr, øːz] n diner.

diocèse [djɔsɛːz] nm diocese.

dioula [diula] nm itinerant pedlar.

diphtérie [difteri] nf diphtheria.

diplomate [diplɔmat] nm diplomat (ist).

diplomatie [diplɔmasi] nf diplomacy, diplomatic service.

diplomatique [diplɔmatik] a diplomatic.

diplôme [diploːm] nm diploma, certificate.

diplômé [diplome] a certificated.

dire [diːr] vt to say, tell, speak; nm assertion, statement, words; **dites donc!** I say!; **ce vin ne me dit rien** I don't care for this wine; **et — que** and to think that; **que dites-vous de cela?** what do you think of that?

direct [dirɛkt] a direct, straight, pointed, flat.

directeur, -trice [dirɛktœːr, tris] a guiding, controlling; n chief, leader, manager, manageress, headmaster, headmistress, superintendent.

direction [dirɛksjɔ̃] nf direction, management, guidance, leadership, steering.

directives [dirɛktiːv] nf pl main or guiding lines.

dirigeant [diriʒã] a directing, guiding, governing.

dirigeable [diriʒabl] nm airship.

diriger [diriʒe] vt to direct, manage, conduct, guide, steer, point; vr to make one's way, proceed.

discernement [disɛrnəmã] nm discernment, discrimination.

discerner [disɛrne] vt to discern, descry, distinguish.

disciple [disipl] nm disciple, follower.

discipline [disiplin] nf discipline, order.

discipliner [disipline] vt to discipline.

discontinuer [diskɔ̃tinɥe] vt to discontinue, leave off, break off.

disconvenance [diskɔ̃vnãːs] nf disparity, unsuitableness.

disconvenir [diskɔ̃vniːr] vi to be unsuitable, deny.

discordance [diskɔrdãːs] nf disagreement, clash.

discordant [diskɔrdã] a harsh, grating, clashing.

discorde [diskɔrd] nf strife, lack of unity.

discourir [diskuriːr] vi to talk

volubly, hold forth, discourse.

discours [diskuːr] nm discourse, speech, talk.

discourtois [diskurtwa] a impolite, discourteous.

discrédit [diskredi] nm disrepute.

discréditer [diskredite] vt to discredit, disparage, bring into disrepute.

discret, -ète [diskrɛ, ɛt] a discreet, unobtrusive.

discrétion [diskresjɔ̃] nf restraint.

discriminer [diskrimine] vt to discriminate.

disculper [diskylpe] vt to exonerate, clear.

discussion [diskysjɔ̃] nf argument, debate.

discutable [diskytabl] a debatable, disputable.

discuter [diskyte] vt to discuss, talk over, question.

disette [dizɛt] nf want, scarcity, dearth.

diseur, -euse [dizœːr, øːz] n — **de bonne aventure** fortune-teller.

disgrâce [disgrɑːs] nf disfavour, misfortune.

disgracieux, -euse [disgrasjø, øːz] a ungraceful, awkward, ungracious.

disjoindre [disʒwɛ̃ːdr] vt to sever, disjoin.

dislocation [dislɔkasjɔ̃] nf dislocation, dismemberment.

disloquer [dislɔke] vt to dislocate, dismember; vr to fall apart, break up.

disparaître [dispareːtr] vi to disappear, vanish.

disparate [disparat] a unlike, illassorted.

disparition [disparisjɔ̃] nf disappearance.

dispendieux, -euse [dispãdjø, øːz] a expensive.

dispensaire [dispãsɛːr] nm dispensary, out-patients' department.

dispensation [dispãsasjɔ̃] nf dispensing.

dispense [dispãːs] nf dispensation, exemption.

dispenser [dispãse] vt to dispense, distribute, excuse, exempt; vr to get exempted (from de), get out (of de).

disperser [dispɛrse] vtr to scatter, disperse.

dispersion [dispɛrsjɔ̃] nf scattering, dispersal.

disponibilité [dispɔnibilite] nf availability; pl available funds; **être en — to** be on half-pay.

disponible [dispɔnibl] a available.

dispos [dispo] a fit, bright, well.

disposé [dispoze] a disposed, agreeable, ready; **être bien (mal) — to** be in a good (bad) temper.

disposer [dispoze] vt to arrange, array, set out, incline; vr to get ready; **— de** to have at one's disposal.

dispositif [dispɔzitif] *nm* apparatus, gadget.

disposition [dispɔzisjɔ̃] *nf* disposition, disposal, arrangement, tendency; *pl* natural gift, provisions.

disproportion [disprɔpɔrsjɔ̃] *nf* lack of proportion.

disproportionné [disprɔpɔrsjɔne] *a* disproportionate, out of proportion.

disputailler [dispytaje] *vi* to cavil, bicker.

dispute [dispyt] *nf* dispute, squabble.

disputer [dispyte] *vt* to discuss, argue about, dispute, challenge; *vi* to quarrel; *vr* to argue wrangle, contend for.

disqualifier [diskalifje] *vt* to disqualify.

disque [disk] *nm* discus, disc, gramophone record.

dissemblable [di(s)sɑ̃blabl] *a* unlike, dissimilar.

dissemblance [dis(s)ɑ̃blɑ̃:s] *nf* unlikeness, dissimilarity.

disséminer [dis(s)emine] *vt* to scatter, spread.

dissension [dis(s)ɑ̃sjɔ̃] *nf* dissension, discord.

dissentiment [dis(s)ɑ̃timɑ̃] *nm* dissent, disagreement.

disséquer [dis(s)eke] *vt* to dissect.

dissertation [disɛrtasjɔ̃] *nf* essay, composition.

disserter [disɛrte] *vi* to dissert, expatiate.

dissident [dis(s)idɑ̃] *a* dissentient, dissident.

dissimulateur, -trice [dis(s)imylatœ:r, tris] *n* dissembler; *a* deceitful.

dissimulation [dis(s)imylasjɔ̃] *nf* deceit, dissimulation, hiding.

dissimuler [dis(s)imyle] *vt* to dissimulate, conceal, disguise; *vr* to hide.

dissipation [disipasjɔ̃] *nf* dissipation, dispersion, wasting, dissolute conduct, inattentiveness.

dissipé [disipe] *a* dissipated, giddy, inattentive.

dissiper [disipe] *vt* to dissipate, dispel, waste, divert; *vr* to disappear, be dispelled, clear, become dissolute.

dissolu [dis(s)ɔly] *a* profligate, abandoned, dissolute.

dissolution [dis(s)ɔlysjɔ̃] *nf* disintegration, dissolving, breaking-up, solution.

dissoudre [dis(s)udr] *vtr* to dissolve, break up.

dissuader [dis(s)ɥade] *vt* to dissuade, talk out of.

distance [distɑ̃:s] *nf* distance, range.

distancer [distɑ̃se] *vt* to outdistance, outstrip.

distant [distɑ̃] *a* distant, aloof.

distillateur [distilatœ:r] *nm* distiller.

distillation [distilasjɔ̃] *nf* distillation, distilling.

distiller [distile] *vt* to distil, drop.

distillerie [distilri] *nf* distillery.

distinct [distɛ̃(:kt)] *a* distinct, clear, audible.

distinctif, -ive [distɛ̃ktif, i:v] *a* distinctive.

distinction [distɛ̃ksjɔ̃] *nf* distinction, honour, distinguished air.

distingué [distɛ̃ge] *a* eminent, distinguished.

distinguer [distɛ̃ge] *vt* to distinguish, discriminate, characterize, perceive, bring to notice; *vr* to distinguish oneself, be distinguishable.

distraction [distraksjɔ̃] *nf* separation, distraction, absent-mindedness, entertainment.

distraire [distrɛ:r] *vt* to separate, distract, take one's mind off, amuse, entertain; *vr* to amuse oneself.

distrait [distrɛ] *a* absent-minded, listless.

distribuer [distribɥe] *vt* to distribute, apportion, share out, hand out, deliver; — **les rôles** to cast a play.

distributeur, -trice [distribytœ:r, tris] *n* dispenser, distributor; — **automatique** slot-machine.

distribution [distribysjɔ̃] *nf* distribution, issue, allotting, delivery; — **des prix** prize-giving; — **des rôles** cast(ing).

dit [di] *a* called, named; **autrement** — alias.

divagation [divagasjɔ̃] *nf* deviation, wandering.

divaguer [divage] *vi* to deviate, wander, rave.

divan [divɑ̃] *nm* couch.

divergence [divɛrʒɑ̃:s] *nf* divergence, spread.

diverger [divɛrʒe] *vi* to diverge.

divers [divɛ:r] *a* various, sundry, divers, different, diverse; *nm pl* sundries.

diversion [divɛrsjɔ̃] *nf* diversion, change.

diversité [divɛrsite] *nf* variety, diversity.

divertir [divɛrti:r] *vt* to entertain, divert; *vr* to amuse oneself.

divertissement [divɛrtismɑ̃] *nm* recreation, entertainment, diversion.

dividende [dividɑ̃:d] *nm* dividend.

divin [divɛ̃] *a* divine, sacred, heavenly, sublime.

divinateur, -trice [divinatœ:r, tris] *n* soothsayer.

divinité [divinite] *nf* divinity, deity.

diviser [divize] *vt* to divide; *vr* to divide, break up.

diviseur [divizœ:r] *nm* divisor.

divisible [divizibl] *a* divisible.

division [divizjɔ̃] *nf* division, section, dissension.

divorce [divɔrs] *nm* divorce.

divorcer [divɔrse] *vti* to divorce.

divulgation [divylgasjɔ̃] *nf* disclosure.

divulguer [divylge] *vt* to divulge, disclose, reveal.

dix [dis] *a nm* ten, tenth.

dixième [dizjɛm] *a nm* tenth.

dizaine [dizɛn] *nf* (about) ten.

docile [dɔsil] *a* compliant, manageable.

docilité [dɔsilite] *nf* docility.

dock [dɔk] dock(s), warehouse.

docte [dɔkt] *a* learned.

docteur [dɔktœːr] *nm* doctor.

doctoral [dɔktɔral] *a* doctoral, pompous.

doctorat [dɔktɔra] *nm* doctorate.

doctrine [dɔktrin] *nf* doctrine, belief, teaching.

document [dɔkymɑ̃] *nm* document.

documentaire [dɔkymɑ̃tɛːr] *a* documentary.

documentation [dɔkymɑ̃tasjɔ̃] *nf* gathering of facts.

documenter [dɔkymɑ̃te] *vt* to document, give information to; *vr* to collect material, information.

dodeliner [dɔdline] *vti* to dandle, nod, shake.

dodo [dɔdo] *nm* sleep; **faire —** to go to bye-bye.

dodu [dɔdy] *a* plump.

dogme [dɔgm] *nm* dogma.

dogue [dɔg] *nm* mastiff.

doigt [dwa] *nm* finger; **— de pied** toe.

doigté [dwate] *nm* tact, (*mus*) fingering.

doigtier [dwatje] *nm* finger-stall.

doit [dwa] *nm* debit.

doléances [dɔleɑ̃s] *nf pl* grievances, sorrows.

dolent [dɔlɑ̃] *a* doleful.

domaine [dɔmɛn] *nm* domain, estate, province, field.

dôme [doːm] *nm* dome.

domesticité [dɔmɛstisite] *nf* domesticity, staff of servants.

domestique [dɔmɛstik] *a* domestic; *n* servant.

domicile [dɔmisil] *nm* abode, residence.

domicilié [dɔmisilje] *a* residing, resident.

domicilier [dɔmisilje] *vr* to settle, take up residence.

dominance [dɔminɑ̃ːs] *nf* dominion, predominance.

dominant [dɔminɑ̃] *a* ruling, (pre)dominant.

dominateur, -trice [dɔminatœːr, tris] *a* domineering.

domination [dɔminasjɔ̃] *nf* rule, sway.

dominer [dɔmine] *vt* to dominate, rule, master, control, overlook; *vi* to rule.

domino [dɔmino] *nm* hood, domino.

dommage [dɔmaːʒ] *nm* harm, injury, pity; *pl* damage, destruction; **dommages et intérêts** damages (*in law*).

dompter [dɔ̃te] *vt* to tame, break in, master.

dompteur, -euse [dɔ̃tœːr, øːz] *n* tamer, trainer.

don [dɔ̃] *nm* donation, giving, gift, present, talent.

donateur, -trice [dɔnatœːr, tris] *n* donor, giver.

donc [dɔ̃ːk] *cj* so, therefore, then; *ad* well, just, ever.

donjon [dɔ̃ʒɔ̃] *nm* (*of castle*) keep.

donne [dɔn] *nf* (*card games*) deal.

donnée [dɔne] *nf* fundamental idea; *pl* data.

donner [dɔne] *vt* to give, furnish, yield, ascribe, deal; *vi* to look out (sur on to); **— dans** to have a taste for, fall into; **s'en —** **à cœur joie** to have a high old time; **c'est donné** it's dirt cheap.

dont [dɔ̃] *pr* of (by, from, with, about) whom or which, whose.

doré [dɔre] *a* gilt, golden.

dorénavant [dɔrenavɑ̃] *ad* henceforth.

dorer [dɔre] *vt* to gild, brown.

dorloter [dɔrlɔte] *vt* to cuddle, pet, coddle, pamper.

dormant [dɔrmɑ̃] *a* dormant, sleeping, stagnant.

dormeur, -euse [dɔrmœːr, øːz] *n* sleeper, sleepy-head.

dormir [dɔrmiːr] *vi* to sleep, be asleep, be stagnant, lie dormant.

dortoir [dɔrtwaːr] *nm* dormitory.

dorure [dɔryːr] *nf* gilt, gilding.

dos [do] *nm* back, bridge.

dose [doːz] *nf* dose, amount.

doser [doze] *vt* to dose, decide the amount of.

dossier [dɔsje] *nm* (*of chair*) back; record, documents, brief.

dot [dɔt] *nf* dowry.

doter [dɔte] *vt* to give a dowry to, endow.

douaire [dwɛːr] *nm* marriage settlement, dower.

douane [dwan] *nf* customs, customhouse, duty; **en —** in bond.

douanier, -ière [dwanje, jɛːr] *a* customs; *n* customs-officer.

double [dubl] *a* double, twofold; *nm* double, duplicate.

doubler [duble] *vt* to double, fold in two, line, overtake, quicken; **— une classe** to repeat a class; **— un rôle** to understudy a part; **— le cap** to round the cape.

doublure [dublyːr] *nf* lining, understudy.

doucement [dusmɑ̃] *ad* gently, quietly, smoothly.

doucereux, -euse [dusrø, øːz] *a* sweetish, cloying, glib, sugary.

douceur [dusœːr] *nf* sweetness, smoothness, gentleness, softness, mildness; *pl* comforts, sweets.

douche [duʃ] *nf* shower-bath, douche.

doué [dwe] *a* gifted, endowed.

douer [dwe] *vt* to endow.

douille [duːj] *nf* case, casing, socket, sleeve.

douillet, -ette [duʒɛ, ɛt] *a* soft, cosy, delicate, tender.

douleur [dulœːr] *nf* suffering, pain, grief, sorrow.

douloureux, -euse [duluɾø, øːz] *a* painful, aching, sad, sorrowful, grievous.

doute [dut] *nm* doubt, misgiving, scruple; **mettre en —** to call in question; **sans —** probably.

douter [dute] *vi* to doubt, suspect; *vr* to suspect, surmise; **je m'en doutais bien** I thought as much.

douteux, -euse [dutø, øːz] *a* doubtful, questionable.

douve [duːv] *nf* ditch, moat.

doux, douce [du, dus] *a* sweet, gentle, smooth, soft, mild, pleasant; **eau douce** fresh water.

douzaine [duzɛn] *nf* dozen.

douze [duːz] *nm* twelve, twelfth.

doyen, -enne [dwajɛ̃, ɛn] *n* dean, doyen, senior.

dragage [dragaːʒ] *nm* dredging, dragging, mine-sweeping.

dragée [draʒe] *nf* sugared almond, comfit.

dragon [dragɔ̃] *nm* dragon, dragoon.

draguer [drage] *vt* to dredge, drag, sweep.

dragueur [dragœːr] *nm* dredger; **— de mines** mine-sweeper.

drainer [drɛne] *vt* to drain.

dramatique [dramatik] *a* dramatic; **auteur —** playwright.

dramatiser [dramatize] *vt* to dramatize.

dramaturge [dramatyrʒ] *nm* dramatist.

drame [dram] *nm* drama, play, sensational event.

drap [dra] *nm* cloth; **— de lit** bed-sheet; **être dans de beaux —s** to be in a mess.

drapeau [drapo] *nm* flag, colours.

draper [drape] *vt* to drape, hang.

draperie [drapri] *nf* cloth-trade, drapery.

drapier, -ière [drapje, jɛːr] *n* draper, clothier.

dresser [drɛse] *vt* to raise, set up, draw up, make out, train, break in; *vr* to rise, sit up, straighten up; **— les oreilles** to cock one's ears; **faire — les cheveux à qn** to make s.o.'s hair stand on end.

dresseur, -euse [drɛsœːr, øːz] *n* trainer, trimmer, adjuster.

dressoir [drɛswaːr] *nm* dresser, sideboard.

drogue [drɔg] *nf* drug.

droguer [drɔge] *vt* to give medicine to, drug, dope.

droguiste [drɔgist] *nm* drysalter.

droit [drwa] *a* straight, direct, upright, right (hand), honest; *ad* straight (on); *nm* right, due, fee, law; **veston —** single-breasted jacket; **— d'auteur** copyright; **—s acquis** vested interests; **à bon —**

with good reason; **— d'aînesse** birthright.

droite [drwat] *nf* right (-hand, side).

droitier, -ière [drwatje, jɛːr] *a* right-handed.

droiture [drwatyːr] *nf* integrity, uprightness.

drôle [droːl] *a* funny, odd, queer; *n* rogue, rascal.

dromadaire [drɔmadɛːr] *nm* dromedary.

dru [dry] *a* thick, dense, strong; *ad* thickly, heavily.

du [dy] = **de + le.**

duc [dyk] *nm* duke.

duché [dyʃe] *nm* duchy, dukedom.

duchesse [dyʃɛs] *nf* duchess.

duelliste [dɥelist] *nm* duellist.

dûment [dymɑ̃] *ad* duly, in due form.

dune [dyn] *nf* dune, sand-hill.

dunette [dynɛt] *nf* (deck) poop.

duo [dyo] *nm* duet.

dupe [dyp] *nf* dupe, catspaw, mug.

duper [dype] *vt* to dupe, trick, take in.

duperie [dypri] *nf* trickery, sell, a piece of double-dealing.

duplicité [dyplisite] *nf* duplicity, falseness, deceit, double-dealing.

dur [dyːr] *a* hard, harsh, difficult, tough, inured; *ad* hard; **avoir l'oreille —e** to be hard of hearing; **avoir la tête —e** to be slow-witted; **œufs —s** hard-boiled eggs; **c'est un — à cuire** he is a tough nut.

durabilité [dyrabilite] *nf* durability, lasting quality.

durable [dyrabl] *a* hard-wearing, lasting, enduring.

durant [dyrɑ̃] *prep* during, for.

durcir [dyrsiːr] *vt* to harden, make hard; *vi* to grow hard.

durcissement [dyrsismɑ̃] *nm* hardening.

durée [dyre] *nf* duration, continuance, wear, life.

durement [dyrmɑ̃] *ad* hard(ly), roughly, harshly.

durer [dyre] *vi* to last, endure, wear well.

dureté [dyrte] *nf* hardness, harshness, callousness.

durillon [dyrijɔ̃] *nm* callosity.

duvet [dyvɛ] *nm* down, fluff.

duveté [dyvte] *a* downy, fluffy.

dynamique [dinamik] *a* dynamic; *nf* dynamics.

dynamite [dinamit] *nf* dynamite.

dynastie [dinasti] *nf* dynasty.

dysenterie [disɑ̃tri] *nf* dysentery.

dyspepsie [dispɛpsi] *nf* dyspepsia.

dyssymétrie [dis(s)imetri] *nf* asymmetry.

E

eau [o] *nf* water; **— oxygénée** hydrogen peroxide; **mortes —x** neap tides; **vives —x** spring tides; **faire — to leak, bilge; faire venir l'— à la bouche** to make one's mouth water; **laver à grande — to swill.**

eau-de-vie [odvi] *nf* brandy, spirits.

eau-forte [ofɔrt] *nf* aqua fortis, etching.

ébahir [ebaiːr] *vt* to amaze, dumbfound; *vr* to be dumbfounded, abashed.

ébahissement [ebaismɑ̃] *nm* amazement, wonder.

ébats [eba] *nm pl* frolic, sport, gambols, revels.

s'ébattre [sebatr] *vr* to frolic, gambol, frisk about.

s'ébaubir [sebobiːr] *vr* to be astounded, flabbergasted.

ébauche [eboːʃ] *nf* sketch, outline.

ébaucher [eboʃe] *vt* to sketch, rough draw, outline.

ébène [ebɛn] *nf* ebony.

ébéniste [ebenist] *nm* cabinet-maker.

ébénisterie [ebenistri] *nf* cabinetmaking.

éberlué [eberlɥe] *a* dumbfounded.

éblouir [ebluiːr] *vt* to dazzle.

éblouissement [ebluismɑ̃] *nm* dazzling, dazzle, dizziness.

ébonite [ebɔnit] *nf* vulcanite.

éborgner [ebɔrɲe] *vt* to put s.o.'s eye out.

ébouillanter [ebujɑ̃te] *vt* to scald.

éboulement [ebulmɑ̃] *nm* falling-in, landslide.

s'ébouler [sebule] *vr* to fall in, cave in, slip.

éboulis [ebuli] *nm* mass of fallen rock and earth.

ébouriffer [eburife] *vt* to dishevel, ruffle, take aback.

ébrancher [ebrɑ̃ʃe] *vt* to lop the branches off.

ébranlement [ebrɑ̃lmɑ̃] *nm* shaking, tottering, shock, commotion.

ébranler [ebrɑ̃le] *vt* to shake, loosen, set in motion; *vr* to totter, start, move off.

ébrécher [ebreʃe] *vt* to notch, chip, make inroads into.

ébriété [ebriete] *nf* intoxication.

s'ébrouer [sebrue] *vr* to snort; (birds) take a dust bath.

ébruiter [ebrɥite] *vt* to noise abroad, spread, make known; *vr* to be noised abroad, spread.

ébullition [ebylisjɔ̃] *nf* boiling, fever, ferment.

écaille [ekaːj] *nf* scale, shell, flake, chip.

écailler [ekaje] *vt* to scale, open; *vr* to peel, flake off.

écailleux, -euse [ekajø, øːz] *a* scaly, flaky.

écale [ekal] *nf* shell, pod.

écaler [ekale] *vt* to shell, husk.

écarlate [ekarlat] *a* scarlet.

écarquiller [ekarkije] *vtr* to open wide, spread wide apart.

écart [ekaːr] *nm* step aside, swerve,

deflection, straying, divergence, difference, error, variation, discarding; **à l'— aside; faire un —** to shy, step aside; **faire le grand —** to do the splits.

écarté [ekarte] *a* lonely, remote, out-of-the-way.

écarteler [ekartəle] *vt* to quarter; **être écartelé** to be torn between.

écartement [ekartəmɑ̃] *nm* separation, spacing, gap, gauge.

écarter [ekarte] *vt* to separate, space, spread, pull aside, fend off, brush aside, discard; *vr* to diverge, stray, step aside.

ecclésiastique [eklezjastik] *a* ecclesiastical, clerical; *nm* clergyman.

écervelé [esɛrvəle] *a* hare-brained, giddy, rash.

échafaud [eʃafo] *nm* scaffold.

échafaudage [eʃafodaːʒ] *nm* scaffolding.

échafauder [eʃafode] *vt* to construct, build up.

échalas [eʃala] *nm* vine-pole, hoppole, spindle-shanks.

échalis [eʃali] *nm* stile.

échancrer [eʃɑ̃kre] *vt* to cut out, scallop, indent.

échancrure [eʃɑ̃kryːr] *nf* cut-out piece, opening.

échange [eʃɑ̃ːʒ] *nm* exchange, barter.

échangeable [eʃɑ̃ʒabl] *a* exchangeable.

échanger [eʃɑ̃ʒe] *vt* to exchange, barter, bandy.

échantillon [eʃɑ̃tijɔ̃] *nm* sample, pattern.

échappatoire [eʃapatwaːr] *nf* loophole, way out.

échappement [eʃapmɑ̃] *nm* escape, leakage, exhaust-pipe.

échapper [eʃape] *vi* to escape; *vr* to run away, escape, leak; **il l'a échappé belle** he had a narrow escape; **— à qn** to elude s.o.

échappée [eʃape] *nf* vista; turning space; (racing) spurt; (cattle) straying.

écharde [eʃard] *nf* splinter.

écharpe [eʃarp] *nf* scarf, sash, sling.

échasse [eʃaːs] *nf* stilt.

échauder [eʃode] *vt* to scald.

échauffant [eʃofɑ̃] *a* heating, exciting.

échauffement [eʃofmɑ̃] *nm* heating, over-heating, over-excitement.

échauffer [eʃofe] *vt* to overheat, heat, warm; *vt* to get overheated, warm up.

échauffourée [eʃofure] *nf* scuffle, skirmish.

échéance [eʃeɑ̃ːs] *nf* date, expiration, falling due.

échec [eʃɛk] *nm* check, set-back, failure; *pl* chess, chessmen; **échec et mat** checkmate.

échelle [eʃɛl] *nf* ladder, scale; **après lui il faut tirer l'—** he always goes one better than anyone else; **faire la courte — à** to give a leg up to; **— de sauvetage** fire-escape.

échelon [eʃlɔ̃] nm rung, step degree, echelon.

échelonner [eʃlɔne] vt to space out, stagger.

écheveau [eʃvo] nm skein, hank.

échevelé [eʃəvle] a dishevelled, wild, frenzied.

échine [eʃin] nf spine.

échiner [eʃine] vt to work to death; vr to slave, wear o.s. out.

échiquier [eʃikje] nm chessboard, exchequer.

écho [eko] nm echo.

échoir [eʃwaːr] vi to fall (due), expire, devolve.

échoppe [eʃɔp] nf stall, booth.

échouage [eʃwaːʒ] nm stranding, grounding.

échouer [eʃwe] vt to beach; vi to run aground, ground fail, miscarry.

éclabousser [eklabuse] vt to splash, spatter.

éclaboussure [eklabusyːr] nf splash, spatter.

éclair [eklɛːr] nm lightning, flash; eclair.

éclairage [eklɛraːʒ] nm lighting (up); **— par projecteurs** floodlighting.

éclaircie [eklɛrsi] nf break, bright interval, clearing.

éclaircir [eklɛrsiːr] vt to clarify, clear up, solve, enlighten, thin out; vr to clear grow thin, be cleared up.

éclaircissement [eklɛrsismɑ̃] nm clearing-up, enlightenment, elucidation.

éclairer [eklɛre] vt to light, brighten, enlighten, reconnoitre; vr to light up, brighten up, clear.

éclaireur, -euse [eklɛrœːr, øːz] n scout, Boy Scout Girl Guide.

éclat [ekla] nm splinter, chip, flash, brilliancy, glamour, burst; **rire aux —s** to laugh uproariously.

éclatant [eklatɑ̃] a bursting, loud, brilliant, resounding, flagrant.

éclater [eklate] vt to burst, split; vi to burst, explode, break out; **— en colère** to fly into a rage; **— de rire** to burst out laughing.

éclectique [eklɛktik] a eclectic, catholic.

éclipse [eklips] nf eclipse.

éclipser [eklipse] vt to eclipse, put in the shade, surpass; vr to vanish.

éclisse [eklis] nf splint; fish-plate.

éclopé [eklɔpe] a lame, limping; nm cripple, lame person.

éclore [eklɔːr] vi to hatch (out), open out, burst.

éclosion [eklozjɔ̃] nf hatching, blossoming, opening out.

écluse [eklyːz] nf lock, sluice-gate.

écœurant [ekœrɑ̃] a sickening, fulsome.

écœurement [ekœrmɑ̃] nm disgust, loathing.

écœurer [ekœre] vt to sicken, disgust.

école [ekɔl] nf school; **— polytechnique** military academy; **— normale** training college.

écolier, -ière [ekɔlje, jɛːr] n schoolboy, -girl.

éconduire [ekɔ̃dɥiːr] vt to show out, put out.

économe [ekɔnɔm] a economical, thrifty; nm steward, housekeeper, bursar.

économie [ekɔnɔmi] nf economy, thrift; pl savings; **faire des —s to** save, retrench.

économique [ekɔnɔmik] a economic (al).

économiser [ekɔnɔmize] vt to economize, save.

économiste [ekɔnɔmist] nm economist.

écope [ekɔp] nf scoop, ladle, bailer.

écoper [ekɔpe] vt to bail out; vi to cop it

écorce [ekɔrs] nf bark, peel, rind, crust.

écorcer [ekɔrse] vt to bark, peel, husk.

écorcher [ekɔrʃe] vt to skin, flay, graze, scratch.

écorchure [ekɔrʃyːr] nf abrasion, scratch.

écorner [ekɔrne] vt to take the horns off, break the corners of, dog's-ear, make inroads in.

écornifler [ekɔrnifle] vt to scrounge, cadge.

Écosse [ekɔs] nf Scotland.

écossais [ekɔsɛ] a Scottish, Scotch, Scots; **étoffe —e** tartan; n Scot, Scotsman, Scotswoman.

écosser [ekɔse] vt to shell, pod, husk.

écot [eko] nm share, quota.

écoulement [ekulmɑ̃] nm flow, discharge, waste-pipe, sale.

écouler [ekule] vt to sell, dispose of; vr to flow, run out, to pass elapse.

écourter [ekurte] vt to shorten, curtail, cut short.

écoute [ekut] nf listening-place, listening-in; **être aux —s** to be on the look-out; **faire, rester à l'—** to listen in.

écouter [ekute] vt to listen to; vi to listen; **— à la porte** to eavesdrop.

écouteur, -euse [ekutœːr, øːz] n listener; nm earphone, receiver.

écoutille [ekutiːj] nf hatchway.

écran [ekrɑ̃] nm screen.

écrasement [ekrazmɑ̃] nm crushing, crashing, defeat.

écraser [ekraze] vt to crush, run over, overburden, dwarf; vr to collapse, crash.

écrémer [ekreme] vt to skim, cream.

écrevisse [ekrəvis] nf crayfish.

s'écrier [sekrie] vr to exclaim, cry out.

écrin [ekrɛ̃] nm case, casket.

écrire [ekriːr] vt to write, note down, spell; **machine à —** typewriter.

écrit [ekri] *a* written; *nm* writing, paper with writing on it.

écriteau [ekrito] *nm* placard, notice.

écritoire [ekritwa:r] *nf* inkwell.

écriture [ekrity:r] *nf* handwriting; *pl* accounts, Scripture.

écrivain [ekrivɛ̃] *nm* writer, author.

écrou [ekru] *nm* screw-nut.

écrouer [ekrue] *vt* to send to prison, lock up.

écroulement [ekrulmɑ̃] *nm* collapse, falling in, crash.

s'écrouler [sekrule] *vr* to collapse, crumble, tumble down.

écru [ekry] *a* unbleached, raw, natural-coloured.

écu [eky] *nm* shield, escutcheon, crown.

écueil [ekœːj] *nm* reef, rock on which one perishes.

écuelle [ekyɛl] *nf* bowl, basin.

éculer [ekyle] *vt* to wear away the heels of (shoes).

écume [ekym] *nf* foam, froth, scum; **— de mer** meerschaum.

écumer [ekyme] *vt* to skim; *vi* to foam, froth; **— les mers** to scour the seas.

écumeux, -euse [ekymø, øːz] *a* foamy, frothy, scummy.

écumoire [ekymwaːr] *nf* skimming ladle.

écurer [ekyre] *vt* to scour.

écureuil [ekyrœːj] *nm* squirrel.

écurie [ekyri] *nf* stable.

écusson [ekysɔ̃] *nm* escutcheon, coat-of-arms shield.

écuyer, -ère [ekɥije, ɛːr] *n* rider, horseman, -woman; *nm* equerry, squire; **bottes à l'écuyère** riding-boots.

édenté [edɑ̃te] *a* toothless.

édenter [edɑ̃te] *vt* to break the teeth of.

édicter [edikte] *vt* to decree, enact.

édification [edifikasjɔ̃] *nf* building, erection; edification.

édifice [edifis] *nm* edifice, building, structure.

édifier [edifje] *vt* to build, erect, edify.

édit [edi] *nm* edict.

éditer [edite] *vt* to edit, publish.

éditeur, -trice [editœːr, tris] *n* editor, editress, publisher.

édition [edisjɔ̃] *nf* edition, publishing trade; **maison d'—** publishing house.

éditorial [editɔrjal] *a* editorial; *nm* leading article, leader.

édredon [edrədɔ̃] *nm* eiderdown, quilt.

éducation [edykasjɔ̃] *nf* training, rearing, breeding, upbringing.

éduquer [edyke] *vt* to educate, bring up.

effacé [ɛfase] *a* unobtrusive, unassuming, retiring.

effacement [ɛfasmɑ̃] *nm* obliteration, wearing out, unobtrusiveness.

effacer [ɛfase] *vt* to efface, blot out, delete; *vr* to wear away, fade, remain in the background.

effarement [ɛfarmɑ̃] *nm* alarm, fright.

effarer [ɛfare] *vt* to scare, alarm; *vr* to be scared, take fright.

effaroucher [ɛfaruʃe] *vt* to scare away; *vr* to be startled.

effectif, -ive [efɛktif, iːv] *a* effective, actual, real; *nm* total strength, manpower.

effectivement [efɛktivmɑ̃] *ad* actually, as a matter of fact, exactly.

effectuer [efɛktɥe] *vt* to bring about, carry out, execute.

efféminé [efemine] *a* effeminate.

effervescence [efɛrvessɑ̃ːs] *nf* excitement, ebullience, turmoil.

effet [efɛ] *nm* effect, result, impression, operation; *pl* effects, possessions, stocks; **à cet —** for this purpose; **en —** indeed, as a matter of fact; **manquer son —** to fall flat; **faire de l'—** to be effective; **mettre à l'—** to put into operation.

effeuiller [efœje] *vt* to remove the leaves from; *vr* to shed its leaves.

efficace [efikas] *a* effective, efficacious, effectual.

efficacité [efikasite] *nf* efficacy, effectiveness, efficiency.

effigie [efiʒi] *nf* image, likeness.

effilé [efile] *a* fringed, slender, slim, tapering.

effiler [efile] *vt* to unravel, taper; *vr* to fray, taper.

effilocher [efilɔʃe] *vt* to unravel; *vr* to fray.

efflanqué [eflɑ̃ke] *a* lean.

effleurer [eflœre] *vt* to graze, brush, skim, touch upon.

effondrement [efɔ̃drəmɑ̃] *nm* collapse, falling in, subsidence, slump, breakdown.

effondrer [efɔ̃dre] *vt* to break down, smash in; *vr* to collapse, fall in, slump.

s'efforcer [sefɔrse] *vr* to strive, endeavour.

effort [efɔːr] *nm* endeavour, exertion, strain.

effraction [efraksjɔ̃] *nf* housebreaking.

effrayer [efrɛje] *vt* to frighten, terrify, scare, daunt; *vr* to get a fright, be frightened.

effréné [efrene] *a* unbridled, frantic, frenzied.

effriter [efrite] *vt* to wear away; *vr* to crumble.

effroi [efrwa] *nm* fright, dread, terror.

effronté [efrɔ̃te] *a* shameless, impudent, cheeky, saucy.

effronterie [efrɔ̃tri] *nf* effrontery, impudence.

effroyable [efrwajabl] *a* frightful, dreadful, appalling.

effusion [efyzjɔ̃] *nf* effusion, outpouring, effusiveness; — **de sang** bloodshed.

égailler [egaje] *vt* to flush, scatter; *vr* to scatter.

égal [egal] *a* equal, level, even; **cela lui est —** it is all the same to him.

également [egalmɑ̃] *ad* equally, likewise, as well.

égaler [egale] *vt* to be equal to, compare with.

égaliser [egalize] *vt* to equalize, regulate, level.

égalitaire [egalitɛ:r] *an* equalitarian.

égalité [egalite] *nf* equality, evenness, smoothness; **être à —** to be all square, equal.

égard [ega:r] *nm* regard, respect, consideration; *pl* esteem, attentions, consideration; **avoir — à** to take into account; **à cet —** in this respect; **à tous les —s** in every respect; **à l'—** de with regard to, towards.

égaré [egare] *a* lost, stray, distracted.

égarement [egarmɑ̃] *nm* loss, mislaying; aberration, frenzy; *pl* disorderly conduct.

égarer [egare] *vt* to lead astray, mislead, mislay; *vr* to go astray, lose one's way.

égayer [egɛje] *vt* to cheer up, brighten (up).

égide [eʒid] *nf* shield, aegis.

églantier [eglɑ̃tje] *nm* wild rose, sweet brier.

églantine [eglɑ̃tin] *nf* wild rose (flower).

église [egli:z] *nf* church.

égoïsme [egɔism] *nm* selfishness, egoism.

égoïste [egɔist] *a* selfish; *n* egoist, egotist.

égorger [egɔrʒe] *vt* to cut the throat of, butcher.

s'égosiller [segozije] *vr* to shout oneself hoarse.

égout [egu] *nm* drain, sewer, gutter; **eaux d'—** sewage.

égoutter [egute] *vt* to drain; *vr* drip, drop, drain.

égratigner [egratiɲe] *vt* to scratch, graze.

égratignure [egratiɲy:r] *nf* scratch, graze.

égrener [egrəne] *vt* to pick out, pick off; *vr* to drop (one by one); **— son chapelet** to tell one's beads.

égrillard [egrija:r] *a* ribald, daring, spicy.

Égypte [eʒipt] *nf* Egypt.

égyptien, -enne [eʒipsjɛ̃, jɛn] *an* Egyptian.

éhonté [eɔ̃te] *a* shameless, brazenfaced.

éjaculer [eʒakyle] *vt* to ejaculate.

élaborer [elabɔre] *vt* to elaborate, draw up, labour.

élaguer [elage] *vt* to lop off, prune, cut down.

élan [elɑ̃] *nm* spring, bound, dash,

impetus, abandon, (out)burst; moose.

élancé [elɑ̃se] *a* slender, slim, tapering.

élancement [elɑ̃smɑ̃] *nm* twinge, stabbing pain.

s'élancer [selɑ̃se] *vr* to dash forward, rush, spring.

élargir [elarʒi:r] *vt* to widen, enlarge, broaden, release, discharge; *vr* to broaden out, extend.

élargissement [elarʒismɑ̃] *nm* broadening, extension, release, discharge.

élasticité [elastisite] *nf* elasticity, resilience, spring.

élastique [elastik] *a* elastic, springy, resilient; *nm* elastic, rubber band.

électeur, -trice [elɛktœːr, tris] *n* voter, constituent.

électif, -ive [elɛktif, i:v] *a* elective.

élection [elɛksjɔ̃] *nf* election, choice; **se présenter aux —s** to stand at the election.

électoral [elɛktɔral] *a* electoral; **collège —** constituency; **campagne —e** electioneering; **corps —** electorate.

électorat [elɛktɔra] *nm* electorate.

électricien [elɛktrisjɛ̃] *nm* electrician.

électricité [elɛktrisite] *nf* electricity.

électrique [elɛktrik] *a* electric.

électriser [elɛktrize] *vt* to electrify.

électrocuter [elɛktrɔkyte] *vt* to electrocute.

électronique [elɛktrɔnik] *a* electronic; *nf* electronics.

élégance [elegɑ̃:s] *nf* stylishness, smartness.

élégant [elegɑ̃] *a* well-dressed, fashionable.

élégiaque [eleʒjak] *a* elegiac.

élégie [eleʒi] *nf* elegy.

élément [elemɑ̃] *nm* component, element, ingredient; *pl* rudiments.

élémentaire [elemɑ̃tɛ:r] *a* elementary, rudimentary.

éléphant [elefɑ̃] *nm* elephant.

élevage [ɛlvaːʒ] *nm* raising, rearing, breeding.

élévation [elevasjɔ̃] *nf* elevation, raising, rise, height, grandeur.

élève [elɛːv] *n* pupil, boy, girl.

élevé [elve] *a* elevated, high, lofty, exalted; **bien (mal) —** well- (ill-) bred, well (badly) behaved.

élever [elve] *vt* to elevate, erect, raise; *vr* to rise up, arise.

éleveur, -euse [elvœːr, øːz] *n* stockbreeder, grower, keeper.

élider [elide] *vt* to elide.

éligibilité [eliʒibilite] *nf* eligibility.

éligible [eliʒibl] *a* eligible.

élimer [elime] *vt* to wear threadbare; *vr* to wear, be worn threadbare.

éliminatoire [eliminatwaːr] *a* eliminatory, preliminary.

éliminer [elimine] *vt* to eliminate, weed out.

élire [eliːr] *vt* to elect, choose, appoint, return.

élision [elizjɔ̃] *nf* elision.

élite [elit] *nf* élite, pick, flower; **a d'—** crack.

ellipse [elips] *nf* ellipse, ellipsis.

élocution [eləkysjɔ̃] *nf* elocution.

éloge [eləʒ] *nm* eulogy, commendation, praise.

élogieux, -euse [eləʒjø, jøːz] *a* laudatory, glowing.

éloigné [elwaɲe] *a* distant, far (away, off).

éloignement [elwaɲmɑ̃] *nm* absence, removal, isolation, postponement, distance.

éloigner [elwaɲe] *vt* to remove, get out of the way, alienate, postpone; *vr* to withdraw, stand further away.

éloquence [eləkɑ̃ːs] *nf* eloquence.

éloquent [eləkɑ̃] *a* eloquent.

élu [ely] *a* chosen; *nm pl* the elect, the elected members.

élucider [elyside] *vt* to elucidate.

éluder [elyde] *vt* to elude, evade.

émacié [emasje] *a* emaciated.

émail [emaːj] *nm* enamel, glaze.

émailler [emaje] *vt* to enamel, glaze, fleck, besprinkle.

émancipé [emɑ̃sipe] *a* full-fledged, having advanced ideas, emancipated.

émanciper [emɑ̃sipe] *vt* to emancipate; *vr* to become emancipated, kick over the traces.

émaner [emane] *vi* to emanate, come, originate (from).

émasculer [emaskyle] *vt* to emasculate, weaken.

emballage [ɑ̃balaːʒ] *nm* packing, wrapping.

emballement [ɑ̃balmɑ̃] *nm (of machine)* racing, enthusiasm, boom, craze.

emballer [ɑ̃bale] *vt* to pack, wrap up, *(motor engine)* race, fill with enthusiasm; *vr (horse)* to bolt, be carried away, rave (with enthusiasm), fly into a temper.

emballeur [ɑ̃balœːr] *nm* packer.

embarcadère [ɑ̃barkadɛːr] *nm* landing-stage, wharf, platform.

embarcation [ɑ̃barkasjɔ̃] *nf* boat, craft.

embardée [ɑ̃barde] *nf* lurch, swerve, skid.

embargo [ɑ̃bargo] *nm* embargo.

embarquement [ɑ̃barkəmɑ̃] *nm* loading, embarking, shipping, entrainment.

embarquer [ɑ̃barke] *vt* to embark, take aboard, entrain; *vir* to go abroad, entrain.

embarras [ɑ̃bara] *nm* embarrassment, difficulty, quandary, superfluity; *pl* fuss.

embarrassé [ɑ̃barase] *a* embarrassed, involved.

embarrasser [ɑ̃barase] *vt* to embarrass, perplex, confound, hamper, obstruct.

embaucher [ɑ̃boʃe] *vt* to engage, take on, employ.

embauchoir [ɑ̃boʃwaːr] *nm* boot-tree.

embaumer [ɑ̃bome] *vt* to embalm, perfume; *vi* to have a lovely perfume, smell of.

embellir [ɑ̃bɛliːr] *vt* to embellish, improve, beautify.

embellissement [ɑ̃belismɑ̃] *nm* embellishment.

embêtant [ɑ̃bɛtɑ̃] *a (fam)* annoying.

embêter [ɑ̃bete] *vt* to annoy.

emblée [ɑ̃ble] *ad* **d'—** straight away.

emblème [ɑ̃blɛːm] *nm* emblem, badge, sign.

emboбеliner [ɑ̃bobline] *vt* to coax, get round.

emboîtement [ɑ̃bwatmɑ̃] *nm* joint, fitting, encasing.

emboîter [ɑ̃bwate] *vt* to joint, fit together, dovetail, encase; **— le pas à** to fall into step with.

embolie [ɑ̃bəli] *nf* embolism, stroke.

embonpoint [ɑ̃bɔ̃pwɛ̃] *nm* corpulence, stoutness.

embouché [ɑ̃buʃe] *a* **mal —** coarse-tongued.

emboucher [ɑ̃buʃe] *vt* to put to one's mouth, blow.

embouchure [ɑ̃buʃyːr] *nf* mouthpiece. *(river, volcano)* mouth.

embourber [ɑ̃burbe] *vt* to bog; *vr* to be bogged, stuck in the mud.

embout [ɑ̃bu] *nm* ferrule, tip.

embouteillage [ɑ̃butɛjaːʒ] *nm* bottling (up), bottleneck, traffic-jam.

embouteiller [ɑ̃butɛje] *vt* to bottle (up), jam, block; *vr* to get jammed.

embranchement [ɑ̃brɑ̃ʃmɑ̃] *nm* branching off, junction, branch-line.

embrancher [ɑ̃brɑ̃ʃe] *vt* to join up, together.

embrasement [ɑ̃brazmɑ̃] *nm* conflagration.

embraser [ɑ̃braze] *vt* to set fire to, fire; *vr* to catch fire.

embrassade [ɑ̃brasad] *nf* embrace, hug.

embrasser [ɑ̃brase] *vt* to embrace, hug, kiss, enfold, take up, include.

embrasure [ɑ̃brazyːr] *nf* recess, embrasure.

embrayage [ɑ̃brɛjaːʒ] *nm* connecting, coupling-gear, putting into gear.

embrayer [ɑ̃brɛje] *vt* to connect, couple, throw into gear; *vi* to let in the clutch.

embrocher [ɑ̃brɔʃe] *vt* to spit, put on the spit.

embrouillement [ɑ̃brujmɑ̃] *nm* entanglement, intricacy, muddle, confusion.

embrouiller [ɑ̃bruje] *vt* to tangle, muddle, embroil, complicate, confuse; *vr* to become entangled, complicated, confused.

embrun [ɑ̃brœ̃] *nm* spray, spindrift.

embryon [ɑ̃briɔ̃] *nm* embryo.

embûche [ăby(ː)ʃ] *nf* ambush; dresser une — à to waylay.

embuer [ăbɥe] *vt* to cloud, cover with vapour.

embuscade [ăbyskad] *nf* ambush, ambuscade.

embusqué [ăbyske] *nm* shirker, dodger, sharpshooter,

embusquer [ăbyske] *vt* to place in ambush, put under cover; *vr* to lie in ambush, take cover, shirk war service.

éméché [emeʃe] *a* slightly tipsy, rather merry.

émeraude [ɛmroːd] *nf* emerald.

émerger [emɛrʒe] *vi* to emerge, come out.

émeri [ɛmri] *nm* emery.

émérite [emerit] *a* emeritus, retired, experienced.

émerveillement [emɛrvɛjmã] *nm* amazement.

émerveiller [emɛrvɛje] *vt* to amaze, astonish; *vr* to marvel, wonder.

émétique [emetik] *nm* emetic.

émetteur -trice [emetœːr, tris] *a* issuing, transmitting, broadcasting; *n* issuer transmitter.

émettre [emɛtr] *vt* to emit, issue, utter, give out express, transmit, broadcast.

émeute [emøːt] *nf* riot disturbance.

émeutier [emøtje] *nm* rioter.

émietter [emjɛte] *vtr* to crumble.

émigrant [emigrã] *a* emigrating, migratory; *n* emigrant.

émigré [emigre] *n* political exile.

émigrer emigre] *vi* to emigrate, migrate.

éminence [eminãːs] *nf* eminence, height, prominence.

éminent [eminã] *a* distinguished.

émissaire [emisɛːr] *nm* emissary; bouc — scapegoat.

émission [emisjɔ̃] *nf* issue transmission, broadcast; **poste d'**—broadcasting station.

emmagasinage [ãmagazinaːʒ] *nm* storing storage.

emmagasiner [ãmagazine] *vt* to store (up).

emmailloter [ãmajɔte] *v.* to swaddle, swathe.

emmancher [ãmãʃe] *vt* to put a handle on; oint; *vr* to fit (into dans), set going.

emmanchure [ãmãʃyːr] *nf* armhole.

emmêler [ãmɛle] *vt* to mix up, muddle, implicate.

emménager [ãmenaʒe] *vt* to move in, furnish; *vi* to move in.

emmener [ãmne] *vt* to lead, take away take

emmitoufler [ãmitufle] *vt* to muffle up.

émoi [emwa] *nm* emotion, excitement, stir flutter; en — agog, astir, in a flutter.

émoluments [emolymã] *nm pl* emoluments, fees.

émonder [emɔ̃de] *vt* to prune, trim.

émotion [emosjɔ̃] *nf* emotion, feeling, excitement.

émotionnable [emosjɔnabl] *a* emotional, excitable.

émotionner [emosjɔne] *vt* to excite, stir thrill; *vr* to get excited.

émoudre [emudr] *vt* to grind.

émoulu [emuly] *a* sharpened; frais — de just out of, fresh from.

émousser [emuse] *vt* to blunt, deaden; *vr* to become blunt, dulled.

émoustillant [emustijã] *a* piquant, exhilarating.

émoustiller [emustije] *vt* to stir (up), rouse, ti illate, stimulate; *vr* to come to life, sparkle.

émouvant [emuvã] *a* moving, exciting, thrilling.

émouvoir [emuvwaːr] *vt* to move, stir up, excite; *vr* to be moved get excited.

empailler [ãpaje] *vt* to pack, cover in straw, stuff.

empailleur, -euse [ãpajœːr, øːz] *n* taxidermist

empaler [ãpale] *vt* to impale.

empaqueter [ãpakte] *vt* to pack up, parcel up, bundle.

s'emparer [sãpare] *vr* to seize, take possession (of de), secure.

empâté [ãpate] *a* coated, clogged, thick.

empâter [ãpate] *vt* to cover with paste, make sticky, fatten; *vr* to put on at.

empêchement [ãpeʃmã] *nm* impediment, obstacle, hindrance.

empêcher [ãpeʃe] *vt* to prevent, impede, hamper; *vr* to refrain; je ne peux m'— de rire I cannot help laughing.

empeigne [ãpɛɲ] *nf* upper (of shoe).

empennage [ãpenaːʒ] *nm* feathers, feathering, fur, vanes.

empereur [ãprœːr] *nm* emperor.

empesé [ãpəze] *a* starched, stiff, starchy.

empeser [ãpəze] *vt* to starch, stiffen.

empester [ãpɛste] *vt* to infect, create a stink in.

empêtrer [ãpɛtre] *vt* to hobble, entangle, hamper; *vr* to get entangled, involved.

emphase [ãfaːz] *nf* grandiloquence, bombast

emphatique [ãfatik] *a* bombastic, grandiloquent.

empierrer [ãpjɛre] *vt* to ballast, metal.

empiètement [ãpjɛtmã] *nm* encroachment. trespassing, infringement.

empiéter [ãpjete] *vi* to encroach infringe.

empiffrer [ãpifre] *vt* to stuff; *vr* to stuff oneself, guzzle.

empiler [ãpile] *vt* to pile. stack.

empire [ãpiːr] *nm* empire sway,

dominion; — **sur soi-même** self-control.

empirer [ăpire] *vt* to make worse, aggravate; *vr* to get worse.

empirique [ăpirik] *a* empirical.

emplacement [ăplasmă] *nm* site, location.

emplâtre [ăpla:tr] *nm* plaster, poultice.

emplette [ăplɛt] *nf* purchase; **faire ses** —**s** to go shopping.

emplir [ăpli:r] *vt* to fill; *vr* to fill (up).

emploi [ăplwa] *nm* use, employment, job, post.

employé [ăplwaje] *n* employee, clerk, attendant.

employer [ăplwaje] *vt* to employ use; *vr* to spend one's time, occupy oneself.

employeur, -euse [ăplwajœ:r, ø:z] *n* employer.

empocher [ăpɔʃe] *vt* to pocket.

empoignant [ăpwaɲă] *a* thrilling, gripping.

empoigner [ăpwaɲe] *vt* to grasp, grab, grip, hold.

empois [ăpwa] *nm* starch.

empoisonnant [ăpwazɔnă] *a* poisonous rotten.

empoisonnement [ăpwazɔnmă] *nm* poisoning.

empoisonner [ăpwazɔne] *vt* to poison, infect, corrupt.

empoisonneur, -euse [ăpwazɔnœ:r, ø:z] *n* poisoner.

emporté [ăpɔrte] *a* hot-tempered, fiery, hasty.

emportement [ăpɔrtəmă] *nm* outburst, anger, rapture, passion.

emporte-pièce [ăpɔrtəpjɛs] *nm* punch; **réponse à l'**— caustic reply.

emporter [ăpɔrte] *vt* to carry away, off, sweep along, away, remove; *vr* to fly into a rage, bolt; **l'**— to carry the day, prevail, have the best of it; — **la balance** to turn the scale.

empoté [ăpɔte] *a* clumsy, unathletic; *n* muff, duffer.

empoter [ăpɔte] *vt* to pot.

empourprer [ăpurpre] *vt* to tinge with crimson; *vr* to turn crimson, grow red.

empreindre [ăprɛ̃:dr] *vt* to imprint, stamp.

empreinte [ăprɛ̃t] *nf* stamp, mark, imprint, print, impression, mould; — **digitale** fingerprint.

empressé [ăprɛse] *a* eager, solicitous, ardent, sedulous.

empressement [ăprɛsmă] *nm* eagerness, alacrity, haste, zeal.

s'empresser [săprese] *vr* to hurry, be eager, be attentive, dance attendance.

emprise [ăpri:z] *nf* expropriation, hold power.

emprisonnement [ăprizɔnmă] *nm* imprisonment.

emprisonner [ăprizɔne] *vt* to imprison, put in prison, confine.

emprunt [ăprœ̃] *nm* borrowing, loan.

emprunté [ăprœ̃te] *a* borrowed, assumed, embarrassed, self-conscious.

emprunter [ăprœ̃te] *vt* to borrow, take, assume.

emprunteur, -euse [ăprœ̃tœ:r, ø:z] *n* borrower.

ému [emy] *a* moved, touched, excited nervous.

émulation [emylasjɔ̃] *nf* emulation, rivalry.

émule [emyl] *n* rival.

en [ă] *prep* in, into, to, as, like, while; *pn* of it, of them, about it, about them, for that, because of that, some, any.

encadrement [ăkadrəmă] *nm* framing, framework, setting, officering.

encadrer [ăkadre] *vt* to frame, set surround, officer.

encaisse [ăkɛs] *nf* cash in hand, cash-balance.

encaissé [ăkese] *a* boxed-in, sunken, steeply embanked, blind (corner).

encaissement [ăkesmă] *nm* encasing, packing in boxes, collection, embankment.

encaisser [ăkese] *vt* to pack in boxes, collect cash, embank, take (blow).

encaisseur [ăkesœ:r] *nm* collector, cashier, payee.

encan [ăkă] *nm* **mettre à l'**— to put up for auction.

encanailler [ăkanaje] *vr* to keep bad company, go to the dogs.

encapuchonner [ăkapyʃɔne] *vt* to put a hood on, put the cover over.

encart [ăka:r] *nm* inset.

en-cas [ăka] *nm* reserve, something to fall back on.

encastrer [ăkastre] *vt* to fit in, imbed, dovetail.

encaustique [ăkostik] *nf* floor, furniture polish.

encaustiquer [ăkostike] *vt* to polish, beeswax.

enceindre [ăsɛ̃:dr] *vt* to encircle, gird, surround.

enceinte [ăsɛ̃t] *a* pregnant; *nf* wall, fence, enclosure, circumference.

encens [ăsă] *nm* incense, flattery.

encenser [ăsăse] *vt* to cense, burn incense before, flatter.

encenseur [ăsăsœ:r] *nm* censer-bearer flatterer.

encensoir [ăsăswa:r] *nm* censer.

encercler [ăsɛrkle] *vt* to encircle, surround.

enchaînement [ăʃɛnmă] *nm* chaining, series, putting together.

enchaîner [ăʃɛne] *vt* to chain, link up, hold in check.

enchantement [ăʃătmă] *nm* magic, enchantment, charm, spell.

enchanter [ăʃăte] *vt* to enchant, delight, bewitch.

enchanteur, -eresse [ăʃătœ:r rɛ:s]

a bewitching, entrancing; *n* enchanter, enchantress.

enchâsser [ɑ̃ʃase] *vt* to enshrine, set, mount.

enchère [ɑ̃ʃɛːr] *nf* bid(ding); vente à l'— auction sale.

enchérir [ɑ̃ʃeriːr] *vt* to raise the price of; *vi* to go up in price, make a higher bid; — sur qn to outbid, outdo s.o.

enchérissement [ɑ̃ʃerismɑ̃] *nm* rise, increase.

enchérisseur, -euse [ɑ̃ʃerisœːr, øːz] *n* bidder.

enchevêtrement [ɑ̃ʃvɛtrəmɑ̃] *nm* tangling up, confusion.

enchevêtrer [ɑ̃ʃvetre] *vt* to halter, confuse, mix up; *vr* to get entangled, mixed up.

enclaver [ɑ̃klave] *vt* to enclose, dovetail.

enclencher [ɑ̃klɑ̃ʃe] *vt* to put into gear, engage.

enclin [ɑ̃klɛ̃] *a* inclined, prone.

enclore [ɑ̃klɔːr] *vt* to enclose, fence in.

enclos [ɑ̃klo] *nm* enclosure, paddock.

enclume [ɑ̃klym] *nf* anvil.

encoche [ɑ̃kɔʃ] *nf* notch, last, slot; avec —s with thumb index.

encocher [ɑ̃kɔʃe] *vt* to notch, nick.

encoignure [ɑ̃kɔɲyːr] *nf* corner, corner cupboard.

encoller [ɑ̃kɔle] *vt* to gum, glue, paste.

encolure [ɑ̃kɔlyːr] *nf* neck and shoulders, (*dress*) neck, (*collar*) size.

encombrant [ɑ̃kɔ̃brɑ̃] *a* clumsy, bulky, cumbersome.

encombre [ɑ̃kɔ̃ːbr] *nm* obstacle, hindrance, mishap.

encombrement [ɑ̃kɔ̃brəmɑ̃] *nm* obstruction, congestion, jam, litter, overcrowding, glut, bulkiness.

encombrer [ɑ̃kɔ̃bre] *vt* to encumber, burden, congest, crowd, glut, litter.

encontre [ɑ̃kɔ̃ːtr] *ad* à l'— to the contrary; *prep* à l'— de contrary to, unlike.

encore [ɑ̃kɔːr] *ad* still, yet, again, furthermore, even, even at that; — que although.

encouragement [ɑ̃kuraʒmɑ̃] *nm* encouragement, incentive, inducement.

encourager [ɑ̃kuraʒe] *vt* to encourage, hearten, foster, abet, egg on.

encourir [ɑ̃kuriːr] *vt* to incur, draw upon oneself.

encrasser [ɑ̃krase] *vt* to dirty, clog, choke; *vr* to become dirty, clog.

encre [ɑ̃ːkr] *nf* ink.

encrier [ɑ̃krie] *nm* inkwell, inkstand.

encroûter [ɑ̃krute] *vt* to encrust, cake; *vr* to become caked, stagnate.

encyclopédie [ɑ̃siklɔpedi] *nf* encyclopedia.

endetter [ɑ̃dste] *vt* to run into debt; *vr* to get into debt.

endiablé [ɑ̃djable] *a* reckless, wild boisterous.

endiguer [ɑ̃dige] *vt* to dam up, bank, dike.

s'endimancher [sɑ̃dimɑ̃ʃe] *vr* to dress in one's Sunday best.

endive [ɑ̃diːv] *nf* chicory.

endolori [ɑ̃dɔlɔri] *a* painful, tender.

endommager [ɑ̃dɔmaʒe] *vt* to damage, injure.

endormi [ɑ̃dɔrmi] *a* asleep, sleeping, drowsy, sluggish, numb; *n* sleepyhead.

endormir [ɑ̃dɔrmiːr] *vt* to put to sleep, make numb, give an anaesthetic to; *vr* to fall asleep, drop off.

endosser [ɑ̃dose] *vt* to put on, endorse.

endroit [ɑ̃drwa] *nm* place, spot, aspect, right side; à l'— de with regard to.

enduire [ɑ̃dɥiːr] *vt* to coat, smear, daub.

enduit [ɑ̃dɥi] *nm* coating, coat, plaster.

endurance [ɑ̃dyrɑ̃ːs] *nf* endurance, long-suffering.

endurant [ɑ̃dyrɑ̃] *a* patient, long-suffering.

endurcir [ɑ̃dyrsiːr] *vt* to harden, inure; *vr* to harden, become hard, obdurate.

endurcissement [ɑ̃dyrsismɑ̃] *nm* hardening, inuring, obduracy, callousness.

endurer [ɑ̃dyre] *vt* to endure, put up with, bear.

énergie [enɛrʒi] *nf* energy, vigour, power, efficacy, drive.

énergique [enɛrʒik] *a* energetic, vigorous, drastic, strong-willed.

énergumène [enɛrgymɛn] *nm* madman.

énervant [enɛrvɑ̃] *a* enervating, annoying, nerve-racking.

énerver [enɛrve] *vt* to enervate, get on one's nerves; *vr* to grow soft, become irritatable, get excited.

enfance [ɑ̃fɑ̃ːs] *nf* childhood, boyhood, children.

enfant [ɑ̃fɑ̃] *n* child, little boy, girl; — trouvé foundling; *a* bon — easygoing.

enfantement [ɑ̃fɑ̃tmɑ̃] *nm* childbirth, production.

enfanter [ɑ̃fɑ̃te] *vt* to bear, give birth to.

enfantillage [ɑ̃fɑ̃tijaːʒ] *nm* childishness.

enfantin [ɑ̃fɑ̃tɛ̃] *a* childish, childlike, children's.

enfer [ɑ̃fɛːr] *nm* hell.

enfermer [ɑ̃fɛrme] *vt* to shut in, lock up, enclose, sequester; *vr* to shut, lock oneself in.

enferrer [ɑ̃fɛre] *vt* to transfix, run s.o. through; *vr* to transfix oneself, swallow the hook, get caught out.

s'enfiévrer [sɑ̃fjevre] *vr* to grow feverish, get excited.

enfilade [ɑ̃filad] *nf* succession, string, raking fire.

enfiler [ãfile] vt to thread, string, pierce, go along, slip on.

enfin [ãfɛ̃] ad at last, finally, at length, in a word, after all.

enflammé [ãflame] a burning, fiery, blaze.

enflammer [ãflame] vt to inflame, set on fire, stir up; vr to catch fire, become inflamed.

enflé [ãfle] a swollen, inflated, grandiloquent.

enfler [ãfle] vt to swell, puff out, bloat; vr to swell.

enflure [ãflyːr] nf swelling, puffiness, grandiloquence.

enfoncement [ãfɔ̃smã] nm driving in, smashing in, depression, recess, bay.

enfoncer [ãfɔ̃se] vt to drive in, thrust, smash in; vi to sink, settle; vr to plunge, dive, sink.

enfouir [ãfwiːr] vt to bury, hide.

enfourcher [ãfurʃe] vt to stick a fork into, mount.

enfourchure [ãfurʃyːr] nf fork, bifurcation.

enfourner [ãfurne] vt to put in the oven, shovel in.

enfreindre [ãfrɛ̃ːdr] vt to infringe, break, contravene.

s'enfuir [sãfyiːr] vr to flee, escape, fly, run away, elope.

enfumé [ãfyme] a smoky, smoke-blackened.

enfumer [ãfyme] vt to fill (blacken) with smoke.

engagé [ãgaʒe] a pledged; n volunteer.

engageant [ãgaʒã] a winning, prepossessing, inviting, ingratiating.

engagement [ãgaʒmã] nm appointment, commitment, pawning, pledge, bond, engagement, enlistment.

engager [ãgaʒe] vt to engage, sign on, pawn, pledge, enter into, urge; vr to undertake, get involved, commit oneself, enlist, fit, jam, foul.

engainer [ãgɛne] vt to sheathe, envelop.

engeance [ãʒãːs] nf breed, race.

engelure [ãʒlyːr] nf chilblain.

engendrer [ãʒãdre] vt to beget, engender, breed.

engin [ãʒɛ̃] nm engine, machine, device; pl tackle, appliances.

englober [ãglɔbe] vt to include, embrace, take in.

engloutir [ãglutiːr] vt to swallow up, gulp down, engulf; vr to be engulfed.

engoncé [ãgɔ̃se] a bunched-up, hunched-up.

engorgement [ãgɔrʒəmã] nm choking up, clogging, stoppage.

engorger [ãgɔrʒe] vt to choke up, clog, obstruct; vr to get choked up.

engouement [ãgumã] nm infatuation, craze.

engouer [ãgwe] vt to obstruct; vr to become infatuated, go crazy, mad

(about **de**), have a passion (for **de**).

engouffrer [ãgufre] vt to engulf, swallow up; vr to be engulfed, rush.

engourdi [ãgurdi] a numb, cramped, sluggish, lethargic; n dullard, sluggard.

engourdir [ãgurdiːr] vt to benumb, cramp, chill, dull; vr to grow numb, sluggish.

engourdissement [ãgurdismã] nm numbness, sluggishness.

engrais [ãgrɛ] nm fattening food, manure, fertilizer.

engraissement [ãgrɛsmã] nm fattening, growing fat, corpulence.

engraisser [ãgrɛse] vt to fatten, fertilize, manure; vi to grow fat, put on weight.

engranger [ãgrãʒe] vt (corn) to get in, to garner.

engrenage [ãgrənaːʒ] nm gearing, gear, mesh; pl gear-wheels, works.

engrener [ãgrəne] vt to connect, engage; vr to interlock.

enhardir [ãardiːr] vt to make bolder, encourage; vr to venture, grow bolder.

enharnacher [ãarnaʃe] vt to put the harness on.

énigmatique [enigmatik] a enigmatic(al).

énigme [enigm] nf enigma, riddle, conundrum.

enivrement [ãnivrəmã] nm intoxication, rapture.

enivrer [ãnivre] vt to intoxicate, send into raptures; vr to get drunk, be carried away, be uplifted.

enjambée [ãʒãbe] nf stride.

enjambement [ãʒãbmã] nm enjambment.

enjamber [ãʒãbe] vt to step over, bestride; vi to stride along, encroach.

enjeu [ãʒø] nm (betting) stake.

enjoindre [ãʒwɛ̃ːdr] vt to enjoin, exhort, call upon.

enjôler [ãʒole] vt to wheedle, cajole, coax.

enjoliver [ãʒɔlive] vt to embellish, embroider upon.

enjoué [ãʒwe] a playful, sportive, vivacious.

enjouement [ãʒumã] nm playfulness.

enlacement [ãlasmã] nm entwining, embrace.

enlacer [ãlase] vt to entwine, intertwine, clasp, embrace; vr to intertwine, twine, embrace each other.

enlaidir [ãlediːr] vt to make ugly; vi to grow ugly.

enlèvement [ãlɛvmã] nm removal, carrying off, kidnapping, storming.

enlever [ãlve] vt to remove, carry off (away), storm, perform brilliantly, kidnap, abduct; vr to come off, boil over; **se laisser —** to elope.

enliser [ãlize] vt to draw in, engulf; vr to sink, get bogged

enluminer [ãlymine] *vt* to illuminate, colour.

enluminure [ãlyminy:r] *nf* illuminating, colouring, illumination.

ennemi [ɛnmi] *a* enemy, hostile; *n* enemy, foe.

ennoblir [ãnɔbli:r] *vt* to ennoble, exalt, elevate.

ennui [ãnɥi] boredom, tediousness, worry, trouble.

ennuyer [ãnɥije] *vt* to bore, bother, worry, annoy; *vr* to weary, be bored.

ennuyeux, -euse [ãnɥijø, ø:z] *a* tedious, irksome, tiresome, dull, drab, annoying.

énoncé [enɔ̃se] *nm* statement, wording, enunciation.

énoncer [enɔ̃se] *vt* to state, express, articulate.

énonciation [enɔ̃sjasjɔ̃] *nf* stating, articulation.

enorgueillir [ãnɔrgœji:r] *vt* to make proud; *vr* to become proud, pride oneself.

énorme [enɔrm] *a* huge, enormous, excessive, heinous.

énormément [enɔrmemã] *ad* enormously, awfully, a great many, a great deal.

énormité [enɔrmite] *nf* hugeness, enormity, incredible lie, excessiveness.

s'enquérir [sãkeri:r] *vr* to inquire, ask, make inquiries.

enquête [ãkɛt] *nf* inquiry, investigation, inquest.

enquêter [ãkɛte] *vi* to make investigations, hold an inquiry.

enraciner [ãrasine] *vt* to plant securely, establish; *vr* to take root, become ingrained.

enragé [ãraʒe] *a* mad, enthusiastic, rabid; *n* fan.

enrager [ãraʒe] *vt* to enrage, madden; *vi* to be mad, be in a rage.

enrayer [ãrɛje] *vt* to lock, check, stop, foul.

enregistrement [ãrəʒistrəmã] *nm* registration, recording; **bureau d'—** registry office, luggage booking-office.

enregistrer [ãrəʒistre] *vt* to register, record, enrol, enter.

enregistreur, -euse [ãrəʒistrœːr, øːz] *a* recording; *nm* registrar.

enrhumer [ãryme] *vt* to give s.o. a cold; *vr* to catch a cold.

enrichir [ãriʃi:r] *vt* to enrich, make wealthy, augment, increase; *vr* to grow wealthy, make money.

enrober [ãrɔbe] *vt* to cover, coat.

enrôler [ãrole] *vtr* to enrol, enlist.

enrouement [ãrumã] *nm* hoarseness, huskiness.

enroué [ãrwe] *a* hoarse, husky.

enrouer [ãrwe] *vt* to make hoarse; *vr* to become hoarse, husky.

enrouler [ãrule] *vt* to roll up, wind, wrap; *vr* to wind, coil.

enrubanner [ãrybane] *vt* to decorate with ribbon.

ensabler [ãsable] *vt* to sand, silt up.

ensanglanter [ãsãglãte] *vt* to stain, cover, with blood.

enseignant [ãsɛɲã] *a* teaching; **corps —** teaching profession.

enseigne [ãsɛɲ] *nf* mark, sign, token, shop-sign, ensign, (sub-) lieutenant; **logés à la même —** in the same boat.

enseignement [ãsɛɲmã] *nm* teaching, education, lesson.

enseigner [ãsɛɲe] *vt* to teach.

ensemble [ãsã:bl] *ad* together, at the same time; *nm* general effect, whole, set; **vue d'—** general view; **dans l'—** on the whole.

ensemencer [ãsmãse] *vt* to sow.

ensevelir [ãsəvli:r] *vt* to bury, entomb, cover.

ensevelissement [ãsəvlismã] *nm* burial, entombment.

ensoleillé [ãsɔleje] *a* sunny.

ensommeillé [ãsɔmeje] *a* sleepy, drowsy.

ensorceler [ãsɔrsəle] *vt* to bewitch, cast a spell upon.

ensorcellement [ãsɔrsɛlmã] *nm* witchcraft, sorcery, spell.

ensuite [ãsɥit] *ad* then, afterwards, next.

s'ensuivre [sãsɥi:vr] *vr* to follow, ensue.

entablement [ãtabləmã] *nm* coping, copestone.

entaille [ãta:j] *nf* notch, nick, slot, dent, gash.

entailler [ãtaje] *vt* to nick, notch, slot, gash.

entamer [ãtame] *vt* to cut, open, break, start.

entassement [ãtasmã] *nm* piling up stacking.

entasser [ãtase] *vt* to heap (up), stack, accumulate, pack together; *vr* to accumulate, pile up, crowd together.

entendement [ãtãdmã] *nm* understanding, reason.

entendre [ãtã:dr] *vt* to hear, understand, mean, intend; *vr* to agree, know (about en), be good (at à); **—parler de** to hear of; **— dire que** to hear that; **laisser —** to imply.

entendu [ãtãdy] *a* capable, knowing, sensible, shrewd; *ad* **bien —** of course; **c'est —** all right, agreed.

entente [ãtã:t] *nf* agreement, understanding, knowledge.

entérite [ãterit] *nf* enteritis.

enterrement [ãtɛrmã] *nm* burial, funeral.

enterrer [ãtɛre] *vt* to bury, inter.

en-tête [ãtɛ:t] *nm* heading.

entêté [ãtɛte] *a* obstinate, stubborn.

entêtement [ãtɛtmã] *nm* obstinacy, doggedness.

s'entêter [sãtɛte] *vr* to be obstinate, persist.

enthousiasme [ătuzjasm] *nm* enthusiasm.

enthousiasmer [ătuzjasme] *vt* to fill with enthusiasm, send into raptures; *vr* to be, become, enthusiastic, rave (about **pour**).

enthousiaste [ătuzjast] *a* enthusiastic; *n* enthusiast.

entiché [ătiʃe] *a* infatuated, keen, mad; — **du théâtre** stage-struck.

entichement [ătiʃmă] *nm* infatuation, craze.

s'enticher [sătiʃe] *vr* to become infatuated (with **de**), take a fancy (to **de**).

entier, -ière [ătje, jɛːr] *a* whole, entire, intact, downright, straightforward, possessive, whole-hearted.

entièrement [ătjɛrmă] *ad* entirely, completely, quite.

entomologie [ătɔmɔlɔʒi] *nf* entomology

entonner [ătɔne] *vt* to put into casks, strike up, intone; *vr* to rush, sweep.

entonnoir [ătɔnwaːr] *nm* tunnel, crater, shell-hole.

entorse [ătɔrs] *nf* sprain, twist, wrench.

entortiller [ătɔrtije] *vt* to twine, twist, wind, coax, get round; *vr* to coil, wind.

entour [ătuːr] *nm pl* neighbourhood, surroundings; *ad* à l'— round about, around.

entourage [ăturaːʒ] *nm* circle of friends, following environment.

entourer [ăture] *vt* to surround, encircle encompass.

entournure [ăturnyːr] *nf* armhole.

entracte [ătrakt] *nm* interval.

entra de [ătrɛːɔd] mutual aid.

s'entraider [sătrɛde] *vr* to help one another.

entrailles [ătraːj] *nf pl* entrails, bowels, feeling.

encrain [ătrɛ̃] *nm* spirit, dash zest, whole-heartedness.

entraînant [ătrɛnă] *a* stirring, rousing catchy.

entraînement [ătrɛnmă] *nm* dragging away enticing away enthusiasm, catchiness, training.

entraîner [ătrɛne] *vt* to drag carry away, entail, involve, lead astray, train, coach; *vr* to train, get into training.

entraîneur [ătrɛnœːr] *nm* trainer, coach.

entrave [ătraːv] *nf* fetter shackle, obstacle, hobble.

entraver [ătrave] *vt* to fetter, shackle, hobble hamper, clog.

entre [ăːtr] *prep* between, among(st).

encrebâillement [ătrəbaimă] *nm* chink, gap slit, narrow opening.

entrebâiller [ătrəbaje] *vt* to half-open, set ajar.

s'entrechoquer [sătrəʃɔke] *vr* to clash, collide, clink.

entrecôte [ătrəkɔt] *nf* (rib-)steak.

entrecouper [ătrəkupe] *vt* to intersect, interrupt; *vr* to intersect, be interrupted.

entrecroiser [ătrəkrwaze] *vt* to intersect, cross; *vr* to intersect.

entre-deux [ătrədø] *nm* space between, partition, insertion.

entrée [ătre] *nf* entry, entrance, way in, admission, inlet, import duty, entrée; — **interdite** no admittance.

entrefaite [ătrəfɛt] *nf* **sur ces —s** meanwhile.

entrefilet [ătrəfilɛ] *nm* paragraph.

entregent [ătrəʒă] *nm* tact, gumption.

entrelacement [ătrəlasmă] *nm* interlacing, interweaving, intertwining.

entrelacer [ătrəlase] *vtr* to interlace, intertwine.

entrelarder [ătrəlarde] *vt* to lard, interlard.

entremêler [ătrəmɛle] *vt* to intermingle intervene.

entremets [ătrəmɛ] *nm* sweet.

entremetteur -euse [ătrəmɛtœːr, øːz] *n* intermediary, go-between, procurer.

s'entremettre [sătrəmɛtr] *vr* to intervene, act as a go-between.

entremise [ătrəmiːz] *nf* intervention, mediation, medium, agency.

entrepont [ătrəpɔ̃] *nm* between-decks.

entreposer [ătrəpoze] *vt* to bond, warehouse, store.

entreposeur [ătrəpozœːr] *nm* warehouseman.

entrepôt [ătrəpo] *nm* bonded warehouse mart, emporium.

entreprendre [ătrəprăːdr] *vt* to undertake, contract for, take on.

entrepreneur -euse [ătrəprənœːr, øːz] *n* contractor; — **en bâtiments** builder building contractor; — **de pompes funèbres** undertaker.

entreprise [ătrəpriːz] *nf* enterprise, undertaking, concern.

entrer [ătre] *vt* to bring in; *vi* to enter, come in, go in.

entresol [ătrəsɔl] *nm* entresol, mezzanine.

entre-temps [ătrətă] *nm* interval.

entretenir [ătrətniːr] *vt* to maintain, keep (up), support, talk to, entertain; *vr* to keep oneself, converse; **s'— la main** to keep one's hand in.

entretien [ătrətjɛ̃] *nm* maintenance, (up)keep, support, conversation, interview.

entrevoir [ătrəvwaːr] *vt* to catch a glimpse of, glimpse, begin to see, foresee vaguely.

entrevue [ătrəvy] *nf* interview, conference.

entr'ouvert [ătruvɛr] *a* half-open, ajar *chasm*) gaping.

entr'ouvrir [ătruvriːr] *vt* to half-open; *vr* to gape.

énumération [enymɛrasjɔ̃] *nf* enumeration, counting up.

énumérer [enymere] *vt* to enumerate, count up, detail.

envahir [ɑ̃vaiːr] *vt* to invade, overrun, spread over.

envahisseur [ɑ̃vaisœːr] *nm* invader.

envaser [ɑ̃vaze] *vt* to silt up, choke up; *vr* to silt up, settle down in the mud.

enveloppe [ɑ̃vlɔp] *nf* envelope, cover, wrapping, sheath, outward appearance.

envelopper [ɑ̃vlɔpe] *vt* to envelop, wrap, cover, surround, shroud.

envenimer [ɑ̃vnime] *vt* to poison, inflame, embitter, aggravate; *vr* to fester, grow more bitter.

envergure [ɑ̃vɛrgyːr] *nf* breadth, span, scope; **de grande —** far-reaching.

envers [ɑ̃vɛːr] *prep* towards; *nm* reverse, wrong side; **à l'—** inside out, wrong way up.

envi [ɑ̃vi] *nm* **à l'—** vying with one another.

enviable [ɑ̃vjabl] *a* enviable.

envie [ɑ̃vi] *nf* desire, longing, inclination, envy; **avoir — de** to want (to); **porter — à** to envy.

envier [ɑ̃vje] *vt* to envy, begrudge, long for, covet, be envious of.

envieux, -euse [ɑ̃vjø, øːz] *a* envious, jaundiced.

environ [ɑ̃virɔ̃] *ad* about; *nm pl* neighbourhood, outskirts, surroundings.

environner [ɑ̃virɔne] *vt* to surround.

envisager [ɑ̃visaʒe] *vt* to look at, face, view, foresee, anticipate.

envoi [ɑ̃vwa] *nm* sending, forwarding, consignment.

envol [ɑ̃vɔl] *nm* taking wing, taking off, take-off.

s'envoler [sɑ̃vɔle] *vr* to fly away, off, take flight.

envoûtement [ɑ̃vutmɑ̃] *nm* (casting of a) spell, hoodoo, passion, craze.

envoûter [ɑ̃vute] *vt* to put a spell, a hoodoo on, hold enthralled.

envoyé [ɑ̃vwaje] *nm* envoy, representative.

envoyer [ɑ̃vwaje] *vt* to send, dispatch; **— chercher** to send for; **— dire** to send word; **— promener** to send about one's business.

épagneul [epaɲœl] *n* spaniel.

épais, -aisse [epɛ, ɛːs] *a* thick, dense.

épaisseur [epɛsœːr] *nf* thickness, density.

épaissir [epɛsiːr] *vt* to thicken, make dense; *vr* to thicken, grow dense, stout.

épanchement [epɑ̃ʃmɑ̃] *nm* pouring out, effusion, outpouring.

épancher [epɑ̃ʃe] *vt* to pour out, pour forth; *vr* to pour out one's heart, expand, unburden oneself.

épandre [epɑ̃ːdr] *vt* to spread, shed; *vr* to spread.

épanoui [epanwi] *a* in full bloom, beaming, wreathed in smiles.

épanouir [epanwiːr] *vt* to make (sth) open, bring forth, **— out;** *vr* to open out, bloom, light up, beam.

épanouissement [epanwismɑ̃] *nm* opening up, blossoming.

épargne [eparɲ] *nf* economy, thrift, saving.

épargner [eparɲe] *vt* to save, economize, be sparing of, spare.

éparpiller [eparpije] *vtr* to scatter, disperse.

épars [epaːr] *a* scattered, stray, scant.

épatant [epatɑ̃] *a* (*fam*) great, splendid, terrific.

épate [epat] *nf* **faire de l'—** to show off.

épater [epate] *vt* to astound, startle, stagger; to break the foot of.

épaule [epoːl] *nf* shoulder; **hausser les —s** to shrug one's shoulders.

épauler [epole] *vt* to shoulder; *vi* (*rifle*) to aim.

épaulette [epolɛt] *nf* shoulder-strap, epaulette.

épave [epaːv] *nf* wreck, waif, unclaimed object; *pl* flotsam, jetsam, wreckage.

épée [epe] *nf* sword.

épeler [eple] *vt* to spell.

éperdu [epɛrdy] *a* distracted, mad.

éperon [eprɔ̃] *nm* spur, buttress.

éperonner [eprɔne] *vt* to spur, urge on.

épervier [epɛrvje] *nm* sparrow-hawk, fishing net.

éphémère [efemɛːr] *a* ephemeral, short-lived, fleeting; *nf* mayfly.

épi [epi] *nm* (*corn*) ear, cluster.

épice [epis] *nf* spice; **pain d'—** (type of) gingerbread.

épicé [epise] *a* spiced, seasoned, spicy.

épicer [epise] *vt* to spice, season.

épicerie [episri] *nf* spices, groceries, grocer's shop.

épicier, -ière [episje, jɛːr] *n* grocer.

épicurien, -ienne [epikyrjɛ̃, jɛn] *a* epicurean; *n* epicure, sybarite.

épicurisme [epikyrism] *nm* epicureanism.

épidémie [epidemi] *nf* epidemic.

épidémique [epidemik] *a* epidemic (al).

épiderme [epidɛrm] *nm* epiderm(is).

épier [epje] *vt* to spy upon, watch for, listen for.

épigramme [epigram] *nf* epigram.

épilepsie [epilɛpsi] *nf* epilepsy.

épiler [epile] *vt* to remove superfluous hair from, pluck.

épilogue [epilɔg] *nm* epilogue.

épiloguer [epilɔge] *vt* to criticize, find fault with; *vi* to carp.

épinard [epinaːr] *nm* spinach.

épine [epin] *nf* thorn-bush, thorn, prickle.

épinette [epinɛt] *nf* spruce, virginal, spinet.

épineux, -euse [epinø, ø:z] *a* thorny, prickly, knotty, ticklish, tricky.

épingle [epɛ̃gl] *nf* pin; — **de nourrice** safety-pin; — **à linge** clothes-peg; **tiré à quatre —s** spruce, dapper.

épingler [epɛ̃gle] *vt* to pin, fasten with a pin.

épique [epik] *a* epic.

épiscopal [episkɔpal] *a* episcopal.

épiscopat [episkɔpa] *nm* episcopate.

épisode [epizɔd] *nm* episode.

épistolaire [epistɔlɛ:r] *a* epistolary.

épitaphe [epitaf] *nf* epitaph.

épithète [epitɛt] *nf* epithet, adjective.

épître [epi:tr] *nf* epistle.

éploré [eplɔre] *a* tearful, in tears, weeping.

éplucher [eplyʃe] *vt* to clean, peel, sift, examine.

épluchures [eplyʃy:r] *nf pl* peelings, refuse.

épointer [epwɛ̃te] *vt* to blunt, break the point of.

éponge [epɔ̃:ʒ] *nf* sponge.

éponger [epɔ̃ʒe] *vt* to mop, sponge, dab, mop up.

épopée [epɔpe] *nf* epic.

époque [epɔk] *nf* epoch, era, age, period, time; **faire — to** mark an epoch, be a landmark.

s'époumoner [sepumɔne] *vr* to talk, shout, till one is out of breath.

épousailles [epuzɑ:j] *nf pl* wedding.

épouser [epuze] *vt* to marry, wed.

épousseter [epuste] *vt* to dust, beat.

époussette [epusɛt] *nf* feather-duster.

épouvantable [epuvɑ̃tabl] *a* dreadful, appalling.

épouvantail [epuvɑ̃tɑ:j] *nm* scarecrow, bogy.

épouvante [epuvɑ̃:t] *nf* terror, dread, fright.

épouvanter [epuvɑ̃te] *vt* to terrify; *vr* to be terror-stricken, take fright.

époux, -ouse [epu, u:z] *n* husband, wife.

s'éprendre [seprɑ̃:dr] *vr* to fall in love (with **de**), take a fancy (to **de**).

épreuve [eprœ:v] *nf* proof, test, trial, ordeal, print, impression, examination paper; **à l'— de** proof against; **à toute —** foolproof.

éprouvé [epruve] *a* well-tried, sorely tried, stricken.

éprouver [epruve] *vt* to test, try, feel, suffer.

éprouvette [epruvɛt] *nf* test-tube, gauge.

épuisement [epɥizmɑ̃] *nm* exhaustion, distress, depletion, using up, emptying.

épuiser [epɥize] *vt* to exhaust, use up, tire out.

épuisette [epɥizɛt] *nf* scoop, landing-net.

épuration [epyrasjɔ̃] *nf* purification,

purging, expurgation, filtering.

épurer [epyre] *vt* to purify, filter.

équarrir [ekari:r] *vt* to square, broach, cut up.

équateur [ekwatœ:r] *nm* equator.

équation [ekwasjɔ̃] *nf* equation.

équerre [ekɛ:r] *nf* square, angle-iron, bevel.

équerrer [ekɛre] *vt* to square, bevel.

équestre [ekɛstr] *a* equestrian.

équilibre [ekilibr] *nm* equilibrium, balance stability.

équilibrer [ekilibre] *vtr* to balance.

équilibriste [ekilibrist] *n* equilibrist, acrobat, tight-rope walker.

équinoxe [ekinɔks] *nm* equinox.

équipage [ekipa:ʒ] *nm* crew, company, retinue, train, carriage and horses, apparel, rig-out, equipment; **maître d'—** master of the hounds, coxswain.

équipe [ekip] *nf* squad, gang, team, crew, shift, train (of barges); **chef d'—** foreman.

équipée [ekipe] *nf* escapade, frolic, lark.

équipement [ekipmɑ̃] *nm* equipment, accoutrement, outfit, fitting out (up).

équiper [ekipe] *vt* to equip, appoint, fit out, man.

équipier [ekipje] *nm* one of a squad, member of a team.

équitable [ekitabl] *a* just, fair.

équitation [ekitasjɔ̃] *nf* horsemanship, riding.

équité [ekite] *nf* equity, fairness, justness.

équivalent [ekivalɑ̃] *a nm* equivalent.

équivaloir [ekivalwa:r] *vi* to be equal, be equivalent, be tantamount.

équivoque [ekivɔk] *a* ambiguous, equivocal, doubtful; *nf* ambiguity.

équivoquer [ekivɔke] *vi* to equivocate, quibble.

érable [erabl] *nm* maple.

érafler [erafle] *vt* to scratch, graze, score.

éraflure [erafly:r] *nf* scratch, graze.

éraillement [erajmɑ̃] *nm* fraying, grazing, hoarseness.

érailler [eraje] *vt* to unravel, graze, roughen; *vr* to fray, become hoarse.

ère [ɛ:r] *nf* era, period, epoch.

érection [erɛksjɔ̃] *nf* putting up.

éreintant [erɛ̃tɑ̃] *a* back-breaking, killing.

éreinter [erɛ̃te] *vt* to break the back of, wear out, knock about, slate; *vr* to wear oneself out, slave.

ergot [ɛrgo] *nm* spur, dewclaw, ergot; **se dresser sur ses —s** to get on one's high horse.

ergotage [ɛrgɔta:ʒ] *nm* cavilling, quibbling.

ergoter [ɛrgɔte] *vi* to cavil, quibble, haggle.

ergoteur, -euse [ɛrgɔtœ:r, ø:z] *a* cavilling, quibbling; *n* quibbler.

ériger [eriʒe] vt to erect, put up, set up; vr to set oneself up (as en).

ermitage [ɛrmita:ʒ] nm hermitage.

ermite [ɛrmit] nm hermit.

éroder [erɔde] vt to erode, eat away.

érosion [erɔzjɔ̃] nf erosion.

érotique [erɔtik] a erotic.

érotisme [erɔtism] nm erotism.

errements [ɛrmɑ̃] nm pl erring ways.

errer [ɛre] vt to wander, roam, ramble.

erreur [ɛrœ:r] nf error, mistake, slip, fallacy.

erroné [ɛrɔne] a erroneous, false, mistaken.

éructer [erykte] vi to belch.

érudit [erydi] a learned, scholarly, erudite; nm scholar scientist

érudition [erydisjɔ̃] nf learning, scholarship.

éruption [erypsjɔ̃] nf eruption.

ès [ɛs] = en + les; docteur — sciences, doctor of science.

escabeau [ɛskabo] nm stool, steps.

escadre [ɛska:dr] nf (naut) squadron.

escadrille [ɛskadri:j] nf (naut) flotilla. (av) squadron.

escadron [ɛskadrɔ̃] nm (cavalry) squadron.

escalade [ɛskalad] nf climb(ing), scaling.

escalader [ɛskalade] vt to climb, scale.

escale [ɛskal] nf port of call, call; faire — à to put in at; sans — non-stop.

escalier [ɛskalje] nm staircase, stairs; — de service backstairs; — roulant escalator; il a l'esprit de l'— he has never a ready answer.

escalope [ɛskalɔp] nf cutlet.

escamotable [ɛskamotabl] a concealable, retractable.

escamotage [ɛskamota:ʒ] nm sleight of hand, conjuring, theft, pinching.

escamoter [ɛskamɔte] vt to conjure away, whisk away, hide, evade, pinch; (av) retract undercarriage.

escamoteur [ɛskamɔtœ:r] nm conjuror.

escampette [ɛskɑ̃pɛt] nf prendre la poudre d'— to clear off, decamp.

escapade [ɛskapad] nf escapade, adventure, prank.

escarbille [ɛskarbi:j] nf cinder, clinker.

escarbot [ɛskarbo] nm cockchafer, blackbeetle.

escarboucle [ɛskarbukl] nf carbuncle.

escargot [ɛskargo] nm snail.

escarmouche [ɛskarmuʃ] nf skirmish.

escarpé [ɛskarpe] a steep, sheer, precipitous.

escarpement [ɛskarpəmɑ̃] nm escarpment.

escarpin [ɛskarpɛ̃] nm dancing-shoe, pump.

escarpolette [ɛskarpɔlɛt] nf swing.

escarre [ɛska:r] nf bedsore, scab.

escient [ɛsjɑ̃] nm knowledge; à mon — to my knowledge; à son — wittingly.

s'esclaffer [sɛsklafe] vr to burst out laughing, guffaw.

esclandre [ɛsklɑ̃:dr] nm scandal.

esclavage [ɛsklava:ʒ] nm slavery, bondage.

esclave [ɛskla:v] n slave.

escompte [ɛskɔ̃:t] nm discount, rebate.

escompter [ɛskɔ̃te] vt to discount, allow for anticipate.

escorte [ɛskɔrt] nf escort, convoy.

escorter [ɛskɔrte] vt to escort.

escouade [ɛskwad] nf squad, section.

escrime [ɛskrim] nf fencing, swordsmanship skirmishing.

escrimer [ɛskrime] vi to fence; vr to try hard, spar.

escrimeur [ɛskrimœ:r] nm fencer, swordsman

escroc [ɛskro] nm swindler, crook.

escroquer [ɛskrɔke] vt to rob, swindle, cheat.

escroquerie [ɛskrɔkri] nf swindling, swindle.

ésotérique [esɔterik] a esoteric.

espace [ɛspas] nm space, interval.

espacer [ɛspase] vt to space (out); vr to become more and more isolated, grow fewer and fewer.

espadrille [ɛspadri:j] nf rope-soled canvas shoe.

Espagne [ɛspaɲ] nf Spain.

espagnol [ɛspaɲɔl] a Spanish; n Spaniard.

espagnolette [ɛspaɲɔlɛt] nf window-catch.

espèce [ɛspɛs] nf kind, sort, species; pl cash.

espérance [ɛsperɑ̃:s] nf hope, expectation.

espérer [ɛspere] vt to hope (for).

espiègle [ɛspjɛgl] a mischievous, arch, roguish.

espièglerie [ɛspjɛgləri] nf mischievousness, roguishness, trick, prank.

espion, -onne [ɛspjɔ̃, ɔn] n spy.

espionnage [ɛspjɔna:ʒ] nm espionage spying.

espionner [ɛspjɔne] vt to spy (on).

esplanade [ɛsplanad] nf esplanade, parade.

espoir [ɛspwa:r] nm hope.

esprit [ɛspri] nm spirit, ghost, soul, mind, wit.

esquif [ɛskif] nm skiff.

esquimau, -aude [ɛskimo] an Eskimo.

esquinter [ɛskɛ̃te] vt to exhaust, run down slate.

esquisse [ɛskis] nf sketch, draft, outline.

esquisser [ɛskise] vt to sketch, draft, outline.

esquiver [ɛskive] vt to evade, dodge, shirk; vr to slip away, dodge (off), abscond.

essai [ɛsɛ] *nm* trial, test, experiment, attempt, try, sample, essay; à l'— on trial, on approval; **coup d'**— first attempt, trial shot.

essaim [ɛsɛ̃] *nm* swarm, cluster, hive.

essaimer [esɛme] *vi* to swarm.

essayage [esɛjaːʒ] *nm* fitting.

essayer [esɛje] *v* to test, try, try on, fit, attempt, assay; *vr* to try one's hand.

essence [esãːs] *nf* essence, extract, petrol; **po**ste d'— filling-station.

essentiel, -elle [esãsjɛl] *a* essential, crucial, key; *n* the main thing, burden.

essieu [esjø] *nm* axle.

essor [esɔːr] *nm* flight, rise, scope.

essoreuse [esɔrøiz] *nf* mangle, wringer, spin-drier.

essoufflé [esufle] *a* breathless, out of breath.

essoufflement [esufləmã] *nm* breathlessness.

essouffler [esufle] *vt* to wind, put out of breath; *vr* to get breathless, winded.

essuie-glace [esɥiglas] *nm* windscreen wiper.

essuie-mains [esɥimɛ̃] *nm* towel.

essuie-pieds [esɥipje] *nm* doormat.

essuyer [esɥije] *vt* to wipe (up), clean, meet with.

est [ɛst] *nm* east.

estacade [ɛstakad] *nf* line of piles, pier, boom, stockade.

estafette [ɛstafɛt] *nf* courier, dispatch-rider.

estafilade [ɛstafilad] *nf* slash gash, rent.

estaminet [ɛstaminɛ] *nm* café, bar, public house.

estampe [ɛstãːp] *nf* print, engraving.

estamper [ɛstãpe] *vt* to stamp, emboss, diddle, sting.

estampille [ɛstãpiːj] *nf* stamp, trade mark, endorsement.

esthète [ɛstɛt] *n* aesthete.

esthétique [ɛstetik] *a* aesthetic.

estimateur -trice [ɛstimatœːr, tris] *n* valuator.

estimation [ɛstimasjɔ̃] *nf* valuation, valuing, estimate.

estime [ɛstim] *nf* esteem, regard, estimation, reckoning.

estimer [ɛstime] *vt* to estimate, valuate, calculate, guess, consider, deem, value, esteem.

estival [ɛstival] *a* summer, estival.

estivant [ɛstivã] *n* summer visitor, holiday-maker.

estoc [ɛstɔk] *nm* stock, point of sword.

estocade [ɛstɔkad] *nf* thrust.

estomac [ɛstɔma] *nm* stomach.

estomaquer [ɛstɔmake] *vt* to take s.o.'s breath away, stagger.

estompé [ɛstɔ̃pe] *a* blurred, soft, hazy.

estomper [ɛstɔ̃pe] *vt* to stump, shade off, soften the outlines of.

estrade [ɛstrad] *nf* platform, stage, dais.

estropier [ɛstrɔpje] *vt* to maim, cripple spoil, murder.

estuaire [ɛstɥɛːr] *nm* estuary, firth.

estudiantin [ɛstydjãtɛ̃] *a* student.

et [e] *cj* and; et . . et both . . and; **et vous?** what about you? do you? are you?; — **alors!** so what!

étable [etabl] *nf* cattle-shed, byre.

établi [etabli] *nm* (work-)bench.

établir [etabliːr] *vt* to establish, put up, set up, install, fix draw up, lay down; *vr* to establish oneself, settle.

établissement [etablismã] *nm* establishment, setting up, installing, drawing up, laying down.

étage [etaːʒ] *nm* story floor, tier, layer, rank.

étager [etaʒe] *vt* to arrange in tiers, terrace, stagger; *vr* to be tiered, terraced.

étagère [etaʒɛːr] *nf* rack, shelves.

étai [etɛ] *nm* stay prop, strut, mainstay.

étain [etɛ̃] *nm* tin, pewter.

étal [etal] *nm* butcher's stall, shop.

étalage [etalaːʒ] *nm* show, display, window-dressing, show window; **faire — de** to display, show off, flaunt.

étaler [etale] *vt* to display, spread out lay out, exhibit, show off, air; *vr* to stretch (oneself out), sprawl, enlarge (upon), expatiate (on).

étalon [etalɔ̃] *nm* standard, stallion.

étalonner [etalɔne] *vt* to stamp, mark standardize.

étamer [etame] *vt* to tinplate, silver, galvanize.

étameur [etamœːr] *nm* tinsmith.

étamine [etamin] *nf* coarse muslin, gauze, bunting, sieve, strainer, stamen.

étampe [etãːp] *n* stamp, die, punch.

étamper [etãpe] *vt* to stamp, mark, punch.

étanche [etãːʃ] *a* impervious, tight, insulated; — **à l'air (à l'eau)** air-(water)tight.

étancher [etãʃe] *vt* to stanch, stop (flow of), quench, make water(air)tight.

étançonner [etãsɔne] *vt* to prop up, shore up.

étang [etã] *nm* pond, pool.

étape [etap] *nf* stage, stopping-place, a day's march.

état [eta] *nm* state, condition, order, list statement, profession; **mettre qn en — de** to enable s.o. to; **être dans tous ses —s** to be in a great state.

étatisme** [etatism] *nm* state control.

état-major [etamaʒɔːr] *nm* general staff, headquarters.

étau [eto] *nm* (tec) vice.

étayer [etɛje] *vt* to prop up, shore up support; *vr* to brace oneself.

été [ete] *nm* summer

éteignoir [etɛɲwaːr] *nm* damper, extinguisher.

éteindre [etɛ̃ːdr] *vt* to extinguish, put out, switch off, dim; *vr* to go out, die (out, away, down), fade (away).

éteint [etɛ̃] *a* extinguished, extinct, dim, faint dull dead.

étendard [etɑ̃daːr] *nm* standard, flag, colours.

étendre [etɑ̃ːdr] *vt* to stretch, spread, extend, enlarge; *vr* to stretch oneself out, lie down, extend, spread, dwell (upon) hold forth (on).

étendu [etɑ̃dy] *a* extensive, wide, far-reaching.

étendue [etɑ̃dy] *nf* extent, size, expanse stretch.

éternel, -elle [etɛrnɛl] *a* eternal, everlasting, endless.

éterniser [etɛrnize] *vt* to perpetuate, drag out, on; *vr* to drag on and on.

éternité [etɛrnite] *nf* eternity.

éternuement [etɛrnymɑ̃] *nm* sneeze, sneezing.

éternuer [etɛrnɥe] *vt* to sneeze.

éthéré [etere] *a* ethereal.

éthique [etik] *a* ethical; *nf* ethics.

ethnique [ɛtnik] *a* ethnical, ethnological.

étinceler [etɛ̃sle] *vi* to sparkle, glitter, flash.

étincelle [etɛ̃sɛl] *nf* spark, flash.

étincellement [etɛ̃sɛlmɑ̃] *nm* sparkling, glittering, twinkling

étioler [etjɔle] *vt* to blanch make wilt, weaken; *vr* to blanch, wilt.

étique [etik] *a* emaciated, skinny, gaunt.

étiqueter [etikte] *vt* to label, ticket, docket.

étiquette [etikɛt] *nf* label, ticket, docket, etiquette, ceremonial; — à œillets tie-on label; — gommée stick on label.

étoffe [etɔf] *nf* material, cloth, fabric, stuff, makings.

étoffé [etɔfe] *a* ample, rich, stuffed, stout meaty.

étoile [etwal] *nf* star, asterisk; dormir à la belle — to sleep in the open.

étole [etɔl] *nf* stole.

étonnement [etɔnmɑ̃] *nm* surprise, astonishment.

étonner [etɔne] *vt* to surprise, astonish, amaze; *vr* to be surprised.

étouffant [etufɑ̃] *a* stifling, stuffy, sultry, airless.

étouffement [etufmɑ̃] *nm* choking, suffocation, attack of breathlessness.

étouffer [etufe] *vti* to suffocate, choke; *vi* damp, stifle, deaden, smother hush up.

étoupe [etup] *nf* tow, oakum.

étourderie [eturdəri] *nf* thoughtlessness giddiness.

étourdi [eturdi] *a* scatterbrained,

hare-brained, dizzy, giddy; *n* scatterbrain.

étourdir [eturdiːr] *vt* to daze, bemuse, make one's head reel, deafen, astound.

étourdissement [eturdismɑ̃] *nm* giddiness, dizziness.

étourneau [eturno] *nm* starling, scatterbrain.

étrange [etrɑ̃ːʒ] *a* strange, queer, odd.

étranger, -ère [etrɑ̃ʒe, ɛːr] *a* foreign, alien, unfamiliar, irrelevant; *n* foreigner, alien, stranger; *nm* abroad.

étranglement [etrɑ̃gləmɑ̃] *nm* strangulation, constriction, narrows, narrowing bottleneck.

étrangler [etrɑ̃gle] *vt* to throttle, strangle, choke, constrict; *vi* to choke; *vr* to narrow, gulp.

étrave [etraːv] *nf* (*naut*) bow, stem.

être [ɛːtr] *vi* to be exist; *nm* being, existence, creature; il est à écrire he is busy writing; où en êtes-vous? how far have you got? il n'en est rien nothing of the kind; le chapeau est à lui the hat is his; comme si de rien n'était as if nothing had happened.

étreindre [etrɛ̃ːdr] *vt* to embrace, clasp, grasp, wring.

étreinte [etrɛ̃ːt] *nf* embrace, hug, clasp, grip, clutch.

étrenne [etrɛn] *nf* New Year's gift.

étrenner [etrɛne] *vt* to be the first to buy from, use for the first time, handsel.

étrier [etrie] *nm* stirrup; coup de l'— stirrup-cup.

étrille [etriːj] *nf* curry-comb.

étriller [etrije] *vt* to curry-comb, thrash give a drubbing to.

étriper [etripe] *vt* to gut, clean, disembowel.

étriqué [etrike] *a* tight, skimped, cramped.

étroit [etrwa] *a* narrow, tight close, hidebound.

étroitesse [etrwatɛs] *nf* narrowness, tightness, closeness.

étude [etyd] *nf* study, research, prep. (lessons), office, chambers; à l'— under consideration; faire ses —s à to be educated at.

étudiant [etydjɑ̃] *n* student, undergraduate.

étudié [etydje] *a* studied, affected, deliberate.

étudier [etydje] *vt* to study, read, investigate; *vr* to strive, make a point (of).

étui [etɥi] *nm* case, box.

étuve [etyːv] *nf* sweating-room, drying-room.

étuver [etyve] *vt* to dry, heat, stew, steam jug.

étymologie [etimɔlɔʒi] *nf* etymology.

étymologique [etimɔlɔʒik] *a* etymological.

étymologiste [etimɔlɔʒist] *n* etymologist.

eucharistie [økaristi] nf Eucharist, Lord's Supper.

eunuque [ønyk] nm eunuch.

euphémisme [øfemism] nm euphemism.

euphonie [øfɔni] nf euphony.

Europe [ørɔp] nf Europe.

européen, -enne [ørɔpeɛ̃, ɛn] an European.

euthanasie [øtanazi] nf euthanasia.

évacuation [evakɥasjɔ̃] nf clearing, withdrawal, vacating.

évacué [evakɥe] n evacuee.

évacuer [evakɥe] vt to evacuate, empty, withdraw, vacate.

évadé [evade] a escaped; n escaped prisoner.

s'évader [sevade] vr to escape, run away, break out.

évaluation [evalɥasjɔ̃] nf valuation, assessment, estimate, appraisal.

évaluer [evalɥe] vt to valuate, assess, appraise.

évangile [evɑ̃ʒil] nm gospel.

évanouir [evanwiːr] vr to vanish, disappear, faint.

évanouissement [evanwismɑ̃] nm disappearance, fading away, swoon.

évaporation [evapɔrasjɔ̃] nf evaporation, frivolousness.

évaporé [evapɔre] a giddy, light-headed.

évaporer [evapɔre] vr to evaporate, pass off, become silly and frivolous.

évasement [evazmɑ̃] nm widening out, flare, bell-mouth.

évaser [evaze] vtr to open out, widen, flare.

évasif, -ive [evazif, iːv] a evasive.

évasion [evazjɔ̃] nf escape, evasion.

évêché [eveʃe] nm bishopric, bishop's palace.

éveil [evɛːj] nm awakening, wide-awake state, alert, alarm.

éveillé [eveje] a awake, alert, bright, alive.

éveiller [eveje] vt to wake up, awake, arouse; vr to wake up, awaken.

événement [evɛnmɑ̃] nm event, incident, happening, occurrence; dans l'— as it transpired; attendre l'— to await the outcome.

éventail [evɑ̃taːj] nm fan.

éventaire [evɑ̃tɛːr] nm flat basket.

éventé [evɑ̃te] a flat, stale, musty.

éventer [evɑ̃te] vt to air, fan, catch the scent of, get wind of; vr to fan oneself, go flat, go stale.

éventrer [evɑ̃tre] vt to disembowel, gut, smash open.

éventualité [evɑ̃tɥalite] nf eventuality, contingency, possibility.

éventuel, -elle [evɑ̃tɥɛl] a contingent, possible.

éventuellement [evɑ̃tɥɛlmɑ̃] ad possibly, should the occasion arise.

évêque [evɛːk] nm bishop.

s'évertuer [severtɥe] vr to strive, make every effort.

éviction [eviksjɔ̃] nf eviction.

évidemment [evidamɑ̃] ad evidently, obviously.

évidence [evidɑ̃ːs] nf obviousness, conspicuousness; se rendre a l'— to accept the facts; être en — to be to the fore, in the limelight.

évident [evidɑ̃] a evident, obvious, clear.

évider [evide] vt to hollow out, groove, cut away.

évier [evje] nm sink.

évincer [evɛ̃se] to evict, turn out.

évitement [evitmɑ̃] nm avoiding, shunting, loop.

éviter [evite] vt to avoid, shun, evade, save (from).

évocateur, -trice [evɔkatœːr, tris] a evocative, picturesque.

évocation [evɔkasjɔ̃] nf evocation, conjuring up, calling to mind.

évoluer [evɔlɥe] vi to manœuvre, evolve, revolve.

évolution [evɔlysjɔ̃] nf evolution, manœuvre.

évoquer [evɔke] vt to evoke, call forth, conjure up, call to mind.

exacerber [ɛgzasɛrbe] vt to exacerbate.

exact [ɛgzakt] a accurate, punctual, strict, express.

exactitude [ɛgzaktityd] nf exactness, accuracy, punctuality.

exagération [ɛgzaʒerasjɔ̃] nf exaggeration, overstatement.

exagérer [ɛgzaʒere] vt to exaggerate, overrate, magnify, overdo, go too far.

exaltation [ɛgzaltasjɔ̃] nf exaltation, extolling, excitement.

exalté [ɛgzalte] a passionate, elated, impassioned, hot-headed, quixotic.

exalter [ɛgzalte] vt to exalt, extol, excite, uplift; vr to grow enthusiastic, excited.

examen [ɛgzamɛ̃] nm examination, inspection, scrutiny; se présenter à un — to sit an examination.

examinateur, -trice [ɛgzaminatœːr, tris] n examiner.

examiner [ɛgzamine] vt to examine, inspect, scrutinize.

exaspération [ɛgzasperasjɔ̃] nf annoyance, aggravation.

exaspérer [ɛgzaspere] vt to exasperate, aggravate; vr to become exasperated.

exaucer [ɛgzose] vt to fulfil, grant.

excavation [ɛkskavasjɔ̃] nf excavation, digging out.

excédent [ɛksedɑ̃] nm surplus, excess.

excéder [ɛksede] vt to exceed, go beyond, overstrain, tire out, exasperate.

excellence [ɛksɛlɑ̃ːs] nf excellence.

excellent [ɛksɛlɑ̃] a excellent.

exceller [ɛksɛle] vi to excel.

excentricité [ɛksɑ̃trisite] nf eccentricity, oddity.

excentrique [ɛksɑ̃trik] *a* eccentric, odd, outlying; *n* eccentric character.

excepté [ɛksɛpte] *prep* except, but, barring.

excepter [ɛksɛpte] *vt* to except, exclude.

exception [ɛksɛpsjɔ̃] *nf* exception; **sauf —** with certain exceptions.

exceptionnel, -elle [ɛksɛpsjɔnɛl] *a* exceptional.

excès [ɛksɛ] *nm* excess; **à l'—** to excess, to a fault. **over-.**

excessif, -ive [ɛksɛsif, iːv] *a* excessive, undue.

excessivement [ɛksɛsivmɑ̃] *a* exceedingly, over-.

excitabilité [ɛksitabilite] *nf* excitability.

excitant [ɛksitɑ̃] *a* stimulating, exciting, hectic; *nm* stimulant.

excitation [ɛksitasjɔ̃] *nf* excitation, stimulation, incitement.

exciter [ɛksite] *vt* to excite, stimulate, arouse urge, incite, spur (on); *vr* to get worked up, roused.

exclamatif, -ive [ɛksklamatif, iːv] *a* exclamative, exclamatory.

exclamation [ɛksklamasjɔ̃] *nf* exclamation.

s'exclamer [sɛksklame] *vr* to exclaim.

exclure [ɛksklyːr] *vt* to exclude, leave out, debar.

exclusif, -ive [ɛksklyzif, iːv] *a* exclusive, sole.

exclusion [ɛksklyzjɔ̃] *nf* exclusion.

exclusivité [ɛksklyzivite] *nf* exclusiveness, sole rights.

excommunier [ɛkskɔmynje] *vt* to excommunicate.

excrément [ɛskremɑ̃] *nm* excrement, scum.

excursion [ɛskyrsjɔ̃] *nf* excursion, trip, outing, raid.

excursionniste [ɛskyrsjɔnist] *nm* excursionist, tripper.

excusable [ɛkskyzabl] *a* pardonable.

excuse [ɛkskyːz] *nf* excuse, apo·ogy.

excuser [ɛkskyze] *vt* to excuse, pardon, make excuses for; *vr* to apologize, excuse oneself; **se faire —** to withdraw, call off.

exécrable [ɛgzɛkrabl] *a* execrable, abominable.

exécration [ɛgzɛkrasjɔ̃] *nf* execration, loathing.

exécrer [ɛgzekre] *vt* to execrate, loathe.

exécutable [ɛgzekytabl] *a* feasible, practicable.

exécutant [ɛgzekytɑ̃] *n* executant, performer.

exécuter [ɛgzekyte] *vt* to execute, carry out perform, enforce; *vr* to comply.

exécuteur, -trice [ɛgzekytœːr, tris] *n* executor, -trix.

exécutif, -ive [ɛgzekytif, iːv] *a* executive.

exécution [ɛgzekysjɔ̃] *nf* execution, accomplishment, performance, en-

forcement; **mettre à —** to put into effect, carry out.

exemplaire [ɛgzɑ̃plɛːr] *a* exemplary; *nm* specimen, copy.

exemple [ɛgzɑ̃pl] *nm* example, precedent, instance, lesson; **par —** for example, fancy that!

exemp [ɛgzɑ̃] *a* exempt, free.

exempter [ɛgzɑ̃te] *vt* to exempt, excuse; *vr* to get out (of).

exemption [ɛgzɑ̃sjɔ̃] *nf* exemption, immunity.

exercé [ɛgzɛrse] *a* trained, practised.

exercer [ɛgzɛrse] *vt* to exercise exert, carry on drill, train; *vr* to be exerted, practise.

exercice [ɛgzɛrsis] *nm* drill, training practice, exercise, carrying out; financial year; **entrer en —** to take up one's duties; **en —** practising, acting.

exhalaison [ɛgzalɛzɔ̃] *nf* exhalation, odour.

exhalation [ɛgzalasjɔ̃] *nf* exhalation, exhaling.

exhaler [ɛgzale] *vt* to exhale, emit vent pour forth.

exhaustif [ɛgzostif] *a* exhaustive.

exhiber [ɛgzibe] *vt* to exhibit, show, flaunt; *vr* to make an exhibition of oneself.

exhibition [ɛgzibisjɔ̃] *nf* show, showing.

exhorter [ɛgzɔrte] *vt* to exhort, urge.

exhumer [ɛgzyme] *vt* to disinter, unearth, exhume.

exigeant [ɛgziʒɑ̃] *a* exacting, hard to please.

exigence [ɛgziʒɑ̃ːs] *nf* demand, requirement.

exiger [ɛgziʒe] *vt* to exact, demand, require call for.

exigu, -uë [ɛgzigy] *a* tiny, slender, scant, exiguous.

exiguïté [ɛgziguite] *nf* smallness, scantiness, exiguity.

exil [ɛgzil] *nm* exile.

exilé [ɛgzile] *n* exile.

exiler [ɛgzile] *vt* to exile, banish.

existence [ɛgzistɑ̃ːs] *nf* existence life, subsistence; *pl* stock on hand.

exister [ɛgziste] *vi* to exist, live, be extant.

exode [ɛgzɔd] *nm* exodus.

exonérer [ɛgzɔnere] *vt* to exonerate, exempt.

exorbitant [ɛgzɔrbitɑ̃] *a* exorbitant, extortionate.

exorciser [ɛgzɔrsize] *vt* to exorcize.

exotique [ɛgzɔtik] *a* exotic.

expansif, -ive [ɛkspɑ̃sif] *a* expansive, effusive, forthcoming.

expansion [ɛkspɑ̃sjɔ̃] *nf* expansion, expansiveness.

expatriation [ɛkspatriasjɔ̃] *nf* expatriation.

expatrier [ɛkspatrie] *vt* to expatriate; *vr* to leave one's country.

expectative [ɛkspɛktatiːv] *nf* expectation, expectancy.

expectorer [ɛkspɛktɔre] *vt* to expectorate, spit.

expédient [ɛkspedjã] *a nm* expedient; *nm* device, way.

expédier [ɛkspedje] *vt* to dispatch, send off, expedite, hurry through, get rid of.

expéditeur, -trice [ɛkspeditœːr, tris] *n* sender, shipper, consigner.

expédition [ɛkspedisjõ] *nf* dispatch, shipping, consignment, expedition.

expéditionnaire [ɛkspedisjɔnɛːr] *a* expeditionary; *nm* forwarding agent.

expérience [ɛksperjãːs] *nf* experience, experiment, test.

expérimental [ɛksperimãtal] *a* experimental, applied.

expérimentateur, -trice [ɛksperimãtatœːr, tris] *n* experimenter.

expérimentation [ɛksperimãtasjõ] *nf* experimenting.

expérimenté [ɛksperimãte] *a* experienced, skilled.

expérimenter [ɛksperimãte] *vt* to test, try; *vi* to experiment.

expert [ɛkspɛːr] *a* expert, skilled; *nm* expert, valuator.

expert-comptable [ɛkspɛrkõtabl] *nm* chartered accountant, auditor.

expertise [ɛkspɛrtiːz] *nf* survey, valuation, assessment.

expertiser [ɛkspɛrtize] *vt* to value, assess, survey.

expiation [ɛkspjasjõ] *nf* expiation.

expier [ɛkspje] *vt* to expiate, atone for.

expiration [ɛkspirasjõ] *nf* breathing out, expiry.

expirer [ɛkspire] *vi* to expire, to die.

explicatif, -ive [ɛksplikatif, iːv] *a* explanatory.

explication [ɛksplikasjõ] *nf* explanation.

explicite [ɛksplisit] *a* explicit, clear.

expliquer [ɛksplike] *vt* to explain, expound, elucidate, account for; *vr* to explain oneself, have it out (with *avec*).

exploit [ɛksplwa] *nm* deed, feat, writ.

exploitation [ɛksplwatasjõ] *nf* exploitation, cultivation, working, trading upon; — **des mines** mining.

exploiter [ɛksplwate] *vt* to exploit, cultivate, work, take advantage of.

explorateur, -trice [ɛksplɔratœːr, tris] *a* exploring; *n* explorer.

exploration [ɛksplɔrasjõ] *nf* exploration.

explorer [ɛksplɔre] *vt* to explore.

exploser [ɛksploze] *vi* to explode, blow up.

explosible [ɛksplozibl] *a* (high) explosive.

explosif, -ive [ɛksplozif, iːv] *a nm* explosive.

explosion [ɛksplozjõ] *nf* explosion.

exportateur, -trice [ɛkspɔrtatœːr, tris] *a* exporting; *n* exporter.

exportation [ɛkspɔrtasjõ] *nf* exportation; *pl* exports, export trade.

exporter [ɛkspɔrte] *vt* to export.

exposant [ɛkspozã] *n* exhibitor, petitioner.

exposé [ɛkspoze] *a* exposed, open; *nm* account, statement.

exposer [ɛkspoze] *vt* to exhibit, display, show, explain, expose, expound, lay bare.

exposition [ɛkspozisjõ] *nf* exhibition, display, show, exposure, statement.

exprès, -esse [ɛksprɛ, ɛːs] *a* express, clear, explicit; *ad* expressly, on purpose.

expressément [ɛksprɛsemã] *ad* expressly.

express [ɛksprɛːs] *nm* express train, repeating rifle.

expressif, -ive [ɛksprɛsif, iːv] *a* expressive, emphatic.

expression [ɛksprɛsjõ] *nf* expression, squeezing, manifestation (of feeling), (turn of) phrase.

exprimer [ɛksprime] *vt* to express, voice, show, squeeze, press; *vr* to express oneself.

expropriation [ɛksprɔpriasjõ] *nf* expropriation.

exproprier [ɛksprɔprie] *vt* to expropriate, dispossess.

expulser [ɛkspylse] *vt* to expel, drive out, evict, eject.

expulsion [ɛkspylsjõ] *nf* expulsion, eviction, ejection.

expurger [ɛkspyrge] *vt* to expurgate, bowdlerize.

exquis [ɛkski] *a* exquisite.

exsangue [ɛksãːg] *a* bloodless.

extase [ɛkstaːz] *nf* ecstasy, rapture, trance.

s'extasier [sɛkstazje] *vr* to go into raptures.

extatique [ɛkstatik] *a* ecstatic, rapturous.

extensible [ɛkstãsibl] *a* extensible, expanding.

extension [ɛkstãsjõ] *nf* stretching, spread, extent.

exténuation [ɛkstenyasjõ] *nf* extenuation, exhaustion.

exténuer [ɛkstenye] *vt* to extenuate, exhaust, wear out; *vr* to wear oneself out.

extérieur [ɛksterjœːr] *a* exterior, outer, external; *nm* outside, exterior, outward appearance.

exterminer [ɛkstɛrmine] *vt* to exterminate, wipe out, annihilate; *vr* to kill oneself.

externat [ɛkstɛrna] *nm* day-school, out-patients' department.

externe [ɛkstɛrn] *a* external, outside, outward; *n* day-pupil, non-resident medical student.

extincteur, -trice [ɛkstɛ̃ktœːr, tris] *a* extinguishing; *nm* fire-extinguisher.

extinction [ɛkstɛ̃ksjõ] *nf* extinction, putting out, suppression, quenching, loss.

extirper [ɛkstirpe] *vt* to extirpate,

eradicate, root out, (*corn*) remove.
extorquer [ɛkstɔrke] *vt* to extort, squeeze (out of).
extorsion [ɛkstɔrsjɔ̃] *nf* extortion.
extra [ɛkstra] *a nm* extra.
extraction [ɛkstraksjɔ̃] *nf* extraction, getting (out), origin.
extradition [ɛkstradisjɔ̃] *nf* extradition.
extraire [ɛkstrɛːr] *vt* to extract, draw (out).
extrait [ɛkstrɛ] *nm* extract, abstract, excerpt, essence; **— de mariage, de naissance** marriage, birth, certificate.
extraordinaire [ɛkstr(a)ɔrdinɛːr] *a* extraordinary, unusual; **par —** for once in a while.
extra-sensoriel [ɛkstrasɑ̃sɔrjɛl] *a* extrasensory.
extravagance [ɛkstravagɑ̃ːs] *nf* folly, wild act or statement, fantasy.
extravagant [ɛkstravagɑ̃] *a* extravagant, foolish, immoderate, far-fetched, tall.
extrême [ɛkstrɛːm] *a* extreme, far, farthest, drastic, dire; *nm* extreme limit.
extrême-onction [ɛkstrɛmɔ̃ksjɔ̃] *nf* extreme unction.
extrémiste [ɛkstremist] *n* extremist.
extrémité [ɛkstremite] *nf* extremity, end, point, tip.
exubérance [ɛgzyberɑ̃ːs] *nf* exuberance, boisterousness, superabundance, ebullience.
exubérant [ɛgzyberɑ̃] *a* exuberant, high spirited, buoyant, ebullient, superabundant.
exultation [ɛgzyltasjɔ̃] *nf* exultation, elation.
exulter [ɛgzylte] *vi* to exult, rejoice, be elated.

F

fable [fɑːbl] *nf* fable, tale; **la — de la ville** laughing-stock.
fabricant [fabrikɑ̃] *n* manufacturer, maker.
fabricateur, -trice [fabrikatœːr, tris] *n* fabricator, forger.
fabrication [fabrikasjɔ̃] *nf* making, manufacture, forging, fabrication; **— en série** mass production.
fabrique [fabrik] *nf* factory works; **marque de —** trade-mark; **conseil de —** church council.
fabriquer [fabrike] *vt* to manufacture, make, fabricate, invent; **qu'est-ce qu'il fabrique là?** what is he up to?
fabuleux, -euse [fabylø, øːz] *a* fabulous, prodigious.
façade [fasad] *nf* façade, front, face, figurehead; **de —** sham, superficial.
face [fas] *nf* face, aspect; **faire — à** to face up to, cope with; **en — de** opposite; **— à** facing.

face-à-main [fasamɛ̃] *nm* lorgnette.
facétie [fasesi] *nf* joke, jest.
facétieux, -euse [fasesjø, øːz] *a* facetious, jocular.
facette [fasɛt] *nf* facet, aspect.
fâché [fɑʃe] *a* angry, cross, annoyed, sorry.
fâcher [fɑʃe] *vt* to anger, make angry, grieve; *vr* to get angry.
fâcherie [fɑʃri] *nf* tiff, bickering.
fâcheux, -euse [fɑʃø, øːz] *a* annoying, tiresome, unfortunate, unwelcome.
facile [fasil] *a* easy, facile, ready, accommodating.
facilité [fasilite] *nf* easiness, ease, readiness, facility.
faciliter [fasilite] *vt* to facilitate, make easier.
façon [fasɔ̃] *nf* manner, fashion, way, making, workmanship; *pl* fuss, ado, ceremony; **on travaille à —** customer's own materials made up; **à — bespoke**, made to measure; **de — à so as to; de — que** so that that.
faconde [fakɔ̃d] *nf* gift of the gab, glibness.
façonner [fasɔne] *vt* to shape, fashion, work, mould.
façonnier, -ière [fasɔnje, jɛːr] *a* ceremonious, fussy; *nm* jobbing tailor.
fac-similé [faksimile] *nm* facsimile.
factage [faktaːʒ] *nm* transport, carriage, delivery.
facteur, -trice [faktœːr, tris] *n* maker of musical instruments, carrier, postman; *nm* factor.
factice [faktis] *a* artificial, imitation, sham, dummy.
factieux, -euse [faksjø, øːz] *a* factious, seditious.
faction [faksjɔ̃] *nf* guard, sentry-duty, faction; **faire — to** be on guard.
factionnaire [faksjɔnɛːr] *nm* sentry, guard.
factorerie [faktɔrəri] *nf* trading station.
facture [faktyːr] *nf* bill, invoice, workmanship, treatment.
facturer [faktyre] *vt* to invoice.
facultatif, -ive [fakyltatif, iːv] *a* optional.
faculté [fakylte] *nf* option, power, property, ability, faculty, university.
fadaise [fadɛːz] *nf* silly remark; *pl* nonsense.
fade [fad] *a* insipid, tasteless, wishy-washy, tame.
fadeur [fadœːr] *nf* insipidity, colourlessness, lifelessness, tameness.
fagot [fago] *nm* faggot, bundle of firewood; **sentir le —** to smack of heresy.
fagoté [fagɔte] *a* **mal —** shabbily dressed, dowdy.
faiblard [fɛblaːr] *a* weakish.
faible [fɛbl] *a* feeble, weak, faint,

slender, scanty; *nm* weakness, liking.

faiblesse [fɛblɛs] *nf* feebleness, weakness, frailty, failing.

faiblir [fɛbliːr] *vi* to weaken, grow weak(er), fail, faulter.

faïence [fajɑ̃ːs] *nf* crockery, delft, earthenware.

failli [faji] *nm* bankrupt.

faillibilité [fajibilite] *nf* fallibility.

faillible [fajibl] *a* fallible.

faillir [fajiːr] *vi* to fail; il faillit tomber he almost fell.

faillite [fajit] *nf* failure, bankruptcy; faire — to go bankrupt, fail.

faim [fɛ̃] *nf* hunger; avoir — to be hungry.

fainéant [fɛneɑ̃] *a* idle, lazy; *n* lazybones.

fainéanter [fɛneɑ̃te] *vi* to idle, laze about, loaf.

fainéantise [fɛneɑ̃tiːz] *nf* idleness, sloth.

faire [fɛːr] *vt* to make, do, get, be etc; il n'y a rien à — there is nothing can be done about it; cela ne fait rien it does not matter; c'est bien fait it serves you right; c'en est fait de lui he is done for; il ne fait que de partir he has just gone; faites-le monter show him up; je lui ai fait écrire la lettre I got him to write the letter; cela fait très chic that looks very smart; *vr* to become, to form, get accustomed, to mature; il se fit un silence silence fell, ensued; comment se fait-il que vous ne l'ayez pas fait? how does it come about that you did not do it?

faire-part [fɛrpaːr] *nm* card, letter.

faisable [fəzabl] *a* feasible.

faisan [fəzɑ̃] *nm* pheasant.

faisandé [fəzɑ̃de] *a* (meat) high.

faisceau [fɛso] *nm* bundle, pile, cluster, (light) beam.

faiseur, -euse [fəzœːr, øːz] *n* maker, doer, boaster.

fait [fɛ] *a* fully grown, developed; *nm* deed, act, fact, exploit; —s et gestes doings; prendre sur le — to catch in the act; dire son — à qn to give s.o. some home-truths; arriver au — to come to the point; mettre qn au — to give s.o. all the facts; de — actual(ly); en — as a matter of fact, actually; en — de as regards, in the way of.

fait-divers [fɛdivɛːr] *nm* news item.

faîte [fɛt] *nm* top, summit, ridge, cope.

falaise [falɛːz] *nf* cliff.

falbalas [falbalɑ] *nm pl* furbelows, flounces.

fallacieux, -euse [falasjø, øːz] *a* fallacious, deceitful, deceptive.

falloir [falwaːr] *v imp* to be necessary, must, need, take, require; *vr* s'en — to be lacking, be far from; il lui faut une voiture he needs a

car; il m'a fallu une heure pour le faire it took me an hour to do it; il nous faut le faire we must do it; tant s'en faut qu'il ait tort he is far from being wrong.

falot [falo] *nm* lantern; *a* dull, tame.

falsificateur, -trice [falsifikatœːr, tris] *n* falsifier, forger.

falsification [falsifikasjɔ̃] *nf* forgery, forging, adulteration.

falsifier [falsifje] *vt* to falsify, adulterate, debase, doctor.

famé [fame] *a* bien (mal) — of good (evil) repute.

famélique [famelik] *a* starving; *n* starveling.

fameux, -euse [famø, øːz] *a* famous, topping, rare, tiptop.

familial [familjal] *a* family.

familiariser [familjarize] *vt* to familiarize, acquaint; *vr* to make oneself become, familiar (with avec).

familiarité [familjarite] *nf* familiarity.

familier, -ière [familje] *a* familiar, well-known, conversant; *n* regular visitor.

famille [famiːj] *nf* family.

famine [famin] *nf* famine, starvation.

fanal [fanal] *nm* lantern, beacon.

fanatique [fanatik] *a* fanatical; *n* fanatic.

fanatisme [fanatism] *nm* fanaticism.

faner [fane] *vt* to wither, (hay) toss; *vr* to wither, wilt, fade.

faneur, -euse [fanœːr, øːz] *n* haymaker.

faneuse [fanøːz] *nf* tedder.

fanfare [fɑ̃faːr] *nf* flourish, brass band.

fanfaron, -onne [fɑ̃farɔ̃, ɔn] *a* boasting; *n* braggart.

fanfaronnade [fɑ̃farɔnad] *nf* brag, bluster.

fange [fɑ̃ːʒ] *nf* mud, mire, filth.

fangeux [fɑ̃ʒø] *a* filthy, abject.

fanion [fanjɔ̃] *nm* flag.

fanon [fanɔ̃] *nm* dewlap, wattle, fetlock.

fantaisie [fɑ̃tɛzi] *nf* imagination, fancy, whim, freak, fantasia; de — fanciful; articles de — fancy goods.

fantaisiste [fɑ̃tɛzist] *a* fanciful, whimsical.

fantasmagorique [fɑ̃tasmagɔrik] *a* weird, fantastic.

fantasque [fɑ̃task] *a* capricious, quaint, odd, temperamental.

fantassin [fɑ̃tasɛ̃] *nm* infantryman.

fantastique [fɑ̃tastik] *a* fanciful, fantastic, eerie.

fantoche [fɑ̃tɔʃ] *nm* puppet, marionette.

fantôme [fɑ̃toːm] *nm* ghost, phantom.

faon [fɑ̃] *nm* fawn.

faraud [faro] *a* dressed up, cocky.

farce [fars] *nf* farce, trick, joke, stuffing, forcemeat.

farceur, -euse [farsœːr, øːz] n wag, humorist, practical joker.

farcir [farsiːr] vt to stuff.

fard [faːr] nm rouge, make-up, paint, deceit, pretence.

fardeau [fardo] nm load, burden.

farder [farde] vt to rouge, make up, disguise; vr to make up.

farfouiller [farfuje] v'i to rummage (in, about), fumble.

faribole [faribɔl] nf idle story, nonsense.

farine [farin] nf flour, meal; **fleur de — wheat flour; — de manioc** garri, cassava flour.

farineux, -euse [farinø, øːz] a floury, mealy.

farouche [faruʃ] a fierce, wild, grim, shy, unsociable.

fascicule [fasikyl] nm fascicle, instalment, part, bunch.

fascinateur, -trice [fasinatœːr, tris] a fascinating, glamorous.

fascination [fasinasjɔ̃] nf charm.

fasciner [fasine] vt to fascinate, bewitch.

fascisme [fas(s)ism] nm fascism.

fasciste [fas(s)ist] an fascist.

faste [fast] nm pomp, show, ostentation.

fastidieux, -euse [fastidjø, øːz] a boring, tedious, dull.

fastueux, -euse [fastɥø, øːz] a showy, ostentatious.

fat [fat] a foppish; nm fop.

fatal [fatal] a fatal, fateful, inevitable; **femme —e** vamp.

fatalisme [fatalism] nm tatalism.

fatalité [fatalite] nf fatality, fate, calamity.

fatidique [fatidik] a fateful, prophetical.

fatigant [fatigɑ̃] a tiring, tiresome, irksome.

fatigue [fatig] nf fatigue, weariness, wear and tear.

fatiguer [fatige] vt to tire, fag, strain; vr to get tired, tire oneself; **— un poisson** to play a fish.

fatras [fatrɑ] nm jumble rubbish.

fatuité [fatɥite] nf fatuity, self-conceit, foppishness.

faubourg [fobuːr] nm suburb, outskirts.

faubourien, -ienne [foburjɛ̃, jɛn] a suburban.

fauché [foʃe] a stony-broke.

faucher [foʃe] vt to mow, reap, cut.

faucheur, -euse [foʃœːr, øːz] n reaper, mower.

faucheuse [foʃøːz] nf reaper, mowing-machine.

faucille [fosiːj] nf sickle.

faucon [fokɔ̃] nm falcon, hawk.

fauconnerie [fokɔnri] nf falconry, hawking, hawk-house.

faufiler [fofile] vt to baste, tack (on), insert, slip in; vr to pick one's way, slip (in, out), sneak (in, out).

faune [foːn] nm faun: nf fauna.

faussaire [fosɛːr] n forger.

fausser [fose] vt to buckle, warp, falsify, pervert.

fausset [fosɛ] nf falsetto, spigot.

fausseté [foste] nf falsity, duplicity, falsehood.

faute [tot] nf mistake, fault, offence, lack, want, foul; **— de** for want of failing.

fauteuil [fotœːj] nm easy-chair, armchair.

fauteur, -trice [fotœːr, tris] n abettor, instigator.

fautif, -ive [fotif, iːv] a faulty, wrong, at fault.

fauve [foːv] a fawn-coloured, tawny; nm fawn (colour), deer, wild beast.

fauvette [fovɛt] nf warbler.

faux, fausse [fo, foːs] a false, wrong, inaccurate, insincere, treacherous, sham, bogus; ad false(ly); nm false, fake, forgery, fabrication; nf scythe.

faux-filet [fofile] nm sirloin.

faux-fuyant [fofɥiɑ̃] nm subterfuge, dodge.

faux-monnayeur [fomɔnɛjœːr] nm coiner forger.

faveur [favœːr] nf favour, boon, kindness, grace; **billet de —** complimentary ticket.

favorable [favɔrabl] a favourable, auspicious.

favori, -ite [favɔri, it] a favourite; nm pl whiskers.

favoriser [favɔrize] vt to favour, encourage, promote.

fébrile [febril] a febrile, feverish.

fécond [fekɔ̃] a fertile, fruitful, prolific, rich.

féconder [fekɔ̃de] vt to fecundate.

fécondité [fekɔ̃dite] nf fertility, fruitfulness.

fécule [fekyl] nf starch.

fédération [federasjɔ̃] nf federation.

fédérer [federe] vtr to federate.

fée [fe] nf fairy.

féerie [feri] nf fairyland, enchantment.

féerique [ferik] a fairylike.

feindre [fɛ̃ːdr] vt to pretend, simulate sham, feign.

feinte [fɛ̃t] nf feint, pretence, sham.

fêlé [fele] a cracked, mad.

fêler [fele] vtr to crack.

félicitations [felisitasjɔ̃] nf pl congratulations.

félicité [felisite] nf bliss, happiness, felicity.

féliciter [felisite] vt to congratulate, compliment; vr to be pleased (about, with de).

félin [felɛ̃] a eline, catlike.

fêlure [felyːr] nf crack, split, rift, flaw.

femelle [fɔmɛl] a nf female, she-, hen-, cow-.

féminin [feminɛ̃] a feminine, female; nm feminine gender.

femme [fam] nf woman, female, wife; **— de ménage** charwoman.

fémur [femy:r] *nm* femur.

fenaison [fənɛzɔ̃] *nf* haymaking.

fendre [fɑ̃:dr] *vtr* to split, cleave, rend.

fenêtre [f(ə)nɛ:tr] *nf* window.

fenouil [fənu:j] *nm* fennel.

fente [fɑ̃:t] *nf* crack, split, cleft, chink, crevice, slot.

féodal [feɔdal] *a* feudal.

féodalité [feɔdalite] *nf* feudal system.

fer [fɛ:r] *nm* iron, sword, shoe; *pl* chains, irons, fetters; (*fig*) de — hard, inflexible; — **rouge** brand; — **à repasser** flat-iron; — **à friser** curling tongs.

fer-blanc [fɛrblɑ̃] *nm* tin.

ferblanterie [fɛrblɑ̃tri] *nf* tinplate, tinsmith's shop.

ferblantier [fɛrblɑ̃tje] *nm* tinsmith.

férié [ferje] *a* **jour** — holiday.

férir [feri:r] *vt* to strike.

fermage [fɛrma:ʒ] *nm* rent.

ferme [fɛrm] *a* firm, solid, steady; *ad* firmly, hard; *nf* farm, lease.

fermé [fɛrme] *a* closed, exclusive, expressionless, hidebound, blind; **être** — **à qch** to have no appreciation of sth.

fermentation [fɛrmɑ̃tasjɔ̃] *nf* fermentation, unrest.

fermenter [fɛrmɑ̃te] *vi* to ferment, be in a ferment.

fermer [fɛrme] *vt* to close, shut, fasten, turn off, switch off; *vir* to shut, to close.

fermeté [fɛrməte] *nf* firmness, steadiness, resolution.

fermeture [fɛrməty:r] *nf* shutting, close, closing(-down); —**éclair**Ⓡzip-fastener.

fermier, -ière [fɛrmje, jɛ:r] *n* farmer, farmer's wife, tenant, lessee.

fermoir [fɛrmwa:r] *nm* clasp, fastener, hasp.

féroce [ferɔs] *a* wild, savage, fierce, ferocious.

férocité [ferɔsite] *nf* ferocity, fierceness, savagery.

ferraille [fɛra:j] *nf* scrap-iron.

ferrant [fɛrɑ̃] *a* **maréchal** — farrier, shoesmith.

ferré [fɛre] *a* iron-shod, hob-nailed, good (at en); **voie** —**e** railway line.

ferrer [fɛre] *vt* to bind with iron, shoe, (*fish*) strike.

ferronnerie [fɛrɔnri] *nf* iron-foundry, ironmongery.

ferronnier [fɛrɔnje] *nm* ironworker, ironmonger.

ferroviaire [fɛrɔvjɛ:r] *a* railway; **réseau** — railway system.

ferrure [fɛry:r] *nf* piece of iron work, iron fitting, shoeing.

fertile [fɛrtil] *a* fruitful, rich.

fertiliser [fɛrtilize] *vt* to fertilize, make fruitful.

fertilité [fɛrtilite] *nf* fertility, fruitfulness.

féru [fery] *a* enamoured, struck (with **de**).

férule [feryl] *nf* ferrule, rod.

fervent [fɛrvɑ̃] *a* fervent, ardent; *n* enthusiast, fan.

ferveur [fɛrvœ:r] *nf* fervour, ardour, enthusiasm.

fesse [fɛs] *nf* buttock.

fessée [fɛse] *nf* spanking, flogging, thrashing, whipping.

fesser [fɛse] *vt* to spank, whip.

festin [fɛstɛ̃] *nm* banquet, feast.

feston [fɛstɔ̃] *nm* festoon, scallop.

festonner [fɛstɔne] *vt* to festoon, scallop.

festoyer [fɛstwaje] *vti* to feast.

fêtard [fɛta:r] *n* reveller.

fête [fɛ:t] *nf* feast, festival, holiday, festivity, treat, entertainment; **faire la** — to celebrate, go on the spree.

Fête-Dieu [fɛtdjø] *nf* Corpus Christi.

fêter [fɛte] *vt* to observe as a holiday, celebrate, entertain.

fétiche [fetiʃ] *nm* fetish, mascot.

fétide [fetid] *a* fetid, stinking.

fétu [fety] *nm* straw, wisp, jot.

feu [fø] *nm* fire, heat, light, beacon, ardour, spirit; *a* late, deceased, dead; — **roulant** drum-fire; **donner du** — **à qn** to give a light to s.o.; **faire long** — to peter out; **n'y voir que du** — to be taken in; — **d'artifice** fireworks.

feuillage [fœja:ʒ] *nm* foliage.

feuille [fœ:j] *nf* leaf, sheet; — **de présence** time-sheet.

feuillée [fœje] *nf* foliage.

feuillet [fœjɛ] *nm* (*book*) leaf, sheet, plate.

feuilleter [fœjte] *vt* to divide into sheets, turn over, thumb.

feuilleton [fœjtɔ̃] *nm* feuilleton, article, serial story.

feuillu [fœjy] *a* leafy.

feutre [fø:tr] *nm* felt, felt hat, padding.

feutrer [føtre] *vt* to felt, cover with felt.

fève [fɛ:v] *nf* bean, broad-bean.

février [fevrie] *nm* February.

fiacre [fjakr] *nm* cab, hackney-carriage.

fiançailles [fjɑ̃sɑ:j] *nf pl* engagement, betrothal.

fiancé [fjɑ̃se] *n* fiancé(e), betrothed.

fiancer [fjɑ̃se] *vt* to betroth; *vr* to become engaged.

fiasco [fjasko] *nm* fiasco; **faire** — to fizzle out, flop.

fibre [fibr] *nf* fibre, grain.

fibreux, -euse [fibrø, ø:z] *a* fibrous, stringy.

ficeler [fisle] *vt* to tie up.

ficelle [fisɛl] *nf* string.

fiche [fiʃ] *nf* pin, slip of paper, form, index-card, chit.

ficher [fiʃe] *vt* to fix, drive in, do, give; — **le camp** to clear out; *vr* **se** — **de qn** to pull s.o.'s leg; **je m'en fiche** I don't care (a damn).

fichier [fiʃje] *nm* card-index, card-index cabinet.

fichu [fiʃy] *nm* neckerchief, shawl, fichu.

fictif, -ive [fiktif, iːv] *a* fictitious, imaginary.

fiction [fiksjɔ̃] *nf* fiction, invention.

fidèle [fidɛl] *a* faithful, true, loyal.

fidélité [fidelite] *nf* fidelity, loyalty, allegiance.

fieffé [fjefe] *a* given in fief, double-dyed, arrant, arch.

fiel [fjɛl] *nm* gall, malice.

fier, fière [fjɛːr] *a* proud, haughty, fine, arrant.

se fier [səfje] *vr* to trust, rely, confide in (à).

fierté [fjɛrte] *nf* pride, haughtiness.

fièvre [fjɛːvr] *nf* fever, heat; **avoir un peu de —** to have a slight temperature; **— paludéenne** ague, malaria.

fiévreux, -euse [fjevrø, øːz] *a* feverish, fevered, hectic.

fifre [fifr] *nm* fife.

figer [fiʒe] *vt* to congeal, coagulate, clot, fix; *vr* to curdle, congeal, set; **il resta figé** he stood rooted to the spot.

fignoler [fiɲɔle] *vt* to fiddle, finick over; *vi* to fiddle about.

figue [fig] *nf* fig.

figuier [figje] *nm* fig-tree.

figurant [figyrɑ̃] *n* walker-on, extra.

figuratif, -ive [figyratif, iːv] *a* figurative.

figure [figyːr] *nf* figure, shape, face; **faire —** to cut a figure, figure (as de).

figuré [figyre] *a* figured, figurative; **ad au —** figuratively.

figurer [figyre] *vt* to represent; *vi* to look, appear, put up a show; *vr* to fancy, imagine, picture.

fil [fil] *nm* thread, yarn, wire, grain, edge, current, clue; **— de la vierge** gossamer; **de — en aiguille** bit by bit, gradually; **au — de l'eau** with the stream.

filage [filaːʒ] *nm* spinning.

filament [filamɑ̃] *nm* filament, fibre.

filandreux, -euse [filɑ̃drø, øːz] *a* stringy, long-winded.

filant [filɑ̃] *a* gluey, ropy; **étoile —e** shooting-star.

filasse [filas] *nf* tow, oakum.

filateur [filatœːr] *nm* mill-owner, spinner, shadower.

filature [filatyːr] *nf* spinning-mill, spinning, shadowing.

file [fil] *nf* file, rank; **chef de —** leader; **à la —** in single file.

filer [file] *vt* to spin, prolong, pay out, shadow; *vi* to flow gently, fly, tear along, buzz off; **— à l'anglaise** to take French leave; **— vingt nœuds** to do twenty knots.

filet [file] *nm* thread, fillet, net, thin stream, streak.

fileur, -euse [filœːr, øːz] *n* spinner.

filial [filjal] *a* filial.

filiale [filjal] *nf* branch, branch-shop, -company.

filière [filjɛːr] *nf* draw-plate, die; **—à vis** screw-plate; **passer par la —** to work one's way up; **— administrative** official channels.

filigrane [filigran] *nm* filigree, water-mark.

fille [fiːj] *nf* daughter; **jeune —** girl; **petite —** little girl; **vieille —** spinster, old maid; **— d'honneur** brides-maid; **— de salle** waitress; **— (publique)** prostitute.

fillette [fijet] *nf* little girl.

filleul [fijœl] *n* godchild.

film [film] *nm* film, picture; **tourner un —** to make a film; **— sonore** talkie.

filmer [filme] *vt* to film.

filon [filɔ̃] *nm* vein, seam.

filou [filu] *nm* pickpocket, thief, rogue.

filouterie [filutri] *nf* cheating, swindle.

fils [fis] *nm* son, boy.

filtration [filtrasjɔ̃] *nf* filtration, percolation.

filtre [filtr] *nm* filter, strainer.

filtrer [filtre] *vt* to strain, filter; *vi* to percolate, filter, seep; **— un poste** to by-pass a station.

fin [fɛ̃] *a* fine, delicate, keen, subtle, choice; *nf* end, conclusion, close, aim, purpose, object; **mener à bonne —** to bring to a successful conclusion; **en — de compte** finally.

final, -als [final] *a* final, last; *nm* finale.

finale [final] *nf* end of syllable, final (round).

finalité [finalite] *nf* finality.

finance [finɑ̃s] *nf* finance; **ministre des —s** Chancellor of the Exchequer; **ministère des —s** exchequer, treasury.

financer [finɑ̃se] *vt* to finance.

financier, -ière [finɑ̃sje, jɛːr] *a* financial; *nm* financier.

finasser [finase] *vi* to dodge, fox, finesse.

finaud [fino] *a* wily, cunning, foxy; *n* wily bird.

finesse [finɛs] *nf* fineness, delicacy, astuteness, discrimination, artful dodge.

fini [fini] *a* finished, ended, over, accomplished, done for, gone, finite; *nm* finish, perfection.

finir [finiːr] *vt* to finish, conclude, end; **cela n'en finit pas** there is no end to it; **en — avec** to have done with.

finlandais [fɛ̃lɑ̃dɛ] *a* Finnish; *n* Finn.

Finlande [fɛ̃lɑ̃d] *nf* Finland.

fiole [fjɔl] *nf* phial, flask.

fioritures [fjɔrityːr] *nf pl* flourish(es), ornamentation.

firmament [firmamã] *nm* firmament, heavens.

firme [firm] *nf* firm.

fisc [fisk] *nm* treasury, exchequer, inland revenue.

fiscal [fiskal] *a* fiscal.

fission [fisjɔ̃] *nf* — **nucléaire** nuclear fission.

fissure [fis(s)yːr] *nf* fissure, cleft.

fissurer [fis(s)yre] *vtr* to crack, split.

fixage [fiksaːʒ] *nm* fixing, fastening.

fixatif [fiksatif] *nm* fixative, hair cream.

fixe [fiks] *a* fixed, firm, steady, settled.

fixé [fikse] *a* fixed, stated, fast; **être — sur** to be clear about.

fixe-chaussettes [fiks(ə)ʃosɛt] *nm* sock suspender, (US) garter.

fixement [fiksəmã] *ad* fixedly, steadily, hard.

fixer [fikse] *vt* to fix, fasten, hold, determine, gaze at, stare at; *vr* to settle down.

flacon [flakɔ̃] *nm* bottle, flask, flagon.

flageller [flaʒɛlle] *vt* to scourge, flog.

flageoler [flaʒɔle] *vi* to tremble, shake.

flageolet [flaʒɔlɛ] *nm* flageolet, kidney-bean.

flagorner [flagɔrne] *vt* to flatter, toady to.

flagorneur, -euse [flagɔrnœːr øːz] *n* flatterer, toady.

flagrant [flagrã] *a* flagrant, glaring; **pris en — délit** caught redhanded.

flair [flɛːr] *nm* scent, flair.

flairer [flɛre] *vt* to scent, smell (out), sniff.

flamant [flamã] *nm* flamingo.

flambant [flãbã] *a* blazing, roaring, flaming; **— neuf** brand new.

flambeau [flãbo] *nm* torch, candlestick.

flambée [flãbe] *nf* blazing fire, blaze.

flamber [flãbe] *vt* to singe; *vi* to blaze, flame, kindle.

flamboyant [flãbwajã] *a* flaming, blazing, flashing, brilliant.

flamboyer [flãbwaje] *vi* to blaze, flash, glow.

flamme [flɑːm] *nf* flame, passion, fire, pennant.

flammèche [flamɛʃ] *nf* spark.

flan [flã] *nm* flan, (tec) mould.

flanc [flã] *nm* flank, side; **tirer au — ** to swing the lead, shirk, dodge the column.

flancher [flãʃe] *vi* to flinch, falter.

flanelle [flanɛl] *nf* flannel.

flâner [flane] *vi* to stroll, dawdle, lounge about, idle.

flânerie [flanri] *nf* stroll, idling, dawdling.

flâneur, -euse [flanœːr øːz] *n* stroller, idler, dawdler.

flanquer [flãke] *vt* to flank, support, throw, chuck.

flaque [flak] *nf* puddle, pool.

flasque [flask] *a* flabby, backboneless, spineless, limp.

flatter [flate] *vt* to flatter, blandish, stroke, delight; *vr* to flatter oneself, pride oneself.

flatterie [flatri] *nf* flattery.

flatteur, -euse [flatœːr, øːz] *a* flattering, pleasing, fond; *n* flatterer.

flatueux, -euse [flatyø, øːz] *a* flatulent, windy.

flatulence [flatylãːs] *nf* flatulence.

fléau [fleo] *nm* flail, scourge, plague, beam.

flèche [flɛʃ] *nf* arrow, dart, spire, pole, indicator; **faire — de tout bois** to make use of every means.

fléchir [fleʃiːr] *vt* to bend, bow, move to pity; *vi* to give way, sag, falter.

flegmatique [flɛgmatik] *a* phlegmatic, stolid.

flegme [flɛgm] *nm* phlegm, stolidness.

flemmard [flɛmaːr] *a* lazy; *n* slacker, loafer, sluggard.

flemme [flɛm] *nf* laziness.

flétrir [fletriːr] *vt* to fade, wither, brand, sully; *vr* to wither, fade.

flétrissure [fletrisyːr] *nf* fading, withering; stigma.

fleur [flœːr] *nf* flower, bloom, blossom, heyday; **fine — ** flower, pick; **à — de** on the surface of.

fleurer [flœre] *vi* to smell of, be redolent of.

fleuret [flœrɛ] *nm* foil.

fleuri [flœri] *a* in bloom, flower, flowery, florid.

fleurir [flœriːr] *vt* to adorn with flowers; *vi* to flower, bloom, flourish.

fleuriste [flœrist] *n* florist.

fleuve [flœːv] *nm* river.

flexible [flɛksibl] *a* flexible, pliant, pliable; *nm* flex.

flexion [flɛksjɔ̃] *nf* bending, buckling.

flibustier [flibystje] *nm* buccaneer, pirate.

flic [flik] *nm* bobby, cop.

flirt [flœrt] *nm* flirtation, flirting, flirt, boy-, girlfriend.

flirter [flœrte] *vi* to flirt.

flocon [flɔkɔ̃] *nm* flake, tuft.

floconneux, -euse [flɔkɔnø, øːz] *a* fleecy, fluffy.

floraison [flɔrɛzɔ̃] *nm* blossoming, flowering (time).

floral [flɔral] *a* floral.

flore [flɔːr] *nf* flora.

florissant [flɔrisã] *a* flourishing, prosperous.

flot [flo] *nm* wave, billow, surge, flood; *pl* sea; **à — afloat; à —s** in streams, in torrents.

flottaison [flɔtɛzɔ̃] *nf* water-line.

flottant [flɔtã] *a* floating, full, wide, irresolute.

flotte [flɔt] *nf* fleet, float, (*fam*) water.

flottement [flɔtmã] *nm* floating, swaying, fluctuation, hesitation.

flotter [flɔte] *vi* to float, wave, waft, waver, fluctuate.
flotteur [flɔtœːr] *nm* raftsman, float.
flotille [flɔtiːj] *nf* flotilla.
flou [flu] *a* blurred, hazy, fluffy.
fluorescent [flyɔres(s)ɑ̃] *a* fluorescent.
fluctuer [flyktɥe] *vi* to fluctuate.
fluet, -ette [flyɛ, ɛt] *a* slender, thin, delicate, spindly.
fluide [flɥid] *a nm* fluid, liquid.
fluidité [flɥidite] *nf* fluidity.
flûte [flyːt] *nf* flute, flutist, long loaf, tall champagne glass.
flûté [flyte] *a* flute-like, reed-like.
flûtiste [flytist] *nm* flautist.
flux [fly] *nm* flow, flood, rush.
fluxion [flyksjɔ̃] *nf* inflammation, swelling; — **de poitrine** pneumonia.
foc [fɔk] *nm* jib, stay-sail.
foi [fwa] *nf* faith, trust, belief, confidence, credit.
foie [fwa] *nm* liver; **crise de —** bilious attack.
foin [fwɛ̃] *nm* hay.
foire [fwaːr] *nf* fair, market.
foireux [fwarø] *a* cowardly.
fois [fwa] *nf* time, occasion; **à la —** at a time, at the same time, both.
foison [fwazɔ̃] *nf* plenty, abundance.
foisonner [fwazɔne] *vi* to abound, multiply.
folâtre [fɔlaːtr] *a* playful, frisky sportive.
folâtrer [fɔlatre] *vi* to romp, gambol, frisk.
folichon, -onne [fɔliʃɔ̃, ɔn] *a* playful, frisky.
folie [fɔli] *nf* folly, piece of folly, madness, craze.
follet, -ette [fɔlɛ, ɛt] *a* merry, gay; **feu —** will o' the wisp.
fomenter [fɔmɑ̃te] *vt* to foment, stir up.
foncé [fɔ̃se] *a* (*colour*) dark, deep.
foncer [fɔ̃se] *vt* to sink (*shaft*), drive in, bottom, darken; *vi* to rush, charge.
foncier, -ière [fɔ̃sje, jɛːr] *a* land(ed), fundamental, ground.
fonction [fɔ̃ksjɔ̃] *nf* function, office; **faire — de** to act as.
fonctionnaire [fɔ̃ksjɔnɛːr] *nm* civil servant.
fonctionnement [fɔ̃ksjɔnmɑ̃] *nm* functioning, working, behaviour.
fonctionner [fɔ̃ksjɔne] *vi* to function, work, act, run.
fond [fɔ̃] *nm* bottom, back, far end, depth, foundation, background, substance; **à —** thoroughly, up to the hilt; **au —** at heart, at bottom; **article de —** leading article; **course de —** long-distance race.
fondamental [fɔ̃damɑ̃tal] *a* basic, fundamental.
fondateur, -trice [fɔ̃datœːr, tris] *n* founder, promoter.
fondation [fɔ̃dasjɔ̃] *nf* foundation, founding.

fondement [fɔ̃dmɑ̃] *nm* foundation, base, grounds, reliance.
fondé [fɔ̃de] *a* founded, entitled, justified; *nm* **— de pouvoir** proxy, attorney.
fonder [fɔ̃de] *vt* to institute, found, lay the foundations of, base, set up; *vr* to place reliance (on **sur**), base one's reasons (on **sur**) be based.
fonderie [fɔ̃dri] *nf* foundry, smelting works, smelting.
fondeur [fɔ̃dœːr] *nm* smelter, founder.
fondre [fɔ̃dr] *vt* to smelt, cast, melt, fuse, dissolve; *vi* melt, dissolve, pounce, fall upon; *vr* to blend, melt.
fondrière [fɔ̃driɛːr] *nf* bog, quagmire.
fonds [fɔ̃] *nm* land, stock, fund, means; **acheter un —** to buy a business; **— publics** government stocks; **— consolidés** consols; **rentrer dans ses —** to get one's money back.
fondu [fɔ̃dy] *nm* fading in and out (of film), melted (butter), molten (metal), cast (bronze), well-blended (colours); **—e** *nf* fondue.
fontaine [fɔ̃tɛn] *nf* fountain, spring.
fonte [fɔ̃t] *nf* smelting, casting, cast iron, melting; **— brute** pig-iron.
fonts [fɔ̃] *nm pl* font.
football [futbɔl] *nm* football.
footing [futiŋ] *nm* walking, hiking.
for [fɔr] *nm* **dans son — intérieur** in his inmost heart.
forage [fɔraːʒ] *nm* sinking, boring, (*min*) drilling.
forain [fɔrɛ̃] *a* itinerant, travelling, *n* pedlar, stall-keeper, travelling showman.
forçat [fɔrsa] *nm* convict.
force [fɔrs] *nf* power, might, strength, prime, compulsion; *pl* strength, spring, shears; *ad* many, a lot of; **à — de** by (means of); **— leur fut d'accepter** they could do nothing but agree.
forcé [fɔrse] *a* forced, strained; **travaux —s** penal servitude.
forcément [fɔrsemɑ̃] *ad* necessarily, perforce.
forcené [fɔrsəne] *a* frenzied, frantic, desperate.
forcer [fɔrse] *vt* to force, compel, break open, strain.
forcir [fɔrsiːr] *vi* to fill out.
forer [fɔre] *vt* to sink, bore, (*min*) drill.
forestier, -ière [fɔrɛstje, jɛːr] *a* forest, forestry; *n* forester, ranger.
foret [fɔrɛ] *nm* drill, broach, brace-bit, gimlet.
forêt [fɔrɛ] *nf* forest.
foreuse [fɔrøːz] *nf* drill.
forfait [fɔrfɛ] *nm* serious crime; contract; forfeit; **déclarer —** to scratch, call off.
forfaiture [fɔrfɛtyːr] *nf* maladministration, breach.
forfanterie [fɔrfɑ̃tri] *nf* bragging, boasting.

forge [fɔrʒ] nf forge, smithy, iron-works.

forger [fɔrʒe] vt to forge, counterfeit, invent, coin.

forgeron [fɔrʒərɔ̃] nm blacksmith.

forgeur. -euse [fɔrʒœːr øːz] n forger inventor, fabricator (of news), coiner (of words).

formaliser [fɔrmalize] vt to give offence to; vr to take offence (at **de**).

formalisme [fɔrmalism] nm conventionality.

formaliste [fɔrmalist] a formal, stiff, ceremonious conventional.

formalité [fɔrmalite] nf formality, (matter of) form, ceremony ceremoniousness.

format [tɔrma] nm format, size.

formation [fɔrmasjɔ̃] nf formation, moulding forming, training.

forme [fɔrm] nf form shape, figure, mould, last boot-tree; **pour la —** as a matter of form; **être en —** to be in form, be fit.

formel -elle [fɔrmɛl, ɛl] a strict, formal definite.

former [fɔrme] vt to shape, form, create, mould, train; vr to take shape set; **le train se forme à Dijon** the train starts from Dijon.

formidable [fɔrmidabl] a fearsome, terrific stupendous.

formule [fɔrmyl] nf formula form.

formuler [fɔrmyle] vt to formulate, draft put into words, state.

forniquer [fɔrnike] vi to fornicate.

fort [fɔːr] a strong large. stout solid, loud violent; ad very. hard, loud, fast; nm strong part strong man, fort; **c'est plus — que moi** I can't help it; **le plus — c'est que the** best (worst) of it is; **se faire — de** to undertake to; **vous y allez un peu —** you are going a bit too far; **au — de l'hiver** in the dead of winter.

forteresse [fɔrtərɛs] nf fortress, stronghold.

fortifiant [fɔrtifjɑ̃] a fortifying, invigorating, bracing; nm tonic.

fortification [ɔrtifikasjɔ̃] nf fortification fortifying

fortifier [fɔrtifje] vt to fortify, strengthen invigorate; vr to grow stronger.

fortuit [fɔrtɥi] a chance, fortuitous, casual, accidental.

fortuité [fɔrtɥite] nf fortuitousness, casual nature

fortune [fɔrtyn] nf fortune, (piece of) luck; **de —** makeshift; **dîner à la — du pot** to take pot luck; **homme à bonnes —s** lady's man, ladykiller.

fortuné [fɔrtyne] a fortunate well-off, wealthy.

fosse [foːs] nf hole, pit, grave; **— d'aisances** cesspool.

fossé [fose] nm ditch drain moat.

fossette [fosɛt, fɔsɛt] nf dimple.

fossile [fosil] nm fossil.

fossoyer [foswaje, fɔswaje] vt to trench, ditch.

fossoyeur [foswajœːr, fɔswajœːr] nm grave-digger.

fou, fol, folle [fu fɔl, fɔl] a mad, insane, foolish, silly, frantic, frenzied; n lunatic, madman, mad-woman, fool, (chess) bishop; **être — de** to be beside oneself with; **succès — terrific success, hit; monde — enormous crowd.

foudre [fudr] nf thunderbolt, light-ning. **coup de — thunderbolt, bolt from the blue, love at first sight.

foudroyant [fudrwajɑ̃] a crushing, overwhelming smashing, lightning.

foudroyé [fudrwaje] a blasted, dumbfounded.

foudroyer [fudrwaje] vt to blast, strike down.

fouet [fwɛ] nm whip, lash, whisk; **coup de — cut, fillip.

fouetter [fwɛte] vt to whip, flog, whisk lash; vi to batter (against), flap.

fougère [fuʒɛːr] nf fern, bracken.

fougue [fug] nf dash fire.

fougueux, -euse [fugø, øːz] a spirited, dashing mettlesome, fiery.

fouille [fuːj] nf excavation, search-ing.

fouiller [fuje] vt to excavate, dig, search, ransack, rifle; vi to rum-mage.

fouillis [fuji] nm confusion, jumble, muddle.

fouine [fwin] nf stone-marten.

fouiner [fwine] vi to ferret, nose about. interfere.

fouir [fwiːr] vt to dig, burrow.

foulard [fulaːr] nm silk handkerchief, foulard, neckerchief, scarf.

foule [ful] nf crowd, throng, mob.

foulée [fule] nf tread, stride; pl spoor track.

fouler [fule] vt to crush, tread on, (ankle sprain.

foulure [fulyːr] nf sprain, wrench.

four [fuːr] nm oven. kiln; failure; **faire — to be a flop.

fourbe [furb] a crafty; n rascal, knave, double-dealer.

fourberie [furbəri] nf double-dealing, deceit, cheating, treachery.

fourbir [furbiːr] vt to polish, rub up.

fourbu [furby] a foundered, dead-beat, done.

fourche [furʃ] nf fork, pitchfork; **faire — (of roads) to fork.

fourcher [furʃe] v to fork; vi to branch off, fork; **la langue lui a fourché** he made a slip of the tongue.

fourchette [furʃɛt] nf (table) fork, wishbone; **c'est une bonne — he is fond of his food

fourchu [furʃy] a forked, cloven.

fourgon [furgɔ̃] nm van, truck, wagon, poker, rake.

fourgonner [furgɔne] *vti* to poke, rake.

fourmi [furmi] *nm* ant; **avoir des —s dans le bras** to have pins and needles in one's arm.

fourmilier [furmilje] *nm* anteater.

fourmilière [furmilje:r] *nf* anthill, ants' nest.

fourmillement [furmijmɑ̃] *nm* tingling, prickly feeling, swarming.

fourmiller [furmije] *vi* to swarm, teem, tingle.

fournaise [furne:z] *nf* furnace.

fourneau [furno] *nm* furnace, stove, (*pipe*) bowl; **haut —** blast furnace.

fournée [furne] *nf* batch (of loaves).

fourni [furni] *a* stocked, plentiful, thick.

fournil [furni] *nm* bakehouse.

fourniment [furnimɑ̃] *nm* equipment, accoutrement.

fournir [furni:r] *vt* to supply, provide, furnish; *vr* to provide oneself (with **de**).

fournisseur, -euse [furnisœ:r, ø:z] *n* purveyor, supplier, caterer, tradesman.

fourniture [furnity:r] *nf* supplying, providing; *pl* supplies, requisites.

fourrage [fura:ʒ] *nm* fodder, forage.

fourrager [furaʒe] *vt* to pillage; *vi* to forage, rummage.

fourragère [furaʒe:r] *nf* lanyard; forage wagon.

fourré [fure] *a* fur-lined; *n* thicket.

fourreau [furo] *nm* scabbard, case, sheath, sleeve.

fourrer [fure] *vt* to line with fur, cram, stuff, poke, stick; *vr* to thrust oneself, butt (into **dans**).

fourre-tout [furtu] *nm* hold-all.

fourreur [furœ:r] *nm* furrier.

fourrier [furje] *nm* quarter-master.

fourrure [fury:r] *nf* fur, lining.

fourvoyer [furvwaje] *vt* to mislead, lead astray; *vr* to lose one's way, go wrong.

foyer [fwaje] *nm* hearth, firebox, seat, home centre.

frac [frak] *nm* dress-coat.

fracas [fraka] *nm* din, uproar, crash, clash.

fracasser [frakase] *vtr* to shatter, smash.

fraction [fraksjɔ̃] *nf* fraction.

fracture [frakty:r] *nf* fracture, break, breaking open.

fracturer [fraktyre] *vt* to fracture, force; *vr* to break, fracture.

fragile [fraʒil] *a* fragile, flimsy, frail, breakable, brittle.

fragilité [fraʒilite] *nf* fragility, frailty, weakness.

fragment [fragmɑ̃] *nm* fragment, chip, snatch.

fragmentaire [fragmɑ̃te:r] *a* fragmentary.

fragmenter [fragmɑ̃te] *vt* to divide into fragments.

frai [frɛ] *nm* spawn(ing).

fraîcheur [frɛʃœ:r] *nf* cool(ness), chilliness, freshness.

fraîchir [frɛʃi:r] *vi* to grow cooler, freshen.

frais, fraîche [frɛ, frɛʃ] *a* cool, fresh, recent, new, new-laid; *nm* coolness, cool air; **prendre le —** to take the air.

frais [frɛ] *nm* *pl* expenses, charge, outlay, cost; **faux —** incidental expenses; **divers —** sundries.

fraise [frɛ:z] *nf* strawberry; ruff; milling cutter.

fraiser [frɛze] *vt* to plait, frill, mill.

framboise [frɑ̃bwa:z] *nf* raspberry.

franc, franche [frɑ̃, frɑ̃:ʃ] *a* free, frank, downright, open, honest, candid, above-board; *ad* frankly, candidly; *nm* (*coin*) franc; **jouer — jeu** to play fair, play the game; **corps —** volunteer corps.

français [frɑ̃sɛ] *a* French; *n* Frenchman, Frenchwoman.

France [frɑ̃:s] *nf* France.

franchement [frɑ̃ʃmɑ̃] *ad* frankly, candidly, really, downright.

franchir [frɑ̃ʃi:r] *vt* to jump (over), clear, cross.

franchise [frɑ̃ʃi:z] *nf* freedom, immunity, frankness, straightforwardness.

franciser [frɑ̃size] *vt* to gallicize, frenchify.

franc-maçon [frɑ̃masɔ̃] *nm* freemason.

franc-maçonnerie [frɑ̃masɔ̃nri] *nf* freemasonry.

franco [frɑ̃ko] *ad* free, carriage-free, duty paid.

franc-parler [frɑ̃parle] *nm* frankness, plain-speaking.

franc-tireur [frɑ̃tirœ:r] *nm* sniper, sharpshooter, freelance (journalist).

frange [frɑ̃:ʒ] *nf* fringe.

franquette [frɑ̃kɛt] *nf* **à la bonne —** simply, without fuss.

frappant [frapɑ̃] *a* striking, impressive.

frappe [frap] *nf* minting, striking, impression.

frapper [frape] *vt* to strike, smite, knock, insist, stamp, mint; **— le champagne** to ice champagne.

frasque [frask] *nf* escapade, prank, trick.

fraternel, -elle [fratɛrnɛl, ɛl] *a* fraternal, brotherly.

fraterniser [fratɛrnize] *vi* to fraternize.

fraternité [fratɛrnite] *nf* fraternity, brotherhood.

fratricide [fratrisid] *a* fratricidal; *nm* fratricide.

fraude [fro:d] *nf* fraud, fraudulence, deceit, deception; **passer en —** to smuggle in, out.

frauder [frode] *vt* to defraud, swindle; *vi* to cheat.

fraudeur, -euse [frodœ:r, ø:z] *n* smuggler, defrauder.

frauduleux, -euse [frodylø, øːz] *a* fraudulent.

frayer [frɛje] *vt* open up, clear; *vi* to spawn, associate (with *avec*).

frayeur [frɛjœːr] *nf* fear, fright, dread.

fredaine [frədɛn] *nf* escapade, prank.

fredonner [frədɔne] *vt* to hum.

frégate [fregat] *nf* frigate.

frein [frɛ̃] *nm* bit, brake, curb; **serrer (desserrer) le —** to put on (release) the brake; **ronger son —** to champ at the bit, fret; **sans —** unbridled.

freiner [frɛne] *vt* to brake, check; *vi* to brake.

frelater [frəlate] *vt* to adulterate, water down.

frêle [frɛːl] *a* frail, delicate, weak, spare.

frelon [frəlɔ̃] *nm* hornet, drone.

frémir [fremiːr] *vi* to quiver, rustle, tremble, flutter.

frémissement [fremismɑ̃] *nm* quivering, rustling, shaking, quaking.

frêne [frɛːn] *nm* ash-tree.

frénésie [frenezi] *nf* frenzy, madness.

frénétique [frenetik] *a* frantic, frenzied.

fréquence [frekɑ̃ːs] *nf* frequency, prevalence, rate.

fréquent [frekɑ̃] *a* frequent, quick.

fréquentation [frekɑ̃tasjɔ̃] *nf* frequenting.

fréquenter [frekɑ̃te] *vt* to frequent, haunt, associate with; *vi* to visit, go to.

frère [frɛːr] *nm* brother, friar.

fresque [frɛsk] *nf* fresco.

fret [frɛ] *nm* freight, chartering, load.

fréter [frete] *vt* to freight, charter.

frétillant [fretijɑ̃] *a* frisky, lively.

frétiller [fretije] *vi* to wag, wriggle, quiver.

fretin [frətɛ̃] *nm* (*of fish*) fry; **menu —** small fry.

frette [frɛt] *nf* hoop, band.

fretter [frɛte] *vt* to hoop.

friable [friabl] *a* crumbly, friable.

friand [friɑ̃] *a* fond of (good things); **morceau —** titbit.

friandise [friɑ̃diːz] *nf* fondness for good food, titbit; *pl* sweets.

fricassée [frikase] *nf* fricassee, hash.

friche [friʃ] *nf* waste land, fallow land.

fricoter [frikɔte] *vti* to stew, cook.

friction [friksjɔ̃] *nf* friction rubbing, massage, rub-down, dry shampoo.

frictionner [friksjɔne] *vt* to rub, massage, rub down, give a dry shampoo to.

frigide [friʒid] *a* frigid.

frigo [frigo] *nm* fridge.

frigorifier [frigɔrifje] *vt* to chill, refrigerate.

frigorifique [frigɔrifik] *a* chilling, refrigerating; *nm* cold store, frozen meat, refrigerator.

frileux, -euse [frilø, øːz] *a* sensitive to the cold, chilly.

frimas [frima] *nm* hoarfrost, rime.

frime [frim] *nf* pretence, sham, eyewash.

frimousse [frimus] *nf* face of child, girl, cat.

fringale [frɛ̃gal] *nf* **avoir la —** to be ravenous.

fringant [frɛ̃gɑ̃] *a* lively, frisky, spruce, smart.

friper [fripe] *vt* to crush, crumple; *vr* to get crushed.

fripier -ière [fripje, jɛːr] *n* old-clothes dealer.

fripon, -onne [fripɔ̃, ɔn] *a* roguish; *n* rogue, rascal, hussy

friponnerie [fripɔnri] *nf* roguery.

fripouille [fripuːj] *nf* rotter, bad egg, cad.

frire [friːr] *vti* to fry.

frit [fri] *a* fried; **(pommes de terres) —es** chips, (US) French fried (potatoes).

frise [friːz] *nf* frieze.

frisé [frize] *a* curly, frizzy.

friser [frize] *vt* to curl, frizz, skim, graze, verge on; *vi* to curl, be curly.

frisoir [frizwaːr] *nm* curling-tongs, curling-pin.

frisson [frisɔ̃] *nm* shudder, thrill, shiver, tremor.

frissonnement [frisɔnmɑ̃] *nm* shudder(ing), shiver(ing).

frissonner [frisɔne] *vt* to shudder, shiver, quiver.

friture [frityːr] *nf* frying, fry; *pl* crackling noises, atmospherics.

frivole [frivɔl] *a* frivolous, empty, flimsy.

frivolité [frivɔlite] *nf* frivolity, emptiness, trifle.

froc [frɔk] *nm* monk's cowl, habit, gown

froid [frwa] *a* cold, chilly, cool, frigid unimpressed; *nm* cold, chill, coldness, coolness; **il fait —** it is cold; **il a —** he is cold; **— de loup** bitter cold; **prendre —** to catch cold; **battre —** à to cold-shoulder.

froideur [frwadœːr] *nf* coldness, chilliness, frigidity.

froissement [frwasmɑ̃] *nm* crumpling, bruising, rustle, causing offence

froisser [frwase] *vt* to bruise, crumple jostle, offend, ruffle; *vr* to take offence, become crumpled.

frôler [frole] *vt* to graze, brush (against).

fromage [frɔmaːʒ] *nm* cheese; **— de tête** brawn.

fromager [frɔmaʒe] *nm* silk cotton tree.

froment [frɔmɑ̃] *nm* wheat.

fronce [frɔ̃ːs] *nf* gather, pucker.

froncement [frɔ̃smɑ̃] *nm* puckering, wrinkling.

froncer [frɔ̃se] *vt* to pucker, wrinkle, gather; **— les sourcils** to knit one's brows, frown, scowl.

frondaison [frɔ̃dɛzɔ̃] *nf* foliation, foliage.

fronde [frɔ̃:d] *nf* catapult, sling, frond.

fronder [frɔ̃de] *vt* to sling, criticize, jeer at.

frondeur, -euse [frɔ̃dœ:r, ø:z] *a* critical always against authority; *n* slinger, critic scoffer.

front [frɔ̃] *nm* brow, forehead, face, front, cheek, effrontery; **de —** abreast.

frontière [frɔ̃tjɛ:r] *nf* frontier, border line boundary

frontispice [frɔ̃tispis] *nm* title page, frontispiece.

fronton [frɔ̃tɔ̃] *nm* pediment, fronton, ornamental front.

frottement [frɔtmɑ̃] *nm* rubbing, chafing, friction

frotter [frɔte] *v* to rub, polish, chafe, (*match*) strike; *vi* to rub; *vr* to rub. come up (against à), keep company (with à).

frottoir [frɔtwa:r] *nm* polisher, scrubbing brush.

frou-frou [frufru] *nm* rustle, swish.

frousse [frus] *nf* funk.

fructifier [fryktifje] *vi* to fructify, bear fruit.

fructueux -euse [fryktɥø ø:z] *a* fruitful, profitable.

frugal [frygal] *a* frugal, thrifty.

frugalité [frygalite] *nf* frugality.

fruit [frɥi] *nm* fruit, *pl* fruits, advantages benefits; **— sec** (*person*) failure.

fruiterie [frɥitri] *nf* fruit trade, fruiterer s, greengrocer's shop.

fruitier -ière [frɥitje ιε:r] *a* fruit; *n* fruiterer greengrocer

frusques [frysk] *nf pl* togs, clothes.

fruste [fryst] *a* worn, defaced, rough, coarse.

frustrer [frystre] *vt* to frustrate deprive, do (out of **de**).

fugace [fygas] *a* fleeting, transient.

fugacité [fygasite] *nf* transience.

fugitif -ive [fyʒitif i:v] *a* fleeting, passing; *n* fugitive.

fugue [fyg] *nf* fugue, escapade, flying visit jaunt.

fuir [fɥi:r] *vt* to run away from, shun, avoid; *vi* to flee, run away recede, leak

fuite [fɥit] *nf* flight, escape, leak(age).

fulgurant [fylgyrɑ̃] *a* flashing, striking.

fuligineux, -euse [fyliʒinø, ø:z] *a* soot-coloured, sooty.

fulminer [fylmine] *vt* to fulminate; *vi* to inveigh.

fume-cigarette [fymsigaret] *nm* cigarette-holder.

fumée [fyme] *nf* smoke, steam; *pl* fumes.

fumer [fyme] *vt* to smoke, cure. manure; *vi* to smoke, fume, steam.

fumet [fymɛ] *nm* smell, bouquet, aroma, scent.

fumeur, -euse [fymœ:r, ø:z] *n* smoker, curer.

fumeux, -euse [fymø, ø:z] *a* smoky, smoking heady hazy.

fumier [fymje] *nm* dung, manure, dunghill, stable-litter.

fumigation [fymigasjɔ̃] *nf* fumigation.

fumiger [fymiʒe] *vt* to fumigate.

fumiste [fymist] *nm* stove-setter practical joke; hoaxer leg-puller.

fumisterie [fymistri] *nf* stove-setting hoax practical joke, leg-pulling

fumoir [fymwa:r] *nm* smoke-room.

funambule [fynɑ̃byl] *n* tight-rope walker

funambulesque [fynɑ̃bylɛsk] *a* fantastic queer.

funèbre [fynɛbr] *a* funeral, funereal, dismal

funérailles [fynɛra:j] *nf pl* funeral.

funéraire [fynɛrɛ:r] *a* funeral, funerary.

funeste [fynɛst] *a* fatal, deadly, disastrous baleful.

funiculaire [fynikylɛ:r] *a* funicular; *nm* cable-railway.

fur [fy:r] *cj* **au — et à mesure que** (gradually) as, in proportion as; **ad au — et à mesure** gradually as one goes along

furet [fyrɛ] *nm* ferret, Nosy Parker.

fureter [fyrte] *vi* to ferret, pry, cast about.

fureur [fyrœ:r] *nf* fury, rage, madness, passion craze; **faire —** to be all the rage.

furibond [fyribɔ̃] *a* furious.

furie [fyri] *n* fury, rage passion.

furieux, -euse [fyrjø, jø:z] *a* furious, wild, raging in a rage.

furoncle [fyrɔ̃:kl] *nm* boil.

furtif -ive [fyrtif i:v] *a* stealthy covert furtive secret, sneaking.

fusain [fyzɛ̃] *nm* spindletree, charcoal sketch.

fuseau [fyzo] *nm* spindle, bobbin.

fusée [fyze] *nf* spindle, fuse, rocket; **— à pétard** maroon; **— éclairante** flare; **— porte-amarre** rocket apparatus.

fuselage [fyzla:ʒ] *nm* uselage.

fuseler [fyzle] *vt* to taper.

fuser [fyze] *vi* to fuse, melt, run, spread.

fusible [fyzibl] *a* fusible, easily melted.

fusil [fyzi] *nm* gun, rifle, steel; **coup de —** gunshot, report; **attraper un coup de —** to get stung, overcharged.

fusilier [fyzilje] *nm* fusilier; **— marin** marine.

fusillade [fyzijad] *nf* firing, volley.

fusiller [fyzije] *vt* to shoot, execute.

fusion [fyzjɔ̃] *nf* fusion, melting, smelting, union, amalgamation.

fusionner [fyzjɔne] *vti* to merge, unite, amalgamate.

fustiger [fysti3e] *vt* to flog, thrash.

fût [fy] *nm* stock, shaft, handle, barrel cask, bole.

futaie [fytɛ] *nf* wood, forest, very large tree.

futaille [fytɑːj] *nf* cask. barrel, tun.

futé [fyte] *a* crafty, smart.

futile [fytil] *a* futile, frivolous, trivial.

futilité [fytilite] *nf* futility, triviality.

futur [fytyːr] *a* future, to come; *nm* future tense; *n* future husband, wife.

fuyant [fɥijɑ̃] *a* fleeing, fleeting, receding, elusive, shifty.

fuyard [fɥijaːr] *n* fugitive, runaway.

G

gabardine [gabardin] *nf* raincoat, gaberdine.

gabarit [gabari] *nm* gauge, templet, model, mould, stamp.

gabegie [gabʒi] *nf* dishonesty, underhand dealings, muddle, mismanagement.

gabier [gabje] *nm* topman, seaman.

gâche [gɑːʃ] *nf* staple, wall-hook.

gâcher [gɑʃe] *vt* to mix, waste, spoil, bungle, make a mess of.

gâchette [gɑʃɛt] *nf* trigger.

gâchis [gɑʃi] *nm* wet mortar, mud, slush, mess.

gaffe [gaf] *nf* boat-hook, gaff, blunder, bloomer.

gaffer [gafe] *vt* to hook, gaff; *vi* blunder.

gaga [gaga] *a* doddering; *nm* dodderer.

gage [gaːʒ] *nm* pledge, pawn, security, token, forfeit; *pl* wages, pay.

gager [gaʒe] *vt* to wager, bet, pay, hire.

gageure [gaʒyːr] *nf* wager, bet.

gagnant [gaɲɑ̃] *a* winning; *n* winner.

gagne-pain [gaɲpɛ̃] *nm* livelihood, bread-winner.

gagner [gaɲe] *vt* to earn, gain, win (over), get, reach, overtake, catch up (on); *vr* to be catching, be infectious.

gai [ge, gɛ] *a* gay, merry, blithe, cheerful, bright.

gaieté [gete, gɛte] *nf* gaiety, mirth, merriment, cheerfulness.

gaillard [gajaːr] *a* strong, stalwart, hearty, merry, spicy; *nm* fellow, fine, jolly fellow; — **d'avant** forecastle; — **d'arrière** quarter-deck; —e *nf* wench, strapping, bold young woman.

gaillardise [gajardiːz] *nf* jollity, gaiety; *pl* broad humour, suggestive stories.

gain [gɛ̃] *nm* gain, profit, earnings, winning(s); — **de cause** decision in one's favour.

gaine [gɛːn] *nf* case, cover, sheath, corset.

gala [gala] *nm* gala, fête.

galamment [galamɑ̃] *ad* gallantly, courteously, bravely.

galant [galɑ̃] *a* attentive to women, gay, amatory; **intrigue** —e loveaffair; — **homme** gentleman; *nm* lover, ladies' man.

galanterie [galɑ̃tri] *nf* attention to women, love affair, compliment, gift.

galbe [galb] *nm* contour, outline, figure.

gale [gal] *nf* itch, scabies, mange, scab.

galère [galɛːr] *nf* galley.

galerie [galri] *nf* gallery, arcade, balcony, circle.

galet [galɛ] *nm* pebble, shingle, roller, pulley.

galette [galɛt] *nf* cake, ship's biscuit; (*fam*) money, dough.

galeux, -euse [galø, øːz] *a* itchy, mangy, scabby; **brebis** —**se** black sheep.

galimatias [galimatja] *nm* nonsense, gibberish.

Galles [gal] *nm* **pays de** — Wales.

gallois [galwa] *a nm* Welsh; *n* Welshman.

galon [galɔ̃] *nm* braid, stripe, band.

galonner [galɔne] *vt* to trim with braid, lace.

galop [galo] *nm* gallop.

galoper [galɔpe] *vti* to gallop.

galopin [galɔpɛ̃] *nm* urchin, young scamp.

galvaniser [galvanize] *vt* to galvanize.

galvauder [galvode] *vt* to botch, besmirch; *vr* to sully one's name.

gambade [gɑ̃bad] *nf* gambol, caper.

gambader [gɑ̃bade] *vi* to gambol, caper, romp.

gamelle [gamɛl] *nf* tin-can, messtin dixie.

gamin [gamɛ̃] *nm* urchin, youngster, nipper; —e *nf* (pert) little girl.

gamme [gam] *nf* gamut, scale, range.

gammée [game] *a* **croix** — swastika.

ganache [ganaʃ] *nf* lower jaw; duffer, old fogey.

gangrène [gɑ̃grɛn] *nf* gangrene, canker.

gangrener [gɑ̃grəne] *vt* to gangrene, canker; *vr* to mortify, become cankered.

gangreneux, -euse [gɑ̃grənø, øːz] *a* gangrenous, cankerous.

ganse [gɑːs] *nf* braid, gimp, piping, loop.

gant [gɑ̃] *nm* glove, gauntlet.

gantelé [gɑ̃tle] *a* gauntleted, mailed.

ganter [gɑ̃te] *vt* to glove, *vr* to put on one's gloves.

ganterie [gɑ̃tri] *nf* glove-making, -factory, -shop.

gantier [gɑ̃tje] *nm* glover.

garage [gara:ʒ] nm garage, shed, depot, storage, parking, shunting; **voie de** — siding.

garagiste [garaʒist] nm garage-keeper proprietor.

garant [garɑ̃] nm guarantor, surety, bail, authority warrant, guarantee.

garantie [garɑ̃ti] nf guarantee, pledge, security, safeguard, underwriting.

garantir [garɑ̃ti:r] vt to guarantee, warrant, vouch for, underwrite, shield, insure.

garçon [garsɔ̃] nm boy, lad, son, young man, chap, fellow, bachelor, servant, assistant, waiter; — **d'honneur** groomsman, best man; — **manqué** tomboy.

garçonnet [garsɔnɛ] nm little boy.

garçonnière [garsɔnjɛ:r] nf bachelor's, single man's flat.

garde [gard] nf guardianship, care, guard, watch(ing), keeping, charge, flyleaf, the Guards; **prendre** — to take care, beware (à of), be careful (à of), to take good care (à to), be careful not (de to); **sans y prendre** — inadvertently; nm keeper, guard, watchman, guardsman.

garde-à-vous [gardavu] nm au — at attention.

garde-barrière [gardbarjɛ:r] n (level-crossing) gatekeeper.

garde-boue [gardəbu] nm mudguard, splash board.

garde-champêtre [gardʃɑ̃pɛtr] nm village policeman.

garde-chasse [gardəʃas] nm gamekeeper.

garde-corps [gardəkɔr] nm parapet, balustrade, rail.

garde-feu [gardəfø] nm fireguard, fender.

garde-fou [gardəfu] nm parapet, rail(ing).

garde-malade [gardmalad] n nurse.

garde-manger [gardmɑ̃ʒe] nm larder, pantry.

garder [garde] vt to guard, protect, look after, preserve, keep, remain in, observe, respect; vr to protect oneself, beware (de of), take care not (de to), refrain (de from).

garde-robe [gardərɔb] nf wardrobe, clothes.

gardeur, -euse [gardœ:r, ø:z] n keeper, herdsman.

gardien, -ienne [gardjɛ̃, jɛn] n guardian, caretaker, warder, attendant, goalkeeper; — **de la paix** policeman.

gare [ga:r] excl look out! take care! mind!; nf station; — **maritime** harbour station.

garer [gare] vt to shunt, garage, park; vr to stand aside take cover, pull to one side shunt.

se gargariser [səgargarize] vr to gargle.

gargarisme [gargarism] nm gargle.

gargouille [gargu:j] nf gargoyle.

garnement [garnəmɑ̃] nm **mauvais** — scamp, rascal.

garni [garni] a well-filled, garnished, furnished; nm furnished room(s).

garnir [garni:r] vt to furnish, provide, fill, stock, fit out, trim, garnish, garrison.

garnison [garnizɔ̃] nf garrison.

garniture [garnity:r] nf fittings, furnishings, trimming(s), decoration, lining, lagging, packing.

garrotter [garɔte] vt to strangle, to bind tightly.

gars [ga] nm boy, lad, young fellow.

Gascogne [gaskɔɲ] nf Gascony.

gascon, -onne [gaskɔ̃, ɔn] an Gascon.

gaspiller [gaspije] vt to waste, squander, spoil.

gastrique [gastrik] a gastric.

gastronome [gastrɔnɔm] nm gastronome.

gastronomie [gastrɔnɔmi] nf gastronomy.

gastronomique [gastrɔnɔmik] a gastronomical.

gâteau [gɑto] nm cake, tart; — **de miel** honeycomb.

gâter [gɑte] vt to spoil, pamper, damage, taint, mar; vr to deteriorate; **enfant gâté** spoilt child.

gâterie [gɑtri] nf excessive indulgence, spoiling; pl treats, dainties, delicacies.

gâteux, -euse [gɑtø, ø:z] a senile, in one's dotage; n dotard.

gauche [go:ʃ] a left, warped, clumsy, awkward; nf left.

gaucher [goʃe] a left-handed; n left-hander.

gaucherie [goʃri] nf clumsiness, awkwardness.

gauchir [goʃi:r] vti to warp, buckle.

gaudriole [godriɔl] nf broad joke.

gaufre [go:fr] nf waffle.

gaufrer [gofre] vt to crimp, emboss, crinkle

gaufrette [gofrɛt] nf water biscuit.

gaule [go:l] nf pole, stick, fishing-rod.

gaulois [golwa] a Gallic; **esprit** — free, broad, Gallic wit; n Gaul.

gauloiserie [golwazri] nf broad, free joke.

se gausser [səgose] vr to poke fun (de at), taunt.

gaver [gave] vt to cram, stuff; vr to gorge.

gaz [ga:z] nm gas; pl flatulence, wind; **à pleins** — flat out.

gaze [ga:z] nf gauze.

gazelle [gazɛl] nf gazelle.

gazer [gaze] vt to cover with gauze, gloss over, tone down, veil, gas; vi to speed, cause ructions go well.

gazeux, -euse [gazø, ø:z] a gaseous, aerated, gassy.

gazogène [gazɔʒɛn] a gas-producing; nm gazogene, gas-generator.

gazomètre [gazɔmɛtr] *nm* gasometer.

gazon [gazɔ̃] *nm* grass, turf, sod, lawn, green.

gazouillement [gazujmɑ̃] *nm* twittering, warbling, babbling, prattling.

gazouiller [gazuje] *vi* to twitter, warble, babble, prattle.

geai [ʒe] *nm* jay.

géant [ʒeɑ̃] *a* gigantic, giant; *n* giant, giantess.

geignard [ʒeɲaːr] *a* whining, fretful; *nm* whiner, sniveller.

geindre [ʒɛ̃dr] *vi* to whine, whimper.

gélatine [ʒelatin] *nf* gelatine.

gelé [ʒ(ə)le] *a* frozen, frostbitten.

gelée [ʒ(ə)le] *nf* frost, jelly.

geler [ʒ(ə)le] *vti* to freeze; *vr* to freeze, solidify.

gelure [ʒəlyːr] *nf* frostbite.

gémir [ʒemiːr] *vi* to moan, groan, wail.

gémissement [ʒemismɑ̃] *nm* moan (ing), groan(ing), wail(ing).

gênant [ʒɛnɑ̃] *a* in the way, awkward, embarrassing.

gencive [ʒãsiːv] *nf* gum.

gendarme [ʒãdarm] *nm* gendarme, policeman.

gendre [ʒãːdr] *nm* son-in-law.

gêne [ʒɛn] *nf* embarrassment, discomfort, constraint, want, straitened circumstances; **sans —** free and easy.

gêné [ʒene] *a* embarrassed, ill at ease, awkward, hard up.

généalogie [ʒenealɔʒi] *nf* genealogy, pedigree.

généalogique [ʒenealɔʒik] *a* genealogical, family.

gêner [ʒene] *vt* to cramp, constrain, pinch, hamper, inconvenience, embarrass; *vr* to inconvenience oneself; **ne pas se —** not to put oneself out, to make oneself at home.

général [ʒeneral] *a* general, prevailing; *nm* general; **— de division** major-general; **— de brigade** brigadier-general.

généralement [ʒeneralmɑ̃] *ad* generally.

généralisation [ʒeneralizasjɔ̃] *nf* generalization.

généraliser [ʒeneralize] *vt* to generalize; *vr* to become general, spread.

généralissime [ʒeneralisim] *nm* generalissimo, commander-in-chief.

généralité [ʒeneralite] *nf* generality.

générateur, -trice [ʒeneratœːr, tris] *a* generating, generative; *nm* generator.

génération [ʒenerasjɔ̃] *nf* generation.

généreux, -euse [ʒenerø, øːz] *a* generous.

générique [ʒenerik] *a* generic; *nm* (*film*) credits.

générosité [ʒenerozite] *nf* generosity.

genèse [ʒənɛːz] *nf* genesis.

genêt [ʒ(ə)nɛ] *nm* (*bot*) broom.

genévrier [ʒənevrie] *nm* juniper.

génial [ʒenjal] *a* inspired, bright, brilliant.

génie [ʒeni] *nm* genius, spirit, (army) engineers; **— civil** civil engineering.

genièvre [ʒənjɛːvr] *nm* juniper, gin.

génisse [ʒenis] *nf* heifer.

genou [ʒənu] *nm* knee.

genre [ʒãːr] *nm* kind, sort, type, genus, family, style.

gens [ʒã] *n pl* people, folk(s), men, servants.

gentiane [ʒãsjan] *nf* gentian.

gentil, -ille [ʒãti, iːj] *a* nice, pretty, kind, sweet, good.

gentilhomme [ʒãtijɔm] *nm* nobleman.

gentillesse [ʒãtijɛs] *nf* prettiness, graciousness, kindness; *pl* nice things.

gentiment [ʒãtimɑ̃] *ad* nicely, prettily, sweetly.

géographie [ʒeɔgrafi] *nf* geography.

géographique [ʒeɔgrafik] *a* geographical.

geôle [ʒoːl] *nf* gaol, prison.

geôlier [ʒolje] *nm* gaoler, warder.

géologie [ʒeɔlɔʒi] *nf* geology.

géologue [ʒeɔlɔg] *nm* geologist.

géométrie [ʒeɔmetri] *nf* geometry.

géométrique [ʒeɔmetrik] *a* geometrical.

gérance [ʒerãːs] *nf* management, managership.

géranium [ʒeranjɔm] *nm* geranium.

gérant [ʒerã] *n* manager(ess), director, managing-.

gerbe [ʒɛrb] *nf* sheaf, spray, shower.

gerçure [ʒɛrsyːr] *nf* chap, crack, fissure.

gérer [ʒere] *vt* to manage.

germain [ʒɛrmɛ̃] *a* full, first.

germanique [ʒɛrmanik] *a* Germanic.

germe [ʒɛrm] *nm* germ, (*potato*) eye, seed.

germer [ʒɛrme] *vi* to germinate, sprout, shoot.

germination [ʒɛrminasjɔ̃] *nf* germination.

gésier [ʒezje] *nm* gizzard.

gésir [ʒeziːr] *vi* to lie.

geste [ʒɛst] *nm* gesture, movement, motion, wave.

gesticuler [ʒɛstikyle] *vi* to gesticulate.

gestion [ʒɛstjɔ̃] *nf* management, administration, care.

gibecière [ʒipsjɛːr] *nf* game-bag, satchel.

giberne [ʒibɛrn] *nf* wallet, pouch, satchel.

gibier [ʒibje] *nm* game.

giboulée [ʒibule] *nf* (hail) shower.

giboyeux, -euse [ʒibwajø, øːz] *a* well stocked with game.

giclement [ʒikləmɑ̃] *nm* splashing, spirting.

gicler [ʒikle] *vi* to splash (up), squelch, spurt (out).

gicleur [ʒiklœːr] *nm* spray, jet.

gifle [ʒifl] *nf* slap, smack, cuff.

gifler [ʒifle] *vt* to slap, smack.

gigantesque [ʒigātɛsk] *a* gigantic, huge.

gigot [ʒigo] *nm* leg of mutton.

gigue [ʒig] *nf* jig.

gilet [ʒilɛ] *nm* waistcoat, vest, jacket; — tricoté cardigan.

gingembre [ʒēʒãːbr] *nm* ginger.

girafe [ʒiraf] *nf* giraffe.

giratoire [ʒiratwaːr] *a* gyratory, roundabout.

girofle [ʒirɔfl] *nm* clove.

giroflée [ʒirɔfle] *nf* stock, wallflower.

giron [ʒirɔ̃] *nm* lap.

girouette [ʒirwɛt] *nf* weathercock, turncoat.

gisant [ʒizã] *a* lying, recumbent.

gisement [ʒizmã] *nm* layer, seam, stratum, bearing.

gîte [ʒit] *nm* resting-place, lair, home, shelter, bed, seam, leg of beef.

givre [ʒiːvr] *nm* hoarfrost.

glabre [glɑːbr] *a* smooth, hairless, clean-shaven.

glace [glas] *nf* ice, glass, mirror, window, icing, ice-cream.

glacé [glase] *a* frozen, icy, chilled, stony, iced, glossy.

glacer [glase] *vt* to freeze, chill, ice, glaze.

glacial [glasjal] *a* icy, frozen, frigid, stony.

glacier [glasje] *nm* glacier, ice-cream vendor, manufacturer of mirrors.

glacière [glasjɛːr] *nf* ice-house, ice-box, freezer.

glacis [glasi] *nm* slope, bank, glaze.

glaçon [glasɔ̃] *nm* block of ice, ice-floe, icicle.

gladiateur [gladjatœːr] *nm* gladiator.

glaïeul [glajœl] *nm* gladiolus.

glaise [glɛːz] *nf* clay.

glaive [glɛv] *nm* sword, sword-fish.

gland [glã] *nm* acorn, tassel.

glande [glãːd] *nf* gland.

glaner [glane] *vt* to glean.

glaneur, -euse [glanœːr, øːz] *n* gleaner.

glapir [glapiːr] *vi* to yelp, yap, (fox) bark.

glas [glɑ] *nm* knell, passing-bell.

glauque [gloːk] *a* glaucous, seagreen.

glissade [glisad] *nf* slip, slide, sliding.

glissant [glisã] *a* slippery, sliding.

glissement [glismã] *nm* sliding, slip, gliding, glide.

glisser [glise] *vi* to slip, skid, slide, glide, pass over; *vt* to slip; *vr* to glide, creep, steal into (dans).

glisseur, -euse [glisœːr, øːz] *n* slider; *nm* speedboat, glider.

glissière [glisjɛːr] *nf* groove, slide, shoot; à —s sliding.

global [glɔbal] *a* total, inclusive, lump.

globe [glɔb] *nm* globe, orb, ball.

globulaire [glɔbylɛːr] *a* globular.

globule [glɔbyl] *nm* globule.

gloire [glwaːr] *nf* glory, fame, boast, pride, halo.

glorieux. -euse [glɔrjø, øːz] *a* glorious, proud, conceited, boastful: *nm* braggart.

glorifier [glɔrifje] *vt* to glorify praise; *vr* to boast.

gloriole [glɔrjɔl] *nf* notoriety, vainglory, credit.

glose [gloːz] *nf* gloss, note, comment, criticism.

gloser [gloze] *vt* to gloss, criticize.

glossaire [glɔsɛːr] *nm* glossary.

glouglou [gluglu] *nm* gurgle, gobblegobble.

glousser [gluse] *vi* to cluck, gobble, gurgle, chuckle.

glouton, -onne [glutɔ̃, ɔn] *a* greedy gluttonous; *n* glutton.

gloutonnerie [glutɔnri] *nf* gluttony.

glu [gly] *nf* bird-lime.

gluant [glyã] *a* gluey, sticky.

glutineux [glytinø] *a* glutinous.

glycérine [gliserin] *nf* glycerine.

glycine [glisin] *nf* wistaria.

go [go] *ad* tout de — straight off.

gobelet [gɔblɛ] *nm* goblet, cup, tumbler.

gobe-mouches [gɔbmuʃ] *nm* flycatcher, ninny wiseacre.

gober [gɔbe] *vt* to swallow, gulp down; *vr* to fancy oneself.

gobeur, -euse [gɔbœːr, øːz] *n* conceited person.

godasses [gɔdas] *nfpl* boots.

godet [gɔde] *nm* mug, cup, flare, gore.

godille [gɔdiːj] *nf* scull.

godiller [gɔdije] *vi* to scull.

goéland [gɔelã] *nm* seagull.

goélette [gɔelɛt] *nf* schooner.

goémon [gɔemɔ̃] *nm* seaweed.

goguenard [gɔgnaːr] *a* bantering, joking, jeering.

goinfre [gwɛ̃ːfr] *nm* glutton.

goinfrerie [gwɛ̃frəri] *nf* gluttony, guzzling.

goitre [gwaːtr] *nm* goitre.

golf [gɔlf] *nm* golf, golf-course.

golfe [gɔlf] *nm* gulf, bay.

gombo [gɔ̃bo] *nm* okro.

gomme [gɔm] *nf* gum, (india)rubber, eraser.

gommeux, -euse [gɔmø, øːz] *a* gummy, sticky; *nm* pretentious man dude.

gond [gɔ̃] *nm* hinge.

gondolant [gɔ̃dɔlã] *a* funny, killing.

gondole [gɔ̃dɔl] *nf* gondola.

gondoler [gɔ̃dɔle] *vi* to warp, buckle, sag; *vr* to warp, buckle, shake with laughter.

gondolier [gɔ̃dɔlje] *nm* gondolier.

gonflage [gɔ̃flaːʒ] *nm* inflation, tyrepressure.

gonflement [gɔ̃fləmã] *nm* inflating, inflation, distension.

gonfler [gɔ̃fle] *vt* to swell, inflate, blow up; *vir* to swell, become distended.

gonfleur [gɔ̃flœ:r] nm inflator, air-pump.

goret [gɔrɛ] nm piglet.

gorge [gɔrʒ] nf throat, gullet, breast, gorge, (mountain) pass; **rire à —** déployée to laugh heartily; **rendre — to disgorge; faire des —s chaudes de** to laugh heartily at the expense of.

gorgée [gɔrʒe] nf mouthful, gulp.

gorger [gɔrʒe] vt to stuff, gorge.

gorille [gɔri:j] nm gorilla.

gosier [gozje] nm throat, gullet.

gosse [gɔs] n youngster, child, kid.

gothique [gɔtik] a gothic.

goudron [gudrɔ̃] nm tar.

goudronner [gudrɔne] vt to tar, spray with tar.

gouffre [gufr] nm gulf, abyss, chasm.

goujat [guʒa] nm boor, cad, black-guard.

goujaterie [guʒatri] nf boorishness, churlish act.

goujon [guʒɔ̃] nm gudgeon, stud, pin.

goulet [gulɛ] nm gully, narrows, narrow channel.

goulot [gulo] nm (bottle)neck.

goulu [guly] a greedy, gluttonous.

goupille [gupi:j] nf (linch)pin.

goupillon [gupijɔ̃] nm holy-water sprinkler.

gourde [gurd] nf gourd, water-bottle, flask, fool.

gourdin [gurdɛ̃] nm cudgel.

gourmand [gurmɑ̃] a greedy, very fond (of); n gourmand, glutton.

gourmander [gurmɑ̃de] vi to guzzle; vt to scold.

gourmandise [gurmɑ̃di:z] nf greediness, gluttony; pl sweet things.

gourme [gurm] nf impetigo, wild oats.

gourmet [gurmɛ] nm epicure.

gousse [gus] nf pod, shell; **— d'ail** clove of garlic.

gousset [gusɛ] nm waistcoat pocket, gusset.

goût [gu] nm taste, flavour, relish, liking, style, manner.

goûter [gute] vt to taste, enjoy, relish, take a snack between meals; nm (afternoon) snack, tea.

goutte [gut] nf drop, drip, dram, splash, spot, sip, gout.

goutteux, -euse [gutø, ø:z] a gouty.

gouttière [gutjɛ:r] nf gutter, rain-pipe, spout.

gouvernail [guvɛrna:j] nm rudder, helm.

gouvernante [guvɛrnɑ̃:t] nf gover-ness, housekeeper.

gouverne [guvɛrn] nf guidance, direction, steering; pl controls.

gouvernement [guvɛrnəmɑ̃] nm government.

gouverner [guvɛrne] vt to govern, control, steer.

gouverneur [guvɛrnœ:r] nm gover-nor.

goyavier [gwajavje] nm guava tree.

grabuge [graby:ʒ] nm quarrel, row.

grâce [gras] nf grace, gracefulness, favour, pardon, mercy; **de bonne, de mauvaise —** willingly, un-willingly; **— à** thanks to.

gracier [grasje] vt to pardon, reprieve.

gracieux, -euse [grasjø, ø:z] a graceful, gracious, free.

gracile [grasil] a slim, slender.

gradation [gradasjɔ̃] nf gradation.

grade [grad] nm grade, rank, degree.

gradé [grade] nm noncommissioned officer.

gradin [gradɛ̃] nm step, tier.

graduel, -elle [gradɥɛl] a gradual.

graduer [gradɥe] vt to graduate, grade.

grain [grɛ̃] nm grain, corn, berry, bean, particle, speck, squall; **— de beauté** beauty spot, mole; **— de plomb** pellet; **— de raisin** grape.

graine [grɛn] nf seed.

grainetier [grɛntje] nm seedsman, corn-chandler.

graissage [grɛsa:ʒ] nm greasing, lubrication.

graisse [grɛs] nf grease, fat; **— de rognon** suet; **— de rôti** dripping.

graisser [grɛse] vt to grease, lubricate.

graisseux, -euse [grɛsø, ø:z] a greasy, oily, fatty.

grammaire [gramɛ:r] nf grammar.

grammairien, -ienne [grammɛrjɛ̃, jɛn] nm grammarian.

grammatical [grammatikal] a gram-matical.

gramme [gram] nm gram(me).

gramophone [gramɔfɔn] nm gramo-phone.

grand [grɑ̃] a tall, large, big, main, great, noble, high, grown up, grand; **en —** on a large scale, full size; nm grandee; pl grown-ups, great ones.

grand'chose [grɑ̃ʃo:z] pr much.

grandement [grɑ̃dmɑ̃] ad greatly, largely, grandly, ample, high.

grandeur [grɑ̃dœ:r] nf size, height, magnitude, grandeur, Highness.

grandiloquence [grɑ̃dilɔkɑ̃:s] nf grandiloquence.

grandiose [grɑ̃djo:z] a grandiose, imposing.

grandir [grɑ̃di:r] vi to grow (up, tall); vt to increase, make taller, magnify.

grand'mère [grɑ̃mɛ:r] nf grand-mother.

grand'messe [grɑ̃mɛs] nf high mass.

grand'peine [grɑ̃pɛn] ad **à —** with great difficulty.

grand-père [grɑ̃pɛ:r] nm grand-father.

grand'route [grɑ̃rut] nf highway, high road, main road.

grand'rue [grɑ̃ry] nf main street, high street.

grands-parents [grɑ̃parɑ̃] nm pl grandparents.

grange [grɑ̃:ʒ] nf barn.

granit [grani(t)] *nm* granite.

graphique [grafik] *a* graphic; *nm* diagram, graph.

graphite [grafit] *nm* graphite, plumbago.

grappe [grap] *nf* bunch, cluster.

grappin [grapɛ̃] *nm* grapnel, hook, grab; *pl* climbing-irons.

gras, -se [grɑ, grɑːs] *a* fat(ty), fatted, rich, oily, greasy, thick, ribald, heavy; **faire —** to eat meat; **jour —** meat day; *nm* fat.

grassement [grɑsmɑ̃] *ad* generously.

grasset, -ette [grasɛ, ɛt] *a* plump, fattish, chubby.

grasseyer [grɑseje] *vi* to burr, roll one's 'r's.

grassouillet, -ette [grɑsujɛ, ɛt] *a* plump, chubby.

gratification [gratifikasjɔ̃] *n* †bonus, gratuity.

gratifier [gratifje] *vt* to bestow, confer.

gratin [gratɛ̃] *nm* burnt part, upper ten; **au —** with bread-crumbs and grated cheese.

gratiné [gratine] *a* with bread-crumbs.

gratis [gratis] *ad* gratis, free (of charge).

gratitude [gratityd] *nf* gratitude, gratefulness.

gratte-ciel [gratsjɛl] *nm* skyscraper.

gratte-pieds [gratpje] *nm* scraper.

gratter [grate] *vt* to scratch, scrape (out).

gratuit [gratɥi] *a* gratuitous, free, uncalled for.

gratuité [gratɥite] *nf* gratuitousness.

grave [grɑːv] *a* grave, solemn, serious, low-pitched.

graveleux, -euse [gravlø, øːz] *a* gritty, ribald.

graver [grave] *vt* to engrave, cut, carve; **— à l'eau-forte** to etch.

graveur [gravœːr] *nm* engraver, carver.

gravier [gravje] *nm* gravel, grit.

gravir [graviːr] *vt* to climb.

gravitation [gravitasjɔ̃] *nf* gravitation.

gravité [gravite] *nf* gravity, severity, seriousness, weight, low pitch.

graviter [gravite] *vi* to gravitate, revolve.

gravure [gravyːr] *nf* engraving, print, illustration; **— à l'eau-forte** etching; **— sur bois** wood-cut.

gré [gre] *nm* liking, taste, will; **au — de** according to, at the mercy of; **bon —, mal —** willy-nilly; **de — à —** by mutual consent; **de — ou de force** by fair means or foul; **savoir — à** to be grateful to; **savoir mauvais — à** to be angry with.

grec, grecque [grɛk] *a nm* Greek; *n* Greek.

Grèce [grɛs] *nf* Greece.

gredin [grədɛ̃] *nm* rogue.

gréement [gremɑ̃] *nm* rigging, gear.

gréer [gree] *vt* to rig, sling.

greffe [grɛf] *nf* graft, grafting.

greffer [grefe] *vt* to graft.

greffier [grɛfje] *nm* clerk of court.

grêle [grɛːl] *a* small, slender, thin, high-pitched; *nf* hail, shower.

grêlé [grɛle] *a* pock-marked.

grêler [grɛle] *v imp* to hail.

grêlon [grɛlɔ̃] *nm* hailstone.

grelot [grəlo] *nm* bell.

grelotter [grələte] *vi* to tremble, shake, shiver.

grenade [grənad] *nf* pomegranate, grenade; **— à main** hand-grenade; **— sous-marine** depth-charge.

grenadine [grənadin] *nf* grenadine.

grenier [grənje] *nm* granary, loft, attic, garret.

grenouille [grənuːj] *nf* frog, funds.

grès [grɛ] *nm* sandstone.

grésiller [grezije] *vi* to crackle, sputter, sizzle.

grève [grɛːv] *nf* beach, shore, strand, strike; **se mettre en —** to go on strike; **faire —** to be on strike; **— de solidarité** strike in sympathy; **— perlée** go-slow; **— sur le tas** sit-down strike; **— de zèle** work to rule.

grever [grəve] *vt* to burden, mortgage

gréviste [grevist] *n* striker.

gri(s)-gri(s) [grigri] *nm* amulet.

gribouillage [gribujaːʒ] *nm* scrawl, scribble.

gribouiller [gribuje] *vt* to scrawl, scribble.

grief [griɛf] *nm* grievance.

grièvement [griɛvmɑ̃] *ad* severely, seriously, deeply.

griffe [grif] *nf* claw, talon, clip, facsimile signature, writing; *pl* clutches.

griffer [grife] *vt* to scratch, claw, stamp.

griffonnage [grifɔnaːʒ] *nm* scrawl, scribble.

griffonner [grifɔne] *vt* to scrawl, scribble.

grignoter [griɲɔte] *vt* nibble, pick at.

grigou [grigu] *nm* skinflint, miser.

gril [gri] *nm* gridiron, grill.

grillade [grijad] *nf* grilled meat, grill.

grillage [grijaːʒ] *nm* grilling, toasting, roasting, grating, netting, lattice-work.

grille [griːj] *nf* grating, railings, iron-barred gate, entrance gate, grid.

griller [grije] *vt* to grill, roast, scorch, rail in, grate.

grillon [grijɔ̃] *nm* (*insect*) cricket.

grimace [grimas] *nf* grimace, wry face.

grimacer [grimase] *vi* to grimace, make faces.

grimacier, -ière [grimasje, jɛːr] *a* grimacing, grinning, simpering.

se grimer [səgrime] *vr* to make up (one's face).

grimper [grɛpe] *vti* to climb.

grimpeur, -euse [grɛ̃pœːr, øːz] *a* climbing; *n* climber.

grincer [grɛ̃se] *vi* to grate, grind, gnash, creak.

grincheux, -euse [grɛ̃ʃø, øːz] *a* grumpy, surly; *n* grumbler.

griot [grio] *nm* storyteller, praise singer.

grippe [grip] *nf* dislike, influenza.

grippé [gripe] *a* suffering from influenza.

grippe-sou [gripsu] *nm* skinflint, miser.

gris [gri] *a* grey, dull, cloudy, intoxicated.

grisâtre [grizɑːtr] *a* greyish.

griser [grize] *vt* to make tipsy, intoxicate; *vr* to become intoxicated, be carried away (with de).

griserie [grizri] *nf* tipsiness, intoxication, rapture.

grisonner [grizɔne] *vi* to turn grey.

grisou [grizu] *nm* firedamp.

grive [griːv] *nf* thrush.

grivois [grivwa] *a* broad, ribald, licentious.

grivoiserie [grivwazri] *nf* ribald, broad joke.

grog [grɔg] *nm* grog, toddy.

grognard [grɔɲaːr] *a* grumbling; *n* grumbler.

grognement [grɔɲəmɑ̃] *nm* grunt (ing), growl(ing), grumbling.

grogner [grɔɲe] *vi* to grunt, growl, snarl, grumble.

grognon [grɔɲɔ̃] *a* grumbling, querulous; *n* grumbler.

groin [grwɛ̃] *nm* snout.

grommeler [grɔmle] *vi* to grumble, mutter.

grondement [grɔ̃dmɑ̃] *nm* growl (ing), snarl(ing), rumble, roaring.

gronder [grɔ̃de] *vi* to growl, snarl, rumble, mutter, roar, grumble; *vt* to scold, rebuke.

gronderie [grɔ̃dri] *nf* scolding.

grondeur, -euse [grɔ̃dœːr, øːz] *a* grumbling, scolding; *n* grumbler, scold.

groom [grum] *nm* groom, page(boy).

gros, -se [gro, groːs] *a* big, large, heavy, stout, thick, coarse, plain, rough, loud, gruff, gross, pregnant; — **bonnets** bigwigs; — **mots** bad language; *nm* bulk, mass, chief part, hardest part; **en** — in bulk, wholesale.

groseille [grozɛːj] *nf* currant (red, white); — **à maquereau** gooseberry.

groseillier [grozɛje] *nm* currant-bush.

grossesse [grosɛs] *nf* pregnancy.

grosseur [grosœːr] *nf* size, bulk, thickness, swelling.

grossier, -ière [grosje, jɛːr] *a* coarse, rough, gross, vulgar, rude.

grossièreté [grosjerte] *nf* coarseness, roughness, rudeness, offensive remark.

grossir [grosiːr] *vt* to enlarge, magnify; *vi* to increase, swell, grow bigger.

grossissement [grosismɑ̃] *nm* increase, swelling, magnifying, enlargement.

grotesque [grɔtɛsk] *a* ludicrous.

grotte [grɔt] *nf* grotto.

grouiller [gruje] *vi* to swarm, be alive (with de); *vr* to get a move on, hurry up.

groupe [grup] *nm* group, clump, cluster, party.

groupement [grupmɑ̃] *nm* grouping, group.

grouper [grupe] *vt* to group, arrange; *vr* to form a group, gather.

gruau [gryo] *nm* wheat flour; — **d'avoine** oatmeal, gruel.

grue [gry] *nf* crane, prostitute.

gruger [gryʒe] *vt* to fleece, plunder, sponge on.

grumeau [grymo] *nm* clot, lump.

gué [ge] *nm* ford.

guenille [gəniːj] *nf* rag, tatter.

guenon [gənɔ̃] *nf* she-monkey, ugly woman.

guêpe [gɛːp] *nf* wasp; — **maçonne** mason wasp.

guêpier [gepje] *nm* wasps' nest, hornets' nest.

guère [gɛːr] *ad* hardly (any, ever), barely, not much, not many, but little, but few.

guéridon [geridɔ̃] *nm* pedestal table, occasional table.

guérilla [gerija, -illa] *nf* guerrilla.

guérir [geriːr] *vt* to cure, heal; *vi* to recover, heal.

guérison [gerizɔ̃] *nf* recovery, cure, healing.

guérissable [gerisabl] *a* curable.

guérite [gerit] *nf* sentry-box, signalbox.

guerre [gɛːr] *nf* war(fare), fighting, strife, quarrel, feud; — **d'usure** war of attrition; — **de mouvement** open warfare; — **de position** trench warfare; — **éclair** blitz war; **de bonne** — quite fair; **de** — **lasse** for the sake of peace.

guerrier, -ière [gerje, jɛːr] *a* warlike, war-; *nm* warrior.

guerroyer [gerwaje] *vi* to wage war.

guet [ge] *nm* watch, look-out.

guet-apens [getapɑ̃] *nm* ambush, trap.

guêtre [gɛːtr] *nf* gaiter, spat.

guetter [gete] *vt* to lie in wait for, watch, be on the look-out for, listen for.

guetteur [getœːr] *nm* lookout (man).

gueule [gœl] *nf* mouth, muzzle, face, mug; **ta** — ! shut up! **casser la** — à qn to knock s.o.'s face in; **avoir la** — **de bois** to feel parched after excess of alcohol.

gueuler [gœle] *vti* to bawl, shout.

gueuleton [gœltɔ̃] *nm* blow-out, binge, tuck-in.

gueux, -euse [gø, ø:z] *a* poor, beggarly; *n* beggar.

gui [gi] *nm* mistletoe.

guichet [gifɛ] *nm* wicket-gate, grating, turnstile, barrier, pay-desk, booking-office window.

guide [gid] *nm* guide, conductor, guidebook; *nf* rein.

guider [gide] *vt* to guide, conduct, drive, steer.

guidon [gidɔ̃] *nm* handlebar, mark flag, pennant, (on gun) foresight.

guigne [giɲ] *nf* gean; bad luck.

guigner [giɲe] *vt* to peep at, cast an eye over, to leer, ogle.

guignol [giɲɔl] *nm* Punch and Judy show Punch.

guillemets [gijmɛ] *nm pl* inverted commas, quotation marks.

guilleret, -ette [gijrɛ, ɛt] *a* lively, gay, perky, broad.

guillotine [gijɔtin] *nf* guillotine.

guillotiner [gijɔtine] *vt* to guillotine.

guimauve [gimo:v] *nf* marshmallow.

guimbarde [gɛ̃bard] *nf* Jew's harp, ramshackle vehicle.

guimpe [gɛ̃:p] *nf* wimple, blouse front.

guindé [gɛ̃de] *a* stiff, strained, starchy.

guingois [gɛ̃gwa] *nm* crookedness, skew, twistedness; **de —** askew, awry.

guinguette [gɛ̃gɛt] *nf* suburban tavern with music and dancing.

guipure [gipy:r] *nf* guipure, pointlace, pillow-lace.

guirlande [girlɑ̃:d] *nf* garland, festoon.

guirlander [girlɑ̃de] *vt* to garland, festoon.

guise [gi:z] *nf* way, manner; **à sa —** as one pleases; **en — de** by way of.

guitare [gita:r] *nf* guitar.

guttural [gytyral] *a* guttural.

gymnaste [ʒimnast] *nm* gymnast.

gymnastique [ʒimnastik] *a* gymnastic; **au pas —** at the double; *nf* gymnastics.

gynécologue [ʒinekɔlɔg] *n* gynecologist.

gypse [ʒips] *nm* gypsum, plaster o i Paris.

gyroscope [ʒirɔskɔp] *nm* gyroscope.

H

The asterisk denotes that the initial h, which is never pronounced is aspirate, i.e. there is no liaison or elision.

habile [abil] *a* clever, skilful smart.

habileté [abilte] *nf* cleverness, skill, sk fulness, capability, smartness.

habillé [abije] *a* dressed (up), clad, smart, dressy.

habillement [abijmɑ̃] *nm* clothing, clothes, dress.

habiller [abije] *vt* to dress, clothe;

vr to dress, put one's clothes on.

habilleur, -euse [abijœ:r, ø:z] *n* dresser.

habit [abi] *nm* dress, coat, evening-dress; *pl* clothes.

habitable [abitabl] *a* (in)habitable.

habitant [abitɑ̃] *nm* inhabitant, dweller, resident, occupier; **loger chez l'—** to billet privately.

habitation [abitasjɔ̃] *nf* dwelling, residence, abode.

habiter [abite] *vt* to inhabit, live in, occupy; *vi* to live, reside, dwell.

habitude [abityd] *nf* habit, custom, use, practice, wont, knack; **d'—** usually; **comme d'—** as usual.

habitué [abitɥe] *nm* regular attendant, frequenter regular customer.

habituel, -elle [abitɥɛl] *a* usual, habitual, customary.

habituer [abitɥe] *vt* to accustom, get into the habit; *vr* to get used, grow accustomed.

***hâbleur** [ablœ:r] *nm* braggart, boaster.

***hache** [aʃ] *nf* axe, hatchet.

***haché** [aʃe] *a* staccato, jerky, minced.

***hacher** [aʃe] *vt* to chop (up), hash, hack, mince.

***hachis** [aʃi] *nm* minced meat, mince, hash.

***hachoir** [aʃwa:r] *nm* c hopper, mincer, chopping-board.

***hagard** [aga:r] *a* haggard, wild, drawn.

***haie** [ɛ] *nf* hedge(row), hurdle, line.

***haillon** [ajɔ̃] *nm* rag, tatter.

***haine** [ɛn] *nf* hatred, aversion.

***haineux, -euse** [ɛnø, ø:z] *a* full of hatred.

***haïr** [ai:r] *vt* to hate, detest, loathe.

***haïssable** [aisabl] *a* hateful, detestable.

***halage** [ala:ʒ] *nm* towing.

***hâle** [ɑ:l] *nm* sunburn, tan.

***hâlé** [ɑle] *a* sunburnt, tanned, weather-beaten.

haleine [alɛn] *nf* breath, wind; **travail de longue —** work requiring a long effort; **tenir en —** to keep in suspense.

haler [ale] *vt* to tow, pull, heave, haul up, in.

***hâler** [ale] *vt* to sunburn, tan, brown.

***haleter** [alte] *vi* to pant, gasp for breath.

***hall** [al, ɔl] *nm* (entrance) hall, hotel lounge.

***halle** [al] *nf* (covered) market.

***hallebarde** [albard] *nf* halberd; **il pleut des —s** it's raining cats and dogs.

***hallier** [alje] *nm* thicket.

hallucination [al(l)ysinasjɔ̃] *nf* hallucination.

***halte** [alt] *nf* stop, halt.

haltère [altɛ:r] *nm* dumb-bell.

***hamac** [amak] *nm* hammock.

hameau [amo] *nm* hamlet.
hameçon [amsɔ̃] *nm* hook, bait.
hampe [ɑ̃:p] *nf* staff pole, handle, shaft.
hanche [ɑ̃:ʃ] *nf* hip, haunch.
handicaper [ɑ̃dikape] *vt* to handicap.
hangar [ɑ̃gɑ:r] *nm* shed, outhouse.
hanneton [antɔ̃] *nm* cockchafer.
hanter [ɑ̃te] *vt* to frequent, haunt.
hantise [ɑ̃ti:z] *nf* obsession.
happer [ape] *vt* to snap up, catch, seize.
haranguer [arɑ̃ge] *vt* to harangue, lecture.
haras [arɑ] *nm* stud farm, stud.
harasser [arase] *vt* to exhaust, wear out.
harceler [arsəle] *vt* to harass, worry, harry, pester.
hardes [ard] *nf pl* old clothes, get-up, gear.
hardi [ardi] *a* bold, daring, fearless, rash, forward.
hardiesse [ardjɛs] *nf* boldness, daring, fearlessness, forwardness, impudence.
hareng [arɑ̃] *nm* herring; — salé et fumé kipper; — saur red herring.
hargneux [arɲø] *a* snarling, ill-tempered, peevish, snappish.
haricot [ariko] *nm* kidney bean, haricot bean; —s verts french beans.
harmonie [armɔni] *nf* harmony, accord, band; en — harmoniously, in keeping.
harmonieux, -euse [armɔnjø, ø:z] *a* harmonious, melodious.
harmonique [armɔnik] *a nm* harmonic.
harmoniser [armɔnize] *vt* to harmonize, attune; *vr* to be in keeping tone in.
harnachement [arnaʃmɑ̃] *nm* harnessing, trappings.
harnais [arnɛ] *nm* harness, gear, tackle.
harpe [arp] *nf* harp.
harpie [arpi] *nf* harpy, shrew.
harpiste [arpist] *n* harpist.
harpon [arpɔ̃] *nm* harpoon.
harponner [arpɔne] *vt* to harpoon.
hasard [azɑ:r] *nm* chance, luck, accident, risk, hazard; au — at random; à tout — on the off chance.
hasarder [azarde] *vt* to hazard, risk, venture; *vr* to take risks, venture.
hasardeux, -euse [azardø, ø:z] *a* hazardous, risky, daring.
hâte [ɑ:t] *nf* haste, hurry; avoir — de to be in a hurry to, be eager to; à la — hastily, hurriedly.
hâter [ɑte] *vt* to hasten, hurry on, quicken; *vr* to hurry, make haste.
hâtif, -ive [ɑtif, i:v] *a* hasty, hurried, early, premature.
hausse [o:s] *nf* rise, rising, elevation, range, sight; jouer à la — to speculate on a rise.

haussement [osmɑ̃] *nm* raising, lifting, shrug(ging).
hausser [ose] *vt* to raise, lift, shrug; *vi* to rise.
haussier [osje] *nm* (*Stock Exchange*) bull.
haut [o] *a* high, tall, lofty raised, loud, upper, higher, important, remote; *ad* high, up, above, aloud, back; — les mains hands up; *nm* height, top, head; en — above, aloft, upstairs; de — en bas from top to bottom, downward, up and down; les —s et les bas ups and downs.
hautain [otɛ̃] *a* haughty.
hautbois [obwa] *nm* oboe.
hauteur [otœ:r] *nf* height, elevation, altitude, eminence, hill(top), haughtiness, loftiness, pitch (of note); à la — de level with, equal to.
haut-le-cœur [olǝkœ:r] *nm* heave, retch.
haut-le-corps [olǝkɔ:r] *nm* start, jump.
haut-parleur [oparlœ:r] *nm* loud-speaker.
hauturier, -ière [otyrje, jɛ:r] *a* of the high seas; pilote — deep-sea pilot.
hâve [ɑ:v] *a* hollow, gaunt.
havre [ɑ:vr] *nm* haven, harbour.
havresac [ɑvrǝsak] *nm* knapsack.
hé [e] *excl* hi! hullo! I say!
hebdomadaire [ɛbdɔmadɛ:r] *a nm* weekly.
héberger [ebɛrʒe] *vt* to harbour, lodge, put up, shelter.
hébéter [ebete] *vt* to daze, dull, stupefy, bewilder.
hébreu [ebrø] *a nm* Hebrew.
hécatombe [ekatɔ̃:b] *nf* hecatomb, slaughter.
hégémonie [eʒemɔni] *nf* hegemony.
hein [ɛ̃] *excl* eh! what!
hélas [elɑ:s] *excl* alas!
héler [ele] *vt* to hail, call.
hélice [elis] *nf* spiral, propellor, (of ship) screw.
hélicoptère [elikɔptɛ:r] *nm* helicopter.
héliotrope [eljɔtrɔp] *a nm* heliotrope, sunflower.
hellénique [slenik] *a* Hellenic.
helvétique [ɛlvetik] *a* Swiss.
hémicycle [emisikl] *nm* hemicycle.
hémisphère [emisfɛ:r] *nm* hemisphere.
hémorragie [emɔraʒi] *nf* haemorrhage, bleeding.
hémorroïdes [emɔrɔid] *nf pl* piles.
hennir [eni:r] *vi* to neigh, whinny.
héraldique [eraldik] *a* heraldic; *nf* heraldry.
héraut [ero] *nm* herald.
herbage [ɛrba:ʒ] *nm* grassland, pasture, greens.
herbe [ɛrb] *nf* herb, plant, weed, grass; en — budding, in embryo.
herbeux, -euse [ɛrbø, ø:z] *a* grassy.
herbivore [ɛrbivɔ:r] *a* herbivorous.

herboriser [ɛrbɔrize] *vi* to herborize, botanize.

herboriste [ɛrbɔrist] *n* herbalist.

herculéen, -enne [ɛrkyleɛ̃, ɛn] *a* herculean.

héréditaire [eredite:r] *a* hereditary.

hérédité [eredite] *nf* heredity, right of inheritance.

hérésie [erezi] *nf* heresy.

hérétique [eretik] *a* heretical; *n* heretic.

*****hérissé** [erise] *a* bristly, prickly, bristling.

*****hérisser** [erise] *vt* to bristle (up), ruffle; *vr* to bristle, stand on end.

*****hérisson** [erisɔ̃] *nm* hedgehog, (sea)urchin.

héritage [erita:ʒ] *nm* inheritance, heritage.

hériter [erite] *vti* to inherit.

héritier, -ière [eritje, jɛ:r] *n* heir, heiress.

hermétique [ɛrmetik] *a* hermetically sealed, tight.

hermine [ɛrmin] *nf* stoat, ermine.

herniaire [ɛrnjɛ:r] *a* hernial; **bandage — truss.**

*****hernie** [ɛrni] *nf* hernia, rupture.

héroïne [erɔin] *nf* heroine.

héroïque [erɔik] *a* heroic.

héroïsme [erɔism] *nm* heroism.

*****héron** [erɔ̃] *nm* heron.

*****héros** [ero] *nm* hero.

*****herse** [ɛrs] *nf* harrow, portcullis.

hésitation [ezitasjɔ̃] *nf* hesitation.

hésiter [ezite] *vi* to hesitate, falter.

hétéroclite [eterɔklit] *a* odd, queer.

hétérodoxe [eterɔdɔks] *a* heterodox.

hétérogène [eterɔʒɛn] *a* heterogeneous, mixed.

*****hêtre** [ɛ:tr] *nm* beech.

heure [œ:r] *nf* hour, time, o'clock; **la dernière —** stop-press news; **de bonne —** early, in good time; **sur l'—** at once; **tout à l'—** just now, a few minutes ago, presently; **à tout à l'—** see you later; **à la bonne —** that's right, well done!

heureusement [œrøzmɑ̃] *ad* happily, luckily.

heureux, -euse [œrø, ø:z] *a* happy, pleased, lucky, s uccessful, blessed.

*****heurt** [œ:r] *nm* knock, shock, bump; **sans heurt** smoothly.

*****heurter** [œrte] *vt* to knock against, run against, shock; *vr* to run (into), knock up (against), collide.

*****heurtoir** [œrtwa:r] *nm* doorknocker, buffer.

hévéa [evea] *nm* rubber tree.

hexagone [ɛksagɔn] *a* hexagonal; *nm* hexagon.

*****hibou** [ibu] *nm* owl.

*****hideur** [idœ:r] *nf* hideousness.

*****hideux, -euse** [idø, ø:z] *a* hideous.

hier [iɛ:r] *ad* yesterday.

*****hiérarchie** [jerarʃi] *nf* hierarchy.

*****hiérarchique** [jerarʃik] *a* hierarchical; **par voie —** through official channels.

hiéroglyphe [jerɔglif] *nm* hieroglyph.

hilarité [ilarite] *nf* hilarity, merriment.

hindou [ɛ̃du] *an* Hindu.

hippique [ippik] *a* horse, equine; **concours — horse-show.**

hippodrome [ip(p)ɔdrom] *nm* racecourse.

hippopotame [ippɔpɔtam] *nm* hippopotamus.

hirondelle [irɔ̃dɛl] *nf* swallow.

hirsute [irsyt] *a* hairy, hirsute, shaggy.

*****hisser** [ise] *vt* to hoist (up), pull up, run up; *vr* to pull oneself up, raise oneself.

histoire [istwa:r] *nf* history, story, tale; **faire des —s** to make a fuss; **— de s'amuser** just for a lark.

historien, -ienne [istɔrjɛ̃, jɛn] *n* historian.

historique [istɔrik] *a* historic(al); *nm* statement, account.

hiver [ivɛ:r] *nm* winter .

hivernant [ivɛrnɑ̃] *a* wintering; *nm* winter visitor.

hiverner [ivɛrne] *vi* to (lie up for) winter, hibernate.

*****hocher** [ɔʃe] *vt* to shake, nod.

hoirie [wari] *nf* succession, inheritance.

*****hollandais** [ɔlɑ̃dɛ] *a nm* Dutch; *n* Dutchman, Dutchwoman.

*****Hollande** [ɔlɑ̃:d] *nf* Holland.

holocauste [ɔlɔkɔst] *nm* holocaust, sacrifice.

*****homard** [ɔma:r] *nm* lobster.

homicide [ɔmisid] *a* homicidal; *n* homicide; *nm* homicide (crime).

hommage [ɔmaːʒ] *nm* tribute, token of esteem; *pl* respects.

hommasse [ɔmas] *a* masculine, mannish.

homme [ɔm] *nm* man, mankind, husband

homogène [ɔmɔʒɛn] *a* homogeneous.

homologuer [ɔmɔlɔge] *vt* to confirm, endorse, ratify, prove, record.

homonyme [ɔmɔnim] *nm* homonym, namesake.

homosexuel [ɔmɔsɛksyɛl] *a* homosexual.

*****Hongrie** [ʒɔ̃gri] *nf* Hungary.

*****hongrois** [ʒɔ̃grwa] *a nm* Hungarian.

honnête [ɔnɛt] *a* honest upright decent, well-bred, seemly, reasonable.

honnêteté [ɔnɛtte] *nf* honesty, uprightness, decency, courtesy.

honneur [ɔnœ:r] *nm* honour, credit; **faire — à** to honour, meet.

honorable [ɔnɔrabl] *a* honourable, respectable.

honoraire [ɔnɔrɛ:r] *a* honorary; *nm pl* fees, honorarium.

honorer [ɔnɔre] *vt* to honour, respect, favour, do credit to.

honorifique [ɔnɔrifik] *a* honorary, honorific.

***honté** [ɔ̃:t] nf shame, disgrace, scandal; **avoir —** to be ashamed; **faire —** à to put to shame, disgrace.

***honteux, -euse** [ɔ̃tø, ø:z] a ashamed, shamefaced, bashful, disgraceful.

hôpital [ɔpital] nm hospital, infirmary.

***hoquet** [ɔkɛ] nm hiccup, gasp.

horaire [ɔrɛːr] nm timetable.

***horde** [ɔrd] nf horde.

horizon [ɔriz5] nm horizon.

horizontal [ɔriz5tal] a horizontal.

horloge [ɔrlɔ:ʒ] nf clock.

horloger [ɔrlɔʒe] nm clock and watchmaker.

horlogerie [ɔrlɔʒri] nf clock and watchmaking, clockwork.

***hormis** [ɔrmi] prep except, but, save.

hormone [ɔrmɔn] nf hormone.

horreur [ɔrrœːr] nf horror, abhorrence; pl horrid things, atrocities.

horrible [ɔrribl] a horrid, frightful.

horrifier [ɔrrifje] vt to horrify.

horrifique [ɔrrifik] a horrific, hair-raising.

horripilant [ɔrripilɑ̃] a hair-raising.

horripiler [ɔrripile] vt to make someone's flesh creep, irritate.

***hors** [ɔ:r] prep out of, outside, except, all but; **— de** out(side) of; **— de combat** out of action, disabled; **être — de soi** to be beside oneself.

***hors-bord** [ɔrbɔːr] nm outboard motor boat.

***hors-d'œuvre** [ɔrdøːvr] nm extraneous matter, hors-d'œuvre.

hortensia [ɔrtɑ̃sja] nm hydrangea.

horticole [ɔrtikɔl] a horticultural, flower-.

horticulteur [ɔrtikyltœːr] nm horticulturist.

horticulture [ɔrtikylty:r] nf horticulture.

hospice [ɔspis] nm hospice, home, asylum, poorhouse.

hospitalier, -ière [ɔspitalje, jɛːr] a hospitable.

hospitaliser [ɔspitalize] vt to send, admit to a hospital, a poorhouse.

hospitalité [ɔspitalite] nf hospitality.

hostie [ɔsti] nf (Eucharistic) host.

hostile [ɔstil] a adverse, inimical, unfriendly.

hostilité [ɔstilite] nf hostility, enmity.

hôte, -esse [o:t, otɛs] n host, hostess, landlord, landlady, guest, visitor, inmate, dweller.

hôtel [otɛl] nm hotel, mansion, townhouse; **— de ville** town hall; **— des postes** general post office; **— des ventes** auction rooms; **— meublé, garni** lodging house, furnished apartments.

hôtel-Dieu [otɛldjø] nm hospital.

hôtelier, -ière [otəlje, jɛːr] n hotelkeeper, landlord.

hôtellerie [otɛlri] nf inn, restaurant, hotel trade.

***hotte** [ɔt] nf basket (carried on back), hod.

***houblon** [ubl5] nm (bot) hop(s).

***houblonnière** [ublɔnjɛːr] nf hopfield.

***houe** [u] nf hoe.

***houille** [uːj] nf coal; **— blanche** hydro-electric power.

***houiller, -ère** [uje, jɛːr] a coal (bearing).

***houillère** [ujɛːr] nf coalmine, pit, colliery.

***houle** [ul] nf swell, surge, hearing.

***houlette** [ulɛt] nf crook (shepherd's, of umbrella), crozier, trowel.

***houleux, -euse** [ulø, ø:z] a stormy, surging.

***houppe** [up] nf tuft, bunch, crest, powder-puff.

***houppé** [upe] a tufted, crested.

***houppette** [upɛt] nf small tuft, powder-puff.

***houspiller** [uspije] vt to hustle, jostle, maul, abuse.

***housse** [us] nf cover(ing), dust-sheet, horse-cloth.

***houx** [u] nm holly.

***hoyau** [wajo] nm hoe.

***hublot** [yblo] nm scuttle, porthole.

***huche** [yʃ] nf trough, bin.

***hue** [y] excl gee-up!

***huée** [ye] nf boo(ing), hoot(ing), jeer(ing).

***huer** [ye] vi to shout, whoop; vt to boo, hoot.

huile [ɥil] nf oil; **— de copra** coconut oil.

huiler [ɥile] vt to oil.

huileux, -euse [ɥilø, ø:z] a oily, greasy.

huilier [ɥilje] nm oilcan, oil and vinegar cruet.

huis [ɥi] nm **à — clos** in camera, behind closed doors.

huissier [ɥisje] nm usher, bailiff, sheriff's officer.

***huit** [ɥit] a eight; **— jours** week; **d'aujourd'hui en —** this day week; **donner ses — jours** to give a week's notice; nm eight, eighth.

***huitaine** [ɥitɛn] nf (about) eight, week.

***huitième** [ɥitjɛm] a nm eighth.

huître [ɥiːtr] nf oyster.

humain [ymɛ̃] a human, humane.

humaniser [ymanize] vt to humanize; vr to become more humane.

humanitaire [ymanitɛːr] a humanitarian, humane.

humanité [ymanite] nf humanity.

humble [œ̃:bl] a humble, lowly.

humecter [ymɛkte] vt to moisten, damp, wet.

***humer** [yme] vt to suck in, (up), breathe in, sniff.

humeur [ymœːr] nf humour, mood, temper, ill-humour.

humide [ymid] a damp, humid, moist, wet.

humidité [ymidite] nf damp(ness),

humidity, moisture, moistness; craint l'— to be kept dry.

humiliation [ymiljasjɔ̃] *nf* affront.

humilier [ymilje] *vt* to humiliate, humble.

humilité [ymilite] *nf* humility, humbleness.

humoriste [ymɔrist] *a* humorous; *nm* humorist.

humoristique [ymɔristik] *a* humorous.

humour [ymuːr] *nm* humour.

*hune** [yn] *nf* top; — de vigie crow's nest.

*hunier** [ynje] *nm* topsail.

*huppe** [yp] *nf* tuft, crest.

*huppé** [ype] *a* tufted, crested, (*fam*) well-dressed.

*hure** [yːr] *nf* head, brawn, potted head.

*hurlement** [yrləmɑ̃] *nm* howl(ing), yell(ing).

*hurler** [yrle] *vi* to howl, yell, roar; *vt* to bawl out.

*hutte** [yt] *nf* hut, shed.

hybride [ibrid] *a nm* hybrid.

hydrate [idrat] *nm* hydrate.

hydraulique [idrolik] *a* hydraulic, water-; *nf* hydraulics.

hydravion [idravjɔ̃] *nm* sea-plane.

hydrogène [idrɔʒɛn] *nm* hydrogen; bombe à — hydrogen bomb.

hydroglisseur [idroglisœːr] *nm* speed-boat.

hydrophile [idrɔfil] *a* absorbent.

hydrophobie [idrɔfɔbi] *nf* hydrophobia, rabies.

hydropisie [idrɔpizi] *nf* dropsy.

hyène [jɛn] *nf* hyena.

hygiène [iʒjɛn] *nf* hygiene, health, sanitation.

hygiénique [iʒjenik] *a* hygienic, healthy, sanitary; papier — toilet paper.

hymne [im(n)] *nm* song, (national) anthem; *nf* hymn.

hyperbole [iperbɔl] *nf* hyperbole, exaggeration.

hypnose [ipnoːz] *nf* hypnosis, trance.

hypnotiser [ipnɔtize] *vt* to hypnotize.

hypnotisme [ipnɔtism] *nm* hypnotism.

hypocondriaque [ipɔkɔ̃driak] *an* hypochondriac.

hypocrisie [ipɔkrizi] *nf* hypocrisy, cant.

hypocrite [ipɔkrit] *a* hypocritical; *n* hypocrite.

hypodermique [ipɔdermik] *a* hypodermic.

hypothécaire [ipɔtekɛːr] *a* mortgage; *nm* mortgagee.

hypothèque [ipɔtɛk] *nf* mortgage.

hypothéquer [ipɔteke] *vt* to mortgage.

hypothèse [ipɔtɛːz] *nf* hypothesis, assumption.

hystérie [isteri] *nf* hysteria.

hystérique [isterik] *a* hysteric(al).

I

ici [isi] *ad* here, now; par — this way; d'— huit jours a week today; d'— là between now and then; d'— peu before long; jusqu'— hitherto, as far as this; — bas here below.

iconoclaste [ikɔnɔklast] *a* iconoclastic; *nm* iconoclast.

idéal [ideal] *a nm* ideal.

idéaliser [idealize] *vt* to idealize.

idéalisme [idealism] *nm* idealism.

idéaliste [idealist] *a* idealistic; *n* idealist.

idée [ide] *nf* idea, thought, notion, fancy, mind; il lui est venu à l'— que it occurred to him that; — fixe obsession.

identification [idɑ̃tifikasjɔ̃] *nf* identification.

identifier [idɑ̃tifje] *vt* to identify.

identique [idɑ̃tik] *a* identical.

identité [idɑ̃tite] *nf* identity.

idéologie [ideɔlɔʒi] *nf* ideology.

idéologue [ideɔlɔg] *a* ideological; *nm* ideologue.

idiomatique [idjɔmatik] *a* idiomatic.

idiome [idjɔm] *nm* language, idiom.

idiosyncrasie [idjɔsɛ̃krazi] *nf* idiosyncrasy.

idiot [idjo] *a* idiot(ic), senseless; *n* idiot, silly ass.

idiotie [idjɔsi] *nf* idiocy, imbecility, stupidity.

idiotisme [idjɔtism] *nm* idiom, idiomatic expression, idiocy.

idolâtre [idɔlaːtr] *a* idolatrous; *n* idolater, idolatress.

idolâtrer [idɔlatre] *vt* to idolize, worship.

idolâtrie [idɔlatri] *nf* idolatry.

idole [idɔl] *nf* idol, image, god.

idylle [idil] *nf* idyll.

idyllique [idilik] *a* idyllic.

if [if] *nm* yew(tree).

igname [iɲam] *nf* yam.

ignare [iɲaːr] *a* ignorant, uneducated; *n* ignoramus.

ignoble [iɲɔbl] *a* vile, base.

ignominie [iɲɔmini] *nf* ignominy, shame.

ignominieux, -euse [iɲɔminjø, øːz] *a* ignominious, disgraceful.

ignorance [iɲɔrɑ̃ːs] *nf* ignorance.

ignorant [iɲɔrɑ̃] *a* ignorant; *n* ignoramus.

ignorer [iɲɔre] *vt* to be ignorant of, not to know, to be unaware of.

il, ils [il] *pn* he, it, they, there.

île [il, iːl] *nf* island, isle.

illégal [illegal] *a* illegal.

illégalité [illegalite] *nf* illegality, unlawfulness.

illégitime [illeʒitim] *a* illegitimate, unlawful, unreasonable.

illégitimité [illeʒitimite] *nf* illegitimacy, unlawfulness.

illettré [illetre] *a* illiterate, uneducated.

illicite [illisit] *a* illicit, unlawful.

illimité [illimite] *a* unlimited, boundless.

illisibilité [illizibilite] *nf* illegibility.

illisible [illizibl] *a* illegible, unreadable.

illogique [illoʒik] *a* illogical, inconsistent.

illogisme [illoʒism] *nm* illogicality, inconsistency.

illumination [illyminasjɔ̃] *nf* illumination, lighting, understanding; *pl* lights, illuminations.

illuminer [illymine] *vt* to illuminate, enlighten, throw light on.

illusion [illyzjɔ̃] *nf* illusion, delusion.

illusionniste [illyzjɔnist] *n* illusionist, conjurer.

illusoire [illyzwa:r] *a* illusory.

illustration [illystrasjɔ̃] *nf* illustrating, illustration.

illustre [illystr] *a* illustrated, made famous, renowned.

illustré [illystre] *nm* picture-paper, illustrated newspaper.

illustrer [illystre] *vt* to make famous, illustrate; *vr* to win renown

îlot [ilo] *nm* islet.

image [ima:ʒ] *nf* image, picture, likeness, simile, metaphor, reflection; **faire —** to be vivid.

imagé [imaʒe] *a* full of imagery, picturesque.

imaginaire [imaʒinɛ:r] *a* imaginary.

imagination [imaʒinasjɔ̃] *nf* imagination, fancy, invention.

imaginer [imaʒine] *vtr* to imagine, fancy, picture; *vt* invent, devise.

imbattable [ɛ̃batabl] *a* unbeatable, invincible.

imbécile [ɛ̃besil] *a* imbecile, half-witted, silly; *n* fool, half-wit.

imbécilité [ɛ̃besilite] *nf* imbecility, silliness.

imberbe [ɛ̃bɛrb] *a* beardless.

imbiber [ɛ̃bibe] *vt* to imbibe, absorb, soak, impregnate, steep; *vr* to become impregnated, soak in, absorb.

imbrisable [ɛ̃brizabl] *a* unbreakable.

imbu [ɛ̃by] *a* soaked, steeped (**de** in).

imbuvable [ɛ̃byvabl] *a* undrinkable; (*of person*) unbearable.

imitateur, -trice [imitatœ:r, tris] *a* imitative; *n* imitator.

imitation [imitasjɔ̃] *nf* copy, copying, mimicking, impersonation.

imiter [imite] *vt* to imitate, copy, mimic.

immaculé [imakyle] *a* immaculate, pure, spotless.

immangeable [imɑ̃ʒabl] *a* uneatable.

immanquablement [imɑ̃kabləmɑ̃] *ad* inevitably, without fail.

immatériel, -elle [immaterjɛl] *a* immaterial, incorporeal.

immatriculation [immatrikylasjɔ̃] *nf* matriculation, enrolling, registration; **plaque d'—** number plate.

immatriculer [immatrikyle] *vtr* to register, enrol, matriculate.

immaturité [immatyrite] *nf* immaturity.

immédiat [immedja] *a* immediate, direct, urgent.

immémorial [immemɔrjal] *a* immemorial.

immense [immɑ̃:s] *a* immense, vast, huge.

immensité [immɑ̃site] *nf* vastness.

immerger [immɛrʒe] *vt* to immerse, plunge, dip.

immérité [immerite] *a* unmerited, undeserved.

immersion [immɛrsjɔ̃] *nf* immersion, dipping, submersion.

immeuble [immœbl] *a* real, fixed; *nm* real estate, house, tenement, premises.

immigrant [immigrɑ̃] *an* immigrant.

immigré [immigre] *n* immigrant, settler.

imminence [imminɑ̃:s] *nf* imminence.

imminent [imminɑ̃] *a* imminent.

immiscer [immise] *vt* to mix up, involve; *vr* to get involved, interfere.

immixtion [immiksjɔ̃] *nf* interference.

immobile [immɔbil] *a* motionless, still, immovable.

immobilier, -ière [immɔbilje, jɛ:r] *a* real (*estate*), building (*society*).

immobiliser [immɔbilize] *vt* to immobilize, tie up, convert into real estate.

immobilité [immɔbilite] *nf* immobility.

immodéré [immɔdere] *a* immoderate, excessive.

immodeste [immɔdɛst] *a* immodest, shameless.

immoler [immɔle] *vt* to sacrifice, immolate.

immonde [immɔ̃:d] *a* filthy, foul.

immondices [immɔ̃dis] *nf pl* dirt, refuse, filth.

immoral [immɔral] *a* immoral.

immoralité [immɔralite] *nf* immorality immoral act.

immortaliser [immɔrtalize] *vt* to immortalize.

immortalité [immɔrtalite] *nf* immortality.

immortel, -elle [immɔrtɛl] *a* immortal, undying.

immuable [immɥabl] *a* unalterable, unchanging.

immuniser [immynize] *vt* to immunize.

immunité [immynite] *nf* immunity.

immutabilité [immytabilite] *nf* immutability.

impact [ɛ̃pakt] *nm* impact.

impair [ɛ̃pe:r] *a* odd, uneven; *nm* blunder, bloomer.

impalpable [ɛ̃palpabl] *a* intangible.

impardonnable [ɛ̃pardɔnabl] *a* unpardonable, unforgivable.

imparfait [ɛ̃parfɛ] *a* imperfect, defective, incomplete.

impartial [ɛparsjal] *a* impartial, unprejudiced.

impassable [ɛpasabl] *a* impassable, unfordable.

impasse [ɛpɑːs] *nf* blind-alley, dilemma, fix, deadlock, (*cards*) finesse.

impassibilité [ɛpasibilite] *nf* impassiveness.

impassible [ɛpasibl] *a* impassive, unmoved, callous.

impatience [ɛpasjɑ̃ːs] *nf* impatience, eagerness.

impatient [ɛpasjɑ̃] *a* impatient, anxious, eager.

impatienter [ɛpasjɑ̃te] *vt* to make impatient; *vr* to lose patience.

impayable [ɛpɛjabl] *a* invaluable, priceless, terribly funny.

impeccable [ɛpɛkabl] *a* faultless, flawless.

impécunieux [ɛpekynjø] *a* impecunious.

impénétrable [ɛpenɛtrabl] *a* impenetrable, impervious, inscrutable.

impénitence [ɛpenitɑ̃ːs] *nf* impenitence, obduracy.

impénitent [ɛpenitɑ̃] *a* obdurate, unrepentant.

impératif, -ive [ɛperatif, iːv] *a* imperative, imperious; *nm* imperative.

impératrice [ɛperatris] *nf* empress.

imperceptible [ɛpersɛptibl] *a* imperceptible, inaudible.

imperfection [ɛperfɛksjɔ̃] *nf* imperfection, defectiveness, incompleteness, flaw.

impérial [ɛperjal] *a* imperial.

impériale [ɛperjal] *nf* top-deck, top, imperial, double-decker bus.

impérialisme [ɛperjalism] *nm* imperialism.

impérieux [ɛperjø, øːz] *a* imperious, peremptory, domineering, urgent.

impérissable [ɛperisabl] *a* imperishable.

imperméabiliser [ɛpermeabilize] *vt* to proof, make waterproof.

imperméable [ɛpermeabl] *a* impervious; *nm* waterproof.

impersonnel, -elle [ɛpersɔnɛl] *a* impersonal.

impertinence [ɛpertinɑ̃ːs] *nf* impertinence.

impertinent [ɛpertinɑ̃] *a* impertinent, rude.

imperturbable [ɛpertyrbabl] *a* cool, calm and collected.

impétueux [ɛpetɥø, -øːz] *a* impetuous, impulsive.

impétuosité [ɛpetɥozite] *nf* impetuosity, impulsiveness.

impie [ɛpi] *a* impious, blasphemous.

impiété [ɛpjete] *nf* impiety, ungodliness, blasphemy.

impitoyable [ɛpitwajabl] *a* pitiless, ruthless.

implacabilité [ɛplakabilite] *nf* implacability, relentlessness.

implacable [ɛplakabl] *a* implacable, relentless.

implanter [ɛplɑ̃te] *vt* to plant, implant; *vr* to take root, take hold.

implicite [ɛplisit] *a* implicit, absolute.

impliquer [ɛplike] *vt* to implicate, involve.

implorer [ɛplɔre] *vt* to implore, entreat, beseech.

impoli [ɛpɔli] *a* impolite, unmannerly.

impolitesse [ɛpɔlitɛs] *nf* unmannerliness, rude act, word.

impolitique [ɛpɔlitik] *a* impolitic, ill-advised.

impondérable [ɛpɔ̃derabl] *a* imponderable.

impopulaire [ɛpɔpylɛːr] *a* unpopular.

impopularité [ɛpɔpylarite] *nf* unpopularity.

importance [ɛpɔrtɑ̃ːs] *nf* importance, moment, magnitude.

important [ɛpɔrtɑ̃] *a* important, large, extensive, considerable, self-important; *nm* the main thing.

importateur, -trice [ɛpɔrtatœːr, tris] *a* importing; *n* importer.

importation [ɛpɔrtasjɔ̃] *nf* importing, import.

importer [ɛpɔrte] *vt* to import; *vi* to be important, matter; **n'importe** never mind, it does not matter; **n'importe qui, quoi, comment, quand** anyone, anything, anyhow, anytime.

importun [ɛpɔrtœ̃] *a* importunate, tiresome, unwelcome; *n* intruder, nuisance.

importuner [ɛpɔrtyne] *vt* to importune, bother, trouble, dun.

importunité [ɛpɔrtynite] *nf* importunity.

imposable [ɛpozabl] *a* taxable, ratable, assessable.

imposant [ɛpozɑ̃] *a* imposing, impressive.

imposé [ɛpoze] *n* ratepayer, taxpayer.

imposer [ɛpoze] *vt* to impose, set, prescribe, enforce, tax, rate; *vi* to command respect; *vr* to assert oneself, force oneself, itself (upon), be imperative; **en — à** to impose upon, take in, overawe.

imposition [ɛpozisjɔ̃] *nf* imposition, imposing, setting, prescribing, taxation, rates.

impossibilité [ɛpɔsibilite] *nf* impossibility.

impossible [ɛpɔsibl] *a* impossible.

imposteur [ɛpɔstœːr] *nm* imposter, hypocrite.

imposture [ɛpɔstyːr] *nf* imposture, sham, swindle.

impôt [ɛpo] *nm* tax, duty; **frapper d'un —** to tax.

impotence [ɛpotɑ̃ːs] *nf* helplessness, infirmity.

impotent [ɛ̃pɔtɑ̃] *a* infirm, helpless, crippled; *n* cripple, invalid.

impracticable [ɛ̃pratikabl] *a* impracticable, unfeasible, (*road*) impassable.

imprécation [ɛ̃prɛkasjɔ̃] *nf* imprecation, curse.

imprécis [ɛ̃presi] *a* vague, inaccurate.

imprécision [ɛ̃presizjɔ̃] *nf* vagueness, inaccuracy.

imprégner [ɛ̃preɲe] *vt* to impregnate, saturate; *vr* to become saturated, soak up.

imprenable [ɛ̃prənabl] *a* impregnable.

impression [ɛ̃presjɔ̃] *nf* impression, stamp(ing), print(ing).

impressionnable [ɛ̃presjɔnabl] *a* impressionable, nervous, sensitive.

impressionnant [ɛ̃presjɔnɑ̃] *a* impressive.

impressionner [ɛ̃presjɔne] *vt* to impress, make an impression on, move; *vr* to be moved, get nervous.

impressionisme [ɛ̃presjɔnism] *nm* impressionism.

imprévoyable [ɛ̃prevwajabl] *a* unforeseeable.

imprévoyance [ɛ̃prevwajɑ̃:s] *n* lack of foresight.

imprévoyant [ɛ̃prevwajɑ̃] *a* shortsighted, improvident.

imprévu [ɛ̃prevy] *a* unforeseen, unexpected; *nm* unexpected, emergency.

imprimé [ɛ̃prime] *nm* printed matter, paper, form, leaflet; **envoyer en — to send by book-post.**

imprimer [ɛ̃prime] *vt* to (im)print, impress, stamp.

imprimerie [ɛ̃primri] *nf* printing, printing house, press.

imprimeur [ɛ̃primœ:r] *nm* printer.

improbabilité [ɛ̃prɔbabilite] *nf* improbability, unlikelihood.

improbable [ɛ̃prɔbabl] *a* improbable, unlikely.

improbité [ɛ̃prɔbite] *nf* dishonesty.

improductif, -ive [ɛ̃prɔdyktif, i:v] *a* unproductive.

impromptu [ɛ̃prɔ̃(p)ty] *a* extempore; *ad* without preparation; *nm* impromptu.

impropriété [ɛ̃prɔpriete] *nf* impropriety, unsuitableness, incorrectness.

improvisation [ɛ̃prɔvizasjɔ̃] *nf* improvisation, extemporization.

improvisé [ɛ̃prɔvize] *a* improvised, extempore, makeshift.

improviser [ɛ̃prɔvize] *vt* to improvise, put together, make up; *vi* to speak extempore.

improviste (à l') [alɛ̃prɔvist] *ad* unexpected(ly).

imprudence [ɛ̃prydɑ̃:s] *nf* rashness, indiscretion.

impudence [ɛ̃pydɑ̃:s] *nf* insolence, (piece of) impudence.

impudent [ɛ̃pydɑ̃] *a* impudent, insolent, shameless.

impudicité [ɛ̃pydisite] *nf* lewdness, immodesty.

impudique [ɛ̃pydik] *a* lewd, immodest, unchaste.

impuissance [ɛ̃pɥisɑ̃:s] *nf* helplessness, powerlessness, impotence.

impuissant [ɛ̃pɥisɑ̃] *a* helpless, powerless, impotence, futile.

impulsif, -ive [ɛ̃pylsif, i:v] *a* impulsive.

impulsion [ɛ̃pylsjɔ̃] *nf* impulse, impetus.

impunément [ɛ̃pynemɑ̃] *ad* with impunity.

impunité [ɛ̃pynite] *nf* impunity.

impur [ɛ̃py:r] *a* impure, unchaste, unclean, foul.

impureté [ɛ̃pyrte] *nf* impurity, foulness.

imputable [ɛ̃pytabl] *a* imputable, attributable, chargeable.

imputation [ɛ̃pytasjɔ̃] *nf* imputation, charge, attribution.

imputer [ɛ̃pyte] *vt* to impute, ascribe, charge.

inabordable [inabɔrdabl] *a* inaccessible, prohibitive.

inacceptable [inaksɛptabl] *a* unacceptable.

inaccessible [inaksesibl] *a* inaccessible, unapproachable.

inaccoutumé [inakutyme] *a* unaccustomed, unusual, unwonted.

inachevé [inaʃve] *a* unfinished, incomplete.

inactif, -ive [inaktif, i:v] *a* inactive, inert.

inaction [inaksjɔ̃] *nf* inaction, inertia.

inactivité [inaktivite] *nf* inactivity, inertness.

inadmissible [inadmisibl] *a* inadmissible, who has failed in written examination.

inadvertance [inadvɛrtɑ̃:s] *nf* inadvertance, oversight, mistake.

inadvertant [inadvɛrtɑ̃] *a* careless.

inaliénable [inaljenabl] *a* inalienable, untransferable.

inaltérable [inaltɛrabl] *a* unalterable, unfailing.

inamovible [inamɔvibl] *a* irremovable, fixed, held for life.

inanimé [inanime] *a* lifeless, inanimate, unconscious.

inanité [inanite] *nf* inanity, inane remark.

inanition [inanisjɔ̃] *nf* starvation, inanition.

inaperçu [inapɛrsy] *a* unnoticed, unseen.

inapparent [inaparɑ̃] *a* unapparent.

inapplication [inaplikasjɔ̃] *nf* lack of diligence, of assiduity.

inappliqué [inaplike] *a* inattentive, careless, unapplied.

inappréciable [inapresjabl] *a* inappreciable, not perceptible, invaluable.

inapprivoisé [inaprivwaze] *a* untamed, wild.

inapte [inapt] *a* unfit, unsuited, inapt, unemployable

inaptitude [inaptityd] *nf* unfitness.

inarticulé [inartikyle] *a* inarticulate, not jointed.

inassouvi [inasuvi] *a* unappeased, unsatisfied.

inassouvissable [inasuvisabl] *a* insatiable.

inattaquable [inatakabl] *a* unassailable, unquestionable.

inattendu [inatɑ̃dy] *a* unexpected, unlooked for.

inattentif, -ive [inatɑ̃tif, i:v] *a* inattentive, careless, unobservant.

inattention [inatɑ̃sjɔ̃] *nf* inattention, carelessness.

inaugural [inogyral] *a* inaugural, opening.

inauguration [inogyrasjɔ̃] *nf* opening, unveiling.

inaugurer [inogyre] *vt* to inaugurate, open, unveil.

inavouable [inavwabl] *a* shameful, foul, low.

incalculable [ɛ̃kalkylabl] *a* incalculable, countless.

incandescence [ɛ̃kɑ̃dɛssɑ̃:s] *nf* white heat.

incantation [ɛ̃kɑ̃tasjɔ̃] *nf* incantation.

incapable [ɛ̃kapabl] *a* inefficient, unfit, unable.

incapacité [ɛ̃kapasite] *nf* incapacity, inefficiency, inability, disablement.

incarcérer [ɛ̃karsere] *vt* to incarcerate, imprison.

incarnadin [ɛ̃karnadɛ̃] *a* incarnadine, rosy, pink.

incarnat [ɛ̃karna] *a* rosy, pink, flesh coloured; *nm* rosiness, rosy hue.

incarnation [ɛ̃karnasjɔ̃] *nf* embodiment.

incarné [ɛ̃karne] *a* incarnate, ingrowing.

incarner [ɛ̃karne] *vt* to incarnate, embody, be the incarnation of.

incartade [ɛ̃kartad] *nf* outburst, tirade, prank.

incendiaire [ɛ̃sɑ̃djɛ:r] *a* incendiary, inflammatory; *n* incendiary.

incendie [ɛ̃sɑ̃di] *nm* fire, conflagration, burning; **échelle à — fire-escape; pompe à — fire-engine; poste d'— fire-station.

incendier [ɛ̃sɑ̃dje] *vt* to set on fire, burn down.

incertain [ɛ̃sɛrtɛ̃] *a* uncertain, doubtful, unreliable.

incertitude [ɛ̃sɛrtityd] *nf* uncertainty, doubt.

incessamment [ɛ̃sɛsamɑ̃] *ad* immediately.

incessant [ɛ̃sɛsɑ̃] *a* unceasing, ceaseless.

inceste [ɛ̃sɛst] *nm* incest.

incestueux, -euse [ɛ̃sɛstɥø, ø:z] *a* incestuous.

incidence [ɛ̃sidɑ̃:s] *nf* incidence.

incident [ɛ̃sidɑ̃] *a* parenthetical, incidental; *nm* incident, occurrence.

incinérateur [ɛ̃sinɛratœ:r] *nm* incinerator.

incinérer [ɛ̃sinere] *vt* to incinerate, cremate.

incisif [ɛ̃sisif] *a* incisive.

incision [ɛ̃sizjɔ̃] *nf* incision, cutting, lancing, tapping.

inciter [ɛ̃site] *vt* to incite, urge.

incivilisé [ɛ̃sivilize] *a* uncivilized.

incivilité [ɛ̃sivilite] *nf* incivility, (piece of) rudeness.

inclassable [ɛ̃klɑsabl] *a* unclassifiable, nondescript.

inclémence [ɛ̃klemɑ̃:s] *nf* inclemency

inclinaison [ɛ̃klinɛzɔ̃] *nf* inclination, incline, gradient, tilt, slope.

inclination [ɛ̃klinasjɔ̃] *nf* inclination, bending, bow, nod, bent.

incliner [ɛ̃kline] *vt* to incline, slope, bow, tilt, dip, predispose; *vi* to be predisposed, inclined; *vr* to slope, slant, bow, give way.

inclure [ɛ̃kly:r] *vt* to enclose.

inclus [ɛ̃kly] *a* including.

inclusif, -ive [ɛ̃klyzif, i:v] *a* inclusive.

inclusion [ɛ̃klyzjɔ̃] *nf* inclusion, enclosing.

incohérence [ɛ̃kɔɛrɑ̃:s] *nf* incoherence, disjointedness

incohérent [ɛ̃kɔɛrɑ̃] *a* incoherent, disjointed.

incolore [ɛ̃kɔlɔ:r] *a* colourless.

incomber [ɛ̃kɔbe] *vi* to fall, devolve, be incumbent.

incombustible [ɛ̃kɔbystibl] *a* incombustible, uninflammable.

incomestible [ɛ̃kɔmɛstibl] *a* inedible.

incommensurable [ɛ̃kɔm(m)ɑ̃syrabl] *a* incommensurable, incommensurate, immeasurable.

incommode [ɛ̃kɔmɔd] *a* inconvenient, uncomfortable, awkward, tiresome.

incommoder [ɛ̃kɔmɔde] *vt* to inconvenience, upset, disagree with.

incommodité [ɛ̃kɔmɔdite] *nf* inconvenience, discomfort.

incomparable [ɛ̃kɔparabl] *a* incomparable, matchless.

incompatible [ɛ̃kɔpatibl] *a* incompatible.

incompétence [ɛ̃kɔpetɑ̃:s] *nf* incompetence, inefficiency.

incompétent [ɛ̃kɔpetɑ̃] *a* incompetent, inefficient, unqualified.

incompréhensible [ɛ̃kɔpreɑ̃sibl] *a* incomprehensible.

incompréhension [ɛ̃kɔpreɑ̃sjɔ̃] *nf* obtuseness, want of understanding.

incompris [ɛ̃kɔpri] *a* misunderstood, not appreciated.

inconcevable [ɛ̃kɔ̃s(ə)vabl] *a* inconceivable, unthinkable.

inconciliable [ɛ̃kɔ̃siljabl] *a* irreconcilable incompatible.

24

inconduite [ɛ̃kɔ̃dɥit] *nf* bad living, misconduct.

incongru [ɛ̃kɔ̃gry] *a* incongruous, unseemly, stupid.

incongruité [ɛ̃kɔ̃gryite] *nf* incongruity, unseemliness, stupid remark.

inconnu [ɛ̃kɔny] *a* unknown; *n* stranger, unknown person; *nm* (the) unknown.

inconscience [ɛ̃kɔ̃sjɑ̃:s] *nf* unconsciousness, want of principle.

inconscient [ɛ̃kɔ̃sjɑ̃] *a* unconscious, unaware; *nm* subconscious mind.

inconséquent [ɛ̃kɔ̃sekɑ̃] *a* inconsistent, irresponsible, illogical.

inconsidéré [ɛ̃kɔ̃sidere] *a* inconsiderate, thoughtless, heedless.

inconsistant [ɛ̃kɔ̃sistɑ̃] *a* soft, flabby.

inconsolable [ɛ̃kɔ̃sɔlabl] *a* inconsolable.

inconstance [ɛ̃kɔ̃stɑ̃:s] *nf* inconstancy, fickleness, changeableness.

inconstant [ɛ̃kɔ̃stɑ̃] *a* inconstant, fickle, changeable.

incontestable [ɛ̃kɔ̃testabl] *a* indisputable, beyond question.

incontesté [ɛ̃kɔ̃teste] *a* undisputed.

incontinent [ɛ̃kɔ̃tinɑ̃] *a* incontinent; *ad* straightway, forthwith.

incontrôlable [ɛ̃kɔ̃trolȧbl] *a* not verifiable, unable to be checked.

inconvenance [ɛ̃kɔvnɑ̃:s] *nf* unsuitability, impropriety, unseemliness, improper act or word.

inconvenant [ɛ̃kɔ̃vnɑ̃] *a* improper, unseemly.

inconvénient [ɛ̃kɔvenjɑ̃] *nm* disadvantage, drawback, objection.

incorporer [ɛ̃kɔrpɔre] *vt* to incorporate, embody.

incorrect [ɛ̃kɔr(r)ɛkt] *a* wrong, ill-mannered.

incorrection [ɛ̃kɔr(r)ɛksjɔ̃] *nf* incorrectness, inaccuracy, ill-bred act.

incorrigible [ɛ̃kɔr(r)iʒibl] *a* incorrigible, hopeless.

incorruptible [ɛ̃kɔr(r)yptibl] *a* incorruptible.

incrédibilité [ɛ̃kredibilite] *nf* incredibility.

incrédule [ɛ̃kredyl] *a* incredulous; *n* unbeliever.

incrédulité [ɛ̃kredylite] *nf* incredulity.

incriminer [ɛ̃krimine] *vt* to incriminate, accuse.

incroyable [ɛ̃krwajabl] *a* incredible, unbelievable.

incroyant [ɛ̃krwajɑ̃] *a* unbelieving; *n* unbeliever.

incrustation [ɛ̃krystasjɔ̃] *nf* incrustation, inlaying, inlaid work, furring.

incruster [ɛ̃kryste] *vt* to incrust, fur, inlay; *vr* to become incrusted, furred up.

incubation [ɛ̃kybasjɔ̃] *nf* incubation, hatching.

inculpable [ɛ̃kylpabl] *a* chargeable, indictable.

inculpation [ɛ̃kylpasjɔ̃] *nf* charge, indictment.

inculpé [ɛ̃kylpe] *n* accused, defendant.

inculper [ɛ̃kylpe] *vt* to charge, indict.

inculquer [ɛ̃kylke] *vt* to inculcate, instil.

inculte [ɛ̃kylt] *a* uncultivated, wild, uncultured.

incurable [ɛ̃kyrabl] *a* incurable.

incurie [ɛ̃kyri] *nf* carelessness, negligence.

incuriosité [ɛ̃kyrjɔzite] *nf* want of curiosity.

incursion [ɛ̃kyrsjɔ̃] *nf* inroad, raid.

Inde [ɛ̃:d] *nf* India; *pl* Indies.

indébrouillable [ɛ̃debrujabl] *a* tangled, inextricable.

indécence [ɛ̃desɑ̃:s] *nf* immodesty, indecency.

indécent [ɛ̃desɑ̃] *a* immodest, indecent, improper.

indéchiffrable [ɛ̃deʃifrabl] *a* undecipherable, illegible, unintelligible.

indécis [ɛ̃desi] *a* undecided, irresolute, doubtful, open, vague.

indécision [ɛ̃desizjɔ̃] *nf* indecision, irresolution.

indéfendable [ɛ̃defɑ̃dabl] *a* indefensible.

indéfini [ɛ̃defini] *a* indefinite, undefined.

indéfinissable [ɛ̃definisabl] *a* indefinable.

indélébile [ɛ̃delebil] *a* indelible.

indélicat [ɛ̃delika] *a* indelicate, tactless.

indélicatesse [ɛ̃delikatɛs] *nf* indelicacy, tactlessness, coarse act or remark.

indémaillable [ɛ̃demajabl] *a* ladder-proof.

indemne [ɛ̃demn] *a* undamaged, unhurt.

indemniser [ɛ̃dɛmnize] *vt* to compensate, indemnify.

indemnité [ɛ̃dɛmnite] *nf* indemnity, compensation, grant, allowance; — **de chômage** dole.

indéniable [ɛ̃denjabl] *a* undeniable.

indépendance [ɛ̃depɑ̃dɑ̃:s] *nf* independence.

indépendant [ɛ̃depɑ̃dɑ̃] *a* independent, unattached, self-contained.

indescriptible [ɛ̃dɛskriptibl] *a* indescribable.

indésirable [ɛ̃dezirabl] *a* undesirable, objectionable.

indestructible [ɛ̃dɛstryktibl] *a* indestructible.

indéterminé [ɛ̃determine] *a* irresolute, indefinite, indeterminate.

index [ɛ̃dɛks] *nm* forefinger, index, indicator.

indicateur, -trice [ɛ̃dikatœːr, tris] *a* indicatory; *nm* time-table, gauge, indicator, detector, informer; **poteau** — signpost.

indicatif, -ive [ɛ̃dikatif, iːv] *a*

indicative; *nm* indicative (mood), signature tune.

indication [ɛ̃dikasjɔ̃] *nf* indication, information, sign, clue, pointing out; *pl* instructions, directions.

indice [ɛ̃dis] *nm* sign, mark, indication, clue.

indicible [ɛ̃disibl] *a* unspeakable, indescribable.

indien, -ienne [ɛ̃djɛ̃, jɛn] *an* Indian

indienne [ɛ̃djɛn] *nf* chintz, print, overarm stroke.

indifférence [ɛ̃diferɑ̃:s] *nf* indifference, apathy.

indifférent [ɛ̃diferɑ̃] *a* apathetic, immaterial, all the same.

indigence [ɛ̃diʒɑ̃:s] *nf* want, poverty.

indigène [ɛ̃diʒɛn] *a* indigenous, native; *n* native.

indigent [ɛ̃diʒɑ̃] *a* indigent, needy.

indigeste [ɛ̃diʒɛst] *a* indigestible, heavy, undigested.

indigestion [ɛ̃diʒɛstjɔ̃] *nf* attack of indigestion.

indignation [ɛ̃diɲasjɔ̃] *nf* indignation.

indigne [ɛ̃diɲ] *a* unworthy, undeserving, vile.

indigné [ɛ̃diɲe] *a* indignant.

indigner [ɛ̃diɲe] *vt* to make indignant; *vr* to be, to become, indignant.

indignité [ɛ̃diɲite] *nf* indignity, unworthiness, infamy.

indiquer [ɛ̃dike] *vt* to indicate, point (to, out), show, appoint; c'était indiqué it was the obvious thing to do.

indirect [ɛ̃dirɛkt] *a* indirect, devious.

indiscipliné [ɛ̃disipline] *a* unruly, undisciplined.

indiscret, -ète [ɛ̃diskrɛ, ɛt] *a* indiscreet, unguarded, tactless, prying.

indiscrétion [ɛ̃diskresjɔ̃] *nf* indiscretion, tactless remark or action.

indiscutable [ɛ̃diskytabl] *a* unquestionable, indisputable.

indispensable [ɛ̃dispɑ̃sabl] *a* indispensable, necessary, essential, requisite.

indisponibilité [ɛ̃disponibilite] *nf* unavailability.

indisposé [ɛ̃dispoze] *a* indisposed, unwell, ill-disposed.

indisposer [ɛ̃dispoze] *vt* to upset, disagree with, make unwell, antagonize.

indisposition [ɛ̃dispozisjɔ̃] *nf* indisposition.

indissoluble [ɛ̃dissolybl] *a* insoluble (*chem*), indissoluble.

indistinct [ɛ̃distɛ̃(:kt)] *a* indistinct, faint, blurred.

individu [ɛ̃dividy] *nm* individual, fellow, character.

individualiser [ɛ̃dividɥalize] *vt* to individualize, specify.

individuel, -elle [ɛ̃dividɥɛl] *a* individual, personal.

indivisible [ɛ̃divizibl] *a* indivisible.

Indochine [ɛ̃dɔʃin] *nf* Indo-China.

indocile [ɛ̃dɔsil] *a* intractable, wilful, disobedient.

indolence [ɛ̃dɔlɑ̃:s] *nf* apathy.

indolent [ɛ̃dɔlɑ̃] *a* indolent, slack, slothful.

indomptable [ɛ̃dɔ̃tabl] *a* untamable, ungovernable, unmanageable, invincible.

indu [ɛ̃dy] *a* not due, undue, unwarranted, unreasonable

indubitable [ɛ̃dybitabl] *a* unquestionable.

induire [ɛ̃dɥi:r] *vt* to induce, tempt.

indulgence [ɛ̃dylʒɑ̃:s] *nf* indulgence, forbearance, leniency.

indulgent [ɛ̃dylʒɑ̃] *a* forbearing, lenient.

indûment [ɛ̃dymɑ̃] *ad* unduly.

industrialiser [ɛ̃dystrialize] *vt* to industrialize.

industrialisme [ɛ̃dystrialism] *nm* industrialism.

industrie [ɛ̃dystri] *nf* industry, trade, activity, industriousness; vivre d'— to live by one's wits.

industriel, -ielle [ɛ̃dystriɛl] *a* industrial; *nm* industrialist, manufacturer.

industrieux, -euse [ɛ̃dystriø, ø:z] *a* industrious, active.

inébranlable [inebrɑ̃labl] *a* unshakeable, steadfast, unswerving.

inédit [inedi] *a* unpublished, new.

ineffable [inefabl] *a* ineffable, unutterable.

ineffaçable [inefasabl] *a* indelible.

inefficace [inefikas] *a* ineffective, ineffectual.

inefficacité [inefikasite] *nf* inefficacy, ineffectiveness, ineffectualness.

inégal [inegal] *a* unequal, uneven, irregular, unsteady.

inégalité [inegalite] *nf* inequality, unevenness, roughness, unsteadiness.

inéligible [ineliʒibl] *a* ineligible.

inéluctable [inelyktabl] *a* inevitable.

inénarrable [inenarabl] *a* indescribable, beyond words.

inepte [inɛpt] *a* inept, foolish, stupid, futile.

ineptie [inɛpsi] *nf* ineptitude, stupid remark.

inépuisable [inepɥizabl] *a* inexhaustible, abundant.

inéquitable [inekitabl] *a* unfair.

inerte [inɛrt] *a* inert, dull, sluggish, listless.

inespéré [inɛspere] *a* unexpected, unhoped-for.

inestimable [inɛstimabl] *a* priceless, invaluable.

inévitable [inevitabl] *a* inevitable.

inexact [inɛgzakt] *a* inexact, inaccurate, unpunctual.

inexactitude [inɛgzaktityd] *nf* inaccuracy, unpunctuality.

inexcusable [inɛkskyzabl] *a* unpardonable, unwarranted.

inexécutable [inɛgzekytabl] *a* impracticable.

inexercé [inɛgzɛrse] *a* unexercised, unpractised.

inexistant [inɛgzistɑ̃] *a* non-existent.

inexorable [inɛgzɔrabl] *a* inexorable.

inexpérience [inɛksperjɑ̃:s] *nf* inexperience.

inexpérimenté [inɛksperimɑ̃te] *a* inexperienced, unpractised, untried, raw.

inexplicable [inɛksplikabl] *a* inexplicable, unaccountable.

inexpliqué [inɛksplike] *a* unexplained, unaccounted for.

inexploité [inɛksplwate] *a* unworked, undeveloped.

inexpressif, -ive [inɛksprɛsif, i:v] *a* expressionless.

inexprimable [inɛksprimabl] *a* inexpressible, beyond words.

inextricable [inɛkstrikabl] *a* inextricable.

infaillibilité [ɛ̃fajibilite] *nf* infallibility.

infaillible [ɛ̃fajibl] *a* infallible, sure, unerring.

infâme [ɛ̃fɑ:m] *a* infamous, foul.

infamie [ɛ̃fami] infamy, foul deed or word.

infanterie [ɛ̃fɑ̃tri] *nf* infantry.

infatigable [ɛ̃fatigabl] *a* tireless, untiring, indefatigable.

infatuation [ɛ̃fatɥasjɔ̃] *nf* self-conceit, infatuation.

infécond [ɛ̃fekɔ̃] *a* barren, sterile, unfruitful.

infécondité [ɛ̃fekɔ̃dite] *nf* sterility, barrenness.

infect [ɛ̃fɛkt] *a* stinking, tainted, rotten, foul.

infecter [ɛ̃fɛkte] *vt* to infect, taint, stink of.

infectieux, -euse [ɛ̃fɛksjø, ø:z] *a* infectious.

infection [ɛ̃fɛksjɔ̃] *nf* infection, contamination, stink.

s'inféoder [sɛ̃feɔde] *vr* to give one's support, join.

inférer [ɛ̃fere] *vt* to infer.

inférieur [ɛ̃ferjœ:r] *a* inferior, lower; *n* inferior.

infériorité [ɛ̃ferjɔrite] *nf* inferiority.

infernal [ɛ̃fɛrnal] *a* infernal, devilish, diabolical.

infertile [ɛ̃fɛrtil] *a* barren, infertile, unfruitful.

infester [ɛ̃fɛste] *vt* to infest, overrun.

infidèle [ɛ̃fidɛl] *a* unfaithful, faithless, false; *n* infidel, unbeliever.

infidélité [ɛ̃fidelite] *nf* infidelity, unfaithfulness.

infiltration [ɛ̃filtrasjɔ̃] *nf* infiltration, percolation.

s'infiltrer [sɛ̃filtre] *vr* to infiltrate, seep, soak in.

infime [ɛ̃fim] *a* lowly, mean, tiny.

infini [ɛ̃fini] *a* infinite, endless, boundless, countless; *nm* infinite, infinity.

infiniment [ɛ̃finimɑ̃] *ad* infinitely.

infinité [ɛ̃finite] *nf* infinity, infinitude, countless number.

infirme [ɛ̃firm] *a* infirm, disabled, crippled, feeble; *n* cripple, invalid.

infirmer [ɛ̃firme] *vt* to weaken, invalidate, quash.

infirmerie [ɛ̃firməri] *nf* infirmary, sick-room.

infirmier, -ière [ɛ̃firmje, ɛ:r] *n* (male) nurse, hospital orderly.

infirmité [ɛ̃firmite] *nf* infirmity, weakness, disability.

inflammation [ɛ̃flamasjɔ̃] *nf* inflammation.

inflation [ɛ̃flasjɔ̃] *nf* inflation.

inflexible [ɛ̃flɛksibl] *a* inflexible, unbending, rigid.

inflexion [ɛ̃flɛksjɔ̃] *nf* inflection, modulation.

infliger [ɛ̃fliʒe] *vt* to inflict.

influence [ɛ̃flyɑ̃:s] *nf* influence, effect, sway.

influencer [ɛ̃flyɑ̃se] *vt* to influence, sway.

influent [ɛ̃flyɑ̃] *a* influential.

influer [ɛ̃flye] *vi* to have an influence, an effect.

informateur, -trice [ɛ̃fɔrmatœ:r, tris] *n* informant.

information [ɛ̃fɔrmasjɔ̃] *nf* inquiry, preliminary investigation; *pl* news bulletin.

informe [ɛ̃fɔrm] *a* shapeless, illformed, misshapen; (*jur*) irregular.

informer [ɛ̃fɔrme] *vt* to inform, apprise; *vi* to inform (against contre); *vr* to make inquiries.

infortune [ɛ̃fɔrtyn] *nf* misfortune.

infortuné [ɛ̃fɔrtyne] *a* unfortunate, unlucky.

infraction [ɛ̃fraksjɔ̃] *nf* infringement, breach.

infranchissable [ɛ̃frɑ̃ʃisabl] *a* impassable, insuperable.

infructueux, -euse [ɛ̃fryktɥø, ø:z] *a* unsuccessful, barren, fruitless.

infuser [ɛ̃fyse] *vt* to infuse, steep; *vr* to infuse, brew.

infusion [ɛ̃fyzjɔ̃] *nf* infusion.

ingambe [ɛ̃gɑ̃:b] *a* active.

s'ingénier [sɛ̃ʒenje] *vr* to contrive, use all one's wits.

ingénieur [ɛ̃ʒenjœ:r] *nm* engineer.

ingénieux, -euse [ɛ̃ʒenjø, ø:z] *a* ingenious, clever.

ingéniosité [ɛ̃ʒenjɔzite] *nf* ingenuity, ingeniousness.

ingénu [ɛ̃ʒeny] *a* ingenuous, simple, artless, unsophisticated.

ingénuité [ɛ̃ʒenɥite] *nf* ingenuousness, simplicity.

s'ingérer [sɛ̃ʒere] *vr* to interfere, meddle (with dans).

ingouvernable [ɛ̃guvɛrnabl] *a* unmanageable, uncontrollable.

ingrat [ɛ̃gra] *an* ungrateful, thankless, unprofitable, barren.

ingratitude [ɛ̃gratityd] *nf* ingratitude, thanklessness.

ingrédient [ɛ̃gredjɑ̃] *nm* ingredient.
inguérissable [ɛ̃gerisabl] *a* incurable.
ingurgiter [ɛ̃gyrʒite] *vt* to gulp down, swallow.
inhabile [inabil] *a* awkward, unskilled, clumsy.
inhabitable [inabitabl] *a* uninhabitable.
inhabité [inabite] *a* uninhabited, untenanted, vacant.
inhabituel(le) [inabituɛl] *a* unusual, unwonted.
inharmonieux, -euse [inarmɔnjø, øːz] *a* discordant, unmusical.
inhérent [inerɑ̃] *a* inherent.
inhibition [inibisjɔ̃] *nf* inhibition.
inhospitalier, -ière [inɔspitalje, jɛːr] *a* inhospitable.
inhumain [inymɛ̃] *a* inhuman, heartless.
inhumer [inyme] *vt* to bury, inter.
inimaginable [inimaʒinabl] *a* unimaginable, unthinkable.
inimitable [inimitabl] *a* inimitable, peerless.
inimitié [inimitje] *nf* enmity, ill-will, ill-feeling.
ininflammable [inɛ̃flamabl] *a* fireproof.
inintelligent [inɛ̃teliʒɑ̃] *a* unintelligent, obtuse.
inintelligible [inɛ̃teliʒibl] *a* unintelligible.
ininterrompu [inɛ̃tɛrɔ̃py] *a* uninterrupted, unbroken.
iniquité [inikite] *nf* injustice, wickedness.
initial [inisjal] *a* initial, starting.
initiale [inisjal] *nf* initial (letter).
initiateur, -trice [inisjatœːr, tris] *n* initiator.
initiative [inisjatiːv] *nf* initiative, push; **syndicat d'—** information bureau.
initier [inisje] *vt* to initiate.
injecter [ɛ̃ʒɛkte] *vt* to inject; *vr* to become bloodshot.
injection [ɛ̃ʒɛksjɔ̃] *nf* injection.
injonction [ɛ̃ʒɔ̃ksjɔ̃] *nf* injunction, behest.
injudicieux, -euse [ɛ̃ʒydisjø, øːz] *a* injudicious.
injure [ɛ̃ʒyːr] *nf* insult, wrong.
injurier [ɛ̃ʒyrje] *vt* to insult, call names, abuse.
injurieux, -euse [ɛ̃ʒyrjø, øːz] *a* insulting, abusive.
injuste [ɛ̃ʒyst] *a* unfair, unjust.
injustice [ɛ̃ʒystis] *nf* injustice, unfairness, wrong.
injustifiable [ɛ̃ʒystifjabl] *a* unjustifiable.
inlassable [ɛ̃lɑsabl] *a* untiring, tireless.
innavigable [inavigabl] *a* unnavigable, unseaworthy.
inné [inne] *a* innate, inborn.
innocence [inɔsɑ̃ːs] *nf* innocence, harmlessness.
innocent [inɔsɑ̃] *a* innocent, simple,

guileless, harmless; *n* half-wit, idiot.
innocenter [inɔsɑ̃te] *vt* to clear, declare innocent.
innocuité [innɔkɥite] *nf* innocuousness, harmlessness.
innombrable [innɔ̃brabl] *a* countless, innumerable.
innover [innɔve] *vt* to innovate; *vi* to break new ground.
inobservation [inɔpsɛrvasjɔ̃] *nf* disregard, breach.
inobservé [inɔpsɛrve] *a* unnoticed, unobserved.
inoccupé [inɔkype] *a* unoccupied, idle, vacant.
inoculer [inɔkyle] *vt* to inoculate, inject.
inodore [inɔdor] *a* odourless, scentless.
inoffensif, -ive [inɔfɑsif, iːv] *a* inoffensive, harmless.
inondation [inɔ̃dasjɔ̃] *nf* flood.
inonder [inɔ̃de] *vt* to flood, inundate; **être inondé de** to be flooded with, soaked in.
inopiné [inɔpine] *a* unexpected, unforeseen.
inopportun [inɔpɔrtœ̃] *a* inopportune, unseasonable, ill-timed.
inopportunité [inɔpɔrtynite] *nf* inopportuneness, unseasonableness.
inoubliable [inubliabl] *a* unforgettable.
inouï [inui, -w-] *a* unheard of, outrageous.
inoxydable [inɔksidabl] *a* rustproof, stainless; *nm* stainless steel.
inqualifiable [ɛ̃kalifjabl] *a* unspeakable.
inquiet, -ète [ɛ̃kjɛ, ɛt] *a* anxious, uneasy, concerned.
inquiéter [ɛ̃kjete] *vt* to make anxious, disturb, disquiet, alarm; *vr* to worry, grow anxious.
inquiétude [ɛ̃kjetyd] *nf* anxiety, misgivings.
insaisissable [ɛ̃sezisabl] *a* elusive, imperceptible.
insalissable [ɛ̃salisabl] *a* dirtproof.
insalubre [ɛ̃salybr] *a* unhealthy, insanitary.
insanité [ɛ̃sanite] *nf* insanity; *pl* (*fam*) nonsense.
insatiable [ɛ̃sasjabl] *a* insatiable, unquenchable.
inscription [ɛ̃skripsjɔ̃] *nf* inscription, writing down, enrolment; **droit d'—** entrance fee, registration fee.
inscrire [ɛ̃skriːr] *vt* to inscribe, write down, enrol, register; *vr* to enrol, put down one's name.
insecte [ɛ̃sɛkt] *nm* insect.
insécurité [ɛ̃sekyrite] *nf* insecurity.
insensé [ɛ̃sɑ̃se] *a* mad, senseless, wild, crazy.
insensibiliser [ɛ̃sɑ̃sibilize] *vt* to anaesthetize.
insensibilité [ɛ̃sɑ̃sibilite] *nf* insensibility, callousness, lack of feeling.

insensible [ɛ̃sɑ̃sibl] *a* insensitive, callous, unfeeling, imperceptible.

inséparable [ɛ̃separabl] *a* inseparable.

insérer [ɛ̃sere] *vt* to insert.

insidieux, -euse [ɛ̃sidjø, ø:z] *a* insidious.

insigne [ɛ̃siɲ] *a* distinguished, signal, notorious; *nm* badge, emblem; *pl* insignia.

insignifiance [ɛ̃siɲifjɑ̃:s] *nf* insignificance.

insignifiant [ɛ̃siɲifjɑ̃] *a* insignificant, trivial, meaningless.

insinuation [ɛ̃sinɥasjɔ̃] *nf* insinuation, innuendo, insertion.

insinuer [ɛ̃sinɥe] *vt* to insinuate, hint at, insert; *vr* to steal, slip, creep (into **dans**).

insipide [ɛ̃sipid] *a* insipid, tasteless, dull, flat.

insistance [ɛ̃sistɑ̃:s] *nf* insistence, persistence.

insister [ɛ̃siste] *vi* to insist, persist; **— sur** stress.

insociable [ɛ̃sɔsjabl] *a* unsociable.

insolation [ɛ̃sɔlasjɔ̃] *nf* insolation, sunstroke.

insolence [ɛ̃sɔlɑ̃:s] *nf* insolence, impertinence.

insolent [ɛ̃sɔlɑ̃] *an* insolent, impudent, impertinent.

insolite [ɛ̃sɔlit] *a* unusual, strange.

insoluble [ɛ̃sɔlybl] *a* insoluble, unsolvable.

insolvabilité [ɛ̃sɔlvabilite] *nf* insolvency.

insolvable [ɛ̃sɔlvabl] *a* insolvent.

insomnie [ɛ̃sɔmni] *nf* insomnia, sleeplessness.

insondable [ɛ̃sɔ̃dabl] *a* fathomless, bottomless, unfathomable.

insonore [ɛ̃sɔnɔ:r] *a* soundproof.

insouciance [ɛ̃susjɑ̃:s] *nf* unconcern, casualness.

insouciant [ɛ̃susjɑ̃] *a* care-free, heedless.

insoucieux, -euse [ɛ̃susjø, ø:z] *a* heedless, regardless.

insoumis [ɛ̃sumi] *a* unsubdued, unruly, refractory.

insoumission [ɛ̃sumisjɔ̃] *nf* insubordination.

insoupçonnable [ɛ̃supsɔnabl] *a* beyond suspicion.

insoutenable [ɛ̃sutnabl] *a* untenable, indefensible.

inspecter [ɛ̃spɛkte] *vt* to inspect, examine.

inspecteur, -trice [ɛ̃spɛktœ:r, tris] *n* inspector, inspectress, examiner, overseer.

inspection [ɛ̃spɛksjɔ̃] *nf* inspection, examination, survey.

inspiration [ɛ̃spirasjɔ̃] *nf* inspiration, breathing in.

inspirer [ɛ̃spire] *vt* to inspire, breathe in, prompt; *vr* to find inspiration (in **de**).

instabilité [ɛ̃stabilite] *nf* instability,

unsteadiness, uncertainty, fickleness.

instable [ɛ̃stabl] *a* unstable, unsteady, unreliable.

installation [ɛ̃stalasjɔ̃] *nf* setting up, fittings, plant.

installer [ɛ̃stale] *vt* to install, fit up, equip; *vr* to settle down, move in.

instamment [ɛ̃stamɑ̃] *ad* earnestly, urgently.

instance [ɛ̃stɑ̃:s] *nf* solicitation, lawsuit; *pl* entreaties, requests.

instant [ɛ̃stɑ̃] *a* urgent, pressing; *nm* instant, moment; **à l'—** at once, **a moment ago**; **par —s** off and on.

instantané [ɛ̃stɑ̃tane] *a* instantaneous; *nm* snapshot.

instar [ɛ̃sta:r] *prep* **à l'— de** after the manner of, like.

instigateur, -trice [ɛ̃stigatœ:r, tris] *n* instigator.

instigation [ɛ̃stigasjɔ̃] *nf* instigation, incitement.

instinct [ɛ̃stɛ̃] *nm* instinct.

instinctif, -ive [ɛ̃stɛ̃ktif, i:v] *a* instinctive.

instituer [ɛ̃stitɥe] *vt* to institute, set up, appoint.

institut [ɛ̃stity] *nm* institute, institution.

instituteur, -trice [ɛ̃stitytœ:r, tris] *n* primary school-teacher, founder.

institution [ɛ̃stitysjɔ̃] *nf* setting up, institution, establishment.

instructeur [ɛ̃stryktœ:r] *nm* instructor; **sergent —** drill sergeant.

instructif, -ive [ɛ̃stryktif, i:v] *a* instructive.

instruction [ɛ̃stryksjɔ̃] *nf* education, training, (*jur*) preliminary investigation; *pl* directions, orders.

instruire [ɛ̃strɥi:r] *vt* to instruct, train, (*jur*) investigate, inform.

instruit [ɛ̃strɥi] *a* educated, learned, trained.

instrument [ɛ̃strymɑ̃] *nm* instrument, tool.

instrumentation [ɛ̃strymɑ̃tasjɔ̃] *nf* instrumentation, orchestration.

instrumenter [ɛ̃strymɑ̃te] *vt* to score, orchestrate; *vi* to order proceedings to be taken.

insu [ɛ̃sy] *nm* **à l'— de** without the knowledge of; **à son —** without his knowing.

insubmersible [ɛ̃sybmɛrsibl] *a* unsinkable.

insubordination [ɛ̃sybɔrdinasjɔ̃] *nf* insubordination.

insuccès [ɛ̃syksɛ] *nm* failure.

insuffisance [ɛ̃syfizɑ̃:s] *nf* insufficiency, shortage, inadequacy, incompetence.

insuffisant [ɛ̃syfizɑ̃] *a* insufficient, inadequate, incompetent.

insulaire [ɛ̃sylɛ:r] *a* insular; *n* islander.

insularité [ɛ̃sylarite] *nf* insularity.

insulte [ɛ̃sylt] *nf* insult.

insulter [ɛ̃sylte] *vt* to insult; *vi* to be an insult to.

insupportable [ɛ̃sypɔrtabl] *a* unbearable, insufferable, intolerable.

insurgé [ɛ̃syrʒe] *n* rebel, insurgent.

s'insurger [sɛ̃syrʒe] *vr* to revolt, rise in revolt.

insurmontable [ɛ̃syrmɔ̃tabl] *a* insuperable.

insurrection [ɛ̃syrrɛksjɔ̃] *nf* rebellion, insurrection.

intact [ɛ̃takt] *a* intact, whole, undamaged.

intangible [ɛ̃tãʒibl] *a* intangible, inviolable.

intarissable [ɛ̃tarisabl] *a* inexhaustible, endless.

intégral [ɛ̃tegral] *a* integral, full, complete.

intégrant [ɛ̃tegrã] *a* integral.

intègre [ɛ̃tɛgr] *a* upright, honest, just.

intégrer [ɛ̃tegre] *vt* integrate.

intégrité [ɛ̃tegrite] *nf* integrity, honesty, entirety.

intellectuel, -elle [ɛ̃tɛl(l)ɛktɥɛl] *a* intellectual, mental; *n* intellectual, highbrow.

intelligence [ɛ̃tɛl(l)iʒã:s] *nf* intelligence, intellect, understanding; **vivre en bonne — avec** to live on good terms with; **être d'— avec** to be in league with.

intelligent [ɛ̃tɛl(l)iʒã] *a* intelligent, clever.

intelligible [ɛ̃tɛl(l)iʒibl] *a* audible, understandable.

intempérance [ɛ̃tãperã:s] *nf* intemperance, licence.

intempérant [ɛ̃tãperã] *a* intemperate.

intempérie [ɛ̃tãperi] *nf* inclemency (of weather).

intempestif, -ive [ɛ̃tãpɛstif, i:v] *a* unseasonable, inopportune.

intenable [ɛ̃tnabl] *a* untenable.

intendance [ɛ̃tãdã:s] *nf* stewardship, commissariat, Army Service Corps, supply depot, finance office.

intendant [ɛ̃tãdã] *nm* steward (of household); bursar; **— général** quartermaster general.

intense [ɛ̃tã:s] *a* intense, intensive, severe.

intensité [ɛ̃tãsite] *nf* intensity, strength.

intenter [ɛ̃tãte] *vt* **— un procès to** bring an action.

intention [ɛ̃tãsjɔ̃] *nf* intention, purpose; **à votre —** for you, meant for you.

intentionné [ɛ̃tãsjɔne] *a* intentioned, meaning, disposed.

intentionnel, -elle [ɛ̃tãsjɔnɛl] *a* intentional.

inter [ɛ̃tɛ:r] *nm* (*telephone*) trunks.

intercaler [ɛ̃tɛrkale] *vt* to insert, add.

intercéder [ɛ̃tɛrsede] *vi* to intercede.

intercepter [ɛ̃tɛrsɛpte] *vt* to intercept, cut off.

interception [ɛ̃tɛrsɛpsjɔ̃] *nf* interception, tackle.

intercession [ɛ̃tɛrsɛsjɔ̃] *nf* intercession.

interchangeable [ɛ̃tɛrʃãʒabl] *a* interchangeable.

interdiction [ɛ̃tɛrdiksjɔ̃] *nf* interdiction, prohibition.

interdire [ɛ̃tɛrdi:r] *vt* to prohibit, forbid, ban, suspend, nonplus, take aback.

interdit [ɛ̃tɛrdi] *a* suspended, forbidden, taken aback, nonplussed; *nm* interdict; **sens — no entry.**

intéressant [ɛ̃terɛsã] *a* interesting.

intéressé [ɛ̃terɛse] *a* interested, concerned, selfish.

intéresser [ɛ̃terɛse] *vt* to interest, concern; *vr* to be interested, take an interest.

intérêt [ɛ̃terɛ] *nm* interest, advantage, stake; **avoir — à le faire to** be to one's interest to do it; **porter — à** to take an interest in.

interférer [ɛ̃tɛrfere] *vt* to interfere.

intérieur [ɛ̃terjœ:r] *a* interior, inward, home, domestic, inland; *nm* inside, interior, home, house, insideforward; **à l'—** inside.

intérim [ɛ̃terim] *nm* interim.

interjection [ɛ̃tɛrʒɛksjɔ̃] *nf* interjection.

interligne [ɛ̃tɛrliɲ] *nm* space between two lines.

interlocuteur, -trice [ɛ̃tɛrlɔkytœ:r, tris] *n* interlocutor, speaker.

interloquer [ɛ̃tɛrlɔke] *vt* to disconcert, take aback; *vr* to become embarrassed.

intermède [ɛ̃tɛrmɛd] *nm* interlude.

intermédiaire [ɛ̃tɛrmedjɛ:r] *a* intermediate, intervening, middle; *nm* intermediary, agency, agent, gobetween, middleman.

interminable [ɛ̃tɛrminabl] *a* neverending, endless.

intermittent [ɛ̃tɛrmittã] *a* intermittent, irregular.

internat [ɛ̃tɛrna] *nm* boardingschool.

international, -e, -aux [ɛ̃tɛrnasjɔnal, o] *a* international; *nf* the International.

interne [ɛ̃tɛrn] *a* internal, interior, inner, inward; *n* boarder, resident doctor.

interner [ɛ̃tɛrne] *vt* to intern, confine.

interpellation [ɛ̃tɛrpɛl(l)asjɔ̃] *nf* question, interruption, challenge.

interpeller [ɛ̃tɛrpɛl(l)e] *vt* to call upon s.o. for an explanation, challenge.

interplanétaire [ɛ̃tɛrplanetɛ:r] *a* interplanetary.

interpoler [ɛ̃tɛrpɔle] *vt* to interpolate.

interposer [ɛ̃tɛrpoze] *vt* to interpose, place between; *vr* to intervene.

interprétation [ɛ̃tɛrpretasjɔ̃] *nf* interpretation, rendering.

interprète [ɛ̃tɛrprɛt] *n* interpreter, player, actor.

interpréter [ɛ̃tɛrprete] *vt* to interpret, expound, render.

interrogateur, -trice [ɛ̃tɛrɔgatœːr, tris] *a* inquiring, questioning; *n* interrogator, examiner.

interrogatif, -ive [ɛ̃tɛrɔgatif, iːv] *a* interrogative.

interrogation [ɛ̃tɛrɔgasjɔ̃] *nf* interrogation, question(ing), oral test; **point d'—** question mark.

interrogatoire [ɛ̃tɛrɔgatwaːr] *nm* interrogation, cross-examination.

interroger [ɛ̃tɛrɔʒe] *vt* to interrogate, question.

interrompre [ɛ̃tɛrɔ̃ːpr] *vt* to interrupt, break (off), stop.

interrupteur [ɛ̃tɛryptœːr] *nm* switch, cut-out.

interruption [ɛ̃tɛrypsjɔ̃] *nf* interruption, breaking off, switching off.

intersection [ɛ̃tɛrsɛksjɔ̃] *nf* intersection.

interstice [ɛ̃tɛrstis] *nm* chink.

interurbain [ɛ̃tɛryrbɛ̃] *a* interurban, trunk (call).

intervalle [ɛ̃tɛrval] *nm* interval, space, distance, period.

intervenir [ɛ̃tɛrvəniːr] *vi* to intervene, interfere.

intervention [ɛ̃tɛrvɑ̃sjɔ̃] *nf* intervention.

interversion [ɛ̃tɛrvɛrsjɔ̃] *nf* inversion.

intervertir [ɛ̃tɛrvɛrtiːr] *vt* to invert, reverse.

interviewer [ɛ̃tɛrvju(v)e] *vt* to interview.

intestin [ɛ̃tɛstɛ̃] *a* internal, civil; *nm* intestine.

intimation [ɛ̃timasjɔ̃] *nf* notification, notice.

intime [ɛ̃tim] *a* intimate, inner, inmost.

intimer [ɛ̃time] *vt* to notify.

intimider [ɛ̃timide] *vt* to intimidate, frighten.

intimité [ɛ̃timite] *nf* intimacy, privacy.

intituler [ɛ̃tityle] *vi* to entitle.

intolérable [ɛ̃tɔlerabl] *a* intolerable, unbearable.

intolérance [ɛ̃tɔlerɑ̃ːs] *nf* intolerance.

intolérant [ɛ̃tɔlerɑ̃] *a* intolerant.

intonation [ɛ̃tɔnasjɔ̃] *nf* intonation, pitch.

intoxication [ɛ̃tɔksikasjɔ̃] *nf* poisoning.

intoxiquer [ɛ̃tɔksike] *vt* to poison.

intraduisible [ɛ̃tradɥizibl] *a* untranslatable.

intraitable [ɛ̃trɛtabl] *a* unmanageable, uncompromising.

intransigeance [ɛ̃trɑ̃siʒɑ̃ːs] *nf* strictness, intolerance.

intransigeant [ɛ̃trɑ̃siʒɑ̃] *a* uncompromising, unbending, adamant.

intransportable [ɛ̃trɑ̃spɔrtabl] *a* not fit to travel.

intrépide [ɛ̃trepid] *a* intrepid, fearless, dauntless.

intrépidité [ɛ̃trepidite] *nf* fearlessness, dauntlessness.

intrigant [ɛ̃trigɑ̃] *a* intriguing, scheming; *n* intriguer, schemer.

intrigue [ɛ̃trig] *nf* intrigue, scheme, plot.

intriguer [ɛ̃trige] *vt* to intrigue, puzzle; *vi* to plot, scheme.

intrinsèque [ɛ̃trɛ̃sɛk] *a* intrinsic.

introduction [ɛ̃trɔdyksjɔ̃] *nf* introduction, bringing in, admission.

introduire [ɛ̃trɔdɥiːr] *vt* to introduce, put in, show in; *vr* to enter, get in.

introniser [ɛ̃trɔnize] *vt* to enthrone, establish.

introspection [ɛ̃trɔspɛksjɔ̃] *nf* introspection.

introuvable [ɛ̃truvabl] *a* not to be found, untraceable.

intrus [ɛ̃try] *a* intruding; *n* intruder.

intrusion [ɛ̃tryzjɔ̃] *nf* intrusion, trespass.

intuition [ɛ̃tɥisjɔ̃] *nf* intuition.

inusité [inyzite] *a* unusual.

inutile [inytil] *a* useless, vain, unavailing, needless.

inutilisable [inytilizabl] *a* useless, unserviceable.

inutilité [inytilite] *nf* uselessness.

invalide [ɛ̃valid] *a* infirm, disabled, invalid; *nm* disabled soldier.

invalider [ɛ̃valide] *vt* to invalidate, declare void, (*elected member*) unseat.

invalidité [ɛ̃validite] *nf* disablement, disability, invalidity.

invariable [ɛ̃varjabl] *a* invariable, unchanging.

invasion [ɛ̃vazjɔ̃] *nf* invasion.

invective [ɛ̃vɛktiːv] *nf* invective.

invectiver [ɛ̃vɛktive] *vt* to abuse, call s.o. names; *vi* to revile (**contre**).

invendable [ɛ̃vɑ̃dabl] *a* unsaleable.

inventaire [ɛ̃vɑ̃tɛːr] *nm* inventory; **dresser l'—** to take stock.

inventer [ɛ̃vɑ̃te] *vt* to invent, devise, discover, make up.

inventeur [ɛ̃vɑ̃tœːr] *nm* inventor, discoverer.

invention [ɛ̃vɑ̃sjɔ̃] *nf* invention, inventiveness, device, made-up story.

inventorier [ɛ̃vɑ̃tɔrje] *vt* to make a list of, inventory.

inverse [ɛ̃vɛrs] *a* inverse, inverted, opposite; *nm* opposite, reverse.

inversion [ɛ̃vɛrsjɔ̃] *nf* inversion, reversal.

invertir [ɛ̃vɛrtiːr] *vt* to invert, reverse.

investigateur, -trice [ɛ̃vɛstigatœːr, tris] *a* investigating, searching; *n* investigator.

investir [ɛ̃vɛstiːr] *vt* to invest, entrust; beleaguer.

investiture [ɛ̃vɛstityːr] *nf* nomination, induction.

invétéré [ɛ̃vetere] *a* inveterate, deep-rooted, hardened, confirmed.

invincible [ɛ̃vɛ̃sibl] *a* invincible, insuperable.

inviolable [ɛ̃vjɔlabl] *a* inviolable, sacred.

invisibilité [ɛ̃vizibilite] *nf* invisibility.

invisible [ɛ̃vizibl] *a* invisible, never to be seen.

invitation [ɛ̃vitasjɔ̃] *nf* invitation.

invite [ɛ̃vit] *nf* invitation, inducement, (*cards*) lead.

invité [ɛ̃vite] *n* guest.

inviter [ɛ̃vite] *vt* to invite, ask, call for.

involontaire [ɛ̃vɔlɔ̃tɛːr] *a* involuntary, unintentional.

invoquer [ɛ̃vɔke] *vt* to invoke, call upon, bring forward.

invraisemblable [ɛ̃vrɛsɑ̃blabl] *a* unlikely, improbable, extraordinary.

invraisemblance [ɛ̃vrɛsɑ̃blɑːs] *nf* unlikelihood, improbability.

invulnérable [ɛ̃vylnɛrabl] *a* invulnerable.

iode [jɔd, iɔd] *nm* iodine.

irascible [irassibl] *a* crusty, quick-tempered.

iris [iris] *nm* iris.

irisé [irize] *a* iridescent, rainbow-coloured.

irlandais [irlɑ̃dɛ] *an* Irish, Irishman, Irishwoman.

Irlande [irlɑ̃ːd] *nf* Ireland.

ironie [irɔni] *nf* irony.

ironique [irɔnik] *a* ironical.

irradier [irradje] *vi* to radiate, spread, irradiate.

irraisonnable [irrezɔnabl] *a* irrational.

irrecevable [irrəsəvabl] *a* inadmissible.

irréconciliable [irrekɔ̃siljabl] *a* irreconcilable.

irrécusable [irrekyzabl] *a* irrefutable, unimpeachable.

irréel, -elle [irreɛl] *a* unreal.

irréfléchi [irrefleʃi] *a* unconsidered, thoughtless.

irréflexion [irreflɛksjɔ̃] *nf* thoughtlessness.

irréfutable [irrefytabl] *a* irrefutable, indisputable.

irrégularité [irregylarite] *nf* irregularity, unsteadiness, unpunctuality.

irrégulier, -ière [irregylje, jɛːr] *a* irregular, loose (*life*).

irrémédiable [irremedjabl] *a* irremediable, irreparable.

irremplaçable [irrɑ̃plasabl] *a* irreplaceable.

irréparable [irreparabl] *a* irreparable, irretrievable.

irrépressible [irrepresibl] *a* irrepressible.

irréprochable [irreprɔʃabl] *a* irreproachable, faultless, impeccable.

irrésistible [irrezistibl] *a* irresistible.

irrésolu [irrezɔly] *a* irresolute, unsteady, unsolved.

irrésolution [irrezɔlysjɔ̃] *nf* hesitancy, uncertainty, wavering.

irrespectueux, -euse [irrespɛktɥø, øːz] *a* disrespectful.

irresponsable [irrespɔ̃sabl] *a* irresponsible.

irrévérencieux, -euse [irrevɛrɑ̃sjø, øːz] *a* irreverent, disrespectful.

irrévocable [irrevɔkabl] *a* irrevocable, binding.

irrigation [irrigasjɔ̃] *nf* irrigation.

irriguer [irrige] *vt* to irrigate.

irritable [irritabl] *a* irritable short-tempered, sensitive, jumpy.

irritation [irritasjɔ̃] *nf* irritation.

irriter [irrite] *vt* to irritate, annoy, rouse, inflame; *vr* to become angry, inflamed.

irruption [irrypsjɔ̃] *nf* irruption, inrush, raid.

islandais [islɑ̃dɛ] *a* Icelandic; *n* Icelander.

Islande [islɑ̃ːd] *nf* Iceland.

isolateur, -trice [izɔlatœːr, tris] *a* insulating; *nm* insulator.

isolement [izɔlmɑ̃] *nm* isolation, loneliness, insulation.

isolé [izɔle] *a* isolated, lonely, insulated.

isoler [izɔle] *vt* to isolate, insulate.

issu [isy] *a* sprung (from), descended (from).

issue [isy] *nf* issue, outlet exit, end, conclusion.

isthme [ism] *nm* isthmus.

Italie [itali] *nf* Italy.

italien, -ienne [italjɛ̃, jɛn] *an* Italian.

italique [italik] *a* italic; *nm* italics.

item [ˈtɛm] *ad* likewise.

itinéraire [itinerɛːr] *nm* itinerary, route.

itinérant [itinerɑ̃] *a* itinerant.

ivoire [ivwaːr] *nm* ivory.

ivraie [ivrɛ] *nf* tares, chaff.

ivre [iːvr] *a* drunk, tipsy, intoxicated, wild, mad.

ivresse [ivrɛs] *nf* intoxication, rapture.

ivrogne [ivrɔɲ] *a* drunken; *nm* drunkard, drunk man, sot.

ivrognerie [ivrɔɲri] *nf* drunkenness.

J

jabot [ʒabo] *nm* crop, jabot, ruffle, frill.

jacasser [ʒakase] *vi* to chatter, jabber.

jachère [ʒaʃɛːr] *nf* untilled land, fallow.

jacinthe [ʒasɛ̃t] *nf* hyacinth.

Jacques [ʒaːk] James.

jacquet [ʒakɛ] *nm* backgammon.

jactance [ʒaktɑːs] *nf* boasting, brag, boastfulness.

jadis [ʒadis] *ad* once, formerly, in bygone days.

jaillir [ʒajiːr] *vi* to spout, gush (out), spurt, flash.

jaillissement [ʒajismɑ̃] nm spouting, gushing.

jais [ʒɛ] nm jet.

jalon [ʒalɔ̃] nm surveyor's staff, rod; landmark.

jalonner [ʒalɔne] vt to stake out, mark out, blaze.

jalouser [ʒaluze] vt to be jealous of, envy.

jalousie [ʒaluzi] nf jealousy, venetian blind, shutter.

jaloux, -ouse [ʒalu, uːz] a jealous, anxious.

jamais [ʒamɛ] ad ever, never; **ne . . . jamais** never.

jambage [ʒɑ̃baːʒ] nm jamb, leg, downstroke.

jambe [ʒɑ̃ːb] nf leg, strut; **prendre ses —s à son cou** to take to one's heels; **à toute —s** as fast as one can.

jambière [ʒɑ̃bjɛːr] nf elastic stocking; pl leggings, shin-guards, waterproof overtrousers.

jambon [ʒɑ̃bɔ̃] nm ham.

jansénisme [ʒɑ̃senism] nm Jansenism.

jante [ʒɑ̃ːt] nf rim.

janvier [ʒɑ̃vje] nm January.

Japon [ʒapɔ̃] nm Japan.

japonais [ʒapɔnɛ] an Japanese.

jappement [ʒapmɑ̃] nm yelping, yapping.

japper [ʒape] vi to yelp, yap.

jaquette [ʒakɛt] nf (woman's) jacket, morning coat.

jardin [ʒardɛ̃] nm garden; **— public** public park; **— potager** kitchen garden; **— d'enfants** kindergarten.

jardinage [ʒardinaːʒ] nm gardening.

jardiner [ʒardine] vi to garden.

jardinière [ʒardinjɛːr] nf flowerstand, window box, market-gardener's cart mixed vegetables.

jargon [ʒargɔ̃] nm jargon, gibberish.

jarre [ʒaːr] nf earthenware jar.

jarret [ʒarɛ] nm hough, ham, hock.

jarretelle [ʒartɛl] nf suspender, (US) garter; **porte-jarretelles** nm suspender belt (US) garter belt.

jars [ʒaːr] nm gander.

jaser [ʒaze] vi to chatter.

jaseur, -euse [ʒazœːr, øːz] a talkative; n chatterbox.

jasmin [ʒasmɛ̃] nm jasmine.

jaspe [ʒasp] nm asper.

jasper [ʒaspe] vt to mottle, marble.

jatte [ʒat] nf bowl, basin, pan.

jauge [ʒoːʒ] nf gauge, tonnage, dipstick.

jauger [ʒoʒe] vt to gauge, measure, draw.

jaunâtre [ʒonɑːtr] a yellowish.

jaune [ʒoːn] a nm yellow; (slang) blackleg; **— d'œuf** yolk (of an egg); **rire —** to smile wryly.

jaunir [ʒoniːr] vt to make yellow; vi to turn yellow.

jaunisse [ʒonis] nf jaundice.

javel [ʒavɛl] nm **eau de —** (type of) bleach.

javelle [ʒavɛl] nf bundle, swath.

javelot [ʒavlo] nm javelin.

je [ʒə] pn I.

jésuite [ʒezɥit] nm Jesuit.

jet [ʒɛ] nm throw(ing), cast, jet spurt, ray, shoot; **— d'eau** fountain; **d'un seul —** in one piece, at one attempt.

jetée [ʒəte] nf jetty, pier.

jeter [ʒəte] vt to throw (away), cast, fling, utter; vr to throw oneself, attack, fall (upon **sur**), flow (into **dans**).

jeton [ʒətɔ̃] nm counter, token.

jeu [ʒø] nm game, playing, acting, gambling, stake(s), child's play; **— de cartes** pack of cards; **— de mot** pun; **— de société** parlour game; **ce n'est pas de —** it is not fair (play); **prendre du —** to work loose; **hors —** offside.

jeudi [ʒødi] nm Thursday.

jeun [ʒœ̃] ad **à —** fasting, on an empty stomach.

jeune [ʒœn] a young, youthful, junior.

jeûne [ʒøn] nm fast(ing).

jeûner [ʒøne] vi to fast.

jeunesse [ʒœnɛs] nf youth, boyhood, girlhood, youthfulness, young people.

joaillerie [ʒwajri] nf jeweller's trade, jewellery.

joaillier, -ière [ʒwaje, jɛːr] n jeweller.

jobard [ʒɔbaːr] nm simpleton, dupe mug.

joie [ʒwa] nf joy, gladness, mirth, merriment; **à cœur —** to one's heart's content; **feu de —** bonfire.

joindre [ʒwɛ̃ːdr] vtr to join, unite, combine, add.

joint [ʒwɛ̃] nm joint, join.

jointoyer [ʒwɛ̃twaje] vt to point.

jointure [ʒwɛ̃tyːr] nf join, joint.

joli [ʒɔli] a pretty, fine, nice; **c'est du —!** what a mess!

joliment [ʒɔlimɑ̃] ad prettily, nicely, awfully.

jonc [ʒɔ̃] nm rush, reed, cane.

joncher [ʒɔ̃ʃe] vt to strew, litter.

jonction [ʒɔ̃ksjɔ̃] nf junction, joining.

jongler [ʒɔ̃gle] vi to juggle.

jonglerie [ʒɔ̃gləri] nf jugglery, juggling.

jongleur [ʒɔ̃glœːr] nm juggler, tumbler.

jonquille [ʒɔ̃kiːj] nf jonquil, daffodil.

joue [ʒu] nf cheek; **mettre en —** to aim (at).

jouer [ʒwe] vt to play, stake, back, act, feign, cheat; vi to play, gamble, work, be loose; vr to make fun (of **de**); **faire —** to work, set in motion.

jouet [ʒwɛ] nm toy, plaything.

joueur, -euse [ʒwœːr, øːz] a fond of play, fond of gambling; n player, performer, gambler; **être beau —** to be a (good) sport.

joufflu [ʒufly] a chubby.

joug [ʒug] nm yoke.

jouir [ʒwiːr] vi (de) to enjoy.

jouissance [ʒwisãːs] nf pleasure, enjoyment, possession.

jouisseur, -euse [ʒwisœːr, øːz] n pleasure-seeker, sensualist.

joujou [ʒuʒu] nm toy.

jour [ʒuːr] nm day, daylight, light, opening; **en plein —** in broad daylight; **mettre au —** to bring to light; **sous un autre —** in another light; **de — en —** from day to day.

journal [ʒurnal] nm newspaper, diary; **— de bord** logbook.

journalier, -ière [ʒurnalje, jɛːr] a daily; n day-labourer.

journalisme [ʒurnalism] nm journalism.

journaliste [ʒurnalist] n journalist, reporter.

journée [ʒurne] nf day, day's work day's pay.

journellement [ʒurnɛlmã] ad daily, every day.

joute [ʒut] nf joust, tilting.

jouter [ʒute] vi to tilt, joust, fight.

jovial [ʒɔvjal] a jovial, jolly.

jovialité [ʒɔvjalite] nf joviality, jollity.

joyau [ʒwajo] nm jewel.

joyeux, -euse [ʒwajø, øːz] a joyous, joyful, merry.

jubilation [ʒybilasjɔ̃] nf glee.

jubilé [ʒybile] nm jubilee.

jubiler [ʒybile] vi to be gleeful, to gloat.

jucher [ʒyʃe] vti to perch; vr to roost, perch.

juchoir [ʒyʃwaːr] nm perch, roosting-place.

judas [ʒyda] nm traitor, spy-hole.

judiciaire [ʒydisjɛːr] a judicial, legal.

judicieux, -euse [ʒydisjø, øːz] a judicious, sensible.

juge [ʒyːʒ] nm judge, umpire; **— d'instruction** examining magistrate; **— de paix** magistrate.

jugé [ʒyʒe] nm au **—** by guesswork.

jugement [ʒyʒmã] nm judgment, trial, sentence, opinion, discrimination.

jugeote [ʒyʒɔt] nf common sense, gumption.

juger [ʒyʒe] vt to judge, try, sentence, deem, imagine; vi to form an opinion of, imagine.

jugulaire [ʒygylɛːr] a jugular; nf jugular vein, chin-strap.

juif, -ive [ʒyif, ʒyiːv] a Jewish; n Jew, Jewess.

juillet [ʒyije] nm July.

juin [ʒyɛ̃] nm June.

juiverie [ʒyivri] nf Jewry, ghetto.

jujube [ʒyʒyb] nm jujube.

jumeau, -elle [ʒymo, ɛl] an twin.

jumeler [ʒymle] vt to arrange in pairs.

jumelles [ʒymɛl] nf pl opera-glasses, field-glasses, binoculars.

jument [ʒymã] nf mare.

jungle [ʒɔ̃ːgl] nf jungle.

jupe [ʒyp] nf skirt.

jupe-culotte [ʒypkylɔt] nf divided skirt.

jupon [ʒypɔ̃] nm petticoat, underskirt.

juré [ʒyre] a sworn; nm juryman, juror; pl jury.

jurer [ʒyre] vt to vow, pledge, swear; vi to curse, swear, (colours) clash.

juridiction [ʒyridiksjɔ̃] nf jurisdiction.

juridique [ʒyridik] a juridical, legal, judicial.

juriste [ʒyrist] nm jurist.

juron [ʒyrɔ̃] nm oath, curse, swear-word.

jury [ʒyri] nm jury, examining board, selection committee.

jus [ʒy] nm juice, gravy.

jusque [ʒysk(ə)] prep up to, as far as, until, even; jusqu'ici so far, until now; **—là** up to that point, until then; jusqu'à ce que until.

juste [ʒyst] a just, fair, right, righteous, accurate, tight, scanty; ad just, exactly, accurately, barely; au **—** exactly; comme de **—** as is only right.

justement [ʒystəmã] ad justly, precisely, just; as a matter of fact.

justesse [ʒystes] nf correctness, accuracy, exactness, soundness; de **—** only just, just in time.

justice [ʒystis] nf justice, fairness, law; se faire **—** to take the law into one's own hands, to kill oneself.

justicier [ʒystisje] nm justiciary.

justifiable [ʒystifjabl] a justifiable.

justification [ʒystifikasjɔ̃] nf justification, vindication.

justifier [ʒystifje] vt to justify, warrant, vindicate, clear; vr to justify, vindicate, clear oneself.

jute [ʒyt] nm jute.

juteux, -euse [ʒytø, øːz] a juicy.

juvénile [ʒyvenil] a juvenile, youthful.

juxtaposer [ʒykstapoze] vt to place side by side.

K

kangourou [kãguru] nm kangaroo.

kapokier [kapɔkje] nm silk cotton tree.

karité [karite] nm shea butter.

képi [kepi] nm peaked cap.

kermesse [kɛrmes] nf fair.

kif-kif [kifkif] a inv (fam) likewise.

kilogramme [kilɔgram] nm kilogram.

kilomètre [kilɔmɛtr] nm kilometre.

kilométrique [kilɔmetrik] a kilometric; borne **—** milestone.

kiosque [kjɔsk] nm kiosk, stall, stand, conning-tower.

klaxon [klaksɔ̃] nm motor horn.

klaxonner [klaksɔne] *vi* to sound the horn.

kleptomane [klɛptɔman] *an* klepto-maniac.

kolatier [kɔlatje] *nm* kola nut tree.

krack [krak] *nm* (financial) crash, failure.

kyrielle [kirjɛl] *nf* rigmarole , string.

L

l' see **le**.

la [la] *def art pn f* see **le**.

la [la] *nm* musical note A.

là [la] *ad* there, then, that; *excl* there now! c'est — **la question** that is the question; **d'ici** — in the meantime; **oh** — —! oh, I say!

là-bas [laba] *ad* over there, yonder.

labeur [labœ:r] *nm* labour, hard work.

labial [labjal] *a* labial.

laboratoire [labɔratwa:r] *nm* labora-tory.

laborieux, -euse [labɔrjø, ø:z] *a* laborious, hard-working, arduous, hard, slow.

labour [labu:r] *nm pl* ploughed land.

labourable [laburabl] *a* arable.

labourage [labura:ʒ] *nm* ploughing, tilling.

labourer [labure] *vt* to till, plough (up), furrow.

laboureur [laburœ:r] *nm* plough-man.

labyrinthe [labirɛ̃:t] *nm* labyrinth, maze.

lac [lak] *nm* lake, (Scot) loch.

lacer [lase] *vt* to lace (up); *vr* to lace oneself up.

lacérer [lasere] *vt* to lacerate, slash, tear.

lacet [lasɛ] *nm* lace, noose, snare; **en** — winding.

lâchage [lɑʃa:ʒ] *nm* releasing, drop-ping.

lâche [lɑ:ʃ] *a* cowardly, loose, lax, slack; *n* coward.

lâchement [lɑʃmɑ̃] *ad* in a cowardly way.

lâcher [lɑʃe] *vt* to release, drop, let go, let fly, let loose, let out, set free, divulge, blab out; — **pied** to give ground, give way; — **prise** to let go (one's hold); *nm* release.

lâcheté [lɑʃte] *nf* cowardice, craven, cowardly action.

lacis [lasi] *nm* network.

laconique [lakɔnik] *a* laconic.

lacrymogène [lakrimɔʒɛn] *a* **gaz** — tear gas.

lacté [lakte] *a* milky, lacteal.

lacune [lakyn] *nf* lacuna, gap, break, blank.

là-dedans [ladədɑ̃] *ad* in there, within, in it, in them.

là-dehors [ladəɔ:r] *ad* outside, with-out.

là-dessous [latsu] *ad* under there,

under that, under it, under them, underneath.

là-dessus [latsy] *ad* on that, on it, on them, thereupon.

ladre [lɑ:dr] *a* mean, stingy; *nm* miser, skinflint.

ladrerie [lɑdrəri] *nf* meanness, niggardliness.

lagune [lagyn] *nf* lagoon.

là-haut [lao] *ad* up there.

laïciser [laisize] *vt* to secularize.

laid [lɛ] *a* ugly, despicable.

laideron, -onne [lɛdrɔ̃, ɔn] *n* plain person.

laideur [lɛdœ:r] *nf* ugliness, mean-ness.

lainage [lɛna:ʒ] *nm* woollen article, fleece; *pl* woollen goods.

laine [lɛn] *nf* wool; — **filée** yarn; — **peignée** worsted.

lainerie [lɛnri] *nf* woollen mill, -trade, wool-shop.

laineux, -euse [lɛnø, ø:z] *a* woolly, fleecy.

lainier, -ière [lenje, jɛ:r] *a* **industrie lainière** wool trade; *n* woollen-goods manufacturer.

laïque [laik] *a* lay, secular; *nm* layman.

laisse [lɛs] *nf* leash, lead.

laissé-pour-compte [lɛsepu:rkɔ̃:t] *nm* returned goods, rejects, unsold stock.

laisser [lɛse] *vt* to leave, let, allow; **se** — **faire** to submit; — **là quelque-chose** to give up doing something; **ne pas** — **de faire** not to fail to do, to do nevertheless.

laisser-aller [lɛseale] *nm* untidiness, carelessness, neglect.

laisser-faire [lɛsefɛ:r] *nm* non-interference, non-resistance.

laissez-passer [lɛsepase] *nm* pass, permit.

lait [lɛ] *nm* milk; **frère, sœur de** — foster-brother, sister.

laitage [lɛta:ʒ] *nm* dairy produce, milk foods.

laiterie [lɛtri] *nf* dairy.

laiteux, -euse [lɛtø, ø:z] *a* milky.

laitier, -ière [lɛtje, jɛ:r] *a* dairy-, milk-; *n* dairyman, milkman, milk-maid, dairymaid; *nm* slag, dross.

laiton [lɛtɔ̃] *nm* brass.

laitue [lɛty] *nf* lettuce.

laïus [lajy:s] *nm* (fam) speech.

lama [lama] *nm* (animal) llama; (priest) lama.

lambeau [lɑ̃bo] *nm* scrap, shred, rag, tatter.

lambin [lɑ̃bɛ̃] *a* (fam) slow, sluggish; *n* slow-coach.

lambris [lɑ̃bri] *nm* wainscoting, panelling, panelled ceiling.

lambrissage [lɑ̃brisa:ʒ] *nm* wain-scoting, panelling.

lame [lam] *nf* blade, strip, slat, wave; — **de fond** groundswell.

lamé [lame] *a* spangled.

lamentable [lamɑ̃tabl] *a* pitiful,

woeful, lamentable, deplorable.

lamentation [lamãtasjɔ̃] *nf* lament (ation), wail(ing).

se lamenter [səlamãte] *vr* to lament, wail.

laminer [lamine] *vt* to laminate, roll, calender.

laminoir [laminwaːr] *nm* rolling-mill, roller, calender.

lampadaire [lãpadɛːr] *nm* standard lamp, candelabrum.

lampe [lãːp] *nf* lamp, light, torch, valve.

lamper [lãpe] *vt* to gulp, swig.

lampion [lãpjɔ̃] *nm* fairy light, Chinese lantern.

lampiste [lãpist] *n* lampman.

lampisterie [lãpistəri] *nf* lamp-room, lamp works.

lance [lãːs] *n* spear, lance, nozzle.

lancé [lãse] *a* under way, flying; **un homme — a** man who has made his name.

lance-bombes [lãsbɔ̃ːb] *nm* trench mortar, bomb rack.

lance-flammes [lãsflaːm] *nm* flame-thrower.

lancement [lãsmã] *nm* throwing, putting, launching, floating, promoting.

lance-pierres [lãspjɛːr] *nm* catapult.

lancer [lãse] *vt* to throw, cast, drop (*bombs*), launch, float, start, set (on, going, on one's feet), put on the market; *vr* to rush, dash, launch (out), plunge.

lance-torpille [lãstɔrpiːj] *nm* torpedo-tube.

lancette [lãsɛt] *nf* lancet.

lancier [lãsje] *nm* lancer.

lancinant [lãsinã] *a* shooting, throbbing.

lande [lãːd] *nf* heath, moor.

langage [lãgaːʒ] *nm* language, speech, talk.

lange [lãːʒ] *nf* baby's napkin; *pl* swaddling-clothes.

langoureux, -euse [lãgurø, øːz] *a* languorous, languid.

langouste [lãgust] *nf* (spiny) lobster.

langue [lãːg] *nf* tongue, language, speech; **— vivante** modern language; **— verte** slang; **mauvaise — mis**chief-maker, slandermonger; **donner sa — aux chats** to give it up.

languette [lãgɛt] *nf* strip, tongue.

langueur [lãgœːr] *nf* languor, listlessness.

languir [lãgiːr] *vi* to languish, pine.

languissant [lãgisã] *a* listless, languid, dull.

lanière [lanjɛːr] *nf* strip, strap, thong, lash.

lanterne [lãtɛrn] *nf* lantern, lamp, light.

lapalissade [lapalisad] *nf* truism, obvious remark.

laper [lape] *vt* to lap (up).

lapidaire [lapidɛːr] *a* lapidary, concise; *nm* lapidary.

lapider [lapide] *vt* to throw stones at, vilify.

lapin [lapɛ̃] *nm* rabbit, coney; **— de garenne** wild rabbit; **poser un — to** fail to turn up.

laps [laps] *nm* lapse, space of time.

lapsus [lapsyːs] *nm* lapse, mistake, slip.

laquais [lakɛ] *nm* lackey, footman.

laque [lak] *nf* lake, hair-lacquer; **— en écailles** shellac; *nm* lacquer.

laquer [lake] *vt* to lacquer, japan, enamel.

laquelle *rel pn* *see* **lequel**.

larbin [larbɛ̃] *nm* flunkey.

larcin [larsɛ̃] *nm* larceny, petty theft.

lard [laːr] *nm* fat, bacon.

larder [larde] *vt* to lard, inflict, shower, interlard.

large [larʒ] *a* broad, wide, ample, liberal, generous; *nm* space, open sea, breadth; **au — out** at sea; **prendre le — to** put to sea, make off; **au — de** off.

largesse [larʒɛs] *nf* liberality, generosity, largess(e).

largeur [larʒœːr] *nf* breadth, broadness, width.

larguer [large] *vt* to loose, cast off, unfurl, release.

larme [larm] *nf* tear, drop.

larmoyant [larmwajã] *a* tearful, maudlin.

larmoyer [larmwaje] *vi* to snivel, shed tears, (*eyes*) water.

larron [larɔ̃] *nm* thief.

larve [larv] *nf* larva, grub.

laryngite [larɛ̃ʒit] *nf* laryngitis.

larynx [larɛ̃ks] *nm* larynx.

las, lasse [la, laːs] *a* tired, weary.

lascif, -ive [lasif, iːv] *a* lewd.

lasser [lase] *vt* to tire, weary; *vr* to grow tired, weary.

lassitude [lasityd] *nf* weariness.

latent [latã] *a* latent.

latéral [lateral] *a* lateral, side-cross-.

latin [latɛ̃] *a* *nm* Latin; **— de cuisine** dog-Latin.

latitude [latityd] *nf* latitude, scope.

latte [lat] *nf* lath, slat.

lattis [lati] *nm* lathing, lattice-work.

lauréat [lɔrea, -at] *nm* laureate, prize-winner.

laurier [lɔrje] *nm* laurel, bay.

laurier-rose [lɔrjeroːz] *nm* oleander.

lavabo [lavabo] *nm* wash-hand basin, lavatory.

lavande [lavãːd] *nf* lavender.

lavandière [lavãdjɛːr] *nf* washer-woman.

lave [laːv] *nf* lava.

lavement [lavmã] *nm* rectal injection, enema.

laver [lave] *vt* to wash, bathe; *vr* to wash (oneself), have a wash; **— la tête à qn** to give s.o. a good wigging, dressing-down.

lavette [lavɛt] *nf* mop, dish-cloth.

laveur, -euse [lavœːr, øːz] n washer, washerwoman, washer-up.

lavis [lavi] nm washing, wash-tint, wash-drawing.

lavoir [lavwaːr] nm wash-house, washing board.

laxatif, -ive [laksatif, iːv] a nm laxative, aperient.

layette [lɛjɛt] nf layette, outfit of baby linen.

lazzi [lazi, ladzi] nm pl jeers.

le, la, l', les [lə, la, l, lɛ] def art the, a (often untranslated); pn him, her, it, them; neut pn so (often untranslated).

léché [leʃe] a finicking, over-polished.

lécher [leʃe] vt to lick.

lécheur, -euse [leʃœːr, øːz] n toady, parasite.

leçon [ləsɔ̃] nf lesson; — de choses object-lesson; faire la — à qn to lecture, drill s.o.

lecteur, -trice [lɛktœːr, tris] n reader, (foreign) assistant in French university.

lecture [lɛktyːr] nf reading, perusal; salle de — reading room.

ledit, ladite, lesdits, lesdites [lədi, ladi, ledi, ledit] a the aforesaid.

légal [legal] a legal, lawful.

légaliser [legalize] vt to attest, authenticate, legalize.

légalité [legalite] nf legality, lawfulness.

légataire [legateːr] nm legatee, heir.

légation [legasjɔ̃] nf legation.

légendaire [leʒɑ̃dɛːr] a legendary.

légende [leʒɑ̃d] nf legend, inscription, caption, key.

léger, -ère [leʒe, ɛːr] a light, agile, flighty, frivolous, slight, mild, weak; ad à la légère lightly, scantily, without due reflection.

légèreté [leʒɛrte] nf lightness, fickleness, levity, agility, mildness, weakness.

légion [leʒjɔ̃] nf legion.

législateur, -trice [leʒislatœːr, tris] a legislative; n legislator, lawgiver.

législatif, -ive [leʒislatif, iːv] a legislative.

législation [leʒislasjɔ̃] nf legislation, laws.

législature [leʒislatyːr] nf legislative body.

légitime [leʒitim] a legitimate, lawful, justifiable, sound.

légitimer [leʒitime] vt to legitimate, legitimatize, justify.

legs [lɛ] nm legacy, bequest.

léguer [lege] vt to bequeath, leave, will.

légume [legym] nm vegetable; grosse — bigwig.

lendemain [lɑ̃dmɛ̃] nm next day, day after, morrow; sans — shortlived; du jour au — very quickly, from one day to the next.

lénifiant [lenifjɑ̃] a soothing, relaxing.

lent [lɑ̃] a slow, lingering.

lenteur [lɑ̃tœːr] nf slowness, dilatoriness.

lentille [lɑ̃tiːj] nf lentil, lens.

léopard [leɔpaːr] nm leopard.

lèpre [lɛpr] nf leprosy.

lépreux, -euse [leprø, øːz] a leprous; n leper.

lequel, laquelle, lesquels, lesquelles [ləkɛl, lakɛl, lekɛl] rel pn who, whom, which; inter pn which (one).

léser [leze] vt to injure, wrong.

lésiner [lezine] vi to be mean, closefisted, haggle (over).

lésion [lezjɔ̃] nf lesion, injury, wrong.

lessive [lɛsiːv] nf wash(ing).

lessiver [lɛsive] vt to wash, scrub.

lessiveuse [lɛsivøːz] nf clothes boiler, copper.

lest [lɛst] nm ballast.

leste [lɛst] a light, nimble, smart, flippant, free, spicy (humour).

léthargie [letarʒi] nf lethargy.

léthargique [letarʒik] a lethargic, dull.

lettre [lɛtr] nf letter, note; pl literature, letters; — de change bill of exchange; — de voiture consignment note; au pied de la — literally; écrire quelque chose en toutes —s to write something out in full.

lettré [lɛtre] a lettered, literate, wellread; nm scholar.

leu [lø] nm à la queue — — in single file.

leur [lœ(ː)r] pos a their; pos pn le, la —, les —s theirs; nm their own; pl their own people; pn dat (to) them.

leurre [lœːr] nm lure, decoy, bait, allurement, catch.

leurrer [lœre] vt to lure, decoy, allure, entice; vr to be taken in.

levain [ləvɛ̃] nm leaven, yeast.

levant [ləvɑ̃] a rising (sun); nm east, orient.

levé [ləve] a raised, up, out of bed; voter à main —e vote by show of hands; nm survey.

levée [ləve] nf lifting, adjourning, collection, levy, embankment, (cards) trick.

lever [ləve] vt to raise, lift (up), collect, levy, remove, cut off, (camp) strike, adjourn, (anchor) weigh, (survey) effect; vi to shoot, rise; vr to stand up, get up, rise, (day) dawn; nm rising, levee, survey; — de rideau curtain-raiser; — du soleil sunrise.

levier [ləvje] nm lever, crowbar; — de commande control lever.

lèvre [lɛːvr] nf lip, rim; du bout des —s forced, disdainful.

lévrier [levrje] nm greyhound.

levure [ləvyːr] nf yeast.

lexicographe [lɛksikɔgraf] nm lexicographer.

lexique [lɛksik] nm lexicon, glossary,

lézard [lezaːr] nm lizard; **faire le —** to bask in the sun.

lézarde [lezard] nf crevice, crack, chink.

lézarder [lezarde] vt to crack, split; vr to lounge, sun oneself.

liaison [ljɛzɔ̃] nf joining, binding, connection, linking, liaison, slur, (mus) tie.

liant [ljɑ̃] a friendly, engaging, responsive, flexible, pliant; nm friendly disposition, flexibility.

liasse [ljas] nf bundle, wad.

libation [libasjɔ̃] nf libation, drinking.

libelle [libɛl] nm lampoon, libel.

libeller [libɛle] vt to draw up.

libellule [libɛlyl] nf dragonfly.

libéral [liberal] an liberal, broad, generous.

libéralité [liberalite] nf liberality, generosity.

libérateur, -trice [liberatœːr, tris] a liberating; n liberator.

libération [liberasjɔ̃] nf liberation, release, discharge.

libérer [libere] vt to liberate, release, free, discharge.

liberté [libɛrte] nf liberty, freedom.

libertin [libɛrtɛ̃] a licentious, dissolute, wayward; n libertine, rake, free-thinker.

libertinage [libɛrtinaːʒ] nm dissolute ways.

libraire [librɛːr] nm bookseller.

librairie [librɛri] nf book-trade, bookshop.

libre [libr] a free, clear, open, disengaged, unoccupied, vacant, for hire.

libre-échange [libreʃɑ̃ːʒ] nm free-trade.

libre-service [librəsɛrvis] nm self-service.

licence [lisɑ̃ːs] nf licence, excessive liberty, permission, certificate, bachelor's degree.

licencié [lisɑ̃sje] nm licentiate, licensee, licence-holder; **— ès lettres** (approx) B.A.; **— en droit** (approx) LL.B.; **— ès sciences** (approx) B.Sc.

licencier [lisɑ̃sje] vt to disband, sack, dismiss.

licencieux, -euse [lisɑ̃sjø, øːz] a licentious.

licite [lisit] a licit, lawful.

licorne [likɔrn] nf unicorn.

licou [liku] nm halter.

lie [li] nf lees, dregs.

lié [lje] a bound, tied, friendly, intimate.

liebig [libig] nm beef extract.

liège [ljɛːʒ] nm cork.

lien [ljɛ̃] nm bond, tie.

lier [lje] vt to bind, tie (up), link, join, (sauce) thicken; **— amitié avec qn** to strike up an acquaintance with s.o.; vr to become friendly, intimate (with avec).

lierre [ljɛːr] nm ivy.

lieu [ljø] nm place, spot, scene; pl premises; **en premier, dernier —** firstly, lastly; **avoir —** to take place, have every reason (to); **donner —** to give rise (to à); **tenir —** to take the place (of de); **au — de** instead of.

lieue [ljø] nf league.

lieuse [ljøːz] nf (mechanical) binder.

lieutenant [ljøtnɑ̃] nm lieutenant, mate; **— de vaisseau** lieutenant-commander.

lièvre [ljɛːvr] nm hare; **mémoire de —** memory like a sieve.

liftier, -ière [liftje, jɛːr] n lift-man, -boy, -girl, -attendant.

ligaturer [ligatyre] vt to tie up, bind, ligature.

ligne [liɲ] nf line, cord, row; **hors —** outstanding, out of the common; **à la —** new paragraph.

lignée [liɲe] nf issue, stock, descendants.

lignite [liɲit] nf lignite.

ligoter [ligɔte] vt to bind, tie up.

ligue [lig] nf league.

liguer [lige] vt to league; vr to form a league.

lilas [lila] a nm lilac.

limace [limas] nf slug.

limaçon [limasɔ̃] nm snail; **en —** spiral.

limande [limɑ̃ːd] nf dab.

lime [lim] nf file.

limer [lime] vt to file (up, off, down), (verses) polish.

limier [limje] nm bloodhound.

limitation [limitasjɔ̃] nf restriction.

limite [limit] nf limit, boundary; pl bounds; a maximum.

limiter [limite] vt to limit, mark the bounds of.

limitrophe [limitrɔf] a adjacent, bordering.

limoger [limɔʒe] vt to relegate.

limon [limɔ̃] nm mud, silt, lime.

limonade [limɔnad] nf lemonade.

limoneux, -euse [limɔnø, øːz] a muddy.

limpide [lɛ̃pid] a limpid.

limpidité [lɛ̃pidite] nm limpidity, clarity.

lin [lɛ̃] nm flax, linseed, linen.

linceul [lɛ̃sœl] nm shroud.

linéaire [lineɛːr] a linear.

linéal [lineal] a lineal.

linéament [lineamɑ̃] nm lineament, feature.

linge [lɛ̃ːʒ] nm linen.

lingère [lɛ̃ʒɛːr] nf sewing-maid.

lingerie [lɛ̃ʒri] nf underwear, linen-room.

linguiste [lɛ̃gɥist] n linguist.

linguistique [lɛ̃gɥistik] a linguistic; nf linguistics.

linoléum [linɔleɔm] nm linoleum.

linon [linɔ̃] nm lawn, buckram.

linotte [linɔt] nf linnet; **tête de —** feather-brained person.

linteau [lɛ̃to] nm lintel.

lion, -onne [ljɔ̃, ɔn] n lion, lioness.

lionceau [ljɔ̃so] *nm* lion cub.

lippu [lipy] *a* thick-lipped.

liquéfier [likefje] *vt* to liquefy.

liqueur [likœːr] *nm* liquor, drink, liqueur, liquid.

liquidation [likidasjɔ̃] *nf* liquidation, settlement, clearing, selling off.

liquide [likid] *a* liquid, ready; *nm* liquid.

liquider [likide] *vt* to liquidate, settle, sell off, finish off.

liquoreux, -euse [likɔrø, øːz] *a* liqueur-like, sweet.

lire [liːr] *vt* to read.

lis [lis] *nm* lily.

liséré [lizere] *nm* border, edge, piping, binding.

lisérer [lizere] *vt* to border, edge, pipe.

liseron [lizrɔ̃] *nm* bindweed.

liseur, -euse [lizœːr, øːz] *a* reading; *n* reader.

liseuse [lizøːz] *nf* dust-jacket, book-marker, bed-jacket.

lisibilité [lizibilite] *nf* legibility.

lisible [lizibl] *a* legible.

lisière [lizjɛːr] *nf* edge, border, selvedge, list, leading-strings.

lisse [lis] *a* smooth, polished.

lisser [lise] *vt* to smooth, polish, preen.

liste [list] *nf* list, roster, register.

lit [li] *nm* bed, layer, bottom; **— de sangle** camp-bed; **enfant du second —** child of the second marriage.

litanie [litani] *nf* litany, rigmarole.

lit-armoire [liarmwaːr] *nm* box-bed.

literie [litri] *nf* bedding.

lithographie [litɔgrafi] *nf* lithograph(y).

litière [litjɛːr] *nf* litter.

litige [litiːʒ] *nm* litigation, lawsuit; **en —** under dispute.

litigieux, -euse [litiʒjø, øːz] *a* litigious.

litre [litr] *nm* litre.

littéraire [literɛːr] *a* literary.

littéral [literal] *a* literal, written.

littérateur [literatœːr] *nm* man of letters.

littérature [literatyːr] *nf* literature.

littoral [litɔral] *a* littoral, coastal; *nm* seaboard.

liturgie [lityrʒi] *nf* liturgy.

liturgique [lityrʒik] *a* liturgical.

livide [livid] *a* livid, ghastly.

livraison [livrɛzɔ̃] *nf* delivery, part, instalment; **à —** on delivery.

livre [liːvr] *nf* pound; *nm* book; **— de poche** paperback.

livrée [livre] *nf* livery.

livrer [livre] *vt* to deliver, surrender, give up, hand over; **— bataille** to give, join battle; *vr* to give oneself up, confide (in à), indulge (in), take (to).

livresque [livrɛsk] *a* book, bookish.

livret [livrɛ] *nm* small book, booklet, handbook, libretto.

livreur, -euse [livrœːr, øːz] *n* delivery-man, -boy, -girl.

lobe [lɔb] *nm* lobe, flap.

local [lɔkal] *a* local; *nm* premises, building, quarters.

localiser [lɔkalize] *vt* to localize, locate.

localité [lɔkalite] *nf* locality, place, spot.

locataire [lɔkatɛːr] *n* tenant, lessee, lodger.

location [lɔkasjɔ̃] *nf* hiring, letting, renting, booking; **en —** on hire; **agent de —** house-agent.

locomotive [lɔkɔmɔtiv] *nf* locomotive, engine.

locomotion [lɔkɔmosjɔ̃] *nf* locomotion.

locution [lɔkysjɔ̃] *nf* expression, phrase.

lof [lɔf] *nm* (*naut*) windward side.

logarithme [lɔgaritm] *nm* logarithm.

loge [lɔːʒ] *nf* lodge, box, dressing-room.

logement [lɔʒmɑ̃] *nm* lodging(s), accommodation, billet(ing), housing.

loger [lɔʒe] *vi* to lodge, live, be billeted; *vt* to lodge, house, billet, stable, put, place; *vr* to lodge, find a home, a place.

logeur, -euse [lɔʒœːr, øz] *n* land-lord -lady.

logique [lɔʒik] *a* logical, reasoned; *nf* logic.

logis [lɔʒi] *nm* dwelling, home, lodgings, accommodation.

loi [lwa] *nf* law, act, rule; **projet de — bill.**

loin [lwɛ̃] *ad* far, a long way off; **au —** in the distance, far and wide; **de — from** a distance; **de — en —** at long intervals, now and then.

lointain [lwɛ̃tɛ̃] *a* distant, far-off; *nm* distance.

loir [lwaːr] *nm* dormouse.

loisible [lwazibl] *a* permissible, convenient.

loisir [lwaziːr] *nm* leisure, spare time.

londonien, -enne [lɔ̃dɔnjɛ̃, jɛn] *a* Londoner.

Londres [lɔ̃ːdr] *nm* London.

long [lɔ̃] *a* long, lengthy, slow; *nm* length; **à la longue** in the long run; **de — en large** up and down, to and fro; **le — de** along(side); **tout le — du jour** for the whole day long; **en dire — to speak** volumes; **en savoir — to** know a lot.

longe [lɔ̃ːʒ] *nf* halter.

longer [lɔ̃ʒe] *vt* to skirt, hug, run alongside.

longeron [lɔ̃ʒrɔ̃] *nm* girder, beam, tail-boom, spar.

longévité [lɔ̃ʒevite] *nf* longevity, expectation of life.

longitude [lɔ̃ʒityd] *nf* longitude.

longtemps [lɔ̃tɑ̃] *ad* long, a long time.

longuement [lɔ̃gmɑ̃] *ad* for a long time, at length.

longueur [lɔ̃gœːr] *nf* length; *pl* tedious passages; **tirer en —** to drag on, spin out.

longue-vue [lɔ̃gvy] *nf* telescope, field-glass.

looping [lupiŋ] *nm* **faire du —** to loop the loop.

lopin [lɔpɛ̃] *nm* plot, allotment.

loquace [lɔkwas] *a* loquacious, talkative.

loquacité [lɔkwasite] *nf* loquacity, talkativeness.

loque [lɔk] *nf* rag.

loquet [lɔkɛ] *nm* latch.

loqueteux, -euse [lɔktø, øːz] *a* tattered, ragged.

lorgnade [lɔrɲad] *nf* sidelong glance.

lorgner [lɔrɲe] *vt* to cast a (sidelong) glance at, have a covetous eye on, make eyes at, ogle.

lorgnette [lɔrɲɛt] *nf* opera-glasses.

lorgnon [lɔrɲɔ̃] *nm* eyeglasses, pince-nez.

loriot [lɔrjo] *nm* oriole.

lors [lɔːr] *ad* **depuis, dès —** from that time, ever since then; **— même que** even when; **— de** at the time of.

lorsque [lɔrsk(ə)] *cj* when.

losange [lɔzɑ̃ːʒ] *nm* lozenge; **en —** diamond-shaped.

lot [lo] *nm* share, portion, lot, prize; **gros —** first prize.

loterie [lɔtri] *nf* lottery, raffle, draw.

lotion [losjɔ̃] *nf* lotion.

lotir [lɔtiːr] *vt* to divide into lots, sort out, allot.

lotissement [lɔtismɑ̃] *nm* dividing into lots, selling in lots, building site, housing estate.

lotte [lɔt] *nf* burbot.

louable [lwabl, lu-] *a* praiseworthy, commendable.

louage [lwaːʒ, lu-] *nm* hire, hiring, letting out.

louange [lwɑ̃ːʒ] *nf* praise.

louche [luʃ] *a* ambiguous, suspicious, queer; *nf* ladle.

loucher [luʃe] *vi* to squint, (*fam*) to look enviously (at **sur**).

louer [lwe, lue] *vt* to hire (out), let (out), rent, reserve, praise, commend; *vr* to engage, hire oneself, be pleased, satisfied (with), congratulate oneself (upon **de**).

loueur, -euse [lwœːr, lu-, øːz] *n* hirer, renter.

loufoque [lufɔk] *a* cr⸱⸱ked, dippy.

loulou [lulu] *nm* pomeranian dog.

loup [lu] *nm* wolf, black velvet mask, flaw, error; **à pas de —** stealthily; **avoir une faim de —** to be ravenously hungry; **un froid de —** bitter cold; **quand on parle du —, on en voit la queue** talk of the devil and he's sure to appear; **— de mer** old salt, sea dog.

loup-cervier [lusɛrvje] *nm* lynx.

loupe [lup] *nf* lens, magnifying glass, wen.

louper [lupe] *vt* to bungle, make a mess of.

loup-garou [lugaru] *nm* werewolf.

lourd [luːr] *a* heavy, ponderous, ungainly, dull(witted), close, sultry.

lourdaud [lurdo] *a* loutish, clumsy, dullwitted; *n* lout, blockhead.

lourdeur [lurdœːr] *nf* heaviness, ponderousness, ungainliness, dullness, sultriness.

loustic [lustik] *nm* joker, wag.

loutre [lutr] *nf* otter.

louve [luːv] *nf* she-wolf.

louveteau [luvto] *nm* wolf-cub.

louvoyer [luvwaje] *vi* to tack, manoeuvre.

loyal [lwajal] *a* loyal, true, upright, fair.

loyauté [lwajote] *nf* loyalty, fidelity, uprightness, honesty, fairness.

loyer [lwaje] *nm* rent.

lubie [lybi] *nf* whim, fad.

lubricité [lybrisite] *nf* lewdness.

lubrifiant [lybrifjɑ̃] *a* lubricating; *nm* lubricant.

lubrique [lybrik] *a* lewd.

lucarne [lykarn] *nf* attic window, skylight.

lucide [lysid] *a* lucid, clear.

lucidité [lysidite] *nf* lucidity, clearness.

luciole [lysjɔl] *nf* fire-fly.

lucratif, -ive [lykratif, iːv] *a* lucrative, profitable.

luette [lɥɛt] *nf* uvula.

lueur [lɥœːr] *nf* gleam, glimmer, light.

luge [lyːʒ] *nf* toboggan.

lugubre [lygyːbr] *a* lugubrious, gloomy, dismal.

lui [lɥi] *pers pn dat* (to) him, her, it; *from* him, her, it; *disj pn* he; him; **—même** himself.

luire [lɥiːr] *vi* to shine, gleam.

luisant [lɥizɑ̃] *a* shining, gleaming; *nm* gloss, sheen.

lumière [lymjɛːr] *nf* light; *pl* understanding, knowledge, enlightenment.

lumignon [lymiɲɔ̃] *nm* candle-end, dim light.

lumineux, -euse [lyminø, øːz] *a* luminous, bright.

luminosité [lyminozite] *nf* luminosity.

lunaire [lynɛːr] *a* lunar.

lunatique [lynatik] *a* whimsical, capricious, moody.

lundi [lœ̃di] *nm* Monday.

lune [lyn] *nf* moon; **clair de —** moonlight; **être dans la —** to be wool-gathering; **— de miel** honeymoon.

lunetier [lyntje] *nm* spectacle-maker, optician.

lunette [lynɛt] *nf* telescope, wishbone, (w.c.) seat; *pl* spectacles, goggles.

lupin [lypɛ̃] *nm* lupin.

lurette [lyrɛt] *nf* **il y a belle —** a long time ago.

luron, -onne [lyrɔ̃, ɔn] n strapping lad (lass), gay chap, tomboy.

lustre [lystr] nm polish, gloss, chandelier, period of five years.

lustrer [lystre] vt to polish (up), gloss, glaze.

lustrine [lystrin] nf cotton lustre.

luth [lyt] nm lute.

luthier [lytje] nm violin-maker.

lutin [lytɛ̃] a mischievous; nm sprite, imp.

lutiner [lytine] vt to tease, torment.

lutrin [lytrɛ̃] nm lectern.

lutte [lyt] nf struggle, contest, strife, wrestling; de haute — by force (of arms), hard-won.

lutter [lyte] vi to struggle, compete, fight, wrestle.

luxe [lyks] nm luxury, profusion superfluity; de — first-class, luxury.

luxer [lykse] vt to dislocate, put out of joint.

luxueux, -euse [lyksɥø, øːz] a luxurious, sumptuous.

luxure [lyksyːr] nf lewdness.

luxurieux, -euse [lyksyrjø, øːz] a lewd, lustful.

luzerne [lyzɛrn] nf lucerne.

lycée [lise] nm secondary school.

lycéen, -enne [liseɛ̃, ɛn] n pupil, schoolboy, -girl.

lymphatique [lɛ̃fatik] a lymphatic.

lyncher [lɛ̃ʃe] vt to lynch.

lynx [lɛ̃ks] nm lynx.

lyre [liːr] nf lyre.

lyrique [lirik] a lyric(al); nm lyric poet.

lyrisme [lirism] nm lyricism, enthusiasm.

lys [lis] nm lily.

M

ma [ma] af see mon.

maboul [mabul] a dippy, cracked, mad.

macabre [makɑːbr] a grim, gruesome; danse — Dance of Death.

macadamiser [makadamize] vt to macadamize.

macaron [makarɔ̃] nm macaroon, rosette.

macaroni [makarɔni] nm macaroni.

macédoine [masedwan] nf salad, hotch-potch.

macérer [masere] vt to macerate, steep, mortify.

mâchefer [mɑʃfɛːr] nm clinker, slag, dross.

mâché [mɑʃe] a chewed, worn, ragged, frayed.

mâcher [mɑʃe] vt to chew, munch, champ; ne pas — ses mots not to mince one's words.

machiavélique [makjavelik] a Machiavellian.

mâchicoulis [mɑʃikuli] nm machicolation.

machin [maʃɛ̃] nm thing, contraption, thingummy.

machinal [maʃinal] a mechanical.

machinateur, -trice [maʃinatœːr, tris] n machinator, schemer, intriguer.

machination [maʃinasjɔ̃] nf machination, plot.

machine [maʃin] nf machine, engine, contraption; pl machinery; — à écrire typewriter; fait à la — machine made.

machine-outil [maʃinuti] n machine-tool.

machiner [maʃine] vt to plot, scheme.

machinerie [maʃinri] nf machine construction, machinery, plant, engine-room.

machinisme [maʃinism] nm mechanism, (use of) machinery.

machiniste [maʃinist] nm stagehand.

mâchoire [mɑʃwaːr] nf jaw, jawbone.

mâchonner [mɑʃɔne] vt to chew, munch, mumble.

maçon [masɔ̃] nm mason, bricklayer.

maçonner [masɔne] vt to build, face with stone, brick up.

maçonnerie [masɔnri] nf masonry, stonework.

maçonnique [masɔnik] a masonic.

macule [makyl] nf stain, blemish, spot.

maculer [makyle] vti to stain, spot, blur.

madame [madam] nf Mrs, madam.

madeleine [madlɛn] nf sponge-cake.

mademoiselle [madmwazɛl] nf Miss.

madone [madɔn] nf Madonna.

madré [mɑdre] a wily, mottled; n wily bird.

madrier [mɑdrie] nm beam, joist, thick plank.

madrigal [madrigal] nm madrigal.

madrilène [madrilɛn] a of Madrid.

magasin [magazɛ̃] nm shop, store, warehouse, magazine.

magasinage [magazinaːʒ] nm storing, warehouse dues.

magasinier [magazinje] nm warehouseman, storekeeper.

magazine [magazin] nm magazine.

mage [maːʒ] nm seer; pl wise men.

magicien, -ienne [maʒisjɛ̃, ɛn] n magician, wizard.

magie [maʒi] nf magic, wizardry.

magique [maʒik] a magic(al).

magistral [maʒistral] a magisterial, masterly.

magistrat [maʒistra] nm magistrate, judge.

magistrature [maʒistratyːr] nf magistracy.

magnanerie [maɲanri] nf rearinghouse for silkworms, sericulture.

magnanime [maɲanim] a magnanimous great-hearted.

magnanimité [maɲanimite] *nf* magnanimity.

magnésie [maɲezi] *nf* magnesia.

magnétique [maɲetik] *a* magnetic.

magnétiser [maɲetize] *vt* to magnetize, hypnotize, mesmerize.

magnétisme [maɲetism] *nm* magnetism, hypnotism, mesmerism.

magnéto [maɲeto] *nm* magneto.

magnétophone [maɲetɔfɔn] *nm* tape-recorder.

magnificence [maɲifisɑ̃:s] *nf* magnificence, splendour, liberality, munificence.

magnifier [maɲifje] *vt* to glorify, exalt.

magnifique [maɲifik] *a* magnificent, sumptuous, grand.

magot [mago] *nm* small ape, grotesque porcelain figure, ugly man, (*money*) hoard.

mahométan [maɔmetɑ̃] *a* Mohammedan, Moslem.

mai [mɛ] *nm* May.

maigre [mɛ:gr] *a* thin, lean, scanty, frugal, meagre, poor; *nm* lean (of meat); **faire —** to fast; **jour —** fast-day; **repas —** meatless meal.

maigreur [mɛgrœ:r] *nf* leanness, thinness, scantiness.

maigrir [mɛgri:r] *vt* to make thin (ner), thin down; *vi* to grow thin, lose weight.

mail [ma:j] *nm* avenue, public walk, mall.

maille [mɑ:j] *nf* mesh, link, stitch, speckle; **cotte de —s** coat of mail.

maillet [maje] *nm* mallet.

maillon [majɔ̃] *nm* link, shackle; **— tournant** swivel.

maillot [majo] *nm* swaddling-clothes, jersey, singlet, tights; **— de bain** bathing-costume.

main [mɛ̃] *nf* hand, handwriting, (*cards*) hand, quire; **— courante** handrail; **coup de —** surprise attack, helping hand; **sous la —** to, at hand; **à pleines —s** liberally, in handfuls; **fait à la —** handmade; **se faire la —** to get one's hand in; **avoir perdu la —** to be out of practice; **gagner haut la —** to win hands down; **ne pas y aller de —morte** to go at it; **avoir la — dure** to be a martinet; **en venir aux —s** to come to blows; **mettre la dernière — à** to put the finishing touch to.

main d'œuvre [mɛ̃dœ:vr] *nf* man-power, labour.

main-forte [mɛ̃fɔrt] *nf* help, assistance.

mainmise [mɛ̃mi:z] *nf* seizure.

mainmorte [mɛ̃mɔrt] *nf* mortmain.

maint [mɛ̃] *a* many a; **à —es reprises** many a time.

maintenant [mɛ̃tnɑ̃] *ad* now; **dès —** from now on, even now.

maintenir [mɛ̃tni:r] *vt* to support, hold up, maintain, uphold; *vr* to keep, continue, hold one's own.

maintien [mɛ̃tjɛ̃] *nm* maintenance, keeping, demeanour, bearing.

maire [mɛ:r] *nm* mayor.

mairie [mɛri] *nf* town hall, municipal buildings.

mais [mɛ] but; *excl* why! *adv* more; **je n'en peux —** I can't help it.

maïs [mais] *nm* maize, Indian corn.

maison [mɛzɔ̃] *nf* house, household, family, dynasty, firm; **— de santé** nursing-home; **— de fous** lunatic asylum; **— de correction** reformatory; **garder la —** to stay indoors, at home.

maisonnée [mɛzɔne] *nf* household, family.

maisonnette [mɛzɔnɛt] *nf* cottage, small house.

maître, -esse [mɛ:tr, mɛtrɛs] *a* principal, main, chief, out and out, utter; *n* master, mistress; **— de conférences** lecturer; **— d'équipage** boatswain; **premier —** chief petty officer; **— d'hôtel** butler, head-waiter, chief steward; **maîtresse femme** capable woman.

maître-autel [mɛtrotɛl] *nm* high altar.

maîtrise [mɛtri:z] *nf* command, mastery, control, self-control; choir-school.

maîtriser [mɛtrize] *vt* to master, curb, subdue; *vr* to keep control of oneself.

majesté [maʒɛste] *nf* majesty, grandeur.

majestueux, -euse [maʒɛstɥø, ø:z] *a* majestic, stately.

majeur [maʒœ:r] *a* major, greater, chief, important, of age; **force —e** absolute necessity, compulsion.

major [maʒɔ:r] *nm* regimental adjutant, medical officer.

majoration [maʒɔrasjɔ̃] *nf* over-valuation, increase, additional charge.

majordome [maʒɔrdɔm] *nm* major-domo, steward.

majorer [maʒɔre] *vt* to overvalue, raise, put up the price of, make an additional charge.

majorité [maʒɔrite] *nf* majority, coming of age.

majuscule [maʒyskyl] *a nf* capital (letter).

mal [mal] *nm* evil, wrong, harm, hurt, ache, malady, difficulty, trouble; *ad* badly, ill; **— lui en a pris** he had cause to rue it; **prendre en —** to take amiss; **avoir — au cœur** to feel sick; **avoir — à la tête** to have a headache; **se trouver —** to feel faint; **avoir le —.du pays** to be homesick; **se donner du — pour** to take pains to; **tant bien que —** somehow or other; **pas — de** a good lot of, a good many; **elle n'est pas —** she is not bad looking; **on est très — ici** we are very uncomfortable here.

malade [malad] *a* ill, sick, upset, sore, painful; *n* invalid, sick person, patient; **se faire porter —** to report sick.

maladie [maladi] *nf* illness, complaint, ailment, disease, disorder.

maladif, -ive [maladif, i:v] *a* sickly, unhealthy.

maladresse [maladrɛs] *nf* awkwardness, clumsiness, lack of skill, slip, blunder.

maladroit [maladrwa] *a* clumsy, unskilful; *n* blunderer.

malaise [malɛːz] *nm* discomfort, faintness, indisposition, uneasiness.

malappris [malapri] *a* uncouth; *n* ill-bred person.

malavisé [malavize] *a* indiscreet, unwise, rash.

malchance [malʃɑ̃ːs] *nf* (piece of) bad luck.

malchanceux, -euse [malʃɑ̃sø, øːz] *a* unlucky, unfortunate.

maldonne [maldɔn] *nf* misdeal.

mâle [maːl] *a* male, manly, he-, dog-, cock-, buck-; *nm* male.

malédiction [malediksjɔ̃] *nf* curse.

maléfice [malefis] *nm* evil spell.

maléfique [malefik] *a* evil, baleful, maleficent.

malencontreux, -euse [malɑ̃kɔ̃trø, øːz] *a* untoward, unlucky, tiresome.

malentendu [malɑ̃tɑ̃dy] *nm* misunderstanding.

malfaçon [malfasɔ̃] *nf* bad workmanship.

malfaisant [malfəzɑ̃] *a* evil, harmful.

malfaiteur, -trice [malfɛtœːr, tris] *n* malefactor, evil-doer.

malfamé [malfame] *a* of ill repute.

malgache [malgaʃ] *an* Madagascan.

malgré [malgre] *prep* in spite of, notwithstanding; *cj* **— que** in spite of, although.

malhabile [malabil] *a* awkward, clumsy.

malheur [malœːr] *nm* misfortune, ill luck; **jouer de —** to be out of luck.

malheureux, -euse [malœrø, øːz] *a* unhappy, wretched, unfortunate, unlucky.

malhonnête [malɔnɛt] *a* dishonest, rude, improper.

malhonnêteté [malɔnɛtte] *nf* dishonesty, dishonest action, rudeness, rude remark.

malice [malis] *nf* malice, spitefulness, mischievousness, roguishness, trick; **n'y pas entendre —** to mean no harm.

malicieux, -euse [malisjø, øːz] *a* mischievous, naughty.

malignité [maliɲite] *nf* spite, malignancy.

malin, -igne [malɛ̃, iɲ] *a* malicious, mischievous, sly, shrewd, malignant; **ce n'est pas —** that's easy enough.

malingre [malɛ̃ːgr] *a* sickly, weakly, puny.

malintentionné [malɛ̃tɑ̃sjɔne] *a* ill-disposed, evil-minded.

malle [mal] *nf* trunk, box; **faire sa —** to pack one's trunk.

malléable [maleabl] *a* malleable, pliable, soft.

malle-poste [malpɔst] *nf* mail coach.

mallette [malɛt] *nf* small trunk.

malmener [malmɔne] *vt* to ill-treat, ill-use, treat roughly, put through it.

malodorant [malɔdɔrɑ̃] *a* evil-smelling.

malotru [malɔtry] *a* ill-bred, coarse; *nm* boor, lout.

malpeigné [malpɛɲe] *n* slut, slovenly person.

malpropre [malprɔpr] *a* dirty, untidy, indecent, dishonest.

malpropreté [malprɔprəte] *nf* dirtiness, untidiness, unsavouriness, dishonesty.

malsain [malsɛ̃] *a* unhealthy, unwholesome, corrupting.

malséant [malseɑ̃] *a* unseemly, unbecoming.

malt [malt] *nm* malt.

maltraiter [maltrɛte] *vt* to ill-treat.

malveillance [malvɛjɑ̃ːs] *nf* malevolence, spitefulness, foul play.

malveillant [malvɛjɑ̃] *a* malevolent, spiteful.

malvenu [malvəny] *a* ill-advised, unjustified.

malversation [malvɛrsasjɔ̃] *nf* embezzlement.

maman [mamɑ̃] *nf* mummy, mama.

mamelle [mamɛl] *nf* breast, udder.

mamelon [mamlɔ̃] *nf* nipple, teat, rounded hillock.

mammifère [mamifɛːr] *nm* mammal.

mamour [mamuːr] *nm* my love; *pl* **faire des —s à quelqu'un** to cuddle, coax someone.

manche [mɑ̃ːʃ] *nf* sleeve, hose-pipe, game, set, round, heat; **la Manche** the English Channel; *nm* handle, shaft, stock, joy-stick.

mancheron [mɑ̃ʃrɔ̃] *nm* handle (of plough), short sleeve.

manchette [mɑ̃ʃɛt] *nf* cuff, wristband, newspaper headline, marginal note; *pl* handcuffs.

manchon [mɑ̃ʃɔ̃] *nm* muff, socket, sleeve, casing, gas-mantle.

manchot [mɑ̃ʃo] *an* one-armed (person); penguin.

mandarine [mɑ̃darin] *nf* tangerine.

mandat [mɑ̃da] *nm* mandate, commission, money order, warrant; **— de comparution** summons.

mandataire [mɑ̃datɛːr] *n* mandatory, agent, proxy.

mandat-poste [mɑ̃dapɔst] *nm* postal order.

mander [mɑ̃de] *vt* to send for, summon, send word to; *vi* to report.

mandibule [mɑ̃dibyl] *nf* mandible.

mandoline [mɑ̃dɔlin] *nf* mandolin(e).

mandragore [mãdragɔːr] nf mandragora, mandrake.

manège [manɛːʒ] nm training of horses, horsemanship, riding-school, trick, little game; — de chevaux de bois roundabout, merry-go-round.

manette [manɛt] nf hand lever, handle.

manganèse [mãganɛːz] nm manganese.

mangeable [mãʒabl] a eatable, edible.

mangeaille [mãzaːj] nf food, grub.

mangeoire [mãʒwaːr] nf manger, trough.

manger [mãʒe] vt to eat (up, away, into), squander; nm food; **donner à** — à to feed, give sth to eat to.

mange-tout [mãʒtu] nm spendthrift string-bean.

mangouste [mãgust] nf mongoose.

mangue [mãːg] nf mango.

maniable [manjabl] a manageable, easily handled, handy.

maniaque [manjak] a raving mad, faddy; n maniac, crank.

manie [mani] nf mania, craze, fad.

maniement [manimã] nm handling; — d'armes rifle drill.

manier [manje] vt to handle, ply, wield, control, feel.

manière [manjɛːr] nf manner, way; pl manners, affected airs; à sa — in his own way; à la — de after, in the manner of; de cette — in this way; d'une — ou d'une autre somehow or other; en — de by way of; **arranger qn de la belle** — to give s.o. a thorough dressing-down.

maniéré [manjere] a affected, mincing.

maniérisme [manjerism] nm mannerism.

manifestant [manifɛstã] n demonstrator.

manifestation [manifɛstasjɔ̃] nf (public) demonstration, manifestation.

manifeste [manifɛst] a manifest, obvious, evident, patent; nm manifesto.

manifester [manifɛste] vt to manifest, display, reveal, show, express; vi to demonstrate; vr to show, reveal itself, appear, become apparent.

manigance [manigãːs] nf intrigue, scheme, game; pl underhand work, trickery.

manigancer [manigãse] vt to plot, scheme, arrange, be up to.

manille [maniːj] nf ankle-ring, shackle, manille.

manioc [manjɔk] nm cassava.

manipulateur, -trice [manipylatœːr, tris] n manipulator.

manipuler [manipyle] vt to manipulate, operate, handle, arrange.

manitou [manitu] nm le grand — the big boss.

manivelle [manivɛl] nf handle, crank, starting-handle.

manne [man] nf manna, basket, hamper.

mannequin [manikɛ̃] nm small hamper, manikin, dummy, mannequin.

manœuvrable [manœvrabl] a easily handled.

manœuvre [manœːvr] nf working, handling, manœuvre, drill, shunting, scheme, move; nm labourer.

manœuvrer [manœvre] vt to work, operate, handle, manœuvre, shunt; vi to manœuvre, scheme.

manoir [manwaːr] nm manor, country house.

manomètre [manɔmɛtr] nm pressure-gauge.

manquant [mãkã] a missing, wanting, absent; n absentee.

manque [mãːk] nm lack, want, shortage, deficiency, breach; — de mémoire forgetfulness; à la — dud.

manqué [mãke] a unsuccessful, missed, wasted; un garçon — tomboy.

manquement [mãkmã] nm failure, omission, breach, oversight, lapse.

manquer [mãke] vt to miss, waste; vi to be short (of de), lack, run short, be missing, fail; il manqua (de) tomber he almost fell; — à sa parole to break one's word; il leur manque they miss him; ne pas — de to be sure to.

mansarde [mãsard] nf attic, garret.

mansardé [mãsarde] a with sloping ceiling, roof.

mansuétude [mãsyetyd] nf gentleness.

mante [mãːt] nf mantis; — religieuse praying mantis.

manteau [mãto] nm coat, cloak, mantle; mantelpiece.

manucure [manykyːr] n manicurist.

manuel, -elle [manɥɛl] a manual; nm handbook.

manufacture [manyfaktyːr] nf factory, works.

manufacturer [manyfaktyre] vt to manufacture.

manufacturier, -ière [manyfaktyrje, jɛːr] a manufacturing; n manufacturer.

manuscrit [manyskri] nm manuscript.

manutention [manytãsjɔ̃] nf administration, handling, stores.

mappemonde [mapmɔ̃ːd] nf map of the world.

maquereau [makro] nm mackerel.

maquette [makɛt] nf clay model, model, dummy, mock-up.

maquignon, -onne [makiɲɔ̃, ɔn] n horse-dealer, shady dealer, jobber.

maquignonnage [makiɲɔnaːʒ] nm horse-dealing, faking, shady dealing.

maquignonner [makiɲɔne] vt to doctor, arrange, fix.

maquillage [makija:ʒ] *nm* make-up, making-up.

maquiller [makije] *vt* to make up, fake up, doctor, cook; *vr* to make up.

maquis [maki] *nm* bush, scrub; Resistance Movement.

maquisard [makiza:r] *n* member of the Resistance Movement.

maraîcher, -ère [marɛʃe, ɛ:r] *a* market-gardening; *n* market gardener.

marais [marɛ] *nm* marsh, bog; floating vote; — **salant** salt-pan.

marasme [marasm] *nm* wasting, stagnation, depression.

marâtre [marɑ:tr] *nf* stepmother, hard-hearted mother.

maraude [maro:d] *nf* marauding, looting, plundering; **être en** — to be on the scrounge, prowl.

marbre [marbr] *nm* marble.

marbrer [marbre] *vt* to marble, vein, mottle, blotch.

marbrier [marbrie] *nm* monumental mason.

marbrure [marbry:r] *nf* marbling, veining, mottling, blotch.

marc [ma:r] *nm* residue; — **de café** coffee grounds.

marcassin [markasɛ̃] *nm* young wild boar.

marchand [marʃɑ̃] *a* commercial, trading, merchant; *n* shopkeeper, tradesman, dealer; **valeur** —**e** market value; — **des quatre saisons** hawker, costermonger.

marchander [marʃɑ̃de] *vt* to bargain, haggle over, be sparing of, grudge.

marchandise [marʃɑ̃di:z] *nf* merchandise, commodity, wares, goods.

marche [marʃ] *nf* walk(ing), gait, march(ing), working, running, progress, course, step, stair; **en** — moving, running, under way; **mettre en** — to get going, start up; **faire** — **arrière** to reverse, go astern.

marché [marʃe] *nm* market, bargain, deal(ing), contract; **(à) bon** — cheap(ly); **par-dessus le** — into the bargain; **faire bon** — **de** to attach little value to.

marchepied [marʃəpje] *nm* step, running-board.

marcher [marʃe] *vi* to walk, tread, go, run, work, get along; **il ne marche pas** he is not having any, he won't do as he is told; **faire** — **qn** to make s.o. do as he is told, pull s.o.'s leg.

marcheur, -euse [marʃœ:r, ø:z] *n* walker; **vieux** — old rake.

mardi [mardi] *nm* Tuesday; — **gras** Shrove Tuesday.

mare [ma:r] *nf* pool, pond.

marécage [mareka:ʒ] *nm* marsh (land), swamp.

marécageux, -euse [marekaʒø, ø:z] *a* marshy, swampy, boggy.

maréchal [mareʃal] *nm* marshal; — **ferrant** farrier, shoesmith; — **des logis** sergeant; — **de France** field-marshal.

marée [mare] *nf* tide, fresh fish; — **montante** flood tide; — **descendante** ebb tide; **arriver comme** — **en carême** to come at the right time; **train de** — fish-train.

marelle [marɛl] *nf* hopscotch.

mareyeur, -euse [marɛjœ:r, ø:z] *n* fish merchant, fish porter.

margarine [margarin] *nf* margarine.

marge [marʒ] *nf* margin, edge, border, fringe.

margelle [marʒɛl] *nf* edge.

marguerite [margərit] *nf* daisy, marguerite.

marguillier [margije] *nm* churchwarden.

mari [mari] *nm* husband.

mariage [marja:ʒ] *nm* marriage, matrimony.

Marie [mari] Mary.

marié [marje] *a* married; *n* bridegroom, bride.

marier [marje] *vt* to marry, give in marriage, unite, blend, cross; *vr* to get married, marry, harmonize.

marie-salope [marisalɔp] *nf* dredger, slut.

marigot [marigo] *nm* small stream.

marin [marɛ̃] *a* marine, sea-; *nm* sailor, seaman, seafaring man; **avoir le pied** — to be a good sailor; **se faire** — to go to sea; — **d'eau douce** landlubber.

marinade [marinad] *nf* pickle, brine.

marine [marin] *nf* navy, seamanship, seascape; — **marchande** merchant service; **bleu** — navy blue.

mariner [marine] *vt* to pickle, souse, marinate; *vi* to be in pickle.

marinier, -ière [marinje, jɛ:r] *a* naval, marine; *nm* bargee, waterman.

marionnette [marjɔnɛt] *nf* marionnette, puppet.

maritime [maritim] *a* maritime, naval, seaside, sea(borne); **agent** — shipping agent; **courtier** — shipbroker.

marivaudage [marivoda:ʒ] *nm* affected, flippant conversation, mild flirtation.

marlou [marlu] *nm* pimp.

marmaille [marma:j] *nf* (*fam*) brats, children.

marmelade [marməlad] *nf* compote, marmalade.

marmite [marmit] *nf* pot, pan, camp-kettle, heavy shell; — **de géants** pothole.

marmiter [marmite] *vt* to shell, bombard.

marmiton [marmitɔ̃] *nm* cook's boy, scullion.

marmonner [marmɔne] *vt* to mutter, mumble.

marmot [marmo] *nm* brat, child.

marmotte [marmɔt] *nf* marmot, kerchief.

marmotter [marmɔte] *vt* to mumble, mutter.

marne [marn] *nf* marl.

Maroc [marɔk] *nm* Morocco.

marocain [marɔkɛ̃] *an* Moroccan.

maroquinerie [marɔkinri] *nf* (morocco-) leather trade, goods, shop.

marotte [marɔt] *nf* cap and bells, bauble, hobby, fad.

marquant [markɑ̃] *a* outstanding, notable.

marque [mark] *nf* mark, stamp, make, token, proof, marker, tally, score, scoring; — **de fabrique** trademark; — **déposée** registered trademark; **vin de** — first class wine; **personnage de** — prominent person.

marqué [marke] *a* marked, pronounced, appointed.

marquer [marke] *vt* to mark, put a mark on, show, note down, record, score; *vi* to stand out, make one's mark; **elle marque bien** she is a good-looker; — **son âge** to look one's age; — **les points** to keep the score; — **le pas** to mark time.

marqueter [markəte] *vt* to speckle, spot, inlay.

marqueterie [markətri] *nf* marquetry, inlaid-work.

marqueur, -euse [markœːr, øːz] *n* marker, stamper, scorer.

marquis [marki] *nm* marquis, marquess.

marquise [markiːz] *nf* marchioness; awning, glass porch, marquee.

marraine [marɛn] *nf* godmother, sponsor.

marrant [marɑ̃] *a* terribly funny, killing.

marre [maːr] *nf* **j'en ai** — I'm fed up.

marrer [mare] *vr* to split one's sides with laughing.

marron, -onne [marɔ̃, ɔn] *a* chestnut-coloured; unlicensed, quack, sham; *nm* chestnut.

marronnier [marɔnje] *nm* chestnut-tree.

mars [mars] *nm* March, Mars; **champ de** — parade-ground.

marsouin [marswɛ̃] *nm* porpoise, colonial infantry soldier.

marteau [marto] *nm* hammer, door-knocker.

marteler [martəle] *vt* to hammer (out); *vi* to knock.

martial [marsjal] *a* martial, warlike, soldierlike.

martinet [martinɛ] *nm* strap, whip, swift.

martingale [martɛ̃gal] *nf* martingale, half-belt.

martin-pêcheur [martɛ̃pɛʃœːr] *nm* kingfisher.

martre [martr] *nm* marten, sable.

martyr [martiːr] *n* martyr.

martyre [martiːr] *nm* martyrdom.

martyriser [martirize] *vt* to martyr, torture.

marxisme [marksism] *nm* marxism.

mascarade [maskarad] *nf* masquerade.

mascaret [maskarɛ] *nm* bore, tidal wave.

mascotte [maskɔt] *nf* mascot, charm.

masculin [maskylɛ̃] *a* masculine, male, mannish; *nm* masculine gender.

masque [mask] *nm* mask, features, expression, masque.

masquer [maske] *vt* to mask, hide, screen, disguise; **virage masqué** blind corner.

massacre [masakr] *nm* massacre, slaughter; **jeu de** — Aunt Sally (game).

massacrer [masakre] *vt* to massacre, slaughter, butcher, spoil; **être d'une humeur massacrante** to be in a vile temper.

massage [masaːʒ] *nm* massage, rubbing down.

masse [mas] *nf* mass, bulk, crowd, mace, sledge-hammer.

masser [mase] *vt* to mass, massage, rub down; *vr* to mass, throng together.

masseur, -euse [masœːr, øːz] *n* masseur, masseuse.

massif, -ive [masif, iːv] *a* solid, massive, bulky; *nm* clump, group, range.

massue [masy] *nf* club, bludgeon.

mastic [mastik] *nm* mastic, putty, cement.

mastication [mastikasjɔ̃] *nf* mastication, chewing.

mastiquer [mastike] *vt* to masticate, chew, putty, fill with cement.

m'as-tu-vu [matyvy] *nm* swanky, show-off.

masure [mazyːr] *nf* hovel, tumble-down house.

mat [mat] *a* dull, unpolished, mat, checkmated; *nm* checkmate.

mât [mɑ] *nm* mast, pole, strut; — **de cocagne** greasy pole.

match [matʃ] *nm* match; — **de sélection** trial match.

matelas [matlɑ] *nm* mattress.

matelasser [matlase] *vt* to pad, cushion; **porte matelassée** baize-covered door.

matelot [matlo] *nm* sailor, seaman; — **de première (deuxième) classe** leading (able) seaman.

mater [mate] *vt* to dull, mat, checkmate, humble.

matérialiser [materjalize] *vtr* to materialize.

matérialiste [materjalist] *a* materialistic; *n* materialist.

matériaux [materjo] *nm pl* material(s).

matériel, -elle [materjɛl] *a* material, sensual, physical; *nm* material, plant, implements, equipment; — **roulant** rolling stock.

maternel, -elle [matɛrnɛl] *a* maternal, mother(ly); **école —le** infant school.

maternité [matɛrnite] *nf* maternity, motherhood, maternity hospital.

mathématicien, -ienne [matematisjɛ̃, jɛn] *n* mathematician.

mathématique [matematik] *a* mathematical; *nf pl* mathematics.

matière [matjɛːr] *nf* matter, substance, material, subject.

matin [matɛ̃] *nm* morning; **de grand, de bon —** early in the morning.

mâtin [matɛ̃] *nm* mastiff.

matinal [matinal] *a* morning, early rising; **il est —** he is up early.

matinée [matine] *nf* morning, matinee; **faire la grasse —** to lie late in bed.

matines [matin] *nf pl* matins.

matineux, -euse [matinø, øːz] *a* early rising; **il est — ** he gets up early.

matois [matwa] *a* sly, crafty, cunning; *n* cunning person; **fin —** sly, wily, bird.

matou [matu] *nm* tom-cat.

matraque [matrak] *nf* bludgeon.

matrice [matris] *nf* matrix, womb, mould, die.

matricide [matrisid] *a* matricidal; *n* matricide.

matricule [matrikyl] *nf* register, roll, registration (certificate); *nm* (registration) number; **plaque —** number plate.

matriculer [matrikyle] *vt* to enrol, enter in a register, stamp a number on.

matrimonial [matrimɔnjal] *a* matrimonial.

maturation [matyrasjɔ̃] *nf* maturation, ripening.

mâture [matyːr] *nf* masts; **dans la — aloft**.

maturement [matyrmã] *ad* after due deliberation.

maturité [matyrite] *nf* maturity, ripeness, mellowness.

maudire [modiːr] *vt* to curse.

maudit [modi] *a* cursed, damned, damnable, confounded.

maugréer [mogree] *vi* to curse, (fret and) fume.

mausolée [mozɔle] *nm* mausoleum.

maussade [mosad] *a* glum, sullen, dismal, dull.

mauvais [mɔvɛ] *a* bad, wrong, poor, nasty; **ad sentir —** to have a bad smell; **il fait —** the weather is bad.

mauve [moːv] *a nm* mauve.

mauviette [movjɛt] *nf* chit, softy.

maxime [maksim] *nf* maxim.

maximum [maksimɔm] *a nm* maximum.

mazout [mazu] *nm* fuel oil.

me [m(ə)] *pn* me, to me, myself, to myself.

méandre [meɑ̃ːdr] *nm* meander, bend, winding.

mécanicien, -ienne [mekanisjɛ̃, jɛn] *a* mechanical; *n* mechanic, machinist, engineer, engine-driver.

mécanique [mekanik] *a* mechanical, clockwork; *nf* mechanics, machinery, mechanism.

mécanisation [mekanizasjɔ̃] *nf* mechanization.

mécaniser [mekanize] *vt* to mechanize.

mécanisme [mekanism] *nm* mechanism, machinery, works, technique.

mécano [mekano] *nm* (*fam*) mechanic.

méchanceté [meʃɑ̃ste] *nf* wickedness, spitefulness, naughtiness, ill-natured word or act.

méchant [meʃɑ̃] *a* wicked, bad, naughty, ill-natured, spiteful, vicious, wretched, sorry.

mèche [mɛʃ] *nf* wick, fuse, match, (*hair*) lock, wisp, gimlet, spindle, drill; **éventer la —** to give the game away; **être de — avec** to be in league with.

mécompte [mekɔ̃ːt] *nm* miscalculation, error, misjudgment, disappointment.

méconnaissable [mekɔnɛsabl] *a* unrecognizable.

méconnaissance [mekɔnɛsɑ̃ːs] *nf* refusal to recognize or appreciate, ignoring, disavowal.

méconnaître [mekɔnɛːtr] *vt* to fail (refuse) to recognize, not to appreciate, to ignore, misunderstand, disavow.

mécontent [mekɔ̃tɑ̃] *a* discontented, displeased, dissatisfied.

mécontentement [mekɔ̃tɑ̃tmã] *nm* discontent, dissatisfaction.

mécontenter [mekɔ̃tɑ̃te] *vt* to displease, dissatisfy, annoy.

mécréant [mekreɑ̃] *a* misbelieving, unbelieving; *n* infidel.

médaille [medaːj] *nf* medal, badge; **revers de la —** other side of the picture.

médaillon [medajɔ̃] *nm* medallion, locket, inset.

médecin [medsɛ̃] *nm* doctor, physician.

médecine [medsin] *nf* medicine.

médiateur, -trice [medjatœːr, tris] *a* mediatory, mediating; *n* mediator.

médiation [medjasjɔ̃] *nf* mediation.

médical [medikal] *a* medical.

médicament [medikamã] *nm* medicine, medicament.

médicinal [medisinal] *a* medicinal.

médiéval [medjeval] *a* medieval.

médiocre [medjɔkr] *a* mediocre, moderate, second-rate; *nm* mediocrity.

médiocrité [medjɔkrite] *nf* mediocrity, feebleness, nonentity.

médire [mediːr] *vi* to slander, speak ill of.

médisance [medizɑ̃ːs] *nf* calumny, scandal.

médisant [medizã] *a* slanderous, calumnious, backbiting; *n* slanderer.

méditatif, -ive [meditatif, iːv] *a* meditative.

méditation [meditasjɔ̃] *nf* meditation, contemplation.

méditer [medite] *vt* to contemplate, ponder; *vi* to meditate, muse.

Méditerranée [meditɛrane] *nf* Mediterranean.

méditerranéen, -enne [meditɛraneɛ̃, ɛn] *a* Mediterranean.

médium [medjɔm] *nm* medium.

médius [medjys] *nm* middle finger.

méduse [medyːz] *nf* jellyfish.

méduser [medyze] *vt* to petrify, paralyse.

méfait [mefɛ] *nm* misdeed; *pl* damage.

méfiance [mefjãːs] *nf* distrust, mistrust, suspicion.

méfiant [mefjã] *a* distrustful, suspicious.

se méfier [səmefje] *vr* to distrust, mistrust, be watchful, be on one's guard.

mégalomanie [megalɔmani] *nf* megalomania.

mégaphone [megafɔn] *nm* megaphone.

mégarde [megard] *ad* **par —** inadvertently.

mégère [meʒɛːr] *nf* shrew.

mégot [mego] *nm* cigarette-end.

méhari [meari] *nm* racing camel.

meilleur [mɛjœːr] *a* better, best; *comp sup of* **bon**; *nm* best, best thing.

mélancolie [melãkɔli] *nf* melancholy, dejection, melancholia, sadness.

mélange [melãːʒ] *nm* mixing, mingling, blending, mixture, blend.

mélanger [melãʒe] *vtr* to mix, mingle, blend.

mélasse [melas] *nf* molasses, treacle.

mêlée [mele] *nf* conflict, fray, scuffle, scrum, scrimmage; **demi de — scrum-half.**

mêler [mele] *vt* to mix, mingle, blend, tangle, involve, implicate, shuffle; *vr* to mix, mingle, interfere, meddle.

mélèze [melɛːz] *nm* larch.

méli-mélo [melimelo] *nm* jumble.

mélodie [melɔdi] *nf* melody, tune, harmony, song.

mélodieux, -euse [melɔdjø, øːz] *a* melodious, tuneful, harmonious.

mélodique [melɔdik] *a* melodic.

mélodramatique [melɔdramatik] *a* melodramatic.

mélodrame [melɔdram] *nm* melodrama.

mélomane [melɔman] *a* music-loving; *n* music-lover.

melon [məlɔ̃] *nm* melon, bowler hat.

mélopée [melɔpe] *nf* art of recitative, chant, singsong.

membrane [mãbran] *nf* membrane, web.

membre [mãːbr] *nm* member, limb.

membré [mãːbre] *a* -limbed.

membrure [mãbryːr] *nf* limbs, framework.

même [mɛm] *a* same, very, -self; *ad* even; **de lui —** of his own accord; **de — likewise; il en est de — de lui** it is the same with him; **tout de —** all the same; **à — la bouteille** out of the bottle; **revenir au —** to come to the same thing; **à — de** in a position to.

mémento [memɛ̃to] *nm* memorandum, notebook, memento, synopsis.

mémoire [memwaːr] *nm* memoir, paper, memorial, bill, account; *nf* memory, recollection.

mémorable [memɔrabl] *a* memorable, eventful.

mémorandum [memɔrãdɔm] *nm* memorandum, notebook.

mémorial [memɔrjal] *nm* memorial, memoirs, daybook.

menaçant [mənasã] *a* threatening, menacing.

menace [mənas] *nf* threat, menace; *pl* intimidation.

menacer [mənase] *vt* to threaten, menace; **— ruine** to be falling to pieces; **qn du poing** to shake one's fist at s.o.

ménage [menaːʒ] *nm* household, family, married couple, housekeeping, housework; **se mettre en — to** set up house; **faire bon — ensemble** to get on well together; **femme de — housekeeper, charwoman.**

ménagement [menaʒmã] *nm* consideration, caution, care.

ménager [menaʒe] *vt* to be sparing of, save, humour, spare, arrange, contrive; *vr* to take care of oneself.

ménager, -ère [menaʒe, jɛːr] *a* domestic, house-, thrifty, careful, housewifely; **Arts M—s** Ideal Home Exhibition; *nf* housewife, housekeeper, canteen of cutlery.

ménagerie [menaʒri] *nf* menagerie.

mendiant [mãdjã] *a* begging, mendicant; *n* beggar.

mendicité [mãdisite] *nf* begging, beggary.

mendier [mãdje] *vt* to beg (for); *vi* to beg.

menée [məne] *nf* track, intrigue; *pl* manœuvres.

mener [məne] *vt* to lead, take, drive, steer, manage, control; **— à bonne fin** to carry through; **n'en pas — large** to feel small.

ménétrier [menetrie] *nm* (strolling) fiddler.

meneur, -euse [mənœːr, øːz] *n* leader, agitator, ringleader.

méningite [menɛ̃ʒit] *nf* meningitis.

menotte [mənɔt] *nf* tiny hand; *pl* handcuffs, manacles.

menotter [mənɔte] *vt* to manacle, handcuff.

mensonge [mãsɔ̃ːʒ] *nm* lie, falsehood, illusion.

mensonger, -ère [mãsɔ̃ʒe, ɛːr] *a* lying, deceitful, illusory.

mensualité [mãsɥalite] *nf* monthly payment.

mensuel, -elle [mãsɥɛl] *a* monthly.

mensuration [mãsyrasjɔ̃] *nf* measurement, measuring, mensuration.

mental [mãtal] *a* mental.

mentalité [mãtalite] *nf* mentality.

menterie [mãtri] *nf* fib, tale, story.

menteur, -euse [mãtœːr, øːz] *a* lying, deceptive, false; *n* liar.

menthe [mãːt] *nf* mint, peppermint.

mention [mãsjɔ̃] *nf* endorsement; **reçu avec — de** passed with distinction; **faire — de** to mention.

mentionner [mãsjɔne] *vt* to mention, speak of.

mentir [mãtiːr] *vi* to lie, tell lies.

menton [mãtɔ̃] *nm* chin.

mentonnière [mãtɔnjɛːr] *nf* chinstrap, chinpiece, chinrest.

mentor [mɛtɔːr] *nm* mentor, tutor, guide.

menu [məny] *a* small, tiny, fine, minute, slight, trifling, petty; *ad* small, fine; *nm* menu, bill of fare; **par le — in** detail.

menuet [mənɥɛ] *nm* minuet.

menuiserie [mənɥizri] *nf* carpentry, woodwork.

menuisier [mənɥizje] *nm* joiner, carpenter.

méplat [mepla] *a* flat; *nm* flat part, plane.

se méprendre [səmeprãːdr] *vr* to be mistaken, make a mistake (about **sur**); **il n'y a pas à s'y — there is no** mistake about it.

mépris [mepri] *nm* scorn, contempt.

méprisable [meprizabl] *a* contemptible, despicable.

méprisant [meprizã] *a* contemptuous, scornful.

méprise [mepriːz] *nf* error, mistake, misapprehension.

mépriser [meprize] *vt* to despise, scorn.

mer [mɛːr] *nf* sea; **en pleine — on** the high seas; **prendre la — to put** out to sea; **mettre à la — to lower** (a boat).

mercantile [mɛrkãtil] *a* commercial, money-grabbing, mercenary.

mercantilisme [mɛrkãtilism] *nm* profiteering, commercialism.

mercenaire [mɛrsənɛːr] *an* mercenary.

mercerie [mɛrsəri] *nf* haberdashery.

merci [mɛrsi] *nf* mercy; *ad* thanks, thank you, no thanks, no thank you.

mercier, -ière [mɛrsje, jɛːr] *n* haberdasher.

mercredi [mɛrkrədi] *nm* Wednesday; **— des Cendres** Ash Wednesday.

mercure [mɛrkyːr] *nm* mercury, quicksilver.

mercuriale [mɛrkyrjal] *nf* market price-list, reprimand.

merde [mɛrd] *nf* shit, excrement.

mère [mɛːr] *nf* mother, source; *a* main.

méridien, -ienne [meridjɛ̃, jɛn] *a* meridian, meridional; *nm* meridian; *nf* meridian line.

méridional [meridjɔnal] *a* meridional, Southern; *n* Southerner.

meringue [mərɛ̃g] *nf* meringue.

mérinos [merinɔs] *nm* merino.

merisier [mərizje] *nm* wild cherry-tree.

méritant [meritã] *a* deserving, meritorious, worthy.

mérite [merit] *nm* merit, worth, credit, ability.

mériter [merite] *vt* to deserve, merit, earn.

méritoire [meritwaːr] *a* deserving, worthy, meritorious.

merlan [mɛrlã] *nm* whiting; *(fam)* barber.

merle [mɛrl] *nm* blackbird.

merluche [mɛrlyʃ] *nf* hake, dried cod.

merrain [mɛrɛ̃] *nm* caskwood.

merveille [mɛrvɛːj] *nf* marvel, wonder; **à — wonderfully well,** excellently.

merveilleux, -euse [mɛrvɛjø, øːz] *a* marvellous, wonderful; *nm* supernatural.

mes [me] *a pl* see **mon**.

mésalliance [mezaljãːs] *nf* misalliance, unsuitable marriage.

se mésallier [səmezalje] *vr* to marry beneath one.

mésange [mezãːʒ] *nf* tit; **— charbonnière** tomtit, great tit.

mésaventure [mezavãtyːr] *nf* misadventure, mishap.

mésentente [mezãtãt] *nf* misunderstanding, disagreement.

mésestime [mezɛstim] *nf* low esteem, poor opinion.

mésestimer [mezɛstime] *vt* to underestimate, have a poor opinion of.

mésintelligence [mezɛtɛliʒãːs] *nf* misunderstanding, disagreement, discord.

mesquin [mɛskɛ̃] *a* mean, petty, shabby, paltry.

mesquinerie [mɛskinri] *nf* meanness, pettiness, shabbiness, paltriness, stinginess, mean action.

mess [mɛs] *nm* officers' mess.

message [mesaːʒ] *nm* message.

messager, -ère [mesaʒe, ɛr] *n* messenger, carrier.

messagerie [mesaʒri] *nf* freight trade; **les —s** central newsagency; **— maritime** shipping office.

messe [mɛs] *nf* mass; **— des morts** requiem mass.

messie [mɛsi] *nm* Messiah.

mesure [məzyːr] *nf* measure, standard (size), gauge, extent, bounds, moderation; *pl* measures, steps; **en — de** in a position to; **donner sa — to show what one can**

do; **dépasser la —** to overstep the mark; **fait sur —** made to measure; **à — que** as.

mesure-étalon [məzyretalɔ̃] *nf* standard measure.

mesuré [məzyre] *a* measured, moderate, restrained.

mesurer [məzyre] *vt* to measure (out, off), judge, calculate; *vr* to measure oneself (with), tackle; **— qn des yeux** to eye s.o. up and down.

métairie [meteri] *nf* small farm.

métal [metal] *nm* metal.

métallique [metalik] *a* metallic; **toile —** wire gauze.

métalliser [metalize] *vt* to metallize, plate.

métallurgie [metallyrʒi] *nf* metallurgy.

métallurgiste [metallyrʒist] *nm* metallurgist, metal-worker.

métamorphose [metamɔrfoz] *nf* metamorphosis, transformation.

métaphore [metafɔːr] *nf* metaphor.

métaphorique [metafɔrik] *a* metaphorical.

métaphysicien, -ienne [metafizisjɛ̃, jɛn] *n* metaphysician.

métaphysique [metafizik] *a* metaphysical; *nf* metaphysics.

métayer, -ère [meteje, jɛːr] *n* farmer, share-cropper.

métempsychose [metɑ̃psikoːz] *nf* metempsychosis, transmigration of souls.

météore [meteɔːr] *nm* meteor.

météorologie [meteɔrɔlɔʒi] *nf* meteorology.

météorologique [meteɔrɔlɔʒik] *a* meteorological; **bulletin —** weather report.

métèque [metɛk] *nm* (*pej*) foreigner.

méthode [metɔd] *nf* method, system, orderliness, primer.

méthodique [metɔdik] *a* methodical.

méticuleux, -euse [metikylø, øːz] *a* meticulous, particular, punctilious.

métier [metje] *nm* trade, profession, craft(smanship), loom; **homme de — craftsman**; **— manuel** handicraft; **sur le —** on the stocks, in preparation.

métis, -isse [metis] *a* half-bred, cross-bred, mongrel; *n* half-cast, half-breed, mongrel.

métisser [metise] *vt* to cross(breed).

métrage [metraːʒ] *nm* measuring, metric area or volume, length; (**film à**) **court —** a short.

mètre [metr] *nm* metre, rule; **— à ruban** tape-measure.

métrique [metrik] *a* metric(al); *nf* metrics, prosody.

métro [metro] *nm* underground (railway), tube.

métropole [metrɔpɔl] *nf* metropolis, mother country.

métropolitain [metrɔpɔlitɛ̃] *a* metropolitan, home-; *nm* underground (railway).

mets [mɛ] *nm* dish, food.

mettable [metabl] *a* wearable.

metteur, -euse [metœːr, øːz] *n* — **en scène** producer, director.

mettre [metr] *vt* to put (up, on), place, set (up), lay, wear; *vr* to go, stand, sit, put on; **se — à** to begin, set about; **mettons qu'il l'ait fait** suppose he did do it; **se — en colère** to get angry; **—en scène** to produce (*a play*).

meuble [mœbl] *a* movable; *nm* piece or suite of furniture; *pl* furniture.

meublé [mœble] *a* furnished, stocked; *nm* furnished room(s).

meubler [mœble] *vt* to furnish, stock; *vr* to furnish (one's house).

meugler [møgle] *vi* to low.

meule [møːl] *nf* millstone, stack, rick.

meuler [møle] *vt* to grind.

meulière [møljɛːr] *nf* millstone, -quarry.

meunerie [mønri] *nf* milling, milling-trade.

meunier, -ière [mønje, jɛːr] *n* miller.

meurtre [mœrtr] *nm* murder.

meurtrier, -ière [mœrtrie, iɛːr] *a* murderous, deadly; *n* murderer, murderess.

meurtrière [mœrtriɛːr] *nf* loophole.

meurtrir [mœrtriːr] *vt* to bruise, batter.

meurtrissure [mœrtrisyːr] *nf* bruise.

meute [møːt] *nf* pack, mob, crowd.

mexicain [mɛksikɛ̃] *an* Mexican.

Mexique [mɛksik] *nm* Mexico.

mi [mi] *ad* half, semi, mid-; **à la — -septembre** in mid-September; **à — -chemin** half way; **à — -côte** half way up; **à — -corps** to the waist; *nm* note E.

miasme [mjasm] *nm* miasma.

miauler [mjole] *vi* to mew, caterwaul.

mi-carême [mikarɛm] *nm* Mid-Lent.

miche [miʃ] *nf* round loaf.

Michel [miʃɛl] Michael.

micmac [mikmak] *nm* trickery, scheming.

micocoulier [mikɔkulje] *nm* nettle-tree.

micro [mikro] *nm* mike, microphone.

microbe [mikrɔb] *nm* microbe, germ.

microbicide [mikrɔbisid] *a* germ-killing; *nm* germ-killer.

microcosme [mikrɔkɔsm] *nm* microcosm.

microscope [mikrɔskɔp] *nm* microscope.

microsillon [mikrɔsijɔ̃] *nm* long-playing record.

midi [midi] *nm* noon, midday, south; **chercher — à quatorze heures** to see difficulties when there are none.

midinette [midinɛt] *nf* workgirl, young dressmaker.

mie [mi] *nf* crumb, soft part of a loaf.

miel [mjɛl] *nm* honey.

mielleux, -euse [mjɛlø, ø:z] *a* honeyed, sugary, bland.

mien, mienne [mjɛ̃, mjɛn] *pos pn* le(s) —(s), **la mienne, les miennes** mine; *nm* my own; *pl* my own people.

miette [mjɛt] *nf* crumb, morsel, tiny bit, atom.

mieux [mjø] *ad* better, (the) best, *comp sup of* **bien**; *nm* best thing, improvement; **de — en —** better and better; **à qui — —** one more than the other; **c'est on ne peut —** it could not be better; **faire de son —** to do one's best; **être au — avec** to be on the best terms with; **tant —!** all the better!

mièvre [mjɛ:vr] *a* affected, pretty-pretty, delicate.

mièvrerie [mjɛvrəri] *nf* affectation, insipid prettiness.

mignard [miɲa:r] *a* affected, simpering, mincing, pretty-pretty.

mignardise [miɲardi:z] *nf* affectation, mincing manner, prettiness, garden pink.

mignon, -onne [miɲɔ̃, ɔn] *a* dainty, sweet, tiny; *n* darling, pet, favourite; **péché —** besetting sin.

mignonnette [miɲɔnɛt] *nf* mignonnette lace, coarsely ground pepper, London pride.

migraine [migrɛn] *nf* migraine, sick headache.

migrateur, -trice [migratœ:r, tris] *a* migratory, migrant.

migration [migrasjɔ̃] *nf* migration.

mijaurée [miʒɔre] *nf* affected woman.

mijoter [miʒɔte] *vt* to stew slowly, let simmer, plot; *vi* to stew, simmer; *vr* to simmer.

mil [mil] *a* thousand.

milan [milɑ̃] *nm* kite.

milice [milis] *nf* militia.

milieu [miljø] *nm* middle, midst, environment, circle, set, class, mean, middle course; **au beau — de** right in the middle of; **juste —** happy medium.

militaire [milite:r] *a* military, soldierlike; *nm* soldier.

militant [militɑ̃] *an* militant (supporter).

militariser [militarize] *vt* to militarize.

militer [milite] *vi* to militate, tell.

mille [mil] *a* thousand; *nm* thousand; mile; **avoir des — et des cents** to have tons of money.

mille-feuille [milfœ:j] *nf* flaky pastry, yarrow.

millénaire [millenɛ:r] *a* millenial, *nm* thousand years.

millénium [millenjɔm] *nm* millenium.

mille-pattes [milpat] *nm* centipede.

millésime [mil(l)ezim] *nm* date (*coin*), year of manufacture, of vintage.

millet [mijɛ] *nm* millet.

milliardaire [miljardɛ:r] *a nm* multimillionaire.

millier [milje] *nm* thousand.

milligramme [milligram] *nm* milli-gramme.

millimètre [mil(l)imɛtr] *nm* milli-metre.

million [miljɔ̃] *nm* million.

millionnaire [miljɔnɛ:r] *an* million-aire(ss).

mime [mim] *nm* mimic, mime.

mimique [mimik] *a* mimic; *nf* mimicry.

mimosa [mimoza] *nm* mimosa.

minable [minabl] *a* shabby, seedy-looking, pitiable.

minaret [minarɛ] *nm* minaret.

minauder [minode] *vi* to smirk, simper, mince.

minaudier, -ière [minodje, jɛ:r] *a* smirking, simpering, mincing, affected.

mince [mɛ̃:s] *a* thin, slim, slight, scanty; *excl* **— alors!** dash it all, well I never!

minceur [mɛ̃sœ:r] *nf* thinness, slim-ness.

mine [min] *nf* appearance, look, mine, lead; **— de plomb** graphite; **de bonne (mauvaise) —** prepossess-ing (evil-looking); **avoir bonne (mauvaise) —** to look well (ill); **faire — de** to make as if to; **faire bonne — à** to be pleasant to; **cela ne paie pas de —** it is not much to look at.

miner [mine] *vt* to (under)mine, sap.

minerai [minrɛ] *nm* ore.

minéral [mineral] *a nm* mineral.

minet, -ette [minɛ, ɛt] *n* pussy.

mineur, -eure [minœ:r] *a* minor, underage, lesser; *n* minor; *nm* miner, sapper.

miniature [minjaty:r] *nf* miniature, small scale.

minier, -ière [minje, jɛ:r] *a* mining.

minime [minim] *a* small, trifling, trivial.

minimum [minimɔm] *a nm* mini-mum.

ministère [ministɛ:r] *nm* ministry, office, government; **— des Affaires Etrangères** Foreign Office; **— de l'Intérieur** Home Office; **— de l'Armement** Ministry of Supply; **— de la Guerre** War Office.

ministériel, -elle [ministerjɛl] *a* ministerial, cabinet.

ministre [ministr] *nm* minister, clergyman; **premier —** Prime Min-ister; **— des Affaires Etrangères** Foreign Secretary; **— de l'Intérieur** Home Secretary; **— des Finances** Chancellor of the Exchequer.

minois [minwa] *nm* pretty face.

minorité [minɔrite] *nf* minority, infancy.

minoterie [minɔtri] *nf* flour-mill, -milling.

minotier [minɔtje] *nm* miller.

minuit [minɥi] *nm* midnight.

minuscule [minyskyl] *a* small, tiny, diminutive, minute.

minute [minyt] *nf* minute, record, draft; *excl* not so fast! hold on! réparations à la — repairs while you wait.

minuter [minyte] *vt* to minute, record, enter, draw up.

minuterie [minytri] *nf* staircase switch.

minutie [minysi] *nf* minute detail, trifle, fussiness over detail, thoroughness.

minutieux, -euse [minysjø, øːz] *a* minute, detailed, thorough, meticulous.

mioche [mjɔʃ] *n* (*fam*) small child, kid.

mi-parti [miparti] *a* half and half, parti-coloured.

mirabelle [mirabɛl] *nf* mirabelle plum.

miracle [mirakl] *nm* miracle, wonder.

miraculeux, -euse [mirakylø, øːz] *a* miraculous, marvellous, wonderful.

mirage [miraːʒ] *nm* mirage.

mire [miːr] *nf* aiming, sight, surveyor's pole, (TV) test pattern; point de — cynosure.

mirer [mire] *vt* to sight, aim at, have one's eye on, examine; *vr* to look at oneself, admire oneself.

mirifique [mirifik] *a* amazing, wonderful.

mirobolant [mirɔbɔlɑ̃] *a* amazing, astounding.

miroir [mirwaːr] *nm* mirror, looking-glass, speculum; œufs au — eggs cooked in butter.

miroiter [mirwate] *vi* to gleam, sparkle, shimmer; faire — qch to dazzle, entice with sth.

misaine [mizɛn] *nf* foresail; mât de — foremast.

misanthrope [mizɑ̃trɔp] *a* misanthropic; *nm* misanthrope, misanthropist.

misanthropie [mizɑ̃trɔpi] *nf* misanthropy.

mise [miz] *nf* putting, setting, placing, stake, bid, dress; — à l'eau launching; — en scène setting, staging; — en retraite pensioning; — en plis setting (of hair); — en marche starting up; cela n'est pas de — that is not done, (worn, permissible).

miser [mize] *vt* to stake, gamble, lay, bid.

misérable [mizerabl] *a* wretched, miserable, despicable; *n* wretch, scoundrel.

misère [mizeːr] *nf* misery, poverty,

want, distress, trouble, worry, wretchedness, shabbiness, trifle; crier — to plead poverty, be shabby; faire des — à to tease unmercifully.

miséreux, -euse [mizerø, øːz] *an* destitute, poverty-stricken (person).

miséricorde [mizerikɔrd] *nf* mercy; *excl* goodness gracious!

miséricordieux, -euse [mizerikɔrdjø, øːz] *a* merciful.

misogyne [mizɔʒin] *a* misogynous; *nm* misogynist, woman-hater.

misogynie [mizɔʒini] *nf* misogyny.

missel [misɛl] *nm* missal.

missile [misil] *nm* missile.

mission [misjɔ̃] *nf* mission; en — on a mission.

missionnaire [misjɔnɛːr] *nm* missionary.

missive [misiːv] *nf* missive.

mistral [mistral] *nm* mistral (wind).

mitaine [mitɛn] *nf* mitten.

mite [mit] *nf* moth, mite.

mité [mite] *a* moth-eaten.

mi-temps [mitɑ̃] *nf* half-time, interval, half.

miteux, -euse [mitø, øːz] *a* shabby, seedy-looking.

mitigation [mitigasjɔ̃] *nf* mitigation.

mitiger [mitiʒe] *vt* to mitigate.

mitonner [mitɔne] *vt* to let simmer, concoct; *vi* to simmer.

mitoyen, -enne [mitwajɛ̃, ɛn] *a* dividing, intermediate.

mitraille [mitraːj] *nf* grapeshot; (*fam*) coppers.

mitrailler [mitraje] *vt* to machine-gun, (*fam*) take shots of; — de questions to fire questions at.

mitraillette [mitrajɛt] *nf* tommy-gun.

mitrailleur [mitrajœːr] *nm* machine-gunner; fusil — automatic rifle, bren-gun; fusilier — bren-gunner.

mitrailleuse [mitrajøːz] *nf* machine-gun.

mitre [mitr] *nf* mitre, chimney-pot, chimney-cowl.

mi-vitesse [mivitɛs] *ad* à — at half-speed.

mi-voix [mivwa] *ad* à — under one's breath, in an undertone.

mixte [mikst] *a* mixed, composite, joint.

mixture [mikstyːr] *nf* mixture.

mnémonique [mnemɔnik] *a* mnemonic; *nf* mnemonics.

mobile [mɔbil] *a* mobile, moving, movable, detachable, changeable, unstable; *nm* moving body, motive, motive power.

mobilier, -ière [mɔbilje, jɛːr] *a* movable, personal; *nm* (suite of) furniture.

mobilisable [mɔbilizabl] *a* mobilizable, available.

mobilisation [mɔbilizasjɔ̃] *nf* mobilization, liquidation.

mobiliser [mɔbilize] *vt* to mobilize, call up, liquidate.

mobilité [mɔbilite] *nf* mobility, instability.

mocassin [mɔkasɛ̃] *nm* moccasin.

moche [mɔʃ] *a* (*fam*) ugly, lousy, rotten.

modalité [mɔdalite] *nf* modality; *pl* clauses, terms.

mode [mɔd] *nf* fashion, manner, vogue; *pl* millinery, fashions; *nm* mood, mode, method; **à la —** in fashion; **magasin de —s** milliner's shop; **— d'emploi** directions for use.

modèle [mɔdɛl] *a* model, exemplary; *nm* model, pattern; **prendre — sur** to model oneself on.

modelé [mɔdle] *nm* relief, modelling.

modeler [mɔdle] *vt* to model, fashion, shape, mould; *vr* to model oneself.

modérateur, -trice [mɔderatœːr, tris] *a* moderating, restraining; *n* moderator; *nm* regulator, governor, control.

modération [mɔderasjɔ̃] *nf* moderation, temperance, restraint, mitigation, reduction.

modéré [mɔdere] *a* moderate, restrained temperate.

modérer [mɔdere] *vt* to moderate, restrain, temper, control, regulate, mitigate, reduce; *vr* to control oneself, calm down. abate.

moderne [mɔdɛrn] *a* modern.

moderniser [mɔdɛrnize] *vt* to modernize.

modeste [mɔdɛst] *a* modest, quiet, retiring, unpretentious.

modestie [mɔdɛsti] *nf* modesty, unpretentiousness.

modicité [mɔdisite] *nf* moderateness, reasonableness, slenderness (of means).

modificateur, -trice [mɔdifikatœːr, tris] *a* modifying; *n* modifier.

modificatif, -ive [mɔdifikatif, iːv] *a* modifying, modal.

modification [mɔdifikasjɔ̃] *nf* modification, change, alteration.

modifier [mɔdifje] *vt* to modify, change, alter.

modique [mɔdik] *a* moderate, slender, reasonable.

modiste [mɔdist] *n* milliner, modiste.

modulation [mɔdylasjɔ̃] *nf* modulation, inflexion.

module [mɔdyl] *nm* module, unit, modulus

moduler [mɔdyle] *vti* to modulate.

moelle [mwal] *nf* marrow, substance, pith, medulla; **jusqu'à la —** to the backbone, to the core.

moelleux, -euse [mwalø, øːz] *a* mellow, velvety, soft; *nm* mellowness, velvetiness, softness.

moellon [mwalɔ̃] *nm* quarry stone.

mœurs [mœrs] *nf pl* customs, habits, manners, morals.

moi [mwa] *pn* I, me; *nm* self, ego; **moi-même** myself; **à moi!** help! **un ami à —** a friend of mine; **de vous à —** between you and me.

moignon [mwaɲɔ̃] *nm* stump.

moindre [mwɛ̃ːdr] *a* lesser, least, *comp sup* of **petit.**

moine [mwan] *nm* monk, f riar.

moineau [mwano] *nm* sparrow.

moins [mwɛ̃] *ad* less, not so (much, many), (the) least, *comp sup* of **peu**; *prep* less, minus; **— de** less than; **au —** at least; **du —** at least, at any rate; **pas le — du monde** not in the least; **en — de rien** in no time, in a jiffy; **à — de** unless, barring; **à — que** unless; **rien — que** anything but, nothing less than.

moins-value [mwɛ̃valy] *nf* depreciation.

moire [mwaːr] *nf* watered silk.

moiré [mware] *a* moiré, watered.

mois [mwa] *nm* month.

moïse [mɔiːz] *nm* wicker cradle.

moisir [mwaziːr] *vt* to mildew, make mouldy; *vi* to mildew, go mouldy, vegetate.

moisi [mwazi] *a* mildewed, mouldy, musty fusty; *nm* mildew, mould; **sentir le —** to have a musty smell.

moisissure [mwazisyːr] *nf* mildew, mouldiness, mustiness.

moisson [mwasɔ̃] *n f* harvest, harvest-time, crop.

moissonner [mwasɔne] *vt* to harvest, gather (in), reap.

moissonneur, -euse [mwasɔnœːr, øːz] *n* harvester, reaper.

moissonneuse [mwasɔnøːz] *nf* reaping-machine; **— -batteuse** combine-harvester.

moite [mwat] *a* moist, damp, clammy.

moiteur [mwatœːr] *nf* moistness, clamminess.

moitié [mwatje] *nf* half, (*fam*) better half; **plus grand de —** half as big again; **se mettre de —** avec to go halves with; **couper par —** to cut in halves; **— — — fifty-fifty.**

molaire [mɔlɛːr] *a nf* molar.

môle [mol] *nm* mole, breakwater.

molécule [mɔlekyl] *nf* molecule.

moleskine [mɔlɛskin] *nf* imitation leather, rexine.

molester [mɔlɛste] *vt* to molest.

molette [mɔlɛt] *nf* small pestle, knob, (of *spur*) rowel, trimmer.

mollasse [mɔlas] *a* soft, flabby, spineless, apathetic.

mollesse [mɔlɛs] *nf* softness, flabbiness, indolence, apathy.

mollet, -ette [mɔlɛ, ɛt] *a* softish; *nm* (*leg*) calf; **œuf —** soft-boiled egg.

molletière [mɔltjɛːr] *nf* puttee.

molleton [mɔltɔ̃] *nm* flannel, swansdown.

mollir [mɔliːr] *vt* to ease, slacken; *vi* to become soft, abate, slacken, weaken.

mollusque [mɔlysk] *nm* mollusc, spineless person, vegetable.

môme [moːm] *n* (*fam*) kid.

moment [mɔmɑ̃] *nm* moment,

momentum; **en ce —** at the moment, just now; **sur le —** on the spur of the moment, for a moment; **d'un — à l'autre** any moment; **à tout —** constantly; **du — que** from the time when, seeing that.

momentané [mɔmɑ̃tane] *a* momentary.

momie [mɔmi] *nf* mummy.

mon, ma, mes [mɔ̃, ma, me] *a* my; **un de mes amis** a friend of mine.

monacal [mɔnakal] *a* monastic, monkish.

monarchie [mɔnarʃi] *nf* monarchy.

monarchiste [mɔnarʃist] *an* monarchist.

monarque [mɔnark] *nm* monarch.

monastère [mɔnastɛːr] *nm* monastery.

monastique [mɔnastik] *a* monastic.

monceau [mɔ̃so] *nm* heap, pile.

mondain [mɔ̃dɛ̃] *a* worldly, society, fashionable; *n* man about town, society woman.

mondanité [mɔ̃danite] *nf* worldliness, mundaneness; *pl* social events, society news.

monde [mɔ̃ːd] *nm* world, society, company, crowd, people; **tout le —** everybody; **homme du —** society man, socialite; **beau —** society; **aller dans le —** to move in society, go out; **avoir du —** to have company; **être le mieux du — avec** to be on the best of terms with; **savoir son —** to know how to behave in company.

mondial [mɔ̃djal] *a* world-, worldwide.

monégasque [mɔnegask] *an* of Monaco.

monétaire [mɔnetɛːr] *a* monetary, financial.

monétiser [mɔnetize] *vt* to mint.

moniteur, -trice [mɔnitœːr, tris] *n* monitor, instructor, supervisor, coach.

monnaie [mɔnɛ] *nf* money, currency, change; **— du pape** honesty (flower); **rendre à qn la — de sa pièce** to pay s.o. back in his own coin.

monnayer [mɔnɛje] *vt* to coin, mint, exploit.

monnayeur [mɔnɛjœːr] *nm* minter; **faux —** counterfeiter, coiner.

monocle [mɔnɔkl] *nm* monocle.

monogame [mɔnɔgam] *a* monogamous.

monogramme [mɔnɔgram] *nm* monogram.

monographie [mɔnɔgrafi] *nm* monograph.

monolithe [mɔnɔlit] *a* monolithic; *nm* monolith.

monologue [mɔnɔlɔg] *nm* monologue, soliloquy.

monologuer [mɔnɔlɔge] *vi* to soliloquize.

monôme [mɔnoːm] *nm* monomial,

procession of students in single file.

monoplan [mɔnɔplɑ̃] *nm* monoplane.

monopole [mɔnɔpɔl] *nm* monopoly.

monopoliser [mɔnɔpɔlize] *vt* to monopolize.

monoprix [mɔnɔpri] *nm* = Marks and Spencer.

monorail [mɔnɔraːj] *a nm* monorail.

monosyllabe [mɔnɔsillab] *a* monosyllabic; *nm* monosyllable.

monosyllabique [mɔnɔsillabik] *a* monosyllabic.

monotone [mɔnɔtɔn] *a* monotonous, dreary, dull.

monotonie [mɔnɔtɔni] *nf* monotony, sameness, dullness.

monseigneur [mɔ̃sɛnjœːr] *nm* His (Your) Grace, His (Your) Lordship, His (Your) Royal Highness, my Lord; **pince —** nm jemmy.

monsieur [m(ə)sjø] *nm* Mr, master, sir, gentleman.

monstre [mɔ̃ːstr] *a (fam)* huge, monstrous, colossal; *nm* monster, monstrosity.

monstrueux, -euse [mɔ̃stryø, øːz] *a* monstrous, colossal, gigantic, unnatural, scandalous.

mont [mɔ̃] *nm* mount, mountain; **par —s et par vaux** up hill and down dale.

montage [mɔ̃taːʒ] *nm* carrying up, assembling, equipping, fitting up (on, out), setting, staging, producing, editing.

montagnard [mɔ̃taɲaːr] *a* highland, mountain; *n* highlander, mountain-dweller.

montagne [mɔ̃taɲ] *nf* mountain(s); **—s russes** scenic railway.

montagneux, -euse [mɔ̃taɲø, øːz] *a* mountainous.

montant [mɔ̃tɑ̃] *a* rising, climbing, uphill, high-necked; *nm* post, upright, pole, amount, total, pungency.

mont-de-piété [mɔ̃dəpjete] *nm* pawnbroker's office, shop.

monte [mɔ̃ːt] *nf* mating (season), mount(ing), horsemanship.

monte-charge [mɔ̃tʃarʒ] *nm* hoist.

monte-plats [mɔ̃tpla] *nm* servicelift.

monté [mɔ̃te] *a* mounted, fitted, equipped, stocked; **coup —** put-up job, frame-up; **être — contre** have a grudge against.

montée [mɔ̃te] *nf* rise, gradient, slope, climb(ing).

monter [mɔ̃te] *vt* to climb, go up, mount, ride, bring up, carry up, take up, assemble, fit up (out, on), set (up), produce, stage; *vi* to climb, go (come) up, ascend, come (to), rise, get in; *vr* to amount to; **se — la tête** to get excited; **je l'ai fait — à côté de moi** I gave him a lift.

monteur, -euse [mɔ̃tœːr, øːz] *n* mounter, setter, fitter, producer, editor.

monticule [mɔ̃tikyl] *nm* hillock, hummock.

montrable [mɔ̃trabl] *a* presentable, fit to be seen.

montre [mɔ̃:tr] *nf* watch, display, show, show-case; — -bracelet wrist-watch; faire — de to display, show; mettre qch en — to display sth. in the window.

montrer [mɔ̃tre] *vt* to show (how to), display, point out, prove; *vr* to appear, prove, turn out (to be).

montreur, -euse [mɔ̃trœ:r, ɔ:z] *n* showman, -woman.

montueux, -euse [mɔ̃tɥø, ø:z] *a* hilly.

monture [mɔ̃ty:r] *nf* mount, setting, frame, handle.

monument [mɔnymɑ̃] *nm* monument, memorial, historic building.

monumental [mɔnymɑ̃tal] *a* monumental, colossal.

se moquer [səmɔke] *vr* to make fun (of de), laugh at; il s'en moque he doesn't care.

moquerie [mɔkri] *nf* mockery, derision, scoffing.

moquette [mɔkɛt] *nf* moquette.

moqueur, -euse [mɔkœ:r, ø:z] *a* mocking, derisive, scoffing; *n* scoffer.

moral [mɔral] *a* ethical, moral, intellectual, mental; *nm* morale, mind; remonter le — à qn to raise s.o.'s spirits, buck s.o. up.

morale [mɔral] *nf* moral, morals, ethics, moral philosophy, preachifying; faire la — à qn to sermonize, lecture.

moralisateur, -trice [mɔralizatœ:r, tris] *a* moralizing, edifying; *n* moralizer.

moraliser [mɔralize] *vt* to sermonize, raise the morals of, lecture; *vi* to moralize.

moraliste [mɔralist] *n* moralist.

moralité [mɔralite] *nf* morality, morals, moral (lesson).

moratoire [mɔratwa:r] *a* moratory.

morbide [mɔrbid] *a* morbid.

morbidité [mɔrbidite] *nf* morbidity, morbidness.

morceau [mɔrso] *nm* morsel, piece, bit, scrap.

morceler [mɔrsəle] *vt* to cut into small pieces, break up.

morcellement [mɔrsɛlmɑ̃] *nm* cutting up, breaking up, dismemberment.

mordant [mɔrdɑ̃] *a* caustic, biting, pungent, piercing, corrosive; *nm* mordancy, pungency.

mordicus [mɔrdikys] *ad* tenaciously, stoutly.

mordiller [mɔrdije] *vt* to nibble, snap playfully at.

mordoré [mɔrdɔre] *a* bronze; *nm* bronze colour.

mordre [mɔrdr] *vt* to bite; *vi* to bite, catch, take (to à); s'en — les doigts to be sorry for it.

mordu [mɔrdy] *a* mad (on de); *n* fan.

morfondre [mɔrfɔ̃:dr] *vt* to chill to the bone; *vr* to freeze, be bored, wait impatiently.

morganatique [mɔrganatik] *a* morganatic.

morgue [mɔrg] *nf* pride, arrogance, mortuary.

moribond [mɔribɔ̃] *a* moribund, dying.

moricaud [mɔriko] *a* dark-skinned, swarthy; *n* blackamoor, darky.

morigéner [mɔriʒene] *vt* to lecture, haul over the coals.

morne [mɔrn] *a* dismal, dreary, gloomy, dull.

morose [mɔro:z] *a* morose, surly, gloomy.

morosité [mɔrozite] *nf* surliness, gloominess.

morphine [mɔrfin] *nf* morphia, morphine.

morphinomane [mɔrfinɔman] *n* morphia addict, drug addict.

morphologie [mɔrfɔlɔʒi] *nf* morphology.

mors [mɔ:r] *nm* bit, chap, joint.

morse [mɔrs] *nm* walrus, morse code.

morsure [mɔrsy:r] *nf* bite.

mort [mɔ:r] *a* dead, deceased, spent; *nf* death; *n* dead man, dead woman, dummy; arrêt de — death-sentence; avoir la — dans l'âme to be sick at heart; se donner la — to take one's life; point — neutral, deadlock; nature —e still life; eau —e stagnant water; faire le — to pretend to be dead, lie low, (bridge) be dummy.

mortadelle [mɔrtadɛl] *nf* Polony sausage.

mortaise [mɔrtɛ:z] *nf* slot, mortise.

mortalité [mɔrtalite] *nf* mortality.

morte-eau [mɔrto] *nf* neap tide.

mortel, -elle [mɔrtɛl] *a* mortal, fatal, deadly, (fam) deadly dull.

morte-saison [mɔrtsɛzɔ̃] *nf* slack season, off season.

mortier [mɔrtje] *nm* mortar, mortar-board.

mortifier [mɔrtifje] *vt* to hang (game), mortify, hurt.

mort-né [mɔrne] *a* stillborn.

mortuaire [mɔrtɥɛ:r] *a* mortuary, burial, funeral; drap — pall.

morue [mɔry] *nf* cod.

morutier [mɔrytje] *nm* cod-fishing boat, cod-fisher.

morve [mɔrv] *nf* glanders, nasal mucus.

morveux, -euse [mɔrvø, ø:z] *a* glandered, snotty; *n* (fam) brat.

mosaïque [mozaik] *a nf* mosaic.

mosquée [mɔske] *nf* mosque.

mot [mo] *nm* word, term, saying; bon — witticism; — de passe (ralliement) pass word, catchword; — d'ordre watchword, directive; — pour — word for word; —s croisés crossword puzzle; comprendre à demi-— to take the hint.

motard [mɔtaːr] *nm* speed-cop, (*US*) courtesy cop.

motet [mɔtɛ] *nm* motet, anthem.

moteur, -trice [mɔtœːr, tris] *a* motive, driving; *nm* motor, engine.

motif, -ive [mɔtif, iːv] *a* motive; *nm* reason, motive, cause, grounds, theme, pattern, design.

motion [mɔsjɔ̃] *nf* motion, proposal.

motiver [mɔtive] *vt* to motivate, warrant, give cause for, give the reason for.

moto [mɔto] *nf* motorcycle, motorbike.

motocycliste [mɔtɔsiklist] *nm* motor cyclist.

motorisé [mɔtɔrize] *a* fitted with a motor, motorized.

motte [mɔt] *nf* mound, lump, clod, pat; — **de gazon** turf.

motus [mɔtys] *excl* mum's the word!

mou, molle [mu, mɔl] *a* soft, flabby, feeble, limp, slack, close; *nm* slack (*of rope*), lights (*animal lungs*).

mouchard [muʃar] *nm* sneak, spy, informer, telltale.

moucharder [muʃarde] *vt* to spy on, inform against, nark; *vi* to spy.

mouche [muʃ] *nf* fly, speck, spot, bull's eye, beauty-spot; — **bleue** blue-bottle; **bateau** — river steamer; **faire** — to score a bull; **prendre la** — to take the huff.

moucher [muʃe] *vt* to wipe (s.o.'s) nose, snuff, trim, (*fam*) tell off; *vr* to blow one's nose; **il ne se mouche pas du pied** he thinks a lot of himself.

moucheron [muʃrɔ̃] *nm* gnat, midge.

moucheté [muʃte] *a* speckled, flecked, brindle(d).

moucheture [muʃtyːr] *nf* speckle, spot, fleck.

mouchoir [muʃwaːr] *nm* handkerchief, kerchief.

moudre [mudr] *vt* to grind, mill.

moue [mu] *nf* pout; **faire la** — to pout.

mouette [mwɛt] *nf* seagull.

mouflard [muflaːr] *n* fat-faced, heavy-jowled person.

moufle [mufl] *nf* mitten, pulley-block, clamp, muffle-furnace.

mouflon [muflɔ̃] *nm* moufflon, wild sheep.

mouillage [mujaːʒ] *nm* wetting, damping, moistening, mooring, anchorage, watering-down.

mouiller [muje] *vt* to wet, damp, moisten, anchor, moor, lay (*mines*); *vr* to get wet, fill (*eyes*); **poule mouillée** cissy, milksop.

mouilleur [mujœːr] *nm* damper; — **de mines** minelayer.

moulage [mulaːʒ] *nm* milling, grinding, moulding, casting.

moule [mul] *nm* mould, cast, matrix, shape, baking tin; *nf* mussel, blockhead.

moulé [mule] *a* moulded, well-proportioned, copperplate; *nm* print.

mouler [mule] *vt* to mould, cast, fit closely.

mouleur [mulœːr] *nm* moulder, caster.

moulin [mulɛ̃] *nm* mill; **jeter son bonnet par-dessus les —s** to throw propriety to the winds.

moulinet [mulinɛ] *nm* turnstile, current-meter, (*fishing*) reel; **faire le** — to twirl one's stick.

moulure [mulyːr] *nf* moulding.

mourant [murɑ̃] *a* dying, feeble; *n* dying person.

mourir [muriːr] *vi* to die (away); *vr* to be dying, fade (away, out); **c'était à — de rire** it was killingly funny.

mouron [murɔ̃] *nm* chickweed; — **rouge** scarlet pimpernel.

mousquetaire [muskətɛːr] *nm* musketeer.

mousse [mus] *nm* ship's boy, cabin-boy; *nf* moss, froth, foam, cream, lather.

mousseline [muslin] *nf* muslin; — **de soie** chiffon; **gâteau** — sponge cake; **pommes** — mashed potatoes.

mousser [muse] *vi* to froth, foam, effervesce, lather.

mousseux, -euse [musø, øːz] *a* foaming, frothy, sparkling, fizzy.

mousson [musɔ̃] *nm* monsoon.

moussu [musy] *a* mossy, moss-grown.

moustache [mustaʃ] *nf* moustache; *pl* whiskers.

moustachu [mustaʃy] *a* having a moustache, whiskered.

moustiquaire [mustikɛːr] *nf* mosquito net.

moustique [mustik] *nm* mosquito, gnat.

moutard [mutaːr] *nm* small boy, youngster, nipper.

moutarde [mutard] *nf* mustard.

moutardier [mutardje] *nm* mustard-pot, mustard-maker.

mouton [mutɔ̃] *nm* sheep, mutton, sheepskin, (*fam*) nark; *pl* white-horses (*waves*).

moutonnant [mutɔnɑ̃] *a* foam-flecked.

moutonner [mutɔne] *vi* foam, be covered with white horses.

moutonneux, -euse [mutɔnø, øːz] *a* foaming.

mouture [mutyːr] *nf* milling, grinding, milling dues, (*cereals, coffee*) ground mixture, rehash.

mouvant [muvɑ̃] *a* moving, unstable, changeable; **sables —s** quicksands.

mouvement [muvmɑ̃] *nm* movement, motion, change, action, impulse, outburst, thrill, stir, traffic; **de son propre —** of one's own accord; **être dans le —** to be in the swim.

mouvementé [muvmɑ̃te] *a* lively,

exciting, thrilling, eventful, animated.

mouvoir [muvwa:r] *vt* to move, drive, propel, move to action, prompt; *vr* to move.

moyen, -enne [mwajɛ̃, jɛn] *a* medium, average, mean, middle; *nm* means, way, course; *pl* resources, ability; — âge Middle Ages; il n'y a pas — it can't be done; au — de by means of; employer les grands —s to take drastic measures.

moyennant [mwajɛnɑ̃] *prep* for, at (price); — que on condition that; — argent for a consideration.

moyenne [mwajɛn] *nf* average, mean, pass mark; en — on an average.

moyeu [mwajø] *nm* hub, nave, boss.

mû [my] *a* driven, propelled.

muable [mɥabl] *a* changeable, unstable.

mue [my] *nf* moulting, slough(ing), casting of skin or coat, moulting time, breaking of the voice, coop.

muer [mɥe] *vi* to moult, cast skin or coat, slough, break; *vr* se — en to change into.

muet, -ette [mɥɛ, ɛt] *a* mute, dumb, silent, unsounded; *n* mute, dumb person.

mufle [myfl] *nm* muzzle, snout, nose, mug, fathead, swine.

muflerie [myfləri] *nf* vulgar behaviour, mean trick.

mugir [myʒi:r] *vi* to low, bellow, roar, moan, howl.

mugissement [myʒismɑ̃] *nm* lowing, bellowing, roaring, moaning.

muguet [mygɛ] *nm* lily of the valley.

muid [mɥi] *nm* hogshead.

mulâtre [mylɑ:tr] *a* mulatto, halfcast; *n (f* mulâtresse) mulatto.

mule [myl] *nf* (she-)mule; bedroom slipper, mule.

mulet [mylɛ] *nm* (he-)mule; grey mullet.

muletier [myltje] *nm* muleteer, mule-driver.

mulot [mylo] *nm* field mouse.

multicolore [myltikɔlɔ:r] *a* multicoloured.

multiple [myltipl] *a* multiple, multifarious, manifold; *nm* multiple.

multiplicateur, -trice [myltiplikatœ:r, tris] *a* multiplying; *nm* multiplier.

multiplication [myltiplikasjɔ̃] *nf* multiplication.

multiplicité [myltiplisite] *nf* multiplicity, multifariousness.

multiplier [myltiplie] *vti* to multiply; *vr* to be on the increase, be everywhere at once.

multitude [myltityd] *nf* multitude, crowd.

municipal [mynisipal] *a* municipal; conseil — town-council; conseiller — town-councillor; loi —e bye-law.

municipalité [mynisipalite] *nf* municipality, town-council.

munificence [mynifisɑ̃:s] *nf* munificence, bounty.

munificent [mynifisɑ̃] *a* munificent, bountiful.

munir [myni:r] *vt* to provide, supply, furnish, fit.

munition [mynisjɔ̃] *nf* munitioning, provisioning; *pl* ammunition, munitions.

munitionner [mynisjɔne] *vt* to munition, supply.

muqueux, -euse [mykø, ø:z] *a* mucous.

mur [my:r] *nm* wall; mettre qn au pied du — to corner s.o.

mûr [my:r] *a* ripe, mature, mellow.

mûraie [myrɛ] *nf* mulberry plantation.

muraille [myra:j] *nf* wall, rampart, barrier, (of ship) side.

mural [myral] *a* mural, wall-.

mûre [my:r] *nf* mulberry; — sauvage blackberry.

murer [myre] *vt* to wall in, brick up, block up.

mûrier [myrje] *nm* mulberry bush; — sauvage blackberry bush, bramble bush.

mûrir [myri:r] *vt* to ripen, mature, develop; *vi* to grow ripe, reach maturity.

murmure [myrmy:r] *nm* murmur (ing), whisper, babbling.

murmurer [myrmyre] *vti* to murmur, whisper.

musaraigne [myzarɛɲ] *nf* shrewmouse.

musarder [myzarde] *vi* to idle, moon about, dawdle.

musc [mysk] *nm* musk.

muscade [myskad] *nf* nutmeg.

muscat [myska] *nm* muscat grape, muscatel (wine).

muscle [myskl] *nm* muscle.

musclé [myskle] *a* muscular, brawny

musculature [myskylaty:r] *nf* musculation.

muse [my:z] *nf* muse.

museau [myzo] *nm* muzzle, snout; (fam) mug.

musée [myze] *nm* museum; — de peinture picture-gallery.

museler [myzle] *vt* to muzzle.

muselière [myzəljɛ:r] *nf* muzzle.

muser [myze] *vi* to idle, moon about, trifle.

muserolle [myzrɔl] *nf* noseband.

musette [myzɛt] *nf* bagpipe, nosebag, haversack, school-bag; bal — dance with accordion band.

musical [myzikal] *a* musical.

musicien, -enne [myzisjɛ̃, jɛn] *a* musical; *n* musician, bandsman.

musicomane [myzikɔman] *n* musiclover.

musique [myzik] *nf* music, band.

musqué [myske] *a* musk-scented, affected.

musulman [myzylmɑ̃] *an* Moslem, Mohammedan.

mutabilité [mytabilite] *nf* mutability.

mutation [mytasjɔ̃] *nf* mutation, change, transfer.

mutilation [mytilasjɔ̃] *nf* mutilation, defacement.

mutilé [mytile] *a* mutilated, maimed; *nm* disabled soldier.

mutiler [mytile] *vt* to mutilate, maim, deface.

mutin [mytɛ̃] *a* unruly, roguish, arch, *nm* mutineer.

se mutiner [səmytine] *vr* to rebel, mutiny, refuse to obey.

mutinerie [mytinri] *nf* unruliness, mutiny.

mutisme [mytism] *nm* muteness, dumbness.

mutualité [mytɥalite] *nf* mutuality, (system of) friendly societies.

mutuel, -elle [mytɥɛl] *a* mutual; **société de secours** — friendly society.

myope [mjɔp] *a* short-sighted.

myopie [mjɔpi] *nf* short-sightedness.

myosotis [mjɔzɔtis] *nm* forget-me-not.

myriade [mirjad] *nf* myriad.

myrrhe [mi:r] *nf* myrrh.

myrte [mirt] *nm* myrtle.

mystère [mistɛ:r] *nm* mystery, mystery play; **il n'en fait pas** — he makes no bones about it, no secret of it.

mystérieux, -euse [misterjø, ø:z] *a* mysterious, weird, eerie, uncanny.

mysticisme [mistisism] *nm* mysticism.

mystificateur, -trice [mistifikatœ:r, tris] *a* mystifying; *n* hoaxer, leg-puller.

mystification [mistifikasjɔ̃] *nf* mystification, hoax, leg-pull.

mystifier [mistifje] *vt* to mystify, hoax, pull s.o.'s leg.

mystique [mistik] *a* mystical; *n* mystic.

mythe [mit] *nm* myth, legend.

mythique [mitik] *a* mythical, legendary.

mythologie [mitɔlɔʒi] *nf* mythology.

mythologique [mitɔlɔʒik] *a* mythological.

N

nabot [nabo] *n* midget, dwarf.

nacelle [nasɛl] *nf* skiff, gondola.

nacre [nakr] *nf* mother of pearl.

nacré [nakre] *a* pearly.

naevus [nevy:s] *nm* birthmark, mole.

nage [na:ʒ] *nf* swimming, rowing, sculling, stroke; **en** — bathed in perspiration.

nageoire [naʒwa:r] *nf* fin, float.

nager [naʒe] *vi* to swim, float, row, scull.

nageur, -euse [naʒœ:r, ø:z] *n* swimmer, oarsman.

naguère [nagɛ:r] *ad* not long since, a little while ago.

naïf, -ïve [naif, i:v] *a* artless, ingenuous, unaffected.

nain [nɛ̃] *an* dwarf.

naissance [nɛsɑ̃:s] *nf* birth, descent, root, rise, dawn.

naissant [nɛsɑ̃] *a* newborn, dawning, budding, incipient, nascent.

naître [nɛ:tr] *vi* to be born, spring up, grow, originate; **faire** — to give rise to, arouse; **à** — unborn.

naïveté [naivte] *nf* artlessness, ingenuousness.

nantir [nɑ̃ti:r] *vt* to give security to, provide.

naphtaline [naftalin] *nf* moth-balls, naphthaline.

nappe [nap] *nf* tablecloth, cover, cloth, sheet (*of water*).

napperon [naprɔ̃] *nm* traycloth, napkin.

narcisse [narsis] *nm* narcissus.

narcotique [narkɔtik] *a nm* narcotic.

narguer [narge] *vt* to flout.

narine [narin] *nf* nostril.

narquois [narkwa] *a* quizzical, waggish.

narrateur, -trice [narratœ:r, tris] *n* narrator, teller.

narratif, -ive [narratif, i:v] *a* narrative.

narration [narrasjɔ̃] *nf* narration, story, narrative.

nasal [nazal] *a* nasal.

naseau [nazo] *nm* nostril.

nasillard [nazija:r] *a* nasal, through one's nose, with a nasal twang.

nasiller [nazije] *vi* to speak through one's nose.

nasse [nas] *nf* net, trap, eel-pot.

natal [natal] *a* native, natal, birth-.

natalité [natalite] *nf* birth-rate.

natation [natasjɔ̃] *nf* swimming.

natif, -ive [natif, i:v] *a* native, inborn.

nation [nasjɔ̃] *nf* nation.

national [nasjɔnal] *a nm* national; **route—e** main road.

nationaliser [nasjɔnalize] *vt* to nationalize.

nationalisme [nasjɔnalism] *nm* nationalism.

nationalité [nasjɔnalite] *nf* nationality.

nativité [nativite] *nf* nativity.

natte [nat] *nf* mat(ting), plait, braid.

naturalisation [natyralizasjɔ̃] *nf* naturalization.

naturaliser [natyralize] *vt* to naturalize.

naturaliste [natyralist] *a* naturalistic; *n* naturalist.

nature [naty:r] *nf* nature, kind, character, disposition; — **morte** still-life; **grandeur** — life-size; *a* plain, natural; **café** — black coffee.

naturel, -elle [natyrɛl] *a* natural, unaffected, illegitimate; *nm* disposition, naturalness, simplicity.

naufrage [nofra:ʒ] *nm* shipwreck; **faire — to** be shipwrecked.

naufragé [nofraʒe] *a* shipwrecked; *n* castaway.

nauséabond [nozeabɔ̃] *a* nauseous, foul.

nausée [noze] *nf* nausea, sickness, disgust.

nautique [notik] *a* nautical, aquatic.

naval [naval] *a* naval, sea-.

navet [nave] *nm* turnip; (*fam*) rubbish, daub.

navette [navɛt] *nf* shuttle, incense box; rape seed; **faire la — to** go to and fro.

navigable [navigabl] *a* navigable, seaworthy.

navigateur [navigatœ:r] *nm* navigator, seafarer; *a* seafaring.

navigation [navigasjɔ̃] *nf* navigation, sailing, shipping.

naviguer [navige] *vti* to navigate, sail.

navire [navi:r] *nm* ship, vessel, boat.

navrant [navrɑ̃] *a* heartbreaking, -rending.

navrer [navre] *vt* to break one's heart, grieve.

ne [n(ə)] *neg ad used mostly with* pas, point, *etc*, not.

néanmoins [neɑ̃mwɛ̃] *ad* nevertheless, notwithstanding, yet, still.

néant [neɑ̃] *nm* nothing(ness), worthlessness, nought.

nébuleux, -euse [nebylø, ø:z] *a* nebulous, cloudy, hazy.

nécessaire [nesɛsɛ:r] *a* necessary, needful, required, requisite; *nm* necessaries, what is necessary, bag, case, outfit.

nécessité [nesesite] *nf* necessity, straitened circumstances.

nécessiter [nesesite] *vt* to necessitate, entail.

nécessiteux, -euse [nesesitø, ø:z] *a* necessitous, needy.

nécrologie [nekrɔlɔʒi] *nf* obituary notice.

nécromancien, -ienne [nekrɔmɑ̃sjɛ̃, jɛn] *n* necromancer.

nectarine [nɛktarin] *nf* nectarine peach.

nef [nɛf] *nf* nave.

néfaste [nefast] *a* luckless, baneful, ill-fated, evil.

nèfle [nɛfl] *nf* medlar.

négatif, -ive [negatif, i:v] *a nm* negative.

négligé [negliʒe] *a* neglected, careless, slovenly; *nm* undress, négligé, déshabillé.

négligeable [negliʒabl] *a* negligible.

négligence [negliʒɑ̃:s] *nf* negligence, neglect, carelessness.

négligent [negliʒɑ̃] *a* negligent, careless, neglectful, off-hand.

négliger [negliʒe] *vt* to neglect, be neglectful of, disregard, leave undone; *vr* to neglect oneself, be careless of one's appearance.

négoce [negɔs] *nm* trade, business.

négociable [negɔsjabl] *a* negotiable, transferable.

négociant [negɔsjɑ̃] *n* trader, merchant.

négociation [negɔsjasjɔ̃] *nf* negotiation, transaction, treaty, dealing.

négocier [negɔsje] *vt* to negotiate.

nègre [nɛ:gr] *nm* negro, (*fam*) nigger; hackwriter; *a* negro; **parler petit — to** speak pidgin.

négresse [negrɛs] *nf* negress.

neige [nɛ:ʒ] *nf* snow; **— fondue** sleet, slush; **œufs à la — floating islands; tempête de — snowstorm.**

neiger [neʒe] *vi* to snow.

neigeux, -euse [neʒø, ø:z] *a* snowy, snow-covered.

nénufar, nénuphar [nenyfa:r] *nm* water-lily.

néologisme [neɔlɔʒism] *nm* neologism.

néophyte [neɔfit] *nm* neophyte, beginner.

néo-zélandais [neozelɑ̃dɛ] *an* New Zealander, from New Zealand.

néphrite [nefrit] *nf* nephritis.

népotisme [nepotism] *nm* nepotism.

nerf [nɛ:r] *nm* nerve, sinew, (*fig*) energy, stamina; *pl* hysterics; **porter sur les — à qn to** get on s.o.'s nerves.

nerveux, -euse [nɛrvø, ø:z] *a* excitable, highly-strung, sinewy, nervous.

nervosité [nɛrvozite] *nf* irritability, nerves.

nervure [nɛrvy:r] *nf* rib, nervure, vein.

net, nette [nɛt] *a* clean, clear, distinct, plain, sharp, fair, (*of prices*) net; **mettre au — to** make a fair copy of; **faire place nette to** clear out; *ad* plainly, flatly, clearly, dead.

netteté [nɛt(ə)te] *nf* cleanness, cleanliness, distinctness, downrightness.

nettoyage [nɛtwaja:ʒ] *nm* cleaning, cleansing.

nettoyer [nɛtwaje] *vt* to clean (out), clear, mop up.

nettoyeur, -euse [nɛtwajœ:r, ø:z] *n* cleaner.

neuf [nœf] *a nm* nine, ninth.

neuf, neuve [nœf, nœ:v] *a* new; **à — anew, like new; quoi de — what is** the news? what's new?

neurasthénie [nørasteni] *nf* neurasthenia.

neutraliser [nøtralize] *vt* to neutralize, counteract.

neutralité [nøtralite] *nf* neutrality.

neutre [nø:tr] *a nm* neuter; *a* neutral; **zone — no** man's land.

neuvième [nœvjɛm] *a nm* ninth.

neveu [n(ə)vø] *nm* nephew.

névralgie [nevralʒi] *nf* neuralgia.

névrite [nevrit] *nf* neuritis.

névrose [nevro:z] *nf* neurosis.

névrosé [nevroze] *an* neurotic, neurasthenic.

nez [ne] *nm* nose, face, nose-piece, sense of smell.

ni [ni] *cj* nor, or, neither . . . nor.

niais [niɛ, njɛ] *a* simple, foolish, silly; *n* fool, simpleton.

niaiserie [niɛzri, njɛ-] *nf* silliness, foolishness; *pl* nonsense.

niche [niʃ] *nf* niche, recess, dog-kennel, trick, prank.

nichée [niʃe] *nf* nest(ful), brood.

nicher [niʃe] *vi* to nest; *vt* to put, lodge; *vr* to build a nest, nestle, lodge.

nid [ni] *nm* nest.

nièce [njɛs] *nf* niece.

nier [nie, nje] *vt* to deny, plead not guilty.

nigaud [nigo] *a* silly; *n* simpleton, booby, fool.

nimbe [nɛ̃:b] *nm* nimbus, halo.

se nipper [sənipe] *vr* to rig oneself out.

nippes [nip] *nf pl* (old) clothes, things.

nique [nik] *nf* faire la — à to pull a face at, turn up one's nose.

nitouche [nituʃ] *nf* sainte — little prude.

nitrate [nitrat] *nm* nitrate.

niveau [nivo] *nm* level, standard; passage à — level crossing.

niveler [nivle] *vt* to level, even up, survey.

nobiliaire [nɔbiljɛ:r] *n* peerage (-book, -list).

noble [nɔbl] *a* noble, lofty, high-minded; *n* noble(man, woman).

noblesse [nɔblɛs] *nf* nobility, noble birth, nobleness.

noce [nɔs] *nf* wedding, wedding-party; voyage de —s honeymoon; faire la — to live it up.

noceur, -euse [nɔsœr, øːz] *n* fast liver, dissolute man, rake.

nocif, -ive [nɔsif, iːv] *a* noxious, injurious.

noctambule [nɔktãbyl] *nm* sleep-walker, night-prowler.

nocturne [nɔktyrn] *a* nocturnal, night-; *nm* nocturne.

Noë' [nɔɛl] *nm* Christmas, Christmas carol.

nœud [nø] *nm* knot, bow, bond, crux.

noir [nwaːr] *a* black, swarthy, dark, gloomy, dirty, base, foul; *nm* black, black man, bull's eye; broyer du — to be in the dumps.

noire [nwaːr] *nf* crotchet, black ball.

noirâtre [nwarɑːtr] *a* blackish, darkish.

noirceur [nwarsœːr] *nf* blackness, darkness, smut, base action.

noircir [nwarsiːr] *vi* to grow black; *vt* to blacken, darken, sully.

noisetier [nwaztje] *nm* hazel tree.

noisette [nwazɛt] *nf* hazel-nut; *a* hazel, nut-brown.

noix [nwa] *nf* walnut, nut.

nom [nɔ̃] *nm* name, noun; — de famille surname; petit — Christian,

pet name; — de guerre assumed name; qui n'a pas de — beyond words, unspeakable.

nomade [nɔmad] *a* nomadic, wandering

nombre [nɔ̃:br] *nm* number.

nombrer [nɔ̃bre] *vt* to count, number.

nombreux, -euse [nɔ̃brø, øːz] *a* numerous, many.

nombril [nɔ̃bri] *nm* navel.

nominatif, -ive [nɔminatif, iːv] *a* nominal, registered; *nm* nominative.

nomination [nɔminasjɔ̃] *nf* appointment, nomination.

nommément [nɔmemã] *ad* namely, by name.

nommer [nɔme] *vt* to name, call, mention by name, appoint, nominate, elect; *vr* to be called, give one's name.

non [nɔ̃] *ad* no, not; non-, un-, in-; *nm* no; faire signe que — to shake one's head.

nonagénaire [nɔnaʒenɛːr] *n* nonagenarian.

nonchalance [nɔ̃ʃalãːs] *nf* nonchalance, unconcern.

non-lieu [nɔ̃ljø] *nm* no case.

nonne [nɔn] *nf* nun.

nonobstant [nɔnɔbstã] *prep* notwithstanding; *ad* nevertheless.

nonpareil, -eille [nɔ̃parɛj] *a* matchless.

non-sens [nɔ̃sãːs] *nm* meaningless sentence, remark.

non-valeur [nɔ̃valœːr] *nf* valueless object, bad debt, worthless security, unproductiveness, inefficient person, non-effective unit.

nord [nɔːr] *nm* north; *a* north, northern; perdre le — be all at sea.

nord-est [nɔr(d)ɛst] *nm* north-east.

nordique [nɔrdik] *a* Nordic.

nord-ouest [nɔr(d)wɛst] *nm* north-west.

normal [nɔrmal] *a* normal, standard, average.

normalien, -ienne [nɔrmaljɛ̃, jɛn] *n* student at the Ecole Normale Supérieure.

normand [nɔrmã] *a* Norman, non-committal, shrewd; *n* Norman.

Normandie [nɔrmãdi] *nf* Normandy.

norme [nɔrm] *nf* norm, standard.

Norvège [nɔrvɛːʒ] *nf* Norway.

norvégien, -ienne [nɔrveʒjɛ̃, jɛn] *an* Norwegian.

nostalgie [nɔstalʒi] *nf* nostalgia, home-sickness.

notable [nɔtabl] *a* notable, considerable, eminent.

notaire [nɔtɛːr] *nm* notary, solicitor.

notamment [nɔtamã] *ad* notably, especially, among others.

note [nɔt] *nf* note, memorandum, mark, bill, account; changer de — to change one's tune; forcer la — to lay it on, overdo it.

noté [nɔte] *a* **bien, mal —** of good, bad, reputation.

noter [nɔte] *vt* to note, take a note of, write down.

notice [nɔtis] *nf* notice, account, review.

notification [nɔtifikasjɔ̃] *nf* notification, intimation.

notifier [nɔtifje] *vt* to notify, intimate.

notion [nɔsjɔ̃] *nf* notion, idea.

notoire [nɔtwaːr] *a* well-known, notorious.

notoriété [nɔtɔrjete] *nf* notoriety, repute; **— publique** common knowledge.

notre, nos [nɔtr, no] *pos a* our.

nôtre [noːtr] *pos pn* **le, la —, les —s** ours; *nm* ours, our own; *pl* our own people *etc.*

nouer [nwe, nue] *vt* to tie (up), knot; *vr* to become knotted, become stiff; **— conversation avec** to enter into conversation with.

noueux, -euse [nuø, øːz] *a* knotty, gnarled, stiff.

nougat [nuga] *nm* nougat.

nouilles [nuːj] *nf pl* ribbon vermicelli, noodles.

nounou [nunu] *nf* nanny, children's nurse.

nourri [nuri] *a* fed, nourished, furnished, copious, full, sustained, prolonged.

nourrice [nuris] *nf* (wet) nurse; auxiliary tank, feed-pipe.

nourricier, -ière [nurisje, jɛːr] *a* nutritious, nutritive, foster-.

nourrir [nuriːr] *vt* to nourish, feed, suckle, nurse, rear, maintain, board, foster, cherish, fill out.

nourrissant [nurisɑ̃] *a* nourishing, nutritious.

nourrisson [nurisɔ̃] *nm* baby at the breast, infant, foster-child.

nourriture [nurityːr] *nf* food, board, feeding.

nous [nu] *pn* we, us, ourselves, each other; **à —** ours.

nouveau, -elle [nuvo, ɛl] *a* new, recent, fresh, another, further, second; **du —** something new; **de —** again; **à —** afresh, anew.

nouveau-né [nuvone] *an* new-born (child).

nouveauté [nuvote] *nf* novelty, change, innovation, new publication, play *etc*; *pl* new styles, latest fashions; **magasin de —s** drapery store.

nouvelle [nuvɛl] *nf* piece of news, short story.

nouvellement [nuvɛlmɑ̃] *ad* newly, lately.

Nouvelle-Zélande [nuvɛlzelɑ̃d] *nf* New Zealand.

nouvelliste [nuvelist] *nm* short-story writer.

novateur, -trice [nɔvatœːr, tris] *n* innovator.

novembre [nɔvɑ̃ːbr] *nm* November.

novice [nɔvis] *a* inexperienced, new, fresh, unpractised; *n* novice, beginner, probationer, apprentice.

noviciat [nɔvisja] *nm* novitiate, probationary period, apprenticeship.

noyade [nwajad] *nf* drowning.

noyau [nwajo] *nm* stone, kernel, nucleus, cell, hub, core.

noyautage [nwajotaːʒ] *nm* (communist) infiltration.

noyé [nwaje] *a* drowned, flooded, sunken, choked, suffused; *n* drowned, drowning man, woman.

noyer [nwaje] *nm* walnut-tree.

noyer [nwaje] *vt* to drown, sink, flood, swamp, (fish) play; *vr* to drown, be drowned.

nu [ny] *a* naked, nude, bare, plain; *nm* nude; **à —** uncovered, exposed, bareback.

nuage [nɥaːʒ] *nm* cloud, haze, drop (of milk in tea).

nuageux, -euse [nɥaʒø, øːz] *a* cloudy, overcast, hazy.

nuance [nɥɑ̃ːs] *nf* shade, hue, tinge, slight suggestion.

nuancer [nɥɑ̃se] *vt* to blend, shade, vary.

nubile [nybil] *a* nubile; **âge —** age of consent.

nucléaire [nyklɛɛːr] *a* nuclear.

nudisme [nydism] *nm* nudism.

nudité [nydite] *nf* nudity, nakedness, bareness.

nue [ny] *nf* cloud.

nuée [nɥe] *nf* (large) cloud, swarm, host, shower.

nuire [nɥiːr] *vt* to harm, hurt, injure, prejudice.

nuisible [nɥizibl] *a* harmful, injurious.

nuit [nɥi] *nf* night, dark(ness); **cette —** last night, tonight; **à la — tombante** at nightfall.

nul, nulle [nyl] *a* no, not one, not any, worthless, of no account, null, invalid, non-existent; **course nulle** dead heat; **partie nulle** draw, drawn game; **nulle part** nowhere; *pn* no one, none, nobody.

nullement [nylmɑ̃] *ad* not at all, by no means, in no way.

nullité [nyllite] *nf* nullity, invalidity, emptiness, incapacity, nonentity.

nûment [nymɑ̃] *ad* frankly; without embellishment.

numéral [nymeral] *a nm* numeral.

numérique [nymerik] *a* numerical.

numéro [nymero] *nm* number, item, turn; **c'est un —** he is a character.

nuptial [nypsjal] *a* nuptial, bridal, wedding-.

nuque [nyk] *nf* nape of the neck.

nutritif, -ive [nytritif, iːv] *a* nutritious, nourishing, food-.

nymphe [nɛ̃ːf] *nf* nymph.

O

obéir [ɔbeiːr] *vt* to obey, comply (with à).

obéissance [ɔbeisãːs] *nf* obedience, submission.

obéissant [ɔbeisã] *a* obedient, dutiful.

obélisque [ɔbelisk] *nm* obelisk.

obèse [ɔbɛːz] *a* fat, corpulent, stout.

obésité [ɔbezite] *nf* obesity, corpulence.

objecter [ɔbʒɛkte] *vt* to raise (as) an objection.

objecteur [ɔbʒɛktœːr] *nm* (conscientious) objector.

objectif, -ive [ɔbʒɛktif, iːv] *a* objective; *nm* objective, target, lens.

objection [ɔbʒɛksjɔ̃] *nf* objection.

objet [ɔbʒɛ] *nm* object, thing, aim, purpose, subject.

obligation [ɔbligasjɔ̃] *nf* obligation, duty, agreement, bond, debenture.

obligatoire [ɔbligatwaːr] *a* obligatory, compulsory, binding.

obligé [ɔbliʒe] *a* obliged, bound, indispensable, inevitable, grateful.

obligeance [ɔbliʒãːs] *nf* obligingness, kindness.

obliger [ɔbliʒe] *vt* to oblige, compel, do (s.o.) a favour.

oblique [ɔblik] *a* oblique, slanting, indirect, underhand.

obliquer [ɔblike] *vi* to edge, slant, turn off (*direction*).

oblitération [ɔbliterasjɔ̃] *nf* obliteration, cancelling.

oblitérer [ɔblitere] *vt* to obliterate, cancel.

obole [ɔbɔl] *nf* mite.

obscène [ɔpsɛ(ː)n] *a* obscene.

obscénité [ɔpsenite] *nf* obscenity.

obscur [ɔpskyːr] *a* obscure, indistinct, unknown, dark.

obscurcir [ɔpskyrsiːr] *vt* to obscure, darken, dim, make unintelligible; *vr* to grow dark, become obscure, dim.

obscurcissement [ɔpskyrsismã] *nm* darkening, growing dim, blackout.

obscurité [ɔpskyrite] *nf* obscurity, darkness, dimness, unintelligibility.

obséder [ɔpsede] *vt* to obsess, haunt, worry.

obsèques [ɔpsɛk] *nf pl* obsequies, funeral.

obséquieux, -euse [ɔpsekjø, øːz] *a* obsequious.

observance [ɔpsɛrvãːs] *nf* observance.

observateur, -trice [ɔpsɛrvatœːr, tris] *a* observant, observing; *n* observer.

observation [ɔpsɛrvasjɔ̃] *nf* observation, remark, comment, reprimand, observance.

observatoire [ɔpsɛrvatwaːr] *nm* observatory.

observer [ɔpsɛrve] *vt* to observe, keep (to), watch, note; **faire —** to

point out; *vr* to be careful, discreet.

obsession [ɔpsɛsjɔ̃] *nf* obsession.

obstacle [ɔpstakl] *nm* obstacle, impediment.

obstination [ɔpstinasjɔ̃] *nf* obstinacy.

obstiné [ɔpstine] *a* obstinate, stubborn.

obstruction [ɔpstryksjɔ̃] *nf* obstruction, blocking, choking.

obstruer [ɔpstrye] *vt* to obstruct, block, choke; *vr* to become blocked, choked.

obtempérer [ɔptãpere] *vt* to comply (with à).

obtenir [ɔptəniːr] *vt* to obtain, get, procure, achieve.

obtention [ɔptãsjɔ̃] *nf* obtaining.

obtus [ɔpty] *a* obtuse, dull, blunt.

obus [ɔby(ːs)] *nm* shell.

obusier [ɔbyzje] *nm* howitzer.

oc [ɔk] *ad* **langue d'—** dialect of South of France.

occasion [ɔkazjɔ̃, -ka-] *nf* occasion, opportunity, motive, bargain; **à l'—** when the opportunity occurs, in case of need, once in a while, on the occasion of (de), with regard (to de), **d'—** second-hand.

occasionner [ɔkazjɔne, -ka-] *vt* to occasion, give rise to.

occident [ɔksidã] *nm* west.

occidental [ɔksidãtal] *a* west(ern).

occlusion [ɔklyzjɔ̃] *nf* occlusion, closing, obstruction.

occulte [ɔkylt] *a* occult, hidden

occupant [ɔkypã] *a* occupying; *n* occupying (power, army *etc*), occupier.

occupation [ɔkypasjɔ̃] *nf* occupation, occupancy, business, employment.

occupé [ɔkype] *a* occupied, busy, engaged.

occuper [ɔkype] *vt* to occupy, inhabit, fill, hold, employ; *vr* to keep oneself busy, go in (for de), turn one's attention (to de), attend (to de); **occupez-vous de ce qui vous regarde** mind your own business.

occurrence [ɔkyrãːs] *nf* occurrence, event; **en l'—** under the circumstances.

océan [ɔseã] *nm* ocean.

océanique [ɔseanik] *a* ocean(ic).

ocre [ɔkr] *nf* ochre.

octave [ɔktaːv] *nf* octave.

octobre [ɔktɔbr] *nm* October.

octogénaire [ɔktɔʒenɛːr] *an* octogenarian.

octogone [ɔktɔgɔn] *a* octagonal; *nm* octagon.

octroi [ɔktrwa] *nm* concession, tollhouse.

octroyer [ɔktrwaje] *vt* to concede, grant, allow, bestow.

oculaire [ɔkylɛːr] *a* ocular, eye-; *nm* eyepiece.

oculiste [ɔkylist] *nm* oculist.

ode [ɔd] *nf* ode.

odeur [odœːr] *nf* odour, smell, scent.

odieux, -euse [ɔdjø, øːz] *a* odious, hateful, heinous; *nm* odiousness, odium.

odorant [ɔdɔrɑ̃] *a* sweet-smelling.

odorat [ɔdɔra] *nm* sense of smell.

œil [œːj] *nm, pl* yeux [jø] eye, sight, look; **regarder dans le blanc des yeux** to look full in the face; **cela saute aux yeux** it is obvious; **coûter les yeux de la tête** to cost an outrageous price; **à l'—** on tick, free; **à vue d'—** visibly, at a glance; **coup d'—**view, glance; **faire de l'—à** to give the glad eye to, wink at.

œillade [œjad] *nf* glance, *pl* sheep's eyes.

œillère [œjeːr] *nf* blinker, eye-bath, eye-tooth.

œillet [œjɛ] *nm* eyelet, pink, carnation; **— de poète** sweet-william.

œsophage [ezɔfaːʒ] *nm* œsophagus, gullet.

œuf [œf] *nm* egg; *pl* spawn, roe; **— dur** hard-boiled egg; **— sur le plat** egg fried in butter; **faire d'un — un bœuf** to make a mountain out of a molehill.

œuvre [œːvr] *nf* work; **— de bienfaisance** charitable society, charity; **mettre en —** to put in hand, bring into play; *nm* works.

offensant [ɔfɑ̃sɑ̃] *a* offensive, objectionable.

offense [ɔfɑ̃s] *nf* offence.

offenser [ɔfɑ̃se] *vt* to offend, injure, be offensive to; *vr* to take offence.

offensif, -ive [ɔfɑ̃sif, iːv] *a* offensive.

office [ɔfis] *nm* office, functions, service, worship, department; **faire — de** to act as; **d'—** officially, automatically; **— des morts** burialservice; *nf* pantry, servants' hall.

officiel, -elle [ɔfisjɛl] *a* official, formal.

officier [ɔfisje] *nm* officer; **— de l'état civil** registrar; *vi* to officiate.

officieux, -euse [ɔfisjø, øːz] *a* officious, semi-official; **à titre —** unofficially; *n* busybody.

officine [ɔfisin] *nf* chemist's shop, den, hotbed.

offrande [ɔfrɑ̃d] *nf* offering.

offrant [ɔfrɑ̃] *a nm* **le plus —** the highest bidder.

offre [ɔfr] *nf* offer, tender; **l'— et la demande** supply and demand.

offrir [ɔfriːr] *vt* to offer, proffer, stand, bid, afford, put up; *vr* to offer oneself, present itself.

offusquer [ɔfyske] *vt* to offend, shock, be offensive (at de).

ogival [ɔʒival] *a* pointed, ogival, gothic.

ogive [ɔʒiːv] *nf* ogive, pointed arch.

ogre, -esse [ɔgr, ɔgrɛs] *n* ogre, ogress.

oie [wa] *nf* goose.

oignon [ɔɲɔ̃] *nm* onion, bulb, bunion.

oindre [wɛ̃dr] *vt* to oil, anoint.

oiseau [wazo] *nm* bird, individual; **à vol d'—** as the crow flies.

oiseau-mouche [wazomuʃ] *nm* humming-bird.

oiselet [wazlɛ] *nm* small bird.

oiseleur [wazlœːr] *nm* bird-catcher.

oiseux, -euse [wazø, øːz] *a* idle, useless, trifling.

oisif, -ive [wazif, iːv] *a* idle; *n* idler.

oisillon [wazijɔ̃] *nm* fledgling.

oisiveté [wazivte] *nf* idleness.

oison [wazɔ̃] *nm* gosling, simpleton.

oléagineux, -euse [ɔleaʒinø, øːz] *a* oleaginous, oily, oil.

olfactif, -ive [ɔlfaktif, iːv] *a* olfactory.

oligarchie [ɔligarʃi] *nf* oligarchy.

olivâtre [ɔlivaːtr] *a* olive-hued, sallow.

olive [ɔliːv] *a* olive-green, -shaped; *nf* olive.

olivier [ɔlivje] *nm* olive-tree, -wood.

Olympe [ɔlɛ̃p] *nm* Olympus.

olympique [ɔlɛ̃pik] *a* Olympic.

ombilical [ɔ̃bilikal] *a* umbilical, navel.

ombrage [ɔ̃braːʒ] *nm* shade, umbrage.

ombrager [ɔ̃braʒe] *vt* to shade, overshadow.

ombrageux, -euse [ɔ̃braʒø, øːz] *a* touchy, (*horse*) shy.

ombre [ɔ̃br] *nf* shade, shadow, darkness, ghost.

ombrelle [ɔ̃brɛl] *nf* sunshade, parasol.

ombreux, -euse [ɔ̃brø, øːz] *a* shady.

omelette [ɔmlɛt] *nf* omelette; **— aux fines herbes** savoury omelette.

omettre [ɔmɛtr] *vt* to omit.

omission [ɔmisjɔ̃] *nf* omission.

omnibus [ɔmnibyːs] *nm* (omni)bus; **— train** — slow train.

omnipotence [ɔmnipɔtɑ̃ːs] *nf* omnipotence.

omnivore [ɔmnivɔːr] *a* omnivorous.

omoplate [ɔmoplat] *nf* shoulderblade.

on [5] *pn* one, people, a man, we, you, they; **— demande** wanted; **— dit** it is said; **— ne passe pas** no thoroughfare.

oncle [ɔ̃ːkl] *nm* uncle.

onction [ɔ̃ksjɔ̃] *nf* oiling, anointing, unction, unctuousness.

onctueux, -euse [ɔ̃ktɥø, øːz] *a* unctuous, oily, greasy.

onde [ɔ̃ːd] *nf* wave, ocean, water.

ondé [ɔ̃de] *a* wavy, waved, watered.

ondée [ɔ̃de] *nf* heavy shower.

on-dit [ɔ̃di] *nm pl* hearsay, idle talk.

ondoyant [ɔ̃dwajɑ̃] *a* undulating, waving.

ondoyer [ɔ̃dwaje] *vi* to undulate, wave, sway.

ondulant [ɔ̃dylɑ̃] *a* undulating, waving, flowing.

ondulation [ɔ̃dylasjɔ̃] *nf* undulation, wave.

ondulé [ɔ̃dyle] *a* wavy, undulating, corrugated.

onduler [ɔ̃dyle] *vi* to undulate; *vt*

to corrugate, wave; **se faire —** to have one's hair waved.

onéreux, -euse [ɔnerø, øːz] *a* onerous, heavy.

ongle [ɔ̃ːgl] *nm* nail, claw, talon; **se faire les —s** to trim one's nails.

onglée [ɔ̃gle] *nf* numbness, tingling (of the fingers).

onglet [ɔ̃glɛ] *nm* guard, tab.

onguent [ɔ̃gɑ̃] *nm* ointment, salve.

onomatopée [ɔnɔmatɔpe] *nf* onomatopœia.

onyx [ɔniks] *nm* onyx.

onze [ɔ̃ːz] *a nm* eleven, eleventh.

onzième [ɔ̃zjɛm] *an* eleventh.

opacité [ɔpasite] *nf* opacity.

opale [ɔpal] *nf* opal.

opaque [ɔpak] *a* opaque.

opéra [ɔpera] *nm* opera, opera-house.

opérateur [ɔperatœːr] *nm* operator, cameraman.

opération [ɔperasjɔ̃] *nf* operation, process, transaction; **salle d'—** operating-theatre.

opératoire [ɔperatwaːr] *a* operative.

opéré [ɔpere] *n* person operated upon, surgical case.

opérer [ɔpere] *vt* to operate, perform an operation on, effect, work, carry out, make; **se faire —** to undergo an operation.

opérette [ɔperɛt] *nf* operetta, light opera, musical comedy.

ophtalmique [ɔftalmik] *a* ophthalmic.

opiner [ɔpine] *vi* to express an opinion, vote; **— du bonnet** to nod approval.

opiniâtre [ɔpinjɑːtr] *a* obstinate, opinionated, stubborn, dogged, persistent.

opiniâtrer [ɔpinjɑtre] *vr* to be obstinate, persist (in **à**).

opiniâtreté [ɔpinjɑtrəte] *nf* obstinacy.

opinion [ɔpinjɔ̃] *nf* opinion, view.

opium [ɔpjɔm] *nm* opium.

opportun [ɔpɔrtœ̃] *a* opportune, timely, advisable.

opportunisme [ɔpɔrtynism] *nm* opportu ism.

opportuniste [ɔpɔrtynist] *n* opportunist, time-server.

opportunité [ɔpɔrtynite] *nf* opportuneness, timeliness, advisability.

opposé [ɔpoze] *a* opposed. opposite, opposing; *nm* contrary, opposite, reverse; **à l'— de** contrary to.

opposition [ɔpozisjɔ̃] *nf* opposition, objection, injunction, contrast; **par — à** as opposed to, in contradiction to.

oppresser [ɔprese] *vt* to oppress.

oppresseur [ɔprɛsœːr] *a* oppressive, tyrannical; *nm* oppressor.

oppressif, -ive [ɔprɛsif, iv] *a* oppressive.

oppression [ɔprɛsjɔ̃] *nf* oppression.

opprimer [ɔprime] *vt* to oppress.

opprobre [ɔprɔbr] *nm* opprobrium, disgrace.

opter [ɔpte] *vt* to choose, decide (in favour of **pour**).

opticien [ɔptisjɛ̃] *nm* optician.

optimisme [ɔptimism] *nm* optimism.

optimiste [ɔptimist] *a* optimistic; *n* optimist.

option [ɔpsjɔ̃] *nf* choice, option

optique [ɔptik] *a* optic, visual, optical; *nf* optics.

opulence [ɔpylɑ̃ːs] *nf* opulence, affluence.

opulent [ɔpylɑ̃] *a* opulent, affluent, rich.

opuscule [ɔpyskyl] *nm* pamphlet.

or [ɔːr] *nm* gold; **à prix d'—** at an exorbitant price; **affaire d'—** good bargain, good thing; *cj* now.

oracle [ɔraːkl] *nm* oracle.

orage [ɔraːʒ] *nm* (thunder)storm.

orageux, -euse [ɔraʒø, øːz] *a* stormy, thundery.

oraison [ɔrɛzɔ̃] *nf* oration, prayer.

oral [ɔral] *a* oral, verbal; *nm* oral examination, viva.

orange [ɔrɑ̃ːʒ] *nf* orange.

orangé [ɔrɑ̃ʒe] *a* orange(-coloured).

orangeade [ɔrɑ̃ʒad] *nf* orange squash.

oranger [ɔrɑ̃ʒe] *nm* orange-tree; **fleur(s) d'—** orange-flower, -blossom.

orangerie [ɔrɑ̃ʒri] *nf* orange-grove, -greenhouse.

orang-outan(g) [ɔrɑ̃utɑ̃] *nm* orang-outang.

orateur [ɔratœːr] *nm* orator, speaker.

oratoire [ɔratwaːr] *a* oratorical; *nm* chapel, oratory.

orbe [ɔrb] *nm* orb, globe, heavenly body.

orbite [ɔrbit] *nf* orbit, socket.

orchestration [ɔrkɛstrasjɔ̃] *nf* orchestration.

orchestre [ɔrkɛstr] *nm* orchestra; **chef d'—** conductor.

orchestrer [ɔrkɛstre] *vt* to orchestrate, score.

orchidée [ɔrkide] *nf* orchid.

ordinaire [ɔrdinɛːr] *a* usual, common, ordinary, vulgar; **vin —** table wine; *nm* custom, wont, normal habit, daily fare; **d'—** as a rule; **comme d'—** as usual.

ordinal [ɔrdinal] *a* ordinal.

ordinateur [ɔrdinatœːr] *nm* computer.

ordonnance [ɔrdɔnɑ̃ːs] *nf* order, arrangement, ordinance, regulation, ruling orderly, batman, medical prescription; **officier d'—** orderly officer, aide-de-camp.

ordonné [ɔrdɔne] *a* orderly, tidy, methodical.

ordonner [ɔrdɔne] *vt* to arrange, order, command, prescribe, ordain.

ordre [ɔrdr] *nm* order, method, discipline, class, character, command, warrant; **mettre en —** to put in order; **à l'—!** order! **— du jour**

order of the day, agenda; **cité à l'— du jour** mentioned in dispatches; **passer à l'— du jour** to proceed with the business; **jusqu'à nouvel — until** further notice; **billet à — promissory** note.

ordure [ɔrdyːr] nf dirt, filth(iness); pl rubbish, refuse; **boîte à —s** dustbin.

ordurier, -ière [ɔrdyrje, jɛːr] a filthy, obscene.

oreille [ɔrɛːj] nf ear, lug; **avoir l'— dure** to be hard of hearing; **avoir de l'—** to have a good ear; **dresser l'—** to prick up one's ears; **se faire tirer l'—** to have to be asked twice; **rebattre les —s à qn** to din in s.o.'s ears.

oreiller [ɔrɛje] nm pillow.

oreillon [ɔrɛjɔ̃] nm earflap; pl mumps.

ores [ɔːr] ad d'— **et déjà** here and now.

orfèvre [ɔrfɛːvr] nm goldsmith.

orfèvrerie [ɔrfɛvrəri] nf goldsmith's craft, shop, (gold, silver) plate.

orfraie [ɔrfrɛ] nf sea-hawk.

organdi [ɔrgɑ̃di] nm organdie.

organe [ɔrgan] nm organ, agency, mouthpiece.

organique [ɔrganik] a organic.

organisateur, -trice [ɔrganizatœːr, trisl a organizing; n organizer.

organisation [ɔrganizasjɔ̃] nf organization, organizing, constitution, body.

organiser [ɔrganize] vt to organize, arrange.

organisme [ɔrganism] nm organism, constitution, system.

organiste [ɔrganist] nm organist.

orge [ɔrʒ] nf barley.

orgelet [ɔrʒəlɛ] nm sty.

orgie [ɔrʒi] nf orgy, riot.

orgue [ɔrg] nm (pl is f) organ; — **de Barbarie** barrel-organ.

orgueil [ɔrgœj] nm pride.

orgueilleux, -euse [ɔrgœjø, øːz] a proud.

orient [ɔrjɑ̃] nm orient, east.

oriental [ɔrjɑ̃tal] a eastern, east, oriental; n Oriental.

orientation [ɔrjɑ̃tasjɔ̃] nf orientation, guidance, direction, trend.

orienter [ɔrjɑ̃te] vt to orient, guide, direct, point, take the bearings of; vr to find one's bearings, turn (to).

orifice [ɔrifis] nm opening, orifice.

originaire [ɔriʒinɛːr] a original, native, originating.

originairement [ɔriʒinɛrmɑ̃] ad originally.

original [ɔriʒinal] a original, first, novel, odd; nm original, top copy, eccentric.

originalement [ɔriʒinalmɑ̃] ad in an original manner, oddly.

originalité [ɔriʒinalite] nf originality, eccentricity.

origine [ɔriʒin] nf origin, beginning, extraction, source; **à l'—** originally.

originel -elle [ɔriʒinɛl] a original, primordial; **péché —** original sin.

oripeau [ɔripo] nm tinsel; pl gaudy finery.

orme [ɔrm] nm elm-tree.

ornement [ɔrnəmɑ̃] nm ornament, adornment.

ornemental [ɔrnəmɑ̃tal] a ornamental, decorative.

ornementer [ɔrnəmɑ̃te] vt to ornament.

orner [ɔrne] vt to ornament, adorn.

ornière [ɔrnjɛːr] nf rut, groove.

ornithologie [ɔrnitɔlɔʒi] nf ornithology.

orphelin [ɔrfəlɛ̃] a orphan(ed); n orphan; — **de mère** motherless.

orphelinat [ɔrfəlina] nm orphanage.

ortei' [ɔrtɛ:] nm toe.

orthodoxe [ɔrtɔdɔks] a orthodox, conventional.

orthodoxie [ɔrtɔdɔksi] nf orthodoxy.

orthographe [ɔrtɔgraf] nf spelling.

orthographier [ɔrtɔgrafje] vt to spell.

ortie [ɔrti] nf nettle.

os [ɔs, pl o] nm bone; **trempé jusqu'aux —** soaked to the skin.

oscillateur [ɔsil(l)atœːr] nm oscillator.

oscillation [ɔsil(l)asjɔ̃] nf oscillation, fluctuation.

osciller [ɔsije, ɔsile] vi to oscillate, swing, flicker, fluctuate, waver.

osé [oze] a daring, bold.

oseille [ɔzɛːj, o-] nf sorrel.

oser [oze] vt to dare.

osier [osje] nm osier; **panier d'—** wicker-basket.

ossature [ɔssatyːr] nf frame(work), skeleton.

osselet [ɔslɛ] nm knuckle-bone.

ossements [ɔsmɑ̃, os-] nm pl bones.

osseux, -euse [ɔsø, øːz] a bony.

ossifier [ɔssifje] vt to ossify; vr to harden.

ossuaire [ɔssɥɛːr] nm charnel-house.

ostensible [ɔstɑ̃sibl] a ostensible.

ostensoir [ɔstɑ̃swaːr] nm monstrance.

ostentation [ɔstɑ̃tasjɔ̃] nf ostentation, show.

ostraciser [ɔstrasize] vt to ostracize.

ostréiculture [ɔstreikyltyːr] nf oyster-breeding.

otage [ɔtaːʒ] nm hostage.

ôter [ote] vt to remove, take away, take off; vr to remove oneself.

otite [ɔtit] nf otitis.

ottomane [ɔt(t)ɔman] nf divan, ottoman.

ou [u] cj or; — . . . — either . . . or.

où [u] ad inter where?; rel where, in which, to which, when; **n'importe — anywhere**; **d'—?** whence? where? where from? **d'— vient que . . .?** how does it happen that . . .? **jusqu'—?** how far? **partout —** wherever.

ouailles [waːj] nf pl flock.
ouate [wat] nf wadding, cotton wool.
ouaté [wate] a padded, quilted, fleecy, soft.
ouater [wate] vt to pad, line with wadding, quilt.
oubli [ubli] nm forgetfulness, oblivion, omission, oversight; par — inadvertently.
oublie [ubli] nf cone, wafer.
oublier [ublie] vt to forget, neglect, overlook; vr to be unmindful of oneself, forget oneself.
oubliettes [ublist] nf pl dungeon.
oublieux, -euse [ubliø, øːz] a forgetful, oblivious.
oued [wɛd] nm watercourse, wadi.
ouest [wɛst] a west(ern); nm west.
ouf [uf] excl ah! phew!
oui [wi] ad yes, ay(e); je crois que — I think so.
oui-dire [widiːr] nm hearsay.
ouïe [wi] nf (sense of) hearing; pl gills.
ouïr [wiːr, uiːr] vt to hear.
ouragan [uragɑ̃] nm hurricane.
ourdir [urdiːr] vt to warp, hatch, (plot) weave.
ourler [urle] vt to hem.
ourlet [urle] nm hem, edge.
ours [urs] nm bear; — blanc polar bear; — en peluche teddy-bear; — mal léché unlicked cub, boorish fellow; il ne faut pas vendre la peau de l'— avant de l'avoir tué don't count your chickens before they are hatched.
oursin [ursɛ̃] nm sea-urchin.
ourson [ursɔ̃] nm bear's cub.
ouste [ust] excl allez —! off you go! hop it!
outil [uti] nm tool.
outillage [utijaːʒ] nm tools, gear, plant; — national national capital equipment.
outiller [utije] vt to equip, fit out, provide with tools, equip with plant.
outrage [utraːʒ] nm outrage, offence, contempt.
outrageant [utraʒɑ̃] a outrageous, insulting.
outrager [utraʒe] vt to outrage, insult, offend.
outrance [utrɑ̃ːs] nf excess; à — to the utmost, to the bitter end
outre [uːtr] prep beyond, in addition to, ultra-; ad passer — to go on, take no notice (of), disregard; en — besides, over and above; en — de in addition to; d'— en — through and through; — que apart from the fact that.
outré [utre] a exaggerated, overdone.
outrecuidance [utrəkɥidɑ̃ːs] nf presumptuousness.
outre-Manche [utrəmɑ̃ːʃ] ad across the Channel.
outre-mer [utrəmɛːr] ad beyond the sea(s), oversea(s).

outrepasser [utrəpase] vt to exceed, go beyond.
outrer [utre] vt to exaggerate, overdo, carry to excess, revolt, provoke beyond measure.
ouvert [uvɛːr] a open, gaping, unfortified, frank; grand — wide open.
ouvertement [uvɛrtəmɑ̃] ad openly, frankly.
ouverture [uvɛrtyːr] nf opening, outbreak, overture, aperture, gap, width, span; heures d'— business hours, visiting hours.
ouvrable [uvrabl] a workable, working.
ouvrage [uvraːʒ] nm work, workmanship.
ouvragé [uvraʒe] a worked, wrought.
ouvrager [uvraʒe] vt to work, figure.
ouvrant [uvrɑ̃] a opening; nm leaf (of door).
ouvre-boîtes [uvrəbwat] nm tin opener, can opener.
ouvre-bouteilles [uvrəbuteːj] nm bottle-opener, can opener.
ouvrer [uvre] vt to work.
ouvreuse [uvrøːz] nf usher(ette).
ouvrier, -ière [uvrie, ɛːr] a working, labour; n worker, workman, operative, labourer, hand; f factory girl.
ouvrir [uvriːr] vt to open, turn (on), draw back, cut (through, open), lance, begin, start; vi to open (onto sur); vr to open, begin, open one's heart.
ovaire [ɔvɛːr] nm ovary.
ovale [ɔval] a nm oval.
ovation [ɔvasjɔ̃] nf ovation, acclamation.
oxydable [ɔksidabl] a oxidizable, liable to rust.
oxyde [ɔksid] nm oxide.
oxygène [ɔksiʒɛn] nm oxygen.
oxygéné [ɔksiʒene] a oxygenated; eau —e peroxide of hydrogen; cheveux —s peroxided hair.
ozone [ɔzɔn, -oːn] nm ozone.

P

pacage [pakaːʒ] nm pasture, grazing.
pachyderme [paʃidɛrm, paki-] a thick-skinned; nm pachyderm.
pacificateur, -trice [pasifikatœːr, tris] a pacifying; n peace-maker.
pacification [pasifikasjɔ̃] nf pacification, peace-making.
pacifier [pasifje] vt to pacify, appease, quieten, calm down.
pacifique [pasifik] a pacific, peaceful.
pacifisme [pasifism] nm pacifism.
pacotille [pakɔtiːj] nf cheap goods; de — tawdry.
pacte [pakt] nm pact.
pactiser [paktize] vi to come to terms, treat.
pagaie [pagɛ] nf paddle.

pagaïe [paga:j] *nf* rush, disorder, chaos.

paganisme [paganism] *nm* paganism.

pagayer [pageje] *vti* to paddle.

page [pa:ʒ] *nf* page; *nm* page(boy); **à la —** up to date.

pagination [paʒinasjɔ̃] *nf* paging, pagination.

pagne [paɲ] *nm* loincloth, (*Africa*) cloth (*toga*).

païen, -enne [pajɛ̃, jɛn] *a nf* pagan, heathen.

paillard [paja:r] *a* lewd, ribald.

paillardise [pajardi:z] *nf* ribaldry, ribald joke.

paillasse [pajas] *nf* straw mattress, palliasse.

paillasson [pajasɔ̃] *nm* (door)mat, matting.

paille [pa:j] *nf* straw, chaff, mote, flaw; **feu de —** flash in the pan; **homme de —** figurehead.

pailleter [pajte] *vt* to spangle.

paillette [pajɛt] *nf* spangle, flaw, flash, flake.

paillotte [pajɔt] *nf* straw, reed hut.

pain [pɛ̃] *nm* bread, loaf; **petit —** roll; **— de savon** cake of soap; **cela se vend comme du — frais** that sells like hot cakes; **pour une bouchée de —** for a mere song.

pair [pɛ:r] *a* equal, even; *nm* equal, peer, par; **être au —** to have board and lodging but unpaid; **aller de — avec** to be in keeping with; **marcher de — avec** to keep abreast of; **traiter qn de — à égal** to treat someone as an equal.

paire [pɛ:r] *nf* pair, brace.

pairie [peri] *nf* peerage.

paisible [pezibl] *a* peaceful, quiet.

paître [pɛ:tr] *vt* to pasture, graze, crop; *vi* to browse, graze; **envoyer — qn** to send s.o. about his business.

paix [pe] *nf* peace(fulness), quiet (ness).

palabrer [palabre] *vi* to palaver.

palace [palas] *nm* magnificent hotel.

palais [palɛ] *nm* palace, palate; **P— de Justice** law-courts.

palan [palɑ̃] *nm* pulley-block, tackle.

palatal [palatal] *a* palatal.

pale [pal] *nf* blade, sluice.

pâle [pɑ:l] *a* pale, pallid, wan.

palefrenier [palfrənje] *nm* groom, ostler.

palet [palɛ] *nm* quoit, puck.

paletot [palto] *nm* coat, overcoat.

palette [palɛt] *nf* palette, bat, blade; **roue à —s** paddle-wheel.

pâleur [palœ:r] *nf* pallor, paleness.

palier [palje] *nm* landing, stairhead, stage, level stretch.

pâlir [pali:r] *vt* to make pale; *vi* to turn pale, grow dim.

palissade [palisad] *nf* palisade, fence, stockade.

palissandre [palisɑ̃:dr] *nm* rosewood.

palliatif, -ive [palljatif, i:v] *a nm* palliative.

palmarès [palmarɛ:s] *nm* prize list, honours list.

palme [palm] *nf* palm(-branch); **noix de —** palm nut.

palmier [palmje] *nm* palm-tree.

palonnier [palɔnje] *nm* swing-bar, rudder-bar.

pâlot, -otte [palo, ɔt] *a* palish, drawn.

palpable [palpabl] *a* palpable, obvious.

palpabilité [palpabilite] *nf* palpability, obviousness.

palper [palpe] *vt* to feel, finger.

palpitant [palpitɑ̃] *a* quivering, throbbing, fluttering, exciting.

palpiter [palpite] *vi* to palpitate, quiver, throb, flutter.

paludéen, -enne [palydeɛ̃, ɛn] *a* marsh.

paludisme [palydism] *nm* malaria.

pâmer [pame] *vir* to faint, swoon; **se — d'admiration devant** to go into raptures over.

pâmoison [pamwazɔ̃] *nf* swoon, faint.

pamphlet [pɑ̃flɛ] *nm* pamphlet, lampoon.

pamphlétaire [pɑ̃fletɛ:r] *nm* pamphleteer.

pamplemousse [pɑ̃pləmus] *nf* grapefruit.

pampre [pɑ̃:pr] *nm* vine-branch.

pan [pɑ̃] *nm* skirt, tail, flap, side, bit.

pan! [pɑ̃] *excl* bang!

panacée [panase] *nf* panacea.

panache [panaʃ] *nm* plume, tuft, trail, wreath, somersault; **avoir du — to** have style; **avoir son — to** be slightly intoxicated.

panaché [panaʃe] *a* plumed, mixed, motley; **bière —e** shandy.

panade [panad] *nf* **être dans la —** to be in a fix, to be in want.

panard [pana:r] *nm* (*fam*) foot.

panaris [panari] *nm* whitlow.

pancarte [pɑ̃kart] *nf* bill, placard.

panégyrique [paneʒirik] *a* eulogistic; *nm* panegyric.

paner [pane] *vt* to cover with breadcrumbs.

panier [panje] *nm* basket, hamper; **— à salade** salad shaker, black Maria; **— percé** spendthrift.

panique [panik] *a nf* panic.

panne [pan] *nf* plush, fat, breakdown; **en —** hove to, stranded, broken down; **rester en — d'essence** to run out of petrol.

panneau [pano] *nm* panel, board, hoarding, trap.

panoplie [panɔpli] *nf* panoply, suit of armour.

panorama [panɔrama] *nm* panorama.

panoramique [panɔramik] *a* panoramic.

panse [pɑ̃:s] *nf* paunch.

pansement [pɑ̃smɑ̃] nm dressing.
panser [pɑ̃se] vt to dress, groom, rub down.
pansu [pɑ̃sy] a pot-bellied.
pantalon [pɑ̃talɔ̃] nm trousers, knickers.
pantelant [pɑ̃tlɑ̃] a panting.
panthéisme [pɑ̃teism] nm pantheism.
panthère [pɑ̃tɛːr] nf panther.
pantin [pɑ̃tɛ̃] nm jumping-jack, puppet, nobody.
pantois [pɑ̃twa] a flabbergasted, speechless.
pantomime [pɑ̃tɔmim] nf pantomime, dumb show.
pantoufle [pɑ̃tufl] nf slipper.
panure [panyːr] nf bread-crumbs.
paon, -onne [pɑ̃, pan] n peacock, -hen.
papa [papa] nm daddy, papa; à la — unhurriedly; de — old-fashioned.
papauté [papote] nf papacy.
papaye [papɛ] nf pawpaw.
pape [pap] nm Pope.
papelard [paplaːr] a nmf sanctimonious (person).
paperasse [papras] nf official paper, old paper, red tape.
paperassier, -ière [paprasje, jɛːr] a who likes to accumulate papers, bureaucratic.
papeterie [paptri] nf paper manufacture, trade, mill, stationer's shop.
papetier, -ière [paptje, jɛːr] n paper-manufacturer, stationer.
papier [papje] nm paper, document; — à lettres notepaper; — de soie tissue paper; — peint wallpaper; — hygiénique toilet paper.
papillon [papijɔ̃] nm butterfly, moth, leaflet, inset, ticket.
papillonner [papijɔne] vi to flit, flutter about.
papillote [papijɔt] nf curl paper, sweet paper, (cook) papillote.
papilloter [papijɔte] vt to put into curl papers; vi to flicker, blink.
papyrus [papiryːs] nm papyrus.
pâque [pɑːk] nf Passover.
paquebot [pakbo] nm steamer, liner, packet-boat.
pâquerette [pɑkrɛt] nf daisy.
Pâques [pɑːk] nm Easter; nf pl Easter sacrament; — fleuries Palm Sunday.
paquet [pakɛ] nm parcel, package, bundle; — de mer mass of sea water, heavy sea.
par [par] prep by, through, for, with, in, from, out, over, about, on, out of; — où a-t-il passé? which way did he go? — ici (là) this way (that way); — trop difficile far too difficult; —ci, —là here and there.
parabole [parabɔl] nf parable, parabola.
parabolique [parabɔlik] a parabolic.

parachever [paraʃve] vt to finish off, complete.
parachute [paraʃyt] nm parachute.
parachutiste [paraʃytist] n parachutist, paratrooper.
parade [parad] nf parade, show, display, parry.
paradis [paradi] nm paradise, heaven, gallery.
paradoxal [paradɔksal] a paradoxical.
paradoxe [paradɔks] nm paradox.
paraffine [parafin] nf (liquid) paraffin.
parage [paraːʒ] nm trimming, birth, lineage; pl regions, parts, latitudes.
paragraphe [paragraf] nm paragraph.
paraître [parɛːtr] vi to appear, seem, look, be published, show; il y paraît that is quite obvious; à ce qu'il me paraît as far as I can judge.
parallèle [parallɛl] a nm parallel, comparison.
parallélogramme [parallelɔgram] nm parallelogram.
paralyser [paralize] vt to paralyse, cripple.
paralysie [paralizi] nf paralysis.
paralytique [paralitik] a nmf paralytic.
parangon [parɑ̃gɔ̃] nm paragon, flawless gem.
parapet [parapɛ] nm parapet.
paraphe [paraf] nm flourish, initial.
parapher [parafe] vt to initial.
paraphrase [parafraːz] nf paraphrase.
paraphraser [parafraze] vt to paraphrase.
parapluie [paraplɥi] nm umbrella.
parasite [parazit] a parasitic; nm parasite; pl (radio) interference.
parasol [parasɔl] nm sunshade, parasol.
paratonnerre [paratɔnɛːr] nm lightning conductor.
paratyphoïde [paratifɔid] a nf paratyphoid.
paravent [paravɑ̃] nm folding-screen.
parbleu [parblø] excl I should think so! rather!
parc [park] nm park, pen, paddock, carpark; — à huîtres oyster bed.
parcage [parkaːʒ] nm penning, (cars) parking.
parcelle [parsɛl] nf particle, scrap, plot.
parce que [pars(ə)kə] cj because.
parchemin [parʃəmɛ̃] nm parchment, vellum.
parcimonie [parsimɔni] nf parsimony, meanness.
parcimonieux, -euse [parsimɔnjø, øːz] a parsimonious, niggardly.
parcourir [parkuriːr] vt to go through, travel over (through), read through, glance through, cover.

parcours [parku:r] *nm* distance, mileage, run, course.

par-dessous [pardəsu] *prep* under, beneath; *ad* underneath, under it, them.

par-dessus [pardəsy] *prep* over; *ad* over it, them, on top (of it, them); *nm* overcoat.

par-devant [pardəvã] *prep* before, in the presence of.

pardon [pardɔ̃] *nm* pardon, forgiveness, pilgrimage.

pardonner [pardɔne] *vt* to forgive, pardon, excuse.

pare-boue [parbu] *nm* mudguard.

pare-brise [parbri:z] *nm* windscreen.

pare-choc [parʃɔk] *nm* bumper.

pareil, -eille [parɛ:j] *a* similar, like, same, equal, such; *nmf* peer, equal, match; **rendre la —le à qn** to get even with s.o.

pareillement [parɛjmã] *ad* likewise, also.

parement [parmã] *nm* cuff, altar cloth, facing, kerbstone.

parent [parã] *nm* relative, kinsman; *pl* parents, relations.

parenté [parãte] *nf* relationship, kinship.

parenthèse [parãtɛ:z] *nf* parenthesis, digression, bracket; **entre —s** in parentheses, by the way.

parer [pare] *vt* to adorn, deck out, trim, pare, ward off; *vi* **— à qch** to guard against sth.

paresse [parɛs] *nf* laziness, sloth, sluggishness.

paresser [parɛse] *vi* to idle, laze.

paresseux, -euse [parɛsø, ø:z] *a* lazy, idle, sluggish; *n* lazybones.

parfaire [parfɛ:r] *vt* to finish off, complete.

parfait [parfɛ] *a* perfect, real; *nm* perfect tense.

parfaitement [parfɛtmã] *ad* perfectly, absolutely, exactly, quite so.

parfois [parfwa] *ad* sometimes, occasionally, at times.

parfum [parfœ̃] *nm* perfume, scent, flavour.

parfumé [parfyme] *a* perfumed, scented fragrant flavoured.

parfumerie [parfymri] *nf* perfumery.

pari [pari] *nm* bet, wager; **— mutuel** totalizator.

paria [parja] *nm* outcast.

parier [parje] *vt* to bet, lay wager.

parieur, -euse [parjœ:r ø:z] *n* backer, punter.

parisien, -ienne [parizjɛ̃, jɛn] *nmf* Parisian from Paris.

paritaire [paritɛ:r] *a* **représentation — ** equal representation.

parité [parite] *nf* parity, equality, evenness.

parjure [parʒy:r] *a* perjured; *n* perjurer; *nm* perjury.

parlant [parlã] *a* talking; **film — talkie**.

parlement [parləmã] *nm* parliament.

parlementaire [parləmãtɛ:r] *a* parliamentary; **drapeau — ** flag of truce.

parlementer [parləmãte] *vi* to parley.

parler [parle] *vti* to speak, talk; *nm* speech, speaking; **tu parles!** not half!

parleur, -euse [parlœ:r, ø:z] *n* speaker, talker.

parloir [parlwa:r] *nm* parlour.

parmi [parmi] *prep* among(st), amid(st).

Parnasse [parnɑ:s] *nf* Parnassus.

parodie [parɔdi] *nf* parody, skit.

parodier [parɔdje] *vt* to parody, do a skit on.

paroi [parwa] *nf* partition, wall, lining.

paroisse [parwas] *nf* parish.

paroissial [parwasjal] *a* parochial.

paroissien, -enne [parwasjɛ̃, jɛn] *a* parochial; *n* parishioner; *nm* prayerbook.

parole [parɔl] *nf* word, remark, parole, promise, (power of) speech; **po`ter la — ** to be the spokesman.

paroxysme [parɔksism] *nm* paroxysm, fit, outburst.

parquer [parke] *vt* to pen up, imprison, park.

parquet [parkɛ] *nm* floor(ing), public prosecutor's department.

parqueter [parkəte] *vt* to parquet, floor.

parqueterie [parkətri] *nf* laying of floors, parquetry.

parrain [parɛ̃] *nm* godfather, sponsor.

parricide [parisid] *a* parricidal; *nm* parricide.

parsemer [parsəme] *vt* to sprinkle, strew, dot.

part [pa:r] *nf* share, portion, part; **billet de faire — ** invitation, intimation (*wedding, funeral*); **prendre — à** to take part in, join in; **faire — de qch à qn** to acquaint s.o. with sth; **de — en — ** through and through; **de — et d'autre** on both sides; **d'une —, d'autre — ** on the one hand, on the other hand; **à — ** aside, except for.

partage [parta:ʒ] *nm* sharing, portion, allotment.

partager [partaʒe] *vt* to divide, share (out), apportion.

partance [partã:s] *nf* departure; **en — ** (outward) bound, outgoing.

partant [partã] *a* departing; *nm pl* departing guests, starters; *ad* therefore.

partenaire [partənɛ:r] *nm* partner.

parterre [partɛ:r] *nm* flower-bed, pit.

parti [parti] *nm* party, side advantage decision, course, match; **se ranger du — ** to side with; **en prendre son — ** to make the best of it; **tirer — de** to take advantage of;

— **pris** prejudice; *a* gone, away, tipsy.

partial [parsjal] *a* partial, prejudiced.

partialité [parsjalite] *nf* partiality, prejudice.

participation [partisipasjɔ̃] *nf* participation, share.

participe [partisip] *nm* participle.

participer [partisipe] *vi* to participate, share; — **de** to partake of, have something of.

particulariser [partikylarize] *vt* to particularize, specify; *vr* to be different from others.

particularité [partikylarite] *nf* particularity, peculiarity.

particule [partikyl] *nf* particle.

particulier, -ière [partikylje, jɛːr] *a* particular, peculiar, special, personal, private; *n* private individual.

partie [parti] *nf* part, party, game; **faire** — **de** to belong to, be part of; **se mettre de la** — to join in; **prendre à** — to call to account.

partiel [parsjɛl] *a* partial.

partir [partiːr] *vi* to depart, leave, set off, go away, start; — **(d'un éclat) de rire** to burst out laughing.

partisan [partizɑ̃] *nm* partisan, supporter, follower, guerrilla soldier.

partition [partisjɔ̃] *nf* partition, score.

partout [partu] *ad* everywhere; — **où** wherever.

parure [paryːr] *nf* adorning, ornament, dress, set of jewellery.

parution [parysjɔ̃] *nf* appearance, publication.

parvenir [parvəniːr] *vi* to arrive, reach, attain, manage, succeed.

parvenu [parvəny] *n* upstart.

parvis [parvi] *nm* parvis, square.

pas [pɑ] *ad* not; *nm* step, pace, tread, threshold, strait, pass; **mauvais** — awkward predicament; **à deux** — **d'ici** nearby, just round the corner; **au** — at walking pace, dead slow; **prendre le** — **sur** to take precedence over.

passable [pɑsabl] *a* passable, fair.

passage [pɑsaːʒ] *nm* passage, way through, passing, crossing, transition; **être de** — to be passing through; — **interdit** no thoroughfare.

passager, -ère [pɑsaʒe, ɛːr] *a* fleeting, short-lived; *n* passenger.

passant [pɑsɑ̃] *a* busy; *n* passer-by.

passe [pɑːs] *nf* pass(ing), channel, permit, thrust; **en** — **de** in a fair way to.

passementerie [pɑsmɑ̃tri] *nf* lace (trade), trimmings.

passe-montagne [pɑsmɔ̃taɲ] *nm* Balaclava (helmet).

passe-partout [pɑspartu] *nm* master-, (skeleton-)key.

passe-passe [pɑspɑs] *nm* sleight of hand.

passeport [pɑspɔːr] *nm* passport.

passé [pɑse] *a* past, over, faded; *nm* past.

passer [pɑse] *vt* to pass, hand, cross, ferry across, exceed, excuse, spend, strain, slip on; *vi* to pass (on, over, off, by, through), fade, call, to be shown, be promoted; *vr* to happen, take place, go off, be spent; — **un examen** to sit an examination; **faire** — to hand round; **se faire** — **pour** to pose as; **se** — **de** to do without.

passereau [pɑsro] *nm* sparrow.

passerelle [pɑsrɛl] *nf* foot-bridge, (ship) bridge, gangway.

passe-temps [pɑstɑ̃] *nm* pastime.

passeur, -euse [pɑsœːr, øːz] *n* ferryman (woman).

passible [pɑsibl] *a* liable.

passif, -ive [pɑsif, iːv] *a* passive; *nm* debit, liabilities, passive.

passion [pɑsjɔ̃] *nf* passion.

passionnel, -elle [pɑsjɔnɛl] *a* concerning the passions, caused by jealousy.

passionné [pɑsjɔne] *a* passionate, enthusiastic; *nmf* enthusiast.

passionner [pɑsjɔne] *vt* to impassion, thrill, excite, fill with enthusiasm; *vr* to become passionately fond (of **pour**), be enthusiastic (over **pour**).

passivité [pɑsivite] *nf* passivity.

passoire [pɑswaːr] *nf* strainer.

pastel [pɑstɛl] *nm* crayon, pastel (drawing).

pastèque [pɑstɛk] *nf* water-melon.

pasteur [pɑstœːr] *nm* shepherd, pastor, minister.

pasteuriser [pɑstœrize] *vt* to pasteurize.

pastiche [pɑstiʃ] *nm* pastiche, parody.

pastille [pɑstiːj] *nf* lozenge, drop, (rubber) patch.

pastis [pɑstis] *nm* aniseed aperitif, *a* muddle.

pastoral [pɑstɔral] *a* pastoral.

pat [pat] *a nm* stalemate.

pataquès [patakɛːs] *nm* faulty liaison.

patate [patat] *nf* (sweet) potato, (*fam*) spud.

patati [patati] *et* — **et patata** and so on and so forth.

pataud [pato] *a* clumsy, boorish.

patauger [patoʒe] *vi* to splash, flounder, paddle.

pâte [paːt] *nf* paste, dough, fufu (*W. African*); *pl* noodles, spaghetti *etc*; **être de la** — **des héros** to be of the stuff that heroes are made of; **quelle bonne** — **d'homme** what a decent chap.

pâté [pɑte] *nm* pie, blot, block.

patée [pɑte] *nf* mash, food.

patelin [patlɛ̃] *a* glib, wheedling; *nm* village.

patenôtre [patnoːtr] *nf* Lord's prayer.

patent [patɑ̃] *a* patent, obvious.
patente [patɑ̃:t] *nf* licence.
patenter [patɑ̃te] *vt* to license;
faire — to patent.
patère [patɛ:r] *nf* (hat-) coat-peg.
paterne [patɛrn] *a* patronizing.
paternel, -elle [patɛrnɛl] *a* paternal,
fatherly.
paternité [patɛrnite] *nf* paternity,
fatherhood.
pâteux, -euse [patø, ø:z] *a* doughy,
thick, coated.
pathétique [patetik] *a* pathetic,
touching; *nm* pathos.
pathologie [patɔlɔʒi] *nf* pathology.
pathos [patɔs] *nm* bathos.
patibulaire [patibylɛ:r] *a* of the
gallows, hangdog.
patiemment [pasjamɑ̃] *ad* patiently.
patience [pasjɑ̃:s] *nf* patience.
patient [pasjɑ̃] *a* patient, long-
suffering; *n* patient.
patienter [pasjɑ̃te] *vi* to have
patience.
patin [patɛ̃] *nm* skate, runner, skid;
—s à roulettes roller skates.
patine [patin] *nf* patina.
patiner [patine] *vi* to skate, slip.
patineur, -euse [patinœ:r, ø:z] *n*
skater.
patinoire [patinwa:r] *nf* skating-
rink.
pâtir [pɑti:r] *vi* to suffer.
pâtisserie [pɑtisri] *nf* pastry
(-making), cake-shop, tea-room; *pl*
cakes.
pâtissier, -ière [pɑtisje, jɛ:r] *n*
pastry-cook, tea-room proprietor.
patois [patwa] *nm* patois, dialect,
lingo.
patraque [patrak] *a* out of sorts,
seedy, rotten.
pâtre [pɑ:tr] *nm* herdsman, shepherd.
patriarche [patriarʃ] *nm* patriarch.
patrie [patri] *nf* native land, fatherland.
patrimoine [patrimwan] *nm* patrimony, heritage.
patriote [patriɔt] *a* patriotic; *nmf*
patriot.
patriotique [patriɔtik] *a* patriotic.
patriotisme [patriɔtism] *nm* patriotism.
patron, -onne [patrɔ̃, ɔn] *n* patron,
patron saint, protector, head, boss,
skipper; *nm* pattern, model.
patronal [patrɔnal] *a* of a patron
saint, of employers.
patronat [patrɔna] *nm* (body of)
employers.
patronner [patrɔne] *vt* to patronize,
support.
patrouille [patru:j] *nf* patrol.
patrouiller [patruje] *vi* to patrol.
patte [pat] *nf* paw, foot, leg, tab,
flap; **— de mouches** scrawl.
patte-d'oie [patdwa] *nf* crossroads;
pl crow's feet, wrinkles.
pattemouille [patmu:j] *f* damp
cloth (*for ironing*).

pâturage [pɑtyra:ʒ] *nm* grazing,
pasture.
pâture [pɑty:r] *nf* food, pasture.
paturon [patyrɔ̃] *nm* pastern.
paume [po:m] *nf* palm (of hand),
tennis.
paupière [popjɛ:r] *nf* eyelid.
paupiette [popjɛt] *nf* (meat) olive.
pause [po:z] *nf* pause, interval, rest;
—café tea-break.
pauvre [po:vr] *a* poor, scanty, sorry,
wretched, shabby; *n* poor man,
woman.
pauvresse [povrɛs] *nf* poor woman.
pauvreté [povrəte] *nf* poverty, want.
se pavaner [səpavane] *vr* to strut
(about).
pavé [pave] *nm* pavement, paved
road, paving-stone, slab; **battre le
—** to walk the streets; **prendre le
haut du —** to assume lordly airs.
pavillon [pavijɔ̃] *nm* pavilion, lodge,
flag, ear- (mouth)piece, bell (of brass
instrument); **— de jardin** summer-
house.
pavoiser [pavwaze] *vt* to deck with
flags, bunting.
pavot [pavo] *nm* poppy.
payable [pɛjabl] *a* payable.
payant [pɛjɑ̃] *a* paying; *n* payer.
paye [pɛ:j] *nf* pay, wages.
payement [pɛjmɑ̃] *nm* payment.
payer [pɛje] *vt* to pay (for), stand, treat;
vi to pay; **—d'audace** to brazen it out,
put a bold face on it; **— de mots** to
put off with fine talk; **— de la tête de
qn** to take a rise out of s.o.; **il est payé
pour le savoir** he knows it to his cost.
payeur, -euse [pɛjœ:r, ø:z] *n* payer,
teller, paymaster.
pays [pe(j)i] *nm* country, land,
district, locality; *n* (*f* **payse**) fellow-
countryman, -woman.
paysage [peiza:ʒ] *nm* landscape,
scenery.
paysagiste [peizaʒist] *nm* landscape
painter.
paysan, -anne [peizɑ̃, an] *an* peasant;
n countryman.
péage [pea:ʒ] *nm* toll.
peau [po] *nf* skin, hide, peel; **avoir
qn dans la —** to be head over heels
in love with s.o.; **faire — neuve** to
cast its skin, turn over a new leaf.
peau-rouge [poru:ʒ] *nm* redskin,
Red Indian.
peccadille [pɛkadi:j] *nf* peccadillo.
pêche [pɛʃ] *nf* fishing, fishery, catch,
peach.
péché [peʃe] *nm* sin.
pécher [peʃe] *vi* to sin.
pêcher [peʃe] *vt* to fish for, fish up;
vi to fish.
pêcherie [pɛʃri] *nf* fishery, fishing-
ground.
pécheur, -eresse [peʃœ:r, peʃrɛs] *a*
sinning; *n* sinner.
pêcheur, -euse [pɛʃœ:r, ø:z] *a*
fishing; *n* fisher, fisherman, -woman;
— à la ligne angler.

péculateur [pekylatœːr] nm peculator, embezzler.

pécule [pekyl] nf savings, nest-egg, gratuity.

pécuniaire [pekynjɛːr] a pecuniary.

pédagogie [pɛdagɔʒi] nf pedagogy.

pédagogique [pɛdagɔʒik] a pedagogic.

pédale [pɛdal] nf pedal, treadle.

pédaler [pɛdale] vi to pedal, cycle.

pédant [pɛdɑ̃] a pedantic; n pedant.

pédicure [pediky:r] n chiropodist.

pègre [pɛːgr] nf underworld.

peigne [pɛɲ] nm comb, card.

peigné [pɛɲe] a combed; **bien —** well-groomed; **mal —** unkempt, tousled.

peignée [pɛɲe] nf drubbing.

peigner [pɛɲe] vt to comb (out), card, dress down.

peignoir [pɛɲwaːr] nm (woman's) dressing-gown, wrap.

peindre [pɛ̃ːdr] vt to paint, depict.

peine [pɛn] nf penalty, punishment, affliction, sorrow, trouble, difficulty; **homme de —** labourer; **en être pour sa —** to have one's trouble for nothing; **à —** hardly, scarcely.

peiner [pɛne] vt to vex, grieve, pain; vi toil, drudge.

peintre [pɛ̃ːtr] nm painter, artist.

peinture [pɛ̃ty:r] nf painting, picture, paint.

péjoratif, -ive [peʒɔratif, iːv] a pejorative.

pelage [pəlaːʒ] nm coat, fur, wool.

pêle-mêle [pɛlmɛl] ad pell-mell, helter-skelter; nm jumble.

peler [p(ə)le] vt to peel, skin; vi to peel off.

pèlerin [pɛlrɛ̃] n pilgrim.

pèlerine [pɛlrin] nf cape.

pèlerinage [pɛlrinaːʒ] nm pilgrimage.

pélican [pelikɑ̃] nm pelican.

pelisse [p(ə)lis] nf pelisse, fur-lined coat.

pelle [pɛl] nf shovel, scoop.

pelleter [pɛlte] vt to shovel.

pelleterie [pɛltri] nf fur-trade, furriery.

pelletier, -ière [pɛltje, jɛːr] n furrier.

pellicule [pelikyl] nf pellicle, skin, film; pl dandruff.

pelote [plɔt] nf ball, wad, pin-cushion, pelota.

peloton [plɔtɔ̃] nm ball, group, squad, platoon.

pelotonner [plɔtɔne] vt to wind into a ball; vr to curl up, huddle together.

pelouse [pluːz] nf lawn, green, public enclosure.

peluche [plyʃ] nf plush, shag.

pelure [plyːr] nf peel, skin, rind; **papier —** copy paper.

pénal [penal] a penal.

pénalité [penalite] nf penalty.

penaud [pəno] a crestfallen, sheepish, abashed.

penchant [pɑ̃ʃɑ̃] nm slope, tendency.

penché [pɑ̃ʃe] a leaning, stooping.

pencher [pɑ̃ʃe] vt to bend, tilt; vi to lean, incline; vr to stoop, bend, lean.

pendable [pɑ̃dabl] a hanging, abominable.

pendaison [pɑ̃dɛzɔ̃] nf hanging.

pendant [pɑ̃dɑ̃] a hanging, pending, baggy; nm pendant, counterpoint; prep during, for; cj **— que** while, whilst.

pendeloque [pɑ̃dlɔk] nf pendant, drop, shred.

penderie [pɑ̃dri] nf wardrobe.

pendre [pɑ̃ːdr] vt to hang, hang up; vi to hang (down).

pendu [pɑ̃dy] a hanged, hanging.

pendule [pɑ̃dyl] nf clock; nm pendulum, balancer.

pêne [pɛːn] nm bolt, latch.

pénétrable [penetrabl] a penetrable.

pénétrant [penetrɑ̃] a penetrating, piercing, keen.

pénétration [penetrasjɔ̃] nf penetration, shrewdness, insight, perspicacity.

pénétré [penetre] a penetrated, imbued, full, earnest.

pénétrer [penetre] vt to penetrate, pierce, imbue, see through; vi to penetrate, enter, break (into); vr to become imbued, impregnated.

pénible [penibl] a painful, distressing, hard.

péniche [peniʃ] nf barge, lighter.

péninsule [penɛ̃syl] nf peninsula.

pénitence [penitɑ̃ːs] nf penitence, repentance, penance, disgrace.

pénitencier [penitɑ̃sje] nm penitentiary.

pénitent [penitɑ̃] an penitent.

pénitentiaire [penitɑ̃sjɛːr] a penitentiary.

penne [pɛn] nf quill, feather.

pénombre [penɔ̃ːbr] nf half-light, semi-darkness.

pensant [pɑ̃sɑ̃] a thinking; **bien —** orthodox, right-thinking, moral; **mal —** unorthodox, evil-thinking.

pensée [pɑ̃se] nf thought, idea, pansy.

penser [pɑ̃se] vti to think; **— à faire qch** to remember to do sth; **— le voir** to expect to see him; **il pensa mourir** he almost died; **vous n'y pensez pas** you don't mean it.

penseur, -euse [pɑ̃sœːr, øːz] n thinker.

pensif, -ive [pɑ̃sif, iːv] a pensive, thoughtful.

pension [pɑ̃sjɔ̃] nf pension, allowance, board and lodging, boarding-house, -school; **prendre — chez** to board, lodge with; **— de famille** residential hotel.

pensionnaire [pɑ̃sjɔnɛːr] n pensioner, boarder, inmate.

pensionnat [pɑ̃sjɔna] nm boarding-school, hostel.

pensum [pɛ̃sɔm] nm imposition, unpleasant task.

pentagonal [pɛ̃tagɔnal] *a* pentagonal.
pentagone [pɛ̃tagɔn] *a* pentagonal; *nm* pentagon.
pente [pɑ̃:t] *nf* slope, gradient, bent.
Pentecôte [pɑ̃tko:t] *nf* Whitsuntide.
pénurie [penyri] *nf* scarcity, shortage, poverty.
pépère [pepɛ:r] *a* first-class, easy; *nm* granddad, old chap.
pépier [pepje] *vi* to peep, chirp.
pépin [pepɛ̃] *nm* pip, stone, umbrella, (*fam*) hitch, trouble.
pépinière [pepinjɛ:r] *nf* nursery.
pepiniériste [pepinjerist] *nm* nurseryman.
pépite [pepit] *nf* nugget.
percale [pɛrkal] *nf* percale, chintz.
perçant [pɛrsɑ̃] *a* piercing, keen, shrill.
perce-neige [pɛrsnɛ:ʒ] *nm or f inv* snowdrop.
perce-oreille [pɛrsɔrɛ:j] *nm* earwig.
percepteur, -trice [pɛrsɛptœ:r, tris] *n* tax-collector.
perceptible [pɛrsɛptibl] *a* perceptible, audible, collectible.
perceptif, -ive [pɛrsɛptif, i:v] *a* perceptive.
perception [pɛrsɛpsjɔ̃] *nf* perception, collection, tax-office.
percée [pɛrse] *nf* cutting, opening, vista, break(through).
percer [pɛrse] *vt* to pierce, hole, go through, break through, broach, bore; *vi* to come through, break through.
perceuse [pɛrsø:z] *nf* drill.
percevable [pɛrsəvabl] *a* perceivable, leviable.
percevoir [pɛrsəvwa:r] *vt* to perceive, discern, collect.
perche [pɛrʃ] *nf* pole, rod, perch, lanky person.
percher [pɛrʃe] *vi* to roost, perch; *vr* to perch, alight.
percheron [pɛrʃərɔ̃] *nm* percheron, draught horse.
perchoir [pɛrʃwa:r] *nm* perch, roost.
perclus [pɛrkly] *a* stiff, crippled, paralysed.
perçoir [pɛrswa:r] *nm* gimlet, awl, broach.
percolateur [pɛrkɔlatœ:r] *nm* percolator.
percussion [pɛrkysjɔ̃] *nf* percussion.
percutant [pɛrkytɑ̃] *a* percussive, percussion.
percuter [pɛrkyte] *vt* to strike, tap.
perdant [pɛrdɑ̃] *a* losing; *n* loser.
perdition [pɛrdisjɔ̃] *nf* perdition; **en** — sinking, on the road to ruin.
perdre [pɛrdr] *vt* to lose, waste, ruin. *vi* to lose, deteriorate; *vr* to get lost, go to waste, disappear; il s'y **perd** he can't make anything of it.
perdu [pɛrdy] *a* lost, ruined, doomed, wasted, spare, distracted; à **corps** — recklessly.
perdreau [pɛrdro] *nm* young partridge.

perdrix [pɛrdri] *nf* partridge.
père [pɛr] *nm* father, senior.
péremptoire [perɑ̃ptwa:r] *a* peremptory, final.
pérennité [perɛnnite] *nf* perenniality.
perfectible [pɛrfɛktibl] *a* perfectible.
perfection [pɛrfɛksjɔ̃] *nf* perfection, faultlessness.
perfectionnement [pɛrfɛksjɔnmɑ̃] *nm* perfecting, improving.
perfectionner [pɛrfɛksjɔne] *vt* to perfect, improve.
perfide [pɛrfid] *a* perfidious, treacherous.
perfidie [pɛrfidi] *nf* (act of) perfidy, perfidiousness.
perforant [pɛrfɔrɑ̃] *a* perforating, armour-piercing.
perforateur, -trice [pɛrfɔratœ:r, tris] *a* perforating.
perforatrice [pɛrfɔratris] *nf* drill.
perforation [pɛrfɔrasjɔ̃] *nf* perforation, drilling.
performance [pɛrfɔrmɑ̃:s] *nf* performance.
péricliter [periklite] *vi* to be shaky, in jeopardy.
péril [peril] *nm* peril, risk, danger.
périlleux, -euse [perijø, ø:z] *a* perilous, hazardous; **saut** — somersault.
périmé [perime] *a* out of date, not valid, expired.
périmètre [perimɛtr] *nm* perimeter.
période [perjɔd] *nf* period, era, spell.
périodique [perjɔdik] *a* periodical, recurring; *nm* periodical.
péripétie [peripesi] *nf* vicissitude, change.
périphérie [periferi] *nf* periphery, circumference.
périphrase [perifra:z] *nf* periphrasis.
périr [peri:r] *vi* to perish, die, be lost.
périscope [periskɔp] *nm* periscope.
périssable [perisabl] *a* perishable, mortal.
périssoire [periswa:r] *nf* canoe, skiff.
péristyle [peristil] *nm* peristyle.
péritonite [peritɔnit] *nf* peritonitis.
perle [pɛrl] *nf* pearl, bead, drop.
perler [pɛrle] *vt* to pearl, husk; *vi* to form in beads.
permanence [pɛrmanɑ̃:s] *nf* permanence; **en** — continuous, permanent(ly).
permanent [pɛrmanɑ̃] *a* continuous, standing.
permanente [pɛrmanɑ̃t] *nf* permanent wave.
perméable [pɛrmeabl] *a* permeable, pervious.
permettre [pɛrmɛtr] *vt* to permit, allow, enable; *vr* to take the liberty, indulge (in de).
permis [pɛrmi] *a* permitted, allowed, permissible; *nm* permit, licence.
permission [pɛrmisjɔ̃] *nf* permission, leave, pass.

permissionnaire [pɛrmisjɔnɛːr] *nm* person, soldier on leave.

permutation [pɛrmytasjɔ̃] *nf* permutation, exchange.

permuter [pɛrmyte] *vt* to exchange, permute.

pernicieux, -euse [pɛrnisjø, øːz] *a* pernicious, hurtful.

pérorer [perɔre] *vi* to deliver a harangue, expatiate.

perpendiculaire [pɛrpɑ̃dikylɛːr] *a nf* perpendicular.

perpétrer [pɛrpetre] *vt* to perpetrate.

perpétuel, -elle [pɛrpetɥɛl] *a* perpetual, endless.

perpétuer [pɛrpetɥe] *vt* to perpetuate; *vr* to last.

perpétuité [pɛrpetɥite] *nf* perpetuity; à — in perpetuity, for life.

perplexe [pɛrplɛks] *a* perplexed, at a loss, perplexing.

perplexité [pɛrplɛksite] *nf* perplexity, confusion.

perquisition [pɛrkizisjɔ̃] *nf* search, inquiry.

perquisitionner [pɛrkizisjɔne] *vi* to search.

perron [pɛrɔ̃] *nm* (flight of) steps.

perroquet [pɛrɔkɛ] *nm* parrot.

perruche [pɛryʃ] *nf* hen-parrot, parakeet.

perruque [pɛryk] *nf* wig, fogey.

perruquier, -ière [pɛrykje, jɛːr] *n* wigmaker.

pers [pɛːr] *a* bluish-green.

persan [pɛrsɑ̃] *an* Persian.

Perse [pɛrs] *nf* Persia.

persécuter [pɛrsekyte] *vt* to persecute, plague, dun.

persécution [pɛrsekysjɔ̃] *nf* persecution, pestering.

persévérance [pɛrseverɑ̃s] *nf* perseverance, doggedness, steadfastness.

persévérant [pɛrseverɑ̃] *a* persevering, dogged.

persévérer [pɛrsevere] *vi* to persevere, persist.

persienne [pɛrsjɛn] *nf* venetian blind, shutter.

persiflage [pɛrsiflaːʒ] *nm* persiflage, banter, chaff.

persil [pɛrsi] *nm* parsley.

persillé [pɛrsije] *a* blue-moulded, spotted with fat.

persistance [pɛrsistɑ̃s] *nf* persistence, continuance, doggedness.

persistant [pɛrsistɑ̃] *a* persistent, dogged, steady.

persister [pɛrsiste] *vi* to persist, continue.

personnage [pɛrsɔnaːʒ] *nm* personage, character, individual, notability.

personnalité [pɛrsɔnalite] *nf* personality, personal remark, person of note.

personne [pɛrsɔn] *nf* person, individual; *pn* anyone, anybody, no one, nobody.

personnel, -elle [pɛrsɔnɛl] *a* personal, not transferable; *nm* personnel, staff.

personnification [pɛrsɔnifikasjɔ̃] *nf* personification.

personnifier [pɛrsɔnifje] *vt* to personify.

perspective [pɛrspɛktiːv] *nf* perspective, prospect, outlook, vista.

perspicace [pɛrspikas] *a* perspicacious, astute.

perspicacité [pɛrspikasite] *nf* perspicacity, insight, astuteness.

persuader [pɛrsɥade] *vt* to persuade, convince, induce.

persuasif, -ive [pɛrsɥazif, iːv] *a* persuasive.

persuasion [pɛrsɥazjɔ̃] *nf* persuasion, conviction.

perte [pɛrt] *nf* loss, waste, ruin; à — de vue as far as the eye can see.

pertinence [pɛrtinɑ̃s] *nf* pertinence, pertinency, relevancy.

pertinent [pɛrtinɑ̃] *a* pertinent, relevant.

perturbation [pɛrtyrbasjɔ̃] *nf* perturbation, disturbance, trepidation.

pervenche [pɛrvɑ̃ʃ] *nf* periwinkle.

pervers [pɛrvɛːr] *a* perverse, depraved.

perversion [pɛrvɛrsjɔ̃] *nf* perversion, corruption.

perversité [pɛrvɛrsite] *nf* perversity, depravity.

pervertir [pɛrvɛrtiːr] *vt* to pervert, corrupt; *vr* to become depraved, corrupted.

pesage [pəzaːʒ] *nm* weighing, paddock.

pesant [pəzɑ̃] *a* heavy, ponderous; *nm* weight.

pesanteur [pəzɑ̃tœːr] *nf* weight, heaviness.

pesée [pəze] *nf* weighing, leverage.

pèse-lettres [pɛzlɛtr] *nm* letter-balance.

peser [pəze] *vt* to weigh, ponder; *vi* to weigh, hang heavy, be a burden (to **sur**), stress.

pessimisme [pɛsimism] *nm* pessimism, despondency.

pessimiste [pɛsimist] *a* pessimistic; *n* pessimist.

peste [pɛst] *nf* plague, pestilence, pest.

pester [pɛste] *vi* to curse, storm (at **contre**).

pestifère [pɛstifɛːr] *a* pestiferous, pestilential.

pet [pɛ] *nm* fart; — de nonne fritter.

pétale [petal] *nm* petal.

pétarade [petarad] *nf* crackling, backfire, succession of bangs.

pétarader [petarade] *vi* to make a succession of bangs, backfire.

pétard [petaːr] *nm* detonator, blast, squib, fog-signal.

péter [pete] *vi* to fart, pop, bang, crackle, come off.

pétiller [petije] *vi* to spark(le), fizz, bubble, crackle.

petit [pəti] *a* small, little, tiny, petty; *n* little boy, girl, pup, kitten, cub, whelp.

petit-beurre [pətibœːr] *nm* biscuit.

petite-fille [pətitfiːj] *nf* granddaughter.

petitement [pətitmã] *ad* in a limited way, pettily, half-heartedly.

petitesse [pətitɛs] *nf* smallness, tininess, pettiness, mean act, thing.

petit-fils [pətifis] *nm* grandson.

petit-gris [pətigri] *nm* squirrel (fur).

pétition [petisjɔ̃] *nf* petition.

pétitionner [petisjɔne] *vi* to make a petition.

petit-lait [pətilɛ] *nm* whey.

petit-maître [pətimɛtr] *nm* fop, dandy.

petits-enfants [pətizãfã] *nm pl* grandchildren.

pétrifier [petrifje] *vt* to petrify; *vr* to be petrified, turn into stone.

pétrin [petrɛ̃] *nm* kneading-trough; **dans le — in the soup, in a fix.

pétrir [petriːr] *vt* to knead, mould, shape; **pétri d'orgueil** bursting with pride.

pétrole [petrɔl] *nm* petroleum, paraffin, oil.

pétrolier [petrɔlje] *a* oil; *nm* oil-tanker.

pétrolifère [petrɔlifɛːr] *a* oil(bearing).

pétulance [petylãːs] *nf* liveliness, impulsiveness.

peu [pø] *ad* little, not much, few, not many, not very, dis-, un-, -less; **un — a little, rather, just; — à — little by little; avant —, d'ici — before long; à — près almost; quelque — not a little, somewhat; pour — que however little.

peuplade [pœplad] *nf* tribe.

peuple [pœpl] *nm* people, nation, masses; **petit — lower classes.

peupler [pœple] *vt* to populate, stock, throng; *vr* to become populous, peopled.

peuplier [pøplje] *nm* poplar.

peur [pœːr] *nf* fear, fright; **avoir une — bleue** to be in a blue funk; **à faire — frightfully; faire — à** to frighten; **de — que** lest, for fear that.

peureux, -euse [pœrø, øːz] *a* timorous, timid.

peut-être [pøtɛːtr] *ad* perhaps, maybe.

phacochère [fakɔʃɛːr] *nm* warthog.

phalange [falãːʒ] *nf* phalanx, finger, toe-joint; host.

phalène [falɛn] *nf* moth.

pharamineux, -euse [faraminø, øːz] *a* colossal, terrific.

phare [faːr] *nm* lighthouse, beacon, headlight.

pharmaceutique [farmasøtik] *a* pharmaceutic(al).

pharmacie [farmasi] *nf* pharmacy, chemist's shop, dispensary; **armoire à — medicine-chest.

pharmacien, -enne [farmasjɛ̃, jɛn] *n* chemist, druggist.

pharyngite [farɛ̃ʒit] *nf* pharyngitis.

phase [faːz] *n* phase, stage, phasis.

phénique [fenik] *a* carbolic.

phénix [feniks] *nm* phœnix, paragon.

phénoménal [fenɔmenal] *a* phenomenal.

phénomène [fenɔmɛn] *nm* phenomenon, freak, marvel.

philanthrope [filãtrɔp] *nm* philanthropist.

philanthropie [filãtrɔpi] *nf* philanthropy.

philatéliste [filatelist] *n* philatelist, stamp-collector.

philistin [filistɛ̃] *an* Philistine.

philologie [filɔlɔʒi] *nf* philology.

philosophe [filɔzɔf] *a* philosophical; *n* philosopher.

philosophie [filɔzofi] *nf* philosophy.

philosophique [filɔzɔfik] *a* philosophical.

phobie [fɔbi] *nf* phobia.

phonétique [fɔnetik] *a* phonetic; *nf* phonetics.

phonologie [fɔnɔlɔʒi] *nf* phonology, phonemics.

phoque [fɔk] *nm* seal.

phosphate [fɔsfat] *nm* phosphate.

phosphore [fɔsfɔːr] *nm* phosphorus.

phosphorescence [fɔsfɔresãːs] *nf* phosphorescence.

photo [fɔto] *nf* photo.

photogénique [fɔtɔʒenik] *a* photogenic.

photographe [fɔtɔgraf] *nm* photographer.

photographie [fɔtɔgrafi] *nf* photography, photograph.

photographier [fɔtɔgrafje] *vt* to photograph.

phrase [fraːz] *nf* sentence, phrase; **faire des —s** to use flowery language.

phraseur, -euse [frazœːr, øːz] *n* wordy speaker, empty talker.

phtisie [ftizi] *nf* phthisis, consumption.

phtisique [ftizik] *an* consumptive.

physicien, -enne [fizisjɛ̃, jɛn] *n* physicist, natural philosopher.

physiologie [fizjɔlɔʒi] *nf* physiology.

physiologique [fizjɔlɔʒik] *a* physiological.

physionomie [fizjɔnɔmi] *nf* physiognomy, countenance.

physique [fizik] *a* physical, bodily; *nm* physique; *nf* physics, natural philosophy.

piaffer [pjafe] *vi* to prance, paw the ground, swagger.

piailler [pjaje] *vi* to cheep, squeal, squall.

pianiste [pjanist] *n* pianist.

piano [pjano] *nm* piano; **— à queue grand piano.

pianoter [pjanɔte] *vi* to strum, drum, tap.

piauler [pjole] *vi* to cheep, whimper.
piaule [pjol] *nf* digs.
pic [pik] *nm* pick(axe), peak, woodpecker; à — sheer, steep(ly), at the right moment.
pichenette [piʃnɛt] *nf* flick, fillip.
picorer [pikɔre] *vt* to steal, pilfer; *vi* to scratch about for food, pick.
picoter [pikɔte] *vt* to peck (at), prick, sting; *vi* prickle, smart, tingle.
pic-vert [pivɛːr] *nm* green woodpecker.
pie [pi] *a* piebald; *n* piebald horse; *nf* magpie.
pièce [pjɛs] *nf* piece, part, patch, room, coin, document, cask; — de théâtre play; — d'eau ornamental lake; de toutes —s completely, out of nothing; travailler à la — to do piece-work; trois francs la — three francs a piece.
pied [pje] *nm* foot(ing), base, leg (*chair*), stem, scale; — de laitue head of lettuce; au — levé offhand, at a moment's notice; ur — afoot, up; perdre — to lose one's footing, to get out of one's depth; lever le — to clear out, elope.
pied-à-terre [pjetatɛːr] *nm* occasional residence.
pied-d'alouette [pjedalwɛt] *nm* larkspur.
piédestal [pjedɛstal] *nm* pedestal.
piège [pjɛʒ] *nm* snare, trap; tendre un — to set a trap.
pierraille [pjɛraːj] *nf* rubble, roadmetal.
pierre [pjɛːr] *nf* stone; c'est une — dans votre jardin it is a dig at you.
Pierre [pjɛːr] Peter.
pierreries [pjɛrəri] *nf pl* jewels, gems.
pierreux, -euse [pjɛrø, øːz] *a* stony, gritty.
piété [pjete] *nf* piety, godliness.
piétiner [pjetine] *vt* to trample (down), tread, stamp on; *vi* to stamp; — sur place to mark time.
piéton [pjetɔ̃] *nm* pedestrian.
piètre [pjɛtr] *a* poor, paltry, sorry.
pieu [pjø] *nm* post, stake, pile, (*fam*) bed.
pieuvre [pjœːvr] *nf* octopus.
pieux, -euse [pjø, øːz] *a* pious, religious, reverent.
pige [piːʒ] *nf* measuring rod.
pigeon, -onne [piʒɔ̃, ɔn] *n* pigeon, greenhorn.
pigeonnier [piʒɔnje] *nm* dovecote.
piger [piʒe] *vt* to look at, twig, understand, catch; *vi* to understand, get it.
pigment [pigmɑ̃] *nm* pigment.
pignon [piɲɔ̃] *nm* gable, pinion.
pignouf [piɲuf] *nm* 'out, skinflint.
pile [pil] *nf* pile, heap, battery, pier, thrashing; — ou face heads or tails; s'arrêter — to stop dead.
piler [pile] *vt* to crush, pound.

pilier [pilje] *nm* pillar, column, shaft.
pillage [pijaːʒ] *nm* pillage, looting, ransacking.
piller [pije] *vt* to pillage, loot, plunder, ransack, rifle.
pilon [pilɔ̃] *nm* pestle, steamhammer, (*fam*) drumstick.
pilori [pilɔri] *nm* pillory.
pilot [pilo] *nm* pile.
pilotage [pilɔtaːʒ] *nm* pile-driving, piloting, driving.
pilote [pilɔt] *nm* pilot.
piloter [pilɔte] *vt* to pilot, fly, drive.
pilotis [pilɔti] *nm* pile (*foundation*).
pilule [pilyl] *nf* pill.
pimbêche [pɛ̃bɛʃ] *nf* unpleasant, supercilious woman, sour puss, catty woman.
piment [pimɑ̃] *nm* spice, red pepper.
pimenter [pimɑ̃te] *vt* to season, spice.
pimpant [pɛ̃pɑ̃] *a* spruce.
pin [pɛ̃] *nm* pine, fir-tree.
pinacle [pinakl] *nm* pinnacle.
pinard [pinaːr] *nm* wine.
pince [pɛ̃s] *nf* pincers, tongs, pliers, forceps tweezers, clip, peg, claw, grip — monseigneur jemmy.
pinceau [pɛ̃so] *nm* (paint)brush.
pincé [pɛ̃se] *a* supercilious, huffy, prim; *nm* pizzicato.
pincée [pɛ̃se] *nf* pinch.
pince-nez [pɛ̃sne] *nm* eye-glasses, pince-nez.
pincer [pɛ̃se] *vt* to pinch, nip (off), pluck, nab, grip; — les lèvres to purse one's mouth.
pince-sans-rire [pɛ̃sɑ̃riːr] *nm* person with a dry sense of humour.
pingouin [pɛ̃gwɛ̃] *nm* penguin, auk.
pingre [pɛ̃gr] *a* stingy mean; *nm* skinflint, screw.
pinson [pɛ̃sɔ̃] *nm* finch, chaffinch.
pintade [pɛ̃tad] *nf* guinea-fowl.
pioche [pjɔʃ] *nf* pickaxe, mattock.
piocher [pjɔʃe] *vt* to dig (with a pick), wot (up).
piocheur, -euse [pjɔʃœr, øːz] *nm* pickman, navvy digger; *n* swot.
piolet [pjɔlɛ] *nm* ice-axe.
pion [pjɔ̃] *nm* pawn, (*draughts*) piece; monitor.
pioncer [pjɔ̃se] *vi* to sleep, snooze.
pionnier [pjɔnje] *nm* pioneer.
pipe [pip] *nf* pipe, tube.
pipeau [pipo] *nm* reed-pipe, bird-call.
piper [pipe] *vt* to lure, decoy.
pipi [pipi] *nm* faire — to piddle, pee.
piquant [pikɑ̃] *a* stinging, prickly, cutting, pungent, piquant, spicy, tart; *nm* prickle, quill, pungency, point.
pique [pik] *nm* spade(s) (*cards*); *n* pike, spite.
piqué [pike] *a* quilted, padded, (worm)eaten, spotted, dotty, staccato; *nm* pique, quilting, diving; bombarder en — to dive-bomb; pas — des vers first rate.

pique-assiette [pikasjɛt] *nm* sponger.
pique-nique [piknik] *nm* picnic;
faire (un) — to picnic
piquer [pike] *vt* to prick, bite, sting,
make smart, excite, spur, stitch,
nettle, dive, give an injection to;
— une tête to take a header; *vr* to
prick oneself, to get nettled, excited,
become eaten up (with **de**), to pride
oneself (on **de**).
piquet [pike] *nm* stake, peg, picket,
(*cards*) piquet.
piqueter [pikte] *vt* to stake (out),
peg out, picket, spot, dot.
piquette [pikɛt] *nf* poor wine.
piqueur, **-euse** [pikœːr, øːz] *n*
whipper-in, huntsman.
piqûre [pikyːr] *nf* sting, bite, prick,
injection, stitching.
pirate [pirat] *nm* pirate.
pire [piːr] *a* worse, worst; *comp sup*
of **mauvais**; *nm* worst, worst of it.
pirogue [pirɔg] *nf* canoe, surf boat.
pirouette [pirwɛt] *nf* pirouette,
whirligig.
pirouetter [pirwɛte] *vi* to pirouette.
pis [pis] *nm* udder, dug, pap; *ad*
worse, worst; *comp sup* of **mal**; **de mal
en —** from bad to worse.
pis-aller [pizale] *nm* makeshift, last
resource; **au —** at the worst.
piscine [pisin] *nf* swimming-bath,
-pool.
pisé [pize] *nm* puddled clay.
pissenlit [pisɑ̃li] dandelion.
pissotière [pisɔtjɛːr] *nf* public urinal.
pistache [pistaʃ] *nf* pistachio (nut).
piste [pist] *nf* track, trail, race-track,
rink, floor; **— de décollage** runway;
route à double — dual carriageway;
— sonore sound track; **faire fausse
—** to be on the wrong track.
pistolet [pistɔlɛ] *nm* pistol.
piston [pistɔ̃] *nm* piston, ram, valve,
influence.
pistonner [pistɔne] *vt* to push (on),
use one's influence for, help on.
pitance [pitɑ̃s] *nf* allowance,
pittance.
piteux, **-euse** [pitø, øːz] *a* piteous,
sorry; **faire piteuse mine** to look
woe-begone.
pitié [pitje] *nf* pity, mercy, compassion; **avec —** compassionately;
elle lui fait — he is sorry for her;
prendre qn en — to take pity on
s.o.
piton [pitɔ̃] *nm* eyebolt, peak.
pitoyable [pitwajabl] *a* pitiful,
piteous, wretched.
pitre [pitr] *nm* clown.
pittoresque [pitɔrɛsk] *a* picturesque, graphic; *nm* picturesqueness.
pivert [pivɛr] *nm* green woodpecker.
pivoine [pivwan] *nf* peony.
pivot [pivo] *nm* pivot, pin, swivel.
pivoter [pivɔte] *vi* to pivot, swivel,
hinge, turn.
placage [plakaːʒ] *nm* plating, veneer-
ing.

placard [plakaːr] *nm* cupboard, bill,
poster, panel.
placarder [plakarde] *vt* to post up,
stick bills on.
place [plas] *nf* place, seat, post, job,
room, square; **faire —** à to make
room, way, for; **— forte** fortress.
placement [plasmɑ̃] *nm* investing,
investment, placing, sale, employment.
placer [plase] *vt* to place, put, find a
seat (a post) for, invest, sell; *vr* to
take up one's position, take a seat,
get a post.
placet [plasɛ] *nm* petition.
placidité [plasidite] *nf* placidity.
plafond [plafɔ̃] *nm* ceiling, maximum.
plafonnier [plafɔnje] *nm* ceiling
light.
plage [plaːʒ] *nf* beach, shore, seaside
resort.
plagiaire [plaʒjɛːr] *a nm* plagiarist.
plagiat [plaʒja] *nm* plagiarism.
plagier [plaʒje] *vt* to plagiarize.
plaid [plɛ] *nm* plaid, travelling-rug.
plaider [plɛde] *vti* to plead, argue.
plaideur, **-euse** [plɛdœr, øːz] *n*
suitor, litigant.
plaidoirie [plɛdwari] *nf* pleading,
speech.
plaidoyer [plɛdwaje] *nm* speech for
the defence.
plaie [plɛ] *nf* wound, sore, evil.
plaignant [plɛɲɑ̃] *n* plaintiff, prosecutor.
plain-chant [plɛ̃ʃɑ̃] *nm* plainsong.
plaindre [plɛ̃dr] *vt* to pity, be sorry
for; *vr* to complain.
plaine [plɛn] *nf* plain, flat country,
open country.
plain-pied [plɛ̃pje] *ad* **de —** level,
on one floor, smoothly, straight.
plainte [plɛ̃t] *nf* complaint, moan,
lament; **porter — contre** to make
a complaint against.
plaintif, **-ive** [plɛtif, iːv] *a* plaintive,
doleful, mournful.
plaire [plɛːr] *vt* to please, appeal to;
vr to take pleasure, thrive, like it,
be happy; **s'il vous plaît** please;
plaît-il? I beg your pardon?
plaisance [plɛzɑːs] *nf* **maison de —**
country seat; **bateau de —** pleasure
boat
plaisant [plɛzɑ̃] *a* funny, amusing;
nm joker, wag; **mauvais —** practical
joker.
plaisanter [plɛzɑ̃te] *vi* to joke, jest;
vt to banter, chaff.
plaisanterie [plɛzɑ̃tri] *nf* joke,
jest(ing); **entendre la —** to be able
to take a joke.
plaisir [plɛziːr] *nm* pleasure, enjoyment, favour; **à —** without reason,
freely; **au —** I hope we shall meet
again; **par —** for the fun of the
thing; **partie de —** pleasure-trip,
-party, outing, picnic.
plan [plɑ̃] *a* even, flat, level; *nm*
plane, plan, scheme, draft; **gros —**

close-up; **premier —** foreground; **en —** in the lurch.

planche [plɑ̃:ʃ] *nf* plank, board, shelf, plate, engraving; *pl* boards, stage; **— de bord** dashboard; **— de salut** sheet-anchor, last hope; **faire la —** to float on one's back.

planchéier [plɑ̃ʃeje] *vt* to floor, board (over).

plancher [plɑ̃ʃe] *nm* floor(ing), floor-board.

planer [plane] *vt* to plane, smooth; *vi* to hover, glide, soar.

pianète [planɛt] *nf* planet.

planeur [planœ:r] *nm* glider.

planquer [plɑ̃ke] (*fam*) *vt* to hide; *vr* to take cover.

plant [plɑ̃] *nm* plantation, patch, sapling, seedling.

plantain [plɑ̃tɛ̃] *nm* plantain.

plantation [plɑ̃tasjɔ̃] *nf* planting, plantation.

plante [plɑ̃:t] *nf* plant, sole (of foot); **jardin des —s** botanical gardens.

planter [plɑ̃te] *vt* to plant, set, fix, stick; *vr* to station oneself, stand; **— là** to leave in the lurch.

planteur [plɑ̃tœ:r] *nm* planter, grower.

planton [plɑ̃tɔ̃] *nm* orderly.

plantureux, -euse [plɑ̃tyrø, ø:z] *a* abundant, copious, rich, lush.

plaquage [plaka:ʒ] *nm* throwing over, (rugby) tackle.

plaque [plak] *nf* sheet, plate, slab, tablet, plaque, disk.

plaqué [plake] *a* plated, veneered; *nm* veneered wood, plated metal, electroplate.

plaquer [plake] *vt* to plate, veneer, plaster, throw over, drop, tackle, lay flat; *vr* to lie down flat, pancake.

plaquette [plakɛt] *nf* tablet, booklet.

plastique [plastik] *a* plastic; *nf* (art of) modelling, plastic art, plastic.

plastron [plastrɔ̃] *nm* breast-plate, shirt-front.

plastronner [plastrone] *vi* to swagger, strut, pose.

plat [pla] *a* flat, level, dull, tame; *nm* flat, dish, course, flat-racing; **à — flat**, run down, all in; **faire du — à** to toady to, fawn upon; **à — ventre** flat on the ground.

platane [platan] *nm* plane-tree.

plat-bord [plabɔ:r] *nm* gunwale.

plateau [plato] *nm* tray, plateau, platform, turntable.

plate-bande [platbɑ̃:d] *nf* flowerbed.

plate-forme [platform] *nf* platform, footplate.

platine [platin] *nm* platinum.

platiner [platine] *vt* to platinum-plate.

platitude [platityd] *nf* platitude, dullness.

plâtras [plɑtrɑ] *nm* broken plaster, rubbish.

plâtre [plɑ:tr] *nm* plaster; *pl* plaster-work.

plâtrer [plɑtre] *vt* to plaster (up).

plausible [plozibl] *a* plausible.

plébiscite [plebissit] *nm* plebiscite.

plein [plɛ̃] *a* full, big, solid; **en — right** in the middle (of), out and out; *nm* **avoir son —** to be fully loaded; **battre son —** to be in full swing; **faire le —** to fill up (with de).

plénière [plenjɛ:r] *a* plenary, full, complete.

plénipotentiaire [plenipɔtɑ̃sjɛ:r] *a nm* plenipotentiary.

plénitude [plenityd] *nf* plenitude, fullness.

pléonastique [pleɔnastik] *a* pleon-astic.

pleurard [plœra:r] *a* tearful, snivel-ling; *n* sniveller.

pleurer [plœre] *vt* to weep for, mourn (for); *vi* weep, cry, drip.

pleurésie [plœrezi] *nf* pleurisy.

pleureur, -euse [plœrœ:r, ø:z] *a* tearful, whimpering; *n* whimperer, mourner.

pleurnicher [plœrniʃe] *vi* to whine, snivel.

pleutre [plø:tr] *nm* coward.

pleuvoir [plœvwa:r] *vi* to rain; **— à verse** to pour.

pli [pli] *nm* fold, pleat, crease, pucker, envelope, cover, note, habit, trick.

pliant [pliɑ̃] *a* pliant, flexible, collapsible; *nm* camp-stool, folding chair.

plie [pli] *nf* plaice.

plier [plie] *vt* to fold (up), bend; *vi* to bend, give way; *vr* to submit, yield.

plinthe [plɛ̃:t] *nf* plinth, skirting-board.

plissé [plise] *a* pleated; *nm* pleats, pleating.

plissement [plismɑ̃] *nm* pleating, creasing, crumpling.

plisser [plise] *vt* to pleat, crumple, crease, corrugate.

plomb [plɔ̃] *nm* lead, shot, fuse; **de — leaden**; **à — vertical(ly)**; **fil à — plumbline**; **faire sauter les —s** to blow the fuses.

plombage [plɔ̃ba:ʒ] *nm* leading, stopping, (tooth) filling.

plombagine [plɔ̃baʒin] *nf* blacklead, graphite.

plomber [plɔ̃be] *vt* to (cover with) lead, stop (tooth).

plomberie [plɔ̃bri] *nf* plumbing, plumber's shop, lead-works.

plombier [plɔ̃bje] *nm* plumber, lead-worker.

plongeoir [plɔ̃ʒwa:r] *nm* diving-board.

plongeon [plɔ̃ʒɔ̃] *nm* dive, plunge, diver.

plongée [plɔ̃ʒe] *nf* dive, plunge.

plonger [plɔ̃ʒe] *vt* to plunge, im-merse, thrust; *vi* to dive, plunge, dip; *vr* to immerse oneself, devote oneself (to dans).

plongeur, -euse [plɔ̃ʒœːr, øːz] *a* diving; *n* diver, bottlewasher, dishwasher.

ploutocrate [plutɔkrat] *nm* plutocrat.

ployer [plwaje] *vt* to bend; *vi* to give way, bow.

pluie [plɥi] *nf* rain.

plumage [plymaːʒ] *nm* plumage, feathers.

plumard [plymaːr] *nm* (*fam*) bed.

plume [plym] *nf* feather, quill, pen, nib.

plumeau [plymo] *vt* feather duster.

plumer [plyme] *vt* to pluck, fleece.

plumet [plymɛ] *nm* plume, ostrich feather.

plumier [plymje] *nm* pencil-case.

plupart (la) [(la)plypaːr] *nf* (the) most, greatest or greater part, majority; **pour la** — mostly.

plural [plyral] *a* plural.

pluralité [plyralite] *nf* plurality, multiplicity.

pluriel, -elle [plyrjɛl] *a nm* plural.

plus [ply(s)] *ad* more, most, plus, in addition; *nm* more, most; — (**et**) — **the more** . . . **the more**; **tant et** — any amount; — **de** more, more than, no more; **ne** . . . **plus** no more, no longer, not now, not again; **de** — more, besides; **en** — extra, into the bargain; **en** — **de** over and above; **non** — either; **tout au** — at the very most.

plusieurs [plyzjœːr] *a pn* several.

plus-que-parfait [plyskəparfɛ] *nm* pluperfect.

plus-value [plyvaly] *nf* appreciation, increase (in value).

plutôt [plyto] *ad* rather, sooner, on the whole.

pluvier [plyvje] *nm* plover.

pluvieux, -euse [plyvjø, øːz] *a* rainy, wet.

pneu [pnø] *nm* tyre.

pneumatique [pnømatik] *a* pneumatic, air-; *nm* tyre, express letter.

pneumonie [pnømɔni] *nf* pneumonia.

pochard [pɔʃaːr] *n* boozer.

poche [pɔʃ] *nf* pocket, pouch, bag; **acheter chat en** — to buy a pig in a poke; **y être de sa** — to be out of pocket.

pocher [pɔʃe] *vt* to poach, dash off; *vi* to get baggy, to crease; — **l'œil à qn** to give s.o. a black eye.

pochette [pɔʃɛt] *nf* small pocket, handbag, fancy handkerchief, small fiddle.

pochoir [pɔʃwaːr] *nm* stencil.

poêle [pwaːl, pwal] *nm* stove, pall; *nf* frying pan.

poème [pɔɛːm] *nm* poem.

poésie [pɔezi] *nf* poetry, poem.

poète [pɔɛt] *a* poetic; *nm* poet.

poétique [pɔetik] *a* poetic(al); *nf* poetics.

pognon [pɔɲɔ̃] *nm* money, dough.

poids [pwɑ] *nm* weight, burden, importance; **prendre du** — to put on weight.

poignant [pwaɲɑ̃] *a* poignant, soul-stirring.

poignard [pwaɲaːr] *nm* dagger.

poignarder [pwaɲarde] *vt* to stab.

poigne [pwaɲ] *nf* grip, energy, firmness, drive.

poignée [pwaɲe] *nf* handful, handle; — **de main** handshake.

poignet [pwaɲɛ] *nm* wrist, cuff, wrist-band.

poil [pwal] *nm* hair, fur, coat, bristle, nap; **à** — naked, hairy; **au** —! wonderful! **reprendre du** — **de la bête** to take a hair of the dog that bit you.

poilu [pwaly] *a* hairy, shaggy; *nm* soldier, tommy.

poinçon [pwɛ̃sɔ̃] *nm* awl, piercer, punch, stamp.

poinçonner [pwɛ̃sɔne] *vt* to pierce, punch, stamp.

poindre [pwɛ̃ːdr] *vi* to dawn, break, come up.

poing [pwɛ̃] *nm* fist, hand; **coup de** — punch; **dormir à** —**s fermés** to sleep like a log.

point [pwɛ̃] *ad* not, not at all; *nm* point, speck, dot, mark, stitch, full stop; **à** — done to a turn; **à** — **nommé** in the nick of time; **de tous** —**s** in all respects; **mettre au** — to focus, tune up, adjust, clarify, perfect; **mise au** — focusing, tuning up, clarification; **faire le** — to take one's bearings, take stock of one's position.

pointage [pwɛ̃taːʒ] *nm* checking, ticking off, sighting.

pointe [pwɛ̃t] *nf* point, tip, top, head, touch, tinge, twinge, quip; — **sèche** etching-needle, dry-point etching; — **du jour** daybreak; **heures de** — rush hours; **pousser une** — **jusqu'à** to push on to, take a walk over to; **en** — pointed.

pointer [pwɛ̃te] *vt* to prick, stab, sharpen, tick off, check, point, aim; *vi* to appear, soar, rise, sprout.

pointeur [pwɛ̃tœːr] *nm* checker, time-keeper, gun-layer, scorer.

pointillé [pwɛ̃tije] *a* dotted, stippled; *nm* dotted line, stippling.

pointiller [pwɛ̃tije] *vt* to dot, stipple, pester, annoy; *vi* to cavil, quibble.

pointilleux, -euse [pwɛ̃tijø, øːz] *a* captious, critical.

pointu [pwɛ̃ty] *a* pointed, sharp, angular.

pointure [pwɛ̃tyːr] *nf* size.

poire [pwaːr] *nf* pear, bulb; (*fam*) mug; **garder une** — **pour la soif** to put something by for a rainy day.

poireau [pwaro] *nm* leek.

poireauter [pwarote] *vi* to hang about (waiting).

poirier [pwarje] *nm* pear-tree.

pois [pwa] *nm* pea, spot; **petits —** green peas; **— de senteur** sweet peas; **— chiches** chick peas.

poison [pwazɔ̃] *nm* poison.

poissard [pwasaːr] *a* vulgar, coarse.

poisse [pwas] *nf* bad luck.

poisser [pwase] *vt* to coat with pitch, wax, make sticky.

poisson [pwasɔ̃] *nm* fish; **— rouge** goldfish; **— d'avril** April fool.

poissonnerie [pwasɔnri] *nf* fish-market, fish-shop.

poissonneux, -euse [pwasɔnø, øːz] *a* full of fish, stocked with fish.

poissonnier, -ière [pwasɔnje, jɛːr] *n* fishmonger, fishwife.

poissonnière [pwasɔnjɛːr] *nf* fish-kettle.

poitevin, -e [pwatvɛ̃, in] *a* from Poitou or Poitiers.

poitrail [pwatraːj] *nm* chest, breast (strap).

poitrinaire [pwatrinɛːr] *an* consumptive.

poitrine [pwatrin] *nf* chest, breast, bosom, brisket.

poivre [pwaːvr] *nm* pepper, spiciness.

poivré [pwavre] *a* peppery, spicy.

poivrier [pwavrie] *nm* pepper-pot, pepper-plant.

poivron [pwavrɔ̃] *nm* Jamaica pepper, capsicum.

poivrot [pwavro] *nm* boozer, drunkard.

poix [pwa] *nf* pitch, wax.

polaire [pɔlɛːr] *a* polar.

polariser [pɔlarize] *vt* to polarize; *vr* to have a one-track mind.

pôle [poːl] *nm* pole.

polémique [pɔlemik] *a* polemic(al); *nf* controversy.

polémiste [pɔlemist] *nm* polemist.

poli [pɔli] *a* polished, glossy, polite; *nm* polish, gloss.

policer [pɔlise] *vt* to organize, establish order in.

police [pɔlis] *nf* police, policing, policy; **salle de — guard-room; faire la —** to keep order.

polichinelle [pɔliʃinɛl] *nf* punch, turncoat, puppet, buffoon; **théâtre de —** Punch and Judy show; **secret de —** open secret.

policier, -ière [pɔlisje, jɛːr] *a* police; *nm* detective; **roman —** detective story.

polir [pɔliːr] *vt* to polish.

polisson, -onne [pɔlisɔ̃, ɔn] *a* ribald, naughty; *n* scamp, rascal, scapegrace.

polissonnerie [pɔlisɔnri] *nf* naughtiness, smutty remark.

politesse [pɔlitɛs] *nf* politeness, courtesy, manners.

politicien, -enne [pɔlitisjɛ̃, jɛn] *n* politician.

politique [pɔlitik] *a* political, politic, diplomatic; *nm* politician; *nf* politics, policy.

pollen [pɔlɛn] *nm* pollen.

polluer [pɔlɥe] *vt* to pollute, defile.

pollution [pɔlysjɔ̃] *nf* pollution, defilement.

Pologne [pɔlɔɲ] *nf* Poland.

polonais [pɔlɔnɛ] *a nm* Polish; *n* Pole.

poltron, -onne [pɔltrɔ̃, ɔn] *a* cowardly, timid; *n* coward.

polycopié [pɔlikɔpje] *nm* cyclostyled lecture.

polycopier [pɔlikɔpje] *vt* to cyclostyle, stencil.

polygame [pɔligam] *a* polygamous; *n* polygamist.

polyglotte [pɔliglɔt] *an* polyglot.

polygone [pɔligɔn] *nm* polygon, experimental range.

polype [pɔlip] *nm* polyp, polypus.

polytechnicien [pɔliteknisjɛ̃] *nm* student of the *Ecole polytechnique*.

pombe [pɔ̃b] *nm* millet beer.

pommade [pɔmad] *nf* pomade, hair-cream, ointment, lip-salve.

pomme [pɔm] *nf* apple, knob, head; **— de terre** potato; **— d'arrosoir** rose of a watering-can; **— de pin** fir-cone; **tomber dans les —** to pass out.

pommeau [pɔmo] *nm* pommel.

pommeler [pɔmle] *vr* to become dappled, mottled.

pommette [pɔmɛt] *nf* knob, cheek-bone.

pommier [pɔmje] *nm* apple-tree.

pompe [pɔ̃ːp] *nf* pump, pomp, display; **— à incendie** fire-engine; **entrepreneur de —s funèbres** undertaker.

pomper [pɔ̃pe] *vt* to pump, suck up.

pompette [pɔ̃pɛt] *a* slightly tipsy.

pompeux, -euse [pɔ̃pø, øːz] *a* pompous, turgid.

pompier [pɔ̃pje] *nm* fireman, pump-maker; *a* uninspired.

pomponner [pɔ̃pɔne] *vt* to adorn, titivate; *vr* to deck oneself out, titivate.

ponce [pɔ̃ːs] *nf* **pierre —** pumice-stone.

poncer [pɔ̃se] *vt* to pumice, sand-paper, pounce.

poncif [pɔ̃sif] *nm* pounced drawing, conventional work, commonplace effect, image *etc.*

ponctionner [pɔ̃ksjɔne] *vt* to tap, puncture.

ponctualité [pɔ̃ktɥalite] *nf* punctuality.

ponctuation [pɔ̃ktɥasjɔ̃] *nf* punctuation.

ponctuel, -elle [pɔ̃ktɥɛl] *a* punctual.

ponctuer [pɔ̃ktɥe] *vt* to punctuate, emphasize, dot.

pondération [pɔ̃derasjɔ̃] *nf* balance, level-headedness.

pondéré [pɔ̃dere] *a* thoughtful, level-headed.

pondre [pɔ̃ːdr] *vt* to lay, produce.

pont [pɔ̃] *nm* bridge, deck, axle; **— levis** drawbridge; **— roulant** gantry;

faire le — to take the intervening day(s) off.

ponte [pɔ̃t] nf laying, eggs laid.

pontife [pɔ̃tif] nm pontiff, pundit.

pontifier [pɔ̃tifje] vi to lay down the law, dogmatize.

ponton [pɔ̃tɔ̃] nm landing-stage, ramp.

popote [pɔpɔt] nf kitchen, restaurant, cooking, mess.

populace [pɔpylas] nf riff-raff, rabble, mob.

populacier, -ière [pɔpylasje, jɛːr] a vulgar, common.

populaire [pɔpylɛːr] a popular, vulgar; **chanson —** folksong, street song.

populariser [pɔpylarize] vt to popularize.

popularité [pɔpylarite] nf popularity.

population [pɔpylasjɔ̃] nf population.

populeux, -euse [pɔpylø, øːz] a populous.

porc [pɔːr] nm pig, swine, pork.

porcelaine [pɔrsəlɛn] nf porcelain, china.

porc-épic [pɔrkepik] nm porcupine.

porche [pɔrʃ] nm porch.

porcherie [pɔrʃəri] nf pigsty, piggery.

pore [pɔːr] nm pore.

poreux, -euse [pɔrø, øːz] a porous.

pornographie [pɔrnɔgrafi] nf pornography.

porphyre [pɔrfiːr] nm porphyry, slab.

port [pɔːr] nm port, harbour, haven, carriage, postage, carrying, bearing; **se mettre au — d'armes** to shou der arms; **— dû** carriage forward.

portable [pɔrtabl] a portable, presentable, wearable.

portage [pɔrtaːʒ] nm porterage, carrying, transport, portage.

portail [pɔrtaːj] nm portal, door.

portant [pɔrtɑ̃] a carrying, bearing; **être bien (mal) portant** to be well (ill).

portatif, -ive [pɔrtatif, iːv] a portable.

porte [pɔrt] nf door, gate(way); **— battante** swing-door; **— tambour** revolving door; **— cochère** carriage entrance; **mettre à la —** to turn (put) s.o. out; **écouter aux —s** to eavesdrop.

porte-affiches [pɔrtafiʃ] nm noticeboard.

porte-amarre [pɔrtamaːr] nm linerocket.

porte-avions [pɔrtavjɔ̃] nm aircraft carrier.

porte-bagages [pɔrtbagaːʒ] nm luggage-rack.

porte-bonheur [pɔrtbɔnœːr] nm charm, mascot.

porte-clefs [pɔrtkle] nm keyring.

porte-documents [pɔrtdɔkymɑ̃] nm attaché-case.

portée [pɔrte] nf litter, brood, range, reach, scope, span; **à — de la voix** within call; **d'une grande —** farreaching.

portefaix [pɔrtəfɛ] nm porter.

porte-fenêtre [pɔrtfənɛːtr] nf french window.

portefeuille [pɔrtəfœːj] nm portfolio, pocket-book, wallet, letter-case.

porte-flambeau [pɔrtflɑ̃bo] nm torch-bearer.

portemanteau [pɔrtmɑ̃to] nm coatstand.

porte-mine [pɔrtəmin] nm propelling pencil.

porte-monnaie [pɔrtmɔnɛ] nm purse.

porte-parole [pɔrtparɔl] nm spokesman, mouthpiece

porte-plume [pɔrtəplym] nm pen (holder).

porter [pɔrte] vt to carry, bear, wear, take, inscribe, produce, bring (in), induce; vi bear, carry, hit (home), tell; vr to go, proceed, be; **— un coup** to deal, aim a blow; **— manquant** to post as missing; **il me porte sur les nerfs** he gets on my nerves; **se — candidat** to stand as candidate; **se — bien** to be well.

porte-serviettes [pɔrtsɛrvjɛt] nm towel-rail.

porteur, -euse [pɔrtœːr, øːz] n porter, bearer, carrier.

porte-voix [pɔrtəvwa] nm megaphone.

portier, -ière [pɔrtje, jɛːr] n doorkeeper, gate-keeper.

portière [pɔrtjɛːr] nf door.

portillon [pɔrtijɔ̃] nm sidegate, wicket-gate.

portion [pɔrsjɔ̃] nf portion, helping, share.

portique [pɔrtik] nm porch, portico.

porto [pɔrto] nm port (wine).

portrait [pɔrtrɛ] nm portrait, likeness; **— en pied** full-length portrait.

portraitiste [pɔrtrɛtist] nm portraitpainter.

portugais [pɔrtygɛ] an Portuguese.

Portugal [pɔrtygal] nm Portugal.

pose [poːz] nf pose, attitude, posing, affectation, (time) exposure, laying, posting.

posé [poze] a sitting, sedate, staid, steady.

poser [poze] vt to put (down), place, lay (down), set, fix up, admit, suppose; vi to pose, sit, rest; vr to settle, alight, set one_lf up (as en).

poseur, -euse [pozœːr, øːz] n poseur, snob, layer.

positif, -ive [pozitif, iːv] a positive, actual, matter-of-fact; nm positive.

position [pozisjɔ̃] nf position, situation, site, status, posture, post.

possédant [pɔsedɑ̃] a classes **—es** propertied classes.

possédé [pɔsede] a possessed; n person possessed, maniac.

posséder [posede] *vt* to possess, own, know thoroughly; *vr* to contain oneself.

posseseur [posɛsœːr] *nm* possessor, owner.

possessif, -ive [posɛsif, iːv] *a nm* possessive.

possession [posɛsjɔ̃] *nf* possession, ownership.

possibilité [pɔsibilite] *nf* possibility, feasibility.

possible [posibl] *a* possible, feasible; *nm* possible, utmost; **pas —** not really! well I never!

postal [postal] *a* postal.

poste [post] *nm* post, job, appointment, station; **— de T.S.F.** wireless set, -station; *nf* post, post office; **mettre une lettre à la —** to post a letter.

poster [poste] *vt* to post, station; *vr* to take up a position.

postérieur [postərjœːr] *a* posterior, subsequent, rear, back; *nm* posterior, bottom.

postérité [posterite] *nf* posterity, issue.

posthume [postym] *a* posthumous.

postiche [postiʃ] *a* false, imitation, sham, dummy.

postillon [postijɔ̃] *nm* postillon; **envoyer des —s** to splutter.

postscolaire [postskɔlɛːr] *a* further (education), after-school.

postulant [postylɑ̃] *n* applicant, candidate.

postuler [postyle] *vt* to apply for, solicit.

posture [postyːr] *nf* posture, position, attitude.

pot [po] *nm* pot, jar, jug, mug, tankard; **payer les —s cassés** to pay the damage.

potable [potabl] *a* drinkable.

potache [potaʃ] *nm* schoolboy, pupil.

potage [potaːʒ] *nm* soup.

potager, -ère [potaʒe, ɛːr] *a* for the pot; *nm* kitchen-garden.

potasse [potas] *nf* potash.

potasser [potase] *vt* to swot up (for); *vi* to swot.

pot-au-feu [potofø] *a* homely, plain; *nm* stock-pot, soup with boiled beef.

pot-de-vin [podvɛ̃] *nm* bribe.

poteau [poto] *nm* post, pole; **— d'arrivée** winning-post; **— de départ** starting-post.

potelé [potle] *a* chubby, plump.

potence [potɑ̃s] *nf* gibbet, gallows, jib, derrick.

potentiel, -elle [potɑ̃sjɛl] *a* potential; *nm* potentialities.

poterie [potri] *nf* pottery.

poterne [potɛrn] *nf* postern.

potiche [potiʃ] *nf* (Chinese) porcelain vase.

potier, -ière [potje, jɛːr] *n* potter.

potin [potɛ̃] *nm* piece of gossip, (*fam*) noise; *pl* tittle-tattle.

potiron [potirɔ̃] *nm* pumpkin.

pou [pu] *nm* louse.

poubelle [pubɛl] *nf* dustbin.

pouce [pus] *nm* thumb, big toe, inch; **manger sur le —** to take a snack.

poucet [pusɛ] *nm* **le petit —** Tom Thumb.

poucier [pusje] *nm* thumb-stall, -piece.

poudre [puːdr] *nf* powder, dust; **— aux yeux** bluff, eyewash.

poudrer [pudre] *vt* to powder, dust; *vr* to put on powder.

poudreux, -euse [pudrø, øːz] *a* dusty, powdery.

poudrier [pudrie] *nm* powder-box, compact.

poudrière [pudriɛːr] *nf* powder-horn, magazine.

poudroyer [pudrwaje] *vt* to cover with dust; *vi* to form clouds of dust.

pouf [puf] *nm* pout, puff.

pouffer [pufe] *vir* (se) **— de rire** to roar with laughter.

pouilleux, -euse [pujø, øːz] *a* lousy, verminous.

poulailler [pulaje] *nm* hen-house, -roost, (*theatre fam*) the gods.

poulain [pulɛ̃] *nm* colt, foal, pony-skin, skid.

poularde [pulard] *nf* fowl.

poule [pul] *nf* hen, fowl, pool, sweepstake; tart; **— d'eau** moorhen; **— mouillée** coward, chicken.

poulet [pulɛ] *nm* chick(en), love-letter.

poulette [pulɛt] *nf* pullet.

pouliche [puliʃ] *nf* filly.

poulie [puli] *nf* pulley, block.

poulpe [pulp] *nm* octopus.

pouls [pu] *nm* pulse.

poumon [pumɔ̃] *nm* lung; **crier à pleins —s** to shout at the top of one's voice; **respirer à pleins —s** to take a deep breath.

poupe [pup] *nf* poop, stern.

poupée [pupe] *nf* doll, (tailor's) dummy, puppet.

poupon, -onne [pupɔ̃, on] *n* baby, baby-faced boy, girl.

pouponnière [pupɔnjɛːr] *nf* day-nursery.

pour [puːr] *prep* for, on behalf of, in favour of, because of, for the sake of, instead of, as, to, by, in order to, with regard to, although; **— que** in order that, so that; **— dix francs (de)** ten francs worth (of); **je n'y suis — rien** I have nothing to do with it; **il en a — une heure** it will take him an hour; **— ce qui est de l'argent** as far as the money is concerned.

pourboire [purbwaːr] *nm* tip, gratuity.

pourceau [purso] *nm* hog, swine, pig.

pour-cent [pursɑ̃] *nm* (rate) per cent.

pourcentage [pursɑ̃taːʒ] *nm* percentage.

pourchasser [purʃase] *vt* to pursue.

pourlécher [purleʃe] *vt* to lick round; *vr* to run one's tongue over one's lips.

pourparler [purparle] *nm* parley, negotiation.

pourpoint [purpwɛ̃] *nm* doublet.

pourpre [purpr] *a nm* deep red, crimson; *nf* purple.

pourquoi [purkwa] *cj adv* why?

pourri [puri] *a* rotten, bad.

pourrir [puriːr] *vt* to rot; *vir* to decay, rot, go bad.

pourriture [purityːr] *nf* rotting, rot(tenness).

poursuite [pursɥit] *nf* pursuit, tracking (down); *pl* proceedings, prosecution, suing.

poursuivant [pursɥivɑ̃] *n* prosecutor, plaintiff.

poursuivre [pursɥiːvr] *vt* to pursue, chase, prosecute. carry on, continue, dog; *vr* to continue, go on.

pourtant [purtɑ̃] *ad* however, yet, still.

pourtour [purtuːr] *nm* circumference, periphery, precincts, area.

pourvoir [purvwaːr] *vt* to provide (for, with de,) make provision (for à), furnish, supply, equip.

pourvoyeur, -euse [purvwajœːr, øːz] *n* purveyor, caterer, provider.

pousse [pus] *nf* growth, shoot.

poussé [puse] *a* thorough, exhaustive, deep.

pousse-café [puskafe] *nm* liqueur (after coffee), chaser.

poussée [puse] *nf* push(ing), shove, thrust, pressure.

pousse-pousse [puspus] *nm* rickshaw, go-cart (of child).

pousser [puse] *vt* to push (on), thrust, shove, urge (on), drive, impel, prompt, utter; *vi* to grow, shoot, push (on, forward); *vr* to push oneself forward.

poussier [pusje] *nm* coal-dust.

poussière [pusjɛːr] *nf* dust.

poussiéreux, -euse [pusjerø, øːz] *a* dusty.

poussif, -ive [pusif, iːv] *a* broken-winded, wheezy.

poussin [pusɛ̃] *nm* chick.

poutre [putr] *nf* beam, joist, girder.

poutrelle [putrɛl] *nf* small beam, girder, spar.

pouvoir [puvwaːr] *nm* power, influence, authority, power of attorney; *vt* to be able, can, manage, to be allowed, may, might *etc*; *vr* ro be possible; **il n'en peut plus** he is worn out; **on n'y peut rien** it can't be helped, nothing can be done about it; **c'est on ne peut plus difficile** nothing could be more difficult.

prairie [prɛri] *nf* meadow, field, grassland.

praline [pralin] *nf* burnt almond.

praliner [praline] *vt* to bake in sugar, crust.

praticabilité [pratikabilite] *nf* practicability, feasibility.

praticable [pratikabl] *a* practicable, feasible. passable.

praticien, -enne [pratisjɛ̃, jɛn] *n* practitioner, expert; *a* practising.

pratiquant [pratikɑ̃] *a* practising.

pratique [pratik] *a* practical, useful; *nf* practice, practical knowledge, experience, association, custom; *pl* practises, dealings.

pratiquer [pratike] *vti* to practise; *vt* put into practice, employ, make, associate with.

pré [pre] *nm* meadow.

préalable [prealabl] *a* previous, preliminary; **au —** previously, to begin with.

préambule [preɑ̃byl] *nm* preamble (to de).

préau [preo] *nm* yard, covered playground.

préavis [preavi] *nm* (previous) notice, warning.

précaire [prekɛːr] *a* precarious, shaky.

précaution [prekosjɔ̃] *nf* (pre)caution, care, wariness.

précautionneux, -euse [prekosjɔ̃nø, øːz] *a* cautious, wary, guarded.

précédent [presedɑ̃] *a* preceding, previous; *nm* precedent.

précéder [presede] *vt* to precede, take precedence over; *vi* to have precedence.

précepte [presɛpt] *nm* precept.

précepteur, -trice [preseptœːr, tris] *n* tutor, governess.

prêche [prɛːʃ] *nm* sermon.

prêcher [preʃe] *vt* to preach (to), recommend; *vi* to preach; **— d'exemple** to practice what one preaches; **— pour son saint** to talk in one's own interests.

prêchi-prêcha [preʃipreʃa] *nm* going on and on, preachifying.

précieux, -euse [presjø, øːz] *a* precious, valuable, affected.

préciosité [presjosite] *nf* preciosity, affectation.

précipice [presipis] *nm* precipice.

précipitamment [presipitamɑ̃] *ad* precipitately, hurriedly, headlong.

précipitation [presipitasjɔ̃] *nf* precipitancy, overhastiness, precipitation.

précipité [presipite] *a* precipitate, rushed, hurried, headlong; *nm* precipitate.

précipiter [presipite] *vt* to precipitate, rush, hurry, hurl down, into; *vr* to rush, dash, bolt.

précis [presi] *a* precise, definite, accurate; *nm* précis, summary.

précisément [presizemɑ̃] *ad* precisely, just, exactly, as a matter of fact.

préciser [presize] *vt* to state exactly, specify; *vi* to be precise, more explicit.

précision [presizjɔ̃] nf precision, accuracy, preciseness; pl fuller particulars.

précoce [prekɔs] a precocious, early.

précocité [prekɔsite] nf precociousness, earliness.

préconçu [prekɔ̃sy] a preconceived.

préconiser [prekɔnize] vt to advocate.

précurseur [prekyrsœːr] nm forerunner, precursor.

prédécesseur [predesɛsœːr] nm predecessor.

prédestiner [predɛstine] vt to predestine, foredoom, fix beforehand.

prédicateur [predikatœːr] nm preacher.

prédiction [prediksjɔ̃] nf prediction, foretelling.

prédilection [predilɛksjɔ̃] nf liking, fondness.

prédire [prediːr] vt to predict, foretell, forecast.

prédisposer [predispoze] vt to predispose, prejudice.

prédisposition [predispozisjɔ̃] nf predisposition, prejudice, propensity.

prédominance [predɔminɑ̃ːs] nf predominance, prevalence, supremacy.

prédominer [predɔmine] vi to predominate, prevail.

prééminence [preeminɑ̃ːs] nf preeminence, superiority.

prééminent [preeminɑ̃] a pre-eminent, outstanding.

préface [prefas] nf preface.

préfacer [prefase] vt to write a preface for.

préfectoral [prefɛktɔral] a prefectoral, of a prefect.

préfecture [prefɛktyːr] nf prefecture, prefect's house or office; — de police Paris police headquarters.

préférable [preferabl] a preferable, better.

préférence [preferɑ̃ːs] nf preference, priority.

préférer [prefere] vt to prefer, like better.

préfet [prefɛ] nm prefect; — de police chief commissioner of the Paris police.

préfixe [prefiks] nm prefix.

préfixer [prefikse] vt to settle beforehand, prefix.

préhistorique [preistɔrik] a prehistoric.

préjudice [preʒydis] nm injury, detriment, prejudice; porter — à qn to harm, injure, hurt.

préjudiciable [preʒydisjabl] a prejudicial, injurious, detrimental.

préjugé [preʒyʒe] nm prejudice, preconceived idea.

préjuger [preʒyʒe] vti to judge beforehand.

se prélasser [səprɛlase] vr to lounge, loll, laze.

prélat [prɛla] nm prelate.

prélèvement [prelɛvmɑ̃] nm deduction, levy.

prélever [prelve] vt to deduct, levy.

préliminaire [preliminɛːr] a nm preliminary.

prélude [prɛlyd] nm prelude.

prématuré [prematyre] a premature, untimely.

préméditer [premedite] vt to premeditate.

prémices [premis] nf pl first fruits.

premier, -ière [prəmje, jɛːr] a first, foremost, early, original; — rôle leading part, lead; — venu first comer, anybody; du — coup first shot, at the first attempt; nm au — first floor; jeune — juvenile lead.

première [prəmjɛːr] nf first night, first performance, first class, sixth form.

prémisse [premis] nf premise, premiss.

prémonition [premɔnisjɔ̃] nf premonition.

prémunir [premyniːr] vt to (fore) warn; vr to provide.

prendre [prɑ̃ːdr] vt to take (up, on, in), pick up, grasp, catch, assume; vi to freeze, seize, congeal, set, catch on; vr to catch, get caught, begin, clutch, cling; à tout — on the whole; bien lui en a pris de partir it was a good thing for him that he left; s'en — à to attack, blame; se — d'amitié pour to take a liking to; cela ne prend pas that won't take a trick; s'y prendre to set about it.

prénom [prenɔ̃] nm first name Christian name.

préoccupation [preɔkypasjɔ̃] nf preoccupation, anxiety, concern, care.

préoccuper [preɔkype] vt to preoccupy, worry, engross; vr to attend, see (to de).

préparatif [preparatif] nm preparation.

préparation [preparasjɔ̃] nf preparing, preparation.

préparatoire [preparatwaːr] a preparatory.

préparer [prepare] vt to prepare, get ready, read for; vr to get ready, prepare, brew.

prépondérance [prepɔ̃derɑ̃ːs] nf preponderance, prevalency.

prépondérant [prepɔ̃derɑ̃] a preponderant, predominant; voix — casting vote.

préposé [prepoze] n person in charge.

préposer [prepoze] vt to appoint.

préposition [prepozisjɔ̃] nf preposition.

prérogative [prerɔgatiːv] nf prerogative, privilege.

près [prɛ] ad near, near-by, close by; prep — de near, close to, by, on, about; à beaucoup — by far; à peu — nearly, about; à cela — with that exception; **de —** closely, at a short distance; **il n'est pas à cent francs —** 100 francs more or less does not matter to him.

présage [prɛza:ʒ] *nm* presage, foreboding, omen.

présager [prɛzaʒe] *vt* to presage, predict, portend.

pré-salé [presale] *nm* mutton, sheep (fattened in fields near the sea).

presbyte [prɛzbit] *a* long-sighted.

presbytère [prɛzbite:r] *nm* presbytery, rectory, manse.

prescience [presjã:s] *nf* prescience, foreknowledge.

prescription [prɛskripsjɔ̃] *nf* prescription, regulation, direction.

prescrire [prɛskri:r] *vt* to prescribe, stipulate, ordain.

préséance [preseã:s] *nf* precedence, priority.

présence [prezã:s] *nf* presence, attendance; **faire acte de —** to put in an appearance.

présent [prezã] *a* present, ready; *nm* present (time or tense), gift.

présentable [prezãtabl] *a* presentable.

présentation [prezãtasjɔ̃] *nf* presentation, introduction, get-up.

présenter [prezãte] *vt* to present, introduce, show; *vr* to introduce oneself, appear, call, arise, occur; **le livre présente bien** the book is attractively got up; **se bien —** to look promising, well.

préservatif, -ive [preservatif, i:v] *a nm* preservative, preventive.

préservation [prezɛrvasjɔ̃] *nf* preservation, protection, saving.

préserver [prezɛrve] *vt* to preserve, protect, save.

présidence [prezidã:s] *nf* presidency, president's house, chairmanship.

président [prezidã] *n* president, chairman.

présidentiel, -elle [prezidãsjɛl] *a* presidential, of the president.

présider [prezide] *vt* to preside over; *vi* to preside, be in the chair.

présomptif, -ive [prezɔ̃ptif, i:v] *a* presumptive, apparent.

présomption [prezɔ̃psjɔ̃] *nf* presumption, presumptuousness.

présomptueux, -euse [prezɔ̃ptɥø, ø:z] *a* presumptuous, presuming, forward.

presque [prɛsk *ad* nearly, almost, hardly.

presqu'île [prɛskil] *nf* peninsula.

pressant [presã] *a* pressing, urgent.

presse [prɛ:s] *nf* crowd, throng, hurry, press(ing-machine), press, newspapers; **sous —** printing; **heures de —** rush hours.

pressé [prese] *a* pressed, squeezed, crowded, hurried, in a hurry, urgent.

pressentiment [presãtimã] *nm* presentiment, forewarning, feeling.

presser [prese] *vt* to press, squeeze, hasten, hurry (on), quicken, beset; *vi* to be urgent, press; *vr* to hurry (up), crowd.

pression [presjɔ̃] *nf* pressure, tension; **bière à la —** draught beer; **bouton —** press-stud.

pressoir [prɛswa:r] *nm* wine-, cider-press.

pressurer [presyre] *vt* to press (out), squeeze.

prestance [prɛstã:s] *nf* fine presence.

prestation [prɛstasjɔ̃] *nf* loan, lending, prestation; **— de serment** taking an oath.

preste [prɛst] *a* nimble, alert, quick.

prestidigitateur [prɛstidiʒitatœ:r] *nm* conjuror.

prestidigitation [prɛstidiʒitasjɔ̃] *nf* conjuring, sleight of hand.

prestige [prɛsti:ʒ] *nm* prestige, fascination.

prestigieux, -euse [prɛstiʒjø, ø:z] *a* amazing, marvellous, spellbinding.

présumer [prezyme] *vt* to presume, assume; **trop —** to overrate.

présupposer [presypoze] *vt* to presuppose, take for granted.

prêt [prɛ] *a* ready, prepared; *nm* loan, lending.

prêt-bail [prɛbaj] *nm* lend-lease.

prétendant [pretãdã] *n* candidate, applicant, claimant; *nm* suitor.

prétendre [pretã:dr] *vt* to claim, require, intend, state, maintain, aspire.

prétendu [pretãdy] *a* alleged, so-called, would-be; *n* intended.

prétentieux, -euse [pretãsjø, ø:z] *a* pretentious, snobbish, conceited.

prétention [pretãsjɔ̃] *nf* pretension, claim, aspiration, self-conceit.

prêter [prete] *vt* to lend, ascribe, attribute; *vi* lend itself (to à), give scope (for à); *vr* to fall in (with à), be a party (to à), indulge (in à).

prêteur, -euse [pretœ:r, ø:z] *a* (given to) lending; *n* lender; **— sur gages** pawnbroker.

prétexte [pretɛkst] *nm* pretext, excuse; **sous aucun —** on no account.

prétexter [pretɛkste] *vt* to pretext, plead, make the excuse of.

prêtre [prɛ:tr] *nm* priest.

prêtrise [prɛtri:z] *nf* priesthood.

preuve [prœ:v] *nf* proof, token, evidence; **faire — de** to show, display; **faire ses —s** to survive the test, show what one can do.

prévaloir [prevalwa:r] *vi* to prevail; *vr* to avail oneself, take advantage (of **de**).

prévenance [prevnã:s] *nf* attention, kindness.

prévenant [prevnã] *a* attentive, considerate, prepossessing.

prévenir [prevni:r] *vt* to prevent, avert, anticipate, inform, warn, tell, prejudice.

prévenu [prevny] *a* prejudiced, biased; *n* accused.

préventif, -ive [prevãtif, i:v] *a* preventive, deterrent.

prévention [prevãsjɔ̃] *nf* prejudice, detention.

prévision [previzjɔ̃] *nf* forecast(ing), expectation, anticipation, likelihood.

prévoir [prevwa:r] *vt* to foresee, forecast, provide for.

prévoyance [prevwajã:s] *nf* foresight, forethought.

prévoyant [prevwajã] *a* foreseeing, far-sighted.

prie-Dieu [pridjø] *nm* prayer-stool.

prier [prie] *vt* to pray, beg, request ask, invite; **sans se faire —** without having to be coaxed, readily; **je vous en prie** please do, don't mention it.

prière [prie:r] *nf* prayer, entreaty, request; **— de ne pas fumer** please do not smoke.

prieur [priœ:r] *n* prior, prioress.

prieuré [priœre] *nm* priory.

primaire [prime:r] *a* primary.

primat [prima] *nm* primate.

primauté [primote] *nf* primacy, pre-eminence.

prime [prim] *a* first, earliest; *nf* premium, bonus, option, subsidy, reward, free gift; **de — saut** on the first impulse; **faire —** to be at a premium.

primer [prime] *vt* to surpass, outdo, award a prize, bonus to, to give a subsidy, bounty, to.

prime-sautier, -ière [primsotje, je:r] *a* impulsive, spontaneous.

primeur [primœ:r] *nf* newness, freshness; *pl* early vegetables.

primevère [primvɛ:r] *nf* primrose, primula.

primitif, -ive [primitif, i:v] *a* primitive, earliest, original; **les —s** the early masters.

primordial [primɔrdjal] *a* primordial, primeval, of prime importance.

prince [prɛ̃:s] *nm* prince.

princesse [prɛ̃sɛs] *nf* princess; **aux frais de la —** at the expense of the state, free, gratis.

princier, -ière [prɛ̃sje, je:r] *a* princely.

principal [prɛ̃sipal] *a* principal, chief; *nm* chief, head(master), main thing.

principauté [prɛ̃sipote] *nf* principality.

principe [prɛ̃sip] *nm* principle; **sans —s** unscrupulous; **dès le —** from the beginning.

printanier, -ière [prɛ̃tanje, je:r] *a* spring(-like).

printemps [prɛ̃tã] *nm* spring(time).

priorité [priɔrite] *nf* priority.

prise [pri:z] *nf* hold, grip, capture, taking, pinch, prize, setting; **— d'air** air-intake; **— d'eau** hydrant, cock; **— de courant** plug; **— de**

vues filming, shooting; **donner — à** to leave oneself open to; **en venir aux —s** to come to grips; **lâcher —** to let go.

priser [prize] *vt* to snuff (up), value, prize; *vi* to take snuff.

prisme [prism] *nm* prism.

prison [prizɔ̃] *nf* prison, gaol, imprisonment.

prisonnier, -ière [prizɔnje, je:r] *a* captive; *n* prisoner.

privation [privasjɔ̃] *nf* (de)privation, hardship.

privé [prive] *a* private, privy; *nm* private life.

priver [prive] *vt* to deprive; *vr* to deny oneself.

privilège [privilɛ:3] *nm* privilege, prerogative, preference.

privilégié [privilezje] *a* privileged, licensed, preference.

prix [pri] *nm* price, prize, reward, value, cost; **— de revient** cost price; **— du trajet** fare; **au —** de at the price of, compared with; **de —** expensive; **attacher beaucoup de —** à to set a high value on.

probabilité [prɔbabilite] *nf* probability, likelihood.

probable [prɔbabl] *a* probable, likely.

probant [prɔbã] *a* conclusive, convincing.

probe [prɔb] *a* upright, honest.

probité [prɔbite] *nf* integrity, probity.

problématique [prɔblɛmatik] *a* problematical.

problème [prɔblɛm] *nm* problem.

procédé [prɔsede] *nm* process, method, proceeding, conduct, dealing, tip; **bons —s** civilities, fair dealings.

procéder [prɔsede] *vi* to proceed, originate (in de), take proceedings.

procédure [prɔsedy:r] *nf* procedure, proceedings.

procès [prɔsɛ] *nm* (legal) action, proceedings, case; **sans autre forme de —** without further ado, at once.

procession [prɔsesjɔ̃] *nf* procession.

processus [prɔsesy:s] *nm* process, method.

procès-verbal [prɔsɛverbal] *nm* minutes, report, particulars; **dresser un —** à qn to take s.o.'s name and address.

prochain [prɔʃɛ̃] *a* next, nearest, neighbouring, approaching; *n* neighbour.

prochainement [prɔʃɛnmã] *ad* shortly.

proche [prɔʃ] *a* near, at hand; *ad* near.

proclamation [prɔklamasjɔ̃] *nf* proclamation.

proclamer [prɔklame] *vt* to proclaim, declare.

procréer [prɔkree] *vt* to procreate, beget.

procurer [prɔkyre] *vtr* to procure, get, obtain.

procureur, -atrice [prɔkyrœːr, prɔkyratris] *n* procurator, proxy, agent; *nm* attorney.

prodigalité [prɔdigalite] *nf* prodigality, extravagance, lavishness.

prodige [prɔdiːʒ] *nm* prodigy, marvel.

prodigieux, -euse [prɔdiʒjø, øːz] *a* prodigious.

prodigue [prɔdig] *a* prodigal, lavish, profuse, thriftless; *n* waster, prodigal.

prodiguer [prɔdige] *vt* to be prodigal of, be lavish of, waste; *vr* to strive to please, make o.s. cheap.

producteur, -trice [prɔdyktœːr, tris] *a* productive; *n* producer.

productif, -ive [prɔdyktif, iːv] *a* productive.

production [prɔdyksjɔ̃] *nf* product (ion), generation, yield, output.

productivité [prɔdyktivite] *nf* productivity, productiveness.

produire [prɔdɥiːr] *vt* to produce, bear, yield, bring out, forward; *vr* to occur.

produit [prɔdɥi] *nm* product, produce, takings; — **secondaire** by-product.

proéminence [prɔeminãːs] *nf* prominence, protuberance.

profane [prɔfan] *a* profane, lay; *n* layman, outsider.

profaner [prɔfane] *vt* to desecrate, misuse.

proférer [prɔfere] *vt* to utter, speak.

professer [prɔfɛse] *vt* to profess, teach.

professeur [prɔfɛsœːr] *nm* professor, teacher.

profession [prɔfɛsjɔ̃] *nf* profession, occupation, trade.

professionnel, -elle [prɔfɛsjɔnɛl] *an* professional; *a* vocational; **enseignement** — vocational training.

professorat [prɔfɛsɔra] *nm* teaching profession, professorship, body of teachers.

profil [prɔfil] *nm* profile, section.

profiler [prɔfile] *vt* to draw in profile, in section, shape; *vr* to be outlined, stand out.

profit [prɔfi] *nm* profit, advantage, benefit.

profiter [prɔfite] *vi* to profit, be profitable, take advantage (of **de**).

profiteur [prɔfitœːr] *nm* profiteer.

profond [prɔfɔ̃] *a* deep, profound, deep-seated; *nm* depth.

profondeur [prɔfɔ̃dœːr] *nf* depth, profundity.

profusion [prɔfyzjɔ̃] *nf* profusion, abundance.

progéniture [prɔʒenityːr] *nf* progeny, offspring.

programme [prɔgram] *nm* programme, syllabus, curriculum.

progrès [prɔgrɛ] *nm* progress, improvement, headway.

progresser [prɔgrɛse] *vi* to progress, make headway.

progressif, -ive [prɔgrɛsif, iːv] *a* progressive, gradual.

progression [prɔgrɛsjɔ̃] *nf* progress (ion).

prohiber [prɔibe] *vt* to prohibit, forbid.

prohibitif, -ive [prɔibitif, iːv] *a* prohibitive.

proie [prwa] *nf* prey, quarry; **en** — **à** a prey to.

projecteur [prɔʒɛktœːr] *nm* projector, searchlight, spotlight.

projectile [prɔʒɛktil] *nm* projectile, missile.

projection [prɔʒɛksjɔ̃] *nf* projection, throwing out, beam, lantern slide.

projet [prɔʒɛ] *nm* project, scheme, plan, draft; — **de loi** bill.

projeter [prɔʒəte] *vt* to project, throw, plan; *vr* to be thrown, stand out.

prolétaire [prɔletɛːr] *an* proletarian.

prolifique [prɔlifik] *a* prolific.

prolixe [prɔliks] *a* prolix, verbose.

prolixité [prɔliksite] *nf* prolixity, wordiness.

prologue [prɔlɔg] *nm* prologue.

prolongation [prɔlɔ̃gasjɔ̃] *nf* prolongation, protraction, extension; *pl* extra time.

prolongement [prɔlɔ̃ʒmã] *nm* prolongation, lengthening, extension.

prolonger [prɔlɔ̃ʒe] *vt* to prolong, protract, extend; *vr* to be prolonged, continue.

promenade [prɔmnad] *nf* walk(ing), outing, ramble, public walk; — **en auto** car ride, drive; — **en bateau** sail; **emmener en** — to take for a walk.

promener [prɔmne] *vt* to take for a walk, a sail, a run, take about; *vr* to go for a walk *etc*; **envoyer** — **qn** to send s.o. about his business.

promeneur, -euse [prɔmnœːr, øːz] *nmf* walker, rambler.

promenoir [prɔm(ə)nwaːr] *nm* lounge, lobby, promenade.

promesse [prɔmɛs] *nf* promise.

prometteur, -euse [prɔmɛtœːr, øːz] *a* promising, full of promise(s).

promettre [prɔmɛtr] *vt* to promise, look promising.

promiscuité [prɔmiskɥite] *nf* promiscuity.

promontoire [prɔmɔ̃twaːr] *nm* promontory, headland.

promoteur, -trice [prɔmɔtœːr, tris] *a* promoting; *n* promoter.

promotion [prɔmɔsjɔ̃] *nf* promotion.

prompt [prɔ̃] *a* prompt, quick, hasty, ready.

promptitude [prɔ̃tityd] *nf* promptitude, readiness.

promulguer [prɔmylge] *vt* to promulgate, issue.

prôner [prone] *vt* to praise, extol.

pronom [prɔnɔ̃] *nm* pronoun.

prononcer [prɔnɔ̃se] vt to pronounce, say, mention, deliver; vr to declare one's opinion, decision, speak out.

prononciation [prɔnɔ̃sjasjɔ̃] nf pronunciation, utterance, delivery.

pronostic [prɔnɔstik] nm prognostic (ation), forecast.

pronostiquer [prɔnɔstike] vt to forecast.

propagande [prɔpagɑ̃d] nf propaganda, publicity.

propagation [prɔpagasjɔ̃] nf propagation, spreading

propager [prɔpaʒe] vtr to propagate, spread.

propension [prɔpɑ̃sjɔ̃] nf propensity.

prophète, prophétesse [prɔfɛːt, prɔfetɛs] n prophet, prophetess.

prophétie [prɔfesi] nf prophecy, prophesying.

prophétiser [prɔfetize] vt to prophesy, foretell.

propice [prɔpis] a propitious, favourable.

proportion [prɔpɔrsjɔ̃] nf proportion, ratio; pl size; toute — gardée within limits.

proportionné [prɔpɔrsjɔne] a proportionate, proportioned.

proportionnel, -elle [prɔpɔrsjɔnɛl] a proportional.

proportionner [prɔpɔrsjɔne] vt to proportion, adapt.

propos [prɔpo] nm purpose, remark matter, subject; pl talk; à — by the way, appropriate(ly), opportune(ly); mal à — untimely.

proposer [prɔpoze] vt to propose, suggest; vr to come forward, propose (to).

proposition [prɔpozisjɔ̃] nf proposition, proposal, motion, clause.

propre [prɔpr] a own, very; suitable (for à); peculiar (to à); proper; clean, neat; nm characteristic, peculiarity; au — in the literal sense.

proprement [prɔprəmɑ̃] ad properly, nicely, neatly, appropriately.

propreté [prɔprəte] nf clean(li)ness, tidiness.

propriétaire [prɔprietɛːr] n owner, proprietor, landlord, -lady.

propriété [prɔpriete] nf property, estate, ownership, propriety.

propulser [prɔpylse] vt to propel.

propulseur [prɔpylsœːr] a propelling; nm propeller.

propulsion [prɔpylsjɔ̃] nf propulsion, drive.

prorogation [prɔrɔgasjɔ̃] nf prorogation, delay, extension

proroger [prɔrɔʒe] vt to adjourn, extend, delay.

prosaïque [prɔzaik] a prosaic, pedestrian.

prosateur, -trice [prɔzatœːr, tris] n prose writer.

proscription [prɔskripsjɔ̃] nf proscription, outlawing, banishment.

proscrire [prɔskriːr] vt to proscribe, outlaw, banish.

proscrit [prɔskri] a outlawed; n outlaw.

prose [proːz] nf prose.

prospecter [prɔspɛkte] vt to prospect, circularize.

prospectus [prɔspɛktyːs] nm prospectus, handbill.

prospère [prɔspɛːr] a prosperous, flourishing, favourable.

prospérer [prɔspere] vi to prosper, thrive.

prospérité [prɔsperite] nf prosperity.

prosterné [prɔstɛrne] a prostrate, prone.

se prosterner [səprɔstɛrne] vr to prostrate oneself, grovel.

prostituée [prɔstitɥe] nf prostitute, whore.

prostré [prɔstre] a prostrate(d), exhausted.

protagoniste [prɔtagɔnist] nm protagonist.

protecteur, -trice [prɔtɛktœːr, tris] a protective, patronizing; n protector, protectress, patron(ess).

protection [prɔtɛksjɔ̃] nf protection, patronage.

protégé [prɔteʒe] n protégé(e), ward.

protéger [prɔteʒe] vt to protect, patronize, be a patron of.

protéine [prɔtein] nf protein.

protestant [prɔtɛstɑ̃] n Protestant.

protestation [prɔtɛstasjɔ̃] nf protestation, protest.

protester [prɔtɛste] vti to protest.

protêt [prɔtɛ] nm protest.

protocole [prɔtɔkɔl] nm protocol, correct procedure, etiquette.

protubérance [prɔtyberɑ̃s] nf protuberance, projection, bump.

proue [pru] nf prow, bows.

prouesse [prɥɛs] nf prowess, exploit.

prouver [pruve] vt to prove, give proof of.

provenance [prɔvnɑ̃s] nf origin, produce; en — de coming from.

provençal [prɔvɑ̃sal] an Provençal.

Provence [prɔvɑ̃ːs] nf Provence.

provende [prɔvɑ̃ːd] nf provender, fodder, supplies.

provenir [prɔvniːr] vi to originate, come, arise.

proverbe [prɔvɛrb] nm proverb.

proverbial [prɔvɛrbjal] a proverbial.

providence [prɔvidɑ̃ːs] nf providence.

providentiel, -elle [prɔvidɑ̃sjɛl] a providential.

province [prɔvɛ̃ːs] nf province(s).

provincial [prɔvɛ̃sjal] a provincial.

proviseur [prɔvizœːr] nm headmaster (of lycée).

provision [prɔvizjɔ̃] nf provision, supply, reserve, stock.

provisoire [prɔvizwaːr] a temporary, provisional; à titre — provisionally, temporarily.

provocant [prɔvɔkɑ̃] a provocative.

24

provocateur, -trice [prɔvɔkatœːr, tris] *a* provocative; *n* instigator, inciter.

provocation [prɔvɔkasjɔ̃] *nf* provocation, instigation, inciting, challenge.

provoquer [prɔvɔke] *vt* to provoke, arouse, cause, incite, challenge.

proxénète [prɔksenɛt] *n* procurer, procuress.

proximité [prɔksimite] *nf* proximity, nearness.

prude [pryd] *a* prudish; *nf* prude.

prudence [prydɑ̃ːs] *nf* prudence, caution, carefulness.

prudent [prydɑ̃] *a* prudent, careful, cautious.

prune [pryn] *nf* plum; **jouer pour des —s** to play for the fun of the thing.

pruneau [pryno] *nm* prune.

prunelle [prynɛl] *nf* sloe, pupil, apple (of eye).

prunier [prynje] *nm* plum-tree.

Prusse [prys] *nf* Prussia.

prussien, -enne [prysjɛ̃, jɛn] *an* Prussian.

psalmodier [psalmɔdje] *vt* to intone, chant, drone; *vi* to chant.

psaume [psoːm] *nm* psalm.

psautier [psotje] *nm* psalter.

pseudonyme [psødɔnim] *a* pseudonymous; *nm* pseudonym, assumed name.

psychanalyse [psikanaliːz] *nf* psychoanalysis.

psyché [psiʃe] *nf* cheval-mirror.

psychiatrie [psikjatri] *nf* psychiatry.

psychique [psiʃik] *a* psychic.

psychologie [psikɔlɔʒi] *nf* psychology.

psychologique [psikɔlɔʒik] *a* psychological.

psychologue [psikɔlɔg] *nm* psychologist.

psychose [psikoːz] *nf* psychosis.

puanteur [pɥɑ̃tœːr] *nf* stink, stench.

puberté [pybɛrte] *nf* puberty.

public, -ique [pyblik] *a nm* public.

publication [pyblikasjɔ̃] *nf* publication, publishing.

publiciste [pyblisist] *nm* publicist.

publicité [pyblisite] *nf* publicity, advertising; **faire de la — to** advertise.

publier [pyblie] *vt* to publish, proclaim.

puce [pys] *nf* flea; **mettre la — à l'oreille de qn** to arouse s.o.'s suspicions, start s.o. thinking.

pucelle [pysɛl] *nf* virgin, maid(en).

pudeur [pydœːr] *nf* modesty, decorousness, decency.

pudibond [pydibɔ̃] *a* prudish, easily shocked.

pudibonderie [pydibɔ̃dri] *nf* prudishness.

pudique [pydik] *a* modest, chaste, virtuous.

puer [pɥe] *vi* to stink, smell.

puéril [pɥeril] *a* puerile, childish.

puérilité [pɥerilite] *nf* puerility, childishness, childish statement.

pugilat [pyʒila] *nm* boxing, fight.

pugiliste [pyʒilist] *nm* pugilist, boxer.

puiné [pɥine] *a* younger.

puis [pɥi] *ad* then, next, afterwards; **et — après** what about it, what next?

puisard [pɥizaːr] *nm* cesspool, sump.

puiser [pɥize] *vt* to draw, take.

puisette [pɥizɛt] *nf* scoop, ladle.

puisque [pɥisk(ə)] *cj* as, since.

puissance [pɥisɑ̃ːs] *nf* power, strength, force.

puissant [pɥisɑ̃] *a* powerful, strong, mighty, potent.

puits [pɥi] *nm* well, shaft, pit, fount.

pulluler [pyllyle] *vi* to multiply rapidly, teem, swarm.

pulmonaire [pylmɔnɛːr] *a* pulmonary.

pulpe [pylp] *nf* pulp.

pulper [pylpe] *vt* to pulp.

pulpeux, -euse [pylpø, øːz] *a* pulpy.

pulsation [pylsasjɔ̃] *nf* pulsation, throb(bing).

pulvérisateur [pylverizatœːr] *nm* pulverizer, atomizer.

pulvériser [pylverize] *vt* to pulverize, grind (down), spray, atomize.

punaise [pynɛːz] *nf* bug, drawing-pin.

punir [pyniːr] *vt* to punish.

punition [pynisjɔ̃] *nf* punishment, punishing.

pupille [pypil] *n* ward; *nf* pupil (of eye).

pupitre [pypiːtr] *nm* desk, stand, rack.

pur [pyːr] *a* pure, clear, sheer, mere, genuine.

purée [pyre] *nf* purée, thick soup, mash; **— de pommes de terre** mashed potatoes; **être dans la —** to be hard-up.

pureté [pyrte] *nf* pureness, purity, clearness.

purgatif, -ive [pyrgatif, iːv] *a nm* purgative.

purgatoire [pyrgatwaːr] *nm* purgatory.

purge [pyrʒ] *nf* purge, purgative, draining, cleaning.

purger [pyrʒe] *vt* to purge, clean (out), cleanse, clear; *vr* to take medicine; **— sa peine** to serve one's sentence.

purificateur, -trice [pyrifikatœːr, tris] *a* purifying, cleansing; *n* purifier, cleanser.

purification [pyrifikasjɔ̃] *nf* purification.

purifier [pyrifje] *vt* to purify, cleanse, refine; *vr* to clear, become pure.

purin [pyrɛ̃] *nm* liquid manure.

puritanisme [pyritanism] *nm* puritanism.

pur-sang [pyrsɑ̃] nm thoroughbred.
pus [py] nm pus, matter.
pusillanime [pyzillanim] a pusillanimous, faint-hearted.
pustule [pystyl] nf pustule, pimple.
putain [pytɛ̃] nf whore.
putatif, -ive [pytatif, iːv] a putative, supposed.
putois [pytwa] nm pole-cat, skunk.
putréfaction [pytrefaksjɔ̃] nf putrefaction.
putréfier [pytrefye] vtr to putrefy, rot.
putride [pytrid] a putrid, tainted.
pygmée [pigme] n pygmy.
pyjama [piʒama] nm pyjamas.
pylône [piloːn] nm pylon, mast, pole.
pyorrhée [pjɔre] nf pyorrhea.
pyramide [piramid] nf pyramid.
pyromane [pirɔman] n pyromaniac.
python [pitɔ̃] nm python.

Q

quadragénaire [kwadraʒeneːr] an quadragenarian.
quadrangulaire [kwadrɑ̃gylɛːr] a quadrangular.
quadrilatéral [kwadrilatɛral] a quadrilateral.
quadriller [kadrije] vt to rule in squares, cross-rule.
quadrupède [kwadrypɛd] a four-footed; nm quadruped.
quadrupler [kwadryple] vt to quadruple.
quai [ke] nm quay, wharf, embankment, platform.
qualificatif, -ive [kalifikatif, iːv] a qualifying.
qualification [kalifikasjɔ̃] nf qualifying, title.
qualifier [kalifje] vt to qualify, call, describe.
qualité [kalite] nf quality, property, capacity, qualification, rank; **en —** de as, in the capacity of.
quand [kɑ̃] cj ad when; **— même** cj even if; ad all the same.
quant [kɑ̃t] ad **— à** as for, as to, as regards.
quantième [kɑ̃tjɛm] nm day of the month.
quantité [kɑ̃tite] nf quantity, amount, lot.
quarantaine [karɑ̃tɛn] nf (about) forty, quarantine.
quarante [karɑ̃ːt] anm forty.
quarantième [karɑ̃tjɛm] anm fortieth.
quart [kaːr] nm quarter, quarter of a litre watch; **être de —**, to be on watch, on duty.
quarteron [kart(ə)rɔ̃] an quadroon.
quartier [kartje] nm quarter, part, portion, district, ward, quarters; **— général** headquarters.
quartier-maître [kartjemɛːtr] nm quartermaster, leading seaman.

quasi [kazi] ad quasi, almost, all but.
quasiment [kazimɑ̃] ad as it were.
quatorze [katɔrz] anm fourteen, fourteenth.
quatorzième [katɔrzjɛm] anm fourteenth.
quatrain [katrɛ̃] nm quatrain.
quatre [katr] anm four, fourth; **se mettre en quatre**, to do all one can.
quatre-vingt-dix [katrəvɛ̃dis] anm ninety.
quatre-vingts [katrəvɛ̃] anm eighty.
quatrième [katriɛm] fourth.
quatuor [kwatɥɔːr] nm (mus) quartet.
que [k(ə)] cj that, but; ad than, as, how, how many; **ne . . . que**, only; **(soit) — . . . (soit) — . . .**, whether **. . . or; qu'il parle**, let him speak; pr that, whom, which, what; **qu'est-ce qui? qu'est-ce que?** what?
Québec [kebɛk] nm Quebec.
quel, -le [kɛl] a what, which, who, what a; **— que** whoever, whatever.
quelconque [kɛlkɔ̃k] a any, some, whatever, commonplace, ordinary.
quelque [kɛlk(ə)] a some, any; pl some, a few; **— . . . qui, que** whatever, whatsoever; ad some, about; **— . . que** ad however
quelque chose [kɛlkaʃoːz] pn something, anything.
quelquefois [kɛlkəfwa] ad sometimes.
quelque part [kɛlkəpaːr] ad somewhere.
quelqu'un, quelqu'une [kɛlkœ̃, kɛlkyn] pn someone, anyone, one; pl some, a few.
quémander [kemɑ̃de] vi to beg; vt to solicit, beg for.
qu'en dira-t-on [kɑ̃diratɔ̃] nm what people will say, gossip.
quenelle [kənɛl] nf fish ball, forcemeat ball.
quenouille [kənuːj] nf distaff.
querelle [kərɛl] nf quarrel, row.
quereller [kərele] vt to quarrel with; vr to quarrel.
querelleur, -euse [kərelœːr, øːz] a quarrelsome; n quarreller, wrangler.
question [kɛstjɔ̃] nf question, query, matter, point.
questionnaire [kɛstjɔneːr] nm list of questions.
questionner [kɛstjɔne] vt to question.
quête [kɛːt] nf search, quest, collection.
quêter [kɛte] vt to search for, collect.
queue [kø] nf tail, end, train, stalk, stem, rear, queue, file, cue; **finir en — de poisson** to peter out; **piano à — grand** piano; **en, à la — in the** rear.
queue d'aronde [kødarɔ̃ːd] nf dovetail.
queue-de-pie [kødpi] nf tails, evening dress.
queue-de-rat [kødra] nf small taper.
qui [ki] pn who, whom, which, that;

— **que** who(so)ever, whom(so)ever;
— **que ce soit** anyone; — **est-ce que?** whom?

quiconque [kikɔ̃k] *pn* who(so)ever, anyone who.

quiétude [kɥietyd, kje] *nf* quietude.

quignon [kiɲɔ̃] *nm* hunk, chunk.

quille [ki:j] *nf* skittle, ninepin, keel.

quincaillerie [kɛ̃kajri] *nf* ironmongery.

quincaillier [kɛ̃kaje] *nm* ironmonger.

quinine [kinin] *nf* quinine.

quinquennal [kɥɛ̃kɥɛnnal] *a* quinquennial, five-year.

quintal [kɛ̃tal] *nm* quintal, 100 kilogrammes.

quinte [kɛ̃t] *nf* (*mus*) fifth; fit of bad temper; — **de toux** fit of coughing.

quintessence [kɛ̃tɛssɑ̃:s] *nf* quintessence.

quintette [k(ɥ)ɛ̃tɛt] *nm* quintet.

quinteux, -euse [kɛ̃tø, ø:z] *a* fitful, restive, fretful.

quintupler [k(ɥ)ɛ̃typle] *vti* to increase fivefold.

quinzaine [kɛ̃zɛn] *nf* (about) fifteen, fortnight.

quinze [kɛ̃:z] *a nm* fifteen, fifteenth; — **jours** fortnight.

quinzième [kɛ̃zjɛm] *a nm* fifteenth.

quiproquo [kiprɔko] *nm* mistake, misunderstanding.

quittance [kitɑ̃:s] *nf* receipt, discharge.

quitte [kit] *a* quit, rid, free (of); **en être — pour la peur** to get off with a fright; — **à** even though, at the risk of.

quitter [kite] *vt* to quit, leave; **ne quittez pas!** hold the line!

qui-vive [kivi:v] *nm* challenge; **sur le —** on the alert.

quoi [kwa] *pn* what, which; **avoir de — vivre** to have enough to live on; **il n'y a pas de —** don't mention it; **de — écrire** writing materials; **sans —** otherwise; — **qui, que** whatever; — **qu'il en soit be that** as it may; — **que ce soit** anything whatever; **à — bon?** what's the use?

quoique [kwak(ə)] *cj* (al)though.

quolibet [kɔlibɛ] *nm* gibe.

quotidien, -enne [kɔtidjɛ̃, jɛn] *a* daily, everyday; *nm* daily paper.

R

rabâcher [rabɑʃe] *vti* to repeat over and over again.

rabais [rabɛ] *nm* reduction, rebate, allowance; **au —** at a reduced price.

rabaisser [rabɛse] *vt* to lower, reduce, belittle, humble.

rabat-joie [rabaʒwa] *n* killjoy, spoilsport.

rabatteur, -euse [rabatœːr, øːz] *n* tout; *nm* beater.

rabattre [rabatr] *vt* to lower, bring down, turn down, take down, reduce, beat (up); *vi* to turn off; **en —** to climb down; *vr* to fold (down), fall back.

rabbin [rabɛ̃] *nm* rabbi.

rabiot [rabjo] *nm* surplus, buckshee, extra (work).

râble [rɑ:bl] *nm* back, saddle (of hare).

râblé [rɑble] *a* broadbacked, strapping.

rabot [rabo] *nm* plane.

raboter [rabɔte] *vt* to plane, polish.

raboteux, -euse [rabɔtø, øz] *a* rough, bumpy.

rabougrir [rabugriːr] *vt* to stunt; *vir* to become stunted.

rabougrissement [rabugrismɑ̃] *nm* stuntedness.

rabrouer [rabrue] *vt* to scold, rebuke, rebuff, snub.

racaille [rakɑ:j] *nf* rabble, riff-raff, trash.

raccommodage [rakɔmɔdɑ:ʒ] *nm* mend(ing), repair(ing), darn(ing).

raccommodement [rakɔmɔdmɑ̃] *nm* reconciliation.

raccommoder [rakɔmɔde] *vt* to mend, repair, darn, reconcile; *vr* to make it up.

raccord [rakɔ:r] *nm* join, joint, link, connection.

raccorder [rakɔrde] *vt* to join, link up, connect bring into line; *vr* to fit together.

raccourci [rakursi] *a* short(ened), abridged; **à bras —(s)** with might and main, with a vengeance; *nm* abridgement, foreshortening, short cut; **en —** in miniature, in short.

raccourcir [rakursiːr] *vt* to shorten, curtail, foreshorten; *vir* to grow shorter, draw in.

raccroc [rakro] *nm* fluke.

raccrocher [rakrɔʃe] *vt* to hook up, hang up, get hold of again; *vr* to clutch, catch on, recover, cling.

race [ras] *nf* race, descent, strain, stock, breed; **avoir de la —** to be pure-bred, pedigreed; **bon chien chasse de —** what's bred in the bone comes out in the flesh.

racé [rase] *a* thoroughbred.

rachat [raʃa] *a* repurchase, redemption.

rachetable [raʃtabl] *a* redeemable.

racheter [raʃte] *vt* to repurchase, buy back, redeem, ransom, retrieve, atone for.

rachitique [raʃitik] *a* rachitic, rickety.

racine [rasin] *nf* root.

racisme [rasism] *nm* colour bar, colour prejudice.

raclée [rakle] *nf* thrashing.

racler [rɑkle] *vt* to scrape, rake, rasp; **se — la gorge** to clear one's throat.

racloir [rɑklwaːr] *nf* scraper.

racoler [rakɔle] *vt* to recruit, enlist, tout for.

racoleur [rakɔlœːr] *nm* recruiting-sergeant, tout.

racontars [rakɔ̃taːr] *nm pl* gossip, tittle-tattle.

raconter [rakɔ̃te] *vt* to relate, tell (about), recount; *vi* to tel' a story; **en —** to exaggerate, spin a yarn

raconteur, -euse [rakɔ̃tœːr, øːz] *n* (story-)teller, narrator

racornir [rakɔrniːr] *vtr* to harden, toughen.

rade [rad] *nf* roadstead, roads.

radeau [rado] *nm* raft.

radiateur [radjatœːr] *a* radiating; *nm* radiator.

radiation [radjasjɔ̃] *nf* erasure, cancellation, striking off, radiation.

radical [radikal] *a nm* radical.

radier [radje] *vt* to erase, cancel, strike off radiate.

radieux, -euse [radjø, øːz] *a* radiant, beaming.

radio [radjo] *nf* wireless, X-rays; **par —** broadcast; *nm* wireless message, wireless operator.

radio-actif [radjoaktif iːv] *a* radio-active.

radio-diffusion [radjɔdifyzjɔ̃] *nf* broadcast(ing).

radiogramme [radjɔgram] *nm* wireless message, X-ray photograph.

radiographie [radjɔgrafi] *nf* radiography.

radiologie [radjɔlɔʒi] *nf* radiology.

radio-reportage [radjɔrəpɔrtaːʒ] *nm* running commentary.

radiotélégraphie [radjɔtelegrafi] *nf* wireless telegraphy.

radiothérapie [radjɔtɛrapi] *nf* radiotherapy.

radis [radi] *nm* radish.

radium [radjɔm] *nm* radium.

radotage [radɔtaːʒ] *nm* drivel, twaddle.

radoter [radɔte] *vi* to drivel, talk nonsense.

radoteur, -euse [radɔtœːr, øːz] *n* dotard.

radoub [radu] *nm* repair, refitting; **en —** in dry dock.

radoucir [radusiːr] *vt* to calm, soften, mollify; *vr* to grow milder.

rafale [rafal] *nf* squall, gust, burst.

raffermir [rafɛrmiːr] *vt* to harden, strengthen, fortify; *vr* to harden, improve be restored.

raffiné [rafine] *a* refined, subtle, fine, polished.

raffiner [rafine] *vt* to refine; *vi* to be too subtle; *vr* to become refined.

raffinerie [rafinri] *nf* refinery.

raffoler [rafɔle] *vi* to be very fond (of **de**), dote (upon **de**), be mad (on **de**).

rafistoler [rafistɔle] *vt* to patch up, do up.

rafle [raːfl] *nf* raid, clean sweep, round-up.

rafler [rafle] *vt* to make clean sweep of round up, comb out.

rafraichir [rafrɛʃiːr] *vt* to refresh, cool, freshen up, touch up, trim, brush up; *vr* to turn cooler, have sth to drink, rest.

rafraîchissement [rafrɛʃismɑ̃] *nm* refreshing cooling, freshening up, brushing up; *pl* refreshments.

ragaillardir [ragajardiːr] *vtr* to cheer up, revive.

rage [raːʒ] *n* rage, madness, rabies, mania, passion; **— de dents** violent attack of toothache; **faire —** to rage.

rager [raʒe] *vi* to rage; **faire — qn** to make s.o. wild.

rageur, -euse [raʒœːr, øːz] *a* hot-tempered, passionate.

ragot [rago] *nm* gossip.

ragoût [ragu] *nm* stew.

rahat-loukoum [raatlukum] *nm* Turkish delight.

raid [rɛd] *nm* raid, long-distance flight, l.-d. un.

raide [rɛd] *a* stiff, taut, unbending, steep; **coup —** stinging blow; **c'est un peu —!** that's a bit thick! **— mort** stone-dead.

raideur [rɛdœːr] *nf* stiffness, tightness, steepness; **avec —** stiffly, arrogantly.

raidir [rɛdiːr] *vt* to stiffen, tighten; *vr* to stiffen, brace oneself, steel oneself.

raie [rɛ] *nf* line, stroke, streak, stripe, parting, ridge, ray, (*fish*) skate.

railler [raje] *vt* to jeer at, laugh at; *vi* to joke; *vr* to make fun (of **de**), scoff (at **de**).

raillerie [rajri] *nf* raillery, banter, joke.

railleur, -euse [rajœːr, øːz] *a* bantering, mocking; *n* joker, scoffer.

rainure [rɛnyːr] *nf* groove, slot, channel.

rais [rɛ] *nm* spoke.

raisin [rɛzɛ̃] *nm* grape; **—s secs** raisins; **—s de Corinthe** currants.

raison [rɛzɔ̃] *nf* reason, motive, right mind, sense(s), satisfaction, ratio; **avoir — to** be right; **avoir — de qn. de qch** to get the better of s.o., sth; **se faire une —** to make the best of it; **à — de** at the rate of.

raisonnable [rɛzɔnabl] *a* reasonable, fair adequate.

raisonnement [rɛzɔnmɑ̃] *nm* reasoning, argument.

raisonner [rɛzɔne] *vi* to reason, argue; *vt* to reason with, study.

raisonneur, -euse [rɛzɔnœːr, øːz] *a* reasoning, argumentative; *n* reasoner, arguer.

rajeunir [raʒœniːr] *vt* to rejuvenate, make (s.o. look) younger, renovate; *vi* to get younger.

rajuster [raʒyste] *vt* to readjust, put straight.

râle [rɑːl] *nm* rattle (in the throat).
ralenti [ralɑ̃ti] *a* slow(er): *nm* slow motion; **au — dead** slow; **mettre au —** to slow down, throttle down.
ralentir [ralɑ̃tiːr] *vti* to slacken, slow down.
râler [rɑle] *vi* to rattle, be at one's last gasp, be furious.
ralliement [ralimɑ̃] *nm* rally(ing); **mot de —** password.
rallier [ralje] *vt* to rally, rejoin, win over; *vr* to rally, join.
rallonge [ralɔ̃ːʒ] *nf* extension piece, extra leaf.
rallonger [ralɔ̃ʒe] *vt* to lengthen, let down.
rallye [rali] *nm* race-meeting, rally.
ramage [ramaːʒ] *nm* floral design, warbling, singing.
ramassé [ramase] *a* thickset, stocky, compact.
ramasser [ramase] *vt* to gather, collect, pick up; *vr* to gather, crouch.
rame [ram] *nf* oar, ream, string, train.
rameau [ramo] *nm* branch, bough; **le dimanche des R—x** Palm Sunday.
ramener [ramne] *vt* to bring back, bring round, reduce, pull down, restore.
ramer [rame] *vi* to row, pull.
rameur [ramœːr] *n* rower, oarsman.
ramier [ramje] *nm* wood pigeon.
ramification [ramifikasjɔ̃] *nf* ramification, branch(ing).
se ramifier [səramifje] *vr* to branch out.
ramollir [ramɔliːr] *vt* to soften, enervate; *vr* to soften, grow soft (-headed).
ramollissement [ramɔlismɑ̃] *nm* softening.
ramoner [ramɔne] *vt* to sweep, rake out.
ramoneur [ramɔnœːr] *nm* (chimney-) sweep.
rampe [rɑ̃ːp] *nf* slope, gradient, handrail, footlights, ramp.
ramper [rɑ̃pe] *vi* to creep, crawl, grovel, cringe.
rancart [rɑ̃kaːr] *nm* **mettre au —** to cast aside.
rance [rɑ̃ːs] *a* rancid.
rancir [rɑ̃siːr] *vi* to become rancid.
rancœur [rɑ̃kœːr] *nf* rancour, bitterness, resentment.
rançon [rɑ̃sɔ̃] *nf* ransom.
rancune [rɑ̃kyn] *nf* rancour, grudge, spite, ill-feeling.
rancunier, -ière [rɑ̃kynje, jɛːr] *a* vindictive, spiteful.
randonnée [rɑ̃dɔne] *nf* tour, run, excursion.
rang [rɑ̃] *nm* row, line, rank, status; **rompre les —s** to disperse, dismiss; **de premier —** first-class.
rangé [rɑ̃ʒe] *a* orderly, well-ordered, steady, staid; **bataille —e** pitched battle.
rangée [rɑ̃ʒe] *nf* row, line.

ranger [rɑ̃ʒe] *vt* to arrange, draw up, put away, tidy, keep back, rank, range; *vr* to draw up, range, fall in (with à); **se — du côté de** to side with; **se — de côté** to stand aside.
ranimer [ranime] *vt* to revive, rekindle, stir up; *vr* to come to life again.
rapace [rapas] *a* rapacious.
rapacité [rapasite] *nf* rapaciousness.
rapatrier [rapatrie] *v.* to repatriate.
râpe [rɑːp] *nf* rasp, file, grater.
râpé [rɑpe] *a* grated, shabby, threadbare.
râper [rɑpe] *vt* to rasp, grate, wear out.
rapetasser [raptase] *vt* to patch (up).
rapetisser [raptise] *vt* to shorten, make smaller; *vir* to shrink, shorten.
rapide [rapid] *a* rapid, quick, swift, steep; *nm* rapid, express train.
rapidité [rapidite] *nf* rapidity, swiftness, steepness.
rapiécer [rapjese] *vt* to patch.
rapin [rapɛ̃] *nm* (*fam*) art student.
rappareiller [raparɛje] *vt* to match.
rapparier [raparje] *vt* to match.
rappel [rapɛl] *nm* recall, call(ing), reminder, repeal.
rappeler [raple] *vt* to recall, call back, remind, repeal; *vr* to recall, remember; **rappelez-moi à son bon souvenir** remember me kindly to him.
rapport [rapɔːr] *nm* return, yield, profit, report, relation, connection, contact; *pl* relations, terms; **en — avec** in keeping with; **par — à** with regard to; **sous ce —** in this respect.
rapporter [rapɔrte] *vt* to bring back, bring in, yield, report, tell tales, revoke, refer; *vr* to agree, tally, fit together, refer, relate; **s'en — à** to rely on, to leave it to, go by.
rapporteur, -euse [rapɔrtœːr, øːz] *n* tale bearer; *nm* reporter, recorder, protractor.
rapproché [raprɔʃe] *a* near, close (-set), related.
rapprochement [raprɔʃmɑ̃] *nm* bringing together, reconciling, comparing, nearness, reconciliation.
rapprocher [raprɔʃe] *vt* to bring together, bring near(er), draw up, compare, reconcile; *vr* to draw near(er), become reconciled.
rapt [rapt] *nm* kidnapping, abduction.
raquette [rakɛt] *nf* racket, snowshoe, prickly pear.
rare [raːr] *a* rare, unusual, sparse.
rarement [rarmɑ̃] *ad* seldom, rarely.
rareté [rarte] *nf* rarity, scarcity, unusualness, rare happening, curiosity.
ras [rɑ] *a* close-cropped, close-shaven, bare; **en —e campagne** in the open country; **faire table —e**

de to make a clean sweep of; **à, au — de** level with, flush with, up to.

rasade [razad] *n,* bumper.

rase-mottes [razmɔt] *nm* **voler à — to** hedge-hop.

raser [raze] *vt* to shave, bore, raze to the ground, skim (over, along), hug; *vr* to shave, be bored; **se faire — to** have a shave.

rasoir [razwaːr] *nm* razor; **qu'il est —! how** boring, tiresome he is!

rassasier [rasazje] *vt* to satisfy, satiate, surfeit; *vr* to eat one's fill.

rassemblement [rasɑ̃bləmɑ̃] *nm* assembling, gathering, fall-in, crowd.

rassembler [rasɑ̃ble] *vtr* to assemble, gather together, muster.

rasséréner [raserene] *vt* to clear (up); *vr* to clear up, brighten up.

rassis [rasi] *a* settled, staid, sane, stale.

rassurer [rasyre] *vt* to reassure, strengthen; *vr* to feel reassured, set one's mind at rest.

rat [ra] *nm* rat, miser; **— de bibliothèque** bookworm; **— de cave** exciseman, wax taper; **— d'église** excessively pious person; **— d'hôtel** hotel thief; **mort aux —s** rat-poison.

ratatiné [ratatine] *a* shrivelled, wizened.

rate [rat] *nf* spleen; **ne pas se fouler la — to** take things easy.

raté [rate] *a* miscarried, bungled, muffed; *n* failure, misfire.

râteau [rɑto] *nm* rake, cue-rest.

râteler [rɑtle] *vt* to rake up.

râtelier [rɑtəlje] *nm* rack, denture.

rater [rate] *vi* to miscarry, misfire, fail; *vt* to miss, fail, foozle, muff.

ratière [ratjeːr] *nf* rat-trap.

ratifier [ratifje] *vt* to ratify.

ration [rasjɔ̃] *nf* ration, allowance.

rationnel, -elle [rasjɔnɛl] *a* rational.

rationnement [rasjɔnmɑ̃] *nm* rationing.

rationner [rasjɔne] *vt* to ration (out).

ratisser [ratise] *vt* to rake.

ratissoire [ratiswaːr] *nf* rake, hoe, scraper.

rattacher [rataʃe] *vt* to (re)fasten, tie up, bind, connect; *vr* to be connected (with à), fastened (to à).

rattraper [ratrape] *vt* to recapture, catch (again, up), overtake, recover; *vr* to save oneself, recoup oneself, make it up.

rature [ratyːr] *nf* erasure.

raturer [ratyre] *vt* to erase, cross out.

rauque [roːk] *a* raucous, hoarse, harsh.

ravage [ravaːʒ] *nm* (*usu pl*) havoc.

ravager [ravaʒe] *vt* to devastate, lay waste.

ravaler [ravale] *vt* to swallow (again, down), disparage, roughcast; *vr* to lower oneself; **— ses paroles to** eat one's words.

ravauder [ravode] *vt* to mend, darn.

ravi [ravi] *a* delighted, overjoyed, enraptured.

ravigoter [ravigɔte] *vtr* to revive, buck up.

ravin [ravɛ̃] *nm* ravine.

raviner [ravine] *v* to gully, cut up, rut.

ravir [raviːr] *vt* to ravish, carry off, enrapture, delight; **à — ravishingly,** delightfully.

se raviser [səravize] *vr* to change one's mind.

ravissant [ravisɑ̃] *a* lovely, delightful, bewitching, ravishing.

ravitaillement [ravitajmɑ̃] *nm* revictualling, supply(ing); **service du — Army** Service Corps.

ravitailler [ravitaje] *vtr* to revictual; *vt* to supply.

ravitailleur [ravitajœːr] *nm* carrier, supply-ship.

raviver [ravive] *vtr* to revive, brighten.

rayer [rɛje] *vt* to scratch, rule, stripe, delete, strike off.

rayon [rɛjɔ̃] *nm* ray, beam, radius, drill, row, shelf, counter, department; **— visuel** line of sight; **— de miel** honeycomb; **chef de — shop**walker, buyer.

rayonne [rɛjɔn] *nf* rayon.

rayonnement [rɛjɔnmɑ̃] *nm* radiation, radiance.

rayonner [rɛjɔne] *vi* to radiate, beam, be radiant.

rayure [rɛjyːr] *nf* scratch, stripe, erasure, striking off.

raz [rɑ] *nm* strong current; **— de marée** tide-race, tidal wave.

ré [re] *nm* the note D, D string.

réactif [reaktif, iːv] *a* **papier — litmus** paper.

réacteur [reaktœːr] *nm* reactor, (*aut*) choke.

réaction [reaksjɔ̃] *nf* reaction; **avion à — jet-plane.**

réactionnaire [reaksjɔnɛːr] *an* reactionary.

réagir [reaʒiːr] *vi* to react.

réalisation [realizasjɔ̃] *nf* realization, carrying into effect, selling out.

réaliser [realize] *vt* to realize, carry out, sell out; *vr* to materialize, be realized.

réalisme [realism] *nm* realism.

réaliste [realist] *a* realistic; *n* realist.

réalité [realite] *nf* reality.

réarmement [rearməmɑ̃] *nm* rearming, refitting.

réassurer [reasyre] *vt* to reassure, reinsure.

rébarbatif, -ive [rebarbatif, iːv] *a* forbidding, grim, crabbed, repulsive.

rebattre [rəbatr] *vt* to beat again, reshuffle; **— les oreilles à qn** to repeat the same thing over and over again to s.o.

rebattu [rəbaty] *a* hackneyed, trite.

rebelle [rəbɛl] *a* rebellious, obstinate; *n* rebel.

rébellion [rebɛljɔ̃] nf rebellion, rising.

reboiser [rəbwaze] vt to retimber, (re)afforest.

rebondi [rəbɔ̃di] a plump, chubby, rounded.

rebondir [rəbɔ̃diːr] vi to rebound, bounce, start up all over again.

rebord [rəbɔːr] nm edge, hem, border, rim, flange.

rebours [rəbuːr] nm wrong way, contrary; à, au — against the grain, backwards, the wrong way.

rebouteur [rəbutœːr] nm bone-setter.

rebrousse-poil [rəbruspwal] ad à — the wrong way, against the nap or hair.

rebuffade [rəbyfad] nf rebuff.

rébus [rebyːs] nm puzzle, riddle.

rebut [rəby] nm scrap, waste, rubbish, scum; pl rejects; **bureau des** —**s** returned-letter office.

rebutant [rəbytɑ̃] a discouraging, irksome, repulsive, forbidding.

rebuter [rəbyte] vt to rebuff, repulse, discourage; vr to become discouraged, jib.

récalcitrant [rekalsitrɑ̃] a recalcitrant, refractory.

recaler [rəkale] vt to fail.

récapituler [rekapityle] vt to recapitulate.

receler [rəsele] vt to conceal, hide, receive (stolen goods).

receleur, -euse [rəslœːr, øːz] n receiver, fence.

récemment [resamɑ̃] ad recently, lately.

recensement [rəsɑ̃smɑ̃] nm census, counting.

recenser [rəsɑ̃se] vt to take the census of, count, check off.

récent [resɑ̃] a recent, fresh, late.

récépissé [resepise] nm receipt.

réceptacle [resɛptakl] nm receptacle.

récepteur, -trice [resɛptœːr, tris] a receiving; nm receiver.

réception [resɛpsjɔ̃] nf receipt, reception, admission, welcome, receiving desk; **accuser** — **de** to acknowledge receipt of; **avis, (accusé) de** — **advice** (acknowledgement) of delivery; **jour de** — at-home day.

recette [rəsɛt] nf receipt(s), takings, gate-money, recipe.

receveur, -euse [rəsəvœːr, øːz] n receiver, addressee, tax-collector, conductor, -tress; — **des Postes** postmaster.

recevoir [rəsəvwaːr] vt to receive, get, entertain, welcome, take in (boarders), accept, admit; vi be at home.

rechange [rəʃɑ̃ːʒ] nm replacement, spare, change, refill; a **de** — spare.

réchapper [reʃape] vi to escape, recover.

recharger [rəʃarʒe] vt to recharge, reload.

réchaud [reʃo] nm portable stove, (gas-)ring, hot-plate.

réchauffé [reʃofe] nm warmed-up dish, rehash.

réchauffer [reʃofe] vt to reheat, warm up, stir up.

rêche [rɛʃ] a harsh, rough, crabbed, sour.

recherche [rəʃɛrʃ] nf search, pursuit, studied refinement; pl research.

recherché [rəʃɛrʃe] a in great demand, choice, mannered, affected, studied.

rechercher [rəʃɛrʃe] vt to search (for, into), seek.

rechigner [rəʃiɲe] vi to look surly, jib (at à, devant).

rechute [rəʃyt] nf relapse.

récidiver [residive] vi to offend again, recur.

récidiviste [residivist] n old offender.

récif [resif] nm reef.

récipient [resipjɑ̃] nm receiver, container, vessel.

réciprocité [resiprɔsite] nf reprocity.

réciproque [resiprɔk] a reciprocal, mutual; nf the like.

réciproquement [resiprɔkmɑ̃] ad reciprocally, vice-versa, mutually.

récit [resi] nm recital, account, story, narrative.

récitation [resitasjɔ̃] nf reciting, recitation.

réciter [resite] vt to recite, say.

réclamation [reklamasjɔ̃] nf complaint, claim.

réclame [reklaːm] nf publicity, advertising, advertisement, sign.

réclamer [reklame] vi to complain, protest; vt to claim, demand back, beg for, call (out) for; vr — **de qn** to quote s.o. as one's authority, to use s.o.'s name.

reclus [rəkly] n recluse.

réclusion [reklyzjɔ̃] nf reclusion, seclusion.

recoin [rəkwɛ̃] nm nook, recess.

récolte [rekɔlt] nf harvest(ing), crop(s).

récolter [rekɔlte] vt to harvest, gather (in).

recommandation [rəkɔmɑ̃dasjɔ̃] nf recommendation, advice; **lettre de** — letter of introduction, testimonial.

recommander [rəkɔmɑ̃de] vt to (re)commend, advise, register.

recommencer [rəkɔmɑ̃se] vti to recommence, begin again.

récompense [rekɔ̃pɑ̃ːs] nf recompense, reward, prize.

récompenser [rekɔ̃pɑ̃se] vt to recompense, reward, requite.

réconciliation [rekɔ̃siljasjɔ̃] nf reconciliation.

réconcilier [rekɔ̃silje] vt to reconcile; vr to make it up, make one's peace, become friends again.

reconduire [rəkɔ̃dɥiːr] vt to accompany back, escort, see home, show out.

réconfort [rekɔ̃fɔːr] *nm* comfort, consolation.

réconforter [rekɔ̃fɔrte] *vt* to comfort, console, fortify, refresh; *vr* to cheer up.

reconnaissance [rəkɔnɛsɑ̃ːs] *nf* recognition, acknowledgment, admission, reconnoitring, reconnaissance, gratitude, thankfulness.

reconnaissant [rəkɔnɛsɑ̃] *a* grateful, thankful.

reconnaître [rəkɔnɛːtr] *vt* to recognize, acknowledge, reconnoitre; *vr* to acknowledge, get one's bearings; **ne plus s'y —** to be quite lost, bewildered.

reconstituant [rəkɔ̃stituɑ̃] *a nm* restorative.

record [rəkɔːr] *nm* record.

recourbé [rəkurbe] *a* bent (back, down, round) curved, crooked.

recourir [rəkuriːr] *vi* to run (again, back), have recourse (to à), appeal (to à).

recours [rəkuːr] *nm* recourse, resort, claim, appeal.

recouvrement [rəkuvrəmɑ̃] *nm* recovery, collection, recovering, cover (ing), overlapping.

recouvrer [rəkuvre] *vt* to recover, regain, collect.

recouvrir [rəkuvriːr] *vt* to recover, cover (over), overlap; *vr* to become overcast.

récréation [rekreasjɔ̃] *nf* recreation, amusement, relaxation, playtime; **cour de —** playground; **en —** at play.

récréer [rekree] *vt* to enliven, refresh, entertain, amuse; *vr* to take some recreation.

se récrier [sərekrie] *vr* to cry out, exclaim, protest.

récriminer [rekrimine] *vi* to recriminate

se recroqueviller [sərəkrɔkvije] *vr* to curl (up, in), shrivel (up).

recru [rəkry] *a* **— de fatigue** worn out, dead tired.

recrudescence [rəkrydɛssɑ̃ːs] *nf* recrudescence.

recrue [rəkry] *nf* recruit.

recruter [rəkryte] *vt* to recruit, enlist.

rectangle [rɛktɑ̃ːgl] *a* right-angled; *nm* rectangle.

rectangulaire [rɛktɑ̃gylɛːr] *a* rectangular.

recteur [rɛktœːr] *nm* rector.

rectification [rɛktifikasjɔ̃] *nf* rectification, rectifying, straightening, (re)adjustment.

rectifier [rɛktifje] *vt* to rectify, straighten, adjust.

rectiligne [rɛktiliɲ] *a* rectilinear.

rectitude [rɛktityd] *nf* straightness, rectitude.

reçu [rəsy] *pp* of **recevoir**; *nm* receipt.

recueil [rəkœːj] *nm* collection.

recueillement [rəkœjmɑ̃] *nm* meditation, composure, concentration.

recueilli [rəkœji] *a* meditative, rapt, concentrated, still.

recueillir [rəkœjiːr] *vt* to gather, collect, take in; *vr* to collect one's thoughts, commune with oneself.

recul [rəkyl] *nm* recoil, backward movement, room to move back.

reculade [rəkylad] *nf* backward movement, withdrawal.

reculé [rəkyle] *a* remote.

reculer [rəkyle] *vi* to move back, draw back; *vt* to move back, postpone.

reculons [rəkylɔ̃] *ad* **à —** backwards.

récupérer [rekypere] *vt* to recover, recoup, salvage; *vr* to recuperate.

récurer [rekyre] *vt* to scour.

récuser [rekyze] *vt* to challenge, take exception to; *vr* to refuse to give an opinion, disclaim competence, decline.

rédacteur, -trice [redaktœːr, tris] *n* writer, editor.

rédaction [redaksjɔ̃] *nf* writing, editing, editorial staff, newspaper office, composition, wording.

reddition [reddisjɔ̃] *nf* surrender.

rédempteur, -trice [redɑ̃ptœːr, tris] *a* redeeming; *n* redeemer.

rédemption [redɑ̃psjɔ̃] *nf* redemption.

redevable [rədvabl] *a* indebted, obliged.

redevance [rədvɑ̃ːs] *nf* rent, tax, due.

rédiger [rediʒe] *vt* to draft, write, edit.

redingote [rədɛ̃gɔt] *nf* frock-coat.

redire [rədiːr] *vt* to repeat; **trouver à — à** to find fault with.

redite [rədit] *nf* repetition.

redondance [rədɔ̃dɑ̃ːs] *nf* redundance.

redoubler [rəduble] *vt* to redouble, reline, repeat (*a class*); *vi* to redouble.

redoutable [rədutabl] *a* formidable.

redoute [rədut] *nf* redoubt.

redouter [rədute] *vt* to dread.

redressement [rədrɛsmɑ̃] *nm* setting up again, righting, rectifying, straightening, redress.

redresser [rədrɛse] *vt* to set upright again, right, rectify, straighten; *vr* to sit up again, draw oneself up, right oneself.

réductible [redyktibl] *a* reducible.

réduction [redyksjɔ̃] *nf* reduction, cut, conquest.

réduire [redɥiːr] *vt* to reduce; *vr* to be reduced, confine oneself to, boil down.

réduit [redɥi] *nm* retreat, hovel, redoubt.

rééducation [reedykasjɔ̃] *nf* **centre de —** probation centre, borstal.

réel, -elle [reɛl] *a* real, actual; *nm* reality.

réexpédier [reɛkspedje] *vt* to forward, retransmit.

réfaction [refaksjɔ̃] *nf* rebate, allowance.

refaire [rəfɛːr] *vt* to remake, do again, make again, repair, take in; *vr* to recuperate.

réfection [refɛksjɔ̃] *nf* remaking, repairing.

réfectoire [refɛktwaːr] *nm* dining-hall.

référence [referɑ̃ːs] *nf* reference.

référer [refere] *vt* to refer, ascribe; *vir* to refer (to à).

refiler [rəfile] *vt* to fob off, pass on.

réfléchi [refleʃi] *a* thoughtful, considered, reflexive.

réfléchir [refleʃiːr] *vt* to reflect, throw back; *vi* to reflect, consider; *vr* to be reflected.

reflet [rəflɛ] *nm* reflection, gleam.

refléter [rəflete] *vt* to reflect, throw back.

réflexe [reflɛks] *a nm* reflex.

réflexion [reflɛksjɔ̃] *nf* reflection, thought, remark.

refluer [rəflye] *vi* to ebb, surge back.

reflux [rəfly] *nm* ebb(-tide), surging back

refondre [rəfɔ̃ːdr] *vt* to recast, reorganize.

refonte [rəfɔ̃ːt] *nf* recasting, reorganization.

réformateur, -trice [reformatœːr, tris] *a* reforming; *n* reformer.

réformation [reformasjɔ̃] *nf* reformation.

réforme [reform] *nf* reform, reformation, discharge.

réformer [reforme] *vt* to reform, discharge (as unfit).

réformé [reforme] *n* protestant, disabled soldier.

refoulement [rəfulmɑ̃] *nm* forcing back, repression.

refouler [rəfule] *vt* to drive back, repress.

réfractaire [refraktɛːr] *an* refractory, insubordinate.

réfracter [refrakte] *vt* to refract; *vr* to be refracted.

refrain [rərrɛ̃] *nm* refrain, theme, chorus.

réfréner [rəfrene] *vt* to restrain, curb.

réfrigérant [refriʒerɑ̃] *nm* refrigerator, cooler.

réfrigérer [refriʒere] *vt* to refrigerate, cool, chill.

refroidir [rəfrwadiːr] *vt* to chill, cool, damp; *vir* to grow cold, cool down.

refroidissement [rəfrwadismɑ̃] *nm* cooling (down), chill.

refuge [rəfyːʒ] *nm* shelter, refuge, traffic island.

réfugié [refyʒje] *n* refugee.

se réfugier [sərefyʒje] *vr* to take refuge.

refus [rəfy] *nm* refusal; **ce n'est pas de —** it is not to be refused.

refuser [rəfyze] *vtr* to refuse; *vt* to reject, fail, turn away, grudge.

réfuter [refyte] *vt* to refute, disprove.

regagner [rəgaɲe] *vt* to regain, recover, get back to.

regain [rəgɛ̃] *nm* aftercrop, renewal, fresh lease.

régal [regal] *nm* feast, treat.

régaler [regale] *vt* to entertain, treat.

regard [rəgaːr] *nm* look, glance, gaze; **au — de** compared with; **en — de** opposite.

regardant [rəgardɑ̃] *a* particular, mean, stingy.

regarder [rəgarde] *vt* to look at, consider concern, watch; *vi* to look (on to **sur**), be particular (about à).

régate [regat] *nf* regatta, boater.

régence [reʒɑ̃ːs] *nf* regency, fob chain, necktie.

régénérer [reʒenere] *vt* to regenerate.

régen [reʒɑ̃] *n* regent, governor.

régenter [reʒɑ̃te] *vt* to lord it over, domineer.

régie [reʒi] *nf* management, stewardship, excise.

regimber [rəʒɛ̃be] *vi* to kick, jib (at contre).

régime [reʒim] *nm* diet, government, administration, system, rules, flow, bunch object.

régiment [reʒimɑ̃] *nm* regiment.

région [reʒjɔ̃] *nf* region, district.

régional [reʒjonal] *a* regional, local.

régir [reʒiːr] *vt* to govern, manage.

régisseur [reʒisœːr] *nm* agent, steward stage-manager.

registre [rəʒistr] *nm* register, account-book.

réglage [rɛglaːʒ] *nm* ruling, adjusting, turning.

règle [rɛgl] *nf* rule, ruler; **en — in** order; *pl* menses, period.

réglé [regle] *a* ruled, regular, steady.

règlement [rɛgləmɑ̃] *nm* regulation, settlement, rule.

réglementaire [rɛgləmɑ̃tɛːr] *a* statutory, regulation.

réglementer [rɛgləmɑ̃te] *vt* to make rules or, regulate.

régler [regle] *vt* to rule, order, adjust, settle; *vr* to model oneself (on **sur**).

réglisse [reglis] *nf* liquorice.

règne [rɛɲ] *nm* reign, sway, kingdom.

régner [reɲe] *vi* to reign, prevail.

regorger [rəgɔrʒe] *vt* to disgorge; *vi* to overflow (with de), abound (in de).

régression [regresjɔ̃] *nf* regression, recession, drop.

regret [rəgrɛ] *nm* regret, sorrow; **à — regretfully**; **être au — (de)** to be sorry.

regretter [rəgrɛte] *vt* to regret, be sorry (for), miss.

régulariser [regylarize] *vt* to regularize, put in order.

régularité [regylarite] *nf* regularity, steadiness, punctuality.

régulateur, -trice [regylatœːr, tris] *a* regulating; *nm* regulator, governor, throttle.

régulier, -ière [regylje, ɛːr] *a* regular, steady, punctual.

réhabiliter [reabilite] *vt* to rehabilitate, discharge.

rehausser [rəose] *vt* to raise, heighten, enhance, accentuate, bring out.

rein [rɛ̃] *nm* kidney; *pl* back.

reine [rɛn] *nf* queen.

reine-claude [rɛnkloːd] *nf* greengage.

réintégrer [reɛ̃tegre] *vt* to reinstate, take up again.

réitérer [reitere] *vt* to repeat, reiterate.

rejaillir [rəʒajiːr] *vi* to gush out, be reflected come back (upon **sur**).

rejet [rəʒɛ] *nm* rejection, throwing up (out).

rejeter [rəʒ(ə)te] *vt* to reject, throw (back, out); *vr* to fall back (on **sur**).

rejeton [rəʒtɔ̃] *nm* shoot, offspring.

rejoindre [rəʒwɛ̃ːdr] *vt* to (re)join, overtake; *vr* to meet (again).

réjouir [reʒwiːr] *vt* to delight, hearten, amuse; *vr* to rejoice, be delighted.

réjouissance [reʒwisãːs] *nf* rejoicing, merrymaking.

relâche [rəlɑːʃ] *nm* relaxation, respite, no performance; *nf* (port of) call.

relâchement [rəlɑʃmã] *nm* slackening, relaxing, relaxation, looseness.

relâcher [rəlɑʃe] *vt* to slacken, loosen, relax, release; *vr* to slacken, get loose, abate, grow lax, milder.

relais [rəlɛ] *nm* relay, stage, shift, posting-house.

relancer [rəlãse] *vt* to throw back; to go after (s.o.); to be at (s.o.); restart.

relater [rəlate] *vt* to relate, report.

relatif, -ive [rəlatif, iːv] *a* relative, relating (to **à**).

relation [rəlasjɔ̃] *nf* relation, contact, connection, account.

relaxer [rəlakse] *vt* to release; *vr* to relax.

relayer [rəlɛje] *vt* to relay, relieve; *vi* to change horses.

relent [rəlã] *nm* stale smell, mustiness.

relève [rəlɛːv] *nf* relief, changing (of guard).

relevé [rəlve] *a* lofty, spicy; *nm* statement, account.

relever [rəlve] *vt* to raise up (again), turn up, pick up, relieve, set off, point out; *vi* to be dependent (on **de**); *vr* to rise (again), recover.

relief [rəljɛf] *nm* relief, prominence.

relier [rəlje] *vt* to bind (again), join, connect.

relieur, -euse [rəljœːr, øːz] *n* bookbinder.

religieux, -euse [rəliʒjø, øːz] *a* religious; *n* monk, nun.

religion [rəliʒjɔ̃] *nf* religion.

reliquaire [rəlikɛːr] *nm* shrine.

reliquat [rəlika] *nm* remainder, after-effects.

relique [rəlik] *nf* relic.

reliure [rəljyːr] *nf* (book)binding.

reluire [rəlɥiːr] *vi* to shine, gleam.

reluquer [rəlyke] *vt* to eye.

remailler [rəmaje] *vt* to remesh, mend.

remanier [rəmanje] *vt* to rehandle, recast.

remarquable [rəmarkabl] *a* remarkable (for **par**).

remarque [rəmark] *nf* remark.

remarquer [rəmarke] *vt* to remark, notice.

rembarrer [rãbare] *vt* to tell off, snub.

remblai [rãblɛ] *nm* embankment.

rembourrer [rãbure] *vt* to stuff, pad.

rembourser [rãburse] *vt* to refund, repay.

rembrunir [rãbryniːr] *vtr* to darken, become sad; *vt* to sadden.

remède [rəmɛd] *nm* remedy, cure.

remédier [rəmedje] *vt* — **à** to remedy.

remembrement [rəmãbrəmã] *nm* reallocation of land.

remémorer [rəmemɔre] *vt* to remind (of); *vr* to remember.

remerciement [rəmɛrsimã] *nm* thanks.

remercier [rəmɛrsje] *vt* to thank, dismiss, decline.

remettre [rəmɛtr] *vt* to put back (again), hand (over, in), remit, postpone; *vr* to recover, begin; **s'en** — **à qn** to rely on s.o., leave it to s.o.

remise [rəmiːz] *nf* putting back, off, remittance, delivery, rebate, shed.

rémission [remisjɔ̃] *nf* remission, pardon.

remonter [rəmɔ̃te] *vt* to go up (again), carry up, pull up, wind up, buck up; *vi* to go up again, remount, go back (to **à**); *vr* to cheer up, regain strength.

remonte-pente [rəmɔ̃tpãːt] *nm* skilift.

remontoir [rəmɔ̃twaːr] *nm* winder, key.

remontrance [rəmɔ̃trãːs] *nf* remonstrance.

remontrer [rəmɔ̃tre] *vt* to show again; **en** — **à** to remonstrate with, outdo.

remords [rəmɔːr] *nm* remorse.

remorque [rəmɔrk] *nf* tow(ing), tow-line, trailer.

remorqueur [rəmɔrke] *nm* tug (-boat).

rémouleur [remulœːr] *nm* knifegrinder.

remous [rəmu] *nm* eddy, backwash.

rempart [rãpaːr] *nm* rampart.

remplaçant [rãplasã] n substitute.
remplacement [rãplasmã] nm replacing, substitution.
remplacer [rãplase] vt to replace, deputize for.
rempli [rãpli] nm tuck.
remplir [rãpli:r] vtr to fill (up, in); vt fulfil, occupy.
remporter [rãpɔrte] vt to carry away, gain, win.
remuant [rəmɥã] a stirring, restless.
remue-ménage [rəmymena:ʒ] nm bustle, stir.
remuer [rəmɥe] vti to move, stir.
rémunérateur, -trice [remynɛratœ:r, tris] a remunerative, paying.
rémunération [remynerasjɔ̃] nf remuneration.
renâcler [rənakle] vi to snort, hang back.
renaissance [rənɛsã:s] nf rebirth, revival.
renaître [rənɛ:tr] vi to be born again, revive, reappear.
renard [rəna:r] n fox, vixen.
renchérir [rãʃeri:r] vt to raise the price of; vi to rise in price, outbid, outdo.
rencontre [rãkɔ̃:tr] nf meeting, encounter, collision, occasion; de — chance.
rencontrer [rãkɔ̃tre] vt to meet (with), run across; vr to meet, collide, agree.
rendement [rãdmã] nm yield, output, profit, efficiency.
rendez-vous [rãdevu] nm appointment, meeting-place.
rendre [rã:dr] vt to give back (up, out), yield, deliver, surrender, make; vr to proceed, go, surrender, yield.
rêne [rɛn] nf rein.
renégat [rənega] n renegade.
renfermé [rãfɛrme] a uncommunicative, reticent; nm musty smell.
renfermer [rãfɛrme] vt to shut up (again), lock up, include, contain.
renfler [rãfle] vti to swell (out).
renflouer [rãflue] vt to refloat.
renfoncement [rãfɔ̃smã] nm cavity, recess, knocking in.
renfoncer [rãfɔ̃se] vt to drive in, pull down.
renforcer [rãfɔrse] vt to reinforce, strengthen; vir to become stronger.
renfort [rãfɔ:r] nm reinforcement(s).
se renfrogner [sərãfrɔɲe] vr to frown, scowl.
rengaine [rãgɛ:n] nf old story, old refrain, catchword.
rengainer [rãgene] vt to sheathe.
se rengorger [sərãgɔrʒe] vr to puff oneself out, swagger.
renier [rənje] vt to disown, repudiate.
renifler [rənifle] vti to sniff.
renne [rɛn] nm reindeer.
renom [rənɔ̃] nm renown, fame, repute.
renommé [rənɔme] a celebrated, famous.

renommée [rənɔme] nf fame, good name.
renoncement [rənɔ̃smã] nm renouncing, self-denial.
renoncer [rənɔ̃se] vt to renounce.
renoncule [rənɔ̃kyl] nf buttercup.
renouer [rənwe] vt to join again; to resume, renew.
renouveau [rənuvo] nm springtime, renewal.
renouveler [r(ə)nuvle] vt to renew, renovate; vr to be renewed, recur.
rénovation [renɔvasjɔ̃] nf renovation, revival.
renseignement [rãsɛɲmã] nm (piece of) information.
renseigner [rãsɛɲe] vt to inform; vr to inquire (about sur), find out.
rente [rã:t] nf unearned income, pension.
rentier, -ière [rãtje, jɛ:r] n person of private means, stock-holder.
rentrée [rãtre] nf return, reopening, gathering (in).
rentrer [rãtre] vt to bring (take, get, pull) in; vi to come (go) in (again), come (go) home, reopen.
renverse [rãvɛrs] nf change, turn; à la — backwards.
renversement [rãvɛrsəmã] nm overturning, overthrow, reversal, inversion.
renverser [rãvɛrse] vt to knock over (down), overthrow, spill, reverse, invert, flabbergast; vr to overturn, recline.
renvoi [rãvwa] nm sending back, reflecting, dismissal, reference, putting off, belch.
renvoyer [rãvwaje] vt to send back, reflect, dismiss, refer, defer.
repaire [rəpɛ:r] nm lair, den, haunt.
repaître [rəpɛ:tr] vtr to feed.
répandre [repã:dr] vt to spread, pour out, shed, scatter; vr to (be) spread, spill.
répandu [repãdy] a widespread, well-known.
réparation [reparasjɔ̃] nf repair(ing), reparation, amends.
réparer [repare] vt to mend, repair, redress, restore.
repartie [rəparti] nf repartee, retort.
repartir [rəparti:r] vi to set out again, retort.
répartir [reparti:r] vi to distribute, divide, allot.
répartition [repartisjɔ̃] nf distribution, sharing out, allotment.
repas [rəpa] nm meal.
repasser [rəpase] vt to pass again, cross again, go over, iron, sharpen; vi to pass again, call back.
repêcher [rəpeʃe] vt to fish out (again), pick up, rescue; vr to get another chance (examination).
repentir [rəpãti:r] nm repentance; vr to repent, rue.
répercussion [repɛrkysjɔ̃] nf repercussion.

répercuter [reperkyte] *vtr* to reverberate, reflect.

repère [rəpɛːr] *nm* **point de —** reference, guide, landmark.

repérer [rəpere] *vt* to locate, spot; *vr* to take one's bearings.

répertoire [repertwaːr] *nm* repertory, list, collection.

répéter [repete] *vt* to repeat, rehearse; *vr* to recur.

répétiteur, -trice [repetitœːr, tris] *n* assistant-teacher, private tutor, chorus master.

répétition [repetisjɔ̃] *nf* repetition, rehearsal, private lesson; **— générale** dress rehearsal.

répit [repi] *nm* respite.

repli [rəpli] *nm* fold, crease, bend, coil, withdrawal.

replier [rəplie] *vtr* to fold up, turn in (back), coil up; *vr* to wind, withdraw.

réplique [replik] *nf* ready answer, cue, replica.

répliquer [replike] *vi* to retort.

répondre [repɔ̃ːdr] *vt* to answer, reply, respond, comply; *vi* to answer, be answerable (for **de**), correspond (to **à**), come up (to **à**).

réponse [repɔ̃ːs] *nf* answer.

report [rəpɔːr] *nm* carrying-forward, amount brought forward.

reportage [rəpɔrtaːʒ] *nm* report(ing).

reporter [rəpɔrte] *vt* to replace, take back, bring forward; *vr* to refer.

reporter [rəpɔrtœːr, tɛːr] *nm* reporter.

repos [rəpo] *nm* rest, peace.

reposé [rəpoze] *a* refreshed, calm; **à tête —e** at leisure, quietly.

reposer [rəpoze] *vt* to replace, put back, rest; *vi* to rest, lie; *vr* to rest, alight again, rely (on **sur**).

reposoir [rəpozwaːr] *nm* resting-place, temporary altar.

repoussant [rəpusɑ̃] *a* repulsive.

repousser [rəpuse] *vt* to push away (back off), reject, repel; *vi* to grow again, recoil.

repoussoir [rəpuswaːr] *nm* foil, punch.

répréhensible [repreɑ̃sibl] *a* reprehensible.

reprendre [rəprɑ̃ːdr] *vt* to recapture, take back, recover, resume, reprove, correct; *vi* to begin again, set (in) again; *vr* to correct oneself, pull oneself together.

représailles [rəprezaːj] *nf pl* reprisals.

représentant [rəprezɑ̃tɑ̃] *an* representative.

représentatif, -ive [rəprezɑ̃tatif, iːv] *a* representative.

représentation [rəprezɑ̃tasjɔ̃] *nf* representation, performance, agency, protest.

représenter [rəprezɑ̃te] *vt* to represent, portray, perform, act, reintroduce; *vi* to put up a show, have a fine appearance; *vr* to present oneself again, recur, describe oneself (as **comme**).

répression [represjɔ̃] *nf* repression.

réprimande [reprimɑ̃ːd] *nf* reproof, reprimand.

réprimander [reprimɑ̃de] *vt* to reprove, reprimand.

réprimer [reprime] *vt* to repress quell, curb.

repris [rəpri] *n* **— de justice** old offender.

reprise [rəpriːz] *nf* recapture, taking back, resumption, revival, acceleration, darn(ing), round; **à plusieurs —** several times.

repriser [rəprize] *vt* to darn, mend.

réprobateur, -trice [reprɔbatœːr, tris] *a* reproachful, reproving.

réprobation [reprɔbasjɔ̃] *nf* reprobation.

reproche [rəprɔʃ] *nm* reproach, blame.

reprocher [rəprɔʃe] *vt* to reproach (with), begrudge, cast up.

reproduction [rəprɔdyksjɔ̃] *nf* reproduction, copy.

reproduire [rəprɔdɥiːr] *vt* to reproduce; *vr* to breed, recur.

réprouver [repruve] *vt* to disapprove of, reprobate.

reptile [rɛptil] *a nm* reptile.

repu [rəpy] *a* satiated.

républicain [repyblikɛ̃] *an* republican.

république [repyblik] *nf* republic.

répudier [repydje] *vt* to repudiate, renounce.

répugnance [repyɲɑ̃ːs] *nf* repugnance, loathing, reluctance.

répugnant [repyɲɑ̃] *a* repugnant, loathsome.

répugner [repyɲe] *vi* to be repugnant, loathe, be reluctant.

répulsion [repylsjɔ̃] *nf* repulsion.

réputation [repytasjɔ̃] *nf* reputation, repute, name.

réputé [repyte] *a* of repute, well-known.

requérir [rəkeriːr] *vt* to ask (for), demand, summon.

requête [rəkɛːt] *nf* request, petition.

requin [rəkɛ̃] *nm* shark.

requinquer [rəkɛ̃ke] *vt* to smarten up, repair; *vr* to smarten oneself up, recover.

requis [rəki] *a* requisite, necessary.

réquisition [rekizisjɔ̃] *nf* requisition (ing).

réquisitionner [rekizisjɔne] *vt* to requisition.

réquisitoire [rekizitwaːr] *nm* indictment, charge.

rescapé [rɛskape] *a* rescued; *n* survivor.

rescinder [rɛssɛ̃de] *vt* to annul, rescind.

rescousse [rɛskus] *nf* rescue.

réseau [rezo] *nm* net(work), system.

réséda [reseda] *nm* mignonette.

réservation [rezɛrvasjɔ̃] *nf* reservation.

réserve [rezɛrv] *nf* reserve, reservation, aloofness, caution; **de —** spare, reserve.

réservé [rezɛrve] *a* reserved, cautious, aloof, private.

réserver [rezɛrve] *vt* to reserve, save, set aside.

réserviste [rezɛrvist] *nm* reservist.

réservoir [rezɛrvwaːr] *nm* reservoir, tank.

résidence [rezidãːs] *nf* residence, abode.

résider [rezide] *vi* to reside, live, lie.

résidu [rezidy] *nm* res due, balance.

résignation [reziɲasjɔ̃] *nf* resignation.

résigner [reziɲe] *vt* to resign, give up.

résilier [rezilje] *vt* to cancel, annul.

résille [reziːj] *nf* hair-net, snood.

résine [rezin] *nf* resin.

résistance [rezistãːs] *nf* resistance, opposition, endurance, strength; **pièce de —** main dish, feature.

résistant [rezistã] *a* resistant, strong, fast.

résister [reziste] *vt* to resist, withstand; *vi* to be fast.

résolu [rezɔly] *a* resolute.

résolution [rezɔlysjɔ̃] *nf* resolve, determination, solution, cancelling.

résonance [rezɔnãːs] *nf* resonance.

résonner [rezɔne] *vi* to resound, clang, ring.

résoudre [rezuːdr] *vt* to resolve, decide, (dis)solve, settle; *vr* to decide, dissolve.

respect [rɛspɛ] *nm* respect.

respectable [rɛspɛktabl] *a* respectable.

respecter [rɛspɛkte] *vt* to respect, have regard for.

respectif, -ive [rɛspɛktif, iːv] *a* respective.

respectueux, -euse [rɛspɛktɥø, øːz] *a* respectful.

respiration [rɛspirasjɔ̃] *nf* breathing.

respirer [rɛspire] *vt* to breathe (in), inhale; *vi* to breathe.

resplendir [rɛsplãdiːr] *vi* to shine, glow, be resplendent.

responsabilité [rɛspɔ̃sabilite] *nf* responsibility, liability.

responsable [rɛspɔ̃sabl] *a* responsible.

resquilleur, -euse [rɛskijœːr, øːz] *n* gatecrasher, wangler.

ressac [rəsak] *nm* undertow, surf.

ressaisir [rəseziːr] *vt* to seize again; *vr* to pull oneself together, recover one's self-control.

ressasser [rəsase] *vt* repeat, harp on, resift.

ressemblance [rəsãblãːs] *nf* resemblance, likeness.

ressemblant [rəsãblã] *a* (a)like.

ressembler [rəsãble] *vt* to resemble, be like.

ressentiment [rəsãtimã] *nm* resentment.

ressentir [rəsãtiːr] *vt* to feel; *vr* to feel the effects (oi **de**).

resserrement [rəsɛrmã] *nm* contraction, tightness; **— du cœur** pang.

resserrer [rəsɛre] *vt* to ccntract, tighten, draw tight; *vr* to contract, shrink, narrow, retrench.

ressort [rəsɔːr] *nm* spring, resilience, line, province, resort.

ressortir [rəsɔrtiːr] *vt* to bring out again; *vi* to come, (go) out again, stand out, follow (from **de**), belong (to **à**); **faire —** to bring out.

ressortissant [rəsɔrtisã] *nm* national.

ressource [rəsurs] *nf* resource(fulness), expedient; **en dernière —** in the last resort.

ressusciter [resysite] *vti* to resuscitate, revive.

restant [rɛstã] *a* remaining, left; *nm* rest, remainder.

restaurant [rɛstɔrã] *nm* restaurant.

restaura·teur, -trice [rɛstɔratœːr, tris] *n* restorer; *nm* restaurant-keeper.

restauration [rɛstɔrasjɔ̃] *nf* restoring, restoration.

restaurer [rɛstɔre] *vt* to restore, refresh; *vr* to take refreshment, build oneself up.

reste [rɛst] *nm* remainder, rest; *pl* remains, traces, scraps; **au (du) —** moreover; **de —** left.

rester [rɛste] *vi* to remain, stay, keep, stand, be left.

restituer [rɛstitɥe] *vt* to restore, return.

restitution [rɛstitysjɔ̃] *nf* restitution, restoration, refunding.

restreindre [rɛstrɛ̃ːdr] *vt* to restrict, limit; *vr* to restrict oneself, retrench.

restriction [rɛstriksjɔ̃] *nf* restriction, limitation.

résultat [rezylta] *nm* result, outcome.

résulter [rezylte] *vi* to result, be the result (of **de**).

résumé [rezyme] *nm* summary; **en — in brief.**

résumer [rezyme] *vtr* to sum up.

résurrection [rezyrɛksjɔ̃] *nf* resurrection, revival.

rétablir [retabliːr] *vt* to re-establish, restore, reinstate; *vr* to recover, re-establish oneself.

rétablissement [retablismã] *nm* re-establishment, restoration, reinstatement, recovery.

retaper [rətape] *vt* to do up, mend; *vr* to recover.

retard [rətaːr] *nm* delay, lateness; **en —** late, in arrears.

retardataire [rətardatɛːr] *a* late, backward; *n* laggard, straggler.

retarder [rətarde] *vt* to delay, make late, put back; *vi* to be late, lag.

retenir [rətniːr] *vt* to hold (back), retain, detain, restrain, reserve; *vr* to refrain (from **de**), restrain oneself.

retentir [rətɑ̃tiːr] *vi* to echo, reverberate, resound.

retentissement [rətɑ̃tismɑ̃] *nm* reverberation, repercussion.

retenue [rətny] *nf* withholding, deduction, restraint, detention, discretion.

réticence [retisɑ̃ːs] *nf* reserve, reticence.

rétif, -ive [retif, iːv] *a* stubborn.

retiré [rətire] *a* retired, remote.

retirer [rətire] *vt* to withdraw, obtain, remove; *vr* to retire, recede.

retomber [rətɔ̃be] *vi* to fall back, droop, hang down.

rétorquer [retɔrke] *vt* to retort, cast back.

retors [rətɔːr] *a* twisted, bent, crafty, sly.

retouche [rətuʃ] *nf* retouch(ing), small alteration.

retoucher [rətuʃe] *vt* to touch up.

retour [rətuːr] *nm* return, turn, recurrence, change.

retourner [rəturne] *vt* to turn (inside out), turn (back, down, over, round, up), return; *vi* to return, go back; *vr* to turn round, over.

retracer [rətrase] *vt* to retrace, recall.

rétracter [retrakte] *vtr* to retract, withdraw.

retrait [rətrɛ] *nm* withdrawal, shrinkage, recess.

retraite [rətrɛt] *nf* retreat, retirement, refuge, tattoo.

retraité, -e [rətrɛte] *nmf* pensioner.

retranchement [rətrɑ̃ʃmɑ̃] *nm* cutting off (down, out), entrenchment.

retrancher [rətrɑ̃ʃe] *vt* to cut off (out, down); *vr* to entrench oneself, cut down one's expenses.

rétrécissement [retresismɑ̃] *nm* narrowing, shrinking.

rétrécir [retresiːr] *vtir* to narrow, shrink, contract.

rétribuer [retribɥe] *vt* to remunerate, pay.

rétribution [retribysjɔ̃] *nf* remuneration, reward.

rétrograde [retrɔgrad] *a* retrograde, backward.

rétrograder [retrɔgrade] *vt* to reduce in rank; *vi* to go back, change down.

rétrospectif, -ive [retrɔspɛktif, iːv] *a* retrospective.

retrousser [rətruse] *vt* to turn up, roll up, tuck up; **nez retroussé** snub nose.

rétroviseur [retrɔvizœːr] *nm* driving-mirror.

réunion [reynjɔ̃] *nf* reunion, meeting, joining.

réunir [reyniːr] *vt* to reunite, collect, gather; *vr* to unite, meet.

réussi [reysi] *a* successful.

réussir [reysiːr] *vt* to make a success of; *vi* to succeed, be successful.

réussite [reysit] *nf* success, outcome, (*cards*) patience.

revaloir [rəvalwaːr] *vt* to pay back.

revanche [rəvɑ̃ːʃ] *nf* revenge, return game; **en —** in return, on the other hand.

rêvasser [rɛvase] *vi* to daydream.

rêve [rɛːv] *nm* dream.

revêche [rəvɛʃ] *a* rough, difficult, cantankerous.

réveil [revɛj] *nm* awakening.

réveille-matin [revɛjmatɛ̃] *nm* alarm-clock.

réveiller [revɛje] *vtr* to wake (up), revive.

réveillon [revɛjɔ̃] *nm* midnight party (at Christmas, New Year).

révélateur, -trice [revɛlatœːr, tris] *a* revealing, telltale.

révélation [revɛlasjɔ̃] *nf* revelation, disclosure.

révéler [revele] *vt* to reveal, disclose.

revenant [rəvnɑ̃] *nm* ghost.

revendeur, -euse [rəvɑ̃dœːr, øːz] *n* retailer, second-hand dealer.

revendication [rəvɑ̃dikasjɔ̃] *nf* claim(ing).

revendiquer [rəvɑ̃dike] *vt* to claim.

revenir [rəvniːr] *vi* to come back, amount (to **à**), recover (from **de**), go back on; **en —** to get over it; **faire —** (*cooking*) to brown.

revenu [rəvny] *nm* income, revenue.

rêver [rɛve] *vt* to dream (of); *vi* to dream, ponder.

réverbère [reverbeːr] *nm* streetlamp, reflector.

réverbérer [reverbere] *vt* to reverberate, reflect; *vi* to be reverberated, reflected.

révérence [reverɑ̃ːs] *nf* reverence, bow, curtsy.

révérencieux, -euse [reverɑ̃sjø, øːz] *a* ceremonious, deferential.

révérer [revere] *vt* to revere.

rêverie [rɛvri] *nf* dreaming, musing.

revers [rəvɛːr] *nm* reverse, back, lapel, turn-up; backhand.

revêtement [rəvɛtmɑ̃] *nm* coating, facing, casing, surface, revetment.

revêtir [rəvɛtiːr] *vt* to (re)clothe, dress, invest, coat, face, put on.

rêveur, -euse [rɛvœːr, øːz] *a* dreaming, dreamy; *n* dreamer.

revient [rəvjɛ̃] *nm* **prix de —** cost price.

revirement [rəvirmɑ̃] *nm* veering, sudden change.

réviser [revize] *vt* to revise, examine, overhaul.

révision [revizjɔ̃] *nf* revision, inspection, overhaul(ing); **conseil de —** recruiting board.

revivre [rəviːvr] *vt* to relive; *vi* to live again, revive.

révocation [revɔkasjɔ̃] *nf* revocation, repeal, dismissal.

revoir [rəvwaːr] *vt* to see again, revise; **au —** good-bye.

révolte [revɔlt] *nf* revolt.

révolté [revɔlte] *n* rebel.

révolter [revɔlte] *vt* to revolt, shock, disgust; *vr* to revolt, rebel.

révolu [revɔly] *a* completed, past, ended.

révolution [revɔlysjɔ̃] *nf* revolution, complete change.

révolutionnaire [revɔlysjɔnɛːr] *an* revolutionary.

révolutionner [revɔlysjɔne] *vt* to revolutionize.

revolver [revɔlvɛːr] *nm* revolver.

révoquer [revɔke] *vt* to revoke, repeal, dismiss.

revue [rɔvy] *nf* revue, inspection.

rez-de-chaussée [redʃose] *nm* ground floor.

rhabiller [rabije] *vt* to reclothe, repair; *vr* to dress oneself again, buy new clothes.

rhénan [renɑ̃] *a* Rhenish, of the Rhine.

rhétorique [retɔrik] *nf* rhetoric.

rhinocéros [rinɔserɔs] *nm* rhinoceros, rhinoceros beetle.

rhubarbe [rybarb] *nf* rhubarb.

rhum [rɔm] *nm* rum.

rhumatisant [rymatizɑ̃] *an* rheumatic(ky) (person).

rhumatisme [rymatism] *nm* rheumatism.

rhume [rym] *nm* cold; — **de cerveau** cold in the head.

riant [rjɑ̃] *a* laughing, smiling, pleasant.

ribambelle [ribɑ̃bɛl] *nf* (*fam*) long string.

ricaner [rikane] *vi* to sneer, laugh derisively.

riche [riʃ] *a* rich, wealthy, valuable.

richesse [riʃɛs] *nf* richness, wealth, fertility.

ricin [risɛ̃] *nm* castor-oil plant; **huile de** — castor oil.

ricocher [rikɔʃe] *vi* to ricochet, glance off, rebound.

ricochet [rikɔʃɛ] *nm* rebound, ricochet.

rictus [riktyːs] *nm* grin.

ride [rid] *nf* wrinkle, ripple.

ridé [ride] *a* wrinkled, shrivelled, corrugated.

rideau [rido] *nm* curtain, screen, veil.

ridelle [ridɛl] *nf* rail, rack.

rider [ride] *vtr* to wrinkle, pucker, shrivel, ripple.

ridicule [ridikyl] *a* ridiculous, ludicrous; *nm* ridiculousness, absurdity.

ridiculiser [ridikylize] *vt* to ridicule.

rien [rjɛ̃] *pn* nothing, not anything; *nm* trifle, just a little; **comme si de** — **n'était** as if nothing had happened; **il n'en fera** — he will do nothing of the kind; **il n'y est pour** — he has (had) nothing to do with it; **cela ne fait** — it does not matter.

rieur, -euse [rjœːr, øːz] *a* laughing, gay; *n* laughter.

riflard [riflaːr] *nm* paring chisel, file.

rigide [riʒid] *a* tense, rigid, stiff.

rigidité [riʒidite] *nf* tenseness, rigidity, stiffness.

rigolade [rigɔlad] *nf* fun, joke, lark.

rigole [rigɔl] *nf* gutter, drain, channel.

rigoler [rigɔle] *vi* to laugh, have some fun.

rigolo, -ote [rigɔlo, ɔt] *a* funny, comical, queer; *n* wag.

rigoureux, -euse [rigurø, øːz] *a* rigorous, harsh, severe, strict.

rigueur [rigœːr] *nf* rigour, severity, harshness, strictness; **à la** — if need be, at a pinch; **être de** — to be obligatory.

rillettes [rijɛt] *nf pl* potted minced pork.

rime [rim] *nf* rhyme.

rimer [rime] *vt* to put into rhyme; *vi* to rhyme, write verse; **cela ne rime à rien** there is no sense in it.

rinçage [rɛ̃saːʒ] *nm* rinse, rinsing.

rincée [rɛ̃se] *nf* drubbing.

rincer [rɛ̃se] *vt* to rinse (out); **se** — **la dalle** to wet one's whistle.

riquiqui [rikiki] *a* undersized (*pers* or *thing*), runt, shrimp.

ripaille [ripɑːj] *nf* feasting, carousing.

riposte [ripɔst] *nf* retort, counter (stroke), riposte.

riposter [ripɔste] *vi* to retort, counter, riposte.

rire [riːr] *vi* to laugh, joke, smile; *vr* to laugh (at **de**); *nm* laughter, laugh(ing); **vous voulez** — ! you are joking! **pour** — for fun, make-believe; **fou** — *nm* giggle.

ris [ri] *nm* laugh(ter), reef; — **de veau** sweetbread.

risée [rize] *nf* laughing-stock, jeer.

risible [rizibl] *a* laughable, comical, ludicrous.

risque [risk] *nm* risk; **à ses** —**s et périls** at one's own risk.

risquer [riske] *vt* to risk, venture; *vr* to take a risk, venture.

ristourner [risturne] *vt* to repay, return.

rite [rit] *nm* rite.

rituel, -elle [rityɛl] *a nm* ritual.

rivage [rivaːʒ] *nm* bank, shore, side.

rival [rival] *an* rival.

rivaliser [rivalize] *vi* to vie (with), emulate.

rivalité [rivalite] *nf* rivalry.

rive [riːv] *nf* shore, bank, side, edge.

river [rive] *vt* to rivet, clinch.

riverain [rivrɛ̃] *a* water-, river-, wayside; *n* riverside resident.

rivet [rivɛ] *nm* rivet.

rivière [rivjɛːr] *nf* river, stream.

rixe [riks] *nf* brawl, scuffle.

riz [ri] *nm* rice.

rizière [rizjɛːr] *nf* rice-field.

robe [rɔb] *nf* dress, frock, gown, coat, skin; — **de chambre** dressing-gown.

robinet [rɔbinɛ] nm tap, cock, (US) faucet.
robot [rɔbo] nm robot; **portrait—** identikit.
robuste [rɔbyst] a robust, strong, hardy, sturdy.
roc [rɔk] nm rock.
rocaille [rɔkaːj] nf rock.
rocailleux, -euse [rɔkajø, øːz] a rocky, stony, rugged.
roche [rɔʃ] nf rock, boulder.
rocher [rɔʃe] nm rock, crag.
rochet [rɔʃɛ] nm ratchet.
rocheux, -euse [rɔʃø, øːz] a rocky, stony.
rococo [rɔkɔko] a nm rococo, baroque.
rodage [rɔdaːʒ] nm running in.
rôder [rode] vi to prowl, roam.
rôdeur, -euse [rodœːr, øːz] a prowling; n prowler, vagrant.
rogatons [rɔgatɔ̃] nm pl scraps.
rogner [rɔɲe] vt to clip, trim, pare.
rognon [rɔɲɔ̃] nm kidney.
rognures [rɔɲyːr] nf pl clippings, trimmings, parings.
rogomme [rɔgɔm] nm liquor; **voix de — husky**, throaty voice.
rogue [rɔg] a haughty, arrogant.
roi [rwa] nm king; **fêtes des —s** Twelfth Night; **tirer les —s to** celebrate Twelfth Night.
roide, roideur, roidir [rwad] see **raide, raideur, raidir.**
roitelet [rwatlɛ] nm wren.
rôle [roːl] nm rôle, part, register, roster; **à tour de — in turn.**
romain [rɔmɛ̃] a Roman.
romaine [rɔmɛn] nf cos lettuce.
roman [rɔmɑ̃] a romanic, romanesque; nm novel, romance; **— feuilleton** serial story.
romance [rɔmɑ̃ːs] nf sentimental song, ballad.
romancier, -ière [rɔmɑ̃sje, jɛːr] n novelist.
romanesque [rɔmanɛsk] a romantic.
romanichel, -elle [rɔmaniʃɛl] n gipsy, vagrant.
romantique [rɔmɑ̃tik] a romantic; n romanticist.
romantisme [rɔmɑ̃tism] nm romanticism.
romarin [rɔmarɛ̃] nm rosemary.
rompre [rɔ̃ːpr] vt to break (off, up, in, into), snap, burst; vi to break (off, up); vr to break (off, up), break oneself (in, to à).
rompu [rɔ̃py] a broken (in), tired out.
ronce [rɔ̃ːs] nf bramble, blackberry bush; pl thorns.
ronchonner [rɔ̃ʃɔne] vi to grouse, grumble, growl.
rond [rɔ̃] a round(ed), plump; nm ring, circle, round, disc, bean.
rond-de-cuir [rɔ̃dkɥiːr] nm clerk, bureaucrat.
ronde [rɔ̃ːd] nf round, beat, semibreve; **à la — around.**

rondeau [rɔ̃do] nm rondeau, rondo.
rondelet, -ette [rɔ̃dlɛ, ɛt] a plump, roundish, tidy.
rondelle [rɔ̃dɛl] nf slice, small round, ring, disc.
rondement [rɔ̃dmɑ̃] ad roundly, smartly, frankly.
rondeur [rɔ̃dœːr] nf roundness, plumpness, frankness.
rond-point [rɔ̃pwɛ̃] nm circus, roundabout.
ronflement [rɔ̃flɑ̃mɑ̃] nm snore, snoring, rumbling, throbbing, hum.
ronfler [rɔ̃fle] vi to snore, roar, throb, whirr, hum.
ronger [rɔ̃ʒe] vt to gnaw, corrode, erode; **se — le cœur** to fret one's heart out.
rongeur, -euse [rɔ̃ʒœːr, øːz] a rodent, gnawing; nm rodent.
rônier [ronje] nm fan-palm.
ronronnement [rɔ̃rɔnmɑ̃] nm purr (ing), hum(ming).
ronronner [rɔ̃rone] vi to purr, hum.
roquet [rɔkɛ] nm pug-dog, cur.
rosace [rozas] nf rose-window.
rosaire [rozɛːr] nm rosary.
rosâtre [rozɑːtr] a pinkish.
rosbif [rɔsbif] nm roast beef.
rose [roːz] nf rose; a pink, rosy; **— des vents** compass-card; **découvrir le pot aux —s** to discover the secret.
rosé [roze] a rosy, roseate, (wine) rosé.
roseau [rozo] nm reed.
rosée [roze] nf dew.
roseraie [rozrɛ] nf rose-garden.
rosette [rozɛt] nf rosette, bow.
rosier [rozje] nm rose-bush.
rosir [roziːr] vi to turn pink, rosy.
rosse [rɔs] nf nag, nasty person, beast; a nasty, spiteful.
rossée [rɔse] nf thrashing, drubbing, licking.
rosser [rɔse] vt to thrash, beat.
rosserie [rɔsri] nf nasty remark, dirty trick, nastiness.
rossignol [rɔsiɲɔl] nm nightingale, skeleton-key, bit of junk.
rot [ro] nm belch.
rotatif, -ive [rɔtatif, iːv] a rotary.
rotation [rɔtasjɔ̃] nf rotation.
rotatoire [rɔtatwaːr] a rotative, rotatory.
roter [rɔte] vi to belch.
rotin [rɔtɛ̃] nm rattan, cane.
rôti [roti] nm roast (meat).
rôtir [rotiːr] vti to roast, toast, scorch.
rôtisserie [rotisri] nf restaurant.
rotonde [rɔtɔ̃ːd] nf rotunda, circular hall.
rotondité [rɔtɔ̃dite] nf roundness, rotundity, stoutness.
rotule [rɔtyl] nf knee-cap, ball-and-socket joint.
roturier, -ière [rɔtyrje] a of the common people; n commoner.
rouage [rwaːʒ] nm wheel(s), works.
roublard [rublaːr] an crafty, wily (person).

roublardise [rublardi:z] *nf* crafti-ness, wily trick.

roucouler [rukule] *vi* to coo.

roue [ru] *nf* wheel; **faire la — to** turn cartwheels, spread its tail, strut.

roué [rwe] *a* sly, wily; *nm* rake.

rouennerie [rwanri] *nf* printed cotton goods.

rouer [rwe] *vt* to break on the wheel; **— de coups** to beat unmercifully.

rouet [rwɛ] *nm* spinning-wheel, pulley-wheel.

rouf(le) [ruf] *nm* deck-house.

rouge [ru:ʒ] *a* red; *nm* red, rouge; **bâton de —** lipstick.

rougeâtre [ruʒɑ:tr] *a* reddish.

rouge-gorge [ruʒgɔr:ʒ] *nm* robin.

rougeole [ruʒɔl] *nf* measles.

rougeoyer [ruʒwaje] *vi* to glow, turn red.

rouget [ruʒɛ] *nm* gurnard, red mullet.

rougeur [ruʒœ:r] *nf* redness, flush, blush.

rougir [ruʒi:r] *vt* to redden; *vi* blush, flush, turn red.

rouille [ru:j] *nf* rust, blight, mildew.

rouillé [ruje] *a* rusted, rusty.

rouiller [ruje] *vt* to rust, blight, mildew; *vr* to rust, be blighted, mildewed.

rouillure [rujy:r] *nf* rustiness, blight.

roulage [rula:ʒ] *nm* rolling, haulage, cartage.

roulant [rulɑ̃] *a* rolling, moving, sliding, smooth, killingly funny.

rouleau [rulo] *nm* roller, roll, coil, spool; **— compresseur** steamroller.

roulement [rulmɑ̃] *nm* rolling, rumbling, running, rotation; **— à billes** ball-bearing.

rouler [rule] *vt* to roll (up), haul, trick, take in, turn over; *vi* to roll (along, down, over), roam, rumble, run, turn (upon **sur**); *vr* to roll.

roulette [rulet] *nf* roller, caster, roulette.

roulier [rulje] *nm* carrier, carter.

roulis [ruli] *nm* rolling, lurching.

roulotte [rulɔt] *nf* caravan.

roumain [rumɛ̃] *an* Rumanian.

Roumanie [rumani] *nf* Rumania.

roupie [rupi] *nf* drop, rupee.

roupiller [rupije] *vi* (*fam*) to sleep.

rouquin [rukɛ̃] *a* red-haired, carroty; *n* ginger-head, red-head.

rouspéter [ruspete] *vi* (*fam*) to protest, cut up rough, kick.

roussâtre [rusɑ:tr] *a* reddish.

rousseur [rusœ:r] *nf* redness; **tache de —** freckle.

roussir [rusi:r] *vti* to redden, turn brown, singe.

route [rut] *nf* road, track, course, route; **— nationale** main road; **se mettre en —** to set out.

routier, -ière [rutje, jɛ:r] *a* road-; **café —** transport café; *nm* long distance lorry driver, road racer; **vieux —** old campaigner.

routine [rutin] *nf* routine.

routinier, -ière [rutinje, jɛ:r] *a* routine, unenterprising.

rouvrir [ruvri:r] *vti* to reopen.

roux, rousse [ru, rus] *a* reddish-brown, russet, red; *nm* reddish-brown, russet, (*sauce*) roux.

royal [rwajal] *a* royal, regal, crown.

royaliste [rwajalist] *an* royalist.

royaume [rwajo:m] *nm* kingdom, realm.

royauté [rwajote] *nf* royalty.

ruade [rɥad] *nf* kicking.

ruban [rybɑ̃] *nm* ribbon, band, tape.

rubis [rybi] *nm* ruby; **payer — sur l'ongle** to pay on the nail.

rubrique [rybrik] *nf* heading, rubric, column, imprint, red ochre.

ruche [ryʃ] *nf* hive, ruche.

rude [ryd] *a* coarse, rough, harsh, uncouth, gruff, hard.

rudesse [rydɛs] *nf* coarseness, rough-ness, harshness, uncouthness, gruff-ness.

rudiments [rydimɑ̃] *nm pl* rudi-ments, first principles.

rudoyer [rydwaje] *vt* to treat roughly, bully, browbeat.

rue [ry] *nf* street.

ruée [rɥe] *nf* (on)rush.

ruelle [rɥɛl] *nf* lane, alley, space between bed and wall.

ruer [rɥe] *vi* to kick, lash out; *vr* to hurl oneself (upon **sur**).

rugir [ryʒi:r] *vi* to roar, howl.

rugissement [ryʒismɑ̃] *nm* roar(ing), howling.

rugosité [rygɔzite] *nf* ruggedness, wrinkle.

rugueux, -euse [rygø, ø:z] *a* rough, rugged, wrinkled.

ruine [rɥin] *nf* ruin(ation), downfall; **menacer — to** be falling to bits.

ruiner [rɥine] *vt* to ruin, undo, destroy; *vr* to fall to ruin, ruin oneself.

ruisseau [rɥiso] *nm* stream, brook, gutter.

ruisseler [rɥisle] *vi* to stream, run, trickle.

rumeur [rymœ:r] *nf* rumour, hum, confused murmur, din.

ruminant [ryminɑ̃] *a nm* ruminant.

ruminer [rymine] *vti* to chew the cud, ruminate, ponder.

rupture [rypty:r] *nf* breaking (off, down), fracture, rupture.

rural [ryral] *a* rural, country.

ruse [ry:z] *nf* trick, dodge, ruse, stratagem.

rusé [ryze] *a* sly, crafty, artful.

russe [rys] *an* Russian.

Russie [rysi] *nf* Russia.

rustaud [rysto] *a* uncouth, boorish; *n* boor.

rustique [rystik] *a* rustic, robust.

rustre [rystr] *a* boorish, churlish; *nm* boor, bumpkin.

rut [ryt] *nm* rut(ting).

rutabaga [rytabaga] *nm* swede.

rutilant [rytilɑ̃] *a* gleaming, glowing red.

rythme [ritm] *nm* rhythm.

rythmé [ritme] *a* rhythmic(al).

rythmique [ritmik] *a* rhythmic(al).

S

sa [sa] *see* son.

sable [sɑ:bl] *nm* sand, gravel; **—s mouvants** quicksands.

sablé [sable] *a* sanded, gravelled; *nm* shortbread.

sabler [sable] *vt* to sand, cover with gravel, drink.

sableux, -euse [sablø, ø:z] *a* sandy.

sablier [sablie] *nm* hour-glass, egg-timer, sand-dealer.

sablière [sablie:r] *nf* sand-, gravel-pit.

sablonneux, -euse [sablɔnø, ø:z] *a* sandy, gritty.

sablonnière [sablɔnjɛ:r] *nf* sandpit.

sabord [sabɔ:r] *nm* porthole.

saborder [sabɔrde] *vt* to scuttle.

sabot [sabo] *nm* clog, hoof.

sabotage [sabɔta:ʒ] *nm* clog-making, sabotage.

saboter [sabɔte] *vt* to shoe, bungle, scamp, sabotage.

saboteur, -euse [sabɔtœ:r, ø:z] *n* saboteur, bungler.

sabotier [sabɔtje] *nm* clog-maker.

sabre [sɑ:br] *nm* sabre, sword, swordfish.

sabrer [sabre] *vt* to sabre, cut (down), scamp.

sac [sak] *nm* sack, bag, pouch, knapsack, sackcloth, sacking; **— de couchage** sleeping-bag; **— à main** handbag.

saccade [sakad] *nf* jerk, jolt; **par —s** by fits and starts.

saccadé [sakade] *a* jerky.

saccager [sakaʒe] *vt* to pillage, sack, ransack.

saccharine [sakarin] *nf* saccharine.

sacerdoce [sasɛrdɔs] *nm* priesthood, ministry.

sacerdotal [sasɛrdɔtal] *a* sacerdotal, priestly.

sachet [saʃɛ] *nm* small bag, sachet.

sacoche [sakɔʃ] *nf* satchel, wallet, tool-bag, saddle-bag.

sacre [sakr] *nm* coronation, consecration.

sacrement [sakrəmɑ̃] *nm* sacrament.

sacré [sakre] *a* sacred, holy, damned, confounded.

sacrer [sakre] *vt* to crown, consecrate, anoint; *vi* to swear.

sacrifice [sakrifis] *nm* sacrifice.

sacrifier [sakrifje] *vt* to sacrifice, give up.

sacrilège [sakrilɛ:ʒ] *a* sacrilegious; *nm* sacrilege.

sacristain [sakristɛ̃] *nm* sexton, sacristan.

sacristie [sakristi] *nf* vestry, sacristy.

sadique [sadik] *a* sadistic.

sadisme [sadism] *nm* sadism.

safran [safrɑ̃] *a* saffron-coloured; *nm* crocus, saffron.

sagace [sagas] *a* sagacious, shrewd.

sagacité [sagasite] *nf* sagacity, shrewdness.

sagaie [sagɛ] *nf* assegai, spear.

sage [sa:ʒ] *a* wise, sensible, discreet, good, well-behaved.

sage-femme [saʒfam] *nf* midwife.

sagesse [saʒɛs] *nf* wisdom, discretion, good behaviour.

sagou [sagu] *nm* sago.

saignant [sɛɲɑ̃] *a* bleeding, raw, red, underdone.

saignée [sɛɲe] *nf* bleeding, blood-letting, bend of the arm, irrigation ditch.

saigner [sɛɲe] *vt* to bleed, let blood from; *vi* to bleed.

saillant [sajɑ̃] *a* projecting, jutting out, prominent, salient; *nm* salient.

saillie [saji] *nf* projection, protrusion, ledge, spring, bound, flash of wit.

saillir [saji:r] *vi* to jut out, project, spurt out, stand out.

sain [sɛ̃] *a* healthy, wholesome, sound.

saindoux [sɛ̃du] *nm* lard.

saint [sɛ̃] *a* holy, hallowed, godly, saintly, blessed; *n* saint; **il ne sait plus à quel — se vouer** he does not know where to turn.

Saint-Esprit [sɛ̃tɛspri] *nm* Holy Ghost.

sainteté [sɛ̃təte] *nf* holiness, sanctity.

Saint-Martin [sɛ̃martɛ̃] *nf* Martin-mas.

Saint-Michel [sɛ̃miʃɛl] *nf* Michael-mas.

Saint-Siège [sɛ̃sjɛ:ʒ] *nm* Holy See.

Saint-Sylvestre [sɛ̃silvɛstr] *nf* New Year's Eve, (*Scot*) Hogmanay.

saisie [sɛzi] *nf* seizure, distraint, foreclosure.

saisir [sɛzi:r] *vt* to seize, grasp, catch hold of, grip, understand, perceive; *vr* to seize, lay hands (on de).

saisissant [sɛzisɑ̃] *a* thrilling, striking, keen, biting, piercing.

saisissement [sɛzismɑ̃] *nm* seizure, shock, thrill, chill.

saison [sɛzɔ̃] *nf* season.

saisonnier, -ière [sɛzɔnje, jɛ:r] *a* seasonal.

salacité [salasite] *nf* salaciousness.

salade [salad] *nf* salad, lettuce, hotch-potch, mess.

saladier [saladje] *nm* salad-bowl.

salaire [salɛ:r] *nm* wage(s), pay, reward, retribution.

salaison [salɛzɔ̃] *nf* salting, curing.

salamandre [salamɑ̃:dr] *nf* salamander, stove.

salant [salɑ̃] *a* **marais —** salt-pans, salt-marsh.

salarié [salarje] *a* paid, wage-earning; *n* wage-earner.

salaud [salo] *n* dirty dog, rotter, swine, slattern.

sale [sal] *a* dirty, soiled, filthy, foul; — **type** rotter.

salé [sale] *a* salt(y), salted, spicy, exorbitant, stiff; *nm* pickled pork.

saler [sale] *vt* to salt, pickle, overcharge, fleece, punish severely.

saleté [salte] *nf* dirt, trash, dirtiness, dirty trick (act, remark).

salière [saljɛːr] *nf* salt-cellar, saltbox.

saligaud [saligo] *n* rotter, skunk, dirty person.

salin [salɛ̃] *a* saline, salty, briny; *nm* salt-marsh.

saline [salin] *nf* salt-pan, rock-salt mine.

salir [saliːr] *vt* to dirty, soil, defile, tarnish; *vr* to get dirty, soil, besmirch one's reputation.

salive [saliːv] *nf* saliva, spittle.

salle [sal] *nf* room, hall, ward, house, audience; — **à manger** dining-room; — **d'opérations** operating theatre; — **d'attente** waiting room.

salon [salɔ̃] *nm* drawing-room, saloon, cabin; — **de l'automobile** motor show; — **de beauté** beauty parlour; — **de coiffure** hairdressing-saloon; — **de thé** tea-room.

saloperie [salɔpri] *nf* filth(iness), trash, dirty trick.

salopette [salɔpɛt] *nf* overalls, dungarees.

salpêtre [salpeːtr] *nm* saltpetre, nitre.

saltimbanque [saltɛ̃bãːk] *nm* showman, mountebank, charlatan.

salubre [salyːbr] *a* salubrious, wholesome, healthy.

salubrité [salybrite] *nf* salubrity, wholesomeness, healthiness.

saluer [salɥe] *vt* to salute, bow to, greet, acclaim.

salure [salyːr] *nf* saltness, tang.

salut [saly] *nm* greeting, bow, salute, safety, salvation; — **à tout le monde!** hullo, everybody!

salutaire [salytɛːr] *a* salutary, beneficial, wholesome.

salutation [salytasjɔ̃] *nf* salutation, bow, salute, greeting; *pl* kind regards.

salutiste [salytist] *n* member of the Salvation Army.

salve [salv] *nf* salvo, volley, round, salute.

samara [samara] *nm* sandal.

samedi [samdi] *nm* Saturday.

sanatorium [sanatɔrjɔm] *nm* sanatorium, convalescent home.

sanctification [sãktifikasjɔ̃] *nf* sanctification.

sanctifier [sãktifje] *vt* to sanctify, hallow.

sanction [sãksjɔ̃] *nf* sanction, assent, penalty.

sanctionner [sãksjɔne] *vt* to sanction, ratify, approve, penalize.

sanctuaire [sãktɥɛːr] *nm* sanctuary, sanctum.

sandale [sãdal] *nf* sandal, gym-shoe.

sandwich [sãdwitʃ] *nm* sandwich.

sang [sã] *nm* blood, gore, kin(ship), race; **effusion de —** bloodshed; **coup de —** apoplectic fit, stroke; **se faire du mauvais —** to worry, fret; **son — n'a fait qu'un tour** it gave him an awful shock.

sang-froid [sãfrwa] *nm* composure, coolness, self-possession; **de —** coolly.

sanglade [sãglad] *nf* lash, cut.

sanglant [sãglã] *a* bloody, gory, bloodstained, cutting, scathing.

sangle [sãːgl] *nf* strap, band; **lit de —** camp bed.

sangler [sãgle] *vt* to girth, strap (up); *vr* to lace (button) oneself up tightly.

sanglier [sãglie] *nm* wild boar.

sanglot [sãglo] *nm* sob.

sangloter [sãglɔte] *vi* to sob.

sangsue [sãsy] *nf* leech, bloodsucker.

sanguin [sãgɛ̃] *a* blood, full-blooded.

sanguinaire [sãginɛːr] *a* bloodthirsty, bloody.

sanguine [sãgin] *nf* red chalk, drawing in red chalk, bloodstone, blood orange.

sanguinolent [sãginɔlã] *a* tinged with blood.

sanitaire [sanitɛːr] *a* sanitary, medical, ambulance-, hospital-.

sans [sã] *prep* without, but for, were it not for, had it not been for, un-, less, -lessly; — **que** *cj* without.

sans-culotte [sãkylɔt] *nm* sansculotte, rabid republican.

sans-façon [sãfasɔ̃] *a* homely, downright, outspoken, unceremonious, over-familiar, free and easy; *nm* homeliness, outspokenness, over-familiarity.

sans-fil [sãfil] *nm* wireless message, marconigram.

sans-filiste [sãfilist] *n* wireless fan, wireless operator.

sans-gêne [sãʒɛn] *a* offhanded, unceremonious; *nm* offhandedness, over-familiarity, cheek; *nm pl* **il est — he is** a cool customer.

sans-logis [sãlɔʒi] *nm pl* homeless.

sansonnet [sãsɔnɛ] *nm* starling.

sans-souci [sãsusi] *a* carefree, unconcerned; *n* easy-going person; *nm* unconcern.

sans-travail [sãtravaːj] *nm pl* unemployed, workless.

santal [sãtal] *nm* sandalwood.

santé [sãte] *nf* health; **service de —** medical service.

sape [sap] *nf* sap(ping), undermining.

saper [sape] *vt* to sap, undermine.

sapeur [sapœːr] *nm* sapper, pioneer.

sapeur-pompier [sapœrpɔ̃pje] *nm* fireman.

sapeur-télégraphiste [sapœrtelegrafist] *nm* telegraph operator; *pl* signal corps, signals.

saphir [safiːr] *nm* sapphire.

sapin [sapɛ̃] *nm* fir (tree), coffin.

sapinière [sapinjɛːr] *nf* fir plantation.

sapristi [sapristi] *excl* good heavens!

sarbacane [sarbakan] *nf* blowpipe, pea-shooter.

sarcasme [sarkasm] *nm* (piece of) sarcasm, taunt.

sarcastique [sarkastik] *a* sarcastic.

sarcler [sarkle] *vt* to hoe (up), weed, clean.

sarcloir [sarklwaːr] *nm* hoe.

sarcophage [sarkɔfaːʒ] *nm* sarcophagus.

sardine [sardin] *nf* sardine.

sardonique [sardɔnik] *a* sardonic, sarcastic.

sarment [sarmɑ̃] *nm* vine-shoot, -branch, bine.

sarrasin [sarazɛ̃] *nm* buckwheat, Saracen.

sarrau [saro] *nm* overall, smock.

sasser [sɑse] *vt* to sieve, riddle, sift.

satané [satane] *a* confounded, dashed, abominable.

satanique [satanik] *a* satanic, diabolical, fiendish.

satellite [satɛllit] *nm* satellite, henchman, planet.

satiété [sasjete] *nf* satiety, surfeit, repletion.

satin [satɛ̃] *nm* satin.

satiner [satine] *vt* to satin, make glossy, glaze.

satinette [satinɛt] *nf* sateen.

satire [satiːr] *nf* satire, satirizing.

satirique [satirik] *a* satiric(al); *nm* satirist.

satiriser [satirize] *vt* to satirize.

satisfaction [satisfaksjɔ̃] *nf* satisfaction, gratification, atonement, amends.

satisfaire [satisfɛːr] *vt* to satisfy, gratify, fulfil, meet.

satisfait [satisfɛ] *a* satisfied, contented, pleased.

satisfaisant [satisfəzɑ̃] *a* satisfactory, satisfying.

saturation [satyrasjɔ̃] *nf* saturation.

saturer [satyre] *vt* to saturate; *vr* to become saturated.

satyre [satiːr] *nm* satyr.

sauce [sos] *nf* sauce, soft black crayon.

saucée [sose] *nf* (*fam*) drenching, soaking, telling-off.

saucer [sose] *vt* to dip into sauce, drench, souse, tell off; **se faire** — to get soaked, get a wigging.

saucière [sosjɛːr] *nf* sauce-boat.

saucisse [sosis] *nf* sausage, observation or barrage balloon.

saucisson [sosisɔ̃] *nm* large dry sausage.

sauf, sauve [sof, soːv] *a* safe, saved, unhurt; *prep* but, except, save, barring; — **que** except that.

sauf-conduit [sofkɔ̃dɥi] *nm* safe-conduct, pass.

sauge [soːʒ] *nf* sage.

saugrenu [sogrəny] *a* ridiculous, absurd.

saule [soːl] *nm* willow.

saumâtre [somaːtr] *a* briny, brackish, bitter.

saumon [somɔ̃] *a* salmon-pink; *nm* salmon.

saumure [somyːr] *nf* pickle, brine.

saupoudrer [sopudre] *vt* to sprinkle, dust, powder.

saupoudroir [sopudrwaːr] *nm* sugarsifter, castor.

saur [sɔːr] *a* **hareng** — red herring.

saut [so] *nm* leap, jump, bound, vault, falls, jerk; — **périlleux** somersault; — **d'obstacles** hurdling; —**-de-mouton** flyover.

saute [soːt] *nf* sudden rise, jump, change.

saute-mouton [sotmutɔ̃] *nm* leapfrog.

sauter [sote] *vt* to jump (over), leap (over), leave out, miss, skip; *vi* jump, leap, blow up, explode, crash, come off, change, veer, blow out; **faire** — to explode, burst, blow up, blow out.

sauterelle [sotrɛl] *nf* grasshopper, locust.

sauterie [sotri] *nf* dance, hop.

saute-ruisseau [sotrɥiso] *nm* errand-boy.

sauteur, -euse [sotœːr, øːz] *a* jumping; *n* jumper, turncoat, weathercock.

sautiller [sotije] *vi* to hop (about), skip, jump about.

sautoir [sotwaːr] *nm* St Andrew's cross, neck-chain, jumping lathe; **en** — crosswise, over one's shoulder.

sauvage [sovaːʒ] *a* wild, savage, barbarous, uncivilized, shy, unsociable; *n* savage, unsociable person.

sauvagerie [sovaʒri] *nf* savagery, barbarousness, unsociability.

sauvegarde [sovgard] *nf* safeguard, safe-keeping, safe-conduct.

sauvegarder [sovgarde] *vt* to safeguard, protect.

sauve-qui-peut [sovkipø] *nm* stampede, rout, everyone for himself.

sauver [sove] *vt* to save, rescue; *vr* to escape, run away, be off.

sauvetage [sovtaːʒ] *nm* rescue, salvage; **canot de** — lifeboat.

sauveteur [sovtœːr] *nm* rescuer, lifesaver.

sauveur [sovœːr] *nm* deliverer, Saviour, Redeemer.

savamment [savamɑ̃] *ad* learnedly, knowingly, expertly, ably, cleverly.

savane [savan] *nf* savanna.

savant [savɑ̃] *a* learned, scholarly, skilful; *n* scholar, scientist; **chien** — performing dog.

savate [savat] *nf* old shoe, French

boxing; **traîner la —** to be down at heel.

savetier [savtje] *nm* cobbler.

saveur [savœːr] *nf* savour, flavour, taste, raciness, zest.

savoir [savwaːr] *nm* knowledge, learning; *vt* to know (how, of), be able, contrive, manage; **faire — qch à qn** to let s.o. know about sth, inform s.o of sth; **à —** to wit, namely; **sachez que** I would have you know that; **sans le —** unconsciously, unwittingly; **(au)tant que je le sache** as far as I know, to the best of my knowledge; **pas que je sache** not that I am aware of; **je ne sache pas l'avoir dit** I am not aware of having said so; **il n'a rien voulu —** he would not hear of it; **je ne sais qui** someone or other.

savoir-faire [savwarfɛːr] *nm* tact, cleverness, ability.

savoir-vivre [savwarviːvr] *nm* good-breeding, (good) manners, art of living.

savon [savɔ̃] *nm* soap, wigging; **pain de —** cake of soap.

savonner [savɔne] *vt* to soap, wash, dress down.

savonnerie [savɔnri] *nf* soap-factory, soap-trade.

savonnette [savɔnɛt] *nf* cake of toilet soap.

savonneux, -euse [savɔnø, øːz] *a* soapy.

savonnier, -ière [savɔnje, jɛːr] *a* soap-; *nm* soap-manufacturer.

savourer [savure] *vt* to relish, enjoy.

savoureux, -euse [savurø, øːz] *a* savoury, tasty, racy.

saxophone [saksɔfɔn] *nm* saxophone.

saynète [sɛnɛt] *nf* sketch.

sbire [zbiːr] *nm* policeman, hired ruffian.

scabreux, -euse [skabrø, øːz] *a* scabrous, smutty, dangerous, difficult, rough.

scalper [skalpe] *vt* to scalp.

scandale [skɑ̃dal] *nm* scandal, disgrace.

scandaleux, -euse [skɑ̃dalø, øːz] *a* scandalous, disgraceful.

scandaliser [skɑ̃dalize] *vt* to scandalize, shock; *vr* to be shocked, scandalized.

scander [skɑ̃de] *vt* to scan, stress, mark.

scaphandrier [skafɑ̃drie] *nm* diver.

scarabée [skarabe] *nm* beetle.

scarlatine [skarlatin] *nf* scarlet fever.

sceau [so] *nm* seal, stamp, mark.

scélérat [selera] *a* wicked, cunning, nefarious; *n* scoundrel, villain.

scélératesse [seleratɛs] *nf* wickedness, low cunning.

scellé [sele] *a* sealed, under seal; *nm* seal.

sceller [sele] *vt* to seal (up), fix, fasten, confirm.

scène [sɛn] *nf* stage, scene, row; **mettre en —** to produce.

scénique [senik] *a* scenic, stage.

scepticisme [sɛptisism] *nm* scepticism.

sceptique [sɛptik] *a* sceptical; *n* sceptic.

sceptre [sɛptr] *nm* sceptre.

schéma [ʃema] *nm* diagram, outline.

schématique [ʃematik] *a* diagrammatic, schematic.

schisme [ʃism] *nm* schism.

sciatique [sjatik] *a* sciatic; *nm* sciatic nerve; *nf* sciatica.

scie [si] *nf* saw, catchword, bore.

science [sjɑ̃ːs] *nf* knowledge, learning, science.

scientifique [sjɑ̃tifik] *a* scientific.

scier [sje] *vt* to saw (off).

scierie [siri] *nf* sawmill.

scinder [sɛ̃de] *vt* to split up.

scintillation [sɛ̃tijasjɔ̃, -tillɑ-] *nf* scintillation, twinkling, sparkling.

scintiller [sɛ̃tije, -tille] *vi* to scintillate, twinkle, sparkle.

scission [sissjɔ̃] *nf* scission, split, division, secession.

sciure [sjyːr] *nf* **— de bois** sawdust; **— de fer** iron filings.

sclérose [skleroːz] *nf* sclerosis.

sclérosé [skleroze] *a* hardened, (fig) in a rut.

scolaire [skɔlɛːr] *a* school.

scolastique [skɔlastik] *a* scholastic; *nf* scholasticism.

scolopendre [skɔlɔpɑ̃ːdr] *nf* centipede.

scorbut [skɔrby] *nm* scurvy.

scorie [skɔri] *nf* slag, cinders, dross.

scoutisme [skutism] *nm* scouting, Boy Scout movement.

scrofule [skrɔfyl] *nf* scrofula.

scrupule [skrypyl] *nm* scruple; **se faire un — de** to have scruples about.

scrupuleux, -euse [skrypylø, øːz] *a* scrupulous.

scrutateur, -trice [skrytatœːr, tris] *a* searching, keen, scrutinizing; *n* scrutinizer, teller.

scruter [skryte] *vt* to scrutinize, scan.

scrutin [skrytɛ̃] *nm* poll, ballot, voting; **— de liste** multiple voting; **procéder au —** to take the vote; **voter au —** to ballot; **dépouiller le —** to count the votes.

sculpter [skylte] *vt* to carve, sculpture.

sculpteur [skyltœːr] *nm* sculptor, carver.

sculptural [skyltyral] *a* sculptural, statuesque.

sculpture [skyltyːr] *nf* sculpture, carving.

se [s(ə)] *pn* oneself, himself, herself, itself, themselves, each other, one another.

séance [seɑ̃ːs] *nf* session, sitting,

meeting, performance, a seance.

séant [seã] *a* becoming, seemly, proper, sitting; *nm* bottom, behind; **se dresser sur son — ** to sit up.

seau [so] *nm* pail, bucket

sec, sèche [sɛk, sɛʃ] *a* dry, dried, harsh, unfeeling, gaunt, spare, curt, tart, sharp; **boire — ** to drink spirits neat, drink heavily; **parler — ** to clip one's words; **à pied — ** dryshod; **à — ** dry, dried-up, aground, hard-up.

sécateur [sekatœːr] *nm* pruningscissors.

sécession [sesɛsjɔ̃] *nf* secession.

sèche [sɛʃ] *nf (fam)* fag, gasper.

sèchement [sɛʃmã] *ad* drily, boldly, curtly.

sécher [seʃe] *vt* to dry (up), fail, cut, skip; *vi* to become or run dry, dry up, be stumped, stick; *vr* to dry oneself, dry up, run dry; **faire — qn** to stump s.o.; **— sur pied** to pine for.

sécheresse [seʃrɛs] *nf* dryness, drought, harshness, unfeelingness, gauntness, barrenness, curtness.

séchoir [seʃwar] *nm* drying place, drier, airer.

second [səgɔ̃, zgɔ̃] *a* second; *nm* first mate, chief officer, second in command; second floor.

secondaire [səgɔ̃dɛːr, zgɔ̃-] *a* secondary, subordinate, minor.

seconde [səgɔ̃ːd, zgɔ̃ːd] *nf* second, second class, fifth form.

seconder [səgɔ̃de, zgɔ̃-] *vt* to second, support, assist, promote, further.

secouer [səkwe] *vt* to shake (up, down, off), rouse, stir; *vr* to shake oneself, bestir oneself.

secourable [səkurabl] *a* helpful, ready to help, helping.

secourir [səkuriːr] *vt* to help, aid, succour, relieve.

secours [s(ə)kuːr] *nm* help, aid, succour, relief, assistance; **porter — à** to lend assistance to; **apporter les premiers — à** to apply first-aid to; **poste de — ** first-aid post; **de — ** spare, emergency, relief; **au —!** help!

secousse [səkus] *nf* shake, shaking, shock, jolt.

secret [səkrɛ] *a* secret; *nm* secret, secrecy; **au — ** in solitary confinement.

secrétaire [səkretɛːr] *n* secretary; *nm* writing-desk.

secrétariat [səkretarja] *nm* secretaryship, secretariat.

sécréter [sekrete] *vt* to secrete.

sectaire [sɛktɛːr] *n* sectarian.

secte [sɛkt] *nf* sect.

secteur [sɛktœːr] *nm* sector, beat (of policeman).

section [sɛksjɔ̃] *nf* cutting, section, division, branch, stage, platoon.

sectionner [sɛksjɔne] *vt* to divide into sections, cut into pieces.

séculaire [sekylɛːr] *a* century-old, venerable, secular.

séculier, -ière [sekylje, jɛːr] *a* secular; *n* layman, -woman.

sécurité [sekyrite] *nf* security, safety, safeness.

sédatif, -ive [sedatif, iːv] *a nm* sedative.

sédentaire [sedãtɛːr] *a* sedentary, fixed.

sédiment [sedimã] *nm* sediment, deposit.

séditieux, -euse [sedisjø, øːz] *a* seditious; *nm* mutineer, rebel.

sédition [sedisjɔ̃] *nf* sedition, mutiny.

séducteur, -trice [sedyktœːr, tris] *a* seductive, tempting, alluring, enticing; *n* seducer, enticer, tempter.

séduction [sedyksjɔ̃] *nf* seduction, enticement, bribing, seductiveness, charm.

séduire [seduiːr] *vt* to seduce, (al)lure, captivate, charm, suborn, lead astray.

séduisant [seduizã] *a* tempting, captivating, attractive, fascinating, alluring.

ségrégation [segregasjɔ̃] *nf* segregation, separation.

seiche [sɛʃ] *nf* cuttle-fish.

seigle [sɛgl] *nm* rye.

seigneur [sɛɲœːr] *nm* lord, nobleman, God, the Lord.

seigneurie [sɛɲœri] *nf* lordship, manor.

sein [sɛ̃] *nm* bosom, breast.

séisme [seism] *nm* seism, earthquake.

seize [sɛːz] *a nm* sixteen, sixteenth.

seizième [sɛzjɛm] *a nm* sixteenth.

séjour [seʒuːr] *nm* sojourn, stay, residence, abode.

séjourner [seʒurne] *vi* to stay, sojourn, reside.

sel [sɛl] *nm* salt, spice, wit; *pl* smelling salts.

sélection [selɛksjɔ̃] *nf* selection.

selle [sɛl] *nf* saddle, stool, movement of bowels.

seller [sele] *vt* to saddle.

sellette [selɛt] *nf* stool of repentance, small stool; **tenir qn sur la — ** to have s.o. on the carpet.

sellier [selje] *nm* saddler.

selon [s(ə)lɔ̃] *prep* according to, after; **c'est — ** it depends.

Seltz [sɛls] *nm* **eau de S— ** sodawater.

semailles [s(ə)maːj] *nf pl* sowing(s).

semaine [s(ə)mɛn] *nf* week, workingweek, week's pay; **faire la — anglaise** to stop work on Saturdays at midday.

semblable [sãblabl] *a* similar, like, alike, such; *n* fellow-man, like.

semblant [sãblã] *nm* semblance, show, sham, appearance; **faire — de** to pretend.

sembler [sãble] *vi* to seem, appear, look; **à ce qu'il me semble** as far as I can see, to my mind.

semelle [s(ə)mɛl] *nf* sole, foot, tread; **battre la —** to stamp one's feet (for warmth).

semence [s(ə)mã:s] *nf* seed, (tin) tacks.

semer [s(ə)me] *vt* to sow, scatter, spread, dot, outpace, shake off.

semestre [s(ə)mɛstr] *nm* term, half-year.

semestriel, -elle [s(ə)mɛstriɛl] *a* half-yearly.

semeur, -euse [s(ə)mœːr, øːz] *n* sower, spreader.

sémillant [semijã] *a* sprightly, lively, brisk.

séminariste [seminarist] *nm* seminarist.

semis [səmi] *nm* sowing, seed-bed, seedling.

sémitique [semitik] *a* semitic.

semonce [səmɔ̃ːs] *nf* rebuke, scolding, dressing-down.

semoncer [səmɔ̃se] *vt* to scold, rebuke, lecture.

semoule [s(ə)mul] *nf* semolina.

sénat [sɛna] *nm* senate.

sénateur [sɛnatœːr] *nm* senator.

sénile [senil] *a* senile.

sénilité [senilite] *nf* senility.

sens [sã:s] *nm* sense, intelligence, meaning, direction; **bon —** common sense; **rue à — unique** one-way street; **— interdit** no entry; **— dessus dessous** upside down.

sensation [sãsasjɔ̃] *nf* sensation, feeling, stir.

sensationnel, -elle [sãsasjɔnɛl] *a* sensational, super.

sensé [sãse] *a* sensible, judicious.

sensibilisateur, -trice [sãsibilizatœːr, tris] *a* sensitizing; *nm* sensitizer.

sensibilité [sãsibilite] *nf* sensibility, sensitiveness, feeling, tenderness.

sensible [sãsibl] *a* sensitive, susceptible, tender, sore, palpable, perceptible.

sensiblerie [sãsibləri] *nf* mawkish sentiment.

sensitif, -ive [sãsitif] *a* sensitive, sensory.

sensualisme [sãsɥalism] *nm* sensualism.

sensualité [sãsɥalite] *nf* sensuality.

sensuel, -elle [sãsɥɛl] *a* sensual, sensuous, voluptuous; *n* sensualist.

sentence [sãtã:s] *nf* maxim, sentence.

sentencieux, -euse [sãtãsjø, øːz] *a* sententious.

senteur [sãtœːr] *nf* perfume, scent.

senti [sãti] *a* heartfelt, genuine.

sentier [sãtje] *nm* path.

sentiment [sãtimã] *nm* feeling, sense, sensation, sentiment, opinion; **faire du —** to play on the emotions.

sentimental [sãtimãtal] *a* sentimental.

sentimentalité [sãtimãtalite] *nf* sentimentality.

sentine [sãtin] *nf* bilge.

sentinelle [sãtinɛl] *nf* sentry,

sentinel; **en — on** sentry duty.

sentir [sãtiːr] *vt* to feel, smell, be aware (of); *vi* to smell (of), taste of, smack of; *vr* to feel; **je ne peux pas le —** I can't stand him; **ne pas se — de joie** to be beside oneself with joy, overjoyed.

seoir [swaːr] *vi* to become, suit.

séparable [separabl] *a* separable.

séparation [separasjɔ̃] *nf* separation, breaking up, parting.

séparatisme [separatism] *nm* separatism.

séparé [separe] *a* separate, apart, distinct.

séparément [separemã] *ad* separately, apart, singly.

séparer [separe] *vt* to separate, divide, part, be between; *vr* to part, separate, divide, break up.

sept [sɛ(t)] *a* nm seven, seventh.

septembre [sɛptã:br] *nm* September.

septentrional [sɛptãtriɔnal] *a* northern; *n* Northerner.

septième [sɛtjɛm] *a nm* seventh.

septique [sɛptik] *a* septic.

septuagénaire [sɛptɥaʒenɛːr] *an* septuagenarian.

septuor [sɛptɥɔːr] *nm* septet.

sépulcral [sepylkral] *a* sepulchral.

sépulcre [sepylkr] *nm* sepulchre, tomb.

sépulture [sepyltyːr] *nf* burial-place, tomb, interment.

séquelle [sekɛl] *nf* gang, string; *pl* after-effects.

séquence [sekã:s] *nf* sequence, run.

séquestration [sekɛstrasjɔ̃] *nf* sequestration, seclusion, isolation.

séquestre [sekɛstr] *nm* sequestrator, trustee, sequestration, embargo; **sous —** sequestered.

séquestrer [sekɛstre] *vt* to sequester, sequestrate, confine, isolate.

séraphin [serafɛ̃] *nm* seraph.

séraphique [serafik] *a* seraphic, angelic.

serein [sərɛ̃] *a* serene, calm, quiet.

sérénade [serenad] *nf* serenade.

sérénité [serenite] *nf* serenity, calmness.

serf, serve [sɛrf, sɛrv] *a* in bondage; *n* serf.

serge [sɛrʒ] *nm* serge.

sergent [sɛrʒã] *nm* sergeant; **— major** quartermaster-sergeant; **— de ville** policeman.

série [seri] *nf* series, succession, line, set, run, break; **fin de —** remnant; **article hors —** specially made article, outsize; **voiture de —** car of standard model.

sérieux, -euse [serjø, øːz] *a* serious, grave, solemn, earnest, genuine; *nm* seriousness, gravity; **manque de — levity; prendre qch au —** to take sth seriously; **garder son —** to keep a straight face.

serin [s(ə)rɛ̃] *nm* canary, simpleton.

seringue [sərɛ̃:g] *nf* syringe.

serment [sɛrmɑ̃] *nm* oath; **prêter —** to take an oath, be sworn in; **sous —** on oath.

sermon [sɛrmɔ̃] *nm* sermon, talking-to.

sermonner [sɛrmɔne] *vt* to lecture; *vi* to preachify, lay down the law.

sermonneur, -euse [sɛrmɔnœːr, øːz] *a* sermonizing; *n* sermonizer.

serpe [sɛrp] *nf* bill-hook.

serpent [sɛrpɑ̃] *nm* snake, serpent; **— à sonnettes** rattlesnake.

serpenter [sɛrpɑ̃te]̄ *vi* to wind, meander.

serpentin [sɛrpɑ̃tɛ̃] *a* serpentine; *nm* worm (*of still*), coil, streamer.

serpette [sɛrpɛt] *nf* bill-hook, pruning-knife.

serpillière [sɛrpijɛːr] *nf* sacking, apron.

serpolet [sɛrpɔlɛ] *nm* wild thyme.

serrage [sɛraːʒ] *nm* tightening, clamping, grip; **— des freins** braking.

serre [sɛːr] *nf* greenhouse, pressing, talon, claw, grip, clip; **— chaude** hothouse.

serré [sere] *a* tight, close, serried, packed, closely-woven, compact, close-fisted.

serrement [sɛrmɑ̃] *nm* squeezing, pressure; **— de cœur** pang; **— de main(s)** handshake.

serre-papiers [sɛrpapje] *nm* file, paper-clip, -weight.

serrer [sere] *vt* to press, squeeze, clasp, shake (hands), clench, close (up), tighten, condense, put away; *vr* to stand or sit closer, huddle together, crowd, tighten.

serre-tête [sɛrtɛːt] *nm* head-band, crash-helmet, scrum-cap.

serrure [sɛryːr] *nf* lock; **trou de la — keyhole.**

serrurerie [sɛryr(ə)ri] *nf* lock, locksmith's (shop), locksmithing, metal work.

serrurier [sɛryrje] *nm* locksmith, ironsmith.

sertir [sɛrtiːr] *vt* to set.

servage [sɛrvaːʒ] *nm* bondage, serfdom.

serval [sɛrval] *nm* bush-cat.

servant [sɛrvɑ̃] *a* serving; *nm* server; *pl* gun crew.

servante [sɛrvɑ̃ːt] *nf* maid-servant, dumb-waiter, tea-trolley.

serveur, -euse [sɛrvœːr, øːz] *n* carver, barman, barmaid, waitress, server; *f* coffee pot.

serviable [sɛrvjabl] *a* obliging, helpful.

service [sɛrvis] *nm* service, disposition, attendance, good turn, department, course, set; **escalier de —** backstairs; **porte de — tradesmen's** entrance; **entrer en — to go into** service; **entrer au — to go into the** army; **être de — to be on duty;** **assurer le — entre . . . et . . . to run** between . . . and . . .; **bon pour le —** fit for service, serviceable; **libre — self-service.**

serviette [sɛrvjɛt] *nf* napkin, towel, brief-case.

servile [sɛrvil] *a* slavish, servile.

servilité [sɛrvilite] *nf* servility, slavishness.

servir [sɛrviːr] *vt* to serve (up, out), attend to, wait on, help, work, operate; *vi* to serve, be in use, be useful, be used; *vr* to help oneself, shop, deal, use; **— de** to be used as, serve as; **cela ne sert à rien** that is no use.

serviteur [sɛrvitœːr] *nm* servant.

servitude [sɛrvityd] *nf* servitude, slavery, bondage.

ses [se] *see* **son.**

session [sɛsjɔ̃] *nf* session, sitting.

séton [setɔ̃] *nm* **blessure en — flesh** wound.

seuil [sœj] *nm* threshold, doorstep.

seul [sœl] *a* single, alone, sole, one, only, by oneself.

seulement [sœlmɑ̃] *ad* only, merely, solely, even.

sève [sɛːv] *nf* sap, pith, vigour.

sévère [sevɛːr] *a* severe, stern, harsh, strict.

sévérité [severite] *nf* severity, sternness, harshness, strictness.

sévices [sevis] *nm pl* brutality, maltreatment, cruelty.

sévir [seviːr] *vi* to be rife, severe, to rage, dea severeɪy (with **contre).**

sevrer [sevre] *vt* to wean, deprive.

sexagénaire [sɛksaʒenɛːr] *an* sexagenarian.

sexe [sɛks] *nm* sex.

sextant [sɛkstɑ̃] *nm* sextant.

sexualité [sɛksɥalite] *nf* sexuality.

sexuel, -elle [sɛksɥɛl] *a* sexual.

seyant [sɛjɑ̃] *a* becoming.

shampooing [ʃɑ̃pwɛ̃] *nm* shampoo.

si [si] *ad* so, as, such, yes; *cj* if, whether, how, what about; *nm* B (*mus*); **si . . . que** however; **si ce n'était** were it not for.

siamois [sjamwa] *an* Siamese.

sidéré [sidere] *a* struck dumb, dazed, dumbfounded.

sidérurgie [sideryrʒi] *nf* metallurgy, iron smelting.

siècle [sjɛkl] *nm* century, age, period.

siège [sjɛːʒ] *nm* seat, chair, bottom (of chair), centre, siege; **déclarer l'état de — to declare martial law.**

siéger [sjeʒe] *vi* to sit, be seated, be centred.

sien, sienne [sjɛ̃, sjɛn] *pos pn* **le(s) —(s), la sienne, les siennes** his, hers, its, one's; *nm* his, her, its, one's own; *pl* one's own people; **y mettre du — to do one's share; faire des siennes** to be up to one's tricks.

sieste [sjɛst] *nf* siesta, nap.

sifflant [siflɑ̃] *a* whistling, hissing, sibilant.

siffler [sifle] *vt* to whistle (for, to, after), pipe, boo, hiss, swig; *vi* to whistle, hiss, sizzle, whizz, wheeze.

sifflet [siflɛ] *nm* whistle, pipe, hiss, catcall.

siffleur, -euse [sifloeːr, øːz] *a* whistling, hissing, wheezy; *n* whistler, booer.

siffloter [siflɔte] *vti* to whistle softly.

sigle [sigl] *nm* initials, trade-name, trade-mark.

signal [siɲal] *nm* signal.

signalement [siɲalmã] *nm* description, particulars.

signalé [siɲale] *a* signal, well-known, conspicuous.

signaler [siɲale] *vt* to signal, distinguish, point out, report, give a description of; *vr* to distinguish oneself.

signaleur [siɲaloeːr] *nm* signaller, signalman.

signalisateur [siɲalizatoeːr] *nm* signalling apparatus, traffic indicator.

signalisation [siɲalizasjɔ̃] *nf* signalling.

signataire [siɲateːr] *n* signatory.

signature [siɲatyːr] *nf* signature, signing.

signe [siɲ] *nm* sign, mark, symptom, indication, gesture; — **de tête** nod; **faire** — **à qn** to beckon, motion to s.o.

signer [siɲe] *vt* to sign, stamp; *vr* to cross oneself.

signet [siɲɛ] *nm* bookmark(er).

significatif, -ive [siɲifikatif, iːv] *a* significant.

signification [siɲifikasjɔ̃] *nf* signification, significance, meaning, notification.

signifier [siɲifje] *vt* to signify, mean, notify.

silence [silãːs] *nm* silence, stillness, hush, rest; **passer sous** — to ignore.

silencieux, -euse [silãsjø, øːz] *a* silent, still, noiseless; *nm* silencer.

silex [silɛks] *nm* silex, flint.

silhouette [silwɛt] *nf* silhouette, outline, figure.

silhouetter [silwɛte] *vt* to silhouette, outline; *vr* to stand out, show up.

sillage [sijaːʒ] *nm* wake, wash, track.

sillon [sijɔ̃] *nm* furrow, track, trail, wrinkle, groove, streak.

sillonner [sijɔne] *vt* to furrow, plough, cleave, wrinkle.

simagrée [simagre] *nf usu pl* affectation, affected airs.

simiesque [simjɛsk] *a* ape-like, monkey-like.

similaire [similɛːr] *a* similar, like.

similarité [similarite] *nf* similarity, likeness.

simili [simili] *nm* imitation.

similitude [similityd] *nf* similitude, similarity, likeness.

simple [sɛ̃ːpl] *a* simple, easy, mere, ordinary, plain, homely, guileless, sing'e; *nm* single (game); *pl* herbs; — **soldat** private (soldier).

simplicité [sɛ̃plisite] *nf* simplicity plainness, naturalness, simplemindedness.

simplificateur, -trice [sɛ̃plifikatoeːr, tris] *a* simplifying.

simplification [sɛ̃plifikasjɔ̃] *nf* simplification.

simplifier [sɛ̃plifje] *vt* to simplify.

simpliste [sɛ̃plist] *a* over-simple.

simulacre [simylakr] *nm* semblance, sham, show image.

simulateur, -trice [simylatoeːr, tris] *n* simulator, shammer.

simulation [simylasjɔ̃] *nf* simulation, shamming.

simuler [simyle] *vt* to simulate, sham feign.

simultané [simyltane] *a* simultaneous.

sinapisme [sinapism] *nm* mustard plaster.

sincère [sɛ̃sɛːr] *a* sincere, genuine, rank, candid.

sincérité [sɛ̃serite] *nf* sincerity, genuineness, candour.

singe [sɛ̃ːʒ] *nm* monkey, ape, mimic, (*sl*) bully-beef.

singer [sɛ̃ʒe] *vt* to ape, mimic.

singerie [sɛ̃ʒri] *nf* grimace, antic, affected airs, monkey-house.

singulariser [sɛ̃gylarize] *vt* to make conspicuous.

singularité [sɛ̃gylarite] *nf* peculiarity, unusualness, oddness, eccentricity.

singulier, -ière [sɛ̃gylje, iɛːr] *a* peculiar, singular, unusual, remarkable, queer, odd; *nm* singular; **combat** — single combat.

sinistre [sinistr] *a* sinister, ominous, fatal; *nm* catastrophe, disaster, calamity.

sinistré [sinistre] *a* damaged (by fire *etc*); *n* victim.

sinon [sinɔ̃] *cj* if not, otherwise, except.

sinueux, -euse [sinyø, øːz] *a* sinuous, winding, meandering.

sinuosité [sinyɔzite] *nf* winding, meander, bend.

sinusite [sinyzit] *nf* sinusitis.

siphon [sifɔ̃] *nm* siphon, trap.

sire [siːr] *nm* sire; **triste** — sorry fellow.

sirène [sirɛn] *nf* siren, vamp, buzzer, hooter, foghorn.

sirop [siro] *nm* syrup.

siroter [sirɔte] *vt* to sip; *vi* to tipple.

sis [si] *pp* situated.

sismique [sismik] *a* seismic.

site [sit] *nm* beauty spot, site.

sitôt [sito] *ad* — **dit,** — **fait** no sooner said than done; **nous ne le reverrons pas de** — we will not see him for some time to come.

situation [sitɥasjɔ̃] *nf* situation, site, position, post, state.

situer [sitɥe] *vt* to situate, locate, place.

six [si(s)] *a nm* six, sixth.

sixième [sizjɛm] *an* sixth; *nm* sixth (part); *nf* first form (school).

ski [ski] *nm* ski, skiing; — **nautique** water-skiing.

skieur, -euse [skiœːr, øːz] *n* skier.

slip [slip] *nm* slip, slipway, briefs, underpants.

smoking [smɔkiŋ] *nm* dinner jacket.

snob [snɔb] *nm* snob, slavish imitator of popular fashion or opinion; *a* smart, snobbish.

snobisme [snɔbism] *nm* snobbery, slavish imitation of popular fashion or opinion.

sobre [sɔbr] *a* temperate, moderate, sparing, quiet.

sobriété [sɔbriete] *nf* sobriety, temperateness, moderation.

sobriquet [sɔbrikɛ] *nm* nickname.

soc [sɔk] *nm* ploughshare.

sociabilité [sɔsjabilite] *nf* sociability, sociableness.

sociable [sɔsjabl] *a* sociable.

social [sɔsjal] *a* social; **raison —e** name of a firm.

socialisme [sɔsjalism] *nm* socialism.

socialiste [sɔsjalist] *a* socialist(ic); *n* socialist.

sociétaire [sɔsjetɛːr] *n* member, shareholder.

société [sɔsjete] *nf* society, association, club, companionship, company, partnership; **S — des Nations** League of Nations.

sociologie [sɔsjɔlɔʒi] *nf* sociology.

socle [sɔkl] *nm* pedestal, plinth, base, stand.

socque [sɔk] *nm* clog, patten, sock.

socquette [sɔkɛt] *nf* ankle sock.

sodium [sɔdjɔm] *nm* sodium.

sœur [sœːr] *nf* sister, nun.

sofa [sɔfa] *nm* sofa, settee.

soi [swa] *pn* oneself, him-, her-, it-; **— -même** oneself.

soi-disant [swadizɑ̃] *a* would-be, so-called, self-styled; *ad* supposedly.

soie [swa] *nf* silk, bristle; **papier de — ** tissue paper.

soierie [swari] *nf* silk-fabric, silks, silk-trade, -factory.

soif [swaf] *nf* thirst; **avoir —** to be thirsty, eager (for de).

soigné [swaɲe] *a* neat, careful, carefully done, well-groomed, trim.

soigner [swaɲe] *vt* to take care of, attend (to), look after, nurse, take pains with; *vr* to take care of o.s., look after o.s.

soigneux, -euse [swaɲø, øːz] *a* careful, tidy, neat.

soin [swɛ̃] *nm* care, trouble, attention, pains, task; *pl* solicitude, attention(s), aid, treatment; **avoir — to take care; être aux petits —s auprès de qn** to be most attentive to.

soir [swaːr] *nm* evening, night.

soirée [sware] *nf* evening, party, reception.

soit [swa] *excl* right! agreed! *cj* — **l'un — l'autre** either one or the other; — **aujourd'hui ou demain** either today or tomorrow; — **qu'il le fasse ou qu'il ne le fasse pas** whether he does it or not.

soixantaine [swasɑ̃tɛn] *nf* about sixty.

soixante [swasɑ̃ːt] *a nm* sixty.

soixantième [swasɑ̃tjɛm] *a nm* sixtieth.

sol [sɔl] *nm* ground, soil, earth, G (*mus*).

solaire [sɔlɛːr] *a* solar.

soldat [sɔlda] *nm* soldier; **simple — ** private; — **de première classe** lance-corporal; — **de plomb** tin soldier.

solde [sɔld] *nm* balance, settlement, job lot, surplus stock, clearance sale; *nf* pay; **prix de —** bargain price; **être à la — de** to be in the pay of.

solder [sɔlde] *vt* to balance, settle, clear off, sell off.

sole [sɔl] *nf* sole.

solécisme [sɔlesism] *nm* solecism.

soleil [sɔlɛːj] *nm* sun, sunshine, sunflower, monstrance, Catherine wheel; **coup de —** sunburn, sunstroke, sunny interval; **il fait du —** it is sunny.

solennel, -elle [sɔlanɛl] *a* solemn, grave, official.

solenniser [sɔlanize] *vt* to solemnize, celebrate.

solennité [sɔlanite] *nf* solemnity, solemn ceremony.

solfège [sɔlfɛːʒ] *nm* sol-fa.

solidaire [sɔlidɛːr] *a* interdependent, jointly responsible, binding, bound up (with de).

solidariser [sɔlidarize] *vt* to make responsible.

solidarité [sɔlidarite] *nf* joint responsibility, interdependence, solidarity; **faire la grève de —** to strike in sympathy.

solide [sɔlid] *a* solid, secure, sound, strong, hefty, staunch; *nm* solid; **viser au —** to have an eye to the main chance.

solidifier [sɔlidifje] *vtr* to solidify.

solidité [sɔlidite] *nf* solidity, soundness, stability, strength, staunchness.

soliloque [sɔlilɔk] *nm* soliloquy.

soliste [sɔlist] *a* solo; *n* soloist.

solitaire [sɔlitɛːr] *a* solitary, lonely; *nm* hermit, recluse, solitaire.

solitude [sɔlityd] *nf* solitude, loneliness, wilderness.

solive [sɔliːv] *nf* beam, joist, rafter.

sollicitation [sɔllisitasjɔ̃] *nf* solicitation, entreaty, canvassing.

solliciter [sɔllisite] *vt* to solicit, beg for, canvass, apply for, attract.

solliciteur, -euse [sɔllisitœːr, øːz] *n*

petitioner, canvasser, applicant.

sollicitude [sɔllisityd] *nf* solicitude, concern, care, anxiety.

solo [sɔlo] *a nm* solo.

solstice [sɔlstis] *nm* solstice.

soluble [sɔlybl] *a* soluble, solvable.

solution [sɔlysjɔ̃] *nf* solution, answer, settlement.

solvabilité [sɔlvabilite] *nf* solvency.

solvable [sɔlvabl] *a* solvent.

sombre [sɔ̃:br] *a* sombre, dark, dismal, gloomy, dull.

sombrer [sɔ̃bre] *vi* to sink, founder, go down.

sommaire [sɔmmɛːr] *a* summary, succinct, hasty, scant; *nm* summary, synopsis.

sommation [sɔmasjɔ̃] *nf* notice, summons.

somme [sɔm] *nf* sum, amount, pack-saddle; *nm* nap, snooze; **bête de —** beast of burden; **— toute, en —** on the whole, in short.

sommeil [sɔmɛːj] *nm* sleep, slumber, sleepiness; **avoir —** to be sleepy, drowsy; **avoir le — léger (profond),** to be a light (heavy) sleeper.

sommeiller [sɔmeje] *vi* to slumber, be asleep, nod.

sommelier [sɔməlje] *nm* wine-waiter.

sommer [sɔme] *vt* to summon, call upon.

sommet [sɔmɛ] *nm* summit, top, crown, crest, apex; **conférence au —** summit conference.

sommier [sɔmje] *nm* bed-springs, register.

sommité [sɔmmite] *nf* summit, top, leading figure.

somnambule [sɔmnãbyl] *a* somnambulistic; *n* somnambulist, sleep-walker.

somnifère [sɔmnifɛːr] *a nm* sleeping-tablet, soporific.

somnolence [sɔmnɔlãːs] *nf* somnolence, drowsiness.

somnolent [sɔmnɔlã] *a* somnolent, drowsy, sleepy.

somnoler [sɔmnɔle] *vi* to doze, nod, drowse.

somptueux, -euse [sɔ̃ptɥø, øːz] *a* sumptuous.

son, sa, ses [sɔ̃, sa, se] *a* his, her, its, one's.

son [sɔ̃] *nm* sound, bran; **tache de —** freckle.

sonate [sɔnat] *nf* sonata.

sondage [sɔ̃daːʒ] *nm* sounding, boring, probing, bore-hole.

sonde [sɔ̃ːd] *nf* plummet, sounding-line, -rod, boring-machine, probe, taster.

sonder [sɔ̃de] *vt* to sound, bore, probe, investigate, fathom.

sondeuse [sɔ̃døːz] *nf* drilling-machine.

songe [sɔ̃ːʒ] *nm* dream.

songe-creux [sɔ̃ʒkrø] *nm* dreamer, visionary.

songer [sɔ̃ʒe] *vi* to dream, muse, imagine, remember, think.

songerie [sɔ̃ʒri] *nf* reverie, musing, daydream(ing), brown study.

songeur, -euse [sɔ̃ʒœːr, øːz] *a* dreamy, pensive; *n* dreamer.

sonnaille [sɔnaːj] *nf* cattle-bell.

sonnant [sɔnã] *a* ringing, striking; **à une heure —e** on the stroke of one; **espèces —es** hard cash.

sonner [sɔne] *vt* to ring (for), strike; *vi* to ring, sound, toll, strike.

sonnerie [sɔnri] *nf* ringing, chimes, bell system of bells, bugle call; **— électrique** electric bell; **— aux morts** last post.

sonnet [sɔnɛ] *nm* sonnet.

sonnette [sɔnɛt] *nf* small bell, housebell, handbell; **coup de —** ring.

sonneur [sɔnœːr] *nm* bell-ringer.

sonore [sɔnɔːr] *a* sonorous, resounding resonant, ringing, voiced, with good acoustics; **bande —** sound-track.

sonoriser [sɔnɔrize] *vt* to add the sound effects to (*a film*), to install amplifiers.

sonorité [sɔnɔrite] *nf* sonority, resonance.

sophisme [sɔfism] *nm* sophism, fallacy.

sophiste [sɔfist] *nm* sophist.

sophistiqué [sɔfistike] *a* sophisticated, adulterated.

soporifique [sɔpɔrifik] *a* soporific, tiresome.

sorbier [sɔrbje] *nm* service-tree, rowan-tree.

sorcellerie [sɔrsɛlri] *nf* witchcraft, sorcery.

sorcier, -ière [sɔrsje, jɛːr] *n* sorcerer, sorceress, wizard, witch, hag.

sordide [sɔrdid] *a* squalid, sordid, mean, dirty.

sornettes [sɔrnɛt] *nf pl* nonsense, trash.

sort [sɔːr] *nm* fate, chance, lot, spell; **tirer au —** to draw lots, ballot.

sortable [sɔrtabl] *a* suitable, eligible, presentable.

sortant [sɔrtã] *a* outgoing, retiring.

sorte [sɔrt] *nf* kind, sort, way, manner; **de la —** in that way; **de — que** so that; **en quelque —** in a way.

sortie [sɔrti] *nf* going out, coming out, exit, way out, leaving, sortie, trip, outburst; **— de secours** emergency exit; **jour de —** day out; **— de bain** bathing wrap.

sortilège [sɔrtilɛːʒ] *nm* charm, spell.

sortir [sɔrtiːr] *vt* to take (put, bring, pull) out; *vi* to go (come, walk) out, protrude, stand out, spring, descend; *nm* coming out; **— de table** to rise from table; **faire —** to put out, take out; **il est sorti** he is out; **au — de l'école** on coming out of school, on leaving school.

sosie [sozi] nm double.

sot, sotte [so, sɔt] a stupid, foolish, silly; n fool, dolt.

sottise [sɔtiːz] nf stupidity, folly, silliness, foolish thing.

sou [su] nm sou; cent —s five francs; il n'a pas le — he is penniless; il n'a pas pour deux —s de curiosité he is not the least bit curious.

soubassement [subasmɑ̃] nm base, substructure.

soubresaut [subrəso] nm leap, start, jump, jolt, gasp; pl spasmodic movements, convulsions.

soubrette [subrɛt] nf soubrette, waiting-maid.

souche [suʃ] nf stump, log, dolt, counterfoil, origin; faire — to found a family; de bonne — of good stock, pedigree.

souci [susi] nm care, worry, anxiety, solicitude, marigold.

se soucier [səsusje] vr to concern o.s., worry, trouble, care, mind, bother.

soucieux, -euse [susjø, øːz] a anxious, mindful, worried.

soucoupe [sukup] nf saucer.

soudain [sudɛ̃] a sudden; ad suddenly.

soudaineté [sudɛnte] nf suddenness.

soudard [sudaːr] nm old soldier.

soude [sud] nf soda; bicarbonate de — bicarbonate of soda, baking soda.

souder [sude] vt to solder, weld; vr to weld, knit; lampe à — blowlamp.

soudoyer [sudwaje] vt to hire, bribe.

soudure [sudyːr] nf soldering, welding, soldered joint, solder.

soufflage [suflaːʒ] nm blowing, blast.

souffle [sufl] nm breath, breathing, blast, puff, inspiration; couper le — à qn to take s.o.'s breath away; à bout de — out of breath.

soufflé [sufle] a unvoiced; nm soufflé.

souffler [sufle] vt to blow (out, off, up), breathe, utter, filch, pinch; vi to blow, pant, puff, recover one's breath; — (son rôle à) qn to prompt s.o.

soufflet [suflɛ] nm bellows, gore, insult, box on the ear, slap.

souffleter [suflǝte] vt to slap, box s.o.'s ears, insult.

souffleur, -euse [suflœːr, øːz] n prompter; nm blower.

souffrance [sufrɑ̃ːs] nf suffering, pain; en — in suspense, awaiting delivery.

souffrant [sufrɑ̃] a suffering, unwell, ailing.

souffre-douleur [sufrǝdulœːr] nm butt, drudge.

souffreteux, -euse [sufrǝtø, øːz] a sickly, seedy, needy.

souffrir [sufriːr] vt to suffer, endure, bear, allow (of); vi to be in pain, suffer.

soufre [sufr] nm sulphur, brimstone.

soufrer [sufre] vt to sulphurate.

souhait [swɛ] nm wish, desire; à — to one's liking.

souhaitable [swɛtabl] a desirable.

souhaiter [swɛte] vt to wish (for), desire.

souiller [suje] vt to soil, pollute, stain, sully.

souillon [sujɔ̃] n sloven, slut; nf scullery maid.

souillure [sujyːr] nf stain, spot, blemish, blot.

soûl [su] a drunk, surfeited; tout son — one's fill.

soulagement [sulaʒmɑ̃] nm relief, comfort, alleviation.

soulager [sulaʒe] vt to relieve, alleviate, ease; vr to relieve one's feelings, relieve oneself.

soûlard [sulaːr] nm drunkard.

soûler [sule] vt to stuff with food, make drunk; vr to gorge, get drunk.

soûlerie [sulri] nf drinking bout, drunken orgy.

soulèvement [sulɛvmɑ̃] nm rising, upheaval, revolt, indignant outburst.

soulever [sulve] vt to raise, lift, rouse, stir up; vr to revolt, heave.

soulier [sulje] nm shoe.

souligner [suliɲe] vt to underline, stress, emphasize.

soumettre [sumɛtr] vt to subdue, subject, refer, lay, submit; vr to submit, comply, yield, defer.

soumis [sumi] a submissive, amenable, biddable, liable, subject.

soumission [sumisjɔ̃] nf submission, submissiveness, compliance, tender.

soupape [supap] nf valve.

soupçon [supsɔ̃] nm suspicion, touch, dash, flavour.

soupçonner [supsɔne] vt to suspect, guess, conjecture, surmise.

soupçonneux, -euse [supsɔnø, øːz] a suspicious, distrustful.

soupe [sup] nf soup.

soupente [supɑ̃ːt] nf garret, loft, recess, brace, strap.

souper [supe] vi to have supper; nm supper; j'en ai soupé I am fed up (with it).

soupeser [supǝze] vt to weigh in the hand, feel the weight of.

soupière [supjɛːr] nf soup-tureen.

soupir [supiːr] nm sigh.

soupirail [supiraːj] nm ventilator, air-hole.

soupirant [supirɑ̃] nm suitor.

soupirer [supire] vi to sigh, gasp, long (for après).

souple [supl] a supple, flexible, adaptable, pliant.

souplesse [suplɛs] nf suppleness, pliability, flexibility, litheness; — d'esprit adaptability.

source [surs] nf source, spring, well, fount(ain), origin, root; de bonne — on good authority.

sourcier, -ière [sursje, jɛːr] n water-diviner.

sourcil [sursi] *nm* eyebrow.

sourciller [sursije] *vi* to frown, flinch, wince.

sourcilleux, -euse [sursijø, øːz] *a* frowning, supercilious.

sourd [suːr] *a* deaf, muffled, dull, veiled, muted, sound-proof, unvoiced; **bruit** — thud; **lanterne** —**e** dark-lantern; — **comme un pot** as deaf as a door post.

sourdement [surdəmã] *ad* with a dull hollow sound, dully, secretly.

sourdine [surdin] *nf* mute, damper, dimmer; **en** — on the sly.

sourd-muet, sourde-muette [surmɥɛ, surdmɥɛt] *a* deaf-and-dumb; *n* deaf-mute.

sourdre [surdr] *vi* to well up, spring, arise.

souricière [surisjeːr] *nf* mousetrap, trap.

sourire [suriːr] *vi* to smile, appeal; *nm* smile.

souris [suri] *nf* mouse; *nm* smile.

sournois [surnwa] *a* sly, crafty, artful. underhand; *n* sneak, shifty character, sly boots.

sournoiserie [surnwazri] *nf* craftiness, underhand piece of work.

sous [su] *prep* under(neath), below, beneath, within (time), sub-; — **la pluie** in the rain; — **peine de mort** on pain of death.

sous-alimentation [suzalimãtasjõ] *nf* malnutrition.

sous-bois [subwa] *nm* underwood, undergrowth.

sous-chef [suʃɛf] *nm* deputy chief, assistant manager, chief assistant.

souscription [suskripsjõ] *nf* subscription, contribution, signing, signature; **verser une** — to make a contribution.

souscrire [suskriːr] *vt* to subscribe (to), sign.

sous-développé [sudevlɔpe] *a* underdeveloped.

sous-directeur, -trice [sudirɛktœːr, tris] *n* assistant-manager(ess), vice-principal.

sous-entendre [suzãtãːdr] *vt* to imply, understand.

sous-entendu [suzãtãdy] *nm* implication; **parler par** —**s** to hint, insinuate.

sous-entente [suzãtãt] *nf* mental reservation.

sous-estimer [suzɛstime] *vt* to under-estimate.

sous-gouverneur [suguvɛrnœːr] *nm* deputy-, vice-governor.

sous-jacent [suʒasã] *a* subjacent, underlying.

sous-lieutenant [suljøtnã] *nm* second-, sub-lieutenant.

sous-location [sulɔkasjõ] *nf* sublet (ting).

sous-louer [sulwe] *vt* to sub-let, sub-lease.

sous-main [sumɛ̃] *nm* writing-pad, blotting-pad; **en** — behind the scenes.

sous-marin [sumarɛ̃] *a* submarine, submerged; *nm* submarine.

sous-officier [suzɔfisje] *nm* non-commissioned officer, (*naut*) petty officer.

sous-pied [supje] *nm* under-strap.

sous-préfecture [suprefɛktyːr] *nf* sub-prefecture.

sous-produit [suprɔdɥi] *nm* by-product.

sous-secrétaire [susəkrɛteːr] *n* under-secretary.

sous-seing [susɛ̃] *nm* private contract agreement.

soussigner [susiɲe] *vt* to sign, undersign.

sous-sol [susɔl] *nm* basement, sub-soil.

sous-titre [sutiːtr] *nm* sub-title, caption.

soustraction [sustraksjõ] *nf* subtraction, removal.

soustraire [sustreːr] *vt* to subtract, remove, take away, shield, screen; *vr* to elude, avoid, dodge, get out (ot à); **se** — **à la justice** to abscond.

sous-ventrière [suvãtrjeːr] *nf* belly-band, saddle-girth.

sous-vêtement [suvɛtmã] *nm* undergarment.

soutache [sutaʃ] *nf* braid.

soutane [sutan] *nf* cassock.

soute [sut] *nf* store-room, coal-bunker; — **à eau** water-tank; — **à munitions** magazine.

soutenable [sutnabl] *a* bearable, tenable, arguable.

soutenance [sutnãːs] *nf* maintaining (thesis).

souteneur [sutnœːr] *nm* upholder, pimp.

soutenir [sutniːr] *vt* to sustain, support, withstand, maintain, keep, back (up), assert; *vr* to support oneself, keep up, be maintained.

soutenu [sutny] *a* sustained, unflagging, constant, continued, steady, elevated.

souterrain [sutɛrɛ̃] *a* subterranean, underground; *nm* tunnel underground passage.

soutien [sutjɛ̃] *nm* support, prop, supporter.

soutien-gorge [sutjɛ̃gɔrʒ] *nm* brassière.

soutier [sutje] *nm* trimmer.

soutirer [sutire] *vt* to rack, draw off, squeeze.

souvenance [suvnãːs] *nf* recollection.

souven.r [suvniːr] *v imp* to come to mind; *vr* to remember, recall; *nm* memory, recollection, remembrance, memento, souvenir, memorial, keepsake.

souvent [suvã] *ad* often.

souverain [suvrɛ̃] *a* sovereign, supreme; *n* sovereign, ruler.

souveraineté [suvrɛnte] *nf* sovereignty.

soviétique [sɔvjetik] a soviet; n Soviet citizen.

soyeux, -euse [swajø, øːz] a silky, silken.

spacieux, -euse [spasjø, øːz] a spacious, roomy.

sparadrap [sparadra] nm sticking-plaster.

sparte [spart] nm esparto grass.

spartiate [sparsjat] a spartan.

spasme [spasm] nm spasm.

spasmodique [spasmɔdik] a spasmodic.

spatule [spatyl] nf spatula.

speaker, -ine [spikœːr, krin] n (radio) announcer.

spécial [spesjal] a special, particular.

se spécialiser [səspesjalize] vr to specialize.

spécialiste [spesjalist] n specialist, expert.

spécialité [spesjalite] nf specialty, special feature.

spécieux, -euse [spesjø, øːz] a specious.

spécification [spesifikasjɔ̃] nf specification.

spécifier [spesifje] vt to specify, determine.

spécifique [spesifik] a specific, precise.

spécimen [spesimɛn] a nm specimen.

spéciosité [spesjozite] nf speciousness.

spectacle [spɛktakl] nm spectacle, scene sight, display, theatre, show; salle de — theatre; pièce à grand — spectacular play; se donner en — to make an exhibition of o.s.

spectaculaire [spɛktakylɛːr] a spectacular.

spectateur, -trice [spɛktatœːr, tris] n spectator, onlooker, bystander.

spectral [spɛktral] a spectral, ghostly, ghostlike, of the spectrum.

spectre [spɛktr] nm ghost, spectre, apparition, spectrum.

spéculaire [spekylɛːr] a specular.

spéculateur, -trice [spekylatœːr, tris] n speculator, theorizer.

spéculatif, -ive [spekylatif, iːv] a speculative.

spéculation [spekylasjɔ̃] nf speculation, theorizing, conjecture.

spéculer [spekyle] vi to speculate, theorize, cogitate; — à la baisse (hausse) to speculate on a rise (fall).

spermatozoïde [spɛrmatozɔid] nm spermatozoon.

sperme [spɛrm] nm sperm.

sphère [sfɛr] nf sphere, orb, globe.

sphérique [sferik] a spherical.

sphéroïde [sferɔid] nm spheroid.

sphinx [sfɛ̃ks] nm sphinx.

spider [spidɛːr] nm dickey-seat, rumble seat.

spinal [spinal] a spinal.

spiral [spiral] a spiral.

spirale [spiral] nf spiral; escalier en — winding staircase.

spirite [spirit] a spiritualistic; n spiritualist.

spiritisme [spiritism] nm spiritualism.

spiritualiste [spirityalist] a spiritualistic; n spiritualist.

spirituel, -elle [spirityɛl] a spiritual, sacred, witty.

spiritueux, -euse [spirityø, øːz] a spirituous, alcoholic; nm pl spirits.

spleen [splin] nm spleen, depression; avoir le — to have the blues.

splendeur [splɑ̃dœːr] nf splendour, grandeur, magnificence, brilliance, pomp.

splendide [splɑ̃did] a splendid, magnificent, grand, gorgeous, glorious.

spoliateur, -trice [spɔljatœːr, tris] a spoliatory, despoiling; n despoiler, plunderer.

spoliation [spɔljasjɔ̃] nf spoliation, despoiling, plundering.

spolier [spɔlje] vt to despoil, rob, plunder.

spongieux, -euse [spɔ̃ʒjø, øːz] a spongy.

spontané [spɔ̃tane] a spontaneous, involuntary.

spontanéité [spɔ̃taneite] nf spontaneity.

sporadique [spɔradik] a sporadic.

spore [spɔːr] nf spore.

sport [spɔːr] nm sport(s), games; a sporting, casual.

sportif, -ive [spɔrtif, iːv] a sport(ing), athletic; n sportsman, -woman, lover of games; réunion sportive sports, athletic meeting.

sportsman [spɔrt(s)man] nm sportsman, race-goer.

spumeux, -euse [spymø, øːz] a spumy, frothy, foamy.

square [skwɛːr, skwaːr] nm small public garden.

squelette [skəlɛt] nm skeleton, framework, outline.

squelettique [skəlɛtik] a skeleton-like.

stabilisateur, -trice [stabilizatœːr, tris] a stabilizing, steadying; nm stabilizer.

stabiliser [stabilize] vt to stabilize, steady; vr to become steady, stable.

stabilité [stabilite] nf stability, steadiness, firmness, balance, durability.

stable [stabl] a stable, steady, firm, durable.

stade [stad] nm stadium, sports-ground, stage.

stage [staːʒ] nm probationary period, course.

stagiaire [staʒjɛːr] a probationary; n probationer.

stagnant [stagnɑ̃] a stagnant, dull.

stagnation [stagnasjɔ̃] nf stagnation, stagnancy, standstill.

stalactite [stalaktit] nf stalactite.

stalagmite [stalagmit] nf stalagmite.

stalle [stal] *nf* stall, box, seat, pew.

stance [stɑ̃:s] *nf* stanza.

stand [stɑ̃:d] *nm* stand, shooting-gallery.

standard [stɑ̃da:r] *nm* switchboard, standard.

standardisation [stɑ̃dardizasjɔ̃] *nf* standardization.

standardiser [stɑ̃dardize] *vt* to standardize.

station [stasjɔ̃] *nf* stop, station, stage, taxi-rank, position, post, standing; — **centrale** power-house; — **balnéaire** seaside resort, spa; — **thermale** spa, watering place; — **d'hiver** winter resort; **faire une** — à to halt at.

stationnaire [stasjɔnɛ:r] *a* stationary, fixed.

stationnement [stasjɔnmɑ̃] *nm* standing, stopping, stationing, taxi-rank; **parc de** — parking place; — **interdit** no parking.

stationner [stasjɔne] *vi* to stand, park, stop, be stationed.

statique [statik] *a* static.

statistique [statistik] *a* statistical; *nf* statistics.

statuaire [statɥɛ:r] *a* statuary; *n* sculptor; *nf* statuary.

statue [staty] *nf* statue.

statuer [statɥe] *vt* to ordain, decree, enact; — **sur une affaire** to decide, give a decision on a matter.

stature [staty:r] *nf* stature, height.

statut [staty] *nm* statute, regulation, article, ordinance, by(e)-law.

statutaire [statytɛ:r] *a* statutory.

sténodactylo(graphe) [stenɔdaktilɔ(graf)] *n* shorthand-typist.

sténodactylographie [stenɔdaktilɔgrafi] *nf* shorthand and typing.

sténographe [stenɔgraf] *n* stenographer, shorthand writer.

sténographie [stenɔgrafi] *nf* stenography, shorthand.

sténographier [stenɔgrafje] *vt* to take down in shorthand.

stentor [stɑ̃tɔ:r] *nm* **voix de** — stentorian voice.

steppe [stɛp] *n* steppe.

stère [stɛ:r] *nm* stere, cubic metre.

stéréophonie [stereɔfɔni] *nf* stereophony.

stéréotype [stereɔtip] *a* stereotype(d); *nm* stereotype plate.

stérile [steril] *a* sterile, barren, fruitless.

stérilisation [sterilizasjɔ̃] *nf* sterilization.

stériliser [sterilize] *vt* to sterilize.

stérilité [sterilite] *nf* sterility, barrenness, fruitlessness.

sternum [stɛrnɔm] *nm* sternum, breastbone.

stigmate [stigmat] *nm* stigma, scar, brand.

stigmatiser [stigmatize] *vt* to stigmatize, brand (with infamy), pock-mark.

stimulant [stimylɑ̃] *a* stimulating; *nm* stimulant, stimulus, incentive.

stimulation [stimylasjɔ̃] *nf* stimulation.

stimuler [stimyle] *vt* to stimulate, incite, rouse.

stipulation [stipylasjɔ̃] *nf* stipulation.

stipuler [stipyle] *vt* to stipulate, lay down.

stock [stɔk] *nm* stock; — **en magasin** stock in hand.

stockiste [stɔkist] *nm* stocker, wholesale warehouseman, agent; **agence** — service-station.

stoïcien, **-enne** [stɔisjɛ̃, jɛn] *a* stoic(al); *n* stoic.

stoïcisme [stɔisism] *nm* stoicism.

stoïque [stɔik] *a* stoic(al).

stomacal [stɔmakal] *a* gastric.

stomachique [stɔmaʃik] *a* stomach-, stomachic.

stoppage [stɔpaːʒ] *nm* stopping, stoppage, invisible mending.

stopper [stɔpe] *vt* to stop, fine-darn; *vi* to (come to a) stop.

store [stɔ:r] *nm* blind.

strabisme [strabism] *nm* squinting.

strangulation [strɑ̃gylasjɔ̃] *nf* strangulation, throttling, constriction.

strapontin [strapɔ̃tɛ̃] *nm* folding-, bracket-seat.

strass [stras] *nm* strass, paste jewellery.

stratagème [strataʒɛm] *nm* stratagem.

stratégie [strateʒi] *nf* strategy, generalship, craft.

stratégique [strateʒik] *a* strategic (al).

stratosphère [stratɔsfɛ:r] *nf* stratosphere.

strict [strikt] *a* strict, severe; **le** — **nécessaire** the bare necessities.

strident [stridɑ̃] *a* strident, harsh, grating.

strie [stri] *nf* score, streak.

strier [strie] *vt* to score, scratch, streak, groove.

striure [striy:r] *nf* score, scratch, streak, groove, striation.

strophe [strɔf] *nf* stanza, verse.

structure [strykty:r] *nf* structure.

strychnine [striknin] *nf* strychnine.

stuc [styk] *nm* stucco.

studieux, **-euse** [stydjø, ø:z] *a* studious.

studio [stydjo] *nm* (film) studio, artist's studio.

stupéfaction [stypefaksjɔ̃] *nf* stupefaction, amazement, bewilderment.

stupéfait [stypefɛ] *a* stupefied, amazed, astounded.

stupéfiant [stypefjɑ̃] *a* stupefying, astounding; *nm* narcotic, drug.

stupéfier [stypefje] *vt* to stupefy, bemuse, astound.

stupeur [stypœ:r] *nf* stupor, astonishment, amazement.

stupide [stypid] *a* stupid, foolish, silly.

stupidité [stypidite] *nf* stupidity, foolishness, stupid thing.

stupre [stypr] *nm* debauchery.

style [stil] *nm* style, pin, etching-needle; **robe de** — period dress.

styler [stile] *vt* to train, school.

stylet [stilɛ] *nm* stiletto.

styliser [stilize] *vt* to stylize, conventionalize.

stylo(graphe) [stilɔ(graf)] *nm* fountain-pen, stylograph.

styptique [stiptik] *a nm* styptic, astringent.

su [sy] *nm* au — de to the knowledge of; **à mon vu et** — to my certain knowledge.

suaire [sɥɛːr] *nm* shroud, winding-sheet.

suave [sɥaːv] *a* bland, suave, sweet, mild, soft, mellow.

suavité [sɥavite] *nf* blandness, suavity, sweetness, mildness, mellowness.

subalterne [sybaltɛrn] *a* subordinate, junior; *nm* subaltern, underling.

subdiviser [sybdivize] *vtr* to subdivide.

subdivision [sybdivizjɔ̃] *nf* subdivision.

subir [sybiːr] *vt* to undergo, go through, sustain, suffer.

subit [sybi] *a* sudden, unexpected.

subjacent [sybʒasɑ̃] *a* subjacent, underlying.

subjectif, -ive [sybʒɛktif, iːv] *a* subjective.

subjonctif, -ive [sybʒɔ̃ktif, iːv] *a nm* subjunctive.

subjuguer [sybʒyge] *vt* to subjugate, subdue, overcome, captivate.

sublime [syblim] *a* sublime, exalted, lofty; *nm* sublime.

sublimer [syblime] *vt* to sublimate, purify.

submerger [sybmɛrʒe] *vt* to submerge, immerse.

submersible [sybmɛrsibl] *a* submersible, sinkable; *nm* submersible, submarine.

submersion [sybmɛrsjɔ̃] *nf* submersion, immersion.

subordination [sybɔrdinasjɔ̃] *nf* subordination.

subordonné [sybɔrdɔne] *a* subordinate, dependent; *n* subordinate, underling.

subordonner [sybɔrdɔne] *vt* to subordinate.

subornation [sybɔrnasjɔ̃] *nf* subornation, bribing.

suborner [sybɔrne] *vt* to suborn, bribe.

subreptice [sybrɛptis] *a* surreptitious, stealthy.

subrogation [sybrɔgasjɔ̃] *nf* subrogation, substitution, delegation.

subroger [sybrɔʒe] *vt* to subrogate, appoint as deputy.

subséquent [sypsekɑ̃] *a* subsequent, ensuing.

subside [sypsid] *nm* subsidy.

subsidence [sypsidɑ̃ːs] *nf* subsidence.

subsidiaire [sypsidjɛːr] *a* subsidiary, accessory.

subsistance [sypsistɑ̃ːs] *nf* subsistence, keep, sustenance.

subsister [sypsiste] *vi* to subsist, exist, hold good.

substance [sypstɑ̃ːs] *nf* substance, matter, material.

substantiel, -elle [sypstɑ̃sjɛl] *a* substantial.

substantif, -ive [sypstɑ̃tif, iːv] *a* substantive; *nm* noun

substituer [sypstitɥe] *vt* to substitute, entail; *vr* to take the place (of à).

substitut [sypstity] *nm* deputy, assistant, delegate.

substitution [sypstitysjɔ̃] *nf* substitution.

subterfuge [syptɛrfyːʒ] *nm* subterfuge, dodge.

subtil [syptil] *a* subtle, shrewd, discerning, fine, tenuous, thin.

subtiliser [syptilize] *vt* to subtilize, refine, make too subtle, pinch.

subtilité [syptilite] *nf* subtlety, rarity, shrewdness, acuteness.

subvenir [sybvəniːr] *vt* to provide for, supply; — **aux frais d'un voyage** to defray the expenses of a journey.

subvention [sybvɑ̃sjɔ̃] *nf* subsidy, grant.

subventionner [sybvɑ̃sjɔne] *vt* to subsidize; **théâtre subventionné par l'état** state-aided theatre.

subversif, -ive [sybvɛrsif, iːv] *a* subversive.

subversion [sybvɛrsjɔ̃] *nf* subversion, overthrow.

suc [syk] *nm* juice, sap, pith, essence, substance.

succédané [syksedane] *nm* substitute.

succéder [syksede] *vt* to follow, succeed.

succès [syksɛ] *nm* success, (favourable) outcome, result; **remporter un** — **fou** to bring the house down.

successeur [syksesœːr] *nm* successor.

successif, -ive [syksesif, iːv] *a* successive.

succession [syksesjɔ̃] *nf* succession, sequence, estate, inheritance; **prendre la** — **de** to take over (from).

succinct [syksɛ̃] *a* succinct, concise, brief.

succion [syksjɔ̃] *nf* suction, sucking.

succomber [sykɔ̃be] *vi* to succumb, die, yield.

succulent [sykylɑ̃] *a* succulent, juicy, tasty.

succursale [sykyrsal] *nf* branch, sub-office.

sucer [syse] *vt* to suck.

sucette [sysɛt] *nf* dummy, lollipop.

suçoir [syswaːr] *nm* sucker.

16

sucre [sykr] *nm* sugar; — **en pain** loaf sugar; — **en poudre** castor sugar.

sucré [sykre] *a* sugared, sweet(ened), sugary.

sucrer [sykre] *vt* to sugar, sweeten.

sucrerie [sykrəri] *nf* sugar refinery; *pl* confectionery, sweets.

sucrier [sykrie] *nm* sugar-basin.

sud [syd] *a* south, southern, southerly; *nm* south.

sudation [sydasjɔ̃] *nf* sweating.

sud-est [sydɛst] *a* south-east(ern), south-easterly; *nm* south-east.

sud-ouest [sydwɛst] *a* south-west (ern), south-westerly; *nm* south-west.

Suède [sɥɛd] *nf* Sweden.

suédois [sɥedwa] *a* Swedish; *n* Swede.

suer [sɥe] *vi* to sweat, perspire, exude, toil.

sueur [sɥœːr] *nf* sweat, perspiration; **en** — sweating.

suffire [syfiːr] *vi* to suffice, be enough, be adequate, meet, cope (with à); *vr* to be self-sufficient.

suffisance [syfizãːs] *nf* sufficiency, adequacy, (self-)conceit, priggishness.

suffisant [syfizã] *a* sufficient, enough, adequate, conceited, self-satisfied.

suffixe [syfiks] *nm* suffix.

suffocation [syfɔkasjɔ̃] *nf* choking, suffocation.

suffoquer [syfɔke] *vt* to suffocate, choke, stifle; *vi* to choke.

suffrage [syfraːʒ] *nm* suffrage, franchise, vote.

suffusion [syfyzjɔ̃] *nf* suffusion, blush.

suggérer [sygʒere] *vt* to suggest, hint (at).

suggestif, -ive [sygʒɛstif, iːv] *a* suggestive.

suggestion [sygʒɛstjɔ̃] *nf* suggestion, hint.

suicide [sɥisid] *a* suicidal; *nm* suicide.

suicidé [sɥiside] *n* suicide.

se suicider [səsɥiside] *vr* to commit suicide.

suie [sɥi] *nf* soot.

suif [sɥif] *nm* tallow, candle-grease.

suinter [sɥɛ̃te] *vi* to ooze, sweat, run, seep, leak.

Suisse [sɥis] *nf* Switzerland.

suisse [sɥis] *an* Swiss; *nm* church officer; **petit** — cream cheese.

suite [sɥit] *nf* continuation, succession, series, suite, retinue, train, sequel, result, consequence, coherence; **donner** — à to follow up, execute; **faire** — à to be a continuation of, a sequel to; **dans la** — subsequently; **par la** — afterwards, later on; **par** — (de) as a result (of); **tout de suite** immediately; **de** — in succession, one end; **sans** — disconnected, incoherent.

suivant [sɥivã] *a* follow ng, next; *nm* follower, attendant; *prep* according to, following; — **que** according as.

suivi [sɥivi] *a* coherent, steady, continuous, popular.

suivre [sɥiːvr] *vt* to follow (up), pursue, act upon, observe, escort; — **des cours** to attend lectures; **faire** — to forward; **à** — to be continued.

sujet, -ette [syʒɛ, ɛt] *a* subject, dependent, prone, liable, open; *n* subject; *nm* subject, topic, ground, theme, reason, fellow; **bon** — steady person; **mauvais** — bad lot, worthless character; **au** — de about, with regard to.

sujétion [syʒesjɔ̃] *nf* subjection, servitude.

sulfate [sylfat] *nm* sulphate.

sulfater [sylfate] *vt* to sulphate, dress with copper sulphate.

sulfure [sylfyːr] *nm* sulphide.

sulfureux, -euse [sylfyrø, øːz] *a* sulphurous.

sulfurique [sylfyrik] *a* sulphuric.

sultan [syltã] *nm* sultan.

sultane [syltan] *nf* sultana.

superbe [sypɛrb] *a* superb, splendid, magnificent, stately, arrogant, haughty; *nf* arrogance, haughtiness.

super(carburant) [sypɛrkarbyrã] *nm* high-grade petrol.

supercherie [sypɛrʃəri] *nf* fraud, hoax, deceit.

superficie [sypɛrfisi] *nf* area, surface.

superficiel, -elle [sypɛrfisjɛl] *a* superficial, shallow.

superflu [sypɛrfly] *a* superfluous, unnecessary; *nm* superfluity, overabundance.

superfluité [sypɛrflyite] *nf* superfluity.

supérieur [syperjœːr] *a* superior, upper, higher; *n* superior, head.

supériorité [syperjɔrite] *nf* superiority, supremacy, superiorship.

superlatif, -ive [sypɛrlatif, iːv] *a nm* superlative.

superposer [sypɛrpoze] *vt* to super-(im)pose.

superstitieux, -euse [sypɛrstisjø, øːz] *a* superstitious.

superstition [sypɛrstisjɔ̃] *nf* superstition.

supplanter [syplãte] *vt* to supplant, supersede.

suppléance [sypleãːs] *nf* deputyship, substitution.

suppléant [sypleã] *a* temporary, acting; *n* deputy, substitute.

suppléer [syplee] *vt* to deputize for, make up, make good; — à to compensate for.

supplément [syplemã] *nm* supplement, extra, addition, excess fare; **en** — additional, extra.

supplémentaire [syplemãtɛːr] *a* supplementary, extra, additional.

suppliant [syplid̃] *a* suppliant, pleading, beseeching; *n* supplicant, suppliant.

supplication [syplikasjɔ̃] *nf* supplication.

supplice [syplis] *nm* torture, punishment, anguish, torment, agony.

supplier [syplie] *vt* to implore, beseech, beg.

support [sypɔːr] *nm* support, prop, stand, bracket, rest, holder.

supportable [sypɔrtabl] *a* bearable, tolerable.

supporter [sypɔrte] *vt* to hold up, support, prop, endure, suffer, put up with, tolerate.

supposé [sypoze] *a* supposed, alleged, fictitious, assumed, forged; — **que** supposing that.

supposer [sypoze] *vt* to suppose, assume, imply.

supposition [sypɔzisjɔ̃] *nf* supposition, assumption.

suppositoire [sypɔzitwaːr] *nm* suppository.

suppôt [sypo] *nm* tool.

suppression [sypresjɔ̃] *nf* suppression, cancelling, discontinuance.

supprimer [syprime] *vt* to suppress, abolish, cancel, discontinue, omit.

suppurer [sypyre] *vi* to suppurate, run.

supputer [sypyte] *vt* to calculate, compute.

suprématie [sypremasi] *nf* supremacy.

suprême [syprɛːm] *a* supreme, crowning, paramount, last.

sur [syːr] *prep* (up)on, over, above, about, towards, along, over-, super-; **un homme** — **dix** one man out of ten; **dix mètres** — **huit** tén yards by eight; — **ce (quoi)** whereupon.

sûr [syːr] *a* sure, certain, unerring, unfailing, safe, reliable, staunch; **à coup** — without fail, for certain.

surabondant [syrabɔ̃dã] *a* superabundant.

surabonder [syrabɔ̃de] *vi* to superabound, be surfeited (with **de**).

suraigu, -uë [syregy] *a* high-pitched, overshrill.

suralimenter [syralimɑ̃te] *vt* to feed up overfeed.

suranné [syrane] *a* old-fashioned, out of date.

surcharge [syrʃarʒ] *nf* overload(ing), extra load, excess weight, surcharge, overtax.

surcharger [syrʃarʒe] *vt* to overload, overcharge, surcharge, overtax.

surchauffer [syrʃofe] *vt* to overheat, superheat.

surclasser [syrklase] *vt* to outclass.

surcomprimé [syrkɔ̃prime] *a* supercharged.

surcontrer [syrkɔ̃tre] *vt* to redouble.

surcroissance [syrkrwasãːs] *nf* overgrowth.

surcroît [syrkrwa] *nm* increase,

addition; **par** — in addition, into the bargain.

surdité [syrdite] *nf* deafness.

sureau [syro] *nm* elder (tree).

surélever [syrelve] *vt* to raise, heighten.

sûrement [syrmã] *ad* surely, certainly, safely, securely.

surenchère [syrɑ̃ʃɛːr] *nf* higher bid.

surenchérir [syrɑ̃ʃeriːr] *vi* to bid higher; *vt* — **sur** outbid.

surestimer [syrɛstime] *vt* to overestimate.

sûreté [syrte] *nf* sureness, soundness, safety, security, guarantee; **la Sûreté** the Criminal Investigation Department; **pour plus de** — to be on the safe side.

surexcitation [syrɛksitasjɔ̃] *nf* (over)excitement.

surexciter [syrɛksite] *vt* to excite, over-stimulate.

surexposer [syrɛkspoze] *vt* to overexpose.

surface [syrfas] *nf* surface, area.

surfaire [syrfɛːr] *vt* to overcharge, overrate; *vi* to overcharge.

surgir [syrʒiːr] *vi* to (a)rise, loom up, come into sight, crop up.

surhausser [syrose] *vt* to raise, heighten, increase.

surhumain [syrymɛ̃] *a* superhuman.

surimposer [syrɛ̃poze] *vt* to superimpose, increase the tax on.

suriner [syrine] *vt* (fam) to knife, do in.

surintendant [syrɛ̃tɑ̃dɑ̃] *nm* superintendent, steward.

surjet [syrʒɛ] *nm* overcasting, whipping (of seams).

sur-le-champ [syrləʃɑ̃] *ad* immediately.

surlendemain [syrlɑ̃dmɛ̃] *nm* next day but one, day after next; **le** — **de son départ** the second day after his departure.

surmenage [syrmənaːʒ] *nm* overworking, overdriving, strain.

surmené [syrməne] *a* overworked, jaded, fagged.

surmener [syrməne] *vt* to overwork, overexert; *vr* to overwork, overdo it.

surmontable [syrmɔ̃tabl] *a* surmountable.

surmonter [syrmɔ̃te] *vt* to surmount, top, overcome, get over; *vr* to master one's feelings.

surnaturel, -elle [syrnatyrɛl] *a* supernatural, uncanny; *nm* supernatural.

surnom [syrnɔ̃] *nm* nickname.

surnombre [syrnɔ̃ːbr] *nm* excessive number; **en** — supernumerary.

surnommer [syrnɔme] *vt* to nickname, call.

suroît [syrwa] *nm* sou'wester.

surpasser [syrpase] *vt* to surpass, outdo, outshine, exceed, excel, pass one's understanding.

surpayer [syrpɛje] *vt* to overpay, pay too much for.

surpeuplement [syrpœpləmɑ̃] *nm* overcrowding.

surplis [syrpli] *nm* surplice.

surplomb [syrplɔ̃] *nm* overhang; **en —** overhanging.

surplomber [syrplɔ̃be] *vti* to overhang.

surplus [syrply] *nm* surplus, excess; **au —** besides.

surpoids [syrpwɑ] *nm* overweight; **en —** in excess.

surprenant [syrprənɑ̃] *a* surprising, astonishing.

surprendre [syrprɑ̃:dr] *vt* to surprise, astonish, catch unawares, overtake, overhear, intercept, catch, detect.

surprise [syrpriz] *nf* surprise, astonishment, lucky-dip.

surproduction [syrprɔdyksjɔ̃] *nf* overproduction.

sursaut [syrso] *nm* start, jump; **en — with** a start.

sursauter [syrsote] *vi* to start, jump.

surseoir [syrswa:r] *vt* to postpone, delay, suspend.

sursis [syrsi] *nm* postponement, reprieve, deferment.

surtaux [syrto] *nm* overassessment.

surtaxe [syrtaks] *nf* surtax, supertax, surcharge.

surtout [syrtu] *ad* above all, particularly, especially.

surveillance [syrvɛjɑ̃:s] *nf* supervision, vigilance, watching.

surveillant [syrvɛjɑ̃] *n* supervisor, overseer, watchman, usher, invigilator.

surveiller [syrvɛje] *vt* to supervise, superintend, invigilate, look after, watch; *vr* to watch one's step.

survenir [syrv(ə)ni:r] *vi* to happen, arise, crop up.

survêtement [syrvɛtmɑ̃] *nm* tracksuit.

survie [syrvi] *nf* survival, survivorship, after-life.

survivance [syrvivɑ̃:s] *nf* survival.

survivant [syrvivɑ̃] *a* surviving; *n* survivor.

survivre [syrvi:vr] *vi* to survive; *vt* **— à** to outlive.

survoler [syrvɔle] *vt* to fly over.

survolté [syrvɔlte] *a* worked up, het up.

sus [sys] *ad* against, upon; *excl* come on! **courir — à qn** to rush at s.o.; **en —** in addition, besides.

susceptibilité [syseptibilite] *nf* susceptibility, touchiness.

susceptible [syseptibl] *a* susceptible, touchy, likely, liable, apt.

susciter [syssite] *vt* to arouse, stir up, raise up, give rise to, bring on.

susdit [sydi] *a* aforesaid, above-mentioned.

suspect [syspɛ(kt)] *a* suspect, suspicious, doubtful; *nm* suspect.

suspecter [syspɛkte] *vt* to suspect, doubt.

suspendre [syspɑ̃:dr] *vt* to suspend, hang, stop, defer; *vr* to hang (on).

suspendu [syspɑ̃dy] *a* suspended, hanging, sprung; **pont —** suspension bridge.

suspens [syspɑ̃] *ad* **en —** in suspense, undecided, in abeyance.

suspension [syspɑ̃sjɔ̃] *nf* suspension, hanging, interruption, springing, hanging lamp.

suspicion [syspisjɔ̃] *nf* suspicion.

sustenter [systɑ̃te] *vt* to sustain, support.

susurrer [sysyre] *vi* to murmur, rustle, sough.

suture [syty:r] *nf* suture, join; **point de —** stitch.

suturer [sytyre] *vt* to stitch.

suzerain [syzrɛ̃] *a* paramount, sovereign; *n* suzerain(e).

suzeraineté [syzrɛnte] *nf* suzerainty.

svelte [svɛlt] *a* slim, slender, slight.

sveltesse [svɛltɛs] *nf* slimness, slenderness.

sycomore [sikɔmɔ:r] *nm* sycamore.

syllabe [sillab] *nf* syllable.

sylphe [silf] *nm* sylph.

sylphide [silfid] *nf* sylph.

sylvestre [silvɛstr] *a* woodland, sylvan.

sylviculture [silvikylty:r] *nf* forestry.

symbole [sɛ̃bɔl] *nm* symbol, sign.

symbolique [sɛ̃bɔlik] *a* symbolic(al).

symboliser [sɛ̃bɔlize] *vt* to symbolize.

symétrie [simetri] *nf* symmetry.

symétrique [simetrik] *a* symmetrical.

sympathie [sɛ̃pati] *nf* liking, sympathy; **avoir de la — pour qn** to like s.o.

sympathique [sɛ̃patik] *a* likeable, congenial, sympathetic; **encre —** invisible ink.

sympathiser [sɛ̃patize] *vi* to sympathize, have a fellow feeling (for **avec**).

symphonie [sɛ̃fɔni] *nf* symphony, orchestra.

symphonique [sɛ̃fɔnik] *a* symphonic.

symptomatique [sɛ̃ptɔmatik] *a* symptomatic.

symptôme [sɛ̃pto:m] *nm* symptom, sign.

synagogue [sinagɔg] *nf* synagogue.

synchroniser [sɛ̃krɔnize] *vt* to synchronize.

synchronisme [sɛ̃krɔnism] *nm* synchronism.

syncope [sɛ̃kɔp] *nf* faint, syncope.

syncoper [sɛ̃kɔpe] *vt* to syncopate.

syndic [sɛ̃dik] *nm* syndic, assignee, trustee.

syndical [sɛ̃dikal] *a* syndical, trade union.

syndicalisme [sɛ̃dikalism] *nm* trade unionism.

syndicaliste [sɛ̃dikalist] *nm* trade unionist.

syndicat [sɛ̃dika] *nm* syndicate, trusteeship, trade union, federation.

syndiquer [sɛ̃dike] *vt* to syndicate, unite in a trade union; *vr* to form a trade union, combine.

synonyme [sinɔnim] *a* synonymous; *nm* synonym.

syntaxe [sɛ̃taks] *nf* syntax.

synthèse [sɛ̃tɛːz] *nf* synthesis.

synthétique [sɛ̃tetik] *a* synthetic.

synthétiser [sɛ̃tetize] *vt* to synthesize

Syrie [siri] *nf* Syria.

systématique [sistematik] *a* systematic, stereotyped, hidebound.

systématiser [sistematize] *vt* to systematize

système [sistɛm] *nm* system, type; **esprit de —** hidebound mentality, unimaginativeness; **employer le —** D *(fam)* to wangle it.

T

ta [ta] *see* ton.

tabac [taba] *nm* tobacco; **— à priser** snuff.

tabagie [tabaʒi] *nf* place smelling (full) of tobacco-smoke, smoking room.

tabatière [tabatjɛːr] *nf* snuff-box.

tabernacle [tabɛrnakl] *nm* tabernacle.

table [tabl] *nf* table, board, slab; **mettre la —** to set the table.

tableau [tablo] *nm* board, picture, scene, panel, roster; **— de bord** dashboard.

tabler [table] *vi* to reckon, count (on **sur**).

tablette [tablɛt] *nf* tablet, cake, slab, shelf, notebook; **inscrire sur ses —s** to make a note of.

tabletterie [tabletri] *nf* fancy-goods (industry).

tablier [tablie] *nm* apron, pinafore, footplate, floor (of bridge), dashboard.

tabouret [taburɛ] *nm* stool.

tac au tac [takotak] *ad* tit for tat.

tache [taʃ] *nf* spot, stain, blot.

tâche [taːʃ] *nf* task, job; **travail à la —** piecework, jobbing; **prendre à — de** to make a point of.

tacher [taʃe] *vt* to stain, spot; *vr* to stain (one's clothes).

tâcher [taʃe] *vi* to try.

tâcheron [taʃrɔ̃] *nm* pieceworker, jobber.

tacheter [taʃte] *vt* to speckle, mottle, fleck.

tacite [tasit] *a* tacit, understood.

taciturne [tasityrn] *a* taciturn, silent.

taciturnité [tasityrnite] *nf* taciturnity.

tacot [tako] *nm* ramshackle motor car, old crock.

tact [takt] *nm* touch, feel, tact.

tacticien [taktisjɛ̃] *nm* tactician.

tactile [taktil] *a* tactile.

tactique [taktik] *a* tactical; *nf* tactics.

taffetas [tafta] *nm* taffeta.

taie [tɛ] *nf* pillow-slip.

taillade [tajad] *nf* slash, gash, cut.

taillant [tajɑ̃] *nm* (cutting) edge.

taille [taːj] *nf* cut(ting), hewing, clipping, figure, waist, height, tax; **être de —** à to be fit to.

tailler [taje] *vt* to cut (out), hew, clip, carve, sharpen.

tailleur, -euse [tajœːr, øːz] *n* cutter, hewer, tailor(ess); *nm* (woman's) costume, suit.

taillis [taji] *nm* copse, brushwood.

tain [tɛ̃] *nm* silvering, foil.

taire [tɛːr] *vt* to say nothing about, keep dark; *vr* to be silent, hold one's tongue.

talent [talɑ̃] *nm* talent, gift, ability.

taloche [talɔʃ] *nf* cuff, (builder's) mortar-board.

talon [talɔ̃] *nm* heel, counterfoil, beading, flange, butt; **marcher sur les —s de qn** to follow close on s.o.'s heels, close behind s.o.

talonner [talɔne] *vt* to follow, dog, spur on, dun, heel.

talus [taly] *nm* slope, bank, ramp.

tambour [tɑ̃buːr] *nm* drum, drummer, barrel, spool, revolving door; **— de ville** town crier.

tambourin [tɑ̃burɛ̃] *nm* tambourine, tabor.

tambouriner [tɑ̃burine] *vi* to drum, knock.

tambour-major [tɑ̃burmaʒɔːr] *nm* drum-major.

tamis [tami] *nm* sifter, sieve, riddle.

tamiser [tamize] *vt* to sift, strain, filter, screen; *vi* to filter through.

tampon [tɑ̃pɔ̃] *nm* stopper, bung, plug, buffer, pad, stamp.

tamponnement [tɑ̃pɔnmɑ̃] *nm* collision, plugging.

tamponner [tɑ̃pɔne] *vt* to plug, dab. pad, collide with.

tam-tam [tamtam] *nm* African drum, dance.

tancer [tɑ̃se] *vt* to scold, chide.

tandis que [tɑ̃di(s)kə] *cj* while, whereas.

tangage [tɑ̃gaːʒ] *nm* pitching.

tangent [tɑ̃ʒɑ̃] *a* tangent.

tangible [tɑ̃ʒibl] *a* tangible.

tanguer [tɑ̃ge] *vi* to pitch.

tanière [tanjɛːr] *nf* lair, den, hole.

tanin [tanɛ̃] *nm* tannin.

tanner [tane] *vt* to tan.

tannerie [tanri] *nf* tannery.

tanneur [tanœːr] *nm* tanner.

tant [tɑ̃] *ad* so much, so many, as much, so; **— que** as much as, as long as; **si — est que** if it is true that, if it is the case that; **— soit peu** somewhat, ever so little; **en — que** in so far as, as; **— pis** so much the worse, can't be helped, too bad.

tante [tɑ̃:t] *nf* aunt.

tantième [tɑ̃tjɛm] *nm* percentage, quota.

tantinet [tɑ̃tinɛ] *nm* tiny bit, spot.

tantôt [tɑ̃to] *ad* presently, soon, a little while ago; **tantôt . . . tantôt . . .** now . . . now; **à —!** see you later!

taon [tɑ̃] *nm* horse-fly, cleg.

tapage [tapaːʒ] *nm* din, row.

tapageur, -euse [tapaʒœːr, øːz] *a* rowdy, noisy, showy, flashy.

tape [tap] *nf* stopper, tap, pat, slap.

tape-à-l'œil [tapalœːj] *nm* flashy article; *a* flashy.

tapecul [tapky] *nm* pillion-seat, boneshaker.

taper [tape] *vt* to tap, pat, hit, touch, type; **— dans l'œil à qn** to catch, fill s.o.'s eye; **— sur qn** to slate s.o.; (*fam*) **ça tape** it's hot.

tapinois [tapinwa] *ad* **en —** on the sly, slyly.

se tapir [sətapiːr] *vr* to crouch, cower, squat, take cover.

tapis [tapi] *nm* carpet, cloth, cover; **mettre qch sur le —** to bring sth up for discussion; **— roulant** conveyor belt, moving pavement.

tapisser [tapise] *vt* to paper, line, cover.

tapisserie [tapisri] *nf* tapestry (making), wallpaper; **faire —** to be a wallflower.

tapissier, -ière [tapisje, jɛːr] *n* tapestry-worker, upholsterer.

tapoter [tapɔte] *vt* to tap, strum.

taquin [takɛ̃] *a* teasing; *n* tease.

taquiner [takine] *vt* to tease.

taquinerie [takinri] *nf* teasing.

tarabiscoté [tarabiskɔte] *a* ornate, grooved.

tard [taːr] *ad* late; **sur le —** late in the day, late in life; **tôt ou —** sooner or later.

tarder [tarde] *vi* to delay, loiter, be long (in à); **il leur tarde de vous revoir** they are longing to see you.

tardif, -ive [tardif, iːv] *a* late, backward, belated, tardy, slow.

tare [taːr] *nf* blemish, defect, depreciation, tare.

tarer [tare] *vt* to damage, blemish, spoil.

se targuer [sətarge] *vr* to pride oneself (on de).

tarière [tarjɛːr] *nf* auger, drill.

tarif [tarif] *nm* tariff, price list, fare.

tarifer [tarife] *vt* to price.

tarir [tariːr] *vti* to dry up.

tarte [tart] *nf* tart.

tartine [tartin] *nf* slice of bread and butter, long story, rigmarole.

tartre [tartr] *nm* tartar, fur, scale.

tartufe [tartyf] *nm* hypocrite, imposter.

tas [ta] *nm* heap, pile, pack, lot(s); **grève sur le —** stay-in strike.

tasse [taːs] *nf* cup.

tassé [tase] *a* full, heaped, squat.

tasser [tase] *vt* to squeeze, pack, cram; *vr* to crowd together, squeeze up, settle.

tâter [tate] *vt* to feel, taste, try; *vr* to hesitate.

tatillonner [tatijɔne] *vi* to interfere, meddle, fuss, be fussy.

tâtonner [tatɔne] *vi* to feel one's way, grope (about).

tâtons (à) [tatɔ̃] *ad* groping(ly), warily.

tatouer [tatwe] *vt* to tattoo.

taudis [todi] *nm* hovel; *pl* slums.

taupe [toːp] *nf* mole(skin).

taupinière [topinjɛːr] *nf* molehill.

taureau [tɔro] *nm* bull.

tautologie [tɔtɔlɔʒi] *nf* tautology.

taux [to] *nm* rate, scale.

taverne [tavɛrn] *nf* tavern, public house.

taxe [taks] *nf* tax, duty, rate, charge.

taxer [takse] *vt* to tax, charge, fix the price of, accuse.

taxi [taksi] *nm* taxi.

Tchécoslovaquie [tʃekɔslɔvaki] *nf* Czechoslovakia.

tchèque [tʃɛk] *an* Czech.

te [t(ə)] *pn* you, to you, yourself, thee, to thee, thyself.

technicien [tɛknisjɛ̃] *nm* technician.

technique [tɛknik] *a* technical; *nf* technique, technics, engineering.

technologie [tɛknɔlɔʒi] *nf* technology.

technologique [tɛknɔlɔʒik] *a* technological.

teigne [tɛɲ] *nf* moth, scurf, ringworm, vixen.

teigneux, -euse [tɛɲø, øːz] *a* scurfy.

teindre [tɛ̃:dr] *vt* to dye, tinge, stain; *vr* to be tinged, dye one's hair.

teint [tɛ̃] *nm* dye, colour, complexion.

teinte [tɛ̃:t] *nf* shade, hue, tint, tinge, touch.

teinter [tɛ̃te] *vt* to tint, tinge.

teinture [tɛ̃tyːr] *nf* dye(ing), tinting, hue, tincture, smattering.

teinturier, -ière [tɛ̃tyrje, jɛːr] *n* dyer.

tek [tɛk] *nm* teak.

tel, telle [tɛl] *a* such, like; *pn* such a one; **— que** such as, like; **— quel** as it (she, he) is, ordinary; **monsieur un —** Mr So-and-so.

télécinéma [telesinema] *nm* tele-recording.

télécommander [telekɔmɑ̃de] *vt* to operate by remote control.

télégramme [telegram] *nm* telegram.

télégraphe [telegraf] *nm* telegraph.

télégraphie [telegrafi] *nf* telegraphy; **— sans fil** wireless telegraphy.

télégraphier [telegrafje] *vti* to telegraph, cable, wire.

téléguider [telegide] *vt* to radio-control.

télépathie [telepati] *nf* telepathy.

téléphérique [teleferik] *a nm* cable railway.

téléphone [telefɔn] *nm* (tele)phone.
téléphoner [telefɔne] *vti* to (tele) phone, ring up.
téléphonique [telefɔnik] *a* telephonic; **cabine —** callbox.
téléphoniste [telefɔnist] *n* telephonist, operator.
télescope [telɛskɔp] *nm* telescope.
télescoper [telɛskɔpe] *vti* to telescope, crumple up.
télésiège [telesjɛːʒ] *nm* chair-lift.
télévision [televizjɔ̃] *nf* television.
tellement [tɛlmɑ̃] *ad* so, in such a way.
téméraire [temɛrɛːr] *a* rash, reckless, bold.
témérité [temerite] *nf* rashness, temerity, rash act.
témoignage [temwaɲaːʒ] *nm* evidence, testimony, token, mark.
témoigner [temwaɲe] *vt* to show, display, prove, testify to; *vi* to give evidence.
témoin [temwɛ̃] *nm* witness, second, baton.
tempe [tɑ̃ːp] *nf* temple.
tempérament [tɑ̃peramɑ̃] *nm* constitution, nature; **vente à —** hire-purchase.
tempérance [tɑ̃perɑ̃ːs] *nf* moderation.
tempérant [tɑ̃perɑ̃] *a* temperate, moderate.
température [tɑ̃peratyːr] *nf* temperature.
tempéré [tɑ̃pere] *a* moderate, temperate.
tempérer [tɑ̃pere] *vt* to moderate, temper; *vr* to moderate, abate.
tempête [tɑ̃pɛːt] *nf* storm.
tempêter [tɑ̃pɛte] *vi* to storm, rage.
tempétueux, -euse [tɑ̃petɥø, øːz] *a* stormy.
temple [tɑ̃ːpl] *nm* temple, (Protestant) church.
temporaire [tɑ̃pɔrɛːr] *a* provisional, temporary.
temporel, -elle [tɑ̃pɔrɛl] *a* temporal.
temporiser [tɑ̃pɔrize] *vi* to temporize, procrastinate.
temps [tɑ̃] *nm* time, period, age, weather, tense; **à —** in time; **de tout —** at all times; **quel — fait-il?** what is the weather like?
tenable [tənabl] *a* tenable, bearable.
tenace [tənas] *a* tenacious, adhesive, retentive, rooted.
ténacité [tenasite] *nf* tenacity, adhesiveness, retentiveness.
tenaille [tənɑːj] *nf* tongs; *pl* pincers.
tenancier, -ière [tənɑ̃sje, jɛːr] *n* keeper, lessee, tenant.
tenant [tənɑ̃] *a* **séance —e** forthwith; **—s et aboutissants** adjoining properties, ins and outs; **d'un seul —** in one piece.
tendance [tɑ̃dɑ̃ːs] *nf* tendency, trend.
tendancieux, -euse [tɑ̃dɑ̃sjø, øːz] *a* tendentious.

tendre [tɑ̃ːdr] *vt* to stretch (out) strain, hang, set, tighten, spread, hold out; *vi* to lead, tend; *vr* to become tight, strained, taut, tense.
tendre [tɑ̃ːdr] *a* tender, delicate, loving.
tendresse [tɑ̃drɛs] *nf* tenderness, love.
ténèbres [tenɛːbr] *nf pl* darkness.
ténébreux, -euse [tenebrø, øːz] *a* dark, sinister.
teneur [tənœːr, øːz] *n* holder, keeper, taker; *nf* tenor, purport, content.
ténia [tenja] *nm* tapeworm.
tenir [təniːr] *vt* to hold, keep, run, occupy, contain; *vi* to hold, stick, stand, last; *vr* to stand, sit, remain, stay, contain oneself, behave oneself; **— à** to be keen to, be the result of; **s'il ne tient qu'à cela** if that is all; **qu'à cela ne tienne** never mind that; **je n'y tiens plus** I can't stand it any longer; **— de** to have sth of, take after, get from; **— pour** to consider as, be in favour of; **tiens, tiens,** well, well! indeed! **tiens, tenez** (look) here; **on tient quatre dans cette voiture** this car holds four; **se — à** to keep to, hold on to; **s'en — à** to abide by, be content with.
tennis [tenis] *nm* tennis (court).
ténor [tenɔr] *nm* tenor.
tension [tɑ̃sjɔ̃] *nf* tension, pressure, stretching.
tentacule [tɑ̃takyl] *nm* feeler, tentacle.
tentateur, -trice [tɑ̃tatœːr, tris] *a* tempting; *n* tempter, temptress.
tentation [tɑ̃tasjɔ̃] *nf* temptation.
tentative [tɑ̃tatiːv] *nf* attempt.
tente [tɑ̃ːt] *nf* tent, canvas, awning.
tenter [tɑ̃te] *vt* to tempt, try.
tenture [tɑ̃tyːr] *nf* tapestry, hangings, wallpaper.
tenu [təny] *a* kept, bound.
ténu [teny] *a* fine, tenuous, slender, subtle.
tenue [təny] *nf* holding, sitting, upkeep, behaviour, dress, seat; **avoir de la —** to behave oneself; **en grande —** in full dress.
ténuité [tenɥite] *nf* fineness, slenderness, tenuousness.
térébenthine [terebɑ̃tin] *nf* turpentine.
tergiverser [tɛrʒivɛrse] *vi* to beg the question, hesitate.
terme [tɛrm] *nm* term, expression, end, limit, quarter; **mener qch à bon —** to carry sth through.
terminaison [tɛrminɛzɔ̃] *nf* termination, ending.
terminer [tɛrmine] *vtr* to terminate, finish, end.
terminologie [tɛrminɔlɔʒi] *nf* terminology.
terminus [tɛrminyːs] *nm* terminus.
terne [tɛrn] *a* dull, lifeless, flat.

ternir [tɛrniːr] *vt* to tarnish, dim, dull; *vr* to become dim, dull.

terrain [tɛrɛ̃] *nm* land, (piece of) ground, course.

terrasse [tɛras] *nf* terrace, bank.

terrassement [tɛrasmɑ̃] *nm* digging, banking, earthwork.

terrasser [tɛrase] *vt* to bank up, lay low, fell.

terrassier [tɛrasje] *nm* navvy.

terre [tɛːr] *nf* earth, world, land, soil, estate; par — on the ground, on the floor; descendre à — to go ashore; — à — commonplace.

Terre-Neuve [tɛrnœːv] *nf* Newfoundland; *nm* -dog.

terre-neuvien, -enne [tɛrnœvjɛ̃, jɛn] *a* Newfoundland; *n* Newfoundlander; *nm* fisherman, boat that goes to fishing grounds off Newfoundland.

terrestre [tɛrɛstr] *a* terrestrial, earthly.

terreur [tɛrœːr] *nf* terror, dread.

terrible [tɛribl] *a* terrible, dreadful.

terrien, -enne [tɛrjɛ̃, jɛn] *a* landed; landowner, landsman.

terrier [tɛrje] *nm* hole, burrow, terrier.

terrifier [tɛr(r)ifje] *vt* to terrify.

terrine [tɛrin] *nf* earthenware pot, pan, potted meat.

territoire [tɛritwaːr] *nm* territory.

territorial [tɛritɔrjal] *a* territorial.

terroir [tɛrwaːr] *nm* soil.

terroriser [tɛr(r)ɔrize] *vt* to terrorize.

tertre [tɛrtr] *nm* mound, hillock.

tes [te] *see* **ton**.

tesson [tɛsɔ̃] *nm* fragment, broken end.

testament [tɛstamɑ̃] *nm* testament, will.

testateur, -trice [tɛstatœːr, tris] *n* testator, testatrix.

testicule [tɛstikyl] *nm* testicle.

tétanos [tetanɔs] *nm* lockjaw, tetanus.

têtard [tetaːr] *nm* tadpole.

tête [tɛːt] *nf* head, face, top, front; calcul de — mental arithmetic; mauvaise — unruly person; femme de — capable woman; forte — self-willed person; faire une — to pull a long face; en faire à sa — to have one's own way; monter la — à qn to rouse s.o., work s.o. up.

tête-à-queue [tɛtakø] *nm* faire — to swing right round.

tête-à-tête [tɛtatɛːt] *nm* private conversation, tête-à-tête..

tête-bêche [tɛtbɛʃ] *ad* head to foot, head to tail.

tétée [tete] *nf* suck.

téter [tete] *vt* to suck.

tétière [tetjɛːr] *nf* baby's cap, head-stall (*of harness*).

tétin [tetɛ̃] *nm* nipple, dug.

tétine [tetin] *nf* udder, dug, (rubber) teat.

téton [tetɔ̃] *nm* breast.

têtu [tety] *a* obstinate, stubborn.

teuton, -onne [tøtɔ̃, ɔn] *a* Teuton(ic); *n* Teuton.

teutonique [tøtɔnik] *a* Teutonic.

texte [tɛkst] *nm* text.

textile [tɛkstil] *a nm* textile.

textuel, -elle [tɛkstɥɛl] *a* textual.

texture [tɛkstyːr] *nf* texture.

thé [te] *nm* tea, tea-party.

théâtral [teatral] *a* theatrical.

théâtre [teaːtr] *nm* theatre, stage, drama, scene.

théière [tejɛːr] *nf* teapot.

thème [tɛm] *nm* theme, topic, prose composition.

théologie [teɔlɔʒi] *nf* theology, divinity.

théologique [teɔlɔʒik] *a* theological.

théorème [teɔrɛm] *nm* theorem.

théoricien, -enne [teɔrisjɛ̃, jɛn] *n* theorist.

théorie [teɔri] *nf* theory.

théorique [teɔrik] *a* theoretical.

théoriser [teɔrize] *vti* to theorize.

thermal [tɛrmal] *a* thermal; **station** —e spa; eaux —es hot springs.

thermomètre [tɛrmɔmɛtr] *nm* thermometer.

thésauriser [tezɔrize] *vt* to hoard.

thèse [tɛːz] *nf* thesis, argument.

Thierry [tjɛri] *n pr* Theodore.

thon [tɔ̃] *nm* tunny-fish.

thorax [tɔraks] *nm* thorax, chest.

thuriféraire [tyrifɛrɛːr] *nm* incensebearer, flatterer.

thym [tɛ̃] *nm* thyme.

tibia [tibja] *nm* shin-bone, tibia.

tic [tik] *nm* twitching, mannerism.

ticket [tikɛ] *nm* ticket, check, slip.

tic-tac [tiktak] *nm* tick-tock, ticking, pit-a-pat.

tiède [tjɛd] *a* lukewarm, tepid.

tiédeur [tjedœːr] *nf* lukewarmness, tepidity, half-heartedness, coolness.

tiédir [tjediːr] *vt* to make tepid, cool; *vi* to become tepid, cool down, off.

tien, tienne [tjɛ̃, tjɛn] *poss pr* le(s) —(s), la tienne, les tiennes yours, thine; *nm* your own; *pl* your own people.

tierce [tjɛrs] *nf* tierce, third.

tiercé [tjɛrse] *nm* betting (*on horses*).

tiers, tierce [tjɛːr, tjɛrs] *a* third; *nm* third (part), third person, -party.

tige [tiːʒ] *nf* stalk, stem, trunk, shank, shaft.

tignasse [tiɲas] *nf* mop, shock.

tigre, tigresse [tigr, tigrɛs] *n* tiger, tigress.

tilleul [tijœl] *nm* lime-tree, infusion of lime-flowers.

timbale [tɛ̃bal] *nf* kettledrum, metal drinking mug, raised piedish.

timbre [tɛ̃ːbr] *nm* stamp, stamp-duty, bell, timbre.

timbré [tɛ̃bre] *a* stamped, post-marked, sonorous, (*fam*) dotty, cracked.

timbre-poste [tɛ̃brəpɔst] *nm* postage-stamp.

timbre-quittance [tɛ̃brəkitɑ:s] nm receipt-stamp.
timbrer [tɛ̃bre] vt to stamp.
timide [timid] a timid, coy, shy, diffident.
timidité [timidite] nf timidity, shyness, diffidence.
timon [timɔ̃] nm shaft, pole, helm.
timonerie [timɔnri] nf steering (-gear), signalling.
timonier [timɔnje] nm helmsman, signalman.
timoré [timɔre] a timorous, fearful.
tintamarre [tɛ̃tamaːr] nm noise, racket, din.
tinter [tɛ̃te] vti to toll, ring; vi to clink, jingle, tinkle, tingle.
tir [tiːr] nm shooting, gunnery, firing, rifle-range, shooting-gallery.
tirade [tirad] nf (long) speech, tirade.
tirage [tiraːʒ] nm pulling, hauling, draught, drawing, printing, circulation.
tiraillement [tirɑjmɑ̃] nm pulling, tugging, friction, pang, twinge.
tirailler [tirɑje] vt to pull about, tug; vi to fire away.
tirailleur [tirɑjœːr] nm sharpshooter, freelance.
tirant [tirɑ̃] nm purse-string, stay, ship's draught; — **d'air** headroom.
tire [tiːr] nf pull; **voleur à la** — pickpocket.
tiré [tire] a drawn, pinched.
tire-bouchon [tirbuʃɔ̃] nm corkscrew.
tire-bouchonner [tirbuʃɔne] vi to curl up, wrinkle; vt to screw up.
tire-bouton [tirbutɔ̃] nm buttonhook.
tire-d'aile [tirdɛl] ad à — swiftly.
tire-larigot [tirlarigo] ad **boire à** — to drink heavily.
tirelire [tirliːr] nf money-box.
tirer [tire] vt to haul, draw, tug, pull off, out, fire, shoot, let off, print; vi to pull, tug, incline, verge (on **sur**); vr to extricate o.s., get out; **se** — **d'affaire, s'en** — to get out of trouble, manage.
tiret [tirɛ] nm dash, hyphen.
tireur, -euse [tirœːr, øːz] n drawer, marksman, shot.
tiroir [tirwaːr] nm drawer, slide (-valve).
tisane [tizan] nf infusion.
tison [tizɔ̃] nm brand, half-burned log.
tisonner [tizɔne] vt to poke, stir, fan.
tisonnier [tizɔnje] nm poker.
tisser [tise] vt to weave.
tisserand [tisrɑ̃] n weaver.
tissu [tisy] nm cloth, fabric, tissue.
titre [tiːtr] nm title, heading, qualification, right, claim, titledeed, diploma, bond; pl securities; **en** — titular; **à** — **d'office** ex officio; **à quel** —? on what grounds? **à** — **gratuit** free of charge.

titré [titre] a titled, certificated.
titrer [titre] vt to give a title to.
tituber [titybe] vi to stagger, reel.
titulaire [titylɛːr] a titular; n holder.
toaster [toste] vt to toast.
toc [tɔk] nm faked stuff, imitation, rap, knock.
tocsin [tɔksɛ̃] nm alarm-signal, tocsin.
tohu-bohu [tɔyboy] nm hubbub, hurly-burly.
toi [twa] pn you, thou, thee.
toile [twal] nf linen, cloth, canvas, painting; — **cirée** oilcloth, oilskin; — **d'araignée** spider's web, cobweb; — **de fond** back-cloth, -drop.
toilette [twalɛt] nf toilet, dress(ing), dressing-table, wash-stand, lavatory.
toise [twaːz] nf fathom, measuring apparatus.
toiser [twaze] vt to measure, look (s.o.) up and down.
toison [twazɔ̃] nf fleece.
toit [twa] nm roof, home.
toiture [twatyːr] nf roof(ing).
tôle [toːl] nf sheet-iron.
tolérance [tɔlerɑ̃:s] nf tolerance, toleration, allowance.
tolérer [tɔlere] vt to tolerate, suffer.
tolet [tɔlɛ] nm rowlock.
tollé [tɔlle] nm outcry; **crier** — **contre** to raise a hue and cry after.
tomate [tɔmat] nf tomato.
tombe [tɔ̃:b] nf tomb, grave, tombstone.
tombeau [tɔ̃bo] nm tomb, tombstone.
tombée [tɔ̃be] nf fall.
tomber [tɔ̃be] vi to fall, drop, die down, hang; vt to throw, take off; — **sur** to come across, fall upon; — **juste** to arrive, (happen), at the right time, guess right; **laisser** — to drop.
tombereau [tɔ̃bro] nm tip-cart, tumbrel.
tombola [tɔ̃bɔla] nf tombola.
tome [tɔːm] nm volume, tome.
ton, ta, tes [tɔ̃, ta, te] a your, thy.
ton [tɔ̃] nm tone, colour, key, pitch, fashion; **le bon** — good form
tonalité [tɔnalite] nf tonality.
tondeuse [tɔ̃døːz] nf shears, lawnmower.
tondre [tɔ̃:dr] vt to clip, shear, mow, fleece.
tonifier [tɔnifje] vt to tone up, brace.
tonique [tɔnik] a nm tonic; a bracing.
tonitruant [tɔnitryɑ̃] a thunderous, blustering.
tonne [tɔn] nf tun, cask, ton.
tonneau [tɔno] nm barrel, cask, ton.
tonnelier [tɔnəlje] nm cooper.
tonnelle [tɔnɛl] nf arbour, bower.
tonnellerie [tɔnɛlri] nf cooper's shop, cooperage.
tonner [tɔne] vi to thunder.

tonnerre [tɔnɛːr] nm thunder; **du —** marvellous, terrific.

tonsure [tɔ̃syːr] nf tonsure.

tonte [tɔ̃:t] nf clipping, shearing.

topaze [tɔpaːz] nf topaz.

toper [tɔpe] vi to agree, shake hands on it; **tope-là!** done!

topinambour [tɔpinãbuːr] nm Jerusalem artichoke.

topo [tɔpo] nm lecture, demonstration, plan.

topographie [tɔpɔgrafi] nf topography, surveying.

topographique [tɔpɔgrafik] a topographic(al), ordnance.

toquade [tɔkad] nf craze, fancy.

toque [tɔk] nf toque, cap.

toqué [tɔke] a cracked, crazy, infatuated.

toquer [tɔke] vt to infatuate; vr to become infatuated (with de).

torche [tɔrʃ] nf torch, pad.

torchon [tɔrʃɔ̃] nm duster, dishcloth, floor-cloth.

tordant [tɔrdã] a screamingly funny.

tordre [tɔrdr] vt to twist, wring, distort; vr to twist, writhe; **se — de rire** to split one's sides with laughter.

tornade [tɔrnad] nf tornado.

torpédo [tɔrpedo] nm open touring-car.

torpeur [tɔrpœːr] nf torpor.

torpille [tɔrpiːj] nf torpedo.

torpiller [tɔrpije] vt to torpedo.

torréfier [tɔrrefje] vt to roast, scorch.

torrent [tɔr(r)ã] nm torrent, stream.

torrentiel, -elle [tɔr(r)ãsjɛl] a torrential.

torride [tɔrrid] a torrid, broiling.

tors [tɔːr] a twisted, crooked.

torse [tɔrs] nm torso.

torsion [tɔrsjɔ̃] nf twist(ing), torsion.

tort [tɔːr] nm wrong, fault, harm, injury, injustice; **avoir — to be** wrong; **donner — à to decide** against; **à — et à travers** at random.

torticolis [tɔrtikɔli] nm stiff neck.

tortillard [tɔrtijaːr] nm small locomotive, railway.

tortiller [tɔrtije] vt to twist, twirl; vi to wriggle, shilly-shally; vr to wriggle.

tortue [tɔrty] nf tortoise.

tortueux, -euse [tɔrtɥø, øːz] a tortuous, winding.

torture [tɔrtyːr] nf torture, torment.

torturer [tɔrtyre] vt to torture, rack, twist.

tôt [to] ad soon, early; **— ou tard** sooner or later.

total [tɔtal] a nm total, whole.

totalisateur, -trice [tɔtalizatœːr, tris] a adding; nm totalizator.

totaliser [tɔtalize] vt to total up.

totalitaire [tɔtalitɛːr] a totalitarian.

totalité [tɔtalite] nf totality, whole.

touchant [tuʃã] a touching, moving; prep with regard to, concerning.

touche [tuʃ] nf touch, manner, key, bite, hit, look.

touche-à-tout [tuʃatu] n meddler.

toucher [tuʃe] vt to touch (on), hit, draw, cash, move, concern; vi — à to be close to, be in contact with, affect, meddle; vr to adjoin; nm touch, feel.

touer [twe] vt to tow, warp.

touffe [tuf] nf tuft, cluster, clump.

touffu [tufy] a thick, bushy, involved, intricate.

toujours [tuʒuːr] ad always, ever, still, all the same.

toupet [tupɛ] nm forelock, tuft, cheek.

toupie [tupi] nf top.

tour [tuːr] nf tower; nm turn, course, shape, revolution, round, circuit, feat, trick, stroll; **— à — in turn; à — de bras** with all one's might; **mon sang n'a fait qu'un — it gave** me an awful shock.

tourangeau, -elle [turãʒo, ɛl] an (inhabitant) of Touraine.

tourbe [turb] nf peat, rabble.

tourbière [turbjɛːr] nf peat-bog.

tourbillon [turbijɔ̃] nm whirlwind, -pool, eddy, whirl, giddy round.

tourbillonner [turbijɔne] vi to whirl, swirl, eddy.

tourelle [turɛl] nf turret.

tourisme [turism] nm touring, travel.

touriste [turist] n tourist, tripper.

tourment [turmã] nm torment, anguish.

tourmente [turmãːt] nf gale, turmoil.

tourmenter [turmãte] vt to torment, torture, worry, pester, tease, fiddle with; vr to worry, fret.

tournant [turnã] nm bend, corner, turning-point.

tournebroche [turnəbrɔʃ] nm roasting-jack, turnspit.

tournedos [turnedo] nm fillet steak.

tourné [turne] a turned, sour; **bien — shapely, neat.**

tournée [turne] nf circuit, round, tour.

tourner [turne] vt to turn, wind, dodge, get round; vi to turn (out), revolve, result, curdle; vr to turn; **— un film** to make a film, act in a film; **— autour du pot** to beat about the bush.

tournesol [turnəsɔl] nm sunflower.

tournevis [turnəvis] nm screwdriver.

tourniquet [turnikɛ] nm turnstile, tourniquet.

tournoi [turnwa] nm tournament.

tournoyer [turnwaje] vi to whirl, wheel, swirl.

tournure [turnyːr] nf shape, figure, turn, course bustle.

tourte [turt] nf pie, tart.

tourterelle [turtərɛl] nf turtle dove.

Toussaint [tusɛ̃] nf **la — All Saints'** day.

tousser [tuse] vi to cough.

tout [tu] *a* all, whole, every, any; *pr* everything, all, anything; *nm* whole, all, main thing; *ad* very, completely, entirely, quite, right, however, while; **pas du** — not at all; — **à vous** yours truly; — **au plus** at the very most; — **à fait** quite, entirely; — **fait** ready made.

toutefois [tutfwa] *ad* yet, however, nevertheless.

toutou [tutu] *nm* doggie.

tout-puissant [tupɥisɑ̃] *a* omnipotent, all-powerful.

toux [tu] *nf* cough.

toxique [tɔksik] *a* toxic, poisonous.

trac [trak] *nm* funk, stage-fright.

tracas [trakɑ] *nm* worry, bother.

tracasser [trakase] *vtr* to bother, worry.

tracasserie [trakasri] *nf* worry, fuss.

tracassier, -ière [trakasje, jɛːr] *a* meddlesome, fussy.

trace [tras] *nf* trace, track, trail. mark.

tracé [trase] *nm* outline, graph, lay-out, tracing, marking out, plotting.

tracer [trase] *vt* to outline, draw, sketch, plot, lay-out, mark out.

tractation [traktasjɔ̃] *nf* underhand deal(ing).

tracteur [traktœːr] *nm* tractor.

traction [traksjɔ̃] *nf* traction, pulling; — **avant** front-wheel drive (car).

tradition [tradisjɔ̃] *nf* tradition.

traditionnel, -elle [tradisjɔnɛl] *a* traditional.

traducteur, -trice [tradyktœːr, tris] *n* translator.

traduction [tradyksjɔ̃] *nf* translation, translating.

traduire [tradɥiːr] *vt* to translate, express; — **en justice** to prosecute.

trafic [trafik] *nm* traffic, trade, trading.

trafiquant [trafikɑ̃] *nm* trafficker, black-marketeer.

trafiquer [trafike] *vi* to trade, deal, traffic.

tragédie [traʒedi] *nf* tragedy.

tragique [traʒik] *a* tragic; *nm* tragic element, poet.

trahir [traiːr] *vt* to betray, give away, reveal.

trahison [traizɔ̃] *nf* betrayal, treachery, treason.

train [trɛ̃] *nm* train, line, string, suite, mood, movement, pace; **à fond de** — at full speed; **être en** — **de** to be busy, engaged in; **être en** — to be in the mood, in good form; **mener grand** — to live in great style; **mettre en** — to set going.

traînant [trɛnɑ̃] *a* dragging, drawling, listless.

traînard [trɛnaːr] *nm* laggard, straggler.

traîne [trɛ:n] *nf* drag-net, train (*dress*); **à la** — in tow, behind.

traîneau [trɛno] *nm* sleigh, sledge.

traînée [trɛne] *nf* trail, train.

traîner [trɛne] *vt* to drag (out, on), trail, haul, drawl; *vi* to trail, straggle, lag (behind), lie about, drag (on); *vr* to crawl, shuffle along.

train-train [trɛ̃trɛ̃] *nm* routine; **aller son** — to jog along.

traire [trɛːr] *vt* to milk.

trait [trɛ] *nm* dart, shaft, gibe, feature, characteristic, stroke; — **d'union** hyphen; **d'un** — at one gulp, go; **avoir** — **à** to refer to; **cheval de** — draught horse.

traitable [trɛtabl] *a* tractable, docile.

traite [trɛt] *nf* trade, slave-trade, draft, stage, stretch, milking; **d'une** — at a stretch.

traité [trɛte] *nm* treaty, treatise.

traitement [trɛtmɑ̃] *nm* treatment, salary.

traiter [trɛte] *vt* to treat, entertain, discuss, call; *vti* to negotiate; — **de** to deal with, treat for, with.

traiteur [trɛtœːr] *nm* caterer, restaurateur.

traître, -tresse [trɛːtr, trɛtrɛs] *a* treacherous; *n* traitor, traitress.

traîtrise [trɛtriːz] *nf* treachery.

trajectoire [traʒɛktwaːr] *nf* trajectory.

trajet [traʒɛ] *nm* journey, way, passage, course.

trame [tram] *nf* woof, web, plot.

tramer [trame] *vt* to weave.

tramontane [tramɔ̃tan] *nf* north wind, North.

tranchant [trɑ̃ʃɑ̃] *a* sharp, keen, peremptory, contrasting; *nm* edge.

tranche [trɑ̃ʃ] *nf* slice, round, slab, edge, series, chisel.

tranchée [trɑ̃ʃe] *nf* trench.

trancher [trɑ̃ʃe] *vt* to cut (off, short), slice, settle; *vi* to contrast (with); — **le mot** to speak bluntly.

tranquille [trɑ̃kil] *a* calm, quiet, easy; **laisser** — to leave alone.

tranquillisant [trɑ̃kilizɑ̃] *nm* tranquillizer.

tranquilliser [trɑ̃kilize] *vt* to soothe, set at rest; *vr* to set one's mind at rest.

tranquillité [trɑ̃kilite] *nf* peace, calm, quiet.

transaction [trɑ̃zaksjɔ̃] *nf* transaction, compromise.

transatlantique [trɑ̃zatlɑ̃tik] *a* transatlantic; *nm* liner, deck-chair.

transborder [trɑ̃sbɔrde] *vt* to tranship.

transbordeur [trɑ̃sbɔrdœːr] *nm* (**pont**) — transporter-bridge.

transcription [trɑ̃skripsjɔ̃] *nf* transcription, copy.

transcrire [trɑ̃skriːr] *vt* to transcribe, write out.

transe [trɑ̃s] *nf* trance; *pl* fear.

transférer [trɑ̃sfere] *vt* to transfer, remove.

transfert [trɑ̃sfɛːr] *nm* transfer(ence).

transformateur [trãsfɔrmatœːr, -tris] *nm* transformer.

transformer [trãsfɔrme] *vt* to transform; *vr* to change, turn.

transfuge [trãsfyːʒ] *nm* deserter, turncoat.

transfuser [trãsfyze] *vt* to transfuse.

transgresser [trãsgrese] *vt* to transgress, break.

transi [trãsi] *a* frozen, paralysed.

transiger [trãziʒe] *vi* to (come to a) compromise.

transir [trãsiːr] *vt* to benumb, chill.

transition [trãzisjɔ̃] *nf* transition.

transitoire [trãzitwaːr] *a* transitory, temporary.

transmettre [trãsmetr] *vt* to transmit, convey, hand down.

transmission [trãsmisjɔ̃] *nf* transfer, transmission, handing down; — **directe** live broadcast.

transparaître [trãspareːtr] *vi* to show through.

transparent [trãsparã] *a* transparent, clear.

transpercer [trãsperse] *vt* to pierce, transfix.

transpirer [trãspire] *vi* to perspire, transpire.

transplanter [trãsplãte] *vt* to transplant.

transport [trãspɔːr] *nm* transport, carriage, rapture.

transporter [trãspɔrte] *vt* to transport, convey, assign, enrapture.

transporteur [trãspɔrtœːr] *nm* carrier, conveyor.

transposer [trãspoze] *vt* to transpose.

transversal [trãsversal] *a* transversal, cross-, side-.

trapèze [trapeːz] *nm* trapezium, trapeze.

trappe [trap] *nf* trap(door).

trapu [trapy] *a* squat, stocky, thickset.

traquenard [traknaːr] *nm* trap, pitfall.

traquer [trake] *vt* to track down, run to earth, hunt, beat.

travail [travaːj] *nm* (piece of) work, labour, craftsmanship; **travaux forcés** hard labour.

travaillé [travaje] *a* wrought, elaborate.

travailler [travaje] *vt* to work (at, upon), obsess, torment; *vi* to work, toil.

travailleur, -euse [travajœːr, øːz] *a* hard-working; *n* worker.

travailliste [travajist] *a* Labour (Party); *nm* member of the Labour Party.

travée [trave] *nf* girder, bay, span.

travers [traveːr] *nm* breadth, fault, failing; **à** —, **au** — **de** across, through; **en** — across, crosswise; **par le** — amidships; **de** — awry, askance.

traverse [travers] *nf* cross-beam,

-bar, rung, sleeper; **chemin de** — crossroad, side-road.

traversée [traverse] *nf* crossing.

traverser [traverse] *vt* to cross, go through, thwart.

traversin [traversɛ̃] *nm* crossbar, bolster.

travestir [travestiːr] *vt* to disguise, misrepresent; **bal travesti** fancy-dress ball.

travestissement [travestismã] *nm* disguise, disguising, travesty.

trébucher [trebyʃe] *vi* to stumble, trip.

trèfle [trefl] *nm* clover, trefoil, clubs.

treillage [trejaːʒ] *nm* trellis, lattice-work.

treille [treːj] *nf* climbing vine, vine-arbour.

treillis [treji] *nm* lattice, trellis, dungarees; — **métallique** wire-netting.

treize [treːz] *a nm* thirteen, thirteenth.

treizième [trezjem] *an* thirteenth.

tréma [tremɑ] *nm* diaeresis.

tremble [trãːbl] *nm* aspen.

tremblement [trãbləmã] *n* trembling, tremor, quivering, quavering; — **de terre** earthquake.

trembler [trãble] *vi* to tremble, shake, quiver, quaver.

trembloter [trãblɔte] *vi* to quiver, quaver, flicker.

trémière [tremjeːr] *a* **rose** — hollyhock.

trémousser [tremuse] *vir* to flutter; *vr* to fidget; go to a lot of trouble.

trempe [trãːp] *nf* steeping, temper(ing), stamp.

tremper [trãpe] *vt* to steep, soak, drench, temper; *vi* to steep, have a hand (in).

trempette [trãpet] *nf* bread *etc*, dipped in coffee *etc*; quick bath.

tremplin [trãplɛ̃] *nm* spring-, diving-board.

trentaine [trãten] *nf* about thirty.

trente [trãːt] *a nm* thirty, thirtieth.

trente-six [trãtsi, -sis, -siz] *a nm* thirty-six; **ne pas y aller par** — **chemins** not to beat about the bush; **voir** — **chandelles** to see stars.

trentième [trãtjem] *an* thirtieth.

trépaner [trepane] *vt* to drill, bore, trepan.

trépas [trepɑ] *nm* death.

trépasser [trepase] *vi* to die, pass away.

trépidation [trepidasjɔ̃] *nf* shaking, vibration, trepidation.

trépied [trepje] *nm* tripod.

trépigner [trepiɲe] *vi* to stamp, dance.

très [tre] *ad* very, (very) much, most.

trésor [trezɔːr] *nm* treasure, riches, treasury.

trésorerie [trezɔrri] *nf* treasury, treasurer's office.

trésorier, -ière [trezɔrje, jɛːr] *n* treasurer, paymaster, -mistress.

tressaillement [trɛsajmɑ̃] *nm* start, thrill.

tressaillir [trɛsajiːr] *vi* to start, shudder, bound, thrill.

tressauter [tresote] *vi* to start, jump.

tresse [trɛs] *nf* plait, tress.

tresser [trɛse] *vt* to plait, braid, weave.

tréteau [treto] *nm* trestle, stand; *pl* boards, stage.

treuil [trœːj] *nm* windlass, winch.

trêve [trɛːv] *nf* truce, respite; — **de** no more of.

tri [tri] *nm* sorting.

triage [triɑːʒ] *nm* sorting; **gare de —** marshalling yard.

triangle [triɑ̃ːgl] *nm* triangle, set-square.

tribord [tribɔːr] *nm* starboard.

tribu [triby] *nf* tribe.

tribulation [tribylasjɔ̃] *nf* tribulation, trouble.

tribunal [tribynal] *nm* tribunal, (law) court, bench.

tribune [tribyn] *nf* tribune, platform, grandstand.

tribut [triby] *nm* tribute.

tricher [triʃe] *vti* to cheat, trick.

tricherie [triʃri] *nf* cheating, trickery.

tricheur, -euse [triʃœːr, øːz] *n* cheat, trickster.

tricolore [trikɔlɔːr] *a* tricoloured.

tricorne [trikɔrn] *a nm* three-cornered (hat).

tricot [triko] *nm* knitting, cardigan, jumper, jersey.

tricoter [trikɔte] *vt* to knit.

triennal [triɛnnal] *a* triennial.

trier [trie] *vt* to sort (out), pick out.

trigonométrie [trigɔnɔmetri] *nf* trigonometry.

trimbaler [trɛ̃bale] *vt* to lug, trail, drag about.

trimer [trime] *vi* to toil, drudge.

trimestre [trimɛstr] *nm* quarter, term.

trimestriel, -elle [trimɛstriɛl] *a* quarterly.

tringle [trɛ̃ːgl] *nf* (curtain-) rod, bar.

trinquer [trɛ̃ke] *vi* to clink glasses, toast.

triomphal [triɔ̃fal] *a* triumphal.

triomphe [triɔ̃ːf] *nm* triumph.

triompher [triɔ̃fe] *vi* to triumph (over **de**), surmount.

tripatouiller [tripatuje] *vt* to tinker, tamper with.

tripes [trip] *nf pl* tripe, intestines, guts.

triple [tripl] *a nm* treble, triple, threefold.

tripler [triple] *vt* to treble.

tripot [tripo] *nm* gambling house.

tripotage [tripɔtaːʒ] *nm* fiddling about, jobbery.

tripoter [tripɔte] *vt* to fiddle with, tamper with, finger, paw; *vi* to

---

potter, fiddle, mess about, dabble.

trique [trik] *nf* cudgel.

triste [trist] *a* sad, mournful, dismal, bleak, wretched.

tristesse [tristɛs] *nf* sadness, gloom, sorrow, mournfulness.

triturer [trityre] *vt* to grind.

trivial [trivjal] *a* vulgar, common-place, trite.

trivialité [trivjalite] *nf* vulgarity, coarse word, triteness.

troc [trɔk] *nm* barter, exchange, swop(ping).

troène [trɔɛn] *nm* privet.

troglodyte [trɔglɔdit] *nm* cave-dweller.

trogne [trɔɲ] *nf* face, dial.

trognon [trɔɲɔ̃] *nm* core, stump.

trois [trwɑ] *a nm* three, third.

troisième [trwazjɛm] *an* third.

trombe [trɔ̃ːb] *nf* water-spout, cloudburst, whirlwind.

trombone [trɔ̃bɔn] *nm* trombone, paper-clip.

trompe [trɔ̃ːp] *nf* trumpet, horn, hooter, (*elephant*) trunk.

trompe-l'œil [trɔ̃plœːj] *nm* sham, eyewash, window-dressing (*fig*).

tromper [trɔ̃pe] *vt* to deceive, cheat, beguile; *vr* to be mistaken, be wrong.

tromperie [trɔ̃pri] *nf* (piece of) deceit, fraud.

trompette [trɔ̃pɛt] *nf* trumpet, trumpeter.

trompeur, -euse [trɔ̃pœːr, øːz] *a* deceitful, deceptive, misleading; *n* deceiver, cheat.

tronc [trɔ̃] *nm* trunk, bole, collecting-box.

tronçon [trɔ̃sɔ̃] *nm* stump, fragment, section.

tronçonner [trɔ̃sɔne] *vt* to cut into pieces.

trône [troːn] *nm* throne.

trôner [trone] *vi* to sit enthroned, lord it, queen it.

tronquer [trɔ̃ke] *vt* to truncate, mutilate.

trop [tro] *ad* too, too much, over-; **de —** too much, too many, unwanted.

trophée [trɔfe] *nm* trophy.

tropical [trɔpikal] *a* tropical.

tropiques [trɔpik] *nm pl* tropics.

trop-plein [trɔplɛ̃] *nm* overflow, excess.

troquer [trɔke] *vt* to barter, exchange, swop.

trot [tro] *nm* trot.

trotte [trɔt] *nf* stretch, bit, distance, walk.

trotter [trɔte] *vi* to trot, scamper.

trotteuse [trɔtøːz] *nf* go-cart.

trottiner [trɔtine] *vi* to scamper, toddle, jog along.

trottinette [trɔtinɛt] *nf* scooter.

trottoir [trɔtwaːr] *nm* pavement, footpath, platform.

trou [tru] *nm* hole, gap, dead-and-alive place; — **d'air** air-pocket; — **du souffleur** prompter's box.

trouble [trubl] *a* muddy, dim, cloudy; *nm* confusion, uneasiness; *pl* disturbances.

trouble-fête [trubləfɛːt] *nm* spoilsport, killjoy.

troubler [truble] *vt* to disturb, upset, excite, blur, make muddy; *vr* to get upset, become excited, muddy, dim.

trouée [true] *nf* gap.

trouer [true] *vt* to hole, make holes in.

troupe [trup] *nf* troop, gang, company, flock, herd, other ranks; *pl* troops.

troupeau [trupo] *nm* flock, herd, drove.

troupier [trupje] *nm* soldier, seasoned campaigner.

trousse [trus] *nf* outfit, kit, bundle, truss; **à mes —s** after me, at my heels.

trousseau [truso] *nm* bunch, outfit, trousseau.

trousser [truse] *vt* to turn up, tuck up, truss.

trouvaille [truva:j] *nf* find, windfall, godsend.

trouver [truve] *vt* to find, hit upon, think; *vr* to be, be found, happen, feel.

truc [tryk] *nm* knack, dodge, gadget, thingummy.

truchement [tryʃmɑ̃] *nm* intermediary, interpreter.

truculence [trykylɑ̃:s] *nf* truculence.

truelle [tryɛl] *nf* trowel, fish-slice.

truffe [tryf] *nf* truffle, dog's nose.

truie [trɥi] *nf* sow.

truite [trɥit] *nf* trout.

trumeau [trymo] *nm* (*archit*) pier; pier-glass; leg of beef.

truquer [tryke] *vt* to fake, cook, rig.

tsé-tsé [tsetse] *nf* tsetse fly.

T.S.F. *nf* radio.

tu [ty] *pn* you, thou.

tube [tyb] *nm* tube, pipe; (*song*) hit.

tuberculeux, -euse [tybɛrkylø, øːz] *a* tubercular, tuberculous, consumptive.

tuberculose [tybɛrkylo:z] *nf* tuberculosis.

tuer [tɥe] *vt* to kill, slay.

tuerie [tyri] *nf* slaughter, carnage.

tue-tête [tytɛt] *ad* **à —** at the top of one's voice.

tueur [tɥœːr] *nm* killer, slaughterman.

tuile [tɥil] *nf* tile, bit of bad luck.

tulipe [tylip] *nf* tulip.

tulle [tyl] *nm* tulle.

tuméfier [tymefje] *vt* to make swell.

tumulte [tymylt] *nm* tumult, uproar.

tumultueux, -euse [tymyltɥø, øːz] *a* tumultuous, noisy.

tunique [tynik] *nf* tunic.

tunnel [tynɛl] *nm* tunnel.

turbine [tyrbin] *nf* turbine.

turbulence [tyrbylɑ̃:s] *nf* turbulence, boisterousness.

turbulent [tyrbylɑ̃] *a* turbulent, unruly.

turc, turque [tyrk] *a* Turkish; *n* Turk.

turf [tyrf] *nm* racing, race-course.

turfiste [tyrfist] *nm* racegoer.

turpitude [tyrpityd] *nf* turpitude, baseness, base act.

Turquie [tyrki] *nf* Turkey.

turquoise [tyrkwa:z] *a nm* turquoise (colour); *nf* turquoise.

tutelle [tytɛl] *nf* guardianship, protection.

tuteur, -trice [tytœːr, tris] *n* guardian; *nm* stake, trainer.

tutoyer [tytwaje] *vt* to address as 'tu', be familiar with.

tuyau [tɥijo] *nm* tube, (hose-) pipe, stem, goffer, tip, hint.

tuyauter [tɥjote, tɥijote] *vt* to goffer, frill, give a tip, hint to.

tympan [tɛ̃pɑ̃] *nm* eardrum, tympanum.

type [tip] *nm* type, fellow.

typhoïde [tifɔid] *a* typhoid.

typique [tipik] *a* typical.

typo(graphe) [tipɔgraf] *nm* printer, typographer.

typographie [tipɔgrafi] *nf* printing.

tyran [tirɑ̃] *nm* tyrant.

tyrannie [tirani] *nf* tyranny.

tyrannique [tiranik] *a* tyrannical, tyrannous.

tyranniser [tiranize] *vt* to tyrannize, oppress.

tzigane [tsigan] *n* gipsy.

U

ubiquité [ybikɥite] *nf* ubiquity.

ulcère [ylsɛːr] *nm* ulcer, sore.

ulcérer [ylsere] *vt* to ulcerate, hurt, embitter; *vr* to fester, grow embittered.

ultérieur [ylterjœːr] *a* ulterior, subsequent, further

ultimatum [yltimatɔm] *nm* ultimatum.

ultime [yltim] *a* ultimate, last, final.

un, une [œ̃, yn] *indef art* a; *a pn* one; *nm* one; *nf* first page; **— à —** one by one; **en savoir plus d'une** to know a thing or two.

unanime [ynanim] *a* unanimous.

unanimité [ynanimite] *nf* unanimity; **à l'—** unanimously

uni [yni] *a* united, smooth, self-coloured, plain.

unième [ynjɛm] *a* (*in compound numbers only*) first.

unification [ynifikasjɔ̃] *nf* unification, amalgamation.

unifier [ynifje] *vt* to unify, amalgamate.

uniforme [ynifɔrm] *a nm* uniform.

uniformiser [yniformize] *vt* to make uniform, standardize.

uniformité [yniformite] *nf* uniformity.

unilatéral [ynilateral] *a* unilateral, one-sided.

union [ynjɔ̃] *nf* union, unity, association.

uniprix [yniprі] *a* **magasin —** Woolworths.

unique [ynik] *a* single, only, sole, one, unique; **rue à sens —** one-way street.

unir [yn:ir] *vt* to unite, join, make, smooth; *vr* to unite, join, become smooth.

unisson [ynisɔ̃] *nm* unison.

unité [ynite] *nf* unity, consistency, unit.

univers [yniveːr] *nm* universe.

universalité [yniversalite] *nf* universality.

universel, -elle [yniversɛl] *a* universal, world-wide, versatile.

universitaire [yniversiteːr] *a* university; *n* university teacher.

université [yniversite] *nf* university.

uranium [yranjɔm] *nm* uranium.

urbain [yrbɛ̃] *a* urban, town; *n* city-dweller.

urbanisme [yrbanism] *nm* town-planning.

urbanité [yrbanite] *nf* urbanity.

urgence [yrʒɑ̃:s] *nf* urgency, emergency; **d'—** urgently, emergency.

urgent [yrʒɑ̃] *a* urgent, pressing.

urine [yrin] *nf* urine.

uriner [yrine] *vi* to urinate, make water.

urinoir [yrinwaːr] *nm* urinal.

urne [yrn] *nf* urn.

URSS *nf* USSR.

urticaire [yrtikeːr] *nf* nettle-rash.

us [y] *nm pl* **les — et coutumes** ways and customs.

usage [yzaːʒ] *nm* use, using, service, wear, practice, custom, breeding; **d'—** usual, for everyday use.

usagé [yzaʒe] *a* used, worn.

usager, -ère [yzaʒe, ɛːr] *a* for personal use, of everyday use; *n* user.

usé [yze] *a* worn (out, away), threadbare, shabby, stale.

user [yze] *vt* to wear out (away); **— de** to use; *vr* to wear (out, away, down); **en bien (mal) — avec qn** to treat s.o. well (badly).

usine [yzin] *nf* factory, mill, works.

usiner [yzine] *vt* to machine(-finish).

usité [yzite] *a* used, current.

ustensile [ystɑ̃sil] *nm* utensil, tool.

usuel, -elle [yzɥɛl] *a* usual, customary; *nm* reference book.

usufruit [yzyfrɥi] *nm* life interest, usufruct.

usure [yzyːr] *nf* wear (and tear), wearing away, attrition, usury, interest.

usurier, -ière [yzyrje, jeːr] *a* usurious; *n* usurer.

usurpateur, -trice [yzyrpatœːr, tris] *a* usurping; *n* usurper.

usurper [yzyrpe] *vti* to usurp.

ut [yt] *nm* musical note C, do(h).

utile [ytil] *a* useful, handy, serviceable, effective, due.

utilisation [ytilizasjɔ̃] *nf* utilization, using.

utiliser [ytilize] *vt* to utilize, use.

utilitaire [ytiliteːr] *an* utilitarian.

utilité [ytilite] *nf* utility, use(fulness), service.

utopie [ytɔpi] *nf* utopia.

utopique [ytɔpik] *a* utopian.

utopiste [ytɔpist] *an* utopian.

uvule [yvyl] *nf* uvula.

V

vacance [vakɑ̃:s] *nf* vacancy; *pl* holidays, vacation; **en —s** on holiday; **grandes —s** summer holidays.

vacant [vakɑ̃] *a* vacant.

vacarme [vakarm] *nm* din, uproar, hullabaloo.

vaccin [vaksɛ̃] *nm* vaccine, lymph.

vaccination [vaksinasjɔ̃] *nf* vaccination, inoculation.

vacciner [vaksine] *vt* to vaccinate, inoculate.

vache [vaʃ] *nf* cow, cowhide, nasty person, beast; **manger de la — enragée** to have a hard time of it; **parler français comme une — espagnole** to murder the French language.

vachement [vaʃmɑ̃] *ad* damn(ed), terribly.

vacher, -ère [vaʃe, ɛːr] *n* cowherd.

vacherie [vaʃri] *nf* cowshed, dirty trick.

vacillant [vasilɑ̃, -ijɑ̃] *a* wavering, flickering, unsteady, wobbling, uncertain.

vaciller [vasile, -ije] *vi* to waver, flicker, stagger, wobble.

va-comme-je-te-pousse [vakɔmʒətpus] *a* easy-going; *ad* any old how.

vacuité [vakɥite] *nf* emptiness.

vacuum [vakɥɔm] *nm* vacuum.

vadrouille [vadruːj] *nf* spree, swab, mop.

vadrouiller [vadruje] *vi* to rove, roam, gallivant.

vadrouilleur, -euse [vadrujœːr, øːz] *n* gadabout, rake.

va-et-vient [vaevjɛ̃] *nm* coming and going, movement to and fro.

vagabond [vagabɔ̃] *a* vagabond, roving, wandering; *n* vagrant, vagabond, tramp.

vagabondage [vagabɔ̃da:ʒ] *nm* vagabondage, vagrancy.

vagabonder [vagabɔ̃de] *vi* to wander, roam, rove.

vagin [vaʒɛ̃] nm vagina.

vagir [vaʒiːr] vi to wail.

vague [vag] a vague, hazy, indefinite, empty; nm vagueness, space; nf wave; **terrains —s** waste ground.

vaguemestre [vagmɛstr] nm postman, post-orderly.

vaguer [vage] vi to roam, ramble, wander.

vaillance [vajãːs] nf valour, bravery.

vaillant [vajã] a valiant, gallant, brave, stout; **n'avoir pas un sou —** not to have a brass farthing.

vain [vɛ̃] a vain, useless, empty, futile.

vaincre [vɛ̃ːkr] vt to vanquish, defeat, conquer.

vainqueur [vɛ̃kœːr] a inv victorious, conquering; nm victor, conqueror, winner.

vairon [vɛrɔ̃] nm minnow.

vaisseau [vɛso] nm vessel, ship, receptacle.

vaisselier [vɛsəlje] nm dresser.

vaisselle [vɛsɛl] nf plates and dishes, table-service; **faire la —** to wash up.

val [val] nm valley, vale; **par monts et par vaux** up hill and down dale.

valable [valabl] a valid, available, good.

valet [valɛ] nm valet, footman, knave, jack, servant, farm-hand.

valeur [valœːr] nf value, worth, valour, merit, asset; pl securities, bills; **objets de —** valuables; **mettre en —** to bring out, emphasize, develop; **—s actives** assets; **—s passives** liabilities.

valeureux, -euse [valœrø, øːz] a valorous, gallant.

valide [valid] a valid, able-bodied, fit.

valider [valide] vt to ratify, validate.

validité [validite] nf validity.

valise [valiːz] nf suitcase, (US) valise.

vallée [vale] nf valley.

vallon [valɔ̃] nm (small) valley, vale, dale.

vallonné [valɔne] a undulating.

valoir [valwaːr] vti to be worth, be as good (bad) as, deserve, be equivalent to, win, bring (in); **faire —** to assert, make the most of, develop, show off; **se faire —** to show off, push o.s. forward; **cela vaut la peine d'être vu** it is worth seeing; **cela vaut le coup** it is worth while; **il vaut mieux le vendre** it is better to sell it; **ne pas — grand'chose** not to be up to much; **vaille que vaille** at all costs.

valorisation [valɔrizasjɔ̃] nf valorization, stabilization.

valoriser [valɔrize] vt to valorize, stabilize.

valse [vals] nf waltz.

valser [valse] vi to waltz.

valve [valv] nf valve.

vampire [vɑ̃piːr] nm vampire.

vandale [vɑ̃dal] nm vandal.

vandalisme [vɑ̃dalism] nm vandalism.

vanille [vaniːj] nf vanilla.

vanité [vanite] nf vanity, conceit, futility; **tirer — de** to take pride in.

vaniteux, -euse [vanitø, øːz] a vain, conceited.

vanne [van] nf sluice-gate, floodgate.

vanneau [vano] nm lapwing, plover, peewit.

vanner [vane] vt to winnow, sift, tire out.

vannerie [vanri] nf basket-making, basket-, wicker-work.

vanneuse [vanøːz] nf winnowing-machine.

vannier [vanje] nm basket-maker.

vantail [vɑ̃taːj] nm leaf (of door etc).

vantard [vɑ̃taːr] a boastful, bragging; n boaster, braggart.

vantardise [vɑ̃tardiːz] nf boast (fulness), bragging.

vanter [vɑ̃te] vt to praise, extol; vr to brag, boast, pride o.s.

vanterie [vɑ̃tri] nf boast(ing), brag (ging).

va-nu-pieds [vanypje] n barefoot beggar, ragamuffin.

vapeur [vapœːr] nm steamer, steamship; nf steam, vapour, haze, dizziness; **à toute —** full steam (ahead).

vaporeux, -euse [vapɔrø, øːz] a vaporous, steamy, hazy.

vaporisateur [vapɔrizatœːr] nm atomizer, (scent-)spray, evaporator.

vaporisation [vapɔrizasjɔ̃] nf evaporation, atomization, vaporization.

vaporiser [vapɔrize] vt to atomize, vaporize, volatilize, spray; vr to vaporize, spray oneself.

vaquer [vake] vi to be vacant, not to be sitting; **— à** to attend to, look after.

varech [varɛk] nm seaweed, wrack, kelp.

vareuse [varøːz] nf (sailor's) jersey, pea-jacket, short tunic.

variable [varjabl] a variable, changeable, unsettled.

variante [varjãːt] nf variant.

variation [varjasjɔ̃] nf variation, change.

varice [varis] nf varicose vein.

varicelle [varisɛl] nf chicken-pox.

varié [varje] a varied, miscellaneous, variegated.

varier [varje] vt to vary, change; vi to vary, differ, fluctuate.

variété [varjete] nf variety, diversity.

variole [varjɔl] nf smallpox.

vase [vaːz] nm vase, receptacle; **— de nuit** chamber-pot; **en — clos** in isolation; nf mud, slime.

vaseline [vazlin] nf vaseline.

vaseux, -euse [vazø, øːz] a muddy, slimy, off-colour, woolly.

vasistas [vazistɑːs] *nm* fanlight.
vassal [vasal] *an* vassal.
vaste [vast] *a* vast, wide, spacious.
vau [vo] *ad* à — l'eau downstream, to rack and ruin, to the dogs.
vaurien, -enne [vorjɛ̃, jɛn] *n* good-for-nothing, waster, blackguard, scamp.
vautour [votuːr] *nm* vulture.
vautrer [votre] *vr* to wallow, sprawl.
veau [vo] *nm* calf, veal, calf-skin.
vécu [veky] *a* true to life, realistic.
vedette [vədɛt] *nf* mounted sentry, motor launch, small steamer, scout, star; être en — to be in the limelight, in large type; être mis en — sur l'affiche to top the bill.
végétal [veʒetal] *a* vegetable, plant; *nm* plant.
végétarien, -enne [veʒetarjɛ̃, jɛn] *an* vegetarian.
végétarisme [veʒetarism] *nm* vegetarianism.
végétation [veʒetasjɔ̃] *nf* vegetation; *pl* adenoids.
végéter [veʒete] *vi* to vegetate.
véhémence [veemɑ̃ːs] *nf* vehemence.
véhément [veemɑ̃] *a* vehement, violent.
véhicule [veikyl] *nm* vehicle.
veille [vɛːj] *nf* vigil, wakefulness, watch(ing), late night, sitting up, eve, day before; à la — de on the brink of.
veillée [vɛje] *nf* social evening, vigil, wake, night-nursing.
veiller [vɛje] *vt* to sit up with, look after; *vi* to watch, be on the lookout, keep awake, sit up; — à to see to, look after.
veilleur, -euse [vɛjœːr, øːz] *n* watcher, keeper of a vigil; — de nuit night-watchman.
veilleuse [vɛjøːz] *nf* night-light, pilot-light; mettre en — to dim, turn down.
veinard [venaːr] *an* lucky (blighter).
veine [vɛn] *nf* vein, mood, luck; coup de — stroke of luck, fluke.
veineux, -euse [vɛnø, øːz] *a* venous, veined.
vêler [vele] *vi* to calve.
vélin [velɛ̃] *nm* vellum.
velléité [velleite] *nf* inclination, slight desire.
vélo [velo] *nm* bike, cycle; faire du — to go in for cycling.
vélocité [velosite] .., velocity, speed.
vélodrome [velodroːm] *nm* cycle-racing track.
velours [v(ə)luːr] *nm* velvet; — de coton velveteen.
velouté [v(ə)lute] *a* velvety, smooth, soft; *nm* velvetiness, bloom, softness.
velu [vəly] *a* hairy.
venaison [vənɛzɔ̃] *nf* venison, game.
vénal [venal] *a* venal, corrupt(ible).
vénalité [venalite] *nf* venality.
venant [vənɑ̃] *a* thriving; *nm* à tout

— to all comers, to anyone at all.
vendable [vɑ̃dabl] *a* saleable, marketable.
vendange [vɑ̃dɑ̃ːʒ] *nf* grape-gathering, wine harvest, vintage.
vendanger [vɑ̃dɑ̃ʒe] *vti* to gather in the grapes.
vendangeur, -euse [vɑ̃dɑ̃ʒœːr, øːz] *n* vintager, grape-gatherer.
vendeur, -euse [vɑ̃dœːr, øːz] *n* seller, salesman, -woman, shop assistant, vendor.
vendredi [vɑ̃drədi] *nm* Friday; le — saint Good Friday.
vendre [vɑ̃ːdr] *vt* to sell, betray.
vendu [vɑ̃dy] *nm* traitor.
vénéneux, -euse [venenø, øːz] *a* poisonous.
vénérable [venerabl] *a* venerable.
vénération [venerasjɔ̃] *nf* veneration, reverence.
vénérer [venere] *vt* to venerate, revere, worship.
vénérien, -ienne [venerjɛ̃, jɛn] *a* venereal.
vengeance [vɑ̃ʒɑ̃ːs] *nf* vengeance, revenge, retribution; tirer — de to be avenged on.
venger [vɑ̃ʒe] *vt* to avenge; *vr* to revenge oneself, take vengeance.
vengeur, -eresse [vɑ̃ʒœːr, ərɛs] *a* avenging; *n* avenger.
véniel, -elle [venjɛl] *a* venial.
venimeux, -euse [vənimø, øːz] *a* venomous, poisonous, spiteful.
venin [vənɛ̃] *nm* venom, poison, spite.
venir [v(ə)niːr] *vi* to come, reach, grow, be the result (of de); — à apparaître to happen, chance to appear; — de sortir to have just gone out; faire — send for; — chercher to come for; en — à to come to the point of, be reduced to; l'idée me vient que it occurs to me that.
vent [vɑ̃] *nm* wind, blast, flatulence, vent, scent; coup de — gust of wind; il fait du — it is windy; avoir — de to get wind of; mettre au — to hang out to air.
vente [vɑ̃ːt] *nf* sale, selling; en — on sale; — de charité charity bazaar.
venter [vɑ̃te] *vi* to be windy, blow.
venteux, -euse [vɑ̃tø, øːz] *a* windy, windswept.
ventilateur [vɑ̃tilatœːr] *nm* ventilator, fan.
ventiler [vɑ̃tile] *vt* to ventilate.
ventouse [vɑ̃tuːz] *nf* cupping-glass, sucker, vent-hole.
ventre [vɑ̃ːtr] *nm* abdomen, belly, stomach, paunch, bulge; prendre du — to grow stout; n'avoir rien dans le — to be starving, have no guts; se mettre à plat — to lie flat, grovel.
ventriloque [vɑ̃trilɔk] *a* ventriloquous; *nm* ventriloquist.
ventru [vɑ̃try] *a* stout, portly, pot-bellied.

venu [vəny] *n* comer.

venue [vəny] *nf* coming, arrival, advent, growth.

vêpres [vɛːpr] *nf pl* vespers, evensong.

ver [vɛːr] *nm* worm, maggot; — **luisant** glow-worm; — **solitaire** tapeworm; — **à soie** silkworm; **tirer les —s du nez de qn** to worm it out of s.o.

véracité [vɛrasite] *nf* veracity, truth (fulness).

véranda [vɛrɑ̃da] *nf* veranda.

verbal [vɛrbal] *a* verbal.

verbaliser [vɛrbalize] *vi* to make out an official report.

verbe [vɛrb] *nm* verb, word; **avoir le — haut** to be loud-mouthed.

verbeux, -euse [vɛrbø, øːz] *a* verbose, long-winded.

verbiage [vɛrbjaːʒ] *nm* verbiage.

verbosité [vɛrbozite] *nf* verbosity, long-windedness.

verdâtre [vɛrdɑːtr] *a* greenish.

verdeur [vɛrdœːr] *nf* greenness, tartness, vigour.

verdict [vɛrdikt] *nm* verdict, finding.

verdier [vɛrdje] *nm* greenfinch.

verdir [vɛrdiːr] *vt* to paint or make green; *vi* to turn green, become covered with verdigris.

verdoyant [vɛrdwayɑ̃] *a* green, verdant.

verdure [vɛrdyːr] *nf* verdure, greenery, greenness, greens.

véreux, -euse [vɛrø, øːz] *a* worm-eaten, maggoty, shady.

verge [vɛrʒ] *nf* rod, switch, wand.

verger [vɛrʒe] *nm* orchard.

verglas [vɛrglɑ] *nm* ice, black ice.

vergogne [vɛrgɔɲ] *nf* shame; **sans —** shameless.

vergue [vɛrg] *nf* yard.

véridicité [vɛridisite] *nf* truth(fulness).

véridique [vɛridik] *a* veracious, truthful.

vérificateur [vɛrifikatœːr] *nm* inspector, examiner, gauge, auditor.

vérification [vɛrifikasjɔ̃] *nf* inspection, verification, overhauling, checking, auditing.

vérifier [vɛrifje] *vt* to inspect, verify, check, overhaul, audit.

véritable [vɛritabl] *a* real, true, genuine, downright.

vérité [vɛrite] *nf* truth(fulness), sincerity, fact.

vermeil, -eille [vɛrmɛːj] *a* vermilion, bright red, ruby; *nm* silver-gilt.

vermicelle [vɛrmisɛl] *nm* vermicelli.

vermillon [vɛrmijɔ̃] *nm* vermilion, bright red.

vermine [vɛrmin] *nf* vermin.

vermoulu [vɛrmuly] *a* worm-eaten, decrepit.

verni [vɛrni] *a* varnished, patent (*leather*), lucky.

vernir [vɛrniːr] *vt* to varnish, glaze, polish, japan.

vernis [vɛrni] *nm* varnish, glaze, polish, gloss.

vernissage [vɛrnisaːʒ] *nm* varnishing, glazing, polishing, preview.

vernisseur, -euse [vɛrnisœːr] *n* varnisher, glazer, japanner.

vérole [vɛrɔl] *nf* pox; **petite —** smallpox.

verrat [vɛra] *nm* boar.

verre [vɛːr] *nm* glass; — **de lunettes** lens; **papier de —** sandpaper; **tempête dans un — d'eau** storm in a teacup.

verrerie [vɛr(ə)ri] *nf* glassmaking, glassware, glass-factory.

verrier [vɛrje] *nm* glassmaker, -blower.

verrière [vɛrjɛːr] *nf* glass casing, stained glass window.

verroterie [vɛrɔtri] *nf* small glassware, beads.

verrou [vɛru] *nm* bolt, bar, breech-bolt; **pousser (tirer) le —** to bolt (unbolt) the door; **sous les —s** under lock and key.

verrouiller [vɛruje] *vt* to bolt, lock up.

verrue [vɛry] *nf* wart.

vers [vɛːr] *nm* line; *pl* poetry, verse; *prep* towards, to, about.

versant [vɛrsɑ̃] *nm* slope, side.

versatile [vɛrsatil] *a* changeable, unstable, fickle.

versatilité [vɛrsatilite] *nf* instability, fickleness.

verse [vɛrs] *ad* **à —** in torrents.

versé [vɛrse] *a* versed, conversant, well up.

versement [vɛrs(ə)mɑ̃] *nm* pouring (out), payment, instalment, deposit; **bulletin de —** pay-in slip.

verser [vɛrse] *vt* to pour (out), shed, deposit, assign, lay, overturn; *vi* to be laid flat, overturn; — **à boire** to pour out a drink.

verset [vɛrsɛ] *nm* verse.

versification [vɛrsifikasjɔ̃] *nf* versication.

versifier [vɛrsifje] *vt* to put into verse; *vi* to write poetry.

version [vɛrsjɔ̃] *nf* version, account, translation.

verso [vɛrso] *nm* back, verso; **voir au —** see overleaf.

vert [vɛːr] *a* green, unripe, spicy, sharp, vigorous, hale; *nm* green.

vert-de-gris [vɛrdəgri] *nm* verdigris.

vertébral [vɛrtebral] *a* vertebral; **colonne —e** spine

vertèbre [vɛrtɛːbr] *nf* vertebra.

vertement [vɛrtəmɑ̃] *ad* sharply, severely.

vertical [vɛrtikal] *a* vertical, perpendicular, upright.

verticale [vɛrtikal] *nf* vertical.

vertige [vɛrtiːʒ] *nm* giddiness, dizziness, vertigo; **avoir le —** to be giddy.

vertigineux, -euse [vɛrtiʒinø, øːz] *a* giddy, dizzy.

vertu [vɛrty] *nf* virtue chastity, property, quality; **en — de** by virtue of.

vertueux, -euse [vɛrtɥø, øːz] *a* virtuous, chaste.

verve [vɛrv] *nf* verve, zest, go, vigour, high spirits; **être en —** to be in fine fettle.

verveine [vɛrvɛn] *nf* verbena, vervain.

vesce [vɛs] *nf* vetch, tare.

vésicatoire [vezikatwaːr] *a nm* vesicatory.

vésicule [vezikyl] *nf* vesicle, blister, air-cell; **— biliaire** gall-bladder.

vespasienne [vɛspazjɛn] *nf* street urinal.

vespéral [vɛspɛral] *a* evening.

vessie [vɛsi] *nf* bladder; **prendre des —s pour des lanternes** to think the moon is made of green cheese.

veste [vɛst] *nf* jacket.

vestiaire [vɛstjɛːr] *nm* cloakroom, changing-room, robing-room.

vestibule [vɛstibyl] *nm* (entrance-) hall, lobby, vestibule.

vestige [vɛstiːʒ] *nm* trace, mark, vestige.

vestimentaire [vɛstimɑ̃tɛːr] *a* vestimentary.

veston [vɛstɔ̃] *nm* jacket.

vêtement [vɛtmɑ̃] *nm* garment; *pl* clothing, clothes; **—s de dessous** underwear.

vétéran [vetɛrɑ̃] *nm* veteran.

vétérinaire [veterinɛːr] *a* veterinary; *nm* veterinary surgeon.

vétille [vetiːj] *nf* trifle.

vétilleux, -euse [vetijø, øːz] *a* captious, finicky.

vêtir [vetiːr] *vt* to dress, clothe; *vr* to dress oneself.

veto [veto] *nm* veto; **mettre son — à** to veto.

vétusté [vetyste] *nf* decrepitude, old age.

veuf, veuve [vœf, vœːv] *a* widowed; *n* widower, widow.

veule [vœːl] *a* weak, soft, flabby, inert, drab.

veulerie [vœlri] *nf* weakness, flabbiness, drabness.

veuvage [vœvaːʒ] *nm* widow(er)-hood.

vexation [vɛksasjɔ̃] *nf* vexation, annoying word or deed.

vexatoire [vɛksatwaːr] *a* vexatious.

vexer [vɛkse] *vt* to vex, annoy, pester, upset, irritate; *vr* to get annoyed.

viable [vjabl, vjabl] *a* strong enough to live, viable, fit for traffic.

viaduc [vjadyk] *nm* viaduct.

viager, -ère [vjaʒe, ɛːr] *a* for life; *nm* life interest; **rente viagère** life annuity.

viande [vjɑ̃ːd] *nf* meat, flesh.

viatique [vjatik] *nm* viaticum.

vibrant [vibrɑ̃] *a* vibrant, ringing, rousing, vibrating.

vibration [vibrasjɔ̃] *nf* vibration, resonance.

vibratoire [vibratwaːr] *a* vibratory, oscillatory.

vibrer [vibre] *vi* to vibrate, throb; **faire —** to thrill, rouse.

vicaire [vikɛːr] *nm* curate.

vice [vis] *nm* vice, flaw, defect.

vice-consul [viskɔ̃syl] *nm* vice-consul.

vice-roi [visrwa] *nm* viceroy.

vicier [visje] *vt* to vitiate, contaminate, corrupt, taint; *vr* to become corrupted, tainted, foul, spoilt.

vicieux, -euse [visjø, øːz] *a* vicious, depraved, bad-tempered, faulty.

vicinal [visinal] *a* **route —e** local road, by-road.

vicissitude [visissityd] *nf* vicissitude; *pl* ups and downs.

vicomte [vikɔ̃t] *nm* viscount.

vicomtesse [vikɔ̃tɛs] *nf* viscountess.

victime [viktim] *nf* victim, sacrifice.

victoire [viktwaːr] *nf* victory.

victorieux, -euse [viktɔrjø, øːz] *a* victorious.

victuailles [viktɥaːj] *nf pl* victuals, eatables.

vidange [vidɑ̃ːʒ] *nf* emptying, draining, clearing; *nf pl* night-soil.

vidanger [vidɑ̃ʒe] *vt* to empty, drain.

vidangeur [vidɑ̃ʒœːr] *nm* scavenger, cesspool clearer.

vide [vid] *a* empty, unoccupied, blank; *nm* empty space, emptiness, blank, gap, vacuum.

vider [vide] *vt* to empty, drain (off), blow, clean, gut, core, stone, bale, settle; *vr* to empty; **— une question** to settle a question; **— les arçons** to be unsaddled.

vie [vi] *nf* life, existence, lifetime (way of) living, livelihood, vitality; **à — for** life; **avoir la — dure** to die hard, be hard to kill.

vieillard [vjɛjaːr] *nm* old man.

vieilleries [vjɛjri] *nf pl* old things, dated ideas.

vieillesse [vjɛjɛs] *nf* (old) age, old-ness.

vieillissement [vjɛjismɑ̃] *nm* ageing, growing old.

vieillir [vjɛjiːr] *vt* to age, make look older; *vi* to age, grow old, become antiquated.

vieillot, -otte [vjɛjo, ɔt] *a* oldish, old-fashioned.

vierge [vjɛrʒ] *a* virgin(al), pure, blank; *nf* virgin, maiden.

vieux, vieil, vieille [vjø, vjɛ(ː)j] *a* old, ancient, stale; *nm pl* old people; **il est — jeu** he is old-fashioned, antiquated; **mon —** old man; **un — de la vieille** one of the old brigade, an old-timer.

vif, vive [vif, viːv] *a* lively, brisk, sharp, keen, quick, alive, high-spirited, vivid, bright; *nm* living flesh, quick heart; **haie vive** quick-set hedge; **peindre sur le —** to paint from life.

vif-argent [vifarʒã] nm quicksilver, mercury.

vigie [viʒi] nf look-out (man), watch-tower.

vigilance [viʒilã:s] nf vigilance, care.

vigilant [viʒilã] a vigilant, watchful.

vigne [viɲ] nf vine, vineyard; — **vierge** Virginia creeper; **être dans les —s du Seigneur** to be in one's cups.

vigneron, -onne [viɲrɔ̃, ɔn] n vine-grower, vineyard worker.

vignette [viɲɛt] nf excise stamp, road fund licence, vignette.

vignoble [viɲɔbl] nm vineyard.

vigoureux, -euse [vigurø, ø:z] a vigorous, sturdy, strong, hardy.

vigueur [vigœ:r] nf vigour, sturdiness, strength, effect; **entrer en —** to come into effect, force; **mettre en —** to enforce.

vil [vil] a vile, base, low(ly), cheap.

vilain [vilɛ̃] a bad, naughty, nasty, dirty, mean, scurvy, ugly, wretched; nm rascal, villein.

vilebrequin [vilbrəkɛ̃] nm brace (and bit); **arbre à —** crankshaft.

vilenie [viləni] nf nastiness, meanness, foul word, low action.

vilipender [vilipɑ̃de] vt to abuse, run down.

villa [vil(l)a] nf villa.

village [vila:ʒ] nm village.

villageois [vilaʒwa, wa:z] a country, boorish; n villager.

ville [vil] nf town, city; — **d'eau** spa.

villégiateur [vil(l)eʒatœ:r] nm visitor, holiday-maker.

villégiature [vil(l)eʒaty:r] nf holiday, stay in the country.

vin [vɛ̃] nm wine; — **de Bordeaux** claret; — **de Bourgogne** burgundy; — **de Xérès** sherry; — **en cercle** wine in the cask; — **millésimé** vintage wine; **avoir le — triste** to be maudlin in drink.

vinaigre [vinɛ:gr] nm vinegar.

vinaigrette [vinɛgrɛt] nf oil and vinegar dressing.

vinaigrier [vinɛgrie] nm vinegar-maker, vinegar-cruet.

vindicatif, -ive [vɛ̃dikatif, i:v] a vindicative, revengeful.

vineux, -euse [vinø, ø:z] a wine-flavoured, wine-stained, full-bodied, strong, rich in wine.

vingt [vɛ̃] a nm twenty, twentieth.

vingtaine [vɛ̃tɛn] nf about twenty, a score.

vingtième [vɛ̃tjɛm] a nm twentieth.

vinicole [vinikɔl] a wine-growing.

viol [vjɔl] nm rape.

violacé [vjɔlase] a purplish-blue.

violateur, -trice [vjɔlatœ:r, tris] n violator, transgressor.

violation [vjɔlasjɔ̃] nf violation, breach, breaking, infringement.

violence [vjɔlɑ̃:s] nf violence, force, vehemence.

violent [vjɔlɑ̃] a violent, fierce, strong, high.

violenter [vjɔlɑ̃te] vt to do violence to.

violer [vjɔle] vt to violate, break, transgress, rape.

violet, -ette [vjɔlɛ, ɛt] a nm purple, violet.

violette [vjɔlɛt] nf violet.

violon [vjɔlɔ̃] nm violin, fiddle, violinist, gaol, clink.

violoncelle [vjɔlɔ̃sɛl] nm violoncello, 'cello (player).

violoniste [vjɔlɔnist] n violinist.

vipère [vipɛ:r] nf viper, adder.

virage [vira:ʒ] nm turn(ing), swinging round, tacking, cornering, bend.

virement [virmɑ̃] nm turn(ing), transfer; **banque de —** clearing-bank.

virer [vire] vt to turn over, clear, transfer; vi to turn, swing round, tack, veer, corner, bank, change colour.

virevolte [virvɔlt] nf quick circling, sudden change.

virevolter [virvɔlte] vi to circle, spin round.

virginal [virʒinal] a virginal.

virginité [virʒinite] nf virginity, maidenhood.

virgule [virgyl] nf comma, decimal point; **point et —** semi-colon.

viril [viril] a virile, manly, male; **l'âge —** manhood.

virilité [virilite] nf virility, manliness.

virole [virɔl] nf ferrule, binding-ring.

virtuel, -elle [virtɥɛl] a virtual, potential.

virtuose [virtɥo:z] n virtuoso.

virtuosité [virtɥozite] nf virtuosity.

virulence [virylɑ̃:s] nf virulence.

vis [vis] nf screw, thread.

visa [viza] nm visa, initials.

visage [viza:ʒ] nm face, visage, countenance; **trouver — de bois** to find nobody at home, the door shut.

vis-à-vis [vizavi] ad opposite; prep **— de** opposite, facing, with regard to, towards; nm person opposite, partner.

viscère [vissɛ:r] nm viscus; pl viscera.

viscosité [viskozite] nf viscosity, stickiness.

visée [vize] nf aim(ing), sight(ing), design.

viser [vize] vt to aim at, sight, allude to, initial, countersign; vi to aim, aspire.

viseur, -euse [vizœ:r, ø:z] n aimer; nm view-finder, sights, sighting-tube.

visibilité [vizibilite] nf visibility.

visible [vizibl] a visible, obvious, perceptible, open; **il n'est pas —** he is not at home.

visière [vizjɛːr] *nf* visor, eye-shade, peak; **rompre en — avec** to quarrel openly with, attack openly.

vision [vizjɔ̃] *nf* vision, (eye)sight, fantasy.

visionnaire [vizjɔnɛːr] *a* visionary; *n* dreamer.

visite [vizit] *nf* visit, call, inspection, visitor, caller; **faire (rendre) — à** to visit, call on; **rendre à qn sa —** to return s.o.'s visit; **— des bagages** customs inspection.

visiter [vizite] *vt* to visit, attend, inspect, examine, go over, search; **faire — la maison à qn** to show s.o. over the house.

visiteur, -euse [vizitœːr, øːz] *n* visitor, caller, inspector.

vison [vizɔ̃] *nm* vison, mink.

visqueux, -euse [viskø, øːz] *a* viscous, sticky, gluey, thick.

visser [vise] *vt* to screw (down, in, on, up); put the screw on, keep down.

visuel, -elle [vizɥɛl] *a* visual; **champ —** field of vision.

vital [vital] *a* vital.

vitalité [vitalite] *nf* vitality.

vitamine [vitamin] *nf* vitamin.

vite [vit] *a* speedy, fast, fleet, swift; *ad* quickly, fast, soon; **avoir — fait de** to be quick about; **faites vite!** hurry up!

vitesse [vitɛs] *nf* speed, rapidity, -rate; **à toute —** at full speed; **en petite —** by goods train; **gagner qn de —** to outstrip s.o., outrun, steal a march on s.o.; **prendre de la — to gather speed.

viticole [vitikɔl] *a* wine.

viticulteur [vitikyltœːr] *nm* vine-grower.

viticulture [vitikylty:r] *nf* wine-growing.

vitrage [vitra:ʒ] *nm* glazing, windows.

vitrail [vitra:j] *nm* stained glass window.

vitre [vitr] *nf* (window) pane.

vitrer [vitre] *vt* to glaze.

vitreux, -euse [vitrø, øːz] *a* vitreous, glazed, glassy.

vitrier [vitrie] *nm* glazier.

vitrine [vitrin] *nf* shop-window, glass-case, showcase, cabinet.

vitriol [vitriɔl] *nm* vitriol.

vitupération [vityperasjɔ̃] *nf* vituperation.

vitupérer [vitypere] *vt* to blame.

vivace [vivas] *a* long-lived, undying, hardy, perennial.

vivacité [vivasite] *nf* vivacity, vivaciousness, vividness, intensity, hastiness, burst of temper.

vivant [vivɑ̃] *a* living, alive, lively, lifelike, vivid; **langues —es** modern languages; *nm* living person, life-time; **bon —** person who enjoys life, boon companion; **de mon —** in my lifetime.

vivat [vivat] *nm* hurrah.

vive-eau [vivo] *nf* spring-tide.

vivement [vivmɑ̃] *ad* briskly, sharply, warmly.

viveur, -euse [vivœːr, øːz] *n* rake, fast liver.

vivier [vivje] *nm* fish-pond.

vivifiant [vivifjɑ̃] *a* vivifying, bracing, invigorating.

vivisection [vivisɛksjɔ̃] *nf* vivisection.

vivoter [vivɔte] *vi* to live from hand to mouth.

vivre [viːvr] *vi* to live; *nm* food, living; *pl* provisions, supplies; **avoir de quoi —** to have enough to live on; **apprendre à — à qn** to teach s.o. manners; **être commode à — to** be easy to get on with.

vlan [vlɑ̃] *excl* whack! bang!

vocable [vɔkabl] *nm* vocable, word.

vocabulaire [vɔkabylɛːr] *nm* vocabulary.

vocal [vɔkal] *a* vocal.

vocalise [vɔkaliːz] *nf* exercise in vocalization.

vocation [vɔkasjɔ̃] *nf* vocation, bent, call(ing).

vociférant [vɔsiferɑ̃] *a* vociferous.

vociférer [vɔsifere] *vi* to vociferate yell, shout.

voeu [vø] *nm* vow, wish.

vogue [vɔg] *nf* vogue, fashion; **être en —** to be popular; **c'est la grande — it's all the rage.

voguer [vɔge] *vi* to sail.

voici [vwasi] *prep* here is, here are, this is, these are; **me —** here I am; **le — qui arrive** here he comes.

voie [vwa] *nf* way, track(s), thorough-fare, passage; **— d'eau** leak; **ferrée** railway line; **— de garage** siding; **être en — de** to be in a fair way to.

voilà [vwala] *prep* there is, there are, that is, those are; **le —** there he is; **— un an** a year ago; **en — une idée** what an idea! **ne —-t-il pas qu'il pleure** there now, if he isn't crying.

voile [vwal] *nm* veil, cloak; *nf* sail; **mettre à la —** to set sail.

voiler [vwale] *vt* to veil, muffle, cloud, shade, hide; *vr* to cloud over.

voilette [vwalɛt] *nf* (hat) veil, half-veil.

voilier [vwalje] *nm* sailing ship, sail-maker.

voilure [vwalyːr] *nf* sails.

voir [vwaːr] *vt* to see, notice, imagine, look into; *vr* to be seen, show, be obvious; **faire — à** to show, reveal; **faites —** let's see it; **— sur** to look out on; **à ce que je vois** as far as I can see; **il ne peut pas me —** he can't stand the sight of me; **il n'y voit pas** he can't see; **se faire bien —** to get into s.o.'s good books; **vous n'avez rien à — là-dedans** it is none of your business; **cela n'a rien à — à l'affaire** that has nothing to do with it.

voire [vwaːr] *ad* nay, in truth; — **même** and indeed.

voirie [vwari] *nf* roads, refuse (-heap); **le service de** — Highways Department.

voisin [vwazɛ̃] *a* neighbouring, next, adjoining, bordering; *n* neighbour.

voisinage [vwazinaːʒ] *nm* neighbourhood, vicinity, nearness, proximity.

voisiner [vwazine] *vi* to adjoin, be side by side, visit neighbours.

voiturage [vwatyraːʒ] *nm* carriage, cartage.

voiture [vwatyːr] *nf* motor car, vehicle, carriage, cart, van; — **à bras** hand-cart, barrow; — **d'enfant** perambulator, (US) baby carriage; — **de malade** bathchair; — **de place** cab, taxi; **aller en** — to drive; **en** —! all aboard!

voiturer [vwatyre] *vt* to transport, convey.

voiturier, -ière [vwatyrje, jeːr] *a* carriage(able); *nm* carter, carrier.

voix [vwa] *nf* voice, vote; **à haute** — aloud; **à mi-** — under one's breath; **avoir** — **au chapitre** to have a say in the matter; **de vive** — by word of mouth, viva voce; **mettre aux** — to put to the vote.

vol [vɔl] *nm* flight, flying, flock, theft, robbery, stealing, stolen goods; **à** — **d'oiseau** as the crow flies; — **à la roulotte** theft from a motor car; — **à l'étalage** shop-lifting; — **à la tire** pocket-picking, bag-snatching; — **à l'américaine** confidence trick.

volage [vɔlaːʒ] *a* fickle, flighty.

volaille [vɔlaj] *nf* poultry, fowls.

volailler [vɔlaːje] *nm* poultry-yard, poulterer.

volant [vɔlɑ̃] *a* flying, detachable, loose, fluttering; *nm* shuttlecock, flywheel, steering-wheel, flounce.

volatil [vɔlatil] *a* volatile.

volatile [vɔlatil] *nm* winged creature, bird.

volatiliser [vɔlatilize] *vt* to volatilize; *vr* to volatilize, vanish, disappear into thin air.

vol-au-vent [vɔlovɑ̃] *nm* vol-au-vent, puff pastry pie.

volcan [vɔlkɑ̃] *nm* volcano.

volcanique [vɔlkanik] *a* volcanic.

volée [vɔle] *nf* flight, flock, volley, shower, thrashing; **à la** — in flight, on the wing; **semer à la** — to broadcast; **sonner à toute** — to ring a full peal; **de la première** — of the first rank, crack.

voler [vɔle] *vt* to steal, rob, swindle; *vi* to fly, soar; **il ne l'a pas volé** he deserved it.

volet [vɔle] *nm* shutter, sorting-board; **trié sur le** — select, hand-picked.

voleter [vɔlte] *vi* to flutter, flit.

voleur, -euse [vɔlœːr, øːz] *a* flying, thievish, thieving; *nm* thief, robber; **au** —! stop thief!

volière [vɔljeːr] *nf* aviary.

volontaire [vɔlɔ̃teːr] *a* voluntary, wilful, determined, self-willed; *nm* volunteer.

volonté [vɔlɔ̃te] *nf* will; *pl* caprices, whims; **dernières** —s de last will and testament of; **de bonne** — with a good grace, with a will; **à** — ad lib, at will; **de sa propre** — of one's own accord; **faire ses quatre** —s to do as one pleases.

volontiers [vɔlɔ̃tje] *ad* willingly, gladly, readily.

volt [vɔlt] *nm* volt.

voltage [vɔltaːʒ] *nm* voltage.

voltampère [vɔltɑ̃peːr] *nm* watt.

volte-face [vɔltfas] *nf* volte-face, turning-round, right-about-turn; **faire** — to face about, reverse one's opinions.

voltige [vɔltiːʒ] *nf* slack-rope, flying trapeze exercises, trick-riding, vaulting.

voltiger [vɔltiʒe] *vi* to flutter, flit, flap, perform on the flying trapeze or on horseback.

voltigeur, -euse [vɔltiʒœːr, øːz] *n* trapeze artist, trick-rider, equestrian performer; *nm* light infantryman.

volubilité [vɔlybilite] *nf* volubility, fluency.

volume [vɔlym] *nm* volume, bulk, capacity, tome.

volumineux, -euse [vɔlyminø, øːz] *a* voluminous, bulky.

volupté [vɔlypte] *nf* pleasure, delight, sensuousness.

voluptueux, -euse [vɔlyptɥø, øːz] *a* sensuous, voluptuous; *n* sensualist.

volute [vɔlyt] *nf* volute, scroll, wreath.

vomir [vɔmiːr] *vti* to vomit; *vt* bring up, belch forth.

vomissement [vɔmismɑ̃] *nm* vomit (ing).

vomitif, -ive [vɔmitif, iːv] *a nm* emetic.

vorace [vɔras] *a* voracious.

voracité [vɔrasite] *nf* voraciousness, voracity.

votant [vɔtɑ̃] *a* voting, having a vote; *n* voter.

vote [vɔt] *nm* vote, voting, poll, passing; **bulletin de** — voting-paper; **droit de** — franchise.

voter [vɔte] *vt* to vote, pass, carry; *vi* to vote; — **à main levée** to vote by show of hands.

votre, vos [vɔtr, vo] *pos a* your.

vôtre [voːtr] *pos pn* le, la —, les —s yours; *nm* yours, your own; *pl* your own people *etc*; **vous avez encore fait des** —s you have been up to your tricks again.

vouer [vwe] *vt* to vow, devote, pledge, dedicate; **je ne sais à quel saint me** — I don't know what to do next.

vouloir [vulwaːr] *vt* to want, wish, like, will, be willing, consent, be determined, insist, intend, require, need, try; *vr* to try to be; *nm* will; **que voulez-vous?** what can you expect? what do you want? **il ne veut pas de nous** he won't have anything to do with us; **en** — **à** to bear (s.o.) a grudge, be angry with; **je veux bien** I don't mind; **sans le** — unintentionally.

voulu [vuly] *a* required, due, intentional, deliberate.

vous [vu] *pn* you, to you, (to) yourself, (to) each other, one another; ——**même(s)** yourself, yourselves.

voussoir [vuswaːr] *nm* arch-stone.

voussure [vusyːr] *nf* curve, arching.

voûte [vut] *nf* arch, vault, dome, canopy, roof.

voûter [vute] *vt* to arch, vault, bow; *vr* to become bent.

vouvoyer [vuvwaje] *vt* to address as 'vous'.

voyage [vwajaːʒ] *nm* journey, voyage, trip; *pl* travel; **compagnon de** — fellow-traveller, travelling companion; — **de noces** honeymoon.

voyager [vwajaʒe] *vi* to travel, journey, migrate.

voyageur, -euse [vwajaʒœːr, øːz] *a* travelling, migratory; *n* traveller, passenger, fare; **pigeon** — homing pigeon.

voyant [vwajɑ̃] *a* gaudy, conspicuous, loud, showy, clairvoyant; *n* seer, clairvoyant.

voyelle [vwajɛl] *nf* vowel.

voyer [vwaje] *nm* road surveyor.

voyou, -oute [vwaju, ut] *n* hooligan, guttersnipe.

vrac [vrak] *nm* **en** — in bulk, loose, wholesale, pell-mell.

vrai [vrɛ] *a* true, real, genuine, downright; *ad* really, truly; *nm* truth; **à** — **dire** as a matter of fact; **pour de** — in earnest; **il y a du** — there is something in it.

vraiment [vrɛmɑ̃] *ad* truly, really, indeed, is that so?

vraisemblable [vrɛsɑ̃blabl] *a* likely, probable; *nm* what is probable.

vraisemblance [vrɛsɑ̃blɑ̃ːs] *nf* likelihood, probability.

vrille [vriːj] *nf* tendril, gimlet, borer; **descente en** — spiral dive, spin.

vriller [vrije] *vt* to bore; *vi* to twist, corkscrew.

vrombir [vrɔ̃biːr] *vi* to throb, buzz, hum.

vrombissement [vrɔ̃bismɑ̃] *nm* throbbing, buzzing, drone, humming.

vu [vy] *a* seen; *prep* in view of, considering; *cj* — **que** seeing that, whereas; *nm* sight, presentation; **mal** — unpopular, disliked; **bien** — well thought of; **ni** — **ni connu** nobody is any the wiser for it; **au** — **de tous** openly; **au** — **et au su de tous** as everyone knows.

vue [vy] *nf* (eye)sight, view, prospect, purpose, intention, design, slide; **de** — by sight; **en** — **de** in sight of, with a view to; **perdre qn de** — to lose sight of s.o.

vulcaniser [vylkanize] *vt* to vulcanize.

vulcanite [vylkanit] *nf* ebonite, vulcanite.

vulgaire [vylgɛːr] *a* vulgar, common, coarse, low; *nm* common people, vulgarity.

vulgarisation [vylgarizasjɔ̃] *nf* popularization.

vulgariser [vylgarize] *vt* to popularize, vulgarize; *vr* to become popular, vulgar.

vulgarité [vylgarite] *nf* vulgarity.

vulnérabilité [vylnɛrabilite] *nf* vulnerability.

vulnérable [vylnɛrabl] *a* vulnerable.

W

wagon [vagɔ̃] *nm* carriage, coach, truck, waggon.

wagon-couloir [vagɔ̃kulwaːr] *nm* corridor-coach.

wagon-lit [vagɔ̃li] *nm* sleeping-car, sleeper.

wagon-poste [vagɔ̃pɔst] *nm* mailvan.

wagon-restaurant [vagɔ̃rɛstɔrɑ̃] *nm* dining-car.

watt [wat] *nm* watt.

wattman [watman] *nm* driver.

wolfram [vɔlfram] *nm* tungsten ore, wolfram.

X

xérès [kerɛs, gzerɛs] *nm* sherry.

xylographe [ksilɔgraf] *nm* woodengraver.

xylographie [ksilɔgrafi] *nf* woodengraving, wood-cut.

xylophone [ksilɔfɔn] *nm* xylophone.

Y

y [i] *ad* here, there; *pn* at, to, on, in, by, of it or them; **j'y suis** I've got it, I understand; **ça y est** that's it, there you are, right!; **il y a** there is, there are; **il n'y est pour rien** he had nothing to do with it.

yacht [jak(t), jat, jɔt] *nm* yacht.

yaourt [jaurt] *nm* yoghourt.

yeuse [jøːz] *nf* holm-oak.

yole [jɔl] *nf* yawl, skiff.

yougoslave [jugɔslaːv] *an* Yugoslav.

Yougoslavie [jugɔslavi] *nf* Yugoslavia.

youyou [juju] *nm* dinghy.

ypérite [iperit] *nf* mustard-gas.

Z

zazou [zazu] *nm* weirdie, crank.
zèbre [zɛbr] *nm* zebra.
zébré [zebre] *a* striped.
zélateur, -trice [zelatœːr, tris] *a* zealous; *n* zealot, enthusiast.
zèle [zɛːl] *nm* zeal, enthusiasm; **faire du —** to be over-eager, bustle about.
zélé [zele] *a* zealous.
zénith [zenit] *nm* zenith, height.
zéphyr [zefiːr] *nm* zephyr, light breeze.
zéro [zero] *nm* zero, cipher, nought.
zest [zɛst] *nm* **être entre le zist et le —** to be betwixt and between, be so-so.
zeste [zɛst] *nm* peel.
zézayement [zezɛmɑ̃] *nm* lisp(ing).
zézayer [zezɛje] *vi* to lisp.

zibeline [ziblin] *nf* sable.
zigouiller [ziguje] *vt* to kill, knife.
zigzag [zigzag] *nm* zigzag; **faire des —s** to zigzag, stagger along; **éclair en —** forked lightning.
zigzaguer [zigzage] *vi* to zigzag.
zinc [zɛ̃ːg] *nm* zinc, bar, counter.
zinguer [zɛ̃ge] *vt* to (cover with) zinc, galvanize.
zodiaque [zɔdjak] *nm* zodiac.
zona [zɔna] *nm* shingles.
zone [zoːn] *nf* zone, area, belt; **— neutre** no man's land.
zoologie [zɔɔlɔʒi] *nf* zoology.
zoologique [zɔɔlɔʒik] *a* zoological; **jardin —** zoological gardens, zoo.
zoologiste [zɔɔlɔʒist] *nm* zoologist.
zut [zyt] *excl* dash it! hang it all!
zyeuter [zjøte] *vt* to take a squint at.

English — French

A

a [ei, ə] *indef art* un, une.

aback [ə'bæk] *ad* en arrière, par derrière (surprise), abasourdi, interdit.

abandon [ə'bændən] *vt* abandonner, délaisser.

abandoned [ə'bændənd] *a* dissolu, abandonné.

abandonment [ə'bændənmənt] *n* abandon m, dévergondage m.

abase [ə'beis] *vt* abaisser, humilier.

abasement [ə'beismənt] *n* abaissement m, dégradation f.

abash [ə'bæʃ] *vt* déconcerter.

abashment [ə'bæʃmənt] *n* ébahissement m, confusion f.

abate [ə'beit] *vt* diminuer, rabattre; *vi* se calmer.

abatement [ə'beitmənt] *n* apaisement m, diminution f, rabais m.

abbess ['æbis] *n* abbesse f.

abbey ['æbi] *n* abbaye f.

abbot ['æbət] *n* abbé m.

abbreviate [ə'bri:vieit] *vt* abréger.

abbreviation [ə,bri:vi'eiʃən] *n* abréviation f.

abdicate ['æbdikeit] *vti* abdiquer.

abdication [,æbdi'keiʃən] *n* abdication f.

abduct [æb'dʌkt] *vt* enlever.

abduction [æb'dʌkʃən] *n* enlèvement m, rapt m.

abed [ə'bed] *ad* au lit.

aberration [æbə'reiʃən] *n* aberration f, égarement m.

abet [ə'bet] *vt* encourager, assister.

abetment [ə'betmənt] *n* instigation f.

abettor [ə'betə] *n* fauteur, -trice, complice mf.

abeyance [ə'beiəns] *n* suspens m, souffrance f, sommeil m, carence f, vacance f.

abhor [əb'hɔ:] *vt* abhorrer.

abhorrence [əb'hɔrəns] *n* horreur f.

abhorrent [əb'hɔrənt] *a* odieux.

abide [ə'baid] *vt* attendre, souffrir; *vi* rester fidèle (à **by**), demeurer.

abiding [ə'baidiŋ] *a* permanent.

ability [ə'biliti] *n* capacité f, talent m, moyens m pl; **to the best of my — de mon mieux**.

abject ['æbdʒekt] *a* abject.

abjection [æb'dʒekʃən] *n* abjection f.

abjuration [,æbdʒuə'reiʃən] *n* abjuration f.

abjure ['əb'dʒuə] *vt* abjurer, renoncer à.

ablaze [ə'bleiz] *a ad* enflammé, en feu.

able ['eibl] *a* capable, en état (de to); **—bodied** *a* valide.

ablution [ə'blu:ʃən] *n* ablution f.

abnegation [,æbni'geiʃən] *n* abnégation f, renoncement m, r¹pudiation f.

abnormal [æb'nɔ:məl] *a* anormal.

aboard [ə'bɔ:d] *ad* à bord; *prep* à bord de.

abode [ə'boud] *n* demeure f.

abolish [ə'bɔliʃ] *vt* abolir.

abolition [,æbə'liʃən] *n* abolition f.

abominable [ə'bɔminəbl] *a* abominable.

abominate [ə'bɔmineit] *vt* avoir en abomination.

abortion [ə'bɔ:ʃən] *n* avortement m, avorton m.

abound [ə'baund] *vi* abonder, foisonner.

about [ə'baut] *ad* à peu près, environ, çà et là; *prep* autour de, près de, sur le point de, au sujet de.

above [ə'bʌv] *prep* au dessus de, en amont de; *ad* plus que (de), ci-dessus, en amont, au-dessus.

above-board [ə'bʌv'bɔ:d] *ad* net, loyal; *ad* loyalement.

above-named [ə'bʌv'neimd] *a* susnommé.

abrasion [ə'breiʒən] *n* écorchure f.

abreast [ə'brest] *ad* de front.

abridge [ə'bridʒ] *vt* abréger, restreindre.

abridgement [ə'bridʒmənt] *n* raccourcissement m, abrégé m.

abroad [ə'brɔ:d] *ad* à l'étranger, au large, dehors.

abrogate ['æbrougeit] *vt* abroger.

abrogation [,æbrou'geiʃən] *n* abrogation f.

abrupt [ə'brʌpt] *a* brusque.

abruptness [ə'brʌptnis] *n* brusquerie f, escarpement m.

abscess ['æbsis] *n* abcès m.

abscond [əb'skɔnd] *vi* s'esquiver, décamper.

absence ['æbsəns] *n* absence f.

absent [æb'sent] *vi* **to — oneself** s'absenter.

absent ['æbsənt] *a* absent.

absently ['æbsəntli] *ad* d'un air absent, distraitement.

absolute ['æbsəlu:t] *an* absolu m.

absolutely ['æbsəlu:tli] *ad* absolument.

absolution [,æbsə'lu:ʃən] *n* absolution f, acquittement m.

absolutism ['æbsəluːtizəm] *n* absolutisme *m*.

absolutist ['æbsəluːtist] *n* absolutiste *mf*.

absolve [əb'zɔlv] *vt* absoudre, dispenser.

absorb [əb'zɔːb] *vt* absorber.

absorption [əb'zɔːpʃən] *n* absorption *f*.

abstain [əb'stein] *vi* s'abstenir.

abstemious [æb'stiːmjəs] *a* sobre, abstinent.

abstention [æb'stenʃən] *n* abstention *f*.

abstinence ['æbstinəns] *n* abstinence *f*.

abstinent ['æbstinənt] *a* abstinent.

abstract ['æbstrækt] *n* précis *m*, extrait *m*; *a* abstrait.

abstract [æb'strækt] *vt* faire abstraction de, soustraire, distraire, résumer.

abstracted [æb'stræktid] *a* distrait.

abstraction [æb'strækʃən] *n* abstraction *f*.

absurd [əb'səːd] *a* absurde.

absurdity [əb'səːditi] *n* absurdité *f*.

abundance [ə'bʌndəns] *n* abondance *f*.

abundant [ə'bʌndənt] *a* abondant

abundantly [ə'bʌndəntli] *ad* abondamment.

abuse [ə'bjuːs] *n* abus *m*, insulte *f*.

abuse [ə'bjuːz] *vt* abuser de, mésuser de, insulter, injurier.

abusive [ə'bjuːsiv] *a* abusif, outrageant, injurieux.

abut [ə'bʌt] *vi* se toucher.

abyss [ə'bis] *n* abîme *m*.

academy [ə'kædəmi] *n* académie *f*, institution *f*, école *f*.

accede [æk'siːd] *vi* arriver (à to), adhérer (à to).

accelerate [æk'seləreit] *vti* accélérer, activer.

acceleration [æk‚selə'reiʃən] *n* accélération *f*.

accelerator [ək'seləreitə] *n* accélérateur *m*.

accent ['æksənt] *n* accent *m*.

accent [æk'sent] *vt* accentuer.

accentuate [æk'sentjueit] *vt* faire ressortir, souligner, accentuer.

accentuation [æk‚sentju'eiʃən] *n* accentuation *f*.

accept [ək'sept] *vt* accepter, agréer, admettre.

acceptance [ək'septəns] *n* bienvenue *f* acceptation *f*.

access ['ækses] *n* accès *m*, abord *m*.

accessible [æk'sesəbl] *a* accessible.

accessory [æk'sesəri] *n* complice *mf*; *an* accessoire *m*.

accident ['æksidənt] *n* accident *m*, avarie *f*; —**prone** sujet aux accidents.

accidental [‚æksi'dentl] *a* accidentel, fortuit.

accidentally [‚æksi'dentəli] *ad* par accident.

acclaim [ə'kleim] *vt* acclamer.

acclamation [‚æklə'meiʃən] *n* acclamation *f*.

acclimatization [ə'klaimətai'zeiʃən] *n* acclimatation *f*.

acclimatize [ə'klaimətaiz] *vt* acclimater.

acclivity [ə'kliviti] *n* montée *f*, rampe *f*.

accommodate [ə'kɔmədeit] *vt* adapter, arranger, fournir, obliger, loger.

accommodating [ə'kɔmədeitiŋ] *a* accommodant, serviable, complaisant.

accommodation [ə‚kɔmə'deiʃən] *n* adaptation *f*, accommodement *m*, commodités *f pl*, logement *m*, prêt *m*.

accompaniment [ə'kʌmpənimənt] *n* accompagnement *m*.

accompanist [ə'kʌmpənist] *n* accompagnateur, -trice.

accompany [ə'kʌmpəni] *vt* accompagner.

accomplice [ə'kɔmplis] *n* complice *mf*.

accomplish [ə'kʌmpliʃ] *vt* accomplir, parachever, faire.

accomplishment [ə'kʌmpliʃmənt] *n* accomplissement *m*, exécution *f*; *pl* talents *m*, grâces *f pl*.

accord [ə'kɔːd] *n* accord *m*, assentiment *m*; **with one** — d'une seule voix; **of one's own** — de son propre mouvement; *vt* accorder; *vi* s'accorder.

accordance [ə'kɔːdəns] *n* conformité *f*, accord *m*.

according [ə'kɔːdiŋ] *ad* — **to** *prep* selon; — **as** *cj* selon que.

accordingly [ə'kɔːdiŋli] *ad* en conséquence.

accost [ə'kɔst] *vt* accoster, aborder.

account [ə'kaunt] *n* compte *m*, importance *f*, compte-rendu *m*; *vt* regarder (comme); **to** — **for** rendre compte de, répondre de, expliquer; — **rendered** rappel; **on one's own** — à ses risques et périls, de sa propre initiative; **on** — **of** en raison (vue) de; **on no** — à aucun prix.

accountable [ə'kauntəbl] *a* responsable, explicable.

accountancy [ə'kauntənsi] *n* tenue *f* des livres, comptabilité *f*.

accountant [ə'kauntənt] *n* comptable *m*.

accoutrement [ə'kuːtrəmənt] *n* équipement *m*, fourniment *m*, caparaçon *m*.

accredit [ə'kredit] *vt* (ac)créditer.

accrue [ə'kruː] *vi* résulter, s'ajouter (à to), s'accumuler.

accumulate [ə'kjuːmjuleit] *vt* accumuler; *vi* s'accumuler.

accumulation [ə‚kjuːmju'leiʃən] *n* accumulation *f*, amas *m*.

accumulative [ə'kjuːmjulətiv] *a* cumulatif.

accumulator [ə'kju:mjuleitə] *n* (*motor etc*) accu(mulateur) *m*, accumulateur, -trice.

accuracy ['ækjurəsi] *n* exactitude *f*, précision *f*.

accurate ['ækjurit] *a* exact, correct, précis.

accursed [ə'kə:sid] *a* maudit.

accusation [.ækju(:)'zeiʃən] *n* accusation *f*.

accuse [ə'kju:z] *vt* accuser.

accuser [ə'kju:zə] *n* accusateur, -trice.

accustom [ə'kʌstəm] *vt* habituer; **to — oneself** se faire (à), s'habituer.

ace [eis] *n* un *m*, as *m*; **within an — of** à deux doigts de.

acerbity [ə'sə:biti] *n* acerbité *f*.

ache [eik] *n* mal *m*; *vi* avoir mal, souffrir, faire mal.

achieve [ə'tʃi:v] *vt* exécuter, acquérir, atteindre.

achievement [ə'tʃi:vmənt] *n* exécution *f*, succès *m*.

aching ['eikiŋ] *a* douloureux.

acid ['æsid] *a*. acide *m*.

acidity [ə'siditi] *n* acidité *f*.

acidulous [ə'sidjul s] *a* acidulé.

acknowledge [ək'nɔlidʒ] *vt* reconnaître, accuser réception de, répondre à.

acknowledgment [ək'nɔlədʒmənt] *n* reconnaissance *f*, accusé *m* de réception.

acme ['ækmi] *n* apogée *m*.

acne [ækni] *n* acné *f*.

acorn ['eikɔ:n] *n* gland *m*.

acquaint [ə'kweint] *vt* informer; **to — oneself with** se familiariser avec, faire connaissance avec, prendre connaissance de.

acquainted [ə'kweintid] *a* en relation (avec), versé (dans).

acquaintance [ə'kweintəns] *n* connaissance *f*.

acquiesce [.ækwi'es] *vi* acquiescer.

acquiescence [.ækwi'esns] *n* assentiment *m*.

acquire [ə'kwaiə] *vt* acquérir, prendre.

acquirement [ə'kwaiəmənt] *n* acquisition *f*; *pl* talents *m pl*.

acquisition [.ækwi'ziʃən] *n* acquisition *f*.

acquit [ə'kwit] *vti* acquitter, s'acquitter (de).

acquittal [ə'kwitl] *n* quittance *f*, acquittement *m*, accomplissement *m*.

acquittance [ə'kwitəns] *n* paiement *m*, décharge *f*, reçu *m*.

acre ['eikə] *n* acre *f*.

acrid ['ækrid] *a* âcre, acerbe.

acridity [æ'kriditi] *n* âcreté *f*.

acrimonious [.ækri'mounjəs] *a* acrimonieux.

acrimony ['ækriməni] *n* acrimonie *f*.

acrobat ['ækrəbæt] *n* acrobate *mf*.

acrobatics [.ækrə'bætiks] *n* acrobatie *f*.

across [ə'krɔs] *prep* à travers; *ad* en travers, en croix.

act [ækt] *n* acte *m*; *vti* jouer; *vt* représenter; *vi* agir, servir.

acting ['æktiŋ] *n* action *f*, représentation *f*, jeu *m*; *a* qui joue, qui fait semblant, en exercice, suppléant, par intérim.

action ['ækʃən] *n* action *f*.

actionable ['ækʃnəbl] *a* sujet à poursuites.

activate ['æktiveit] *vt* activer, organiser.

active ['æktiv] *a* actif, ingambe.

actively ['æktivli] *ad* **to be — involved in** prendre une part active à.

activity [æk'tiviti] *n* activité *f*, animation *f*.

actor ['æktə] *n* acteur *m*.

actress ['æktris] *n* actrice *f*.

actual ['æktjuəl] *a* réel, de fait, actual.

actuality [.æktju'æliti] *n* réalité *f*.

actually ['æktjuəli] *ad* en fait, présentement.

actuate ['æktjueit] *vt* actionner mettre en marche, motiver, pousser.

acumen [ə'kju:men] *n* sagacité *f*, perspicacité *f*.

acute [ə'kju:t] *a* aigu, -uë.

acuteness [ə'kju:tnis] *n* acuité *f*, vivacité *f*.

adage ['ædidʒ] *n* adage *m*.

adamant ['ædəmənt] *a* inflexible, intransigeant.

adapt [ə'dæpt] *vt* adapter.

adaptability [ə.dæptə'biliti] *n* faculté *f* d'adaptation, souplesse *f*.

adaptable [ə'dæptəbl] *a* adaptable, souple.

adaptation [.ædæp'teiʃən] *n* adaptation *f*.

A.D.C. ['ei'di:'si:] *n* aide de camp *m*.

add [æd] *vt* ajouter, additionner.

adder ['ædə] *n* vipère *f*.

addict ['ædikt] *n* personne adonnée à, -mane *mf*, morphinomane *mf etc*.

addicted [ə'diktid] *a* adonné (à to); **to be — to** s'adonner à.

addiction [ə'dikʃən] *n* besoin *m*, habitude *f*, goût *m*.

addition [ə'diʃən] *n* addition *f*; **in — par** surcroît.

additional [ə'diʃənl] *a* additionnel, supplémentaire.

addle ['ædl] *a* pourri, couvi; confus; *vt* brouiller, pourrir.

address [ə'dres] *n* adresse *f*, tenue *f*, allocution *f*; *pl* avances *f pl*, cour *f*; *vt* s'adresser à, adresser.

addressee [.ædre'si:] *n* destinataire *mf*.

adduce [ə'dju:s] *vt* alléguer.

adept ['ædept] *a* expert (en at); *n* passé maître m.

adequate ['ædikwit] *a* adéquat, suffisant.

adhere [əd'hiə] *vi* adhérer, se coller maintenir (to à).

adherence [əd'hiərəns] *n* adhérence *f*, adhésion *f*.

adherent [əd'hiərənt] *an* adhérent(e) *mf*.

adhesion [əd'hiːʒən] *n* adhésion *f*.

adhesive [əd'hiːsiv] *a* collant.

adjacent [ə'dʒeisənt] *a* adjacent, attenant.

adjective ['ædʒiktiv] *n* adjectif *m*.

adjoin [ə'dʒɔin] *vt* joindre, attenir à; *vi* se toucher.

adjoining [ə'dʒɔiniŋ] *a* contigu, -uë, attenant.

adjourn [ə'dʒəːn] *vt* ajourner, remettre.

adjournment [ə'dʒəːnmənt] *n* ajournement *m*.

adjudge [ə'dʒʌdʒ] *vt* décider, condamner, adjuger.

adjudicate [ə'dʒuːdikeit] *vti* juger.

adjudication [ə,dʒuːdi'keiʃən] *n* jugement *m*.

adjudicator [ə'dʒuːdikeitə] *n* juge *m*.

adjunct ['ædʒʌŋkt] *n* accessoire *m*, auxiliaire *mf*.

adjuration [,ædʒuə'reiʃən] *n* adjuration *f*.

adjure [ə'dʒuə] *vt* adjurer, conjurer.

adjust [ə'dʒʌst] *vt* ajuster, régler.

adjustment [ə'dʒʌstmənt] *n* ajustement *m*, réglage *m*.

ad-lib [æd'lib] *vi* improviser.

administer [əd'ministə] *vt* administrer, (*oath*) déférer, gérer.

administration [əd,minis'treiʃən] *n* administration *f*, gérance *f*.

administrative [əd'ministrətiv] *a* administratif.

administrator [əd'ministreitə] *n* administrateur *m*, gérant *m*.

admirable ['ædmərəbl] *a* admirable.

admiral ['ædmərəl] *n* amiral *m*; **rear—** contre-amiral *m*; **vice—** vice-amiral *m*.

admiralty ['ædmərəlti] *n* Amirauté *f*; **First Lord of the A—** Ministre de la Marine.

admiration [,ædmə'reiʃən] *n* admiration *f*.

admire [əd'maiə] *vt* admirer.

admirer [əd'maiərə] *n* admirateur, -trice.

admiring [əd'maiəriŋ] *a* admiratif.

admiringly [əd'maiəriŋli] *ad* avec admiration.

admissible [əd'misəbl] *a* admissible.

admission [əd'miʃən] *n* confession *f*, admission *f*, aveu *m*, entrée *f*.

admit [əd'mit] *vt* admettre, avouer, laisser entrer; **to — of** permettre, comporter.

admittance [əd'mitəns] *n* entrée *f*, accès *m*.

admittedly [əd'mitidli] *ad* sans conteste.

admonish [əd'mɔniʃ] *vt* admonester, avertir, exhorter.

admonishment [əd'mɔniʃmənt] *n* admonestation *f*, exhortation *f*, avertissement *m*.

ado [ə'duː] *n* affaire *f*, embarras *m*, bruit *m*.

adolescence [,ædə'lesns] *n* adolescence *f*.

adolescent [,ædə'lesnt] *a* adolescent.

adopt [ə'dɔpt] *vt* adopter, suivre, embrasser.

adoption [ə'dɔpʃən] *n* adoption *f*, choix *m*.

adoptive [ə'dɔptiv] *a* adoptif.

adorable [ə'dɔːrəbl] *a* adorable.

adoration [,ædɔː'reiʃən] *n* adoration *f*.

adore [ə'dɔː] *vt* adorer.

adorer [ə'dɔːrə] *n* adorateur, -trice.

adorn [ə'dɔːn] *vt* orner.

adornment [ə'dɔːnmənt] *n* ornement *m*, parure *f*.

adrift [ə'drift] *ad* à la dérive.

adroit [ə'drɔit] *a* adroit.

adroitness [ə'drɔitnis] *n* adresse *f*.

adulation [,ædju'leiʃən] *n* adulation *f*.

adult ['ædʌlt] *an* adulte *mf*.

adulterate [ə'dʌltəreit] *vt* frelater, falsifier.

adulteration [ə,dʌltə'reiʃən] *n* falsification *f*.

adulterer, -ess [ə'dʌltərə, is] *n* homme, femme adultère.

adulterine [ə'dʌltərain] *a* adultérin.

adultery [ə'dʌltəri] *n* adultère *m*.

adumbrate ['ædʌmbreit] *vt* esquisser, ébaucher.

advance [əd'vɑːns] *n* avance *f*, hausse *f*, progrès *m*; *vti* avancer, pousser; *vi* faire des progrès, hausser.

advancement [əd'vɑːnsmənt] *n* avancement *m*, progrès *m*.

advantage [əd'vɑːntidʒ] *n* avantage *m*, dessus *m*; **to take — of** profiter de; *vt* avantager.

advantageous [,ædvən'teidʒəs] *a* avantageux.

advent ['ædvənt] *n* Avent *m*, arrivée *f*, venue *f*.

adventure [əd'ventʃə] *n* aventure *f*, hasard *m*; *vt* risquer; *vi* s'aventurer (à, dans **upon**).

adventurer, -ess [əd'ventʃərə, is] *a* aventurier, -ière, chevalier d'industrie *m*.

adventurous [əd'ventʃərəs] *a* aventureux.

adverb ['ædvəːb] *n* adverbe *m*.

adversary ['ædvəsəri] *n* adversaire *mf*.

adverse ['ædvəːs] *a* adverse, hostile, contraire.

adversity [əd'vəːsiti] *n* adversité *f*.

advert [æd'vəːt] *vi* faire allusion (à **to**).

advertise ['ædvətaiz] *vt* annoncer, faire valoir, faire de la réclame pour; *vi* faire de la publicité.

advertisement [əd'vəːtismənt] *n* publicité *f*, réclame *f*, affiche *f*, annonce *f*.

advertising ['ædvətaiziŋ] n publicité f.

advice [əd'vais] n avis m, conseil(s) m (pl).

advisable [əd'vaizəbl] a recommendable, sage.

advisability [əd,vaizə'biliti] n convenance f, sagesse f.

advise [əd'vaiz] vt conseiller.

advised [əd'vaizd] a (bien, mal) avisé.

advisedly [əd'vaizidli] ad sagement, en connaissance de cause.

adviser [əd'vaizə] n conseiller, -ère.

advisory [əd'vaizəri] a consultatif.

advocacy ['ædvəkəsi] n plaidoyer (en faveur de) m.

advocate ['ædvəkit] n avocat m.

advocate ['ædvəkeit] vt defendre, préconiser.

aerate ['eiəreit] vt aérer.

aerated ['eiəreitid] a gazeux.

aeration [,eiə'reiʃən] n aération f.

aerial ['eəriəl] n antenne f; a aérien, de l'air.

aerobatics [,eərə'bætiks] n acrobatie aérienne f.

aerodrome ['eərədroum] n aérodrome m.

aeronaut ['eərənɔ:t] n aéronaute m.

aeronautics [,eərə'nɔ:tiks] n aéronautique f.

aeroplane ['eərəplein] n avion m.

aesthete ['i:sθi:t] n esthète mf.

aesthetics [i:s'θetiks] n esthétique f.

afar [ə'fɑ:] ad de loin, au loin.

affability [,æfə'biliti] n affabilité f.

affable ['æfəbl] a affable.

affair [ə'fɛə] n affaire f.

affect [ə'fekt] vt affecter, poser à, attaquer, toucher.

affectation [,æfek'teiʃən] n affectation f, simagrées f pl.

affection [ə'fekʃən] n affection f, disposition f.

affectionate [ə'fekʃnit] a affectueux.

affianced [ə'faiənst] a fiancé.

affidavit [,æfi'deivit] n déclaration assermentée f.

affiliate [ə'filieit] vt (s')affilier.

affiliation [ə,fili'eiʃən] n attribution de paternité f, affiliation f.

affinity [ə'finiti] n affinité f.

affirm [ə'fə:m] vt affirmer.

affirmation [,æfə'meiʃən] n affirmation f.

affirmative [ə'fə:mətiv] n affirmative f; a affirmatif.

affix [ə'fiks] vt apposer.

afflict [ə'flikt] vt affliger.

affliction [ə'flikʃən] n affliction f.

afflictive [ə'fliktiv] a affligeant.

affluence ['æfluəns] n affluence f, richesse f.

affluent ['æfluənt] a riche.

afford [ə'fɔ:d] vt s'offrir, se permettre, fournir.

affray [ə'frei] n bagarre f, rixe f.

affright [ə'frait] n effroi m; vt effrayer.

affront [ə'frʌnt] n affront m; vt offenser, faire honte à.

afloat [ə'flout] ad à flot; to get — lancer; to get — again renflouer.

afoot [ə'fut] ad à (sur) pied.

aforesaid [ə'fɔ:sed] a susdit.

aforethought [ə'fɔ:θɔ:t] a with malice — avec préméditation.

afraid [ə'freid] a effrayé; to be — avoir peur.

Africa ['æfrikə] n Afrique f.

African ['æfrikən] a africain.

aft [ɑ:ft] ad à l'arrière.

after ['ɑ:ftə] prep (d')après, selon; ad ensuite; cj après que, quand.

aftermath ['ɑ:ftəmæθ] n regain m, suites f pl.

afternoon ['ɑ:ftə'nu:n] n après-midi m or f inv.

afterthought ['ɑ:ftəθɔ:t] n réflexion f après coup, second mouvement m.

afterwards ['ɑ:ftəwədz] ad ensuite, plus tard.

again [ə'gen] ad encore, de plus, de nouveau; re-; — and — à maintes reprises; now and — de temps à autre; as much — as deux fois autant (plus, aussi).

against [ə'genst] prep contre, sur, à, en vue de.

agape [ə'geip] ad grand ouvert, bouche bée.

age [eidʒ] n âge m, génération f; of — majeur; under — mineur; pl siècles m pl; vti vieillir.

aged ['eidʒid] a âgé, vieux.

agency ['eidʒənsi] n opération f, entremise f, agence f, bureau m.

agenda [ə'dʒendə] n ordre m du jour, agenda m.

agent ['eidʒənt] n agent m, cause f, représentant m.

agglomerate [ə'glɔməreit] n agglomérat m; vt agglomérer.

agglomeration [ə,glɔmə'reiʃən] n agglomération f.

aggravate ['ægrəveit] vt aggraver, exaspérer.

aggravation [,ægrə'veiʃən] n aggravation f, exaspération f, envenimement m.

aggregate ['ægrigit] n agrégat m, ensemble m, total m.

aggregate ['ægrigeit] vt aggréger; vi se monter à.

aggression [ə'greʃən] n aggression f.

aggressive [ə'gresiv] a agressif.

aggressor [ə'gresə] n agresseur m.

aggrieved [ə'gri:vd] a affligé, blessé.

aghast [ə'gɑ:st] a terrifié, stupéfait, interdit.

agile ['ædʒail] a agile.

agility [ə'dʒiliti] n agilité f.

agitate ['ædʒiteit] vt agiter, débattre; vi faire de l'agitation.

agitator ['ædʒiteitə] n agitateur m, meneur m.

aglow [ə'glou] a luisant, rayonnant, embrasé.

ago [ə'gou] ad il y a.

agog [ə'gɔg] *a* ardent, en émoi, impatient.

agonize ['ægənaiz] *vt* torturer.

agony ['ægəni] *n* agonie *f*, angoisse *f*, supplice *m*.

agree [ə'gri:] *vi* consentir (à to), être d'accord, convenir (de to), acce·ter.

agreeable [ə'griəbl] *a* agréable, disposé, qui consent, qui convient, d'accord.

agreed [ə'gri:d] *a* d'accord.

agreement [ə'gri:mənt] *n* accord *m*, convention *f*.

agricultural [ˌægri'kʌltʃərəl] *a* agricole.

agriculture ['ægrikʌltʃə] *n* agriculture *f*.

aground [ə'graund] *ad* à la côte, échoué, par le fond.

ague ['eigju:] *n* fièvre paludéenne *f*.

ahead ['hed] *ad* en tête, l'avant, de l'avant, en avant.

aid [eid] *n* aide *mf*, assistance *f*; *vt* aider, contribuer à.

ail [eil] *vt* tracasser; *vi* avoir mal, souffrir.

ailment ['eilmənt] *n* indisposition *f*.

aim [eim] *n* but *m*, visée *f*; *vt* viser, pointer; **to — at** viser.

aimless ['eimlis] *a* sans but.

aimlessly ['eimlisli] *ad* au hasard, sans but.

air [ɛə] *n* air *m*; *vt* aérer, sécher, étaler, mettre à l'évent; *vi* prendre l'air.

air- (**cushion** *etc*) gonflé d'air.

airborne [ˌ'ɛəbɔ:n] *a* aéroport·.

air-brake ['ɛəbreik] *n* frein *m* pneumatique.

aircraft ['ɛəkrɑ:ft] *n* avion; — **carrier** *n* porte-avions *m*; —**man** *n* mécanicien *m*.

air-cushion ['ɛəˌkuʃin] *m* coussin à air *m*.

Air Force [ˌ'ɛəfɔ:s] *m* Armée de l'Air *f*.

airhole ['ɛəhou] *n* soupirail *m*.

air-hostess ['ɛə'houstis] *n* hôtesse de l'air.

airily [ˌ'ɛərili] *ad* d'un air dégagé.

airing ['ɛəriˌ] *n* aération *f*, éventage *m*, tour *m*.

airless ['ɛəlis] *a* sans air, renfermé, étouffant.

airliner ['ɛəlainə] *n* avion de ligne *m*.

airmail ['ɛəmeil] *n* courrier *m* aérien; **by —** par avion.

airman ['ɛəmən] *n* aviateur *m*.

airplane ['ɛə plein] *n* avion *m*.

air-pump ['ɛə'pʌmp] *n* pompe *f* pneumatique.

air-raid [ˌ'ɛə reid] *n* raid aérien *m*.

airship ['ɛəʃip] *n* aérostat *m*, (ballon) dirigeable *m*.

airtight ['ɛətait] *a* étanche, hermétique.

airworthy [ˌ'ɛə wə:ði] *a* qui tient l'air, bon pour voler, navigable.

airy ['ɛəri] *a* aéré, aérien, gracieux, désinvolte.

aisle [ail] *n* bas-côté *m*.

ajar [ə'dʒɑ:] *ad* entr'ouvert.

akimbo [ə'kimbou] *ad* les poings sur les hanches.

akin [ə'kin] *a* parent (de to), analogue, qui tient (de to).

alacrity [ə'lækriti] *n* vivacité *f*, empressement *m*.

Alan ['ælən] Alain *m*.

alarm [ə'lɑ:m] *n* alarme *f*, alerte *f*; *vt* alarmer, alerter.

alarm-bell [ə'lɑ:mbel] *n* cloche, sonnette d'alarme *f*, tocsin *m*.

alarm-clock [ə'lɑ:mklɔk] *n* réveille-matin *m*.

alarmist [ə'lɑ:mist] *n* alarmiste *mf*.

alas [ə'læs] *excl* hélas!

albeit [ɔ:l'bi:it] *cj* bien que, quoique.

album ['ælbəm] *n* album *m*.

alchemy ['ælkimi] *n* alchimie *f*.

alcohol ['ælkəhɔl] *n* alcool *m*.

alcoholic [ˌælkə'hɔlik] *an* alcoolique.

alcoholism ['ælkəhɔlizəm] *n* alcoolisme *m*.

alcove [ˌ'ælkouv] *n* niche *f*, retrait *m*, renfoncement *m*.

alder [ˌ'ɔ:ldə] *n* aune *m*.

alderman ['ɔ:ldəmən] *n* adjoint au maire *m*.

ale [eil] *n* bière *f*.

ale-house [ˌ'eilhaus] *n* brasserie *f*, cabaret *m*.

alert [ə'lə:t] *n* alerte *f*, qui-vive *m*; *a* v·gilant, alerte, vif.

alertness [ə'lə:tnis] *n* vigilance *f*, promptitude *f*, vivacité *f*.

algebra [ˌ'ældʒibrə] *n* algèbre *f*

alias ['eiljəs] *n* autre nom *m*, faux nom *m*; *ad* autrement dit, connu sous le nom de.

alibi ['ælibai] *n* alibi *m*.

alien ['eiljən] *n* étranger, -ère; *a* étranger, différent, répugnant (à to).

alienate ['eiljəneit] *vt* (s')aliéner, détourner.

alienation [ˌeiljə'neiʃən] *n* aliénation *f*.

alight [ə'lait] *a* allumé, éclairé, en feu; *vi* descendre, atterrir, se poser.

align [ə'lain] *v* aligner.

alignment [ə'lainmənt] *n* alignement *m*.

alike [ə'laik] *a* pareil, ressemblant; *ad* de même, de la même manière.

alimony ['æliməni] *n* pension alimen·aire *f*.

alive [ə'laiv] *a* en vie, vif, éveillé, grouillant; **to be — and kicking** être plein de vie; **to keep —** entretenir, soutenir.

all [ɔ:l] *n* tous *m pl*, tout *m*, tout le monde *m*; *a* tout, tous, toute(s); *ad* tout, entièrement; **— but** à peu près, autant dire; **I — but fell** j'ai failli tomber; **— clear** fin d'alerte *f*; **All Fools' Day** le premier avril; **All Hallows' Day** (le jour de) la Toussaint; **— in** tout compris, à tout prendre; **— of you** vous tous; **— one** tout un; **— out** total, complètement, à plein rendement, à toute vitesse; — **powerful** tout-puissant; — **right** très bien, ça va bien, entendu, soit!; **All Saints' Day** (le jour de) la Toussaint; **All Souls' Day** le jour des Morts *m*; **at** — du tout; **one and** — tous sans exception; **to stake one's** — jouer son va-tout.

allay [ə'lei] *vt* soulager, apaiser.

allegation [ˌæle'geiʃən] *n* allégation *f*.

allege [ə'ledʒ] *vt* alléguer.

allegiance [ə'liːdʒəns] *n* hommage *m*, foi *f*, fidélité *f*.

allegory ['æligəri] *n* allégorie *f*.

alleviate [ə'liːvieit] *vt* alléger, adoucir.

alleviation [ə.liːvi'eiʃən] *n* soulagement *m*, allègement *m*.

alley ['æli] *n* allée *f*, ruelle *f*; **blind** — impasse *f*, cul de sac *m*.

alliance [ə'laiəns] *n* alliance *f*.

allied ['ælaid] *a* allié, connexe.

allocate ['æləkeit] *vt* allouer, assigner, distribuer.

allocation [ˌælə'keiʃən] *n* allocation *f*, attribution *f*.

allot [ə'lɔt] *vt* lotir, assigner, répartir, destiner, attribuer.

allotment [ə'lɔtmənt] *n* attribution *f*, répartition *f*, lot *m*, lopin *m*, lotissement *m*.

allow [ə'lau] *vt* laisser, permettre, admettre, allouer; **to — for** tenir compte de, compter, faire la part de, prévoir.

allowance [ə'lauəns] *n* permission *f*, pension *f*, remise *f*, concession *f*, indemnité *f*, ration *f*; **to make — for** tenir compte de, faire la part de, se montrer indulgent pour.

alloy ['ælɔi] *n* titre *m*, aloi *m*, alliage *m*; *vt* allier, dévaloriser, modérer.

allude [ə'luːd] *vi* faire allusion (à to).

allure [ə'ljuə] *vt* tenter, attirer, aguicher, séduire.

allurement [ə'ljuəmənt] *n* attrait *m*, charme *m*.

alluring [ə'ljuəriŋ] *a* séduisant, attrayant.

allusion [ə'luːʒən] *n* allusion *f*.

ally ['ælai] *n* allié.

ally [ə'lai] *vt* allier, unir; *vi* s'allier.

almanac ['ɔːlmənæk] *n* almanach *m*, annuaire *m*.

almighty [ɔːl'maiti] *an* tout-puissant *m*; *a* (*fam*) formidable.

almond ['aːmənd] *n* amande *f*; **burnt** — praline *f*; **sugared** — dragée *f*; — **tree** *n* amandier *m*.

almoner ['aːmənə] *a* aumônier *m*.

almost ['ɔːlmoust] *ad* presque, à peu près; **he** — **fell** il faillit tomber.

alms [aːmz] *n* aumône *f*; —**house** *n* hospice *m*, asile *m*.

aloft [ə'lɔft] *ad* (en) haut, en l'air.

alone [ə'loun] *a* seul, tranquille; **to let, leave s.o., sth** — laisser tranquille, laisser en paix; **leave me** —

laissez-moi, fichez-moi la paix; **let** — encore moins, loin de, sans compter, sans parler de.

along [ə'lɔŋ] *prep* le long de; *ad* tout au (du) long; **all** — tout le temps; **all — the line** sur toute la ligne.

alongside [ə'lɔŋ'said] *prep* le long de, au bord de, à côté de; *ad* côte à côte; **to come** — accoster, aborder.

aloof [ə'luːf] *a* distant; *ad* à l'écart.

aloofness [ə'luːfnis] *n* réserve *f*, quant à soi *m*.

aloud [ə'laud] *ad* à haute voix, tout haut.

alphabet ['ælfəbit] *n* alphabet *m*.

alphabetical [ˌælfə'betikəl] *a* alphabétique.

already [ɔːl'redi] *ad* déjà.

also ['ɔːlsou] *ad* aussi, en outre.

altar ['ɔːltə] *n* autel *m*.

alter ['ɔːltə] *vt* altérer, changer (de), remanier, transformer, déplacer; **to — for the better** s'améliorer; **to — for the worse** s'altérer.

alteration [ˌɔːltə'reiʃən] *n* retouche *f*, changement *m*, modification *f*.

altercation [ˌɔːltə'keiʃən] *n* altercation *f*, dispute *f*.

alternate [ɔːl'təːnit] *a* alterne, alternatif; **on — days** tous les deux jours.

alternate ['ɔːltəneit] *vt* faire alterner; *vi* alterner.

alternately [ɔːl'təːnitli] *ad* alternativement, tour à tour.

alternation [ˌɔːltə'neiʃən] *n* alternance *f*, alternative *f*.

alternative [ɔːl'təːnətiv] *n* alternative *f*, choix *m*.

although [ɔːl'ðou] *cj* bien que, quoique.

altitude ['æltitjuːd] *n* altitude *f*, hauteur *f*, profondeur *f*.

altogether [ˌɔːltə'geðə] *ad* tout compte fait, en tout, entièrement, absolument.

aluminium [ˌæljuˈminjəm] *n* aluminium *m*.

alumnus [ə'lʌmnəs] *n* (*US*) élève *mf*, pensionnaire *mf*.

always ['ɔːlweiz] *ad* toujours.

amalgam [ə'mælgəm] *n* amalgame *m*.

amalgamate [ə'mælgəmeit] *vt* amalgamer; *vi* s'amalgamer.

amass [ə'mæs] *vt* amasser.

amateur ['æmətə] *n* amateur *m*.

amaze [ə'meiz] *vt* stupéfier, confondre, renverser.

amazement [ə'meizmənt] *n* stupéfaction *f*, stupeur *f*.

amazing [ə'meiziŋ] *a* renversant.

ambassador [æm'bæsədə] *n* ambassadeur *m*.

ambassadress [æm'bæsədris] *n* ambassadrice *f*.

amber ['æmbə] *n* ambre *m*; *a* ambre; — **light** feu jaune *m*.

ambidextrous ['æmbi'dekstrəs] *a* ambidextre.

ambiguity [ˌæmbiˈgjuiti] *n* ambiguité *f*.

ambiguous [æmˈbigjuəs] *a* ambigu, -uë, équivoque, obscur.

ambition [æmˈbiʃən] *n* ambition *f*.

ambitious [æmˈbiʃəs] *a* ambitieux.

amble [ˈæmbl] *vi* aller (à) l'amble; **to — along** marcher d'un pas tranquille, à la papa.

ambulance [ˈæmbjuləns] *n* ambulance *f*.

ambush [ˈæmbuʃ] *n* embuscade *f*; *vt* attirer dans un piège, dans un guet-apens; **to lie in —** *vi* s'embusquer.

ameliorate [əˈmiːljəreit] *vt* améliorer; *vi* s'améliorer, s'amender.

amelioration [əˌmiːljəˈreiʃən] *n* amélioration *f*.

amen [ˈɑːˈmen] *excl* amen, ainsi soit-il.

amenable [əˈmiːnəbl] *a* responsable, sensible (à to), soumis, maniable, passable, docile; **— to reason** raisonnable.

amend [əˈmend] *vt* amender, modifier, corriger; *vi* s'amender, se corriger.

amendment [əˈmendmənt] *n* modification *f*, rectification *f*, amendement *m*.

amends [əˈmendz] *n* dédommagement *m*, réparation *f*; **to make — for** dédommager, réparer

amenity [əˈmiːniti] *n* agrément *m*, aménité *f*; *pl* commodités *f pl*.

America [əˈmerikə] *n* Amérique *f*; **North —, South —** l'Amérique du Nord, l'Amérique du Sud.

American [əˈmerikən] *a* américain: *n* Américain(e) *m(f)*.

amiability [ˌeimjəˈbiliti] *n* amabilité *f*, cordialité *f*, concorde *f*.

amiable [ˈeimjəbl] *a* aimable.

amicable [ˈæmikəbl] *a* amical, à l'amiable.

amid(st) [əˈmid(st)] *prep* au milieu de, parmi.

amidships [əˈmidʃips] *ad* par le travers.

amiss [əˈmis] *a* insuffisant, fâcheux, qui cloche; *ad* (en) mal, de travers.

amity [ˈæmiti] *n* amitié *f*, bonne intelligence *f*.

ammonia [əˈmounjə] *n* ammoniaque *f*.

ammunition [ˌæmjuˈniʃən] *n* munitions *f pl*; *a* de munition, réglementaire.

amnesia [æmˈniːzjə] *n* amnésie *f*.

amnesty [ˈæmnəsti] *n* amnistie *f*; *vt* amnistier.

among(st) [əˈmʌŋ(st)] *prep* parmi, au milieu de, (d')entre.

amorous [ˈæmərəs] *a* porté à l'amour, amoureux.

amorousness [ˈæmərəsnis] *n* penchant à l'amour *m*.

amorphous [əˈmɔːfəs] *a* amorphe.

amount [əˈmaunt] *n* montant *m*,

compte *m*, somme *f*, quantité *f*; *vi* (se) monter (à to), s'élever (à to), revenir (à to).

amour [əˈmuə] *n* liaison *f*, intrigue galante *f*.

ample [ˈæmpl] *a* ample, vaste, abondant.

ampleness [ˈæmplnis] *n* ampleur *f*, abondance *f*.

amplification [ˌæmplifiˈkeiʃən] *n* amplification *f*.

amplifier [ˈæmplifaiə] *n* amplificateur *m*.

amplify [ˈæmplifai] *vt* amplifier, développer.

amplitude [ˈæmplitjuːd] *n* ampleur *f*, abondance *f*, dignité *f*.

amputate [ˈæmpjuteit] *vt* amputer.

amputation [ˌæmpjuˈteiʃən] *n* amputation *f*.

amuck [əˈmʌk] *ad* comme un fou, furieux.

amulet [ˈæmjulit] *n* amulette *f*, gri(s)-gri(s) *m*.

amuse [əˈmjuːz] *vt* amuser, divertir.

amusement [əˈmjuːzmənt] *n* amusement *m*, divertissement *m*, distraction *f*.

Amy [ˈeimi] Aimée *f*.

an [æn, ən, n] *art* un, une.

anaemia [əˈniːmjə] *n* anémie *f*.

anaemic [əˈniːmik] *a* anémique.

anaesthesia [ˌænisˈθiːzjə] *n* anesthésie *f*.

anaesthetic [ˌænisˈθetik] *n* anesthétique *m*.

anaesthetize [æˈniːsθətaiz] *vt* anesthésier, insensibiliser, endormir.

analogous [əˈnæləgəs] *a* analogue.

analogy [əˈnælədʒi] *n* analogie *f*.

analysis [əˈnæləsis] *n* analyse *f*.

analyst [ˈænəlist] *n* analyste *m*.

analytic(al) [ˌænəˈlitik(əl)] *a* analytique.

analyze [ˈænəlaiz] *vt* analyser, faire l'analyse de.

anarchist [ˈænəkist] *n* anarchiste *mf*.

anarchy [ˈænəki] *n* anarchie *f*.

anathema [əˈnæθəmə] *n* anathème *m*.

anathematize [əˈnæθəmətaiz] *vt* jeter l'anathème sur.

anatomist [əˈnætəmist] *n* anatomiste *m*.

anatomize [əˈnætəmaiz] *vt* disséquer.

anatomy [əˈnætəmi] *n* anatomie *f*.

ancestor [ˈænsistə] *n* ancêtre *m*, aïeul, -eux *m*.

ancestral [ænˈsestrəl] *a* ancestral.

ancestry [ˈænsistri] *n* race *f*, lignée *f*.

anchor [ˈæŋkə] *n* ancre *f*; *vt* ancrer, mettre au mouillage; *vi* jeter l'ancre, mouiller; **to cast —** jeter l'ancre; **to weigh —** lever l'ancre.

anchovy [ˈæntʃəvi] *n* anchois *m*.

ancient [ˈeinʃənt] *a* ancien, antique.

ancientness [ˈeinʃəntnis] *n* ancienneté *f*.

and [ænd, ənd, ən] *cj* et; **two(shillings) — six(pence)** deux shillings six pence; **without bread — butter** sans pain ni beurre; **wait — see** attendez voir.

andiron ['ændaiən] *n* chenet *m*.

Andrew ['ændru:] André *m*.

anecdote ['ænikdout] *n* anecdote *f*.

anecdotic(al) [ˌænek'dɔtik(əl)] *a* anecdotique.

anemone [ə'neməni] *n* anémone *f*.

aneurism ['ænjuərizəm] *n* anévrisme *m*.

anew [ə'nju:] *ad* de nouveau, autrement.

angel ['eindʒəl] *n* ange *m*.

Angela ['ændʒələ] Angèle *f*.

angelic [æn'dʒelik] *a* angélique, d'ange.

anger ['æŋgə] *n* colère *f*; *vt* mettre en colère, irriter.

angina [æn'dʒainə] *n* angine *f*; — **pectoris** angine de poitrine.

angle ['æŋgl] *n* angle *m* coin *m*; *vi* pêcher à la ligne.

angler ['æŋglə] *n* pêcheur *m* à la ligne.

anglicanism ['æŋglikənizəm] *n* anglicanisme *m*.

angling ['æŋgliŋ] *n* pêche *f*.

angry ['æŋgri] *a* en colère, fâché, enflammé, douloureux; **to get —** se mettre en colère, se fâcher, s'irriter; **to get — with** s.o. se fâcher contre qn; **I am — with myself for doing it** je m'en veux de l'avoir fait.

anguish ['æŋgwiʃ] *n* angoisse *f*, supplice *m*.

angular ['æŋgjulə] *a* angulaire, anguleux.

animal ['æniməl] *an* animal *m*.

animate ['ænimeit] *vt* animer, inspirer, inciter.

animated ['ænimeitid] *a* animé, vif.

animation [ˌæni'meiʃən] *n* animation *f*, entrain *m*, vivacité *f*, vie *f*, encouragement *m*.

animator ['ænimeitə] *n* animateur, -trice.

animosity [ˌæni'mɔsiti] *n* animosité *f*.

ankle ['æŋkl] *n* cheville *f*.

Ann [æn] Anne *f*.

annals ['ænls] *n* annales *f pl*.

anneal [ə'ni:l] *vt* tremper, tempérer.

annex ['æneks] *n* annexe *f*; [ə'neks] *vt* annexer.

annexation [ˌænek'seiʃən] *n* annexion *f*.

annihilate [ə'naiəleit] *vt* annihiler, anéantir.

annihilation [əˌnaiə'leiʃən] *n* anéantissement *m*.

anniversary [ˌæni'və:səri] *n* anniversaire *m*.

annotate ['ænouteit] *vt* annoter, commenter.

annotation [ˌænou'teiʃən] *n* annotation *f*, commentaire *m*.

annotator ['ænouteitə] *n* annotateur *m*, commentateur *m*.

announce [ə'nauns] *vt* annoncer, faire part de.

announcement [ə'naunsmənt] *n* annonce *f*, avis *n*, faire-part *m*.

announcer [ə'naunsə] *n* annonceur *m*, speaker *m*.

annoy [ə'nɔi] *vt* contrarier, ennuyer.

annoyance [ə'nɔiəns] *n* contrariété *f*, dégoût *m*, ennui *m*.

annoying [ə'nɔiiŋ] *a* contrariant, fâcheux, ennuyeux.

annual ['ænjuəl] *n* annuaire *m*, plante annuelle *f*; *a* annuel.

annuity [ə'nju(:)iti] *n* annuité *f*, rente *f*; **life —** rente viagère *f*.

annul [ə'nʌl] *vt* annuler, abroger, résilier.

annulment [ə'nʌlmənt] *n* annulation *f*, abrogation *f*.

annunciate [ə'nʌnsieit] *vt* annoncer.

annunciation [əˌnʌnsi'eiʃən] *n* annonce *f*, annonciation *f*.

anoint [ə'nɔint] *vt* oindre.

anointing [ə'nɔintiŋ] *n* onction *f*, sacre *m*.

anomalous [ə'nɔmələs] *a* anormal, irrégulier.

anomaly [ə'nɔməli] *n* anomalie *f*.

anon [ə'nɔn] *ad* tantôt; **ever and —** de temps à autre.

anonymity [ˌænə'nimiti] *n* anonymat *m*.

anonymous [ə'nɔniməs] *a* anonyme.

another [ə'nʌðə] *a pron* un (une) autre; encore (un, une); **one —** l'un l'autre, les unes les autres; **one way or —** d'une façon ou d'une autre; **that's — matter** c'est tout autre chose.

answer ['ɑ:nsə] *n* réponse *f*; *vti* répondre; **to — for** répondre de (*vouch*), répondre pour (*instead of*).

answerable ['ɑ:nsərəbl] *a* responsable.

answering ['ɑ:nsəriŋ] *a* sympathique, qui répond à, qui correspond à.

ant [ænt] *n* fourmi *f*; **—eater** fourmilier *m*; **—hill** n fourmilière *f*.

antagonism [ænt'ægənizəm] *n* antagonisme *m*.

antagonist [æn'tægənist] *n* adversaire *m*.

antagonize [æn'tægənaiz] *vt* contrecarrer, se faire un ennemi de.

antecedent [ˌænti'si:dənt] *n* antécédent *m*; *a* antérieur.

antedate [ˌænti'deit] *vt* antidater.

antenatal [ˌænti'neitl] *a* prénatal.

antenna [æn'tenə] *n* antenne *f*.

anterior [æn'tiəriə] *a* antérieur.

anteriority [æntiəri'ɔriti] *n* antériorité *f*.

anthem ['ænθəm] *n* antienne *f*, hymne *m*.

Anthony ['æntəni] Antoine *m*.

anti-aircraft ['ænti'eəkrɑ:ft] *a* contre-avions, anti-aérien.

16

antibiotic ['ænti'baiɔtik] *n* antibiotique *f*.

antibody ['ænti‚bɔdi] *n* anticorps *m*.

Antichrist ['æntikraist] *n* Antéchrist *m*.

anticipate [æn'tisipeit] *vt* anticiper (sur), prévenir, devancer, s'attendre à.

anticipation [æn‚tisi'peiʃən] *n* anticipation *f*, prévision *f*, attente *f*; in — d'avance, par avance.

antics ['æntiks] *n pl* pitreries *f pl*, singeries *f pl*, cabrioles *f pl*.

anti-dazzle [‚ænti'dæzl] *a* anti-aveuglant; — **headlights** phares-code *m pl*.

antidote ['æntidout] *n* antidote *m*.

antipathetic(al) [‚æntipə'θetik(l)] *a* antipathique.

antipathy [æn'tipəθi] *n* antipathie *f*.

antipodes [æn'tipədi:z] *n* antipodes *m pl*.

antiquarian [‚ænti'kwɛəriən] *n* antiquaire *m*; —'s **shop** magasin d'antiquités *m*.

antiquated ['æntikweitid] *a* suranné, vieilli désuet.

antique [æn'ti:k] *a* antique, ancien; *n* antique *m*, objet antique *m*; — **dealer** antiquaire *m*; — **shop** magasin *m* d'antiquités.

antiquity [æn'tikwiti] *n* antiquité *f*.

antiseptic [‚ænti'septik] *an* antiseptique *m*.

antitheft [ænti'θeft] *a* antivol.

antithesis [æn'tiθəsis] *n* antithèse *f*, contraire *m*.

antithetic(al) [‚ænti'θetik(əl)] *a* antithétique.

antler ['æntlə] *n* andouiller *m*; *pl* bois *m pl*.

anvil ['ænvil] *n* enclume *f*.

anxiety [æŋ'zaiəti] *n* anxiété *f*, inquiétude *f*, désir *m*.

anxious ['æŋkʃəs] *a* anxieux, inquiet, soucieux, désireux, inquiétant.

any ['eni] *a* du, de la, des; quelque, tout, un, en; not — ne ... aucun, nul; *pn* quiconque; *ad* en rien.

anybody, anyone ['enibɔdi, 'eni‚wʌn] *pn* quelqu'un, n'importe qui, tout le monde, quiconque; not — ne ... personne.

anyhow ['enihau] *ad* n'importe comment, de toute façon, en tout cas; — **you can try** vous pouvez toujours essayer.

anyone *see* **anybody**.

anything ['eniθiŋ] *pn* quelque chose, n'importe quoi, tout; not — ne ... rien; — **else, sir?** et avec cela, monsieur? — **you like** tout ce que vous voudrez; **I would give** — **to know** je donnerais gros pour savoir; **to run like** — courir à toutes jambes.

anyway ['eniwei] *ad* n'importe comment, de toute façon, en tout cas; en fait, en fin de compte.

anywhere ['eniwɛə] *ad* n'importe où,

dans quelque endroit que ce soit; not — ne ... nulle part.

apace [ə'peis] *ad* vite, vivement, à grands pas.

apart [ə'pɑːt] *ad* à part, de côté, à l'écart, indépendamment (de **from**); **to come** — se détacher; *a* espace; **they are 10 miles** — ils sont à 10 milles l'un de l'autre.

apartment [ə'pɑːtmənt] *n* chambre *f*, pièce *f*, logement *m*, (US) appartement *m*.

apathetic [‚æpə'θetik] *a* apathique, indifférent.

apathy ['æpəθi] *n* apathie *f*.

ape [eip] *n* singe *m*; *vt* singer.

aperient [ə'piəriənt] *n* laxatif *m*, purge *f*.

aperture ['æpətjuə] *n* orifice *m*, ouverture *f*.

apex ['eipeks] *n* sommet *m*.

apiary ['eipjəri] *n* rucher *m*.

apiece [ə'piːs] *ad* (la) pièce, chaque, chacun, par tête.

apish ['eipiʃ] *a* simiesque, de singe, sot.

apogee ['æpoudʒiː] *n* apogée *m*.

apologetic(al) [ə‚pɔlə'dʒetik(əl)] *a* apologétique, d'excuse.

apologetics [ə‚pɔlə'dʒetiks] *n* apologétique *f*.

apologist [ə'pɔlədʒist] *n* apologiste *m*.

apologize [ə'pɔlədʒaiz] *vi* s'excuser, demander pardon.

apology [ə'pɔlədʒi] *n* excuses *f pl*, apologie *f*.

apoplectic [‚æpə'plektik] *a* apoplectique; **an** — **fit, stroke** une attaque (d'apoplexie).

apoplexy ['æpəpleksi] *n* apoplexie *f*, congestion cérébrale *f*.

apostasy [ə'pɔstəsi] *n* apostasie *f*.

apostate [ə'pɔstit] *n* apostat *m*.

apostle [ə'pɔsl] *n* apôtre *m*.

apostleship [ə'pɔslʃip] *n* apostolat *m*.

apostolic [‚æpəs'tɔlik] *a* apostolique.

apothecary [ə'pɔθikəri] *n* apothicaire *m*, pharmacien *m*.

appalling [ə'pɔːliŋ] *a* effroyable, épouvantable.

apparatus [‚æpə'reitəs] *n* dispositif *m*, appareil *m*, attirail *m*.

apparel [ə'pærəl] *n* habit *m*, vêtement(s) *m(pl)*; *vt* habiller, vêtir.

apparent [ə'pærənt] *a* manifeste, évident; (*heir*) présomptif.

apparently [ə'pærəntli] *ad* apparemment.

apparition [‚æpə'riʃən] *n* apparition *f*, fantôme *m*.

appeal [ə'piːl] *n* appel *m*; *vi* interjeter appel; **to** — **to** recourir à, en appeler à, faire appel à, plaire à, s'adresser à; **that doesn't** — **to me** cela ne me dit rien; **the idea** —**s to me** l'idée me sourit.

appear [ə'piə] *vi* apparaître, paraître, sembler, se présenter.

appearance [ə'piərəns] *n* apparition
f, apparence *f*, mine *f*, tournure *f*;
**to put in an — faire acte de
présence; for the sake of —(s)** pour
la forme; **to, by all —(s)** selon toute
apparence.

appease [ə'pi:z] *vt* apaiser, calmer.

appeasement [ə'pi:zmənt] *n* apaisement *m*, conciliation *f*.

append [ə'pend] *vt* attacher, ajouter,
apposer, joindre.

appendage [ə'pendidʒ] *n* addition *f*,
apanage *m*.

appendicitis [ə,pendi'saitis] *n* appendicite *f*.

appendix [ə'pendiks] *n* appendice *m*,
annexe *f*.

appertain [,æpə'tein] *vi* appartenir,
se rapporter.

appertaining [,æpə'teiniŋ] *a* relatif,
qui incombent.

appetite ['æpitait] *n* appétit *m*, soif
f; **to whet someone's —** mettre qn
en appétit.

appetizer ['æpitaizə] *n* apéritif *m*.

appetizing ['æpitaiziŋ] *a* appétissant.

applaud [ə'plɔ:d] *vti* applaudir.

applause [ə'plɔ:z] *n* applaudissements *m pl*.

apple ['æpl] *n* pomme *f*, (*of the eye*)
pupille *f*, prunelle *f*.

apple-dumpling ['æpl'dʌmpliŋ] *n*
chausson *m*.

apple-pie ['æpl'pai] *n* tourte aux
pommes *f*; **in — order** en ordre
parfait; **— bed** *n* lit en porte-feuille
m.

apple tree ['æpltri:] *n* pommier *m*.

appliance [ə'plaiəns] *n* moyen *m*,
dispositif *m*, machine *f*, appareil *m*.

applicable ['æplikəbl] *a* applicable,
approprié.

applicant ['æplikənt] *n* postulant *m*,
requérant *m*.

application [,æpli'keiʃən] *n* application *f*, demande *f*.

apply [ə'plai] *vt* appliquer; *vi*
s'appliquer (à **to**), s'adresser (à **to**),
se présenter; **to — for** demander,
solliciter.

appoint [ə'pɔint] *vt* fixer, nommer,
équiper, meubler.

appointive [ə'pɔintiv] *n* (US) poste
m.

appointment [ə'pɔintmənt] *n*
rendez-vous *m*, nomination *f*, emploi
m; *pl* équipement *m*, installation *f*.

apportion [ə'pɔ:ʃən] *vt* répartir,
assigner.

apportionment [ə'pɔ:ʃənmənt] *n* répartition *f*, distribution *f*, allocation
f.

apposite ['æpəzit] *a* approprié, à
propos.

appositeness ['æpəzitnis] *n* convenance *f*, justesse *f*.

apposition [,æpə'ziʃən] *n* apposition
f.

appraisal [ə'preizəl] *n* évaluation *f*,
mise à prix *f*.

appraise [ə'preiz] *vt* évaluer.

appraiser [ə'preizə] *n* commissaire-
priseur *m*.

appreciate [ə'pri:ʃieit] *vt* évaluer,
apprécier, faire cas de, se rendre
compte de, goûter; *vi* prendre de la
valeur, augmenter de valeur.

appreciation [ə,pri:ʃi'eiʃən] *n*
évaluation *f*, hausse *f*, appréciation
f, compte-rendu *f*, critique *f*.

apprehend [,æpri'hend] *vt* appréhender, comprendre.

apprehension [,æpri'henʃən] *n* compréhension *f*, appréhension *f*, crainte
f, arrestation *f*.

apprehensive [,æpri'hensiv] *a* intelligent, inquiet, craintif.

apprentice [ə'prentis] *n* apprenti *m*;
vt mettre en apprentissage.

apprenticeship [ə'prentiʃip] *n* apprentissage *m*.

apprise [ə'praiz] *vt* informer, apprendre, prévenir.

approach [ə'proutʃ] *n* approche *f*,
approximation *f*, accès *m*; *pl*
avances *f pl*; *vt* approcher de,
aborder, faire des offres à; *vi*
(s')approcher.

approachable [ə'proutʃəbl] *a* abordable.

approbation [,æprə'beiʃən] *n* approbation *f*; **on —** à condition, à
l'essai.

appropriate [ə'proupriit] *a* propre
(à **to**), approprié; [ə'pprouprieit] *vt*
s'approprier, destiner.

approval [ə'pru:vəl] *n* approbation
f; **on —**, (*fam*) **on appro** à condition,
à l'examen, à l'essai.

approve [ə'pru:v] *vt* approuver.

approver [ə'pru:və] *n* approbateur,
-trice.

approximate [ə'prɔksimit] *a* approximatif, proche.

approximation [ə,prɔksi'meiʃən] *n*
approximation *f*.

appurtenance [ə'pə:tinəns] *a* ap-
partenance *f*; *pl* dépendances *f pl*,
accessoires *m pl*.

apricot ['eiprikɔt] *n* abricot *m*; **—
tree** abricotier *m*.

April ['eiprəl] *n* avril *m*; **to make an
— fool of s.o.** donner un poisson
d'avril à qn.

apron ['eiprən] *n* tablier *m*; **to be
tied to one's mother's — strings**
être pendu aux jupes de sa mère.

apt [æpt] *a* approprié, juste, porté
(à **to**), sujet (à **to**), prompt d'esprit,
doué, habile.

aptitude ['æptitju:d] *n* aptitude *f*,
disposition *f*.

aptly ['æptli] *ad* (avec) à propos,
habilement.

aptness ['æptnis] *n* justesse *f*,
tendance *f*, propriété *f*.

aqualung ['ækwə'lʌŋ] *n* scaphandre
m.

aqueduct ['ækwidʌkt] *n* aqueduc *m*.

aqueous ['eikwiəs] *a* aqueux.

aquiline ['ækwilain] *a* aquilin, d'aigle.

Arab ['ærəb] *n* Arabe *m*.

arable ['ærəbl] *a* arable.

arbitrage ['ɑːbitridʒ] *n* arbitrage *m*.

arbitrary ['ɑːbitrəri] *a* arbitraire.

arbitrate ['ɑːbitreit] *vti* arbitrer.

arbitration [.ɑːbi'treiʃən] *n* arbitrage *m*.

arbitrator ['ɑːbitreitə] *n* arbitre *m*.

arbour ['ɑːbə] *n* bosquet *m*, berceau *m* de verdure, tonnelle *f*.

arc [ɑːk] *n* arc *m*.

arcade [ɑː'keid] *n* arcade *f*.

arch [ɑːtʃ] *n* arche *f*, voûte *f*, cintre *m*; *vt* voûter, cintrer, arquer; *vi* former voûte; *a* espiègle, malicieux.

arch- ['ɑːtʃ] *a* maître, fieffé, archi-, consommé.

archaeologist [.ɑːki'ɔlədʒist] *n* archéologue *m*.

archaeology [.ɑːki'ɔlədʒi] *n* archéologie *f*.

archaic [ɑː'keiik] *a* archaïque.

archaism ['ɑːkeiizəm] *n* archaïsme *m*.

archangel ['ɑːk.eindʒəl] *n* archange *m*.

archbishop ['ɑːtʃ'biʃəp] *n* archevêque *m*.

archbishopric [ɑːtʃ'biʃəprik] *n* archevêché *m*.

archdeacon ['ɑːtʃ'diːkən] *n* archidiacre *m*.

archdeaconship [ɑːtʃ'diːkənʃip] *n* archidiaconat *m*.

archduchess ['ɑːtʃ'dʌtʃis] *n* archiduchesse *f*.

archduke ['ɑːtʃ'djuːk] *n* archiduc *m*.

arched [ɑːtʃt] *ad* en arc, voûté, arqué, cintré, busqué, cambré.

archer ['ɑːtʃə] *n* archer *m*.

archery ['ɑːtʃəri] *n* tir à l'arc *m*.

archetype ['ɑːkitaip] *n* archétype *m*.

archipelago [.ɑːki'peligou] *n* archipel *m*.

architect ['ɑːkitekt] *n* architecte *m*.

architecture ['ɑːkitektʃə] *n* architecture *f*.

archives ['ɑːkaivz] *n* archives *f pl*.

archivist ['ɑːkivist] *n* archiviste *mf*.

archness ['ɑːtʃnis] *m* malice *f*, espièglerie *f*.

archway ['ɑːtʃwei] *n* arcades *f pl*.

arctic ['ɑːktik] *a* arctique.

ardent ['ɑːdənt] *a* ardent, fervent.

ardently ['ɑːdəntli] *ad* ardemment, avec ardeur.

ardour ['ɑːdə] *a* ardeur *f*.

arduous ['ɑːdjuəs] *a* ardu, pénible, escarpé, énergique.

area ['ɛəriə] *n* aire *f*, cour en sous-sol *f*, surface *f*, étendue *f*, zone *f*.

arena [ə'riːnə] *n* arène *f*.

arguable ['ɑːgjuəbl] *a* soutenable, discutable.

argue ['ɑːgju] *vt* prouver, soutenir; *vi* argumenter, discuter, raisonner, se disputer.

argument ['ɑːgjumənt] *n* argument *m*, débat *m*, discussion *f*, argumentation *f*.

arid ['ærid] *a* aride.

aridity [æ'riditi] *n* aridité *f*.

aright [ə'rait] *ad* à juste titre, à bon droit.

arise [ə'raiz] *vi* se lever, s'élever, survenir, surgir, se présenter.

arisen [ə'rizen] *pp* of **arise**.

aristocracy [.æris'tɔkrəsi] *n* aristocratie *f*.

aristocrat ['æristəkræt] *n* aristocrate *mf*.

aristocratic [.æristə'krætik] *a* aristocratique, aristocrate.

arithmetic [ə'riθmətik] *n* arithmétique *f*.

ark [ɑːk] *n* coffre *m*, arche *f*.

arm [ɑːm] *n* bras *m*; arme *f*; *pl* armoiries *f pl*; fore— avant-bras *m*; — in — bras dessus bras dessous; with open —s à bras ouverts; at —'s length à longueur de bras; fire— arme à feu *f*; to lay down one's —s mettre bas les armes; *vt* armer.

armament ['ɑːməmənt] *n* armement *m*, artillerie *f*.

armature ['ɑːmətjuə] *n* armature *f*.

armband ['ɑːm'bænd] *n* brassard *m*.

armchair ['ɑːm'tʃɛə] *n* fauteuil *m*.

armful ['ɑːmful] *n* brassée *f*.

armhole ['ɑːmhoul] *n* emmanchure *f*.

armistice ['ɑːmistis] *n* armistice *m*.

armlet ['ɑːmlit] *n* brassard *m*, bracelet *m*.

armour ['ɑːmə] *n* armure *f*, blindage *m*, les blindés *m pl*; —clad *a* cuirassé, blindé; — plates *n* (plaques de) blindage *f pl*.

armourer ['ɑːmərə] *n* armurier *m*.

armoury ['ɑːməri] *n* armurie *f*, arsenal *m*.

armpit ['ɑːmpit] *n* aisselle *f*.

army ['ɑːmi] *n* armée *f*.

aroma [ə'roumə] *n* arome *m*, bouquet *m*.

arose [ə'rouz] *pt* of **arise**.

around [ə'raund] *prep* autour de; *ad* à l'entour, à la ronde.

arouse [ə'rauz] *vt* soulever, exciter, éveiller.

arraign [ə'rein] *vt* mettre en accusation *f*, attaquer.

arraignment [ə'reinmənt] *n* mise en accusation *f*.

arrange [ə'reindʒ] *vt* ranger; *vi* (s')arranger (pour to).

arrangement [ə'reindʒmənt] *n* arrangement *m*, dispositions *f pl*.

arrant ['ærənt] *a* insigne, fieffé, pur.

array [ə'rei] *n* ordre *m*, cortège *m*, atours *m pl*; *vt* rassembler, disposer, parer.

arrear [ə'riə] *n* arrière *m*; *pl* arriéré *m*, arrérages *m pl*; in —s en retard, arriéré.

arrearage [ə'riəridʒ] *n* arrérages *m pl*.

arrest [ə'rest] n arrêt m, saisie f, arrestation f; vt arrêter, suspendre, captiver.

arrival [ə'raivəl] n arrivée f, arrivage m.

arrive [ə'raiv] vi arriver.

arrogance ['ærəgəns] n arrogance f.

arrogant ['ærəgənt] a arrogant, rogue.

arrogantly ['ærəgəntli] ad arrogamment.

arrogate ['ærəgeit] vt s'arroger, attribuer.

arrow ['ærou] n flèche f.

arson ['ɑːsn] n incendie volontaire m.

art [ɑːt] n art m, artifice m; **black — magie** noire f.

arterial [ɑː'tiəriəl] a artériel.

artery ['ɑːtəri] n artère f.

artful ['ɑːtful] a rusé, habile, malin.

artfulness ['ɑːtfulnis] n ingéniosité f, art(ifice) m.

artichoke ['ɑːtitʃouk] n (Jerusalem) topinambour m; (globe) artichaut m.

article ['ɑːtikl] n article m, objet m, pièce f; vt passer un contrat d'apprentissage à.

articulate [ɑː'tikjuleit] vti articuler.

articulation [ɑː.tikju'leiʃən] n articulation f.

artifice ['ɑːtifis] n artifice m, habileté f, ruse f.

artificial [.ɑːti'fiʃəl] a artificiel, simili-, faux, factice.

artillery [ɑː'tiləri] n artillerie f; **—man** artilleur m.

artisan [.ɑːti'zæn] n artisan m; ouvrier qualifié m.

artist ['ɑːtist] n artiste mf.

artistic [ɑː'tistik] a artistique, artiste.

artless ['ɑːtlis] a sans art, naturel, ingénu, innocent.

Aryan ['ɛəriən] an aryen.

as [æz, əz] ad aussi, si, comme, en (qualité de); ci) que, comme, tout . . . que, si . . . que, pendant que, puisque; **so good —,** — to assez bon pour; **— for,** — **to** quant à; — **from** à dater de, provenant de; — **though** comme si; — **it were** pour ainsi dire; — **yet** jusqu'ici.

asbestos [æs'bestɔs] n asbeste m.

ascend [ə'send] vt gravir; vi s'élever; vti (re)monter.

ascendancy [ə'sendənsi] n ascendant m, suprématie f.

ascension [ə'senʃən] n ascension f.

ascent [ə'sent] n escalade f, montée f, ascension f.

ascertain [.æsə'tein] vt constater, s'assurer, savoir.

ascetic [ə'setik] an ascétique mf.

asceticism [ə'setisizəm] n ascétisme m.

ascribe [əs'kraib] vt attribuer, imputer.

asepsis [æ'sepsis] n asepsie f.

aseptic [æ'septik] a aseptique.

ash [æʃ] n frêne m; cendre f; **—bin** n boîte f à ordures; **—tray** n cendrier m.

ashamed [ə'ʃeimd] a honteux; **to be — avoir** honte.

ashen ['æʃn] a en bois de frêne, en cendres, cendré; **—faced** blême.

ashore [ə'ʃɔː] ad à terre, à la côte; **to go —** débarquer; **to run —** s'échouer.

aside [ə'said] n aparté m; ad de côté, à part, à l'écart.

ask [ɑːsk] vti demander; vt inviter, (question) poser; **to —** for chercher, demander; **to — about** se renseigner sur; **to — after** s'informer de; **for the asking** sur demande, pour rien.

askance [əs'kæns] ad de travers, avec méfiance.

askew [əs'kjuː] ad obliquement, de biais, de travers.

aslant [ə'slɑːnt] ad obliquement, de biais.

asleep [ə'sliːp] a endormi; **to be — dormir.**

asp [æsp] n tremble m, aspic m.

asparagus [əs'pærəgəs] n asperge f.

aspect ['æspekt] n aspect m, mine f, exposition f.

aspen ['æspən] n tremble m.

asperity [æs'periti] n rudesse f, aspérité f.

asperse [əs'pəːs] vt calomnier, éclabousser.

aspersion [əs'pəːʃən] n aspersion f, calomnie f.

asphalt ['æsfælt] n asphalte m.

asphyxia [æs'fiksiə] n asphyxie f.

asphyxiate [æs'fiksieit] vt asphyxier.

aspirate ['æspərit] vt aspirer.

aspiration [.æspə'reiʃən] n aspiration.

aspire [əs'paiə] vi aspirer.

aspirin ['æspərin] n aspirine f.

aspiring [əs'paiəriŋ] a ambitieux, qui aspire (à to).

ass [æs] n âne m; **she —** ânesse f; **young — ânon** m; **to behave like an — faire** l'âne, le sot, l'idiot.

assail [ə'seil] vt assaillir.

assailable [ə'seiləbl] a attaquable.

assailant [ə'seilənt] n assaillant m.

assassin [ə'sæsin] n assassin m.

assassinate [ə'sæsineit] vt assassiner.

assassination [ə.sæsi'neiʃən] n assassinat m.

assault [ə'sɔːlt] n assaut m, agression f, attentat m; **by —** d'assaut; vt attaquer, donner l'assaut à, attenter (à la pudeur).

assay [ə'sei] n essai m; vt essayer, titrer.

assegai ['æsigai] n sagaie f.

assemblage [ə'semblidʒ] n assemblage m, réunion f.

assemble [ə'sembl] vt assembler; vi s'assembler, se rassembler.

assembly [ə'sembli] n assemblée f, rassemblement m.

assent [ə'sent] n assentiment m,

consentement m; vi consentir, déférer (à to), convenir (de to).

assert [ə'sɔːt] vt revendiquer, affirmer, faire valoir.

assertion [ə'səːʃən] n revendication f, affirmation f.

assertive [ə'səːtiv] a péremptoire, autoritaire.

assertiveness [ə'səːtivnis] n ton péremptoire m.

assess [ə'ses] vt imposer, taxer, évaluer, estimer.

assessable [ə'sesəbl] a imposable, évaluable.

assessment[ə'sesmənt]nrépartition f, évaluation f, taxation f, imposition f.

assessor [ə'sesə] n répartiteur m, assesseur m, contrôleur m.

assets ['æsets] n actif m, biens m pl.

asseverate [ə'sevəreit] vt attester, affirmer.

asseveration [ə,sevə'reiʃən] n attestation f.

assiduity [,æsi'dju(ː)iti] n assiduité f.

assiduous [ə'sidjuəs] a assidu.

assign [ə'sain] vt assigner, attribuer, fixer, transférer.

assignation [,æsig'neiʃən] n assignation f, transfert m, rendez-vous m, attribution f.

assignment [ə'sainmənt] n assignation f, attribution f, allocation f.

assimilable [ə'similəbl] a assimilable.

assimilate [ə'simileit] vt assimiler.

assimilation [ə,simi'leiʃən] n assimilation f.

assist [ə'sist] vt assister, aider; vi assister (à at).

assistance [ə'sistəns] n assistance f, aide f.

assistant [ə'sistənt] a adjoint, sous-; n aide mf, assistant(e) mf, adjoint(e) mf, employé(e) mf.

assize [ə'saiz] n assises f pl.

associate [ə'souʃiit] an associé m, camarade mf.

associate [ə'souʃieit] vt associer, mettre en contact; vi fréquenter, frayer (avec with) s'associer, s'allier (à with).

association [ə,sousi'eiʃən] n association f, fréquentation f, société f, amicale f.

assort [ə'sɔːt] vt classer, assortir; vi s'associer.

assortment [ə'sɔːtmənt] n assortiment m, classement m.

assuage [ə'sweidʒ] vt apaiser.

assuagement [ə'sweidʒmənt] n apaisement m.

assume [ə'sjuːm] vt prendre, assumer, affecter, présumer.

assuming [ə'sjuːmiŋ] a arrogant, prétentieux; cj en admettant que.

assumption [ə'sʌmpʃən] n hypothèse f, arrogance f, Assomption f; — of office entrée en fonctions f.

assurance [ə'ʃuərans] n assurance f.

assure [ə'ʃuə] vt assurer.

assuredly [ə'ʃuəridli] ad assurément.

asterisk ['æstərisk] n astérisque m.

astern [əs'təːn] ad (naut) à l'arrière, derrière.

asthma ['æsmə] n asthme m.

astir [əs'təː] ad en mouvement, en émoi, levé, debout.

astonish [əs'tɔniʃ] vt étonner.

astonishing [əs'tɔniʃiŋ] a étonnant.

astonishingly [əs'tɔniʃiŋli] ad étonnamment.

astonishment [əs'tɔniʃmənt] n étonnement m.

astound [əs'taund] vt stupéfier, abasourdir.

astraddle [ə'strædl] ad à califourchon, à cheval.

astray [əs'trei] a égaré; ad hors du droit chemin; to go — s'égarer, faire fausse route, se dévoyer; to lead — égarer, dévoyer.

astride [əs'traid] ad à califourchon, à cheval.

astrologer [əs'trɔledʒə] n astrologue m.

astrology [əs'trɔledʒi] n astrologie f.

astronaut ['æstrənɔːt] n astronaute m.

astronautics [,æstrə'nɔːtiks] n astronautique f.

astronomer [əs'trɔnəmə] n astronome m.

astronomy [əs'trɔnəmi] n astronomie f.

astute [əs'tjuːt] a sagace, astucieux, fin.

astuteness [əs'tjuːtnis] n finesse f, astuce f.

asunder [ə'sʌndə] ad à part, en pièces, en deux.

asylum [ə'sailəm] n asile m.

at [æt] prep à, chez etc; — one d'accord; — that et de plus, tel quel; — hand sous la main; — all events en tout cas; to be — s.o. s'en prendre à qn.

ate [et] pt of eat.

atheism ['eiθiizəm] n athéisme m.

atheist ['eiθiist] n athée mf.

athlete ['æθliːt] n athlète m.

athletic [æθ'letik] a athlétique, sportif, bien taillé.

athleticism [æθ'letisizəm] n athlétisme m.

athletics [æθ'letiks] n pl sports m pl, culture physique f.

at-home [ət'houm] n réception f, jour m.

athwart [ə'θwɔːt] prep en travers de; ad en travers, par le travers.

atmosphere ['ætməsfiə] n atmosphère f, ambiance f.

atmospheric [,ætməs'ferik] a atmosphérique; n pl parasites m pl, fritures f pl, perturbations f pl.

atom ['ætəm] n atome m.

atomic [ə'tɔmik] a atomique.

atomize ['ætəmaiz] vt vaporiser, pulvériser.

atone [ə'toun] vti expier.

atonement [ə'tounmənt] n expiation f, réparation f.

atrocious [ə'troufəs] a atroce, exécrable, affreux.

atrocity [ə'trɔsiti] **atrociousness** [ə'troufsnis] n atrocité f.

attach [ə'tætʃ] vt attacher, fixer, lier, saisir.

attaché [ə'tæʃei] n attaché m; — **case** serviette f, mallette f, porte-documents m.

attachment [ə'tætʃmənt] n attachement m, attache f, saisie f.

attack [ə'tæk] n attaque f, assaut m, accès m, crise f; vt attaquer, s'attaquer à.

attain [ə'tein] vt atteindre.

attainable [ə'teinəbl] a accessible, à portée.

attainder [ə'teində] n mort civile f.

attainment [ə'teinmənt] n réalisation f, arrivée f; pl talents m pl, succès m pl, connaissances f pl.

attempt [ə'tempt] n tentative f, coup de main m, essai m, attentat m; vt tenter, essayer, attaquer.

attend [ə'tend] vt s'occuper de, soigner, assister à; vi faire attention; **to** — se charger de, s'occuper de.

attendance [ə'tendəns] n présence f, service m, assistance f.

attendant [ə'tendənt] n employé(e) mf, appariteur m, gardien, -ienne, ouvreuse f; a présent, qui sui(ven)t.

attention [ə'tenʃən] n attention f, garde-à-vous m.

attentive [ə'tentiv] a attentif, plein d'attentions, prévenant, soucieux.

attenuate [ə'tenjueit] vt atténuer.

attenuation [ə,tenju'eiʃən] n atténuation f.

attest [ə'test] vt attester, déférer le serment à.

attestation [,ætes'teiʃən] n attestation f, déposition f.

attic ['ætik] n mansarde f, grenier m, combles m pl.

attire [ə'taiə] n habit m, atours m pl, costume m; vt habiller, parer.

attitude ['ætitjuːd] n attitude f, pose f.

attorney [ə'təːni] n fondé de pouvois m, procureur (général) m, avoué m; **power of** — procuration f.

attract [ə'trækt] vt attirer.

attraction [ə'trækʃən] n attraction f, séduction f.

attractive [ə'træktiv] a attrayant, séduisant.

attractiveness [ə'træktivnis] n attrait m, charme m.

attribute ['ætribjuːt] n attribut m, apanage m, qualité f.

attribute [ə'tribjuːt] vt attribuer, prêter.

attribution [,ætri'bjuːʃən] n attribution f.

attrition [ə'triʃən] n attrition f, usure f.

attune [ə'tjuːn] vt accorder.

auburn ['ɔːbən] a châtain, auburn (no f).

auction ['ɔːkʃən] n vente aux enchères f; vt mettre aux enchères.

auctioneer [,ɔːkʃə'niə] n commissaire-priseur m, crieur m.

audacious [ɔː'deifəs] a audacieux, hardi.

audacity [ɔː'dæsiti] n audace f.

audible ['ɔːdəbl] a qui s'entend, intelligible, perceptible.

audibly ['ɔːdəbli] ad distinctement.

audience ['ɔːdjəns] n audience f, auditoire m, assistance f.

audio-visual ['ɔːdiou'vizjuəl] a audio-visuel.

audit ['ɔːdit] n apurement de comptes m; vt apurer, vérifier.

audition [ɔː'diʃən] n ouïe f, audition f, séance f.

auditor ['ɔːditə] n expert-comptable m.

auger ['ɔːgə] n tarière f.

aught [ɔːt] n **for** — I know autant que je sache.

augment [ɔːg'ment] vti augmenter.

augmentation [,ɔːgmen'teiʃən] n augmentation f.

augur ['ɔːgə] n augure m; vti augurer.

augury ['ɔːgjuri] n augure m, présage m.

August ['ɔːgəst] n août m.

august [ɔː'gʌst] a auguste.

aunt [ɑːnt] n tante f.

aurora [ɔː'rɔːrə] n aurore f, aube f.

auspices ['ɔːspisiz] n pl auspices m pl.

auspicious [ɔːs'piʃəs] a favorable, propice.

austere [ɔs'tiə] a austere, âpre.

austerity [ɔs'teriti] n austérité f.

Australia [ɔs'treiljə] n Australie f.

Austria ['ɔstriə] n Autriche f.

Austrian ['ɔstriən] a autrichien.

authentic [ɔː'θentik] a authentique.

authenticate [ɔː'θentikeit] vt authentiquer, certifier, légaliser.

authenticity [,ɔːθen'tisiti] n authenticité f.

author ['ɔːθə] n auteur m.

authoritative [ɔː'θɔritətiv] a qui fait autorité, autorisé, péremptoire, autoritaire.

authority [ɔː'θɔriti] n autorité f, mandat m.

authorization [,ɔːθərai'zeiʃən] n autorisation f, mandat m.

authorize ['ɔːθəraiz] vt autoriser.

authorship ['ɔːθəʃip] n paternité f.

autocracy [ɔː'tɔkrəsi] n autocratie f.

autocrat ['ɔːtəkræt] n autocrate m.

autograph ['ɔːtəgrɑːf] n autographe m; vt signer, autographier.

automatic [,ɔːtə'mætik] a automatique, machinal.

automation [,ɔːtə'meiʃən] n automatisation f.

automaton [ɔː'tɔmətən] n automate m.

automobile ['ɔ:təməbi:l] n (*especially US*) automobile f.

autonomous [ɔ:'tɔnəməs] a autonome.

autonomy [ɔ:'tɔnəmi] n autonomie f.

autumn ['ɔ:təm] n automne m.

autumnal [ɔ:'tʌmnəl] a automnal, d'automne.

auxiliary [ɔ:g'ziljəri] an auxiliaire mf.

avail [ə'veil] n utilité f; **without —** sans effet; *vti* servir à, être utile à; **to — oneself of** profiter de.

available [ə'veiləbl] a utile, accessible, disponible, existant, valable.

avarice ['ævəris] n cupidité f.

avaricious [.ævə'riʃəs] a cupide, avaricieux, avare.

avenge [ə'vendʒ] vt venger.

avenger [ə'vendʒə] n vengeur, -eresse.

avenue ['ævinju:] n avenue f.

aver [ə'və:] vt affirmer.

average ['ævəridʒ] n moyenne f; a moyen, courant; vt compter (faire) en moyenne, établir la moyenne de.

averse [ə'və:s] a opposé, hostile (à to).

aversion [ə'və:ʃən] n aversion f; **pet — bête** f noire.

avert [ə'və:t] vt détourner, écarter, prévenir.

aviary ['eivjəri] n volière f.

aviation [.eivi'eiʃən] n aviation f.

aviator ['eivieitə] n aviateur, -trice.

avid ['ævid] a avide.

avidity [ə'viditi] n avidité f.

avocation [.ævou'keiʃən] n vocation f, métier m.

avoid [ə'vɔid] vt éviter.

avoidable [ə'vɔidəbl] a évitable.

avoirdupois [.ævədə'pɔiz] n système m des poids et mesures.

avow [ə'vau] vt avouer.

avowal [ə'vauəl] n aveu m.

avowedly [ə'vauidli] ad franchement.

await [ə'weit] vt attendre.

awake [ə'weik] vi s'éveiller, se réveiller; vt éveiller, réveiller; a éveillé, vigilant, averti, informé (de to).

awakening [ə'weikniŋ] n (r)éveil m.

award [ə'wɔ:d] n jugement m, attribution f; vt adjuger, accorder, décerner.

aware [ə'wɛə] a instruit (de of), informé (de of); **to be — of** savoir, avoir conscience de.

awash [ə'wɔʃ] a baigné, lavé, inondé, à fleur d'eau.

away [ə'wei] ad à distance, au loin; **go —!** sortez!; **out and —** de loin, sans arrêter; **to make — with** détruire, enlever; **far and — de** beaucoup; **right — sur-le-champ, tout de suite.

awe [ɔ:] n stupeur sacrée f, respect craintif m, effroi m, terreur f; **— stricken, —struck** frappé de terreur, intimidé.

awful ['ɔ:ful] a terrible, affreux solennel.

awfully ['ɔ:fuli] ad terriblement, infiniment; **thanks —** merci mille fois.

awhile [ə'wail] ad un moment.

awkward ['ɔ:kwəd] a gauche, gêné, embarrassant, peu commode.

awkwardness ['ɔ:kwədnis] n gaucherie f, embarras m, inconvénient m, gêne f.

awl [ɔ:l] n alène f.

awn [ɔ:n] n barbe f.

awning ['ɔ:niŋ] n marquise f, tente f, bâche f, abri m.

awoke [ə'wouk] pt of **awake.**

awry [ə'rai] a tortueux, pervers; ad de travers.

axe [æks] n hache f; vt porter la hache dans; **to have an — to grind** avoir un intérêt au jeu.

axiom ['æksiəm] n axiome m.

axis ['æksis] n axe m.

axle ['æksl] n essieu m.

ay(e) [ai] n oui; [ei] ad toujours.

azure ['eiʒə] n azur m; a d'azur, azure.

B

babble ['bæbl] n babil m; vi babiller.

baboon [bə'bu:n] n babouin m, cynocéphale m.

baby ['beibi] n bébé m; (*US*) **— carriage** voiture f d'enfant.

babyhood ['beibihud] n enfance f, bas âge m.

babyish ['beibiiʃ] a enfantin, puéril.

bachelor ['bætʃələ] n célibataire m, garçon m, bachelier, -ière.

bachelorhood ['bætʃələhud] n célibat m.

back [bæk] n dos m, arrière m, dossier m, envers m, verso m, fond m; vt (faire) reculer, appuyer, parier pour, endosser; vi reculer, faire marche arrière; **to — down** descendre à reculons, en rabattre; **to — out** sortir à reculons, se dégonfler, s'excuser; a arrière, de derrière; ad en arrière, à l'arrière, dans le sens contraire, de retour; **there and —** aller et retour.

backbite ['bækbait] vt médire de.

backbiter ['bæk.baitə] n mauvaise langue f.

backbiting ['bækbaitiŋ] n médisance f.

backbone ['bækboun] n épine dorsale f; **to the —** jusqu'à la moelle des os.

backdate ['bæk'deit] vt antidater.

backdoor ['bæk'dɔ:] n porte de service f, porte basse f; a souterrain.

backfiring ['bæk'faiəriŋ] n retour de flamme m, (*aut*) pétarade f.

backgammon [bæk'gæmən] n trictrac m.

background ['bækgraund] n arrière-plan m, fond m.

backing ['bækiŋ] n recul m, appui m, soutien m.

back-marker ['bæk'mɑːkə] n scratch m.

backsliding ['bæk'slaidiŋ] n rechute f.

backstairs ['bæk'stɛəz] n escalier de service m.

backward ['bækwəd] a rétrograde, arriéré, en retard, en arrière.

backwardness ['bækwədnis] n lenteur f, retard m, état m arriéré.

backwards ['bækwədz] ad à reculons, à la renverse, à rebours, en arrière.

bacon ['beikən] n lard m, bacon m.

bad [bæd] n mauvais m, ruine f; a mauvais, méchant, malade, fort, gros.

bade [beid] pt of **bid**.

badge [bædʒ] n (in)signe m.

badger ['bædʒə] n blaireau m.

badly ['bædli] ad mal, gravement; — off gêné.

badness ['bædnis] n méchanceté f, pauvreté f, maladie f.

baffle ['bæfl] vt déjouer, contrecarrer, défier.

bag [bæg] n sac m, gibecière f, tableau m, (cows) pis m, (eyes) poche f, pl pantalon m; vt mettre en sac, empocher, chiper, prendre; vi bouffer, s'enfler.

bagful ['bægful] n sac m, sachée f.

baggage ['bægidʒ] n bagage m; donzelle f.

baggy ['bægi] a bouffant.

bagpipe ['bægpaip] n cornemuse f, biniou m.

bail [beil] n caution f; batflanc m, anse f; vt se porter (donner) caution pour, vider, écoper.

bailiff ['beilif] n bailli m, huissier m, régisseur m.

bait [beit] n amorce f; vt amorcer, tourmenter.

baize [beiz] n serge f.

bake [beik] vt (faire) cuire au four, rissoler; vi cuire, se rôtir.

bakehouse ['beikhaus] n fournil m.

baker ['beikə] n boulanger, -ère.

baker's (shop) ['beikəz] n boulangerie f.

baking ['beikiŋ] n cuisson m; — powder levure f, poudre f à lever.

balance ['bæləns] n équilibre m, balance f, bilan m; — in hand avoir; — due manque; vt peser, équilibrer, balancer; vi osciller, s'équilibrer, se faire contre-poids.

balance-sheet ['bælənsfiːt] n bilan m.

balance-wheel ['bælənswiːl] n balancier m.

balcony ['bælkəni] n balcon m.

bald [bɔːld] a chauve, pelé, dégarni.

balderdash ['bɔːldədæʃ] n balivernes f pl.

baldness ['bɔːldnis] n calvitie f.

bale [beil] n ballot m, paquet m, malheur m.

baleful ['beilful] a funeste.

ba(u)lk [bɔːk] n obstacle m, poutre f; vt contrecarrer, contrarier, esquiver; vi se dérober, reculer (devant at).

ball [bɔːl] n bal m, boule f, bille f, ballon m, balle f, boulet m, peloton m.

ballade [bæ'lɑːd] n ballade f.

ballast ['bæləst] n lest m, ballast m; vt lester, empierrer.

ball-bearing ['bɔːl'bɛəriŋ] n roulement à billes m.

balloon [bə'luːn] n ballon m.

ballot ['bælət] n boule f, scrutin m, bulletin m; (US) vote à main levée m; vt voter; vti tirer au sort.

ballot-box ['bælətbɔks] n urne f.

balm [bɑːm] n baume m.

balmy ['bɑːmi] a embaumé, toqué.

baluster ['bæləstə] n rampe f, balustre m.

balustrade [,bæləs'treid] n balustrade f.

bamboo [bæm'buː] n bambou m.

bamboozle [bæm'buːzl] vt mystifier, filouter.

bamboozlement [bæm'buːzlmənt] n mystification f.

ban [bæn] n ban m, interdit m, mise hors la loi f, malédiction f; vt mettre au ban, interdire, mettre à l'index.

banana [bə'nɑːnə] n banane f.

band [bænd] n bande f, musique f, orchestre m; vt bander; vi to — together s'associer, se bander.

bandage ['bændidʒ] n bandage m, bandeau m.

bandbox ['bændbɔks] n carton à chapeaux m.

bandmaster ['bænd,mɑːstə] n chef m de musique.

bandstand ['bændstænd] n kiosque m, estrade f.

bandy ['bændi] vt échanger; a bancal, arqué.

bane [bein] n poison m, ruine f.

baneful ['beinful] a empoisonné, ruineux, funeste.

bang [bæŋ] n coup sonore m, claquement m, détonation f; vti claquer, frapper; excl pan! v'lan!

bangle ['bæŋgl] n anneau m, bracelet m.

banish ['bæniʃ] vt bannir, proscrire, exiler.

banishment ['bæniʃmənt] n bannissement m, exil m.

banister ['bænistə] n rampe f.

bank [bæŋk] n rive f, berge f, bord m, banque f, talus m, banc m; vt endiguer, relever, mettre en banque; vi virer, miser (sur on).

banker ['bæŋkə] n banquier m.

banknote ['bæŋknout] n billet de banque m.

bankrupt ['bæŋkrəpt] n banqueroutier, -ière, failli(e) m; vt réduire à la faillite.

bankruptcy ['bæŋkrəptsi] n banqueroute f, faillite f.

banner ['bænə] n bannière f, étandard m.

banns [bænz] n bans m pl.

banquet ['bæŋkwit] n banquet m; vt traiter; vi banqueter.

banter ['bæntə] n plaisanterie f; vti plaisanter.

baptism ['bæptizəm] n baptême m.

baptismal [bæp'tizməl] a baptismal, de baptême.

baptize [bæp'taiz] vt baptiser.

bar [bɑ:] n barre f, bar m, comptoir m, barrière f, (law) barreau m; vt barrer, exclure; prep moins, sauf.

barb [bɑ:b] n barbe f, pointe f.

barbarian [bɑ:'bɛəriən] an barbare mf.

barbarism ['bɑ:bərizəm] n barbarie f.

barbarous ['bɑ:bərəs] a cruel, grossier.

barbed [bɑ:bd] a barbelé, acéré.

barbed-wire ['bɑ:bd'waiə] n fil de fer barbelé m.

barber ['bɑ:bə] n barbier m, coiffeur m.

bard [bɑ:d] n barde f.

bare [bɛə] a nu, vide, seul, simple; vt mettre à nu, dégainer, dépouiller.

bareback ['bɛəbæk] ad à cru.

barefaced ['bɛəfeist] a impudent, cynique, effronté.

barefooted ['bɛə'futid] a nu-pieds.

bareheaded ['bɛə'hedid] a nu-tête, découvert.

barely ['bɛəli] ad à peine, tout juste.

bareness ['bɛənis] n nudité f, dénuement m.

bargain ['bɑ:gin] n marché m, occasion f; into the — par dessus le marché; vi traiter, négocier; to — over, with marchander.

barge [bɑ:dʒ] n chaland m, barque f, péniche f.

bargee [bɑ:'dʒi:] n batelier m.

baritone ['bæritoun] n (mus) baryton m.

bark [bɑ:k] n écorce f, aboiement m, trois-mâts m; vt écorcer, écorcher; vi aboyer.

barley ['bɑ:li] n orge m.

barm ['bɑ:m] n levure f.

barmaid ['bɑ:meid] n serveuse f.

barman ['bɑ:mən] n garçon m de comptoir, barman m.

barn [bɑ:n] n grange f; (US) écurie f, étable f, hangar m.

barometer [bə'rɔmitə] n baromètre m.

baron ['bærən] n baron m.

baroness ['bærənis] n baronne f.

baronet ['bærənit] n baronnet m.

baronetcy ['bærənitsi] n baronnie f.

barrack(s) ['bærəks] n caserne f, baraque f.

barrage ['bærɑ:ʒ] n barrage m.

barrel ['bærəl] n baril m, barrique f, canon de fusil m, barillet m; **double-barrelled** à deux coups.

barren ['bærən] a stérile, aride.

barrenness ['bærənnis] n stérilité f, aridité f.

barricade [.bæri'keid] n barricade f; vt barricader.

barrier ['bæriə] n barrière f; **sound** — mur m du son.

barring ['bɑ:riŋ] prep excepté.

barrister ['bæristə] n avocat m.

barrow ['bærou] n brouette f, charrette f à bras.

bartender ['bɑ:tendə] n (US) barman m.

barter ['bɑ:tə] n troc m, échange m; vt troquer.

base [beis] n base f; vt baser, fonder; a bas, vil.

baseless ['beislis] a sans fondement, sans base.

basement ['beismənt] n soubassement m, sous-sol m.

baseness ['beisnis] n bassesse f.

bash [bæʃ] vt cogner; to — in enfoncer.

bashful ['bæʃful] a timide.

bashfulness ['bæʃfulnis] n timidité f, fausse honte f.

basic ['beisik] a fondamental, de base.

basin ['beisn] n cuvette f, bassine f, bassin m, jatte f.

basis ['beisis] n see **base**.

bask [bɑ:sk] vi se chauffer.

basket ['bɑ:skit] n panier m, corbeille f; éventaire m; vt mettre dans un (au) panier.

bass [beis] n basse f, bar m; a de basse, grave.

bastard ['bæstəd] an bâtard(e) mf.

bastardy ['bæstədi] n bâtardise f.

baste [beist] vt faufiler, bâtir, arroser, rosser.

bat [bæt] n chauve-souris f, crosse f.

batch [bætʃ] n fournée f; tas m.

bath [bɑ:θ] n bain m, baignoire f.

bathe [beið] vt baigner; vi se baigner.

bather ['beiðə] n baigneur, -euse.

bathos ['beiθɔs] n chute f, dégringolade f.

bathroom ['bɑ:θrum] n salle de bain f.

batman ['bætmən] n ordonnance f, brosseur m.

battalion [bə'tæljən] n bataillon m.

batten ['bætn] vi s'empiffrer, s'engraisser, se repaître.

batter ['bætə] n pâte f; vt battre, malmener, cabosser.

battering-ram ['bætəriŋræm] n bélier m.

battery ['bætəri] n batterie f, pile f, voies de fait f pl.

battle ['bætl] n bataille f; vi se battre, lutter.

battle-axe ['bætlæks] n hache f d'armes.

battledore ['bætldɔ:] n raquette f.

battlement ['bætlmənt] *n* créneau *m*.

battleship ['bætlʃip] *n* cuirassé *m*.

bauble ['bɔːbl] *n* babiole *f*, (*fool's*) marotte *f*.

bawdiness ['bɔːdinis] *n* obscénité *f*.

bawdy ['bɔːdi] *a* obscène.

bawl [bɔːl] *vi* vociférer, gueuler, brailler; *vt* — **out** (*US*) engueuler.

bay [bei] *n* laurier *m*, baie *f*; entre-deux *m*; aboiement *m*, abois *m pl*; *vi* aboyer, hurler; *a* bai, en saillie.

bayonet ['beiənit] *n* baïonnette *f*; *vt* embrocher.

bazaar [bəˈzaː] *n* bazar *m*.

be [biː] *vi* être, exister, avoir, aller, faire (froid *etc*).

beach [biːtʃ] *n* plage *f*, grève *f*; *vt* atterrir, échouer.

beacon ['biːkən] *n* balise *f*, feu *m*, poteau *m*.

bead [biːd] *n* grain *m*, perle *f*, bulle *f*; *pl* chapelet *m*.

beadle ['biːdl] *n* bedeau *m*, appari-teur *m*.

beak [biːk] *n* bec *m*, éperon *m*, magistrat *m*.

beaker ['biːkə] *n* coupe *f*.

beam [biːm] *n* poutre *f*, fléau *m*, rayon *m*; *vi* rayonner.

bean [biːn] *n* haricot *m*; **broad** — fève *f*, **french** — haricot vert *m*.

bear ['bɛə] *n* ours *m*; baissier *m*; *vi* jouer à la baisse; *vt* (em-, rem-, sup-, se com-)porter, souffrir, en-durer, mettre au jour; **to** — **out** confirmer.

bearable ['bɛərəbl] *a* supportable.

beard [biəd] *n* barbe *f*; *vt* défier, narguer.

bearded ['biədid] *a* barbu.

beardless ['biədlis] *a* imberbe, sans barbe.

bearer ['bɛərə] *n* porteur, -euse.

bearing ['bɛəriŋ] *n* conduite *f*; rapport *m*, aspect *m*, maintien *m*, port *m*, position *f*.

beast [biːst] *n* bête *f*, bétail *m*, brute *f*, porc *m*.

beastliness ['biːstlinis] *n* glouton-nerie *f*, bestialité *f*.

beastly ['biːstli] *a* bestial, répugnant; *ad* terriblement.

beat [biːt] *n* coup de baguette *m*, cadence *f*; battement *m*, ronde *f*, tournée *f*; (*mus*) mesure *f*; *vti* battre; **to** — **about the bush** tourner autour du pot; **to** — **one's brains** se creuser la cervelle.

beaten ['biːtn] *a* (re)battu.

beater ['biːtə] *n* rabatteur *m*, battoir *m*, fléau *m*.

beatification [bi(ː)ˌætifiˈkeiʃən] *n* béatification *f*.

beatify [bi(ː)ˈætifai] *vt* béatifier.

beatitude [bi(ː)ˈætitjuːd] *n* béatitude *f*.

beau [bou] *n* dandy *m*.

beautiful ['bjuːtəful] *a* beau, (*before vowels*) bel, belle.

beauty ['bjuːti] *n* beauté *f*; — **spot** *n* mouche *f*, site *m*.

beaver ['biːvə] *n* castor *m*.

becalm [biˈkaːm] *vt* déventer.

became [biˈkeim] *pt of* **become**.

because [biˈkɔz] *cj* parce que; *prep* — **of** à cause de.

beck [bek] *n* signe *m*, ordre *m*.

beckon ['bekən] *vt* faire signe à, appeler; *vi* faire signe.

become [biˈkʌm] *vi* devenir; *vt* aller bien à.

becoming [biˈkʌmiŋ] *a* seyant, convenable.

becomingly [biˈkʌmiŋli] *ad* avec grâce, convenablement.

bed [bed] *n* lit *m*, plate-bande *f*, banc *m*, gisement *m*; *a* de lit; *vt* coucher, repiquer, déposter, sceller.

bed-chamber ['bedˌtʃeimbə] *n* chambre *f*.

bedclothes ['bedklouðz] *n pl* draps *m pl* de lit.

bedding ['bediŋ] *n* literie *f*.

bedizen [biˈdaizn] *vt* pomponner, affubler.

bed-ridden ['bedˌridn] *a* alité.

bedroom ['bedrum] *n* chambre *f* à coucher.

bedside ['bedsaid] *n* chevet *m*.

bedsore ['bedsɔː] *n* escarre *f*.

bedspread ['bedspred] *n* couvre-lit *m*.

bedstead ['bedsted] *n* bois de lit *m*.

bedtime ['bedtaim] *n* heure *f* d'aller au lit.

bee [biː] *n* abeille *f*.

beech [biːtʃ] *n* hêtre *m*.

beef [biːf] *n* bœuf *m*, bifteck *m*.

beehive ['biːhaiv] *n* ruche *f*.

beekeeper ['biːkiːpə] *n* apiculteur *m*.

beeline ['biːlain] *n* ligne *f* droite.

been [biːn] *pp of* **be**.

beer [biə] *n* bière *f*; **millet** — pombe *m*.

beerhouse ['biəhaus] *n* brasserie *f*.

beet [biːt] *n* (côtes de) bette(s) *f*.

beetle ['biːtl] *n* (*tool*) maillet *m*, masse *f*, demoiselle *f*, (*insect*) blatte *f*, scarabée *m*; *vi* surplomber.

beetling ['biːtliŋ] *a* saillant, mena-çant, bombé, broussailleux, en sur-plomb.

beetroot ['biːtruːt] *n* betterave *f*.

befall [biˈfɔːl] *vt* arriver (à), advenir, survenir.

befit [biˈfit] *vt* aller à, convenir à.

befitting [biˈfitiŋ] *a* seyant, con-venable.

before [biˈfɔː] *prep* avant, devant, par-devant; *ad* (aupar)avant, devant, en avant; *cj* avant que, plutôt que.

beforehand [biˈfɔːhænd] *ad* d'avance, au préalable, par avance, déjà.

befriend [biˈfrend] *vt* traiter (*etc*) en ami, protéger, venir en aide à.

beg [beg] *vt* prier, supplier, demander, solliciter, mendier; *vi* faire le beau, mendier.

began [biˈgæn] *pt of* **begin**.

beget [bi'get] *vt* engendrer, procréer, enfanter.

begetter [bi'getə] *n* père *m*.

beggar ['begə] *n* mendiant(e) *mf*, gueux, -se, quémandeur, -euse; *vt* réduire à la misère, mettre sur la paille, défier.

beggarliness ['begəlinis] *n* misère *f*, mesquinerie *f*.

beggarly ['begəli] *a* miséreux, misérable, mesquin.

beggary ['begəri] *n* misère *f*, mendicité *f*.

begin [bi'gin] *vti* commencer; **to — with** pour commencer; *vt* amorcer, entamer, se mettre à.

beginner [bi'ginə] *n* débutant(e) *mf*, novice *mf*, auteur *m*.

beginning [bi'giniŋ] *n* commencement *m*, début *m*, origine *f*.

begone [bi'gɔn] *excl* sortez! allez-vous en!

begot(ten) [bi'gɔt(n)] *pt of* beget.

begrudge [bi'grʌdʒ] *vt* mesurer, envier, donner à contre-cœur.

beguile [bi'gail] *vt* tromper, charmer, distraire, séduire.

begun [bi'gʌn] *pp of* begin.

behalf [bi'hɑːf] *n* **in**, **on — of** au nom de, de la part de, au compte de.

behave [bi'heiv] *vi* se conduire, se comporter, fonctionner.

behaved [bi'heivd] *a* **well — sage**, bien élevé; **badly — mal** élevé.

behaviour [bi'heivjə] *n* conduite *f*, maintien *m*, tenue *f*, manières *f pl*, fonctionnement *m*.

behead [bi'hed] *vt* décapiter.

beheading [bi'hediŋ] *n* décapitation *f*, décollation *f*.

beheld [bi'held] *pt of* behold.

behest [bi'hest] *n* commandement *m*, ordre *m*.

behind [bi'haind] *prep* derrière, en arrière de, en retard sur; *ad* (par) derrière, en arrière.

behold [bi'hould] *vt* apercevoir, voir, regarder.

beholden [bi'houldən] *a* obligé, redevable.

beholder [bi'houldə] *n* spectateur, -trice, témoin *m*.

behoof [bi'huːf] *n* bien *m*; **on s.o.'s — à** l'intention de, à l'avantage de.

behove [bi'houv] *vt* incomber à, seoir à, appartenir à.

being ['biːiŋ] *n* être *m*.

belabour [bi'leibə] *vt* rosser, rouer de coups.

belated [bi'leitid] *a* retardé, en retard, attardé, tardif.

belch [beltʃ] *n* rot *m*, renvoi *m*, grondement *m*, jet de flamme *m*; *vi* roter, éructer; *vt* vomir.

beleaguer [bi'liːgə] *vt* assiéger.

belfry ['belfri] *n* beffroi *m*.

Belgian ['beldʒən] *an* belge *mf*.

Belgium ['beldʒəm] *n* Belgique *f*.

belie [bi'lai] *vt* démentir, donner un démenti à.

belief [bi'liːf] *n* foi *f*, croyance *f*, conviction *f*.

believe [bi'liːv] *vti* croire; *vt* ajouter foi à; **to make —** faire semblant.

believer [bi'liːvə] *n* croyant(e) *mf*, partisan *m*.

belittle [bi'litl] *vt* diminuer, décrier, rabaisser.

bell [bel] *n* cloche *f*, sonnette *f*, sonnerie *f*, timbre *m*, grelot *m*, clochette *f*.

bellboy ['belbɔi], **bellhop** ['belhɔp] *n* (US) groom *m*.

bellied ['belid] *a* ventru.

belligerency [bi'lidʒərənsi] *n* état de guerre *m*.

belligerent [bi'lidʒərənt] *an* belligérant(e) *mf*.

bellow ['belou] *n* mugissement *m*, beuglement *m*, grondement *m*; *vi* mugir, gronder; *vti* beugler, brailler.

bellows ['belouz] *n* soufflet *m*.

belly ['beli] *n* ventre *m*, panse *f*, bedaine *f*; *vt* gonfler; *vi* se gonfler, s'enfler.

bellyful ['beliful] *n* ventrée *f*; **to have had one's — en** avoir plein le dos.

belong [bi'lɔŋ] *vi* appartenir (à **to**), être (à **to**).

belongings [bi'lɔŋiŋz] *n* biens *m pl*, affaires *f pl*, effets *m pl*.

beloved [bi'lʌvd] *an* (bien-)aimé(e) *mf*, chéri(e) *mf*.

below [bi'lou] *prep* au dessous de, en aval de; *ad* (au, en, là-) dessous, ci-dessous, plus loin, en bas, en aval.

belt [belt] *n* ceinture *f*, ceinturon *m*, courroie *f*, bande *f*, zone *f*; *vt* ceindre, entourer.

bemoan [bi'moun] *vt* pleurer, se lamenter de.

bemuse [bi'mjuːz] *vt* étourdir, stupéfier.

bench [bentʃ] *n* banc *m*, banquette *f*, gradin *m*; établi *m*, tribunal *m*, magistrature *f*.

bend [bend] *n* nœud *m*, courbe *f*, virage *m*, tournant *m*, coude *m*; *pl* (US) mal *m* des caissons; *vti* courber, ployer, plier, fléchir, pencher, arquer; *vi* se courber, s'incliner, tourner, faire un coude (*road etc*); **to — back** *vt* replier, recourber; *vi* se replier, se recourber; **to — down** *vi* se baisser, se courber.

beneath [bi'niːθ] *prep* au dessous de, sous; *ad* (au-)dessous, en bas.

benedictine [,beni'diktiːn] *an* bénédictin(e) *mf*; *n* (liqueur) bénédictine.

benediction [,beni'dikʃən] *n* bénédiction *f*.

benefaction [,beni'fækʃən] *n* bienfait *m*, don *m*.

benefactor, -tress ['benifæktə, tris] *n* bienfaiteur, -trice, donateur, -trice.

beneficence [bi'nefisəns] *n* bienfaisance *f*.

beneficent [bi'nefisənt] *a* bienfaisant, salutaire.

beneficently [bi'nefisəntli] *ad* généreusement, salutairement.

beneficial [.beni'fiʃəl] *a* avantageux, salutaire.

beneficiary [.beni'fiʃəri] *n* bénéficiaire *m*, bénéficier, -ière.

benefit ['benifit] *n* bénéfice *m*, bien *m*, gouverne *f*, secours (mutuels) *m pl*; *vt* profiter à; *vi* bénéficier, profiter (de by).

benevolence [bi'nevələns] *n* bienveillance *f*, bienfait *m*.

benevolent [bi'nevələnt] *a* bienveillant; — **society** société *f* de secours mutuels.

benighted [bi'naitid] *a* surpris par la nuit, aveuglé, plongé dans l'ignorance.

benign [bi'nain] *a* bénin, -igne, affable, heureux, doux.

benignity [bi'nigniti] *n* bénignité *f*; bienveillance *f*.

bent [bent] *pt of* **bend**; *n* pli *m*, tour *m*, penchant *m*, dispositions *f pl*; *a* courbé, plié, voûté, arqué, résolu.

benumb [bi'nam] *vt* engourdir, transir, frapper de stupeur.

benzine ['benzi:n] *n* benzine *f*.

bequeath [bi'kwi:ð] *vt* léguer.

bequest [bi'kwest] *n* legs *m*.

bereave [bi'ri:v] *vt* enlever, ravir, priver.

bereaved [bi'ri:vd] *pp a* affligé, en deuil.

bereavement [bi'ri:vmənt] *n* perte *f*, deuil *m*.

bereft [bi'reft] *pp of* **bereave**.

berry ['beri] *n* baie *f*, grain *m*.

berth [bə:θ] *n* cabine *f*, couchette *f*; mouillage *m*, place *f*; *vi* mouiller; *vt* amarrer à quai.

beseech [bi'si:tʃ] *vt* supplier, implorer, conjurer.

beset [bi'set] *vt* cerner, entourer, assaillir, obséder.

besetting [bi'setiŋ] — **sin** *n* péché mignon *m*.

beside [bi'said] *prep* à côté de, près de; **to be** — **o.s.** être hors de soi.

besides [bi'saidz] *ad* d'ailleurs, en outre, en plus, du reste; *prep* en outre de, sans compter.

besiege [bi'si:dʒ] *vt* assiéger.

besieger [bi'si:dʒə] *n* assiégeant *m*.

besmear [bi'smiə] *vt* graisser, tacher, barbouiller.

besmirch [bi'smə:tʃ] *vt* salir, obscurcir, ternir, souiller.

besom ['bi:zəm] *n* balai de bruyère *m*.

besot [bi'sɔt] *vt* abrutir.

besought [bi'sɔ:t] *pt of* **beseech**.

bespatter [bi'spætə] *vt* éclabousser.

bespeak [bi'spi:k] *vt* commander, retenir, annoncer.

bespoke [bi'spouk] *a* sur mesure, à façon.

best [best] *a* le meilleur; *ad* le mieux; *n* le mieux *m*; **to do one's** — faire de son mieux; **to look one's** — être

à son avantage; **to the** — **of one's ability** de son mieux; **to get the** — **of it** avoir le dessus; **to make the** — **of it** en prendre son parti; **to the** — **of my knowledge** autant que je sache; **the** — **of it is that . . .** le plus beau de l'affaire, c'est que...; — **man** garçon d'honneur.

best-seller ['best'selə] *n* best-seller *m*, livre à succès *m*, grand favori *m*.

bestir [bi'stə:] *vi* **to** — **o.s.** se remuer.

bestow [bi'stou] *vt* conférer, octroyer.

bestowal [bi'stouəl] *n* octroi *m*, don *m*.

bestrew [bi'stru:] *vt* joncher, parsemer.

bestride [bi'straid] *vt* enfourcher, enjamber, se mettre à califourchon sur.

bet [bet] *n* pari *m*; *vt* parier; *pt of* **bet**.

betake [bi'teik] *vt* **to** — **o.s.** se rendre.

betimes [bi'taimz] *ad* de bonne heure, à temps.

betoken [bi'toukən] *vt* indiquer, annoncer, révéler.

betray [bi'trei] *vt* livrer, vendre, trahir, montrer.

betrayal [bi'treiəl] *n* trahison *f*, révélation *f*.

betrayer [bi'treiə] *n* traître, -esse.

betrothal [bi'trouðəl] *n* fiançailles *f pl*.

betrothed [bi'trouðd] *an* fiancé(e) *mf*.

better ['betə] *n* parieur *m*; *a* meilleur; *ad* mieux; *vt* améliorer, surpasser; **to be** — aller mieux, valoir mieux; **to get** — s'améliorer, se rétablir, guérir; **to get the** — **of** l'emporter sur; **to think** — **se raviser**; — **and** — de mieux en mieux.

betterment ['betəmənt] *n* amélioration *f*.

between [bi'twi:n] *prep* entre; **far** — clairsemé, rare.

bevel ['bevəl] *n* équerre *f*, biais *m*, biseau *m*; *vt* biseauter, tailler en biais, chanfreiner.

bevelled ['bevəld] *a* biseauté, de biais.

beverage ['bevəridʒ] *n* breuvage *m*, boisson *f*.

bevy ['bevi] *n* compagnie *f*, troupe *f*, bande *f*.

bewail [bi'weil] *vt* se lamenter sur, pleurer.

bewailing [bi'weiliŋ] *n* lamentation *f*.

beware [bi'wɛə] *vi* prendre garde; *vt* **to** — **of** prendre garde à (de), se garder de, se méfier de.

bewilder [bi'wildə] *vt* abasourdir, ahurir, dérouter, désorienter, confondre.

bewilderment [bi'wildəmənt] *n* ahurissement *m*, confusion *f*.

bewitch [bi'witʃ] *vt* ensorceler, charmer, enchanter.

bewitchment [bi'witʃmənt] n ensorcellement m.

beyond [bi'iɔnd] n l'au-delà m; prep au-delà de, après, par-delà, derrière, outre; ad au-delà, plus loin, par-delà.

bias ['baiəs] n biais m, penchant m, tendance f, prévention f, parti-pris m.

biassed ['baiəst] a prévenu, tendancieux, partial.

bib [bib] n bavette f, bavoir m.

bibber ['bibə] n soiffard m, buveur m.

Bible ['baibl] n bible f.

biblical ['biblikəl] a biblique.

bibliographer [,bibli'ɔgrəfə]n bibliographe m.

bibliographical ,biblə'græfikəl] a bibliographique.

bibliography [,bibli'ɔgrəfi] n bibliographie f.

bibliophile ['biblioufail] n bibliophile m.

bicker ['bikə] vi se quereller, se chamailler, murmurer, crépiter, briller.

bickering 'bikəriŋ] n prise de bec f, chamailleries f pl, bisbille f.

bicycle ['baisikl] n bicyclette f.

bid [bid] n offre f, enchère f, demande f; vti commander, dire, inviter, offrir, demander; to — for faire une offre pour; to — s.o. good-day donner le bonjour à qn.

bidden ['bidn] pp of bid.

bidder ['bidə] n enchérisseur m; to the highest — au plus offrant.

bide [baid] vti attendre.

biennial [bai'eniəl] a bisannuel, biennal.

bier [biə] n brancard m, civière f.

big [big] a gros(se), grand.

bigamist ['bigəmist] n bigame mf.

bigamous ['bigəməs] a bigame mf.

bigamy ['bigəmi] n bigamie f.

bight [bait] n baie f, anse f, crique f.

bigness ['bignis] n grosseur f, importance f, grandeur f.

bigot ['bigət] n bigot(e) mf, fanatique mf.

bigotry ['bigətri] n bigoterie f, fanatisme f.

bigwig ['bigwig] n gros bonnet m.

bike [baik] n bécane f, vélo m.

bile ['bail] n bile f.

bilge [bildʒ] n sentine f, fond de cale m; vi faire eau; to talk — dire des balivernes.

bilious ['biljəs]a bilieux, cholérique; — attack, crise f de foie.

bilk [bilk] vt filouter, éluder, tromper.

bill [bil] n bec m, facture f, note f, traite f, effet m, addition f; — of fare carte f, affiche f; hand-— prospectus m; vt annoncer, afficher, placarder; vi se becqueter; to — and coo faire les tourtereaux.

billet ['bilit] n bûche f, (billet m de) logement m, place f; vt loger, cantonner.

billiard-ball ['biljədbɔːl] n bille f.

billiard-cloth ['biljədklɔθ] n drap m.

billiard-cue ['biljədkjuː] n queue f.

billiard-room ['biljədrum] n salle de billard f.

billiards ['biljədz] n billard m.

billiard-table ['biljəd,teibl] n billard m.

billion ['biljən] n milliard m, trillion m.

billow ['bilou] n grande vague f, houle f, lame f; vi se soulever, s'enfler.

billowy ['biloui] a houleux.

bill-poster, -sticker ['bil,poustə, ,stikə] n afficheur m.

bill-posting ['bil,poustiŋ] n affichage m.

billy-goat ['biligout] n bouc m.

bin [bin] n seau m, huche f, boîte à ordures f, panier m, coffre m.

bind [baind] vt lier, attacher, ligoter, bander, obliger, relier, engager.

binder ['baində] n (re)lieur, -euse, botteleur, -euse, bandage m, lieuse f, ceinture f.

binding ['baindiŋ] n reliure f, bordure f, bandage m, liséré m; a obligatoire.

binoculars [bi'nɔkjuləz] n pl jumelle(s) f pl.

biographer [bai'ɔgrəfə] n biographe m.

biographical [,baiou'græfikəl] a biographique.

biography [bai'ɔgrəfi] n biographie f.

biological [baiə'lɔdʒikəl] a biologique.

biologist [bai'ɔlədʒist] n biologue m

biology [bai'ɔlədʒi] n biologie f.

biped ['baiped] an bipède m.

biplane ['baiplein] n biplan m.

birch [bəːtʃ] n bouleau m, verges f pl; vt donner les verges à, flageoler.

bird [bəːd] n oiseau m, perdreau m, volaille f, type m; a — in the hand is worth two in the bush un 'tiens' vaut mieux que deux 'tu l'auras'; to give s.o. the — siffler qn, envoyer promener qn; bird's-eye view vue à vol d'oiseau.

bird-call ['bəːdkɔːl] n appeau m.

bird-catcher ['bəːd,kætʃə] n oiseleur m.

bird-lime ['bəːdlaim] n glu f.

bird-seed ['bəːdsiːd] n mouron m.

birth [bəːθ] n naissance f, origine f, lignée f; to give — to donner le jour à, enfanter, mettre bas; — certificate acte m de naissance.

birthday ['bəːθdei] n anniversaire m, fête f.

birthplace ['bəːθpleis] n lieu natal m, lieu de naissance, berceau m.

birth-rate ['bəːθreit] n natalité f.

birthright ['bəːθrait] n droit m d'aînesse, de naissance.

biscuit ['biskit] n biscuit m, gateau sec m.

bishop ['biʃəp] n évêque m, (chess) fou m.

bishopric ['biʃəprik] n évêché m.

bison ['baisn] n bison m.

bissextile [bi'sekstail] a bissextile.

bit(ten) [bit, 'bitn] pt (pp) of bite.

bit [bit] n mors m, frein m; morceau m, brin m, miette f, bout m, (US) pièce f de ¼ dollar.

bitch [bitʃ] n chienne f etc, femelle f.

bite [bait] n morsure f, piqûre f, bouchée f, touche f, coup de dent m, mordant m; vt mordre, piquer, sucer, prendre, donner un coup de dent à, attraper; vi mordre.

biting ['baitiŋ] a mordant, piquant, cuisant, cinglant, âpre.

bitter ['bitə] a amer, aigre, âpre, rude, cruel, acharné; — cold n froid de loup m; to the — end jusqu'au bout.

bittern ['bitə(:)n] n butor m.

bitterness ['bitənis] n amertume f, acrimonie f, aigreur f, âpreté f, rancune f.

bitumen ['bitjumin] n bitume m.

bituminous [bi'tju:minəs] a bitumineux.

bivouac ['bivuæk] n bivouac m; vi bivouaquer.

blab [blæb] vt révéler; vi parler au bout vendre la mèche.

blabber ['blæbə] n bavard(e) mf, indiscret, -ète mf.

black [blæk] a noir, triste, sombre; to be — and blue être couvert de bleus; — eye œil poché m, œil au beurre noir m; — Maria panier m à salade; — pudding boudin m; — sheep brebis f galeuse; n noir(e) mf, nègre, négresse f; vt noircir, cirer.

blackball ['blækbɔ:l] n boule f noire; vt blackbouler.

blackbeetle ['blækbi:tl] n cafard m.

blackberry ['blækbəri] n mûre f; — bush ronce f, mûrier m.

blackbird ['blækbə:d] n merle m.

blackboard ['blækbɔ:d] n tableau noir m.

blackcurrant(s) ['blæk'kʌrənt(s)] n cassis m.

blacken ['blækən] vt noircir, assombrir, obscurcir; vi (se) noircir, s'assombrir.

blackfriar ['blæk'fraiə] n dominicain m.

blackguard ['blæga:d] n canaille f, vaurien m.

blacking ['blækiŋ] n cirage noir m.

blackish ['blækiʃ] a noirâtre.

blacklead ['blæk'led] n mine f de plomb, plombagine f.

blackleg ['blækleg] n escroc m, renard m, jaune m.

blackmail ['blækmeil] n chantage m; vt faire chanter.

blackmailer ['blækmeilə] n maître chanteur m.

blackness ['blæknis] n noirceur f, obscurité f.

blackout ['blækaut] n couvre-feu m, obscurcissement m, black-out m; vt obscurcir.

blacksmith ['blæksmiθ] n forgeron m, maréchal ferrant m; — 's forge f.

blackthorn ['blækθɔ:n] n prunellier m, épine noire f.

bladder ['blædə] n vessie f, outre f gonflée de vent, vésicule f.

blade [bleid] n feuille f, brin m, plat m, pale f, lame f; tranchant m, omoplate f, épaule f, boute-en-train m, luron m.

blame [bleim] n blâme m, faute f; vt blâmer, reprocher, attribuer.

blameless ['bleimlis] a irréprochable, innocent.

blameworthy ['bleim,wə:ði] a blâmable, répréhensible.

blanch [bla:ntʃ] vti blanchir, pâlir; vi blêmir.

bland [blænd] a aimable, flatteur, doux, affable, doucereux, suave.

blandish ['blændiʃ] vt flatter, cajoler, amadouer.

blandishment ['blændiʃmənt] n flatterie f, cajolerie f.

blank [blæŋk] n blanc m, billet blanc m, vide m, trou m; a blanc, en (à) blanc, inexpressif, vide, confondu, net.

blanket ['blæŋkit] n couverture f; to toss s.o. in a — verner qn; wet — rabat-joie m.

blankly ['blæŋkli] ad vaguement, d'un air déconcerté.

blare [blɛə] n sonnerie f, accents cuivrés m pl; vi sonner, retentir; vt faire retentir, brailler.

blarney ['bla:ni] n eau f bénite de cour, boniments m pl, flagornerie f, pommade f.

blaspheme [blæs'fi:m] vti blasphémer.

blasphemer [blæs'fi:mə] n blasphémateur, -trice.

blasphemous ['blæsfiməs] a blasphématoire, blasphémateur, impie.

blasphemy ['blæsfimi] n blasphème m.

blast [bla:st] n souffle m, coup de vent m, charge explosive f, rafale f, sonnerie f; vt faire sauter, foudroyer, flétrir, brûler, détruire, anéantir.

blast-furnace ['bla:st,fə:nis] n haut-fourneau m.

blasting ['bla:stiŋ] n sautage m, coups m pl de mine, foudroiement m, anéantissement m.

blast-off ['bla:stɔ:f] n mise f à feu.

blatant ['bleitənt] a bruyant, criard, criant.

blaze [bleiz] n flamme f, flambée f, éclat m, conflagration f; go to —s! allez au diable! vi trompeter; vi flamber, flamboyer, resplendir; to — up s'enflammer, s'emporter, se révolter.

blazon ['bleizn] n blason m, armoiries f pl; vt blasonner; to — forth proclamer, publier, crier du haut des toits.

bleach [bliːtʃ] *vti* blanchir; *vi* décolorer; *n* décolorant m, agent de blanchiment m.

bleak [bliːk] *n* ablette *f*; *a* blême, battu des vents, désolé, glacial, désert.

blear [bliə] *a* confus, vague, chassieux; *vt* brouiller, estomper, rendre trouble.

bleat [bliːt] *n* bêlement m; *vi* bêler.

bleed [bliːd] *vti* saigner.

bleeding [bliːdiŋ] *n* saignement m, saignée *f*; *a* saignant, ensanglanté.

blemish [blemiʃ] *n* tache *f*, défaut m, tare *f*; *vt* gâter, (en)tacher, souiller.

blench [blentʃ] *vi* broncher, pâlir, blêmir.

blend [blend] *n* mélange m, alliance *f*; *vt* mêler, mélanger, fondre, marier; *vi* se mêler, se mélanger, se marier, se confondre.

bless [bles] *vt* bénir, consacrer, accorder.

blessed [blesid] *a* béni, comble, bienheureux, saint, fichu.

blessedness [blesidnis] *n* félicité *f*.

blessing [blesiŋ] *n* bénédiction *f*, bénédicité m.

blew [bluː] *pt of* **blow**.

blight [blait] *n* mildiou m, rouille *f*, nielle *f*, brouissure *f*, fléau m; *vt* frapper de mildiou, rouiller, nieller, brouir, moisir, flétrir.

blind [blaind] *n* store m, jalousie *f*, feinte *f*; *a* aveugle, invisible, masqué; sans issue; *vt* aveugler, crever les yeux à, éblouir.

blindfold [blaindfould] *a* ad les yeux bandés; *vt* bander les yeux à.

blindly [blaindli] *ad* aveuglément, à l'aveugle(tte).

blindman's buff [blaindmænz'bʌf] *n* colin-maillard m.

blindness [blaindnis] *n* cécité *f*, aveuglement m.

blink [bliŋk] *n* lueur *f*, coup d'œil m, clignement d'yeux m, échappée *f*; *vi* ciller, cligner, clignoter, papilloter; to — at fermer les yeux sur.

blinkers [bliŋkəz] *n* œillères *f pl*.

bliss [blis] *n* félicité *f*, béatitude *f*.

blister [blistə] *n* ampoule *f*, cloque *f*, boursuflure *f*.

blithe [blaið] *a* joyeux.

blitz [blits] *n* guerre-éclair *f*; bombardement m.

blizzard [blizəd] *n* tempête *f*, tourmente de neige *f*.

bloat [blout] *vt* saler et fumer, enfler, gonfler, bouffir.

bloated [bloutid] *a* bouffi, gonflé, congestionné.

bloater [bloutə] *n* hareng saur m.

blob [blɔb] *n* tache *f*, pâté d'encre m.

block [blɔk] *n* bûche *f*, souche *f*, billot m, bloc m, obstruction *f*, tronçon m; **traffic** — embouteillage

m; — **of houses** pâté de maisons m; — **of flats** immeuble m; *vt* bloquer, obstruer, boucher, encombrer, barrer.

blockade [blɔ'keid] *n* blocus m; **to run the** — braver le blocus; *vt* bloquer, obstruer, faire le blocus de.

blockhead [blɔkhed] *n* tête *f* de bois, bûche *f*.

blockhouse [blɔkhaus] *n* blokhaus m.

bloke [blouk] *n* (*fam*) type m, individu m, coco m.

blood [blʌd] *n* sang m; **in cold** — de sang-froid; **his** — **was up** il était monté.

blood-donor [blʌd'dounə] *n* donneur de sang m.

bloodhound [blʌdhaund] *n* limier m, détective m.

bloodless [blʌdlis] *a* exsangue, anémié, sans effusion de sang.

bloodletting [blʌd'letiŋ] *n* saignée *f*.

blood poisoning [blʌd,pɔizniŋ] *n* empoisonnement m du sang, toxémie *f*.

bloodshed [blʌdʃed] *n* massacre m, carnage m.

bloodshot [blʌdʃɔt] *a* injecté de sang.

bloodsucker [blʌd,sʌkə] *n* sangsue *f*.

bloodthirsty [blʌd,θəːsti] *a* sanguinaire, assoiffé de sang.

bloodvessel [blʌd,vesl] *n* vaisseau sanguin m.

bloody [blʌdi] *a* sanglant, en (de, du) sang, ensanglanté, sanguinaire; *ad* rudement, diablement.

bloom [bluːm] *n* fleur *f*, épanouissement m, duvet m, velouté m; *vi* fleurir, être dans sa, en, fleur.

bloomer [bluːmə] *n* gaffe *f*, bévue *f*, bourde *f*.

blooming [bluːmiŋ] *n* fleuraison *f*; *a* en fleur, fleurissant, florissant, sacré.

blossom [blɔsəm] *n* fleur *f*; *vi* fleurir; to — out s'épanouir.

blot [blɔt] *n* tache *f*, pâté m, défaut m; *vt* faire des taches sur, noircir (du papier), sécher, boire; to — out effacer, anéantir.

blotch [blɔtʃ] *n* pustule *f*, tache *f*; *vt* marbrer, couvrir de taches.

blotchy [blɔtʃi] *a* marbré, couperosé.

blotting-paper [blɔtiŋ,peipə] *n* buvard m.

blouse [blauz] *n* blouse *f*, chemisette *f*; camisole *f*, chemisier m.

blow [blou] *n* coup m, souffle m d'air, floraison *f*; *vi* souffler, venter, fleurir, fondre, sauter; *vt* souffler, essoufler, chasser, faire sauter; **to** — **a kiss** envoyer un baiser; to — **one's nose** se moucher; to — **away** emporter; to — **down** (r)abattre, renverser; **to** — **out** souffler, éteindre, enfler; *vi* s'éteindre; to — **up** *vi* sauter; *vt* faire sauter, gonfler.

blower ['bloʊə] n souffleur m, tablier de cheminée m.

blowfly ['bloʊflaɪ] n mouche f à viande.

blown [bloʊn] pp of **blow**.

blowpipe ['bloʊpaɪp] n chalumeau m, canne f, sarbacane f.

blowy ['bloʊɪ] a venteux, balayé par le vent.

blubber ['blʌbə] n graisse f de baleine, vi pleurer bruyamment, pleurnicher, pleurer comme un veau.

blubberer ['blʌbərə] n pleurnicheur, -euse, pleurard(e) mf.

bludgeon ['blʌdʒən] n trique f, matraque f; vt assommer, asséner un coup de matraque à.

blue [bluː] a bleu; n bleu m, ciel m, la grande bleue f; to have the — avoir le cafard, les papillons noirs; light — bleu clair; dark — bleu foncé; navy — bleu marine; Prussian — bleu de Prusse; sky — bleu de ciel; vt bleuir, passer au bleu, gaspiller.

bluebell ['bluːbel] n clochette f, campanule f.

bluebottle ['bluː bɔtl] n bluet m, mouche bleue f.

bluejacket ['bluːdʒækɪt] n matelot m.

blue-stocking ['bluːstɔkɪŋ] n bas-bleu m.

bluff [blʌf] n cap escarpé m, bluff m; vti bluffer; vi faire du bluff; a à pic, brusque, cordial.

bluffness ['blʌfnɪs] n brusquerie f cordiale, franc-parler m.

bluish ['bluːɪʃ] a bleuâtre, bleuté.

blunder ['blʌndə] n bévue f, gaffe f; vi faire une gaffe, gaffer; to — into heurter; to — along marcher à l'aveuglette.

blunderbuss ['blʌndəbʌs] n tromblon m.

blundering ['blʌndərɪŋ] a maladroit, brouillon.

blunt [blʌnt] a émoussé, brusque, franc; vt émousser.

bluntly ['blʌntlɪ] ad rudement, carrément.

bluntness ['blʌntnɪs] n rudesse f, brusquerie f, état émoussé m.

blur [bləː] n tache f, macule f, buée f, effet confus m; vt tacher, obscurcir, troubler, brouiller, voiler, estomper.

blurb [bləːb] n annonce f, fadaises f pl.

blurt [bləːt] vt to — out lâcher, raconter de but en blanc.

blush [blʌʃ] n rougeur f; vi rougir.

blushingly ['blʌʃɪŋlɪ] ad en rougissant.

bluster ['blʌstə] n fracas m, rodomontades f pl, jactance f, menaces f pl; vi faire rage, s'emporter, le prendre de haut, fanfaronner, faire du fracas.

blusterer ['blʌstərə] n fanfaron m, rodmont m.

blustering ['blʌstərɪŋ] a soufflant en rafales, bravache.

boa ['boʊə] n boa m.

boar [bɔː] n verrat m, sanglier m.

board [bɔːd] n planche f, madrier m, tableau m, carton m, pension f, commission f, ministère m, conseil m, comité m; above — franc, net; on — à bord (de); vi être en pension, prendre pension; vt planchéier, prendre en pension, aborder, aller à bord de, s'embarquer sur; to — out mettre en pension; to — up condamner, boucher.

boarder ['bɔːdə] n pensionnaire mf.

boarding-house ['bɔːdɪŋhaus] n pension f.

boarding-school ['bɔːdɪŋskuːl] n pensionnat m, internat m.

boast [boust] n hâblerie f, vanterie f; vi se vanter, se faire gloire (de about).

boaster ['boustə] n vantard m, fanfaron m, hâbleur m.

boastful ['boustful] a vantard, glorieux.

boat [bout] n bateau m, barque f, canot m, embarcation f; to be in the same — être logés à la même enseigne; vi aller, se promener en bateau, faire du canotage.

boater ['boutə] n (hat) canotier m.

boat-hook ['bouthuk] n gaffe f.

boating ['boutɪŋ] n canotage m, partie de canotage f.

boatman ['boutmən] n batelier m, loueur de canots m.

boat-race ['boutreis] n course de bateaux f, match d'aviron m, régate f.

boatswain ['bousn] n maître d'équipage m.

bob [bɔb] n bouche f, bonchon m, plomb m, coiffure f à la Ninon, courbette f, petit bond m; vt couper court, écourter; vi danser, s'agiter, faire la courbette.

bobbin ['bɔbin] n bobine f.

bobby ['bɔbi] n (fam) sergot m, flic m.

bode [boud] vt présager.

bodice ['bɔdis] n corsage m, cache-corset m.

bodily ['bɔdili] a corporel, physique; ad corporellement, en corps.

boding ['boudɪŋ] n présage m, pressentiment m.

bodkin ['bɔdkin] n passelacet m, épingle f.

body ['bɔdi] n corps m, cadavre m, carrosserie f, fuselage m, substance f, consistance f.

bog [bɔg] n marais m, bourbier m, fondrière f, marécage m; vt enliser, embourber; to get bogged s'enliser.

bogey ['bougi] n épouvantail m, lutin m, croquemitaine m, le Père Fouettard m.

boggle ['bɔgl] vi to — at, over rechigner à, devant, reculer, hésiter devant.

boggy ['bɔgi] *a* marécageux, tourbeux.

bogle ['bougl] *n* fantôme *m*, épouvantail *m*.

bogus ['bougəs] *a* faux, véreux.

boil [bɔil] *n* furoncle *m*, clou *m*; *vi* bouillir, bouillonner; *vt* faire bouillir, faire cuire; to — **down** *vt* condenser, réduire; to — se réduire; to — **over** déborder.

boiler ['bɔilə] *n* chaudière *f*, bouilloire *f*, lessiveuse *f*.

boiler-maker ['bɔiləmeikə] *n* chaudronnier *m*.

boiling ['bɔiliŋ] *n* ébullition *f*, remous *m*, bouillonnement *m*.

boisterous ['bɔistərəs] *a* violent, exuberant, tapageur, bruyant, tempétueux.

boisterousness ['bɔistərəsnis] *n* violence *f*, exubérance *f*, turbulence *f*.

bold [bould] *a* hardi, téméraire, audacieux, effronté; to **make** — to se permettre de, oser.

boldness ['bouldnis] *n* hardiesse *f*, effronterie *f*, audace *f*.

bole [boul] *n* tronc *m*, fût *m*.

Bolshevism ['bɔlʃivizəm] *n* bolchevisme *m*.

Bolshevist ['bɔlʃivist] *n* bolcheviste *mf*.

bolster ['boulstə] *n* traversin *m*, coussinet *m*; *vt* soutenir, préserver, appuyer.

bolt [boult] *n* verrou *m*, pêne *m*, boulon *m*, coup de foudre *m*, culasse *f*; *vt* verrouiller, enfermer, boulonner, avaler tout rond, gober, bouffer; *vi* s'emballer, détaler, déguerpir, décamper, filer, lever le pied.

bolter ['boultə] *n* blutoir *m*; *vt* bluter.

boltering ['boultəriŋ] *n* blutage *m*.

bomb [bɔm] *n* bombe *f*; **time** — bombe *f* à retardement; —**proof** à l'abri des bombes.

bombard [bɔm'bɑːd] *vt* bombarder, pilonner.

bombast ['bɔmbæst] *n* emphase *f*, grandiloquence *f*.

bombastic [bɔm'bæstik] *a* ampoulé, emphatique.

bomb-crater ['bɔmkreitə] *n* entonnoir *m*.

bomber ['bɔmə] *n* bombardier *m*.

bond [bɔnd] *n* attache *f*, lien *m*, engagement *m*, obligation *f*, depôt *m*, bon *m*, entrepôt *m*, douane *f*; *pl* fers *m pl*; *vt* assembler, entreposer, mettre en dépôt.

bondage ['bɔndidʒ] *n* servitude *f*, esclavage *m*, emprisonnement *m*.

bondholder ['bɔnd.houldə] *n* obligataire *m*, porteur *m* de bons.

bondsman ['bɔndzmən] *n* esclave *m*.

bone [boun] *n* os *m*, (*fish*) arêt˃ *f*; ossements *m pl*; *vt* désosser, escamoter.

boneless ['bounlis] *a* mou, désossé, sans arêtes.

bonfire ['bɔn.faiə] *n* feu *m* de joie.

bonnet ['bɔnit] *n* bonnet *m*, béguin *m*, capot *m*; **bee in the** — araignée dans le plafond.

bonny ['bɔni] *a* beau, joli.

bonus ['bounəs] *n* boni *m*, prime *f*, gratification *f*.

bony ['bouni] *a* osseux, décharné, anguleux, tout os, plein d'arêtes.

boo [buː] *n* huée *f*; *vti* huer.

booby ['buːbi] *n* niais(e) *mf*, nigaud(e) *mf*.

booby-trap ['buːbitræp] *n* attrapenigaud *m*.

book [buk] *n* livre *m*, bouquin *m*, livret *m*, cahier *m*, carnet *m*; *vt* entrer, inscrire, retenir, louer.

bookbinder ['buk.baində] *n* relieur *m*.

bookbinding ['buk.baindiŋ] *n* reliure *f*.

bookcase ['bukkeis] *n* bibliothèque *f*.

book-ends ['bukendz] *n pl* serrelivres *m inv*.

booking ['bukiŋ] *n* location *f*, inscription *f*, réservation *f*.

booking-office ['bukiŋ.ɔfis] *n* bureau *m* de location, guichet *m*.

bookish ['bukiʃ] *a* livresque.

book-keeper ['buk.kiːpə] *n* teneur *m* de livres, comptable *m*.

book-keeping ['buk.kiːpiŋ] *n* tenue *f* de livres, comptabilité *f*.

booklet ['buklit] *n* livret *m*, brochure *f*.

bookmaker ['buk.meikə] *n* bookmaker *m*.

bookmark ['bukmɑːk] *n* signet *m*.

bookseller ['buk.selə] *n* libraire *m*.

book-sewer ['buk.souə] *n* brocheur *m*.

bookshop ['bukʃɔp] *n* librairie *f*.

bookstall ['bukstɔːl] *n* étalage *m* de livres, (*station*) bibliothèque *f*.

bookworm ['bukwəːm] *n* rat de bibliothèque *m*.

boom [buːm] *n* emballement *m*, vogue *f*, hausse rapide *f*, boom *m*, grondement *m*, ronflement *m*, barrage *m*; *vt* faire de la réclame pour, faire du tapage, du battage, autour de; *vi* entrer en hausse, s'emballer, trouver la grande vente, retentir, ronfler, tonner.

boon [buːn] *n* faveur *f*, don *m*, bénédiction *f*, avantage *m*; — **companion** bon vivant *m*, bon compagnon *m*.

boor [buə] *n* rustre *m*, goujat *m*, paysan *m*.

boorishness ['buəriʃnis] *n* rusticité *f*, grossièreté *f*.

boost [buːst] *vt* faire du tapage autour de, faire de la réclame pour, lancer, chauffer.

boot [buːt] *n* bottine *f*, botte *f*, brodequin *m*, coffre *m*.

bootblack ['buːtblæk] n cireur m.
booth [buːθ] n tente f, baraque f, salle f de scrutin.
boot-jack ['buːtdʒæk] n tirebottes m.
bootleg ['buːt.leg] vi faire la contrebande des boissons alcooliques.
bootmaker ['buːt.meikə] n bottier m, cordonnier m.
boot polish ['buːt.pɔliʃ] n cirage m, crème f à chaussures.
boots [buːts] n garçon m d'étage, cireur m de chaussures.
booty ['buːti] n butin m.
booze [buːz] n (fam) boisson f; vi chopiner, être en ribote.
bopeep [bou'piːp] n cache-cache m.
border ['bɔːdə] n bord m, bordure f, marge f, lisière f, frontière f; vt border; to — upon frôler, toucher à, tirer sur, friser, côtoyer.
borderer ['bɔːdərə] n frontalier, -ière.
borderline ['bɔːdəlain] n ligne de démarcation f; — case cas limite m.
bore [bɔː] pt of bear; n (gun) âme f, calibre m, trou m, mascaret m, raseur m, importun(e) mf, corvée f, scie f; vt forer, percer, assommer, ennuyer; vi (horse) encenser.
boredom ['bɔːdəm] n ennui m.
boring ['bɔːriŋ] a ennuyeux, assommant.
born [bɔːn] pp né; to be — naître; he was — il est né, il naquit; to be — again renaître.
borne [bɔːn] pp of bear.
borough ['bʌrə] n bourg m.
borrow ['bɔrou] vt emprunter.
borrower ['bɔrouə] n emprunteur, -euse.
borrowing ['bɔrouiŋ] n emprunt m.
bosh [bɔʃ] n blague f, fariboles f pl, chansons f pl.
bosom ['buzəm] n sein m, giron m, poitrine f, cœur m, surface f; a intime.
boss [bɔs] n bosse f, patron, -onne.
bossy ['bɔsi] a autoritaire.
botanist ['bɔtənist] n botaniste mf.
botany ['bɔtəni] n botanique f.
botch [bɔtʃ] n travail malfait m, ravaudage m; vt ravauder, saboter; to — up retaper, rafistoler.
both [bouθ] pn tous (les) deux, l'un et l'autre; a deux; ad à la fois, tant ... que ...
bother ['bɔðə] n ennui m, tracas m, embêtement m; vt ennuyer, tourmenter, tracasser, embêter; vi s'inquiéter, se faire de la bile; excl zut!
bottle ['bɔtl] n bouteille f, flacon m, bocal m, (hay) botte f, (baby's) biberon m; hot-water — bouillotte f, moine m; vt mettre en bouteilles, botteler; to — up ravaler, refouler, étouffer, embouteiller.
bottleneck ['bɔtlnek] n étranglement m, goulot m, embouteillage m.

bottle-washer ['bɔtl.wɔʃə] n plongeur m.
bottom ['bɔtəm] n fond m, derrière m, siège m, lit m, bas bout m, queue f, bas m, dessous m; vt mettre un fond, siège, à; vi toucher le fond; to get to the — of approfondir.
bottomless ['bɔtəmlis] a sans fond, insondable.
bough [bau] n rameau m, branche f.
boulder ['bouldə] n gros galet m, roche f, pierre f roulée.
bounce [bauns] n bond m, vantardise f, épate f; vt faire rebondir; vi (re)bondir, se vanter, faire de l'épate.
bouncer ['baunsə] n hâbleur m, épateur m, mensonge impudent m, expulseur m, videur m.
bound [baund] pt pp of bind; n limite f, bornes f pl, saut m, bond m; vt borner, limiter; vi (re)bondir, (sur)sauter; a à destination de, en route (pour), lié (à to), tenu (de to); he is — to come il ne peut pas manquer de venir.
boundary ['baundəri] n frontière f, limite f, bornes f pl.
bounden ['baundən] a sacré, impérieux.
boundless ['baundlis] a illimité, infini, sans bornes.
bounteous ['bauntiəs] a abondant, généreux.
bountiful ['bauntiful] a généreux, bienfaisant.
bounty ['baunti] n générosité f, munificence f, fondation f, prime f, subvention f.
bouquet [bu'kei] n bouquet m.
bout [baut] n tour m, orgie f, crise f, accès m, lutte f.
bow [bou] n courbe f, arc m, (coup d')archet m, nœud m; a arqué, cintré.
bow [bau] n révérence f, salut m, avant m, étrave f; vt courber, incliner, baisser, plier, voûter; vi s'incliner, faire une révérence.
bowels ['bauəlz] n boyaux m pl, entrailles f pl, intestins m pl.
bower ['bauə] n charmille f, tonnelle f.
bowl [boul] n bol m, jatte f, coupe f, (pipe) fourneau m, boule f; pl (jeu de) boules f pl; vt rouler, lancer; vi jouer aux boules; to — over renverser.
bowler ['boulə] n joueur m de boules, (hat) melon m.
bowling-green ['bouliŋgriːn] n boulingrin m, jeu m de boules.
bowman ['boumən] n archer m.
bowsprit ['bousprit] n beaupré m.
bow-window ['bou'windou] n fenêtre cintrée f, en saillie.
box [bɔks] n boîte f, caisse f, coffre m, carton m, tirelire f, tronc m, loge f, barre f, siège m du cocher, guérite f, pavillon m de chasse

(*horse*) box *m*, stalle *f*; — **on the ear** gifle *f*, claque *f*; *vt* to — s.o.'s ears gifler qn, calotter; *vi* boxer, faire de la boxe.

boxer ['bɔksə] *n* boxeur *m*.

boxing ['bɔksiŋ] *n* boxe *f*.

box-office ['bɔks'ɔfis] *n* bureau *m* de location.

box-room ['bɔksrum] *n* (chambre *f* de) débarras *m*.

boxwood ['bɔkswud] *n* buis *m*.

boy [bɔi] *n* enfant *m*, garçon *m*, gars *m*, élève *m*, gamin *m*, boy *m*.

boycott ['bɔikət] *vt* boycotter.

boycotting ['bɔikətiŋ] *n* boycottage *m*.

boyhood ['bɔihud] *n* enfance *f*, adolescence *f*.

boyish ['bɔiiʃ] *a* garçonnier, puéril, enfantin, de garçon, d'enfant.

brace [breis] *n* attache *f*, croisillon *m*, acolade *f*, vilebrequin *m*, paire *f*, couple *f*; *pl* bretelles *f pl*; *vt* attacher, armer, ancrer, tendre, coupler, fortifier; to — **up** ravigoter, remonter, retremper; to — o.s. se raidir.

bracelet ['breislit] *n* bracelet *m*.

bracing ['breisiŋ] *a* fortifiant, tonique, tonifiant.

bracken ['brækən] *n* fougère *f*.

bracket ['brækit] *n* applique *f*, console *f*, tasseau *m*, (*gas*) bras *m*, parenthèse *f*, crochet *m*; *vt* mettre entre parenthèses, accoler.

bracket-seat ['brækit,si:t] *n* strapontin *m*.

brackish ['brækiʃ] *a* saumâtre.

brag [bræg] *n* vantardise *f*, fanfaronnade *f*; *vi* se vanter.

braggart ['brægət] *n* vantard *m*, fanfaron *m*.

braid [breid] *n* natte *f*, tresse *f*, galon *m*, lacet *m*, ganse *f*, soutache *f*; *vt* natter, border, soutacher, galonner, passementer.

brain [brein] *n* cerveau *m*, cervelle *f*; to rack one's —s se creuser la cervelle; *a* cérébral; *vt* assommer, casser la tête à.

brain-child ['breintʃaild] *n* conception personnelle *f*.

brain-drain ['breindrein] *n* brain-drain *m*.

brain-fever ['brein,fi:və] *n* fièvre cérébrale *f*.

brainless ['breinlis] *a* idiot, stupide.

brainwave ['breinweiv] *n* idée géniale *f*, trouvaille *f*, inspiration *f*.

brainy ['breini] *a* (*fam*) intelligent; to be — avoir de la tête.

braise [breiz] *vt* braiser.

brake [breik] *n* fourré *m*, hallier *m*, frein *m*; *vti* freiner; *vi* serrer le frein.

brakesman ['breikzmən] *n* serre-frein *m*.

bramble ['bræmbl] *n* ronce *f*, mûrier *m* des haies; — **berry** mûre sauvage *f*.

bran [bræn] *n* son *m*.

branch [bra:ntʃ] *n* branche *f*, rameau *m*, bras *m*, embranchement *m*, filiale *f*, succursale *f*; *vi* to — **out** se ramifier; to — **off** bifurquer.

branch-line, -road ['bra:ntʃlain, roud] *n* embranchement *m*, bifurcation *f*.

brand [brænd] *n* tison *m*, brandon *m*, marque *f*, fer rouge *m*; *vt* marquer au fer rouge, cautériser, stigmatiser, flétrir.

brandish ['brændiʃ] *vt* brandir.

brand-new ['brænd'nju:] *a* flambant neuf.

brandy ['brændi] *n* cognac *m*, eau *f* de vie; **liqueur** — fine champagne *f*.

brass [bra:s] *n* cuivre jaune *m*, laiton *m*, les cuivres *m pl*, toupet *m*, (*sl*) galette *f*.

brass-band ['bra:s'bænd] *n* fanfare *f*.

brass-hat ['bra:s'hæt] *n* officier d'état-major *m*, galonnard *m*.

brassière ['bræsiə] *n* soutien-gorge *m*.

brass-plate ['bra:s'pleit] *n* plaque *f*.

brassware ['bra:sweə] *n* dinanderie *f*.

brat [bræt] *n* mioche *mf*, moutard *m*.

bravado [brə'va:dou] *n* crânerie *f*, bravade *f*.

brave [breiv] *a* brave, courageux, beau, élégant; *vt* braver, affronter; to — it out payer d'audace.

bravery ['breivəri] *n* bravoure *f*, courage *m*, élégance *f*, atours *m pl*.

brawl [brɔ:l] *n* dispute *f*, rixe *f*, bagarre *f*, murmure *m*, bruissement *m*; *vi* se chamailler, se bagarrer, brailler, bruire, murmurer.

brawn [brɔ:n] *n* muscle *m*, fromage *m* de tête.

brawny ['brɔ:ni] *a* musclé, costaud.

bray [brei] *n* braiment *m*; *vti* braire; *vt* broyer.

braze [breiz] *vt* souder, braser.

brazen ['breizn] *a* d'airain, effronté, cynique.

brazier ['breizjə] *n* chaudronnier *m*, brasero *m*.

breach [bri:tʃ] *n* brèche *f*, rupture *f*, contravention *f* violation *f*, infraction *f*; *vt* faire (une) brèche dans, percer.

bread [bred] *n* pain *m*; **new** — pain frais; **stale** — pain rassis; **brown** — pain bis; **wholemeal** — pain complet; — **bin** huche *f* au pain, maie *f*.

bread-crumbs ['bredkrʌmz] *n pl* chapelure *f*, gratin *m*.

breadth [bredθ] *n* largeur *f*, ampleur *f*.

break [breik] *n* fracture *f*, cassure *f*, rupture *f*, alinéa *m*, percée *f*, trouée *f*, lacune *f*, trou *m*, arrêt *m*, répit *m*; — **of day** point du jour *m*; *vt* (inter)rompre, casser, briser, entamer, violer, manquer à, amortir, résilier; *vi* (se) briser, (se) rompre (se) casser, poindre, muer, s'altérer, déferler; **to — down** vt démolir, supprimer, venir à bout de; vi s'effrondrer, échouer, demeurer court, fondre en larmes, rester en panne; **to — in** vt défoncer, enfoncer, dresser; vi intervenir, entrer par effraction, faire irruption; **to — off** vt détacher, casser, (inter) rompre; vi se détacher, s'(inter) rompre; **to — out** s'évader, se déclarer, éclater; **to — through** vt enfoncer, percer, trouer; vi faire une percée, se frayer un passage; **to — up** vt démolir, séparer, désarmer, démembrer, morceler, disperser, rompre; vi se désagréger, se séparer, se disperser, se démembrer, entrer en vacances.

breakable ['breikəbl] a fragile.

breakage ['breikidʒ] n casse f, fracture f.

breakdown ['breikdaun] n panne f, effondrement nerveux m, rupture f, insuccès m, interruption f.

breaker ['breikə] n dresseur, -euse, dompteur, -euse, brisant m, violateur, -trice.

breakfast ['brekfəst] n petit déjeuner m; vi déjeuner.

breakneck ['breiknek] a à se rompre le cou.

break-through ['breik'θru:] n percée f, trouée f.

break-up ['breik'ʌp] n dissolution f, dispersion f, affaissement m, entrée f en vacances.

breakwater ['breik.wɔ:tə] n brise-lames m, môle m.

bream [bri:m] n brème f.

breast [brest] n poitrine f, sein m, poitrail m, blanc m, devant m.

breastbone ['brestboun] n sternum m.

breasted ['brestid] a **single—** droit; **double—** croisé.

breastplate ['brestpleit] n cuirasse f, plastron m.

breast-stroke ['breststrouk] n brasse (sur le ventre).

breath [breθ] n souffle m, haleine f, bouffée f; **last —** dernier soupir m, âme f; **under one's —** à mi-voix, en sourdine.

breathe [bri:ð] vti souffler, respirer; vt exhaler, murmurer; **to — in** aspirer; **to — out** exhaler.

breather ['bri:ðə] n moment de répit m; **to give a — to** s.o. laisser souffler qn; **to go for a —** aller prendre l'air.

breathing ['bri:ðiŋ] n respiration f.

breathless ['breθlis] a essouflé.

breathlessness ['breθlisnis] n essouflement m.

bred [bred] pp pt of **breed**.

breech [bri:tʃ] n culasse f, derrière m; pl culotte f.

breed [bri:d] n race f, lignée f, couvée f, espèce f; vt porter, élever,

produire, engendrer, procréer; vi multiplier, se réproduire, faire de l'élevage.

breeder ['bri:də] n éleveur m, réproducteur, -trice.

breeding ['bri:diŋ] n élevage m, reproduction f, éducation f, savoir vivre m.

breeze [bri:z] n brise f, grabuge m.

breezy ['bri:zi] a venteux, désinvolte, bruyant.

brethren ['breðrin] n pl frères m pl.

Breton ['bretən] an Breton, -onne.

breviary ['bri:vjəri] n bréviaire m.

brevity ['breviti] n brièveté f.

brew [bru:] vt brasser, faire infuser, fomenter; vi fermenter, s'infuser, se préparer, se mijoter, se tramer.

brewer ['bru:ə] n brasseur m.

brewery ['bruəri] n brasserie f.

brewing ['bru:iŋ] n brassage m.

briar ['braiə] n ronce f, bruyère f, églantier m; **— rose** églantine f.

bribe [braib] n pot-de-vin m; vt acheter, soudoyer, graisser la patte à.

bribery ['braibəri] n corruption f.

bribing ['braibiŋ] n corruption f, subornation f.

brick [brik] n brique f; **to drop a —** faire une gaffe.

brick-kiln ['brikkiln] n four m à briques.

bricklayer ['brikleiə] n maçon m.

brickwork ['brikwə:k] n maçonnerie f.

bridal ['braidl] a de noce, de mariée, nuptial, de mariage.

bride [braid] n mariée f, jeune mariée f.

bridegroom ['braidgrum] n marié m.

bridesmaid ['braidzmeid] n demoiselle d'honneur f.

bridge [bridʒ] n pont m, passerelle f, (nose) dos m, (violin) chevalet m, (cards) bridge m; vt jeter un pont sur, relier, combler.

bridgehead ['bridʒhed] n tête de pont f, point d'appui m.

Bridget ['bridʒit] Brigitte f.

bridge-train ['bridʒtrein] n les pontonniers m pl, train de pontons m.

bridle ['braidl] n bridon m, bride f, frein m; vt brider, refréner; vi se rebiffer, se redresser, regimber.

brief [bri:f] n bref m, dossier m, exposé m, cause f; vt engager, constituer, rédiger; a bref, court; **in —** bref, en résumé.

briefless ['bri:flis] a sans cause.

briefly ['bri:fli] ad brièvement.

brig [brig] n brick m.

brigade [bri'geid] n brigade f.

brigadier [brigə'diə] n général m de brigade.

brigand ['brigənd] n bandit m, brigand m.

bright ['brait] a clair, vif, éclatant, lumineux, brillant, éveillé.

brighten ['braitn] vt animer, éclairer, égayer, dérider, fourbir; vi s'animer, s'éclairer, se dérider, s'épanouir, s'éclaircir.

brightness ['braitnis] n éclat m, splendeur f, vivacité f.

brilliant ['briljənt] a brillant.

brilliantly ['briljəntli] ad brillamment, avec brio.

brim [brim] n bord m, vt remplir jusqu'au bord; to — over déborder.

brimstone ['brimstən] n soufre m.

brine [brain] n saumure f; vt saler.

bring [briŋ] vt apporter, amener, faire venir; to — about causer, amener, produire, effectuer, opérer, entraîner, occasionner; to — down abattre, (r)abaisser, terrasser, faire crouler, descendre; to — forth produire, mettre au monde, mettre bas, provoquer; to — forward avancer, reporter; to — in introduire, faire entrer, rapporter, faire intervenir; to — off mener à bien, réussir, sauver, renflouer; to — out faire (res)sortir, faire valoir, mettre en relief, lancer; to — round ranimer, (r)amener; to — together réunir, réconcilier; to — up élever, (faire) monter, avancer, mettre sur le tapis, rendre.

brink [briŋk] n bord m; on the — of près de, à la veille de.

briny ['braini] a salé, saumâtre; n (fam) mer f.

brisk [brisk] a vif, actif, fringant, animé, gazeux, vivifiant, frais.

brisket ['briskit] n poitrine f (de bœuf).

briskness ['brisknis] n vivacité f, activité f.

bristle ['brisl] n soie f, crin m, poil m; vt faire dresser, hérisser; vi se hérisser, se rebiffer, regimber.

bristling ['brisliŋ] a hérissé.

Britain ['britn] n Angleterre f; Great — Grande Bretagne f.

British ['britiʃ] a anglais, britannique.

Briton ['britn] n Anglais(e) mf.

Brittany ['britəni] n Bretagne f.

brittle ['britl] a fragile, cassant.

brittleness ['britlnis] n fragilité f.

broach [broutʃ] n broche f, flèche f, perçoir m, foret m; vt percer, mettre en perce, entamer, embrocher.

broad [brɔːd] a large, plein, grivois, hardi, libre, marqué; n (US) (sl) poupée f.

broadcast ['brɔːdkɑːst] vt radio-diffuser, répandre, disséminer; n émission f, radio-reportage m, audition f.

broadcaster ['brɔːdkɑːstə] n micro-phoniste mf, artiste mf de la radio.

broadcasting ['brɔːdkɑːstiŋ] n radio-diffusion f; — station poste émetteur m.

broaden ['brɔːdn] vt élargir; vi s'élargir, s'évaser.

broadening ['brɔːdniŋ] n élargissement m.

broad-minded ['brɔːdmaindid] a tolérant, aux idées larges.

broadness ['brɔːdnis] n largeur f, grossièrté f.

broadside ['brɔːdsaid] n bordée f, flanc m, travers m.

brocade [brə'keid] n brocart m.

broil [brɔil] n dispute f, rixe f; vti (faire) griller.

broiling ['brɔiliŋ] a ardent, torride.

broke [brouk] pt of **break**; a sans le sou, dans la dèche.

broken ['broukən] pp of **break**; a brisé, détraqué, raboteux, incertain, en pièces, (entre)coupé, agité, décousu.

brokenly ['broukənli] ad sans suite, par à-coups.

broken-winded ['broukən'windid] a poussif.

broker ['broukə] n revendeur, -euse, courtier m, agent m de change, brocanteur m.

brokerage ['broukəridʒ] n courtage m.

bronchitis [brɔŋ'kaitis] n bronchite f.

bronze [brɔnz] n bronze m; vt bronzer; vi se bronzer.

brooch [broutʃ] n broche f.

brood ['bruːd] n couvée f, nichée f, volée f; vi couver, méditer, rêver; to — over remâcher, couver.

brook [bruk] n ruisseau m; vt souffrir.

brooklet ['bruklit] n ruisselet m.

broom [bruːm] n genêt m; balai m; —stick manche m à balai.

broth [brɔθ] n bouillon m, potage m.

brother ['brʌðə] n frère m, confrère m.

brotherhood ['brʌðəhud] n confrérie f, société f, fraternité f.

brother-in-law ['brʌðərinlɔ:] n beau-frère m.

brotherly ['brʌðəli] a fraternel.

brought [brɔːt] pt of **bring**.

brow [brau] n sourcil m, front m, surplomb m, crête f.

browbeat ['braubiːt] vt malmener, intimider, rabrouer.

brown [braun] an brun m, marron m; a châtain, fauve; vt brunir, faire dorer, rissoler.

brownish ['brauniʃ] a brunâtre.

browse [brauz] vti brouter, bouquiner.

bruise [bruːz] n meurtrissure f, contusion f, bleu n, noir m; vt meurtrir, contusionner.

brunette [bruː'net] an brune f.

brunt [brʌnt] n choc m, poids m, fort m.

brush [brʌʃ] n brosse f, balai m, pinceau m, coup m de brosse, (fox) queue f; échauffourée f; vt brosser, balayer; to — aside écarter; to — out balayer; to — up, down donner un coup de brosse à;

to — **up** repolir, rafraîchir, dérouiller; to — **against** frôler, effleurer.

brushwood ['brʌʃwud] n broussailles f pl, fourré m, brindilles f pl.

brusque [brusk] a brusque, bourru, rude.

Brussels ['brʌslz] n Bruxelles; — **sprouts** choux m pl de Bruxelles.

brutal ['bru:tl] a brutal, de brute, sensuel.

brutality [bru:'tæliti] n brutalité f.

brutalize ['bru:təlaiz] vt abrutir.

brute [bru:t] n bête f, brute f; a brut, stupide.

brutish ['bru:tiʃ] a bestial, de brute, abruti.

bubble ['bʌbl] n bulle f, bouillon m, chimère f; vi bouillonner, pétiller, glouglouter; to — **over** déborder.

buccaneer [,bʌkə'niə] n flibustier m, pirate m.

buck [bʌk] n daim m, chevreuil m, mâle m, dandy m; to — **off** désarçonner; vt to — **up** remonter le courage à, ravigoter; vi reprendre courage, se remuer.

bucket ['bʌkit] n seau m, baquet m.

buckle ['bʌkl] n boucle f, agrafe f, voile m, benne f; vt boucler, agrafer, serrer, voiler; vi se mettre (à to), s'appliquer (à to); to — **up** se voiler, se gondoler.

buckler ['bʌklə] n bouclier m.

buckram ['bʌkrəm] n bougran m.

buckshee ['bʌk'ʃiː] ad à l'œil, gratis.

buckskin ['bʌkskin] n peau f de daim.

buckwheat ['bʌkwiːt] n sarrasin m.

bud [bʌd] n bourgeon m, bouton m; vi bourgeonner, boutonner.

budding ['bʌdiŋ] a qui bourgeonne, qui boutonne, en herbe.

budge [bʌdʒ] vi bouger, remuer, reculer.

budget ['bʌdʒit] n sac m, budget m; to — **for sth** porter qch au budget.

buff [bʌf] n buffle m; a couleur buffle; vt polir; to strip to the — se mettre à poil.

buffalo ['bʌfəlou] n buffle m.

buffer ['bʌfə] n tampon m, amortisseur m; —**state** état-tampon m.

buffer-stop ['bʌfəstɔp] n butoir m.

buffet ['bʌfit] n soufflet m; vt souffleter, ballotter, secouer; vi lutter.

buffet ['bufei] n buffet m.

buffoon [bʌ'fuːn] n bouffon m.

buffoonery [bʌ'fuːnəri] n bouffonnerie f.

bug [bʌg] n punaise f, (US) insecte m; **big** — grosse légume.

bugbear ['bʌgbeə] n épouvantail m, cauchemar m, bête noire f, loup-garou m.

bugle ['bjuːgl] n clairon m; vi sonner du clairon.

bugler ['bjuːglə] n clairon m.

build [bild] vt construire, bâtir, fonder; to — **up** échafauder,

affermir, créer; n construction f, charpente f.

builder ['bildə] n entrepreneur m, constructeur m, fondateur, -trice.

building ['bildiŋ] n bâtiment m, édifice m, construction f.

built [bilt] pp pt of **build**; —**up area** agglomération urbaine f.

bulb [bʌlb] n bulbe m, ampoule f, poire f, oignon m.

Bulgaria [bʌl'gɛəriə] n Bulgarie f.

Bulgarian [bʌl'gɛəriən] an bulgare m; n Bulgare mf.

bulge [bʌldʒ] n gonflement m, renflement m, bombement m; vti bomber, ballonner; vi faire saillie.

bulk [bʌlk] n chargement m, grande carcasse f, masse f, gros m, volume m, grandeur f, — **in** — en vrac, en gros; vt empiler, grouper; to — **large** occuper une place importante.

bulkhead ['bʌlkhed] n cloison f étanche.

bulky ['bʌlki] a volumineux, encombrant.

bull [bul] n taureau m, mâle m, haussier m, bulle f, bourde f, mouche f.

bulldog ['buldɔg] n bouledogue m.

bulldozer ['bul douzə] n niveleuse f, bulldozer m.

bullet ['bulit] n balle f.

bulletin ['bulitin] n bulletin m, communiqué m; **news** — informations f pl, journal parlé m.

bullfight ['bulfait] n course f de taureaux.

bullfinch ['bulfintʃ] n bouvreuil m.

bullheaded ['bul'hedid] a têtu, gaffeur, impétueux.

bullion ['buljən] n lingot m.

bullock ['bulək] n bœuf m.

bull's eye ['bulzai] n noir m, mouche f, hublot m, œil de bœuf m, lanterne sourde f, lentille f.

bully ['buli] n brute f, brimeur m, souteneur m; vt rudoyer, brutaliser, malmener.

bully-beef ['buli'biːf] n (fam) singe m.

bulwark ['bulwək] n rempart m, bastingage m.

bumble-bee ['bʌmblbiː] n bourdon m.

bump [bʌmp] n heurt m, secousse f, cahot m, bosse f; vt heurter, cogner, secouer; vi (se) heurter, (se) cogner, buter; to — **along** cahoter; to — **into** tamponner, buter contre; excl pan!

bumper ['bʌmpə] n (aut) parechoc m; rasade f; a monstre, comble etc.

bumpkin ['bʌmpkin] n rustre m.

bumptious ['bʌmpʃəs] a arrogant, présomptueux.

bumptiousness ['bʌmpʃəsnis] n arrogance f, suffisance f, outrecuidance f.

bumpy ['bʌmpi] a en creux et en bosses, cahoteux, inégal.

bunch [bʌntʃ] n bouquet m (grapes)

grappe *f*, (*radishes*) botte *f*, (*bananas*)
régime *m*, (*keys*) trousseau *m*,
(*people*) bande *f*, groupe *m*, peloton
m; *vt* lier, attacher, botteler, réunir,
grouper; *vi* se pelotonner, se serrer.

bundle ['bʌndl] *n* paquet *m*, fagot
m, liasse *f*, ballot *m*, faisceau *m*; *vt*
mettre en paquet, empaqueter,
fourrer; to — off envoyer paître;
to — out flanquer à la porte.

bungle ['bʌŋgl] *n* gâchis *m*; *vt*
gâcher, bousiller, rater, massacrer.

bungler ['bʌŋglə] *n* maladroit(e) *mf*,
bousilleur *m*.

bunion ['bʌnjən] *n* oignon *m*.

bunk [bʌŋk] *n* couchette *f*; *vi*
décamper, filer.

bunker ['bʌŋkə] *n* soute *f*, banquette
f, (*golf*) bunker *m*.

bunkum ['bʌŋkəm] *n* blague *f*,
balivernes *f pl*.

bunting ['bʌntiŋ] *n* étamine *f*,
drapeaux *m pl*.

buoy [bɔi] *n* bouée *f*.

buoyancy ['bɔiənsi] *n* insubmersibi-
lité *f*, élasticité *f*, entrain *m*, ressort
m.

buoyant ['bɔiənt] *a* élastique,
exubérant, flottable, insubmersible,
qui a du ressort.

burble ['bə:bl] *n* murmure *m*,
gloussement *m*; *vi* murmurer,
glousser.

burden ['bə:dn] *n* charge *f*, fardeau
m, tonnage *m*, poids *m*, refrain *m*,
essentiel *m*, fond *m*; *vt* charger,
encombrer.

burdensome ['bə:dnsəm] *a* pesant,
encombrant, fâcheux, onéreux.

bureau ['bjuərou] *n* bureau *m*,
secrétaire *m*.

bureaucracy [bjuə'rɔkrəsi] *n* bureaucratie *f*.

bureaucrat ['bjuəroukræt] *n* bureaucrate *m*, rond-de-cuir *m*.

burgess ['bə:dʒis] *n* bourgeois *m*,
citoyen *m*.

burgh ['bʌrə] *n* (*Scot*) bourg *m*.

burglar ['bə:glə] *n* cambrioleur *m*.

burglary ['bə:gləri] *n* cambriolage
m.

burgle ['bə:gl] *vt* cambrioler.

burgomaster ['bə:gə,maːstə] *n*
bourgmestre *m*.

Burgundian [bə:'gʌndjən] *a* bourguignon; *n* Bourguignon, -onne.

Burgundy ['bə:gəndi] *n* Bourgogne
f, (*wine*) bourgogne *m*.

burial ['beriəl] *n* enterrement *m*.

burlesque [bə:'lesk] *an* burlesque
m; *n* parodie *f*; *vt* parodier.

burly ['bə:li] *a* massif, solide, costaud.

Burma ['bə:mə] *n* Birmanie *f*.

Burmese [bə:'miːz] *an* birman.

burn [bə:n] *n* brûlure *f*; *vti* brûler.

burner ['bə:nə] *n* brûleur, -euse, bec
m, brûleur *m*.

burnish ['bə:niʃ] *vt* polir.

burnt [bə:nt] *pp of* **burn**; —
offering holocauste *m*.

burrow ['bʌrou] *n* terrier *m*; *vt*
creuser; *vi* se terrer, fouiller.

bursar ['bə:sə] *n* économe *mf*,
boursier, -ière.

burst [bə:st] *n* éclatement *m*,
explosion *f*, salve *f*, éclat *m*; *vti*
éclater, crever; *vt* faire éclater, faire
sauter, percer, rompre; *vi* faire
explosion, exploser, sauter, se
rompre, éclore, regorger; to — in
vt enfoncer; *vi* faire irruption; to —
out jaillir, éclater, s'exclamer, sortir
en coup de vent.

bury ['beri] *vt* enterrer, enfouir,
ensevelir, enfoncer, plonger.

bus [bʌs] *n* autobus *m*, (*auto*)car *m*;
to miss the — manquer l'autobus,
manquer le coche.

bush [buʃ] *n* arbuste *m*, arbrisseau
m, buisson *m*, brousse *f*, coussinet
m, bague *f*; —cat serval *m*.

bushel ['buʃl] *n* boisseau *m*.

bushy ['buʃi] *a* touffu, broussailleux,
épais.

busily ['bizili] *ad* activement, avec
affairement.

business ['biznis] *n* affaire(s) *f pl*,
occupation *f*, établissement *m*; it is
none of your — cela ne vous regarde
pas; to make it one's — to se faire
un devoir de; to send s.o. about his
— envoyer promener qn; big —man
brasseur d'affaires; —man homme
d'affaires.

businesslike ['biznislaik] *a* actif,
pratique, sérieux.

buskin ['bʌskin] *n* cothurne *m*.

bust [bʌst] *n* buste *m*, gorge *f*.

bustle ['bʌsl] *n* agitation *f*, remue-
ménage *m*; *vi* s'agiter, s'affairer,
faire l'empressé; *vt* bousculer.

busy ['bizi] *a* occupé, actif, affairé;
vt occuper.

busybody ['bizibɔdi] *n* mouche *f* du
coche, officieux, -euse *mf*.

but [bʌt] *cj* mais, sans (que), que . . .
ne (*after a negative*); *ad* seulement,
ne . . . que, excepté, autre que,
sinon, si ce n'est; — for sans, à part;
all — presque, autant dire; anything
— riens moins que.

butcher ['butʃə] *n* boucher *m*; *vt*
massacrer, égorger; —'s boucherie *f*.

butchery ['butʃəri] *n* boucherie *f*,
massacre *m*, tuerie *f*.

butler ['bʌtlə] *n* sommelier *m*,
dépensier *m*, maître d'hôtel *m*.

butt [bʌt] *n* crosse *f*, gros bout *m*,
(*US*) mégot *m*, butte *f*, coup *m* de tête,
tête *f* de turc, souffre-douleur *m*,
cible *f*; *pl* champ *m* de tir; *vt*
donner un coup de tête à; *vi* fourrer
le nez (dans into), foncer (dans into),
donner de la tête (contre against).

butter ['bʌtə] *n* beurre *m*; shea —
karité *f*; *vt* beurrer; — would not
melt in his mouth c'est une sainte
nitouche.

butter-bean ['bʌtəbiːn] *n* haricot
beurre *m*.

buttercup ['bʌtəkʌp] n bouton m d'or.

butter-dish ['bʌtədiʃ] n beurrier m.

butter-fingers ['bʌtə fiŋgəz] n empoté(e) mf, maladroit(e) mf.

butterfly ['bʌtəflai] n papillon m.

buttermilk ['bʌtəmilk] n petit-lait m, babeurre m.

buttock ['bʌtək] n fesse f.

button ['bʌtn] n bouton m; vt boutonner; — -hook tire-bouton m.

buttonhole ['bʌtnhoul] n boutonnière f; vt accrocher, cueillir.

buttress ['bʌtris] n contrefort m, arc-boutant m; vt soutenir, renforcer, étayer.

buxom ['bʌksəm] a rebondi, avenant

buy [bai] vt acheter; to — back racheter; to — over acheter; to — out désintéresser; to — up accaparer.

buyer ['baiə] n acheteur, -euse, chef m de rayon.

buzz [bʌz] n bourdonnement m, brouhaha m, fritures f pl; vi bourdonner, tinter; to — off déguerpir, filer.

buzzard ['bʌzəd] n buse f.

by [bai] prep par, près de, à côté de, à, en, pour, avec, de, sur, envers; ad près, à (de) côté; — and — avant peu, tout à l'heure.

bygone ['baigɔn] an passé m.

by(e)-law ['bailɔ:] n arrêté municipal m

by-name ['baineim] n sobriquet m.

by-pass ['baipɑ:s] n route f d'évitement m; vt éviter, contourner, filtrer.

by-product ['bai prɔdəkt] n sous-produit m.

by-road ['bairoud] n rue écartée f.

bystander ['bai stændə] n spectateur, -trice, curieux -euse.

byway ['baiwei] n chemin détourné m, raccourci m; pl à-côtés m pl.

byword ['baiwə:d] n proverbe m, risée f, fable f.

C

cab [kæb] n fiacre m, voiture de place f, cabine f.

cabbage ['kæbidʒ] n chou m.

cabbage-patch ['kæbidʒpætʃ] n plant m, carré de choux m.

cabin ['kæbin] n cabane f, cabine f, case f, poste m de conduite.

cabinet ['kæbinit] n vitrine f, bonheur du jour m, coffret m, ministère m; a ministériel, d'état.

cabinet-maker ['kæbinit meikə] n ébéniste m.

cabinet-work ['kæbinit wə:k] n ébénisterie f.

cabin-trunk ['kæbin trʌnk] n malle f (de) paquebot.

cable ['keibl] n câble m, chaîne f, câblogramme m; vt câbler, aviser par câble.

cable-railway ['keibl'reilwei] n funiculaire m.

cabman ['kæbmən] n cocher m, chauffeur m.

caboodle [kə'bu:dl] n the whole — tout le bazar, tout le fourbi.

caboose [kə'bu:s] n (US) wagon m de queue.

cabstand ['kæbstænd] n station f de voitures.

ca' canny [kɔ'kæni] a tout doux, hésitant; vi faire la grève perlée.

cackle ['kækl] n caquet m; vi caqueter.

cacophony [kæ'kɔfəni] n cacophonie f.

cad [kæd] n goujat m, mufle m, canaille f.

caddie ['kædi] n cadet m, caddie m.

caddishness ['kædiʃnis] n goujaterie f, muflerie f.

caddy ['kædi] n boîte f à thé.

cadence ['keidəns] n cadence f, rythme m.

cadet [kə'det] n cadet m, élève officier, m membre m d'un bataillon scolaire.

cadge [kædʒ] vti colporter, mendier, écornifler.

cadger ['kædʒə] n colporteur m, camelot m, mendiant(e) mf, écornifleur m.

cage [keidʒ] n cage f.

cahoot [kə'hu:t] n to be in —s with (sl) être de mèche avec.

cajole [kə'dʒoul] vt cajoler, enjôler.

cajolery [kə'dʒouləri] n cajolerie f, enjôlement m.

cajoling [kə'dʒouliŋ] a enjôleur.

cake [keik] n gâteau m, tablette f, morceau m, pain m; to sell like hot —s se vendre comme du pain frais.

cake-shop ['keikʃɔp] n pâtisserie f.

calabash ['kæləbæʃ] n calebasse f, gou. de f.

calamitous [kə'læmitəs] a désastreux.

calamity [kə'læmiti] n calamité f, désastre m, malheur m.

calculate ['kælkjuleit] vti calculer, estimer, évaluer; vi faire un (des) calcul(s).

calculated ['kælkjuleitid] a délibéré, calculé, propre (à to).

calculating ['kælkjuleitiŋ] a calculateur, avisé, réfléchi.

calculation [kælkju'leiʃən] n calcul m.

calendar ['kælində] n calendrier m, répertoire m.

calf [kɑ:f] n veau m, mollet m.

calibrate ['kælibreit] vt calibrer, étalonner, graduer.

calibre ['kælibə] n calibre m, alésage m.

call [kɔ:l] n appel m, cri m, rappel m, visite f, invitation f, demande f, invite f, communication f, coup de téléphone m; at — sur demande; within — à portée de la voix; vti crier, appeler; *vt* héler, convoquer; ordonner, déclarer; *vi* faire escale, toucher (à at); **to — aside** prendre à part; **to — back** *vt* rappeler; *vi* repasser; **to — for** demander, venir chercher; **to — forth** évoquer, provoquer, faire appel à; **to — off** *vt* décommander, rompre, rappeler; *vi* s'excuser, se retirer; **to — on** faire une visite à, passer chez, se présenter chez; **to — out** *vti* appeler; *vt* provoquer réquisitionner; **to — together** réunir, convoquer; **to — up** évoquer, appeler au téléphone, mobiliser; **to — upon** sommer.

callbox ['kɔːlbɒks] *n* cabine téléphonique *f*.

caller ['kɔːlə] *n* visiteur, -euse, visite *f*.

calling ['kɔːliŋ] *n* appel *m*, vocation *f*, profession *f*.

callosity [kæ'lɒsiti] *n* callosité *f*, durillon *m*.

call-up ['kɔːlʌp] *n* mobilisation *f*.

callous ['kæləs] *a* calleux, brutal, dur, endurci.

callousness ['kæləsnis] *n* dureté *f*, manque *m* de cœur.

callow ['kælou] *a* sans plumes, novice, inexpérimenté; **a — youth** un blancbec.

calm [kɑːm] *a* calme, tranquille; *n* calme *m*, tranquillité *f*; *vt* calmer, tranquilliser, apaiser; **to — down** s'apaiser, se calmer.

calumniate [kə'lʌmnieit] *vt* calomnier.

calumniator [kə'lʌmnieitə] *n* calomniateur, -trice.

calumny ['kæləmni] *n* calomnie *f*.

calvary ['kælvəri] *n* calvaire *m*.

calve [kɑːv] *vi* vêler.

cam [kæm] *n* came *f*.

camber ['kæmbə] *n* cambrure *f*, bombement *m*.

Cambodia [kæm'boudjə] *n* Cambodge *m*.

cambric ['keimbrik] *n* batiste *f*.

came [keim] *pt of* **come**.

camel ['kæməl] *n* chameau *m*.

cameo ['kæmiou] *n* camée *m*.

camera ['kæmərə] *n* appareil *m* photographique; **in —** à huis clos; **ciné —** caméra *f*.

cameraman ['kæmərəmæn] *n* photographe *m*, opérateur *m*.

cami-knickers ['kæminikəz] *n* chemise-culotte *f*.

camouflage ['kæməflɑːʒ] *n* camouflage *m*; *vt* camoufler.

camp [kæmp] *n* camp *m*, campement *m*; *vti* camper; **to go —ing** faire du camping.

campaign [kæm'pein] *n* campagne *f*; *vi* faire campagne.

camper ['kæmpə] *n* amateur (-trice) de camping, campeur *m*.

camphor ['kæmfə] *n* camphre *m*.

can [kæn] *n* broc *m*, pot *m*, bidon *m*, boîte *f*, (oil) burette *f*, (beer)

canette *f*; *vt* mettre, conserver, en boîte.

can [kæn] *vi* pouvoir, savoir; **all one — de son mieux**; **he cannot but do** it il ne peut pas ne pas le faire.

Canada ['kænədə] *n* Canada *m*.

Canadian [kə'neidjən] *a* canadien; *n* Canadien, -ienne.

canal [kə'næl] *n* canal *m*.

canalization [,kænəlai'zeiʃən] *n* canalisation *f*.

canalize ['kænəlaiz] *vt* canaliser.

canary [kə'nɛəri] *n* canari *m*, serin *m*.

cancel ['kænsəl] *vt* annuler, biffer, révoquer, résilier, supprimer, décommander, contremander; **to — out** s'éliminer.

cancellation [,kænse'leiʃən] *n* annulation *f*, résiliation *f*, révocation *f*, contre-ordre *m*.

cancer ['kænsə] *n* cancer *m*.

cancerous ['kænsərəs] *a* cancéreux.

candid ['kændid] *a* franc, sincère, impartial, sans malice.

candidate ['kændidit] *n* candidat(e) *mf*, aspirant *m*, pretendant(e) *mf*.

candidature ['kænditʃə] *n* candidature *f*.

candle ['kændl] *n* bougie *f*, chandelle *f*, cierge *f*.

candlestick ['kændlstik] *n* chandelier *m*, bougeoir *m*.

candour [,'kændə] *n* franchise *f*, impartialité *f* bonne foi *f*.

candy ['kændi] *n* sucre candi *m*; *vt* glacer, faire candir, confire.

cane [kein] *n* tige *f*, canne *f*, badine *f*, rotin *m*; **— chair** chaise cannée *f*. **—rat** agouti *m*; *vt* bâtonner, fouetter.

canine ['keinain] *n* canine *f*; *a* canin.

caning ['keiniŋ] *n* bastonnade *f*, correction *f*.

canister ['kænistə] *n* boîte *f*.

canker ['kæŋkə] *n* chancre *m*, fléau *m*, plaie *f*; *vt* ronger, corrompre.

canned [kænd] *a* en boîte; en conserve.

cannibal ['kænibəl] *an* cannibale *mf*.

cannibalism ['kænibəlizəm] *n* cannibalisme *m*.

cannon ['kænən] *n* canon *m*, pièce *f*, carambolage *m*; *vi* caramboler, se heurter.

cannonade [,kænə'neid] *n* canonnade *f*; *vt* canonner.

cannon-ball ['kænənbɔːl] *n* boulet *m*.

cannon-fodder ['kænənfɒdə] *n* chair à canon *f*.

canny ['kæni] *a* avisé, sûr, rusé, finaud, économe.

canoe [kə'nuː] *n* canoë *m*, pirogue *f*, périssoire *f*.

canon ['kænən] *n* canon *m*, chanoine *m*, règle *f*.

canoness ['kænənis] *n* chanoinesse *f*.

canonize ['kænənaiz] *vt* canoniser.

canonry ['kænənri] *n* canonicat *m*.

can-opener ['kænoupnə] n ouvre-boîte m.

canopy ['kænəpi] n dais m, baldaquin m, ciel m, marquise f.

cant [kænt] n argot m, pharisaïsme m, tartuferie f, plan incliné m; vt incliner.

cantankerous [kən'tæŋkərəs] a revêche, batailleur, acariâtre.

canteen [kæn'ti:n] n cantine f, gamelle f, bidon m, caisse f; — of cutlery service m de table en coffre.

canter ['kæntə] n petit galop m; vi aller au petit galop.

canticle ['kæntikl] n cantique m.

cantilever ['kæntili:və] n encorbellement m, cantilever m.

canto ['kæntou] n chant m.

canvas ['kænvəs] n toile f, tente f, voile f; under — sous voile, sous la tente.

canvass ['kænvəs] vt discuter, solliciter, briguer; vi (com) faire la place, faire une tournée électorale.

canvasser ['kænvəsə] n agent électoral m, solliciteur, -euse, placier m.

cap [kæp] n bonnet m, casquette f, toque f, calotte f; vt coiffer, couronner, surpasser, saluer; to — it pour comble; if the — fits, wear it qui se sent morveux, se mouche.

capability [‚keipə'biliti] n pouvoir m, moyens m pl, capacité f, faculté f.

capable ['keipəbl] a capable, compétent, susceptible (de).

capacious [kə'peiʃəs] a spacieux, ample, grand.

capacity [kə'pæsiti] n capacité f, contenance f, débit m, rendement m, aptitude f, qualité f, mesure f; to — à plein, comble.

cape [keip] n cap m, collet m, pèlerine f, cape f.

caper ['keipə] n câpre f, cabriole f; vi cabrioler, gambader.

capital ['kæpitl] n capitale f, majuscule f, capital m, chapiteau m; a capital, fameux.

capitalism ['kæpitəlizəm] n capitalisme m.

capitalist ['kæpitəlist] n capitaliste mf.

capitalize ['kæpitəlaiz] vt capitaliser.

capitulate [kə'pitjuleit] vi capituler.

capitulation [kə‚pitju'leiʃən] n capitulation f.

capon ['keipən] n chapon m.

caprice [kə'pri:s] b caprice m.

capricious [kə'priʃəs] a capricieux.

capriciousness [kə'priʃəsnis] n humeur capricieuse f, inconstance f.

capsize [kæp'saiz] vi chavirer, capoter; vt faire chavirer.

capstan ['kæpstən] n cabestan m.

capsule ['kæpsju:l] n capsule f, (of spaceship) cabine f.

captain ['kæptin] n capitaine m, chef m (d'équipe); vt commander, diriger.

caption ['kæpʃən] n arrestation f,

légende f, soustitre m, rubrique f, manchette f.

captious ['kæpʃəs] a captieux, chicaneur, pointilleux.

captivate ['kæptiveit] vt séduire, captiver, charmer.

captive ['kæptiv] an prisonnier, -ière, captif, -ive.

captivity [kæp'tiviti] n captivité f.

capture ['kæptʃə] n capture f, prise f; vt prendre, capturer, capter.

car [ka:] n char m, wagon m, voiture f, auto f; dining — wagon-restaurant m; sleeping — wagon-lit m.

carafe [kə'ra:f] n carafe f.

caramel ['kærəmel] n caramel m, bonbon m au caramel.

caravan ['kærəvæn] n caravane f, roulotte f.

carbide ['ka:baid] n carbure m.

carbine ['ka:bain] n carabine f.

carbon ['ka:bən] n (papier) carbone m.

carbonize ['ka:bənaiz] vt carboniser, carburer.

carboy ['ka:bɔi] n bonbonne f.

carbuncle ['ka:bʌŋkl] n anthrax m, escarboucle f.

carburettor ['ka:bjuretə] n carburateur m.

carcass ['ka:kəs] n corps m, cadavre m, carcasse f.

card [ka:d] n carte f; visiting — carte f de visite; he is a — c'est un numéro; a queer — un drôle de type.

cardboard ['ka:dbɔ:d] n carton m.

card-case ['ka:dkeis] n porte-cartes m.

cardigan ['ka:digən] n tricot m, cardigan m.

cardinal ['ka:dinl] an cardinal m.

card-index ['ka:d'indeks] n classeur m, fichier m.

card-sharper ['ka:d‚ʃa:pə] n bonneteur m, tricheur, -euse, escroc m.

care [kɛə] n soin m, souci m, attention f, peine f, solicitude f, préoccupation f, entretien m; vi s'inquiéter, se soucier; c/o (care of) aux bons soins de; with — fragile; to take — prendre garde; to take — not to se garder de, prendre garde de; to take — of prendre soin de, se charger de; to — for vt aimer, soigner; I don't — a rap je m'en fiche, je m'en moque pas mal; I don't — for this tobacco ce tabac ne me dit rien.

career [kə'riə] n course f, cours m, carrière f; vi marcher (courir) comme un fou.

careerist [kə'riərist] n arriviste mf.

careful ['kɛəful] a soigneux, prudent, attentif.

carefulness ['kɛəfulnis] n soin m, attention f, prudence f, circonspection f.

careless ['kɛəlis] a sans soin, négligent, insouciant.

carelessness ['kɛəlisnis] n négligence f, insouciance f.

caress [kə'res] n caresse f; vt caresser.

caretaker ['kɛə,teikə] n concierge mf, gardien, -ienne.

cargo ['kɑːgou] n cargaison f.

cargo-boat ['kɑːgoubout] n cargo m.

caricature [,kærikə'tjuə] n caricature f, charge f; vt caricaturer, charger.

carmine ['kɑːmain] an carmin m; a carminé.

carnage ['kɑːnidʒ] n carnage m, tuerie f.

carnal ['kɑːnl] a charnel, sensuel, de la chair.

carnation [kɑː'neiʃən] n œillet m; an incarnat m.

carnival ['kɑːnivəl] n carnaval m.

carnivore ['kɑːnivɔː] n carnassier m.

carnivorous [kɑː'nivərəs] a carnassier, carnivore.

carol ['kærəl] n chant m; **Christmas** — (chant de) Noël m; vti chanter, tirelirer.

carousal [kə'rauzəl] n buverie f, orgie f, bombe f.

carouse [kə'rauz] vi faire la noce, faire la bombe.

carp [kɑːp] n carpe f; vi mordre sur tout; **to** — **at** crier après, gloser sur, chicaner.

carpenter ['kɑːpintə] n charpentier m.

carpet ['kɑːpit] n tapis m; **to be on the** — être sur la sellette; vt poser un (des) tapis sur, recouvrir d'un tapis.

carping ['kɑːpiŋ] a mordant, chicanier, malveillant, pointilleux.

carport ['kɑːpɔːt] n abri m.

carriage ['kæridʒ] n (trans)port m, voiture f, wagon m, affût m, allure f, maintien m; — **free** franco; — **forward** en port dû; — **paid** franco de port.

carriageway ['kæridzwei] n dual — route jumelée f.

carrier ['kæriə] n camionneur m, roulier m, porteur, -euse, porte-avions m, porte-bagages m.

carrion ['kæriən] n charogne f.

carrot ['kærət] n carotte f.

carroty ['kærəti] a rouquin, roux, rouge de carotte.

carry ['kæri] n trajet m, trajectoire f, portée f; vti porter; vt transporter, rouler, amener, conduire, emporter, enlever, supporter, voter, adopter; **to** — **away** emporter, enlever, entraîner; **to** — **back** rapporter, ramener, reporter; **to** — **down** descendre; **to** — **forward** avancer, reporter; **to** — **off** enlever, (r)emporter; **to** — **on** vt soutenir, entretenir, poursuivre; vi continuer, persister, se conduire; **to** — **out** exécuter, mettre à exécution, appliquer, réussir, exercer, porter dehors; **to** — **through** mener à bonne fin;

to — **weight** peser, avoir de l'influence, avoir du poids, être handicapé.

cart [kɑːt] n charrette f, tombereau m, camion m; vt transporter, charroyer, charrier; **to** — **about** trimbaler.

cartage ['kɑːtidʒ] n charroi m, charriage m, transport m.

carter ['kɑːtə] n charretier m, roulier m, camionneur m.

cart-horse ['kɑːthɔːs] n cheval m de trait.

cart-load ['kɑːtloud] n charretée f, tombereau m.

cart-shed ['kɑːtʃed] n remise f, hangar m.

Carthusian [kɑː'θjuːzjən] an chartreux m.

cartilage ['kɑːtilidʒ] n cartilage m.

cartoon [kɑː'tuːn] n carton m, dessin m (satirique, humoristique, animé), portrait caricaturé m.

cartridge ['kɑːtridʒ] n cartouche f.

cartwright ['kɑːtrait] n charron m.

carve [kɑːv] vt tailler, sculpter (sur bois), ciseler, découper.

carver ['kɑːvə] n ciseleur m, serveur m, découpeur m, couteau m à découper.

carving ['kɑːviŋ] n sculpture f, découpage m.

cascade [kæs'keid] n cascade f, chute f d'eau; vi tomber en cascade.

case [keis] n cas m, affaire f, cause f, boîte f, caisse f, trousse f, fourreau m, étui m, écrin m, vitrine f, boîtier m; **in** — au cas où; **in any (no)** — en tout (aucun) cas; vt emballer, encaisser, envelopper.

casement ['keismənt] n battant m, croisée f.

cash [kæʃ] n monnaie f, argent comptant m, espèces f pl; vt encaisser, toucher; — **account** compte m en banque; **petty** — argent m de poche, petite caisse f; — **down** comptant; — **on delivery** paiement m à la livraison; — **book** livre m de caisse; — **box** n caisse f.

cashier [kæ'ʃiə] n caissier, -ière; vt casser.

cashmere ['kæʃmiə] n cachemire m.

casino [kə'siːnou] n casino m.

cask [kɑːsk] n tonneau m, fût m.

casket ['kɑːskit] n écrin m, boîte f, coffret m, cassette f.

cassava [kə'sɑːvə] n manioc m.

cassock ['kæsək] n soutane f.

cast [kɑːst] n lancement m, jet m, calcul m, moule m, moulage m, modèle m, coulée f, bas de ligne m, (dice) coup m, (eye) faux-trait m, (mind) type m, trempe f, qualité f, (theatre) troupe f, distribution f des rôles; vt lancer, (pro)jeter, ôter, couler, mouler, fondre, assigner un rôle à; **to** — **about** fureter; **to** — **aside** rejeter, se débarrasser de, mettre de côté; **to** — **away** jeter (au loin); **to — back** renvoyer, reporter; **to — down** déprimer, abattre, jeter bas; **to — off** rejeter, larguer, renier; **to — up** rejeter, reprocher.

castaway ['kɑːstəwei] n naufragé(e) mf, réprouvé(e) mf, proscrit(e) mf.

caste [kɑːst] n caste f; **half— an,** metis, -isse.

castigate ['kæstigeit] vt corriger, châtier.

castigation [ˌkæsti'geiʃən] n correction f, châtiment m.

casting ['kɑːstiŋ] n jet m, fronte f, moulage m, modelage m, distribution des rôles; f a (vote) qui départage.

cast-iron ['kɑːst'aiən] n fonte f; a de fer, de fonte.

castle ['kɑːsl] n château m; **—s in the air** des châteaux en Espagne; vi (chess) roquer.

castor ['kɑːstə] n saupoudroir m, poivrière f, roulette f.

castor-oil ['kɑːstər'ɔil] n huile f de ricin.

castrate [kæs'treit] vt châtrer, émasculer.

casual ['kæʒuəl] a fortuit, accidentel, banal, désinvolte, insouciant.

casually ['kæʒuəli] ad en passant, avec désinvolture.

casualty ['kæʒuəlti] n accident m, blessé(e) mf, mort(e) mf, malheur m; pl pertes f pl.

cat [kæt] n chat, -tte; **tom —** matou m.

cataclysm ['kætəklizəm] n cataclysme m.

catacombs ['kætəkoumz] n catacombes f pl.

catalepsy ['kætəlepsi] n catalepsie f.

catalogue ['kætələg] n catalogue m, liste f, prix-courant m; vt cataloguer.

catapult ['kætəpʌlt] n lance-pierres m inv, fronde f, catapulte f; vt lancer.

cataract ['kætərækt] n cataracte f.

catarrh [kə'tɑː] n catarrhe m.

catastrophe [kə'tæstrəfi] n catastrophe f, désastre m, dénouement m.

catcalls ['kætkɔːlz] n pl miaulements m pl, sifflets m pl, huées f pl.

catch [kætʃ] n prise f, capture f, pêche f, attrape f, piège m, agrafe f, loquet m, déclic m, cran d'arrêt m; vti prendre; vt attraper, saisir, accrocher, surprendre; vi se prendre, s'engager, mordre; **to — on** prendre, réussir; **to — up** saisir, rattraper, rejoindre.

catching ['kætʃiŋ] a séduisant, contagieux, communicatif.

catchword ['kætʃwəːd] n mot m d'ordre, mot m de ralliement, slogan m scie f.

catchy ['kætʃi] a entraînant, insidieux.

catechism ['kætikizəm] n catéchisme m.

categorical [ˌkæti'gɔrikəl] a catégorique.

category ['kætigəri] n catégorie f.

cater ['keitə] vi pourvoir; **to — for** pourvoir à, approvisionner.

caterer ['keitərə] n fournisseur, -euse, pourvoyeur, -euse, traiteur m.

catering ['keitəriŋ] n approvisionnement m; **to do the —** fournir le buffet.

caterpillar ['kætəpilə] n chenille f.

caterwaul ['kætəwɔːl] vi miauler, faire du tapage.

caterwauling ['kætəwɔːliŋ] n miaulements m pl, tapage m, sabbat m de chats.

catgut ['kætgʌt] n catgut m.

cathedral [kə'θiːdrəl] n cathédrale f.

catholic ['kæθəlik] an catholique mf; a universel, tolérant.

catholicism [kə'θɔlisizəm] n catholicisme m.

catholicity [ˌkæθə'lisiti] n catholicité f, orthodoxie f, universalité f, tolérance f.

cat-o'-nine-tails ['kætə'nainteilz] n garcette f.

cat's-paw ['kætspɔː] n instrument m, dupe f.

cattish ['kætiʃ] a méchant, rosse.

cattle ['kætl] n bétail m, bestiaux m pl; **— show** comice agricole m.

cattle-drover ['kætldrouvə] n bouvier m.

cattle-shed ['kætlʃed] n étable f.

caucus ['kɔːkəs] n comité m, clique politique f.

caught [kɔːt] pt pp of **catch.**

cauldron ['kɔːldrən] n chaudron m, chaudière f.

cauliflower ['kɔliflauə] n chou-fleur m.

caulk [kɔːk] vt calfater, calfeutrer, mater.

cause [kɔːz] n cause f, motif m, occasion f, raison f, sujet m; vt causer, occasionner, provoquer.

causeway ['kɔːzwei] n chaussée f, digue f.

caustic ['kɔːstik] a caustique, mordant.

cauterize ['kɔːtəraiz] vt cautériser.

caution ['kɔːʃən] n prudence f, précaution f, circonspection f, réprimande f, avertissement m; vt avertir, mettre sur ses gardes.

cautious ['kɔːʃəs] a prudent, circonspect.

cautiousness ['kɔːʃəsnis] n prudence f, circonspection f.

cavalier [ˌkævə'liə] n cavalier m, gentilhomme m, cavalier servant m, galant m; a cavalier, désinvolte.

cavalry ['kævəlri] n cavalerie f.

cavalryman ['kævəlrimən] n cavalier m, soldat m de cavalerie.

cave [keiv] n caverne f, grotte f; **to — in** s'affaisser, s'effondrer, s'enfoncer, céder.

cavern ['kævən] *n* souterrain *m*, caverne *f*.
cavil ['kævil] *vi* ergoter, chicaner.
cavilling ['kæviliŋ] *n* argutie *f*, ergotage *m*, chicanerie *f*; *a* ergoteur.
cavity ['kæviti] *n* cavité *f*, creux *m*, trou *m*, fosse *f*.
caw [kɔː] *vi* croasser.
cease [siːs] *n* cesse *f*; *vti* cesser.
cease-fire [siːsˈfaiə] *n* cessez-le-feu *m*.
ceaseless ['siːslis] *a* incessant.
ceaselessly ['siːslisli] *ad* incessamment, sans cesse.
Cecilia ['siljə] Cécile *f*.
cedar ['siːdə] *n* cèdre *m*.
ceiling ['siːliŋ] *n* plafond *m*.
celebrate ['selibreit] *vt* célébrer, fêter, commémorer; *vi* faire la fête.
celebration [ˌseliˈbreiʃən] *n* fête *f*, commémoration *f*.
celebrity [siˈlebriti] *n* célébrité *f*, renommée *f*, sommité *f*.
celeriac [səˈleriæk] *n* céleri-rave *m*.
celery ['seləri] *n* céleri *m*.
celestial [siˈlestjəl] *a* céleste.
celibacy ['selibəsi] *n* célibat *m*.
celibate ['selibit] *n* célibataire *mf*.
cell [sel] *n* cellule *f*, cachot *m*.
cellar ['selə] *n* cave *f*, caveau *m*.
cellophane ['seləfein] *n* cellophane *f*.
celluloid ['seljulɔid] *n* celluloïde *m*.
cellulose ['seljulous] *n* cellulose *f*.
Celtic ['keltik] *a* celtique, celte.
cement [siˈment] *n* ciment *m*; *vt* cimenter.
cemetery ['semitri] *n* cimetière *m*.
cense [sens] *vt* encenser.
censer ['sensə] *n* encensoir *m*.
censor ['sensə] *n* censeur *m*, *vt* interdire, supprimer, contrôler; **to be —ed** passer par la censure.
censoring ['sensəriŋ] *n* censure *f*.
censorious [senˈsɔːriəs] *a* réprobateur, dénigrant, sévère.
censorship ['sensəʃip] *n* censure *f*, contrôle *m*.
censurable ['senʃərəbl] *a* répréhensible, censurable.
censure ['senʃə] *n* censure *f*, blâme *m*; *vt* censurer, condamner, critiquer.
census ['sensəs] *n* recensement *m*.
cent [sent] *n* cent *m*; **he hasn't a —** il n'a pas le sou.
centenarian [ˌsentiˈnɛəriən] *an* centenaire *mf*.
centenary [senˈtiːnəri] *an* centenaire *m*.
centigramme ['sentigræm] *n* centigramme *m*.
centimetre ['sentiˌmiːtə] *n* centimètre *m*.
centipede ['sentipiːd] *n* mille-pattes *m inv*.
central ['sentrəl] *a* central.
centralize ['sentrəlaiz] *vt* centraliser.
centre ['sentə] *n* centre *m*, milieu *m*, foyer *m*; *vt* centrer, concentrer; *vi* se centrer, se concentrer.
centre-forward [ˌsentəˈfɔːwəd] *n* avant-centre *m*.

centre-half [ˌsentəˈhɑːf] *n* demi-centre *m*.
centrifugal [senˈtrifjugəl] *a* centrifuge.
centripetal [senˈtripitl] *a* centripète.
centuple ['sentjupl] *an* centuple *m*; *vt* centupler.
century ['sentʃuri] *n* siècle *m*.
cereal ['siəriəl] *an* céréale *f*.
cerebral ['seribrəl] *a* cérébral.
ceremonial [ˌseriˈmounjəl] *n* cérémonial *m*, étiquette *f*; *a* de cérémonie.
ceremonious [ˌseriˈmounjəs] *a* cérémonieux.
ceremony ['seriməni] *n* cérémonie *f*, façon(s) *f pl*.
cert ['səːt] *n* (*sl*) certitude *f*, affaire sûre *f*; **it's a —** c'est couru.
certain ['səːtn] *a* certain, sûr; **to make —** s'assurer.
certainly ['səːtnli] *ad* certainement, certes, assurément, à coup sûr.
certainty ['səːtnti] *n* certitude *f*.
certificate [səˈtifikit] *n* certificat *m*, attestation *f*, titre *m*, diplôme *m*; diplômer.
certify ['səːtifai] *vt* certifier, déclarer, attester.
certifying ['səːtifaiiŋ] *n* attestation *f*, homologation *f*, approbation *f*.
certitude ['səːtitjuːd] *n* certitude *f*.
cessation [seˈseiʃən] *n* cessation *f*, arrêt *m*.
cession ['seʃən] *n* cession *f*, abandon *m*.
cesspool ['sespuːl] *n* fosse *f*, puisard *m*.
chafe [tʃeif] *vt* frotter, irriter, écorcher, frictionner, érailler; *vi* se frotter, s'irriter, s'énerver, s'agiter.
chaff [tʃɑːf] *n* balle *f*, paille *f*, blague *f*, persiflage *m*; *vt* blaguer, railler.
chaffinch ['tʃæfintʃ] *n* pinson *m*.
chafing ['tʃeifiŋ] *n* irritation *f*, frottement *m*, friction *f*, écorchement *m*.
chagrin ['ʃægrin] *n* chagrin *m*, dépit *m*; *vt* chagriner, mortifier.
chain [tʃein] *n* chaîne *f*, enchaînement *m*, série *f*, suite *f*; *vt* enchaîner, attacher.
chair [tʃɛə] *n* chaise *f*, siège *m*, fauteuil *m*, chaire *f*; **to be in the —** présider.
chairman ['tʃɛəmən] *n* président *m*.
chalice ['tʃælis] *n* calice *m*.
chalk [tʃɔːk] *n* craie *f*, pastel *m*, blanc *m*; *vt* marquer, tracer *etc* à la craie.
chalky ['tʃɔːki] *a* crayeux.
challenge ['tʃælindʒ] *n* défi *m*, provocation *f*, qui vive *m*, interpellation *f*, récusation *f*; *vt* défier, crier qui vive à, porter un défi à, provoquer (en duel), mettre en question, récuser.
chamber ['tʃeimbə] *n* chambre *f*, cabinet *m*, salle *f*, étude *f*.

chamberlain ['tʃeimbəlin] n chambellan m.

chambermaid ['tʃeimbəmeid] n femme f de chambre.

chamber-pot ['tʃeimbəpɔt] n pot m de chambre.

champ [tʃæmp] vt mâcher, ronger.

Champagne [ʃæm'pein] n Champagne f; (wine) champagne m.

champion ['tʃæmpjən] n champion, -onne; vt soutenir.

championship ['tʃæmpjənʃip] n championnat m.

chance [tʃɑːns] n chance f, sort m, occasion f, hasard m; a fortuit, de rencontre; vt risquer; vi venir (à to); to — upon rencontrer (par hasard); to — tomber sur.

chancel ['tʃɑːnsəl] n chœur m.

chancellor ['tʃɑːnsələ] n chancelier m.

chancellory ['tʃɑːnsələri] n chancellerie f.

chancy ['tʃɑːnsi] a chanceux, incertain, risqué.

chandelier [‚ʃændi'liə] n lustre m, candélabre m.

change [tʃeindʒ] n changement m, change f, revirement m, monnaie f; vt changer, transformer, modifier; vi (se) changer, se modifier, se transformer.

changeable ['tʃeindʒəbl] a changeant, variable.

changeableness ['tʃeindʒəblnis] n mobilité f, inconstance f, variabilité f.

channel ['tʃænl] n lit m, canal m, rainure f, voie f; the Channel la Manche; Irish Channel mer d'Irlande f.

chant [tʃɑːnt] n (plain-)chant m, psalmodie f; vt chanter, psalmodier.

chanty ['tʃɑːnti] n chanson de bord f.

chaos ['keiɔs] n chaos m.

chaotic [keiˈɔtik] a chaotique, sans ordre, désorganisé.

chap [tʃæp] n gerçure f, crevasse f, bajoue f, type m; vt gercer, crevasser.

chapel ['tʃæpl] n chapelle f, oratoire m.

chaperon ['ʃæpəroun] n chaperon m; vt chaperonner.

chaplain [keiˈɔtik] n aumônier m.

chaplet ['tʃæplit] n guirlande f, chapelet m.

chapter ['tʃæptə] n chapitre m, suite f.

char [tʃɑː] vt carboniser; vi aller en journée, faire des ménages; n femme f de ménage, femme f de journée.

character ['kærɪktə] n caractère m, moralité f, certificat m (de moralité), réputation f, numéro m, original(e) mf, personnage m, individu m.

characteristic [‚kærɪktəˈristik] n trait m (de caractère), particularité f; a caractéristique.

characterize ['kærɪktəraiz] vt caractériser, être caractéristique de.

charcoal ['tʃɑːkoul] n charbon m de bois, fusain m.

charcoal-burner ['tʃɑːkoul‚bəːnə] n charbonnier m.

charge [tʃɑːdʒ] vti charger; vt accuser, demander; n charge f, prix m, frais m pl, fonction f, emploi m, soin m, garde f, accusation f; to — s.o. with sth accuser qn de qch, reprocher qch à qn; to — sth to s.o. mettre qch au compte de qn; on a — of sous l'inculpation de; free of — franco, gratuitement, gratis.

chargeable ['tʃɑːdʒəbl] a imputable, inculpable.

charger ['tʃɑːdʒə] n chargeur m, plateau m, cheval m de bataille.

charily ['tʃɛərili] ad prudemment, chichement.

chariness ['tʃɛərinis] n prudence f, parcimonie f.

chariot ['tʃæriət] n char m.

charitable ['tʃæritəbl] a charitable, de bienfaisance.

charity ['tʃæriti] n charité f, bienfaisance f, aumônes f pl.

charm [tʃɑːm] n charme m, agrément m, sort m, sortilège m, portebónheur m, fétiche m; vt charmer, enchanter, jeter un sort sur.

charnel-house ['tʃɑːnlhaus] n charnier m.

chart [tʃɑːt] n carte f, diagramme m; vt relever la carte de, porter sur une carte, établir le graphique de, l'hydrographie de, explorer.

charter ['tʃɑːtə] n charte f; vt accorder une charte à, affréter, louer.

chartering ['tʃɑːtəriŋ] n nolisement m, affrètement m.

charwoman ['tʃɑːwumən] n femme de ménage f.

chary ['tʃɛəri] a prudent, chiche, avare.

chase [tʃeis] n chasse f, poursuite f; vt poursuivre, (pour)chasser, ciseler, repousser.

chaser ['tʃeisə] n chasseur m, pousse-café m.

chasing ['tʃeisiŋ] n ciselure f, repoussage m.

chasm ['kæzəm] n crevasse f, abîme m, gouffre m, vide m.

chassis ['ʃæsi] n chassis m.

chaste [tʃeist] a chaste, pudique, pur.

chasten ['tʃeisn] vt châtier, assagir, dégonfler.

chastise [tʃæs'taiz] vt châtier, corriger.

chastisement ['tʃæstizmənt] n châtiment m.

chastity ['tʃæstiti] n chasteté f, pureté f, sobriété f.

chat [tʃæt] n (brin de) causerie f, causette f; vi bavarder, causer.

chattel ['tʃætl] n propriété f, bien

m, mobilier *m*; **goods and —s** biens et effets *m pl*.

chatter ['tʃætə] *n* babil *m*, caquetage *m*, bavardage *m*, claquement *m*; *vi* bavarder, jaser, caqueter, claquer.

chatterbox ['tʃætəbɔks] *n* moulin *m* à paroles, bavard *m*.

chatty ['tʃæti] *a* bavard, causant, causeur.

chauffeur ['ʃoufə] *n* chauffeur *m*.

cheap [tʃi:p] *a* bon marché, (à prix) réduit, trivial, facile; **it's dirt —** c'est donné.

cheapen ['tʃi:pən] *vt* déprécier, baisser le prix de.

cheaply ['tʃi:pli] *ad* (à) bon marché, à peu de frais, à bon compte.

cheat [tʃi:t] *n* tricheur, -euse, escroc *m*, filou *m*; *vti* tricher; *vt* tromper, voler.

cheating ['tʃi:tiŋ] *n* tricherie *f*, tromperie *f*, fourberie *f*.

check [tʃek] *n* échec *m*, arrêt (brusque) *m*, contrôle *m*, contremarque *f*, rebuffade *f*, bulletin *m*, ticket *m*, étoffe à carreaux *f*; *vt* tenir en échec, arrêter, retenir, contenir, freiner, réprimer, réprimander, contrôler, vérifier, réviser, compulser.

checker ['tʃekə] *n* contrôleur *m*, pointeur *m*.

checker-board ['tʃekəbɔːd] *n* damier *m*.

checkmate ['tʃek'meit] *vt* faire échec et mat à, déjouer, contrecarrer.

cheek [tʃi:k] *n* joue *f*, toupet *m*, effronterie *f*.

cheekbone ['tʃi:kboun] *n* pommette *f*.

cheekiness ['tʃi:kinis] *n* effronterie *f*.

cheeky ['tʃi:ki] *a* effronté.

cheep [tʃi:p] *vi* piauler, pépier.

cheer [tʃiə] *n* belle humeur *f*, bonne chère *f*, acclamations *f pl*, applaudissements *m pl*, vivats *m pl*; *vt* réconforter, égayer, acclamer; **to give three —s for** accorder un ban à; *vti* applaudir; **to — up** *vi* reprendre courage, se regaillardir; *vt* réconforter, remonter le moral à; **— up!** courage!

cheerful ['tʃiəful] *a* joyeux, gai, réconfortant, égayant.

cheerfully ['tʃiəfuli] *ad* gaîment, de bon cœur.

cheerfulness ['tʃiəfulnis] *n* gaieté *f*, belle humeur *f*, entrain *m*.

cheering ['tʃiəriŋ] *n* applaudissements *m pl*, acclamation *f*; *a* réjouissant, encourageant.

cheerio ['tʃiəri'ou] *excl* à bientôt! à tantôt! à la vôtre!

cheerless ['tʃiəlis] *a* sombre, morne.

cheery ['tʃiəri] *a* gai, joyeux.

cheese [tʃi:z] *n* fromage *m*.

chef [ʃef] *n* chef *m* (de cuisine).

chemical ['kemikəl] *a* chimique; *n pl* produits chimiques *m pl*.

chemist ['kemist] *n* chimiste *m*, pharmacien *m*; **—'s shop** pharmacie *f*.

chemistry ['kemistri] *n* chimie *f*.

cheque [tʃek] *n* chèque *m*; **blank —** chèque en blanc; **traveller's —** chèque de voyage; **to cross a —** barrer un chèque.

cheque-book ['tʃekbuk] *n* carnet *m* de chèques, chéquier *m*.

chequer ['tʃekə] *n* damier *m*; *pl* carreaux *m pl*, quadrillage *m*; *vt* disposer en damier, quadriller, diaprer, varier.

chequered ['tʃekəd] *a* varié, diapré, inégal, quadrillé, en damier, à carreaux, accidenté.

cherish ['tʃeriʃ] *vt* chérir, soigner, caresser.

cherry ['tʃeri] *n* cerise *f*.

cherry tree ['tʃeritri] *n* cerisier *m*.

cherub ['tʃerəb] *n* chérubin *m*.

chervil ['tʃɔːvil] *n* cerfeuil *m*.

chess [tʃes] *n* échecs *m pl*.

chessboard ['tʃesbɔːd] *n* échiquier *m*.

chest [tʃest] *n* poitrine *f*, poitrail *m*, coffre *m*, caisse *f*; **— of drawers** commode *f*.

chestnut ['tʃesnʌt] *n* châtaigne *f*, marron *m*; *a* châtain, marron, alezan.

chestnut tree ['tʃesnʌttri] *n* châtaignier *m*, marronnier *m*.

chew [tʃu:] *vt* (re)mâcher, mastiquer, chiquer, ruminer.

chicanery [ʃi'keinəri] *n* chicanerie *f*, arguties *f pl*.

chick [tʃik] *n* poussin *m*.

chicken ['tʃikin] *n* poulet *m*.

chicken-pox ['tʃikinpɔks] *n* varicelle *f*.

chickweed ['tʃikwi:d] *n* mouron *m* des oiseaux.

chicory ['tʃikəri] *n* endive *f*.

chidden ['tʃidn] *pp* of **chide**.

chide [tʃaid] *vti* gronder.

chief [tʃi:f] *n* chef *m*, patron *m*; *a* en chef, principal.

chiefly ['tʃi:fli] *ad* notamment.

chilblain ['tʃilblein] *n* engelure *f*.

child [tʃaild] *n* enfant *mf*.

childbed ['tʃaildbed] *n* couches *f pl*.

childbirth ['tʃaildbɔːθ] *n* accouchement *m*.

childhood ['tʃaildhud] *n* enfance *f*.

childish ['tʃaildiʃ] *a* enfantin, d'enfant, puéril.

childishness ['tʃaildiʃnis] *n* puérilité *f*, enfantillage *m*.

childless ['tʃaildlis] *a* sans enfant, stérile.

childlike ['tʃaildlaik] *a* enfantin, d'enfant.

children ['tʃildrən] *pl* of **child**.

chill [tʃil] *n* froid *m*, refroidissement *m*, chaud et froid *m*, frisson *m*; *a* glacial, froid; *vt* glacer, refroidir; *vi* se glacer, se refroidir.

chilled [tʃild] *a* transi de froid, glacé, frigorifié.

chilly ['tʃili] *a* froid, frileux, glacial, frisquet.

chime [tʃaim] *n* carillon *m*; *vti* sonner, carillonner; *vi* s'harmoniser (avec **with**); **to — in** placer son mot, intervenir.

chimera [kai'miərə] *n* chimère *f*.

chimney ['tʃimni] *n* cheminée *f*.

chimney-pot ['tʃimnipɔt] *n* cheminée *f*.

chimney-sweep ['tʃimniswiːp] *n* ramoneur *m*.

chin [tʃin] *n* menton *m*.

chinstrap ['tʃinstræp] *n* jugulaire *f*.

china ['tʃainə] *n* porcelaine *f*.

China ['tʃainə] *n* Chine *f*.

Chinaman ['tʃainəmən] *n* Chinois *m*.

Chinese ['tʃai'niːz] *an* chinois *m*; *n* Chinois(e) *mf*.

chink [tʃiŋk] *n* fente *f*, crevasse *f*, lézarde *f*, entrebâillement *m*, tintement *m*; *vi* sonner, tinter; *vt* faire sonner, faire tinter.

chintz [tʃints] *n* perse *f*.

chip [tʃip] *n* copeau *m*, éclat *m*, tranche *f*, écornure *f*, écaille *f*, jeton *m*; *vt* couper, ébrécher, écorner; *vi* s'ébrécher, s'écorner; **to — in** intervenir, placer son mot.

chips [tʃips] *n pl* (pommes *f pl* de terre) frites *f pl*.

chiropodist [ki'rɔpədist] *n* pédicure *m*.

chirp [tʃəːp] **chirrup** ['tʃirəp] *n* pépiement *m*, gazouillement *m*; *vi* pépier, gazouiller, grésiller.

chisel ['tʃizl] *n* ciseau *m*, burin *m*; *vt* ciseler, sculpter.

chit [tʃit] *n* marmot *m*, mioche *mf*, brin *m*.

chit-chat ['tʃittʃæt] *n* commérages *m pl*.

chivalrous ['ʃivəlrəs] *a* chevaleresque.

chivalry ['ʃivəlri] *n* chevalerie *f*, courtoisie *f*.

chive [tʃaiv] *n* ciboulette *f*.

chlorine ['klɔːriːn] *n* chlore *m*.

chloroform ['klɔrəfɔːm] *n* chloroforme *m*.

chock [tʃɔk] *n* cale *f*; *vt* caler, mettre sur cale, bourrer.

chock-full ['tʃɔkful] *a* bourré, bondé.

chocolate ['tʃɔkəlit] *n* chocolat *m*; **— button, candy** crotte de chocolat *f*.

choice [tʃɔis] *n* choix *m*, préférence *f*, élection *f*; *a* de choix, choisi.

choir ['kwaiə] *n* chœur *m*, maîtrise *f*.

choke [tʃouk] *n* étranglement *m*, étrangleur *m*, (*aut*) starter *m*; *vti* étrangler, suffoquer, étouffer; *vt* boucher, obstruer; *vi* se boucher, obstruer; *vi* se boucher, s'obstruer; **to — back** refouler; **to — down** avaler.

choking ['tʃoukiŋ] *n* suffocation *f*, étranglement *m*, étouffement *m*, obstruction *f*.

cholera ['kɔlərə] *n* choléra *m*.

choleric ['kɔlərik] *a* cholérique, irascible.

choose [tʃuːz] *vt* choisir, opter, élire, adopter.

choosy ['tʃuːzi] *a* difficile, chipoteur.

chop [tʃɔp] *n* coup *m* (de hache), côtelette *f*, clapotis *m*; *vt* hacher, tailler, couper, fendre; *vi* clapoter; **to — down** abattre; **to — off** couper, trancher.

chopper ['tʃɔpə] *n* hachoir *m*, couperet *m*; (*US*) hélicoptère *m*.

choppy ['tʃɔpi] *a* agité, haché.

chopstick ['tʃɔpstik] *n* baguette *f*.

chord [kɔːd] *n* corde *f*, accord *m*.

chorister ['kɔristə] *n* choriste *m*, chantre *m*, enfant de chœur *m*.

chorus ['kɔːrəs] *n* chœur *m*, refrain *m*; **—girl** girl *f*.

chose [tʃouz] *pt of* **choose**.

Christ [kraist] *n* le Christ.

christen ['krisn] *vt* baptiser.

Christendom ['krisndəm] *n* chrétienté *f*.

christening ['krisniŋ] *n* baptême *m*.

Christian ['kristjən] *an* chrétien, -ienne.

Christianity [.kristi'æniti] *n* christianisme *m*.

Christmas ['krisməs] *n* Noël *m*; **Father —** le Père Noël.

Christmas-box ['krisməsbɔks] *n* étrennes *f pl*.

Christmas-carol ['krisməs'kærəl] *n* noël *m*.

Christopher ['kristəfə] Christophe *m*.

chromium ['kroumjəm] *n* chrome *m*.

chromium-plated ['kroumjəm.pleitid] *a* chromé.

chronic ['krɔnik] *a* chronique, constant.

chronicle ['krɔnikl] *n* chronique *f*; *vt* relater, faire la chronique de.

chronicler ['krɔniklə] *n* chroniqueur *m*.

chronological [.krɔnə'lɔdʒikl] *a* chronologique.

chronology [krə'nɔlədʒi] *n* chronologie *f*.

chronometer [krə'nɔmitə] *n* chronomètre *m*.

chrysalis ['krisəlis] *n* chrysalide *f*.

chrysanthemum [kri'sænθəməm] *n* chrysanthème *m*.

chubby ['tʃʌbi] *a* joufflu, potelé.

chuck [tʃʌk] *n* tape *f*; *vt* jeter, plaquer; **to — out** flanquer à la porte; **to — up** abandonner, balancer.

chuckle ['tʃʌkl] *n* rire étouffé *m*, gloussement *m*; *vi* rire sous cape, glousser.

chum [tʃʌm] *n* copain *m*, copine *f*, camarade *mf*.

chunk [tʃʌnk] *n* gros morceau *m*, (*bread*) quignon *m*.

church [tʃəːtʃ] *n* église *f*, temple *m*.

churchwarden ['tʃəːtʃ'wɔːdn] n marguillier m.

churchyard ['tʃəːtʃ'jaːd] n cimetière m.

churl [tʃəːl] n rustre m, ladre m.

churlish ['tʃəːliʃ] a grossier, mal élevé, grincheux, hargneux, bourru.

churlishness ['tʃəːliʃnis] n rusticité f, grossièreté f.

churn [tʃəːn] n baratte f; vt battre; vi (sea) bouillir, bouillonner.

cicada [si'kɑːdə] n cigale f.

cider ['saidə] n cidre m.

cigar [si'gɑː] n cigare m.

cigarette [ˌsigə'ret] n cigarette f.

cigarette-case [ˌsigəːretkeis] n étui m à cigarettes.

cigarette-holder [ˌsigəːret.houldə] n fume-cigarette m.

cinder ['sində] n cendre f; pl cendres f pl, escarbilles f pl.

Cinderella [ˌsindəˈrelə] n Cendrillon.

cine-camera ['siniˈkæmərə] n caméra f.

cinema ['sinimə] n cinéma m.

cine-projector ['sinipɹəˈdʒektə] n ciné-projecteur m.

cinnamon ['sinəmən] n canelle f.

cipher ['saifə] n zéro m, chiffre m, clé f; vt chiffrer.

circle ['səːkl] n cercle m, milieu m; vicious — cercle vicieux; vt encercler, entourer, faire le tour de; vi tourner en rond, tournoyer.

circuit ['səːkit] n circuit m, ressort m, tournée f, tour m, enceinte f, parcours m, pourtour m, détour m.

circuitous [səˈkjuitəs] a tournant, détourné.

circular ['səːkjulə] an circulaire f.

circularize ['səːkjuləraiz] vt envoyer des circulaires à.

circulate ['səːkjuleit] vi circuler; vt faire circuler.

circulation [ˌsəːkjuˈleiʃən] n circulation f, (of newspaper) tirage m.

circumcise ['səːkəmsaiz] vt circoncire.

circumcision [ˌsəːkəmˈsiʒən] n circoncision f.

circumference [səˈkʌmfərəns] n circonférence f.

circumflex ['səːkəmfleks] an circonflexe m.

circumlocution [ˌsəːkəmləˈkjuːʃən] n circonlocution f, ambages f pl.

circumscribe ['səːkəmskraib] vt circonscrire.

circumspect ['səːkəmspekt] a circonspect.

circumspection [ˌsəːkəmˈspekʃən] n circonspection f.

circumstance ['səːkəmstəns] n circonstance f, situation f, cérémonie f.

circumstantial [ˌsəːkəmˈstænʃəl] a indirect, circonstancié, circonstanciel.

circumvent [ˌsəːkəmˈvent] vt circonvenir.

circus ['səːkəs] n cirque m, rondpoint m.

cistern ['sistən] n réservoir m, citerne f.

citadel ['sitədl] n citadelle f.

citation [sai'teiʃən] n citation f.

cite [sait] vt citer, assigner.

citizen ['sitizn] n citoyen, citadin(e) mf bourgeois(e) mf.

citizenship ['sitiznʃip] n civisme m.

citron ['sitrən] n cédrat m.

city ['siti] n (grande)ville f, cité f; garden — cité jardin f.

civic ['sivik] a civique, municipal.

civics ['siviks] n instruction civique f.

civil ['sivil] a civil, poli, honnête; C— Service n administration f; — servant n fonctionnaire m; in — life dans le civil; (US) C— War Guerre f de sécession.

civilian [si'viljən] n civil m, pékin m.

civility [si'viliti] n politesse f, civilité f.

civilization [ˌsivilaiˈzeiʃən] n civilisation f.

civilize ['sivilaiz] vt civiliser.

clack [klæk] n claquement m; vi claquer, caqueter.

clad [klæd] pt pp of **clothe**.

claim [kleim] n revendication f, réclamation f, titre m, droit m, demande f, prétention f; vt réclamer, revendiquer, prétendre (à), demander.

claimant ['kleimənt] n demandeur, -eresse, réclamant(e) mf, prétendant(e) mf, revendicateur m.

clairvoyant [klɛəˈvɔiənt] a clairvoyant, doué de seconde vue; n voyant(e) mf.

clam [klæm] n palourde f.

clamant ['kleimənt] a bruyant, criant, urgent.

clamber ['klæmbə] vi grimper; n escalade f.

clammy ['klæmi] a moite, humide, gluant.

clamorous ['klæmərəs] a bruyant, braillard.

clamour ['klæmə] n clameur f; vi pousser des cris, vociférer; to — for demander, réclamer, à grand cris.

clamp [klæmp] n crampon m, mordache f, patte f d'attache, (potato) silo m; vt consolider, brider, agrafer.

clan [klæn] n clan m.

clandestine [klæn'destin] a clandestin.

clang [klæŋ] n bruit m retentissant, son m métallique; vt résonner, retentir; vt faire résonner.

clank [klæŋk] n cliquetis m; vi sonner; vt faire sonner.

clap [klæp] n éclat m, battement m, applaudissements m pl, tape f; vi battre (des mains); vti applaudir; vt camper, fourrer.

clapper ['klæpə] n battant m,

crécelle *f*, claquet *m*, claqueur *m*.

claptrap ['klæptræp] *n* tape-à-l'œil *m*, boniment *m*.

claret ['klærət] *n* bordeaux *m* rouge.

clarify ['klærifai] *vt* clarifier, éclaircir; *vi* se clarifier, s'éclaircir.

clarinet [‚klæri'net] *n* clarinette *f*.

clarion ['klæriən] *n* clairon *m*; *a* claironnant.

clarity ['klæriti] *n* clarté *f*, lucidité *f*.

clash [klæʃ] *n* choc *m*, heurt *m*, fracas, cliquetis *m*, confit *m*; *vi* faire du fracas, se heurter, s'entrechoquer, jurer; *vt* faire résonner.

clasp [klɑːsp] *n* agrafe *f*, fermoir *m*, fermeture *f*, étreinte *f*; *vt* agrafer, serrer, étreindre.

clasp-knife ['klɑːspnaif] *n* couteau fermant, pliant *m*.

class [klɑːs] *n* classe *f*, catégorie *f*, type *m*, sorte *f*; *vt* classer.

classic ['klæsik] *an* classique *m*.

classicism ['klæsisizəm] *n* classicisme *m*.

classification [‚klæsifi'keiʃən] *n* classement *m*.

classify ['klæsifai] *vt* classer.

clatter ['klætə] *n* bruit *m*, fracas *m*, brouhaha *m*, ferraillement *m*.

clause [klɔːz] *n* clause *f*, article *m*, proposition *f*.

clavicle ['klævikl] *n* clavicule *f*.

claw [klɔː] *n* serre *f*, pince *f*, griffe *f*; *vt* gratter, griffer, déchirer, égratigner.

clay [klei] *n* argile *f*, glaise *f*, pisé *m*.

clean [kliːn] *a* propre, net, bien fait, complet; *vt* nettoyer, vider, mettre en ordre, balayer, (re)curer, décrotter, décrasser.

cleaner ['kliːnə] *n* teinturier *m*, nettoyeur, -euse, décrotteur *m*, balayeur, -euse.

cleaning ['kliːniŋ] *n* nettoyage *m*, dégraissage *m*.

clean(li)ness ['klenlinis] *n* propreté *f*, netteté *f*.

cleanse [klenz] *vt* purifier, laver, curer, assainir.

clear [kliə] *a* clair, net, évident, libre, dégagé, sûr; **all** — fin d'alerte *f*; *vt* éclaircir, disculper, déblayer, dégager, franchir, solder, acquitter, gagner net, desservir, (*forest*, *bush*) débrousser; *vi* s'éclaircir, se dégager, se dissiper; **to** — **away** *vt* écarter, enlever; *vi* se dissiper; **to** — **off** enlever, solder; **to** — **out** *vt* nettoyer, balayer, vider; *vi* filer, ficher le camp, se sauver; **to** — **up** *vt* tirer au clair, éclaircir; *vi* s'éclaircir.

clearance ['kliərəns] *n* déblayage *m*, liquidation *f*, congé *m*, jeu *m*.

clear-cut ['kliə'kʌt] *a* distinct, net ciselé.

clear-headed ['kliə'hedid] *a* lucide, perspicace.

clearing ['kliəriŋ] *n* clairière *f*, levée *f*, dégagement *m*, déblaiement *m*, évacuation *f*, défrichement *m*.

clearness ['kliənis] *n* clarté *f*, netteté *f*.

clear-sighted ['kliə'saitid] *a* clairvoyant.

cleavage ['kliːvidʒ] *n* division *f*, scission *f*, (*fam*) décolleté *m*.

cleave [kliːv] *vt* fendre; *vi* se fendre, s'attacher.

cleaver ['kliːvə] *n* couperet *m*, fendoir *m*.

cleft [kleft] *pt pp* of **cleave**; *n* fente *f*, crevasse *f*, fissure *f*; *a* fourchu, (*palate*) fendu; **in a** — **stick** dans une impasse, mal pris.

clemency ['klemənsi] *n* clémence *f*, douceur *f*, indulgence *f*.

clement ['klemənt] *a* clément, indulgent, doux.

clench [klentʃ] *see* **clinch**; *vt* serrer; *vi* se serrer.

clergy ['kləːdʒi] *n* clergé *m*.

clergyman ['kləːdʒimən] *n* ecclésiastique *m*, pasteur *m*.

clerical ['klerikəl] *a* de clerc, d'écriture, de copiste.

clerk [klɑːk] *n* clerc *m*, commis *m*, employé(e) de bureau *mf*.

clever ['klevə] *a* habile, adroit, intelligent, ingénieux.

cleverness ['klevənis] *n* habileté *f*, adresse *f*, intelligence *f*, ingéniosité *f*.

click [klik] *n* (dé)clic *m*, cliquetis *m*; *vti* cliqueter, claquer; *vi* avoir de la veine, avoir des touches, cadrer.

client ['klaiənt] *n* client(e) *mf*.

clientele [‚kliːɑːn'tel] *n* clientèle *f*.

cliff [klif] *n* falaise *f*, paroi *f* rocheuse, rochers *m pl*.

climate ['klaimit] *n* climat *m*.

climatic [klai'mætik] *a* climat(ér)que.

climax ['klaimæks] *n* gradation *f*, comble *m*, apogée *f*.

climb [klaim] *n* escalade *f*, montée *f*, ascension *f*, côte *f*; *vti* monter, grimper; *vt* escalader, gravir, monter à, sur, grimper à, sur, faire l'ascension de; *vi* prendre de l'altitude; **to** — **down** *vti* descendre; *vi* baisser pavillon, en rabattre, se dégonfler; **to** — **over** escalader, franchir.

climber ['klaimə] *n* grimpeur *m*, alpiniste, plante grimpante *f*, arriviste *mf*.

clinch [klintʃ] *n* crampon *m*, corps à corps *m*; *vt* river, serrer, conclure.

clincher ['klintʃə] *n* argument décisif *m*.

cling [kliŋ] *vi* se cramponner, s'accrocher, se prendre, coller.

clinging ['kliŋiŋ] *a* étroit, collant.

clinic ['klinik] *n* clinique *f*.

clink [kliŋk] *n* tintement *m*, cliquetis *m*; prison *f*; *vi* tinter, s'entrechoquer; *vt* faire tinter, choquer; **to** — **glasses** trinquer.

clip [klip] *n* agrafe *f*, pince *f*, attache *f*; *vt* agrafer, pincer, tondre, rogner, tailler.

clippers ['klipəz] n tondeuse f.
clipping ['klipiŋ] n tonte f, tondage m, taille f, coupure f; pl rognures f pl.
cloak [klouk] n manteau m, masque m; vt couvrir, masquer.
cloakroom ['kloukrum] n consigne f, vestiaire m.
clock [klɔk] n pendule f, horloge f, baguette f; vt chronométrer.
clock-maker ['klɔk'meikə] n horloger m.
clock-making ['klɔk'meikiŋ] n horlogerie f.
clockwise ['klɔkwaiz] a dans le sens des aiguilles d'une montre, à droite.
clockwork ['klɔkwəːk] n mouvement d'horlogerie m, rouage m d'horloge; **to go like** — marcher comme sur des roulettes.
clod [klɔd] n motte f de terre, rustre m.
clog [klɔg] n entrave f, galoche f, sabot m; vt entraver, obstruer, arrêter, boucher; vi s'obstruer, se boucher.
cloister ['klɔistə] n cloître m; pl ambulatoire m.
close [klous] n (en)clos m, clôture f, enceinte f; a fermé, clos, confiné, lourd, compact, serré, secret, proche, étroit, exact, intime, avare; ad de près, étroitement; — **by** tout près; — **to** prep tout près de.
close [klouz] n clôture f, fermeture f, conclusion f, fin f; **to draw to a** — tirer à sa fin; vt fermer, clore, conclure, terminer, (res)serrer; vi (se) fermer, se terminer, faire relâche, en venir aux prises; **to** — **down** vti fermer; **to** — **up** vt boucher, barrer, obturer; vi s'obturer, se serrer.
closely ['klousli] ad de près.
closeness ['klousnis] n proximité f, rapprochement m, étroitesse f, intimité f, lourdeur f, avarice f, exactitude f, réserve f.
closet ['klɔzit] n cabinet m, armoire f; vt enfermer.
close-up ['klousʌp] n gros, premier plan m.
closing ['klouziŋ] n fermeture f, clôture f.
closure ['klouʒə] n clôture f.
clot [klɔt] n caillot m, grumeau m; vi se prendre, se coaguler, se figer, se cailler.
cloth [klɔθ] n toile f, étoffe f, nappe f, napperon m, linge m, torchon m, drap m, tapis m, habit ecclésiastique m; **to lay the** — mettre la nappe, le couvert.
clothe [klouð] vt (re)vêtir, habiller, couvrir.
clothes [klouðz] n pl habits m pl, vêtements m pl, effets m pl.
clothes-horse ['klouðzhɔːs] n séchoir; (US) mannequin m.
clothes-peg ['klouðzpeg] n patère f.
clothier ['klouðiə] n drapier m.

clothing ['klouðiŋ] n habillement m, vêtements m pl.
cloud [klaud] n nuage m, nue f, nuée f, buée f; vt assombrir, couvrir, obscurcir, voiler, ternir, embuer, troubler; vi s'assombrir, se couvrir, s'obscurcir, se voiler, se troubler, se ternir.
cloudy ['klaudi] a nuageux. couvert, trouble.
clout [klaut] n torchon m, linge m, chiffon m, taloche f.
clove [klouv] pt of **cleave**; n clou m de girofle; — **of garlic** gousse f d'ail.
cloven ['klouvn] pp of **cleave**; a fendu, fourchu.
clover ['klouvə] n trèfle m; **to be in** — être comme un coq en pâte.
clown [klaun] n clown m, bouffon m, pitre m; vi faire le clown.
cloy [klɔi] vt ressasier, affadir.
club [klʌb] n massue f, crosse f, gourdin m, club m, cercle m, (cards) trèfle m; vt frapper avec un gourdin, assommer; vi s'associer; **to** — **together** se cotiser.
club-foot ['klʌb'fut] n pied-bot m.
cluck [klʌk] n gloussement m; vi glousser.
clue [kluː] n indice m, indication f.
clump [klʌmp] n massif m, bouquet m, masse f; vi sonner, marcher lourdement.
clumsiness ['klʌmzinis] n gaucherie f, balourdise f, maladresse f.
clumsy ['klʌmzi] a gauche, maladroit.
clung [klʌŋ] pt pp of **cling**.
cluster ['klʌstə] n groupe m, grappe f, essaim m, bouquet m; vt grouper; vi se grouper.
clutch [klʌtʃ] n prise f, étreinte f, poigne f, griffes f pl, couvée f, (cheville d')embrayage f; **to let in** (out) **the** — embrayer, (débrayer); vt empoigner, étreindre, saisir; **to** — **at** s'agripper à, se raccrocher à.
clutter ['klʌtə] n encombrement m, pagaïe f; — **up** encombrer.
coach [koutʃ] n coche m, carrosse m, voiture f, autocar m, répétiteur m, entraîneur m; vt donner des leçons à, entraîner.
coach-builder ['koutʃ'bildə] n carrossier m.
coach-building ['koutʃ'bildiŋ] n carrosserie f.
coach-house ['koutʃhaus] n remise f.
coaching ['koutʃiŋ] n leçons f pl, répétitions f pl, dressage m, entraînement m.
coachman ['koutʃmən] n cocher m.
coachwork ['koutʃwəːk] n carrosserie f.
coagulate [kou'ægjuleit] vt (faire) coaguler, figer; vi s e coaguler, se figer.
coal [koul] n charbon m, houille f; **to haul** s.o. **over the** —s laver la tête à qn; vi faire le charbon.

coal-bed ['koul'bed] *n* banc *m*, couche *f* de houille.

coalesce [,kouə'les] *vi* s'unir, fusionner.

coalfield ['koulfi:ld] *n* bassin houiller *m*.

coalition [,koulə'lijən] *n* coalition *f*.

coalmine ['koulmain] *n* mine *f* de houille, houillère *f*.

coalminer ['koulmainə] *n* mineur *m*, houilleur *m*.

coal-tar ['koul'tɑː] *n* goudron *m*.

coarse [kɔːs] *a* gros(sier), rude, rêche.

coarseness ['kɔːsnis] *n* grossièreté *f*, rudesse *f*, grosseur *f*, brutalité *f*.

coast [koust] *n* côte *f*, rivage *m*, littoral *m*; *vi* côtoyer le rivage, faire le cabotage; **to — down a hill** descendre une côte en roue libre, le moteur débrayé.

coastal ['koustəl] *a* côtier.

coaster ['koustə] *n* caboteur *m*.

coasting ['koustiŋ] *n* cabotage *m*, navigation côtière.

coat [kout] *n* pardessus *m*, manteau *m*, habit *m*, robe *f*, poil *m*, couche *f*, revêtement *m*; *vt* couvrir, enduire, revêtir.

coat-hanger ['kout,hæŋə] *n* porte-vêtements *m*.

coat-peg ['koutpeg] *n* patère *f*.

coax [kouks] *vt* amadouer, câliner, cajoler, amener (à to).

coaxing ['kouksiŋ] *n* cajoleries *f pl*, enjôlement *m*; *a* cajoleur, câlin.

cob [kɔb] *n* cygne *m*, bidet *m*, torchis *m*, (*bread*) miche *f*, (*nut*) aveline *f*.

cobble ['kɔbl] *n* galet *m*, caillou *m*; *vt* paver, rapiécer.

cobbler ['kɔblə] *n* savetier *m*, cordonnier *m*.

cobra ['koubrə] *n* cobra *m*, serpent à lunettes *m*.

cobweb ['kɔbweb] *n* toile d'araignée *f*.

cock [kɔk] *n* coq *m*, mâle *m*, robinet *m*, (*gun*) chien *m*, (*hay*) meule *f*, (*scales*) aiguille *f*, retroussis *m*; *vt* dresser, retrousser, mettre de travers, armer.

cockade [kɔ'keid] *n* cocarde *f*.

cock-a-doodle-doo ['kɔkəduːdl'duː] *excl* cocorico!

cock-and-bull story ['kɔkən'bul-'stɔːri] *n* coq à l'âne *m*.

cockatoo [,kɔkə'tuː] *n* cacatoès *m*.

cockchafer ['kɔk,tʃeifə] *n* hanneton *m*.

cockle ['kɔkl] *n* coque *f*, bucarde *f*.

cockney ['kɔkni] *an* londonien, -ienne.

cockpit ['kɔkpit] *n* arène *f*, carlingue *f*.

cockroach ['kɔkroutʃ] *n* cafard *m*, blatte *f*, cancrelet *m*.

cockscomb ['kɔkskoum] *n* crête *f* de coq.

cocksure ['kɔk'ʃuə] *a* qui ne doute de rien, outrecuidant, très assuré.

cocky ['kɔki] *a* faraud, outrecuidant.

cocoa ['koukou] *n* cacao *m*; **— tree** cacaoyer *m*; **— plantation** cacaotière *f*.

coconut ['koukənʌt] *n* noix de coco *f*; **— palm** cocotier *m*; **— plantation** cocoteraie *f*; **— oil** huile *f* de copra.

cocoon [kə'kuːn] *n* cocon *m*.

cod [kɔd] *n* morue *f*, cabillaud *m*.

coddle ['kɔdl] *vt* dorloter, choyer.

code [koud] *n* code *m*, chiffre *m*; *vt* codifier, chiffrer.

codicil ['kɔdisil] *n* codicille *m*.

codliver-oil ['kɔdlivər'ɔil] *n* huile *f* de foie de morue.

coerce [kou'əːs] *vt* forcer, contraindre.

coercion [kou'əːʃən] *n* coercition *f*, contrainte *f*.

coercive [kou'əːsiv] *a* coercitif.

coffee ['kɔfi] *n* café *m*; **— bean** grain *m* de café; **— grounds** marc *m* de café; **black —** café noir; **white —** café au lait, café crème.

coffee-mill ['kɔfimil] *n* moulin à café *m*.

coffee plant ['kɔfiplɑːnt] *n* caféier *m*.

coffee plantation ['kɔfiplæn,teiʃən] *n* caféière *f*.

coffeepot ['kɔfipɔt] *n* cafetière *f*.

coffer ['kɔfə] *n* coffre *m*.

coffin ['kɔfin] *n* cercueil *m*, bière *f*.

cog [kɔg] *n* dent *f*; **he's only a — in the wheel** il n'est qu'un rouage de la machine.

cogency ['koudʒənsi] *n* force *f*, puissance *f*, urgence *f*.

cogent ['koudʒənt] *a* décisif, valable, urgent.

cogitate ['kɔdʒiteit] *vi* réfléchir; *vti* méditer.

cogitation [,kɔdʒi'teiʃən] *n* réflexion *f*, délibération.

cognate ['kɔgneit] *a* parent, connexe, analogue, qui a du rapport, de même origine.

cognizance ['kɔgnizəns] *n* connaissance *f* compétence *f* ressort *m*.

cogwheel ['kɔgwiːl] *n* roue dentée *f*.

cohabit [kou'hæbit] *vi* cohabiter.

cohabitation [,kouhæbi'teiʃən] *n* cohabitation *f*.

coheir ['kou'ɛə] *n* cohéritier, -ière.

cohere [kou'hiə] *vi* se tenir ensemble, adhérer, s'agglomérer, être conséquent, se tenir.

coherence [kou'hiərəns] *n* cohésion *f*, cohérence *f*, suite *f*.

coherent [kou'hiərənt] *a* cohérent, qui a de la suite conséquent.

cohesion [kou'hiːʒən] *n* cohésion *f*.

cohesive [kou'hiːsiv] *a* adhérent, cohésif.

coil [kɔil] *n* rouleau *m*, bobine *f*, anneau *m*, repli *m*; *vt* embobiner, (en)rouler; **to — up** *vi* s'enrouler, se lover, se mettre en rond, serpenter; *vi* enrouler.

coin [kɔin] *n* pièce *f*, monnaie *f*; *vt* frapper, forger, inventer.

coinage ['kɔinidʒ] *n* frappe *f*, monnaie *f*.

coincide [ˌkouin'said] *vi* coïncider, s'accorder.

coincidence [kou'insidəns] *n* coïncidence *f*, concours *m*.

coiner ['kɔinə] *n* faux-monnayeur *m*, forgeur *m*, inventeur *m*.

coke [kouk] *n* coke *m*.

colander ['kɔləndə] *n* passoire *f*.

cold [kould] *a* froid, insensible; *n* froid *m*, rhume *m*; — **in the head** rhume de cerveau *m*; **it is** — il fait froid; **he is** — il a froid; **to catch** — prendre froid, s'enrhumer, attraper un rhume; **to grow** — se refroidir.

coldness ['kouldnis] *n* froideur *f*, froid *m*, froidure *f*.

cold-shoulder ['kould'ʃouldə] *vt* battre froid à.

colic ['kɔlik] *n* colique *f*.

collaborate [kə'læbəreit] *vi* collaborer.

collaboration [kə,læbə'reiʃən] *n* collaboration *f*.

collaborator [kə'læbəreitə] *n* collaborateur, -trice.

collapse [kə'læps] *n* effondrement *m*, écroulement *m*, dégringolade *f*, débâcle *f*; *vi* s'effondrer, s'écrouler, s'affaiser, se rabattre.

collapsible [kə'læpsəbl] *a* pliant, démontable, rabattable.

collar ['kɔlə] *n* (faux-)col *m*, collier *m*, collerette *f*, collet *m*; *vt* prendre au collet, saisir.

collarbone ['kɔləboun] *n* clavicule *f*.

colleague ['kɔliːg] *n* collègue *mf*.

collect [kə'lekt] *vr* rassembler, réunir, percevoir, ramasser; *vi* se rassembler, s'amasser, faire la quête.

collected [kə'lektid] *a* froid, posé, recueilli, de sang-froid.

collection [kə'lekʃən] *n* collecte *f*, quête *f*, levée *f*, collection *f*, rassemblement *m*, collectionnement *m*, recueil *m*, perception *f*.

collective [kə'lektiv] *a* collectif.

collector [kə'lektə] *n* collecteur, -trice, collectionneur, -euse, quêteur, -euse, percepteur, -trice, receveur, -euse, encaisseur *m*; **ticket** — contrôleur *m*.

college ['kɔlidʒ] *n* collège *m*, école *f*.

collide [kə'laid] *vi* se heurter.

collier ['kɔliə] *n* mineur *m* (de charbon), (navire) charbonnier *m*.

colliery ['kɔljəri] *n* mine *f* de houille.

collision [kə'liʒən] *n* collision *f*, tamponnement *m*.

colloquial [kə'loukwiəl] *a* familier, parlé.

colloquy ['kɔləkwi] *n* colloque *m*.

collusion [kə'luːʒən] *n* collusion *f*, connivence *f*.

colon ['koulən] *n* deux-points *m*.

colonel ['kəːnl] *n* colonel *m*.

colonial [kə'lounjəl] *a* colonial.

colonist ['kɔlənist] *n* colon *m*.

colonization [ˌkɔlənai'zeiʃən] *n* colonisation *f*.

colonize ['kɔlənaiz] *vt* coloniser.

colony ['kɔləni] *n* colonie *f*.

colossal [kə'bsl] *a* colossal.

colossus [kə'bsəs] *n* colosse *m*.

colour ['kʌlə] *n* couleur *f*, coloris *m*, teint *m*; *pl* drapeau *m*, cocarde *f*, livrée *f*; *vt* colorer, colorier, présenter sous un faux jour; *vi* rougir, se colorer; **in its true** —s sous son vrai jour; **to be off** — n'être pas dans son assiette; **with flying** —s haut la main.

colour-bar ['kʌləbaː] *n* racisme *m*.

colour-blind ['kʌləblaind] *a* daltonien.

colour-blindness ['kʌləblaindnis] *n* daltonisme *m*.

coloured ['kʌləd] *a* coloré, de couleur.

colourful ['kʌləful] *a* pittoresque, coloré.

colouring ['kʌləriŋ] *n* coloris *m*, coloration *f*, teint *m*.

colourless ['kʌləlis] *a* incolore, terne, pâle.

colt [koult] *n* poulain *m*, pouliche *f*.

column ['kɔləm] *n* colonne *f*.

comb [koum] *n* peigne *m*, étrille *f*, carde *f*, crête *f*; *vt* peigner, étriller, carder, fouiller; *vi* déferler; **to** — **out** démêler, faire une rafle dans.

combat ['kɔmbæt] *n* combat *m*; *vt* combattre, lutter contre, s'opposer à.

combatant ['kɔmbətənt] *n* combattant *m*.

combative ['kɔmbətiv] *a* combatif, batailleur.

combination [ˌkɔmbi'neiʃən] *n* combinaison *f*, mélange *m*, combiné *m*.

combine ['kɔmbain] *n* combinaison *f*, cartel *m*; [kəm'bain] *vt* combiner, unir, joindre, allier; *vi* se combiner, s'unir, fusionner, se syndiquer.

combined [kəm'baind] *a* combiné, joint (à with).

combustible [kəm'bʌstibl] *a* inflammable; *an* combustible *m*.

combustion [kəm'bʌstʃən] *n* combustion *f*.

come [kʌm] *vi* venir, arriver, en venir (à), en arriver (à); **to** — **about** arriver, se passer, se faire; **to** — **across** tomber sur, rencontrer, trouver; **to** — **along** s'en venir, s'amener, se dépêcher; **to** — **away** partir, se détacher; **to** — **back** revenir, en revenir (à); **to** — **by** *vi* passer par; *vt* obtenir; **to** — **down** *vti* descendre; *vi* baisser, s'abaisser, s'écrouler; **to** — **forward** (s')avancer; **to** — **in** entrer; **to** — **off** descendre, se détacher, s'effacer, avoir lieu, réussir, aboutir; **to** — **out** sortir, débuter, paraître, se montrer, s'effacer, se mettre en grève; **to** — **to** revenir à soi, reprendre connaissance; **to** — **up to** s'approcher de, venir à, répondre à, s'élever à; **to** — **up against** entrer en conflit avec, se heurter avec; **to — upon** tomber sur, surprendre.

come-back ['kʌmbæk] n retour m (à la charge), réplique f, réapparition f.

comedian [kə'miːdjən] n auteur m, (acteur) comique, comédien, -ienne.

comedy ['kɔmidi] n comédie f.

comeliness ['kʌmlinis] n grâce f.

comely ['kʌmli] a gracieux, avenant.

comer ['kʌmə] n (premier, -ière, nouveau, -elle) venu(e) mf arrivant(e) mf, venant(e) mf.

comet ['kɔmit] n comète f.

comfit ['kʌmfit] n dragée f, bonbon m.

comfort ['kʌmfət] n (ré)confort m, aisance f, bienêtre m, confortable m, consolation f, soulagement m; pl douceurs f pl, gâteries f pl; vt réconforter, consoler, soulager, mettre à l'aise.

comfortable ['kʌmfətəbl] a à l'aise, bien, confortable, aisé, commode.

comforter ['kʌmfətə] n consolateur, -trice, cache-nez m, écharpe f, tétine f, sucette f.

comic ['kɔmik] an comique m.

comical ['kɔmikəl] a comique, drôle.

coming ['kʌmiŋ] a prochain, à venir, futur, d'avenir; n venue f, arrivée f, approche f, avènement m; — **of age** majorité f.

comity ['kɔmiti] n affabilité f.

comma ['kɔmə] n virgule f; **inverted —s** guillemets m pl.

command [kə'mɑːnd] n ordre m, commandement m, maîtrise f; vt ordonner, commander (à), dominer.

commandeer [ˌkɔmən'diə] vt réquisitionner.

commander [kə'mɑːndə] n commandeur m, commandant m (en chef) capitaine de frégate m.

commanding [kə'mɑːndiŋ] a imposant, dominateur, dominant.

commandment [kə'mɑːndmənt] n commandement m.

commemorate [kə'meməreit] vt commémorer.

commemoration [kəˌmemə'reiʃən] n commémoration f.

commemorative [kə'memərətiv] a commémoratif.

commence [kə'mens] vti commencer.

commencement [kə'mensmənt] n commencement m.

commend [kə'mend] vt confier, recommander, louer.

commendable [kə'mendəbl] a recommandable, louable.

commendation [ˌkɔmen'deiʃən] n recommendation f, éloge m, louange f.

commensurate [kə'menʃərit] a proportionné, commensurable.

comment ['kɔment] vi commenter, faire des observations; n commentaire m, observation f.

commentary ['kɔmentəri] n commentaire m, glose f; **running —** radio-reportage m.

commentator ['kɔmenteitə] n commentateur, -trice, radio-reporter m.

commerce ['kɔməːs] n commerce m, les affaires f pl.

commercial [kə'məːʃəl] a commercial, mercantile; n annonce publicitaire f; — **traveller** n commis-voyageur m.

commiserate [kə'mizəreit] vi compatir (à **with**), s'apitoyer (sur **with**).

commiseration [kəˌmizə'reiʃən] n commisération f.

commissary ['kɔmisəri] n délégué m, intendant m.

commission [kə'miʃən] n commission f, courtage m, guelte f, délégation f, mandat m, brevet m, nomination f, perpétration f; vt mandater, nommer, charger (de), commissionner, déléguer, (ship) armer.

commissionaire [kəˌmiʃə'nɛə] n commissionnaire m, chasseur m.

commissioned [kə'miʃənd] a commissionné; **non— officer** sous-officier m.

commissioner [kə'miʃənə] n commissaire m, délégué m.

commit [kə'mit] vt confier, remettre, commettre, compromettre, renvoyer, engager; — **to memory** apprendre par cœur; — **suicide** se suicider.

commitment [kə'mitmənt] n engagement m.

committal [kə'mitl] n engagement m, perpétration f.

committee [kə'miti] n comité m, commission f, conseil m.

commode [kə'moud] n commode f, chaise percée f.

commodious [kə'moudjəs] a spacieux, ample.

commodiousness [kə'moudjəsnis] n grandeur f.

commodity [kə'mɔditi] n denrée f, marchandise f, article m.

common ['kɔmən] a commun, public, vulgaire, ordinaire, courant, coutumier, (mil) simple, communal.

commonalty ['kɔmənəlti] n commun m des hommes, les roturiers m pl.

commoner ['kɔmənə] n bourgeois(e) mf, homme du peuple, roturier, -ière.

commonly ['kɔmənli] ad communément, vulgairement.

commonness ['kɔmənnis] n vulgarité f, trivialité f, frequence f.

commonplace ['kɔmənpleis] n lieu commun m; a banal, terre à terre.

commons ['kɔmənz] n peuple m; **the House of Commons** = la Chambre des Députés.

commonsense ['kɔmən,sens] n bon sens m, sens commun m.

commonweal ['kɔmənwiːl] n bien public m, chose publique f.

commonwealth ['kɔmənwelθ] n république f, commonwealth m.

commotion [kə'mouʃən] n commotion f, émoi m, agitation f, ébranlement m, brouhaha m, troubles m pl.

communal ['kɔmjuːnl] a communal, public, (life) collectif.

commune [kə'mjuːn] vi communier s'entretenir; to — with oneself se recueillir, vivre en soi.

communicable [kə'mjuːnikəbl] a communicable, contagieux.

communicant [kə'mjuːnikənt] n communiant(e) mf, informateur, -trice.

communicate [kə'mjuːnikeit] vti communiquer; vi communier, faire part de.

communication [kə.mjuːni'keiʃən] n communication f, rapports m pl.

communicative [kə'mjuːnikətiv] a communicatif, expansif.

communion [kə'mjuːnjən] n communion f, relations f pl.

communism ['kɔmjunizəm] n communisme m.

communist ['kɔmjunist] an communiste mf.

community [kə'mjuːniti] n communauté f, solidarité f, société f.

communize ['kɔmjunaiz] vt socialiser, communiser.

commutable [kə'mjuːtəbl] a échangeable, permutable, commuable.

commutation [.kɔmjuː'teiʃən] n commutation f.

commute [kə'mjuːt] vt (é)changer, commuer.

compact ['kɔmpækt] n contrat m, accord m, pacte m, poudrier m; [kəm'pækt] a compact, tassé, serré, concis.

compactness [kəm'pæktnis] n compacité f, concision f.

companion [kəm'pænjən] n compagnon m, compagne f, demoiselle (dame) de compagnie f.

companionable [kəm'pænjənəbl] a sociable.

companionship [kəm'pænjənʃip] n camaraderie f.

company ['kʌmpəni] n compagnie f, (ship) équipage m, société f, corporation f, bande f, troupe f; to have — for dinner avoir du monde à dîner.

comparable ['kɔmpərəbl] a comparable.

comparative [kəm'pærətiv] a comparatif, relatif.

comparatively [kəm'pærətivli] ad par comparaison, relativement.

compare [kəm'pɛə] vt comparer, confronter, collationner, échanger.

compared [kəm'pɛəd] pt pp of compare; — with prep à côte de, par rapport à, au prix de, par comparaison à.

comparison [kəm'pærisn] n comparaison f.

compartment [kəm'pɑːtmənt] n compartiment m, case f.

compass ['kʌmpəs] n compas m, boussole f, portée f, limites f pl, détour m; vt faire le tour de, entourer, saisir, tramer, exécuter.

compassion [kəm'pæʃən] n compassion f, pitié f.

compassionate [kəm'pæʃənit] a compatissant.

compatibility [kəm.pæti'biliti] n compatibilité f.

compatible [kəm'pætibl] a compatible.

compatriot [kəm'pætriət] n compatriote mf.

compel [kəm'pel] vt contraindre, forcer, obliger, imposer.

compendious [kəm'pendiəs] a succinct.

compendium [kəm'pendiəm] n abrégé m.

compensate ['kɔmpenseit] vt (ré) compenser, rémunérer, dédommager; to — for racheter, compenser.

compensation [.kɔmpen'seiʃən] n dédommagement m, indemnité f.

compete [kəm'piːt] vi rivaliser, concourir, faire concurrence, disputer.

competence ['kɔmpitəns] n compétence f, aisance f.

competent ['kɔmpitənt] a compétent, capable.

competition [.kɔmpi'tiʃən] n concurrence f, concours m.

competitive [kəm'petitiv] a de concours, de concurrence.

competitor [kəm'petitə] n compétiteur, -trice, concurrent(e) mf, émule mf.

compilation [.kɔmpi'leiʃən] n compilation f.

compile [kəm'pail] vt compiler, dresser.

compiler [kəm'pailə] n compilateur, -trice.

complacency [kəm'pleisnsi] n contentement m (de soi), suffisance f.

complacent [kəm'pleisnt] a suffisant, content de soi-même.

complain [kəm'plein] vi se plaindre, porter plainte.

complainer [kəm'pleinə] n réclamant(e) mf, mécontent(e) mf.

complaint [kəm'pleint] n plainte f, grief m, maladie f.

complaisance [kəm'pleizəns] n complaisance f.

complaisant [kəm'pleizənt] a complaisant, obligeant.

complement ['kɔmplimənt] n complément m; [.kɔmpli'ment] vt compléter.

complete [kəm'pliːt] a complet, entier, total, absolu, accompli, achevé, au complet; vt compléter, accomplir, achever, mettre le comble à.

completion [kəm'pliːʃən] n achèvement m, accomplissement m, satisfaction f.

complex ['kɔmpleks] an complexe m.

complexion [kəm'plekʃən] n teint m, jour m, couleur f, caractère m.

complexity [kəm'pleksiti] n complexité f.

compliance [kəm'plaiəns] n déférence f, acquiescement m; **in —with** conformément à.

compliant [kəm'plaiənt] a obligeant, docile.

complicate ['kɔmplikeit] vt compliquer.

complication [ˌkɔmpli'keiʃən] n complication f.

complicity [kəm'plisiti] n complicité f.

compliment ['kɔmplimənt] n compliment m; [ˌkɔmpli'ment] vt féliciter, complimenter.

complimentary [ˌkɔmpli'mentəri] a flatteur (ticket) de faveur, (book) en hommage.

comply [kəm'plai] vi se conformer (à with), accéder (à with), obéir (à with). observer, se soumettre (à with) s'exécuter.

component [kəm'pounənt] n élément m, composant m; a constitutif, constituant.

compose [kəm'pouz] vt composer, arranger; **to — oneself** se calmer, se remettre.

composed [kəm'pouzd] a calme, posé composé.

composer [kəm'pouzə] n compositeur, -trice.

composite ['kɔmpəzit] a composite, composé.

composition [ˌkɔmpə'ziʃən] n composition f, constitution f, arrangement m, composé m, mélange m, rédaction f, dissertation f.

compositor [kəm'pɔzitə] n typographe m, compositeur m.

composure [kəm'pouʒə] n calme m, maîtrise de soi sang-froid m.

compound ['kɔmpaund] an composé m, concession f; **— interest** intérêts composés; a complexe; n masti m.

compound [kəm'paund] vt mélanger, combiner, arranger, composer; vi s'arranger, transiger.

comprehend [ˌkɔmpri'hend] vt comprendre.

comprehensible [ˌkɔmpri'hensəbl] a compréhensible.

comprehension [ˌkɔmpri'henʃən] n compréhension f.

comprehensive [ˌkɔmpri'hensiv] a compréhensif; **— school** collège pilote (m xte) f.

comprehensiveness [ˌkɔmpri'hensivnis] n étendue f, portée f.

compress ['kɔmpres] n compresse f.

compress [kəm'pres] vi comprimer, bander, condenser, concentrer.

comprise [kəm'praiz] vt comprendre, comporter, renfermer.

compromise ['kɔmprəmaiz] n compromis m; vi transiger; vti compromettre; **to — oneself** se compromettre.

compulsion [kəm'pʌlʃən] n force f, contrainte f.

compulsory [kəm'pʌlsəri] a obligatoire, coercitif.

compunction [kəm'pʌŋkʃən] n remords m regret m, componction f.

computation [ˌkɔmpju'teiʃən] n calcul m, estimation f.

compute [kəm'pjuːt] vt calculer, estimer.

computer [kəm'pjuːtə] n ordinateur m, calculateur m.

comrade ['kɔmrid] n camarade m, compagnon m.

comradeship ['kɔmridʃip] n camaraderie f.

con [kɔn] vt étudier, diriger, (US) escroquer.

concave ['kɔn'keiv] a concave, incurvé.

conceal [kən'siːl] vt cacher, dissimuler, céler, voiler, dérober, masquer.

concealment [kən'siːlmənt] n dissimulation f, réticence f.

concede [kən'siːd] vt accorder, concéder, admettre.

conceit [kən'siːt] n vanité f, suffisance f, pointe f, jugement m.

conceited [kən'siːtid] a vaniteux, suffisant, glorieux.

conceivable [kən'siːvəbl] a concevable.

conceive [kən'siːv] vt concevoir; vi s'imaginer.

concentrate ['kɔnsəntreit] vt concentrer; vi se concentrer.

concentration [ˌkɔnsən'treiʃən] n concentration f, application f, rassemblement m.

conception [kən'sepʃən] n conception f idée f.

concern [kən'səːn] n intérêt m, sympathie f, affaire f, souci m, sollicitude f, maison f de commerce, entreprise f; **the whole —** toute la boutique; vt regarder, concerner, intéresser, importer; **to — oneself with** s'occuper de, s'intéresser à.

concerned [kən'səːnd] a préoccupé (de with), intéressé, (à with), inquiet, soucieux.

concerning [kən'səːniŋ] prep quant à, au sujet de, en ce qui concerne, pour ce qui est de.

concert ['kɔnsət] n concert m, accord m, unisson m; **— hall** salle f de concert; **in — with** de concert avec.

concert [kən'səːt] vt concerter; vi se concerter.

concession [kən'seʃən] n concession f.

conciliate [kən'silieit] vt (ré)concilier

conciliation [kən,sili'eiʃən] *n* conciliation *f*.

conciliatory [kən'siliətəri] *a* conciliant. conciliatoire.

concise [kən'sais] *a* concis.

concision [kən'siʒən] *n* concision *f*.

conclude [kən'kluːd] *vti* conclure; *vi* se terminer; *vt* terminer, achever, régler.

conclusion [kən'kluːʒən] *n* conclusion *f*, fin *f*.

conclusive [kən'kluːsiv] *a* concluant, décisif.

conclusiveness [kən'kluːsivnis] *n* force décisive *f*.

concoct [kən'kɔkt] *vt* confectionner, composer, combiner, imaginer, concevoir.

concoction [kən'kɔkʃən] *n* potpourri *m*, boisson *f*, confectionnement *m*, conception *f*, tissu *m*.

concord ['kɔŋkɔːd] *n* harmonie *f*, accord *m*.

concordance [kən'kɔːdəns] *n* concordance *f*, harmonie *f*, accord *m*.

concordant [kən'kɔːdənt] *a* concordant.

concourse ['kɔŋkɔːs] *n* concourse *m*, affluence *f*, foule *f*.

concrete ['kɔnkriːt] *n* ciment *m*, béton *m*; **reinforced** — béton armé; *a* concret *m*.

concrete [kən'kriːt] *vt* solidifier, cimenter, bétonner; *vi* se solidifier.

concur [kən'kəː] *vi* s'accorder, contribuer, concourir, être d'accord.

concurrence [kən'kʌrəns] *n* concours *m*, approbation *f*, assentiment *m*.

concurrent [kən'kʌrənt] *a* concurrent, simultané.

concurrently [kən'kʌrəntli] *ad* concurremment.

concussion [kən'kʌʃən] *n* commotion *f*, secousse *f*, ébranlement *m* choc *m*.

condemn [kən'dem] *vt* condamner, censurer.

condemnation [,kɔndem'neiʃən] *n* condamnation *f*, censure *f*.

condensation [,kɔnden'seiʃən] *n* condensation *f*.

condense [kən'dens] *vt* condenser, concentrer; serrer; *vi* se condenser.

condenser [kən'densə] *n* condenseur *m*, distillateur *m*.

condescend [,kɔndi'send] *vi* condescendre s'abaisser.

condescending [,kɔndi'sendiŋ] *a* condescendant.

condescension [,kɔndi'senʃən] *n* condescendance *f*, déférence *f*.

condign [kən'dain] *a* juste, merité, exemplaire.

condiment ['kɔndimənt] *n* assaisonnement *m*, condiment *m*.

condition [kən'diʃən] *n* condition *f*, situation *f*, état *m*; *vt* conditionner.

conditional [kən'diʃənl] *a* conditionnel, dépendant.

condolatory [kən'doulətəri] *a* de condoléance.

condole [kən'doul] *vi* sympathiser (avec **with**), exprimer ses condoléances (à **with**).

condolence [kən'douləns] *n* condoléances *f pl*.

condone [kən'doun] *vt* pardonner.

conduce [kən'djuːs] *vi* aboutir, contribuer.

conducive [kən'djuːsiv] *a* qui conduit (à **to**), qui contribue (à **to**), favorable (à **to**).

conduct ['kɔndəkt] *n* conduite *f*, gestion *f*.

conduct [kən'dʌkt] *vt* conduire, mener, diriger, gérer; **to — oneself** se conduire, se comporter.

conduction [kən'dʌkʃən] *n* conduction *f* transmission *f*.

conductor [kən'dʌktə] *n* guide *m*, conducteur *m*, chef *m* d'orchestre, (*bus*) receveur *m*.

conductress [kən'dʌktris] *n* conductrice *f*, receveuse *f*.

conduit ['kɔndit] *n* conduit *m*.

cone [koun] *n* cône *m*, pomme de pin *f*.

confection [kən'fekʃən] *n* confection *f*; bonbons *m pl*, confits *m pl*.

confectioner [kən'tekʃənə] *n* confiseur *m*.

confectioner's [kən'fekʃənəz] *n* confiserie *f*.

confectionery [kən'fekʃnəri] *n* confiserie *f*.

confederacy [kən'fedərəsi] *n* confédération *f*, conspiration *f*.

confederate [kən'fedərit] *an* confédéré *m*; *n* complice *m*, comparse *m*.

confer [kən'fəː] *vti* conférer; *vt* accorder. octroyer.

conference ['kɔnfərəns] *n* conférence *f*. congrès *m*, consultation *f*.

conferment [kən'təːmənt] *n* octroi *m*, attribution *f*.

confess [kən'fes] *vt* confesser, avouer; *vi* se confesser faire des aveux.

confession [kən'teʃən] *n* confession *f*, aveu *m*; **to go to —** aller à confesse.

confessional [kən'feʃənl] *n* confessional *m*; *a* confessionnel.

confessor [kən'fesə] *n* confesseur *m*.

confide [kən'faid] *vt* confier, avouer en confidence; *vi* se fier (à **in**).

confidence ['kɔnfidəns] *n* confidence *f*, confiance *f* (*en* soi), assurance *f*; (*US* — **game** fraude *f*.

confident ['kɔn idənt] *a* confiant, assuré sûr.

confidential [,kɔnfi'denʃəl] *a* confidential, de confiance.

confidentially [,kɔnfi'denʃəli] *ad* en confidence, à titre confidentiel.

confidently ['kɔnfidəntli] *ad* avec confiance.

confine [kən'fain] *vt* limiter, confiner, borner, emprisonner, renfermer.

confined [kən'faind] *a* (*space*) resserré; — **to bed** alité, (*woman*) en couches.

confinement [kən'fainmənt] *n* réclusion *f*, emprisonnement *m*, restriction *f*, accouchement *m*, couches *f pl*.

confines ['kɔnfainz] *n pl* confins *m pl*.

confirm [kən'fəːm] *vt* confirmer, fortifier, raffermir.

confirmation [,kɔnfə'meiʃən] *n* confirmation *f*, raffermissement *m*.

confirmed [kən'fəːmd] *a* invétéré, endurci, incorrigible.

confiscate ['kɔnfiskeit] *vt* confisquer.

confiscation [,kɔnfis'keiʃən] *n* confiscation *f*.

conflagration [,kɔnflə'greiʃən] *n* conflagration *f*, incendie *m*, embrasement *m*.

conflict ['kɔnflikt] *n* conflit *m*, lutte *f*.

conflict [kən'flikt] *vi* être en conflit, jurer, se heurter.

confluent ['kɔnfluənt] *n* confluent *m*, affluent *m*.

conform [kən'fɔːm] *vt* conformer; *vi* se conformer, obéir, s'adapter.

conformation [,kɔnfɔː'meiʃən] *n* conformation *f*, structure *f*.

conformity [kən'fɔːmiti] *n* conformité *f*; **in** — **with** conformément à.

confound [kən'faund] *vt* confondre, embarrasser, déconcerter.

confounded [kən'faundid] *a* maudit, sacré.

confraternity [,kɔnfrə'təːniti] *n* confrérie *f*, bande *f*.

confront [kən'frʌnt] *vt* affronter, confronter, faire face à, se trouver en presence de.

confuse [kən'fjuːz] *vt* mettre en désordre, confondre, embrouiller, (em)mêler.

confused [kən'fjuːzd] *a* confus, interdit, ahuri, bouleversé, trouble.

confusedly [kən'fjuːzidli] *ad* confusément.

confusion [kən'fjuːʒən] *n* confusion *f*, désordre *m*, désarroi *m*, remue-ménage *m*.

confutation [,kɔnfjuː'teiʃən] *n* réfutation *f*.

confute [kən'fjuːt] *vt* réfuter, démolir les arguments de.

congeal [kən'dʒiːl] *vt* (con)geler, coaguler, figer; *vi* se congeler, se coaguler, se figer, se prendre.

congenial [kən'dʒiːnjəl] *a* du même caractère que, au goût de, sympathique, agréable, convenable.

congeniality [kən,dʒiːni'æliti] *n* sympathie *f*, caractère agréable *m*, accord *m* de sentiments.

congest [kən'dʒest] *vt* congestionner, encombrer, embouteiller.

congestion [kən'dʒestʃən] *n* congestion *f*, encombrement *m*, embouteillage *m*, surpeuplement *m*.

conglomerate [kən'glɔməreit] *vt* conglomérer; *vi* se conglomérer, s'agglomérer.

congratulate [kən'grætjuleit] *vt* féliciter.

congratulation [kən,grætju'leiʃən] *n* félicitation *f*.

congregate ['kɔngrigeit] *vt* rassembler, réunir; *vi* se réunir, se rassembler.

congregation [,kɔngri'geiʃən] *n* congrégation *f*, assemblée *f*, amas *m*, rassemblement *m*.

congress ['kɔngres] *n* congrès *m*, réunion *f*.

congruency ['kɔngruənsi] *n* accord *m*, conformité *f*.

congruous ['kɔngruəs] *a* approprié, conforme.

conifer ['kɔnifə] *n* conifère *m*.

conjecture [kən'dʒektʃə] *n* conjecture *f*; *vt* conjecturer.

conjugal ['kɔndʒugəl] *a* conjugal.

conjugate ['kɔndʒugeit] *vt* conjuguer.

conjugation [,kɔndʒu'geiʃən] *n* conjugaison *f*.

conjunction [kən'dʒʌŋkʃən] *n* connexion *f*, jonction *f*, coïncidence *f*; **in** — **with** conjointement avec.

conjuncture [kən'dʒʌŋktʃə] *n* conjoncture *f*, circonstance *f*.

conjuration [,kɔndʒuə'reiʃən] *n* conjuration *f*, évocation *f*.

conjure [kən'dʒuə] *vt* conjurer, évoquer.

conjure ['kʌndʒə] *vi* faire des tours de prestidigitation; **to** — **away** escamoter.

conjurer ['kʌndʒərə] *n* prestidigitateur *m*.

connect [kə'nekt] *vt* (re)lier, rattacher, réunir, associer; *vi* se (re)lier, se réunir, faire correspondance.

connection [kə'nekʃən] *n* lien *m*, rapport *m*, sens *m*, égard *m*, parenté *f*, clientèle *f*, correspondance *f*, prise *f* de courant.

conning-tower ['kɔniŋ,tauə] *n* kiosque *m*.

connivance [kə'naivəns] *n* connivence *f*, complicité *f*.

connive [kə'naiv] *vi* être de connivence (avec **with**), fermer les yeux (sur **at**).

connubial [kə'njuːbjəl] *a* conjugal.

conquer ['kɔŋkə] *vt* conquérir, vaincre.

conqueror ['kɔŋkərə] *n* conquérant *m*, vainqueur *m*.

conquest ['kɔŋkwest] *n* conquête *f*.

conscience ['kɔnʃəns] *n* conscience *f*.

conscientious [,kɔnʃi'enʃəs] *a* consciencieux, scrupuleux.

conscientiousness [,kɔnʃi'enʃəsnis] *n* conscience *f*.

conscious ['kɔnʃəs] *a* conscient; **to be** — **of** sentir, avoir conscience de, s'apercevoir de; **to become** — reprendre connaissance.

consciously ['kɔnʃəsli] *ad* consciemment.

consciousness ['kɔnʃəsnis] *n* conscience *f*, connaissance *f*, sens *m*.

conscript ['kɔnskript] *an* conscrit *m*.

conscript [kən'skript] *vt* engager, enrôler.

conscription [kən'skripʃən] *n* conscription *f*.

consecrate ['kɔnsikreit] *vt* consacrer, bénir.

consecration [ˌkɔnsi'kreiʃən] *n* consécration *f*.

consecutive [kən'sekjutiv] *a* consécutif, de suite.

consensus [kən'sensəs] *n* accord *m*, unanimité *f*, consensus *m*.

consent [kən'sent] *n* consentement *m*, assentiment *m*, agrément *m*; *vi* consentir.

consequence ['kɔnsikwəns] *n* conséquence *f*, importance *f*.

consequent ['kɔnsikwənt] *a* résultant.

consequential [ˌkɔnsi'kwenʃəl] *a* conséquent, consécutif, important, plein de soi.

consequently ['kɔnsikwəntli] *ad* conséquemment, en conséquence.

conservation [ˌkɔnsə'veiʃən] *n* conservation *f*.

conservative [kən'səːvətiv] *an* conservateur, -trice.

conservatory [kən'səːvətri] *n* serre *f*, jardin *m* d'hiver.

conserve [kən'səːv] *vt* conserver, préserver.

conserves [kən'səːvz] *n pl* confitures *f pl*, conserves *f pl*.

consider [kən'sidə] *vt* considérer, réfléchir à, regarder, estimer, examiner, envisager, avoir égard à.

considerable [kən'sidərəbl] *a* considérable.

considerate [kən'sidərit] *a* attentif, prévenant.

considerately [kən'sidəritli] *ad* avec égards, avec prévenance.

consideration [kənˌsidə'reiʃən] *n* considération *f*, réflexion *f*, récompense *f*, importance *f*; **in — of** eu égard à; **under — ** à l'étude, en délibération; **after due —** tout bien considéré, après mûre réflection; **for a —** moyennant finance; **on no —** pour rien au monde, à aucun prix.

considering [kən'sidəriŋ] *ad* somme toute; *prep* étant donné, vu, eu égard à; *cj* vu que, attendu que.

consign [kən'sain] *vt* livrer, expédier, déposer, consigner.

consignment [kən'sainmənt] *n* expédition *f*, envoi *m*, dépôt *m*; — **note** récépissé *m*, lettre de voiture *f*.

consist [kən'sist] *vi* consister (en, à of), se composer (de of).

consistence [kən'sistəns] *n* consistance *f*.

consistency [kən'sistənsi] *n* suite *f*,

logique *f*, uniformité *f*, régularité *f*.

consistent [kən'sistənt] *a* compatible, fidèle (à with), conséquent, logique, régulier.

consolation [ˌkɔnsə'leiʃən] *n* consolation *f*.

console [kən'soul] *vt* consoler.

console ['kɔnsoul] *n* console *f*.

consolidate [kən'sɔlideit] *vt* consolider, raffermir, unifier.

consolidation [kənˌsɔli'deiʃən] *n* consolidation *f*, raffermissement *m*.

consols [kən'sɔlz] *n pl* fonds consolidés *m pl*.

consonance ['kɔnsənəns] *n* consonance *f*, accord *m*.

consonant ['kɔnsənənt] *n* consonne *f*; *a* compatible, harmonieux, qui s'accorde.

consort ['kɔnsɔːt] *n* consort(e) *mf*, époux, -se *mf*.

consort [kən'sɔːt] *vi* **to — with** fréquenter, frayer avec.

conspicuous [kən'spikjuəs] *a* marquant, insigne, remarquable, en vue, en évidence; **to make oneself —** se faire remarquer, se signaler.

conspiracy [kən'spirəsi] *n* conspiration *f*, conjuration *f*.

conspirator [kən'spirətə] *n* conspirateur, -trice, conjuré *m*.

conspire [kən'spaiə] *vi* conspirer, comploter, agir de concert, concourir.

constable ['kʌnstəbl] *n* agent *m* de police, gendarme *m*; **chief —** commissaire *m* de police.

constabulary [kən'stæbjuləri] *n* police *f*, gendarmerie *f*.

constancy ['kɔnstənsi] *n* constance *f*, régularité *f*, fidelité *f*, fermeté *f*.

constant ['kɔnstənt] *a* constant, continuel, fidèle, invariable.

constantly ['kɔnstəntli] *ad* constamment, toujours.

constellation [ˌkɔnstə'leiʃən] *n* constellation *f*.

consternation [ˌkɔnstə'neiʃən] *n* consternation *f*.

constipate ['kɔnstipeit] *vt* constiper.

constipation [ˌkɔnsti'peiʃən] *n* constipation *f*.

constituency [kən'stitjuənsi] *n* circonscription *f*, collège électoral *m*.

constituent [kən'stitjuənt] *n* électeur, -trice, élément *m*; *a* constituant, constitutif.

constitute ['kɔnstitjuːt] *vt* constituer.

constitution [ˌkɔnsti'tjuːʃən] *n* constitution *f*, composition *f*, santé *f*.

constitutional [ˌkɔnsti'tjuːʃənl] *a* constitutionnel.

constrain [kən'strein] *vt* contraindre, forcer.

constraint [kən'streint] *n* contrainte *f*, retenue *f*.

constrict [kən'strikt] *vt* rétrécir, (res)serrer, étrangler.

constriction [kən'strikʃən] *n* étranglement *m*, resserrement *m*.

construct [kən'strʌkt] vt construire, établir, charpenter.

construction [kən'strʌkʃən] n construction f, établissement m, édifice m, interprétation f.

construe [kən'struː] vt traduire, interpréter, expliquer, analyser.

consul ['kɔnsəl] n consul m.

consular ['kɔnsjulə] a consulaire.

consulate ['kɔnsjulit] n consulat m.

consult [kən'sʌlt] vti consulter.

consultation [,kɔnsəl'teiʃən] n consultation f, délibération f.

consume [kən'sjum] vt consumer, consommer, épuiser, perdre.

consumer [kən'sjumə] n consommateur, -trice.

consummate [kən'sʌmit] a consommé, achevé.

consummate ['kɔnsʌmeit] vt consommer.

consummation [,kɔnsʌ'meiʃən] n consommation f, comble m.

consumption [kən'sʌmpʃən] n consomption f, phtisie f, consommation f.

consumptive [kən'sʌmptiv] a phtisique, tuberculeux.

contact ['kɔntækt] n contact m, rapport m; vt se mettre en rapport avec, contacter.

contagion [kən'teidʒən] n contagion f.

contagious [kən'teidʒəs] a contagieux, communicatif.

contain [kən'tein] vt contenir, comporter, renfermer, retenir.

container [kən'teinə] n récipient m.

contaminate [kən'tæmineit] vt contaminer, vicier, corrompre.

contamination [kən,tæmi'neiʃən] n contamination f.

contemplate ['kɔntempleit] vt contempler, considérer, envisager; vi méditer, se recueillir.

contemplation [,kɔntem'pleiʃən] n contemplation f, recueillement m.

contemplative ['kɔntempleitiv] a contemplatif, recueilli.

contemporary [kən'tempərəri] an contemporain(e) mf.

contempt [kən'tempt] n mépris m.

contemptible [kən'temptəbl] a méprisable.

contemptuous [kən'temptjuəs] a méprisant, de mépris.

contend [kən'tend] vi lutter, disputer, rivaliser; vt soutenir, prétendre.

content [kən'tent] n contentement m, contenance f; a content; vt contenter.

contentedly [kən'tentidli] ad avec plaisir.

contention [kən'tenʃən] n discussion f, rivalité f, idée f, prétention f.

contentious [kən'tenʃəs] a disputeur, chicanier, discutable.

contentment [kən'tentmənt] n contentement m.

contents ['kɔntents] n pl contenu m, table des matières f.

contest ['kɔntest] n lutte f, concours m.

contest [kən'test] vt contester, disputer, débattre.

contestation [,kɔntes'teiʃən] n contestation f.

context ['kɔntekst] n contexte m.

contiguous [kən'tigjuəs] a contigu, -uë.

continence ['kɔntinəns] n continence f.

continent ['kɔntinənt] an continent m.

continental [,kɔnti'nentl] a continental.

contingent [kən'tindʒənt] n contingent m; a éventuel, subordonné.

continual [kən'tinjuəl] a continuel, sans cesse.

continuation [kən,tinju'eiʃən] n continuation f, durée f, suite f.

continue [kən'tinju] vti continuer; vt maintenir, poursuivre, prolonger; vi se prolonger.

continuity [,kɔnti'njuiti] n continuité f.

continuous [kən'tinjuəs] a continu, permanent.

continuously [kən'tinjuəsli] ad continûment, sans arrêt, sans désemparer.

contort [kən'tɔːt] vt tordre, crisper.

contortion [kən'tɔːʃən] n contorsion f, crispation f.

contour ['kɔntuə] n contour m, profil m, tracé m.

contraband ['kɔntrəbænd] n contrebande f.

contraceptive [,kɔntrə'septiv] n préservatif m; a anticonceptionnel.

contract ['kɔntrækt] n contrat m, entreprise f.

contract [kən'trækt] vt contracter, resserrer, crisper; vi s'engager, se rétrécir, se crisper, se contracter.

contraction [kən'trækʃən] n contraction f, rétrécissement m, crispement m.

contractor [kən'træktə] n entrepreneur m, (mil) fournisseur m.

contradict [,kɔntrə'dikt] vt démentir, contredire.

contradiction [,kɔntrə'dikʃən] n contradiction f, démenti m.

contradictory [,kɔntrə'diktəri] a contradictoire.

contraption [kən'træpʃən] n machin m, truc m, dispositif m.

contrary ['kɔntrəri] a contraire, opposé; **on the** — au contraire.

contrast ['kɔntrɑːst] n contraste m.

contrast [kən'rɑːst] vi contraster; vt mettre en contraste, opposer.

contravene [,kɔntrə'viːn] vt enfreindre, contrevenir à, s'opposer à.

contravention [,kɔntrə'venʃən] n violation f, contravention f.

contribute [kən'tribjut] vti contribuer (à **to**), souscrire; **to — to a newspaper** collaborer à un journal.

contribution [ˌkɔntri'bjuːʃən] n contribution f.

contrite [ˈkɔntrait] a contrit.

contrivance [kən'traivəns] n invention f, manigance f, ingéniosité f, dispositif m.

contrive [kən'traiv] vt inventer, combiner; vi s'arranger (pour **to**), trouver moyen (de **to**).

control [kən'troul] n contrôle m, maîtrise f, autorité f; vt contrôler, maîtriser, diriger.

controller [kən'troulə] n contrôleur, -euse, commande f.

controversial [ˌkɔntrə'vəːʃəl] a controversable, (person) disputeur.

controversy [ˈkɔntrəvəːsi] n controverse f.

contumacious [ˌkɔntju'meiʃəs] a rebelle, contumace.

contuse [kən'tjuːz] vt contusionner.

contusion [kən'tjuːʒən] n contusion f.

conundrum [kə'nʌndrəm] n énigme f, problème m, devinette f.

convalesce [ˌkɔnvə'les] vi être en convalescence, relever de maladie.

convalescence [ˌkɔnvə'lesns] n convalescence f.

convalescent [ˌkɔnvə'lesnt] a convalescent.

convector [kən'vektə] n appareil m de chauffage par convection.

convene [kən'viːn] vt convoquer; vi se réunir.

convenience [kən'viːnjəns] n convenance f, commodité f, avantage m; pl commodités f pl, agréments m pl.

convenient [kən'viːnjənt] a commode.

conveniently [kən'viːnjəntli] ad commodément, sans inconvénient.

convent [ˈkɔnvənt] n couvent m.

convention [kən'venʃən] n convention f, convocation f, usage m; pl bienséances f pl.

conventional [kən'venʃənl] a conventionnel, normal, ordinaire, classique, stylisé.

conventionality [kənˌvenʃə'næliti] n formalisme m, bienséances f pl.

converge [kən'vəːdʒ] vi converger.

convergence [kən'vəːdʒəns] n convergence f.

conversant [kən'vəːsənt] a familiar, versé au courant (de **with**).

conversation [ˌkɔnvə'seiʃən] n conversation f, entretien m.

converse [ˈkɔnvəːs] an réciproque f, converse f.

converse [kən'vəːs] vi causer, s'entretenir.

conversely [ˈkɔnvəːsli] ad réciproquement.

conversion [kən'vəːʃən] n conversion f.

convert [ˈkɔnvəːt] n converti(e) mf.

convert [kən'vəːt] vt convertir, transformer.

convex [ˈkɔn'veks] a convexe, bombé.

convey [kən'vei] vt (trans)porter, transmettre, communiquer.

conveyance [kən'veiəns] n transport m, voiture f, transmission f.

convict [ˈkɔnvikt] n forçat m.

convict [kən'vikt] vt convaincre, condamner.

conviction [kən'vikʃən] n conviction f, condamnation f.

convince [kən'vins] vt convaincre, persuader.

convivial [kən'viviəl] a plein d'entrain, jovial, de fête.

convocation [ˌkɔnvə'keiʃən] n convocation f, assemblée f.

convoke [kən'vouk] vt convoquer.

convoy [ˈkɔnvɔi] n convoi m, escorte f.

convoy [ˈkɔnvɔi] vt convoyer, escorter.

convulse [kən'vʌls] vt bouleverser, décomposer, tordre, convulser.

convulsion [kən'vʌlʃən] n convulsion f, bouleversement m.

convulsive [kən'vʌlsiv] a convulsif.

coo [kuː] vi roucouler.

cook [kuk] n cuisinier, -ière; vti cuire, cuisiner; vt faire cuire; maquiller, truquer.

cooker [ˈkukə] n réchaud m, cuisinière f.

cookery [ˈkukəri] n cuisine f.

cool [kuːl] n frais m, fraîcheur f; a frais, rafraîchissant, impudent, imperturbable; vt rafraîchir, refroidir; vi se rafraîchir, se refroidir.

cooler [ˈkuːlə] n seau m à glace, refroidisseur m, (US) taule f.

coolly [ˈkuːli] ad froidement, avec sang-froid.

coolness [ˈkuːlnis] n fraîcheur f, sang-froid m.

coop [kuːp] n mue f; vt enfermer, claustrer.

co-operate [kou'ɔpəreit] vi coopérer, collaborer.

co-operation [kouˌɔpə'reiʃən] n. collaboration f, coopération f, concours m.

co-operative stores [kou'ɔpərətiv ˌstɔːz] n coopérative f.

co-opt [kou'ɔpt] vt coopter.

co-ordinate [kou'ɔːdineit] vt coordonner.

co-ordination [kouˌɔːdi'neiʃən] n coordination f.

cop [kɔp] n fuseau m, flic m; vt pincer, attraper, écoper.

cope [koup] **to — with** faire face à, tenir tête à, venir à bout de

copious [ˈkoupjəs] a copieux, abondant.

copiousness [ˈkoupjəsnis] n abondance f.

copper [ˈkɔpə] n cuivre m, billon m, sou m, lessiveuse f, sergot m.

copse [kɔps] n taillis m.

copy ['kɔpi] *n* copie *f*, exemplaire *m*, numéro *m*; *vt* copier, imiter, se modeler sur.

copyist ['kɔpiist] *n* copiste *mf*.

copyright ['kɔpirait] *n* propriété littéraire *f*, droit d'auteur *m*.

coral ['kɔrəl] *n* corail *m*.

cord [kɔːd] *n* cordelette *f*, cordon *m*, (*vocal*) cordes *f pl*, étoffe *f* à côtes, ganse *f*; *vt* corder.

corded ['kɔːdid] *a* côtelé, à côtes.

cordial ['kɔːdjəl] *an* cordial *m*; *a* chaleureux.

cordiality [.kɔːdi'æliti] *n* cordialité *f*.

cordon ['kɔːdn] *n* cordon *m*; to — off *vt* isoler, entourer d'un cordon.

corduroy ['kɔːdərɔi] *n* velours côtelé *m*.

core [kɔː] *n* cœur *m*, trognon *m*.

co-respondent ['kouris.pɔndənt] *n* complice *mf* (d'adultère).

cork [kɔːk] *n* liège *m*, bouchon *m*; *vt* boucher.

corked [kɔːkt] *a* qui sent le bouchon.

corkscrew ['kɔːkskruː] *n* tire-bouchon *m*.

corn [kɔːn] *n* grain *m*, blé *m*, (US) maïs *m*; (*foot*) cor *m*.

cornea ['kɔːniə] *n* cornée *f*.

corned [kɔːnd] *a* salé, de conserve.

corner ['kɔːnə] *n* coin *m*, angle *m*, tournant *m*, virage *m*, accaparement *m*; *vt* acculer, mettre au pied du mur, accaparer; *vi* virer.

corner-stone ['kɔːnəstoun] *n* pierre angulaire *f*.

cornet ['kɔːnit] *n* cornet *m* (à piston).

corn exchange ['kɔːniks'tʃeindʒ] *n* halle *f* aux blés.

cornflour ['kɔːnflauə] *n* farine *f* de riz, *etc*.

cornflower ['kɔːnflauə] *n* bluet *m*.

cornice ['kɔːnis] *n* corniche *f*.

coronation [.kɔrə'neiʃən] *n* couronnement *m*, sacre *m*.

corporal ['kɔːpərəl] *n* caporal *m*, brigadier *m*; *a* corporel.

corporate ['kɔːpərit] *a* constitué; — spirit esprit de corps *m*, solidarité *f*.

corporation [.kɔːpə'reiʃən] *n* corporation *f*, conseil municipal *m*, bedaine *f*.

corpse [kɔːps] *n* cadavre *m*.

corpuscle ['kɔːpʌsl] *n* corpuscle *m*.

Corpus Christi ['kɔːpəs'kristi] *n* Fête-Dieu *f*.

correct [kə'rekt] *a* correct, juste, exact; *vt* corriger, reprendre, rectifier.

correction [kə'rekʃən] *n* correction *f*, redressement *m*.

corrector [kə'rektə] *n* correcteur, -trice.

correspond [.kɔris'pɔnd] *vi* correspondre (à **with**, to).

correspondence [.kɔris'pɔndəns] *n* correspondance *f*.

correspondent [.kɔris'pɔndənt] *n* correspondant(e) *mf*, envoyé *m*.

corridor ['kɔridɔː] *n* couloir *m*, corridor *m*.

corroborate [kə'rɔbəreit] *vt* corroborer, confirmer.

corroboration [kə.rɔbə'reiʃən] *n* corroboration *f*.

corrode [kə'roud] *vt* corroder, ronger; *vi* se corroder.

corrosion [kə'rouʒən] *n* corrosion *f*.

corrosive [kə'rousiv] *an* corrosif *m*.

corrugated ['kɔrugeitid] *a* ondulé, cannelé, gaufré.

corrupt [kə'rʌpt] *vt* corrompre, altérer; *a* corrompu.

corruption [kə'rʌpʃən] *n* corruption *f*, subornation *f*.

corsair ['kɔːsɛə] *n* corsaire *m*.

corset ['kɔːsit] *n* corset *m*.

Corsica ['kɔːsikə] *n* la Corse *f*.

Corsican ['kɔːsikən] *a nm* corse; *n* Corse *mf*.

cosmic ['kɔzmik] *a* cosmique.

cosmonaut ['kɔzmənɔːt] *n* cosmonaute *mf*.

cosmopolitan [.kɔsmə'pɔlitən] *an* cosmopolite *mf*.

cosmopolitanism [.kɔzmə'pɔlitənizəm] *n* cosmopolitisme *m*.

cost [kɔst] *n* prix *m*, coût *m*, dépens *m pl*, frais *m pl*; *vi* coûter; *vt* établir le prix de.

costermonger ['kɔstə.mʌŋgə] *n* marchand *m* des quatre saisons.

costly ['kɔstli] *a* coûteux, dispendieux, précieux, somptueux.

cosy ['kouzi] *n* couvre-théière *m*; *a* tiède, douillet, bon.

cot [kɔt] *n* abri *m*, berceau *m*, couchette *f*, hutte *f*.

cottage ['kɔtidʒ] *n* chaumière *f*.

cotton ['kɔtn] *n* coton *m*, fil *m*; — **plant** cotonnier *m*; — **plantation** cotonneraie *f*.

cotton-wool ['kɔtn'wul] *n* ouate *f*, coton hydrophile *m*.

couch [kautʃ] *n* lit *m*, divan *m*; *vt* coucher; *vi* se tapir, s'embusquer.

cough [kɔf] *n* toux *f*; *vi* tousser.

could [kud] *pt of* **can.**

council ['kaunsl] *n* concile *m*, conseil *m*.

councillor ['kaunsilə] *n* conseiller *m* (municipal).

counsel ['kaunsəl] *n* conseil *m*, délibération *f*, avocat *m*; *vt* conseiller, recommander.

counsellor ['kaunsələ] *n* conseiller *m*.

count [kaunt] *n* compte *m*, calcul *m*, comte *m*; *vti* compter.

countdown ['kauntdaun] *n* compte à rebours *m*.

countenance ['kauntinəns] *n* expression *f*, visage *m*, sérieux *m*, contenance *f*, appui *m*; *vt* sanctionner, appuyer, approuver.

counter ['kauntə] *n* comptoir *m*, jeton *m*, contre *m*; *a* opposé; *vt* contrarier, contredire, aller à l'encontre de; *vi* riposter; *ad* en sens contraire.

counteract [ˌkauntə'rækt] vt neutraliser.

counterbalance [ˌkauntə'bæləns] n contre-poids m; vt contrebalancer, faire contrepoids à, compenser.

countercharge ['kauntətʃaːdʒ] n contre-accusation f.

counterfeit ['kauntəfit] n contrefaçon f; — **coin** pièce fausse f; vt feindre, contrefaire, forger.

counterfoil ['kauntəfɔil] n talon m, souche f.

countermand [ˌkauntə'maːnd] vt contremander, rappeler, décommander.

counterpane ['kauntəpein] n couvre-pied m, courtepointe f.

counterpart ['kauntəpaːt] n contrepartie f, pendant m.

countersign ['kauntəsain] n mot m de passe, mot m d'ordre; vt viser, contresigner.

countess ['kauntis] n comtesse f.

countless ['kauntlis] a innombrable.

country ['kʌntri] n contrée f, pays m, campagne f, province f, patrie f.

country-house ['kʌntri'haus] n maison de campagne f.

countryman ['kʌntrimən] n campagnard m, compatriote m.

countryside ['kʌntrisaid] n campagne f, pays m.

county ['kaunti] n comté m.

couple ['kʌpl] n couple mf, laisse f; vt (ac)coupler, unir, associer.

coupon ['kuːpɔn] n coupon m, ticket m, estampille officielle f, bon(-prime) m.

courage ['kʌridʒ] n courage m.

courageous [kə'reidʒəs] a courageux.

courier ['kuriə] n courrier m.

course [kɔːs] n course f, cours m, champ de courses m, carrière f, série f, marche f, direction f, route f, plat m, service m; of — naturellement; **matter of** — chose qui va de soi, positif, prosaïque.

court [kɔːt] n cour f, terrain de jeux m, court m (tennis); vt courtiser, inviter, chercher, solliciter, aller au-devant de.

courteous ['kəːtiəs] a courtois.

courtesy ['kəːtiːi] n courtoisie f, politesses f pl.

courtesan [ˌkɔːti'zæn] n courtisane f.

courtier ['kɔːtjə] n courtisan m.

courtliness ['kɔːtlinis] n élégance f, raffinement m.

courtly ['kɔːtli] a élégant, courtois.

courtship ['kɔːtʃip] n cour f.

courtyard ['kɔːtjaːd] n cour f.

cousin ['kʌzn] n cousin(e) mf; **first** — cousin germain; **second** — issu de germain; **third** — au 3ᵉ degré etc.

cove [kouv] n (sea) anse f, crique f, type m.

covenant ['kʌvinənt] n pacte m, alliance f, contrat m.

cover ['kʌvə] n couverture f, housse f, bâche f, dessus m, couvercle m,

abri m; couvert m, voile m, masque m; (US) contre-rendu m; vt (re)couvrir, revêtir, embrasser; (US) faire un compte-rendu.

covering ['kʌvəriŋ] a de couverture, confirmatif.

coverlet ['kʌvəlit] n couvre-pied m, dessus m de lit, couvre-lit m.

covert ['kʌvət] a couvert, furtif, voile, indirect.

covet ['kʌvit] vt convoiter.

covetous ['kʌvitəs] a convoiteux, avide.

covetousness ['kʌvitəsnis] n convoitise f, cupidité f.

covey ['kʌvi] n couvée f, compagnie f, vol m, troupe f.

cow [kau] n vache f femelle f; vt intimider.

coward ['kauəd] an lâche mf.

cowardice ['kauədis] n lâcheté f.

cowardly ['kauədli] a lâche, poltron; ad lâchement.

cower ['kauə] vi s'accroupir, se blottir, se faire petit.

cowl [kaul] n capuchon m, capot m, mitre f, champignon m.

cowrie-shell ['kauriʃel] n cauri m.

coxcomb ['kɔkskoum] n poseur m, fat m, petit-maître m.

coxswain ['kɔksn] n homme de barre m, maître m d'équipage.

coy [kɔi] a timide, réservé, écarté.

coyness ['kɔinis] n timidité f, réserve f.

crab [kræb] n crabe m, (apple) pomme sauvage f, (tool) chèvre f.

crabbed ['kræbd] a revêche, raboteux, grincheux, aigre.

crack [kræk] n craquement m, coup sec m, fêlure f, lézarde f, fente f; a (fam) d'élite; —**brained** fêlé, timbré, toqué; vi craquer, claquer, se casser, se gercer, se fêler, muer; vt faire craquer (claquer), casser, fêler, (joke) faire.

cracker ['krækə] n pétard m, casse-noix m, diablotin m.

crackle ['krækl] n craquement m, crépitement m, friture f, craquelure f; vi crépiter, craqueter, grésiller, pétiller.

cracksman ['kræksmən] n (sl) cambrioleur m.

cradle ['kreidl] n berceau m; —**song** berceuse f; vt coucher, bercer.

craft [kraːft] n habileté f, ruse f, art m, métier m, vaisseau m, avion m.

craftsman ['kraːftsmən] n ouvrier qualifié m, artisan m.

crafty ['kraːfti] a rusé, cauteleux, fin.

crag [kræg] n rocher m.

craggy ['krægi] a rocheux, rocailleux.

cram [kræm] vt remplir, gaver, fourrer, enfoncer, bourrer, chauffer; vi se gaver, s'empiffrer, s'entasser.

cramming ['kræmiŋ] n gavage m, bourrage m, chauffage m.

cramp [kræmp] n crampe f, crampon m; vt donner des crampes à, engourdir.

cramped [kræmpt] a crispé, gêné, à l'étroit.

crane [krein] n grue f; vt tendre, soulever.

crank [kræŋk] n manivelle f, coude m, meule f, original(e) mf, toque(e) mf.

crape [kreip] n crêpe m.

crash [kræʃ] n fracas m, crac m, krach m, accident m; vt briser, fracasser, écraser; vi dégringoler, s'abattre, s'écraser, casser du bois; to — into heurter, tamponner, accrocher.

crass [kræs] a grossier, crasse.

crate [kreit] n manne f, cageot m.

crater ['kreitə] n cratère m, entonnoir m.

crave [kreiv] vt solliciter; to — for désirer violemment, avoir soif de.

craven ['kreivən] an lâche mf.

craving ['kreiviŋ] n besoin m, faim f, soif f.

crawl [krɔːl] vi se traîner, ramper, grouiller; n rampement m, (swimming) crawl m.

crawler ['krɔːlə] n (cab) maraudeur m, reptile m.

crayfish ['kreifiʃ] n langouste f, écrevisse f.

crayon ['kreiən] n fusain m, pastel m.

craze [kreiz] n folie f, manie f, toquade f.

crazy ['kreizi] a branlant, toqué, affolé, insensé.

creak [kriːk] n grincement m; vi grincer, craquer, crier.

cream [kriːm] n crème f; vi crêmer, mousser; vt écrémer.

creamery ['kriːməri] n crémerie f.

creamy ['kriːmi] a crêmeux.

crease [kriːs] n pli m; vt plisser, froisser; vi se plisser, prendre un faux pli, se froisser.

create [kriː'eit] vt créer.

creation [kriː'eiʃən] n création f.

creator [kriː'eitə] n créateur, -trice.

creature ['kriːtʃə] n créature f, être m, homme m.

credentials [kri'denʃəlz] n lettres de créance f, certificat m.

credibility [ˌkredi'biliti] n crédibilité f.

credible ['kredibl] a croyable, digne de foi.

credibly ['kredibli] ad vraisemblablement.

credit ['kredit] n foi f, mérite m, honneur m, crédit m; tax — s déductions fiscales; vt croire, ajouter foi à, créditer, accorder, reconnaître.

creditable ['kreditəbl] a honorable, qui fait honneur (à to).

creditor ['kreditə] n créancier, -ière.

credulity [kri'djuːliti] n crédulité f.

credulous ['kredjuləs] a crédule.

creed [kriːd] n crédo m, foi f.

creek [kriːk] n crique f, anse f.

creep [kriːp] vi ramper, se glisser, grimper.

creeper ['kriːpə] n plante rampante f, grimpante.

creeps [kriːps] n chair f de poule.

cremate [kri'meit] vt brûler, incinérer.

cremation [kri'meiʃən] n incinération f.

crematorium [ˌkremə'tɔːriəm] n four crématoire m.

crept [krept] pt pp of **creep**.

crescent ['kresnt] n croissant m.

cress [kres] n cresson m.

crest [krest] n crête f, huppe f, plumet m, cimier m, armoiries f pl.

crestfallen ['krest.fɔːlən] a penaud, découragé.

crevice ['krevis] n crevasse f, fente f, fissure f.

crew [kruː] n équipage m, équipe f, bande f.

crib [krib] n mangeoire f, crèche f, lit d'enfant m, poste m; to — from plagier, copier sur.

crick [krik] n torticolis m.

cricket ['krikit] n cricket m, grillon m.

crier ['kraiə] n crieur m.

crime [kraim] n crime m, délit m.

criminal ['kriminl] an criminel, -elle.

criminality [ˌkrimi'næliti] n criminalité f.

crimp [krimp] vt plisser, onduler, friser, racoler.

crimson ['krimzn] an cramoisi m, pourpre m.

cringe [krindʒ] n courbette obséquieuse f; vi s'aplatir, se tapir, faire le chien couchant.

crinkle ['kriŋkl] n pli m, ride f; vt chiffonner, froisser; vi se froisser.

cripple ['kripl] n ⸱estropié(e) mf, infirme mf; vt estropier, paralyser.

crisis ['kraisis] n crise f.

crisp [krisp] a cassant, croquant, vif, brusque, bouclé; vti boucler; vt crêper.

criss-cross ['kriskrɔs] n entrecroisement m; a entrecroisé, revêche; vt entrecroiser; vi ⸱'entrecroiser.

criterion [krai'tiəriən] n critérium m, critère m.

critic ['kritik] n critique m.

critical ['kritikəl] a critique.

criticism ['kritisizəm] n critique f.

criticize ['kritisaiz] vt critiquer, censurer.

croak [krouk] n c(r)oassement m; vi c(r)oasser.

crochet ['krouʃei] n crochet m.

crockery ['krɔkəri] n faïence f, vaisselle f.

crocodile ['krɔkədail] n crocodile m, caïman m.

crocus ['kroukəs] n crocus m, safran m.

croft [krɔft] n clos m.

crook [kruk] n houlette f, crosse f,

croc *m*, crochet *m*, courbe *f*, escroc *m*; *vt* (re)courber.

crooked ['krukid] *a* courbé, tordu, tortueux, malhonnête.

croon [kru:n] *n* bourdonnement *m*, fredonnement *m*, plainte *f*; *vti* bourdonner, fredonner.

crop [krɔp] *n* récolte *f*, jabot *m*, manche *f* de fouet, cravache *f*, coupe *f* de cheveux (à ras); *vt* récolter, brouter, écourter, tondre, couper ras, planter; **to — up** *vi* affleurer, surgir, se présenter.

cross [krɔs] *n* croix *f*, barre *f*, croisement *m*; *a* croisé, fâché; *vt* croiser, traverser, barrer; *vi* se croiser; **to — out** *vt* biffer; **to — oneself** se signer.

crossbar ['krɔsbɑː] *n* traverse *f*.

cross-belt ['krɔsbelt] *n* cartouchière *f*, bandoulière *f*.

crossbreed ['krɔsbriːd] *n* hybride *m*, métis, -isse.

cross-examination ['krɔsig͵zæmi'-neiʃən] *n* contre-interrogatoire *m*.

cross-eyed ['krɔsaid] *a* louche.

cross-grained ['krɔsgreind] *a* à contre-fil, revêche, grincheux.

crossing ['krɔsiŋ] *n* croisement *m*, traversée *f*.

cross-legged ['krɔs'legd] *a* les jambes croisées.

crossroads ['krɔsroudz] *n* carrefour *m*.

cross-section ['krɔs'sekʃən] *n* coupe *f*, tranche *f*, catégorie *f*.

crossword ['krɔswəːd] *n* mots croisés *m pl*.

crotchet ['krɔtʃit] *n* noire *f*, caprice *m*.

crotchety ['krɔtʃiti] *a* fantasque, difficile.

crouch [krautʃ] *vi* s'accroupir, se blottir, se ramasser.

croup [kru:p] *n* croupe *f*, croup *m*.

crow [krou] *n* corneille *f*, corbeau *m*, cri du coq *m*; **as the — flies** à vol d'oiseau; *vi* chanter, crier de joie, chanter victoire, crâner.

crowbar ['kroubɑː] *n* levier *m*, pince *f*.

crowd [kraud] *n* foule *f*, affluence *f*, bande *f*, monde *m*; *vt* remplir, tasser, serrer; *vi* se presser, s'entasser, s'empiler, affluer, s'attrouper.

crowded ['kraudid] *a* comble, bondé, encombré.

crown [kraun] *n* couronne *f*; *vt* couronner.

crucial ['kru:ʃəl] *a* essentiel, décisif, critique.

crucible ['kru:sibl] *n* creuset *m*.

crucifix ['kru:sifiks] *n* crucifix *m*.

crucifixion [͵kru:si'fikʃən] *n* crucifiement *m*.

crucify ['kru:sifai] *vt* crucifier.

crude [kru:d] *a* cru, mal digéré, vert, rude, sommaire, brutal, frustre.

crudely ['kru:dli] *ad* crûment, rudement, grossièrement.

crudity ['kru:diti] *n* crudité *f*, grossièreté *f*.

cruel ['kruəl] *a* cruel.

cruelty ['kruəlti] *n* cruauté *f*.

cruet ['kru:it] *n* burette *f*.

cruet-stand ['kru:itstænd] *n* huilier *m*.

cruise [kru:z] *n* croisière *f*; *vi* croiser, marauder.

cruiser ['kru:zə] *n* croiseur *m*.

crumb [krʌm] *n* mie *f*, miette *f*.

crumble ['krʌmbl] *vt* briser en morceaux, émietter, effriter; *vi* s'écrouler, s'émietter, s'effriter.

crumple ['krʌmpl] *vt* froisser, chiffonner; *vi* se froisser, se friper, se télescoper.

crunch [krʌntʃ] *vt* croquer, écraser; *vi* craquer, grincer, crier.

crusade [kru:'seid] *n* croisade *f*, campagne *f*.

crush [krʌʃ] *n* écrasement *m*, cohue *f*, béguin *m*; *vt* écraser, froisser, terrasser, broyer.

crust [krʌst] *n* croûte *f*, croûton *m*, dépôt *m*.

crutch [krʌtʃ] *n* béquille *f*.

crux [krʌks] *n* nœud *m*.

cry [krai] *n* cri *m*, crise *f* de larmes; *vi* crier, pleurer; **to — down** décrier; **to — off** renoncer, se faire excuser; **to — out** s'écrier; **to — up** louer.

crypt [kript] *n* crypte *f*.

crystal ['kristl] *n* cristal *m*, boule de cristal *f*; *a* cristallin, limpide.

cub [kʌb] *n* petit *m*, ourson *m*, ours mal léché, louveteau *m*.

Cuba ['kju:bə] *n* Cuba *m*.

Cuban ['kju:bən] *an* cubain.

cube [kju:b] *n* cube *m*.

cubic ['kju:bik] *a* cubique.

cuckoo ['kuku] *n* coucou *m*.

cucumber ['kju:kʌmbə] *n* concombre *m*.

cud [kʌd] **to chew the — ** ruminer.

cuddle ['kʌdl] *vt* mignoter, peloter; **to — into** se pelotonner contre.

cudgel ['kʌdʒəl] *n* gourdin *m*; *vt* rosser.

cue [kju:] *n* queue *f*, invite *f*, indication *f*, mot *m*.

cuff [kʌf] *n* taloche *f*, claque *f*, manchette *f*; *vt* gifler, calotter.

cull [kʌl] *vt* (re)cueillir.

culling ['kʌliŋ] *n* cueillette *f*; *pl* glanures *f pl*.

culminant ['kʌlminənt] *a* culminant.

culminate ['kʌlmineit] *vi* s'achever (en in), se couronner (par in).

culmination [͵kʌlmi'neiʃən] *n* point culminant *m*.

culpability [͵kʌlpə'biliti] *n* culpabilité *f*.

cult [kʌlt] *n* culte *m*.

cultivate ['kʌltiveit] *vt* cultiver.

cultivation [͵kʌlti'veiʃən] *n* cultivation *f*.

cultivator ['kʌltiveitə] *n* cultivateur, motoculteur *m*.

culture ['kʌltʃə] *n* culture *f*.

culvert ['kʌlvət] n canal m, canalisation f, tranchée f, cassis m.

cumbersome ['kʌmbəsəm] a encombrant, gênant.

cumbrous ['kʌmbrəs] a encombrant, gênant.

cumulate ['kju:mjuleit] vt (ac)cumuler.

cumulation [‚kju:mju'leiʃən] n accumulation f, cumul m.

cumulative ['kju:mjulətiv] a cumulatif.

cunning ['kʌniŋ] n finesse f, ruse f, habileté f, rouerie f; a entendu, retors, rusé, cauteleux.

cup [kʌp] n tasse f, coupe f, calice m.

cupboard ['kʌbəd] n buffet m, armoire f, placard m.

cupidity [kju:'piditi] n cupidité f.

cur [kə:] n roquet m, cuistre m.

curable ['kjuərəbl] a guérissable.

curate ['kjuərit] n vicaire m, abbé m.

curator [kjuə'reitə] n curateur m, conservateur m.

curb [kə:b] n gourmette f, margelle f, bordure f, frein m; vt refréner, brider.

curd [kə:d] n lait caillé m.

curdle ['kə:dl] vi se cailler, se figer, tourner.

cure [kjuə] n guérison f, remède m, cure f, soin m; vt guérir, saler, fumer, mariner.

curfew ['kə:fju:] n couvre-feu m.

curio ['kjuəriou] n pièce rare f, bibelot m, curiosité f.

curiosity [‚kjuəri'ɔsiti] n curiosité f.

curious ['kjuəriəs] a curieux, singulier, indiscret.

curl [kə:l] n boucle f, (lips) ourlet m; vt (en)rouler, friser; vi déferler, monter en spirale, friser.

curlew ['kə:lu:] n courlis m.

curling-tongs ['kə:liŋtɔŋz] n fer m à friser.

curl-paper ['kə:lpeipə] n papillotte f.

curly ['kə:li] a bouclé, frisé.

currant ['kʌrənt] n groseille f, raisin de Corinthe m.

currency ['kʌrənsi] n cours m, circulation monétaire f, monnaie (courante) f.

current ['kʌrənt] n courant m, cours m, tendance f; a à courant, en cours.

currently ['kʌrəntli] ad couramment.

curry ['kʌri] n cari m; to — favour with amadouer, se mettre bien avec.

curse [kə:s] n malédiction f, fléau m, juron m; vt maudire; vi sacrer, blasphémer, jurer, pester.

cursory ['kə:səri] a superficiel, rapide.

curt [kə:t] a bref, sec.

curtail [kə:'teil] vt écourter, restreindre, réduire.

curtailment [kə:'teilmənt] n retranchement m, restriction f, réduction f.

curtain [kə:tn] n rideau m; excl tableau! **fireproof** — rideau de fer m; —**raiser** lever de rideau m.

curtly ['kə:tli] ad brièvement, sèchement.

curtness ['kə:tnis] n sécheresse f, brièveté f, rudesse f.

curtsy ['kə:tsi] n révérence f; vi faire une révérence.

curve [kə:v] n courbe f; vt (re)courber; vi se courber.

cushion ['kuʃən] n coussin m, (billiards) bande f.

cushy ['kuʃi] a (fam) moelleux, pépère, de tout repos.

custard ['kʌstəd] n flan de lait m, crème cuite f.

custody ['kʌstədi] n garde f, prison f.

custom ['kʌstəm] n usage m, coutume f, clientèle f; pl (droits m de) douane f.

customary ['kʌstəməri] a d'usage, habituel.

customarily ['kʌstəmərili] ad d'habitude.

customer ['kʌstəmə] n client(e) mf, chaland(‿) mf, type m, coco m.

custom-house ['kʌstəmhaus] n bureau m de la douane.

customs-officer ['kʌstəmz'ɔfisə] n douanier m.

cut [kʌt] n coupure f, coupe f, tranche f, incision f, coup m; vti couper; vt blesser, (teeth) faire, percer, (lecture) sécher, couper (au) court; to — down réduire; to — off amputer, trancher; to — up tailler en pièces.

cute [kju:t] a rusé, malin, coquet, mignon.

cutlass ['kʌtləs] n coutelas m, coupe-coupe m.

cutler ['kʌtlə] n coutelier m.

cutlery ['kʌtləri] n coutellerie f.

cutlet ['kʌtlit] n côtelette f.

cut-throat ['kʌtθrout] n coupe-jarret m.

cutting ['kʌtiŋ] n taille f, (dé)coupage m, incision f, coupure f, bouture f; a tranchant, mordant.

cycle ['saikl] n cycle m, bicyclette f; **motor** — motocyclette f; vi faire de la (aller à) bicyclette.

cycling ['saikliŋ] n cyclisme m.

cyclist ['saiklist] n cycliste mf.

cyclone ['saikloun] n cyclone m.

cygnet ['signit] n jeune cygne m.

cylinder ['silində] n cylindre m.

cylindrical [si'lindrikəl] a cylindrique.

cynic ['sinik] n cynique m, sceptique m.

cynical ['sinikəl] a cynique, sceptique.

cynicism ['sinisizəm] n cynisme m, scepticisme m.

cynosure ['sinəzjuə] n point de mire m.

cypress ['saipris] n cyprès m.

Cyprus ['saiprəs] n Chypre f.

cyst [sist] n kyste m.

czar [zɑː] n czar m, tsar m.

czarina [zɑːˈriːnə] n tsarine f.

D

D-Day [ˈdiːdei] n Jour J. m.

dab [dæb] n limande f, tape f, coup d'éponge m; vt tamponner, éponger, tapoter.

dabble [ˈdæbl] vt mouiller; vi patauger, jouer (à in), faire, s'occuper (de in).

dabbler [ˈdæblə] n amateur, -trice.

dad(dy) [ˈdædi] n papa m.

daddy-long-legs [ˈdædiˈlɒŋlegz] n faucheux m.

daffodil [ˈdæfədil] n narcisse des bois m, jonquille f.

daft [dɑːft] a toqué, entiché.

dagger [ˈdægə] n poignard m; at —s drawn à couteaux tirés; to look —s at s.o. foudroyer qn du regard.

daily [ˈdeili] an quotidien m; journalier; ad tous les jours.

daintiness [ˈdeintinis] n délicatesse f, beauté fine f.

dainty [ˈdeinti] n morceau de choix, friandise f; a délicat, mignon, exquis.

dairy [ˈdɛəri] n laiterie f.

dairymaid [ˈdɛərimeid] n laitière f.

dairyman [ˈdɛərimən] n laitier m.

dais [ˈdeiis] n estrade f, dais m.

daisy [ˈdeizi] n marguerite f, pâquerette f.

dale [deil] n vallée f, combe f.

dalliance [ˈdæliəns] n coquetteries f pl, flânerie f, badinage m, délai m.

dally [ˈdæli] vi jouer, coqueter, badiner, tarder.

dam [dæm] n barrage m, digue f; vt barrer, endiguer.

damage [ˈdæmidʒ] n dégats m pl, dommages m pl, préjudice m; pl dommages-intérêts m pl; vt endommager, nuire à, abîmer, faire tort à.

damaging [ˈdæmidʒiŋ] a dévastateur, nuisible.

dame [deim] n dame f.

damn [dæm] vt (con)damner, perdre, maudire, envoyer au diable; excl zut!; I don't care a — je m'en fiche.

damnable [ˈdæmnəbl] a damnable, maudit.

damnation [dæmˈneiʃən] n damnation f.

damned [dæmd] a damné, perdu, sacré; ad vachement.

damp [dæmp] n humidité f; a humide, moite; vt mouiller, étouffer, décourager, refroidir.

damper [ˈdæmpə] n éteignoir m, sourdine f, rabat-joie m.

damson [ˈdæmzən] n prune f de Damas.

dance [dɑːns] n danse f, bal m, (African) tam-tam; vti danser; vi sauter, trépigner; vt faire danser.

dance-hall [ˈdɑːnshɔːl] n dancing m, salle f de danse.

dancer [ˈdɑːnsə] n danseur, -euse.

dandelion [ˈdændilaiən] n pissenlit m.

dandle [ˈdændl] vt dodeliner, dorloter.

dandruff [ˈdændrəf] n pellicules f pl.

dandy [ˈdændi] n dandy m.

Dane [dein] n Danois(e) mf.

danger [ˈdeindʒə] n danger m, péril m, risque m.

dangerous [ˈdeindʒrəs] a dangereux, périlleux.

dangle [ˈdæŋgl] vi pendre, se balancer, agiter, pendiller; vt faire balancer.

Danish [ˈdeiniʃ] an danois m.

dapper [ˈdæpə] a net, soigné, tiré à quatre épingles.

dappled [ˈdæpld] a pommelé, tacheté.

dare [dɛə] vt oser, risquer, défier, braver.

dare-devil [ˈdɛəˌdevil] n casse-cou m.

daring [ˈdɛəriŋ] n audace f; a hardi, audacieux.

dark [dɑːk] n noir m, nuit f, obscurité f; a sombre, noir, foncé.

darken [ˈdɑːkən] vt assombrir, obscurcir, attrister; vi s'assombrir, s'obscurcir.

darkness [ˈdɑːknis] n obscurité f, ténèbres f pl.

darling [ˈdɑːliŋ] n chéri(e) mf, amour m.

darn [dɑːn] n reprise f; vt repriser, ravauder.

dart [dɑːt] n flèche f, dard m, fléchette f, .ancement m; vt lancer, darder; vi s'élancer, foncer.

dash [dæʃ] n fougue f, allant m, brio m, trait m, tiret m, pointe f, (fig) goutte f, filet m; vt lancer, éclabousser, diluer, étendre, décevoir; vi se précipiter, s'élancer; to — off vt bâcler; vi filer en vitesse, se sauver.

dashboard [ˈdæʃbɔːd] n tablier m.

dashing [ˈdæʃiŋ] a fougueux, impétueux, tapageur, plein d'entrain, galant.

dastardly [ˈdæstədli] a infâme, lâche.

date [deit] n date f, rendezvous m, datte f; vti dater; out of — démodé, périmé; up to — au courant, à la page.

dating [ˈdeitiŋ] dating from à dater de.

daub [dɔːb] n barbouillage m, croûte f, navet m; vt enduire, barbouiller.

daughter [ˈdɔːtə] n fille f.

daughter-in-law [ˈdɔːtərinlɔː] n belle-fille f.

daunt [dɔːnt] vt effrayer, intimider, décourager.

dauntless [ˈdɔːntlis] a intrépide courageux.

dawdle [ˈdɔːdl] vi traîner, flâner; t — away gaspiller.

dawdler ['dɔːdlə] n lambin(e) mf, flâneur, -euse.

dawn [dɔːn] n aube f, aurore f; vi poindre, naître, se faire jour.

day [dei] n jour m, journée f; — before veille f; — after lendemain m; a week today d'aujourd'hui en huit.

day-boarder ['dei,bɔːdə] n demi-pensionnaire mf.

day-boy ['deibɔi] n externe m.

daybreak ['deibreik] n point du jour m.

daydream ['deidriːm] n rêve (éveillé) m, rêverie f; vi rêver, rêvasser.

day-labourer ['dei'leibərə] n ouvrier m à la journée.

daylight ['deilait] n (lumière f du) jour m, publicité f, notoriété f.

day-nursery ['dei,nəːsri] n crèche f, garderie f.

daze [deiz] vt ébahir, ahurir, étourdir, hébéter.

dazzle ['dæzl] vt éblouir, aveugler.

dazzling ['dæzliŋ] n éblouissement m; a éblouissant.

deacon ['diːkən] n diacre m.

deaconess ['diːkənis] n diaconesse f.

dead [ded] n morts m pl; a mort, défunt, feu, funèbre, éteint, amorti, (loss) net, sec, plat; ad droit, en plein, à fond; in the — of au cœur de, au plus fort de, au milieu de.

deaden ['dedn] vt étouffer, amortir, émousser, feutrer.

dead-end ['ded'end] n cul de sac m, impasse f.

dead-letter ['ded'letə] n lettre morte f, mise au rebut f.

deadline ['dedlain] n dernière limite f, date limite f.

deadlock ['dedlɔk] n point mort m, impasse f.

deadly ['dedli] a mortel.

deaf [def] a sourd.

deafen ['defn] vt rendre sourd, assourdir.

deafness ['defnis] n surdité f.

deal [diːl] n planche f, bois blanc m, sapin m, quantité f, nombre m, affaire f, (cards) donne f; vt donner, distribuer, asséner; vi avoir affaire (à, avec with), s'occuper (de with), traiter (de with), faire le commerce (de in), se conduire.

dealer ['diːlə] n marchand(e) mf, fournisseur m, donneur m.

dealing(s) ['diːliŋz] n relations f pl, affaire f, agissements m pl, menées f pl.

dean [diːn] n doyen m.

deanery ['diːnəri] n doyenne f.

dear ['diə] a cher, coûteux.

dearly ['diəli] ad cher, chèrement.

dearness ['diənis] n cherté f.

dearth [dəːθ] n disette f, pénurie f.

death [deθ] n mort f, décès m; — certificate acte m de décès.

deathbed ['deθbed] n lit m de mort.

death-bell ['deθbel] n glas m.

death-rate ['deθreit] n taux de mortalité m.

death-trap ['deθtræp] n souricière f, casse-cou m.

death-warrant ['deθwɔrənt] n ordre m d'exécution, arrêt m de mort.

debar [di'baː] vt exclure.

debase [di'beis] vt avilir, altérer.

debatable [di'beitəbl] a discutable.

debate [di'beit] n débat m, discussion f; vt débattre; vti discuter.

debauch [di'bɔːtʃ] n débauche f; vt débaucher, corrompre.

debauchee [,debɔː'tʃiː] n débauché(e) mf.

debilitate [di'biliteit] vt débiliter.

debility [di'biliti] n débilité f.

debit ['debit] n débit m, doit m; vt porter au débit (de with), débiter.

debouch [di'bautʃ] vi déboucher.

debt [det] n dette f, passif m.

debt-collector ['detkəlektə] n huissier m.

debtor ['detə] n débiteur, -trice.

debunk [di'bʌŋk] vt dégonfler.

debut ['deibuː] n début m.

decade ['dekeid] n décade f.

decadence ['dekədəns] n décadence f.

decadent ['dekədənt] a décadent.

decamp [di'kæmp] vi décamper, filer.

decant [di'kænt] vt décanter.

decanter [di'kæntə] n carafe f.

decapitate [di'kæpiteit] vt décapiter.

decapitation [di,kæpi'teiʃən] n décapitation f.

decay [di'kei] n déclin m, décadence f, décomposition f; vi tomber en décadence, décliner, pourrir.

decease [di'siːs] n décès m; vi décéder.

deceased [di'siːst] an défunt(e) mf.

deceit [di'siːt] n fourberie f, apparence trompeuse f.

deceitful [di'siːtful] a trompeur, faux, perfide.

deceitfulness [di'siːtfulnis] n fausseté f, perfidie f.

deceive [di'siːv] vt tromper, décevoir.

December [di'sembə] n décembre m.

decency ['diːsnsi] n bienséance f, décence f.

decent ['diːsnt] a décent, passable, honnête.

decently ['diːsntli] ad décemment.

decentralization [diː,sentrəlai'zeiʃn] n décentralisation f.

decentralize [diː'sentrəlaiz] vt décentraliser.

deception [di'sepʃən] n tromperie f, déception f, fraude f.

deceptive [di'septiv] a trompeur.

decide [di'said] vti décider; vt régler, trancher; vi se décider.

decided [di'saidid] a décidé, net, arrêté.

decidedly [di'saididli] ad catégoriquement, incontestablement.

decimal ['desiməl] n décimale f; a décimal.

decimate ['desimeit] *vt* décimer.

decipher [di'saifə] *vt* déchiffrer.

deciphering [di'saifəriŋ] *n* déchiffrement *m*.

decision [di'siʒən] *n* décision *f*, arrêt *m*.

decisive [di'saisiv] *a* décisif, net, tranchant.

deck [dek] *n* pont *m*; *vt* orner, couvrir, pavoiser.

deck-chair ['dek'tʃɛə] *n* transatlantique *m*.

deck-house ['dekhaus] *n* (*naut*) rouf *m*.

declaim [di'kleim] *vti* déclamer.

declamation [,deklə'meiʃən] *n* déclamation *f*.

declamatory [di'klæmətəri] *a* déclamatoire.

declaration [,deklə'reiʃən] *n* déclaration *f*, (*pol*) proclamation *f*, annonce *f*.

declare [di'klɛə] *vt* déclarer, annoncer.

decline [di'klain] *n* déclin *m*, baisse *f*, phtisie *f*; *vti* décliner; *vt* refuser, repousser; *vi* baisser, s'incliner, descendre.

declivity [di'kliviti] *n* pente *f*.

decode ['di:'koud] *vt* déchiffrer.

decompose [,di:kəm'pouz] *vt* décomposer; *vi* se décomposer, pourrir.

decomposition [,di:kɔmpə'ziʃən] *n* décomposition *f*, putréfaction *f*.

decontrol ['di:kən'troul] *vt* décontrôler.

decorate ['dekəreit] *vt* décorer, pavoiser.

decoration [,dekə'reiʃən] *n* décoration *f*, décor *m*.

decorator ['dekəreitə] *n* décorateur *m*.

decorative ['dekərətiv] *a* décoratif.

decorous ['dekərəs] *a* séant.

decorum [di'kɔːrəm] *n* décorum *m*, bienséance *f*.

decoy [di'kɔi] *n* piège *m*, amorce *f*, appeau *m*, appât *m*, agent provocateur *m*; *vt* attraper, induire (à into), leurrer, attirer.

decrease ['di:kriːs] *n* diminution *f*, décroissance *f*.

decrease [di:'kriːs] *vti* diminuer; *vi* décroître.

decree [di'kriː] *n* décret *m*, arrêt *m*, édit *m*; *vt* décréter; — **nisi** divorce *m* sous conditions.

decrepit [di'krepit] *a* décrépit, caduc, délabré.

decrepitude [di'krepitjuːd] *n* décrépitude *f*, caducité *f*.

decry [di'krai] *vt* décrier, dénigrer, huer.

dedication [,dedi'keiʃən] *n* consécration *f*, dédicace *f*.

dedicate ['dedikeit] *vt* consacrer, dédier.

deduce [di'djuːs] *vt* déduire, conclure.

deduct [di'dʌkt] *vt* retrancher, rabattre.

deduction [di'dʌkʃən] *n* déduction *f*, rabais *m*, conclusion *f*.

deed [di:d] *n* acte *m*, (haut) fait *m*, exploit *m*.

deem [di:m] *vt* estimer, juger.

deep [di:p] *n* fond *m*, profondeur *f*, mer *f*, abîme *m*, gouffre *m*; *a* profond, (*mourning*) grand, (*colour*) chaud, foncé, (*sound*) riche, bas.

deepen ['di:pən] *vt* approfondir, creuser, augmenter; *vi* devenir plus profond *etc*.

deepening ['di:pniŋ] *n* approfondissement *m*.

deeply ['di:pli] *ad* profondément.

deer [diə] *n* daim *m*, cerf *m*.

deerskin ['diəskin] *n* peau *f* de daim.

deface [di'feis] *vt* défigurer, discréditer, mutiler, oblitérer.

defalcation [,di:fæl'keiʃən] *n* défalcation *f*, détournement *m*.

defalcate ['di:fælkeit] *vi* défalquer, détourner des fonds.

defamation [,defə'meiʃən] *n* diffamation *f*.

defamatory [di'fæmətəri] *a* diffamatoire.

defame [di'feim] *vt* diffamer.

default [di'fɔːlt] *n* défaut *m*, forfait *m*; *vi* faire défaut.

defaulter [di'fɔːltə] *n* défaillant *m*, contumace *mf*.

defeat [di'fiːt] *n* défaite *f*, annulation *f*; *vt* déjouer, battre, vaincre, contrarier.

defeatism [di'fiːtizəm] *n* défaitisme *m*.

defeatist [di'fiːtist] *n* défaitiste *mf*.

defect [di'fekt] *n* défaut *m*, manque *m*.

defection [di'fekʃən] *n* défection *f*.

defective [di'fektiv] *a* défectueux, anormal.

defence [di'fens] *n* défense *f*.

defend [di'fend] *vt* défendre, protéger.

defendant [di'fendənt] *n* défendeur, -eresse.

defender [di'fendə] *n* défenseur *m*.

defensible [di'fensəbl] *a* défendable.

defensive [di'fensiv] *n* défensive *f*; *a* défensif.

defer [di'fəː] *vt* différer, ajourner; *vi* déférer (à to).

deference ['defərəns] *n* déférence *f*.

deferment [di'fəːmənt] *n* ajournement *m*, remise *f*.

defiance [di'faiəns] *n* défi *m*, révolte *f*.

defiant [di'faiənt] *a* rebelle, défiant, provocant.

deficiency [di'fiʃənsi] *n* insuffisance *f*, manque *m*, défaut *m*, manquant *m*.

deficient [di'fiʃənt] *a* qui manque de, déficitaire, défectueux.

deficit ['defisit] *n* déficit *m*.

defile ['di:fail] *n* défilé *m*; [di'fail] *vi* marcher par files, défiler; *vt* souiller, profaner.

defilement [di'failmənt] n souillure f, profanation f.

definable [di'fainəbl] a définissable.

define [di'fain] vt définir, (dé)limiter.

definite ['definit] a défini, net, précis, définitif.

definiteness ['definitnis] n netteté f, précision f.

definition [,defi'niʃən] n définition f.

definitive [di'finitiv] a définitif.

deflate [di'fleit] vt dégonfler; vi pratiquer la déflation.

deflect [di'flekt] vt (faire) dévier, détourner.

deflection [di'flekʃən] n déviation f, déjettement m.

deform [di'fɔːm] vt déformer, défigurer.

deformed [di'fɔːmd] a difforme.

deformity [di'fɔːmiti] n difformité f.

deformation [,diːfɔː'meiʃən] n déformation f.

defraud [di'frɔːd] vt voler, frauder, frustrer.

defray [di'frei] vt défrayer, couvrir.

deft [deft] a adroit.

deftness ['deftnis] n adresse f.

defunct [di'fʌŋkt] a défunt.

defy [di'fai] vt défier.

degenerate [di'dʒenəreit] an dégénéré(e) mf; vi dégénérer.

degeneration [di,dʒenə'reiʃən] n dégénérescence f.

degradation [,degrə'deiʃən] n dégradation f, abrutissement m.

degrade [di'greid] vt avilir, dégrader, casser.

degree [di'griː] n degré m, grade m, titre m, échelon m, condition f; to a — au dernier point.

dehydrate [diː'haidreit] vt déshydrater.

deign [dein] vi daigner.

deity ['diːiti] n divinité f.

dejected [di'dʒektid] a déprimé, abattu.

dejection [di'dʒekʃən] n abattement m.

delay [di'lei] n délai m, retard m; vt remettre, retarder, différer.

delegate ['deligit] n délégué(e) mf.

delegate ['deligeit] vt déléguer.

delegation [,deli'geiʃən] n délégation f.

delete [di'liːt] vt effacer, rayer.

deleterious [,deli'tiəriəs] a délétère, nuisible.

deletion [di'liːʃən] n radiation f, rature f, suppression f.

deliberate [di'libərit] a délibéré, voulu, réfléchi.

deliberate [di'libəreit] vti délibérer.

deliberately [di'libəritli] ad délibérément, exprès.

deliberation [di,libə'reiʃən] n délibération f.

delicacy ['delikəsi] n délicatesse f, finesse f, friandise f.

delicate ['delikit] a délicat, fin, raffiné, épineux.

delicious [di'liʃəs] a délicieux, exquis.

delight [di'lait] n délices f, pl joie f; vt enchanter, ravir.

delightful [di'laitful] a délicieux, ravissant.

delineate [di'linieit] vt tracer, esquisser.

delineation [di,lini'eiʃən] n délinéation f, description f, tracé m.

delinquency [di'liŋkwənsi] n délit m, faute f, négligence f.

delinquent [di'liŋkwənt] an délinquant(e) mf, coupable mf.

delirious [di'liriəs] a délirant, en délire.

delirium [di'liriəm] n délire m.

deliver [di'livə] vt (dé)livrer, remettre, (letters) distribuer, (blow) asséner, (ball) lancer, (lectures) faire.

deliverance [di'livərəns] n délivrance f, libération f.

deliverer [di'livərə] n libérateur, -trice, livreur, -euse.

delivery [di'livəri] n livraison f, distribution f, remise f, débit m.

dell [del] n vallon m, combe f.

delude [di'luːd] vt tromper, duper.

deluge ['deljuːdʒ] n déluge m; vt inonder.

delusion [di'luːʒən] n leurre m, illusion f, hallucination f.

demand [di'maːnd] n requête f, (com) demande f, revendication f; vt requérir, exiger, réclamer.

demarcation [,diːmaː'keiʃən] n démarcation f.

demarcate ['diːmaːkeit] vt délimiter.

demean [di'miːn] vi to — oneself s'abaisser.

demeanour [di'miːnə] n conduite f, tenue f.

demented [di'mentid] a (tombé) en démence, fou.

demise [di'maiz] n transfert m, carence f, mort f; vt transférer, céder.

demobilization ['diː,moubilai'zeiʃən] n démobilisation f.

demobilize [diː'moubilaiz] vt démobiliser.

democracy [di'mɔkrəsi] n démocratie f.

democrat ['deməkræt] n démocrate mf; (US) membre mf du parti démocrate.

democratic [,demə'krætik] a démocratique, démocrate.

demolish [di'mɔliʃ] vt démolir.

demolition [,demə'liʃən] n démolition f.

demon ['diːmən] n démon m.

demonetize [diː'mʌnitaiz] vt démonétiser.

demonstrate ['demənstreit] vt démontrer; vi manifester.

demonstration [,demɔns'treiʃən] n démonstration f, manifestation f.

demonstrative [di'mɔnstrətiv] a démonstratif, expansif.

demonstrator ['demənstreitə] n dé-

monstrateur *m*, **préparateur** *m*, **manifestant** *m*.

demoralization [di,morəlai'zeiʃən] *n* démoralisation *f*.

demoralize [di'morəlaiz] *vt* démoraliser.

demur [di'mə:] *n* objection *f*; *vi* objecter, hésiter.

demure [di'mjuə] *a* réservé, composé, faussement modeste, prude.

demureness [di'mjuənis] *n* ingénuité feinte *f*, air prude *m*.

den [den] *n* tanière *f*, antre *m*, retraite *f*, turne *f*, cagibi *m*; (*fam*) cabinet *m* de travail.

denial [di'naiəl] *n* refus *m*, démenti *m*, désaveu *m*, reniement *m*.

denizen ['denizn] *n* habitant(e) *mf*, hôte *m*.

Denmark ['denmɑːk] *n* Danemark *m*.

denominate [di'nomineit] *vt* dénommer.

denote [di'nout] *vt* dénoter, accuser, respirer.

denounce [di'nauns] *vt* dénoncer, déblatérer contre.

dense [dens] *a* dense, épais, lourd, bouché.

density ['densiti] *n* densité *f*, lourdeur *f*.

dent [dent] *n* entaille *f*, bosselure *f*; *vt* entailler, bosseler.

dental ['dentl] *n* dentale *f*; *a* dentaire.

dentifrice ['dentifris] *n* dentifrice *m*.

dentist ['dentist] *n* dentiste *m*.

dentition [den'tiʃən] *n* dentition *f*.

denture ['dentʃə] *n* dentier *m*, denture *f*.

denude [di'njuːd] *vt* dénuder, dépouiller.

denunciation [di,nʌnsi'eiʃən] *n* dénonciation *f*.

deny [di'nai] *vt* (re)nier, refuser, démentir, désavouer.

depart [di'pɑːt] *vi* partir, trépasser, se départir (de **from**).

department [di'pɑːtmənt] *n* département *m*, rayon *m*, service *m*, bureau *m*; — **store** bazar *m*, grand magasin *m*.

departmental [,diːpɑːt'mentl] *a* départemental, de service.

departure [di'pɑːtʃə] *n* départ *m*, déviation *f*.

depend [di'pend] *vi* dépendre (de **on**), compter (sur **on**), tenir (à **on**).

dependable [di'pendəbl] *a* sûr, (digne) de confiance.

dependence [di'pendəns] *n* dépendance *f*, confiance *f*.

dependency [di'pendənsi] *n* dépendance *f*.

dependent [di'pendənt] *a* dépendant, subordonné.

depict [di'pikt] *vt* (dé)peindre.

deplenish [di'pleniʃ] *vt* vider, dégarnir.

deplete [di'pliːt] *vt* vider, épuiser.

depletion [di'pliːʃən] *n* épuisement *m*.

deplorable [di'plɔːrəbl] *a* déplorable, lamentable.

deplore [di'plɔː] *vt* déplorer.

deploy [di'plɔi] *vt* déployer.

deployment [di'plɔimənt] *n* déploiement *m*.

depopulate [diː'pɔpjuleit] *vt* dépeupler.

depopulation [diː,pɔpju'leiʃən] *n* dépopulation *f*.

deport [di'pɔːt] *vt* déporter, expulser (*aliens*); **to — oneself** se comporter.

deportation [,diːpɔː'teiʃən] *n* déportation *f*, expulsion *f*.

deportment [di'pɔːtmənt] *n* comportement *m*, tenue *f*.

depose [di'pouz] *vt* déposer.

deposit [di'pɔzit] *n* dépôt *m*, sédiment *m*, gisement *m*, gage *m*; *vt* déposer, verser en gage.

depositary [di'pɔzitəri] *n* dépositaire *m*.

deposition [,diːpə'ziʃən] *n* déposition *f*.

depository [di'pɔzitəri] *n* gardemeubles *m*, entrepôt *m*.

depot ['depou] *n* dépôt *m*, entrepôt *m*, garage *m*; (*US*) gare *f*.

depravation [,deprə'veiʃən] *n* dépravation *f*.

deprave [di'preiv] *vt* dépraver.

deprecate ['deprikeit] *vt* déconseiller (fortement), désapprouver.

depreciate [di'priːʃieit] *vt* déprécier; *vi* se déprécier.

depreciation [di,priːʃi'eiʃən] *n* dépréciation *f*, amortissement *m*.

depredation [,depri'deiʃən] *n* déprédation *f*.

depress [di'pres] *vt* (a)baisser, appuyer, déprimer, attrister.

depression [di'preʃən] *n* dépression *f*, abattement *m*.

deprival [di'praivəl] *n* privation *f*.

deprive [di'praiv] *vt* priver.

depth [depθ] *n* profondeur *f*, fond *m*, fort *m*, cœur *m*; **to get out of one's — ** perdre pied.

deputation [,depju'teiʃən] *n* délégation *f*.

depute [di'pjuːt] *vt* déléguer.

deputize ['depjutaiz] **to — for** *vt* représenter, remplacer.

deputy ['depjuti] *n* délégué *m*, suppléant *m*, sous-.

derail [di'reil] *vt* (faire) dérailler.

derailment [di'reilmənt] *n* déraillement *m*.

derange [di'reindʒ] *vt* déranger.

derangement [di'reindʒmənt] *n* dérangement *m*.

derelict ['derilikt] *n* épave *f*; *a* abandonné.

dereliction [,deri'likʃən] *n* abandon *m*, négligence *f*.

deride [di'raid] *vt* tourner en dérision, bafouer, se gausser de.

derision [di'riʒən] n dérision f, objet m de dérision.

derisive [di'raisiv] a ironique, dérisoire, railleur.

derivation [‚deri'veiʃən] n dérivation f.

derivative [di'rivətiv] an dérivatif m.

derive [di'raiv] vti tirer; vi dériver, provenir.

derogate ['derəgeit] vi déroger (à **from**), diminuer.

derogation [‚derə'geiʃən] n dérogation f, abaissement m.

derogatory [di'rogətəri] a dérogatoire.

descend [di'send] vti descendre, dévaler; vi s'abaisser.

descent [di'sent] n desc nte f, lignage m, parage m, transmission f.

describe [dis'kraib] vt dépeindre, décrire, donner pour, qualifier, signaler.

description [dis'kripʃən] n description f, signalement m, espèce f.

descriptive [dis'kriptiv] a descriptif, de description.

descry [dis'krai] vt apercevoir, aviser.

desecrate ['desikreit] vt profaner.

desert [di'zə:t] n mérite m, dû m; vt abandonner; vti déserter.

desert ['dezət] an désert m.

deserter [di'zə:tə] n déserteur m.

desertion [di'zə:ʃən] n désertion f, abandon m.

deserve [di'zə:v] vt mériter.

deservedly [di'zə:vidli] ad à juste titre.

deserving [di'zə:viŋ] a méritant, méritoire.

desiccate ['desikeit] vt dessécher.

desiccation [‚desi'keiʃən] n desiccation f.

design [di'zain] n dess(e)in m, esquisse f, modèle m, projet m; vt désigner, esquisser, projeter, créer, former, destiner.

designate ['dezigneit] vt désigner, nommer.

designation [‚dezig'neiʃən] n désignation f, nom m.

designedly [di'zainidli] ad à dessein.

designer [di'zainə] n dessinateur, -trice, créateur, -trice, décorateur m.

designing [di'zainiŋ] a intrigant.

desirable [di'zaiərəbl] a désirable, souhaitable.

desire [di'zaiə] n désir m, souhait m; vt désirer, avoir envie de.

desirous [di'zaiərəs] a désireux.

desist [di'zist] vi renoncer (à **from**), cesser (de **from**).

desk [desk] n pupitre m, bureau m.

desolate ['desəlit] a solitaire, abandonné, désert, désolé.

desolate ['desəleit] vt dépeupler, dévaster, désoler.

desolation [‚desə'leiʃən] n désolation f, solitude f.

despair [dis'pɛə] n désespoir m; vi désespérer.

despairingly [dis pɛəriŋli] ad désespérément.

desperate ['despərit] a désespéré, forcené, acharné, affreux.

desperation [‚despə'reiʃən] n désespoir m.

despicable [dis'pikəbl] a méprisable.

despise [dis'paiz] vt mépriser.

despite [dis'pait] ad malgré.

despoil [dis'poil] vt dépouiller, spolier.

despoiler [dis'poilə] n spoliateur, -trice.

despoliation [‚dispoli'eiʃən] n spoliation f.

despond [dis'pond] vi se décourager.

despondency [dis'pondensi] n découragement m, abattement m.

despondent [dis'pondənt] a découragé, abattu.

despot ['despot] n despote m.

despotic [des'potik] a despotique, arbitraire.

despotism ['despətizəm] n despotisme m.

dessert [di'zə:t] n dessert m, (US) entremets m.

dessert-spoon [di'zə:tspu:n] n cuiller f à entremets.

destination [‚desti'neiʃən] n destination f.

destine ['destin] vt destiner.

destiny ['destini] n destinée f, destin m, sort m.

destitute ['destitju:t] a sans ressources, dénué, indigent.

destitution [‚desti'tju:ʃən] n dénuement m, misère f, indigence f.

destroy [dis'troi] vt détruire.

destroyer [dis'troiə] n destructeur, -trice, (naut) contre-torpilleur m.

destruction [dis'trʌkʃən] n destruction f.

destructive [dis'trʌktiv] a destructeur, destructif.

desultorily ['desəltərili] ad sans suite, à bâtons rompus.

desultoriness ['desəltərinis] n incohérence f, décousu m, manque de suite m.

desultory ['desəltəri] a décousu, sans suite.

detach [di'tætʃ] vt détacher, dételer.

detachedly [di'tætʃədli] ad d'un ton (air) détaché, avec désinvolture.

detachment [di'tætʃmənt] n détachement m, indifférence f.

detail ['di:teil] n détail m, détachement m; vt détailler, affecter (à **for**).

detailed ['di:teild] a détaillé, circonstancie; — **work** travail très fouillé.

detain [di'tein] vt retenir, empêcher, détenir.

detect [di'tekt] vt découvrir, apercevoir, repérer, détecter.

detection [di'tekʃən] n découverte f, détection f, repérage m.

detective [di'tektiv] n détective m; — **novel** roman policier m.

detention [di'tenʃən] n détention f,

arrestation *f*, arrêts *m pl*, retard *m*, retenue *f*.

deter [di'tə:] *vt* détourner, décourager, retenir.

deteriorate [di'tiəriəreit] *vt* détériorer; *vi* se détériorer, dégénérer, se gâter.

deterioration [di.tiəriə'reiʃən] *n* détérioration *f*, dégénération *f*.

determination [di.tə:mi'neiʃən] *n* détermination *f*, résolution *f*.

determine [di'tə:min] *vti* déterminer, décider; *vt* constater.

determined [di'tə:mind] *a* résolu.

deterrent [di'terənt] *n* mesure préventive *f*, arme *f* de dissuasion.

detest [di'test] *vt* détester.

detestation [.di:tes'teiʃən] *n* horreur *f*, haine *f*.

detonate ['detəneit] *vi* détoner; *vt* faire détoner.

detonation [.detə'neiʃən] *n* détonation *f*.

detract [di'trækt] **to — from** retrancher, déprécier, diminuer.

detraction [di'trækʃən] *n* dénigrement *m*, détraction *f*.

detractor [di'træktə] *n* détracteur, -trice.

detriment ['detrimənt] *n* détriment *m*, préjudice *m*.

detrimental [.detri'məntl] *a* préjudiciable, nuisible.

deuce [dju:s] *n* deux *m*, diable *m*, diantre *m*.

deuced [dju:st] *a* sacré, satané.

devastate ['devəsteit] *vt* ravager, dévaster.

devastation [.devəs'teiʃən] *n* dévastation *f*.

devastating ['devəsteitiŋ] *a* dévastateur.

develop [di'veləp] *vt* exploiter, développer; *vi* se développer, se produire.

development [di'veləpmənt] *n* développement *m*.

deviate ['di:vieit] *vi* dévier, s'écarter.

deviation [.di:vi'eiʃən] *n* déviation *f*, écart *m*.

device [di'vais] *n* plan *m*, ruse *f*, moyen *m*, invention *f*, dispositif *m*, devise *f*.

devil ['devl] *n* diable *m*.

devilish ['deviliʃ] *a* diabolique.

devilry ['devlri] *n* diablerie *f*, méchanceté *f*.

devious ['di:vjəs] *a* détourné, tortueux.

devise [di'vaiz] *vt* imaginer, combiner, tramer.

deviser [di'vaizə] *n* inventeur, -trice.

devoid [di'vɔid] *a* dénué, dépourvu.

devolve [di'vɔlv] *vt* passer (à **upon**), rejeter (sur **upon**), transmettre; *vi* échoir, incomber.

devote [di'vout] *vt* vouer, dévouer, consacrer.

devotee [.devou'ti:] *n* fanatique *mf*, fervent(e) *mf*.

devotion [di'vouʃən] *n* dévotion *f*, dévouement *m*, consécration *f*.

devour [di'vauə] *vt* dévorer.

devout [di'vaut] *an* dévôt, fervent, zélé.

dew [dju:] *n* rosée *f*.

dewy ['dju:i] *a* couvert de rosée.

dexterity [deks'teriti] *n* dextérité *f*.

dexterous ['dekstrəs] *a* adroit.

diabetes [.daiə'bi:ti:z] *n* diabète *m*.

diabetic [.daiə'betik] *an* diabétique *mf*.

diabolic(al) [.daiə'bɔlik(əl)] *a* diabolique, infernal.

diadem ['daiədem] *n* diadème *m*.

diagnose ['daiəgnouz] *vt* diagnostiquer.

diagnosis [.daiəg'nousis] *n* diagnostic *m*.

diagonal [dai'ægənl] *n* diagonale *f*; *a* diagonal.

diagram ['daiəgræm] *n* diagramme *m*, tracé *m*, schéma *m*.

dial ['daiəl] *n* cadran *m*.

dialogue ['daiəlɔg] *n* dialogue *m*.

diameter [dai'æmitə] *n* diamètre *m*.

diametrical [.daiə'metrikəl] *a* diamétral.

diamond ['daiəmənd] *n* diamant *m*, losange *m*, (*cards*) carreau *m*.

diaper ['daiəpə] *n* linge damassé *m*; (*US*) couches *fpl*; *vt* damasser.

diaphragm ['daiəfræm] *n* diaphragme *m*, membrane *m*.

diary ['daiəri] *n* journal *m*, agenda *m*.

dibble ['dibl] *n* plantoir *m*.

dice [dais] *n* dés *m pl*; — **box** cornet *m*.

dicky ['diki] *n* faux-plastron *m*, tablier *m*, (*aut*) spider *m*; *a* flanchard.

dictate ['dikteit] *n* dictat *m*, ordre *m*, voix *f*; [dik'teit] *vt* dicter, ordonner; *vi* faire la loi.

dictation [dik'teiʃən] *n* dictée *f*.

dictator [dik'teitə] *n* dictateur *m*.

dictatorial [.diktə'tɔ:riəl] *a* dictatorial.

dictatorship [dik'teitəʃip] *n* dictature *f*.

diction ['dikʃən] *n* diction *f*, style *m*.

dictionary ['dikʃənri] *n* dictionnaire *m*.

did [did] *pt of* **do**.

die [dai] *n* (*pl* **dice**) dé *m*, (*pl* **dies**) coin *m*, matrice *f*· *vi* mourir, crever; **to — away**, **out** s'éteindre, tomber.

diehard ['daiha:d] *n* jusqu'au boutiste *m*; **the —s** le dernier carré *m*, les irréductibles *m pl*; *a* — **conservative** conservateur intransigeant.

diet ['daiət] *n* régime *m*, diète *f*; *vt* mettre au régime; *vi* suivre un régime.

differ ['difə] *vi* différer.

difference ['difrəns] *n* différence *f*, écart *m*, différend *m*.

different ['difrənt] *a* différent, divers.

differentiate [.difə'renʃieit] *vt* différencier; *vi* faire la différence.

differently ['difrəntli] *ad* différemment.

difficult ['difikəlt] *a* difficile.

difficulty ['difikəlti] *n* difficulté *f*, ennui *m*, peine *f*, gêne *f*.

diffidence ['difidəns] *n* défiance de soi *f*, timidité *f*.

diffident ['difidənt] *a* modeste, timide, qui manque d'assurance.

diffuse [di'fjuːz] *vt* diffuser, répandre.

diffuse [di'fjuːs] *a* diffus.

diffusion [di'fjuːʒən] *n* diffusion *f*.

dig [dig] *vt* creuser, bêcher, piocher, piquer; **to — up** déterrer, déraciner.

digest [dai'dʒest] *vt* digérer, assimiler; *vi* se digérer, s'assimiler.

digestible [di'dʒestəbl] *a* digestible.

digestion [di'dʒestʃən] *n* digestion *f*.

digestive [di'dʒestiv] *a* digestif.

dignified ['dignifaid] *a* digne, majestueux.

dignify ['dignifai] *vt* honorer, donner un air de majesté à.

dignity ['digniti] *n* dignité *f*.

digress [dai'gres] *vi* s'écarter (de from), faire une digression.

digression [dai'greʃən] *n* digression *f*.

digs [digz] *n pl* garni *m*, logement *m*, piaule *f*.

dike [daik] *n* levée *f*, digue *f*, remblai *m*; *vt* endiguer, remblayer.

dilapidated [di'læpideitid] *a* délabré, décrépit.

dilapidation [di,læpi'deiʃən] *n* délabrement *m*, dégradation *f*.

dilatation [,dailei'teiʃən] *n* dilatation *f*.

dilate [dai'leit] *vt* dilater; *vi* se dilater, s'étendre (sur upon).

dilatoriness ['dilətərinis] *n* temporisation *f*, tergiversation *f*, lenteur *f*.

dilatory ['dilətəri] *a* lent, tardif.

dilemma [dai'lemə] *n* dilemme *m*.

diligence ['dilidʒəns] *n* diligence *f*, application *f*.

diligent ['dilidʒənt] *a* diligent, appliqué.

diligently ['dilidʒəntli] *ad* diligemment.

dilute [dai'ljuːt] *a* dilué, atténué; *vt* diluer, arroser, atténuer.

dim [dim] *a* indistinct, voilé, faible, sourd; *vt* assombrir, éclipser, ternir, mettre en veilleuse; *vi* s'affaiblir, baisser.

dime [daim] *n* (*US*) dîme; **— store** prix unique *m*.

dimension [di'menʃən] *n* dimension *f*.

diminish [di'miniʃ] *vti* diminuer.

diminution [,dimi'njuːʃən] *n* diminution *f*.

diminutive [di'minjutiv] *an* diminutif *m*.

dimmer ['dimə] *n* phare code *m*.

dimness ['dimnis] *n* pénombre *f*, faiblesse *f*, imprécision *f*.

dim-out ['dimaut] *n* obscurcissement *m*.

dimple ['dimpl] *n* fossette *f*, ride *f*, creux *m*.

din [din] *n* tintamarre *m*, vacarme *m*; *vt* corner, rabattre.

dine [dain] *vi* dîner; **to — out** dîner en ville.

dinghy ['dingi] *n* canot *m*.

dingy ['dindʒi] *a* sale, crasseux, terne, sombre.

dining-room ['daininrum] *n* salle *f* à manger.

dinner ['dinə] *n* dîner *m*.

dinner-jacket ['dinə,dʒækit] *n* smoking *m*.

dint [dint] **by — of** à force de.

diocese ['daiəsis] *n* diocèse *m*.

dip [dip] *n* plongeon *m*, pente *f*, immersion *f*, bain *m*; *vti* plonger, baisser, (*headlights*) basculer; *vt* puiser, tremper, baigner; *vi* pencher.

diphtheria [dip'θiəriə] *n* diphtérie *f*.

diphthong ['dipθɔŋ] *n* diphtongue *f*.

diploma [di'ploumə] *n* diplôme *m*.

diplomacy [di'plouməsi] *n* diplomatie *f*.

diplomat ['dipləmæt] *n* diplomate *m*.

diplomatic [,diplə'mætik] *a* diplomatique, prudent.

dire ['daiə] *a* affreux, cruel, dernier, extrême.

direct [dai'rekt] *a* direct, droit, catégorique, formel, franc; *vt* adresser, diriger, attirer, ordonner, indiquer.

direction [di'rekʃən] *n* direction *f*, sens *m*, adresse *f*; *pl* instructions *f pl*.

directly [di'rektli] *ad* tout de suite, (tout) droit, directement, tout à l'heure, bientôt, personnellement.

director [di'rektə] *n* directeur *m*, gérant *m*, administrateur *m*.

directorship [di'rektəʃip] *n* directorat *m*.

directory [di'rektəri] *n* indicateur *m*, annuaire *m*, bottin *m*, directoire *m*.

dirge [dəːdʒ] *n* misérère *m*, chant funèbre *m*.

dirk [dəːk] *n* poignard *m*.

dirt [dəːt] *n* boue *f*, saleté *f*, ordure *f*, crasse *f*.

dirtiness ['dəːtinis] *n* crasse *f*, saleté *f*.

dirty ['dəːti] *vt* salir; *vi* se salir; *a* sale, malpropre, crasseux, vilain, polisson.

disability [,disə'biliti] *n* incapacité *f* (de travail), infirmité *f*.

disable [dis'eibl] *vt* rendre impropre au travail, mettre hors de combat, désemparer.

disabled [dis'eibld] *a* invalide, estropié, désemparé.

disabuse [,disə'bjuːz] *vt* désabuser.

disaffected [,disə'fektid] *a* détaché, refroidi.

disaffection [ˌdisə'fekʃən] n désaffection f.

disagree [ˌdisə'griː] vi n'être pas d'accord, ne pas convenir.

disagreeable [ˌdisə'griːəbl] a désagréable, fâcheux.

disagreement [ˌdisə'griːmənt] n disconvenance f, désaccord m, mésentente f.

disallow ['disə'lau] vt désavouer, interdire, ne pas admettre, rejeter.

disappear [ˌdisə'piə] vi disparaître.

disappearance [ˌdisə'piərəns] n disparition f.

disappoint [ˌdisə'pɔint] vt désappointer, décevoir.

disappointed [ˌdisə'pɔintəd] a déçu; (US) manqué.

disappointment [ˌdisə'pɔintmənt] n déception f, désappointement m, déboire m.

disapproval [ˌdisə'pruːvəl] n désapprobation f.

disapprove [ˌdisə'pruːv] vti désapprouver.

disapproving [ˌdisə'pruːviŋ] a désapprobateur.

disarm [dis'aːm] vti désarmer.

disarmament [dis'aːməmənt] n désarmement m.

disarrange ['disə'reindʒ] vt déranger.

disarrangement [ˌdisə'reindʒmənt] n désorganisation f, désordre m, dérangement m.

disarray ['disə'rei] n désarroi m, désordre m, déroute f.

disaster [di'zaːstə] n désastre m, sinistre m, catastrophe f.

disastrous [di'zaːstrəs] a désastreux, funeste.

disavow ['disə'vau] vt désavouer, renier.

disavowal [ˌdisə'vauəl] n désaveu m, reniement m.

disband [dis'bænd] vt licencier; vi se débander.

disbanding [dis'bændiŋ] n licenciement m.

disbelief ['disbi'liːf] n incrédulité f.

disc [disk] n disque m, plaque f; slipped — hernie discale f.

discard [dis'kaːd] n écart m, défausse f; vt se défausser de, écarter, mettre au rancart, laisser de côté.

discern [di'səːn] vt distinguer, discerner.

discernible [di'səːnəbl] a discernable, perceptible.

discerning [di'səːniŋ] a perspicace, judicieux.

discernment [di'səːnmənt] n discernement m.

discharge [dis'tʃaːdʒ] n déchargement m, décharge f, acquittement m, élargissement m, renvoi m, exécution f, paiement m; vt décharger, élargir, renvoyer, (s')acquitter (de), lancer; vi se jeter, se dégorger.

disciple [di'saipl] n disciple m.

disciplinary ['disiplinəri] a disciplinaire.

discipline ['disiplin] n discipline f; vt discipliner, mater, former.

disclaim [dis'kleim] vt répudier, désavouer, renoncer à, dénier.

disclaimer [dis'kleimə] n répudiation f, désaveu m, déni m.

disclose [dis'klouz] vt découvrir, divulguer, révéler.

disclosure [dis'klouʒə] n révélation f, divulgation f.

discolour [dis'kʌlə] vt décolorer, ternir, délaver; vi se décolorer, se ternir.

discoloration [disˌkʌlə'reiʃən] n décoloration f.

discomfit [dis'kʌmfit] vt déconcerter, déconfire.

discomfiture [dis'kʌmfitʃə] n déconfiture f, déconvenue f.

discomfort [dis'kʌmfət] n malaise m, gêne f.

discomposure [ˌdiskəm'pouʒə] n confusion f, trouble m.

disconcert [ˌdiskən'səːt] vt déranger, déconcerter, interloquer.

disconnect ['diskə'nekt] vt couper, décrocher, disjoindre, débrayer.

disconnected ['diskə'nektid] a décousu, sans suite.

disconnection [ˌdiskə'nekʃən] n disjonction f, débrayage m.

disconsolate [dis'kɔnsəlit] a inconsolable, désolé.

discontent ['diskən'tent] n mécontentement m.

discontented ['diskən'tentid] a mécontent, insatisfait (de with).

discontinuance [ˌdiskən'tinjuəns] n discontinuation f, fin f.

discontinue ['diskən'tinju] vt discontinuer; vti cesser.

discontinuity ['dis,kɔnti'njuiti] n discontinuité f.

discontinuous ['diskən'tinjuəs] a discontinu.

discord ['diskɔːd] n discorde f, discordance f, dissonance f.

discount ['diskaunt] n rabais m, escompte m; [dis'kaunt] vt escompter, laisser hors de compte.

discountenance [dis'kauntinəns] vt désapprouver, décontenancer.

discourage [dis'kʌridʒ] vt décourager, déconseiller.

discouragement [dis'kʌridʒmənt] n découragement m.

discourse ['diskɔːs] n traité m, sermon m, essai m, dissertation f.

discourse [dis'kɔːs] vi causer, discourir.

discourteous [dis'kəːtjəs] a discourtois, impoli.

discourtesy [dis'kəːtisi] n discourtoisie f, impolitesse f.

discover [dis'kʌvə] vt découvrir, révéler, s'apercevoir (de), constater.

discovery [dis'kʌvəri] n révélation f, découverte f, trouvaille f.

discredit [dis'kredit] *n* déconsidération *f*, discrédit *m*, doute *m*; *vt* discréditer, déconsidérer, mettre en doute.

discreditable [dis'kreditəbl] *a* indigne, déshonorant.

discreet [dis'kri:t] *a* discret, prudent.

discrepancy [dis'krepənsi] *n* désaccord *m*, inconsistance *f*, écart *m*.

discretion [dis'kreʃən] *n* prudence *f*, discrétion *f*, choix *m*.

discriminate [dis'krimineit] *vt* distinguer.

discriminating [dis'krimineitiŋ] *a* sagace, avisé, fin.

discrimination [dis,krimi'neiʃən] *n* finesse *f*, goût *m*, discernement *m*.

discuss [dis'kʌs] *vt* discuter, délibérer, débattre.

discussion [dis'kʌʃən] *n* discussion *f*.

disdain [dis'dein] *n* dédain *m*; *vt* dédaigner.

disdainful [dis'deinful] *a* dédaigneux.

disease [di'zi:z] *n* maladie *f*, affection *f*.

diseased [di'zi:zd] *a* malade; — **mind** esprit morbide *m*.

disembark ['disim'ba:k] *vti* débarquer.

disembarkation [,disemba:'keiʃən] *n* débarquement *m*.

disembody ['disim'bɔdi] *vt* désincarner, désincorporer, licencier.

disembowel [,disim'bauəl] *vt* éventrer.

disengage ['disin'geidʒ] *vt* dégager, rompre, débrayer, déclencher; *vi* se dégager, rompre.

disengaged ['disin'geidʒd] *a* libre, visible.

disengagement ['disin'geidʒmənt] *n* dégagement *m*, rupture *f*.

disentangle ['disin'tæŋgl] *vt* débrouiller, démêler, dépêtrer.

disentanglement ['disin'tæŋglmənt] *n* débrouillement *m*, démêlage *m*.

disfavour [dis'feivə] *n* défaveur *f*, disgrâce *f*.

disfigure [dis'figə] *vt* défigurer, gâter.

disfranchise ['dis'fræntʃaiz] *vt* priver de droits politiques, de représentation parlementaire.

disgorge [dis'gɔ:dʒ] *vt* rendre, dégorger; *vi* se jeter.

disgrace [dis'greis] *n* disgrâce *f*, honte *f*; *vt* disgrâcier, déshonorer.

disgraceful [dis'greisful] *a* honteux, scandaleux.

disgruntled [dis'grʌntld] *a* mécontent, bougon.

disguise [dis'gaiz] *n* déguisement *m*, feinte *f*; **in** — déguisé; *vt* déguiser, travestir.

disgust [dis'gʌst] *n* dégoût *m*; *vt* dégoûter, écœurer.

disgusting [dis'gʌstiŋ] *a* dégoûtant, dégueulasse.

dish [diʃ] *n* plat *m*, mets *m*, récipient *m*, bol *m*; *vt* servir, supplanter, rouler, déjouer.

dish-cloth ['diʃklɔθ] *n* lavette *f*, torchon *m*.

dish-cover ['diʃ,kʌvə] *n* couvre-plat *m*.

dishearten [dis'ha:tn] *vt* décourager, démoraliser.

dishevelled [di'ʃevəld] *a* débraillé, dépeigné.

dishonest [dis'ɔnist] *a* malhonnête, déloyal.

dishonesty [dis'ɔnisti] *n* malhonnêteté *f*, improbité *f*.

dishonour [dis'ɔnə] *n* déshonneur *m*; *vt* déshonorer.

dishonourable [dis'ɔnərəbl] *a* déshonorant, sans honneur.

dishwasher ['diʃ,wɔʃə] *n* plongeur *m*.

dishwater ['diʃ,wɔ:tə] *n* eau de vaisselle *f*.

disillusion [,disi'lu:ʒən] *vt* désillusionner, désabuser.

disillusionment [,disi'lu:ʒənmənt] *n* désenchantement *m*, désillusionnement *m*.

disinclination [,disinkli'neiʃən] *n* aversion *f*, répugnance *f*.

disinfect [,disin'fekt] *vt* désinfecter.

disinfectant [,disin'fektənt] *an* désinfectant *m*.

disinfection [,disin'fekʃən] *n* désinfection *f*.

disingenuous [,disin'dʒenjuəs] *a* faux.

disingenuousness [,disin'dʒenjuəsnis] *n* fausseté *f*.

disinherit ['disin'herit] *vt* déshériter.

disintegrate [dis'intigreit] *vt* désintégrer, désagréger; *vi* se désintégrer, se désagréger.

disintegration [dis,inti'greiʃən] *n* désintégration *f*, désagrégation *f*.

disinterested [dis'intristid] *a* désintéressé.

disinterestedness [dis'intristidnis] *n* désintéressement *m*.

disjoin [dis'dʒɔin] *vt* disjoindre, désunir.

disjoint [dis'dʒɔint] *vt* disjoindre, disloquer, démettre, désarticuler.

disjointed [dis'dʒɔintid] *a* disloqué, décousu, incohérent.

dislike [dis'laik] *n* antipathie *f*; *vt* ne pas aimer, trouver antipathique, détester.

dislodge [dis'lɔdʒ] *vt* déloger, détacher, dénicher.

disloyal ['dis'lɔiəl] *a* déloyal, infidèle.

disloyalty ['dis'lɔiəlti] *n* déloyauté *f*, infidélité *f*.

dismal ['dizməl] *a* morne, lugubre.

dismantle [dis'mæntl] *vt* démanteler, démonter.

dismantling [dis'mæntliŋ] *n* démantèlement *m*, démontage *m*.

dismay [dis'mei] *n* consternation *f*, épouvante *f*, gêne *f*; *vt* effrayer, consterner, affoler.

dismember [dis'membə] *vt* démembrer.

dismiss [dis'mis] *vt* renvoyer, congédier, révoquer, rejeter, écarter, acquitter.

dismissal [dis'misəl] *n* renvoi *m*, révocation *f*, acquittement *m*.

disobedience [.disə'bi:djəns] *n* désobéissance *f*.

disobedient [.disə'bi:djənt] *a* désobéissant.

disobey [.disə'bei] *vt* désobéir à; *vi* désobéir.

disoblige ['disə'blaidʒ] *vt* désobliger.

disobliging ['disə'blaidʒiŋ] *a* désobligeant.

disorder [dis'ɔːdə] *n* désordre *m*, confusion *f*.

disorderly [dis'ɔːdəli] *a* désordonné, turbulent, déréglé, en désordre.

disorganization [dis.ɔːgənai'zeiʃən] *n* désorganisation *f*.

disorganize [dis'ɔːgənaiz] *vt* désorganiser.

disown [dis'oun] *vt* désavouer, renier.

disparage [dis'pæridʒ] *vt* dénigrer déprécier.

disparagement [dis'pæridʒmənt] *n* dénigrement *m*, dépréciation *f*.

disparity [dis'pæriti] *n* inégalité *f*, différence *f*.

dispassionate [dis'pæʃnit] *a* calme, impartial, désintéressé.

dispatch [dis'pætʃ] *n* envoi *m*, rapidité *f*, dépêche *f*, expédition *f*, promptitude *f*; *vt* expédier, envoyer, dépêcher.

dispatch-rider [dis'pætʃ.raidə] *n* estafette *f*.

dispel [dis'pel] *vt* dissiper, chasser.

dispensary [dis'pensəri] *n* dispensaire *m*, pharmacie *f*.

dispensation [.dispen'seiʃən] *n* distribution *f*, dispensation *f*, dispense *f*.

dispense [dis'pens] *vt* distribuer, administrer; *vi* se dispenser (de with), se passer (de with).

disperse [dis'pəːs] *vt* disperser, dissiper; *vi* se disperser.

dispersion [dis'pəːʃən] *n* dispersion *f*.

dispirit [dis'pirit] *vt* décourager.

displace [dis'pleis] *vt* déplacer, remplacer.

displacement [dis'pleismənt] *n* déplacement *m*.

display [dis'plei] *n* déploiement *m*, étalage *m*, parade *f*, manifestation *f*, montre *f*; *vt* déployer, faire parade, (montre, preuve) de, manifester, afficher.

displease [dis'pliːz] *vt* déplaire à, mécontenter.

displeasure [dis'pleʒə] *n* déplaisir *m*, mécontentement *m*.

disport [dis'pɔːt] *vr* se divertir.

disposal [dis'pouzəl] *n* disposition *f*, vente *f*, cession *f*.

dispose [dis'pouz] *vt* disposer,

arranger, expédier; *vi* se disposer (de of), se débarrasser (de of).

dispossess [.dispə'zes] *vt* déposséder.

dispossession [.dispə'zeʃən] *n* dépossession *f*.

disproof [dis'pruːf] *n* réfutation *f*.

disproportion [.disprə'pɔːʃən] *n* disproportion *f*.

disproportionate [.disprə'pɔːʃnit] *a* disproportionné.

disprove [dis'pruːv] *vt* réfuter.

disputable [dis'pjuːtəbl] *a* discutable, contestable.

dispute [dis'pjuːt] *n* dispute *f*, discussion *f*; *vt* discuter, débattre, contester; *vi* se disputer.

disqualification [dis.kwɔlifi'keiʃən] *n* disqualification *f*, inhabilité *f*.

disqualify [dis'kwɔlifai] *vt* disqualifier.

disquiet [dis'kwaiət] *n* inquiétude *f*; *vt* inquiéter.

disregard [.disri'gaːd] *n* indifférence *f*, mépris *m*; *vt* laisser de côté, ne tenir aucun compte de, mépriser.

disregarding [.disri'gaːdiŋ] *prep* sans égard à (pour).

disrepair [.disri'pɛə] *n* délabrement *m*.

disreputable [dis'repjutəbl] *a* déconsidéré, de mauvaise réputation, minable.

disrepute ['disri'pjuːt] *n* mauvaise réputation *f*, discrédit *m*.

disrespect ['disris'pekt] *n* manque de respect *m*.

disrespectful [.disris'pektful] *a* irrespectueux, irrévérencieux.

disruption [dis'rʌpʃən] *n* dislocation *f*, scission *f*, démembrement *m*.

dissatisfaction ['dis.sætis'fækʃən] *n* mécontentement *m*.

dissatisfy [dis'sætisfai] *vt* mécontenter.

dissect [di'sekt] *vt* disséquer.

dissection [di'sekʃən] *n* dissection *f*.

dissemble [di'sembl] *vt* dissimuler.

dissembler [di'semblə] *n* hypocrite *mf*.

disseminate [di'semineit] *vt* disséminer.

dissemination [di.semi'neiʃən] *n* dissémination *f*.

dissension [di'senʃən] *n* dissension *f*.

dissent [di'sent] *n* dissentiment *m*, dissidence *f*; *vi* différer.

dissenter [di'sentə] *n* dissident *m*.

dissipate ['disipeit] *vt* dissiper; *vi* se dissiper.

dissipation [.disi'peiʃən] *n* dissipation *f*, dispersion *f*, gaspillage *m*, dérèglement *m*.

dissolute ['disəluːt] *a* dissolu, débauché.

dissoluteness ['disəluːtnis] *n* dérèglement *m*, débauche *f*.

dissolution [.disə'luːʃən] *n* dissolution *f*, dissipation *f*.

dissolve [di'zɔlv] *vt* dissoudre; *vi* se dissoudre.

dissolvent [di'zɔlvənt] *an* dissolvant m.

distaff ['distɑ:f] *n* quenouille *f*.

distance ['distəns] *n* distance *f*, lointain *m*, intervalle *m*, éloignement *m*.

distant ['distənt] *a* éloigné, lointain, distant, réservé.

distaste ['dis'teist] *n* répugnance *f*, aversion *f*.

distasteful [dis'teistful] *a* répugnant, antipathique.

distemper [dis'tempə] *n* maladie *f* (des chiens), badigeon *m*, détrempe *f*; *vt* badigeonner.

distend [dis'tend] *vt* gonfler, dilater; *vi* enfler, se dilater.

distil [dis'til] *vti* distiller; *vi* s'égoutter, se distiller.

distillation [disti'leiʃən] *n* distillation *f*.

distiller [dis'tilə] *n* distillateur *m*.

distillery [dis'tiləri] *n* distillerie *f*.

distinct [dis'tiŋkt] *a* distinct, net, clair.

distinction [dis'tiŋkʃən] *n* distinction *f*.

distinctive [dis'tiŋktiv] *a* distinctif.

distinctness [dis'tiŋktnis] *n* netteté *f*.

distinguish [dis'tiŋgwiʃ] *vt* distinguer; *vi* faire la distinction.

distinguishable [dis'tiŋgwiʃəbl] *a* perceptible, sensible.

distort [dis'tɔ:t] *vt* déformer, travestir, tordre, convulser, fausser.

distract [dis'trækt] *vt* distraire, détourner, diviser, déranger.

distracted [dis'træktid] *a* fou, furieux, affolé.

distraction [dis'trækʃən] *n* distraction *f*, dérangement *m*, folie *f*, affolement *m*.

distress [dis'tres] *n* détresse *f*, dénuement *m*, misère *f*, angoisse *f*; *vt* tourmenter, affliger, épuiser.

distribute [dis'tribju:t] *vt* distribuer, répartir.

distribution [distri'bju:ʃən] *n* distribution *f*, répartition *f*.

district ['distrikt] *n* district *m*, région *f*.

distrust [dis'trʌst] *n* méfiance *f*; *vt* se méfier de.

distrustful [dis'trʌstful] *a* méfiant, soupçonneux.

disturb [dis'tə:b] *vt* troubler, agiter, déranger.

disturbance [dis'tə:bəns] *n* trouble *m*, bagarre *f*, émeute *f*, tapage *m*.

disunion [dis'ju:njən] *n* désunion *f*.

disuse ['dis'ju:s] *n* désuétude *f*.

disused [dis'ju:zd] *a* hors de service, hors d'usage.

ditch [ditʃ] *n* tranchée *f*, fossé *m*; *vt* creuser, draîner; (*US*) faire dérailler (train); **to be —ed** échouer, être dans le pétrin.

ditcher ['ditʃə] *n* fossoyeur *m*.

ditto ['ditou] *an* idem, amen.

ditty ['diti] *n* chanson (nette) *f*.

divagate ['daivəgeit] *vi* divaguer.

divagation [daivə'geiʃən] *n* divagation *f*.

divan [di'væn] *n* divan *m*; **—bed** divan-lit *m*.

dive [daiv] *n* plongeon *m*, plongée *f*, pique *m*; *vi* se plonger, piquer (une tête, du nez).

diver ['daivə] *n* plongeur *m*, scaphandrier *m*.

diverge [dai'və:dʒ] *vi* diverger, s'écarter.

divergence [dai'və:dʒəns] *n* divergence *f*.

diverse [dai'və:s] *a* divers, différent.

diversify [dai'və:sifai] *vt* diversifier.

diversion [dai'və:ʃən] *n* diversion *f*, divertissement *m*, détournement *m*.

divert [dai'və:t] *vt* détourner, divertir, écarter, distraire.

divest [dai'vest] *vt* dévêtir, dépouiller, priver.

divide [di'vaid] *vt* partager, diviser; *vi* aller aux voix, se diviser, se partager, fourcher.

dividend ['dividend] *n* dividende *m*.

dividers [di'vaidəz] *n* compas *m*.

divine [di'vain] *n* théologien *m*, prêtre *m*; *a* divin; *vt* deviner, prédire.

diviner [di'vainə] *n* devin *m*, sourcier *m*.

diving ['daiviŋ] *n* (*sport*) plongeon *m*, (*av*) piqué *m*; **— board** plongeoire *m*.

divinity [di'viniti] *n* divinité *f*, théologie *f*.

division [di'viʒən] *n* division *f*, partage *m*, répartition *f*, frontière *f*, vote *m*.

divorce [di'vɔ:s] *n* divorce *m*; *vt* divorcer.

divulge [dai'vʌldʒ] *vt* divulguer.

divulgement [dai'vʌldʒmənt] *n* divulgation *f*.

dizziness ['dizinis] *n* vertige *m*, étourdissement *m*.

dizzy ['dizi] *a* étourdi, vertigineux.

do [du:] *vt* faire, finir, cuire à point, rouler, refaire; *vi* se porter, aller, s'acquitter; **to — away with** supprimer, abolir, tuer; **to — up** remettre à neuf, retaper.

docile ['dousail] *a* docile.

docility [dou'siliti] *n* docilité *f*.

dock [dɔk] *n* bassin *m*, dock *m*, cale *f*, banc *m* des accusés, box *m*; *vt* mettre en bassin; *vi* entrer au bassin.

docker ['dɔkə] *n* débardeur *m*.

docket ['dɔkit] *n* bordereau *m*, fiche *f*, étiquette *f*; *vt* classer, étiqueter.

dockyard ['dɔkjɑ:d] *n* chantier maritime *m*.

doctor ['dɔktə] *n* docteur *m*, médecin *m*; *vt* soigner, falsifier, cuisiner, doper, truquer, maquiller.

document ['dɔkjumənt] *n* document *m*; **—case** porte-documents *m*.

documentary [,dɔkju'mentəri] *a* documentaire

documentation [,dɔkjumen'teiʃən] *n* documentation *f*.

dodge [dɔdʒ] *n* tour *m*, faux-fuyant *m*, truc *m*, esquive *f*; *vi* se jeter de côté, s'esquiver, finasser; *vt* esquiver, éviter, tourner, éluder.

dodger ['dɔdʒə] *n* finaud *m*, tire-au-flanc *m*.

doe [dou] *n* daine *f*, lapine *f*.

doff [dɔf] *vt* ôter.

dog [dɔg] *n* chien *m*, chenet *m*, gaillard *m*; **dirty—** salaud *m*; **—tired** (*fam*) claqué.

dog-days ['dɔgdeiz] *n* canicule *f*.

dogged ['dɔgid] *a* tenace.

doggedness ['dɔgidnis] *n* ténacité *f*, persévérance *f*.

doggerel ['dɔgərəl] *n* poésie burlesque *f*; *a* trivial, boiteux, de mirliton.

dogma ['dɔgmə] *n* dogme *m*.

dogmatic [dɔg'mætik] *a* dogmatique, tranchant.

dog's ear ['dɔgz'iə] *n* corne *f*; *vt* faire une corne à, corner.

doily ['dɔili] *n* napperon *m*.

doings ['duːiŋz] *n pl* faits et gestes *m pl*, agissements *m pl*, exploits *m pl*.

doldrums ['dɔldrəmz] *n pl* **to be in the —** avoir le cafard, être dans le marasme.

dole [doul] *n* don *m*, aumône *f*, allocation de chômage *f*; **to — out** *vt* donner au compte-goutte.

doleful ['doulful] *a* triste, sombre, dolent, lugubre.

doll [dɔl] *n* poupée *f*.

dolphin ['dɔlfin] *n* dauphin *m*.

dolt [doult] *n* niais *m*, sot *m*.

domain [də'mein] *n* domaine *m*, propriété *f*.

dome [doum] *n* dôme *m*, coupole *f*.

domestic [də'mestik] *an* domestique *mf*; *a* d'intérieur, national, de ménage.

domesticate [də'mestikeit] *vt* domestiquer, apprivoiser.

domesticated [də'mestikeitid] *a* soumis, d'intérieur.

domesticity [,dɔmes'tisiti] *n* amour *m* du foyer, vie privée *f*, soumission *f*.

domicile ['dɔmisail] *n* domicile *m*.

dominate ['dɔmineit] *vti* dominer; *vt* commander.

domination [,dɔmi'neiʃən] *n* domination *f*.

domineer [,dɔmi'niə] *vt* tyranniser.

domineering [,dɔmi'niəriŋ] *a* dominateur, autoritaire.

dominican [də'minikən] *an* dominicain(e) *mf*.

dominion [də'minjən] *n* domination *f*, empire *m*; *pl* dominions *m pl*, colonies *f pl*.

don [dɔn] *vt* enfiler, endosser, revêtir; *n* professeur *m*.

Donald ['dɔnld] Daniel *m*.

donation [dou'neiʃən] *n* donation *f*, don *m*.

done [dʌn] *pp of* do; *a* fourbu, fini, conclu! tope là, cuit à point; **over—** trop cuit; **under—** saignant; **well —!** bravo! bien cuit.

donkey ['dɔŋki] *n* âne *m*, baudet *m*.

doom [duːm] *n* jugement *m* (dernier), ruine *f*, malheur *m*, sort *m*; *vt* condamner, vouer, perdre.

door [dɔː] *n* porte *f*, portière *f*.

doorkeeper ['dɔː,kiːpə] *n* concierge *mf*, portier *m*.

doormat ['dɔːmæt] *n* paillasson *m*.

doorstep ['dɔːstep] *n* pas *m*, seuil *m*.

dope [doup] *n* narcotique *m*, stupéfiant *m*, tuyau *m*, bourrage de crâne *m*; *vt* droguer, doper, endormir.

dormer ['dɔːmə] *n* lucarne *f*.

dormitory ['dɔːmitri] *n* dortoir *m*.

dormouse ['dɔːmaus] *n* loir *m*.

Dorothy ['dɔrəθi] Dorothée *f*.

dose [dous] *n* dose *f*; *vt* doser, droguer.

dot [dɔt] *n* point *m*; *vt* mettre les points sur, semer, pointiller, piquer.

dotage ['doutidʒ] *n* radotage *m*, seconde enfance *f*.

dotard ['doutəd] *n* gaga *m*, gâteux *m*.

dote [dout] *vt* radoter, raffoler (de on).

double ['dʌbl] *n* double *m*, crochet *m*, sosie *m*; *a* double; *ad* double (ment), deux fois, à double sens, en partie double; *vt* doubler, plier en deux; *vi* (se) doubler, prendre le pas de gymnastique.

double-dealer ['dʌbl'diːlə] *n* fourbe *m*.

double-dealing ['dʌbl'diːliŋ] *m* duplicité *f*.

double-declutch [,dʌbl'diː'klʌtʃ] *vi* (*aut*) faire un double débrayage.

double-dyed ['dʌbl'daid] *a* fieffé, achevé.

double-edged ['dʌbl'edʒd] *a* à deux tranchants.

double-lock ['dʌbl'lɔk] *vt* fermer à double tour.

double-quick ['dʌbl'kwik] *ad* au pas de course.

doubt [daut] *n* doute *m*; *vt* douter.

doubtful ['dautful] *a* douteux, incertain.

doubtless ['dautlis] *ad* sans doute.

dough [dou] *n* pâte *f*; (*sl*) fric *m*.

doughnut ['dounʌt] *n* beignet soufflé *m*, pet de nonne *m*.

doughy ['doui] *a* pâteux.

dour [duə] *a* sévère, obstiné, buté.

dove [dʌv] *n* colombe *f*.

dovecot(e) ['dʌvkɔt] *n* colombier *m*.

dovetail ['dʌvteil] *n* queue d'aronde *f*; *vi* s'encastrer; *vt* encastrer, assembler à queue d'aronde.

dowager ['dauədʒə] *n* douairière *f*.

dowdy ['daudi] *a* mal fagoté.

down [daun] *n* dune *f*; duvet *m*; bas *m*; *a* en bas, en pente, descendant; *prep* au (en) bas de; *ad* en bas, en aval, à bas! comptant, par écrit, en baisse; *vt* abattre, terrasser, descendre.

down-and-outer ['daunən'autə] *n* (US) pouilleux *m*, miséreux.

downcast ['daunka:st] *a* abattu, déprimé.

downfall ['daunfɔ:l] *n* chute *f*, ruine *f*.

downhearted ['daun'ha:tid] *a* découragé, abattu.

downpour ['daunpɔ:] *n* déluge *m*, forte pluie *f*.

downright ['daunrait] *a* franc, droit, net; *ad* carrément, catégoriquement.

downstairs ['daun'stɛəz] *ad* en bas.

downtrodden ['daun,trɔdn] *a* opprimé, foulé aux pieds.

downwards ['daunwədz] *ad* en aval, en descendant.

downy ['dauni] *a* duveté.

dowry ['dauri] *n* dot *f*, douaire *m*.

doze [douz] *n* somme *m*; *vi* sommeiller, s'assoupir.

dozen ['dʌzn] *n* douzaine *f*.

drab [dræb] *a* brunâtre, terne, ennuyeux, prosaïque.

draft [dra:ft] *n* détachement *m*, traite *f*, effet *m*, tracé *m*, brouillon *m*, projet *m*; (US) conscription *f*; *vt* détacher, désigner, esquisser, rédiger.

draftsman ['dra:ftsmən] *n* dessinateur *m*, rédacteur *m*.

drag [dræg] *n* drague *f*, herse *f*, traîneau *m*, obstacle *m*, grappin *m*, sabot *m*, résistance *f*; *vt* draguer, (en)traîner; *vi* tirer, traîner.

dragon ['drægən] *n* dragon *m*.

dragonfly ['drægənflai] *n* libellule *f*.

dragoon [drə'gu:n] *n* dragon *m*; *vt* persécuter, contraindre.

drain [drein] *n* fossé *m*, caniveau *m*, égout *m*, perte *f*, (*fig*) saignée *f*; *vt* drainer, assécher, assainir; *vi* s'écouler, s'égoutter.

drake [dreik] *n* canard *m*.

drama ['dra:mə] *n* drame *m*, le théâtre *m*.

dramatic [drə'mætik] *a* dramatique.

dramatist ['dræmətist] *n* dramaturge *m*.

dramatize ['dræmətaiz] *vt* mettre au théâtre, adapter à la scène, dramatiser.

drank ['dræŋk] *pt of* **drink**.

drape [dreip] *vt* draper.

draper ['dreipə] *n* drapier *m*, marchand *m* de nouveautés.

drapery ['dreipəri] *n* draperie *f*.

drastic ['dræstik] *a* radical, énergique.

draught [dra:ft] *n* traction *f*, courant d'air *m*, tirant d'eau *m*, coup *m* (de vin *etc*), esquisse *f*, traite *f*; *pl* jeu de dames *m*; **on** — à la pression.

draught-board ['dra:ftbɔ:d] *n* damier *m*.

draught-horse ['dra:fthɔ:s] *n* cheval *m* de trait.

draughtsman ['dra:ftsmən] *n* dessinateur *m*, rédacteur *m*, pion *m*.

draw [drɔ:] *n* tirage *m*, partie nulle *f*, question insidieuse *f*, loterie *f*, clou *m*, attraction *f*; *vt* (at-, re)tirer, traîner, tendre, aspirer, (*tooth*) extraire, (*salary*) toucher, faire parler, dessiner, rédiger; **to** — **aside** *vt* écarter, tirer; *vi* s'écarter; **to** — **back** *vt* retirer; *vi* reculer; **to** — **up** *vt* (re)lever, approcher; *vi* s'arrêter.

drawback ['drɔ:bæk] *n* remise *f*, mécompte *m*, échec *m*, inconvénient *m*.

drawbridge ['drɔ:bridʒ] *n* pont-levis *m*.

drawer ['drɔ:ə] *n* tiroir *m*; *pl* caleçon *m*, pantalon *m* de femme.

drawing ['drɔ:iŋ] *n* dessin *m*.

drawing-board ['drɔ:iŋbɔ:d] *n* planche *f*.

drawing-pin ['drɔ:iŋpin] *n* punaise *f*.

drawing-room ['drɔ:iŋrum] *n* salon *m*.

drawl [drɔ:l] *n* voix traînante *f*; *vt* traîner; *vi* parler d'une voix traînante

drawn [drɔ:n] *pp of* **draw**; *a* tiré, nul.

dray [drei] *n* camion *m*, haquet *m*.

dread [dred] *n* effroi *m*; *vt* redouter.

dreadful ['dredful] *a* terrible, horrible.

dreadnought ['drednɔ:t] *n* cuirassé *m*.

dream [dri:m] *n* rêve *m*, songe *m*; *vt* rêver.

dreamer ['dri:mə] *n* rêveur, -euse, songe-creux *m*.

dreamy ['dri:mi] *a* rêveur, songeur, vague.

dreary ['driəri] *a* lugubre, morne, ennuyeux, terne.

dredge [dredʒ] *n* drague *f*; *vt* draguer, curer, saupoudrer.

dredger ['dredʒə] *n* curemôle *m*, drague *f*.

dregs [dregz] *n* lie *f*.

drench [drentʃ] *vt* tremper, mouiller.

dress [dres] *n* vêtement *m*, tenue *f*, costume *m*, robe *f*, toilette *f*; **full** — grande tenue; *vt* habiller, vêtir, coiffer, pavoiser, aligner, parer, panser, tailler; *vi* s'habiller, faire sa toilette, se mettre (en habit), s'aligner.

dress-circle ['dres'sə:kl] *n* fauteuils *m pl* de balcon.

dresser ['dresə] *n* dressoir *m*, habilleuse *f*, apprêteur, -euse; (US) commode-toilette *f*.

dressing ['dresiŋ] *n* habillage *m*, toilette *f*, pansement *m*, assaisonnement *m*, apprêt *m*, alignement *m*.

dressing-case ['dresiŋkeis] *n* nécessaire *m* de toilette.

dressing-down ['dresiŋ'daun] *n* semonce *f*, savonnage *m*.

dressing-gown ['dresiŋgaun] *n* robe *f* de chambre, peignoir *m*.

dressing-room ['dresiŋrum] *n* cabinet *m* de toilette.

dressing-table ['dresiŋˌteibl] *n* coiffeuse *f*.

dressmaker ['dresˌmeikə] *n* couturier, -ière.

dressy ['dresi] *a* élégant, chic, qui aime la toilette.

drew [druː] *pt of* **draw**.

dribble ['dribl] *n* goutte *f*, dégouttement *m*, dribble *m*; *vi* dégoutter, baver, dribbler.

drift [drift] *n* débâcle *f*, dérive *f*, laisser-aller *m*, direction *f*, portée *f*, amas *m*; *vi* être emporté, dériver, s'amasser, se laisser aller; *vt* flotter, charrier.

drifter ['driftə] *n* chalutier *m*.

drill [dril] *n* foret *m*, mèche *f*, perforateur *m*, perceuse *f*, sillon *m*, semoir *m*, exercice *m*, manœuvre *f*; — **sergeant** sergent instructeur *m*; *vt* forer, semer, instruire, faire faire l'exercice à; *vi* faire l'exercice, manœuvrer.

drink [driŋk] *n* boisson *f*, alcool *m*, un verre *m*, ivrognerie *f*, boire *m*; *vt* boire.

drinkable ['driŋkəbl] *a* buvable, potable.

drinker ['driŋkə] *n* buveur, -euse, alcoolique *mf*.

drinking ['driŋkiŋ] *n* boire *m*, boisson *f*; —**water** eau potable *f*.

drip [drip] *vt* verser goutte à goutte; *vi* s'égoutter, dégoutter, dégouliner, suinter; *n* (d)égouttement *m*, dégoulinement *m*.

dripping ['dripiŋ] *n* graisse (à frire) *f*, (d)égouttement *m*; — **pan** lèchefrite *f*.

drive [draiv] *n* avance *f*, poussée *f*, randonnée *f*, promenade *f*, avenue *f*, tendance *f*, mouvement *m*, énergie *f*; *vt* pousser, entraîner, conduire, chasser, forcer, surmener, actionner; *vi* se promener, chasser, conduire; **driving school** auto-école *f*.

drivel ['drivl] *n* bave *f*, roupie *f*, radotage *n*; *vi* radoter, baver.

driver ['draivə] *n* mécanicien *m*, conducteur *m*, chauffeur, -euse.

drizzle ['drizl] *n* bruine *f*; *vi* bruiner.

droll [droul] *a* drôle.

drollery ['drouləri] *n* drôlerie *f*, bouffonnerie *f*.

dromedary ['drɔmədəri] *n* dromadaire *m*.

drone [droun] *n* bourdon *m*, bourdonnement *m*, ronronnement *m*, fainéant *m*; *vi* bourdonner, ronronner.

droop [druːp] *n* attitude penchée *f*, découragement *m*; *vt* laisser tomber, pendre, (a)baisser, pencher; *vi*

languir, se pencher, retomber, s'affaisser.

drop [drɔp] *n* goutte *f*, pastille *f*, chute *f*, baisse *f*, rideau *m*, pendant *m*; *vi* s'égoutter, se laisser tomber, tomber, plonger, baisser; *vt* laisser tomber, baisser, lâcher, abandonner, laisser, verser goutte à goutte; **to — in** entrer en passant; **to — off** partir, s'endormir.

dropsy ['drɔpsi] *n* hydropisie *f*.

drought [draut] *n* sécheresse *f*.

drove [drouv] *n* troupeau *m*, foule *f*.

drover ['drouvə] *n* toucheur de bœufs *m*.

drown [draun] *vt* noyer, tremper, inonder, couvrir; *vi* se noyer.

drowsiness ['drauzinis] *n* somnolence *f*.

drowsy ['drauzi] *a* assoupi, endormi, soporifique.

drubbing ['drʌbiŋ] *n* (*fam*) raclée *f*, tripotée *f*.

drudge [drʌdʒ] *n* tâcheron *m*, femme de peine *f*, souffre-douleur *mf*; *vi* trimer.

drudgery ['drʌdʒəri] *n* corvée *f*, travail ingrat *m*.

drug [drʌg] *n* drogue *f*, stupéfiant *m*, (*fig*) rossignol *m*; *vt* droguer, endormir.

druggist ['drʌgist] *n* droguiste *m*, pharmacien *m*.

drum [drʌm] *n* tympan *m*; bonbonne *f*, tambour *m*; **big —** grosse caisse; **African —** tam-tam *m*.

drummer ['drʌmə] *n* tambour *m*.

drum-fire ['drʌm'faiə] *m* feu roulant *m*.

drumming ['drʌmiŋ] *n* bourdonnement *m*, battement *m*, tambourinage *m*.

drunk [drʌŋk] *pp of* **drink**; *a* ivre, saoûl.

drunkard ['drʌŋkəd] *n* ivrogne, ivrognesse.

drunkenness ['drʌŋkənnis] *n* ivresse *f*, ivrognerie *f*.

dry [drai] *a* sec, à sec, tari, caustique; *n* (*US*) prohibitionniste *m*; *vt* (faire) sécher, essuyer; *vi* sécher, se dessécher, tarir.

dryness ['drainis] *n* sécheresse *f*.

dub [dʌb] *vt* armer, traiter (de), doubler.

dubious ['djuːbjəs] *a* douteux, louche, incertain.

duchess ['dʌtʃis] *n* duchesse *f*.

duchy ['dʌtʃi] *n* duché *m*.

duck [dʌk] *n* canard *m*, cane *f*, plongeon *m*, courbette *f*, esquive *f*, coutil *m*; *vti* plonger; *vi* se baisser, esquiver de la tête.

duckling ['dʌkliŋ] *n* caneton *m*.

duct [dʌkt] *n* conduit *m*, conduite *f*.

dud [dʌd] *n* raté *m*; *pl* nippes *f pl*; *a* moche, faux.

dudgeon ['dʌdʒən] *n* colère *f*.

due [djuː] *n* dû *m*, dettes *f pl*, droits *m pl*; *a* dû, attendu.

duel ['djuəl] n duel m; vi se battre en duel.

duellist ['djuəlist] n duelliste m, bretteur m.

duet [dju'et] n duo m.

duffer ['dʌfə] n cancre m, empoté(e) mf, maladroit(e) mf.

dug [dʌg] pt pp of **dig**; n pis m, téton m.

dug-out ['dʌgaut] n trou m, abri m, cagna m.

duke [djuːk] n duc m.

dull [dʌl] a ennuyeux, stupide, insensible, émoussé, terne, sourd, mat, sombre; vt amortir, émousser, ternir, hébéter.

dullard ['dʌləd] n balourd(e) mf, cancre m.

dullness ['dʌlnis] n hébétude f, lourdeur f, monotonie f, marasme m.

duly ['djuːli] ad dûment, à point.

dumb [dʌm] a muet, sot; ——**bell** haltère f; — **show** pantomime f.

dumbfounded [dʌm'faundid] a éberlué, interdit.

dumbness ['dʌmnis] n mutisme m.

dummy ['dʌmi] n homme de paille m, mannequin m, silhouette f, mort m, (of baby) sucette f, maquette f; a faux, postiche.

dump [dʌmp] n dépôt m (de munitions), (fam) trou m; vt décharger, déposer (avec un bruit sourd); vi faire du dumping.

dumpling ['dʌmpliŋ] n chausson m.

dumps [dʌmps] n pl cafard m; **to be in the** —s avoir le cafard, broyer du noir.

dumpy ['dʌmpi] a trapu, replet, boulot.

dun [dʌn] a gris-brun; vt relancer, importuner.

dunce [dʌns] n endormi(e) mf, cancre m, crétin m; —'s **cap** bonnet m d'âne.

dung [dʌŋ] n bouse f, fiente f, crottin m.

dungeon ['dʌndʒn] n cul-de-basse-fosse m, cachot m.

dunghill ['dʌŋhil] n fumier m.

dunk ['dʌŋk] vt tremper; vi faire trempette.

dupe [djuːp] n dupe f; vt duper.

duplex ['djuːpleks] a double.

duplicate ['djuːplikit] n double m; a double de rechange.

duplicate ['djuːplikeit] vt établir en double.

duplicity [dju'plisiti] n duplicité f.

durable ['djuərəbl] a durable, résistant.

duration [djuə'reiʃən] n durée f.

duress [djuə'res] n contrainte f, emprisonnement m.

during ['djuəriŋ] prep pendant, au cours de.

durst [dəːst] pt (old) of **dare**.

dusk [dʌsk] n crépuscule m.

dusky ['dʌski] a sombre, brun, foncé, noiraud.

dust [dʌst] n poussière f; vt saupoudrer, couvrir de poussière, épousseter; — **coat** cache-poussière m; — **jacket** protège-livre m.

dustbin ['dʌstbin] n boîte à ordures f, poubelle f.

duster ['dʌstə] n torchon m, chiffon à épousseter m.

dustman ['dʌstmən] n balayeur m, boueux m.

dusty ['dʌsti] a poussiéreux, poudreux.

dutiable ['djuːtjəbl] a imposable, taxable.

dutiful ['djuːtiful] a respectueux, soumis.

duty ['djuːti] n devoir m, taxe f, droits m pl; **on** — de service; — **paid** franco, franc de douane.

dwarf [dwɔːf] n nain m.

dwell [dwel] vi demeurer, s'étendre (sur **on**).

dwelling ['dweliŋ] n maison f, demeure f.

dwelt [dwelt] pt of **dwell**.

dwindle ['dwindl] vi fondre, dépérir.

dye [dai] n teinte f, teinture f, teint m; — **works** teinturerie f; vt teindre, teinter; vi se teindre.

dyer ['daiə] n teinturier m.

dying ['daiiŋ] a mourant, de mort.

dynamite ['dainəmait] n dynamite f; vt faire sauter à la dynamite.

dynasty ['dinəsti] n dynastie f.

dysentery ['disntri] n dysenterie f.

dyspepsia [dis'pepsiə] n dyspepsie f.

dyspeptic [dis'peptik] a dyspeptique.

E

each [iːtʃ] a chaque; pn chacun(e); **two francs** — deux francs la pièce; — **other** l'un l'autre, entre eux.

eager ['iːgə] a empressé, ardent, avide, impatient.

eagerly ['iːgəli] ad ardemment, avec empressement.

eagerness ['iːgənis] n ardeur f, empressement m.

eagle ['iːgl] n aigle m.

eaglet ['iːglit] n aiglon m.

ear [iə] n oreille f, (corn) épi m, (tec) anse f.

ear-drop ['iədrɔp] n pendant d'oreille m.

ear-drum ['iədrʌm] n tympan m.

early ['əːli] a matinal, précoce, prochain, premier; **in** — **summer** au début de l'été; ad de bonne heure, tôt.

ear-mark ['iəmaːk] vt réserver, assigner.

earn [əːn] vt gagner.

earnest ['əːnist] n présage m, (com) arrhes f pl, avant-goût m; a sérieux, sincère, consciencieux; **in** — pour de bon.

earnestly ['əːnistli] ad sérieusement, instamment.

earnestness ['ə:nistnis] n sérieux m, sincérité f, ardeur f, ferveur f.

earnings ['ə:niŋz] n gain(s) m, gages m pl.

earring ['iəriŋ] n boucle f d'oreille.

earshot ['iəʃɔt] n portée f de la voix.

earth [ə:θ] n terre f, terrier m; vt relier au sol.

earthen ['ə:θən] a de (en) terre.

earthenware ['ə:θənwɛə] n faïence f, poterie f; — pot canari m.

earthliness ['ə:θlinis] n mondanité f.

earthly ['ə:θli] a terrestre.

earthquake ['ə:θkweik] n tremblement m de terre.

earthworks ['ə:θwə:ks] n terrassements m pl.

earthworm ['ə:θwə:m] n ver m de terre.

earthy ['ə:θi] a terreux.

ear-trumpet ['iə.trʌmpit] n cornet acoustique m.

earwig ['iəwig] n perce-oreille(s) m.

ease [i:z] n facilité f, tranquillité f, aise f, soulagement m; (mil) repos m; vt soulager, calmer, détendre; to — up ralentir, freiner, se relâcher.

easel ['i:zl] n chevalet m.

easily ['i:zili] ad facilement, aisément, tranquillement.

east [i:st] n est m, levant m, orient m; Near E— proche Orient; Middle E— moyen Orient; Far E— extrême Orient.

Easter ['i:stə] n Pâques f pl.

easterly ['i:stəli] a oriental, d'est; ad vers l'est.

eastern ['i:stən] a oriental, de l'est.

eastward ['i:stwəd] ad vers l'est; a à l'est.

easy ['i:zi] a facile, aisé, à l'aise, tranquille, accommodant, dégagé.

easy-chair ['i:zi'tʃɛə] n fauteuil m.

easy-going ['i:zi.gouiŋ] a débonnaire, qui ne s'en fait pas, accommodant.

eat [i:t] vt manger.

eatable ['i:təbl] a mangeable.

eatables ['i:təblz] n pl comestibles m pl, provisions f pl.

eaten ['i:tn] pp of eat; — up with dévoré de, consumé par, pétri de.

eating ['i:tiŋ] n manger m; a à croquer, de dessert.

eaves [i:vz] n avance f de toit.

eavesdrop ['i:vzdrɔp] vi écouter aux portes.

ebb [eb] n reflux m, déclin m; vi refluer, décliner.

E-boat ['i:bout] n vedette lance-torpilles f.

ebony ['ebəni] n ébène f.

ebullience [i'bʌljəns] n exubérance f, effervescence f.

ebullient [i'bʌljənt] a exubérant, bouillant.

ebullition [.ebə'liʃən] n ébullition f, effervescence f.

eccentric [ik'sentrik] a excentrique, original.

eccentricity [.eksen'trisiti] n excentricité f.

echo ['ekou] n écho m; vt faire écho à, se faire l'écho de, répéter; vi faire écho, retentir.

eclipse [i'klips] n éclipse f; vt éclipser.

economic [.i:kə'nɔmik] a économique.

economical [.i:kə'nɔmikəl] a économe, économique.

economics [.i:kə'nɔmiks] n économie politique f, régime économique m.

economist [i:'kɔnəmist] n économiste m.

economize [i:'kɔnəmaiz] vt économiser; vi faire des économies.

economy [i:'kɔnəmi] n économie f.

ecstasy ['ekstəsi] n extase f, transe f, ravissement m.

ecstatic [eks'tætik] a extatique, en extase.

eddy ['edi] n remous m, volute f, tourbillon m.

edge [edʒ] n bord m, bordure f, fil m, tranchant m; on — agacé, énervé; vt border, aiguiser; to — (in); to — one's way (in) se faufiler (dans); to — away s'écarter tout doucement.

edgeless ['edʒlis] a émoussé.

edgeways ['edʒweiz] ad de côté, de champ; to get a word in — glisser un mot dans la conversation.

edible ['edibl] a mangeable, comestible, bon à manger.

edict ['i:dikt] n édit m.

edify ['edifai] vt édifier.

edit ['edit] vt éditer, rédiger.

edition [i'diʃən] n édition f.

editor ['editə] n éditeur m, rédacteur en chef m, directeur m.

editorial [.edi'tɔ:riəl] an éditorial m; n article de fond m.

educate ['edju:keit] vt instruire, élever, former; he was educated in Paris il a fait ses études à Paris.

education [.edju:'keiʃən] n éducation f, instruction f, enseignement m.

educational [.edju:'keiʃənl] a d'enseignement, éducateur.

educative ['edju:kətiv] a éducatif.

educator ['edju:keitə] n éducateur, -trice.

Edward ['edwəd] Edouard m.

eel [i:l] n anguille f.

eerie ['iəri] a étrange, fantastique, surnaturel.

efface [i'feis] vt effacer, oblitérer.

effect [i'fekt] n effet m, influence f, conséquence f; of no — inutile, inefficace; to no — en vain; for — à effet; to the same — dans le même sens; in — en fait, en réalité; vt exécuter, accomplir.

effective [i'fektiv] n effectif m; a effectif, efficace, valide.

effectively [i'fektivli] ad en réalité, efficacement.

effectiveness [i'fektivnis] n efficacité f.

effeminate [i'feminit] *a* efféminé.

effervesce [,efə'ves] *vi* bouillonner, mousser.

effervescence [,efə'vesns] *n* effervescence *f*.

effete [e'fi:t] *a* épuisé, caduc.

efficacious [,efi'keiʃəs] *a* efficace.

efficaciousness [,efi'keiʃəsnis] *n* efficacité *f*.

efficacy ['efikəsi] *n* efficacité *f*, rapidité *f*.

efficiency [i'fiʃənsi] *n* efficience *f*, efficacité *f*, rendement *m*, capacité *f*, valeur *f*.

efficient [i'fiʃənt] *a* efficace, compétent, effectif, capable.

efficiently [i'fiʃəntli] *ad* efficacement.

effigy ['efidʒi] *n* effigie *f*.

effort ['efət] *n* effort m.

effortless ['efətlis] *a* sans effort, passif, facile.

effrontery [e'frʌntəri] *n* effronterie *f*.

effulgence [e'fʌldʒəns] *n* éclat m, splendeur *f*.

effulgent [e'fʌldʒənt] *a* resplendissant, éclatant.

effusion [i'fju:ʒən] *n* effusion *f*, épanchement m.

effusive [i'fju:siv] *a* expansif, démonstratif.

effusiveness [i'fju:sivnis] *n* exubérance *f*, effusion *f*.

egg [eg] *n* œuf m; **new-laid —** œuf frais; **boiled —** œuf à la coque; **hard-boiled —** œuf dur; **soft-boiled —** œuf mollet; **fried —** œuf sur le plat; **poached —** œuf poché; **scrambled —s** œufs brouillés; *vt* **to — on** encourager.

egg-cup ['egkʌp] *n* coquetier m.

egg-spoon ['egspu:n] *n* petite cuiller *f*.

egg-whisk ['egwisk] *n* fouet m.

eglantine ['egləntain] *n* églantine *f*, églantier m.

ego ['egou] *n* le moi.

egoist ['egouist] *an* égoïste *mf*.

egregious [i'gri:dʒəs] *a* énorme, insigne.

egret ['i:gret] *n* aigrette *f*.

Egyptian [i'dʒipʃən] *an* égyptien.

eiderdown ['aidədaun] *n* édredon m.

eight [eit] *an* huit m.

eighteen ['ei'ti:n] *an* dixhuit m.

eighteenth ['ei'ti:nθ] *an* dixhuit m, dix-huitième *mf*.

eighth [eitθ] *an* huit m, huitième *mf*.

eightieth ['eitiiθ] *an* quatre-vingts m, quatre-vingtième *mf*.

eighty ['eiti] *an* quatre-vingts m.

either ['aiðə] *pn* l'un et (ou) l'autre; *a* chaque; **on — side** de chaque côté; *cj* ou, soit, non plus; **— ... or** ou ... ou, soit ... soit; **not ... —** ne ... non plus.

eject [i:'dʒekt] *vt* jeter (dehors), expulser, émettre.

eke out ['i:k 'aut] *vt* ajouter à, compléter, faire durer.

elaborate [i'læbəreit] *vt* élaborer.

elaborate [i'læbərit] *a* compliqué, soigné, tiré, recherché.

elaboration [i,læbə'reiʃən] *n* élaboration *f*.

elapse [i'læps] *vi* s'écouler.

elastic [i'læstik] *an* élastique m.

elasticity [,elæs'tisiti] *n* élasticité *f*.

elated [i'leitid] *a* gonflé, transporté, exultant, enivré.

elation [i'leiʃən] *n* orgueil m, ivresse *f*, exaltation *f*.

elbow ['elbou] *n* coude m; *vt* coudoyer, pousser des coudes; *vi* jouer des coudes; **to have — room** avoir ses coudées franches.

elder ['eldə] *n* (*bot*) sureau m; aîné(e) *mf*, Ancien m; *a* plus âgé, aîné.

elderly ['eldəli] *a* d'un certain âge.

eldest ['eldist] *a* aîné.

elect [i'lekt] *vt* choisir, élire; *a* désigné, élu.

election [i'lekʃən] *n* élection *f*.

electioneer [i lekʃə'niə] *vi* mener une campagne électorale.

electioneering [i,lekʃə'niəriŋ] *n* campagne *f* (propagande *f*) électorale.

elector [i'lektə] *n* électeur m, votant m.

electorate [i'lektərit] *n* corps électoral m.

electric [i'lektrik] *a* électrique.

electrical [i'lektrikəl] *a* électrique.

electrician [ilek'triʃən] *n* électricien m.

electricity [ilek'trisiti] *n* électricité *f*.

electrification [i lektrifi'keiʃən] *n* électrification *f*.

electrify [i'lektrifai] *vt* électrifier, électriser.

electrocute [i'lektrəkju:t] *vt* électrocuter.

electrocution [i,lektrə'kju:ʃən] *n* électrocution *f*.

electrolier [i,lektrou'liə] *n* lustre électrique m.

electron [i'lektrɔn] *n* électron m.

electroplate [i'lektroupleit] *n* ruolz m, articles m *pl* argentés; *vt* plaquer.

electrotyping [i'lektrou'taipiŋ] *n* galvanoplastie *f*.

elegance ['eligəns] *n* élégance *f*.

elegant ['eligənt] *a* élégant.

elegantly ['eligəntli] *ad* élégamment.

elegy ['elidʒi] *n* élégie *f*.

element ['elimənt] *n* élément m, facteur m; *pl* rudiments m *pl*.

elementary [,eli'mentəri] *a* élémentaire, primaire.

elephant ['elifənt] *n* éléphant m.

elevate ['eliveit] *vt* élever.

elevation [,eli'veiʃən] *n* élévation *f*, altitude *f*.

elevator ['eliveitə] *n* (*US*) ascenseur m.

eleven [i'levn] *an* onze m.

eleventh [i'levnθ] *n* onze; *an* onzième *mf*.

elf [elf] *n* elfe m, lutin m.

elicit [i'lisit] *vt* extraire, tirer.

elide [i'laid] *vt* élider.

eligible ['elidʒəbl] *a* éligible, admissible, désirable.

eliminate [i'limineit] *vt* éliminer.

elimination [i,limi'neiʃən] *n* élimination *f*.

elision [i'liʒən] *n* élision *f*.

elixir [i'liksə] *n* élixir *m*.

elk [elk] *n* élan *m*.

ell [el] *n* aûne *f*.

elm [elm] *n* orme *m*.

elongate ['iːlɔŋgeit] *vt* allonger; *vi* s'allonger.

elope [i'loup] *vi* se laisser (se faire) enlever, prendre la fuite.

elopement [i'loupmənt] *n* enlèvement *m*, fuite *f*.

eloquence ['eləkwəns] *n* éloquence *f*.

eloquent ['eləkwənt] *a* éloquent.

eloquently ['eləkwəntli] *ad* éloquemment.

else [els] *a* (d')autre de plus; *ad* autrement, ou bien; **something** — autre chose *m*; **everywhere** — partout ailleurs; **anybody** — quelqu'un d'autre.

elsewhere ['els'wɛə] *ad* ailleurs, autre part.

elucidate [i'luːsideit] *vt* élucider, éclaircir.

elucidation [i,luːsi'deiʃən] *n* élucidation *f*.

elude [i'luːd] *vt* éluder, échapper à, esquiver.

elusive [i'luːsiv] *a* fuyant, insaisissable, évasif, souple.

elusiveness [i'luːsivnis] *n* souplesse fuyante *f*, intangibilité *f*.

emaciated [i'meiʃieitid] *a* émacié, décharné.

emaciation [i,meisi'eiʃən] *n* maigreur extrême *f*.

emanate ['eməneit] *vi* émaner.

emanation [,emə'neiʃən] *n* émanation *f*.

emancipate [i'mænsipeit] *vt* émanciper.

emancipator [i'mænsipeitə] *n* émancipateur, -trice.

emasculate [i'mæskjuleit] *vt* châtrer, expurger.

embalm [im'baːm] *vt* embaumer.

embalming [im'baːmiŋ] *n* embaumement *m*.

embank [im'bæŋk] *vt* endiguer, remblayer.

embankment [im'bæŋkmənt] *n* quai *m*, remblai *m*, levée *f*.

embargo [em'baːgou] *n* embargo *m*, séquestre *m*; **to put an — on** mettre l'embargo sur, interdire.

embark [im'baːk] *vt* embarquer; *vi* s'embarquer.

embarkation [,embaː'keiʃən] *n* embarquement *m*.

embarrass [im'bærəs] *vt* gêner, embarrasser.

embarrassment [im'bærəsmənt] *n* embarrass *m*, gêne *f*.

embassy ['embəsi] *n* ambassade *f*.

embedded [im'bedid] *a* pris, enfoncé.

embellish [im'beliʃ] *vt* embellir, enjoliver.

embellishment [im'beliʃmənt] *n* embellissement *m*.

ember ['embə] *n* braise *f*; **— days** Quatre-Temps *m pl*.

embezzle [im'bezl] *vt* détourner.

embezzlement [im'bezlmənt] *n* détournement *m*.

embitter [im'bitə] *vt* envenimer, aigrir, aggraver.

embitterment [im'bitəmənt] *n* aigreur *f*, aggravation *f*, envenimement *m*.

emblem ['embləm] *n* emblème *m*, symbole *m*.

emblematic [,embli'mætik] *a* emblématique, figuratif.

embodiment [im'bɔdimənt] *n* incarnation *f*.

embody [im'bɔdi] *vt* incarner, donner corps à, exprimer, incorporer.

embolden [im'bouldən] *vt* enhardir.

embolism ['embəlizəm] *n* embolie *f*.

emboss [im'bɔs] *vt* estamper, repousser.

embossing [im'bɔsiŋ] *n* relief *m*, brochage *m* (d'étoffes), repoussage *m*.

embrace [im'breis] *n* embrassement *m*, étreinte *f*; *vt* embrasser, étreindre, saisir, adopter, comporter.

embrasure [im'breiʒə] *n* embrasure *f*.

embroider [im'brɔidə] *vt* broder.

embroidery [im'brɔidəri] *n* broderie *f*.

embroil [im'brɔil] *vt* (em)brouiller, envelopper, entraîner.

embroilment [im'brɔilmənt] *n* imbroglio *m*.

embryo ['embriou] *n* embryon *m*.

embryonic [,embri'ɔnik] *a* embryonnaire, en herbe.

emend [iː'mend] *vt* corriger.

emendation [,iːmen'deiʃən] *n* correction *f*, émendation *f*.

emerald ['emərəld] *n* émeraude *f*.

emerge [i'məːdʒ] *vi* émerger, sortir.

emergency [i'məːdʒənsi] *n* crise *f*, éventualité *f*; **— brake,** — **exit** frein *m*, sortie *f* de secours.

emery ['eməri] *n* émeri *m*; **— cloth** toile *f* d'émeri.

emetic [i'metik] *n* vomitif *m*.

emigrant ['emigrənt] *n* émigrant(e) *mf*, émigré *m*.

emigrate ['emigreit] *vi* émigrer.

emigration [,emi'greiʃən] *n* émigration *f*.

eminence ['eminəns] *n* éminence *f*, distinction *f*.

eminent ['eminənt] *a* éminent.

eminently ['eminəntli] *ad* éminemment, par excellence.

emissary ['emisəri] *n* émissaire *m*.

emission [i'miʃən] *n* émission *f*.

emit [i'mit] *vt* émettre.

emoluments [i'mɔljumənts] *n pl* émoluments *m pl*, traitement *m*, appointements *m pl*.

emotion [i'mouʃən] *n* émotion *f*, trouble *m*.

emotive [i'moutiv] *a* émotif.

emperor ['empərə] *n* empereur *m*.

emphasis ['emfəsis] *n* accent *m*, intensité *f*, insistance *f*, force *f*.

emphasize ['emfəsaiz] *vt* mettre en relief, souligner.

emphatic [im'fætik] *a* expressif, accentué, significatif, énergique, positif, net.

empire ['empaiə] *n* empire *m*.

employ [im'plɔi] *n* service *m*; *vt* employer.

employee [ˌemplɔi'iː] *n* employé(e) *mf*.

employer [im'plɔiə] *n* patron, -onne, employeur *m*, maître, -tresse.

employment [im'plɔimənt] *n* situation *f*, travail *m*, emploi *m*.

empower [im'pauə] *vt* autoriser, donner pouvoir à.

empress ['empris] *n* impératrice *f*.

emptiness ['emptinis] *n* vide *m*, néant *m*.

empty ['empti] *a* vide, vain, inoccupé; **to come back ——handed** revenir bredouille; *vt* vider; *vi* se décharger, se vider.

emulate ['emjuleit] *vt* rivaliser avec, imiter.

emulation [ˌemju'leiʃən] *n* émulation *f*.

enable [i'neibl] *vt* mettre à même (de to), permettre (à), autoriser.

enact [i'nækt] *vt* ordonner, décréter, jouer.

enactment [i'næktmənt] *n* décret *m*, promulgation *f*.

enamel [i'næməl] *n* émail *m*, vernis *m*; *vt* émailler, vernir.

enameller [i'næmələ] *n* émailleur *m*.

encamp [in'kæmp] *vt* (faire) camper; *vi* camper.

encampment [in'kæmpmənt] *n* campement *m*, camp *m*.

encase [in'keis] *vt* enfermer, encaisser, revêtir.

enchant [in'tʃɑːnt] *vt* enchanter, ensorceler.

enchanting [in'tʃɑːntiŋ] *a* enchanteur, ravissant.

enchantment [in'tʃɑːntmənt] *n* enchantement *m*, ravissement *m*.

encircle [in'səːkl] *vt* encercler, entourer, cerner.

enclave [in'kleiv] *n* enclave *f*.

enclose [in'klouz] *vt* enclore, entourer, (r)enfermer, insérer.

enclosed [in'klouzd] *a* ci-inclus, ci-joint.

enclosure [in'klouʒə] *n* clôture *f*, enceinte *f*, (en)clos *m*, pièce incluse *f*.

encompass [in'kʌmpəs] *vt* entourer, contenir, renfermer.

encore [ɔŋ'kɔː] *excl* bis *m*; *vt* bisser.

encounter [in'kauntə] *n* rencontre *f*, combat *n*, assaut *m*; *vt* rencontrer, affronter, essuyer.

encourage [in'kʌridʒ] *vt* encourager, favoriser.

encouragement [in'kʌridʒmənt] *n* encouragement *m*.

encroach [in'kroutʃ] *vi* empiéter (sur **upon**).

encroachment [in'kroutʃmənt] *n* empiètement *m*, usurpation *f*.

encrust [in'krʌst] *vt* incruster, encroûter.

encumber [in'kʌmbə] *vt* gêner, embarrasser, encombrer, grever.

encumbrance [in'kʌmbrəns] *n* charge *f*, encombrement *m*, embarras *m*.

encyclic [en'siklik] *an* encyclique *f*.

encyclopedia [en'saiklou'piːdjə] *n* encyclopédie *f*.

encyclopedic [enˌsaiklou'piːdik] *a* encyclopédique.

end [end] *n* fin *f*, bout *m*, extrémité *f*; *vti* finir; *vt* terminer, achever; *vi* se terminer; **on** — debout, de suite; **in the** — au bout du compte, à la fin; **to the bitter** — jusqu'au bout.

endanger [in'deindʒə] *vt* mettre en danger, exposer.

endear [in'diə] *vt* rendre cher, faire aimer.

endeavour [in'devə] *n* effort *m*, tentative *f*; *vi* s'efforcer, tenter.

ending ['endiŋ] *n* fin *f*, conclusion *f*, dénouement *m*, terminaison *f*; *a* final, dernier.

endive ['endiv] *n* chicorée *f*.

endless ['endlis] *a* sans fin, interminable.

endorse [in'dɔːs] *vt* appuyer, endosser, estampiller.

endorsement [in'dɔːsmənt] *n* (*fin*) endossement *m*, (*passport*) mention *f*, approbation *f*.

endow [in'dau] *vt* doter, investir.

endowed [in'daud] *a* doué, muni.

endowment [in'daumənt] *n* dotation *f*, fondation *f*.

endurable [in'djuərəbl] *a* supportable.

endurance [in'djuərəns] *n* résistance *f*, endurance *f*.

endure [in'djuə] *vt* supporter, endurer.

enduring [in'duəriŋ] *a* durable, qui persiste.

enemy ['enimi] *an* ennemi(e) *mf*.

energetic [ˌenə'dʒetik] *a* énergique.

energy ['enədʒi] *n* énergie *f*, vigueur *f*, nerf *m*.

enervate ['enəːveit] *vt* énerver, amollir.

enervation [ˌenəː'veiʃən] *n* énervement *m*, mollesse *f*.

enfeeble [in'fiːbl] *vt* affaiblir.

enfeeblement [in'fiːblmənt] *n* affaiblissement *m*.

enfilade [ˌenfi'leid] *n* enfilade *f*; *vt* prendre d'enfilade.

enforce [in'fɔːs] *vt* imposer, faire respecter, mettre en vigueur, appliquer.

enforcement [in'fɔːsmənt] *n* application *f*, mise *f* en vigueur.

enfranchise [in'fræntʃaiz] *vt* donner le droit de vote à, ériger en circonscription.

engage [in'geidʒ] *vt* occuper, engager, retenir, embaucher, attirer.

engaged [in'geidʒd] *a* occupé, retenu, fiancé.

engagement [in'geidʒmənt] *n* engagement *m*, fiançailles *f pl*, combat *m*.

engender [in'dʒendə] *vt* engendrer, faire naître.

engine ['endʒin] *n* engin *m*, machine *f*, locomotive *f*, moteur *m*.

engine-driver ['endʒin,draivə] *n* mécanicien *m*.

engineer [,endʒi'niə] *n* ingénieur *m*, mécanicien *m*; *pl* (*mil*) le génie *m*; *vt* construire, machiner, combiner.

engineering [,endʒi'niəriŋ] *n* génie *m*, construction *f*, mécanique *f*.

England ['iŋglənd] *n* Angleterre *f*.

English ['iŋgliʃ] *n* Anglais(e) *mf*; *an* anglais *m*.

Englishman ['iŋgliʃmən] *n* Anglais *m*.

engrave [in'greiv] *vt* graver.

engraver [in'greivə] *n* graveur *m*.

engraving [in'greiviŋ] *n* gravure *f*.

engross [in'grous] *vt* accaparer, absorber.

engulf [in'gʌlf] *vt* engloutir.

enhance [in'haːns] *vt* (re)hausser, relever, mettre en valeur, accroître.

enhancement [in'haːnsmənt] *n* mise *f* en valeur.

enigma [i'nigmə] *n* énigme *f*.

enigmatic [,enig'mætik] *a* énigmatique.

enjoin [in'dʒɔin] *vt* enjoindre, recommander.

enjoy [in'dʒɔi] *vt* aimer, goûter, jouir de, prendre plaisir à; **to — oneself** s'amuser.

enjoyable [in'dʒɔiəbl] *a* agréable.

enjoyment [in'dʒɔimənt] *n* plaisir *m*, jouissance *f*.

enlarge [in'laːdʒ] *vt* accroître, agrandir, élargir, développer; *vi* s'élargir, s'agrandir; **to — upon** s'étendre sur.

enlargement [in'laːdʒmənt] *n* agrandissement *m*, accroissement *m*.

enlighten [in'laitn] *vt* éclairer.

enlightenment [in'laitnmənt] *n* lumières *f pl*.

enlist [in'list] *vt* enrôler; *vi* s'engager.

enlistment [in'listmənt] *n* enrôlement *m*.

enliven [in'laivn] *vt* animer, inspirer, égayer.

enmity ['enmiti] *n* hostilité *f*, inimitié *f*.

ennoble [i'noubl] *vt* anoblir, ennoblir.

enormity [i'nɔːmiti] *n* énormité *f*.

enormous [i'nɔːməs] *a* énorme, gigantesque.

enormously [i'nɔːməsli] *ad* énormément.

enough [i'nʌf] *a n ad* assez (de), suffisamment.

enquire [in'kwaiə] *vi* se renseigner (sur **about**), s'informer (de **about**).

enrage [in'reidʒ] *vt* exaspérer, faire enrager.

enrapture [in'ræptʃə] *vt* ravir, transporter.

enrich [in'ritʃ] *vt* enrichir.

enrol [in'roul] *vt* enrôler, immatriculer, enregistrer.

enrolment [in'roulmənt] *n* enrôlement *m*, enregistrement *m*, embauche *f*.

ensconce [in'skɔns] **to — oneself** se nicher, s'installer, se carrer.

enshrine [in'ʃrain] *vt* enchâsser.

enshroud [in'ʃraud] *vt* cacher, voiler, envelopper.

ensign ['ensain] *n* insigne *m*, pavillon *m*, porte-drapeau *m*.

enslave [in'sleiv] *vt* asservir.

enslavement [in'sleivmənt] *n* asservissement *m*.

ensnare [in'snɛə] *vt* prendre au piège, dans ses filets.

ensue [in'sjuː] *vi* s'ensuivre.

ensure [in'ʃuə] *vt* mettre en sûreté, (s')assurer.

entail [in'teil] *vt* impliquer, entraîner, occasionner.

entangle [in'tæŋgl] *vt* embrouiller, emmêler, empêtrer.

entanglement [in'tæŋglmənt] *n* enchevêtrement *m*; *pl* complications *f pl*.

enter ['entə] *vt* entrer dans; *vi* entrer, se faire inscrire; *vt* enregistrer, inscrire.

enterprise ['entəpraiz] *n* entreprise *f*, initiative *f*.

enterprising ['entəpraiziŋ] *a* entreprenant.

entertain [,entə'tein] *vt* recevoir, entretenir, caresser, amuser, régaler.

entertaining [,entə'teiniŋ] *a* amusant, divertissant.

entertainment [,entə'teinmənt] *n* amusement *m*, fête *f*, divertissement *m*.

enthrall [in'θrɔːl] *vt* ensorceler, charmer, envoûter.

enthrone [in'θroun] *vt* mettre sur le trône, introniser.

enthronement [in'θrounmənt] *n* couronnement *m*, intronisation *f*.

enthusiasm [in'θjuːziæzəm] *n* enthousiasme *m*.

enthusiast [in'θjuːziæst] *n* enthousiaste *mf*, fervent(e) *mf*.

enthusiastic [in,θjuːzi'æstik] *a* enthousiaste, passionné.

entice [in'tais] *vt* attirer, séduire; **enticing** séduisant.

enticement [in'taismənt] *n* attrait *m*, séduction *f*.

entire [in'taiə] *a* entier, complet, tout, pur.

entirely [in'taiəli] *ad* entièrement, tout à fait.

entirety [in'taiəti] n totalité f, intégralité f.

entitle [in'taitl] vt intituler, donner le titre, le droit, à, autoriser.

entomb [in'tu:m] vt enterrer.

entrails ['entreilz] n entrailles f pl.

entrain [en'trein] vt embarquer (dans le train).

entrance ['entrəns] n entrée f, accès m, admission f; — **examination** examen m d'entrée.

entrance [in'tra:ns] vt ravir, transporter.

entreat [in'tri:t] vt supplier.

entreaty [in'tri:ti] n supplication f; pl instances f pl.

entrench [in'trentʃ] vt retrancher.

entrust [in'trʌst] vt charger (de with), confier (à).

entry ['entri] n entrée f, inscription f; by double (single) — en partie double (simple).

entwine [in'twain] vt entrelacer, enlacer; vi s'entrelacer.

enumerate [i'nju:məreit] vt énumérer, dénombrer.

enumeration [i,nju:mə'reiʃən] n énumération f.

enunciate [i'nʌnsieit] vt articuler, énoncer.

enunciation [i,nʌnsi'eiʃən] n énonciation f.

envelop [in'veləp] vt envelopper.

envelope ['envəloup] n enveloppe f.

enviable ['enviəbl] a enviable, digne d'envie.

envious ['enviəs] a envieux, d'envie; **to be** — **of** porter envie à.

environment [in'vaiərənmənt] n milieu m, entourage m, ambiance f, atmosphère f.

environs [en'vaiərənz] n pl environs m pl.

envisage [in'vizidʒ] vt regarder en face, envisager.

envoy ['envɔi] n envoyé m.

envy ['envi] n envie f; vt envier, porter envie à.

epic ['epic] n épopée f; a épique.

epicure ['epikjuə] n gourmet m.

epidem.c [,epi'demik] n épidémie f; a épidémique.

epidermis [,epi'də:mis] n épiderme m.

epigram ['epigræm] n épigramme f.

epigraph ['epigra:f] n épigraphe f.

epilepsy ['epilepsi] n épilepsie f.

epileptic [,epi'leptik] a épileptique.

episcopacy [i'piskəpəsi] n épiscopat m.

episcopal [i'piskəpəl] a épiscopal.

episode ['episoud] n épisode m.

episodic [,epi'sɔdik] a épisodique.

epistle [i'pisl] n épître f.

epistolary [i'pistələri] a épistolaire.

epitaph ['epita:f] n épitaphe f.

epithet ['epiθet] n épithète f.

epitome [i'pitəmi] n abrégé m, résumé m.

epoch ['i:pɔk] n époque f.

equable ['ekwəbl] a égal, uni(forme), régulier.

equal ['i:kwəl] n égal(e) mf, pareil(le) mf; a égal, de taille (à to); vt égaler.

equal.ty [i:'kwɔliti] n égalité f.

equalization [,i:kwəlai'zeiʃən] n égalisation f.

equalize ['i:kwəlaiz] vt égaliser.

equally ['i:kwəli] ad également, pareillement.

equator [i'kweitə] n équateur m.

equatorial [,ekwə'tɔ:riəl] a équatorial.

equerry ['ekwəri] n écuyer m.

equestrian [i'kwestriən] a équestre.

equilibrate [,i:kwi'laibreit] vt équilibrer.

equilibrium [,i:kwi'libriəm] n équilibre m.

equinox ['i:kwinɔks] n équinoxe m.

equip [i'kwip] vt munir, équiper, monter.

equipage ['ekwipidʒ] n équipage m.

equipment [i'kwipmənt] n équipement m, outillage m, installation f, matériel m.

equipoise ['ekwipɔiz] n équilibre m, contre-poids m.

equitable ['ekwitəbl] a équitable.

equity ['ekwiti] n équité f.

equivalence [i'kwivələns] n équivalance f.

equivalent [i'kwivələnt] an équivalent m.

equivocal [i'kwivəkəl] a équivoque, ambigu -uë, douteux.

equivocate [i'kwivəkeit] vi jouer sur les mots, tergiverser.

era ['iərə] n ère f.

eradicate [i'rædikeit] vt extirper, déraciner.

eradication [i,rædi'keiʃən] n déracinement m.

erase [i'reiz] vt effacer, raturer.

eraser [i'reizə] n gomme f.

erasure [i'reizə] n rature f.

ere [εə] prep avant; cj avant que.

erect [i'rekt] a droit; vt dresser, bâtir, ériger.

erection [i'rekʃən] n érection f, construction f, montage m, édifice m.

ermine ['ə:min] n hermine f.

erode [i'roud] vt ronger, éroder, corroder.

erosion [i'rouʒən] n érosion f, usure f.

err [ə:] vi se tromper, faire erreur, être erroné, pécher.

errand ['erənd] n course f, commission f.

errand-boy ['erəndbɔi] n commissionnaire m, chasseur m.

erroneous [i'rounjəs] a erroné, faux.

error ['erə] n erreur f, faute f, méprise f.

erupt [i'rʌpt] vi faire éruption.

eruption [i'rʌpʃən] n éruption f.

escalator ['eskəleitə] n escalier mouvant m.

escapade [ˌeskəˈpeid] n escapade f, frasque f.

escape [isˈkeip] n évasion f, fuite f; vi s'évader, s'esquiver, (s')échapper; vt échapper à.

eschew [isˈtʃuː] vt éviter, s'abstenir de, renoncer à.

escort [ˈeskɔːt] n escorte f, cavalier m.

escort [isˈkɔːt] vt escorter, accompagner, reconduire.

escutcheon [isˈkʌtʃən] n écu(sson) m, blason m.

Eskimo [ˈeskimou] an Esquimau m; — **woman** femme esquimau.

especial [isˈpeʃəl] a (tout) particulier, propre.

espouse [isˈpauz] vt se marier avec, épouser.

espy [isˈpai] vt apercevoir, aviser.

essay [ˈesei] n tentative f, essai m, dissertation f.

essay [eˈsei] vt essayer, éprouver.

essence [ˈesns] n essence f, extrait m, fond m, suc m.

essential [iˈsenʃəl] an essentiel m, indispensable m.

establish [isˈtæbliʃ] vt fonder, créer, établir.

establishment [isˈtæbliʃmənt] n établissement m, fondation f, pied m (de guerre), train m de maison.

estate [isˈteit] n condition f, rang m, succession f, domaine m, immeuble m.

esteem [isˈtiːm] n estime f; vt estimer, tenir (pour).

estimate [ˈestimit] n estimation f, devis m, appréciation f; [ˈestimeit] vt évaluer, apprécier.

estimation [ˌestiˈmeiʃən] n estime f, jugement m.

estrange [isˈtreindʒ] vt (s')aliéner, indisposer.

estrangement [isˈtreindʒmənt] n désaffection f, refroidissement m, aliénation f.

estuary [ˈestjuəri] n estuaire m.

etch [etʃ] vt graver à l'eau forte.

etching [ˈetʃiŋ] n eau-forte f.

eternal [iˈtəːnl] a éternel.

eternity [iˈtəːniti] n éternité f.

ether [ˈiːθə] n éther m.

ethereal [iˈθiəriəl] a éthéré.

ethical [ˈeθikəl] a moral.

ethics [ˈeθiks] n morale f.

etiquette [ˈetiket] n étiquette f, convenances f pl, cérémonial m, protocole m.

etymology [ˌetiˈmɔlədʒi] n étymologie f.

eucharist [ˈjuːkərist] n eucharistie f.

eulogize [ˈjuːlədʒaiz] vt faire l'éloge de.

eulogy [ˈjuːlədʒi] n éloge m, panégyrique m.

eunuch [ˈjuːnək] n eunuque m.

Europe [ˈjuərəp] n l'Europe f.

European [ˌjuərəˈpiːən] n Européen, -enne mf; a européen.

evacuate [iˈvækjueit] vt évacuer, expulser.

evacuation [iˌvækjuˈeiʃən] n évacuation f.

evade [iˈveid] vt esquiver, déjouer, éviter, tourner.

evaluate [iˈvæljueit] vt évaluer, estimer.

evangelic [ˌiːvænˈdʒelik] a évangélique.

evangelist [iˈvændʒəlist] n évangéliste mf.

evaporate [iˈvæpəreit] vt faire évaporer; vi s'évaporer, se vaporiser.

evaporation [iˌvæpəˈreiʃən] n évaporation f.

evasion [iˈveiʒən] n subterfuge m, faux-fuyant m, échappatoire f.

evasive [iˈveiziv] a évasif.

eve [iːv] n veille f.

even [ˈiːvən] a égal, uni, plat, pair; ad même, seulement, encore; vt égaliser, aplanir.

evening [ˈiːvniŋ] n soir m, soirée f.

evening-dress [ˈiːvniŋdres] n habit m, robe f de soirée, tenue f de soirée.

evenly [ˈiːvənli] ad également, régulièrement.

evensong [ˈiːvənsɔŋ] n office du soir m, vêpres f pl.

event [iˈvent] n événement m, cas m, chance f, résultat m, épreuve f; in the — of au cas où; at all —s à tout hasard.

eventful [iˈventful] a mouvementé, mémorable, tourmenté.

ever [ˈevə] ad toujours, jamais.

everlasting [ˌevəˈlaːstiŋ] a éternel.

evermore [ˈevəˈmɔː] ad pour toujours, à jamais.

every [ˈevri] a chaque, tout; — **other** day tous les deux jours.

everybody [ˈevribɔdi] pn tout le monde, tous, chacun.

everyday [ˈevridei] a quotidien, journalier, banal.

everyone [ˈevriwʌn] pn tout le monde, chacun, tous.

everything [ˈevriθiŋ] pn tout.

everywhere [ˈevriweə] ad partout.

evict [iˈvikt] vt expulser.

eviction [iˈvikʃən] n expulsion f, éviction f.

evidence [ˈevidəns] n évidence f, signe m, preuve f, témoignage m; v. indiquer, attester, manifester.

evident [ˈevidənt] a évident.

evil [ˈiːvl] n mal m, péché m; a mauvais méchant, malin.

evilly [ˈiːvili] ad mal.

evince [iˈvins] vt montrer.

evocation [ˌevouˈkeiʃən] n évocation f.

evoke [iˈvouk] vt évoquer.

evolution [ˌiːvəˈluːʃən] n évolution f, développement m.

evolve [iˈvɔlv] vt dérouler, développer, élaborer; vi évoluer, se dérouler, se développer.

ewe [juː] n brebis f.

ewer ['juːə] n aiguière f, pot m à eau, broc m.

exact [ig'zækt] a juste, exact, précis; vt exiger, extorquer.

exacting [ig'zæktin] a exigeant, fatigant.

exaction [ig'zækʃən] n exigence f, exaction f.

exactitude [ig'zæktitjuːd] n exactitude f, précision f.

exactly [ig'zæktli] ad précisément, justement, tout juste, juste.

exaggerate [ig'zædʒəreit] vti exagérer.

exaggeration [ig.zædʒə'reiʃən] n exagération f.

exalt [ig'zɔːlt] vt exalter, porter aux nues, élever.

exaltation [.egzɔːl'teiʃən] n exaltation f, élévation f.

examination [ig.zæmi'neiʃən] n examen m, inspection f, visite f, interrogatoire m, (term) composition f.

examine [ig'zæmin] vt examiner, visiter, vérifier.

examiner [ig'zæminə] n examinateur, -trice, inspecteur, -trice.

example [ig'zaːmpl] n exemple m, précédent m.

exasperate [ig'zæspəreit] vt exaspérer, aggraver.

exasperation [ig.zæspə'reiʃən] n exaspération f.

excavate ['ekskəveit] vt fouiller, creuser, déterrer.

excavation [.ekskə'veiʃən] n excavation f, fouille f.

exceed [ik'siːd] vt dépasser, excéder, aller au-delà de.

exceedingly [ik'siːdiŋli] ad excessivement, extrêmement.

excel [ik'sel] vt surpasser, dépasser; vi exceller.

excellence ['eksələns] n excellence f, mérite m.

excellent ['eksələnt] a excellent, parfait.

except [ik'sept] vt excepter, exclure; prep excepté; cj sauf que.

exception [ik'sepʃən] n exception f, objection f.

exceptionable [ik'sepʃnəbl] a répréhensible.

exceptional [ik'sepʃənl] a exceptionnel.

excerpt ['eksəːpt] n extrait m.

excess [ik'ses] n excès m, surplus m, excédent m, supplément m.

excessive [ik'sesiv] a excessif, immodéré.

excessively [ik'sesivli] ad excessivement, démesurément, à l'excès.

exchange [iks'tʃeindʒ] n échange m, Bourse f, change m; vt (é)changer; vi permuter.

exchangeable [iks'tʃeindʒəbl] a échangeable.

exchequer [iks'tʃekə] n Echiquier m, ministère des finances m, Trésor m, fisc m.

excise ['eksaiz] n contributions indirectes f pl; E— Office Régie f; vt couper, retrancher.

excision [ek'siʒən] n excision f, coupure f.

excitable [ik'saitəbl] a (sur)excitable, émotionnable.

excitation [.eksi'teiʃən] n excitation f.

excite [ik'sait] vt exciter, susciter, émouvoir, agiter.

excitement [ik'saitmənt] n agitation f, émotion f, surexcitation f, sensation(s) f pl.

exciting [ik'saitin] a passionant, palpitant, mouvementé.

exclaim [iks'kleim] vi (s'é)crier, se récrier.

exclamation [.eksklə'meiʃən] n exclamation f.

exclude [iks'kluːd] vt exclure.

excluding [iks'kluːdin] a sans compter.

exclusion [iks'kluːʒən] n exclusion f.

exclusive [iks'kluːsiv] a non compris, à l'exclusion (de of), exclusif, unique.

exclusively [iks'kluːsivli] ad exclusivement.

excommunicate [.ekskə'mjuːnikeit] vt excommunier.

excommunication ['ekskə.mjuːni-'keiʃən] n excommunication f.

excoriate [eks'kɔːrieit] vt écorcher.

excrescence [iks'kresns] n excroissance f.

excruciating [iks'kruːʃieitin] a atroce, déchirant.

excursion [iks'kəːʃən] n sortie f, excursion f.

excusable [iks'kjuːzəbl] a excusable, pardonnable.

excuse [iks'kjuːs] n excuse f, prétexte m.

excuse [iks'kjuːz] vt excuser, dispenser (de from).

executant [ig'zekjutənt] n exécutant(e) mf.

execute ['eksikjuːt] vt exécuter, valider, s'acquitter de.

execution [.eksi'kjuːʃən] n exécution f, validation f, saisie f.

executioner [.eksi'kjuːʃnə] n bourreau m.

executive [ig'zekjutiv] an exécutif m.

executor [ig'zekjutə] n exécuteur, -trice.

exemplar [ig'zemplə] n modèle m, exemplaire m.

exemplary [ig'zempləri] a exemplaire, caractérisque.

exemplify [ig'zemplifai] vt illustrer d'exemples, être l'exemple de.

exempt [ig'zempt] a exempt; vt dispenser.

exemption [ig'zempʃən] n exemption f, dispense f.

exercise ['eksəsaiz] n exercice m, devoir m; vt exercer, pratiquer, éprouver; vi s'entraîner.

exert [ig'zə:t] *vt* déployer, faire sentir, employer, exercer.

exertion [ig'zə:ʃən] *n* effort *m*, efforts *m pl*, fatigues *f pl*, emploi *m*.

exhalation [,ekshə'leiʃən] *n* exhalaison *f*, bouffée *f*, effluve *m*.

exhale [eks'heil] *vt* exhaler; *vi* se dilater, s'exhaler.

exhaust [ig'zɔ:st] *n* échappement *m*; *vt* épuiser, exténuer.

exhaustion [ig'zɔ:stʃən] *n* épuisement *m*.

exhaustive [ig'zɔ:stiv] *a* qui épuise, complet, minutieux.

exhibit [ig'zibit] *n* pièce à conviction *f*, objet exposé *m*; *vt* montrer, étaler, exhiber.

exhibition [,eksi'biʃən] *n* exposition *f*, exhibition *f*, spectacle *m*, étalage *m*.

exhort [ig'zɔ:t] *vt* exhorter.

exhortation [,egzɔ:'teiʃən] *n* exhortation *f*.

exhumation [,ekshju:'meiʃən] *n* exhumation *f*.

exhume [eks'hju:m] *vt* exhumer.

exigence ['eksidʒəns] *n* exigence *f*, nécessité *f*.

exigent ['eksidʒənt] *a* urgent, exigeant.

exiguity [,eksi'gju(:)iti] *n* exiguïté *f*.

exiguous [eg'zigjuəs] *a* exigu, -uë.

exile ['eksail] *n* exil *m*, exilé(e) *mf*; *vt* exiler, bannir.

exist [ig'zist] *vi* exister.

existence [ig'zistəns] *n* existence *f*, vie *f*.

existing [ig'zistiŋ] *a* existant, actuel.

exit ['eksit] *n* sortie *f*.

exodus ['eksədəs] *n* exode *m*, sortie *f*.

exonerate [ig'zɔnəreit] *vt* exonérer, décharger.

exoneration [ig,zɔnə'reiʃən] *n* exonération *f*.

exorbitance [ig'zɔ:bitəns] *n* énormité *f*, exorbitance *f*.

exorbitant [ig'zɔ:bitənt] *a* exorbitant, extravagant.

exorcise ['eksɔ:saiz] *vt* exorciser.

exorcising ['eksɔ:saiziŋ] *n* exorcisme *m*.

exotic [ig'zɔtik] *a* exotique.

expand [iks'pænd] *vt* étendre, dilater, épancher; *vi* se dilater, se développer.

expanse [iks'pæns] *n* étendue *f*.

expansion [iks'pænʃən] *n* expansion *f*, développement *m*.

expansive [iks'pænsiv] *a* expansif, étendu.

expatiate [eks'peiʃieit] *vi* s'étendre (sur **on**), pérorer.

expatriate [eks'pætrieit] *vt* expatrier.

expect [iks'pekt] *vt* (s')attendre (à), compter sur.

expectancy [iks'pektənsi] *n* attente *f*, expectative *f*.

expectation [,ekspek'teiʃən] *n* attente *f*, espérances *f pl*, prévision *f*.

expediency [iks'pi:djənsi] *n* convenance *f*, opportunité *f*.

expedient [iks'pi:djənt] *an* expédient *m*.

expedite ['ekspidait] *vt* hâter, expédier.

expedition [,ekspi'diʃən] *n* expédition *f*, rapidité *f*.

expeditious [,ekspi'diʃəs] *a* expéditif, prompt.

expel [iks'pel] *vt* chasser, expulser.

expend [iks'pend] *vt* dépenser, consommer, épuiser.

expenditure [iks'penditʃə] *n* dépense(s) *f pl*.

expense [iks'pens] *n* débours *m pl*, dépens *m pl*, frais *m pl*.

expensive [iks'pensiv] *a* cher, coûteux, dispendieux.

experience [iks'piəriəns] *n* expérience *f*, épreuve *f*.

experienced [iks'piəriənst] *a* expérimenté, exercé.

experiment [iks'perimənt] *n* essai *m*, expérience *f*; *vi* expérimenter, faire une expérience.

experimental [eks,peri'mentl] *a* expérimental.

experimentally [eks,peri'mentəli] *ad* expérimentalement, à titre d'essai.

expert ['ekspə:t] *an* expert *m*; *a* habile.

expiate ['ekspieit] *vt* expier.

expiation [,ekspi'eiʃən] *n* expiation *f*.

expiration [,ekspaiə'reiʃən] *n* expiration *f*, (d)échéance *f*.

expire [iks'paiə] *vti* exhaler, expirer; *vi* s'éteindre.

expiry [iks'paiəri] *n* fin *f*, terminaison *f*.

explain [iks'plein] *vt* expliquer, éclaircir.

explanation [,eksplə'neiʃən] *n* explication *f*.

explanatory [iks'plænətəri] *a* explicatif; explicateur, -trice.

explicable [eks'plikəbl] *a* explicable.

explicit [iks'plisit] *a* formel, clair.

explode [iks'ploud] *vt* faire sauter, dégonfler; *vi* sauter, faire explosion, éclater.

exploit ['eksplɔit] *n* exploit *m*; *vt* exploiter.

exploitation [,eksplɔi'teiʃən] *n* exploitation *f*.

exploration [,eksplɔ:'reiʃən] *n* exploration *f*.

explore [iks'plɔ:] *vt* explorer.

explorer [iks'plɔ:rə] *n* explorateur, -trice.

explosion [iks'plouʒən] *n* explosion *f*, détonation *f*.

explosive [iks'plouziv] *a* explosible, explosif, détonnant.

export [eks'pɔ:t] *vt* exporter.

export ['ekspɔ:t] *n* exportation *f*; *pl* exportations *f pl*.

exportation [,ekspɔ:'teiʃən] *n* exportation *f*

exporter [eks'pɔːtə] *n* exportateur, -trice.

expose [iks'pouz] *vt* exposer, mettre à nu, démasquer.

expostulate [iks'pɔstjuleit] *vi* en remontrer (à with), faire des remontrances (à with).

expostulation [iks,pɔstju'leiʃən] *n* rémontrance *f*.

expound [iks'paund] *vt* exposer, expliquer.

express [iks'pres] *n* exprès *m*, rapide *m*, express *m*; (US) compagnie *f* de messageries; *a* exact, exprès; *vt* exprimer.

expression [iks'preʃən] *n* expression *f*.

expressive [iks'presiv] *a* expressif.

expressly [iks'presli] *ad* expressément, formellement.

expropriate [eks'prouprieit] *vt* exproprier.

expropriation [eks,proupri'eiʃən] *n* expropriation *f*.

expulsion [iks'pʌlʃən] *n* expulsion *f*.

expunge [iks'pʌndʒ] *vt* biffer, rayer.

expurgate ['ekspɔːgeit] *vt* expurger, épurer.

exquisite [eks'kwizit] *n* élégant *m*; *a* exquis, raffiné.

exquisiteness [eks'kwizitnis] *n* finesse exquise *f*, raffinement *m*.

extant [eks'tænt] *a* subsistant.

extempore [eks'tempəri] *a* improvisé; *ad* d'abondance.

extemporization [eks,tempərai'zeiʃən] *n* improvisation *f*.

extemporize [iks'tempəraiz] *vti* improviser.

extend [iks'tend] *vt* étendre, prolonger, accorder; *vi* se déployer, s'étendre.

extensible [iks'tensibl] *a* extensible.

extension [iks'tenʃən] *n* extension *f*, prolongement *m*, prolongation *f*, agrandissement *m*.

extensive [iks'tensiv] *a* extensif, étendu, ample.

extensively [iks'tensivli] *ad* to use — se servir largement, beaucoup.

extent [iks'tent] *n* étendue *f*, mesure *f*, point *m*.

extenuate [eks'tenjueit] *vt* atténuer, excuser.

extenuation [eks,tenju'eiʃən] *n* atténuation *f*, affaiblissement *m*, exténuation *f*.

exterior [eks'tiəriə] *an* extérieur *m*; *n* dehors *m*.

exterminate [eks'təːmineit] *vt* exterminer, extirper.

extermination [eks,təːmi'neiʃən] *n* extermination *f*, extirpation *f*.

external [eks'təːnl] *a* externe, extérieur.

extinct [iks'tiŋkt] *a* éteint.

extinction [iks'tiŋkʃən] *n* extinction *f*.

extinguish [iks'tiŋgwiʃ] *vt* éteindre, éclipser, anéantir.

extinguisher [iks'tiŋgwiʃə] *n* éteignoir *m*, extincteur *m*.

extirpate ['ekstəːpeit] *vt* extirper.

extol [iks'tɔl] *vt* porter aux nues, exalter.

extort [iks'tɔːt] *vt* extorquer, arracher.

extortion [iks'tɔːʃən] *n* extorsion *f*, arrachement *m*.

extortionate [iks'tɔːʃnit] *a* exorbitant, de pirate.

extra ['ekstrə] *a* supplémentaire, d'extra, de plus; *ad* extra, super, ultra, en plus; *n* supplément *m*; *pl* à-côtés *m pl*.

extract ['ekstrækt] *n* extrait *m*.

extract [iks'trækt] *vt* extraire, (sou) tirer.

extraction [iks'trækʃən] *n* extraction *f*, origine *f*.

extradite ['ekstrədait] *vt* extrader.

extradition [,ekstrə'diʃən] *n* extradition *f*.

extraneous [eks'treinjəs] *a* étranger, en dehors de.

extraordinary [iks'trɔːdnri] *a* extraordinaire.

extravagance [iks'trævəgəns] *n* extravagance *f*, folle dépense *f*, gaspillage *m*.

extravagant [iks'trævəgənt] *a* extravagant, dépensier.

extreme [iks'triːm] *an* extrême *m*.

extremely [iks'triːmli] *ad* extrêmement, au dernier point.

extremist [iks'triːmist] *n* extrémiste *mf*.

extremity [iks'tremiti] *n* extrémité *f*, bout *m*.

extricate ['ekstrikeit] *vt* tirer, sortir, dégager.

exuberance [ig'zuːbərəns] *n* exubérance *f*, luxuriance *f*.

exuberant [ig'zuːbərənt] *a* exubérant.

exult [ig'zʌlt] *vi* exulter.

exultation [egzʌl'teiʃən] *n* jubilation *f*, exultation *f*.

eye [ai] *n* œil *m*, *pl* yeux *m pl*, (needle) chas *m*; *vt* regarder, lorgner.

eyeball ['aibɔːl] *n* pupille *f*, prunelle *f*.

eyebrow ['aibrau] *n* sourcil *m*.

eyeglass ['aiglɑːs] *n* monocle *m*; *pl* lorgnon *m*.

eyelash ['ailæʃ] *n* cil *m*.

eyelet ['ailit] *n* œillet *m*.

eyelid ['ailid] *n* paupière *f*.

eyeshot ['aiʃɔt] *n* portée *f* de vue.

eyesight ['aisait] *n* vue *f*.

eyesore ['aisɔːr] *n* mal *m* d'yeux, tache *f*, hideur *f*.

eyetooth ['aituːθ] *n* canine *f*.

eyewash ['aiwɔʃ] *n* poudre aux yeux *f*.

eyewitness ['ai,witnis] *n* témoin oculaire *m*.

F

fable ['feibl] n fable f, conte m.

fabric ['fæbrik] n construction f, édifice m, tissu m.

fabricate ['fæbrikeit] vt fabriquer, inventer.

fabrication [fæbri'keiʃən] n faux m, fabrication f.

fabulist ['fæbjulist] n fabuliste m.

fabulous ['fæbjuləs] a fabuleux, légendaire, prodigieux.

face [feis] n visage m, figure f, face f, air m, mine f, grimace f, tour.et m, façade f, cadran m; — **cream** crème f de beauté; —**pack** masque m anti-ride; — **value** valeur f nominale; vt regarder en face, faire face à, confronter garnir, couvrir, donner sur; — **up to** affronter.

facet ['fæsit] n facette f.

facetious [fə'si:ʃəs] a facétieux, bouffon.

facial ['feiʃəl] a facial.

facile ['fæsail] a facile.

facility [fa'siliti] n facilité f.

facing ['feisiŋ] n parement m, revers m, revêt m.

fact [fækt] n fait m; **matter-of-—** (of person) pratique; **as a matter of —** en effet, en réalité.

faction ['fækʃən] n faction cabale f.

factious ['fækʃəs] a factieux.

facticious [fæk'tiʃəs] a factice, artificiel.

factor ['fæktə] n facteur m, agent m, (Scot) régisseur m.

factory ['fæktəri] n usine f, manufacture f, fabrique f, factorerie f.

factotum [fæk'toutəm] n factotum m.

facultative ['fækəltətiv] a facultatif.

faculty ['fækəlti] n faculté f, pouvoir m, liberté f.

fad [fæd] n lubie f, manie f, marotte f.

faddist ['fædist] n maniaque mf.

fade [feid] vi se faner, se détendre, s'éteindre; vt faner, décolorer.

faded ['feidid] a fané, décoloré, défra.chi.

fade-out ['feidaut] n fondu m.

fading [feidiŋ] a pâlissant, estompé; n flétrissure f, décoloration f, (of sound) chute f d'intensité.

fag [fæg] n corvée f, (sl) sèche f; vi turbiner, trimer; vt fatiguer, éreinter.

fag-end ['fægend] n mégot m.

faggot ['fægət] n fagot m.

fail [feil] vi manquer, échouer, faire faillite, baisser; vt refuser, coller, manquer à; ad without — sans faute.

failing ['feiliŋ] prep faute de; n défaut m, défaillance f.

failure ['feiljə] n échec m, manque (ment) m, faillite f, raté(e) mf, four m, panne f.

fain [fein] a heureux; ad volontiers.

faint [feint] n défaillance f, syncope f; vi s'évanouir; a faible, pâle, vague, léger.

fair [fɛə] a beau, blond, clair, loyal, juste, passable, moyen; n foire f.

fair-copy ['fɛə'kɔpi] n mise au net f, copie au net f.

fairly ['fɛəli] ad absolument, assez, loyalement.

fairness ['fɛənis] n justice f, loyauté f, impartialité f; n blancheur f, fraicheur f; **in all —** en bonne conscience.

fair-play ['fɛə'plei] n franc jeu m.

fairy ['fɛəri] n fée f.

fairyland ['fɛərilænd] n féerie f.

fairy-like ['fɛərilaik] a féerique.

faith [feiθ] n foi f, parole f.

faithful ['feiθful] a fidèle.

faithfully ['feiθfuli] adv fidèlement; **yours —** agréez l'expression de nos sentiments distingués.

faithless ['feiθlis] a sans foi.

fake [feik] n truquage m, faux m; vt truquer, maquiller.

falcon ['fɔːlkən] n faucon m.

fall [fɔːl] n chute f, tombée f; (US) automne m; vi tomber, baisser, échoir.

fallacy ['fæləsi] n illusion f, fausseté f, erreur f.

fallacious [fə'leiʃəs] a fallacieux, trompeur.

fallen ['fɔːlən] pp of **fall**.

fallibility [fæli'biliti] n faillibilité f.

fallible ['fæləbl] a faillible.

fall-out ['fɔːlaut] n retombée f.

fallow ['fælou] n friche f, jachère f.

false [fɔːls] a faux, trompeur, perfide.

falsehood ['fɔlshud] n fausseté f, mensonge m.

falseness ['fɔlsnis] n duplicité f, mauvaise foi f.

falsification [fɔlsifi'keiʃən] n falsification f.

falsify ['fɔlsifai] vt falsifier, tromper, rendre faux.

falter ['fɔltə] vi trébucher, balbutier, hésiter, flancher.

fame [eim] n réputation f, renom m, renommée f.

famed [feimd] a célèbre, famé.

familiar [fə'miljə] a familier, intime.

familiarity [fə mili'æriti] n familiarité f connaissance f.

familiarize [fə'miljəraiz] vt familiariser, habituer.

family ['tæmili] n famille f.

famine ['fæmin] n famine f.

famish ['fæmiʃ] vi être affamé.

famous ['feiməs] a célèbre fameux.

fan [fæn] n éventail m, ventilateur m, aérateur m, fan m, fervent(e) mf enragé(e) mf; — **palm** rôner m; vt éventer, souffler (sur), attiser, vanner.

fanatic [fə'nætik] n fanatique mf, enragé(e) mf.

fanatical [fə'nætikəl] a fanatique.

fanaticism [fə'nætisizəm] n fanatisme m.

fanciful ['fænsiful] *a* capricieux, fantaisiste, chimérique.

fancy ['fænsi] *n* imagination *f*, fantaisie *f*, chimère *f*, caprice *m*; *vt* (s')imaginer, se toquer de; **to — oneself** se gober.

fang [fæŋ] *n* croc *m*, crochet *m*, défense *f*, racine *f*.

fanner ['fænə] *n* vanneur, -euse.

fantastic [fæn'tæstik] *a* fantastique, fantasque.

fantasy ['fæntəzi] *n* imagination *f*, extravagance *f*.

far [fɑː] *a* éloigné, lointain; *ad* loin, au loin, avant, (de) beaucoup; **so —** jusqu'ici; **in so — as** dans la mesure où; **— afield** très loin.

faraway ['fɑːrəwei] *a* éloigné, lointain.

far-between ['fɑːbi'twiːn] *a* espacé.

far-fetched ['fɑː'fetʃt] *a* outré, tiré par les cheveux, extravagant.

far-off ['fɑːr'ɔf] *a* éloigné.

far-reaching ['fɑː'riːtʃiŋ] *a* de longue portée, de grande envergure.

far-sighted ['fɑː'saitid] *a* presbyte, à longue vue, prévoyant.

farce [fɑːs] *n* farce *f*.

farcical ['fɑːsikəl] *a* grotesque.

fare [fɛə] *n* prix *m* (du voyage), places *f pl*, voyageur, -euse, client(e) *mf*; **good —** bonne chère *f*; *vi* se faire, se porter, se trouver; **single —** aller *m*; **return —** aller et retour *m*.

farewell ['fɛə'wel] *n* adieu *m*.

farm [fɑːm] *n* ferme *f*; *vt* affermer, cultiver, exploiter; *vi* être cultivateur.

farmer ['fɑːmə] *n* fermier *m*, cultivateur *m*.

farming ['fɑːmiŋ] *n* culture *f*, affermage *m*, exploitation *f*.

farrier ['færiə] *n* maréchal ferrant *m*, vétérinaire *m*.

farther ['fɑːðə] *see* **further**.

farthing ['fɑːðiŋ] *n* liard *m*, sou *m*.

fascinate ['fæsineit] *vt* séduire, fasciner.

fascination [ˌfæsi'neiʃən] *n* fascination *f*, charme *m*.

fascism ['fæʃizm] *n* fascisme *m*.

fascist ['fæʃist] *an* fasciste *mf*.

fashion ['fæʃən] *n* mode *f*, façon *f*, coutume *f*; *vt* façonner, former.

fashionable ['fæʃnəbl] *a* à la mode, élégant.

fast [fɑːst] *n* jeûne *m*; *vi* jeûner; *a* fixé, confiné, sûr, solide, bon teint, rapide, qui va fort, qui avance; *ad* solidement, rapidement, fort, vite.

fasten ['fɑːsn] *vt* attacher, ficeler, fermer, fixer, saisir; *vi* se cramponner, se fixer.

fastener ['fɑːsnə] *n* attache *f*, agrafe *f*, fermeture *f*.

fastidious [fæs'tidjəs] *a* difficile, délicat.

fastidiousness [fæs'tidjəsnis] *n* goût difficile *m*.

fastness ['fɑːstnis] *n* rapidité *f*,

vitesse *f*, fermeté *f*, solidité *f*, forteresse *f*.

fat [fæt] *n* gros *m*, graisse *f*; *a* gras, gros.

fatal ['feitl] *a* fatal, mortel, funeste.

fatalism ['feitəlizəm] *n* fatalisme *m*.

fatalist ['feitəlist] *n* fataliste *mf*.

fatality [fə'tæliti] *n* fatalité *f*, sinistre *m*, accident mortel *m*.

fate [feit] *n* destin *m*, sort *m*, destinée *f*.

fateful ['feitful] *a* décisif, gros d'avenir, fatidique, fatal.

father ['fɑːðə] *n* père *m*; **—-in-law** beau-père *m*; *vt* reconnaître, avouer, imputer, patronner, engendrer.

fatherhood ['fɑːðəhud] *n* paternité *f*.

fatherland ['fɑːðəlænd] *n* patrie *f*.

fatherless ['fɑːðəlis] *a* sans père.

fatherly ['fɑːðəli] *a* paternel.

fathom ['fæðəm] *n* toise *f*, brasse *f*; *vt* sonder, approfondir.

fathomless ['fæðəmlis] *a* insondable, sans fond.

fatigue [fə'tiːg] *n* fatigue *f*, corvée *f*; *vt* fatiguer.

fatten ['fætn] *vtn* engraisser.

fatty ['fæti] *a* graisseux, onctueux, gras, gros.

fatuous ['fætjuəs] *a* sot, idiot.

fatuousness ['fætjuəsnis] *n* stupidité *f*.

faucet ['fɔːsit] *n* (US) robinet *m*.

fault [fɔlt] *n* défaut *m*, faute *f*, faille *f*; **to a —** jusqu'à l'excès.

faultless ['fɔltlis] *a* impeccable, sans faute.

faulty ['fɔlti] *a* fautif, défectueux, inexact.

favour ['feivə] *n* faveur *f*; *vt* favoriser, approuver, appuyer.

favourable ['feivərəbl] *a* favorable, propice, avantageux.

favourite ['feivərit] *an* favori, -ite; *a* préféré.

favouritism ['feivəritizəm] *n* favoritisme *m*.

fawn [fɔːn] *n* faon *m*; *a* fauve; *vt* **to — upon** caresser, flagorner, faire le chien couchant devant.

fear [fiə] *n* peur *f*, crainte *f*; *vt* craindre, avoir peur de.

fearful ['fiəful] *a* terrible, affreux, craintif, peureux.

fearless ['fiəlis] *a* sans peur, intrépide.

fearsome ['fiəsəm] *a* hideux, redoutable.

feasible ['fiːzəbl] *a* faisable, praticable, probable.

feasibility [ˌfiːzə'biliti] *n* possibilité *f*, praticabilité *f*.

feast [fiːst] *n* fête *f*, régal *m*, festin *m*; *vt* fêter, régaler; *vi* se régaler, faire festin.

feat [fiːt] *n* exploit *m*, prouesse *f*, haut fait *m*, tour de force *m*.

feather ['feðə] *n* plume *f*, penne *f*, plumage *m*; *vt* garnir de plumes, empenner.

feathery ['feðəri] a léger comme une plume, plumeux.

feather-weight ['feðəweit] n poids plume m.

feature ['fi:tʃə] n trait m (saillant), caractéristique f, spécialité f; (US) grand film m, long-métrage m; vt caractériser, esquisser, mettre en manchette, mettre en vedette.

featureless ['fi:tʃəlis] a terne.

February ['februəri] n février m.

fecund ['fi:kənd] a fécond.

fecundate ['fi:kəndeit] vt féconder.

fecundation [,fi:kən'deiʃən] n fécondation f.

fecundity [fi'kʌnditi] n fécondité f.

fed [fed] pt pp of **feed**; **to be — up** en avoir assez, marre.

federal ['fedərəl] a fédéral.

federalism [,fedərəlizəm] n fédéralisme m.

federate ['fedəreit] vt fédérer; vi se fédérer; a fédéré.

federation [,fede'reiʃən] n fédération f.

fee [fi:] n fief m, frais m pl, cachet m, honoraires m pl.

feeble ['fi:bl] a faible, infirme, chétif.

feebleness ['fi:blnis] n faiblesse f.

feeblish ['fi:bliʃ] a faiblard.

feed [fi:d] n repas m, tétée f, pâture f, picotin m, alimentation f, fourrage m; vt nourrir, alimenter, donner à manger à, ravitailler; vi manger, se nourrir, s'alimenter, brouter.

feeder ['fi:də] n mangeur, -euse, biberon m, tétine f, bavette f.

feed-back ['fi:dbæk] n rétroaction f, réaction f.

feel [fi:l] n toucher m, sensation f; vt toucher, tâter, palper, sentir; vi se sentir, tâtonner, fouiller.

feeler ['fi:lə] n antenne f, éclaireur m, sondage m.

feeling ['fi:liŋ] n toucher m, maniement m, sensation f, sentiment m, sensibilité f; a sensible.

feelingly ['fi:liŋli] ad avec émotion.

feign [fein] vt feindre, simuler.

feint [feint] n feinte f; vi faire une fausse attaque, feinter.

felicitous [fi'lisitəs] a heureux, bien trouvé.

felicity [fi'lisiti] n félicité f.

fell [fel] n peau f, toison f; vt abattre; a sinistre, cruel.

fellow ['felou] n type m, gars m, individu m, membre m, confrère m, pareil m.

fellowship ['felouʃip] n société f, amitié f, association f, camaraderie f.

felon ['felən] n auteur d'un crime m, criminel, -elle.

felonious [fi'lounjəs] a criminel.

felt [felt] pp pt of **feel**; n feutre m, vt feutrer, couvrir de carton goudronné.

female ['fi:meil] n femelle f, femme f; a féminin.

feminine ['feminin] a féminin, femelle.

fen [fen] n marais m.

fence [fens] n barrière f, clôture f, receleur, -euse; vi faire de l'escrime, s'escrimer; vt enclore, clôturer.

fencing ['fensiŋ] n escrime f, clôture f.

fend [fend] vt **to — for oneself** se débrouiller; vt **to — off** parer, écarter.

fender ['fendə] n garde-feu m, pare-choc m, baderne f.

ferment ['fə:ment] n ferment m.

ferment [fə'ment] vt faire fermenter, fomenter; vi fermenter, travailler.

fermentation [,fə:men'teiʃən] n fermentation f, travail m, effervescence f.

fern [fə:n] n fougère f.

ferocious [fə'rouʃəs] a féroce.

ferocity [fə'rɔsiti] n férocité f.

ferret ['ferit] n furet m; vi fureter; vt **to — out** débusquer, dénicher.

ferro-concrete ['ferou'kɔŋkri:t] n ciment armé m.

ferrule ['feru:l] n virole f, embout m.

ferry ['feri] n bac m; vti passer.

ferryman ['ferimən] n passeur m.

fertile ['fə:tail] a fertile.

fertility [fə'tiliti] n fertilité f, fécondité f.

fertilize ['fə:tilaiz] vt fertiliser, féconder.

fertilizer ['fə:tilaizə] n engrais m.

fervent ['fə:vənt] a brûlant, fervent, ardent.

fervour ['fə:və] n chaleur f, ferveur f, zèle m.

fester ['festə] n abcès m; vi suppurer; vt empoisonner, ulcérer.

festival ['festəvəl] n festival m, fête f.

festive ['festiv] a joyeux, de fête.

festivity [fes'tiviti] n festivité f, fête f.

festoon [fes'tu:n] n feston m; vt festonner.

fetch [fetʃ] vt aller chercher, apporter, atteindre, (blow) envoyer, (sigh) pousser, (breath) reprendre.

fetching ['fetʃiŋ] a intéressant.

fetid ['fetid] a fétide.

fetidness ['fetidnis] n fétidité f, puanteur f.

fetter ['fetə] n lien m; pl fers m pl, entraves f pl; vt enchaîner, entraver.

fettle ['fetl] n état m; **in good — en train**, en forme.

feud [fju:d] n vendetta f.

feudal ['fju:dl] a féodal.

feudalism ['fju:dəlizəm] n féodalité f.

fever ['fi:və] n fièvre f.

feverish ['fi:vəriʃ] a fiévreux, fébrile.

few [fju:] a peu de, un (le) petit nombre; **a — quelques**.

fewer ['fju:ə] a moins de, moins nombreux.

fewest ['fju:ist] a le moins de, le moins nombreux.

fez [fez] *n* chéchia *m*.

fiasco [fi'æskou] *n* fiasco *m*, four *m*.

fib [fib] *n* petit mensonge *m*, craque *f*, colle *f*; *vi* enconter (à to).

fibre ['faibə] *n* fibre *f*; **staple —** fibrane *f*.

fibrous ['faibrəs] *a* fibreux.

fickle ['fikl] *a* volage, changeant, inconstant.

fickleness ['fiklnis] *n* inconstance *f*.

fiction ['fikʃən] *n* fiction *f*, romans *m pl*.

fictitious [fik'tiʃəs] *a* fictif, imaginaire.

fiddle ['fidl] *n* violon *m*, crin-crin *m*; *vi* jouer du violon, râcler du violon; **to — with** tripoter, tourmenter.

fiddler ['fidlə] *n* ménétrier *m*, violoneux *m*; violiniste.

fiddlestick ['fidlstik] *n* archet *m*; *pl* sottises *f pl*.

fidelity [fi'deliti] *n* fidélité *f*, loyauté *f*, exactitude *f*.

fidget ['fidʒit] *n* **to have the —s** avoir la bougeotte; *vi* s'agiter, se trémousser.

fie [fai] *excl* fi!

field [fi:ld] *n* champ *m*, (*mil*) campagne *f*, terrain de jeux *m*, domaine *m*, candidatures *f pl*; *a* de campagne.

field glasses ['fi:ldglɑ:siz] *n* jumelles *f pl*.

field-marshal ['fi:ld'mɑ:ʃəl] *n* maréchal *m*.

field-mouse ['fi:ldmaus] *n* mulot *m*.

fiend [fi:nd] *n* démon *m*.

fiendish ['fi:ndiʃ] *a* diabolique, infernal.

fierce [fiəs] *a* féroce, violent.

fiercely ['fiəsli] *ad* violemment, âprement.

fierceness ['fiəsnis] *n* férocité *f*, sauvagerie *f*, violence *f*.

fiery ['faiəri] *a* de feu, ardent, emporté, fougueux.

fife [faif] *n* fifre *m*.

fifteen ['fif'ti:n] *an* quinze *m*.

fifteenth ['fif'ti:nθ] *an* quinzième *mf*, quinze *m*.

fifth [fifθ] *an* cinquième *mf*, cinq *m*.

fiftieth ['fiftiəθ] *an* cinquantième *mf*.

fifty ['fifti] *an* cinquante *m*.

fig [fig] *n* figue *f*, tenue *f*, forme *f*.

fight [fait] *n* lutte *f*, combat *m*, combat(t)ivité *f*; *vi* se battre, lutter, combattre; *vt* combattre, se battre avec.

fighter ['faitə] *n* combattant *m*, militant *m*, avion de combat *m*.

figment ['figmənt] *n* invention *f*, rêve *m*.

fig-tree ['figtri:] *n* figuier *m*.

figure ['figə] *n* forme *f*, corps *m*, taille *f*, personne *f*, ligne *f*, galbe *m*, chiffre *m*, emblème *m*, figure *f*; *vt* (se) figurer, estimer; *vi* calculer, faire figure, se chiffrer, figurer.

figurehead ['figəhed] *n* façade *f*, prête-nom *m*, figure de proue *f*.

filbert ['filbə(:)t] *n* noisette *f*.

filch [filtʃ] *vt* voler, escamoter.

file [fail] *n* lime *f*, piquenotes *m*, classeur *m*, dossier *m*, liasse *f*, file *f*; *vt* limer, enfiler, classer, (US) soumettre; *vi* défiler.

filial ['filjəl] *a* filial.

filiation [fili'eiʃən] *n* filiation *f*.

filibuster ['filibʌstə] *n* flibustier *m*; *vi* flibuster.

filigree ['filigri:] *n* filigrane *m*.

filing ['failiŋ] *n* limaille *f*, limage *m*; classement *m*.

fill [fil] *n* plein *m*, soûl *m*, pipée *f*; *vt* remplir, plomber, compléter, combler; *vi* se remplir, se garnir; **to — up** *vi* faire le plein.

filling ['filiŋ] *n* plombage *m*, chargement *m*, remplissage *m*.

filling-station ['filiŋ,steiʃən] *n* poste d'essence *m*.

fillet ['filit] *n* bandeau *m*, filet *m*.

fillip ['filip] *n* chiquenaude *f*, stimulant *m*, coup de fouet *m*.

filly ['fili] *n* pouliche *f*.

film [film] *n* pellicule *f*, film *m*, voile *m*, (*eye*) taie *f*; *vt* filmer, tourner.

film-star ['filmstɑ:] *n* vedette du cinéma *f*.

filter ['filtə] *n* filtre *m*; *vti* filtrer; *vt* tamiser.

filth [filθ] *n* saleté *f*, ordure *f*.

filthy ['fil0i] *a* sale, crasseux, immonde.

fin [fin] *n* nageoire *f*, aileron *m*.

final ['fainl] *a* final, dernier, définitif, décisif.

finally ['fainəli] *ad* enfin, finalement.

finance [fai'næns] *n* finance *f*; *vt* financer.

financial [fai'nænʃəl] *a* financier.

financier [fai'nænsiə] *n* financier *m*.

finch [fintʃ] *n* pinson *m*.

find [faind] *n* trouvaille *f*, découverte *f*; *vt* trouver, constater, pourvoir, fournir; **all found** tout compris.

fine [fain] *n* amende *f*; *vt* mettre à l'amende; *a* beau, bon, fin, délié, élégant.

finely ['fainli] *ad* habilement, subtilement, magnifiquement, fin.

fineness ['fainnis] *n* beauté *f*, élégance *f*, finesse *f*, excellence *f*.

finery ['fainəri] *n* atours *m pl*, parure *f*.

finesse [fi'nes] *n* finesse *f*; *vi* user de finesse, faire une impasse.

finger ['fiŋgə] *n* doigt *m*; **fore—index** *m*; **middle —** médius *m*; **ring—** annulaire *m*; **little —** petit doigt *m*, auriculaire *m*; *vt* toucher, manier, jouer, tripoter.

fingering ['fiŋgəriŋ] *n* maniement *m*, touche *f*, doigté *m*.

finger-bowl ['fiŋgəboul] *n* rince-doigts *m*.

fingerpost ['fiŋgəpoust] *n* poteau indicateur *m*.

fingerprint ['fiŋgəprint] *n* empreinte digitale *f*.

finish ['finiʃ] n fini m, dernière touche f; to a — à mort; vti finir, terminer; vt achever; vi prendre fin, se terminer.

finished ['finiʃt] a accompli.

Finland ['finlənd] n Finlande f.

Finn [fin] n Finlandais(e) mf.

Finnish ['finiʃ] an finlandais m.

fir [fəː] n sapin m.

fire ['faiə] n feu m, incendie m, tir m, ardeur f; vt allumer, incendier, mettre le feu à, enflammer; vi faire feu; — away allez!

fire-alarm ['faiərə,laːm] n avertisseur d'incendie m.

firearm ['faiəraːm] n arme à feu f.

firebrand ['faiəbrænd] n incendiaire m, boutefeu m, brandon m.

fire-brigade ['faiəbri,geid] n compagnie de sapeurs-pompiers f.

firedamp ['faiədæmp] n grisou m.

firedog ['faiədɔg] n chenet m.

fire-engine ['faiər,endʒin] n pompe à incendie f.

fire-escape ['faiəris,keip] n échelle de sauvetage f.

fireguard ['faiəgaːd] n garde-feu m.

fireman ['faiəmən] n pompier m, chauffeur m.

fireplace ['faiəpleis] n cheminée f.

fireproof ['faiəpruːf] a ignifuge.

fireside ['faiəsaid] n coin du feu m.

firework ['faiəwəːk] n feu d'artifice m.

firing-party ['faiəriŋ,paːti] n peloton d'exécution m.

firm [fəːm] n firme f, maison de commerce f; a ferme, solide, résolu.

firmly ['fəːmli] ad fermement.

firmness ['fəːmnis] n fermeté f, solidité f.

first [fəːst] a premier; ad premièrement, primo.

first-aid ['fəːst'eid] n premiers secours m pl.

first-class ['fəːstklaːs] a de première classe, qualité.

first-rate ['fəːst'reit] a de premier ordre.

firth [fəːθ] n estuaire m.

fish [fiʃ] n poisson m; vti pêcher.

fishbone ['fiʃboun] n arête f.

fisherman ['fiʃəmən] n pêcheur m.

fishery ['fiʃəri] n pêcherie f.

fishing ['fiʃiŋ] n pêche f.

fishing-ground ['fiʃiŋgraund] n pêcherie f.

fishing-net n ['fiʃiŋnet] n épervier.

fishing-rod ['fiʃiŋrɔd] n canne à pêche f.

fish-kettle ['fiʃ'ketl] n poissonnière f.

fishmonger ['fiʃ,mʌŋgə] n marchand de poisson m.

fishmonger's ['fiʃ,mʌŋgəz] n poissonnerie f.

fish-pond ['fiʃpɔnd] n vivier m.

fishy ['fiʃi] a poissonneux, louche.

fissionable ['fiʃnəbl] a fissile.

fissure ['fiʃə] n fissure f.

fist [fist] n poing m.

fit [fit] n attaque f, accès m, ajustement m, coupe f; a apte, bon, convenable, en forme; vt aller à, ajuster, garnir, munir, préparer, équiper; vi s'adapter, s'ajuster; to — on monter, essayer; to — out garnir, équiper; to — up monter.

fitful ['fitful] a capricieux.

fitfully ['fitfuli] ad par accès, par à-coups.

fitly ['fitli] ad à propos, à point.

fitness ['fitnis] n parfait état m convenance f, aptitude f.

fitter ['fitə] n ajusteur m, essayeur m.

fitting ['fitiŋ] n ajustage m, essayage m; pl garnitures f pl; a bon, juste, approprié.

five [faiv] an cinq m.

fivefold ['faivfould] a quintuple.

fix [fiks] n embarras m, situation fâcheuse f; vt fixer, établir, arrêter, assujettir.

fixed [fikst] a fixe, arrêté.

fixedly ['fiksidli] ad fixement.

fixity ['fiksiti] n fixité f.

fixture(s) ['fikstʃə(s)] n garniture(s) fixe(s) f (pl), (fig) meuble m, match m.

fizz [fiz] n bruit de fusée m, pétillement m, (fam) champagne m; vi pétiller, siffler.

fizzle ['fizl] n pétillement m, grésillement m; vi fuser, grésiller; to — out faire long feu, faire four.

flabbergast ['flæbəgaːst] vt renverser, stupéfier.

flabby ['flæbi] a flasque, pendant.

flag [flæg] n drapeau m, pavillon m, dalle f, glaïeul m; vi pendre, languir, fléchir, se relâcher; vt jalonner, signaler, pavoiser.

flagbearer ['flæg'bɛərə] n porte-drapeau m.

flagging ['flægiŋ] n dallage m, ralentissement m.

flagon ['flægən] n flacon m, burette f.

flagrancy ['fleigrənsi] n éclat m, énormité f.

flagrant ['fleigrənt] a flagrant, énorme, scandaleux.

flagship ['flægʃip] n vaisseau-amiral m.

flagstaff ['flægstaːf] n mât m.

flail [fleil] n fléau m.

flair [flɛə] n flair m.

flak [flæk] n tir m contre avion, la DCA.

flake [fleik] n flocon m, flammèche f, lamelle f, pelure f, écaille f; vi tomber à flocons, (s')écailler.

flaky ['fleiki] a floconneux, écailleux, feuilleté.

flame [fleim] n flamme f; vi flamber, s'enflammer.

flame-thrower ['fleim,θrouə] n lance-flammes m.

flaming ['fleimiŋ] a flambant.

Flanders ['flaːndəz] n Flandre f.

flank [flæŋk] n flanc m; vt flanquer, prendre de flanc.

flannel ['flænl] n flanelle f.

flap [flæp] n tape f, battement d'ailes m, patte f, claquement m, pan m, bord m; vti battre; vi s'agiter, claquer.

flare [flɛə] n flambée f, fusée éclairante f, flamme f, feu d'atterrissage m; vi flamber, s'évaser; vt évaser; **to — up** s'emporter, s'enflammer.

flash [flæʃ] n éclair m, lueur f; **in a —** en un clin d'œil; vi flamboyer, jeter des éclairs; vt faire étinceler, télégraphier.

flashing ['flæʃiŋ] n éclat m, clignotement m, projection f.

flashy ['flæʃi] a voyant, tapageur.

flask [flɑːsk] n gourde f, fiole f.

flat [flæt] n appartement m, plat m, plaine f, (mus) bémol m; a plat, tout sec, pur, éventé, catégorique, insipide.

flat-iron ['flæt,aiən] n fer à repasser m.

flatness ['flætnis] n platitude f, monotonie f, égalité f.

flatten ['flætn] vt aplatir, aplanir, niveler, laminer; vi s'aplatir, s'aplanir.

flatter ['flætə] vt flatter.

flatterer ['flætərə] n flatteur m.

flattery ['flætəri] n flatterie f.

flaunt [flɔːnt] vi s'exhiber, se pavaner; vt afficher, faire étalage de, étaler.

flautist ['flɔːtist] n flûtiste mf.

flavour ['fleivə] n saveur f, bouquet m, fumet m, goût m; vt assaisonner, relever, aromatiser.

flavouring ['fleivəriŋ] n assaisonnement m.

flaw [flɔː] n fêlure f, défaut m, paille f, tache f.

flawless ['flɔːlis] a impeccable, sans défaut.

flax [flæks] n lin m.

flaxen ['flæksən] a en (de) lin, blond, filasse.

flay [flei] vt étriller, écorcher, massacrer, rosser.

flea [fliː] n puce f, vétille f.

fleabite ['fliːbait] n morsure de puce f, rien m.

fleck [flek] n tache de son f, grain m, moucheture f; vt tacheter, moucheter.

fled [fled] pt pp of **flee**.

fledged [fledʒd] a couvert de plumes; **fully—** a dru, émancipé.

flee [fliː] vi fuir, se sauver.

fleece [fliːs] n toison f; vt tondre, estamper.

fleecy ['fliːsi] a laineux, cotonneux, moutonné.

fleet [fliːt] n flotte f; train m; vi passer, s'enfuir.

fleeting ['fliːtiŋ] a fugitif, éphémère.

flesh [fleʃ] n chair f.

fleshy ['fleʃi] a charnu, pulpeux.

flew [fluː] pt of **fly**.

flex [fleks] n flexible m; vti fléchir.

flexibility [,fleksi'biliti] n flexibilité f, souplesse f.

flexible ['fleksəbl] a flexible, souple.

flexion ['flekʃən] n flexion f, courbe f.

flick [flik] n chiquenaude f, pichenette f, petit coup m.

flicker ['flikə] n frémissement m, éclair m, clignement m; vi frémir, vaciller, flotter.

flight [flait] n fuite f, vol m, ligne f, essor m, saillie f, volée f, raid m; **— deck** pont m d'envol.

flighty ['flaiti] a volage, écervelé, frivole, pauvre.

flimsy ['flimzi] a fragile, trivial, frivole.

flinch [flintʃ] vi broncher, reculer, fléchir.

fling [fliŋ] n jet m, impulsion f; vt (re)jeter, lancer, émettre; vi se jeter, se précipiter.

flint ['flint] n silex m, pierre à briquet f.

flinty ['flinti] a dur comme pierre, caillouteux.

flip [flip] n chiquenaude f, tape f, petit tour de vol m; vt lancer, tapoter, (ear) pincer.

flippancy ['flipənsi] n désinvolture f, irrévérence f.

flippant ['flipənt] a impertinent, désinvolte.

flirt [flɜːt] n coquette f, flirt m; vi flirter, conter fleurette (à with).

flit [flit] vi voltiger, passer, déménager; n déménagement m.

float [flout] n radeau m, bouchon m, flotteur m, rampe f; vt lancer, émettre, porter, mettre à flot, flotter; vi flotter, nager, faire la planche.

floatation [flou'teiʃən] n lancement m, émission f.

flock [flɔk] n troupeau m, troupe f, bourre m, flocon m; vi s'assembler, s'attrouper.

floe [flou] n banquise f.

flog [flɔg] vt fouetter, fouailler, bazarder.

flogging ['flɔgiŋ] n fessée f, flagellation f.

flood [flʌd] n inondation f, crue f, déluge m, flux m, marée f; vt inonder, irriguer, grossir; vi déborder, se noyer, être en crue.

floodgate ['flʌdgeit] n vanne f.

floodlight ['flʌdlait] vt illuminer par projecteurs.

floor [flɔː] n plancher m, parquet m, étage m; vt planchéier, terrasser, renverser.

floorcloth ['flɔːklɔθ] n torchon m.

flop [flɔp] n plouf!, bruit m sourd, four m; vi s'affaler, faire four.

florid ['flɔrid] a rubicond, fleuri, flamboyant.

florist ['flɔrist] n fleuriste mf.

floss [flɔs] n bourre f.

flotilla [flə'tilə] n flottille f.

flotsam ['flɔtsəm] n épave f flottante.

flounce [flauns] n sursaut m, volant m; **to — out** sortir en colère.

flounder ['flaundə] n carrelet m; vi patauger.

flour ['flauə] n farine f; **cassava —, garri** farine f de manioc.

flourish ['flʌriʃ] n fioritures f pl, parafe m, grand geste m, fanfare f; vi prospérer, embellir; vt brandir.

flourishing ['flʌriʃiŋ] a florissant, prospère.

flout [flaut] vt narguer, se moquer de.

flow [flou] n écoulement m, arrivée f, courant m, flux m, flot m; vi couler, affluer, flotter, résulter, se jeter.

flower ['flauə] n fleur f; vi fleurir; **— garden** jardin m d'agrément; **— shop** boutique f de fleuriste.

flowery ['flauəri] a fleuri.

flowing ['flouiŋ] a coulant, flottant, aisé.

flown [floun] pp of **fly**; a **high —** ampoulé.

flu [flu:] n see **influenza**.

fluctuate ['flʌktjueit] vi fluctuer, vaciller, flotter.

fluctuation [,flʌktju'eiʃən] n fluctuation f, variations f pl.

flue [flu:] n tuyau m (de cheminée).

fluency ['flu:ənsi] n aisance f, facilité f.

fluent ['flu:ənt] a coulant, facile.

fluently ['flu:əntli] ad avec facilité, couramment.

fluff [flʌf] n duvet m.

fluffy ['flʌfi] a duveté, pelucheux.

fluid ['flu:id] an fluide m.

fluidity [flu:'iditi] n fluidité f, inconstance f.

fluke [flu:k] n fer m, pointe f, (coup m de) raccroc m.

flung [flʌŋ] pt pp of **fling**.

flurry ['flʌri] n coup de vent m, excitation f, émoi m, rafale f, vt agiter, étourdir.

flush [flʌʃ] n rougeur f, accès m, transport m, flot m, jet m, vol m d'oiseau, chasse f (d'eau); a débordant, regorgeant, abondant, de niveau; vi jaillir, rougir; vt enivrer, inonder, laver à grande eau.

fluster ['flʌstə] n agitation f; vt énerver, agiter, faire perdre la tête à.

flute [flu:t] n flûte f, cannelure f; vi jouer de la flûte, parler d'une voix flûtée; vt canneler, rainurer.

flutist ['flu:tist] n flûtiste mf.

flutter ['flʌtə] n battement m (d'ailes), émoi m, sensation f, palpitation f, voltigement m; vti battre faiblement; vi palpiter, s'agiter, frémir, trémousser; vt agiter, secouer.

flux [flʌks] n flux m.

fly [flai] n mouche f, fiacre m, braguette f; a malin; vi voler,

courir, se sauver; vti fuir; vt faire voler, piloter; **to — away** s'envoler.

flyer ['flaiə] n aviateur, -trice.

flying ['flaiiŋ] n vol m, aviation f; a flottant, au vent, volant **— visit** visite-éclair f.

flying-boat ['flaiiŋbout] n hydravion m.

flying-bomb ['flaiiŋ'bɔm] n bombe volante f.

flying-club ['flaiiŋ,klʌb] n aéro-club m.

flying-squad ['flaiiŋ'skwɔd] n brigade volante f.

flysheet ['flaiʃi:t] n circulaire m, papillon m.

flywheel ['flaiwi:l] n volant m (de commande).

foal [foul] n poulain m.

foam [foum] n écume f; vi écumer, bouillonner, baver.

fob [fɔb] n gousset m, régence f; **to — off** vt refiler.

focus ['foukəs] n foyer m; vt mettre au point, concentrer; vi converger; **out of —** brouillé.

fodder ['fɔdə] n fourrage m.

foe [fou] n ennemi m.

fog [fɔg] n brouillard m, voile m; vt embrumer, voiler.

foggy ['fɔgi] a épais, brumeux, brouillé.

foghorn ['fɔghɔ:n] n sirène f.

fog-signal ['fɔg,signl] n pétard m.

foil [fɔil] n feuille f, tain m, repoussoir m, fleuret m, piste f; vt donner le change à, tromper, déjouer, faire échouer.

foist [fɔist] vt repasser, refiler.

fold [fould] n parc à bestiaux m, bercail m, troupeau m, (re)pli m, creux m, battant m; vt parquer, plier, envelopper, serrer, croiser; vi se (re)plier.

folding ['fouldiŋ] n (re)pliage m; a pliant, rabattable.

foliage ['fouliidʒ] n feuillage n, feuillée f.

folk(s) [fouk(s)] n gens mf pl.

folksong ['fouksɔŋ] n chanson f populaire.

follow ['fɔlou] vti suivre; vt succéder à; vi s'ensuivre.

follower ['fɔlouə] n partisan m, serviteur m.

following ['fɔlouiŋ] n suite f; a suivant.

folly ['fɔli] n folie f.

foment [fou'ment] vt fomenter.

fond [fɔnd] a tendre, affectueux, indulgent, friand, amateur; **to be — of** aimer.

fondle ['fɔndl] vt câliner.

font [fɔnt] n fonts baptismaux m pl.

food [fu:d] n nourriture f, alimentation f, vivres m pl, pâture f, pâtée f; a alimentaire, nutritif.

fool [fu:l] n sot, sotte, fou, folle imbécile mf, idiot(e) mf, bouffon m vt rouler, duper; vi faire la bête.

foolhardiness ['fuːlˌhɑːdinis] n témérité f.

foolhardy ['fuːlˌhɑːdi] a téméraire, casse-cou.

foolish ['fuːliʃ] a stupide, fou, absurde, insensé.

foolishness ['fuːliʃnis] n folie f, bêtise f.

foolproof ['fuːlpruːf] a de sureté, à toute épreuve.

foot [fut] n pied m, patte f, base f, fond m, bas m, bas-bout m; vt danser, payer.

foot-and-mouth disease ['futən'mauθdi'ziːz] n fièvre aphteuse f.

football ['futbɔːl] n ballon m, football m.

footboard ['futbɔːd] n marchepied m.

footbridge ['futbridʒ] n passerelle f.

foothold ['futhould] n prise f, pied m.

footing ['futiŋ] n pied m, prise f.

footlights ['futlaits] n rampe f.

footman ['futmən] n valet de pied m, laquais m.

footmuff ['futmʌf] n chancelière f.

footnote ['futnout] n note f.

footpath ['futpaːθ] n sentier m, trottoir m.

footplate ['futpleit] n plateforme f.

footprint ['futprint] n empreinte f.

footslogger ['futslɔgə] n piéton m, fantassin m, biffin m.

footstep ['futstep] n pas m; pl traces f pl, brisées f pl.

footstool ['futstuːl] n tabouret m.

foot-warmer ['futˌwɔːmə] n bouillotte f, chaufferette f.

footwear ['futwɛə] n chaussures f pl.

foozle ['fuːzl] vt rater.

fop [fɔp] n gandin m, fat m.

for [fɔ] prep pour, à, quant à, comme, pendant, malgré; cj car.

forage ['fɔridʒ] n fourrage m; vt fourrager marauder; vi aller au fourrage.

forage-cap ['fɔridʒ,kæp] n calot m.

forasmuch [fərəz'mʌtʃ] cj vu que, d'autant que.

foray ['fɔrei] n raid m, incursion f.

forbear [fɔ'bɛə] vt tolérer, s'abstenir de; vi patienter.

forbearance [fɔ'bɛərəns] n indulgence f, patience f.

forbid [fə'bid] vt défendre.

forbidden [fə'bidn] a interdit, défendu, prohibé; **smoking** — défense de fumer.

forbidding [fə'bidiŋ] a sévère, rébarbatif, sinistre.

force [fɔːs] n force f, contrainte f, violence f, puissance f, vigueur f; **task** — corps m expéditionnaire; vt forcer.

forced [fɔːst] a forcé, inévitable, faux.

forceful ['fɔːsful] a énergique, puissant.

force-land ['fɔːslænd] vi faire un atterrissage forcé.

forcible ['fɔːsəbl] a puissant, vigoureux.

ford [fɔːd] n gué m; vt passer à gué.

fordable ['fɔːdəbl] a guéable.

fore [fɔː] n avant m, premier plan m; **to the** — en vue.

forearm ['fɔːrɑːm] n avant-bras m.

forebear ['fɔːbɛə] n ancêtre m.

forebode [fɔː'boud] vt pressentir, augurer.

foreboding [fɔː'boudiŋ] n pressentiment m, mauvais augure m.

forecast ['fɔːkɑːst] n prévision f, pronostic m; vt prévoir.

forecastle ['fouksl] n gaillard d'avant m.

foreclose [fɔː'klouz] vt défendre; (law) forclore, saisir.

forefather ['fɔːˌfɑːðə] n ancêtre m, aïeul m.

forefinger ['fɔːˌfiŋgə] n index m.

forefront ['fɔːfrʌnt] n premier rang m, premier plan m.

foregone ['fɔːgɔn] a acquis (couru) d'avance, prévu.

foreground ['fɔːgraund] n premier plan m.

forehead ['fɔrid] n front m.

foreign ['fɔrin] a étranger.

foreigner ['fɔrinə] n étranger, -ère.

foreland ['fɔːlənd] n promontoire m, cap m, pointe f.

forelock ['fɔːlɔk] n mèche f.

foreman ['fɔːmən] n contremaître n, chef d'équipe m, président du jury m.

foremost ['fɔːmoust] a premier, en tête.

forenoon ['fɔːnuːn] n matinée f.

forerunner ['fɔːˌrʌnə] n précurseur m, avant-coureur m, avant-courrier, -ière.

foresee [fɔː'siː] vt prévoir.

foreshadow [fɔː'ʃædou] vt laisser prévoir, présager.

foresight ['fɔːsait] n prevoyance f, prévision f, (gun) bouton m de mire.

forest ['fɔrist] n forêt f.

forestall [fɔː'stɔːl] vt anticiper, devancer, prévenir.

forester ['fɔristə] n garde-forestier m.

foretaste ['fɔːteist] n avant-goût m.

foretell [fɔː'tel] vt prédire, présager.

forethought ['fɔːθɔːt] n prévoyance f, préméditation f.

forever [fə'revə] ad pour toujours, à jamais.

forewarn [fɔː'wɔːn] vt prévenir, avertir.

foreword ['fɔːwəːd] n avant-propos m, préface f.

forfeit ['fɔːfit] n prix m, rançon f, amende f, confiscation f, forfait m; vt perdre, avoir à payer, forfaire à.

forgave [fə'geiv] pt of **forgive**.

forge [fɔːdʒ] n forge f; vt forger, contrefaire, fabriquer; **to** — **ahead** prendre de l'avance, pousser de l'avant.

forger ['fɔːdʒə] n faussaire mf, forgeron m.

forgery ['fɔːdʒəri] n faux m, contre-façon f.

forget [fə'get] vt oublier, négliger.

forgetful [fə'getful] a oublieux, négligent.

forgetfulness [fə'getfulnis] n oubli m.

forget-me-not [fə'getminɔt] n myosotis m.

forgivable [fə'givabl] a pardonnable.

forgive [fə'giv] vt pardonner.

forgiveness [fə'givnis] n pardon m.

forgiving [fə'givin] a indulgent.

forgo [fɔː'gou] vt renoncer à.

forgot, -ten [fə'gɔt, -n] pt pp of **forget**.

fork [fɔːk] n fourche f, fourchette f, branche f, (em)branchement m; vi fourcher, bifurquer.

forked [fɔːkt] a fourchu.

forlorn [fə'lɔːn] a abandonné, désespéré, désolé.

form [fɔːm] n forme f, formule f, formulaire m, formalité f, manières f pl, classe f, banc m, gite f; vt former, façonner, contracter; vi prendre forme, se former, se faire.

formal ['fɔːməl] a formel, formaliste, gourmé, de cérémonie, protocolaire.

formality [fɔː'mæliti] n formalité f, cérémonie f.

formally ['fɔːməli] ad formellement.

formation [fɔː'meiʃən] n formation f, disposition f.

former ['fɔːmə] a antérieur, ancien, premier, précédent, celui-là, ceux-là, celle(s)-là.

formerly ['fɔːməli] ad antérieurement, autrefois.

formidable ['fɔːmidəbl] a formidable, redoutable.

formless ['fɔːmlis] a informe.

formula ['fɔːmjulə] n formule f.

formulate ['fɔːmjuleit] vt formuler.

forsake [fə'seik] vt renoncer à, retirer, abandonner.

forsaken [fə'seikən] pp of **forsake**.

forsook [fə'suk] pt of **forsake**.

forswear [fɔː'swɛə] vt renoncer sous serment à, renier.

fort [fɔːt] n fort m; **small — fortin** m.

forth [fɔːθ] ad en avant, en route; **and so — et ainsi de suite, et caetera.**

forthcoming [fɔːθ'kʌmiŋ] a proche, prochain, tout prêt, à venir.

forthright ['fɔːθrait] a droit, franc; ad tout droit.

forthwith ['fɔːθwiθ] ad sur-le-champ.

fortieth ['fɔːtiiθ] an quarantième mf.

fortification [,fɔːtifi'keiʃən] n fortification f.

fortify ['fɔːtifai] vt fortifier, affermir, armer.

fortitude ['fɔːtitjuːd] n force d'âme f, courage m.

fortnight ['fɔːtnait] n quinzaine f; **today — d'aujourd'hui en quinze.**

fortnightly ['fɔːtnaitli] ad tous les quinze jours; a bimensuel.

fortress ['fɔːtris] n forteresse f.

fortuitous [fɔː'tjuːitəs] a fortuit, imprévu.

fortunate ['fɔːtʃənit] a heureux, qui a de la chance.

fortunately ['fɔːtʃənitli] ad heureusement.

fortune ['fɔːtʃən] n fortune f, chance f, hasard m.

fortune-teller ['fɔːtʃən,telə] n diseuse de bonne aventure f.

forty ['fɔːti] an quarante m.

forward ['fɔːwəd] n avant m; a qui va de l'avant, précoce, avancé, effronté, présomptueux; ad en avant; vt promouvoir, hâter, faire suivre, expédier.

forwardness ['fɔːwədnis] n audace f, présomption f.

fossil ['fɔsil] an fossile m.

foster ['fɔstə] vt nourrir, élever, encourager.

foster-brother ['fɔstə,brʌðə] n frère de lait m.

foster-child ['fɔstətʃaild] n nourrisson, -onne.

foster-father ['fɔstə,faːðə] n père nourricier m.

foster-mother ['fɔstə,mʌðə] n nourrice f.

foster-sister ['fɔstə,sistə] n sœur de lait f.

fought [fɔːt] pt pp of **fight**.

foul [faul] n coup bas m, faute f; a sale, nauséabond, vicié, obscène, traître, ordurier, déloyal, emmêlé, enrayé; vt salir, enrayer, emmêler, obstruer; vi se rencontrer s'enrayer, s'encrasser.

found [faund] pp pt of **find**; vt fonder, établir.

foundation [faun'deiʃən] n fondation f, fondement m, établissement m, assise f.

founder ['faundə] n fondateur m, fondeur m; vi s'effondrer, sombrer, couler.

foundling ['faundliŋ] n enfant trouvé(e) mf.

foundry ['faundri] n fonderie f.

fountain ['fauntin] n fontaine f, source f, jet d'eau m, réservoir m.

fountain-pen ['fauntinpen] n stylo m.

four [fɔː] an quatre m; **—engined** quadriréacteur.

fourfold ['fɔːfould] a quadruple.

fourteen [fɔː'tiːn] an quatorze m.

fourteenth ['fɔː'tiːnθ] an quatorzième mf, quatorze m.

fourth [fɔːθ] an quatrième mf, quatre m.

fowl [faul] n volaille f, oiseau m.

fox [fɔks] n renard m, rusé m, roublard m.

foxy ['fɔksi] a roublard, rusé.

fraction ['frækʃən] n fraction f, fragment m.

fractious ['frækʃəs] a hargneux, rétif.

fracture ['fræktʃə] n fracture f; vt fracturer, casser; vi se casser, se fracturer.

fragile ['frædʒail] a fragile.

fragility [frə'dʒiliti] n fragilité f.

fragment ['frægmənt] n fragment m.

fragrance ['freigrəns] n parfum m.

fragrant ['freigrənt] a embaumé, odorant, parfumé.

frail [freil] n bannette f; a frêle, éphémère.

frailty ['freilti] n fragilité f.

frame [freim] n cadre m, fuselage m, châssis m, charpente f, corps m, carcasse f; (US) — house maison f démontable (en bois); vt encadrer, façonner, ajuster, construire, concevoir, monter un coup contre.

frame-up ['freimʌp] n coup monté m.

framework ['freimwə:k] n cadre m, charpente f.

France [frɑːns] n France f.

franchise ['fræntʃaiz] n droit de vote m, franchise f.

Frances ['frɑːnsis] Françoise f, Francine f.

Francis ['frɑːnsis] Francis m, François m.

frank [fræŋk] a franc.

frankincense ['fræŋkinsens] n encens m.

frantic ['fræntik] a frénétique, effréné.

fraternal [frə'tə:nl] a fraternel.

fraternity [frə'tə:niti] n amour fraternel m, confrérie f, compagnie f.

fraternize ['frætənaiz] vi fraterniser.

fraternizing ['frætə'naiziŋ] n fraternisation f.

fratricide ['frætrisaid] n fratricide mf.

fraud [frɔːd] n fraude f, supercherie f, imposteur m.

fraudulent ['frɔːdjulənt] a frauduleux.

fraught [frɔːt] a gros (de with).

fray [frei] n bagarre f; vt effilocher, effiler; vi s'effilocher, s'effiler.

frayed [freid] a frangeux.

freak [friːk] n caprice m, phénomène m, monstre m.

freakish ['friːkiʃ] a capricieux, fantasque.

freckle ['frekl] n tache de rousseur f.

freckled ['frekld] a couvert de taches de rousseur.

free [friː] a libre, exempt, gratuit, franco; vt affranchir, libérer, élargir.

freedom ['friːdəm] n liberté f.

freehold ['friːhould] n propriété libre f.

freelance ['friːlɑːns] n franc-tireur m, indépendant(e) mf.

freely ['friːli] ad librement, largement, franchement.

freemason ['friː,meisn] n francmaçon m.

freemasonry ['friː'meisnri] n francmaçonnerie f.

free-trade ['friː'treid] n libre échange m.

free-will ['friː'wil] n libre arbitre m; of one's own — de son propre gré.

freeze [friːz] vti geler; vi se figer, se congeler; vt glacer, congeler; n austerité f, blocage m des prix.

freezing ['friːziŋ] a de congélation, glacial; n gel m, réfrigération f.

freight [freit] n fret m, cargaison f, (US) marchandises f pl; vt (af)fréter, charger, noliser.

French [frentʃ] an français m.

Frenchman ['frentʃmən] n Français m.

French-speaking ['frentʃ'spiːkiŋ] a francophone.

Frenchwoman ['frentʃ,wumən] n Française f.

frenzied ['frenzid] a fou, affolé, délirant, frénétique.

frenzy ['frenzi] n frénésie f, transport m.

frequency ['friːkwənsi] n fréquence f.

frequent ['friːkwənt] a fréquent, répandu.

frequent [friː'kwent] vt fréquenter, courir, hanter.

frequentation [°friːkwen'teiʃən] n fréquentation f.

frequently ['friːkwəntli] ad fréquamment, souvent.

fresco ['freskou] n fresque f.

fresh [freʃ] a frais, nouveau, novice, récent, (water) doux, (wind) vif, alerte, effronté.

freshen ['freʃn] vi rafraîchir, raviver.

freshness ['freʃnis] n fraîcheur f, vigueur f.

fret [fret] n grecque f, irritation f; vt ronger, irriter; vi s'agiter, se faire du mauvais sang.

fretful ['fretful] a irritable, agité.

fretfulness ['fretfulnis] n irritabilité f.

fretsaw ['fretsɔː] n scie à découper f.

fretwork ['fretwə:k] n découpage m, bois découpé m.

friable ['fraiəbl] a friable.

friar ['fraiə] n moine m, frère m.

friction ['frikʃən] n friction f, frottement m, tirage m.

Friday ['fraidi] n vendredi m; Good — vendredi saint.

friend [frend] n ami(e) mf.

friendly ['frendli] a amical.

friendship ['frendʃip] n amitié f.

frieze [friːz] n frise f.

frigate ['frigit] n frégate f.

fright [frait] n frayeur f, épouvante f, peur f.

frighten ['fraitn] vt terrifier, faire peur à.

frightful ['fraitful] a effrayant, affreux.

frightfulness ['fraitfulnis] n terreur f, horreur f.

frigid ['fridʒid] a glacial, froid, réfrigérant.

frill [fril] n ruche f, jabot m, volant m; vt plisser, tuyauter.

fringe [frindʒ] n frange f, bord m, zone f limitrophe.

frippery ['fripəri] n tralala m, fioritures f pl, babioles f pl.

frisk [frisk] vi gambader.

frisky ['friski] a fringant, frétillant, folâtre.

fritter ['fritə] n beignet m; to — away gaspiller.

frivolous ['frivələs] a frivole, futile.

frizz [friz] n frisette f, vti friser.

frizzle ['frizl] vi crépiter, grésiller; vt faire frire.

frock [frɔk] n blouse f, robe f.

frockcoat ['frɔk'kout] n redingote f.

frog [frɔg] n grenouille f.

frolic ['frɔlik] n cabriole f; pl gambades f pl; vi batifoler, s'ébattre.

frolicsome ['frɔliksəm] a espiègle, folâtre.

from [frɔm] prep de, avec, d'après, de chez, à, contre.

front [frʌnt] n front m, façade f, devant m, plastron m, devanture f; in — of devant, en avant de; vt affronter, donner sur.

frontage ['frʌntidʒ] n exposition f, vue f, façade f, devanture f.

frontier ['frʌntjə] n frontière f.

frontispiece ['frʌntispi:s] n frontispice m.

frost [frɔst] n gelée f, gel m, givre m, verglas m; vt geler, glacer, givrer, ferrer à glace.

frostbite ['frɔstbait] n gelure f, congélation f.

frostbitten ['frɔst,bitn] a gelé, brûlé par le froid.

frosty ['frɔsti] a gelé, givré, poudré, glacial.

froth [frɔθ] n écume f, mousse f.

frothy ['frɔθi] a écumeux, mousseux.

frown [fraun] n froncement de sourcils m, vi froncer les sourcils, se renfrogner; to — upon désapprouver.

frowzy ['frauzi] a moisi, renfermé, négligé.

froze, -zen [frouz, -n] pp pt of **freeze**.

fructify ['frʌktifai] vi porter fruit, fructifier; vt faire fructifier.

frugal ['fru:gəl] a frugal, économe, simple.

frugality [fru:'gæliti] n frugalité f, économie f.

fruit [fru:t] n fruit m.

fruiterer ['fru:tərə] n frutier, -ière.

fruiterer's ['fru:tərəz] n fruiterie f.

fruitful ['fru:tful] a fécond, fructueux, fertile.

fruitfulness ['fru:tfulnis] n fécondité f, productivité f.

fruition [fru:'iʃən] n jouissance f, maturation f.

fruitless ['fru:tlis] a stérile.

fruitlessness ['fru:tlisnis] n stérilité f.

fruit-tree ['fru:ttri:] n arbre fruitier m.

frustrate [frʌs'treit] vt frustrer, déjouer, faire échouer.

frustration [frʌs'treiʃən] n frustration f, anéantissement m.

fry [frai] n fretin m, frai m; vt faire frire; vi frire.

frying-pan ['fraiŋ,pæn] n poêle f.

fuddle ['fʌdl] n cuite f; vt griser, brouiller, enfumer.

fuel ['fjuəl] n combustible m, carburant m.

fufu [fufu] n pâte f.

fugacious [fju:'geiʃəs] a fugace.

fugitive ['fju:dʒitiv] an fugitif, -ive mf; a éphémère.

fulcrum ['fʌlkrəm] m point m d'appui.

fulfil [ful'fil] vt remplir, accomplir, exaucer, exécuter.

fulfilment [ful'filmənt] n accomplissement m, exécution f, réalisation f.

full [ful] a plein, rempli, complet, riche, vigoureux, rond, ample, bouffant.

full-blown ['ful'bloun] a épanoui.

full-dress ['ful'dres] n grande tenue f; — rehearsal répétition générale f.

full-debate ['fuldi:'beit] n débat en règle m.

full-length ['ful'leŋθ] a en pied.

full-speed ['ful'spi:d] ad à toute vitesse, à fond de train.

full-stop ['ful'stɔp] n point m.

fullness ['fulnis] n plénitude f, ampleur f, rondeur f.

fully ['fuli] ad pleinement, en plein.

fulminate ['fulmineit] vti fulminer.

fulsome ['fulsəm] a écœurant, excessif.

fumble ['fʌmbl] vi tâtonner, fouiller; to — with tripoter.

fume [fju:m] n fumée f, vapeur f; vi fumer (de rage), rager.

fun [fʌn] n plaisanterie f, amusement m; for — pour rire, histoire de rire.

function ['fʌŋkʃən] n fonction f, cérémonie f; vi fonctionner, marcher.

functionary ['fʌŋkʃənəri] n fonctionnaire m.

fund [fʌnd] n fonds m, caisse f, rente f; vt convertir, consolider.

fundamental [,fʌndə'mentl] a fondamental, essentiel, foncier; n pl essentiel m, principe m.

funeral ['fju:nərəl] n enterrement m, funérailles f pl.

funereal [fju:'niəriəl] a funéraire, funèbre, sépulcral.

funicular [fju:'nikju:lə] n funiculaire m.

funk [fʌŋk] n frousse f, trouille f, trac m, froussard(e) mf; vt esquiver; vi avoir la frousse, se dégonfler.

funnel ['fʌnl] n entonnoir m, cheminée f.

funny ['fʌni] a drôle, marrant, comique.

fur [fəː] n fourrure f, dépôt m.

furbish ['fəːbiʃ] vt fourbir, astiquer.

furious ['fjuəriəs] a furieux, furibond, acharné.

furl [fəːl] vt rouler, serrer, plier, ferler

furlough ['fəːlou] n permission f.

furnace ['fəːnis] n fourneau m, fournaise f, calorifère m, brasier m.

furnish ['fəːniʃ] vt fournir, garnir, meubler.

furniture ['fəːnitʃə] n mobilier m, meubles m pl; **piece of** — meuble m; — **polish** encaustique f.

furrier ['fʌriə] n fourreur m, pelletier, -ière.

furrow ['fʌrou] n sillon m, rainure f; vt labourer, sillonner.

furry ['fəːri] a fourré, garni de fourrure, sale, chargé, encrassé.

further ['fəːðə] a nouveau, supplémentaire, plus ample, plus éloigné; ad plus loin, d'ailleurs, davantage; vt appuyer, favoriser, avancer.

furtherance ['fəːðərəns] n avancement m.

furthermore ['fəːðə'mɔː] ad en outre, de plus.

furtive ['fəːtiv] a furtif.

fury ['fjuəri] n fureur f, rage f, furie f.

furze [fəːz] n genêt m, ajonc m.

fuse [fjuːz] n plomb m, amorce f, fusée f; vti tondre, fusionner; **the lights fused** les plombs ont sauté.

fuselage ['fjuːzəlɑːʒ] n fuselage m.

fusion ['fjuːʒən] n fusion f.

fuss [fʌs] n bruit m, agitation f, embarras m pl; vt tracasser; vi faire des embarras, faire des histoires.

fussy ['fʌsi] a agité, tracassier, méticuleux, tatillon.

fusty ['fʌsti] a moisi, ranci, renfermé, démodé.

futile ['fjuːtail] a futile, vain.

futility [fiuːtiliti] n futilité f, inutilité f.

future ['fjuːtʃə] n avenir m, futur m; a futur.

fuzzy ['fʌzi] a crépu, duveté, frisé, brouillé.

G

gab [gæb] n parole f; **gift of the** — bagout m, faconde f.

gabble ['gæbl] n bafouillage m; vi bredouiller, jacasser.

gable ['geibl] n pignon m.

gad [gæd] vi **to** — **about** courir (la prétentaine), papillonner.

gadfly ['gædflai] n taon m.

gadget ['gædʒit] n truc m, dispositif m.

gaff [gæf] n gaffe f.

gag [gæg] n bâillon m, gag m; vt bâillonner.

gage [geidʒ] n gage m, garantie f, défi m; vt gager offrir en gage.

gaiety ['geiəti] n gaieté f, allégresse f.

gain [gein] n gain m, bénéfice m, avantage m; vt gagner.

gainer ['geinə] n gagnant(e) mf.

gainsay ['gein'sei] vt nier, démentir, contredire.

gait [geit] n port m, allure f, démarche f.

gaiter ['geitə] n guêtre f.

galaxy [gæləksi] n voie f lactée, constellation f.

gale [geil] n rafale f–tempête f.

gall [gɔːl] n fiel m, rancœur f, amertume f, écorchure f; (US) effronterie f, aplomb m; vt écorcher, blesser, irriter.

gallant ['gælənt] n élégant m, galant m; a vaillant, galant, brave, noble

gallantly ['gæləntli] ad vaillamment, galamment.

gallantry ['gæləntri] n vaillance f, galanterie f.

gall-bladder ['gɔːl,blædə] n vésicule biliaire f.

gallery ['gæləri] n galerie f, tribune f, musée m.

galley ['gæli] n galère f, cambuse f, placard m.

galley-slave ['gælisleiv] n galérien m.

gallop ['gæləp] n galop m; vi galoper; vt faire galoper.

gallows ['gælouz] n potence f.

gallstone ['gɔːlstoun] n calcul biliaire m.

galore [gəˈlɔː] n abondance f, ad en abondance, à profusion, à gogo.

galosh [gəˈlɔʃ] n caoutchouc m.

galvanize ['gælvənaiz] vt galvaniser.

gamble ['gæmbl] n jeu m, spéculation f; vti jouer; vt risquer.

gambler ['gæmblə] n joueur, -euse.

gambol ['gæmbəl] n gambade f; vi gambader, s'ébattre.

game [geim] n jeu m, partie f, tour m, manche f, gibier m.

game-bag ['geimbæg] n gibecière f.

gamekeeper ['geim'kiːpə] n gardechasse m.

game-licence ['geim'laisəns] n permis de chasse m.

gammon ['gæmən] n jambon m, blague f attrape f; vt saler, fumer, mystifier.

gamp [gæmp] n pépin m, riflard m.

gamut ['gæmət] n gamme f.

gander ['gændə] n jars m.

gang [gæŋ] n équipe f, bande f.

ganger ['gæŋə] n brigadier m, chef d'équipe m.

gangrene ['gæŋgriːn] n gangrène f; vt gangrener; vi se gangrener.

gangrenous ['gæŋgrənəs] a gangreneux.

gangster ['gæŋstə] n bandit m, gangster m.

gangway ['gæŋwei] n passage m, passerelle f.

gaol [dʒeil] n prison f, geôle f; vt écrouer.

gaolbird ['dʒeil.bəːd] n gibier de potence m.

gaoler ['dʒeilə] n gardien de prison m, geôlier m.

gap [gæp] n trou m, trouée f, brèche f, lacune f, différence f, écart m, intervalle f.

gape [geip] vi bâiller, rester bouche bée, être béant, s'ouvrir.

gaping ['geipiŋ] a béant, bouche bée.

garage ['gærɑːʒ] n garage m; vt remiser, garer.

garb [gɑːb] n costume m, tenue f; vt habiller, vêtir.

garbage ['gɑːbidʒ] n ordures f pl, détritus m pl, tripaille f.

garble ['gɑːbl] vt dénaturer, tronquer, mutiler.

garden ['gɑːdn] n jardin m; vi jardiner.

gardener ['gɑːdnə] n jardinier m.

gargle ['gɑːgl] n gargarisme m; vi se gargariser.

gargoyle ['gɑːgɔil] n gargouille f.

garish ['gɛəriʃ] a criard, voyant.

garland ['gɑːlənd] n guirlande f, couronne f.

garlic ['gɑːlik] n ail m.

garment ['gɑːmənt] n vêtement m.

garner ['gɑːnə] n grenier m; vt accumuler, rentrer, engranger.

garnet ['gɑːnit] n grenat m.

garnish ['gɑːniʃ] n garniture f, vt parer, garnir.

garotte [gə'rɔt] n tourniquet m, garotte f; vt étrangler, garrotter.

garret ['gærit] n mansarde f.

garrison ['gærisən] n garnison f; vt tenir garnison à, garnir de troupes.

garrulity [gə'ruːliti] n loquacité f.

garrulous ['gæruləs] a bavard, loquace.

garter ['gɑːtə] n jarretière f.

gas [gæs] n gaz m, (poison-gaᵉ) les gaz m pl, (US) essence f; vt gazer, asphyxier.

gas-burner ['gæs.bəːnə] n bec de gaz m.

gaseous ['geisiəs] a gazeux.

gas-fitter ['gæs.fitə] n gazier m.

gash [gæʃ] n balafre f, taillade f, entaille f; vt balafrer, entailler.

gas-holder ['gæshouldə] n gazomètre m.

gasket ['gæskit] n joint m.

gas-lamp ['gæs'læmp] n réverbère m.

gasman ['gæsmæn] n employé du gaz m.

gas-mantle ['gæs.mæntl] n manchon à gaz m.

gas-mask ['gæsmɑːsk] n masque à gaz m.

gas-meter ['gæs.miːtə] n compteur à gaz m, gazomètre m.

gasoline ['gæsəliːn] n (US) essence f.

gasp [gɑːsp] n aspiration f convulsive, dernier soupir m; vi panteler, en rester bouche bée, avoir un hoquet.

gassy ['gæsi] a gazeux, mousseux.

gastronomy [gæs'trɔnəmi] n gastronomie f.

gasworks ['gæswəːks] n usine à gaz f.

gate [geit] n porte f grille f, barrière f, vanne f; — **money** recette f.

gatecrasher ['geitkræʃə] n resquilleur m.

gateway ['geitwei] n portail m, porte f.

gather ['gæðə] vt réunir, rassembler, cueillir, moissonner, amasser, gagner, froncer imaginer; vi grossir, se réunir, s'accumuler, s'amonceler.

gathering ['gæðəriŋ] n réunion f, amoncellement m, moisson f, cueillette f, quête f, abcès m, fronçure f.

gathers ['gæðəz] n pl fronces f pl.

gaudy ['gɔːdi] a criard, voyant, éclatant.

gauge [geidʒ] n jauge f, mesure f, calibre m, indicateur m, (rails) écartement m; vt jauger, mesurer, estimer.

gaunt [gɔːnt] a hâve, hagard, décharné.

gauntlet ['gɔːntlit] n gantelet m, gant m (à manchette).

gauze [gɔːz] n gaze f.

gave [geiv] pt of **give**.

gawky ['gɔːki] a dégingandé.

gay [gei] a gai, resplendissant.

gaze [geiz] n regard fixe m; vt regarder fixement; to — at fixer, contempler.

gazette [gə'zet] n gazette f, journal officiel m; vt publier à l'Officiel.

gazetteer [.gæzə'tiə] n gazetier m, dictionnaire m de géographie.

gear [giə] n harnais m, attirail m, ustensiles m pl, engrenage m, marche f, vitesse f; to throw into—, embrayer; to put out of — débrayer.

gearbox ['giəbɔks] n boîte de vitesses f, carter m.

gearing ['giəriŋ] n engrenage m, embrayage m.

gearless ['giəles] a sans engrenage.

gear-lever ['giəliːvə] n levier m de vitesse.

gear-shift ['giəʃift] n (US) levier m de vitesse.

gearwheel ['giəwiːl] n roue dentée f, rouage m.

gecko ['gekou] n margouillat m.

gel [dʒel] n gèle m; vi coaguler.

gelatine [.dʒelə'tiːn] n gélatine f; **explosive** — plastic m.

geld [geld] vt châtrer.

gelding ['geldiŋ] n hougre m, eunuque m.

gem [dʒem] n gemme f, perle f, joyau m.

gender ['dʒendə] n genre m

general ['dʒenərəl] an général m.

generalissimo [.dʒenəri'lisimou] n généralissime m.

generality [.dʒenə'ræliti] n généralité f, portée générale f.

generalization [,dʒenərəlai'zeiʃən] n généralisation f.

generalize ['dʒenərəlaiz] vt généraliser.

generalship ['dʒenərəlʃip] n stratégie f.

generate ['dʒenəreit] vt produire, générer.

generation [,dʒenə'reiʃən] n génération f, production f.

generosity [,dʒenə'rɔsiti] n générosité f.

generous ['dʒenərəs] a généreux, copieux.

genesis ['dʒenisis] n genèse f.

genial ['dʒiːnjəl] a jovial, cordial, doux, chaud.

geniality [,dʒiːni'æliti] n belle humeur f, cordialité f.

genius ['dʒiːnjəs] n génie m, aptitude f.

genteel [dʒen'tiːl] a distingué, élégant, qui affecte de la distinction.

Gentile ['dʒentail] n Gentil(e) mf.

gentility [dʒen'tiliti] n bonne société f.

gentle ['dʒentl] a bien né, doux, aimable.

gently ['dʒentli] ad doucement.

gentlefolk ['dʒentlfouk] n personnes de distinction f pl.

gentleman ['dʒentlmən] n monsieur m, homme comme il faut m, gentleman m.

gentlemanly ['dʒentlmənli] a comme il faut, distingué, convenable.

gentleness ['dʒentlnis] n gentillesse f, douceur f.

gentry ['dʒentri] n haute bourgeoisie f, petite noblesse f.

genuine ['dʒenjuin] a authentique, naturel, sincère, franc, véritable.

geographer [dʒi'ɔgrəfə] n géographe m.

geographical [dʒiə'græfikəl] a géographique.

geography [dʒi'ɔgrəfi] n géographie f.

geologist [dʒi'ɔlədʒist] n géologue m.

geology [dʒi'ɔlədʒi] n géologie f.

geometric [dʒiə'metrik] a géométrique; — **drawing** dessin m géométrique, linéaire.

geometrician [,dʒioume'triʃən] n géometre m.

geometry [dʒi'ɔmitri] n géométrie f.

geomorphic [dʒiou'mɔːfik] a semblable à la terre.

geophysics ['dʒiou'fiziks] n pl géophysique, physique f du globe.

George [dʒɔːdʒ] Georges m.

germ [dʒəːm] n germe m, bacille m, microbe m.

German ['dʒəːmən] n Allemand(e) mf; an allemand m.

Germany ['dʒəːməni] n Allemagne f.

germinate ['dʒəːmineit] vi germer.

germination [,dʒəːmi'neiʃən] n germination f.

gerrymander ['dʒerimændə] vt manipuler, truquer.

gesticulate [dʒes'tikjuleit] vi gesticuler.

gesticulation [dʒes,tikju'leiʃən] n gesticulation f.

gesture ['dʒestʃə] n geste m; vi faire des gestes.

get [get] vt se procurer, obtenir, acquérir, chercher, comprendre, piger, tenir, attraper, avoir, faire; vi devenir, arriver, aboutir; (US fam) **get!** fiche le camp!; **to — across** vt traverser, franchir; vi passer la rampe; **to —away** partir, s'échapper; **to — back** revenir, reculer; **to — in** (r)entrer (dans), monter; **to — on** monter (sur); **to — up** se lever, monter.

ghastly ['gɑːstli] a livide, horrible.

gherkin ['gəːkin] n cornichon m.

ghost [goust] n fantôme m, revenant m, ombre f, esprit m.

ghostly ['goustli] a spectral, fantomatique, spirituel.

ghoul [guːl] n vampire m, strige f.

giant ['dʒaiənt] n géant m.

gibber ['dʒibə] vi baragouiner.

gibberish ['gibəriʃ] n baragouin m, charabia m.

gibbet ['dʒibit] n gibet m, potence f.

gibe [dʒaib] n sarcasme m, quolibet m; vt railler.

giblets ['dʒiblits] n pl abat(t)is m pl.

giddiness ['gidinis] n vertige m.

giddy ['gidi] a étourdi, vertigineux, volage.

gift [gift] n don m, cadeau m, prime f.

gifted ['giftid] a (bien) doué.

gig [gig] n cabriolet m, canot m.

gigantic [dʒai'gæntik] a gigantesque, colossal.

giggle ['gigl] n gloussement m, petit rire m; vi glousser, pousser des petits rires.

gild [gild] vt dorer.

gilder ['gildə] n doreur m.

gilding ['gildiŋ] n dorure f.

gill [gil] n ouïe(s) f pl, branchie(s) f pl, bajoues f pl.

gilt [gilt] n dorure f; a doré.

gimlet ['gimlit] n vrille f.

gimmick ['gimik] n machin, truc.

gin [dʒin] n trappe f, genièvre m, gin m, piège m.

ginger ['dʒindʒə] n gingembre m, énergie f; a roux.

gingerbread ['dʒindʒəbred] n (espèce de) pain d'épice m.

gingerly ['dʒindʒəli] ad avec précaution.

gingham ['giŋəm] n ginnham m.

gipsy ['dʒipsi] n bohémien, -ienne, romanichel, -elle.

giraffe [dʒi'rɑːf] n girafe f.

gird [gəːd] vt ceindre, entourer; **to — at** railler.

girder ['gəːdə] n poutre f, poutrelle f.

girdle ['gəːdl] n gaine f, ceinture f, cordelière f.

girl [gə:l] *n* (jeune) fille *f*, amie *f*.
girlish ['gə:liʃ] *a* de jeune fille, efféminé.
girth [gə:θ] *n* sangle *f*, tour *m*.
gist [dʒist] *n* fin mot *m*, fond *m*, essentiel *m*.
give [giv] *vti* donner; to — away trahir, conduire à l'autel; — in céder, se laisser faire; — out annoncer, distribuer; — over cesser, abandonner; to — up renoncer à, livrer.
given ['givn] *pp of* **give**; *cj* étant donné que.
giver ['givə] *n* donneur, -euse, donateur, -trice.
gizzard ['gizəd] *n* gésier *m*.
glacial ['gleisjəl] *a* glacial.
glacier ['glæsjə] *n* glacier *m*.
glad [glæd] *a* content, heureux, joyeux.
gladden ['glædn] *vt* réjouir.
glade [gleid] *n* clairière *f*.
gladly ['glædli] *ad* volontiers.
gladness ['glædnis] *n* plaisir *m*, joie *f*.
glamorous ['glæmərəs] *a* fascinant, charmeur, enchanteur.
glamour ['glæmə] *n* éclat *m*, charme *m*, fascination *f*.
glance [glɑːns] *n* coup d'œil *m*, regard *m*; *vi* jeter un coup d'œil (sur at); to — through parcourir; to — off glisser, ricocher, dévier.
gland [glænd] *n* glande *f*.
glare [gleə] *n* lumière aveuglante *f*, éclat *m*, regard de défi *m*; *vi* flamboyer; to — at *vt* regarder d'un œil furibond.
glaring ['gleəriŋ] *a* aveuglant, flagrant, éclatant, cru.
glass [glɑːs] *n* verre *m*, (beer) bock *m*, vitre *f*, baromètre *m*; *pl* lunettes *f pl*.
glassblower ['glɑːs,blouə] *n* verrier *m*.
glasscase ['glɑːs'keis] *n* vitrine *f*.
glasscutter ['glɑːs,kʌtə] *n* diamant *m*, tournette *f*.
glass-paper ['glɑːs,peipə] *n* papier de verre *m*.
glassware ['glɑːswɛə] *n* verrerie *f*.
glassy ['glɑːsi] *a* vitreux, transparent.
glaze [gleiz] *n* glacis *m*, lustre *m*; *vt* vitrer, glacer, lustrer, devenir vitreux.
glazier ['gleizjə] *n* vitrier *m*.
gleam [gliːm] *n* rayon *m*, lueur *f*, reflet *m*; *vi* luire, miroiter.
glean [gliːn] *vt* glaner.
gleaner ['gliːnə] *n* glaneur, -euse.
gleaning ['gliːniŋ] *n* glanage *m*; *pl* glanures *f pl*.
glee [gliː] *n* joie *f*, gaîté *f*.
glen [glen] *n* vallon *m*.
glib [glib] *a* spécieux, qui a de la faconde.
glibness ['glibnis] *n* faconde *f*, spéciosité *f*.
glide [glaid] *n* glissement *m*, glissade *f*, vol plané *m*; *vi* glisser, planer.

glider ['glaidə] *n* avion e remorque *m*, planeur *m*.
glimmer ['glimə] *n* lueur *f*; *vi* luire.
glimpse [glimps] *n* lueur passagère *f*, coup d'œil *m*, échappée *f*, aperçu *m*; *vt* entrevoir.
glint [glint] *vi* entreluire, étinceler; *n* trait *m*, meur *f*.
glisten ['glisn] *vi* étinceler, scintiller, luire.
glitter ['glitə] *n* scintillement *m*; *vi* scintiller, étinceler.
gloat [glout] to — over manger (couvrer) des yeux, se réjouir de.
globe [gloub] *n* globe *m*, sphère *f*.
gloom [gluːm] *n* obscurité *f*, dépression *f*.
gloomy ['gluːmi] *a* obscur, sombre, lugubre.
glorification [,glɔːrifi'keiʃən] *n* glorification *f*.
glorify ['glɔːrifai] *vt* glorifier.
glorious ['glɔːriəs] *a* glorieux.
glory ['glɔːri] *n* gloire *f*; to — in se faire gloire de.
gloss [glɔs] *n* lustre *m*, vernis *m*; *vt* lustrer, glacer; to — over glisser sur.
glossary ['glɔsəri] *n* glossaire *m*, lexique *m*.
glossy ['glɔsi] *a* lustré, brillant, glacé.
glove [glʌv] *n* gant *m*; *vt* ganter.
glow [glou] *n* rougeur (diffuse) *f*, ardeur *f*, éclat *m*, rougeoiement *m*; *vi* briller, luire, rougeoyer, s'embraser brûler.
glow-worm ['glouwəːm] *n* luciole *f*, ver luisant *m*.
glue [gluː] *n* colle forte *f*; *vt* coller.
glum [glʌm] *a* renfrogné, maussade.
glut [glʌt] *n* surabondance *f*, encombrement *m*; *vt* gorger, gaver, encombrer.
glutton ['glʌtn] *n* goinfre *m*, gourmand(e) *mf*.
gluttonous ['glʌtənəs] *a* vorace, goulu.
gnarled [nɑːld] *a* noueux, tordu.
gnash [næʃ] *vt* to — one's teeth grincer des dents.
gnashing ['næʃiŋ] *n* grincement *m*.
gnat [næt] *n* cousin *m*, moustique *m*.
gnaw [nɔː] *vti* grignoter ronger.
go [gou] *n* aller *m*, allant *m*, affaire *f*; *vi* (s'en) aller, marcher, partir, tendre à, passer, faire loi, disparaître, devenir; to — away partir; to — back revenir, retourner, reculer; to — down descendre, se coucher, sombrer; to — for aller chercher; to — in(to) entrer (dans); to — off partir; to — on avancer, continuer; to — out sortir; to — through traverser, parcourir.
goad [goud] *n* aiguillon *m*; *vt* piquer, exciter.
goal [goul] *n* but *m*.
goalkeeper ['goul,kiːpə] *n* goal *m*, gardien de but *m*.
goat [gout] *n* chèvre *f*; he-— bouc *m*.

go-between ['goubi'twi:n] *n* entremetteur *m*, truchement *m*.

gobble ['gɔbl] *vt* bâfrer, bouffer; *vi* glouglouter, glousser.

goblet ['gɔblit] *n* gobelet *m*, coupe *f*.

goblin ['gɔblin] *n* lutin *m*.

God [gɔd] *n* Dieu *m*.

godchild ['gɔdtʃaild] *n* filleul(e) *mf*.

goddess ['gɔːdis] *n* déesse *f*.

godfather ['gɔd,faːðə] *n* parrain *m*.

godmother ['gɔd,mʌðə] *n* marraine *f*.

godless ['gɔdlis] *a* athée, impie.

godliness ['gɔdlinis] *n* piété *f*.

godly ['gɔdli] *a* pieux, saint.

godsend ['gɔdsend] *n* aubaine *f*.

godspeed ['gɔd'spiːd] *excl* bonne chance! bon voyage!

goggle ['gɔgl] *vi* rouler les yeux; *n pl* lunettes d'automobile *f pl*; (*fam*) —box télé(vision) *f*.

goggle-eyed ['gɔglaid] *a* aux yeux saillants, de homard.

going ['gouiŋ] *n* terrain *m*, circonstances *m pl*.

gold [gould] *n* or *m*; — **dust** poudre *f* d'or.

gold-digger ['gould,digə] *n* chercheur d'or *m*.

golden ['gouldən] *a* d'or, doré.

goldfinch ['gouldfintʃ] *n* chardonneret *m*.

goldfish ['gouldfiʃ] *n* dorade *f*, poisson rouge *m*.

goldsmith ['gouldsmiθ] *n* orfèvre *m*.

gold-standard ['gould,stændəd] *n* étalon-or *m*.

golf [gɔlf] *n* golf *m*; —**course** (terrain *m* de) golf *m*.

gondola ['gɔndələ] *n* gondole *f*, nacelle *f*.

gone [gɔn] *pp* of **go**; *a* parti, fini, disparu, épris (de on).

good [gud] *n* bien *m*, bon *m*, profit *m*; *pl* marchandises *f pl*, effets *m pl*; *a* bon, sage; — **for nothing** propre à rien; **for** — pour de bon; — **Heavens!** Ciel! — **gracious!** bonté divine!

good-bye ['gud'bai] *excl n* au revoir *m*, adieu *m*.

good-looking ['gud'lukiŋ] *a* de bonne mine, bien, beau.

goodly ['gudli] *a* large, ample.

goodness ['gudnis] *n* bonté *f*, vertu *f*.

goodwill [gud'wil] *n* bon vouloir *m*, clientèle *f*.

goody ['gudi] *n* commère *f*; *a* édifiant; **to be a** — la faire à la vertu.

goose [guːs] *n* oie *f*.

gooseberry ['guzbəri] *n* groseille à maquereau *f*.

gooseflesh ['guːsfleʃ] *n* chair de poule *f*.

goose-step ['guːsstep] *n* pas de l'oie *m*.

gore [gɔː] *n* sang *m* (caillé), pointe *f*, pièce *f*, soufflet *m*, godet *m*; *vt* encorner, blesser d'un coup de cornes.

gorge [gɔːdʒ] *n* gorge *f*, défilé *m*, cœur *m*; *vt* rassasier, gorger; *vi* s'empiffrer, se gorger.

gorgeous ['gɔːdʒəs] *a* splendide, superbe.

gorgeousness ['gɔːdʒəsnis] *n* splendeur *f*.

gorilla [gə'rilə] *n* gorille *m*.

gormandize ['gɔːməndaiz] *vi* bâfrer.

gormandizer ['gɔːməndaizə] *n* gourmand(e) *mf*, goinfre *m*.

gorse [gɔːs] *n* ajonc *m*, genêt *m*.

gory ['gɔːri] *a* ensanglanté.

gosling ['gɔzliŋ] *n* oison *m*.

gospel ['gɔspəl] *n* évangile *m*.

gossamer ['gɔsəmə] *n* fils de la Vierge *m pl*, gaze *f*; *a* léger, ténu.

gossip ['gɔsip] *n* commérage *m*, mauvaise langue *f*, bavette *f*; *vi* cancaner, bavarder.

gouge [gaudʒ] *n* gouge *f*; *vt* arracher.

gourd [guəd] *n* potiron *m*, gourde *f*, calebasse *f*.

gourmet ['guəmei] *n* gourmet *m*, fine fourchette *f*.

gout [gaut] *n* goutte *f*.

gouty ['gauti] *a* goutteux.

govern ['gʌvən] *vt* gouverner, administrer.

governess ['gʌvənis] *n* gouvernante *f*.

governing ['gʌvəniŋ] *a* gouvernant, au pouvoir.

government ['gʌvnmənt] *n* gouvernement *m*, régime *m*, ministère *m*.

governor ['gʌvənə] *n* gouverneur *m*, gouvernant *m*, patron *m*.

gown [gaun] *n* robe *f*.

grab [græb] *n* rapacité *f*; *vt* saisir, happer, arracher.

grace [greis] *n* grâce *f*, bénédicité *m*; *pl* grâces *f pl*; *vt* orner, honorer.

graceful ['greisful] *a* gracieux.

graceless ['greislis] *a* sans grâce.

gracious ['greiʃəs] *a* gracieux, accueillant, bow; **good** —! bonté divine! mon Dieu!

gradation [grə'deiʃən] *n* gradation *f*.

grade [greid] *n* degré *m*, rang *m*, qualité *f*, (US) pente *f*, rampe *f*; *vt* graduer, fondre, classer.

grade crossing ['greid'krɔsiŋ] *n* (US) passage *m* à niveau.

gradient ['greidjənt] *n* pente *f*, rampe *f*, variation *f*.

gradual ['grædjuəl] *a* graduel.

gradually ['grædjuəli] *ad* doucement, peu à peu.

graduate ['grædjueit] *n* licencié(e) *mf*; *vt* passer sa licence, recevoir ses diplômes, conférer (un diplôme).

graft [graːft] *n* greffe *f*, tripotage *m*, gratte *f*, corruption *f*; *vt* greffer; *vi* tripoter, rabioter.

grain [grein] *n* grain *m*; **against the** — à contre-fil, à contre-cœur; **with a** — **of salt** avec réserve.

grammar ['græmə] *n* grammaire *f*; — **school** lycée.

gramophone ['græməfoun] n phonographe m.

granary ['grænəri] n grenier m.

grand [grænd] a grand(iose).

grandchildren ['græn,tʃildrən] n pl petits-enfants m pl.

grand-daughter ['græn,dɔːtə] n petite-fille f.

:randee [,græn'diː] n Grand m.

grandeur ['grændjə] n grandeur f, splendeur f.

grandfather ['grænd,fɑːðə] n grand-père m.

grandiloquence ɪgræn'diləkwəns] n emphase f.

grandiose ['grændiouz] a grandiose, magnifique, pompeux.

grandmother ['græn,mʌðə] n grand'mère f.

grandson ['grænsʌn] n petit-fils m.

grandstand ['grændstænd] n tribune f.

grange [greindʒ] n maison avec ferme f.

granite ['grænit] n granit m; a granitique.

granny ['græni] n bonne-maman f.

grant [grɑːnt] n subvention f, allocation f; vt accorder, admettre, octroyer.

grape [greip] n raisin m.

grapefruit ['greipfruːt] n pamplemousse f.

grape-harvest ['greip,hɑːvist] n vendange f.

grapeshot ['greipʃɔt] n mitraille f.

graphic ['græfik] a graphique, vivant.

grapnel ['græpnəl] n grappin m, ancre f.

grapple ['græpl] n grappin m, prise f, étreinte f; to — with empoigner, colleter, en venir aux prises avec.

grasp [grɑːsp] n prise f, étreinte f, serre f, portée de ɪa main f, compréhension f; vt saisir, serrer, empoigner.

grasping ['grɑːspiŋ] a rapace, cupide.

grass [grɑːs] n herbe f.

grasshopper ['grɑːs,hɔpə] n sauterelle f

grassy ['grɑːsi] a herbu, herbeux, verdoyant.

grate [greit] vt râper, racler; vi grincer, crier, crisser; to — on choquer, agacer.

grater ['greitə] n râpe f.

grateful ['greitful] n reconnaissant.

gratefully ['greitfuli] ad avec reconnaissance.

gratefulness ['greitfulnis] n reconnaissance f.

grating ' greitiŋ] a grinçant; n grille f, grillage m, râpage m, grincement m.

gratification [,grætifi'keiʃən] n plaisir m, satisfaction f.

gratify ['grætifai] vt contenter, rémunérer, satisfaire.

gratis ['grɑːtis] ad gratis; a gratuit.

gratitude ['grætitjuːd] n gratitude f, reconnaissance f.

gratuitous [grə'tjuːitəs] a gratuit.

gratuity [grə'tjuːiti] n gratification f, pourboire m, pot de vin m.

gravamen [grə'veimen] n poids m, fond m.

grave [greiv] n fosse f, tombe f, tombeau m; a sérieux, grave; vt graver, radouber.

grave-digger ['greiv,digə] n fossoyeur m.

gravel ['grævəl] n gravier m.

gravestone ['greivstoun] n pierre tombale f.

graveyard ['greivjɑːd] n cimetière m.

graving-dock ['greiviŋdɔk] n bassin de ɪadoub m.

graving-tool ['greiviŋtuːl] n burin m.

gravitate ['græviteit] vi graviter.

gravity ['græviti] n gravité f, sérieux m.

gravitation ɪ grævi'teiʃən] n gravitation f pesanteur f.

gravy ['greivi] n sauce f, jus m.

graze [greiz] n égratignure f; vt égratigner effleurer; vti brouter, paître.

grease [griːs] n graisse f; vt graisser.

greasy ['griːsi] a graisseux, gras.

great [greit] a grand, gros, fort.

greatcoat ['greitkout] n par-dessus m, capote f.

greatly ['greitli] ad énormément, puissamment, beaucoup.

greatness ['greitnis] n grandeur f, noblesse f.

Greece [griːs] n Grèce f.

greed ɪgriːd] n convoitise f, cupidité f.

greediness ['griːdinis] n cupidité f, gloutonnerie f.

greedy ['griːdi] a gourmand, glouton, cupide, avide.

Greek [griːk] n Grec, Grecque; an grec m.

green [griːn] an vert m; a naïf, sot, inexpérimenté.

greengage ['griːngeidʒ] n reine-claude f.

greengrocer ['griːn,grousə] n fruitier, -ière.

greenhorn ['griːnhɔːn] n blanc-bec m, bleu m.

greenhouse ['griːnhaus] n serre f.

greenish ['griːniʃ] a verdâtre.

Greenland ['griːnlənd] n Groenland m.

greet [griːt] vt saluer, accueillir.

greeting ['griːtiŋ] n salut m, salutation ɪ

gregarious [gri'gɛəriəs] a grégaire, de troupeau.

grenade ɪgri'neid] n grenade ɪ.

grenadier [,grenə'diə] n grenadier m.

grew [gruː] pt of grow.

grey [grei] an gris m; to grow — grisonner.

greyish ['greiiʃ] a grisâtre.

greyhound ['greihaund] n lévrier m, levrette f.

grid [grid] n grille f.

gridiron ['grid,aiən] n gril m, (US) terrain m de football.

grief [gri:f] n chagrin m, mal m, peine f.

grievance ['gri:vəns] n grief m, tort m.

grieve [gri:v] vt affliger, faire de la peine à; vi se désoler, s'affliger.

grievous ['gri:vəs] a affligeant, douloureux.

grill [gril] n gril m, grillade f, grille f, grillage m; vt griller, cuisiner.

grim [grim] a sévère, farouche, sardonique, sinistre.

grimace [gri'meis] n grimace f; vi grimacer, faire la grimace.

grime [graim] n crasse f; vt salir.

grimy ['graimi] a crasseux, encrassé, noir.

grin [grin] n rictus m, sourire épanoui m; vi découvrir ses dents, sourire à belles dents.

grind [graind] vt moudre, broyer, écraser, affiler; vi grincer, (fig) piocher; n grincement m, turbin m.

grinder ['graində] n rémouleur m, broyeur m.

grinding ['graindiŋ] n broyage m, mouture f, grincement m.

grindstone ['graindstoun] n meule f.

grip [grip] n prise f, étreinte f, serre f; pl prises f pl, mains f pl; vt agripper, empoigner, saisir, serrer.

gripe [graip] vi donner la colique à.

grisly ['grizli] a terrifiant, macabre.

grist [grist] n blé m; to bring — to the mill faire venir l'eau au moulin.

gristle ['grisl] n cartilage m, croquant m.

grit [grit] n gravier m, sable m, grès m, cran m; vi grincer; vt sabler.

gritty ['griti] a graveleux, sablonneux.

grizzled ['grizld] a gris, grisonnant.

groan [groun] n gémissement m, grognement m; vi gémir, grogner.

grocer ['grousə] n épicier, -ière.

grocery ['grousəri] n épicerie f.

groggy ['grɔgi] a ivre, étourdi, titubant.

groin [grɔin] n aine f.

groom [gru:m] n palefrenier m, valet d'écurie m; vt panser.

groomed [gru:md] a well—— (bien) soigné, tiré à quatre épingles.

grooming ['gru:miŋ] n pansage m.

groomsman ['gru:mzmən] n garçon d'honneur m.

groove [gru:v] n sillon m, rainure f, glissière f; vt rayer, sillonner; **micro-**
— microsillon m.

grope [group] vi tâtonner; **to — for** chercher à tâtons.

gross [grous] n grosse f; a dru, obèse, grossier, brut, gros.

ground [graund] pp of **grind**; a moulu, broyé; n sol m, terrain m,

fond m, fondement m raison f; vt fonder, appuyer, instruire, (arms) reposer, maintenir au sol; vi s'échouer.

ground floor ['graundflɔ:] n rez-de-chaussée m.

groundless ['graundlis] a sans fondement, immotivé.

groundnut ['graundnʌt] n arachide f.

grounds [graundz] n pl lie f, marc m.

groundsheet ['graundʃi:t] n bâche f de campement.

groundswell ['graundswel] n lame f de fond.

groundwork ['graundwə:k] n fond m, base f, assise f, plan m.

group [gru:p] n groupe m; vt grouper; vi se grouper.

grouse [graus] n coq m de bruyère; vi grogner, ronchonner, rouspéter.

grove [grouv] n bosquet m.

grovel ['grɔvl] vi s'aplatir, ramper.

groveller ['grɔvlə] n flagorneur m, sycophante m, piedplat m.

grow [grou] vt cultiver; vi pousser, grandir, croître, devenir.

growl [graul] n grondement m; vi gronder, grommeler, grogner.

grown [groun] pp of **grow**.

grown-up ['groun'ʌp] n adulte mf, grande personne f.

growth [grouθ] n croissance f, accroissement m, tumeur f.

grub [grʌb] n larve f, (sl) boustifaille f; vt bêcher, nettoyer; vi fouiller.

grudge [grʌdʒ] n dent f, rancune f; vt donner à contre-cœur, mesurer.

grudgingly ['grʌdʒiŋli] ad à contre-cœur.

gruel ['gruəl] n gruau m, brouet m.

gruelling ['gruəliŋ] a éreintant, épuisant.

gruesome ['gru:səm] a macabre, répugnant.

gruff [grʌf] a bourru, revêche, rude, gros.

gruffly ['grʌfli] ad rudement.

gruffness ['grʌfnis] n rudesse f, ton bourru m.

grumble ['grʌmbl] n grognement m; vti grommeler, bougonner.

grumbler ['grʌmblə] n ronchonneur, -euse, grognard(e) mf, rouspéteur, -euse.

grumpy ['grʌmpi] a maussade, grincheux.

grunt [grʌnt] n grognement m; vi grogner.

guarantee [,gærən'ti:] n garant(e) mf, garantie f, caution f; vt garantir, se porter garant pour.

guard [gɑ:d] n garde mf, chef de train m, (US) geôlier m; vt garder, protéger; vi mettre (se tenir) en garde.

guarded ['gɑ:did] a circonspect.

guardedly ['gɑ:didli] ad prudemment, avec réserve.

guardian ['gɑ:djən] n gardien, -ienne, tuteur, -trice.

guardianship ['gɑːdjənʃip] n garde f, tutelle f.

guava ['gwɑːvə] n goyave f; — **tree** goyavier m.

gudgeon ['gʌdʒən] n goujon m.

guess [ges] n conjecture f; vti deviner; vt estimer; **at a** — au jugé.

guesswork ['geswəːk] n hypothèse f, conjecture f.

guest [gest] n invité(e) mf; **paying—** pensionnaire mf; — **house** pension f.

guffaw [gʌˈfɔː] n gros rire m; vi s'esclaffer.

guidance ['gaidəns] n conduite f, direction f, gouverne f, orientation f.

guide [gaid] n guide m; vt guider, conduire, diriger.

guidebook ['gaidbuk] n guide m.

guided ['gaidid] a (of rockets) télé-guidé.

guidepost ['gaidpoust] n poteau indicateur m.

guild [gild] n corporation f, confrérie f.

guildhall ['gildhɔːl] n hôtel de ville m.

guile [gail] n astuce f.

guileful ['gailful] a retors.

guileless ['gaillis] a sans malice, naïf.

guilt [gilt] n culpabilité f.

guiltless ['giltlis] a innocent.

guilty ['gilti] a coupable.

guinea-fowl ['ginifaul] n pintade f.

guinea-pig ['ginipig] n cobaye m, cochon d'Inde m.

guise [gaiz] n forme f, apparence f, costume m.

guitar [giˈtɑː] n guitare f.

gulf [gʌlf] n golfe m, gouffre m, abîme m.

gull [gʌl] n mouette f, jobard m, gogo m; vt rouler.

gullet ['gʌlit] n œsophage m, gosier m.

gullibility [ˌgʌliˈbiliti] n crédulité f, jobardise f.

gullible ['gʌlibl] a crédule, jobard.

gully ['gʌli] n ravin m.

gulp [gʌlp] n lampée f, trait m; vti boire, avaler d'un trait; vi s'étrangler.

gum [gʌm] n gencive f, gomme f; vt gommer, coller.

gumboil ['gʌmbɔil] n abcès à la gencive m.

gumption ['gʌmpʃən] n jugeotte f, gingin m.

gun [gʌn] n fusil m, canon m, pièce f.

gunboat ['gʌnbout] n canonnière f.

gun-carriage ['gʌnˌkæridʒ] n affût de canon m.

gunner ['gʌnə] n canonnier m, artilleur m.

gunnery ['gʌnəri] n tir au canon m.

gunpowder ['gʌnˌpaudə] n poudre f.

gunshot ['gʌnʃɔt] n portée de fusil f (canon), coup de feu m.

gunsmith ['gʌnsmiθ] n armurier m.

gurgle ['gəːgl] n glouglou m, gar-gouillement m; vi glouglouter, gargouiller; vti glousser.

gush [gʌʃ] n jaillissement m, jet m, projection f, effusion f; vi jaillir, saillir, se répandre, la faire au sentiment.

gust [gʌst] n rafale f, ondée f, accès m.

gusto ['gʌstou] n brio m, entrain m.

gut [gʌt] n boyau m; pl entrailles f pl, cran m; vt vider, dévaster.

gutter ['gʌtə] n gouttière f, ruisseau m, rigole f.

guy [gai] n corde f, hauban m, type m, épouvantail m; vt railler, travestir.

guzzle ['gʌzl] vt boire à tire-larigot, bouffer; vi s'empiffrer, se gaver.

gymnasium [dʒimˈneizjəm] n gym-nase m.

gymnast ['dʒimnæst] n gymnaste mf.

gymnastics [dʒimˈnæstiks] n pl gymnastique f.

H

haberdasher ['hæbədæʃə] n mercier m.

haberdasher's ['hæbədæʃəz] n mer-cerie f.

habit ['hæbit] n habitude f, état m, constitution f.

habitable ['hæbitəbl] a habitable.

habitation [ˌhæbiˈteiʃən] n habita-tion f, demeure f.

habitual [həˈbitjuəl] a habituel, invétéré.

hack [hæk] n pioche f, pic m, blessure f, cheval m (de louage), rosse f, corvée f, (US) veilleur m de nuit, agent m de police, écrivassier m; vt couper, frapper, hacher, taillader; vi tousser sèchement.

hackneyed ['hæknid] a usé, rebattu, banal.

had [hæd] pp pt of **have**.

haddock ['hædək] n aiglefin m, aigrefin m.

haft [hɑːft] n manche m, poignée f.

hag [hæg] n sorcière f, chiple f.

haggard ['hægəd] a hagard, hâve, décharné, égaré.

haggle ['hægl] vi ergoter, chicaner.

hail [heil] n grêle f, salut m; vi grêler; vt saluer, héler, venir (de from), descendre (de from).

hailstone ['heilstoun] n grêlon m.

hair [hɛə] n cheveu m, chevelure f, poil m, crin m.

hair-cutting ['hɛəˌkʌtiŋ] n coupe de cheveux f.

hairdresser ['hɛəˌdresə] n coiffeur, -euse.

hairless ['hɛəlis] a chauve, sans poils, glabre.

hairline ['hɛəlain] n — **crack** gerçure f; (fig) distinction f subtile.

hairpin ['hɛəpin] *n* épingle à cheveux *f*.

hair-raising ['hɛə‚reiziŋ] *a* horrifique, horripilant.

hair's breadth ['hɛəz'bredθ] *ad* à un cheveu (près).

hair-splitting ['hɛə‚splitiŋ] *n* chinoiserie *f*, ergotage *m*.

hairy ['hɛəri] *a* chevelu, poilu, velu.

hake [heik] *n* merluche *f*, colin *m*.

hale [heil] *a* robuste; — **and hearty** frais et dispos.

half [hɑːf] *n* moitié *f*; *a* demi, mi-; *ad* à moitié, demi, en deux; — **as much again** une fois et demie autant, la moitié en plus; — **hearted** *a* tiède: **at tide** à mi-marée.

half-back ['hɑːfbæk] *n* demi(-arrière) *m*.

half-bred ['hɑːfbred] *a* métis, demi-sang.

half-brother ['hɑːf‚brʌðə] *n* demi-frère *m*.

half-caste ['hɑːfkɑːst] *a* demi-sang; *an* métis, -isse, hybride *m*.

half-dozen ['hɑːf'dʌzn] *n* demi-douzaine *f*.

half-hour ['hɑːf'auə] *n* demi-heure *f*.

half-mast ['hɑːf'mɑːst] *ad* en berne, à mi-mât.

half-measure ['hɑːf'meʒə] *n* demi-mesure *f*.

half-pay ['hɑːf'pei] *n* demi-solde *f*.

halfway ['hɑːf'wei] *ad* à mi-chemin.

halibut ['hælibət] *n* flétan *m*.

hall [hɔːl] *n* salle *f*, vestibule *m*, hall *m*.

hallmark ['hɔːlmɑːk] *n* contrôle *m*, poinçon *m*, empreinte *f*.

hallow ['hælou] *vt* sanctifier, bénir.

hallucinate [hə'luːsineit] *vt* halluciner.

hallucination [hə‚luːsi'neiʃən] *n* hallucination *f*.

halo ['heilou] *n* halo *m*, nimbe *m*, auréole *f*.

halt [hɔlt] *n* halte *f*; *vi* s'arrêter, hésiter, boiter; *a* boiteux.

halter ['hɔltə] *n* licou *m*, corde *f*.

halve [hɑːv] *vt* couper en deux, partager.

ham [hæm] *n* jambon *m*, jarret *m*.

hamlet ['hæmlit] *n* hameau *m*.

hammer ['hæmə] *n* marteau *m*; *vt* marteler, battre.

hammock ['hæmək] *n* hamac *m*.

hamper ['hæmpə] *n* corbeille *f*, manne *f*, banne *f*; *vt* gêner, empêcher.

hand [hænd] *n* main *f*, (*watch*) aiguille *f*, jeu *m*, ouvrier, — **to** — corps à corps; **out of** — hors de contrôle; **on the one** — d'une part; **old** — vieux routier *m*; *vt* tendre, passer, remettre.

handbag ['hændbæg] *n* sac à main *m*, pochette *f*.

handbook ['hændbuk] *n* manuel *m*, guide *m*.

handcuff ['hændkʌf] *vt* passer les menottes à.

handcuffs ['hændkʌfs] *n pl* menottes *f pl*.

handful ['hændful] *n* poignée *f*.

handicap ['hændikæp] *n* handicap *m*, désavantage *m*; *vt* handicaper, désavantager.

handicraft ['hændikrɑːft] *n* habileté manuelle *f*, métier manuel *m*, travail manuel *m*.

handiwork ['hændiwəːk] *n* travail manuel *m*, ouvrage *m*.

handkerchief ['hæŋkətʃif] *n* mouchoir *m*, pochette *f*.

handle ['hændl] *n* poignée *f*, manche *m*, anse *f*, bouton *m*, bras *m*; *vt* manier, traiter, prendre en main.

handlebar ['hændlbɑː] *n* guidon *m*.

handling ['hændliŋ] *n* maniement *m*, manœuvre *f*.

handrail ['hændreil] *n* rampe *f*, main courante *f*.

handshake ['hændʃeik] *n* poignée de main *f*.

handsome ['hænsəm] *a* beau, élégant, généreux.

handsomely ['hænsəmli] *ad* élégamment, libéralement.

handwriting ['hænd‚raitiŋ] *n* écriture *f*, main *f*.

handy ['hændi] *a* sous la main, commode, adroit, maniable.

hang [hæŋ] *vt* pendre, accrocher, tapisser, poser; *vi* pendre, planer, peser, tomber; **to** — **about** rôder, flâner; **to** — **back** hésiter, rester en arrière.

hangar ['hæŋə] *n* hangar *m*.

hanger ['hæŋə] *n* portemanteau *m*, cintre *m*, crochet *m*.

hanging ['hæŋiŋ] *n* pose *f*, tenture *f*, suspension *f*, montage *m*, pendaison *f*.

hangman ['hæŋmən] *n* bourreau *m*.

hanker ['hæŋkə] *vi* aspirer (à **after**).

hankering ['hæŋkəriŋ] *n* aspiration *f*, forte envie *f*.

hanky-panky ['hæŋki'pæŋki] *n* boniment *m*, tour de passe-passe *m*.

hansom ['hænsəm] *n* cabriolet *m*.

haphazard ['hæp'hæzəd] *a* fortuit; *ad* au petit bonheur, à l'aveuglette.

hapless ['hæplis] *a* malchanceux, infortuné.

happen ['hæpən] *vi* arriver, se passer, se produire.

happening ['hæpniŋ] *n* événement *m*.

happily ['hæpili] *ad* heureusement, par bonheur.

happiness ['hæpinis] *n* bonheur *m*.

happy ['hæpi] *a* heureux.

harangue [hə'ræŋ] *n* harangue *f*, *vt* haranguer.

harass ['hærəs] *vt* harceler, tracasser, tourmenter.

harbinger ['hɑːbindʒə] *n* précurseur *m*, avant-coureur *m*, messager, -ère.

24

harbour ['hɑːbə] n port m, asile m; vt recéler, nourrir, abriter.

hard [hɑːd] a dur, difficile, sévère; — by tout près; — up à sec; — upon de près, sur les talons; ad dur, fort, durement.

hardboard ['hɑːdbɔːd] n Isorel m (Protected Trade Name).

harden ['hɑːdn] vt (en)durcir, tremper; vi durcir, s'endurcir, devenir dur.

hardfisted ['hɑːd'fistid] a pingre, radin.

hardihood ['hɑːdihud] n audace f.

hard labour ['hɑːd'leibə] n travaux forcés m pl.

hardly ['hɑːdli] ad à (avec) peine, ne . . . guère, sévèrement.

hardness ['hɑːdnis] n dureté f, difficulté f.

hardship ['hɑːdʃip] n privation f, épreuve f.

hardware ['hɑːdwɛə] n quincaillerie f.

hardwareman ['hɑːdwɛəmən] n quincailler m.

hardy ['hɑːdi] a résistant, robuste, vigoureux.

hare [hɛə] n lièvre m.

hare-brained ['hɛəbreind] a écervelé, insensé.

harelip ['hɛə'lip] n bec-de-lièvre m.

haricot ['hærikou] n — bean haricot blanc m; — mutton haricot de mouton m.

hark [hɑːk] vti écouter; to — back to revenir à.

harm [hɑːm] n mal m, tort m; vt faire tort à, faire (du) mal à, porter préjudice à.

harmful ['hɑːmful] a nuisible, pénible, nocif.

harmless ['hɑːmlis] a inoffensif.

harmlessly ['hɑːmlisli] ad innocemment.

harmonious [hɑːˈmounjəs] a harmonieux.

harmonize ['hɑːmənaiz] vt harmoniser, concilier; vi s'harmoniser, s'accorder.

harmony ['hɑːməni] n harmonie f, accord m.

harness ['hɑːnis] n harnais m; vt harnacher, capter, aménager.

harness-maker ['hɑːnis,meikə] n bourrelier m.

Harold ['hærəld] Henri m.

harp [hɑːp] n harpe f; vi jouer de la harpe; to — on ressasser, rabâcher.

harpoon [hɑːˈpuːn] n harpon m; vt harponner.

harpsichord ['hɑːpsikɔːd] n clavecin m.

harrow ['hærou] n herse f; vt herser, blesser, déchirer.

harrowing ['hærouiŋ] a déchirant, navrant.

harry ['hæri] vt ravaget, tracasser, harceler.

harsh [hɑːʃ] a rèche, âpre, cruel.

harshness ['hɑːʃnis] n rudesse f, âpreté f, rigueur f.

hart [hɑːt] n cerf m.

harum-scarum ['hɛərəmˈskɛərəm] an hurluberlu(e) mf, écervelé(e) mf.

harvest ['hɑːvist] n moisson f, récolte f, vendange f, fenaison f; vt moissonner, récolter; vi faire la moisson.

harvester ['hɑːvistə] n moissonneur, -euse, (machine) moissonneuse f.

hash [hæʃ] n hachis m, gâchis m, compte m; vt hacher, gâcher.

hassock ['hæsək] n coussin m.

haste [heist] n hâte f.

hasten ['heisn] vt presser, hâter, avancer; vi se presser, se dépêcher se hâter.

hastily ['heistili] ad à la hâte.

hasty ['heisti] a hâtif, vif, emporté.

hat [hæt] n chapeau m.

hat-box ['hætbɔks] n carton à chapeau m.

hatch [hætʃ] n écoutille f, couvaison f, couvée f, éclosion f; vt couver, tramer; vi éclore, se tramer.

hatchet ['hætʃit] n hachette f, cognée f.

hatching ['hætʃiŋ] n éclosion f, machination f.

hate [heit] n haine f, aversion f; vt haïr, détester.

hateful ['heitful] a haïssable, odieux.

hat-peg ['hætpeg] n patère f.

hatred ['heitrid] n haine f.

hatter ['hætə] n chapelier m.

hatter's ['hætəz] n chapellerie f.

haughtiness ['hɔːtinis] n hauteur f, morgue f.

haughty ['hɔːti] a hautain.

haul [hɔːl] n traction f, coup de filet m, butin m; vt haler, tirer, traîner.

haulage ['hɔːlidʒ] n halage m, roulage m, charriage m.

haunch [hɔːntʃ] n hanche f, cuissot m, quartier m.

haunt [hɔːnt] n rendez-vous m, repaire m; vt fréquenter, hanter, obséder.

have [hæv] vt avoir, permettre, savoir, soutenir, admettre, prendre, faire, tenir; I had better, rather je ferais (aimerais) mieux; to — it out with s'expliquer avec.

haven ['heivn] n port m.

haversack ['hævəsæk] n musette f, havresac m.

haves [hævz] n pl les possédants m pl.

havoc ['hævək] n ravage m, dégâts m pl.

hawk [hɔːk] n faucon m; vt colporter; vi chasser au faucon.

hawker ['hɔːkə] n camelot m, colporteur m, (fruit) marchand des quatre saisons m.

hawser ['hɔːzə] n haussière f, amarre f.

hawthorn ['hɔːθɔːn] n aubépine f.

hay [hei] n foin m.

hayloft ['heilɔft] n fenil m.

haymaker ['heimeikə] n faneur, -euse.

haymaking ['heimeikiŋ] n fenaison f.

haystack ['heistæk] n meule de foin f.

hazard ['hæzəd] n hasard m; vt hasarder, risquer.

haze [heiz] n brume f (de chaleur), (US) harassement m, brimade f; vt brimer, bizuter.

hazel ['heizl] n noisetier m.

hazel-nut ['heizlnʌt] n noisette f.

hazy ['heizi] a brumeux, vague, estompé.

he [hi:] pr il, lui, celui; an mâle m.

head [hed] n tête f, face f, sommet m, source f, haut bout m, chef m, crise f; a premier, principal, (en) chef; vt conduire, intituler, venir en tête de; to — for se diriger vers, mettre le cap sur.

headache ['hedeik] n mal de tête m.

headdress ['heddres] n coiffure f.

heading ['hediŋ] n titre m, en-tête m, rubrique f.

headland ['hedlənd] n cap m, promontoire m.

headlight ['hedlait] n phare m.

headline ['hedlain] n titre m, manchette f.

headlong ['hedlɔŋ] a impétueux; ad la tête la première, tête baissée.

headman ['hedmən] n chef m.

headmaster ['hed'ma:stə] n proviseur m, directeur m.

headmistress ['hed'mistris] n directrice f.

headphone ['hedfoun] n récepteur m, écouteur m.

headquarters ['hed'kwɔ:təz] n quartier général m, état major m.

headstone ['hedstoun] n pierre angulaire f, pierre tombale f.

headstrong ['hedstrɔŋ] a têtu, volontaire.

headway ['hedwei] n progrès m (pl), erre f.

heady ['hedi] a violent, capiteux.

heal [hi:l] vti guérir; vi se cicatriser.

healing ['hi:liŋ] n guérison f.

health [helθ] n santé f.

healthy ['helθi] a sain, bien portant, salubre.

heap [hi:p] n tas m, monceau m; vt entasser, amonceler, combler.

heaped ['hi:pd] a entassé, amoncelé, comble.

hear [hiə] vt entendre, entendre dire, apprendre, faire répéter; to — from recevoir des nouvelles de.

heard [hə:d] pp pt of **hear**.

hearer ['hiərə] n auditeur, -trice.

hearing ['hiəriŋ] n ouïe f, oreille f, audition f, audience f.

hearken ['ha:kən] vi écouter, prêter l'oreille (à to).

hearsay ['hiəsei] n ouï-dire m.

hearse [hə:s] n corbillard m.

heart [ha:t] n cœur m, courage m.

heartbeat ['ha:tbi:t] n battement de cœur m.

heartbreaking ['ha:tbreikiŋ] a navrant, accablant, déchirant.

heartbroken ['ha:t,broukən] a navré, accablé.

heartburn ['ha:tbə:n] n aigreurs f pl.

hearten ['ha:tn] vt réconforter, remonter le moral à.

heartfelt ['ha:tfelt] a sincère, senti.

heartily ['ha:tili] ad de bon cœur, avec appétit

heartiness ['ha:tinis] n cordialité f, vigueur f.

heartless ['ha:tlis] a sans cœur, cruel.

heartlessness ['ha:tlisnis] n dureté f, manque de cœur m.

hearth [ha:θ] n foyer m.

hearty ['ha:ti] a cordial, copieux, solide.

heat [hi:t] n chaleur f, colère f, épreuve f, manche f; vti chauffer; vt (r)échauffer, enflammer; vi s'échauffer.

heated ['hi:tid] a chaud, chauffé, animé.

heater ['hi:tə] n radiateur m.

heath [hi:θ] n lande f, bruyère f.

heathen ['hi:ðən] an paien, -ienne.

heather ['heðə] n bruyère f.

heating ['hi:tiŋ] n chauffage m, chauffe f.

heave [hi:v] n soulèvement m, effort m; vt soulever, pousser; vi palpiter, avoir des haut-le-cœur, se soulever, battre du flanc; to — to mettre en panne.

heaven ['hevn] n ciel m.

heavenly ['hevnli] a céleste, divin.

heavily ['hevili] ad pesamment, lourdement.

heaviness ['hevinis] n lourdeur f, poids m, lassitude f.

heavy ['hevi] a lourd, (sea) dur, violent, gros, triste.

Hebrew ['hi:bru:] an hébreu.

heckle ['hekl] vt harceler.

hectic ['hektik] a fiévreux, excitant.

hector ['hektə] vt rudoyer.

hedge [hedʒ] n haie f, (fig) mur m; vt enclore; vi se couvrir, esquiver la question.

hedgehog ['hedʒhɔg] n hérisson m.

heed [hi:d] n attention f; vt faire attention à.

heedful ['hi:dful] a attentif.

heedless ['hi:dlis] a inattentif, léger, insouciant.

heedlessly ['hi:dlisli] ad étourdiment.

heel [hi:l] n talon m; vt réparer le talon de; vti talonner; to bring to — mettre au pas; to —! ici! down at — éculé.

hefty ['hefti] a solide, costaud.

heifer ['hefə] n génisse f.

height [hait] n hauteur f, comble m.

heighten ['haitn] vt rehausser, faire ressortir.

heinous ['heinəs] a atroce, odieux.

heinousness ['heinəsnis] n atrocité f, énormité f.
heir [ɛə] n héritier m.
heiress ['ɛəris] n héritière f.
heirloom ['ɛəlu:m] n bien inaliénable m, meuble m de famille.
held [held] pt pp of **hold**.
Helen ['helin] Hélène f.
hell [hel] n enfer m, diable m.
hellish ['heliʃ] a infernal.
helm [helm] n barre f, gouvernail m.
helmet ['helmit] n casque m.
helmsman ['helmzmən] n timonier m, homme de barre m.
help [help] n aide f, secours m, domestique mf, auxiliaire mf, collaborateur, -trice; vt aider, secourir, servir; **I can't — laughing** je ne peux m'empêcher de rire; **I can't — it** je n'y peux rien.
helpful ['helpful] a secourable, serviable, utile.
helpfulness ['helpfulnis] n serviabilité f.
helping ['helpiŋ] n portion f, morceau m.
helpless ['helplis] a sans défense désemparé, sans ressource.
helplessness ['helplisnis] n impuissance f, faiblesse f.
helter-skelter ['heltə'skeltə] ad pêle mêle, à la débandade.
hem [hem] n ourlet m; vt ourler; **to — in** cerner.
hemlock ['hemlɔk] n ciguë f.
hemp [hemp] n chanvre m.
hen [hen] n poule f, femelle f.
hence [hens] ad d'ici.
henceforth ['hens'fɔ:θ] ad à l'avenir dorénavant.
henchman ['hentʃmən] n partisan m, bras droit m.
henhouse ['hen'haus] n poulailler m.
henpecked ['henpekt] a dominé par sa femme.
henroost ['henrust] n perchoir m.
Henry ['henri] Henri m.
her [hə:] a son, sa, ses; pn la, lui, à elle; **—self** elle-même; **—s** pn le sien, la sienne, les siens, les siennes.
herald ['herəld] n héraut m, messager, -ère, avant-coureur m, avant-courrier, -ière.
heraldry ['herəldri] n blason m, art héraldique m.
herb [hə:b] n herbe f; pl simples m pl.
herbaceous [hə:'beiʃəs] a herbacé.
herbalist ['hə:bəlist] n herboriste mf.
herd [hə:d] n troupeau m; vi vivre en troupe.
herdsman ['hə:dzmən] n pâtre m, bouvier m.
here [hiə] ad ici.
hereafter [hiər'ɑ:ftə] n vie future f, au-delà m; ad à l'avenir, désormais, ci-dessous.
hereditary [hi'reditəri] a héréditaire.
heredity [hi'rediti] n hérédité f.

herein ['hiərin] ad ici, ci-dedans, ci-inclus.
heresy ['herəsi] n hérésie f.
heretic ['herətik] n hérétique mf.
heritage ['heritidʒ] n héritage m.
hermit ['hə:mit] n ermite m.
hernia ['hə:njə] n hernie f.
hero ['hiərou] n héros m.
heroic [hi'rouik] a héroïque.
heroine ['herouin] n héroïne f.
heron ['herən] n héron m.
herring ['heriŋ] n hareng m; **red —** (fig) diversion.
hesitate ['heziteit] vi hésiter.
hesitation [,hezi'teiʃən] n hésitation f.
hew [hju:] vt couper, ouvrir, tailler.
hewer ['hju:ə] n bûcheron m, tailleur m.
heyday ['heidei] n fleur f, apogée m, beaux jours m pl.
hiccup ['hikʌp] n hoquet m; vi avoir le hoquet.
hid, hidden [hid, 'hidn] pt pp of **hide**.
hide [haid] n peau f, cuir m; vt cacher; vi se cacher.
hide-and-seek ['haidan'si:k] n cache-cache m.
hidebound ['haidbaund] a étroit, fermé, systématique.
hideous ['hidjəs] a hideux, horrible, affreux, odieux.
hiding ['haidiŋ] n râclée f, dissimulation f.
hiding-place ['haidiŋpleis] n cachette f.
higgledy-piggledy ['higldi'pigldi] ad en confusion, pêle-mêle.
high [hai] a haut (placé), élevé, grand, gros, avancé, faisandé, (US) (of drug addict) parti, en voyage; **— altar** maître-autel m; **— school** lycée m, collège m.
highborn ['haibɔ:n] a de haute naissance.
highbrow ['haibrau] n intellectuel, -elle, pontife m, snob m.
highflown ['haifloun] a ampoulé, extravagant.
high-handed ['hai'hændid] a impérieux, arbitraire.
highly ['haili] ad fortement, hautement, fort, très; **—strung** exalté, nerveux.
highness ['hainis] n Altesse f, hauteur f.
high-pitched ['hai'pitʃt] a aigu, -un
highroad, -way ['hairoud, -wei] ë route f nationale, grand'route ff voie f; a routier; **dual — route** , jumelée.
high-spirited ['hai'spiritid] a exubérant, courageux, enthousiaste.
highwayman ['haiweimən] n voleur de grand chemin m.
hike [haik] n excursion f à pied; vi faire du footing, trimarder.
hilarious [hi'lɛəriəs] a hilaire.
hilarity [hi'læriti] n hilarité f.
hill [hil] n colline f, côte f, coteau m, montée f.

hillock ['hilək] n tertre m, butte f.

hilltop ['hiltɔp] n sommet m.

hilly ['hili] a accidenté, montueux.

hilt [hilt] n poignée f, garde f, crosse f.

him [him] pn le, lui; —**self** lui-même.

hind [haind] n biche f; a de derrière.

hinder ['hində] vt gêner, empêcher, entraver.

hindmost ['haindmoust] a dernier.

hindquarters ['haind'kwɔːtəz] n arrière train m.

hindrance ['hindrəns] n entrave f, obstacle m, empêchement m.

hinge [hindʒ] n gond m, pivot m, charnière f; vi tourner, dépendre.

hint [hint] n allusion f, insinuation f, mot m; vt insinuer, faire entendre; vi faire allusion (à at).

hip [hip] n hanche f.

hire ['haiə] n louage m, location f; on, for — à louer; vt louer, embaucher.

hireling ['haiəliŋ] n mercenaire m.

hire-purchase ['haiə'pəːtʃis] n paiements échelonnés m pl, vente à tempérament f.

hirsute ['həːsjuːt] a hirsute, velu.

his [hiz] a son, sa, ses; pn le sien, la sienne, les siens, les siennes, à lui.

hiss [his] n sifflement m, sifflets m pl; vti siffler.

historian [his'tɔːriən] n historien m.

historic [his'tɔrik] a historique.

history ['histəri] n histoire f.

hit [hit] n coup m (au but), succès m; vt frapper, atteindre, mettre le doigt sur; vi se cogner, donner.

hitch [hitʃ] n secousse f, accroc m, nœud m; vt pousser (tirer) brusquement, attacher, accrocher.

hitchhike ['hitʃhaik] vi faire de l'autostop.

hither ['hiðə] ad ici, y, çà.

hitherto ['hiðə'tuː] ad jusqu'ici.

hive [haiv] n ruche f, essaim m.

hoard [hɔːd] n stock m, magot m; vt amasser, thésauriser.

hoarding ['hɔːdiŋ] n palissade f, panneau-réclame m, thésaurisation f, amassage m.

hoarfrost ['hɔː'frɔst] n gelée blanche f, givre m.

hoarse [hɔːs] a rauque, enroué.

hoarseness ['hɔːsnis] n enrouement m.

hoary ['hɔːri] a chenu, vénérable, blanchâtre.

hoax [houks] n mystification f, vt mystifier.

hobble ['hɔbl] n boiterie f, entrave f, embarras m; vt entraver; vi aller clopin-clopant.

hobby ['hɔbi] n marotte f, dada m.

hobnail ['hɔbneil] n clou à ferrer m.

hock [hɔk] n jarret m, vin du Rhin m.

hod [hɔd] n hotte f, auge f.

hoe [hou] n houe f, sarcloir m, hoyeau m, daba m; vt biner, sarcler.

hog [hɔg] n porc m, pourceau m, cochon m.

hogshead ['hɔgzhed] n barrique f.

hoist [hɔist] n poulie f, treuil m, monte-charge m; vt hisser.

hold [hould] n prise f, mainmise f, influence f, empire m, cale f; vt (con-, dé-, main-, re-, sou-, tenir, porter; vi tenir (bon), se maintenir, persister, subsister; **to — back** vt retenir; vi hésiter, rester en arrière; **to — on** tenir bon, s'accrocher.

holdall ['houldɔːl] n valise f, fourre-tout m.

holder ['houldə] n manche m, poignée f, récipient m, porteur, -euse, détenteur, -trice, titulaire mf.

holdfast ['houldfɑːst] n crampon m.

holding ['houldiŋ] n propriété f, tenue f, conservation f, tenure f.

hold-up ['houldʌp] n embouteillage m, panne f, attaque f, coup à main armée m.

hole [houl] n trou m; vt trouer, percer.

holiday ['hɔlədi] n jour férié m, congé m, vacances f pl.

holiness ['houlinis] n sainteté f.

Holland ['hɔlənd] n la Hollande f.

hollow ['hɔlou] n creux m, cavité f, cuvette f; a creux, faux, sourd; vt creuser.

holly ['hɔli] n houx m.

hollyhock ['hɔlihɔk] n rose trémière f.

holm [houm] n îlot m, berge f; —**oak** chêne vert m.

holster ['houlstə] n fontes f pl, étui m.

holy ['houli] a saint, bénit, sacré; **the H— Ghost** le Saint-Esprit.

home [houm] n chez-soi m, maison f, foyer m, pays m, asile m, clinique f; a domestique, de famille, indigène, métropolitain, national, (coup) direct, bien appliqué; ad chez soi, de retour; **not at —** sorti; **to drive —** pousser à fond; **to strike —** frapper juste.

homecoming ['houm͵kʌmiŋ] n retour m, rentrée f.

homeless ['houmlis] a sans logis.

homely ['houmli] a simple, commun.

home-made ['houm'meid] a fait chez soi, bricolé.

Home Office ['houm͵ɔfis] n ministère de l'Intérieur m.

home rule ['houm'ruːl] n autonomie f.

Home Secretary ['houm'sekrətri] n ministre de l'Intérieur m.

homesickness ['houmsiknis] n mal du pays m.

homespun ['houmspʌn] a filé à la maison.

homeward ['houmwəd] ad vers la maison, vers le pays.

homily ['hɔmili] n homélie f.

homogeneity [͵hɔmoudʒə'niːiti] n homogénéité f.

homogeneous [͵hɔmə'dʒiːnjəs] a homogène.

hone [houn] *n* pierre *f* à aiguiser, (*razors*) cuir *m*.

honest ['ɔnist] *a* honnête, probe, loyal.

honestly ['ɔnistli] *ad* sincèrement, de bonne foi, honnêtement.

honesty ['ɔnisti] *n* honnêteté *f*, sincérité *f*.

honey ['hʌni] *n* miel *m*.

honeycomb ['hʌnikoum] *n* rayon de miel *m*; *vt* cribler.

honeydew ['hʌnidjuː] *n* miellée *f*.

honeymoon ['hʌnimuːn] *n* lune de miel *f*, voyage de noces *m*.

honeysuckle ['hʌni.sʌkl] *n* chèvrefeuille *m*.

honorary ['ɔnərəri] *a* honoraire, honorifique.

honour ['ɔnə] *n* honneur *m*, distinction *f*; *vt* honorer.

honourable ['ɔnərəbl] *a* honorable, honnête.

hood [hud] *n* capuchon *m*, cape (line) *f*, capote *f*, (US) capot *m* (*de moteur*).

hooded ['hudid] *a* encapuchonné, mantelé.

hoodwink ['hudwiŋk] *vt* égarer, donner le change à.

hoof [huːf] *n* sabot *m*.

hook [huk] *n* croc *m*, crochet *m*, hameçon *m*, faucille *f*; (US) —up (*radio*) combinaison *f* d'intérêts, conjugaison *f* de postes; *vt* (ac) crocher, agrafer, (*fish*) ferrer.

hooked [hukt] *a* crochu, busqué.

hooligan ['huːligən] *n* voyou *m*.

hoop [huːp] *n* cercle *m*, cerceau *f*, arceau *m*.

hooping-cough ['huːpiŋkɔf] *n* coqueluche *f*.

hoot [huːt] *n* hululement *m*, huée *f*, coup de klaxon *m*; *vi* hululer, corner, klaxonner; *vti* huer; *vt* siffler.

hooter ['huːtə] *n* sirène *f*, corne *f*.

hop [hɔp] *n* houblon *m*, petit saut *m*, sauterie *f*; *vi* saut(ill)er; **to** — **it** ficher le camp.

hope [houp] *n* espoir *m*, espérance *f*, attente *f*; *vt* espérer; **to** — **for** espérer.

hopeful ['houpful] *a* qui a bon espoir, qui donne espoir.

hopefully ['houpfuli] *ad* avec confiance.

hopeless ['houplis] *a* désespéré, incurable.

hop-garden ['hɔp'gɑːdn] *n* houblonnière *f*.

hopping ['hɔpiŋ] *n* sautillement *m*, cueillette du houblon *f*.

horde [hɔːd] *n* horde *f*.

horizon [hə'raizn] *n* horizon *m*.

horizontal [,hɔri'zɔntl] *a* horizontal.

horn [hɔːn] *n* cor *m*, corne *f*.

hornbill ['hɔːnbil] *n* calao *m*.

hornet ['hɔːnit] *n* frelon *m*.

horrible ['hɔribl] *a* horrible, affreux.

horrid ['hɔrid] *a* affreux.

horrify ['hɔrifai] *vt* horrifier.

horror ['hɔrə] *n* horreur *f*.

horror-struck ['hɔrəstrʌk] *a* saisi, glacé.

horse [hɔːs] *n* cheval *m*, cavalerie *f*, chevalet *m*.

horseback ['hɔːsbæk] *ad* **on** — à cheval.

horse-dealer ['hɔːs.diːlə] *n* maquignon *m*.

horsefly ['hɔːsflai] *n* taon *m*.

horseman ['hɔːsmən] *n* écuyer *m*, cavalier *m*.

horsemanship ['hɔːsmənʃip] *n* équitation *f*.

horseplay ['hɔːsplei] *n* jeu de vilain *m*, jeu brutal *m*.

horsepower ['hɔːs.pauə] *n* chevalvapeur *m*.

horse-radish ['hɔːs.rædiʃ] *n* raifort *m*.

horseshoe ['hɔːsʃuː] *n* fer à cheval *m*.

horsewoman ['hɔːs.wumən] *n* cavalière *f*, écuyère *f*, amazone *f*.

hose [houz] *n* tuyau *m*, bas *m* *pl*.

hosier's ['houʒəz] *n* bonneterie *f*.

hospitable [hɔs'pitəbl] *a* hospitalier.

hospitably [hɔs'pitəbli] *ad* à bras ouverts.

hospital ['hɔspitl] *n* hôpital *m*.

hospitality [,hɔspi'tæliti] *n* hospitalité *f*.

host ['houst] *n* hôte *m*, hostie *f*, armée *f*.

hostage ['hɔstidʒ] *n* ôtage *m*.

hostel ['hɔstəl] *n* foyer *m*, pension *f*; **youth** — auberge de la jeunesse *f*.

hostess ['houstes] *n* hôtesse *f*, maîtresse *f* de maison.

hostile ['hɔstail] *a* hostile, ennemi.

hostility [hɔs'tiliti] *n* hostilité *f*.

hot [hɔt] *a* très chaud, brûlant, qui emporte la bouche.

hotch-potch ['hɔtʃpɔtʃ] *n* salmigondis *m*, macédoine *f*.

hotel [hou'tel] *n* hôtel *m*.

hot-headed ['hɔt'hedid] *a* exalté, impétueux, emporté.

hothouse ['hɔthaus] *n* serre chaude *f*.

hot-line ['hɔtlain] *n* téléphone rouge *m*.

hotpot ['hɔtpɔt] *n* ragoût *m*.

hot-water bottle [hɔt'wɔːtə.bɔtl] *n* bouillotte *f*, moine *m*.

hough [hɔk] *n* jarret *m*.

hound [haund] *n* chien courant *m*; *pl* meute *f*; *vt* chasser.

hour ['auə] *n* heure *f*; — **hand** petite aiguille *f*.

hourly ['auəli] *ad* à toute heure, à l'heure.

house [haus] *n* maison *f*, Chambre *f*; [hauz] *vt* loger, abriter, garer.

house-agent ['haus.eidʒənt] *n* agent de location *m*.

housebreaking ['haus.breikiŋ] *n* vol *m* avec effraction, cambriolage *m*.

household ['haushould] *n* maisonnée *f*, ménage *m*, maison *f*.

householder ['haus.houldə] *n* occupant(e) *mf*.

housekeeper ['haus,ki:pə] n femme de charge f, ménagère f.

housekeeping ['haus,ki:piŋ] n ménage m.

housemaid ['hausmeid] n femme de chambre f, bonne f.

housetop ['haustɔp] n toit m; **to shout from the —s** crier qch sur les toits.

housewarming ['haus,wɔ:miŋ] n **to hold a —** pendre la crémaillère.

housewife ['hauswaif] n ménagère f.

housework ['hauswə:k] n ménage m.

housing ['hauziŋ] n logement m, rentrée f; **— problem** crise de logement f.

hovel ['hɔvəl] n masure f, taudis m.

hover ['hɔvə] vi planer, flâner, hésiter; **—craft** n aéroglisseur m.

how [hau] ad comment, comme, combien.

however [hau'evə] ad cependant; cj quelque (si) . . . que, de quelque manière que.

howitzer ['hauitsə] n obusier m.

howl [haul] n hurlement m; vi hurler, rugir, mugir.

hub [hʌb] n moyeu m, centre m.

huddle ['hʌdl] n tas m, fouillis m; vt entasser, serrer; vi se blottir, s'entasser, se serrer.

hue [hju:] n teinte f, nuance f; **to raise a — and cry against** crier tollé contre.

huff [hʌf] vt offusquer, froisser, souffler; **to take the —** prendre la mouche, s'offusquer; **to be in the —** être offusqué.

hug [hʌg] n étreinte f; vt étreindre, presser, embrasser, serrer, longer, s'accrocher à.

huge [hju:dʒ] a immense, énorme.

hugeness ['hju:dʒnis] n énormité f, immensité f.

hulk [hʌlk] n carcasse f; pl pontons m pl.

hull [hʌl] n cosse f, coque f.

hullabaloo [,hʌləbə:'lu:] n vacarme m, charivari m.

hum [hʌm] n bourdonnement m, fredonnement m, ronron(nement) m; vi bourdonner, fredonner, ronronner.

human ['hju:mən] a humain.

humane [hju:'mein] a humain, humanitaire.

humanist ['hju:mənist] n humaniste m.

humanity [hju:'mæniti] n humanité f, genre humain m.

humanize ['hju:mənaiz] vt humaniser.

humble ['hʌmbl] a humble; vt humilier, rabattre.

humbug ['hʌmbʌg] n blagueur m, fumiste m, blague f, fumisterie f.

humdrum ['hʌmdrum] a plat, assommant, monotone, quotidien.

humid ['hju:mid] a humide.

humidity [hju:'miditi] n humidité f.

humiliate [hju:'milieit] vt humilier.

humiliation [hju:,mili'eifən] n humiliation f.

humility [hju:'militi] n humilité f.

hummock ['hʌmək] n mamelon m, monticule m.

humorist ['hju:mərist] n plaisant m, humoriste m, comique m.

humorous ['hju:mərəs] a humoristique, comique, plaisant, drôle.

humour ['hju:mə] n humeur f, humour m; vt flatter, se prêter à.

hump [hʌmp] n bosse f, cafard m.

humpback(ed) ['hʌmpbæk(t)] an bossu(e) mf.

hunch [hʌntʃ] n bosse f, pressentiment m; vt incurver, voûter.

hundred ['hʌndrid] an cent m.

hundredth ['hʌndridθ] a centième.

hung [hʌŋ] pp pt of **hang**.

Hungarian [hʌŋ'gɛəriən] a hongrois.

Hungary ['hʌŋgəri] n Hongrie f.

hunger ['hʌŋgə] n faim f; vi avoir faim, être affamé.

hunger-strike ['hʌŋgəstraik] n grève f de la faim.

hungry ['hʌŋgri] a qui a (donne) faim, affamé.

hunt [hʌnt] n chasse f; vti chasser; vi chasser à courre.

hunter ['hʌntə] n chasseur m, monture f.

hunting-box ['hʌntiŋbɔks] n pavillon de chasse m.

hunting-ground ['hʌntiŋgraund] n terrain de chasse m.

hunting-horn ['hʌntiŋhɔːn] n cor de chasse m.

huntsman ['hʌntsmən] n piqueur m, veneur m, chasseur m.

hurdle ['hə:dl] n claie f, haie f, obstacle m; **— race** course de haies f, steeple-chase m.

hurl [hə:l] vt lancer, précipiter.

hurrah [hu'rɑ:] int n hourra m.

hurricane ['hʌrikən] n ouragan m; **—lamp** lampe-tempête f.

hurried ['hʌrid] a pressé, hâtif.

hurriedly ['hʌridli] ad précipitamment, à la hâte.

hurry ['hʌri] n hâte f, urgence f; vt hâter, presser; vi (se) presser, se dépêcher; **in a —** pressé, en toute hâte, de si tôt; **there is no —** rien ne presse.

hurt [hə:t] n mal m, blessure f, tort m, préjudice m; vt faire (du) mal à, blesser, faire tort à; vi faire mal.

hurtful ['hə:tful] a préjudiciable, nocif, nuisible.

husband ['hʌzbənd] n mari m; vt ménager, gérer sagement.

husbandman ['hʌzbəndmən] n fermier m, laboureur m.

husbandry ['hʌzbəndri] n culture f, gestion habile f.

hush [hʌʃ] n silence m, accalmie f; vt faire taire, étouffer; vi se taire; excl chut !

husk [hʌsk] n cosse f, gousse f, balle

f, peau *f*; *vt* écosser, décortiquer, éplucher.

husky ['hʌski] *a* enroué, altéré, (US) fort, costaud; *n* chien esquimau *m*.

hussar [hu'zaː] *n* hussard *m*.

hussy ['hʌsi] *n* effrontée *f*, luronne *f*.

hustle ['hʌsl] *n* bousculade *f*, activité *f*, *vt* bousculer, presser; *vi* jouer des coudes, se hâter.

hut [hʌt] *n* cabane *f*, baraque *f*; (*mil*) baraquement *m*; **straw —** paillotte.

hutch [hʌtʃ] *n* clapier *m*.

hyacinth ['haiəsinθ] *n* jacinthe *f*, hyacinthe *f*.

hybrid ['haibrid] *an* hybride *m*.

hydrangea [hai'dreindʒə] *n* hortensia *m*.

hydrant ['haidrənt] *n* prise d'eau *f*.

hydro-electric [,haidroui'lektrik] *a* hydraulique; **—power** houille *f* blanche.

hydrogen ['haidrədʒən] *n* hydrogène *m*.

hydrophobia [,haidrə'foubjə] *n* hydrophobie *f*, rage *f*.

hyena [hai'iːnə] *n* hyène *f*.

hygiene ['haidʒiːn] *n* hygiène *f*.

hygienic [hai'dʒiːnik] *a* hygiénique.

hymn [him] *n* hymne *m*.

hyphen ['haifən] *n* trait d'union *m*.

hypnosis [hip'nousis] *n* hypnose *f*.

hypnotic [hip'nɔtik] *a* hypnotique.

hypnotism ['hipnətizəm] *n* hypnotisme *m*.

hypnotize ['hipnətaiz] *vt* hypnotiser.

hypocrisy [hi'pɔkrisi] *n* hypocrisie *f*.

hypocrite ['hipəkrit] *n* hypocrite *mf*.

hypocritical [,hipə'kritikəl] *a* hypocrite.

hypothesis [hai'pɔθisis] *n* hypothèse *f*.

hypothetical [,haipou'θetikəl] *a* hypothétique.

hysteria [his'tiəriə] *n* hystérie *f*.

hysterical [his'terikəl] *a* hystérique, sujet à des crises de nerfs.

hysterics [his'teriks] *n* crise de nerfs *f*.

I

I [ai] *pn* je, moi.

Iain ['iən] (*Scot*) Jean *m*.

Iberia [ai'biəriə] *n* Ibérie *f*.

Iberian [ai'biəriən] *a* ibérique; *an* ibérien, -ienne.

ibex ['aibeks] *n* chamois *m*.

ice [ais] *n* glace *f*; *vt* (con)geler, glacer, (*wine*) frapper.

iceberg ['aisbəːg] *n* iceberg *m*, glaçon *m*.

icebound ['aisbaund] *a* pris par les glaces.

icecream ['ais'kriːm] *n* glace *f*.

ice-floe ['aisflou] *n* banquise *f*.

ice-house ['aishaus] *n* glacière *f*.

icicle ['aisikl] *n* glaçon *m*.

icy ['aisi] *a* glacial, couvert de glace.

idea [ai'diə] *n* idée *f*, notion *f*.

ideal [ai'diəl] *an* idéal *m*.

idealize [ai'diəlaiz] *vt* idéaliser.

identical [ai'dentikəl] *a* identique, conforme.

identify [ai'dentifai] *vt* identifier, établir l'identité de.

identikit [ai'dentikit] *a* portrait *m* robot.

identity [ai'dentiti] *n* identité *f*.

idiocy ['idiəsi] *n* idiotie *f*.

idiom ['idiəm] *n* dialecte *m*, locution *f*.

idiot ['idiət] *n* idiot(e) *mf*.

idiotic [,idi'ɔtik] *a* idiot, bête.

idle ['aidl] *a* paresseux, désœuvré, perdu, vain; *vi* paresser, muser, marcher au ralenti.

idleness ['aidlnis] *n* paresse *f*, oisiveté *f*, chômage *m*, futilité *f*.

idler ['aidlə] *n* fainéant(e) *mf*, flâneur, -euse, désœuvré(e) *mf*.

idly ['aidli] *ad* paresseusement, vainement.

idol ['aidl] *n* idole *f*.

idolatrous [ai'dɔlətrəs] *a* idolâtre.

idolatry [ai'dɔlətri] *n* idolâtrie *f*.

idolize [ai'dɔlaiz] *vt* idolâtrer, adorer.

if [if] *cj* si.

igloo ['igluː] *n* igloo *m*.

ignite [ig'nait] *vt* allumer, mettre le feu à; *vi* prendre feu.

ignition [ig'niʃən] *n* allumage *m*, ignition *f*.

ignoble [ig'noubl] *a* né bas, ignoble, infâme.

ignominious [,ignə'miniəs] *a* ignominieux.

ignominy ['ignəmini] *n* ignominie *f*.

ignorance ['ignərəns] *n* ignorance *f*.

ignorant ['ignərənt] *a* ignorant.

ignore [ig'nɔː] *vt* passer sous silence, méconnaître, ne pas tenir compte de.

ill [il] *n* mal *m*, tort *m*; *a* malade, mauvais; *ad* mal.

ill-bred ['il'bred] *a* mal élevé.

ill-considered ['ilkən'sidəd] *a* peu réfléchi, hâtif, -ive.

ill-disposed ['ildis'pouzd] *a* malveillant.

illegal [i'liːgəl] *a* illégal.

illegality [,iliː'gæliti] *n* illégalité *f*.

illegible [i'ledʒəbl] *a* illisible.

illegitimacy [,ili'dʒitiməsi] *n* illégitimité *f*.

illegitimate [,ili'dʒitimit] *a* illégitime.

ill-fated ['il'feitid] *a* malchanceux, néfaste.

ill-feeling ['il'fiːliŋ] *m* rancune *f*, ressentiment *m*.

ill-gotten ['il'gɔtn] *a* mal acquis.

illiberal [i'libərəl] *a* borné, grossier, mesquin.

illicit [i'lisit] *a* illicite.

ill-informed ['ilin'fɔːmd] *a* mal renseigné.

illiterate [i'litərit] *an* illettré(e) *mf*.

illness ['ilnis] *n* maladie *f*.

ill-starred ['il'stɑːd] *a* né sous une mauvaise étoile, néfaste.

ill-timed ['il'taimd] *a* inopportun, malencontreux.

illuminate [i'luːmineit] *vt* illuminer, éclairer, enluminer.

illumination [i,luːmi'neiʃən] *n* illumination *f*, enluminure *f*.

ill-used ['il'juːzd] *a* malmené, maltraité.

illusion [i'luːʒən] *n* illusion *f*.

illusionist [i'luːʒənist] *n* prestidigitateur *m*.

illusive [i'luːsiv] *a* trompeur, mensonger.

illustrate ['iləstreit] *vt* éclairer, illustrer.

illustration [,iləs'treiʃən] *n* illustration *f*, explication *f*, exemple *m*.

illustrator ['iləstreitə] *n* illustrateur *m*.

illustrious [i'lʌstriəs] *a* illustre, célèbre.

image ['imidʒ] *n* image *f*, statuette *f*.

imagery ['imədʒəri] *n* images *fpl*.

imaginable [i'mædʒinəbl] *a* imaginable.

imaginary [i'mædʒinəri] *a* imaginaire.

imagination [i,mædʒi'neiʃən] *n* imagination *f*.

imaginative [i'mædʒinətiv] *a* imaginatif.

imagine [i'mædʒin] *vt* s'imaginer, se figurer, concevoir, croire, imaginer.

imbecile [im'bəsiːl] *an* imbécile *mf*; *a* faible.

imbecility [,imbi'siliti] *n* imbécillité *f*.

imbibe [im'baib] *vt* boire, absorber, imbiber, adopter.

imbue [im'bjuː] *vt* imprégner, inspirer.

imitate ['imiteit] *vt* imiter.

imitation [,imi'teiʃən] *n* imitation *f*.

imitative ['imitətiv] *a* imitatif, imitateur.

imitator ['imitəitə] *n* imitateur, -trice.

immaculate [i'mækjulit] *a* immaculé, irréprochable.

immaterial [,imə'tiəriəl] *a* immatériel, sans importance.

immature [,imə'tjuə] *a* pas mûr.

immeasurable [i'meʒərəbl] *a* incommensurable, infini.

immediate [i'miːdjət] *a* immédiat, direct, premier.

immediately [i'miːdjətli] *ad* aussitôt, tout de suite.

immemorial [,imi'mɔːriəl] *a* immémorial.

immense [i'mens] *a* immense, vaste.

immensely [i'mensli] *ad* énormément, immensément.

immensity [i'mensiti] *n* immensité *f*.

immerse [i'məːs] *vt* immerger, plonger.

immigrant ['imigrənt] *an* immigrant(e) *mf*, immigré(e) *mf*.

immigrate ['imigreit] *vi* immigrer.

immigration [,imi'greiʃən] *n* immigration *f*.

imminence ['iminəns] *n* imminence *f*.

imminent ['iminənt] *a* imminent.

immobility [,imou'biliti] *n* immobilité *f*, fixité *f*.

immoderate [i'mɔdərit] *a* immodéré, démesuré.

immoderately [i'mɔdəritli] *ad* démesurément, immodérément.

immoderation [i,mɔdər'eiʃən] *n* manque de mesure *m*.

immoral [i'mɔrəl] *a* immoral.

immorality [,imə'ræliti] *n* immoralité *f*.

immortal [i'mɔːtl] *a* immortel.

immortality [,imɔːˈtæliti] *n* immortalité *f*.

immortalize [i'mɔːtəlaiz] *vt* immortaliser.

immovable [i'muːvəbl] *a* immuable, inébranlable, insensible.

immune [i'mjuːn] *a* à l'abri (de to), réfractaire (à to).

immunity [i'mjuːniti] *n* immunité *f*, exemption *f*.

immunize ['imjunaiz] *vt* immuniser.

immutability [i,mjuːtə'biliti] *n* immutabilité *f*.

immutable [i'mjuːtəbl] *a* immuable.

imp [imp] *n* diablotin *m*.

impact ['impækt] *n* choc *m*, collision *f*, impression *f*.

impair [im'pɛə] *vt* affaiblir, altérer.

impairment [im'pɛəmənt] *n* affaiblissement *m*, altération *f*.

impale [im'peil] *vt* empaler.

impart [im'pɑːt] *vt* faire part de, communiquer.

impartial [im'pɑːʃəl] *a* impartial, équitable.

impassable [im'pɑːsəbl] *a* infranchissable, impraticable.

impassibility [,impɑːsə'biliti] *n* impassibilité *f*.

impassioned [im'pæʃnd] *a* passionné.

impassive [im'pæsiv] *a* impassible.

impatience [im'peiʃəns] *n* impatience *f*.

impatient [im'peiʃənt] *a* impatient.

impeach [im'piːtʃ] *vt* mettre en accusation, mettre en cause, attaquer, blâmer.

impeccable [im'pekəbl] *a* impeccable.

impecuniosity [,impikjuːnj'ɔsiti] *n* dénuement *m*.

impecunious [,impi'kjuːnjəs] *a* sans le sou, besogneux.

impede [im'piːd] *vt* entraver, retarder.

impediment [im'pedimənt] *n* empêchement *m*, entrave *f*, obstacle *m*, embarras *m*.

impedimenta [im,pedi'mentə] *n pl* bagage *m pl*.

impel [im'pel] *vt* pousser.

impend [im'pend] *vt* menacer, être imminent.

impenetrable [im'penitrəbl] *a* impénétrable.

impenitence [im'penitəns] *n* impénitence *f*.

impenitent [im'penitənt] *a* impénitent.

imperative [im'perətiv] *an* impératif *m*; *a* péremptoire, impérieux.

imperceptible [impə'septəbl] *a* imperceptible, insensible, insaisissable.

imperfect [im'pə:fikt] *a* imparfait, défectueux.

imperfection [,impə'fekʃən] *n* imperfection *f*, défectuosité *f*.

imperial [im'piəriəl] *a* impérial, majestueux.

imperialism [im'piəriəlizəm] *n* impérialisme *m*.

imperialist [im'piəriəlist] *an* impérialiste *mf*.

imperil [im'peril] *vt* mettre en danger.

imperious [im'piəriəs] *a* impérieux.

imperishable [im'periʃəbl] *a* impérissable.

impermeable [im'pə:mjəbl] *a* imperméable.

impersonal [im'pə:snl] *a* impersonnel.

impersonate [im'pə:səneit] *vt* se faire passer pour, représenter.

impersonation [im,pə:sə'neiʃən] *n* personnification *f*, incarnation *f*, imitation *f*.

impertinence [im'pə:tinəns] *n* insolence *f*, impertinence *f*.

impertinent [im'pə:tinənt] *a* impertinent, insolent.

imperturbability [,impətə:bə'biliti] *n* flegme *m*, imperturbabilité *f*, sang-froid *m*.

imperturbable [,impə'tə:bəbl] *a* imperturbable, inaltérable, serein.

impervious [im'pə:vjəs] *a* impénétrable, imperméable.

impetuosity [im,petju'ɔsiti] *n* impétuosité *f*.

impetuous [im'petjuəs] *a* impétueux.

impetus ['impitəs] *n* impulsion *f*, élan *m*.

impiety [im'paiəti] *n* impiété *f*.

impinge [im'pindʒ] *vi* to — upon frapper, se heurter à.

impious ['impiəs] *a* impie.

implant [im'plɑ:nt] *vt* implanter, inspirer, inculquer.

implement ['implimənt] *n* instrument *m*, article *m*, outil *m*; *pl* attirail *m*, matériel *m*.

implement ['impliment] *vt* remplir, exécuter.

implicate ['implikeit] *vt* mettre en cause, emmêler, impliquer.

implication [,impli'keiʃən] *n* implication *f*, insinuation *f*, portée *f*.

implicit [im'plisit] *a* implicite, tacite, absolu.

implore [im'plɔ:] *vt* implorer, supplier.

imploring [im'plɔ:riŋ] *a* suppliant.

imply [im'plai] *vt* impliquer, (faire) supposer.

impolite [,impə'lait] *a* impoli.

impolitely [impə'laitli] *ad* impoliment.

impoliteness [,impə'laitnis] *n* impolitesse *f*.

import ['impɔ:t] *n* portée *f*, signification *f*; *pl* importations *f pl*.

import [im'pɔ:t] *vt* importer, introduire, signifier, dénoter.

importance [im'pɔ:təns] *n* importance *f*, conséquence *f*.

important [im'pɔ:tənt] *a* important.

importing [im'pɔ:tiŋ] *n* importation *f*.

importunate [im'pɔ:tjunit] *a* importun, ennuyeux.

importune [,impɔ:'tju:n] *vt* importuner, solliciter.

impose [im'pouz] *vt* imposer, infliger; to — upon abuser de, en imposer à.

imposition [,impə'ziʃən] *n* imposition *f*, impôt *m*, imposture *f*, supercherie, pensum *m*.

impossibility [im,pɔsə'biliti] *n* impossibilité *f*.

impossible [im'pɔsəbl] *a* impossible.

impostor [im'pɔstə] *n* imposteur *m*.

imposture [im'pɔstʃə] *n* imposture *f*.

impotence ['impətəns] *n* impuissance *f*.

impotent ['impətənt] *a* impuissant, impotent.

impound [im'paund] *vt* mettre à la fourrière, saisir, confisquer, enfermer.

impoverish [im'pɔvəriʃ] *vt* appauvrir.

impoverishment [im'pɔvəriʃmənt] *n* appauvrissement *m*.

impracticability [im,præktikə'biliti] *n* impossibilité *f*.

impracticable [im'præktikəbl] *a* impraticable, intraitable, infaisable.

impregnable [im'pregnəbl] *a* imprenable, inexpugnable.

impregnate ['impregneit] *vt* saturer, imprégner.

impress ['impres] *n* empreinte *f*.

impress [im'pres] *vt* empreindre, timbrer, imprimer impressionner, enrôler de force.

impression [im'preʃən] *n* impression *f*, tirage *m*.

impressionable [im preʃnəbl] *a* impressionnable, susceptible.

impressionism [im'preʃənizəm] *n* impressionnisme *m*.

impressive [im'presiv] *a* frappant, impressionnant.

imprint ['imprint] *n* empreinte *f*, griffe *f*.

imprint [im'print] *vt* imprimer.

imprison [im'prizn] *vt* emprisonner.

imprisonment [im'priznmənt] *n* emprisonnement *m*, prison *f*.

improbability [im,prɔbə'biliti] *n* invraisemblance *f*, improbabilité *f*.

improbable [im'prɔbəbl] *a* improbable, invraisemblable.
improper [im'prɔpə] *a* impropre, indécent.
impropriety [,imprə'praiəti] *n* impropriété *f*, inconvenance *f*.
improve [im'pruːv] *vt* améliorer, profiter de; *vi* s'améliorer, faire des progrès.
improved [im'pruːvd] *a* amélioré, perfectionné.
improvement [im'pruːvmənt] *n* amélioration *f*, progrès *m pl*, mieux *m*.
improvidence [im'prɔvidəns] *n* imprévoyance *f*.
improvident [im'prɔvidənt] *a* imprévoyant.
improvisation [,imprɔvai'zeiʃən] *n* improvisation *f*.
improvise ['imprəvaiz] *vti* improviser.
imprudence [im'pruːdəns] *n* imprudence *f*.
imprudent [im'pruːdənt] *a* imprudent.
impudent ['impjudənt] *a* impudent.
impudently ['impjudəntli] *ad* impudemment.
impugn [im'pjuːn] *vt* critiquer, contester.
impulse ['impʌls] *n* impulsion *f*, mouvement *m*, poussée *f*.
impulsive [im'pʌlsiv] *a* impulsif, prime-sautier.
impulsiveness [im'pʌlsivnis] *n* impulsivité *f*.
impunity [im'pjuniti] *n* impunité *f*; with — impunément.
impure [im'pjuə] *a* impur, rouillé.
impurity [im'pjuəriti] *n* impureté *f*.
imputable [im'pjuːtəbl] *a* imputable.
imputation [,impju'teiʃən] *n* imputation *f*, attribution *f*.
impute [im'pjuːt] *vt* imputer, attribuer.
in [in] *prep* en, dans, pendant; à, de, sur, par; *ad* y, là, rentré, de retour, à la maison.
inability [,inə'biliti] *n* incapacité *f*, impuissance *f*.
inaccessibility ['inæk,sesə'biliti] *n* inaccessibilité *f*.
inaccessible [,inæk'sesəbil] *a* inaccessible, inabordable.
inaccuracy [in'ækjurəsi] *n* inexactitude *f*.
inaccurate [in'ækjurit] *a* inexact.
inaction [in'ækʃən] *n* inaction *f*, inertie *f*.
inactive [in'æktiv] *a* inactif, inerte.
inactivity [,inæk'tiviti] *n* inactivité *f*.
inadequacy [in'ædikwəsi] *n* insuffisance *f*.
inadequate [in'ædikwit] *a* inadéquat, insuffisant.
inadvertency [,inəd'vəːtənsi] *n* inadvertance *f*.
inadvertent [,inəd'vəːtənt] *a* inattentif, involontaire.

inadvertently [,inəd'vəːtəntli] *ad* par mégarde.
inane [i'nein] *a* vide, stupide, inepte.
inanimate ['inænimit] *a* inanimé.
inanity [in'æniti] *n* inanité *f*, niaiserie *f*.
inapposite [in'æpəzit] *a* déplacé.
inappropriate [,inə'proupriit] *a* déplacé, impropre.
inapt [in'æpt] *a* impropre, inapte, inexpert.
inarticulate [,inɑː'tikjulit] *a* inarticulé, muet.
inasmuch as [inəz'mʌtʃ,æz] *cj* en tant que, vu que.
inattention [,inə'tenʃən] *n* inattention *f*.
inaudible [in'ɔːdəbl] *a* insaisissable, imperceptible, faible.
inaugural [i'nɔːgjurəl] *a* inaugural.
inaugurate [i'nɔːgjureit] *vt* inaugurer, introniser.
inauguration [i,nɔːgju'reiʃən] *n* inauguration *f*.
inauspicious [,inɔːs'piʃəs] *a* de mauvais augure, malencontreux.
inborn ['in'bɔːn] *a* inné, infus.
incandescent [,inkæn'desənt] *a* incandescent.
incapable [in'keipəbl] *a* incapable, incompétent, inaccessible.
incarcerate [in'kɑːsəreit] *vt* incarcérer, emprisonner.
incarceration [in,kɑːsə'reiʃən] *n* incarcération *f*.
incarnate [in'kɑːnit] *vt* incarner; *a* incarné.
incarnation [,inkɑː'neiʃən] *n* incarnation *f*.
incendiary [in'sendjəri] *an* incendiaire *m*.
incense ['insens] *n* encens *m*.
incense [in'sens] *vt* offenser, exaspérer.
incentive [in'sentiv] *n* encouragement *m*, stimulant *m*; *a* stimulant.
inception [in'sepʃən] *n* commencement *m*, début *m*.
incessant [in'sesnt] *a* incessant, continuel.
incessantly [in'sesntli] *ad* incessamment, sans cesse.
incest ['insest] *n* inceste *m*.
incestuous [in'sestjuəs] *a* incestueux.
inch [intʃ] *n* pouce *m*; *vi* avancer, reculer, peu à peu.
incidence ['insidəns] *n* incidence *f*.
incident ['insidənt] *n* incident *m*.
incidental [,insi'dentl] *a* accessoire, fortuit, commun (à to); — **expenses** faux frais.
incidentally [,insi'dentəli] *ad* incidemment, en passant.
incinerator [in'sinəreitə] *n* incinérateur *m*.
incise [in'saiz] *vt* inciser.
incision [in'siʒən] *n* incision *f*, entaille *f*.
incisive [in'saisiv] *a* incisif, mordant, pénétrant.

incite [in'sait] *vt* inciter, pousser, exciter.

incitement [in'saitmənt] *n* incitation *f*, instigation *f*.

incivility [,insi'viliti] *n* impolitesse *f*.

inclemency [in'klemənsi] *n* inclémence *f*, rigueur *f*.

inclination [,inkli'neiʃən] *n* inclinaison *f*, pente *f*, inclination *f*.

incline ['inklain] *n* pente *f*, rampe *f*.

incline [in'klain] *vti* incliner, pencher.

include [in'klu:d] *vt* comprendre, englober.

inclusive [in'klu:siv] *a* inclus, tout compris; — **sum** somme globale.

inclusively [in'klu:sivli] *ad* inclusivement.

incoherence [,inkou'hiərəns] *n* incohérence *f*.

incoherent [,inkou'hiərənt] *a* décousu, incohérent.

income ['inkʌm] *n* revenu *m*; — **tax** impôt *m* sur le revenu.

incomparable [in'kɔmpərəbl] *a* incomparable, hors ligne.

incompatible [,inkəm'pætibl] *a* incompatible, inconciliable.

incompetence [in'kɔmpitəns] *n* incapacité *f*, incompétence *f*.

incomplete [,inkəm'pli:t] *a* incomplet, inachevé.

incomprehensible [,inkɔmpri'hensibl] *a* incompréhensible.

incomprehension [,inkɔmpri'henʃən] *n* inintelligence *f*, incompréhension *f*.

inconceivable [,inkən'si:vəbl] *a* inconcevable.

inconclusive [,inkən'klu:siv] *a* pas (non) concluant.

incongruity [,inkɔŋ'gru:iti] *n* incongruité *f*.

incongruous [in'kɔŋgruəs] *a* incongru, déplacé.

incongruously [in'kɔŋgruəsli] *ad* incongrûment.

inconsiderable [,inkən'sidərəbl] *a* négligeable, insignifiant.

inconsiderate [,inkən'sidərit] *a* irréflechi, étourdi, sans égard.

inconsistency [,inkən'sistənsi] *n* inconséquence, inconsistance.

inconsistent [,inkən'sistənt] *a* décousu, inconsistant, inconséquent, contradictoire.

inconsolable [,inkən'souləbl] *a* inconsolable.

inconspicuous [,inkən'spikjuəs] *a* effacé, discret.

inconstancy [in'kɔnstənsi] *n* inconstance *f*, instabilité *f*.

inconstant [in'kɔnstənt] *a* inconstant, volage.

incontinently [in'kɔntinəntli] *ad* incontinent, sur-le-champ.

inconvenience [in'kən'vi:njəns] *n* inconvénient *m*, incommodité *f*.

inconvenient [,inkən'vi:njənt] *a* incommode, inopportun.

incorporate [in'kɔ:pəreit] *vt* incorporer; *vi* se former en société.

incorrect [,inkə'rekt] *a* inexact, incorrect.

incorrigible [in'kɔridʒəbl] *a* incorrigible.

increase ['inkri:s] *n* augmentation *f*,

increase [in'kri:s] *vt* accroître; *vti* augmenter; *vi* s'accroître, s'agrandir.

increasingly [in'kri:siŋli] *ad* de plus en plus.

incredible [in'kredəbl] *a* incroyable.

incredulous [in'krediuləs] *a* incrédule, sceptique.

increment ['inkrimənt] *n* accroissement *m*, plus-value *f*.

incriminate [in'krimineit] *vt* inculper, incriminer.

incriminating [in'krimineitiŋ] *a* accusateur, à conviction.

incubate ['inkjubeit] *vti* couver.

incubation [,inkju'beiʃən] *n* couvaison *f*, incubation *f*.

incubator ['inkju,beitə] *n* couveuse artificielle *f*.

inculcate ['inkʌlkeit] *vt* inculquer.

inculpate ['inkʌlpeit] *vt* inculper.

inculpation [,inkʌl'peiʃən] *n* inculpation *f*.

incumbent [in'kʌmbənt] *a* qu'incombe (à **upon**).

incur [in'kə:] *vt* encourir, s'attirer contracter.

incurable [in'kjuərəbl] *a* incurable.

incursion [in'kə:ʃən] *n* incursion *f*.

indebted [in'detid] *a* endetté, redevable, obligé.

indebtedness [in'detidnis] *n* dette *f*, obligation *f*.

indecent [in'di:snt] *a* indécent, inconvenant.

indecision [indi'siʒən] *n* indécision *f*, irrésolution *f*.

indecisive [,indi'saisiv] *a* indécis(if), peu concluant.

indecorous [in'dekərəs] *a* inconvenant, malséant.

indecorousness [in'dekərəsnis] *n* inconvenance *f*.

indeed [in'di:d] *ad* vraiment, en vérité, en effet, de fait.

indefatigable [,indi'fætigəbl] *a* infatigable.

indefensible [,indi'fensibl] *a* insoutenable, indéfendable.

indefinable [,indi'fainəbl] *a* indéfinissable.

indefinite [in'definit] *a* indéfini, vague, indéterminé.

indelible [in'delibl] *a* indélébile, ineffaçable.

indelicate [in'delikit] *a* indélicat, inconvenant.

indemnify [in'demnifai] *vt* indemniser dédommager.

indemnity [in'demniti] *n* indemnité *f*, sécurités *f pl*.

indent ['indent] *n* commande *f*, ordre de requisition *m*; [in'dent] *vt* entailler, échancrer; **to — for** commander. réquisitionner.

indentation [,inden'teiʃən] n échancrure f, entaille f.

indenture [in'dentʃə] n contrat m; vt lier par contrat.

independence [,indi'pendəns] n indépendance f.

independent [,indi'pendənt] a indépendant.

independently [,indi'pendəntli] ad indépendamment, séparément.

indescribable [,indis'kraibəbl] a indescriptible, indicible.

indestructible [,indis'trʌktəbl] a indestructible.

index ['indeks] n table f alphabétique, indice m; classeur m; vt classer, repertorier.

index-card ['indeks,kɑːd] n fiche f.

India ['indjə] n l'Inde f.

Indian ['indjən] an Indien, -ienne.

india-rubber ['indjə'rʌbə] n caoutchouc m, gomme f (à effacer).

indicate ['indikeit] vt indiquer, désigner, dénoter.

indication [,indi'keiʃən] n indication f, signe m, indice m.

indicative [in'dikətiv] an indicatif m; a suggestif.

indicator ['indikeitə] n indicateur m, aiguille f.

indict [in'dait] vt accuser, traduire en justice.

indictment [in'daitmənt] n accusation f, inculpation f.

Indies ['indiz] n pl Indes f pl; East — les Grandes Indes f; West — les Antilles.

indifference [in'difrəns] n indifférence f, médiocrité f, impartialité.

indifferent [in'difrənt] a indifférent, égal, médiocre, impartial.

indigence ['indidʒəns] n indigence f, misère f.

indigenous [in'didʒinəs] a indigène, du pays, autochtone.

indigent ['indidʒənt] a indigène, nécessiteux.

indigestible [,indi'dʒestəbl] a indigeste.

indigestion [,indi'dʒestʃən] n indigestion f, mauvaise digestion f.

indignant [in'dignənt] a indigné.

indignation [,indig'neiʃən] n indignation f.

indignity [in'digniti] n indignité f, affront m.

indigo ['indigou] n indigo m.

indirect [,indi'rekt] a indirect, détourné.

indiscernible [,indi'səːnəbl] a imperceptible.

indiscreet [,indis'kriːt] a indiscret, imprudent.

indiscretion [,indis'kreʃən] n indiscrétion f, imprudence f, sottise f.

indiscriminate [,indis'kriminit] a fait au hasard.

indiscriminately [,indis'kriminitli] ad au petit bonheur, au hasard.

indispensable [,indis'pensəbl] a indispensable, de première nécessité.

indispose [,indis'pouz] vt indisposer (contre), incommoder; to be —d être indisposé, souffrant.

indisposition [,indispə'ziʃən] n indisposition f, aversion f, malaise m.

indisputable [,indis'pjuːtəbl] a indiscutable, incontestable.

indissoluble [,indi'sɔljubl] a indissoluble.

indistinct [,indis'tiŋkt] a confus, vague, indistinct.

indistinctness [,indis'tiŋktnis] n confusion f.

indistinguishable [,indis'tiŋgwiʃəbl] a impossible à distinguer, imperceptible, insaisissable.

individual [,indi'vidjuəl] n individu m; a individuel, particulier.

individuality [,indi,vidju'æliti] n individualité f.

indivisible [,indi'vizəbl] a indivisible.

Indochina ['indo'tʃainə] n Indochine f.

indoctrinate [in'dɔktrineit] vt endoctriner, instruire.

indolence ['indoləns] n indolence f.

indolent ['indolənt] a indolent, paresseux.

indomitable [in'dɔmitəbl] a indomptable.

indoor ['indɔː] a de salon, de société, d'intérieur; ad —s à l'intérieur, à la maison.

induce [in'djuːs] vt induire, amener, provoquer, décider.

inducement [in'djuːsmənt] n invite f, encouragement m.

induct [in'dʌkt] vt installer, initier.

induction [in'dʌkʃən] n installation f, induction f.

indulge [in'dʌldʒ] vt satisfaire, nourrir, gâter; to — in s'abandonner à, se livrer à.

indulgence [in'dʌldʒəns] n goût excessif m, indulgence f.

indulgent [in'dʌldʒənt] a faible, indulgent.

industrial [in'dʌstriəl] a industriel.

industrialism [in'dʌstriəlizəm] n industrialisme m.

industrialist [in'dʌstriəlist] n industriel m.

industrialize [in'dʌstriəlaiz] vt industrialiser.

industrious [in'dʌstriəs] a actif, industrieux, laborieux.

industry ['indəstri] n industrie f, activité f, application f.

inebriate [i'niːbrieit] vt griser, enivrer; n ivrogne m.

inebriated [i'niːbrieitid] a ivre, enivré, grisé.

inebriety [,iniː'braiəti] n ébriété f, ivresse f.

ineffable [in'efəbl] a ineffable, indicible.

ineffective [,ini'fektiv] a inefficace, impuissant.

ineffectual [,ini'fektjuəl] *a* vain, stérile, inefficace.

nefficacious [,inefi'keiʃəs] *a* inefficace.

inefficiency [,ini'fiʃənsi] *n* inefficacité *f*, incapacité *f*.

inefficient [,ini'fiʃənt] *a* inefficace, incompétent.

inelastic [ini'læstik] *a* raide, inélastique, fixe.

inept [i'nept] *a* déplacé, inepte.

ineptitude [i'neptitju:d] *n* ineptie *f*.

inequality [,ini'kwɔliti] *n* négalité *f*, irrégularité *f*.

ineradicable [,ini'rædikəbl] *a* indéracinable, inextirpable.

inert [i'nə:t] *a* inerte.

inertia [i'nə:ʃə] *n* inertie *f*, paresse *f*.

inestimable [in'estiməbl] *a* inestimable, incalculable.

inevitable [in'evitəbl] *a* inévitable, fatal.

inexact [,inig'zækt] *a* inexact.

inexcusable [,iniks'kju:zəbl] *a* impardonnable, inexcusable.

inexhaustible [,inig'zɔ:stəbl] *a* inépuisable, intarissable.

inexorable [in'eksərəbl] *a* inexorable.

inexpedience [,iniks'pi:djəns] *n* inopportunité *f*.

inexpedient [,iniks'pi:djənt] *a* inopportun, malavisé.

inexpensive [,iniks'pensiv] *a* bon marché, pas cher.

inexperienced [iniks'piəriənst] *a* inexpérimenté, inexercé.

inexpert [in'ekspə:t] *a* inexpert, maladroit.

inexpiable [in'ekspiəbl] *a* inexpiable.

inexplicable [,iniks'plikəbl] *a* inexplicable.

inexpressible [,iniks'presəbl] *a* inexprimable.

inextinguishable [,iniks'tiŋgwiʃəbl] *a* inextinguible, inassouvissable.

inextricable [in'ekstrikəbl] *a* inextricable.

infallible [in'fæləbl] *a* infaillible.

infallibility [in,fæli'biliti] *n* infaillibilité *f*

infamous ['infəməs] *a* infâme, abominable.

infamy ['infəmi] *n* infamie *f*.

infancy ['infənsi] *n* première enfance *f*, minorité *f*.

infant ['infənt] *n* (petit) enfant *mf*, mineur(e) *mf*.

infantile ['infəntail] *a* infantile, enfantin, d'enfant.

infantry ['infəntri] *n* infanterie *f*.

infantryman ['infəntrimən] *n* fantassin *m*.

infatuate [in'fætjueit] *vt* engouer, affoler.

infatuation [in,fætju'eiʃən] *n* folie *f*, engouement *m*.

infect [in'tekt] *vt* infecter, vicier, contagionner.

infection [in'fekʃən] *n* infection *f*, contagion *f*.

infectious [in'fekʃəs] *a* contagieux, infectieux.

infer [in'fə:] *vi* inférer.

inference ['infərəns] *n* inférence *f*, conclusion *f*.

inferior [in'fiəriə] *an* inférieur(e) *mf*; *n* subalterne *m*, subordonné(e) *mf*.

inferiority [in,fiəri'ɔriti] *n* infériorité *f*.

infernal [in'fə:nl] *a* infernal.

infest [in'fest] *vt* infester.

infide ['infidəl] *an* infidèle *mf*.

infidelity [,infi'deliti] *n* infidélité *f*.

infinite ['infinit] *an* infini *m*.

infinity [in'finiti] *n* infinité *f*.

infirm [in'fə:m] *a* faible, infirme.

infirmary [in'fə:məri] *n* infirmerie *f*, hôpital *m*.

infirmity [in'fə:miti] *n* faiblesse *f*, infirmité *f*.

inflame [in'fleim] *vt* enflammer, mettre le feu à; *vi* s'enflammer.

inflammable [in'flæməbl] *a* inflammable.

inflammation [,inflə'meiʃən] *n* inflammation *f*.

inflammatory [in'flæmətəri] *a* inflammatoire, incendiaire.

inflate [in'fleit] *v* gonfler, grossir, hausser; *vi* faire de l'inflation.

inflated [in'fleitid] *a* enflé, gonflé, bouffi.

inflation [in'fleiʃən] *n* gonflement *m*, inflation *f*, hausse *f*. enflure *f*.

inflect [in'flekt] *vt* courber, fléchir, moduler.

inflexible [in'fleksəbl] *a* inflexible, inébranlable.

inflict [in'flikt] *vt* infliger imposer.

influence ['influəns] *n* influence *f*; *vt* influencer.

influential [,influ'enʃəl] *a* influent.

influenza [,influ'enzə] *n* grippe *f*, influenza *f*.

influx ['inflʌks] *n* afflux *m*, affluence *f*.

inform [in'fɔ:m] *vt* informer, avertir, faire savoir à.

informal [in'fɔ:məl] *a* irrégulier, sans cérémonie.

informant [in'fɔ:mənt] *n* informateur -trice.

information [,infə'meiʃən] *n* informations *f* *pl*, renseignements *m* *pl*: **a piece of** — un renseignement.

informative [in'fɔ:mətiv] *a* instructif.

informer [in'fɔ:mə] *n* dénonciateur, -trice délateur *m*, mouchard *m*.

infraction [in'frækʃən] *n* infraction *f*, violation *f*.

infringe [in'frindʒ] *vt* violer, enfreindre empiéter sur.

infringement [in'frindʒmənt] *n* infraction *f*, atteinte *f*, violation *f*.

infuriate [in'fjuərieit] *vt* mettre en fureur.

infuriated [in'fjuərieitid] *a* furieux, en fureur.

infuse [in'fju:z] *vti* infuser.

infusion [in'fju:ʒən] n infusion f,
tisane f.

ingenious [in'dʒi:njəs] a ingénieux.

ingeniousness [in'dʒi:njəsnis] n ingéniosité f.

ingenuity [,indʒə'nju:iti] n ingéniosité
f.

ingenuous [in'dʒenjuəs] a franc,
ingénu, candide.

ingenuousness [in'dʒenjuəsnis] n
franchise f, naïveté f.

inglorious [in'glɔ:riəs] a ignominieux.

ingot ['iŋgət] n lingot m.

ingrained [in'greind] a enraciné,
encrassé.

ingratiate [in'greiʃieit] vt to —
oneself with se pousser dans les
bonnes grâces de.

ingratiating [in'greiʃieitiŋ] a in-
sinuant, doucereux.

ingratitude [in'grætitju:d] n ingratitude f.

ingredient [in'gri:djənt] n ingrédient
m, élément m.

ingress ['ingres] n entrée f.

ingrowing ['in,grouiŋ] a incarné.

ingrown ['ingroun] a incarné, invétéré.

inhabit [in'hæbit] vt habiter.

inhabitable [in'hæbitəbl] a
habitable.

inhabitant [in'hæbitənt] n habitant
(e) mf.

inhalation [,inhə'leiʃən] n inhalation
f, aspiration f.

inhale [in'heil] vt inhaler, aspirer,
avaler.

inherent [in'hiərənt] a inhérent,
propre.

inherit [in'herit] vt hériter (de),
succéder à.

inheritance [in'heritəns] n héritage
m.

inhibit [in'hibit] vt reprimer, in-
hiber, défendre à.

inhibition [,inhi'biʃən] n inhibition
f, défense f.

inhospitable [,inhɔs'pitəbl] a inhospitalier.

inhuman [in'hju:mən] a inhumain.

inhumanity [,inhju'mæniti] n in-
humanité f, cruauté f.

inhume [in'hju:m] vt inhumer,
enterrer.

inimical [i'nimikəl] a hostile, ennemi.

inimitable [i'nimitəbl] a inimitable.

iniquitous [i'nikwitəs] a inique.

iniquity [i'nikwiti] n iniquité f.

initial [i'niʃəl] n initiale f; pl parafe
m; a initial.

initiate [i'niʃieit] vt initier.

initiation [i,niʃi'eiʃən] n initiation f.

initiative [i'niʃətiv] n initiative f.

initiator [i'niʃieitə] n initiateur,
-trice.

inject [in'dʒekt] vt injecter, faire une
piqûre à, piquer.

injection [in'dʒekʃən] n injection f,
piqûre f.

injudicious [,indʒu:'diʃəs] a malavisé, peu judicieux.

injunction [in'dʒʌŋkʃən] n injonction f.

injure ['indʒə] vt blesser, faire tort à,
léser, offenser.

injurious [in'dʒuəriəs] a préjudiciable, nocif, injurieux.

injury ['indʒəri] n préjudice m,
blessure f, mal m, tort m.

injustice [in'dʒʌstis] n injustice f.

ink [iŋk] n encre f.

inkling ['iŋkliŋ] n vague idée f,
soupçon m.

inkwell ['iŋkwel] n encrier.

inky ['iŋki] a taché d'encre, noir.

inlaid ['in'leid] a incrusté.

inland ['inlænd] an intérieur m; ad
à (de) l'intérieur.

inlay ['in'lei] vt incruster, marqueter,
encastrer.

inlaying ['in'leiiŋ] n marqueterie f,
incrustation f.

inlet ['inlət] n crique f, arrivée f.

inmate ['inmeit] n habitant(e) mf,
pensionnaire mf.

inmost ['inmoust] a le plus profond,
intime.

inn [in] n auberge f.

innate [i'neit] a inné.

inner ['inə] a intérieur, intime.

innings ['iniŋz] n manche f.

innkeeper ['inki:pə] n aubergiste mf.

innocence ['inəsns] n innocence f,
candeur f.

innocent ['inəsnt] a innocent, pur,
vierge.

innocuous [i'nɔkjuəs] a inoffensif.

innovate ['inouveit] vi innover.

innovation [,inou'veiʃən] n innovation f, changement m.

innovator ['inouveitə] n (in)nova-
teur -trice.

innuendo [,inju:'endou] n insinuation
f, sous-entendu m.

innumerable [i'nju:mərəbl] a innombrable.

inoculate [i'nɔkjuleit] vt inoculer,
vacciner.

inoculation [i,nɔkju'leiʃən] n inoculation f.

inodorous [in'oudərəs] a inodore.

inoffensive [,inə'fensiv] a inoffensif.

inoperative [in'ɔpərətiv] a sans
action (effet).

inopportune [in'ɔpətju:n] a intempestif, inopportun.

inopportunely [in'ɔpətju:nli] ad hors
de propos.

inordinate [i'nɔ:dinit] a démesuré,
déréglé.

inquest ['inkwest] n enquête f.

inquire [in'kwaiə] vti s'informer
(de about), demander, se renseigner
(sur about).

inquiry [in'kwaiəri] n question f,
enquête f.

inquisition [,inkwi'ziʃən] n investigation f, inquisition f.

inquisitive [in'kwizitiv] a curieux.

inquisitiveness [in'kwizitivnis] *n* curiosité aiguë *f*.

inroad ['inroud] *n* incursion *f*; **to make —s upon** entamer.

inrush ['inrʌʃ] *n* irruption *f*.

insane [in'sein] *a* fou, aliéné.

insanity [in'sæniti] *n* insanité *f*, démence *f*, folie *f*.

insatiable [in'seiʃəbl] *a* insatiable, inassouvissable.

inscribe [in'skraib] *vt* inscrire, graver.

inscription [in'skripʃən] *n* inscription *f*.

inscrutable [in'skru:təbl] *a* impénétrable, fermé.

insect ['insekt] *n* insecte *m*.

insecticide [in'sektisaid] *n* insecticide *m*.

insecure [‚insi'kjuə] *a* peu sûr, mal affermi, incertain.

insensible [in'sensəbl] *a* insensible, sans connaissance.

insensibility [in‚sensə'biliti] *n* défaillance *f*, insensibilité *f*.

insert [in'sə:t] *vt* insérer, introduire.

insertion [in'sə:ʃən] *n* insertion *f*.

inset ['inset] *n* médaillon *m*, hors-texte *m*.

inside [in'said] *an* intérieur *m*; *n* dedans *m*; *ad* à l'intérieur, au dedans; *prep* à l'intérieur de, au dedans de, dans.

insidious [in'sidiəs] *a* insidieux, captieux.

insight ['insait] *n* intuition *f*, perspicacité *f*, aperçu *m*.

insignificance [‚insig'nifikəns] *n* insignifiance *f*.

insignificant [‚insig'nifikənt] *a* insignifiant.

insincere [‚insin'siə] *a* faux, de mauvaise foi.

insincerity [‚insin'seriti] *n* insincérité *f*.

insinuate [in'sinjueit] *vt* insinuer.

insinuation [in‚sinju'eiʃən] *n* insinuation *f*.

insipid [in'sipid] *a* insipide, fade.

insipidity [‚insi'piditi] *n* fadeur *f*, insipidité *f*.

insist [in'sist] *vi* insister, appuyer, soutenir, vouloir.

insistence [in'sistəns] *n* insistance *f*.

insistent [in'sistənt] *a* pressant, importun.

insolence ['insələns] *n* insolence *f*.

insolent ['insələnt] *a* insolent.

insolently ['insələntli] *ad* insolemment.

insoluble [in'sɔljubl] *a* insoluble.

insolvent [in'sɔlvənt] *a* insolvable.

insomnia [in'sɔmniə] *n* insomnie *f*.

inspect [in'spekt] *vt* inspecter, examiner, vérifier, visiter.

inspection [in'spekʃən] *n* inspection *f*, contrôle *m*, revue *f*, visite *f*.

inspector [in'spektə] *n* inspecteur *m*.

inspiration [‚inspə'reiʃən] *n* inspiration *f*.

inspire [in'spaiə] *vt* inspirer, aspirer.

inspirit [in'spirit] *vt* animer, enflammer.

instability [‚instə'biliti] *n* instabilité *f*.

install [in'stɔ:l] *vt* installer, monter.

installation [‚instə'leiʃən] *n* installation *f*, montage *m*.

instalment [in'stɔ:lmənt] *n* acompte *m*, tranche *f*; **on the — system** *a* tempérament.

instance ['instəns] *n* exemple *m*, cas *m*, instance(s) *f pl*; *vt* citer en exemple.

instancy ['instənsi] *n* urgence *f*, imminence *f*.

instant ['instənt] *n* instant *m*; *a* pressant, urgent, du courant.

instantaneous [‚instən'teinjəs] *a* instantané.

instantly ['instəntli] *ad* à l'instant, sur-le-champ.

instead [in'sted] *ad* au lieu de cela; *prep* au lieu de (of).

instep [in'step] *n* cou de pied *m*, cambrure *f*

instigate ['instigeit] *vt* inciter, provoquer.

instigation [‚insti'geiʃən] *n* instigation *f*.

instigator ['instigeitə] *n* instigateur, -trice, fauteur *m*.

instil [in'stil] *vt* verser goutte à goutte, infiltrer, inculquer.

instinct ['instiŋkt] *n* instinct *m*; *a* plein.

instinctive [in'stiŋktiv] *a* instinctif.

institute ['institju:t] *n* institut *m*; *vt* fonder, ouvrir.

institution [‚insti'tju:ʃən] *n* institution *f*, établissement *m*.

instruct [in'strʌkt] *vt* former, instruire, ordonner.

instruction [in'strʌkʃən] *n* instruction(s) *f pl*; *pl* indications *f pl*, ordres *m pl*.

instructive [in'strʌktiv] *a* instructif.

instructor [in'strʌktə] *n* instructeur *m*, précepteur *m*.

instrument ['instrumənt] *n* instrument *m*, mécanisme *m*, appareil *m*; **— panel** tableau de bord *m*.

instrumental [‚instrə'mentl] *a* qui trouve le moyen de, instrumental, contributif.

insubordinate [‚insə'bɔ:dinit] *a* insubordonné, mutin.

insubordination ['insə‚bɔ:di'neiʃən] *n* insubordination *f*, insoumission *f*.

insufferable [in'sʌfərəbl] *a* intolérable, insupportable.

insufficiency [‚insə'fiʃənsi] *n* insuffisance *f*.

insufficient [‚insə'fiʃənt] *a* insuffisant.

insular ['insjələ] *a* insulaire.

insularity [‚insju'læriti] *n* insularité *f*.

insulate ['insjuleit] *vt* isoler.

insult ['insʌlt] *n* insulte *f*, affront *m*; [in'sʌlt] *vt* insulter, injurier.

insuperable [in'sjurpərəbl] *a* insurmontable.

insurance [in'ʃɔːrəns] *n* assurance *f*; life — assurance sur la vie *f*; — company compagnie *f* d'assurance(s).

insure [in'ʃɔː] *vt* assurer, garantir.

insurer [in'ʃɔːrə] *n* assureur *m*.

insurgent [in'səːdʒənt] *n* insurgé(e) *mf*.

insurrection [ˌinsə'rekʃən] *n* soulèvement *m*, émeute *f*.

intact [in'tækt] *a* intact, indemne.

intangibility [inˌtændʒi'biliti] *n* intangibilité *f*.

intangible [in'tændʒəbl] *a* intangible, impalpable.

integral ['intigrəl] *a* intégral, intégrant.

integrate ['intigreit] *vt* compléter, intégrer.

integrity [in'tegriti] *n* intégrité *f*, probité *f*.

intellect ['intilekt] *n* intellect *m*, intelligence *f*.

intellectual [ˌinti'lektjuəl] *a* intellectuel.

intelligence [in'telidʒəns] *n* intelligence *f*, esprit *m*, sagacité *f*.

intelligent [in'telidʒənt] *a* intelligent.

intelligible [in'telidʒəbl] *a* intelligible, compréhensible.

intemperance [in'tempərəns] *n* intempérance *f*, alcoolisme *m*.

intemperate [in'tempərit] *a* immodéré, intempérant.

intend [in'tend] *vt* avoir l'intention (de to), entendre, projeter (de to), vouloir (dire), destiner (à to).

intended [in'tendid] *n* futur(e) *mf*, prétendu(e) *mf*; *a* voulu, projeté.

intense [in'tens] *a* intense, vif, profond.

intensity [in'tensiti] *n* intensité *f*, violence *f*.

intent [in'tent] *n* intention *f*; *a* appliqué, absorbé, profond.

intention [in'tenʃən] *n* intention *f*, dessein *m*, but *m*.

intentional [in'tenʃənl] *a* intentionnel, voulu, fait exprès.

inter [in'təː] *vt* enterrer.

interaction [ˌintər'ækʃən] *n* interaction *f*.

intercede [ˌintəː'siːd] *vi* intercéder.

intercept [ˌintəː'sept] *vt* intercepter, arrêter, couper, capter.

interception [ˌintəː'sepʃən] *n* interception *f*.

intercession [ˌintə'seʃən] *n* intercession *f*.

interchange [ˌintə'tʃeindʒ] *n* échange *m*, communication *f*, *vt* échanger.

intercourse ['intəkɔːs] *n* commerce *m*, relations *f pl*.

interdict ['intədikt] *n* interdit *m*, interdiction *f*; *vt* interdire (à).

interdiction [ˌintə'dikʃən] *n* interdiction *f*.

interest ['intrist] *n* intérêt *m*; participation *f*, crédit *m*; *vt* intéres-

ser; to be —ed in s'intéresser à, s'occuper de.

interesting ['intristiŋ] *a* intéressant.

interfere [ˌintə'fiə] *vi* se mêler (de in, with), s'immiscer (dans in), toucher (à with), intervenir; don't — mêlez-vous de vos affaires.

interference [ˌintə'fiərəns] *n* ingérence *f*, intervention *f*, brouillage *m*.

interfering [ˌintə'fiəriŋ] *a* indiscret, fouinard, importun.

interim ['intərim] *n* intérim *m*; *a* intérimaire; *ad* en attendant.

interior [in'tiəriə] *an* intérieur *m*; *a* interne.

interject [ˌintə'dʒekt] *vt* interjeter; *vi* s'écrier.

interjection [ˌintə'dʒekʃən] *n* interjection *f*.

interlace [ˌintə'leis] *vt* entrelacer, entrecroiser.

interlard [ˌintə'laːd] *vt* bigarrer, entremêler.

interlinear [ˌintə'liniə] *a* interlinéaire.

interlock [ˌintə'lɔk] *vt* emboîter, enclencher; *vi* s'emboîter, s'enclencher, s'engrener.

interlocutor [ˌintə'lɔkjutə] *n* interlocuteur *m*.

interloper ['intəloupə] *n* intrus(e) *mf*, courtier marron *m*, resquilleur, -euse.

interlude ['intəluːd] *n* intermède *m*.

intermediary [ˌintə'miːdjəri] *an* intermédiaire *m*.

intermediate [ˌintə'miːdjət] *a* intermédiaire, intermédiat.

interment [in'təːmənt] *n* enterrement *m*.

intermission [ˌintə'miʃən] *n* interruption *f*, relache *f*, pause *f*, (US) entr'acte *m*, (school) récréation *f*.

intermit [ˌintə'mit] *vt* arrêter, suspendre.

intermittence [ˌintə'mitəns] *n* intermittence *f*.

intermittent [ˌintə'mitənt] *a* intermittent.

intern [in'təːn] *vt* interner; ['intəːn] *n* (US) interne.

internal [in'təːnl] *a* interne, intérieur, intime; (US) — revenue *n* fisc *m*.

international [ˌintə'næʃnəl] *a* international; *n* match international *m*.

internecine [ˌintə'niːsain] *a* — war guerre *f* d'extermination réciproque.

internee [ˌintəː'niː] *n* interné(e) *mf*.

interplay ['intəplei] *n* jeu croisé *m*, effet *m* réciproque (combiné).

interpolate [in'təːpəleit] *vt* intercaler, interpoler.

interpose [ˌintə'pouz] *vt* interposer; *vi* s'interposer.

interpret [in'təːprit] *vt* interpréter; *vi* faire l'interprète.

interpretation [inˌtəːpri'teiʃən] *n* interprétation *f*.

interpreter [in'təːpritə] *n* interprète *mf*.

interrogate [in'terəgeit] *vt* interroger, questionner.

interrogation [in͵terə'geiʃən] *n* interrogation *f*; — **mark** point d'interrogation *m*.

interrogative [͵intə'rɔgətiv] *a* interrogateur.

interrupt [͵intə'rʌpt] *vti* interrompre.

interrupter [͵intə'rʌptə] *n* interrupteur, -trice, coupe-circuit *m*.

interruption [͵intə'rʌpʃən] *n* interruption *f*.

intersect [͵intə'sekt] *vt* entrecouper, entrecroiser.

intersection [͵intə'sekʃən] *n* intersection *f*, croisement *m*.

interstice [in'tə:stis] *n* interstice *m*, alvéole *m*.

interval ['intəvəl] *n* intervalle *m*, entr'acte *m*, mi-temps *f*, récréation *f*.

intervene [͵intə'vi:n] *vi* intervenir, séparer, s'interposer.

intervening [͵intə'vi:niŋ] *a* qui sépare, qui intervient.

intervention [͵intə'venʃən] *n* intervention *f*.

interview ['intəvju:] *n* interview *f*, entrevue *f*; *vt* interviewer, avoir une entrevue avec.

intestinal [in'testinl] *a* intestinal.

intestine [in'testin] *an* intestin *m*.

intimacy ['intiməsi] *n* intimité *f*.

intimate ['intimit] *an* intime *mf*; ['intimeit] *vt* intimer, indiquer, notifier.

intimation [͵inti'meiʃən] *n* intimation *f*, avis *m*.

intimidate [in'timideit] *vt* intimider.

intimidation [in͵timi'deiʃən] *n* intimidation *f*.

into ['intu] *prep* dans, en, entre.

intolerable [in'tɔlərəbl] *a* insupportable, intolérable.

intolerance [in'tɔlərəns] *n* intolérance *f*.

intolerant [in'tɔlərənt] *a* intolérant.

intonation [͵intou'neiʃən] *n* intonation *f*.

intone [in'toun] *vt* psalmodier, entonner.

intoxicate [in'tɔksikeit] *vt* enivrer, tourner la tête à.

intoxication [in͵tɔksi'keiʃən] *n* ivresse *f*, intoxication *f*, enivrement *m*.

intractable [in'træktəbl] *a* intraitable, opiniâtre.

intrepid [in'trepid] *a* intrépide.

intrepidity [͵intri'piditi] *n* intrépidité *f*.

intricacy ['intrikəsi] *n* complication *f*, complexité *f*.

intricate ['intrikit] *a* compliqué, embrouillé.

intrigue [in'tri:g] *n* intrigue *f*, cabale *f*; *vi* intriguer.

intrinsic [in'trinsik] *a* intrinsèque.

introduce [͵intrə'dju:s] *vt* introduire, présenter, initier.

introduction [͵intrə'dʌkʃən] *n* introduction *f*, présentation *f*, avant-propos *m*.

introspection [͵introu'spekʃən] *n* introspection *f*.

introverted [͵introu'və:tid] *a* recueil'i, introverti.

intrude [in'tru:d] *vi* faire intrusion, être importun, empiéter (sur **upon**).

intruder [in'tru:də] *n* intrus(e) *mf*, resquilleur, -euse.

intrusion [in'tru:ʒən] *n* intrusion *f*.

intuition [͵intju:'iʃən] *n* intuition *f*.

inundate ['inʌndeit] *vt* inonder, déborder.

inundation [͵inʌn'deiʃən] *n* inondation *f*.

inure [in'juə] *vt* habituer, endurcir.

invade [in'veid] *vt* envahir, violer.

invader [in'veidə] *n* envahisseur *m*.

invalid [in'vælid] *a* invalide.

invalid [in'vælid] *an* malade *mf*, infirme *mf*; *vt* réformer.

invalidate [in'vælideit] *vt* invalider, casser.

invalidation [in͵væli'deiʃən] *n* invalidation *f*.

invalidity [͵invə'liditi] *n* invalidité *f*.

invaluable [in'væljuəbl] *a* inestimable.

invariable [in'vɛəriəbl] *a* invariable.

invasion [in'veiʒən] *n* invasion *f*, envahissement *m*.

invective [in'vektiv] *n* invective *f*.

inveigh [in'vei] *vi* se déchaîner, invectiver.

inveigle [in'vi:gl] *vt* séduire, attirer, entraîner.

inveiglement [in'vi:glmənt] *n* séduction *f*, leurre *m*.

invent [in'vent] *vt* inventer.

invention [in'venʃən] *n* invention *f*.

inventiveness [in'ventivnis] *n* imagination *f*.

inventor [in'ventə] *n* inventeur *m*.

inverse [in'və:s] *an* inverse *m*; contraire *m*.

inversion [in'və:ʃən] *n* renversement *m*, inversion *f*.

invert [in'və:t] *vt* retourner, renverser.

invest [in'vest] *vt* (re)vêtir, investir, placer.

investigate [in'vestigeit] *vt* examiner, faire une enquête sur, informer sur.

investigation [in͵vesti'geiʃən] *n* investigation *f*, enquête *f*.

investment [in'vestmənt] *n* placement *m*, investissement *m*.

investor [in'vestə] *n* actionnaire *m*, capitaliste *m*.

inveterate [in'vetərit] *a* invétéré, acharné.

invidious [in'vidiəs] *a* odieux, qui fait envie.

invigilate [in'vidʒileit] *vt* surveiller.

invigilation [in͵vidʒi'leiʃən] *n* surveillance *f*.

invigilator [in'vidʒileitə] *n* surveillant(e) *mf*.

invigorating [in'vigəreitiŋ] *a* fortifiant, tonifiant.
invincibility [in,vinsi'biliti] *n* in-
vincibilité *f.*
invincible [in'vinsəbl] *a* invincible.
inviolability [in,vaiələ'biliti] *n* inviolabilité *f.*
invio'able [in'vaiələbl] *a* inviolable.
invisibility [in,vizə'biliti] *n* invisibilité *f.*
invisible [in'vizəbl] *a* invisible, (ink)
sympathique.
invitation [,invi'teiʃən] *n* invitation
f.
invite [in'vait] *vt* inviter, demander.
invitingly [in'vaitiŋli] *ad* de manière
engageante, tentante.
invocation [,invou'keiʃən] *n* invocation *f.*
invoice ['invɔis] *n* facture *f.*
invoke [in'vouk] *vt* invoquer, évoquer.
involuntary [in'vɔləntəri] *a* involontaire.
involve [in'vɔlv] *vt* envelopper, impliquer, engager, entraîner, nécessiter.
inward ['inwəd] *a* intérieur, interne.
iodine ['aiədiːn] *n* (teinture *f* d')iode
m.
irascibility [i,ræsi'biliti] *n* irascibilité *m.*
irascible [i'ræsibl] *a* irascible, colérique.
irate [ai'reit] *a* en colère, courroucé.
Ireland ['aiələnd] *n* Irlande *f.*
iris ['aiəris] *n* iris *m.*
Irish ['aiəriʃ] *an* irlandais *m.*
Irishman ['aiəriʃmən] *n* Irelandais *m.*
irksome ['əːksəm] *a* ennuyeux,
fatigant, ingrat.
iron ['aiən] *n* fer *m*; *a* de fer; *vt*
repasser; to — **out** aplatir, effacer
au fer chaud.
iron age ['aiəneidʒ] *n* âge *m* de fer.
ironclad ['aiənklæd] *an* cuirassé *m.*
iron-foundry ['aiən,faundri] *n* fonderie *f.*
iron-grey ['aiəngrei] *a* gris-fer.
ironical [ai'rɔnikəl] *a* ironique.
ironing ['aiəniŋ] *n* repassage *m.*
ironmonger ['aiən,mʌŋgə] *n* quincailler *m.*
ironmonger's ['aiən,mʌŋgəz] *n* quincaillerie *f.*
iron-ore ['aiən'ɔː] *n* minéral *m* de fer.
iron rations ['aiən'ræʃənz] *n pl*
vivres de réserve *m pl.*
ironwork ['aiənwəːk] *n* serrurerie *f*,
charpenterie *f* en fer.
irony ['aiərəni] *n* ironie *f.*
irradiate [i'reidieit] *vi* rayonner,
iradier.
irradiation [i,reidi'eiʃən] *n* irradiation *f*, rayonnement *m.*
irrational [i'ræʃənl] *a* absurde,
déraisonnable, irrationnel.
irrecognizable [i'rekəgnaizəbl] *a*
méconnaissable.
irreconcilable [i,rekən'sailəbl] *a*

irréconciliable, inconciliable, implacable.
irrecoverable [,iri'kʌvərəbl] *a* irré-
couvrable.
irredeemable [,iri'diːməbl] *a* non
remboursable, irréparable, incorrigible.
irreducible [,iri'djuːsəbl] *a* irré-
ductible.
irrefutable [,iri'fjuːtəbl] *a* irréfutable irrécusable.
irregular [i'regjulə] *a* irrégulier,
inégal.
irrelevant [i'reləvənt] *a* à côté de la
question, hors de propos.
irreligious [,iri'lidʒəs] *a* irréligieux.
irremediable [,iri'miːdiəbl] *a* irrémédiable, sans remède.
irremovable [,iri'muːvəbl] *a* inamovible.
irreparable [i'repərəbl] *a* irréparable.
irreplaceable [,iri'pleisəbl] *a* irremplaçable.
irreproachable [,iri'proutʃəbl] *a*
irréprochable.
irresistible [,iri'zistəbl] *a* irrésistible.
irresolute [i'rezəluːt] *a* irrésolu,
hésitant, indécis.
irresoluteness [i'rezəluːtnis] *n* irrésolution *f*, indécision *f.*
irrespective [,iri'spektiv] *a* sans
égard (à **of**), indépendamment (de
of), indépendant.
irresponsible [,iris'pɔnsəbl] *a* irréfléchi, étourdi.
irresponsive [,iris'pɔnsiv] *a* figé,
froid.
irretentive [,iri'tentiv] *a* peu fidèle,
peu sûr.
irretrievable [,iri'triːvəbl] *a* irréparable.
irreverence [i'revərəns] *n* irrévérence *f.*
irreverent [i'revərənt] *a* irrévérencieux, irrévérent.
irrevocable [i'revəkəbl] *a* irrévocable.
irrigate ['irigeit] *vt* irriguer, arroser.
irrigation [,iri'geiʃən] *n* irrigation *f.*
irritability [,irita'biliti] *n* irritabilité
f.
irritable ['iritəbl] *a* irritable.
irritate ['iriteit] *vt* irriter.
irritating ['iriteitiŋ] *a* irritant,
agaçant.
irritation [,iri'teiʃən] *n* irritation *f.*
irruption [i'rʌpʃən] *n* irruption *f.*
Isabel ['izəbel] Isabelle *f.*
island ['ailənd] *n* île *f*, (street) refuge
m.
islander ['ailəndə] *n* insulaire *mf.*
isle [ail] *n* îlot *m.*
islet ['ailit] *n* îlot *m.*
isolate ['aisouleit] *vt* isoler.
isolation [,aisə'leiʃən] *n* isolement *m*,
solitude *f.*
issue ['isjuː] *n* issue *f*, progéniture *f*,
question *f*, émission *f*, discussion *f*,
débouché *m*, terme *m*, tirage *m*,

numéro m; vti sortir, résulter; vt émettre, publier, lancer.

isthmus ['isθməs] n isthme m.

Italian [i'tæliən] n Italien, -ienne; an italien m.

italics [i'tæliks] n italiques f pl.

it [it] pn il, le; ce, c', cela, ça.

Italy ['itəli] n Italie f.

itch [itʃ] n démangeaison f, prurit m, gale f; vi démanger.

itchy ['itʃi] a galeux, qui démange.

item ['aitəm] n item m de plus, article m, détail m, rubrique f.

itinerant [i'tinərənt] a ambulant, forain.

itinerary [ai'tinərəri] n itinéraire m.

its [its] a son, sa, ses.

itself [it'self] pn soi, lui-, elle-même, se.

ivory ['aivəri] n ivoire m.

ivy ['aivi] n lierre m.

J

jabber ['dʒæbə] n bafouillage m; vi bredouiller, baragouiner.

jack [dʒæk] n valet m, cric m, tourne-broche m, cochonnet m, pavillon m, brochet m; to — up hisser, soulever avec un cric; — of all trades n bricoleur m; — o' lantern n feu follet m.

jackal ['dʒækɔ:l] n chacal m.

jackdaw ['dʒækdɔ:] n choucas m.

jacket ['dʒækit] n veston m, veste f, (women) jaquette f, (books) chemise f; potatoes in their —s pommes de terre en robe de chambre.

jade [dʒeid] n jade m, rosse f, effrontée f.

jaded ['dʒeidid] a éreinté, fourbu, excédé.

jag [dʒæg] n dent f, pointe f; vt denteler, déchiqueter.

jaguar ['dʒægjuə] n jaguar m.

jail [dʒeil] n prison f.

jam [dʒæm] n confiture f, embarras m, embouteillage m, encombrement m; vt presser, bloquer, coincer, caler, enfoncer, fourrer, brouiller; vi se bloquer, se coincer, se caler.

Jane [dʒein] Jeanne f.

Janet ['dʒænit] Jeannette f.

jangle ['dʒæŋgl] vi crier, grincer, cliqueter, s'entrechoquer.

January ['dʒænjuəri] n janvier m.

Japan [dʒə'pæn] n Japon m.

japan [dʒə'pæn] n laque m; vt laquer.

Japanese [ˌdʒæpə'ni:z] n Japonais(e) mf; an japonais m.

jar [dʒɑ:] n jarre f, cruche f, bocal m, pot m, choc m, secousse f, grincement m; vt secouer, ébranler, agacer; vi jurer, détonner.

jargon ['dʒɑ:gən] n jargon m, baragouin m.

jasmine ['dʒæzmin] n jasmin m.

jasper ['dʒæspə] n jaspe m.

jaundice ['dʒɔ:ndis] n jaunisse f.

jaundiced ['dʒɔ:ndist] a envieux, bilieux.

jaunt [dʒɔ:nt] n excursion f, sortie f, balade f.

jaunty ['dʒɔ:nti] a enjoué, désinvolte, vaniteux.

jaw [dʒɔ:] n mâchoire f, mords m, bec m, bouche f; vi bavarder, jaser; vt semoncer.

jay [dʒei] n geai m.

jazz [dʒæz] n jazz m; — band jazz m; vi danser le jazz.

jealous ['dʒeləs] a jaloux.

jealousy ['dʒeləsi] n jalousie f.

jeep [dʒi:p] n jeep f.

jeer [dʒiə] n sarcasme m, huée f; vi ricaner; to — at se moquer de, huer.

jelly ['dʒeli] n gelée f.

jellyfish ['dʒelifiʃ] n méduse f.

jemmy ['dʒemi] n pince-monseigneur f.

jeopardize ['dʒepədaiz] vt mettre en danger.

jeopardy ['dʒepədi] n danger m.

jerk [dʒə:k] n saccade f, à-coup m, secousse f, contraction f, convulsion f; vt secouer, tirer d'un coup sec, tirer par saccades.

jerkily ['dʒə:kili] ad par saccades.

jerky ['dʒə:ki] a saccadé.

jersey ['dʒə:zi] n jersey m, tricot m, maillot m, vareuse f.

jest [dʒest] n plaisanterie f; vi plaisanter.

jester ['dʒestə] n bouffon m, fou m.

jet [dʒet] n jais m, jet m, gicleur m, bec m; — propulsion autopropulsion f; —-propelled plane avion à réaction m.

jetsam ['dʒetsəm] n choses fpl jetées par-dessus bord, épaves f pl.

jettison ['dʒetizn] vt jeter par-dessus bord, se délester de.

jetty ['dʒeti] n jetée f, digue f.

Jew [dʒu:] n Juif m.

jewel ['dʒu:əl] n bijou m, joyau m.

jeweller ['dʒu:ələ] n bijoutier m, joaillier m.

jewellery ['dʒu:əlri] n bijouterie f, joaillerie f.

Jewess ['dʒu:is] n Juive f.

Jewish ['dʒu:iʃ] a juif.

Jewry ['dʒuəri] n monde juif m, juiverie f.

jib [dʒib] n foc m; vi se refuser, renâcler, regimber.

jiffy ['dʒifi] n clin d'œil m; in a — en un clin d'œil.

jig [dʒig] n gigue f, calibre m; vi danser la gigue, gigoter.

jigsaw puzzle ['dʒigsɔ:'pʌzl] n puzzle m, jeu m de patience.

jilt [dʒilt] n coquette f; vt planter là, plaquer.

jingle ['dʒiŋgl] n tintement m, cliquetis m; vi cliqueter, tinter; vt faire sonner.

jingoism ['dʒiŋgouizəm] n chauvinisme m.

jitters ['dʒitəz] n frousse f, trouille f.

Joan [dʒoun] Jeanne f.

job [dʒɔb] n besogne f, affaire f, travail m, place f; vi bricoler.

jobber ['dʒɔbə] n tâcheron m, bricoleur m, tripoteur m.

jobbery ['dʒɔbəri] n tripotage m.

jockey ['dʒɔki] n jockey m; vt duper; vi manœuvrer.

jocose [dʒə'kous] a goguenard, facétieux.

jocular ['dʒɔkjulə] a rieur, badin.

jocund ['dʒɔkʌnd] a enjoué, jovial.

jog [dʒɔg] n cahot m, coup de coude m, petit trot m; vt secouer; vi to — along aller son (petit) train.

John [dʒɔn] Jean m.

join [dʒɔin] n point m, (ligne f de) jonction f, jointure f; vt se joindre à, (re)joindre, (ré)unir, s'inscrire à, relier; vi se (re)joindre; to — up s'engager.

joiner ['dʒɔinə] n menuisier m.

joint [dʒɔint] n joint m, jointure f, articulation f, gond m, pièce f (de viande), rôti m; (US) boîte f (malfamée); **gambling** — tripot m; **juice** — cabaret m borgne; a (con)joint, (ré)uni, en commun; **out of** — déboîté, démis, déréglé.

jointed ['dʒɔintid] a articulé.

joint-heir ['dʒɔint'ɛə] n cohéritier m.

jointly ['dʒɔintli] ad conjointement.

joint-stock company ['dʒɔintstɔk'kʌmpəni] n société anonyme f.

joist [dʒɔist] n solive f, poutre f.

joke [dʒouk] n farce f, bon mot m, plaisanterie f, blague f; vi plaisanter; **practical** — farce f.

joker ['dʒoukə] n plaisant m, farceur, -euse; **practical** — mauvais plaisant m.

jollity ['dʒɔliti] n fête f, réjouissance f.

jolly ['dʒɔli] a gai, joyeux, éméché; ad (fam) drôlement, rudement.

jolt [dʒoult] n cahot m, secousse f; vt secouer; vti cahoter.

jonquil ['dʒɔnkwil] n jonquille f.

Jordan ['dʒɔːdn] n Jordanie f.

jostle ['dʒɔsl] vt pousser, bousculer; vi jouer des coudes.

jot [dʒɔt] n fétu m, brin m; vt to — down noter, griffonner.

journal ['dʒəːnl] n journal m.

journalism ['dʒəːnəlizəm] n journalisme m.

journalist ['dʒəːnəlist] n journaliste mf.

journey ['dʒəːni] n voyage m, trajet m; vi voyager.

journeyman ['dʒəːnimən] n journalier m, compagnon m.

jovial ['dʒouviəl] a jovial.

joviality [dʒouvi'æliti] n jovialité f.

jowl [dʒaul] n mâchoire f, (ba)joue f.

joy [dʒɔi] n joie f.

joyful ['dʒɔiful] a joyeux.

jubilant ['dʒuːbilənt] a joyeux, réjoui; **to be** — jubiler, exulter.

jubilation [dʒuːbi'leiʃən] n jubilation f.

jubilee ['dʒuːbiliː] n jubilé m.

Judas ['dʒuːdəs] n judas m.

judge [dʒʌdʒ] n juge m, arbitre m, connaisseur, -euse; vt juger, estimer.

judgement ['dʒʌdʒmənt] n jugement m, avis m, arrêt m, discernement m.

judicature ['dʒuːdikətʃə] n Justice f, Cour f.

judicial [dʒuːˈdiʃəl] a juridique, judiciaire, légal, impartial.

judicious [dʒuːˈdiʃəs] a judicieux.

jug [dʒʌg] n broc m, cruche f, (fam) violon m.

jugged [dʒʌgd] a cuit à l'étuvée, en civet; emprisonné, coffré.

juggle ['dʒʌgl] vi jongler, faire des tours de passe-passe; to — away escamoter.

juggler ['dʒʌglə] n jongleur m, bateleur m.

juggling ['dʒʌgliŋ] n jonglerie f, tours de passe-passe m pl.

juice [dʒuːs] n jus m.

juicy ['dʒuːsi] a juteux.

Julian ['dʒuːliən] Julien m.

July [dʒuːˈlai] n juillet m.

jumble ['dʒʌmbl] n fouillis m; vt mêler, brouiller.

jump [dʒʌmp] n saut m, bond m, haut-le-corps m; vi sauter, bondir, tressaillir; vt sauter, franchir.

jumper ['dʒʌmpə] n sauteur, -euse, tricot m, vareuse f.

jumpiness ['dʒʌmpinis] n nervosité f.

jumping rope ['dʒʌmpiŋroup] n (US) corde f à sauter.

junction ['dʒʌŋkʃən] n jonction f, bifurcation f, gare d'embranchement f.

juncture ['dʒʌŋktʃə] n jointure f, conjoncture f.

June [dʒuːn] n juin m.

jungle ['dʒʌŋgl] n jungle f.

junior ['dʒuːniə] an cadet, -ette; a jeune; n subalterne m.

juniper ['dʒuːnipə] n genièvre m.

junk [dʒʌŋk] n vieilleries f pl, jonque f; **piece of** — rossignol m; (US) drogue f.

junket ['dʒʌŋkit] n lait caillé m, bombance f.

jurisdiction [dʒuəris'dikʃən] n juridiction f, ressort m.

jurist ['dʒuərist] n juriste m.

jury ['dʒuəri] n jury m.

just [dʒʌst] a juste, équitable; ad (tout) juste, au juste, justement, précisément, seulement, simplement, à l'instant, rien que; **I have** — **seen him** je viens de le voir; **he** — **laughed** il ne fit que rire; — **as** tout comme.

justice ['dʒʌstis] n justice f, juge m.

justifiable [dʒʌsti'faiəbl] a justifiable légitime.

justification [dʒʌstifi'keiʃən] n justification f.

justify ['dʒʌstifai] *vt* justifier.
justness ['dʒʌstnis] *n* justice *f*, justesse *f*.
jut [dʒʌt] *vi* — out faire saillie, avancer.
jute [dʒuːt] *n* jute *m*
juvenile ['dʒuːvənail] *a* juvenile, jeune.
juxtapose ['dʒʌkstəpouz] *vt* juxtaposer.

K

kangaroo [ˌkæŋgə'ruː] *n* kangourou *m*.
keel [kiːl] *n* quille *f*.
keen [kiːn] *a* (*objet*) aiguisé, affilé; vif, acerbe; fin, perçant; (*pers*) zélé, passionné (de on), enragé (de); I am not — on it je n'y tiens pas.
keenness ['kiːnnis] *n* (*obj*) acuité *f*; (*pers*) empressement *m*, ardeur *f*, enthousiasme *m*.
keep [kiːp] *n* donjon *m*, subsistance *f*; *vt* garder, tenir, observer, célébrer; — s.o. waiting faire attendre qn; *vi* se tenir rester, se conserver, continuer (de); — from — s'empêcher de; — in entretenir; kept in en retenue; — on continuer de, à; — to tenir, garder.
keeper ['kiːpə] *n* gardien, -ienne, conservateur *m*, garde *mf*.
keeping ['kiːpiŋ] *n* garde *f*, harmonie *f*, observation *f*, célébration *f*.
keg [keg] *n* barillet *m*, caque *f*.
ken [ken] *n* portée *f*, connaissances *f pl*.
kennel ['kenl] *n* chenil *m*, niche *f*.
kept [kept] *pp pt of* keep.
kerb [kəːb] *n* bordure *f*, margelle *f*.
kerchief ['kəːtʃif] *n* fichu *m*, mouchoir de tête *m*.
kernel ['kəːnl] *n* amande *f*, chair *f*, grain *m*, noyau *m*, essentiel *m*.
kettle ['ketl] *n* bouilloire *f*.
kettledrum ['ketldrʌm] *n* timbale *f*.
key [kiː] *n* clé *f*, clef *f*, touche *f*, mot *m*, corrigé *m*; *a* essentiel, clé; *vt* accorder; to — up stimuler.
keyboard ['kiːbɔːd] *n* clavier *m*.
keyhole ['kiːhoul] *n* trou de la serrure *m*.
keynote ['kiːnout] *n* clé *f*, tonique *f*, note dominante *f*.
key-ring ['kiːriŋ] *n* porte-clefs *m inv*.
keystone ['kiːstoun] *n* clé de voûte *f*.
kick [kik] *n* coup de pied *m*, ruade *f*, recul *m*, ressort *m*; (*US*) plaintes *f pl*, critiques *f pl*; *vi* donner un coup de pied, ruer, reculer; *vt* pousser du pied, donner un coup de pied à, botter.
kick-off ['kikɔf] *n* coup d'envoi *m*.
kid [kid] *n* chevreau *m*, (*fam*) gosse *mf*.
kidnap ['kidnæp] *vt* enlever.
kidnapper ['kidnæpə] *n* ravisseur, -euse.

kidney ['kidni] *n* rein *m*, rognon *m*, acabit *m*, trempe *f*.
kill [kil] *n* mise à mort *f*; *vt* tuer, abattre.
killing ['kiliŋ] *n* tuerie *f*, massacre *m*; *a* meurtrier, tuant, mortel, tordant.
killjoy ['kildʒɔi] *n* rabat-joie *m*.
kiln [kiln] *n* four *m*.
kin [kin] *n* race *f*, souche *f*, parenté *f*, parents *m pl*; *a* allié, apparenté; next of — le plus proche parent, famille *f*.
kind [kaind] *n* espèce *f*, sorte *f*, genre *m*; in — en nature; *a* bon, aimable.
kindergarten ['kindəˌgaːtn] *n* école *f* maternelle, jardin *m* d'enfants.
kindle [kindl] *vt* allumer, enflammer; *vi* s'allumer, prendre feu, flamber.
kindly ['kaindli] *ad* avec bonté, ayez l'obligeance de; *a* bon, bienveillant.
kindness ['kaindnis] *n* bonté *f*, amabilité *f*.
kindred ['kindrid] *n* parenté *f*; *a* analogue.
king [kiŋ] *n* roi *m*, (*draughts*) dame *f*.
kingdom ['kiŋdəm] *n* royaume *m*, règne *m*.
kingfisher ['kiŋfiʃə] *n* martin-pêcheur *m*.
kingly ['kiŋli] *a* royal.
kingship ['kiŋʃip] *n* art de régner *m*, royauté *f*.
kink [kiŋk] *n* nœud *m*, lubie *f*.
kinsfolk ['kinzfouk] *n* parenté *f*, famille *f*.
kipper ['kipə] *n* hareng fumé *m*; *vt* saler, fumer.
kirk [kəːk] *n* (*Scot*) église *f*.
kiss [kis] *n* baiser *m*; *vt* embrasser, baiser.
kissing ['kisiŋ] *n* embrassade.
kit [kit] *n* fourniment *m*, effets *m pl*, fourbi *m*, baluchon *m*, trousse *f*.
kit-bag ['kitbæg] *n* sac *m*.
kitchen ['kitʃin] *n* cuisine *f*.
kitchen-garden ['kitʃin'gaːdn] *n* jardin potager *m*.
kitchen-maid ['kitʃinmeid] *n* fille de cuisine *f*.
kitchen-range ['kitʃin'reindʒ] *n* fourneau *m*, cuisinière *f*.
kite [kait] *n* milan *m*, ballon d'essai *m*, cerf-volant *m*.
kitten ['kitn] *n* chaton *m*.
knack [næk] *n* tour *m* de main, adresse *f*, coup *m*, truc *m*.
knacker ['nækə] *n* équarisseur *m*.
knapsack ['næpsæk] *n* sac *m*, havre-sac *m*.
knave [neiv] *n* gredin *m*, (*cards*) valet *m*.
knead [niːd] *vt* pétrir, masser.
kneading-trough ['niːdiŋ.trɔf] *n* pétrin *m*.
knee [niː] *n* genou *m*.
knee-breeches ['niː.briːtʃiz] *n* culotte *f*.
knee-cap ['niːkæp] *n* rotule *f*; genouillère *f*.

kneel [niːl] *vi* s'agenouiller.

knell [nel] *n* glas *m*.

knew [njuː] *pt of* **know**.

knickerbockers ['nikəbɔkəz] *n* culotte *f*.

knickers ['nikəz] *n* pantalon *m* (de femme), culotte *f*.

knife [naif] *n* couteau *m*; *vt* donner un coup de couteau à, suriner.

knife-board ['naifbɔːd] *n* planche à couteaux *f*.

knife-grinder ['naif,graində] *n* rémouleur *m*.

knight [nait] *n* chevalier *m*; *vt* créer (armer) chevalier.

knighthood ['naithud] *n* rang de chevalier *m*

knit [nit] *vt* tricoter; **to — one's brows** froncer les sourcils; **well—** serré.

knitting ['nitiŋ] *n* tricotage *m*, tricot *m*; **— needle** aiguille à tricoter *f*.

knob [nɔb] *n* bosse *f*, bouton *m*, morceau *m*, pomme *f*.

knock [nɔk] *n* coup *m*; *vti* frapper, cogner; **to — about** *vt* bousculer, malmener; *vi* rouler sa bosse; **to — down** renverser, abattre, adjuger; **to — off** quitter le travail; **to — out** mettre hors de combat, mettre knock-out.

knocker ['nɔkə] *n* marteau *m*.

knock-kneed ['nɔk'niːd] *a* cagneux.

knoll [noul] *n* monticule *m*, tertre *m*.

knot [nɔt] *n* nœud *m*, groupe *m*; *vt* nouer, embrouiller.

knotty ['nɔti] *a* noueux, compliqué.

know [nou] *vt* connaître, reconnaître, savoir; **to be in the —** être dans le secret.

knowing ['nouiŋ] *a* averti, éveillé, fin, rusé, entendu.

knowingly ['nouiŋli] *ad* sciemment, finement, à bon escient.

knowledge ['nɔlidʒ] *n* connaissance *f*, savoir *m*, science *f*; **not to my —** pas que je sache; **without my —** à mon insu; **to have a thorough — of** connaître à fond.

knuckle ['nʌkl] *n* phalange *f*, articulation *f*, jointure *f*; **— of veal** jarret de veau *m*.

knuckle-bone ['nʌkl'boun] *n* osselet *m*.

knuckleduster ['nʌkl,dʌstə] *n* coup-de-poing américain *m*.

kola ['koulə] *n* **— nut** noix *f* de kola; **— tree** kolatier *m*.

Koran [kɔ'ræn] *n* Coran *m*.

L

label ['leibl] *n* étiquette *f*; *vt* étiqueter, classer.

laboratory [lə'bɔrətəri] *n* laboratoire *m*.

laborious [lə'bɔːriəs] *a* laborieux, ardu, pénible.

laboriousness [lə'bɔːriəsnis] *n* application *f*.

labour ['leibə] *n* travail *m*, classe ouvrière *f*, main-d'œuvre *f*; **— exchange** bureau de placement *m*, bourse du Travail *f*; **— party** parti travailliste *m*; *vt* élaborer, travailler; *vi* travailler, peiner.

laboured ['leibəd] *a* cherché, travaillé, pénible.

labourer ['leibərə] *n* manœuvre *m*.

laburnum [lə'bəːnəm] *n* cytise *m*.

labyrinth ['læbərinθ] *n* labyrinthe *m*, dédale *m*.

lace [leis] *n* lacet *m*, galon *m*, dentelle *f*, point *m*; *vt* lacer, galonner, garnir de dentelle, nuancer, corser.

lace-maker ['leis'meikə] *n* fabricant de dentelles *m*, dentellière *f*.

lacerate ['læsəreit] *vt* lacérer.

lachrymal ['lækriməl] *a* lacrymal.

lachrymatory ['lækrimətəri] *a* lacrymogène.

lachrymose ['lækrimous] *a* larmoyant.

lack [læk] *n* manque *m*, défaut *m*, besoin *m*; **for — of** faute de; *vt* manquer de.

lackadaisical [,lækə'deizikəl] *a* maniéré, affecté, langoureux.

lackey ['læki] *n* laquais *m*.

lacking ['lækiŋ] *a* qui manque, en défaut; *prep* à défaut de, faute de.

lacquer ['lækə] *n* laque *m*, vernis-laque *m*; *vt* laquer.

lad [læd] *n* (jeune) garçon *m*, gars *m*, gaillard *m*.

ladder ['lædə] *n* échelle *f*, maille *f* filée.

lade [leid] *vt* charger; *n* bief *m*.

lading ['leidiŋ] *n* chargement *m*.

ladle ['leidl] *n* louche *f*.

lady ['leidi] *n* dame *f*, Lady; *pl* mesdames, mesdemoiselles; **—in-waiting** dame d'honneur *f*; **L— Day** Annonciation *f*.

ladybird ['leidibɔːd] *n* bête à bon Dieu *f*, coccinelle *f*.

ladylike ['leidilaik] *a* de dame, comme il faut.

lag [læg] *n* retard *m*, décalage *m*, cheval de retour *m*, repris de justice *m*; *vi* traîner, rester en arrière.

laggard ['lægəd] *n* traînard *m*, lambin(e) *mf*; *a* lent.

lagging ['lægiŋ] *n* revêtement calorifuge *m*.

lagoon [lə'guːn] *n* lagune *f*.

laic ['leiik] *n* laïque.

laicize ['leiisaiz] *vt* laïciser.

laid [leid] *pt pp of* **lay**; **— up** mis en réserve, remisé, alité.

lain [lein] *pp of* **lie** (être couché).

lair [lɛə] *n* tanière *f*, repaire *m*.

laity ['leiiti] *n* laïques *m pl*, amateurs *m pl*.

lake [leik] *n* lac *m*; *a* lacustre.

lamb [læm] *n* agneau *m*.

lambkin ['læmkin] *n* agnelet *m*.

lame [leim] *a* boiteux, faible; *vt* rendre boiteux, estropier.

lameness ['leimnis] *n* boiterie *f*, claudication *f*, faiblesse *f*.

lament [lə'ment] *n* lamentation *f*; *vt* déplorer, pleurer; *vi* se lamenter.

lamentable ['læməntəbl] *a* lamentable, déplorable.

lamented [lə'mentid] *a* regretté.

lamp [læmp] *n* lampe *f*, lanterne *f*; **standard** — lampadaire *m*, lampe *f* de parquet.

lamplighter ['læmp'laitə] *n* allumeur de réverbères *m*.

lampoon [læm'puːn] *n* libelle *m*; *vt* déchirer, chansonner.

lampoonist [læm'puːnist] *n* libelliste *m*.

lamp-post ['læmppoust] *n* réverbère *m*.

lampshade ['læmpʃeid] *n* abat-jour *m*.

lance [lɑːns] *n* lance *f*.

lancer ['lɑːnsə] *n* lancier *m*.

lancet ['lɑːnsit] *n* lancette *f*.

land [lænd] *n* terre *f*, sol *m*, pays *m*; *vti* débarquer; *vi* atterrir, descendre; *vt* asséner.

landed ['lændid] *a* foncier.

land-holder ['lænd,houldə] *n* propriétaire *mf*, foncier, -ière.

landing ['lændiŋ] *n* débarquement *m*, atterrissage *m*, palier *m*; **forced** — atterrissage forcé *m*.

landing-place ['lændiŋpleis] *n* débarcadère *m*, terrain d'atterrissage *m*.

landing-net ['lændiŋnet] *n* épuisette *f*.

landlady ['læn,leidi] *n* propriétaire *f*.

landlord ['lænlɔːd] *n* propriétaire *m*, patron *m*.

landowner ['lænd,ounə] *n* propriétaire *mf*, foncier, -ière.

landscape ['lænskeip] *n* paysage *m*.

landslide ['lændslaid] *n* éboulement *m*.

land-tax ['lændtæks] *n* impôt foncier *m*.

lane [lein] *n* sentier *m*, ruelle *f*.

language ['læŋgwidʒ] *n* langage *m*, langue *f*.

languid ['læŋgwid] *a* languissant, mou.

languidly ['læŋgwidli] *ad* languissamment, mollement.

languish ['læŋgwiʃ] *vi* languir.

languishing ['læŋgwiʃiŋ] *a* langoureux.

languor ['læŋgə] *n* langueur *f*.

languorous ['læŋgərəs] *a* langoureux.

lank [læŋk] *a* efflanqué, plat.

lantern ['læntən] *n* lanterne *f*, fanal *m*, falot *m*.

lap [læp] *n* giron *m*, sein *m*, pan *m*, lobe *m*, creux *m*, tour *m* (de piste), lapement *m*, lampée *f*, clapotis *m*; *vt* laper, lamper, (*sea*) lécher, faire le tour de; *vi* clapoter.

lapdog ['læpdɔg] *n* bichon *m*.

lapel [lə'pel] *n* revers *m*.

lapidary ['læpidəri] *n* lapidaire *m*.

Lapland ['læplænd] *n* Laponie *f*.

lapse [læps] *n* faux-pas *m*, lapsus *m*, laps de temps *m*, déchéance *f*; *vi* s'écouler, déchoir, manquer (à **from**).

lapsed [læpst] *a* déchu, périmé, caduc.

larboard ['lɑːbəd] *n* bâbord *m*.

larceny ['lɑːsni] *n* larcin *m*.

larch [lɑːtʃ] *n* mélèze *m*.

lard [lɑːd] *n* saindoux *m*.

larder ['lɑːdə] *n* garde-manger *m*.

large [lɑːdʒ] *a* large, gros, grand, vaste; **at** — au large, en liberté.

largeness ['lɑːdʒnis] *n* (**width**) largeur *f*, grandeur *f*, grosseur *f*.

lark [lɑːk] *n* alouette *f*, farce *f*.

larkspur ['lɑːkspə] *n* pied-d'alouette *m*.

laser ['leizə] *n* laser *m*.

lash [læʃ] *n* coup de fouet *m*, lanière *f*; *vti* fouailler, cingler; *vt* attacher, amarrer; **to** — **out** éclater, se ruer.

lass [læs] *n* fille *f*, bonne amie *f*.

lassitude ['læsitjuːd] *n* lassitude *f*.

last [lɑːst] *n* forme *f*, fin *f*; *a* dernier; — **but one** avant-dernier; — **night** cette nuit, la nuit dernière, hier soir; *vi* durer, tenir, faire.

lastly ['lɑːstli] *ad* enfin.

latch [lætʃ] *n* loquet *m*; — **key** passe-partout *m*; *vt* fermer au loquet.

late [leit] *a* tard, tardif, en retard, dernier, feu; —**comer** retardataire; **to be** — **for** être en retard pour; **the train is** — le train a du retard; **it is getting** — il se fait tard.

lately ['leitli] *ad* récemment.

lateness ['leitnis] *n* heure tardive *f*, retard *m*.

latent ['leitənt] *a* latent.

lateral ['lætərəl] *a* latéral, transversal.

laterite ['lætərait] *n* terre de barre *f*, latérite *f*.

lath [lɑːθ] *n* latte *f*.

lathe [leið] *n* tour *m*.

lather ['lɑːðə] *n* mousse *f*, écume *f*; *vt* savonner, rosser; *vi* mousser, écumer.

latitude ['lætitjuːd] *n* largeur *f*, latitude *f*, liberté *f*.

latter ['lætə] *a* dernier, second, celui-ci, celle-ci, ceux-ci, celles-ci.

lattice ['lætis] *n* treillis *m*, treillage *m*.

laudable ['lɔːdəbl] *a* louable.

laudatory ['lɔːdətəri] *a* élogieux.

laugh [lɑːf] *n* rire *m*; *vi* rire.

laughable ['lɑːfəbl] *a* risible, ridicule.

laughing ['lɑːfiŋ] *n* rire *m*; *a* à rire; — **gas** gaz hilarant *m*; — **stock** risée *f*.

laughter ['lɑːftə] *n* rire *m*; **to roar with** — rire aux éclats, rire à gorge déployée.

launch [lɔːntʃ] *n* lancement *m*, chaloupe *f*; *vt* lancer, déclencher; *vi* se lancer.

launderette [lɔːndəˈret] n laverie f, blanchisserie f automatique.

laundress [ˈlɔːndris] n blanchisseuse f.

laundry [ˈlɔːndri] n blanchissage m, blanchisserie f, linge n.

laureate [ˈlɔːriit] n lauréat m.

laurel [ˈlɔrəl] n laurier m.

lava [ˈlɑːvə] n lave f.

lavatory [ˈlævətəri] n lavabo m, cabinets m pl, toilette f.

lavender [ˈlævində] n lavande f.

lavish [ˈlæviʃ] a prodigue, somptueux; vt prodiguer, gaspiller.

lavishness [ˈlæviʃnis] n prodigalité f.

law [lɔː] n loi f droit m; —abiding a respectueux de la loi; L— Courts Palais de Justice m.

lawful [ˈlɔːful] a légal, légitime.

lawfulness [ˈlɔːfulnis] n respect de la loi m, légalité f.

lawless [ˈlɔːlis] a sans foi ni loi, effréné, déréglé, anarchique.

lawlessness [ˈlɔːlisnis] n mépris de la loi m, anarchie f.

lawn [lɔːn] n pelouse f, gazon m.

lawn-mower [ˈlɔːn.mouə] n tondeuse f.

lawsuit [ˈlɔːsjuːt] n procès m.

lawyer [ˈlɔːjə] n homme de loi m, jurisconsulte m.

lax [læks] a lâche, relâché, vague, mou, inexact.

laxity [ˈlæksiti] n laxité f, relâchement m, mollesse f.

lay [lei] pt of lie (être couché); n lai m, spécialité m; a lai, laïque, profane, amateur; vt coucher, étendre, abattre, placer, mettre, déposer, parier, pondre; to — the table mettre le couvert; to — aside se défaire de, mettre de côté; to — down déposer, quitter; to — off congédier; to — out étaler, aménager, assomer, tracer.

lay-by [ˈleibai] n refuge m, parking m.

layer [ˈleiə] n couche f, marcotte f, banc m, pondeuse f.

lay-figure [ˈleiˈfigə] n mannequin m.

laying [ˈleiiŋ] n pose f, ponte f.

layout [ˈleiaut] n tracé m, dessin m, disposition f typographique.

lazily [ˈleizili] ad nonchalamment, paresseusement.

laziness [ˈleizinis] n paresse f.

lazy [ˈleizi] a paresseux.

lead [liːd] n exemple m, tête f, (dogs) laisse f, (cards) main f, câble m, premier rôle m; vti mener, conduire; vt diriger, porter; vi (cards) avoir la main.

lead [led] n plomb m.

leaden [ˈledn] a de plomb, plombé, lourd.

leader [ˈliːdə] n chef m, directeur m, meneur m guide m, éditorial m.

leadership [ˈliːdəʃip] n direction f, commandement m.

leading [ˈliːdiŋ] a principal, de tête;

— case précédent n; — question question qui postule la réponse; — strings lisière f pl.

leaf, pl **leaves** [liːf, liːvz] n feuille f, rallonge f.

leafless [ˈliːflis] a sans feuilles, effeuillé, dépouillé.

leaflet [ˈliːflit] n feuillet m, prospectus m, papillon m.

leafy [ˈliːfi] a feuillu, touffu.

league [liːg] n lieue f, ligne f; L— of Nations Société des Nations f; vi se liguer.

leak [liːk] n fuite f, voie d'eau f; vi fuir, avoir une fuite, faire eau; to — out transpirer.

leakage [ˈliːkidʒ] n fuite f.

lean [liːn] a maigre; n inclinaison f; vt pencher, appuyer; vi s'appuyer, se pencher, ncliner.

leaning [ˈliːniŋ] n penchant m, penchement m, tendance f.

leanness [ˈliːnnis] n maigreur f.

leant [lent] pt pp of lean.

leap [liːp] n saut m; —frog saute-mouton m; — year année bissextile f; vti sauter.

leapt [lept] pt pp of leap.

learn [ləːn] vt apprendre.

learned [ˈləːnid] a savant.

learning [ˈləːniŋ] n savoir m, érudition f.

lease [liːs] n bail m; on — à bail; vt louer, affermer.

leaseholder [ˈliːshouldə] n locataire mf.

leash [liːʃ] n laisse f; vt tenir en laisse.

least [liːst] n le moins; a le, la moindre; at — au (du) moins; not in the — pas le moins du monde; ad (le) moins.

leather [ˈleðə] n cuir m; patent — cuir verni m.

leave [liːv] n permission f, congé m; on — en permission, en congé; —taking départ m, adieu m; vt laisser quitter; vi partir.

leaven [ˈlevn] n levain m; vt faire lever, tempérer.

Lebanon [ˈlebənən] n Liban m.

lecherous [ˈletʃərəs] a lascif, lubrique.

lechery [ˈletʃəri] n lasciveté f, luxure f.

lectern [ˈlektə(ː)n] n lutrin m.

lecture [ˈlektʃə] n conférence f, semonce f; vi faire des conférences; vt faire la leçon à; to — on faire un cours de.

lecturer [ˈlektʃərə] n conférencier m, maître de conférences m, chargé de cours m.

lectureship [ˈlektʃəʃip] n maîtrise de conférences f.

led [led] pt pp of lead.

ledge [ledʒ] n rebord m, corniche f, banc de rochers m.

ledger [ˈledʒə] n grand-livre m.

lee [liː] n abri m; a abrité.

leech [liːtʃ] n sangsue f.

leek [liːk] n poireau m.

leer [liə] n regard de côté m, œillade f; vi regarder de côté, faire de l'œil (à at).

lees [liːz] n lie f.

leeward ['liːwəd] a ad sous le vent.

leeway ['liːwei] n dérive f, retard m.

left [left] pt pp of **leave**; n gauche f; a gauche; **on the —** à gauche; **—handed** gaucher, morganatique, de la main gauche; **—wing** de gauche; **— over** laissé de côté; **—overs** restes m pl.

leg [leg] n jambe f cuisse f, gigot m, pied m.

legacy ['legəsi] n legs m.

legal ['liːgəl] a légal, judiciaire, licite.

legality [liː(ː)'gæliti] n légalité f.

legalize ['liːgəlaiz] vt légaliser, autoriser.

legate ['legit] n légat m.

legatee [,legə'tiː] n légataire mf.

legation [li'geiʃən] n légation f.

legator ['legitə] n testateur m.

legend ['ledʒənd] n légende f.

leggings ['leginz] n jambières f pl, guêtres f pl.

leggy ['legi] a haut sur pattes, dégingandé.

legibility [,ledʒi'biliti] n lisibilité f.

legible ['ledʒəbl] a lisible.

legion ['liːdʒən] n légion f.

legionary ['liːdʒənəri] n légionnaire m.

legislate ['ledʒisleit] vi légiférer.

legislation [,ledʒis'leiʃən] n législation f.

legislative ['ledʒislətiv] a législatif.

legislator ['ledʒisleitə] n législateur m.

legislature ['ledʒisleitʃə] n législature f.

legitimacy [li'dʒitiməsi] n légitimité f.

legitimate [li'dʒitimit] a légitime.

legitimation [li dʒiti'meiʃən] n légitimation f.

legitimize [li'dʒitimaiz] vt légitimer, reconnaître.

leisure ['leʒə] n loisir m.

leisurely ['leʒəli] a qui n'est jamais pressé, tranquille; ad à loisir, à tête reposée.

lemon ['lemən] n citron m.

lemonade [,lemə'neid] n limonade f.

lend [lend] vt prêter; **— lease** prêt-bail m.

lender ['lendə] n prêteur, -euse.

length [leŋθ] n longueur f; **full —** en pied; **at —** longuement, enfin.

lengthwise ['leŋθwaiz] a ad dans le sens de la longueur.

lengthy ['leŋθi] long.

leniency ['liːniənsi] n douceur f, indulgence f.

lenient ['liːniənt] a indulgent, doux.

leniently ['liːniəntli] ad avec douceur (indulgence).

lenity ['leniti] n clémence f.

lens [lenz] n lentille f, loupe f.

lent [lent] pt pp of **lend**.

Lent [lent] n carême m.

lentil [lentil] n lentille f.

leopard ['lepəd] n léopard m.

leper ['lepə] n lépreux -euse.

leprosy ['leprəsi] n lèpre f.

lesbian ['lezbiən] an lesbien, -enne, saphiste.

lesion ['liːʒən] n lésion f.

less [les] n (le) moins; a moindre, moins de; prep ad moins, (in many compounds) sans.

lessee [le'siː] n locataire mf, tenancier, -ière, preneur m.

lessen ['lesn] vti diminuer; vi décroître.

lesser ['lesə] a moindre.

lesson ['lesn] n leçon f.

lessor [le'sɔː] n bailleur, -eresse.

lest [lest] cj de peur que.

let [let] vt laisser, louer; **— us go** partons; **— him do it** qu'il le fasse; **— alone** sans parler de; **to — alone** laisser tranquille; **to — down** baisser, descendre, laisser tomber; **to — in** faire, laisser entrer; **to — on** cafarder; **to — off** décharger; **to — out** laisser echapper, (re)lâcher; **to — through** laisser passer; (US) **to — up** (rain) diminuer; se relâcher.

lethal ['liːθəl] a mortel, meurtrier.

lethargic [le'θɑːdʒik] a léthargique.

lethargy ['leθədʒi] n léthargie f.

letter ['letə] n lettre f; **— bound** a esclave de la lettre; **—box** boîte aux lettres f; **—card** carte-lettre f; **— pad** bloc-notes m.

lettuce ['letis] n laitue f.

leukaemia [ljuː'kiːmiə] n leucémie f.

levee ['levi] n lever m.

level [levl] n niveau m; a uni, régulier, en palier; **— with** au même niveau que, au ras de; **—crossing** passage m à niveau; **—headed** pondéré; vt niveler, viser.

leveller ['levələ] n niveleur m.

levelling ['levliŋ] n nivellement m.

lever ['liːvə] n levier m, manette f.

leveret ['levərit] n levraut m.

levity ['leviti] n légèreté f.

levy ['levi] n levée f; vt lever, imposer, percevoir.

lewd [ljuːd] a luxurieux.

lewdness ['ljuːdnis] n luxure f, lasciveté f.

Lewis ['luː(ː)is] Louis m.

lexicon ['leksikən] n lexique m.

liability [laiə'biliti] n responsabilité f; pl engagements m pl, passif m.

liable ['laiəbl] a passible (de for), responsable, sujet (à to).

liar ['laiə] n menteur, -euse.

libel ['laibəl] n diffamation f, libelle m; vt diffamer.

libeller ['laibələ] n diffamateur, -trice.

libellous ['laibələs] a diffamatoire, calomnieux.

liberal ['libərəl] n libéral m; a large, libéral, prodigue.

liberalism ['libərəlizəm] n libéralisme m.

liberality [,libə'ræliti] n libéralité f, générosité f.

liberate ['libəreit] vt libérer.

liberation [,libə'reiʃən] n libération f.

liberator ['libəreitə] n libérateur, -trice.

libertine ['libə(:)tiin] an libertin m; n débauché m.

liberty ['libəti] n liberté f.

librarian [lai'brɛəriən] n bibliothécaire m.

library ['laibrəri] n bibliothèque f; lending — b. de prêt; free — b. publique; circulating — b. circulante.

lice [lais] n pl poux m pl.

licence ['laisəns] n permission f, autorisation f, permis m, licence f, patente f.

license ['laisəns] vt autoriser, patenter, accorder un permis à.

licentious [lai'senʃəs] a libre, licencieux.

licentiousness [lai'senʃəsnis] n licence f.

lichen ['laikən] n lichen m.

licit ['lisit] a licite.

lick [lik] n coup m de langue; vt lécher, rosser, battre à plate couture, (sur)passer; to — up laper; to — into shape dégrossir.

licking ['likiŋ] n râclée f.

lid [lid] n couvercle m.

lie [lai] n mensonge m, démenti m; disposition f, tracé m, gîte m; vi mentir, être couché, étendu, être resté, se trouver, (bank) déposer; it lies with cela dépend de; to — down se coucher, filer doux; to — up garder la chambre, désarmer; — in n (fam) grasse matinée f.

lieutenant [lef'tenənt] n lieutenant m; second— sous-lieutenant m.

life [laif] n vie f; —boat canot m de sauvetage; —buoy bouée m de sauvetage; — estate propriété f en viager; — saving sauvetage m; — savings économies f pl.

lifeless ['laiflis] a inanimé.

lifelike ['laiflaik] a d'après nature, vivant.

life-size ['laif'saiz] a en pied.

lifetime ['laiftaim] n vie f, vivant m.

lift [lift] n ascenseur m, montecharge m, montée f, (in a car) place f, coup d'épaule m; vt lever, soulever, pendre, voler; vi s'élever, se dissiper.

light [lait] n lumière f, clarté f, jour m, phare m, feu m; vt allumer, éclairer; vi s'allumer, s'éclairer, s'abattre, tomber; a léger, clair; —handedness légèreté de main f; —headed étourdi; —hearted gai, allègre; — minded frivole.

lighten ['laitn] vt alléger, soulager, éclairer, éclaircir; vi s'éclairer, faire des éclairs.

lighter ['laitə] n briquet m, chaland m.

lighthouse ['laithaus] n phare m.

lighting ['laitiŋ] n allumage m, éclairage m.

lightness ['laitnis] n légèreté f.

lightning ['laitniŋ] n éclair m, foudre f; a prompt comme l'éclair, foudroyant; — conductor paratonerre m.

light-ship ['laitʃip] n bateau-feu m, bouée lumineuse f.

lightweight ['laitweit] a léger, poids léger.

like [laik] an semblable mf, pareil, -eille mf; a ressemblant; prep comme; vt aimer, vouloir, désirer.

likeable ['laikəbl] a sympathique.

likelihood ['laiklihud] n vraisemblance f, probabilité f.

likely ['laikli] a probable, propre, susceptible, plein de promesse; ad probablement.

liken ['laikən] vt comparer.

likeness ['laiknis] n ressemblance f, portrait m.

likewise ['laikwaiz] ad de même, aussi.

liking ['laikiŋ] n goût m, penchant m, sympathie f, gré m.

lilac ['lailək] n lilas m.

lily ['lili] n lis m; a de lis; — of the valley muguet m.

limb [lim] n membre m, bras m, branche maîtresse f.

limber ['limbə] n avant-train m; vt atteler; a souple.

limbo ['limbou] n limbes m pl.

lime [laim] n glu f, chaux f, tilleul m, limon m.

lime-juice ['laimdʒuːs] n limonade f, jus de limon m.

lime-kiln ['laimkiln] n four à chaux m.

limelight ['laimlait] n rampe f, feu de la publicité m, vedette f.

limestone ['laimstoun] n pierre à chaux f.

limit ['limit] n limite f, borne f; comble m; vt limiter, borner, restreindre.

limitation [,limi'teiʃən] n limitation f.

limited ['limitid] a à responsabilité limitée, restreint.

limp [limp] n claudication f; vi boiter; a souple, mou.

limpid ['limpid] a limpide.

limpidity [lim'piditi] n limpidité f.

limy ['laimi] a gluant, calcaire.

linden ['lindən] n tilleul m.

line [lain] n ligne f, file f, voie f, trait m, corde f, câble m, fil m, vers m; vt tracer, régler, sillonner, rider, aligner, border, doubler, remplir, garnir; vi s'aligner; to become lined se rider.

lineage ['liniidʒ] n lignage m, lignée f.

lineament ['liniəmənt] n lineament m.

linear ['liniə] a linéaire.

linen ['linin] n toile f (de lin), linge m.

liner ['lainə] n paquebot m.

linger ['liŋgə] vi tarder, trainer, subsister, s'attarder.

lingerer ['liŋgərə] n lambin(e) mf, retardataire mf.

lining ['lainiŋ] n doublure f, coiffe f, garniture f.

link [liŋk] n chaînon m, anneau m, lien m, maille f; vt (re)lier, enchaîner, unir, serrer; vi s'attacher (à to); to — **arms** se donner le bras.

links [liŋks] n (terrain m de) golf.

linnet ['linit] n linotte f.

linseed ['linsi:d] n graîne de lin f.

lint [lint] n charpie f.

lintel ['lintl] n linteau m.

lion ['laiən] n lion m; — **cub** lionceau m.

lioness ['laiənis] n lionne f.

lip [lip] n lèvre f, babine f, bord m; vt toucher des lèvres.

lipstick ['lipstik] n rouge à lèvres m, bâton de rouge m

liquefaction [ˌlikwi'fækʃən] n liquéfaction f.

liquefy ['likwifai] vt liquéfier.

liqueur [li'kjuə] n liqueur f; — **stand** cabaret m, cave à liqueurs f.

liquid ['likwid] an liquide m.

liquidate ['likwideit] vt liquider.

liquidation [ˌlikwi'deiʃən] n liquidation f.

liquidator ['likwideitə] n liquidateur m.

liquidizer ['likwidaizə] m, mixe(u)r m.

liquor ['likə] n boisson alcoolique f.

liquorice ['likəris] n réglisse f.

lisp [lisp] n zézaiement m, bruissement m; vti zézayer.

lissom ['lisəm] a souple.

list [list] n liste f, tableau m, lisière f, bourrelet m, gîte f, (pl) lice f; **wine** — carte f des vins; **honours** — palmarès m; vt cataloguer; vi donner de la bande.

listen ['lisn] vti écouter.

listener ['lisnə] n écouteur, -euse, auditeur, -trice.

listless ['listlis] a apathique.

listlessness ['listlisnis] n apathie f.

lit [lit] pt pp of **light**.

litany ['litəni] n litanie f.

literal ['litərəl] a littéral.

literary ['litərəri] a littéraire; — **man** littérateur m, homme de lettres m.

literature ['litəritʃə] n littérature f.

lithe [laið] a souple.

litheness ['laiðnis] n souplesse f.

litigant ['litigənt] n plaideur, -euse, partie f.

litigate ['litigeit] vi plaider, être en procès.

litigation [ˌliti'geiʃən] n litige m.

litigious [li'tidʒəs] a litigieux, processif.

litter ['litə] n litière f, détritus m,

fouillis m, portée f; —**bin** poubelle f; vt encombrer.

little ['litl] n peu m (de chose); ad peu; a petit; **a** — un peu.

live [laiv] a vivant, vrai, vital, ardent, chargé.

live [liv] vi vivre, demeurer, habiter, durer; **to** — **down** user, faire oublier; **to** — **up to** se hausser à, faire honneur à; **long** —! vive!

livelihood ['laivlihud] n gagne-pain m, vie f.

liveliness ['laivlinis] n vivacité f, entrain m.

lively ['laivli] a vivant, vif, animé, plein de vie.

liven ['laivn] vt animer; **to** — **up** vi s'animer.

liver ['livə] n foie m.

liverish ['livəriʃ] a bilieux, amer.

livery ['livəri] n livrée f, compagnie f.

livestock ['laivstɔk] n bétail m, bestiaux m pl.

livid ['livid] a livide.

living ['liviŋ] n vie f, gagne-pain m, poste m, cure f; —**room** salle f de séjour, living-room m.

lizard ['lizəd] n lézard m.

load [loud] n charge f, chargement m, poids m, tas m; vt charger, accabler, combler; vi prendre charge.

loaded ['loudid] a chargé; — **cane** canne plombée f; — **dice** dés pipés m pl.

loadstone ['loudstoun] n aimant m.

loaf [louf] n pain m; vi fainéanter.

loafer ['loufə] n fainéant m, voyou m.

loam [loum] n glaise f, torchis m.

loan [loun] n prêt m, emprunt m.

loath [louθ] a qui répugne à.

loathe [louð] vt détester, abhorrer.

loathsome ['louðsəm] a répugnant, écœurant.

lobby ['lɔbi] n salle f, vestibule m, couloirs m pl; vi (US) intriguer.

lobster ['lɔbstə] n homard m; — **pot** casier à homard m, langouste f.

local ['loukəl] a local, du lieu, du pays, en ville; — **road** route vicinale f; n pl examens locaux m pl.

locality [lou'kæliti] n localité f, emplacement m, parages m pl, région f, endroit m.

localize ['loukəlaiz] vt localiser.

locate [lou'keit] vt situer, repérer; vi (US) s'établir.

location [lou'keiʃən] n position f, repérage m.

loch [lɔx] n (Scot) lac m, bras de mer m.

lock [lɔk] n flocon m, mèche f, serrure f, écluse f, embouteillage m, enrayure f; vt fermer à clef, mettre sous clef, caler, serrer, écluser; vi se bloquer, s'empoigner.

locker ['lɔkə] n casier m, caisson m, armoire f.

locket ['lɔkit] n médaillon m.

lockjaw ['lɔkdʒɔ:] n tétanos m.

lock-out ['lɔkaut] *n* lockout *m*.

locksmith ['lɔksmiθ] *n* serrurier *m*.

lock-up ['lɔkʌp] *n* fermeture *f*, (*jail*) violon *m*, garage *m*, box *m*.

locomotive ['loukə,moutiv] *n* locomotive *f*.

locum ['loukəm] *n* remplaçant(e) *mf*.

locust ['loukəst] *n* sauterelle *f*, locuste *f*.

lode [loud] *n* filon *m*; **—stone** aimant *m*.

lodge [lɔdʒ] *n* loge *f*, atelier *m*, pavillon *m*; *vt* loger, (con)tenir, déposer; to — **a complaint** porter plainte; to — *s*) loger.

lodger ['lɔdʒə] *n* locataire *mf*, pensionnaire *mf*.

lodging ['lɔdʒiŋ] *n* logement *m*, chambres *f pl* meublées, garni *m*; — **house** hôtel meublé *m*, hôtel à la nuit *m*.

loft [lɔft] *n* grenier *m*, soupente *f*, galerie *f*, pigeonnier *m*.

loftiness ['lɔftinis] *n* hauteur *f*, sublimité *f*, élévation *f*.

lofty ['lɔfti] *a* haut, hautain, élevé, sublime.

log [lɔg] *n* bûche *f*; *vt* débiter en bûches, enregistrer; — **book** livre de bord *m*, carnet de route *m*.

loggerhead ['lɔgəhed] *n* bûche *f*; at —*s* à couteaux tirés.

logic ['lɔdʒik] *n* logique *f*.

logical ['lɔdʒikəl] *a* logique.

loin [lɔin] *n* rein *m*, (*meat*) longe *f*; —**chop** côtelette de filet *f*; —**cloth** pagne *m*.

loiter ['lɔitə] *vi* traîner (en route), s'attarder.

loiterer ['lɔitərə] *n* flâneur, -euse, rôdeur *m*.

loll [lɔl] *vi* pendre, se prélasser; to — **back** se renverser, s'appuyer; to — **about** flâner, fainéanter; to — **out** its tongue tirer la langue.

lollipop ['lɔlipɔp] *n* sucette *f*, sucre d'orge *m*.

London ['lʌndən] *n* Londres *m*.

lone [loun] *a* solitaire.

loneliness ['lounlinis] *n* solitude *f*, isolement *m*.

lonely ['lounli] *ad* esseulé, seul, solitaire.

loner ['lounə] *n* solitaire *m*.

long [lɔŋ] *a* long; *ad* (depuis, pendant, pour) longtemps; *vi* aspirer (à **to**, **for**), avoir bien envie (de **to**, **for**), attendre avec impatience; —**sightedness** presbytie *f*, prévoyance *f*; —**suffering** *a* patient.

longevity [lɔn'dʒeviti] *n* longévité *f*.

longhand ['lɔŋhænd] *n* écriture *f* ordinaire, courante.

longing ['lɔŋiŋ] *n* aspiration *f*, nostalgie *f*, grande envie *f*.

longitude ['lɔŋgitjuːd] *n* longitude *f*.

long-standing [lɔŋ'stændiŋ] *a* de longue terme, durée, connaissance, date *f*.

longways ['lɔŋweiz] *ad* dans le sens de la longueur.

look [luk] *n* regard *m*, air *m*, mine *f*; *vi* regarder, avoir l'air (de); to — **after** prendre soin de; to — **at** regarder; to — **for** attendre, chercher, guetter; to — **in** regarder dans, entrer en passant; to — **out** regarder au dehors, prendre garde; to — **out on** donner sur; to — **through** parcourir, repasser.

looker-on ['lukər'ɔn] *n* spectateur, -trice, badaud(e) *mf*.

look-out ['luk'aut] *n* qui-vive *m*, guet *m*, poste d'observation *m*, vigie *f*, guetteur *m*, perspective *f*.

looking-glass ['lukiŋglɑːs] *n* miroir *m*, glace *f*.

loom [luːm] *n* métier *m*; *vi* se montrer à l'horizon, surgir; to — **ahead**, **large** paraître imminent, menacer.

loony ['luːni] *a* (*fam*) cinglé.

loop [luːp] *n* boucle *f*, anse *f*, huit *m*; *vt* boucler.

loophole ['luːphoul] *n* meurtrière *f*, trou *m*, échappatoire *f*.

loose [luːs] *a* libre, lâche, décousu, dissolu, desserré, détaché; *vt* délier, dénouer, défaire, détacher.

loosen ['luːsn] *vt* relâcher, desserrer, dénouer; *vi* se défaire, se relâcher, se desserrer.

loot [luːt] *n* butin *m*; *vt* piller, saccager.

lop [lɔp] *n* branchette *f*; *vt* élaguer, couper; *vi* pendre.

lopsided ['lɔp'saidid] *a* bancal, déjeté, de guingois.

lord [lɔːd] *n* Seigneur *m*, Lord *m*, maître *m*; *vi* to — **it** faire son grand seigneur.

lordly ['lɔːdli] *a* seigneurial, hautain.

lore [lɔː] *n* savoir *m*, science *f*.

lorry ['lɔri] *n* camion *m*.

lose [luːz] *vt* perdre.

loser ['luːzə] *n* perdant(e) *mf*.

loss [lɔs] *n* perte *f*; at **a** — à perte, désorienté; at **a** — to en peine de.

lost [lɔst] *pt pp of* lose; — **property office** bureau des objets trouvés *m*.

lot [lɔt] *n* (tirage **a** **au**) sort *m*, partage *m*, lot *m* tas *m*; *ad* beaucoup de, nombre de, quantité de.

lotion ['loušən] *n* lotion *f*.

lottery ['lɔtəri] *n* loterie *f*.

loud [laud] *a* haut, fort, bruyant, criard, tapageur.

loudly ['laudli] *ad* à voix haute, bruyamment.

loudness ['laudnis] *n* hauteur *f*, force *f*, fracas *m*.

loudspeaker ['laud'spiːkə] *n* haut-parleur *m*.

lounge [łaundʒ] *n* flânerie *f*, divan *m*, hall *m*, salon *m* (d'attente); *vi* flâner, tuer le temps, se prélasser.

lounger ['laundʒə] *n* flâneur, -euse.

lour ['lauə] *vi* se renfrogner, se couvrir, menacer.

ouse [laus] n pou m; pl poux m pl.

lousy ['lauzi] a pouilleux; — trick sale coup m, cochonnerie f.

lout [laut] n butor m, rustre m, lourdaud m.

ove [lʌv] n amour m, amitiés f pl; vt aimer; —letter billet-doux m, lettre d'amour f; —making cour f; —match mariage d'amour m.

oveliness ''lʌvlinis] n charme m, beauté f, fraîcheur f.

lovely ['lʌvli] a ravissant, charmant, adorable.

over ['lʌvə] n amant m, amoureux m, fiancé m.

loving ['lʌviŋ] a affectueux, tendre.

lovingly ['lʌviŋli] ad tendrement, affectueusement.

ow [lou] n beuglement m; vi beugler, meugler, mugir; a bas, décolleté, commun; (US) —down n to give s.o. the —down renseigner qn; —grade de qualité inférieure; ad bas; at — level à rase-mottes, bas, en contre-bas.

lower ['louə] a (plus) bas; vt baisser, abaisser, affaiblir.

lowliness ['loulinis] n humilité f.

lowly ['louli] a humble.

loyal ['bɪəl] a loyal, fidèle.

loyalty ['bɪəlti] n loyauté f, fidélité f.

lozenge ['bzindʒ] n losange m, tablette f.

lubber ['lʌbə] n pataud m, empoté m; land— terrien m, marin d'eau douce m.

ubricate ['lu:brikeit] vt lubrifier, graisser.

lucerne [lur'sə:n] n luzerne f.

lucid ['lu:sid] a lucide.

lucidity [lur'siditi] n lucidité f, transparence f.

luck [lʌk] n chance f, veine f; bad — malchance f, déveine f, guignon m.

luckily ['lʌkili] ad heureusement, par bonheur.

lucky ['lʌki] a heureux; — dog veinard(e) mf; — penny porte-bonheur m.

lucrative ['lu:krətiv] a lucratif.

lucre ['lu:kə] n lucre m.

Lucy ['lu:si] Lucie f, Luce f.

ludicrous ['lu:dikrəs] a absurde, grotesque.

lug [lʌg] vt traîner, trimbaler.

luggage ['lʌgidʒ] n bagages m pl; — rack filet m; — room salle des bagages f; — ticket bulletin m; — van fourgon m.

lugubrious [lur'gu:briəs] a lugubre.

lukewarm ['lu:kwɔ:m] a tiède.

lull [lʌl] n accalmie f, trève f; vt bercer, endormir; vi se calmer, s'apaiser.

lullaby ['lʌləbai] n berceuse f.

lumbago [lʌm'beigou] n lumbago m.

lumber-['lʌmbə] n vieilleries f pl, fatras m, gros bois m; vt encombrer, entasser, embarrasser; vi marcher gauchement; — mill scierie f;

—room chambre de débarras f, capharnaüm m.

lumberjack ['lʌmbədʒæk] n bûcheron m.

luminosity [,lu:mi'nɔsiti] n luminosité f.

luminous ['lu:minəs] a lumineux.

lump [lʌmp] n morceau m, bosse f, (in the throat) boule f, tas m, enflure f, contusion f; in the — en bloc; — sum somme globale f; vt mettre dans le même sac, en tas.

lunacy ['lu:nəsi] n folie f.

lunar ['lu:nə] a lunaire.

lunatic ['lu:nətik] n fou, folle, aliéné(e) mf; a lunatique.

lunch [lʌntʃ] n déjeuner m; (US) petit repas m.

lung [lʌŋ] n poumon m.

lunge [lʌndʒ] n longe f, (fencing) botte f, ruée f; vi se fendre, se ruer, lancer un coup (à at).

lurch [lə:tʃ] n embardée f, embarras m; in the — en plan; vi embarder, tituber.

lure [ljuə] n leurre m, appât m, fascination f; vt entraîner, leurrer, séduire.

lurid ['ljuərid] a sinistre.

lurk [lə:k] vi se tapir.

lurking ['lə:kiŋ] a furtif, vague; —place cachette f.

luscious ['lʌʃəs] a doux, savoureux, écœurant, fleuri.

lush [lʌʃ] a succulent.

lust [lʌst] n concupiscence f, désir m, soif f; vt to — for désirer violemment, avoir soif de, convoiter.

lustily ['lʌstili] ad de toutes ses forces, à pleins poumons.

lustre ['lʌstə] n lustre m, lustrine f, éclat m.

lustrous ['lʌstrəs] a lustré, glacé, éclatant.

lusty ['lʌsti] a robuste.

lute [lu:t] n luth m.

luxuriance [lʌg'zjuəriəns] n luxuriance f.

luxuriant [lʌg'zjuəriənt] a luxuriant, abondant.

luxurious [lʌg'zjuəriəs] a somptueux, luxueux.

luxury ['lʌkʃəri] n luxe m, amour du luxe m, objet de luxe m.

lying ['laiŋ] a menteur, étendu, couché; — in en couches.

lymph [limf] n lymphe f.

lymphatic [lim'fætik] a lymphatique.

lynch [lintʃ] vt lyncher.

lynx [liŋks] n lynx m.

lyre ['laiə] n lyre f.

lyrical ['lirikəl] a lyrique.

lyricism ['lirisizəm] n lyrisme m.

M

macaroni [,mækə'rouni] n macaroni m.

macaroon [ˌmækə'ruːn] n macaron m.

mace [meis] n masse f, (spice) macis m.

macebearer ['meisbɛərə] n massier m.

macerate ['mæsəreit] vt macérer.

maceration [ˌmæsə'reiʃən] n macération f.

machine [mə'ʃiːn] n machine f, automate m, appareil m; vt usiner, façonner.

machine-gun [mə'ʃiːngʌn] n mitrailleuse f.

machinery [mə'ʃiːnəri] n machinerie f, machines f pl, mécanisme m, rouages m pl.

machinist [mə'ʃiːnist] n mécanicien m, machiniste m.

mackerel ['mækrəl] n maquereau m.

mac(kintosh) ['mæk(intɔʃ)] n imper (méable) m.

mad [mæd] a fou, fol, insensé, enragé, effrené.

madam ['mædəm] n Madame f.

madcap ['mædkæp] an étourdi(e) mf, écervelé(e) mf.

madden ['mædn] vt rendre fou, exaspérer.

maddeningly ['mædniŋli] ad à en devenir fou.

made [meid] pt pp of make.

madhouse ['mædhaus] n asile d'aliénés m.

made [meid] pt pp of make.

madman ['mædmən] n fou m, aliéné m, forcené.

madness ['mædnis] n folie f.

madonna [mə'dɔnə] n madone f.

magazine [mægə'ziːn] n magasin m, dépôt m, magazine m, revue f; — gun fusil m à répétition.

Magdelene ['mægdəlin] Madeleine f.

maggot ['mægət] n larve f, ver m, asticot m.

magic ['mædʒik] n magie f; a magique, enchanté.

magician [mə'dʒiʃən] n magicien, -ienne.

magisterial [ˌmædʒis'tiəriəl] a magistral, de magistrat.

magistracy ['mædʒistrəsi] n magistrature f.

magistrate ['mædʒistreit] n magistrat m, juge m.

magnanimity [ˌmægnə'nimiti] n magnanimité f.

magnanimous [ˌmæg'næniməs] a magnanime.

magnate ['mægneit] n magnat m, gros bonnet m.

magnesia [mæg'niːʃə] n magnésie f.

magnet ['mægnit] n aimant m.

magnetic [mæg'netik] a magnétique, hypnotique.

magnetism ['mægnitizəm] n magnétisme m.

magnetize ['mægnitaiz] vt magnétiser, aimanter.

magneto [mæg'niːtou] n magnéto f.

magnificence [mæg'nifisns] n magnificence f.

magnificent [mæg'nifisnt] a magnifique, somptueux.

magnify ['mægnifai] vt (a)grandir, grossir, exalter.

magnifying glass ['mægnifaiiŋˌglɑːs] n loupe f.

magniloquent [mæg'niləkwənt] a grandiloquent.

magnitude ['mægnitjuːd] n grandeur f, ampleur f.

magpie ['mægpai] n pie f.

mahogany [mə'hɔgəni] n acajou m.

maid [meid] n fille f, pucelle f, bonne f; — of all work bonne à tout faire f; — of honour demoiselle d'honneur f.

maiden ['meidn] n jeune fille f, vierge f; a de jeune fille, non mariée; — voyage voyage de baptème m; — speech début à la tribune m.

maidenhood ['meidnhud] n célibat m.

maidenly ['meidnli] a chaste, modeste.

mail [meil] n (cotte de) mailles f pl, courrier m, poste f; vt expédier; — coach wagon postal m; — train train poste m.

maim [meim] vt mutiler.

main [mein] n force f, conduite principale f, océan m; in the — en gros; a principal, premier, essentiel.

mainland ['meinlənd] n continent m, terre ferme m.

mainly ['meinli] ad surtout, en grande partie, pour la plupart.

mainstay ['meinstei] n armature f, soutien m.

maintain [men'tein] vt soutenir, maintenir, entretenir, garder, conserver.

maintenance ['meintinəns] n moyens d'existence m pl, soutien m, maintien m, entretien m, pension f.

maize [meiz] n maïs m.

majestic [mə'dʒestik] a majestueux, auguste.

majesty ['mædʒisti] n majesté f.

major ['meidʒə] n commandant m, chef d'escadron m, majeure f; (US, school) sujet m special; a majeur, principal, plus grand, ainé; (US) vti passer les examens universitaires.

major-general ['meidʒə'dʒenərəl] n général de brigade m.

majority [mə'dʒɔriti] n majorité f, la plus grande partie.

make [meik] n fabrication f, marque f, taille f, façon f; vt faire, façonner, fabriquer, confectionner, rendre, gagner, arriver à; to — away with se débarrasser de; to — off décamper, se sauver; to — out comprendre, distinguer, dresser, établir; to — over transférer, céder; to — up compléter, compenser, combler, rattraper, arranger, préparer, dresser, inventer; **to — up to** faire des avances à.

make-believe ['meikbi,li:v] n trompe-l'œil m, feinte f.

maker ['meikə] n faiseur, -euse, fabricant m, Créateur m.

makeshift ['meikʃift] n pis-aller m, expédient m; a de fortune.

make-up ['meikʌp] n maquillage m; composition f; vi se maquiller, se grimer.

making ['meikiŋ] n fabrication f, façon f, construction f, création f, main d'œuvre f; pl étoffe f, gains m pl.

maladjusted ['mælə'dʒʌstid] a inadapté.

malaria [mə'lɛəriə] n malaria f, paludisme m.

male [meil] an mâle m.

malefactor ['mælifæktə] n malfaiteur, -trice.

maleficent [mə'lefisnt] a malfaisant, criminel.

malevolence [mə'levələns] n malveillance f.

malevolent [mə'levələnt] a malveillant.

malice ['mælis] n méchanceté f, malice f.

malicious [mə'liʃəs] a méchant, malveillant.

malign [mə'lain] vt calomnier, diffamer.

malignancy [mə'lignənsi] n méchanceté f, malignité f.

malignant [mə'lignənt] a malin, -gne, méchant.

malinger [mə'liŋgə] vi tirer au flanc.

malingerer [mə'liŋgərə] n tireur au flanc m.

mall [mɔ:l] n mail m.

mallard ['mæləd] n canard sauvage m.

mallet ['mælit] n maillet m.

mallow ['mælou] n mauve f.

malnutrition ['mælnju'triʃən] n sous-alimentation f, malnutrition f.

malodorous [mæ'loudərəs] a malodorant.

malpractice ['mæl'præktis] n négligence f, incurie f, malversation f.

malt [mɔ:lt] n malt m.

maltreat [mæl'tri:t] vt maltraiter.

maltreatment [mæl'tri:tmənt] n mauvais traitement m.

man [mæn] n homme m, domestique m, pion m, pièce f; **— in the street** homme moyen; **— of war** vaisseau m de guerre; vt servir, occuper, garnir (d'hommes), armer, équiper.

manacle(s) ['mænəkl(z)] n menotte(s) f pl; vt passer les menottes à.

manage ['mænidʒ] vt manier, diriger, mener, arranger, manœuvrer, maîtriser, réussir à, venir à bout de; vi s'arranger, en venir à bout, se débrouiller.

managed ['mænidʒd] pp of **manage** réussi, gouverné.

management ['mænidʒmənt] n direction f, conduite f, gestion f.

manager ['mænidʒə] n directeur m, régisseur m, gérant m, imprésario m.

manageress ['mænidʒəres] n directrice f, gérante f.

mandate ['mændeit] n mandat m.

mandate ['mændeit] vt mandater.

mandatory ['mændətəri] an mandataire mf, (US) obligatoire.

mandible ['mændibl] n mandibule f.

mandrake ['mændreik] n mandragore f.

mane [mein] n crinière f.

man-eater ['mæn,i:tə] n cannibale m, mangeur d'hommes m.

manful ['mænful] a viril, courageux.

mange [meindʒ] n gale f.

mangel-wurzel ['mæŋgl'wə:zl] n betterave f.

manger ['meindʒə] n mangeoire f, crèche f.

mangle ['mæŋgl] n calandreuse f; vt déchiqueter, estropier, défigurer, calandrer.

mango ['mæŋgou] n mangue f.

mangy ['meindʒi] a galeux.

manhandle ['mænhændl] vt faire à bras d'hommes, manutentionner, malmener.

manhood ['mænhud] n âge viril m, virilité f, humanité.

mania ['meiniə] n manie f.

maniac ['meiniæk] n fou furieux, maniaque mf, enragé(e) mf.

maniacal [mə'naiəkəl] a maniaque, de fou.

manicure ['mænikjuə] vt se faire faire les mains; n manicure f.

manicurist ['mænikjuərist] n manucure mf.

manifest ['mænifest] a manifeste; vti (se) manifester.

manifestation [,mænifes'teiʃən] n manifestation f.

manifesto [,mæni'festou] n manifeste m.

manifold ['mænifould] a divers, multiple; vt polycopier.

manikin ['mænikin] n mannequin m, gringalet m.

manipulate [mə'nipjuleit] vt manipuler, actionner, manœuvrer.

mankind [mæn'kaind] n humanité f, genre humain m.

manliness ['mænlinis] n virilité f.

manly ['mænli] a viril, mâle, d'homme.

manner ['mænə] n manière f, sorte f; pl manières f pl, mœurs f pl, savoir-vivre m.

mannered ['mænəd] a élevé, maniéré.

mannerism ['mænərizəm] n maniérisme m, particularité f, tic m.

mannerly ['mænəli] a poli, bien, courtois.

mannish ['mæniʃ] a masculin, hommassé, d'homme.

manœuvre [mə'nuːvə] *vti* manœuvrer.

manor-house ['mænəhaus] *n* manoir *m*.

manpower ['mæn'pauə] *n* main d'œuvre *f*.

manse [mæns] *n* cure *f*, presbytère *m*.

mansion ['mænʃən] *n* résidence *f*, château *m*; hôtel *m*.

manslaughter ['mæn,slɔːtə] *n* homicide involontaire *m*.

mantelpiece ['mæntlpiːs] *n* manteau de cheminée *m*.

mantis ['mæntis] *n* mante *f*; **praying — mante religieuse.**

mantle ['mæntl] *n* mante *f*, manteau *m*, (*gas*) manchon *m*; *vt* couvrir, dissimuler.

manual ['mænjuəl] *an* manuel *m*; *n* clavier *m*.

manufacture [,mænju'fæktʃə] *n* fabrication *f*; *vt* fabriquer, confectionner.

manufacturer [,mænju'fæktʃərə] *n* manufacturier *m*, fabricant *m*, industriel *m*.

manure [mə'njuə] *n* fumier *m*, engrais *m*; *vt* fumer, engraisser.

manuscript ['mænjuskript] *an* manuscrit *m*.

many ['meni] *n* foule *f*, masse *f*; *a* beaucoup de, bien des, nombre de, nombreux; **as —** autant de, que; **how —?** combien? **too —** trop (de), de trop.

many-sided ['meni'saidid] *a* complexe, multilatère.

many-sidedness ['meni'saididnis] *n* complexité *f*.

map [mæp] *n* carte *f*, (*world*) mappemonde *f*, plan *m*.

maple ['meipl] *n* érable *m*.

mar [maː] *vt* ruiner, troubler, gâter.

maraud [mə'rɔːd] *vti* marauder.

marauder [mə'rɔːdə] *n* maraudeur *m*.

marble ['maːbl] *n* marbre *m*, bille *f*.

March [maːtʃ] *n* mars *m*.

march [maːtʃ] *vi* marcher, défiler; *vt* faire marcher; *n* marche *f*, pas *m*, frontière *f*; **forced —** marche forcée *f*; **quick —** pas accéléré *m*; **— past** défilé *m*.

marchioness ['maːʃənis] *n* marquise *f*.

mare [mɛə] *n* jument *f*.

Margaret ['maːgərit] Marguerite *f*.

margarine [,maːdʒə'riːn] *n* margarine *f*.

margin ['maːdʒin] *n* bordure *f*, lisière *f*, marge *f*.

marginal ['maːdʒinl] *a* marginal.

marigold ['mærigould] *n* souci *m*.

marine [mə'riːn] *n* marine *f*, fusilier marin *m*; *a* marin, maritime.

mariner ['mærinə] *n* marin *m*.

mark [maːk] *n* but *m*, point *m*, note *f*, marque *f*, empreinte *f*, signe *m*, repère *m*; **up to the —** à la hauteur; **of — —** d'importance; *vt* marquer.

repérer, montrer; **— you** remarquez bien.

markedly ['maːkidli] *ad* nettement.

marker ['maːkə] *n* marqueur *m*, signet *m*, jeton *m*, carnet-bloc *m*.

market ['maːkit] *n* marché *m*, débouché *m*; *vt* trouver un débouché pour; *vi* faire son marché.

marketable ['maːkitəbl] *a* qui a un marché, d'un débit facile.

market-gardener ['maːkit'gaːdnə] *n* maraîcher, -ère.

market research ['maːkitri'səːtʃ] *n* étude *f* des marchés.

marksman ['maːksmən] *n* bon tireur *m*.

marl [maːl] *n* marne *f*.

marmalade ['maːməleid] *n* marmelade *f*.

marmoset ['maːməzet] *n* ouistiti *m*.

marmot ['maːmət] *n* marmotte *f*.

maroon [mə'ruːn] *an* marron pourpré *m*; *n* pétard *m*, nègre marron *m*; **to be —ed** être coupé, isolé.

marquee [maː'kiː] *n* (tente-)marquise *f*.

marquess, marquis ['maːkwis] *n* marquis *m*.

marriage ['mæridʒ] *n* mariage *m*; **— lines** extrait de mariage *m*.

marriageable ['mæridʒəbl] *a* nubile, mariable, à marier.

married ['mærid] *a* en ménage.

marrow ['mærou] *n* moelle *f*, courge *f*.

marry ['mæri] *vt* épouser, (*of parent, priest*) marier; *vi* se marier.

marsh [maːʃ] *n* marais *m*.

marshal ['maːʃəl] *n* maréchal *m*, maître des cérémonies *m*; *vt* ranger, rassembler, introduire, trier.

marshmallow [maːʃ'mælou] *n* guimauve *f*.

marshy ['maːʃi] *a* marécageux.

marten ['maːtin] *n* martre *f*: **stone- — fouine** *f*; **pine — martre** *m* des pins.

martial ['maːʃəl] *a* martial, guerrier.

martin ['maːtin] *n* martinet *m*

martinet [,maːti'net] *n* **to be a —** être à cheval sur la discipline.

martyr ['maːtə] *n* martyr(e) *mf*.

martyrdom ['maːtədəm] *n* martyre *m*.

marvel ['maːvəl] *n* merveille *f*, prodige *m*; *vi* s'étonner, s'émerveiller (de **at**).

marvellous ['maːviləs] *a* merveilleux, prodigieux.

Mary ['mɛəri] Marie *f*.

masculine ['mæskjulin] *an* masculin *m*.

mash [mæʃ] *n* moût *m*, mixture *f*, pâtée *f*; *vt* brasser, écraser, mettre en purée, broyer.

mask [maːsk] *n* masque *m*; *vt* masquer, déguiser, voiler.

mason ['meisn] *n* maçon *m*.

masquerade [,mæskə'reid] *n* bal

masqué m, déguisement m, masca-
rade f; vi se déguiser, poser (pour **as**).
mass [mæs] n messe f; **high** —
grand'messe; **low** — messe basse;
foule f, masse f; — **meeting** meeting
m; vt masser; vi se masser, s'amonceler.
massacre ['mæsəkə] n massacre m;
vt massacrer.
massage ['mæsɑːʒ] n massage m; vt
masser, malaxer.
massive ['mæsiv] a massif.
mass-production [ˌmæsprə'dʌkʃən]
m fabrication f en série.
mast [mɑːst] n mât m, faîne f.
master ['mɑːstə] n maître m; vt
maîtriser, surmonter, dompter, posséder à fond
masterful ['mɑːstəful] a impérieux,
autoritaire.
master-key ['mɑːstəkiː] n passe-
partout m.
masterly ['mɑːstəli] ad de maître.
masterpiece ['mɑːstəpiːs] n chef
d'œuvre m.
masterstroke ['mɑːstəstrouk] n
coup de maître m.
mastery ['mɑːstəri] n maîtrise f,
connaissance parfaite f.
mastic ['mæstik] n mastic m.
masticate ['mæstikeit] vt mâcher.
mastication [ˌmæsti'keiʃən] n mastication f.
mastiff ['mæstif] n mâtin m, dogue
m.
mat [mæt] n natte f, paillasson m,
dessous de plat m; vt emmêler,
tresser; vi s'emmêler.
match [mætʃ] n allumette f, match
m, partie f; assortiment m, parti m,
égal(e) m, pareil, -eille; vt unir (à
with), opposer (à), assortir, apparier,
rivaliser avec, égaler; vi s'assortir;
well—ed bien assorti.
matchet ['mætʃet] n coupe-coupe.
matchless ['mætʃlis] a sans égal,
incomparable.
match-maker ['mætʃˌmeikə] n ma-
rieuse f.
mate [meit] n camarade mf, copain
m, compagnon m, compagne f,
second m, aide m, époux m, épouse
f; vi se marier, s'accoupler; vt
accoupler.
material [mə'tiəriəl] n matériaux
m pl, matière(s) f pl, matériel m,
fournitures f pl; **raw** — matières
premières f pl; a matériel, important,
sensible.
materialism [mə'tiəriəlizəm] n
matérialisme m.
materialist [mə'tiəriəlist] n matérialiste mf.
materialize [mə'tiəriəlaiz] vi se
matérialiser, prendre corps, se
réaliser.
maternal [mə'təːnl] a maternel.
maternity [mə'təːniti] n maternité f.
mathematician [ˌmæθimə'tiʃən] n
mathématicien, -ienne.

mathematics [ˌmæθi'mætiks] n ma-
thématiques f pl.
matriculate [mə'trikjuleit] vt immatriculer; vi s'inscrire (à l'université).
matriculation [məˌtrikju'leiʃən] n
(*university*) inscription f.
matrimonial [ˌmætri'mouniəl] a
matrimonial, conjugal.
matrimony ['mætriməni] n mariage
m.
matron ['meitrən] n mère f, matrone
f, infirmière en chef f.
matter ['mætə] n matière f, pus m,
affaire f, question f; vi importer,
suppurer; — **of course** a tout
naturel, positif, prosaïque; **no** —
n'importe; **what is the** — qu'est ce
qu'il y a; **for that** — quant à cela;
—**of-fact** pratique.
Matthew ['mæθjuː] Mathieu m.
mattock ['mætək] n hoyau m.
mattress ['mætris] n matelas m;
spring — sommier m.
mature [mə'tjuə] a mûr; vti mûrir;
vi échoir.
maturity [mə'tjuəriti] n maturité f,
échéance f.
Maud [mɔːd] Mathilde f.
maudlin ['mɔːdlin] a larmoyant,
pompette.
maul [mɔːl] n maillet m; vt battre,
abîmer, malmener.
mausoleum [ˌmɔːsə'liəm] n mausolée
m.
maw [mɔː] n panse f, gueule f.
mawkish ['mɔːkiʃ] a fade.
mawkishness ['mɔːkiʃnis] n fadeur
f, sensiblerie f.
maxim ['mæksim] n maxime f.
maximum ['mæksiməm] n maximum m.
May [mei] n mai m.
may [mei] n aubépine f; v aux
pouvoir; **maybe** peut-être.
mayor [mεə] n maire m.
mayoress ['mεəris] n mairesse f.
maze [meiz] n labyrinthe m, dédale
m.
me [miː] pn me, moi.
meadow ['medou] n pré m, prairie f.
meagre ['miːgə] a maigre, rare,
chiche.
meagreness ['miːgənis] n maigreur
f, rareté f.
meal [miːl] n repas m, farine f.
mealy ['miːli] a farineux, en bouillie,
doucereux.
mean [miːn] n milieu m, moyen-
terme m, moyenne f; pl moyens
m pl, ressources f pl; a moyen,
intermédiaire, minable, médiocre;
— **job** besogne ennuyeuse; **to feel** —
se sentir mal en train, mesquin,
vilain, ladre; vt signifier, vouloir
dire, avoir l'intention (de **to**),
destiner, adresser.
meander [mi'ændə] n méandre m;
vi serpenter.
meaning ['miːniŋ] n sens f.
meanness ['miːnnis] n mesquinerie f,

ladrerie f, médiocrité f, bassesse f.

means [mi:nz] n moyens m pl.

means-test ['mi:nztest] n relevé m des revenus.

meantime, -while ['mi:ntaim, -wail] ad en attendant, cependant.

measles ['mi:zlz] n rougeole f.

measure ['meʒə] n mesure f, démarche f; vt mesurer; vi (US) — **up** égaler qn, être l'égal de.

measurement ['meʒəmənt] n mesurage m, dimension f, tour m, mesure f.

meat [mi:t] n viande f.

Mecca ['mekə] n La Mecque.

mechanic [mi'kænik] n mécanicien m; pl mécanique f.

mechanical [mi'kænikəl] a mécanique, machinal, automatique.

mechanism ['mekənizəm] n mécanisme m, appareil m.

medal ['medl] n médaille f.

medallion [mi'dæljən] n médaillon m.

meddle ['medl] vi se mêler (de with), s'immiscer (dans in), toucher (à with).

meddlesome ['medlsəm] a indiscret, fouinard, officieux.

mediaeval [‚medi'i:vəl] a médiéval, moyenâgeux.

mediate ['mi:dieit] vi s'entremettre, s'interposer.

mediator ['mi:dieitə] n médiateur, -trice.

medical ['medikəl] a médical, de (en) médecine.

medicine ['medsin] n médecine f, médicament m, purgatif m, sorcellerie f.

medicinal [me'disnl] a médicinal.

mediocre [‚mi:di'oukə] a médiocre, quelconque.

meditate ['medifeit] vti méditer; vi se recueillir.

meditation [‚medi'teiʃən] n méditation f, recueillement m.

meditative ['meditətiv] a méditatif, pensif, recueilli.

Mediterranean [‚meditə'reiniən] a méditerranéen; — **Sea** n Méditerranée f.

medium ['mi:djəm] n milieu m, moyen m, médium m, intermédiaire m; a moyen.

medlar ['medlə] n nèfle f.

medley ['medli] n mélange m, bigarrure f, pot pourri m.

meek [mi:k] a doux, résigné.

meekness ['mi:knis] n douceur f, humilité.

meet [mi:t] n rendez-vous m de chasse; vt faire la connaissance de, se retrouver, aller à la rencontre, joindre, se croiser, payer; to — **with** trouver, subir; vi se rencontrer, se retrouver, se rejoindre, a convenable, séant.

meeting ['mi:tiŋ] n rencontre f, réunion f, meeting m.

megalomania ['megəlou'meiniə] n mégalomanie f.

megaton ['megətʌn] n mégatonne f.

melancholy ['melənkəli] n mélancolie f; a mélancolique, triste.

mellow ['melou] a succulent, moëlleux, adouci, mûr, cordial; vti mûrir; vt adoucir; vi s'adoucir.

melodious [mi'loudiəs] a mélodieux, harmonieux.

melodrama ['melə‚dra:mə] n mélodrame m.

melodramatic [‚meloudrə'mætik] a mélodramatique.

melody ['melədi] n mélodie f, air m.

melon ['melən] n melon m.

melt [melt] vti fondre; vt attendrir; vi se fondre, s'attendrir.

melting ['meltiŋ] n fonte f.

melting-pot ['meltiŋpɔt] n creuset m.

member ['membə] n membre m.

membership ['membəʃip] n nombre des membres m, qualité de membre f.

memento [mi'mentou] n mémento m, souvenir m.

memoir ['memwɑ:] n mémoire m.

memorable ['memərəbl] a mémorable.

memorandum [‚memə'rændəm] n mémorandum m.

memorial [mi'mɔ:riəl] n monument m, pétition f; a commémoratif.

memorize ['meməraiz] vt apprendre par cœur.

memory ['meməri] n mémoire f.

menace ['menəs] n menace f; vt menacer.

mend [mend] n réparation f; vt raccommoder réparer, (fig) améliorer, arranger vi se rétablir, se corriger.

mendacious [men'deiʃəs] a menteur, mensonger.

mendacity [men'dæsiti] n penchant au mensonge m, fausseté f.

mendicant ['mendikənt] an mendiant(e) mf.

mendicity [men'disiti] n mendicité f.

menial ['mi:niəl] n domestique mf; a servile.

meningitis [‚menin'dʒaitis] n méningite f.

menses ['mensi:z] n pl menstrues f, règles f.

mental ['mentl] a mental, de tête.

mentality [men'tæliti] n mentalité f.

mention ['menʃən] n mention f; vt mentionner, citer, prononcer, faire mention de.

mercantile ['mə:kəntail] a marchand, mercantile, commerçant.

mercenary ['mə:sinəri] an mercenaire m.

mercer ['mə:sə] n mercier, -ière.

merchandise ['mə:tʃəndaiz] n marchandise f.

merchant ['mə:tʃənt] n négociant(e), commerçant(e); a marchand.

merciful ['mə:siful] *a* clément.

mercifulness ['mə:sifulnis] *n* clémence *f*.

merciless ['mə:silis] *a* inexorable, impitoyable.

mercilessness ['mə:silisnis] *n* implacabilité *f*.

mercurial [mə:'kjuəriəl] *a* vif, inconstant, (*med*) mercuriel.

mercury ['mə:kjuri] *n* mercure *m*, vif-argent *m*.

mercy ['mə:si] *n* pitié *f*, merci *f*, grâce *f*.

mere ['miə] *a* pur, simple, seul; *n* lac *m*.

merely ['miəli] *ad* tout simplement.

merge [mə:dʒ] *vt* fondre, fusionner, amalgamer; *vi* se (con)fondre, s'amalgamer.

merger ['mə:dʒə] *n* fusion *f*, combine *f*.

meridian [mə'ridiən] *n* méridian *m*.

merino [mə'ri:nou] *n* mérinos *m*.

merit ['merit] *n* mérite *m*, valeur *f*; *vt* mériter.

meritorious [.meri'tɔ:riəs] *a* méritoire, méritant.

mermaid ['mə:meid] *n* sirène *f*.

merriment ['merimənt] *n* gaieté *f*, réjouissance *f*.

merry ['meri] *a* joyeux, gai.

merry-go-round ['merigou.raund] *n* chevaux de bois *m* *pl*, carrousel *m*.

mesh [meʃ] *n* maille *f*, filets *m* *pl*; *vt* prendre, engrener; *vi* s'engrener.

mesmerize ['mezməraiz] *vt* hypnotiser.

mess [mes] *n* (*food*) plat *m*, pâtée *f*; saleté *f*, désordre *m*, pétrin *m*; (*army*) mess *m*; *vt* salir, gâcher; *vi* manger au mess, faire table.

message ['mesidʒ] *n* message *m*, course *f*, commission *f*.

messenger ['mesindʒə] *n* messager, -ère, chasseur *m*.

Messiah [mi'saiə] *n* Messie *m*.

metal ['metl] *n* métal *m*; — **fatigue** fatigue *f* des métaux.

metallic [mi'tælik] *a* métallique.

metallurgy [me'tælədʒi] *n* métallurgie *f*.

metamorphosis [.metə'mɔ:fəsis] *n* métamorphose *f*.

metaphor ['metəfə] *n* métaphore *f*, image *f*.

meteor ['mi:tiə] *n* météore *m*.

meteorology [.mi:tjə'rɔlədʒi] *n* météorologie *f*.

meter ['mi:tə] *n* compteur *m*.

method ['meθəd] *n* méthode *f*, ordre *m*, façon *f*, procédé *m*, manière *f*.

methodical [mi'θɔdikəl] *a* méthodique, réglé, qui a de l'ordre.

methylated spirits ['meθileitid 'spiritz] *n* alcool à brûler *m*.

meticulous [mi'tikjuləs] *a* méticuleux, exact.

metre ['mi:tə] *a* mètre *m*, mesure *f*.

metric ['metrik] *a* métrique.

metropolis [mi'trɔpəlis] *n* métropole *f*.

metropolitan [.metrə'pɔlitən] *an* métropolitain *m*.

mettle ['metl] *n* fougue *f*, ardeur *f*, courage *m*.

mettlesome ['metlsəm] *a* fougueux, ardent.

mew [mju:] *n* mue *f*, mouette *f*, miaulement *m*, piaillement *m*; *vt* enfermer; *vi* miauler, piailler.

mew *see* **miaow**.

Mexican ['meksikən] *a* mexicain.

miaow [mi'au] *vi* miauler, piailler; *n* miaulement, piaillement.

miasma [mi'æzmə] *n* miasme *m*.

mice [mais] *n* *pl* souris *f* *pl*.

Michael ['maikl] Michel *m*.

microbe ['maikroub] *n* microbe *m*.

microphone ['maikrəfoun] *n* micro *m*.

microscope ['maikrəskoup] *n* microscope *m*.

microscopic [.maikrəs'kɔpik] *a* microscopique.

midday ['middei] *n* midi *m*.

middle ['midl] *n* milieu *f*; *a* du milieu, moyen.

middle-aged ['midl'eidʒd] *a* d'âge mûr.

middle class ['midl'klɑ:s] *n* (haute) bourgeoisie *f*.

middleman ['midlmæn] *n* intermédiaire *mf*.

middling ['midliŋ] *a* passable.

midge [midʒ] *n* moucheron *m*, cousin *m*.

midget ['midʒit] *n* nain(e) *mf*, nabot(e) *mf*.

midlands ['midləndz] *n* comtés *m* *pl* du centre (de l'Angleterre).

midnight ['midnait] *n* minuit *m*.

midshipman ['midʃipmən] *n* aspirant *m*, midship *m*.

midsummer ['mid.sʌmə] *n* mi-été *f*, la Saint-Jean.

midwife ['midwaif] *n* sage-femme *f*.

mien [mi:n] *n* mine *f*, air *m*.

might [mait] *pt of* **may**; *n* puissance *f*, force *f*.

mighty ['maiti] *a* puissant; (*US*) *ad* très.

migrate [mai'greit] *vi* émigrer.

migratory ['maigrətəri] *a* — **bird**(s), oiseau(x) migrateur(s).

milch-cow ['miltʃkau] *n* vache à lait *f*.

mild [maild] *a* doux, faible, mou.

mildness ['maildnis] *n* douceur *f*, clémence *f*.

mile [mail] *n* mille *m*.

mileage ['mailidʒ] *n* indemnité *f* de déplacement; carnets de billets de chemin de fer.

milestone ['mailstoun] *n* borne milliaire *f*, étape *f*, événement *m*.

militant ['militənt] *a* militant, activiste.

militarist ['militərist] *n* militariste *m*.

military ['militəri] *a* militaire; *n* armée *f*.

militate ['militeit] *vi* militer.

militia [mi'liʃə] *n* milice *f*.

milk [milk] *n* lait *m*; *vt* traire; *a* de lait, lacté.

milkman,-maid ['milkmən,-meid] *n* laitier, -ière.

milksop ['milksɔp] *n* poule mouillée *f*.

milky ['milki] *a* laiteux, lacté; **the M— Way** la Voie Lactée.

mill [mil] *n* moulin *m*, pugilat *m*; *(US)* moteur *m* d'avion; *vti* moudre; *vt* fouler, fraiser, battre; *vi* tourner en rond.

millenary [mi'lenəri] *an* millénaire *m*.

miller ['milə] *n* meunier *m*, minotier *m*.

millet ['milit] *n* mil *m*, millet *m*.

milliard ['miljɑ:d] *n* milliard *m*.

milliner ['milinə] *n* modiste *f*.

millinery ['milinəri] *n* modes *f pl*.

million ['miljən] *n* million *m*.

millionaire [,miljə'nɛə] *n* millionnaire *mf*, milliardaire *mf*.

millstone ['milstoun] *n* meule *f*; *(fig)* boulet *m*.

mimeograph ['mimiəgrɑ:f] *n* autocopiste *m* (au stencil).

mimic ['mimik] *n* imitateur -trice, mime *m*; *vt* contrefaire, singer, imiter.

mimicry ['mimikri] *n* mimique *f*, imitation *f*.

mince [mins] *n* hachis *m*; *vt* hacher; **not to — one's words** ne pas mâcher ses mots.

mincing ['minsiŋ] *a* affecté, minaudier.

mind [maind] *n* pensée *f*, esprit *m*, avis *m*, décision *f*, attention *f*, souvenir *m*, parti *m*; *vi* s'occuper de, garder, avoir soin de, faire attention à, regarder à, soigner, s'inquiéter de; **I don't —** cela m'est égal, je veux bien, ça ne me fait rien.

minded ['maindid] *a* disposé.

mindful ['maindful] *a* réfléchi, attentif, soucieux.

mine [main] *n* mine *f*; *vt* miner, creuser, mouiller des mines dans; *pn* le(s) mien(s), la mienne, les miennes, à moi.

minefield ['mainfi:ld] *n* région *f* minière, champ *m* de mines.

minelayer ['main,leiə] *n* mouilleur *m* de mines.

miner ['mainə] *n* mineur *m*.

mineralogy [,minə'rælədʒi] *n* minéralogie *f*.

minesweeper ['main,swi:pə] *n* dragueur *m* de mines.

mingle ['miŋgl] *vt* mêler, mélanger; *vi* se mêler, se mélanger.

miniature ['minətʃə] *n* miniature *f*; *a* en miniature, en petit.

miniaturist ['minətjuərist] *n* miniaturiste *mf*.

minimize ['minimaiz] *vt* diminuer, minimiser.

minimum ['miniməm] *n* minimum *m*.

mining ['mainiŋ] *a* minier; *n* industrie *f* minière.

minion ['minjən] *n* favori, -ite.

minister ['ministə] *n* ministre *m*, pasteur *m*; **to — to** soigner, veiller, subvenir à.

ministerial [,minis'tiəriəl] *a* ministériel, exécutif.

ministration [,minis'treiʃən] *n* bons soins *m pl*, bons offices *m pl*.

ministry ['ministri] *n* ministère *m*.

mink [miŋk] *n* vison *m*.

minor ['mainə] *an* mineur(e) *mf*; *a* moindre, jeune.

minority [mai'nɔriti] *n* minorité *f*.

minster ['minstə] *n* cathédrale *f*.

minstrel ['minstrəl] *n* ménestrel *m*, chanteur *m*.

mint [mint] *n* Monnaie *f*, trésor *m*, menthe *f*; *vt* frapper, forger.

minuet [,minju'et] *n* menuet *m*.

minus ['mainəs] *prep* moins, en moins; *a* négatif.

minute ['minit] *n* minute *f*; *pl* procès-verbal *m*.

minute [mai'nju:t] *a* menu, tout petit, minutieux.

minuteness [mai'nju:tnis] *n* minutie *f*, petitesse *f*.

minx [miŋks] *n* luronne *f*, friponne *f*.

miracle ['mirəkl] *n* miracle *m*, prodige *m*.

miraculous [mi'rækjuləs] *n* miraculeux, extraordinaire.

mirage ['mirɑ:ʒ] *n* mirage *m*.

mire ['maiə] *n* bourbier *m*, fange *f*, bourbe *f*, boue *f*.

mirror ['mirə] *n* miroir *m*, glace *f*; *vt* refléter.

mirth [mə:θ] *n* gaieté *f*.

misadventure ['misəd'ventʃə] *n* mésaventure *f*.

misalliance ['misə'laiəns] *n* mésalliance *f*.

misanthrope ['mizənθroup] *n* misanthrope *m*.

misapprehend ['mis,æpri'hend] *vt* comprendre de travers, se méprendre sur.

misapprehension ['mis,æpri'henʃən] *n* malentendu *m*, méprise *f*.

misappropriate ['misə'prouprieit] *vt* détourner.

misbegotten ['misbi'gɔtn] *a* illégitime.

misbehave ['misbi'heiv] *vi* se conduire mal.

miscalculate ['mis'kælkjuleit] *vt* mal calculer; *vi* se tromper.

miscarriage [mis'kæridʒ] *n* fausse couche *f*, égarement *m*, déni de justice *m*.

miscarry [mis'kæri] *vi* échouer, faire une fausse couche.

miscellaneous [,misi'leinəis] *a* varié, divers.

miscellany [mi'seləni] n mélange m, recueil m.

mischance [mis'tʃɑːns] n malchance f, malheur m.

mischief ['mistʃif] n malice f, méchant tour m, tort m, mal m.

mischievous ['mistʃivəs] a malicieux, malfaisant, méchant.

misconduct [mis'kɔndəkt] n inconduite f, mauvaise gestion f.

misconduct ['miskən'dʌkt] vt mal gérer.

misconstrue ['miskən'struː] vt interpréter de travers.

miscount ['mis'kaunt] n malcompte m, erreur d'addition f; vi mal compter.

miscreant ['miskriənt] n mécréant m, gredin m.

misdeal ['mis'diːl] n mal donne f; vt mal donner.

misdeed ['mis'diːd] n méfait m, crime m.

misdemeanour [.misdi'miːnə] n délit m, méfait m.

misdirect ['misdi'rekt] vt mal diriger, mal adresser.

miser ['maizə] n avare mf.

miserable ['mizərəbl] a malheureux, misérable.

miserliness ['maizəlinis] n avarice f.

miserly ['maizəli] a avare, sordide.

misery ['mizəri] n misère f.

misfire ['mis'faiə] vi rater, faire long feu, manquer son effet.

misfit ['misfit] n malfaçon f, laissé-pour-compte m, misfit m.

misfortune [mis'fɔːtʃən] n malchance f, malheur m.

misgiving [mis'giviŋ] n défiance f, soupçon m, inquiétude f.

misguided ['mis'gaidid] a mal dirigé.

mishap ['mishæp] n accident m, mésaventure f.

misinformed ['misin'fɔːmd] a mal informé.

misjudge ['mis'dʒʌdʒ] v t maljuger.

mislay, -lead [mis'lei, -'liːd] vt égarer.

mismanage ['mis'mænidʒ] vt mal diriger, gâcher.

mismanagement ['mis'mænidʒmənt] n gestion inhabile f.

misplace ['mis'pleis] vt mal placer, déplacer, égarer.

misprint ['misprint] n coquille f, faute d'impression f.

misrepresent ['mis.repri'zent] vt fausser, dénaturer, travestir.

miss [mis] n Mademoiselle f; ratage m, raté m, coup manqué m; vt manquer, rater.

missal ['misəl] n missel m.

missile ['misail] n projectile m, missile m.

missing ['misiŋ] a manquant, qui manque.

mission ['miʃən] n mission f.

missionary ['miʃnəri] m missionnaire mf.

miss out [mis'aut] vt oublier, omettre; n omission f.

misspell ['mis'spel] vt mal orthographier.

misspent ['mis'spent] a dissipé, dépensé à tort et à travers, mal employé.

mist [mist] n brume f, brouillard m.

mistake [mis'teik] n erreur f, méprise f, faute f; vt mal comprendre, se méprendre sur, se tromper de, confondre.

mistaken [mis'teikn] a dans l'erreur, faux, erroné.

mistakenly [mis'teiknli] ad par erreur.

mister ['mistə] n Monsieur m.

mistletoe ['misltou] n gui m.

mistress ['mistris] n maîtresse f.

mistrust ['mistrʌst] n méfiance f; vt se méfier de.

misty ['misti] a brumeux, confus, vague, estompé.

misunderstand ['misʌndə'stænd] vt mal comprendre, se méprendre sur.

misunderstanding ['misʌndə'stændiŋ] n malentendu m, mésintelligence f.

misuse ['mis'juːs] n mauvais usage m, abus m.

misuse ['mis'juːz] vt mésuser de, maltraiter.

mite [mait] n obole f, brin m, un rien m, (fam) môme mf.

mitigate ['mitigeit] vt apaiser, soulager, mitiger, atténuer.

mitigation [.miti'geiʃən] n adoucissement m, atténuation f.

mitre ['maitə] n mitre f.

mitten ['mitn] n mitaine f.

mix [miks] vt mêler, mélanger, brasser, confondre; vi se mêler, se mélanger, frayer.

mixture ['mikstʃə] n mélange m, mixture f, panaché m.

mix-up ['miks'ʌp] n mélange f; vi confondre.

moan [moun] n gémissement m, plainte f; vt gémir.

moat [mout] n fossé m, douves f pl.

mob [mɔb] n foule f, racaille f, ramassis m; vt faire foule autour de, malmener.

mobile ['moubail] a mobile.

mobilization [.moubilai'zeiʃən] n mobilisation f.

mock [mɔk] a d'imitation, simili, faux; vt se moquer de, narguer, en imposer à, contrefaire.

mockery ['mɔkəri] n raillerie f, parodie f, farce f.

mode [moud] n (fashion) mode f, mode m, manière f.

model ['mɔdl] n modèle m, (fashion) mannequin; vt modeler, copier.

modelling ['mɔdliŋ] n modelage m.

moderate ['mɔdərit] a modéré, médiocre, moyen, sobre.

moderate ['mɔdəreit] vt modérer, tempèrer; vi se modérer.

moderation [ˌmɔdə'reiʃən] n modération f, sobriété f, mesure f.

modern ['mɔdən] a moderne.

modernize ['mɔdənaiz] vt moderniser, renover.

modest ['mɔdist] a modeste, chaste, modéré.

modesty ['mɔdisti] n modestie f, modération f.

modification [ˌmɔdifi'keiʃən] n modification f.

modify ['mɔdifai] vt modifier, atténuer.

modish ['moudiʃ] a à la mode, faraud.

modulate ['mɔdjuleit] vt moduler, ajuster.

modulation [ˌmɔdju'leiʃən] n modulation f.

mohair ['mouhɛə] n mohair m.

moist [mɔist] a humide, moite, mouillé.

moisten ['mɔisn] vt humecter, mouiller.

moisture ['mɔistʃə] n humidité f, buée f, moiteur f.

molar ['moulə] an molaire f.

molasses [mə'læsiz] n pl mélasse f.

mole [moul] n jetée f, môle m, taupe f, grain de beauté m.

molecular [mou'lekjulə] a moléculaire.

molecule ['mɔlikjuːl] n molécule m.

molehill ['moulhil] n taupinière f.

molest [mou'lest] vt molester.

mollify ['mɔlifai] vt apaiser, adoucir.

mollusc ['mɔləsk] n mollusque m.

molten ['moultən] a fondu.

moment ['moumənt] n moment m, instant m, importance f; of — d'importance.

momentarily ['moumən tərili] ad momentanément, pour l'instant.

momentary ['mouməntəri] a momentané, passager.

momentous [mou'mentəs] a important, de conséquence.

monarch ['mɔnək] n monarque m.

monarchy ['mɔnəki] n monarchie f.

monastery ['mɔnəstəri] n monastère m.

monastic [mə'næstik] a monastique, monacal.

Monday ['mʌndi] n lundi m.

money ['mʌni] n argent m; monnaie f, —box n tire-lire f, caisse f; —changer n changeur m; —grubber n grippe-sous m; —lender n usurier m, bailleur de fonds m; —market n marché financier m; —order n mandat m; ready — argent comptant; public — trésor m public.

moneyed ['mʌnid] a riche.

monger ['mʌŋgə] n marchand (de . . .).

mongrel ['mʌŋgrəl] n métis, -isse, bâtard(e) mf.

monk [mʌŋk] n moine m.

monkey ['mʌŋki] n singe m (f guenon); vti singer; vi jouer des tours; — business filouterie f; — wrench clé anglaise f.

monkish ['mʌŋkiʃ] a monastique, monacal.

monogamy [mɔ'nɔgəmi] n monogamie f.

monogram ['mɔnəgræm] n monogramme m.

monologue ['mɔnəlɔg] n monologue m.

monomania ['mɔnou'meiniə] n monomanie f.

monopolist [mə'nɔpəlist] n accapareur, -euse.

monopoly [mə'nɔpəli] n monopole m.

monosyllabic ['mɔnəsi'læbik] a monosyllabique.

monosyllable ['mɔnə,siləbl] n monosyllabe m.

monotonous [mə'nɔtənəs] a monotone.

monotony [mə'nɔtəni] n monotonie f.

monsoon [mɔn'suːn] n mousson f.

monster ['mɔnstə] n monstre m.

monstrance ['mɔnstrəns] n ostensoir m.

monstrosity [mɔns'trɔsiti] n monstruosité f, énormité f.

monstrous ['mɔnstrəs] a monstrueux, énorme.

month [mʌnθ] n mois m.

monthly ['mʌnθli] a mensuel; ad mensuellement.

monument ['mɔnjumənt] n monument m.

monumental [ˌmɔnju'mentl] a monumental.

mood [muːd] n humeur f, mode m, disposition f.

moody ['muːdi] a morose, qui a des lubies, mal luné.

moon [muːn] n lune f; vi rêvasser; to — about musarder.

moonlight ['muːnlait] n clair de lune m.

moonshine ['muːnʃain] n clair de lune m, blague f.

moonstruck ['muːnstrʌk] a lunatique, toqué.

moor [muə] n lande f, bruyère f; vt amarrer; vi s'amarrer.

Moor [muə] n Maure m, Mauresque f.

moorhen ['muəhen] n poule f d'eau.

mooring ['muəriŋ] n amarrage m, mouillage m; pl amarres f pl.

mooring rope ['muəriŋroup] n amarre f.

Moorish ['muəriʃ] a maure, mauresque.

moot [muːt] a discutable.

mop [mɔp] n balai m à laver, lavette f, (hair) tignasse, (naut) faubert; vt éponger, s'essuyer, fauberder.

mope [moup] n ennuyé(e) mf, pl cafard; vi s'ennuyer, avoir le spleen.

moral ['mɔrəl] a moral; n moralité f; pl mœurs f pl.

morale [mɔ'rɑːl] n moral m.
moralist ['mɔrəlist] n moraliste mf.
moralize ['mɔrəlaiz] vi moraliser.
morass [mə'ræs] n marais m, fondrière f.
morbid ['mɔːbid] a morbide, maladif.
more [mɔː] a ad plus (de); prep davantage; — and — de plus en plus; the — . . . the — . . . plus . . . plus . . .
moreover [mɔː'rouvə] ad en outre, d'ailleurs.
morning ['mɔːniŋ] n matin m, matinée f; a du matin, matinal.
Moroccan [mə'rɔkən] an marocain m; n Marocain(e) mf.
Morocco [mə'rɔkou] n Maroc m, (leather) maroquin m.
morose [mə'rous] a morose.
moroseness [mə'rousnis] n maussaderie f, morosité f.
morphia ['mɔːfiə] n morphine f.
morrow ['mɔrou] n lendemain m.
morsel ['mɔːsəl] n morceau m, bouchée f.
mortal ['mɔːtl] a mortel, funeste; — fear peur jaune f.
mortality [mɔː'tæliti] n mortalité f.
mortar ['mɔːtə] n mortier m; vt cimenter.
mortgage ['mɔːgidʒ] n hypothèque f; vt hypothéquer.
mortification [ˌmɔːtifi'keiʃən] n mortification f, (med) gangrène f.
mortify ['mɔːtifai] vti mortifier, (med) se gangrener.
mortise ['mɔːtis] n mortaise f.
mortuary ['mɔːtjuəri] n morgue f; a mortuaire.
mosaic [mə'zeiik] a n mosaïque f.
Moscow ['mɔskou] n Moscou m.
Moslem ['mɔzlem] an musulman(ne).
mosque [mɔsk] n mosquée f.
mosquito [məs'kiːtou] n moustique m; — net moustiquaire f.
moss [mɔs] n mousse f.
mossy ['mɔsi] a moussu.
most [moust] a le plus, la plupart de; ad le (au) plus, très; (US) presque.
mostly ['moustli] ad surtout, pour la plupart.
motel [mou'tel] n motel m.
moth [mɔθ] n phalène f, mite f.
moth-ball ['mɔθbɔːl] n boule de naphtaline f.
moth-eaten ['mɔθˌiːtn] a mangé aux mites, des vers.
mother ['mʌðə] n mère f; vt choyer, servir de mère à; — country mère-patrie f; —-in-law belle-mère f; —-of-pearl nacre f; — tongue langue maternelle f.
motherhood ['mʌðəhud] n maternité f.
motion ['mouʃən] n mouvement m, geste m, signe m; motion f, proposition f; vt diriger d'un geste, faire signe à.
motionless ['mouʃənlis] a immobile.
motivate ['moutiveit] vt motiver.

motivating ['moutiveitiŋ] a moteur.
motive ['moutiv] n motif m, mobile m.
motley ['mɔtli] n bariolage m; a bariolé, mêlé.
motor ['moutə] a moteur, automobile; n moteur m, automobile f; vt conduire en automobile; vi voyager, aller, en automobile; — car n auto(mobile) f; —-cycle n motocyclette f.
motoring ['moutriŋ] n automobilisme m.
motorist ['moutərist] n automobiliste mf.
motorway ['moutəwei] n autoroute f.
mottle ['mɔtl] n marbrure f, veine f; vt marbrer, veiner.
motto ['mɔtou] n devise f.
mould (mould) ['mould] n terreau m, moule m, moisissure f; vt mouler, façonner, pétrir, former.
moulder ['mouldə] vi tomber en poussière, pourrir; n mouleur m.
moulding ['mouldiŋ] n moulage m, moulure f, formation f.
mouldy ['mouldi] a moisi.
moult [moult] n mue f; vi muer.
mound [maund] n tertre m.
mount [maunt] n mont m, monture f, cadre m; vti monter; vt monter sur.
mountain ['mauntin] n montagne f.
mountaineer [ˌmaunti'niə] n alpiniste mf, montagnard(e) m(f).
mountaineering [ˌmaunti'niəriŋ] n alpinisme m.
mountainous ['mauntinəs] a de montagne, montagneux.
mountebank ['mauntibæŋk] n saltimbanque m, charlatan m.
mourn [mɔːn] vti pleurer; vi se lamenter, être en deuil.
mourners ['mɔːnəz] n pl le cortège m funèbre.
mournful ['mɔːnful] a triste, lugubre, endeuillé.
mournfulness ['mɔːnfulnis] n tristesse f.
mourning ['mɔːniŋ] n deuil m.
mouse [maus] n souris f; vi chasser les souris, fureter.
mousetrap ['maustræp] n souricière f.
mouth [mauθ] n bouche f, embouchure f, orifice m, grimace f, gueule f; vti déclamer; vi grimacer, discourir.
mouthful ['mauθful] n bouchée f.
mouthpiece ['mauθpiːs] n embouchure f, porte-parole m.
movable ['muːvəbl] a mobile, mobilier; n pl biens meubles m pl, effets mobiliers m pl.
move [muːv] n mouvement m, coup m, démarche f; vt (é)mouvoir, exciter, pousser, proposer, déplacer; vi bouger, déménager; to — on (faire) circuler; to — back vt faire reculer; vi (se) reculer; to — forward vti avancer; to — in

emménager; to — on s'avancer, circuler; to — out déménager.

movement ['mu:vmənt] n mouvement m, déplacement m.

movies ['mu:viz] n ciné(ma) m.

moving ['mu:viŋ] a émouvant, mobile, en marche.

mow [mou] vt faucher.

mower ['mouə] n faucheur, -euse, (machine) tondeuse f.

mown [moun] pp of **mow**.

Mr ['mistə] Monsieur m.

Mrs ['misiz] n Madame f.

much [mʌtʃ] a beaucoup de; pn beaucoup; ad de beaucoup, très; too — pn trop; a trop de.

mucilage ['mju:silidʒ] n colle f (de bureau).

muck [mʌk] n fumier m, ordure f; vt salir, gâcher.

mud [mʌd] n boue f, banco m; **mud walls** murs en banco.

muddle ['mʌdl] n confusion f, désordre m, pagaille f, gâchis m; vt (em)brouiller, emmêler, to — **through** se débrouiller, finir par s'en tirer.

muddleheaded ['mʌdl,hedid] a brouillon.

muddy ['mʌdi] a boueux, terne, épais, trouble, limoneux.

mudguard ['mʌdgɑ:d] n pareboue m.

muff [mʌf] n manchon m, pataud(e) mf, empoté(e) mf; vt rater.

muffle ['mʌfl] n mufle m, moufle m; vt emmitoufler, assourdir, étouffer.

muffled ['mʌfld] a étouffé, feutré, voilé.

muffler ['mʌflə] n cache-nez m inv.

mug [mʌg] n gobelet m, chope f, poire , nigaud(e) mf.

muggy ['mʌgi] a étouffant, lourd et humide.

mulatto [mju'lætou] n mulâtre, -esse.

mulberry ['mʌlbəri] n mûre f.

mulberry-tree ['mʌlbəritri:] n mûrier m.

mulct [mʌlkt] n amende f; vt mettre à l'amende.

mule [mju:l] n mule f, mulet m.

multifarious [,mʌlti'fɛəriəs] a multiple, divers, varié.

multiple ['mʌltipl] an multiple m.

multiplication [,mʌltipli'keiʃən] n multiplication f.

multiplicity [,mʌlti'plisiti] n multiplicité f.

multiply ['mʌltiplai] vt multiplier; vi se multiplier.

multitude ['mʌltitju:d] n multitude f, foule f.

mum [mʌm] a silencieux; n maman f; excl ilence! motus!

mumble [mʌmbl] n marmottage m; vti marmonner marmotter.

mummify ['mʌmifai] vt momifier.

mummy ['mʌmi] n maman f; momie f.

mumps [mʌmps] n pl oreillons m pl.

munch [mʌnʃ] vti mastiquer; vt mâcher.

mundane ['mʌndein] a mondain, terrestre.

municipal [mju'nisipəl] a municipal.

municipality [mju,nisi'pæliti] n municipalité f.

munificent [mju'nifisnt] a généreux, munificent.

munitions [mju'niʃəns] n pl munitions f pl.

mural ['mjuərəl] a mural.

murder ['mə:də] n meurtre m, assassinat m; vt assassiner, (fig) massacrer

murderer ['mə:dərə] n meurtrier m, assassin m.

murderous ['mə:dərəs] a meurtrier, homicide.

murky ['mə:ki] a sombre, épais, ténébreux.

murmur ['mə:mə] n murmure m; vti murmurer.

muscle ['mʌsl] n muscle m; vi (US) s'immiscer (dans **in**), usurper.

muscular ['mʌskjulə] a musclé, musculaire.

muse [mju:z] n muse f; vi méditer, rêver.

museum [mju'ziəm] n musée m.

mushroom ['mʌʃrum] n champignon m; vi champignonner.

music ['mju:zik] n musique f; — **stand** pupitre m; — **stool** tabouret m.

musical ['mju:zikəl] a musical, mélodieux, musicien; n opérette f.

musician [mju'ziʃən] n musicien, -ienne.

musing ['mju:ziŋ] n rêverie f, méditation f.

musk [mʌsk] n musc m.

musket ['mʌskit] n mousquet m.

musketeer [,mʌski'tiə] n mousquetaire m.

muslin ['mʌzlin] n mousseline f.

musquash ['mʌskwɔʃ] n rat musqué m, castor m.

mussel ['mʌsl] n moule f.

mussy ['mʌsi] a (US) dérangé, sale.

must [mʌst] n moût m moisissure f; v aux devoir, falloir; **they — go** il leur faut partir, ils doivent partir.

mustard ['mʌstəd] n moutarde f; — **plaster** sinapisme m.

muster ['mʌstə] n appel m, rassemblement m; vt rassembler, faire l'appel de compter; vi se rassembler.

musty ['mʌsti] a moisi, désuet.

mutable ['mju:təbl] a sujet à déplacement, changeant.

mutation [mju'teiʃən] n mutation f.

mute [mju:t] a muet sourd; vt assourdir, mettre a sourdine à.

mutilate ['mju:tileit] vt mutiler.

mutilation [mju:ti'leiʃən] n mutilation f.

mutineer [,mju:ti'niə] n révolté m, mutiné m.

mutinous ['mju:tinəs] *a* mutin, rebelle.

mutiny ['mju:tini] *n* mutinerie *f*, révolte *f*.

mutter ['mʌtə] *n* murmure *m*; *vti* murmurer, marmotter.

mutton ['mʌtn] *n* mouton *m*; — **chop** côtelette *f*.

mutual ['mju:tjuəl] *a* mutuel, réciproque, respectif, commun.

mutuality [,mju:tju'æliti] *n* mutualité *f*.

muzzle ['mʌzl] *n* museau *m*, (gun) gueule *f*, muselière *f*; *vt* museler, bâillonner.

my [mai] *a* mon, ma, mes.

myrtle ['mə:tl] *n* myrte *m*.

myself [mai'self] *pn* moi-même.

mysterious [mis'tiəriəs] *a* mystérieux.

mystery ['mistəri] *n* mystère *m*.

mystic ['mistik] *an* mystique *mf*.

mysticism ['mistisizəm] *n* mysticisme *m*.

mystification [,mistifi'keiʃən] *n* mystification *f*, fumisterie *f*.

myth [miθ] *n* mythe *m*.

mythical ['miθikəl] *a* mythique.

mythology [mi'θɔlədʒi] *n* mythologie *f*

myxomatosis [,miksəmə'tousis] *n* myxomatose *f*.

N

nab [næb] *vt* pincer.

nabob ['neibɔb] *n* nabab *m*.

nag [næg] *n* bidet *m*; *vt* chamailler; *vi* grogner sur tout.

nagging ['nægiŋ] *a* hargneux; — **woman** chipie *f*.

nai' [neil] *n* clou *m*, ongle *m*; *vt* clouer, fixer empoigner.

naïve [nɑː'iːv] *a* naïf ingénu.

naked ['neikid] *a* nu, a poil.

nakedness ['neikidnis] *n* nudité *f*.

name [neim] *n* nom *m*, renom *m*, mot *m*; *vt* nommer dire, fixer; **Christian — prénom** *m*, **assumed —** nom d'emprunt, pseudonyme *m*.

nameless ['neimlis] *a* sans nom, innommable, anonyme.

namely ['neimli] *ad* à savoir.

namesake ['neimseik] *n* homonyme *m*.

nap næpj *n* somme *m*, poil *m*; *vi* sommeiller.

napalm ['neipɑːm] *n* napalm *m*.

nape [neip] *n* nuque *f*.

napkin ['næpkin] *n* serviette *f*, (baby's) couche *f*.

napping ['næpiŋ] *a* endormi, hors de garde, au dépourvu.

nappy ['næpi] *n* (fam) couche *f*.

narcissus [nɑː'sisəs] *n* narcisse *m*.

narcotic [nɑː'kɔtik] *n* narcotique *m*; *an* stupéfiant *m*.

narrate [næ'reit] *vt* conter.

narration [næ'reiʃən] *n* narration *f*, récit *m*.

narrative ['nærətiv] *n* récit *m*, narration *f*.

narrator [næ'reitə] *n* narrateur, -trice.

narrow ['nærou] *a* étroit, étranglé; *vt* rétrécir, resserrer, restreindre; *vi* se resserrer, se rétrécir, s'étrangler.

narrowness ['nærounis] *n* étroitesse *f*, exiguïté *f*.

narrows ['nærouz] *n* détroit *m*, défilé *m*, étranglement *m*.

nasal ['neizəl] *n* nasale *f*; *a* nasal, de nez.

nastily ['nɑːstili] *ad* méchamment.

nastiness ['nɑːstinis] *n* méchanceté *f*, saleté *f*.

nasty ['nɑːsti] *a* méchant, vilain, sale.

natal ['neitl] *a* natal.

nation ['neiʃən] *n* nation *f*.

national ['næʃənl] *a* national.

nationalism ['næʃnəlizəm] *n* nationalisme *m*.

nationality [,næʃə'næliti] *n* nationalité *f*.

nationalize ['næʃnəlaiz] *vt* nationaliser.

native ['neitiv] *n* originaire *mf*, indigène *mf*; *a* naturel, de naissance, natif du pays.

nativity [nə'tiviti] *n* nativité *f*.

natty ['næti] *a* soigné, adroit.

natural ['nætʃrəl] *a* naturel, inné, foncier.

naturalism ['nætʃrəlizəm] *n* naturalisme *m*.

naturalist ['nætʃrəlist] *n* naturaliste *m*.

naturalization [,nætʃrəlai'zeiʃən] *n* naturalisation *f*.

naturalize ['nætʃrəlaiz] *vt* naturaliser

naturally ['nætʃrəli] *ad* naturellement, bien sûr.

naturalness ['nætʃrəlnis] *n* naturel *m*, simplicité *f*.

nature ['neitʃə] *n* nature *f*, sorte *f*, tempérament *m*.

naught [nɔːt] *n* rien *m*, zéro *m*; **to come to —** échouer.

naughtiness ['nɔːtinis] *n* méchanceté *f*.

naughty ['nɔːti] *a* vilain, méchant, polisson.

nausea ['nɔːsiə] *n* nausée *f*.

nauseating ['nɔːsieitiŋ] *a* écœurant, nauséabond.

nauseous ['nɔːsiəs] *a* nauséabond, dégoûtant.

naval ['neivəl] *a* naval, maritime, de marine; — **base** port de guerre *m*.

nave [neiv] *n* nef moyeu *m*.

navel ['neivəl] *n* nombril *m*.

navigate ['nævigeit] *v* naviguer; *vt* diriger, gouverner, piloter.

navigation [,nævi'geiʃən] *n* navigation *f*, manœuvre *f*, conduite *f*.

navigator ['nævigeitə] n navigateur m, pilote m.

navvy ['nævi] n terrassier m.

navy ['neivi] n marine f.

nay [nei] ad non, ou plutôt, voire.

near [niə] a proche, prochain, (r)approché; prep près de; ad (de) près, à peu de chose près.

nearly ['niəli] ad de près, presque.

nearness ['niənis] n proximité f, ladrerie f. fidélité f.

neat [ni:t] a net, élégant, bien tenu, en ordre, adroit, nature, (drink) pur.

neatness ['ni:tnis] n netteté f, (bon) ordre m, finesse f.

nebulous ['nebjuləs] n nébuleux.

necessary ['nesisəri] n nécessaire, indispensable.

necessitate [ni'sesiteit] vt nécessiter.

necessitous [ni'sesitəs] a nécessiteux, besogneux.

necessity [ni'sesiti] n nécessité f, besoin m, contrainte f.

neck [nek] n cou m, col m, collet m, encolure f, goulot m.

neckerchief ['nekətʃif] n fichu m, foulard m.

necklace ['neklis] n collier m.

necktie ['nektai] n cravate f.

need [ni:d] n besoin m, nécessité f; vt avoir besoin de, exiger, réclamer, falloir; **he needs a pound** il lui faut une livre.

needful ['ni:dful] an nécessaire m.

needle ['ni:dl] n aiguille f; **—woman** n lingère f, couturière f.

needless ['ni:dlis] a inutile.

needs [ni:dz] ad nécessairement; **he must — refuse** force lui est de refuser.

needy ['ni:di] a nécessiteux, besogneux.

nefarious [ni'fɛəriəs] a inique, abominable.

negative ['negətiv] a négatif; n négative f négatif m, cliché m; vt rejeter, nier, neutraliser.

neglect [ni'glekt] n négligence f, incurie f; vt négliger.

neglectful [ni'glektful] a négligent, insoucieux.

negligently ['neglidʒəntli] ad négligemment.

negligible ['neglidʒəbl] a négligeable.

negotiable [ni'gouʃjəbl] a négociable.

negotiate [ni'gouʃieit] vti négocier; vt conclure, surmonter, franchir.

negotiation [ni,gouʃi'eiʃən] n négociation f.

negotiator [ni'gouʃieitə] n négociateur, -trice.

Negress ['ni:gris] n négresse f.

Negro ['ni:grou] n nègre m.

neigh [nei] n hennissement; vt hennir.

neighbour ['neibə] n voisin(e) mf.

neighbourhood ['neibəhud] n voisinage m, région f.

neighbouring ['neibəriŋ] a voisin, avoisinant.

neither ['naiðə] pn ni l'un ni l'autre; ad ni, non plus.

neo-colonialism [,nioukə'louniəlizm] n néo-colonialisme m.

nephew ['nevju] n neveu m.

nephritis [ne'fraitis] n néphrite f.

nepotism ['nepətizəm] n népotisme m.

nerve ['nə:v] n nerf m, sang-froid m, toupet m; vt fortifier; **to — oneself** se raidir, s'armer de courage.

nerveless ['nə:vlis] a mou, inerte.

nervous ['nə:vəs] a nerveux, excitable.

nervousness ['nə:vəsnis] n timidité f, nervosité f, peur f.

nest [nest] n nid m, nichée f; vi faire son nid, (se) nicher.

nestle ['nesl] vi se blottir, se nicher.

nestling ['nesliŋ] n oisillon m.

net [net] n filet m, réseau m, résille f, tulle m; vt rapporter net, prendre au filet, tendre des filets sur, dans; vi faire du filet; vt prendre au filet, couvrir de filets, tendre des filets dans; a net.

nether ['neðə] a inférieur, infernal.

Netherlands ['neðələndz] n Pays-Bas m pl.

netting ['netiŋ] n filet m, treillis m, pose de filets f.

nettle ['netl] n ortie f; vt piquer, irriter; **—rash** n urticaire f.

network ['netwə:k] n réseau m, ligne f.

neuralgia [njuə'rældʒə] n neuralgie f.

neurasthenia [,njuərəs'θi:niə] n neurasthénie f.

neurasthenic ['njuərəs'θenik] a neurasthénique.

neuritis [njuə'raitis] n névrite f.

neurology [njuə'rɔlədʒi] n neurologie f.

neuropath [njuərə'pɑ:θ] n névropathe m.

neurosis [njuə'rousis] n névrose f.

neurotic [njuə'rɔtik] a névrosé.

neuter ['nju:tə] an neutre m.

neutral ['nju:trəl] a neutre.

neutrality [nju'træliti] n neutralité f.

neutralize ['nju:trəlaiz] vt neutraliser.

neutron ['nju:trɔn] n neutron m.

never ['nevə] ad jamais, ne . . . jamais.

nevertheless [,nevəðə'les] ad cependant, néanmoins.

new [nju:] a neuf, nouveau, jeune, frais; **—born** nouveau-né; **New Year** Le Nouvel An; **New Year's Day** n le jour de l'an.

newly ['nju:li] ad nouvellement, fraîchement.

newness ['nju:nis] n nouveauté f, fraîcheur f.

news [nju:z] n nouvelle(s) f pl, (radio) informations f pl; **a piece of —** une nouvelle; **—agent**, (US) **—dealer** marchand m de journaux; **—boy** n vendeur de journaux m.

newspaper ['njuːs,peipə] *n* journal *m*.

news-reel ['njuːzriːl] *n* informations *f pl*, actualités *f pl*.

news-stand ['njuːzstænd] *n* kiosque à journaux *m*.

newt [njuːt] *n* salamandre *f*.

next [nekst] *a* le plus proche, prochain, suivant; *prep* près de, sur, à même; *ad* ensuite, après près.

nib [nib] *n* bec *m*, pointe *f*.

nibble ['nibl] *vt* grignoter, mordiller, égratigner.

nice [nais] *a* délicat, gentil, joli, doux, fin, subtil.

nicely ['naisli] *ad* gentiment, précisément, bien.

nicety ['naisiti] *n* subtilité *f*; to a — exactement, à point.

niche [nitʃ] *n* niche *f*.

nick [nik] *n* entaille *f*, encoche *f*; *vt* entailler, deviner, attraper, pincer, couper au court; in the — of time juste à temps.

nickname ['nikneim] *n* surnom *m*, sobriquet *m*; *vt* baptiser, surnommer.

niece [niːs] *n* nièce *f*.

niggard ['nigəd] *n* ladre *m*, pingre *m*.

niggardliness ['nigədlinis] *n* ladrerie *f*, pingrerie *f*.

niggardly ['nigədli] *a* ladre, pingre, mesquin.

nigger ['nigə] *n* moricaud(e) *mf*; nègre *m*, négresse *f*.

nigh [nai] *a* proche; *ad* presque.

night [nait] *n* nuit *f*, soir *m*.

night-club ['naitklʌb] *n* boîte de nuit *f*.

nightdress ['naitdres] *n* chemise de nuit *f*.

nightfall ['naitfɔːl] *n* tombée de la nuit *f*.

nightingale ['naitiŋgeil] *n* rossignol *m*.

nightlight ['naitlait] *n* veilleuse *f*.

nightly ['naitli] *a* nocturne, de nuit.

nightmare ['naitmɛə] *n* cauchemar *m*.

night-watchman ['nait'wɔtʃmən] *n* veilleur de nuit *m*.

nil [nil] *n* rien *m*, zéro *m*; *a* nul.

nimble ['nimbl] *a* agile, délié, ingambe.

nincompoop ['ninkəmpuːp] *n* gros bêta *m*, nigaud *m*.

nine [nain] *an* neuf *m*, (US) équipe *f* de baseball.

ninepins ['nainpinz] *n* quilles *f pl*.

nineteen ['nain'tiːn] *an* dix-neuf *m*.

nineteenth ['nain'tiːnθ] *an* dix-neuvième *mf*.

ninetieth ['naintiiθ] *an* quatre-vingt-dixième *mf*.

ninety ['nainti] *an* quatre-vingt-dix *m*.

ninny ['nini] *n* benêt *m*, niais(e) *mf*.

ninth [nainθ] *a* neuvième.

nip [nip] *n* pincement *m*, pinçon *m*, morsure *f*, sarcasme *m*, goutte *f*; *vt* pincer, mordre, piquer, flétrir.

nipper ['nipə] *n* gosse *m*; *pl* pince *f*, tenailles *f pl*.

nipple ['nipl] *n* tétin *m*, mamelon *m*.

no [nou] *nm* *ad* non; *a* aucun, nul; — longer ne . . . plus.

nobility [nou'biliti] *n* noblesse *f*.

noble ['noubl] *an* noble *mf*; *a* grandiose, majestueux.

nobody ['noubədi] *pn* personne; *n* nullité *m*, pauvre type *m*.

nocturnal [nɔk'təːnl] *a* nocturne.

nod [nɔd] *n* signe de tête *m*; *vi* faire un signe de tête, dodeliner, somnoler.

nodding ['nɔdiŋ] *a* à la tête dodelinante.

node [noud] *n* nœud *m*.

noise [nɔiz] *n* bruit *m*, vacarme *m*; *vt* répandre, ébruiter.

noiseless ['nɔizlis] *a* sans bruit, silencieux.

noisily ['nɔizili] *ad* bruyamment.

noisome ['nɔisəm] *a* nuisible, offensant, malodorant, désagréable.

noisy ['nɔizi] *a* bruyant.

no-man's-land ['noumænzlænd] *n* zone neutre *m*, terrains *mpl* vagues, zone *m*.

nominal ['nɔminl] *a* nominal.

nominally ['nɔminəli] *ad* de nom, soi-disant.

nominate ['nɔmineit] *vt* proposer, désigner, nommer.

nomination [,nɔmi'neiʃən] *n* nomination *f*.

non-aligned countries *npl* le tiers monde *m*.

non-alignement ['nɔnə'lainmənt] *n* neutralisme.

non-appearance ['nɔnə'piərəns] *n* absence *f*; (*law*) défaut *m*.

non-committal ['nɔnkə'mitl] *a* évasif, (de) nominal *m*.

nondescript ['nɔndiskript] *a* vague, hétéroclite.

none [nʌn] *a* *pn* aucun, nul; *pn* pas une personne; *ad* en rien, pas.

nonentity [nɔ'nentiti] *n* nullité *f*, zéro *m*.

non-intervention ['nɔn,intə'venʃən] *n* non-intervention *f*.

non-payment ['nɔn'peimənt] *n* défaut de payement *m*.

nonplus ['nɔn'plʌs] *vt* interloquer, interdire.

nonsense ['nɔnsəns] *n* nonsens *m*, galimatias *m*, absurdité *f*, bêtise *f*.

nonsensical [nɔn'sensikəl] *a* absurde.

non-stop ['nɔn'stɔp] *a* sans arrêt, direct

noodle ['nuːdl] *n* nigaud(e) *mf*, benêt *m*; *pl* nouilles *f pl*.

nook [nuk] *n* (re)coin *m*.

noon [nuːn] *n* midi *m*.

noose [nuːs] *n* nœud coulant *m*.

nor [nɔː] *ad* ni, et ne pas.

normal ['nɔːməl] *a* normal, moyen, ordinaire.

Norman ['nɔːmən] *n* Normand(e) *mf*; *a* normand.

Normandy ['nɔːməndi] n Normandie f.

north [nɔːθ] an nord m; a du nord, septentrional.

northwards ['nɔːθwədz] a vers le nord, au nord.

Norway ['nɔːwei] n Norvège f.

nose [nouz] n nez m, flair m; vt sentir, flairer; **to — about** fureter; **to — out** éventer, flairer; **—bag** musette f; **—dive** descente en piqué f; vi piquer du nez.

nosegay ['nouzgei] n bouquet m.

nostril ['nɔstril] n narine f, naseau m.

nostrum ['nɔstrəm] n orviétan m, panacée f.

Nosey Parker ['nouzi'pɑːkə] n fouinard(e) mf, fouille-au-pot m.

not [nɔt] ad ne . . . pas, pas, non.

notable ['noutəbl] a notable, éminent, insigne.

notch [nɔtʃ] n (en)coche f, (US) défilé m, gorge f; vt encocher, faire une coche à.

note [nout] n note f, ton m, signe m, mot m, marque f, réputation f; vt noter.

notebook ['noutbuk] n carnet m, bloc-notes m.

noted ['noutid] a connu, remarquable, célèbre (par for).

notepaper ['nout,peipə] n papier à lettres m.

noteworthy ['nout,wəːði] a remarquable.

nothing ['nʌθiŋ] n pn rien m; n zéro m, néant m; ad en rien, nullement.

nothingness ['nʌθiŋnis] n néant m.

notice ['noutis] n avis m, informé m, avertissement m, affiche f, annonce f, compte m, connaissance f, congé m, notice f; vt remarquer, prendre garde à, s'apercevoir de, apercevoir.

noticeable ['noutisəbl] a sensible, perceptible, digne de remarque.

noticeboard ['noutisbɔːd] n panneau m, écriteau m.

notifiable ['noutifaiəbl] a à déclarer.

notification [,noutifi'keiʃən] n avis m, déclaration f, notification f.

notify ['noutifai] vt avertir, notifier, déclarer.

notion ['nouʃən] n notion f, idée f.

notoriety [,noutə'raiəti] n notoriété f.

notorious [nou'tɔːriəs] a notoire, malfamé.

notwithstanding [,nɔtwiθ'stændiŋ] prep malgré; ad néanmoins; cj bien que.

nought [nɔːt] n rien m, zéro m.

noun [naun] n nom m.

nourish ['nʌriʃ] vt nourrir, sustenter, alimenter.

nourishment ['nʌriʃmənt] n nourriture f.

novel ['nɔvəl] a original, étrange, nouveau; n roman m.

novelist ['nɔvəlist] n romancier m.

novelty ['nɔvəlti] n nouveauté f, innovation f.

November [nou'vembə] n novembre m.

novice ['nɔvis] a apprenti(e) mf, débutant(e) mf, novice mf.

now [nau] ad à présent, maintenant, tout de suite, dès lors, alors, tantôt, or; cj maintenant que.

nowadays ['nauədeiz] ad de nos jours, aujourd'hui.

nowhere ['nouwɛə] ad nulle part.

noxious ['nɔkʃəs] a nuisible, nocif.

nozzle ['nɔzl] n bec m, lance f, tuyau m, buse f.

nuclear ['njuːkliə] a nucléaire, atomique.

nucleus ['njuːkliəs] n noyau m.

nude [njuːd] an nu m.

nudge [nʌdʒ] n coup de coude m; vt pousser du coude.

nudity ['njuːditi] n nudité f.

nugget ['nʌgit] n pépite f.

nuisance ['njuːsns] n délit m, ennui m; **to be a —** être gênant, assommant.

null [nʌl] a nul, nulle.

nullify ['nʌlifai] vt annuler, infirmer.

numb [nʌm] a engourdi; vt engourdir.

number ['nʌmbə] n nombre m, numéro m, chiffre m; vt compter, numéroter.

numberless ['nʌmbəlis] a innombrable.

numbness ['nʌmnis] n engourdissement m.

numerator ['njuːməreitə] n numérateur m.

numerical [nju(ː)'merikəl] a numérique.

numerous ['njuːmərəs] a nombreux.

nun [nʌn] n nonne f, religieuse f.

nunnery ['nʌnəri] n couvent m.

nuptial ['nʌpʃəl] a nuptial; pl noces f pl.

nurse [nəːs] n infirmière f, nurse f, nourrice f, bonne f; vt nourrir, élever, soigner, bercer, ménager, entretenir.

nursery ['nəːsri] n (plants) pépinière f, garderie f, nursery f.

nurseryman ['nəːsrimən] n pépiniériste m.

nursing-home ['nəːsiŋhoum] n clinique f, maison f de santé.

nursling ['nəːsliŋ] n nourrisson m, poupon, -onne.

nurture ['nəːtʃə] n éducation f, soin m, nourriture f, soin m, nourriture f; vt nourrir, élever, soigner.

nut [nʌt] n noix f, écrou m, (fam) tête f, caboche f; cinglé m; **—-crackers** n casse-noix m.

nutmeg ['nʌtmeg] n muscade f.

nutrition [nju(ː)'triʃən] n nutrition f.

nutritious [nju(ː)'triʃəs] a nourrissant.

nutritive ['njuːtritiv] a nutritif.

nutshell ['nʌtʃel] n coquille de noix f; **in a —** en deux mots.

nut-tree ['nʌttriː] n noyer m.

nutty ['nʌti] *a* à goût de noisette, toqué.

nuzzle ['nʌzl] *vt* flairer, fouiller, fourrer son nez dans, (contre); *vi* se blottir.

nymph [nimf] *n* nymphe *f*.

O

oak [ouk] *n* chêne *m*.

oakum ['oukəm] *n* étoupe *f*.

oar [ɔː] *n* rame *f*, aviron *m*; *vi* ramer.

oarsman ['ɔːzmən] *n* rameur *m*, nageur *m*.

oasis [ou'eisis *n* oasis *f*.

oats [outs] *n* avoine *f*; to sow one's wild — jeter sa gourme.

oath [ouθ] *n* serment *m*, juron *m*.

oatmeal ['outmiːl] *n* gruau *m*.

obduracy ['ɔbdjurəsi] *n* endurcissement *m*, obstination *f*.

obdurate ['ɔbdjurit] *a* endurci, obstiné.

obedience [ə'biːdjəns] *n* obéissance *f*, obédience *f*.

obedient [ə'biːdjənt] *a* obéissant, docile.

obeisance [ou'beisəns] *n* révérence *f*, hommage *m*.

obelisk ['ɔbilisk] *n* obélisque *m*.

obese [ou'biːs] *a* obèse.

obesity [ou'biːsiti] *n* obésité *f*.

obey [ə'bei] *vt* obéir; *v* obéir à.

obituary [ə'bitjuəri] *n* notice nécrologique *f*.

object ['ɔbdʒikt] *n* objet *m*, but *m*, complément *m*.

object [əb'dʒekt] *vt* objecter; *vi* to — to trouver à redire à, s'opposer à, désapprouver

objection [əb'dʒekʃən] *n* objection *f*, inconvénient *m*.

objectionable [əb'dʒekʃnəbl] *a* choquant, répugnant, désagréable.

objective [ɔb'dʒektiv] *an* objectif *m*; *n* but *m*.

objectivity [ˌɔbdʒek'tiviti] *n* objectivité *f*.

obligation [ˌɔbli'geiʃən] *n* obligation *f*, engagement *m*.

obligatory [ɔ'bligətəri] *a* obligatoire, de rigueur.

oblige [ə'blaidʒ] *vt* obliger, rendre service à.

obliging [ə'blaidʒiŋ] *a* obligeant, serviable.

oblique [ə'bliːk] *a* oblique.

obliterate [ə'blitəreit] *vt* effacer, oblitérer.

oblivion [ə'bliviən] *n* oubli *m*.

oblivious [ə'bliviəs] *a* oublieux.

oblong ['ɔblɔŋ] *a* oblong.

obloquy ['ɔbləkwi] *n* blâme *m*, opprobre *m*.

obnoxious [əb'nɔkʃəs] *a* offensant, déplaisant, odieux.

oboe ['oubou] *n* hautbois *m*.

obscene [əb'siːn] *a* impur, immonde, obscène.

obscenity [əb'seniti] *n* obscénité *f*, impiété *f*.

obscure [əb'skjuə] *a* obscur; *vt* obscurcir, éclipser, cacher.

obscurity [əb'skjuəriti] *n* obscurité *f*.

obsequies ['ɔbsikwiz] *n* obsèques *f pl*.

obsequious [əb'siːkwiəs] *a* obséquieux.

obsequiousness [əb'siːkwiəsnis] *n* obséquiosité *f*.

observable [əb'zəːvəbl] *a* observable.

observance [əb'zəːvəns] *n* observation *f*, observance *f*.

observant [əb'zəːvənt] *a* observateur.

observation [ˌɔbzə'veiʃən] *n* observation *f*.

observatory [əb'zəːvətri] *n* observatoire *m*.

observe [əb'zəːv] *vt* observer, faire remarquer.

obsess [əb'ses] *vt* obséder.

obsession [əb'seʃən] *n* obsession *f*, hantise *f*.

obsolete ['ɔbsəliːt] *a* désuet, hors d'usage.

obstacle ['ɔbstəkl] *n* obstacle *m*.

obstinacy ['ɔbstənəsi] *n* obstination *f*.

obstinate ['ɔbstinit] *a* obstiné, têtu, acharné.

obstinately ['ɔbstinitli] *ad* obstinément.

obstreperous [əb'strepərəs] *a* bruyant turbulent.

obstreperousness [əb'strepərisnis] *n* rouspétance *f*.

obstruct [əb'strʌkt] *vt* obstruer, boucher, entraver, encombrer.

obstruction [əb'strʌkʃən] *a* obstruction *f*, encombrement *m*, obstacle *m*.

obtain [əb'tein] *vt* se procurer, obtenir; *vi* prévaloir, régner.

obtainable [əb'teinəbl] *a* qui peut s'obtenir procurable.

obtrude [əb'truːd] *vti* (s')imposer, (se) mettre en avant.

obtrusion [əb'truːʒən] *n* ingérence *f*, intrusion *f*.

obtrusive [əb'truːsiv] *a* importun, indiscret.

obtuse [əb'tjuːs] *a* émoussé, obtus.

obtuseness [əb'tjuːsnis] *n* stupidité *f*.

obviate ['ɔbvieit] *vt* parer à, prévenir.

obvious ['ɔbviəs] *a* évident, manifeste, indiqué.

occasion [ə keiʒən] *n* cause *f*, occasion *f*, sujet *m*, affaires *f pl*; *vt* occasionner.

occasional [ə'keiʒənl] *a* de circonstance, occasionnel; — hand extra *m*; épars.

occasionally [ə'keiʒənəli] *ad* à l'occasion, de temps en temps.

occident ['ɔksidənt] *n* occident *m*.

occult [ɔ'kʌlt] *a* occulte.

occultism ['ɔkəltizəm] *n* occultisme *m*.

occupant ['ɔkjupənt] *n* occupant(e) *mf*, habitant(e) *mf*, locataire *mf*.
occupation [.ɔkju'peiʃən] *n* métier *m*, occupation *f*.
occupy ['ɔkjupai] *vt* occuper, habiter, tenir.
occur [ə'kəɪ] *vi* arriver, se produire, venir à l'esprit.
occurrence [ə'kʌrəns] *n* occurrence *f*, événement *m*.
ocean ['ouʃən] *n* océan *m*.
October [ɔk'toubə] *n* octobre *m*.
octopus ['ɔktəpəs] *n* pieuvre *f*.
ocular ['ɔkjulə] *a* oculaire.
oculist ['ɔkjulist] *n* oculiste *mf*.
odd [ɔd] *a* impair, de plus, de reste, dépareillé, curieux, bizarre.
oddity ['ɔditi] *n* bizarrerie *f*, curiosité *f*, excentricité *f*.
oddments ['ɔdmənts] *n pl* fins de série *f pl*, articles soldés *m pl*, fonds de boutique *m pl*.
odds [ɔdz] *n* inégalité *f*, avantage *m*, chances *f pl*; — **and ends** pièces et morceaux.
odious ['oudiəs] *a* odieux.
odorous ['oudərəs] *a* odorant.
odour ['oudə] *n* odeur *f*.
odourless ['oudəlis] *a* inodore, sans odeur.
of [ɔv] *prep* de, d'entre, depuis, par, à, en.
off [ɔf] *prep* de, sur, sans, de dessus, au large de, à la hauteur de; *a* éloigné, extérieur, de liberté; *ad* coupé, fermé, libre, parti, éloigné; **I'm** — je m'en vais; **day** — jour de congé.
offal ['ɔfəl] *n* abats *m pl*, rebut *m*.
offence [ə'fens] *n* contravention *f*, délit *m*, offense *f*.
offend [ə'fend] *vt* offenser, enfreindre, blesser.
offender [ə'fendə] *n* délinquant(e) *mf*, coupable *mf*.
offensive [ə'fensiv] *n* offensive *f*; *a* offensant, répugnant, offensif.
offer ['ɔfə] *n* offre *f*; *vt* offrir; *vi* s'offrir, se présenter.
offering ['ɔfəriŋ] *n* offrande *f*.
offertory ['ɔfətəri] *n* quête *f*.
offhand ['ɔf'hænd] *a* improvisé, désinvolte.
offhandedly ['ɔf'hændidli] *ad* de haut, avec désinvolture.
office ['ɔfis] *n* poste *m*, bureau *m*, office *m*; **good** —**s** bons offices *m pl*.
officer ['ɔfisə] *n* officier *m*.
official [ə'fiʃəl] *a* officiel, réglementaire; *n* employé *m*, fonctionnaire *m*.
officialdom [ə'fiʃəldəm] *n* monde officiel *m*, bureaucratie *f*.
officiate [ə'fiʃieit] *vi* officier, remplir les fonctions (de **as**).
officious [ə'fiʃəs] *a* trop zélé, officieux.
officiousness [ə'fiʃəsnis] *n* excès de zèle *m*.
offing ['ɔfiŋ] *n* (*sea*) large *m*, perspective *f*.

off-peak ['ɔfpiːk] *a* — **hours** heures creuses *f pl*; — **tariff** tarif de nuit *m*.
off-season ['ɔf'siːzn] *n* morte saison *f*.
offset ['ɔfset] *n* œilleton *m*, rejeton *m*, éperon *m*, compensation *f*, repoussoir *m*.
offshoot ['ɔfʃuːt] *n* rejeton *m*.
offshore ['ɔfʃɔː] *ad a* de terre, éloigné de la côte.
offside ['ɔf'said] *a* hors jeu.
offspring ['ɔfspriŋ] *n* rejeton *m*, résultat *m*.
often ['ɔfn] *ad* souvent; — **and** — à mainte reprise.
ogle ['ougl] *n* œillade *f*; *vt* lorgner, faire de l'œil à.
oil [ɔil] *n* huile *f*, pétrole *m*; **crude** — mazout *m*; *vt* huiler, graisser; *vi* faire son plein de mazout; —**can** *n* burette *f*; —**painting** *n* peinture à l'huile; **coconut** — huile *f* de copra.
oilcake ['ɔilkeik] *n* tourteau *m*.
oilcloth ['ɔilklɔθ] *n* toile cirée *f*.
oiliness ['ɔilinis] *n* onctuosité *f*, état graisseux *m*.
oilskin ['ɔilskin] *n* ciré *m*.
oil-tanker ['ɔiltæŋkə] *n* pétrolier *m*.
oil-well ['ɔilwel] *n* puits pétrolifère *m*.
oily ['ɔili] *a* huileux, onctueux.
ointment ['ɔintmənt] *n* onguent *m*, pommade *f*.
old [ould] *a* vieux, vieil, vieille, ancien, âgé; **to grow** — vieillir; — **age** vieillesse *f*; —**timer** (*US*) *n* vieillard *m*.
old-fashioned ['ould'fæʃənd] *a* démodé, suranné.
oldish ['ouldiʃ] *a* vieillot.
olive ['ɔliv] *n* olive *f*; *a* d'olive; — **tree** olivier *m*.
omen ['oumen] *n* présage *m*, augure *m*.
ominous ['ɔminəs] *a* menaçant, de mauvais augure.
omission [ou'miʃən] *n* omission *f*, oubli *m*.
omit [ou'mit] *vt* omettre, oublier.
omnifarious [.ɔmni'fɛəriəs] *a* de toute espèce.
omnipotence [ɔm'nipətəns] *n* toute-puissance *f*.
omnivorous [ɔm'nivərəs] *a* omnivore.
on [ɔn] *prep* sur, à, lors de, en, sous, par, contre; *ad* en cours, en avant! mis, passé, allumé, ouvert.
once [wʌns] *ad* une fois; **at** — immédiatement, à la fois; —**over** *n* (*US*) un coup d'œil scrutateur.
one [wʌn] *a* un, un seul; *pn* on.
one-eyed ['wʌn'aid] *a* borgne.
one's [wʌnz] *a* son, sa, ses.
oneself [wʌn'self] *pn* soi-même.
one-sided ['wʌn'saidid] *a* unilatéral, borné.
one-way ['wʌn'wei] *n* sens unique *m*; *a* à sens unique.
onerous ['ounɔrəs] *a* onéreux.

onion ['ʌnjən] n oignon m.

only ['ounli] a unique, seul; ad seulement; cj sauf que, mais.

onset ['onset] n attaque f, assaut m, départ m, début m.

onslaught ['ɔnslɔːt] see **onset**.

onus ['ounəs] n poids m, charge f, responsabilité f.

onward ['ɔnwəd] a progressif, avancé, avançant; ad en avant, dorénavant.

ooze [uːz] n boue f, limon m, suintement m; vi suinter, dégoutter.

opal ['oupəl] n opale f; a opalin.

opaque [ou'peik] a opaque.

opaqueness [ou'peiknis] n opacité f.

open ['oupən] a ouvert, public, exposé, franc, débouché libre; **in the — (air)** en plein air, au grand air; vt ouvrir, entamer, déboucher, percer, engager; vi s'ouvrir, débuter, commencer, s'épanouir.

opening ['oupəniŋ] n ouverture f, début m, débouché m, inauguration f.

opera ['ɔpərə] n opéra m.

operate ['ɔpəreit] vti opérer; vt accomplir, actionner, faire marcher; vi fonctionner, agir; (US) gérer, exploiter.

operation [,ɔpə'reiʃən] n opération f, action f, fonctionnement m.

operative ['ɔpərətiv] n ouvrier, -ière; a efficace, actif, opératif, en vigueur.

opinion [ə'pinjən] n opinion f, avis m.

opinionated [ə'pinjəneitəd] a obstiné, entier.

opium ['oupjəm] n opium m.

opponent [ə'pounənt] n adversaire m, antagoniste mf.

opportune ['ɔpətjuːn] a opportun.

opportunely ['ɔpətjuːnli] ad à propos, en temps opportun.

opportunism ['ɔpətjuːnizəm] n opportunisme m.

opportunity [,ɔpə'tjuːniti] n occasion f, chance f.

oppose [ə'pouz] vt s'opposer à, opposer.

opposite ['ɔpəzit] a opposé, correspondant; prep face à, en face de; ad en face, en regard; n contraire m, contre-pied m.

opposition [,ɔpə'ziʃən] n opposition f, concurrence f.

oppress [ə'pres] vt opprimer.

oppression [ə'preʃən] n oppression f.

oppressive [ə'presiv] a oppressif, lourd.

oppressor [ə'presə] n oppresseur m.

opprobrious [ə'proubriəs] a déshonorant, injurieux.

opprobrium [ə'proubriəm] n opprobre m.

opt [ɔpt] vi opter; **— out** s'esquiver.

optic ['ɔptik] a optique.

optician [ɔp'tiʃən] n opticien m

optics ['ɔptiks] n optique f.

optimism ['ɔptimizəm] n optimisme m.

optimistic [,ɔpti'mistik] a optimiste.

option ['ɔpʃən] n option f, choix m.

optional ['ɔpʃənl] a facultatif.

opulence ['ɔpjuləns] n opulence f.

opulent ['ɔpjulənt] a opulent.

or [ɔː] cj ou, sinon.

oracle ['ɔrəkl] n oracle m.

oracular [ɔ'rækjulə] a oraculaire, obscur.

oral ['ɔːrəl] a oral.

orange ['ɔrindʒ] n orange f.

oration [ɔː'reiʃən] n discours m, harangue f.

orator ['ɔrətə] n orateur m.

oratorical [,ɔrə'tɔrikəl] a oratoire, ampoulé, disert.

orb [ɔːb] n orbe m, globe m, sphère f.

orbit ['ɔːbit] n orbite f.

orchard ['ɔːtʃəd] n verger m.

orchestra ['ɔːkistrə] n orchestre m.

orchestrate ['ɔːkistreit] vt orchestrer.

orchid ['ɔːkid] n orchidée f.

ordain [ɔː'dein] vt ordonner, conférer les ordres à.

ordeal [ɔː'diːl] n épreuve f.

order ['ɔːdə] n ordre m; **to — sur commande; out of — détraqué, déplacé, irrégulier; in — to afin de;** vt commander ordonner.

orderliness ['ɔːdəlinis] n (esprit m d') ordre m.

orderly ['ɔːdəli] n infirmier militaire m, planton m; a en ordre, rangé, discipliné.

ordinary ['ɔːdnri] a ordinaire, typique, normal.

ordnance ['ɔːdnəns] n artillerie f, intendance f.

ore [ɔː] n mineral m.

organ ['ɔːgən] n organe m, orgue m.

organic [ɔː'gænik] a organique.

organism ['ɔːgənizəm] n organisme m.

organist ['ɔːgənist] n organiste mf.

organization [,ɔːgənai'zeiʃən] n organisation f, organisme m.

organize ['ɔːgənaiz] vt organiser, arranger.

organizer ['ɔːgənaizə] n organisateur, -trice.

orient ['ɔːriənt] n orient m.

oriental [,ɔːri'entl] a oriental, d'orient.

orientation [,ɔːrien'teiʃən] n orientation f.

orifice ['ɔrifis] n orifice m, ouverture f.

origin ['ɔridʒin] n origine f.

original [ə'ridʒənl] an original m; a originel.

originality [ə,ridʒi'næliti] n originalité f.

originate [ə'ridʒineit] vt donner naissance à; vt descendre, provenir, naître.

originator [ə'ridʒineitə] n auteur m, source f.

ornament ['ɔːnəmənt] n ornement m.

ornament [ɔːnə'ment] vt orner, agrémenter.

ornamental [,ɔːnə'mentl] *a* orne-mental, décoratif.

ornamentation [,ɔːnəmen'teiʃən] *n* ornementation *f*, décoration *f*.

orphan ['ɔːfən] *n* orphelin(e) *mf*.

orphanage ['ɔːfənidʒ] *n* orphelinat *m*.

orthodox ['ɔːθədɔks] *a* orthodoxe.

orthodoxy ['ɔːθədɔksi] *n* orthodoxie *f*.

orthography [ɔː'θɔgrəfi] *n* ortho-graphe *f*.

oscillate ['ɔsileit] *vi* osciller.

osier ['ouʒə] *n* osier *m*.

ostensible [ɔs'tensəbl] *a* soi-disant, prétendu.

ostentation [,ɔsten'teiʃən] *n* ostenta-tion *f*, faste *m*.

ostentatious [,ɔsten'teiʃəs] *a* fastueux.

ostler ['ɔslə] *n* garçon d'écurie *m*.

ostracize ['ɔstrəsaiz] *vt* òstraciser, mettre au ban.

ostrich ['ɔstritʃ] *n* autruche *f*.

other ['ʌðə] *an* *pn* autre; *pl* d'autres, les autres.

otherwise ['ʌðəwaiz] *ad* autrement, sans quoi.

otter ['ɔtə] *n* loutre *f*.

ought [ɔːt] *v aux* devoir.

ounce [auns] *n* once *f*.

our ['auə] *a* notre, nos; **—self,** (selves) *pn* nous-même(s), nous.

ours ['auəz] *pn* le, la, les nôtre(s), à nous, nôtre.

oust [aust] *vt* jeter dehors, évincer, supplanter.

out [aut] *ad* dehors, au dehors, au large, sur pied, en grève; *a* épuisé, à bout, sorti, éteint, éclos; **— of** *prep* hors de, à l'abri de, dans, à, par, d'entre, parmi.

outbid [aut'bid] *vt* (r)enchérir sur.

outboard ['autbɔːd] *an* hors bord *m*.

outbreak ['autbreik] *n* explosion *f*, éruption *f*, émeute *f*, accès *m*.

outbuilding ['autbildiŋ] *n* dépen-dance *f*, annexe *f*.

outburst ['autbəːst] *n* explosion *f*, éclat *m*, élan *m*.

outcast ['autkɑːst] *n* paria *m*, proscrit(e) *mf*, exilé(e) *mf*.

outclass [aut'klɑːs] *vt* surclasser, surpasser.

outcome ['autkʌm] *n* résultat *m*, issue *f*.

outcrop ['autkrɔp] *n* affleurement *m*.

outcry ['autkrai] *n* clameur *f*, tollé *m*.

outdo [aut'duː] *vt* surpasser.

outer ['autə] *a* plus éloigné, extérieur, externe.

outfall ['autfɔːl] *n* embouchure *f*.

outfit ['autfit] *n* équipement *m*, trousseau *m*, trousse *f*, attirail *m*, (US) équipe *f* d'ouvriers.

outflank [aut'flæŋk] *vt* déborder, circonvenir.

outflow ['autflou] *n* écoulement *m*, décharge *f*; *vi* provenir.

outgrow [aut'grou] *vt* dépasser, devenir trop grand pour, faire craquer.

outhouse ['authaus] *n* dépendance *f*.

outing ['autiŋ] *n* sortie *f*, excursion *f*.

outlandish [aut'lændiʃ] *a* étranger, étrange, barbare, écarté, reculé.

outlaw ['autlɔː] *n* hors-la-loi *m*, proscrit(e) *mf*; *vt* proscrire.

ouflay ['autlei] *n* dépenses *f pl*, frais *m pl*.

outlet ['autlet] *n* issue *f*, débouché *m*, départ *m*.

outline ['autlain] *n* contour *m*, esquisse *f*, silhouette *f*; *vt* esquisser, silhouetter.

outlive [aut'liv] *vt* survivre à.

outlook ['autluk] *n* (point *m* de) vue *f*, perspective *f*, philosophie *f*, aguets *m pl*.

outlying ['aut,laiiŋ] *a* éloigné, ex-centrique.

outmatch ['autmætʃ] *vt* (US) sur-passer en finesse.

outpost ['autpoust] *n* avant poste *m*.

outpouring ['aut,pɔːriŋ] *n* effusion *f*, débordement *m*.

output ['autput] *n* production *f*, rendement *m*.

outrage ['autreidʒ] *n* outrage *m*; *vt* outrager, violenter.

outrageous [aut'reidʒəs] *a* outra-geux, outrageant, excessif, indigne.

outrageously [aut'reidʒəsli] *ad* outre mesure, immodérément.

outright ['autrait] *a* net, direct; *ad* du (sur le) coup, complètement; *a* franc.

outset ['autset] *n* début *m*.

outshine [aut'ʃain] *vt* éclipser, dé-passer.

outside ['aut'said] *n* dehors *m*, impériale *f*, extérieur *m*, maximum *m*; *a* extérieur, du dehors; *ad* (en) dehors, à l'extérieur; *prep* hors de, en (au) dehors de.

outsider ['aut'saidə] *n* étranger, -ère, intrus(e) *mf*, outsider *m*.

outskirts ['autskəːts] *n* lisière *f*, banlieue *f*, faubourgs *m pl*.

outspoken [aut'spoukən] *a* franc, brutal, rond, entier.

outstanding [aut'stændiŋ] *a* émi-nent, marquant, en suspens, à recouvrer.

outstretch [aut'stretʃ] *vt* (é)tendre, déployer.

outstrip [aut'strip] *vt* dé-,sur-passer, distancer.

outward ['autwəd] *a* extérieur, de dehors, externe; *ad* pour l'étranger, vers le dehors.

outwards ['autwədz] *ad see* **outward**.

outwit [aut'wit] *vt* déjouer, rouler, dépister.

outworn [aut'wɔːn] *a* usé jusqu'à la corde, désuet.

oval ['ouvəl] *an* ovale *m*.

ovary ['ouvəri] *n* ovaire *m*.

ovation [ou'veiʃən] *n* ovation *f*.

oven ['ʌvn] *n* four *m*.

over ['ouvə] *prep* sur, contre, par dessus, au dessus de, plus de; *ad* au dessus, et plus, au delà, de trop, à l'excès.

overall ['ouvərɔːl] *n* salopette *f*, combinaison *f*, bleu *m* de travail, blouse *f*; *a* général.

overawe [,ouvər'ɔː] *vt* en imposer à, intimider.

overbalance [,ouvə'bæləns] *vi* perdre l'équilibre; *vt* renverser.

overbearing [,ouvə'bɛəriŋ] *a* arrogant, autoritaire.

overboard ['ouvəbɔːd] *ad* par dessus bord, à la mer.

overcast ['ouvəkɑːst] *a* couvert, assombri.

overcharge ['ouvə'tʃɑːdʒ] *n* majoration *f*, prix excessif *m*, surcharge *f*; *vt* surfaire, faire payer trop cher à, surcharger.

overcoat ['ouvəkout] *n* pardessus *m*.

overcome [,ouvə'kʌm] *vt* surmonter, dominer, venir à bout de, triompher de, vaincre, accabler.

overdo [,ouvə'duː] *vt* exagérer, outrer, trop cuire.

overdose ['ouvədous] *n* dose excessive *f*.

overdraft ['ouvədrɑːft] *n* dépassement de crédit *m*, découvert *m*.

overdraw ['ouvə'drɔː] *vt* tirer à découvert, charger.

overdrive ['ouvə'draiv] *n* vitesse surmultipliée *f*.

overdue ['ouvə'djuː] *a* en retard, périmé, échu.

overestimate ['ouvər'estimeit] *vt* surestimer.

overflow ['ouvəflou] *n* trop plein *m*, déversoir *m*; [ouvə'flou] *vi* déborder; *vt* inonder.

overflowing [,ouvə'flouiŋ] *n* débordement *m*, inondation *f*; *a* débordant.

overgrow ['ouvə'grou] *vt* envahir; *vi* trop grandir.

overhang ['ouvə'hæŋ] *vt* surplomber.

overhaul ['ouvəhɔːl] *vt* réviser, remettre en état, rattraper; *n* remise en état *f*, révision *f*, examen détaillé *m*.

overhead ['ouvəhed] *a ad* aérien; *n pl* frais généraux *m pl*.

overhear [,ouvə'hiə] *vt* surprendre.

overheat ['ouvə'hiːt] *vt* surchauffer.

overjoyed [,ouvə'dʒɔid] *a* transporté de joie, enchanté.

overland ['ouvəlænd] *a ad* par voie de terre.

overlap ['ouvəlæp] *vt* chevaucher; *vi* se chevaucher.

overleaf ['ouvə'liːf] *ad* au revers, au verso.

overlook [,ouvə'luk] *vt* avoir vue sur, dominer, oublier, laisser passer, négliger, surveiller.

overmuch ['ouvə'mʌtʃ] *ad* par trop, excessif.

overpass ['ouvəpɑːs] *n* enjambement *m*.

overpopulated ['ouvə'pɔpjuleitid] *a* surpeuplé.

overpower [,ouvə'pauə] *vt* terrasser, subjuger, maîtriser, accabler.

overpowering [,ouvə'pauəriŋ] *a* irrésistible, accablant.

overproduction ['ouvəprə'dʌkʃən] surproduction *f*.

overrate ['ouvə'reit] *vt* surfaire, surtaxer, présumer de.

overreach [,ouvə'riːtʃ] *vt* duper, dépasser; **to — oneself** se surmener, se donner un effort.

overri ..... trop fait, blet.

overrule [,ouvə'ruːl] *vt* annuler par autorité supérieure, casser, passer outre à.

overrun [,ouvə'rʌn] *vt* envahir, infester, excéder, dépasser, mener.

oversea(s) ['ouvə'siː(z)] *a* d'outremer; *ad* outre-mer.

oversee ['ouvə'siː] *vt* surveiller.

overseer ['ouvəsiə] *n* surveillant(e) *mf*, contremaître, -tresse.

overshadow [,ouvə'ʃædou] *vt* ombrager, éclipser.

overshoes ['ouvəʃuːz] *n pl* caoutchoucs *m pl*.

overshoot ['ouvə'ʃuːt] *vi* tirer trop loin; *vt* dépasser.

oversight ['ouvəsait] *n* inadvertance *f*, oubli *m*.

overspill ['ouvəspil] *n* déversement *m* de population.

overstate ['ouvə'steit] *vt* exagérer.

overstatement ['ouvə'steitmənt] *n* exagération *f*.

overstep ['ouvə'step] *vt* outrepasser, dépasser.

overstrain ['ouvəstrein] *vt* tendre à l'excès, surmener.

overstrung ['ouvə'strʌŋ] *a* hypertendu.

overt ['ouvəːt] *a* public, évident.

overtake [,ouvə'teik] *vt* dépasser, doubler, rattraper, surprendre.

overthrow [,ouvə'θrou] *vt* renverser, mettre à bas.

overtime ['ouvətaim] *n* heures supplémentaires *f pl*; *ad* au delà du temps normal.

overtly ['ouvəːtli] *ad* au grand jour.

overture ['ouvətjuə] *n* ouverture *f*.

overturn ['ouvətəːn] *vt* tourner sens dessus dessous, renverser; *vi* verser, chavirer, se renverser, capoter.

overvaluation ['ouvə,vælju'eiʃən] *n* surestimation *f*.

overvalue ['ouvə'væljuː] *vt* surestimer.

overweening [,ouvə'wiːniŋ] *a* présomptueux.

overweight ['ouvə'weit] *n* excédent *m*, prépondérance *f*.

overwhelm [,ouvə'welm] *vt* accabler, écraser, combler.

overwork ['ouvə'wəːk] n surmenage m.

overwork ['ouvə'wəːk] vt surmener; vi se surmener.

overwrought ['ouvə'rɔːt] a surmené, surexcité.

owe [ou] vt devoir.

owing ['ouiŋ] a dû; — to grâce à.

owl [aul] n hibou m, chouette f.

owlish ['auliʃ] a solennel, prétentieux, de hibou.

own [oun] a propre, à moi etc; vt posséder, admettre, reconnaître, avouer.

ownership ['ounəʃip] n propriété f, possession f.

ox [ɔks] (pl oxen) n bœuf m.

oxide ['ɔksaid] n oxyde m.

oxidize ['ɔksidaiz] vt oxyder; vi s'oxyder.

oxygen ['ɔksidʒən] n oxygène m.

oxygenate [ɔk'sidʒineit] vt oxygéner.

oyster ['ɔistə] n huître f; — bed banc d'huîtres m.

P

pace [peis] n pas m, allure f, vitesse f; vt arpenter, mesurer au pas, entraîner; vi marcher (à pas mesurés).

pacific [pə'sifik] a pacifique, paisible; n Pacifique m.

pacification [ˌpæsifi'keiʃən] n pacification f.

pacifier ['pæsifaiə] n pacificateur, -trice.

pacifism ['pæsifizəm] n pacifisme m.

pacifist ['pæsifist] n pacifiste mf.

pacify ['pæsifai] vt pacifier, apaiser.

pack [pæk] n paquet m, ballot m, jeu m (de cartes), bande f, meute f; ——ice banquise f; vt empaqueter, emballer, envelopper, entasser, bourrer; vi se presser, s'attrouper, se tasser, faire ses malles.

package ['pækidʒ] n empaquetage m, paquet m; — tour voyage organisé m.

packer ['pækə] n emballeur m.

packet ['pækit] n paquet m, colis m, paquebot m.

packing ['pækiŋ] n emballage m, tassement m.

pact [pækt] n pacte m.

pad [pæd] n bourrelet m, tampon m, coussin m, sous-main m, (paper) bloc m, (fam) pieu m; vt rembourrer, capitonner, garnir.

padding ['pædiŋ] n rembourrage m, capitonnage m, remplissage m.

paddle ['pædl] n pagaie f, palette f, aube f; vti pagayer; vi patauger, barboter, faire trempette.

paddock ['pædək] n pré m, paddock m, pesage m.

padlock ['pædlɔk] n cadenas m; vt cadenasser.

pagan ['peigən] an païen, -ienne.

paganism ['peigənizəm] n paganisme m.

page [peidʒ] n page f, (boy) page m, chasseur m, groom m; vt paginer.

pageant ['pædʒənt] n cortège m, cavalcade f, fête f, spectacle m.

pail(ful) ['peil(ful)] n seau m.

pain [pein] n peine f, douleur f; vt faire mal à, faire de la peine à.

painful ['peinful] a douloureux, pénible.

pain-killer ['peinkilə] n calmant m, anodin m.

painless ['peinlis] a indolore, sans douleur.

painstaking ['peinzˌteikiŋ] a laborieux, assidu, soigné.

paint [peint] n peinture f; vti peindre; vi faire de la peinture.

painter ['peintə] n peintre m, peintre décorateur m.

pair [peə] n paire f, couple mf; vt accoupler, apparier, assortir.

pal [pæl] n copain m, copine f.

palace ['pælis] n palais m.

palatable ['pælətəbl] a délectable, agréable.

palate ['pælit] n palais m.

palaver [pə'lɑːvə] n palabre f; vi palabrer.

pale [peil] n pieu m, pal m; a pâle; vi pâlir.

palette ['pælit] n palette f.

paling ['peiliŋ] n palissade f, clôture f.

palish ['peiliʃ] a pâlot.

pall [pɔːl] n drap mortuaire m, voile m; vi s'affadir, se blaser.

pallbearer ['pɔːlˌbeərə] n qui tient un cordon du poêle.

pallet ['pælit] n paillasse f.

palliate ['pælieit] vt pallier, atténuer.

palliative ['pæliətiv] an palliatif m.

pallid ['pælid] a blême, pâle.

palm [pɑːm] n paume f, palmier m, palme f, rameau m; P— Sunday dimanche des Rameaux; —-nut noix f de palme; — wine vin n de palme; vt escamoter; to — off repasser, refiler.

palmist ['pɑːmist] n chiromancien, -ienne.

palmistry ['pɑːmistri] n chiromancie f.

palmy ['pɑːmi] a triomphant, beau, heureux.

palpable ['pælpəbl] a palpable, évident.

palpitate ['pælpiteit] vi palpiter.

palsy ['pɔːlzi] n paralysie f.

paltry ['pɔːltri] a mesquin, pauvre, malheureux.

pamper ['pæmpə] vt dorloter, gâter.

pamphlet ['pæmflit] n brochure f, opuscule m.

pamphleteer [ˌpæmfli'tiə] n publiciste m, auteur m de brochures.

pan [pæn] n casserole f, sauteuse f, poêle f, bac m; to — out se passer, s'arranger.

panacea [,pænə'siə] n panacée f.

pancake ['pænkeik] n crêpe f.

pandemonium [,pændi'mouniəm] n charivari m, tapage infernal m.

pander ['pændə] **to — to** se prêter à, encourager.

pane [pein] n carreau m, vitre f.

panel ['pænl] n tableau m, panneau m, lambris m, jury m; vt lambrisser, plaquer.

panelling ['pænliŋ] n lambrissage m.

pang [pæŋ] n serrement de cœur m, douleur f; **—s of death** affres de la mort f pl.

panic ['pænik] an panique f; vi s'affoler; **—monger** n fauteur m de panique, paniquard m.

panicky ['pæniki] a alarmiste, qui s'affole pour rien.

panoply ['pænəpli] n panoplie f.

pansy ['pænzi] n pensée f.

pant [pænt] vi haleter, panteler, aspirer (à **after**).

panties ['pæntiz] n pl slip m, culotte f.

pantheism ['pænθiizəm] n panthéisme m.

panther ['pænθə] n panthère f.

pantry ['pæntri] n office m, garde-manger m.

pants [pænts] n caleçon m, (US) pantalon m.

pap [pæp] n tétin m, mamelon m, bouillie f.

papacy ['peipəsi] n papauté f.

paper ['peipə] n papier m, journal m, article m, essai m, épreuve f, copie f; vt tapisser; **—hanger** n colleur de papier m; **—knife** n coupe-papier m; **—weight** n presse-papier m; **—clip** n trombone m; pince f.

papermill ['peipəmil] n papeterie f.

papist ['peipist] n papiste mf.

par [pɑː] n égalité f, pair m, moyenne f.

parable ['pærəbl] n parabole f.

parachute ['pærəʃuːt] n parachute m.

parachutist ['pærəʃuːtist] n parachutiste mf.

parade [pə'reid] n parade f, revue f, défilé m; vt faire étalage de, faire défiler, passer en revue; vi défiler, parader.

paradise ['pærədais] n paradis m.

paradox ['pærədɔks] n paradoxe m.

paradoxical [,pærə'dɔksikəl] a paradoxal.

paraffin ['pærəfin] n paraffine f, pétrole m.

paragon ['pærəgən] n parangon m.

paragraph ['pærəgrɑːf] n paragraphe m, alinéa m, entrefilet m.

parakeet ['pærəkiːt] n perruche f.

parallel ['pærəlel] a parallèle, pareil; n parallèle mf; vt mettre en parallèle, comparer.

paralyse ['pærəlaiz] vt paralyser.

paralysis [pə'rælisis] n paralysie f.

paramount ['pærəmaunt] a suprême.

parapet ['pærəpit] n parapet m, garde-fou m.

paraphernalia [,pærəfə'neiljə] n attirail m, boutique f, bataclan m, affaires f pl.

paraphrase ['pærəfreiz] n paraphrase f; vt paraphraser.

parasite ['pærəsait] n parasite m, pique-assiette m.

paratrooper ['pærətruːpə] n parachutiste m.

parasol ['pærəsɔl] n parasol m, ombrelle f.

parcel ['pɑːsl] n paquet m, colis m, parcelle f, bande f; vt morceler, emballer.

parch [pɑːtʃ] vt rôtir, (des)sécher, griller.

parchment ['pɑːtʃmənt] n parchemin m.

parde [pɑːd] n (US) libération f conditionnelle.

pardon ['pɑːdn] n pardon m; vt pardonner.

pardonable ['pɑːdnəbl] a pardonnable, excusable.

pare [pɛə] vt peler, rogner, tailler.

parent ['pɛərənt] n père m, mère f; pl parents m pl.

parentage ['pɛərəntidʒ] n extraction f, naissance f.

parenthesis [pə'renθisis] n parenthèse f.

pariah ['pæriə] n paria m.

parish ['pæriʃ] n paroisse f.

parishioner [pə'riʃənə] n paroissien, -ienne.

Parisian [pə'riziən] an parisien.

park [pɑːk] n parc m, jardin public m; vt parquer; vi stationner.

parking ['pɑːkiŋ] n stationnement m, parcage m; **— meter** n parcomètre m, compteur m.

parley ['pɑːli] n pourparlers m pl; vi parlementer, entrer en pourparlers.

parliament ['pɑːləmənt] n parlement m.

parliamentary [,pɑːlə'mentəri] a parlementaire.

parlour ['pɑːlə] n salle f, petit salon m, parloir m, (US) salon de coiffure m.

parochial [pə'roukiəl] a paroissial, étroit.

parochialism [pə'roukiəlizem] n esprit de clocher m.

parody ['pærədi] n parodie f, pastiche m; vt parodier, pasticher

parole [pə'roul] n parole f.

paroxysm ['pærəksizəm] n paroxysme m, crise f.

parricide ['pærisaid] n parricide (crime) m, (person) mf.

parrot ['pærət] n perroquet m.

parry ['pæri] n parade f; vt parer, détourner.

parse [pɑːz] vt analyser.

parsimonious [ˌpɑːsiˈmouniəs] *a* parcimonieux, ladre.

parsimony [ˈpɑːsiməni] *n* parcimonie *f*, ladrerie *f*.

parsley [ˈpɑːsli] *n* persil *m*.

parsnip [ˈpɑːsnip] *n* panais *m*.

parson [ˈpɑːsn] *n* prêtre *m* pasteur *m*.

parsonage [ˈpɑːsnidʒ] *n* cure *f*, presbytère *m*.

part [pɑːt] *n* partie *f*, parti *m*, région *f*, (theatre) rôle *m*, côté *m*; *vt* diviser, séparer; *vi* se séparer, se rompre; **to — with** céder, se séparer de.

partake [pɑːˈteik] **to — of** participer à, prendre part à, partager, tenir de, sentir.

partial [ˈpɑːʃəl] *a* partial, qui a un faible (pour to).

partiality [ˌpɑːʃiˈæliti] *n* partialité *f*, penchant *m*.

participate [pɑːˈtisipeit] *vi* participer (à, de in).

participation [pɑːˌtisiˈpeiʃən] *n* participation *f*.

participle [ˈpɑːtsipl] *n* participe *m*.

particle [ˈpɑːtikl] *n* particule *f*, parcelle *f*, brin *m*, semblant *m*.

particular [pəˈtikjulə] *a* spécial, minutieux, difficile; *n pl* détails *m pl*, renseignements *m pl*.

particularity [pəˌtikjuˈlæriti] *n* particularité *f*, minutie *f*.

particularize [pəˈtikjuləraiz] *vt* spécifier; *vi* préciser.

parting [ˈpɑːtiŋ] *n* séparation *f*, rupture *f*, (hair) raie *f*, (ways) croisée *f*; *a* de départ, d'adieu.

partisan [ˌpɑːtiˈzæn] *n* partisan *m*.

partition [pɑːˈtiʃən] *n* partage *m*, démembrement *m*, morcellement *m*, cloison *f*; *vt* démembrer, morceler, partager, cloisonner.

partner [ˈpɑːtnə] *n* partenaire *mf*, associé(e) *mf*, cavalier *m*, danseuse *f*; *vt* associer, être associé à mener, être le partenaire de

partnership [ˈpɑːtnəʃip] *n* association *f*, société *f*.

partridge [ˈpɑːtridʒ] *n* perdrix *f*.

part-time [ˈpɑːtˈtaim] *a* à mi-temps.

party [ˈpɑːti] *n* parti *m*, réception *f*, partie *f*, bande *f*, détachement *m*.

pass [pɑːs] *n* défilé *m*, col *m*, permission *f*, passe *f*, (school) moyenne *f*; *vt* (faire) passer, passer près de, disparaître, dépasser, franchir, doubler, voter, approuver, réussir à (un examen), recevoir; *vi* passer, s'écouler, se passer être reçu.

passable [ˈpɑːsəbl] *a* passable, praticable, traversable.

passage [ˈpæsidʒ] *n* passage *m*, corridor *m*, échange *m*, passe d'armes *f*, traversée *f*.

pass-book [ˈpɑːsbuk] *n* carnet de comptes *m*.

passenger [ˈpæsindʒə] *n* passager, -ère, voyageur, -euse.

passer-by [ˈpɑːsəˈbai] *n* passant(e) *mf*.

passing [ˈpɑːsiŋ] *n* passage *m*, mort *f*, écoulement *m*; *a* passager, fugitif.

passion [ˈpæʃən] *n* passion *f*, colère *f*.

passionate [ˈpæʃənit] *a* ardent, passionné, irascible

passionately [ˈpæʃənitli] *ad* passionnément.

passive [ˈpæsiv] *a* passif.

passiveness [ˈpæsivnis] *n* passivité *f*, inertie *f*.

pass-key [ˈpɑːskiː] *n* passe-partout *m*.

passport [ˈpɑːspɔːt] *n* passeport *m*.

password [ˈpɑːswɔːd] *n* mot de passe *m*.

past [pɑːst] *an* passé *m*; *a* ancien, ex—; *prep* après, au delà de, plus loin que

paste [peist] *n* pâte *f*, colle *f*; *vt* coller (fam) rosser.

pasteboard [ˈpeistbɔːd] *n* carton *m*.

pastel [ˈpæstəl] *n* pastel *m*.

pasteurize [ˈpæstəraiz] *vt* pasteuriser.

pastime [ˈpɑːstaim] *n* passetemps *m*, distraction *f*.

pastor [ˈpɑːstə] *n* pasteur *m*.

pastoral [ˈpɑːstərəl] *a* pastoral.

pastry [ˈpeistri] *n* pâtisserie *f*, pâte *f*; **—cook** *n* pâtissier, -ière; **—shop** *n* pâtisserie *f*.

pasture [ˈpɑːstʃə] *n* pâture *f*, pâturage *m*, pacage *m*; *vt* faire paître.

pasty [ˈpeisti] *n* pâté *m*; *a* pâteux, terreux.

pat [pæt] *n* tape *f*, coquille *f*, motte *f*, rondelle *f*; *vt* tapoter caresser; *ad* à point, du tac au tac, tout prêt.

patch [pætʃ] *n* pièce *f*, emplâtre *m*, mouche *f*, tache *f*, (peas) planche *f*, carré *m*; *vt* rapiécer; **to — up** replâtrer, rafistoler.

patchwork [ˈpætʃwɔːk] *n* rapiéçage *m*, mosaïque *f*.

patchy [ˈpætʃi] *a* fait de pièces et de morceaux, inégal, irrégulier.

paten [ˈpætən] *n* patène *f*.

patent [ˈpeitənt] *n* brevet *m*, lettres patentes *pl*; *a* breveté, patenté, manifeste; *vt* faire breveter.

paternal [pəˈtəːnl] *a* paternel.

paternity [pəˈtəːniti] *n* paternité *f*.

path [pɑːθ] *n* sentier *m*, course *f*, chemin *m*.

pathetic [pəˈθetik] *a* pathétique, triste, attendrissant.

pathfinder [ˈpɑːθˌfaində] *n* éclaireur *m*, pionnier *m*.

patience [ˈpeiʃəns] *n* patience *f*, (cards) réussite *f*.

patient [ˈpeiʃənt] *n* malade *mf*, patient(e) *mf*; *a* patient.

patiently [ˈpeiʃəntli] *ad* patiemment, avec patience.

patriarch [ˈpeitriɑːk] *n* patriarche *m*.

patriarchal [,peitri'ɑːkəl] *a* patriarcal.

Patrick ['pætrik] Patrice *m.*

patrimony ['pætriməni] *n* patrimoine *m.*

patriot ['peitriət] *n* patriote *mf.*

patriotic [,pætri'ɔtik] *a* patriotique, (*person*) patriote.

patriotism ['pætriətizəm] *n* patriotisme *m.*

patrol [pə'troul] *n* patrouille *f*, ronde *f*; *vti* patrouiller.

patron, -ess ['peitrən, is] *n* patron, -onne, protecteur, -trice, client(e) *mf*, habitué(e) *mf.*

patronage ['pætrənidʒ] *n* patronage *m*, protection *f*, clientèle *f*, airs protecteurs *m pl.*

patronize ['pætrənaiz] *vt* patronner, protéger, traiter de haut, accorder sa clientèle à, se fournir chez.

patter ['pætə] *n* crépitement *m*, trottinement *m*, piétinement *m*, fouettement *m*, bagout *m*, boniment *m*; *vi* crépiter, trottiner, jaser.

pattern ['pætən] *n* modèle *m*, échantillon *m*, dessin *m.*

patty ['pæti] *n* petit pâté *m.*

paucity ['pɔːsiti] *n* rareté *f*, disette *f*, manque *m.*

Paul [pɔːl] Paul *m.*

paunch ['pɔːntʃ] *n* panse *f*, bedaine *f.*

pauper ['pɔːpə] *n* indigent(e) *mf*, mendiant(e) *mf.*

pause [pɔːz] *n* pause *f*, arrêt *m*, silence *m*, point d'orgue *m*; *vi* s'arrêter, faire la pause, hésiter.

pave [peiv] *vt* paver, carreler, frayer (la voie).

pavement ['peivmənt] *n* pavé *m*, pavage *m*, trottoir *m*; (US) chaussée *f.*

pavilion [pə'viljən] *n* tente *f*, pavillon *m.*

paw [pɔː] *n* patte *f*; *vt* frapper du pied, tripoter; *vi* piaffer.

pawn [pɔːn] *n* pion *m*, gage *m*; *vt* mettre en gage.

pawnbroker ['pɔːn,broukə] *n* prêteur *m* sur gages.

pawnshop ['pɔːnʃɔp] *n* mont-depiété *m*; (*fam*) tante *f.*

pawpaw ['pɔːpɔː] *n* papaye *f.*

pay [pei] *n* paie *f*, gages *m pl*, salaire *m*, solde *f*; *vt* payer, rétribuer, acquitter, faire; — *in* verser, encaisser; — **a visit** rendre visite (à **to**).

payer ['peiə] *n* payeur, -euse, payant(e) *mf.*

paying-guest ['peiiŋ,gest] *n* hôte payant *m.*

paymaster ['pei,mɑːstə] *n* trésorier *m*, payeur *m.*

payment ['peimənt] *n* paiement *m*, rémunération *f*, règlement *m*, versement *m.*

pea [piː] *n* pois *m*; **green — s** petits pois; **sweet —** pois de senteur.

peace [piːs] *n* paix *f.*

peaceful ['piːsful] *a* paisible, pacifique.

peacefulness ['piːsfulnis] *n* paix *f*, humeur paisible *f.*

peacemaker ['piːs,meikə] *n* pacificateur, -trice.

peach [piːtʃ] *n* pêche *f.*

peach-tree ['piːtʃtriː] *n* pêcher *m.*

peacock ['piːkɔk] *n* paon *m.*

peahen ['piːhen] *n* paonne *f.*

peak [piːk] *n* pic *m*, cime *f*, pointe *f*, visière *f*, apogée *f*, plus fort *m*; *a* maximum, de pointe.

peaked [piːkt] *a* à (en) pointe, pointu, hâve.

peal [piːl] *n* carillon *m*, volée de cloches *f*, coup *m*, grondement *m*; *vti* sonner; *vi* carillonner, gronder.

peanut ['piːnʌt] *n* caca(h)ouète *f.*

pear [pɛə] *n* poire *f.*

pearl [pəːl] *n* perle *f.*

pearly ['pəːli] *a* nacré, perlé.

pear-tree ['pɛətriː] *n* poirier *m.*

peasant ['pezənt] *n* paysan, -anne.

peasantry ['pezəntri] *n* paysannerie *f.*

peat [piːt] *n* tourbe *f*; — **bog** tourbière.

pebble ['pebl] *n* galet *m*, caillou *m.*

peck [pek] *n* coup de bec *m*, bécot *m*; *vt* picoter, donner un coup de bec à, bécoter; *vti* manger du bout des lèvres; *vi* picorer.

pecker ['pekə] *n* **to keep one's — up** ne pas se laisser décourager.

peculiar [pi'kjuːliə] *a* particulier, excentrique, singulier.

peculiarity [pi,kjuːli'æriti] *n* singularité *f*, particularité *f.*

pecuniary [pi'kjuːniəri] *a* pécuniaire, d'argent.

pedal ['pedl] *n* pédale *f*; *vi* pédaler.

pedant ['pedənt] *n* pédant(e) *mf.*

pedantic [pi'dæntik] *a* pédantesque, pédant.

pedantry ['pedəntri] *n* pédantisme *m.*

peddle ['pedl] *vt* colporter; *vi* faire le colportage.

pedestrian [pi'destriən] *n* piéton *m*; *a* à pied, terre à terre, banal; — **crossing** passage clouté *m.*

pedigree ['pedigriː] *n* généalogie *f*, pedigree *m.*

pediment ['pedimənt] *n* fronton *m.*

pedlar ['pedlə] *n* colporteur *m*, porteballe *m*; **itinerant —** dioula *m.*

peel [piːl] *n* peau *f*, écorce *f*, pelure *f*; *vti* peler; *vt* éplucher; *vi* s'écailler.

peep [piːp] *n* coup d'œil *m*, point du jour *m*, pépiement *m*, piaulement *m*; *vi* pépier, risquer un coup d'œil, se montrer; —**hole** *n* judas *m.*

peer [piə] *n* pair *m*, pareil, -eille, égal(e) *mf*; *vi* risquer un coup d'œil; **to — at** scruter.

peerage ['piəridʒ] *n* pairie *f.*

peerless ['piəlis] *a* incomparable, sans pareil.

peevish ['piːviʃ] *a* bougon, revêche, irritable, maussade.

peevishness ['piːviʃnis] *n* humeur bourrue *f*.

peg [peg] *n* cheville *f*, patère *f*, piquet *m*; **to come down a —** en rabattre; *vt* cheviller, marquer, accrocher; **— away** bûcher.

pellet ['pelit] *n* boulette *f*, pilule *f*, grain de plomb *m*.

pelt [pelt] *n* peau *f*; **at full —** à toutes jambes; *vt* bombarder; *vi* (*rain*) tomber à verse.

pen [pen] *n* parc *m*, plume *f*, stylo *m*; *vt* enfermer, parquer, écrire.

penal ['piːnl] *a* pénal, punissable; **— servitude** *n* travaux forcés *m pl*.

penalty ['penlti] *n* amende *f*, peine *f*, sanction *f*, pénalité *f*; (*football*) penalty *m*; inconvénient *m*, rançon *f*.

penance ['penəns] *n* pénitence *f*.

pencil ['pensl] *n* crayon *m*, faisceau *m*; *vt* crayonner, marquer au crayon.

pendant ['pendənt] *n* pendant(if) *m*, pendeloque *f*, (*flag*) flamme *f*.

pending ['pendiŋ] *prep* pendant, en attendant.

pendulum ['pendjuləm] *n* pendule *m*, balancier *m*.

penetrate ['penitreit] *vti* pénétrer.

penetrating ['penitreitiŋ] *a* pénétrant, perçant.

penguin ['peŋgwin] *n* pingouin *m*.

penholder ['pen,houldə] *n* porte-plume *m*.

penicillin [,peni'silin] *n* pénicilline *f*.

peninsula [pi'ninsjulə] *n* péninsule *f*.

penitence ['penitəns] *n* pénitence *f*.

penitent ['penitənt] *an* pénitent(e) *mf*; *a* contrit.

penitentiary [,peni'tenʃəri] *n* pénitencier *m*, prison *f*.

penknife ['pennaif] *n* canif *m*.

pen-name ['penneim] *n* pseudonyme *m*.

pennant ['penənt] *n* flamme *f*, banderole *f*.

penniless ['penilis] *a* sans le sou.

penny ['peni] *n* sou *m*, deux sous *m pl*; **—worth** pour deux sous; **—wise** *a* lésineur.

pension ['penʃən] *n* pension *f*, retraite *f*; *vt* pensionner; **to — off** mettre à la retraite.

pensive ['pensiv] *a* pensif.

pensiveness ['pensivnis] *n* rêverie *f*, air rêveur *m*.

pent [pent] *a* **— in** renfermé, confiné; **— up** contenu, refoulé.

Pentecost ['pentikɔst] *n* Pentecôte *f*.

penthouse ['penthaus] *n* appentis *m*, auvent *m*.

penurious [pi'njuəriəs] *a* pauvre, avare.

penury ['penjuri] *n* pénurie *f*, misère *f*.

peony ['piəni] *n* pivoine *f*.

people ['piːpl] *n* peuple *m*, habitants *m pl*, gens *m pl*, personnes *f pl*, monde *m*, famille *f*, on, vous; *vt* peupler.

pep [pep] *n* vigueur *f*, allant *m*; **to — up** remonter.

pepper ['pepə] *n* poivre *m*; *vt* poivrer, cribler.

pepper-box, -pot ['pepəbɔks, -pɔt] *n* poivrière *f*.

peppermint ['pepəmint] *n* menthe poivrée *f*.

peppery ['pepəri] *a* poivré, emporté, colérique.

pep-pill ['pep'pil] *n* remontant *m*.

per [pəː] *prep* par, pour, à, par l'entremise de.

peradventure [pərəd'ventʃə] *ad* d'aventure, par hasard.

perambulate [pə'ræmbjuleit] *vi* déambuler, se promener.

perambulator ['præmbjuleitə] *n* voiture d'enfant *f*.

perceive [pə'siːv] *vt* percevoir, comprendre, s'apercevoir (de).

percentage [pə'sentidʒ] *n* pourcentage *m*, proportion *f*.

perceptible [pə'septəbl] *a* perceptible, sensible.

perception [pə'sepʃən] *n* perception *f*.

perch [pəːtʃ] *n* perche *f*, perchoir *m*; *vi* se percher, se jucher.

perchance [pə'tʃɑːns] *ad* par hasard.

percolate ['pəːkəleit] *vt* filtrer.

percolator ['pəːkəleitə] *n* percolateur *m*, filtre *m*.

percussion [pəː'kʌʃən] *n* percussion *f*, choc *m*.

perdition [pəː'diʃən] *n* ruine *f*, perte *f*.

peremptory [pə'remptəri] *a* péremptoire, catégorique, absolu.

perennial [pə'reniəl] *a* perpétuel, vivace.

perfect ['pəːfikt] *a* parfait.

perfect [pə'fekt] *vt* perfectionner, parfaire, achever.

perfection [pə'fekʃən] *n* perfection *f*.

perfidious [pəː'fidiəs] *a* perfide, traître.

perfidy ['pəːfidi] *n* perfidie *f*.

perforate ['pəːfəreit] *vt* perforer, percer.

perforation [,pəːfə'reiʃən] *n* perforation *f*, percement *m*.

perforce [pə'fɔːs] *ad* de (par) force.

perform [pə'fɔːm] *vt* remplir, exécuter; *vti* jouer.

performance [pə'fɔːməns] *n* exécution *f*, (*theatre*) représentation *f*, (*cine*) séance *f*, exploit *m*, fonctionnement *m*, performance *f*.

performer [pə'fɔːmə] *n* exécutant(e) *mf*, artiste *mf*.

perfume ['pəːfjuːm] *n* parfum *m*.

perfume [pə'fjuːm] *vt* parfumer.

perfumery [pə'fjuːməri] *n* parfumerie *f*.

perfunctory [pə'fʌŋktəri] *a* de pure forme, superficiel, négligent.

perhaps [pə'hæps] *ad* peut-être.

peril ['peril] *n* péril *m*, danger *m*; **at your —** à vos risques et périls.

perilous ['periləs] *a* périlleux, dangereux.

period ['piəriəd] *n* période *f*, délai *m*, époque *f*, point *m*, phase *f*, style *m*; *pl (med)* règles *f pl*.

perish ['periʃ] *vi* périr, mourir, se détériorer.

perishable ['periʃəbl] *a* périssable, éphémère.

perished ['periʃt] *a* mort, détérioré.

peritonitis [.peritə'naitis] *n* péritonite *f*.

periwinkle ['peri.wiŋkl] *n* pervenche *f*, bigorneau *m*.

perjure ['pə:dʒə] *vt* **to — oneself** se parjurer.

perjurer ['pə:dʒərə] *n* parjure *mf*.

perjury ['pə:dʒəri] *n* parjure *m*, faux témoignage *m*.

perk [pə:k] *vt* **to — up** ravigoter, remettre le moral à; *vi* se ranimer, se retaper; *n (fam) see* **perquisite**.

perky ['pə:ki] *a* impertinent, coquet, dégagé, guilleret.

perm(anent-wave) ['pə:m(ənənt 'weiv)] *n* (ondulation *f*) permanente.

permanent ['pə:mənənt] *a* permanent, fixe.

permanently ['pə:mənəntli] *ad* de façon permanente, à titre définitif.

permeable ['pə:miəbl] *a* perméable.

permeate ['pə:mieit] *vt* pénétrer; *vi* s'insinuer, filtrer.

permission [pə'miʃən] *n* permission *f*, autorisation *f*.

permit ['pə:mit] *n* permis *m*, autorisation *f*.

permit [pə'mit] *vt* permettre (à), autoriser.

pernicious [pə:'niʃəs] *a* pernicieux, fatal.

perpendicular [.pə:pən'dikjulə] *an* perpendiculaire *f*.

perpetrate ['pə:pitreit] *vt* commettre, perpétrer.

perpetration [.pə:pi'treiʃən] *n* perpétration *f*.

perpetrator ['pə:pitreitə] *n* auteur *m*.

perpetual [pə'petjuəl] *a* éternel, perpétuel.

perpetuate [pə'petjueit] *vt* perpétuer.

perpetuity [.pə:pi'tju(:)iti] *n* perpétuité *f*.

perplex [pə'pleks] *vt* embarrasser.

perplexed [pə'plekst] *a* perplexe, embarrassé.

perplexity [pə'pleksiti] *n* perplexité *f*.

perquisite ['pe:kwizit] *n* profit *m*, pourboire *m*, casuel *m*, gratte *f*.

persecute ['pə:sikju:t] *vt* persécuter.

persecution [.pə:si'kju:ʃən] *n* persécution *f*.

perseverance [.pə:si'viərəns] *n* persévérance *f*.

persevere [.pə:si'viə] *vi* persévérer, s'obstiner.

persevering [.pə:si'viəriŋ] *a* persévérant, assidu.

Persia ['pə:ʃə] *n* Perse *f*.

Persian ['pə:ʃən] *n* Persan(e) *mf*; *an* persan *m*.

persist [pə'sist] *vi* persister, s'obstiner, s'entêter.

persistency [pə'sistənsi] *n* persistance *f*, obstination *f*.

person ['pə:sn] *n* personne *f*.

personage ['pə:snidʒ] *n* personnage *m*.

personal ['pə:snl] *a* personnel, individuel.

personality [.pə:sə'næliti] *n* personnalité *f*, personnage *m*.

personification [pə:.sɔnifi'keiʃən] *n* personnification *f*.

personify [pə:'sɔnifai] *vt* personnifier.

personnel [.pə:sə'nel] *n* personnel *m*.

perspective [pə'spektiv] *n* perspective *f*.

perspicacious [.pə:spi'keiʃəs] *a* perspicace.

perspicacity [.pə:spi'kæsiti] *n* perspicacité *f*.

perspicuity [.pə:spi'kju(:)iti] *n* clarté *f*, netteté *f*.

perspicuous [pə'spikjuəs] *a* clair, évident.

perspiration [.pə:spə'reiʃən] *n* transpiration *f*.

perspire [pəs'paiə] *vi* transpirer.

persuade [pə'sweid] *vt* persuader, décider.

persuasion [pə'sweiʒən] *n* persuasion *f*, conviction *f*, confession *f*.

persuasive [pə'sweisiv] *a* persuasif.

pert [pə:t] *a* effronté, impertinent.

pertinacious [.pə:ti'neiʃəs] *a* opiniâtre, entêté, obstiné.

pertinacity [.pə:ti'næsiti] *n* opiniâtreté *f*.

pertinence ['pə:tinəns] *n* pertinence *f*, à-propos *m*.

pertinent ['pə:tinənt] *a* pertinent, juste.

pertinently ['pə:tinəntli] *ad* pertinemment, à-propos.

perturb [pə'tə:b] *vt* bouleverser, troubler, inquiéter.

perturbation [.pə:tə:'beiʃən] *n* bouleversement *m*, inquiétude *f*, trouble *m*.

perusal [pə'ru:zəl] *n* examen *m*, lecture *f*.

peruse [pə'ru:z] *vt* étudier, prendre connaissance de.

pervade [pə:'veid] *vt* pénétrer, animer, régner dans.

perverse [pə'və:s] *a* pervers, contrariant.

perversion [pə'və:ʃən] *n* perversion *f*, travestissement *m*.

perversity [pə'və:siti] *n* perversité *f*, esprit de contradiction *m*.

pervert ['pə:və:t] *n* perverti(e) *mf*, apostat *m*.

pervert [pə'vəːt] *vt* pervertir, fausser.

pervious ['pəːviəs] *a* perméable, accessible.

pessimism ['pesimizəm] *n* pessimisme *m*.

pessimistic [,pesi'mistik] *a* pessimiste.

pest [pest] *n* peste *f*, fléau *m*.

pester ['pestə] *vt* tracasser, importuner, infester.

pestilence ['pestiləns] *n* pestilence *f*.

pestilential [,pesti'lenʃəl] *a* pestilentiel. pernicieux.

pestle ['pesl] *n* pilon *m*; *vt* piler, broyer.

pet [pet] *a* animal *m* familier, favori *m*, chouchou *m*; **to take the —** prendre la mouche; *vt* caresser, choyer.

petal ['petl] *n* pétale *m*.

Peter ['piːtə] Pierre *m*.

peter out ['piːtə'aut] *vi* faire long feu, s'épuiser, s'arrêter.

petition [pə'tiʃən] *n* pétition *f*, prière *f*, demande *f*; *vt* adresser une pétition à.

petitioner [pə'tiʃənə] *n* pétitionnaire *mf*, requérant(e) *mf*.

petrel ['petrəl] *n* pétrel *m*.

petrify ['petrifai] *vt* pétrifier.

petrol ['petrəl] *n* essence *f*.

petroleum [pi'trouliəm] *n* pétrole *m*.

petticoat ['petikout] *n* jupon *m*, jupe *f*.

pettifoggery ['petifɔgəri] *n* chicane *f*.

pettiness ['petinis] *n* mesquinerie *f*.

pettish ['petiʃ] *a* grincheux.

petty ['peti] *a* petit mesquin; **— cash** menue monnaie *f*.

petty-officer ['peti'ɔfisə] *n* contremaître *m*; *pl* maistrance *f*.

petulance ['petjuləns] *n* pétulance *f*, vivacité *f*.

petulant ['petjulənt] *a* pétulant, vif.

pew [pjuː] *n* banc *m*.

pewit ['piːwit] *n* vanneau *m*.

pewter ['pjuːtə] *n* étain *m*.

phantom ['fæntəm] *n* fantôme *m*; *a* illusoire.

Pharisee ['færisiː] *n* pharisien *m*.

pharyngitis [,færin'dʒaitis] *n* pharingite *f*.

pharynx ['færiŋks] *n* pharynx *m*.

phase [feiz] *n* phase *f*.

pheasant ['feznt] *n* faisan *m*, faisane *f*.

phenomenal [fi'nɔminl] *a* phénoménal.

phenomenon [fi'nɔminən] *n* phénomène *m*.

phial ['faiəl] *n* fiole *f*.

philander [fi'lændə] *vi* papillonner, conter fleurette (à).

philanderer [fi'lændərə] *n* flirteur *m*.

philologist [fi'blədʒist] *n* philologue *m*.

philology [fi'blədʒi] *n* philologie *f*.

philosopher [fi'lɔsəfə] *n* philosophe *m*.

philosophy [fi'lɔsəfi] *n* philosophie

f; **moral —** morale *f*; **natural —** physique *f*.

philtre ['filtə] *n* philtre *m*.

phlebitis [fli'baitis] *n* phlébite *f*.

phlegm [flem] *n* flegme *m*.

phlegmatic [fleg'mætik] *a* flegmatique.

phonetician [,fɔni'tiʃən] *n* phonéticien *m*.

phonetics [fə'netiks] *n* phonétique *f*.

phoney ['founi] *a* drôle, faux.

phosphate ['fɔsfeit] *n* phosphate *m*.

phosphorous ['fɔsfərəs] *a* phosphoreux.

phosphorus ['fɔsfərəs] *n* phosphore *m*.

photograph ['foutəgrɑːf] *n* photographie *f*, *vi* photographier.

photographer [fə'tɔgrəfə] *n* photographe *m*.

photographic [,foutə'græfik] *a* photographique.

phrase [freiz] *n* phrase *f* locution *f*, expression *f*; *vi* exprimer, rédiger.

phraseology [,freizi'ɔlədʒi] *n* phraséologie *f*.

phthisis ['θaisis] *n* phtisie *f*.

physic ['fizik] *n (fam)* médecine *f*, médicament *m pl*.

physical ['fizikəl] *a* physique.

physician [fi'ziʃən] *n* médecin *m*.

physicist ['fizisist] *n* physicien, -ienne.

physics ['fiziks] *n* physique *f*.

physiognomy [,fizi'ɔnəmi] *n* physionomie *f*.

pianist ['piənist] *n* pianiste *mf*.

piano ['piænou] *n* piano *m*; *ad* piano; **grand —** piano à queue; **upright —** piano droit.

pick [pik] *n* pic *m*, pioche *f*, élite *f*, dessus du panier *m*; *vt* piocher, picorer, cueillir, choisir, trier, *(lock)* crocheter; **to — out** repérer choisir, faire le tri de; **to — up** ramasser, prendre, relever, racoler, draguer; *vi* reprendre des forces.

pickaback ['pikəbæk] *ad* sur le dos.

pickaxe ['pikæks] *n* pioche *f*.

picket ['pikit] *n* piquet *m*, pieu *m*.

picking ['pikiŋ] *n* cueillette *f*, épluchage *m* crochetage *m*; *pl* bribes *f pl* glanures *f pl*, gratte *f*.

pickle ['pikl] *n* saumure *f*, marinade *f*; *pl* condiments *m pl* conserves au vinaigre *f pl*; *vt* conserver, mariner.

pickpocket ['pikpɔkit] *n* pickpocket *m* voleur à la tire *m*.

picnic ['piknik] *n* piquenique *m*; *vi* faire un piquenique.

pictorial [pik'tɔːriəl] *a* illustré, pittoresque.

picture ['piktʃə] *n* tableau *m*, image *f*; *pl* cinéma *m*; *vt* représenter, se figurer.

picturesque [,piktʃə'resk] *a* pittoresque.

picturesqueness [,piktʃə'resknis] *n* pittoresque *m*.

pie [pai] n pâté m, tourte f, (US) tarte f.

piece [piːs] n morceau m, pièce f; vt assembler, rapiécer.

piecemeal ['piːsmiːl] ad pièce à pièce, un à un.

piecework ['piːswəːk] n travail à la pièce m.

pier [piə] n jetée f, pile f, pilier m.

pierce [piəs] vt percer, pénétrer.

piety ['paiəti] n piété f.

pig [pig] n porc m, pourceau m, cochon m.

pigeon ['pidʒin] n pigeon m; —hole n casier m; to —hole vt classer.

pigheaded ['pig'hedid] a buté, têtu.

pigsty ['pigstai] n porcherie f, étable f, bauge f.

pigtail ['pigteil] n natte f.

pike [paik] n pique f, brochet m, tourniquet m.

pikestaff ['paikstɑːf] n hampe f.

pile [pail] n pieu m, p otis m, pile f, (fam) fortune f, poil m; pl hémorroïdes f pl; vt empiler, entasser, (fam) charrier.

pilfer ['pilfə] vt chaparder.

pilferer ['pilfərə] n chapardeur, -euse.

pilfering ['pilfəriŋ] n chapardage m.

pilgrim ['pilgrim] n pèlerin(e) mf.

pilgrimage ['pilgrimidʒ] n pèlerinage m.

pill [pil] n pilule f.

pillage ['pilidʒ] n pillage m; vt piller, saccager.

pillar ['pilə] n pilier m, colonne f.

pillar-box ['piləbɔks] n boîte aux lettres f.

pill-box ['pilbɔks] n blockhaus m, boîte à pilules.

pillow ['pilou] n oreiller m.

pillow-case ['piloukeis] n taie f.

pilot ['pailət] n pilote m; vi piloter.

pimple ['pimpl] n bouton m, pustule f.

pimply ['pimpli] a boutonneux.

pin [pin] n épingle f, cheville f, (fam) quille f; vt épingler, clouer, fier, accrocher, goupiller; —s and needles fourmis f pl.

pinafore ['pinəfɔː] n tablier m.

pincer ['pinsəz] n pince f, tenailles f pl.

pinch [pintʃ] n pincée f, prise f, pincement m; vt pincer, blesser, gêner, chiper.

pincushion ['pin.kuʃin] n pelote à épingles f.

pine [pain] n pin m; vi languir, dépérir; to — for soupirer après, aspirer à.

pineapple ['pain.æpl] n ananas m.

pinion ['pinjən] n aileron m, aile f, (tec) pignon m; vi couper les ailes à, lier.

pink [pink] n œillet m; an rose m; vt percer; vi (motor) cliqueter.

pin-money ['pin mʌni] n argent de poche m.

pinnacle ['pinəkl] n clocheton m, cime f, apogée f.

pinprick ['pinprik] n piqûre d'épingle f.

pint [paint] n pinte f.

pioneer [,paiə'niə] n pionnier m.

pious ['paiəs] a pieux.

pip [pip] n pépie f, pépin m, point m, cafard m.

pipe [paip] n tuyau m, pipe f, pipée f, sifflet m, chalumeau m; pl cornemuse f; vi jouer de la cornemuse, siffler, crier; vt jouer sur la cornemuse.

piper ['paipə] n joueur de cornemuse m.

pippin ['pipin] n reinette f.

piquancy ['piːkənsi] n piquant m, sel m.

pique [piːk] n pique f, dépit m; vt piquer, dépiter.

pirate ['paiərit] n pirate m.

pistol ['pistl] n pistolet m.

piston ['pistən] n piston m.

pit [pit] n trou m, puits m, fosse f, creux m, marque f, arène f, parterre m, aisselle f; vt enfouir, mettre face à face, marquer, opposer.

pitch [pitʃ] n poix m, degré m, hauteur f, diapason m, comble m, terrain m, tangage m; a noir; vt dresser, poisser, régler le ton de, lancer, jeter; vi tanguer, tomber.

pitched [pitʃt] a rangé, en règle.

pitcher ['pitʃə] n cruche f, broc m.

pitchfork ['pitʃfɔːk] n fourche f.

piteous ['pitiəs] a lamentable, piteux.

pitfall ['pitfɔːl] n trappe f, traquenard m piège m.

pith [piθ] n moelle f, essence f, vigueur f, sève f.

pitiable ['pitiəbl] a pitoyable.

pitiful ['pitiful] a compatissant, lamentable, qui fait pitié.

pitiless ['pitilis] a impitoyable, cruel.

pittance ['pitəns] n pitance f.

pitted ['pitid] a troué, marqué.

pity ['piti] n pitié f; it is a — c'est dommage f; vt plaindre.

pivot ['pivət] n pivot m; vt monter sur pivot, fair pivoter; vi pivoter.

placard ['plækɑːd] n affiche f; vt placarder afficher, couvrir d'affiches.

placate [plə'keit] vt calmer, apaiser.

place [pleis] n place f, endroit m, lieu m résidence f; vt placer, mettre, situer, poser, classer.

placebo [plə'siːbou] n remède factice m.

plagiarism ['pleidʒərizəm] n plagiat m.

plagiarist ['pleidʒərist] n plagiaire m.

plagiarize ['pleidʒəraiz] vt plagier, contrefaire.

plague [pleig] n peste f, fléau m; vt tracasser.

plaice [pleis] n plie f, carrelet m.

plain [plein] n plaine f; a plan, plat,

clair, uni, franc, simple, commun, ordinaire; **in — clothes** en civil; **she is —** elle n'est pas belle; **—dealing** n loyauté f; **—spoken** a franc, rond, carré.

plainly ['pleinli] ad clairement, simplement, sans détours.

plainness ['pleinnis] n air m, commun, clarté f, netteté f, franchise f, simplicité f.

plaint [pleint] n plainte f.

plaintiff ['pleintif] n plaignant(e) mf, demandeur, -eresse.

plaintive ['pleintiv] a plaintif.

plait [plæt] n pli m, tresse f, natte f; vt plisser, natter.

plan [plæn] n plan m, projet m; vt relever, projeter, arrêter le plan de, combiner.

plane [plein] n platane m, rabot m, plan m, niveau m, avion m; a plan, uni; vt raboter, aplanir; vi voler, planer.

planet ['plænit] n planète f.

plank [plæŋk] n planche f, programme m.

plant [plɑːnt] n plante f, outillage m, machinerie f; vt planter (là), établir, fonder; **to — out** dépoter, déplanter.

plantation [plæn'teiʃən] n plantation f, bosquet m.

planter ['plɑːntə] n planteur m.

plash [plæʃ] n flac m, clapotis m, éclaboussure f; vi faire flac, clapoter, éclabousser.

plaster ['plɑːstə] n (em)plâtre m; vt plâtrer, enduire, couvrir.

plasterer ['plɑːstərə] n plâtrier m.

plastic ['plæstik] an plastique f.

plate [pleit] n plaque f, planche f, assiette f, vaisselle f, dentier m; vt plaquer; **—ful** n assiettée f; **—rack** n égouttoir m.

platform ['plætfɔːm] n plate-forme f, estrade f, quai m, trottoir m.

platinum ['plætinəm] n platine m.

platitude ['plætitjuːd] n platitude f, lieu commun m.

platoon [plə'tuːn] n peloton m, section f.

plausible ['plɔːzəbl] a plausible, vraisemblable.

plausibility [ˌplɔːzə'biliti] n plausibilité f.

play [plei] n jeu m, pièce f (de théâtre), carrière f; **fair —** franc jeu m; vti jouer; v' folâtrer, gambader.

player ['pleiə] n joueur m, -euse, acteur, -trice, exécutant(e) mf.

playful ['pleiful] a enjoué.

playground ['pleigraund] n terrain de jeu m, cour f.

playmate ['pleimeit] n camarade mf de jeu, ami(e) d'enfance.

playpen ['pleipen] n parc m (d'enfant).

playtime ['pleitaim] n récréation f.

plaything ['pleiθiŋ] n jouet m.

playwright ['pleirait] n auteur dramatique m.

plea [pliː] n argument m, plaidoyer m. excuse f.

plead [pliːd] vti plaider; vt prétexter, invoquer; vi s'avouer.

pleader ['pliːdə] n défenseur m, plaideur m.

pleasant ['pleznt] a agréable, aimable.

pleasantly ['plezntli] ad agréablement.

pleasantness ['plezntnis] n agrément m, affabilité m, charme m.

please [pliːz] vt plaire à; vi plaire; s'il vous plaît.

pleased [pliːzd] a très heureux, content.

pleasure ['pleʒə] n plaisir m, gré m, plaisance f.

pleat [pliːt] n pli m: vt plisser.

plebiscite ['plebisit] n plébiscite m.

pledge [pledʒ] n gage m, promesse f, toast m; vt mettre en gage, engager, porter un toast à.

plenipotentiary [ˌplenipə'tenʃəri] an plénipotentiaire m.

plentiful ['plentiful] a abondant, copieux.

plenty ['plenti] n abondance f.

pleurisy ['pluərisi] n pleurésie f.

pliability [ˌplaiə'biliti] n souplesse f, flexibilité f.

pliant ['plaiənt] a souple, flexible, complaisant.

pliers ['plaiəz] n pince f.

plight [plait] n (triste) état m; vt engager.

plighted ['plaitid] a engagé, lié.

plod [plɔd] n lourde tâche f; vi avancer (cheminer) péniblement, travailler laborieusement, bûcher.

plot [plɔt] n lopin m, complot m, intrigue f; vt tracer, relever; vti comploter; vi conspirer.

plotter ['plɔtə] n intrigant(e) mf, conspirateur, -trice.

plough [plau] n charrue f; vt labourer, rider, sillonner, (exam) refuser, recaler.

ploughman ['plaumən] n laboureur m.

ploughshare ['plaufʃeə] n soc m

plover ['plʌvə] n pluvier m.

pluck [plʌk] n courage m, cran m; vt cueillir, arracher, plumer, tirer; **to — up courage** prendre courage.

plug [plʌg] n cheville f, bouchon m, tampon m, prise de courant f; vt boucher, tamponner.

plum [plʌm] n prune f, meilleur morceau m, poste etc.

plumage ['pluːmidʒ] n plumage m.

plumb [plʌm] n plomb m; a d'aplomb, vertical, tout pur; vt sonder; ad d'aplomb, juste, en plein.

plumber ['plʌmə] n plombier m.

plumb-line ['plʌmlain] n fil à plomb m.

plume [pluːm] n plume f, plumet m, panache m; **to — oneself on** se piquer de, se flatter de.

plummet ['plʌmit] n plomb m, sonde f.

plump [plʌmp] a rondelet, dodu, bien en chair; n chute f, bruit sourd m, plouf m; ad tout net; vt laisser tomber, flanquer; vi tomber, se laisser tomber lourdement.

plum-tree ['plʌmtri:] n prunier m.

plunder ['plʌndə] n pillage m, butin m; vt piller.

plunderer ['plʌndərə] n pillard m.

plunge [plʌndʒ] n plongeon m; vti plonger; vi se jeter, s'enfoncer, piquer du nez, tanguer.

plural ['pluərəl] an pluriel m; a plural.

plus [plʌs] n prep plus; a positif, actif.

plush [plʌʃ] n peluche f.

plutocracy [plu:'tɔkrəsi] n ploutocratie f.

ply [plai] n pli m, épaisseur f; vt manier, exercer, travailler, gorger, assaillir; vi faire la navette, faire le service.

plywood ['plaiwud] n contre-plaqué m.

pneumatic [nju(:)'mætik] an pneumatique m.

pneumonia [nju(:)'mouniə] n pneumonie f.

poach [poutʃ] vt pocher; vi braconner; vt braconner (dans); vi to — upon empiéter sur.

poacher ['poutʃə] n braconnier m.

poaching ['poutʃiŋ] n braconnage m.

pocket ['pɔkit] n poche f, sac m; —-book calepin m, portefeuille m; vt empocher, mettre dans sa poche.

pock-marked ['pɔk,mɑ:kt] a grêlé.

pod [pɔd] n cosse f, (coco) cabosse f; vt écosser, écaler.

poem ['pouim] n poème m.

poet ['pouit] n poète m.

poetry ['pouətri] n poésie f.

poignant ['pɔinənt] a âpre, piquant, poignant.

point [pɔint] n point m, pointe f, extrémité f, sujet m; (rl) aiguille f; —-blank à bout portant; on — duty de faction; vt tailler, aiguiser, pointer, diriger, braquer; to — out indiquer, représenter, montrer du doigt, faire observer; to — at montrer du doigt; to — to annoncer, laisser supposer.

pointed ['pɔintid] a pointu, aigu, en pointe, mordant, direct.

pointer ['pɔintə] n aiguille f, baguette f, chien d'arrêt m, tuyau m, indication f.

pointless ['pɔintlis] a émoussé, qui manque d'à-propos, fade.

pointsman ['pɔintsmən] n aiguilleur m.

poise [pɔiz] n équilibre m, port m, dignité f, attente f; vt équilibrer, soupeser, balancer.

poison ['pɔizn] n poison m; vt empoisonner, intoxiquer.

poisoning ['pɔizniŋ] n empoisonnement m, intoxication f.

poisonous ['pɔiznəs] a empoisonné, toxique, (plant) vénéneux, (animal) venimeux.

poke [pouk] n coup m (de coude etc), poussée f; vt piquer, pousser du coude, tisonner, fourrer, passer; to — about fureter, fouiller; to — fun at se moquer de.

poker ['poukə] n tisonnier m, (game) poker m.

Poland ['pouland] n Pologne f.

polar ['poulə] a polaire; — bear ours m blanc.

pole [poul] n perche f, échalas m, mât m, poteau m, montant m, timon m, pôle m; —-jump saut m à la perche.

Pole [poul] n Polonais(e) mf.

police [pə'li:s] n police f; vt maintenir l'ordre dans, policer.

policeman [pə'li:smən] n agent m.

police station [pə'li:s'steiʃən] n commissariat m de police, poste m.

policy ['pɔlisi] n politique f, police d'assurance f.

polish ['pɔliʃ] n poli m, éclat m, cirage m, encaustique f, vernis m, blanc d'Espagne m, raffinement m; vt cirer, astiquer, fourbir, polir; to — off finir, régler son compte à, expédier.

Polish ['pouliʃ] an polonais m.

polite [pə'lait] a poli, cultivé, élégant.

politely [pə'laitli] ad poliment.

politeness [pə'laitnis] n politesse f, courtoisie f.

political [pə'litikəl] a politique.

politician [,pɔli'tiʃən] n homme politique m, politicien m.

politics ['pɔlitiks] n politique f.

poll [poul] n scrutin m, vote m; vt obtenir les voix, étêter, écorner; vi voter.

pollute [pə'lu:t] vt polluer, profaner.

poltroon [pɔl'tru:n] n poltron m.

polygamist [pɔ'ligəmist] n polygame m.

polygamy [pɔ'ligəmi] n polygamie f.

polyglot ['pɔliglɔt] an polyglotte mf.

polygon ['pɔligən] n polygone m.

pomegranate ['pɔmi,grænit] n grenade f.

pomp [pɔmp] n pompe f, faste m, apparat m.

pomposity [pɔm'pɔsiti] n solennité f, pompe f, suffisance f, emphase f.

pompous ['pɔmpəs] a pompeux, suffisant, ampoulé.

pond [pɔnd] n bassin m, étang m, vivier m.

ponder ['pɔndə] vt peser, réfléchir sur, considérer; vi ruminer, réfléchir.

ponderous ['pɔndərəs] a pesant, lourd.

pontiff ['pɔntif] n pontife m, prélat m.

pontificate [pɔn'tifikeit] n pontificat m; vi pontifier.

pontoon [pɔn'tu:n] n ponton m.

pontoon bridge [pɔn'tu:nbridʒ] n pont de bateaux m.

pony ['pouni] n poney m.

poodle ['pu:dl] n caniche mf.

pooh-pooh [pu:'pu:] vt tourner en dérision; excl bah!

pool [pu:l] n mare f, flaque f, (swimming-) piscine f, (games) poule f, fonds commun m, cartel m; vt mettre en commun, répartir.

poop [pu:p] n poupe f, dunette f.

poor [puə] a pauvre, malheureux, médiocre, maigre, piètre, faible; the — les pauvres.

poorly ['puəli] ad tout doucement, pas fort, médiocrement; a souffrant.

poorness ['puənis] n pauvreté f, manque m, infériorité f.

pop [pɔp] n bruit sec m; excl pan! vi sauter, péter, éclater; vt faire sauter, fourrer, mettre au clou.

pope [poup] n pape m, pope m.

popery ['poupəri] n papisme m.

poplar ['pɔplə] n peuplier m.

poplin ['pɔplin] n popeline f.

poppy ['pɔpi] n coquelicot m, pavot m.

pop-song ['pɔpsɔŋ] n chanson f (à la mode).

populace ['pɔpjuləs] n peuple m, populace f.

popular ['pɔpjulə] a populaire, aimé, couru, à la mode.

popularity [,pɔpju'læriti] n popularité f.

popularize ['pɔpjuləraiz] vt populariser, vulgariser.

populate ['pɔpjuleit] vt peupler.

population [,pɔpju'leiʃən] n population f.

populous ['pɔpjuləs] a populeux.

porch [pɔːtʃ] n porche m, marquise f.

porcupine ['pɔːkjupain] n porc-épic m.

pore [pɔː] n pore m; vi to — over s'absorber dans.

pork [pɔːk] n porc m; —-butcher n charcutier m.

porous ['pɔːrəs] a poreux, perméable.

porpoise ['pɔːpəs] n marsouin m.

porridge ['pɔridʒ] n bouillie d'avoine f.

porringer ['pɔrindʒə] n écuelle f.

port [pɔːt] n port m; home — port d'attache; sabord m, bâbord m, allure f; (wine) porto m; vt mettre à bâbord, présenter; vi venir sur bâbord.

portable ['pɔːtəbl] a portatif, transportable.

portal ['pɔːtl] n portail m.

portcullis [pɔːt'kʌlis] n herse f.

portend [pɔː'tend] vt présager, faire pressentir, annoncer.

portent ['pɔːtent] n présage m.

portentous [pɔː'tentəs] a formidable, menaçant, de mauvais augure.

porter ['pɔːtə] n portier m, concierge m, porteur m, chasseur m.

porterage ['pɔːtəridʒ] n factage m, transport m.

portfolio [pɔːt'fouliou] n portefeuille m, chemise f, serviette f, carton m.

porthole ['pɔːthoul] n hublot m, sabord m.

portico ['pɔːtikou] n portique m.

portion ['pɔːʃən] n portion f, part f, partie f, dot f; vt partager, doter.

portly ['pɔːtli] a corpulent, imposant.

portmanteau [pɔːt'mæntou] n valise f.

portrait ['pɔːtrit] n portrait m.

portray [pɔː'trei] vt faire le portrait de, (dé)peindre.

Portugal ['pɔːtjugəl] n Portugal m.

Portuguese [,pɔːtju'giːz] an Portugais(e).

pose [pouz] n pose f, affectation f; vti poser, (fam) coller; to — as s'ériger en, se faire passer pour.

poser ['pouzə] n question embarrassante f, colle f.

position [pə'ziʃən] n position f, condition f, place f, état m.

positive ['pɔzətiv] a positif, catégorique, formel, authentique.

possess [pə'zes] vt posséder, tenir, s'approprier, avoir.

possession [pə'zeʃən] n possession f.

possessive [pə'zesiv] a possessif.

possibility [,pɔsə'biliti] n possibilité f, éventualité f.

possible ['pɔsəbl] an possible m; a éventuel.

possibly ['pɔsəbli] ad peut-être.

post [poust] n poste f, courrier m, levée f, mât m, poteau m, place f, emploi m; vt mettre à la poste, poster, affecter; first — appel m; last — sonnerie aux morts f, retraite f; (US) — no bills défense d'afficher.

postage ['poustidʒ] n affranchissement m; — stamp timbre (-poste) m.

postcard ['poustkɑːd] n carte postale f.

post-date ['poust'deit] vt postdater.

poster ['poustə] n affiche f, afficheur m.

posterior [pɔs'tiəriə] an postérieur m.

posterity [pɔs'teriti] n postérité f.

postern ['poustəːn] n poterne f, porte de derrière f.

post-free ['poust'friː] a franco, en franchise.

posthumous ['pɔstjuməs] a posthume.

postman ['poustmən] n facteur m.

postmark ['poustmɑːk] n timbre d'oblitération m; vt timbrer.

postmaster ['poust,mɑːstə] n receveur m, directeur des postes m.

post-mortem ['poust'mɔːtəm] n autopsie f.

post office ['poust,ɔfis] n (bureau m de) poste f.

post-paid ['poust'peid] *a* port payé.

postpone [poust'poun] *vt* ajourner, remettre, reculer.

postscript ['pousskript] *n* post-scriptum *m*.

postulate ['postjulit] *n* postulat *m*; ['postjuleit] *vt* postuler, demander, stipuler.

posture ['postʃə] *n* posture *f*, état *m*, attitude *f*.

posy ['pouzi] *n* petit bouquet *m*.

pot [pot] *n* pot *m*, marmite *f*.

potash ['potæʃ] *n* potasse *f*.

potato [pə'teitou] *n* pomme de terre *f*.

pot-bellied ['pot,belid] *a* ventru, bedonnant.

pot-boiler ['pot,boilə] *n* besogne *f* alimentaire.

potent ['poutənt] *a* puissant, fort, violent.

potential [pə'tenʃəl] *an* potentiel *m*, possible *m*; *a* en puissance, latent.

potentiality [pə,tenʃi'æliti] *n* virtualité *f*, potentialité *f*, potentiel *m*.

pother ['poðə] *n* nuage *m*, tapage *m*, embarras *m pl*.

potion ['pouʃən] *n* potion *f*, sirop *m*, philtre *m*.

pot-luck ['pot'lʌk] *n* fortune du pot *f*.

potter ['potə] *n* potier *m*; *vi* baguenauder, bricoler.

pottery ['potəri] *n* poterie *f*.

pouch [pautʃ] *n* blague *f*, cartouchière *f*, sac *m*, poche *f*, bourse *f*.

poulterer ['poultərə] *n* marchand de volailles *m*.

poultice ['poultis] *n* cataplasme *m*.

poultry ['poultri] *n* volaille *f*; —**yard** *n* basse-cour *f*.

pounce [pauns] *n* serre *f*, attaque *f*; *vt* poncer; **to —** **on** fondre sur, sauter sur.

pound [paund] *n* livre *f*, fourrière *f*, enclos *m*; *vt* piler, broyer, *(mil)* pilonner.

pour [po:] *n* pluie torrentielle *f*; *vt* verser; *vi* se jeter, pleuvoir à verse.

pout [paut] *n* moue *f*, bouderie *f*; *vi* faire la moue, bouder.

poverty ['povəti] *n* pauvreté *f*, rareté *f*, misère *f*.

powder ['paudə] *n* poudre *f*; *vt* (sau)poudrer, pulvériser.

powdered ['paudəd] *a* en poudre.

powder-magazine ['paudəmægə,zi:n] *n* poudrière *f*.

powder-puff ['paudəpʌf] *n* houppe *f*.

powdery ['paudəri] *a* poudreux, friable.

power ['pauə] *n* pouvoir *m*, puissance *f*, faculté *f*, vigueur *f*, *(el)* force *f*; *vt* actionner.

powerful ['pauəful] *a* puissant, énergique, vigoureux.

powerlessness ['pauəlisnis] *n* impuissance *f*, inefficacité *f*.

practicable ['præktikəbl] *a* praticable, faisable, pratique.

practical ['præktikəl] *a* pratique.

practice ['præktis] *n* pratique *f*, étude *f*, clientèle *f*, usage *m*, habitude *f*, exercice *m*, entraînement *m*.

practise ['præktis] *vt* pratiquer, exercer, s'exercer à, étudier; *vi* s'entraîner, faire des exercices.

practitioner [præk'tiʃnə] *n* praticien *m*; **general —** omnipraticien *m*.

prairie ɪ'prɛəri] *n* prairie *f*, savane *f*.

praise [preiz] *n* éloge *m*, louange *f*; *vt* louer, glorifier.

praiseworthy ['preiz,wə:ði] *a* louable.

prance [pra:ns] *vi* se cabrer, piaffer, se pavaner.

prank [præŋk] *n* farce *f*, niche *f*, fredaine *f*, les cents coups *m pl*; *vt* orner pavoiser.

prate [preit] *n* bavardage *m*; *vi* bavarder.

prattle ['prætl] *n* babil *m*; *vi* babiller, jaser.

prattling ['prætliŋ] *a* jaseur.

prawn [pro:n] *n* crevette rose *f*.

pray [prei] *vti* prier.

prayer [prɛə] *n* prière *f*.

prayer book ['prɛəbuk] *n* rituel *m*, livre de messe *m*, paroissien *m*.

preach [pri:tʃ] *vti* prêcher.

preamble [pri:'æmbl] *n* préambule *m*.

precarious [pri'kɛəriəs] *a* précaire, incertain.

precariousness [pri'kɛəriəsnis] *n* précarité *f*.

precaution [pri'ko:ʃən] *n* précaution *f*.

precede [pri(:)'si:d] *vt* précéder, préfacer.

precedence ['presidəns] *n* préséance *f*, pas *m*.

precedent ['presidənt] *n* précédent *m*.

precept ['pri:sept] *n* précepte *m*.

preceptor [pri'septə] *n* précepteur *m*.

precincts ['pri:siŋkts] *n pl* enceinte *f*, limites *f pl*, *(US)* circonscription *f* électorale.

precious ['preʃəs] *a* précieux, de grand prix.

preciousness ['preʃəsnis] *n* haute valeur *f*, préciosité *f*.

precipice ['presipis] *n* précipice *m*.

precipitate [pri'sipitit] *n* précipité *m*; [pri'sipiteit] *vt* précipiter, brusquer.

precipitation [pri,sipi'teiʃən] *n* précipitation *f*.

precipitous [pri'sipitəs] *a* à pic, escarpé.

precise [pri'sais] *a* précis, exact, pointilleux.

precisely [pri'saisli] *ad* précisément, avec précision.

precision [pri'siʒən] *n* précision *f*.

preclude [pri'klu:d] *vt* exclure, prévenir, priver.

precocious [pri'kouʃəs] *a* précoce.

precociousness [pri'kouʃəsnis] *n* précocité *f*.

precursor [pri(ː)'kəːsə] n précurseur m, avant-coureur m, devancier m.
predate [pri'deit] vt antidater.
predatory ['predətəri] a rapace, de proie, de brigand.
predecessor ['priːdisesə] n prédécesseur m.
predicament [pri'dikəmənt] n difficulté f, situation fâcheuse f.
predict [pri'dikt] vt prédire.
predilection [ˌpriːdi'lekʃən] n prédilection f.
predispose ['priːdis'pouz] vt prédisposer.
predisposition ['priːˌdispə'ziʃən] n prédisposition f.
predominate [pri'dɔmineit] vi prédominer.
pre-eminence [pri(ː)'eminəns] n prééminence f.
preen [priːn] to — oneself se bichonner, se faire beau, faire des grâces, se piquer (de on).
preface ['prefis] n préface f; vt préfacer, préluder à.
prefect ['priːfekt] n préfet m.
prefer [pri'fəː] vt préférer, aimer mieux, avancer.
preferably ['prefərəbli] ad de préférence.
preference ['prefərəns] n préférence f.
preferential [ˌprefə'renʃəl] a préférentiel, de faveur.
preferment [pri'fəːmənt] n avancement m.
pregnancy ['pregnənsi] n grossesse f.
pregnant ['pregnənt] a enceinte, grosse, fertile, plein.
prejudice ['predʒudis] n préjudice m, tort m, préjugé m; vt faire tort à, prévenir.
prejudicial [ˌpredʒu'diʃəl] a préjudiciable, nuisible.
prelate ['prelit] n prélat m.
preliminary [pri'liminəri] an préliminaire m; a préalable; n prélude m; pl préliminaires m pl.
prelude ['preljuːd] n prélude m; vi préluder (à); vt annoncer.
premature [ˌpremə'tjuə] a prématuré.
prematurely [ˌpremə'tjuəli] ad prématurément.
premeditate [pri(ː)'mediteit] vt préméditer.
premeditation [pri(ː)ˌmedi'teiʃən] n préméditation f.
premier ['premjə] a premier; n premier ministre m, président du conseil m.
premise ['premis] n prémisse f; pl maison f, lieux m pl, local m.
premium ['priːmjem] n prime f, boni m; **to be at a** — faire prime.
preoccupation [pri(ː)ˌɔkju'peiʃən] n préoccupation f.
preoccupied [pri(ː)'ɔkjupaid] a préoccupé.
preparation [ˌprepə'reiʃən] n pré-

paration f; pl préparatifs m pl.
preparatory [pri'pærətəri], a préparatoire, préalable.
prepare [pri'pɛə] vt préparer, apprêter; vi se préparer, se disposer (à).
prepay ['priː'pei] vt payer d'avance.
preponderance [pri'pɔndərəns] n prépondérance f.
preponderate [pri'pɔndəreit] vi l'emporter (sur over).
preposition [ˌprepə'ziʃən] n préposition f.
prepossessing [ˌpriːpə'zesiŋ] a captivant, prévenant.
preposterous [pri'pɔstərəs] a absurde, saugrenu.
prerequisite ['priː'rekwizit] n condition préalable f; a nécessaire.
prerogative [pri'rɔgətiv] n prérogative f, apanage m.
presage ['presidʒ] n présage m, pressentiment m, vt présager, annoncer, augurer.
prescribe [pris'kraib] vt prescrire, ordonner.
prescription [pris'kripʃən] n ordonnance f, prescription f, ordre m.
presence ['prezns] n présence f, distinction f, maintien m, prestance f.
present ['preznt] n cadeau m, présent m; a présent.
present [pri'zent] vt présenter, offrir, faire cadeau de, soumettre.
presentation [ˌprezen'teiʃən] n présentation f, don m, remise f, cadeau-souvenir m.
presentiment [pri'zentimənt] n pressentiment m.
presently ['prezntli] ad avant (sous) peu, tout à l'heure, bientôt.
preservation [ˌprezə(ː)'veiʃən] n préservation f, conservation f.
preservative [pri'zəːvətiv] an préservatif m.
preserve [pri'zəːv] n chasse (pêche) gardée f; pl conserves f pl, confiture f; vt préserver, conserver, confire, maintenir, garder, observer, garantir (de from).
preside [pri'zaid] vi présider.
presidency ['prezidənsi] n présidence f.
president ['prezidənt] n président(e) mf.
press [pres] n presse f, pressoir m, pression f, foule f, hâte f, placard m, imprimerie f; vt appuyer sur, presser, serrer, pressurer, donner un coup de fer à; vi appuyer, se serrer, peser.
press-stud ['pres'stʌd] n bouton pression m.
pressing ['presiŋ] a pressant, urgent; n pressage m, pression f.
pressure ['preʃə] n pression f, poussée f, urgence f.
pressure-cooker ['preʃəˌkukə] n cocotte minute f.
prestige [pres'tiːʒ] n prestige, embarras m, tension f.

prestressed ['pri'strest] *a* précontraint.

presume [pri'zju:m] *vt* présumer, supposer, se permettre de croire, aimer à croire; to — on se prévaloir de, abuser de.

presumption [pri'zʌmpʃən] *n* présomption *f*.

presumptive [pri'zʌmptiv] *a* présomptif.

presumptuous [pri'zʌmptjuəs] *a* présomptueux.

pretence [pri'tens] *n* prétence *f*, prétexte *m*, (faux) semblant *m*.

pretend [pri'tend] *vt* feindre, faire semblant de, simuler, prétendre.

pretender [pri'tendə] *n* prétendant *m*, soupirant *m*.

pretension [pri'tenʃən] *n* prétention *f*.

pretentious [pri'tenʃəs] *a* prétentieux.

pretext ['pri:tekst] *n* prétexte *m*.

prettiness ['pritinis] *n* joliesse *f*, mignardise *f*.

pretty ['priti] *a* joli, beau, mignon, gentil; *ad* à peu près, assez.

prevail [pri'veil] *vi* l'emporter (sur over), prévaloir (contre, sur over), régner; to — upon s.o. to amener qn à, décider qn à, persuader à qn de.

prevailing [pri'veiliŋ] *a* courant, régnant, général.

prevalent ['prevələnt] *a* prédominant, répandu.

prevaricate [pri'værikeit] *vi* tergiverser, ergoter, mentir.

prevarication [pri,væri'keiʃən] *n* chicane *f*, tergiversation *f*, mensonge *m*.

prevent [pri:'vent] *vt* empêcher, prévenir.

prevention [pri'venʃən] *n* empêchement *m*, protection *f*.

preventive [pri'ventiv] *an* préventif *m*.

preview ['pri:'vju:] *n* exhibition préalable *f*, avant-première *f*.

previous ['pri:viəs] *a* précédent, préalable, antérieur.

previously ['pri:viəsli] *ad* précédemment, auparavant, au préalable.

prey [prei] *n* proie *f*; to — upon vivre sur, dévorer.

price [prais] *n* prix *m*; *vt* mettre un prix à, estimer.

priceless ['praislis] *a* sans prix, impayable.

prick [prik] *n* piqûre *f*, remords *m*; *vt* piquer, tendre, dresser.

pricker ['prikə] *n* poinçon *m*.

prickle ['prikl] *n* épine *f*, piquant *m*, picotement *m*; *vti* piquer, picoter.

pride [praid] *n* orgueil *m*, fierté *f*; to — oneself on s'enorgueillir de, se piquer de.

priest [pri:st] *n* prêtre *m*, prêtresse *f*.

priesthood ['pri:sthud] *n* prêtrise *f*.

prig [prig] *n* poseur *m*.

priggish ['prigiʃ] *a* pédantesque, poseur, bégueule, suffisant.

priggishness ['prigiʃnis] *n* béguelerie *f*, suffisance *f*.

prim [prim] *a* affecté, collet monté, compassé.

primary ['praiməri] *a* primaire, premier, primitif, brut.

primate ['praimit] *n* primat *m*.

prime [praim] *n* fleur *f* (de l'âge), force *f*, commencement *m*; *a* premier, primordial, de première qualité; *vt* préparer, (engine) amorcer.

primer ['praimə] *n* abécédaire *m*, éléments *m pl*.

primeval [prai'mi:vəl] *a* primordial, primitif, vierge.

primitive ['primitiv] *a* primitif (-ve), primaire.

primness ['primnis] *n* affectation *f*, air pincé *m*, air collet monté *m*.

primrose ['primrouz] *n* primevère *f*.

prince [prins] *n* prince *m*.

princely ['prinsli] *a* princier, royal.

princess ['prinses] *n* princesse *f*.

principal ['prinsəpəl] *an* principal *m*; *n* directeur *m*, chef *m*.

principality [,prinsi'pæliti] *n* principauté *f*.

principle ['prinsəpl] *n* principe *m*.

print [print] *n* empreinte *f*, imprimé *m*, gravure *f*, estampe *f*, impression *f*, épreuve *f*, (tissu *m*) imprimé (*m*).

printer ['printə] *n* imprimeur *m*, typographe *m*.

printing ['printiŋ] *n* impression *f*, imprimerie *f*, tirage *m*, typographie *f*; — office *n* imprimerie *f*.

prior ['praiə] *n* prieur *m*; *a* antérieur, préalable; *ad* antérieurement (à to).

prism ['prizəm] *n* prisme *m*.

prison ['prizn] *n* prison *f*.

prisoner ['priznə] *n* prisonnier, -ière.

privacy ['privəsi] *n* intimité *f*, solitude *f*, secret *m*.

private ['praivit] *n* soldat *m* sans grade, particulier, -ière; *a* privé, personnel, intime, confidentiel, retiré, particulier.

privately ['praivitli] *ad* en particulier, dans l'intimité, en confidence.

privation [prai'veiʃən] *n* privation *f*, manque *m*.

privet ['privit] *n* troène *m*.

privilege ['privilidʒ] *n* privilège *m*, bonne fortune *f*.

privileged ['privilidʒd] *a* privilégié.

privy ['privi] *n* privé *m*, cabinets *m pl*.

prize [praiz] *n* prix *m*, (at sea) prise *f*; *vt* apprécier, évaluer, faire grand cas de.

pro [prou] *prep* pour; *an* professionel, -elle.

probability [,prɔbə'biliti] *n* probabilité *f*, vraisemblance *f*.

probable ['prɔbəbl] *a* probable, vraisemblable.

probation [prə'beiʃən] *n* noviciat *m*,

épreuve *f*, surveillance *f*, stage *m*.
probe [proub] *n* sonde *f*; (US)
enquête *f*, sondage *m*; *vt* sonder,
examiner, approfondir.
probity ['proubiti] *n* probité *f*.
problem ['problem] *n* problème *m*.
problematic [,probli'mætik] *a* problématique, incertain.
procedure [pro'si:dʒə] *n* procédure *f*,
~r *f*.
proceed [pro'si:d] *vi* continuer,
poursuivre, passer, se rendre, venir,
procéder, se prendre.
proceeding [pro'si:diŋ] *n* procédé *m*,
façon d'agir *f*; *pl* poursuites *f pl*,
débats *m pl*, réunion *f*, cérémonie *f*.
proceeds ['prousi:dz] *n pl* produit *m*,
recette *f*.
process ['prouses] *n* cours *m*, marche
f, procédé *m*, processus *m*; *vt*
apprêter.
procession [pro'seʃən] *n* procession
f, défilé *m*, cortège *m*.
proclaim [pro'kleim] *vt* proclamer,
déclarer, trahir.
proclamation [,proklə'meiʃən] *n*
proclamation *f*.
procrastinate [prou'kræstineit] *vi*
temporiser.
procrastination [prou,kræsti'neiʃən]
n temporisation *f*.
procuration [,prokjuə'reiʃən] *n* procuration *f*, commission *f*, obtention *f*.
procure [pro'kjuə] *vt* obtenir, (se)
procurer.
procurement [pro'kjuəmənt] *n* (US)
approvisionnement *m* (d'un service).
procurer [pro'kjuərə] *n* proxénète *m*.
prod [prod] *vt* bourrer les côtes à,
pousser.
prodigal ['prodigəl] *an* prodigue *mf*.
prodigality [,prodi'gæliti] *n* prodigalité *f*.
prodigious [pro'didʒəs] *a* prodigieux,
mirobolant.
prodigy ['prodidʒi] *n* prodige *m*,
merveille *f*.
produce ['prodju:s] *n* produit *m*,
rendement *m*, fruits *m pl*, denrées
f pl.
produce [pro'dju:s] *vt* produire,
présenter, provoquer, (*theatre*) monter, mettre en scène.
producer [pro'dju:sə] *n* producteur *m*,
-trice, metteur en scène *m*.
product ['prodəkt] *n* produit *m*,
résultat *m*.
production [pro'dʌkʃən] *n* production *f*, produit *m*, œuvre *f*, (re)pré-
sentation *f*, mise en scène *f*, fabrication *f*.
productive [pro'dʌktiv] *a* productif,
qui rapporte, fécond.
profane [pro'fein] *a* profane, impie;
vi profaner, violer.
profanity [pro'fæniti] *n* impiété *f*,
blasphème *m*.
profess [pro'fes] *vt* professer, faire
profession de, exercer, prétendre;
to — to be se faire passer pour.

professed [pro'fest] *a* déclaré, avoué,
soi-disant.
profession [pro'feʃən] *n* profession *f*,
carrière *f*, métier *m*, déclaration *f*,
affirmation *f*.
professional [pro'feʃənl] *an* professionel, -elle; *a* de carrière, de métier.
professor [pro'fesə] *n* professeur *m*
(d'université).
proffer ['profə] *vt* offrir, présenter.
proficiency [pro'fiʃənsi] *n* aptitude
f, compétence *f*.
proficient [pro'fiʃənt] *a* bon, fort,
compétent, capable.
profile ['proufail] *n* profil *m*.
profit ['profit] *n* profit *m*, gain *m*,
bénéfice(s) *m* (*pl*); *vti* profiter (à, de
by).
profitable ['profitəbl] *a* profitable,
lucratif, avantageux.
profiteer [,profi'tiə] *n* mercanti *m*,
exploitation *f*, mercantilisme *m*.
profligacy ['profligəsi] *n* débauche *f*.
profligate ['profligit] *an* débauché(e)
mf, libertin(e) *mf*.
profound [pro'faund] *a* profond,
approfondi.
profoundly [pro'faundli] *ad* profondément.
profuse [pro'fju:s] *a* prodigue, copieux, excessif.
profusely [pro'fu:sli] abondamment.
profusion [pro'fju:ʒən] *n* profusion
f, abondance *f*.
progeny ['prodʒini] *n* rejeton *m*,
progéniture *f*.
prognostic [prog'nostik] *n* prognostic
m.
prognosticate [prog'nostikeit] *vt* pro-
gnostiquer, prédire.
program(me) ['prougræm] *n* programme *m*.
progress ['prougres] *n* progrès *m*,
cours *m*.
progress [pro'gres] *vi* (s')avancer,
progresser.
progression [pro'greʃən] *n* progression *f*.
progressive [pro'gresiv] *a* progressif,
de progrès, progressiste, d'avant-
garde.
prohibit [pro'hibit] *vt* défendre,
interdire (de).
prohibition [,proui'biʃən] *n* prohibition *f*, défense *f*, interdiction *f*.
prohibitive [pro'hibitiv] *a* prohibitif,
inabordable.
project ['prodʒekt] *n* projet *m*.
project [pro'dʒekt] *vt* projeter; *vi*
s'avancer, faire saillie.
projectile [pro'dʒektail] *n* projectile
m.
projection [pro'dʒekʃən] *n* projection
f, saillie *f*.
projector [pro'dʒektə] *n* lanceur *m*,
projecteur *m*.
proletarian [,proule'tɛəriən] *an* prolétaire *mf*.
proletariat [,proule'tɛəriət] *n* prolétariat *m*.

prolific [prə'lifik] *a* prolifique, fécond.

prolix ['prouliks] *a* prolixe.

prolong [prə'lɔŋ] *vt* allonger, prolonger.

prolongation [,proulɔŋ'geiʃən] *n* prolongation *f*, prolongement *m*.

promenade [,prɔmi'naːd] *n* promenade *f*, esplanade *f*, promenoir *m*; *vi* se promener.

prominence ['prɔminəns] *n* (pro) éminence *f*, importance *f*.

prominent ['prɔminənt] *a* saillant, éminent, en vue, proéminent.

promiscuity [,prɔmis'kju(ː)iti] *n* promiscuité *f*.

promiscuous [prə'miskjuəs] *a* confus, mêlé, en commun.

promise ['prɔmis] *n* promesse *f*; *vt* promettre.

promising ['prɔmisiŋ] *a* qui promet, prometteur.

promontory ['prɔməntri] *n* promontoire *m*.

promote [prə'mout] *vt* promouvoir, nommer, avancer, encourager, soutenir.

promoter [prə'moutə] *n* promoteur *m*, lanceur *m*, auteur *m*.

promotion [prə'mouʃən] *n* avancement *m*, promotion *f*.

prompt [prɔmpt] *a* actif, prompt; *vt* pousser, inspirer, souffler.

prompter ['prɔmptə] *n* souffleur *m*; **—'s box** trou du souffleur *m*.

promptitude ['prɔmptitjuːd] *n* promptitude *f*, empressement *m*.

prone [proun] *a* couché sur le ventre, porté (à **to**).

prong [prɔŋ] *n* branche *f*, dent *f*, fourchon *m*.

pronoun ['prounaun] *n* pronom *m*.

pronounce [prə'nauns] *vt* prononcer, déclarer.

pronouncement [prə'naunsmənt] *n* déclaration *f*.

pronunciation [prə,nʌnsi'eiʃən] *n* prononciation *f*.

proof [pruːf] *n* preuve *f*, épreuve *f*; *a* à l'épreuve de, à l'abri (de **against**), imperméable, étanche, insensible; *vt* imperméabiliser.

prop [prɔp] *n* étai *m*, tuteur *m*, soutien *m*; *vt* étayer, soutenir, appuyer.

propaganda [,prɔpə'gændə] *n* propagande *f*.

propagate ['prɔpəgeit] *vt* propager, répandre.

propagation [,prɔpə'geiʃən] *n* propagation *f*, dissémination *f*.

propel [prə'pel] *vt* lancer, propulser.

propeller [prə'pelə] *n* hélice *f*.

propensity [prə'pensiti] *n* penchant *m*, inclination *f*, tendance *f* (à, vers **to**, **towards**).

proper ['prɔpə] *a* propre, approprié, décent, vrai, correct, convenable, bon, opportun.

properly ['prɔpəli] *ad* bien, comme il faut, convenablement, correctement, complètement.

property ['prɔpəti] *n* propriété *f*, biens *m pl*, immeuble *m*; *pl* accesoires *m pl*; **—man** *n* machiniste *m*.

prophecy ['prɔfisi] *n* prophétie *f*.

prophesy ['prɔfisai] *vti* prophétiser; *vt* prédire.

prophet ['prɔfit] *n* prophète *m*.

propinquity [prə'piŋkwiti] *n* voisinage *m*, proche parenté *f*, ressemblance *f*.

propitiate [prə'piʃieit] *vt* apaiser, se concilier.

propitious [prə'piʃəs] *a* propice, favorable.

proportion [prə'pɔːʃən] *n* proportion *f*, rapport *m*, part *f*; *vt* proportionner.

proportional [prə'pɔːʃənl] *a* proportionnel, proportionné.

proposal [prə'pouzəl] *n* offre *f*, proposition *f*, projet *m*, demande en mariage *f*.

propose [prə'pouz] *vt* (se) proposer; *vi* demander en mariage.

proposition [,prɔpə'ziʃən] *n* proposition *f*, affaire *f*, entreprise *f*.

propound [prə'paund] *vt* proposer, produire, exposer, émettre.

proprietary [prə'praiətəri] *a* possédant, de propriétaire, de propriété.

proprietor [prə'praiətə] *n* propriétaire *mf*.

propriety [prə'praiəti] *n* convenances *f pl*, bienséance *f*, propriété *f*, correction *f*.

proscribe [prəs'kraib] *vt* proscrire, interdire.

proscription [prəs'kripʃən] *n* proscription *f*, interdiction *f*.

prose [prouz] *n* prose *f*, thème *m*.

prosecute ['prɔsikjuːt] *vt* poursuivre, mener.

prosecution [prɔsi'kjuːʃən] *n* poursuite(s) *f* (*pl*), accusation *f*, ministère public *m*, plaignants *m pl*, exercice *m* (d'un métier).

prosecutor ['prɔsikjuːtə] *n* demandeur *m*, le ministère public *m*, procureur du roi *m*.

prose-writer ['prouz'raitə] *n* prosateur *m*.

prospect ['prɔspekt] *n* vue *f*, perspective *f*, chance *f*; *pl* espérances *f pl*.

prospect [prəs'pekt] *vti* prospecter.

prospective [prəs'pektiv] *a* futur, à venir, éventuel.

prospector [prəs'pektə] *n* prospecteur *m*.

prosper ['prɔspə] *vi* prospérer, réussir.

prosperity [prɔs'periti] *n* prospérité *f*.

prosperous ['prɔspərəs] *a* prospère.

prostitute ['prɔstitjuːt] *n* prostituée *f*; *vt* (se) prostituer, se vendre.

prostrate ['prɔstreit] *a* prosterné, prostré, abattu.

prostrate [prɔs'treit] *vt* abattre, accabler; **to — oneself** se prosterner.

prostration [prɔs'treiʃən] *n* prostration *f*, prosternement *m*, abattement *m*.

prosy ['prouzi] *a* prosaïque, fastidieux.

protect [prə'tekt] *vt* protéger, défendre, sauvegarder.

protection [prə'tekʃən] *n* protection *f*, défense *f*, sauvegarde *f*.

protective [prə'tektiv] *a* protecteur.

protein ['prouti:n] *n* protéine *f*.

protest ['proutest] *n* protestation *f*, protêt *m*.

protest [prə'test] *vti* protester; *vt* protester de.

protestant ['prɔtistənt] *n* protestant (e) *mf*.

protocol ['proutəkɔl] *n* protocole *m*.

prototype ['proutətaip] *n* prototype *m*, archétype *m*.

protract [prə'trækt] *vt* prolonger.

protraction [prə'trækʃən] *n* prolongation *f*.

protrude [prə'tru:d] *vi* faire saillie, s'avancer.

proud [praud] *a* fier, orgueilleux.

prove [pru:v] *vt* prouver, démontrer; *vi* se montrer, s'avérer.

provender ['prɔvində] *n* fourrage *m*.

proverb ['prɔvəb] *n* proverbe *m*.

provide [prə'vaid] *vt* fournir, pourvoir, munir, stipuler; *vi* **to — against** se prémunir contre.

provided [prə'vaidid] *cj* pourvu que.

providence ['prɔvidəns] *n* prévoyance *f*, économie *f*, Providence *f*.

provident ['prɔvidənt] *a* prévoyant, économe.

providential [,prɔvi'denʃəl] *a* providentiel.

province ['prɔvins] *n* province *f*.

provincial [prə'vinʃəl] *an* provincial (e) *mf*.

provision [prə'viʒən] *n* provision *f*, approvisionnement *m*, stipulation *f*.

proviso [prə'vaizou] *n* condition *f*, clause *f*.

provocation [,prɔvə'keiʃən] *n* provocation *f*.

provocative [prə'vɔkətiv] *a* provoquant, provocateur.

provoke [prə'vouk] *vt* provoquer, exciter, exaspérer.

provost ['prɔvəst] *n* prévôt *m*, maire *m*.

prow [prau] *n* proue *f*.

prowess ['prauis] *n* courage *m*, prouesse *f*.

prowl [praul] *vi* rôder.

proximate ['prɔksimit] *a* prochain, proche.

proximity [prɔk'simiti] *n* proximité *f*.

proxy ['prɔksi] *n* procuration *f*, mandataire *mf*, fondé *m* de pouvoir(s).

prudence ['pru:dəns] *n* prudence *f*, sagesse *f*.

prudent ['pru:dənt] *a* prudent, sage.

prudery ['pru:dəri] *n* pruderie *f*, pudibonderie *f*.

prudish ['pru:diʃ] *a* prude, bégueule, pudibond.

prune [pru:n] *n* pruneau *m*; *vt* émonder, tailler, élaguer (de off).

pruning ['pru:niŋ] *n* élagage *m*, émondage *m*, taille *f*; **—shears** *n* sécateur *m*.

pry [prai] *vi* fureter, fourrer le nez (dans into).

psalm [sɑ:m] *n* psaume *m*.

psalmody ['sælmədi] *n* psalmodie *f*.

pseudonym ['psju:dənim] *n* pseudonyme *m*.

psychiatrist [sai'kaiətrist] *n* psychiatre *m*.

psychoanalysis [,saikouə'nælisis] *n* psychanalyse *f*.

psychologist [sai'kɔlədʒist] *n* psychologue *m*.

psychology [sai'kɔlədʒi] *n* psychologie *f*.

pub [pʌb] *n* bistro *m*, bar *m*.

puberty ['pju:bəti] *n* puberté *f*.

public ['pʌblik] *an* public *m*.

publication [,pʌbli'keiʃən] *n* publication *f*.

publicist ['pʌblisist] *n* publiciste *m*.

publicity [pʌb'lisiti] *n* publicité *f*, réclame *f*.

publish ['pʌbliʃ] *vt* publier, faire paraître.

publisher ['pʌbliʃə] *n* éditeur *m*.

publishing ['pʌbliʃiŋ] *n* publication *f*; **— house** maison *f* d'édition.

puck [pʌk] *n* lutin *m*, palet *m*.

pucker ['pʌkə] *n* ride *f*, pli *m*, fronce *f*; *vt* plisser, rider, froncer; *vi* se froncer.

pudding ['pudiŋ] *n* pudding *m*; **black —** boudin *m*.

puddle ['pʌdl] *n* flaque *f*, gâchis *m*; *vi* barboter; *vt* brasser, corroyer.

puff [pʌf] *n* souffle *m*, bouffée *f*, houppe *f*, bouffant *m*, feuilleté *m*, réclame *f*; *vi* haleter, souffler, lancer des bouffées; *vt* vanter, gonfler, essouffler.

puffed ['pʌft] *a* essoufflé, bouffant.

puffy ['pʌfi] *a* gonflé, bouffi.

pug(-nose) ['pʌgnouz] *n* nez *m* épaté.

pugnacious [pʌg'neiʃəs] *a* batailleur.

pull [pul] *n* tirage *m*, influence *f*, avantage *m*, piston *m*, lampée *f*, effort *m*; *vt* traîner; *vti* tirer; **to — down** démolir, baisser, renverser; **to — off** enlever, gagner; **to — out** *vt* tirer, arracher; *vi* démarrer, sortir; **to — through** *vt* tirer d'affaire; *vi* se tirer d'affaire; **to — up** *vt* arracher, relever, arrêter; *vi* s'arrêter; **to — oneself together** se ressaisir.

pullet ['pulit] *n* poulette *f*.

pulley ['puli] *n* poulie *f*.

pullover ['pul,ouvə] *n* pull-over *m*, tricot *m*.

pulp [pʌlp] *n* pulpe *f*, pâte *f*, chair *f*.

pulpit ['pulpit] *n* chaire *f*.

pulsate [pʌl'seit] *vi* battre, palpiter, vibrer.

pulse [pʌls] *n* pouls *m*, pulsation *f*, battement *m*; *vi* battre, palpiter.

pulverize ['pʌlvəraiz] *vt* pulvériser, broyer.

pumice(-stone) ['pʌmis(stoun)] *n* pierre ponce *f*.

pump [pʌmp] *n* pompe *f*; *vt* pomper, tirer les vers du nez à.

pumpkin ['pʌmpkin] *n* citrouille *f*.

pun [pʌn] *n* jeu de mots *m*, calembour *m*.

punch [pʌntʃ] *n* poinçon *m*, Polichinelle *m*, coup de poing *m*; *vt* poinçonner, trouer, étamper, donner un coup de poing à.

punctilious [pʌŋk'tiliəs] *a* pointilleux, chatouilleux.

punctual ['pʌŋktjuəl] *a* exact, ponctuel.

punctuality [,pʌŋktju'æliti] *n* ponctualité *f*, exactitude *f*.

punctuate ['pʌŋktjueit] *vt* ponctuer.

punctuation [,pʌŋktju'eiʃən] *n* ponctuation *f*.

puncture ['pʌŋktʃə] *n* piqûre *f*, crevaison *f*; *vti* crever.

pundit [pʌndit] *n* pontife *m*.

pungency ['pʌndʒənsi] *n* âcreté *f*, mordant *m*, saveur *f*.

pungent ['pʌndʒənt] *a* aigu, -uë, mordant, piquant, âcre.

punish ['pʌniʃ] *vt* punir, corriger.

punishable ['pʌniʃəbl] *a* punissable, délictueux.

punishment ['pʌniʃmənt] *n* punition *f*.

punt [pʌnt] *n* bachot *m*, coup de volée *m*.

puny ['pju:ni] *a* chétif, mesquin.

pup(py) ['pʌp(i)] *n* chiot *m*, petit chien *m*.

pupil ['pju:pl] *n* élève *mf*, (eye) pupille *f*.

puppet ['pʌpit] *n* marionnette *f*, pantin *m*.

purblind ['pə:blaind] *a* myope, obtus.

purchase ['pə:tʃəs] *n* achat *m*, acquisition *f*, prise *f*, point d'appui *m*; *vt* acheter.

purchaser ['pə:tʃəsə] *n* acheteur, -euse, acquéreur, -euse.

pure [pjuə] *a* pur.

purgation [pə:'geiʃən] *n* purification *f*, purgation *f*, purge *f*.

purgative ['pə:gətiv] *an* purgatif *m*.

purgatory ['pə:gətəri] *n* purgatoire *m*.

purge [pə:dʒ] *n* purge *f*, épuration *f*; *vt* purger, épurer.

purify ['pjuərifai] *vt* purifier.

Puritan ['pjuəritən] *an* puritain(e) *mf*.

purity ['pjuəriti] *n* pureté *f*.

purl [pə:l] *n* murmure *m*; *vi* murmurer.

purlieu ['pə:lju:] *n* lisière *f*, alentours *m pl*, bornes *f pl*.

purloin ['pə:lɔin] *vt* voler, soustraire.

purple ['pə:pl] *an* violet *m*, cramoisi *m*, pourpre *m*; *n* pourpre *f*.

purport ['pə:pət] *n* sens *m*, teneur *f*.

purport [pə:'pɔ:t] *vt* signifier, impliquer.

purpose ['pə:pəs] *n* dessein *m*, intention *f*, objet *m*; *vt* se proposer (de).

purposeful ['pə:pəsful] *a* calculé, réfléchi, énergique, avisé.

purposeless ['pə:pəslis] *a* sans objet, inutile.

purposely ['pə:pəsli] *ad* à dessein.

purr [pə:] *n* ronronnement *m*; *vi* ronronner.

purse [pə:s] *n* porte-monnaie *m*, bourse *f*; *vt* plisser, serrer, froncer.

purser ['pə:sə] *n* commissaire *m*.

pursuance [pə'sju(:)əns] *n* exécution *f*, conséquence *f*; in — of conformément à.

pursue [pə'sju:] *vti* poursuivre.

pursuit [pə'sju:t] *n* poursuite *f*, occupation *f*, recherche *f*.

purvey [pə:'vei] *vt* fournir.

purveyor [pə:'veiə] *n* fournisseur, -euse.

purview ['pə:vju:] *n* teneur *f*, portée *f*.

pus [pʌs] *n* pus *m*.

push [puʃ] *n* poussée *f*, coup *m* (d'épaule), effort *m*, pression *f*, crise *f*, entregent *m*; *vti* pousser; *vt* presser, appuyer.

pushing ['puʃiŋ] *a* intrigant, entreprenant, débrouillard, ambitieux.

puss [pus] *n* minet, -ette, minou *m*.

put [put] *vt* mettre, remettre, placer, estimer, lancer, verser; to — back retarder, remettre à sa place; to — by mettre de côté; to — down (dé) poser, réprimer, supprimer, noter, attribuer, rabattre; to — in *vt* installer, introduire, glisser, passer; *vi* to — in at faire escale à; to — off *vt* ajourner, remettre, ôter, dérouter; *vi* démarrer; to — on mettre, passer, revêtir, feindre; to — out éteindre, tendre, déconcerter, mettre à la porte, sortir, démettre, publier; to — through exécuter, mettre en communication; to — up *vt* (faire) dresser, construire, monter, hausser, lever, apposer, présenter, loger, héberger, proposer; *vi* descendre, loger; to — up with s'accommoder de, supporter.

putrefy ['pju:trifai] *vi* pourrir, se putréfier.

putrid ['pju:trid] *a* putride, infect.

putty ['pʌti] *n* mastic *m*.

puzzle ['pʌzl] *n* enigme *f*, devinette *f*, embarras *m*; **jigsaw — puzzle** *m*; *vt* intriguer, embarrasser; *vi* se creuser la tête.

pygmy ['pigmi] *n* pygmée *m*.

pyjamas [pə'dʒɑ:məz] *n* pyjama(s) *m* (*pl*).

pylon ['pailən] *n* pylône *m*.

pyramid ['pirəmid] *n* pyramide *f*.
pyre ['paiə] *n* bûcher *m*.
pyx [piks] *n* ciboire *m*.

Q

quack [kwæk] *n* charlatan *m*, couin-couin *m*.
quackery ['kwækəri] *n* charlatanisme *m*.
quadrangle ['kwɔˌdræŋgl] *n* quadrilatère *m*, cour *f*.
quadruple ['kwɔdrupl] *an* quadruple *m*.
quaff [kwɑːf] *vt* lamper, vider d'un seul trait.
quagmire ['kwægmaiə] *n* fondrière *f*.
quail [kweil] *n* caille *f*; *vi* flancher, défaillir.
quaint [kweint] *a* désuet, délicat, étrange, archaïque, fantasque, vieux jeu.
quake [kweik] *vi* trembler.
qualification [ˌkwɔlifi'keiʃən] *n* réserve *f*, atténuation *f*, condition *f*, nom *m*; *pl* titres *m*.
qualify ['kwɔlifai] *vt* qualifier, traiter (de), atténuer, modifier, modérer; *vi* acquérir les titres, se qualifier.
quality ['kwɔliti] *n* qualité *f*.
qualm [kwɔːm] *n* scrupule *m*, remords *m*.
quandary ['kwɔndəri] *n* embarras *m*, impasse *f*.
quantity ['kwɔntiti] *n* quantité *f*.
quarantine ['kwɔrəntiːn] *n* quarantaine *f*.
quarrel ['kwɔrəl] *n* querelle *f*, dispute *f*; *vi* se quereller, se disputer.
quarrelsome ['kwɔrəlsəm] *a* querelleur.
quarry ['kwɔri] *n* proie *f*, carrière *f*; *vt* extraire.
quarter ['kwɔːtə] *n* quart *m*, trimestre *m*, région *f*, logement *m*, quartier *m*, (US) pièce d'1 dollar; *vt* couper en quatre, loger, équarrir, écarteler; — **of an hour** quart d'heure *m*; **a** — to moins le quart; **a** — **past** et quart; —**deck** *n* gaillard d'arrière *m*; —**master-sergeant** *n* maréchal des logis *m*.
quarterly ['kwɔːtəli] *a* trimestriel.
quartet [kwɔː'tet] *n* quatuor *m*.
quarto ['kwɔːtou] *n* inquarto *m*.
quash [kwɔʃ] *vt* casser, annuler.
quaver ['kweivə] *n* chevrotement *m*, trille *m*, croche *f*; *vi* faire des trilles, trembloter, chevroter.
quay [kiː] *n* quai *m*.
queasy ['kwiːzi] *a* barbouillé, scrupuleux.
queen ['kwiːn] *n* reine *f*, (*cards*) dame *f*.
queer ['kwiə] *a* étrange, bizarre, louche.
quell [kwel] *vt* réprimer, écraser, apaiser.

quench [kwentʃ] *vt* éteindre, étancher.
querulous ['kweruləs] *a* plaintif, grognon.
query ['kwiəri] *n* question *f*, (point *m* d')interrogation *f*; *vt* demander, mettre en question.
quest [kwest] *n* quête *f*, recherche *f*.
question ['kwestʃən] *n* question *f*, hésitation *f*, doute *m*; *excl* c'est à savoir! *vt* interroger, questionner, mettre en doute, contester; — **mark** *n* point d'interrogation *m*.
questionable ['kwestʃənəbl] *a* douteux, contestable.
queue [kjuː] *n* queue *f*; *vi* faire la queue.
quibble ['kwibl] *n* jeu *m* de mots, faux-fuyant *m*, équivoque *f*; *vi* ergoter.
quibbler ['kwiblə] *n* ergoteur, -euse.
quick [kwik] *n* vif *m*, fond *m*, moelle *f*; *a* vif, éveillé, rapide, fin; *ad* rapidement, vite; —**tempered** emporté; —**witted** vif.
quicken ['kwikən] *vt* hâter, exciter, animer; *vi* s'animer, s'accélérer.
quicklime ['kwiklaim] *n* chaux vive *f*.
quickly ['kwikli] *ad* vite.
quickness ['kwiknis] *n* vivacité *f*, promptitude *f*, rapidité *f*, acuité *f*.
quicksand ['kwik sænd] *n* sable mouvant *m*.
quicksilver ['kwik silvə] *n* mercure *m*, vif-argent *m*.
quiet ['kwaiət] *n* calme *m*; paix *f*; *a* tranquille, en paix; *vt* apaiser, calmer.
quietly ['kwaiətli] *ad* doucement, silencieusement.
quietness ['kwaiətnis] *n* tranquillité *f*, repos *m*, quiétude *f*, sagesse *f*.
quill [kwil] *n* plume *f* (d'oie), curedent *m*, bobine *f*; *vt* gaufrer, enrouler, rucher.
quilt [kwilt] *n* couverture piquée *f*, édredon *m*; *vt* piquer, ouater.
quince [kwins] *n* coing *m*.
quinine [kwi'niːn] *n* quinine.
quinsy ['kwinzi] *n* angine *f*.
quip [kwip] *n* sarcasme *m*, mot fin *m*, pointe *f*.
quire ['kwaiə] *n* main *f* (de papier).
quirk [kwəːk] *n* argutie *f*, méchant tour *m*, fioriture *f*.
quit [kwit] *a* libre, quitte, débarrassé; *vt* quitter; *vi* démissionner, abandonner la partie.
quite ['kwait] *ad* tout (à fait), bien.
quits [kwits] *n ad* quitte(s).
quiver ['kwivə] *n* carquois *m*, tremblement *m*; *vi* trembler, frémir.
quiz [kwiz] *n* jeu *m*, colle *f*, mystification *f*, original *m*; *vt* dévisager, lorgner, railler.
quizzical ['kwizikəl] *a* ironique, railleur.
quoit [kɔit] *n* anneau *m*, palet *m*.
quota ['kwoutə] *n* quotepart *f*.

quotation [kwou'teiʃən] n citation f,
cote f, cours m; — **marks** n pl
guillemets m pl.
quote [kwout] vt citer, coter; n
citation f.
quotient ['kwouʃənt] n quotient m.

R

rabbi ['ræbai] n rabbin m.
rabbit ['ræbit] n lapin m.
rabble ['ræbl] n canaille f.
rabid ['ræbid] a enragé, acharné,
fanatique.
rabies ['reibiz] n rage f.
race [reis] n race f, course f, courant
m, cours m; vi faire une course,
lutter de vitesse, courir; vt faire
courir, (engine) emballer; —course
n champ de course m; —horse n
cheval de course m.
raciness ['reisinis] n verve f, saveur
f, goût de terroir m.
rack [ræk] n râtelier m, filet m,
égouttoir m, étagère f, chevalet m;
vt torturer, pressurer; to — one's
brains se creuser la cervelle; —ed
by hunger tenaillé par la faim.
racket ['rækit] n raquette f, vacarme
m, vie joyeuse f, affaire véreuse f,
combine f.
racketeer [.ræki'tiə] n gangster m,
combinard m.
racy ['reisi] a de terroir, savoureux,
piquant, salé.
radiance ['reidiəns] n rayonnement
m, éclat m.
radiant ['reidiənt] a rayonnant,
radieux, resplendissant.
radiate ['reidieit] vi rayonner, irradier; vt dégager, émettre.
radiator ['reidieitə] n radiateur m.
radical ['rædikəl] a radical, foncier.
radicalism ['rædikəlizəm] n radica-
lisme m.
radio ['reidiou] n radio f; vt émettre
par la radio; — **control** téléguidage;
vt téléguider.
radioactive ['reidiou'æktiv] a radio-
actif; — **material** matière f rayon-
nante.
radiograph ['reidiougrɑːf] vt radiographier; n-radio(graphie) f.
radiography [reidi'ɔgrəfi] n radiographie f.
radish ['rædiʃ] n radis m.
radius ['reidiəs] n rayon m.
raffle ['ræfl] n loterie f, tombola f;
vt mettre en loterie, en tombola.
raft [rɑːft] n radeau m, train de bois
m.
rafter ['rɑːftə] n chevron m.
rag [ræg] n chiffon m, haillon m,
chahut m, monôme m, brimade f;
vt chahuter, brimer.
ragamuffin ['rægə,mʌfin] n loqueteux, -euse, va-nu-pieds m.
rage [reidʒ] n rage f, fureur f; vi

rager, faire rage; **to be all the** —
faire fureur.
ragged ['rægid] a en loques, déchiqueté, désordonné.
raging ['reidʒiŋ] a furieux, démonté,
fou, brûlant.
ragman ['rægmæn] n chiffonnier m.
raid [reid] n raid m, rafle f; vt
razzier, faire une rafle dans, bombarder.
rail [reil] n rail m, rampe f, balustrade f, barrière f, parapet m,
garde-fou m; pl bastingages m pl;
vi se déchaîner (contre at).
railhead ['reilhed] n tête f de ligne.
railing(s) ['reiliŋ(z)] n grille f,
clôture f.
railroad ['reilroud] n (US) chemin m
de fer; vt faire voter en vitesse un
projet de loi.
railway ['reilwei] n chemin de fer m;
— **line** n voie ferrée f; — **station** n
gare f, station f.
rain [rein] n pluie f; vi pleuvoir.
rainbow ['reinbou] n arc-en-ciel m.
raincoat ['reinkout] n imperméable
m.
rainfall ['reinfɔːl] n précipitation f.
rain-pipe ['rein.paip] n (tuyeau m
de) descente f.
rainy ['reini] a pluvieux.
raise [reiz] vt (é-, sou-, re-)lever,
faire pousser, cultiver, (res)susciter,
provoquer, dresser, hausser, augmenter; (US) n augmentation f (de
salaire).
raisin ['reizn] n raisin sec m.
rake [reik] n râteau m, roué m; vt
ratisser, râcler, balayer; — **off** gratte
f; to — **up** vt attiser, raviver.
rakish ['reikiʃ] a coquin, dissolu,
désinvolte, bravache.
rally ['ræli] n ralliement m, réunion
f, rallye m, rétablissement m,
dernier effort m; vt rallier, rétablir;
vi se rallier, se reformer, retrouver
des forces, se reprendre.
Ralph [rælf] Raoul, Rodolphe m.
ram [ræm] n bélier m, éperon m,
marteau-pilon m; vt éperonner,
pilonner, tasser, bourrer, enfoncer,
tamponner.
ramble ['ræmbl] n flânerie f,
promenade f, divagation f; vi
errer, flâner, divaguer.
rambler ['ræmblə] n flâneur, -euse,
plante grimpante f.
rambling ['ræmbliŋ] a errant, vagabond, décousu; n pl promenades
f pl, divagations f pl.
ramp [ræmp] n rampe f, pente f,
scandale m, affaire véreuse f,
supercherie f, coup monté m.
rampant ['ræmpənt] a forcené,
répandu, envahissant, rampant.
rampart ['ræmpɑːt] n rempart m.
ramshackle ['ræm.ʃækl] a branlant,
délabré.
ran [ræn] pt of **run**.
ranch [rɑːntʃ] n ranch m, prairie f

d'élevage; *vi* faire de l'élevage.

rancid ['rænsid] *a* rance.

rancidness ['rænsidnis] *n* rancidité *f*.

rancorous ['ræŋkərəs] *a* rancunier.

rancour ['ræŋkə] *n* rancœur *f*, rancune *f*.

random ['rændəm] *n* at — à l'aventure, au hasard.

rang [ræŋ] *pt* of **ring**.

range ['reindʒ] *n* rangée *f*, étendue *f*, gamme *f*, rang *m*, direction *f*, portée *f*, fourneau *m* de cuisine, champ de tir *m*, grand pâturage *m*; *vt* ranger, (*gun*) porter, braquer; *vi* s'étendre, errer.

rank ['ræŋk] *n* rang *m*, classe *f*, grade *m*; *vt* ranger; *vi* se ranger, compter; *a* luxuriant, rance, fort, absolu, flagrant, criant, pur.

rankle ['ræŋkl] *vi* s'envenimer, laisser une rancœur.

ransack ['rænsæk] *vt* fouiller, piller.

ransom ['rænsəm] *n* rançon *f*; *vt* rançonner, racheter.

rant [rænt] *n* tirade enflammée *f*, rodomontades *f pl*; *vi* pérorer.

rap [ræp] *n* tape *f*, coup sec *m*, (*fig*) pomme *f*; *vt* donner sur les doigts à; *vti* frapper.

rapacious [rə'peiʃəs] *a* rapace.

rape [reip] *n* viol *m*, (*bot*) colza *m*; *vt* violer.

rapid ['ræpid] *a* rapide.

rapt [ræpt] *a* ravi, recueilli.

rapture ['ræptʃə] *n* ravissement *m*, ivresse *f*.

rapturous ['ræptʃərəs] *a* ravissant, frénétique, extasié.

rare [rɛə] *a* rare.

rarefaction [ˌrɛəri'fækʃən] *n* raréfaction *f*.

rarefy ['rɛərifai] *vt* raréfier.

rarity ['rɛəriti] *n* rareté *f*.

rascal ['rɑːskəl] *n* gredin *m*, fripon *m*, coquin *m*.

rash [ræʃ] *n* éruption *f*; *a* impulsif, casse-cou, irréfléchi.

rasher ['ræʃə] *n* tranche de lard *f*.

rashness ['ræʃnis] *n* impulsivité *f*, témérité *f*.

rasp [rɑːsp] *n* râpe *f*; *vt* râper, racler; *vi* grincer.

raspberry ['rɑːzbəri] *n* framboise *f*.

rat [ræt] *n* rat *m*, faux frère *m*, mouchard *n*; **to smell a** — soupçonner anguille sous roche; *vi* tourner casaque.

ratchet ['rætʃit] *n* cliquet *m*, rochet *m*.

rate [reit] *n* taux *m*, prix *m*, raison *f*, vitesse *f*, impôt municipal *m*, cas *m*; **at any** — en tout cas; *vt* estimer, compter, considérer, classer, imposer; *vi* passer, être classé.

ratepayer ['reit,peiə] *n* contribuable *mf*.

rather ['rɑːðə] *ad* plutôt, assez.

ratification [ˌrætifi'keiʃən] *n* ratification *f*.

ratify ['rætifai] *vt* ratifier, approuver.

ratio ['reiʃiou] *n* proportion *f*, raison *f*.

ration ['ræʃən] *n* ration *f*; *vt* rationner.

rational ['ræʃənl] *a* raisonnable, raisonné, rationnel.

rationalist ['ræʃnəlist] *an* rationaliste *mf*.

rationing ['ræʃniŋ] *n* rationnement *m*.

rat-race ['rætreis] *n* course *f* aux sous.

rattle ['rætl] *n* (bruit de) crécelle *f*, hochet *m*, râle *m*, cliquetis *m*, tintamarre *m*, fracas *m*, crépitement *m*; *vt* faire cliqueter, faire sonner, bouleverser; *vi* ferrailler, cliqueter, crépiter, trembler; **—snake** *n* serpent *m* à sonnettes.

raucous ['rɔːkəs] *a* rauque.

ravage ['rævidʒ] *n* ravage *m*; *vt* ravager, dévaster.

rave [reiv] *vi* hurler, délirer, radoter, s'extasier (sur **about**), raffoler (de **about**).

ravel ['rævəl] *vt* embrouiller; **to — out** débrouiller, effilocher.

raven ['reivn] *n* corbeau *m*.

ravenous ['rævinəs] *a* dévorant, vorace, affamé.

ravine [rə'viːn] *n* ravin *m*.

raving ['reiviŋ] *n* hurlement *m*, délire *m*, *a* délirant; **— mad** fou à lier.

ravish ['ræviʃ] *vt* ravir, violer.

raw [rɔː] *n* vif *m*; *a* cru, (*oil*) brut, âpre, mal dégrossi, inexpérimenté; **— materials** matières premières *f pl*.

rawness ['rɔːnis] *n* crudité *f*, âpreté *f*, inexpérience *f*.

ray [rei] *n* rayon *m*, (*fish*) raie *f*.

rayon ['reiən] *n* soie artificielle *f*, rayonne *f*.

raze [reiz] *vt* raser.

razor ['reizə] *n* rasoir *m*.

reach [riːtʃ] *n* portée *f*, (*sport*) allonge *f*, brief *m*; *vt* atteindre, arriver à, parvenir à, (é)tendre; *vi* s'étendre.

react [riː'ækt] *vi* réagir.

reaction [riː'ækʃən] *n* réaction *f*, contre-coup *m*.

reactor [riː'æktə] *n* réacteur *m* atomique; **breeder** — pile couvreuse.

read [riːd, *pp* red] *vt* lire, étudier; **to — through** parcourir.

readable ['riːdəbl] *a* lisible, d'une lecture facile.

reader ['riːdə] *n* lecteur, -trice, liseur, -euse, professeur adjoint *m*, livre de lecture *m*.

readily ['redili] *ad* volontiers, facilement.

readiness ['redinis] *n* empressement *m*, alacrité *f*, facilité *f*.

reading ['riːdiŋ] *n* lecture *f*, interprétation *f*.

readjust ['riːə'dʒʌst] *vt* rajuster, rectifier.

ready ['redi] *a* prêt, facile, prompt ;
—**made** *a* prêt à porter, tout fait ;
— **reckoner** *n* barême *m*.

real [riəl] *n* réel *m*; *a* vrai, naturel,
réel, foncier; *ad* (US) vraiment.

reality [ri'æliti] *n* réalité *f*.

realization [,riəlai'zeiʃən] *n* réalisation *f*.

realize ['riəlaiz] *vt* comprendre, se
rendre compte de, réaliser.

really ['riəli] *ad* vraiment, en effet.

realm [relm] *n* royaume *m*, domaine
m.

realtor ['riːəltə] *n* (US) agent *m* immobilier.

ream [riːm] *n* rame *f*.

reap [riːp] *vt* moissonner, récolter.

reaper ['riːpə] *n* moissonneur, -euse,
(machine *f*) moissonneuse *f*.

reaping-hook ['riːpiŋhuk] *n* faucille
f.

reappear ['riːə'piə] *vi* réapparaître.

rear [riə] *n* arrière(s) *m* (*pl*), derrière
m, queue *f*, dernier rang *m*; *a* (d')
arrière, de queue; *vt* élever, dresser, ériger; *vi* se cabrer, s'élever, se
dresser; —**guard** *n* arrière-garde *f*.

reason ['riːzn] *n* raison *f*, motif *m*;
vi raisonner.

reasonable ['riːznəbl] *a* raisonnable.

reassemble ['riːə'sembl] *vt* rassembler, remonter.

rebate ['riːbeit] *n* rabais *m*, ristourne
f, escompte *m*.

rebel ['rebl] *n* rebelle *mf*; *a* insurgé.

rebel [ri'bel] *vi* se révolter.

rebellion [ri'beljən] *n* rébellion *f*,
révolte *f*.

rebellious [ri'beljəs] *a* rebelle.

rebound [ri'baund] *n* recul *m*,
ricochet *m*, réaction *f*; *vi* rebondir,
ricocher.

rebuff [ri'bʌf] *n* rebuffade *f*, échec
m; *vt* rabrouer, repousser.

rebuke [ri'bjuːk] *n* semonce *f*,
réprimande *f*; *vt* rembarrer, réprimander.

rebut [ri'bʌt] *vt* repousser, réfuter.

recall [ri'kɔːl] *n* rappel *m*, annulation
f; *vt* (se) rappeler, révoquer, reprendre.

recant [ri'kænt] *vt* retirer, rétracter ;
vi se rétracter.

recapitulate [,riːkə'pitjuleit] *vt* récapituler.

recede [ri'siːd] *vi* reculer, se retirer,
baisser, s'enfuir, fuir.

receipt [ri'siːt] *n* réception *f*,
recette *f*, reçu *m*, récépissé *m*,
quittance *f*; *vt* acquitter.

receive [ri'siːv] *vt* recevoir, admettre,
accueillir.

receiver [ri'siːvə] *n* receleur, -euse,
recepteur *m*, destinataire *mf*; **official**
— syndic.

recent ['riːsnt] *a* récent.

recently ['riːsntli] *ad* récemment,
dernièrement.

receptacle [ri'septəkl] *n* réceptacle
m, récipient *m*.

reception [ri'sepʃən] *n* réception *f*,
accueil *m*.

recess [ri'ses] *n* vacances parlemen-
taires *f pl*, repli *m*, recoin *m*, alcôve *f*.

recipe ['resipi] *n* recette *f*, ordonnance *f*, formule *f*.

reciprocal [ri'siprəkəl] *a* réciproque.

reciprocate [ri'siprəkeit] *vt* (se)
rendre, payer de retour; *vi* rendre la
pareille.

recital [ri'saitl] *n* exposé *m*, recitation *f*, récital *m*.

recite [ri'sait] *vt* réciter, énumérer.

reckless ['reklis] *a* imprudent,
forcené, casse-cou.

recklessness ['reklisnis] *n* imprudence *f*, témérité *f*.

reckon ['rekən] *vt* calculer, compter;
vi estimer.

reckoning ['rekniŋ] *n* règlement de
comptes *m*, calcul *m*, compte *m*.

reclaim [ri'kleim] *vt* reprendre,
réformer, récupérer.

recline [ri'klain] *vt* pencher, étendre,
reposer; *vi* (se) reposer, être appuyé.

recluse [ri'kluːs] *an* reclus(e) *mf*; *n*
anachorète *m*.

recognition [,rekəg'niʃən] *n* reconnaissance *f*.

recognizable [,rekəg'naizəbl] *a* re-
connaissable.

recognizance [ri'kɔgnizəns] *n* engagement *m*, caution *f*.

recognize ['rekəgnaiz] *vt* reconnaître,
avouer.

recoil [ri'kɔil] *n* recul *m*, rebondisse-
ment *m*; *vi* reculer, retomber,
rejaillir, se détendre.

recollect [,rekə'lekt] *vt* se rappeler,
se souvenir de.

recollection [,rekə'lekʃən] *n* mémoire *f*, souvenir *m*.

recommend [,rekə'mend] *vt* confier,
recommander, conseiller.

recompense ['rekəmpens] *n* récompense *f*, compensation *f*; *vt* récompenser, dédommager.

reconcilable ['rekənsailəbl] *a* con-
ciliable.

reconcile ['rekənsail] *vt* (ré)concilier
(à, avec).

reconciliation [,rekənsili'eiʃən] *n*
(ré)conciliation *f*.

recondite [ri'kɔndait] *a* abstrus,
obscur.

recondition [,riːkən'diʃən] *vt* remettre en état, à neuf.

reconnoitre [,rekə'nɔitə] *vt* reconnaître; *vi* faire une reconnaissance.

record ['rekɔːd] *n* document *m*,
dossier *m*, casier *m*, record *m*,
disque *m*, enregistrement *m*, passé
m; — **player** tourne-disques *m inv*.

record [ri'kɔːd] *vt* rapporter, enregistrer, prendre acte de.

recorder [ri'kɔːdə] *n* archiviste *m*,
greffier, appareil enregistreur *m*,
flûte à bec *f*.

recount [ri'kaunt] *vt* raconter.

recoup [ri'kuːp] *vt* défalquer, dédommager; to — one's losses se rattraper de ses pertes.

recourse [ri'kɔːs] n recours m.

recover [ri'kʌvə] vt recouvrer, récupérer, reprendre, rattraper; vi se rétablir, se remettre, se ressaisir.

recovery [ri'kʌvəri] n recouvrement m, récupération f, rétablissement m, relèvement m.

recreation [ˌrekri'eiʃən] n délassement m, divertissement m.

recriminate [ri'krimineit] vi récriminer.

recruit [ri'kruːt] n recrue f; vt recruter, racoler.

recruiting [ri'kruːtiŋ] n recrutement m.

rectangle ['rek,tæŋgl] an rectangle m.

rectification [ˌrektifi'keiʃən] n rectification f, redressement m.

rectify ['rektifai] vt rectifier, réparer, redresser.

rector ['rektə] n recteur m.

recumbent [ri'kʌmbənt] a couché.

recuperate [ri'kjuːpəreit] vt récupérer; vi se rétablir.

recur [ri'kəː] vi revenir, se reproduire.

red [red] a rouge, roux; —handed a pris sur le fait; — herring n hareng saur m, diversion f; —hot chauffé au rouge; —letter a heureux, mémorable; — tape n paperasserie f, bureaucratie f.

redbreast ['redbrest] n rouge-gorge m.

Red Cross ['red'krɔs] n Croix Rouge f.

redden ['redn] vti rougir.

reddish ['rediʃ] a rougeâtre.

redeem [ri'diːm] vt racheter, sauver.

redeemer [ri'diːmə] n sauveur m, rédempteur m.

redemption [ri'dempʃən] n rédemption), salut m, rachat m.

redness ['rednis] n rougeur f, rousseur f.

redolent ['redələnt] a qui sent, parfumé.

redouble [ri'dʌbl] vti redoubler; vt plier en quatre, (bridge) surcontrer.

redoubt [ri'daut] n redoute f.

redoubtable [ri'dautəbl] a redoutable.

redress [riː'dres] n réparation f; vt redresser, réparer.

reduce [ri'djuːs] vt réduire, diminuer, ravaler, ramener; vi maigrir.

reduced [ri'djuːst] a diminué, appauvri.

reducible [ri'djuːsəbl] a réductible.

reduction [ri'dʌkʃən] n réduction f, baisse f, rabais m.

redundant [ri'dʌndənt] a redondant, superflu.

reed [riːd] n roseau m, pipeau m, anche f.

reef [riːf] n récif m, écueil m, filon m, ris m.

reek [riːk] n fumée f, vapeur f,

relent m; vi fumer; to — of empester.

reel ['riːl] n bobine f, dévidoir m, moulinet m; vt enrouler, dévider; vi tituber, tourner, être ébranlé.

re-elect ['riːi'lekt] vt réélire.

re-embark ['riːim'baːk] vti rembarquer.

re-embarkation ['riː emba'keiʃən] n rembarquement m.

re-enter ['ri'entə] vi rentrer, se présenter de nouveau.

re-establish [riːis'tæbliʃ] vt rétablir.

re-establishment ['riːis'tæbliʃmənt] n rétablissement m.

refection [ri'fekʃən] n réfection f, collation f

refectory [ri'tektəri] n réfectoire m.

refer [ri'fəː] vt rapporter référer, renvoyer, attribuer; vi se reporter, se référer, se référer, avoir trait (à to), faire allusion (à to).

referee [ˌretə'riː] n arbitre m, répondant m; vti arbitrer.

reference ['refrəns] n référence f, renvoi m, rapport m, allusion f, mention f.

refine [ri'fain] vt purifier, (r)affiner.

refinement [ri'fainmənt] n (r)affinage m, finesse f, raffinement m.

refinery [ri'fainəri] n raffinerie f.

refit ['riː'fit] vt radouber, rééquiper, réarmer, rajuster remonter.

reflect [ri'flekt] vti réfléchir; vt refléter, renvoyer; vi méditer, rejaillir, faire du tort (à upon).

reflection [ri'flekʃən] n réflexion f, reflet m, image f, critique f, atteinte f.

reflector [ri'flektə] n réflecteur m, cabochon m.

reflex ['riːfleks] n réflexe m, reflet m.

reflexive [ri'fleksiv] a réfléchi.

reform [ri'fɔːm] n réforme f; vt réformer; vi se retormer.

reformation [retə'meiʃən' n réforme f, réformation f.

reformer [ri'fɔːmə] n réformateur, -trice.

refract [ri'frækt] vt réfracter.

refraction [ri'frækʃən] n réfraction f.

refractory [ri'fræktəri] a réfractaire, insoumis.

refrain [ri'frein] n refrain m; vi s'abstenir, s'empêcher.

refresh [ri'freʃ] vt rafraîchir, ranimer.

refreshment [ri'freʃmənt] n rafraîchissement m; — room n buffet m, buvette f.

refrigerator [ri'fridʒəreitə] n réfrigérateur m, glacière f.

refuel [ri'fjuəl] vt ravitailler en combustible; vi se ravitailler en combustible, faire le plein (d'essence).

refuge [ˈrefjuːdʒ] n refuge m, abri m.

refugee ['refjuː'dʒiː] n réfugié(e) mf.

refund ['riːfʌnd] n remboursement m; ['riː'fʌnd] vt rembourser.

refusal [ri'fju:zəl] n refus m.
refuse ['refju:s] n rebut m, ordures f pl, déchets m pl, détritus m.
refuse [ri'fju:z] vt refuser, repousser.
refutation [,refju:'teiʃən] n réfutation f.
refute [ri'fju:t] vt réfuter.
regain [ri'gein] vt regagner, reprendre, recouvrer.
regal ['rigəl] a royal.
regale [ri'geil] vt régaler.
regalia [ri'geiliə] n joyaux m pl, insignes m pl.
regard [ri'ga:d] vt regarder, considérer, concerner, tenir compte de; n égard m, attention f, estime f; pl compliments m pl; with — to quant à, en égard à.
regardless [ri'ga:dlis] a inattentif; — of sans égard à, sans regarder à.
regency ['ri:dʒənsi] n régence f.
regenerate [ri'dʒenəreit] vt régénérer.
regent ['ri:dʒənt] n régent(e) mf.
regiment [,redʒiment] n régiment m; vt enrégimenter.
regimentals [,redʒi'mentlz] n uniforme m.
region ['ri:dʒən] n région f.
register ['redʒistə] n registre m; vt enregistrer, inscrire, (post) recommander, immatriculer.
registrar [,redʒis'tra:] n secrétaire m, greffier m, officier de l'état civil m.
registry ['redʒistri] n mairie f, bureau de l'état civil m, bureau de placement m.
regret [ri'gret] n regret m; vt regretter.
regretful [ri'gretful] a désolé.
regretfully [ri'gretfuli] ad à (avec) regret.
regular ['regjulə] a régulier, habituel, réglé, rangé, normal. réglementaire, permanent.
regularity [,regju'læriti] n régularité f.
regularize ['regjuləraiz] vt régulariser.
regulate ['regiuleit] vt régler, ajuster, réglementer.
regulation [regju'leiʃən] n règlement m, réglementation f, réglage m; a réglementaire, d'ordonnance.
rehearsal [ri'hə:səl] n répétition f, dress — répétition générale.
rehearse [ri'hə:s] vt répéter, énumérer.
reign [rein] n règne m; vi régner.
rein [rein] n rêne f, guide f.
reindeer ['reindiə] n renne m.
reinforce [,ri:in'fo:s] vt renforcer, appuyer.
reinforced [,ri:in'fo:st] a renforcé, armé.
reinforcement [,ri:in'fo:smənt] n renforcement m.
reinstate ['ri:in'steit] vt rétablir, réintégrer.
reinstatement ['ri:in'steitmənt] n rétablissement m, réintégration f.

reinvest ['ri:in'vest] vt replacer.
reiterate [ri:'itəreit] vt réitérer.
reiteration [,ri:itə'reiʃən] n réitération f.
reject [ri'dʒekt] vt rejeter, refuser, repousser; ['ri:dʒekt] n rebut m, article de rebut m.
rejection [ri'dʒekʃən] n rejet m, refus m, rebut m.
rejoice [ri'dʒois] vt réjouir; vi se réjouir.
rejoicing [ri'dʒoisiŋ] n réjouissance f, allégresse f.
rejoin ['ri:'dʒoin] vi riposter, répliquer.
rejoin ['ri:'dʒoin] vt rejoindre, rallier; vi se rejoindre, se réunir.
rejoinder [ri'dʒoində] n riposte f, réplique f.
relapse [ri'læps] n rechute f; vi retomber, avoir une rechute.
relate [ri'leit] vt (ra)conter relater, rapporter, rattacher; vi avoir rapport (a to), se rapporter (à to).
related [ri'leitid] a apparenté, connexe, parent.
relation [ri'leiʃən] n relation f, rapport m, récit m, parent(e) m(f).
relationship [ri'leiʃənʃip] n parenté f, connexion f, rapport m.
relative ['relətiv] n parent(e) m(f); a relatif.
relax [ri'læks] vt détendre, relâcher, délasser, adoucir; vi se détendre, se relâcher, s'adoucir.
relaxation [ri:læk'seiʃən] n distraction f, détente, adoucissement m.
relaxing [ri:'læksiŋ] a apaisant, reposant, énervant.
relay [ri'lei] vt relayer; n relais m, relève f.
release [ri'li:s] n délivrance f, élargissement m, décharge f déclenchement m, lancement m, reçu m transfert m; vt remettre, déclencher, lâcher, dégager, desserrer, faire jouer.
relegate ['religeit] vt reléguer, confier.
relent [ri'lent] vi se radoucir.
relentless [ri'lentlis] a inexorable, implacable, acharné.
relentlessness [ri'lentlisnis] n inflexibilité f, acharnement m.
relevant ['relivənt] a pertinent, qui a rapport (à to).
reliability [ri,laiə'biliti] n sûreté f, régularité f.
reliable [ri'laiəbl] a sûr, de confiance, sérieux, solide, digne de foi.
reliance [ri'laiəns] n confiance f.
relic ['relik] n relique f; pl restes m pl, souvenirs m pl.
relief [ri'li:f] n soulagement m, secours m, délivrance f, relève f, relief m.
relieve [ri'li:v] vt soulager, secourir, délivrer, relever, mettre en relief.
religion [ri'lidʒən] n religion f, culte m.

religious [ri'lidʒəs] *a* religieux, pieux, dévot.

relinquish [ri'liŋkwiʃ] *vt* abandonner, renoncer à.

relinquishment [ri'liŋkwiʃmənt] *n* abandon *m*, renonciation *f*.

relish ['reliʃ] *n* saveur *f*, goût *m*, assaisonnement *m*; *vt* relever, aimer, goûter.

reluctance [ri'lʌktəns] *n* répugnance *f*.

reluctantly [ri'lʌktəntli] *ad* à contrecœur, à regret.

rely [ri'lai] *vi* s'appuyer (sur **on**), compter (sur **on**).

remain [ri'mein] *vi* rester, demeurer.

remainder [ri'meində] *n* reste *m*, restant *m*.

remains [ri'meinz] *n* restes *m pl*, dépouille mortelle *f*.

remand [ri'maːnd] *n* renvoi *m*; *vt* renvoyer en prison.

remark [ri'maːk] *n* attention *f*, remarque *f*, observation *f*; *vt* remarquer, (faire) observer.

remarkable [ri'maːkəbl] *a* remarquable, frappant.

remedy ['remidi] *n* remède *m*; *vt* remédier à.

remember [ri'membə] *vt* se souvenir de, se rappeler, penser à.

remembrance [ri'membrəns] *n* mémoire *f*, souvenir *m*.

remind [ri'maind] *vt* rappeler, faire penser.

reminder [ri'maində] *n* agenda *m*, rappel *m*.

remiss [ri'mis] *a* négligent, lent, apathique.

remission [ri'miʃən] *n* rémission *f*, remise *f*, relâchement *m*, pardon *m*.

remit [ri'mit] *vt* remettre, relâcher, (r)envoyer.

remittance [ri'mitəns] *n* envoi de fonds *m*.

remnant ['remnənt] *n* reste *m*, (*cloth*) coupon *m*.

remonstrance [ri'mɔnstrəns] *n* remontrance *f*.

remonstrate [ri'mɔnstreit] **to —** **with** faire des représentations à.

remorse [ri'mɔːs] *n* remords *m*.

remorseful [ri'mɔːsful] *a* plein de remords.

remorseless [ri'mɔːslis] *a* sans remords, implacable.

remote [ri'mout] *a* lointain, reculé, écarté, vague, peu probable, distant.

remoteness [ri'moutnis] *n* éloignement *m*.

removable [ri'muːvəbl] *a* amovible, détachable.

removal [ri'muːvəl] *n* déménagement *m*, enlèvement *m*, suppression *f*.

remove [ri'muːv] *vt* enlever, supprimer, déplacer, effacer, révoquer, retirer, écarter, déménager.

remunerate [ri'mjuːnəreit] *vt* rémunérer.

remuneration [ri,mjuːnə'reiʃən] *n* rémunération *f*.

remunerative [ri'mjuːnərətiv] *a* rémunérateur.

rend [rend] *vt* déchirer, arracher, fendre.

render ['rendə] *vt* rendre, remettre, fondre.

renegade ['renəgeid] *n* renégat *m*.

renew [ri'njuː] *vt* renouveler, rafraîchir.

renewal [ri'njuːəl] *n* renouvellement *m*, reprise *f*.

renounce [ri'nauns] *vt* renoncer à, dénoncer, répudier, renier.

renouncement [ri'naunsmənt] *n* renoncement *m*.

renovate ['renəveit] *vt* rénover, remettre à neuf.

renovation [,renə'veiʃən] *n* rénovation *f*, remise à neuf *f*.

renown [ri'naun] *n* renom *m*, renommée *f*.

renowned [ri'naund] *a* célèbre, illustre.

rent [rent] *n* déchirure *f*, accroc *m*, loyer *m*; *vt* louer, affermer.

renunciation [ri,nʌnsi'eiʃən] *n* renoncement *m*, renonciation *f*, reniement *m*.

reopen [riː'oupən] *vti* rouvrir; *vi* se rouvrir, rentrer.

reopening ['riː'oupniŋ] *n* rentrée *f*, réouverture *f*.

repair [ri'pɛə] *n* (état de) réparation *f*, radoub *m*; *vt* réparer, raccommoder; *vi* se rendre.

repartee [repaːˈtiː] *n* repartie *f*.

repast [ri'paːst] *n* repas *m*.

repatriate [riː'pætrieit] *vt* rapatrier.

repatriation ['riːpætri'eiʃən] *n* rapatriement *m*.

repay [riː'pei] *vt* rembourser, rendre, s'acquitter envers.

repayment [riː'peimənt] *n* remboursement *m*, récompense *f*.

repeal [ri'piːl] *n* abrogation *f*; *vt* abroger, révoquer.

repeat [ri'piːt] *vt* répéter, rapporter, renouveler.

repeatedly [ri'piːtidli] *ad* à mainte reprise.

repeating [ri'piːtiŋ] *a* à répétition.

repel [ri'pel] *vt* repousser, répugner à.

repellent [ri'pelənt] *a* répugnant, repoussant.

repent [ri'pent] *vt* regretter, se repentir de; *vi* se repentir.

repentance [ri'pentəns] *n* repentir *m*.

repertory ['repətəri] *n* répertoire *m*.

repetition [,repi'tiʃən] *n* répétition *f*, reprise *f*, récitation *f*.

replace [ri'pleis] *vt* remplacer, replacer, remettre en place.

replaceable [ri'pleisəbl] *a* remplaçable.

replacement [ri'pleismənt] *n* remplacement *m*, pièce de rechange *f*.

replenish [ri'pleniʃ] *vt* remplir de nouveau, regarnir, remonter.

replete [ri'pli:t] *a* plein, bondé, rassasié.

reply [ri'plai] *n* réponse *f; vi* répondre.

report [ri'po:t] *n* bruit *m*, nouvelle *f*, compte-rendu *m*, bulletin *m*, rapport *m*, réputation *f*, détonation *f; vt* faire un rapport sur, rendre compte de, signaler, faire le reportage de; *vi* se présenter, dénoncer.

reporter [ri'po:tə] *n* reporter *m*, journaliste *mf*, rapporteur *m*.

repose [ri'pouz] *n* repos *m; vi* (se) reposer.

reposeful [ri'pouzful] *a* reposant.

reprehend [‚repri'hend] *vt* blâmer, reprendre.

reprehensible [repri'hensəbl] *a* répréhensible.

represent [repri'zent] *vt* représenter.

representative [‚repri'zentətiv] *n* représentant(e) *mf; a* représentatif.

repress [ri'pres] *vt* réprimer, refouler, étouffer.

repression [ri'preʃən] *n* répression *f*.

reprieve [ri'pri:v] *n* sursis *m*, grâce *f*, répit *m; vt* surseoir à, grâcier.

reprimand ['reprima:nd] *n* réprimande *f; vt* réprimander.

reprint [ˈri:'print] *n* réimpression *f; vt* réimprimer.

reprisal [ri'praizəl] *n* représaille(s) *f (pl)*.

reproach [ri'proutʃ] *n* honte *f*, reproche *m; vt* reprocher, faire des reproches à.

reproachfully [ri'proutʃfuli] *ad* sur un ton de reproche.

reprobate ['reproubeit] *n* réprouvé(e) *mf*, scélérat *m*.

reproduce [‚ri:prə'dju:s] *vt* reproduire.

reproduction [‚ri:prə'dʌkʃən] *n* reproduction *f*.

reproof [ri'pru:f] *n* blâme *m*, reproche *m*, rebuffade *f*.

reprove [ri'pru:v] *vt* blâmer, réprouver, réprimander, reprendre, condamner.

reptile ['reptail] *n* reptile *m*.

republic [ri'pʌblik] *n* république *f*.

republican [ri'pʌblikən] *an* républicain(e) *mf*.

repudiate [ri'pju:dieit] *vt* répudier, désavouer, renier.

repudiation [ri‚pju:di'eiʃən] *n* répudiation *f*, reniement *m*.

repugnance [ri'pʌgnəns] *n* répugnance *f*, antipathie *f*.

repugnant [ri'pʌgnənt] *a* répugnant, incompatible.

repulse [ri'pʌls] *n* échec *m*, rebuffade *f; vt* repousser.

repulsion [ri'pʌlʃən] *n* répulsion *f*, aversion *f*.

repulsive [ri'pʌlsiv] *a* répulsif, repoussant.

reputable ['repjutəbl] *a* honorable, estimable.

reputation [‚repju:'teiʃən] *n* réputation *f*, renom *m*.

repute [ri'pju:t] *n* réputation *f*, renommée *f*, renom *m*.

reputed [ri'pju:təd] *a* réputé, censé, putatif.

request [ri'kwest] *n* requête *f*, prière *f; vt* demander, prier.

require [ri'kwaiə] *vt* requérir, exiger, réclamer, avoir besoin de, falloir.

requirement [ri'kwaiəmənt] *n* exigence *f*, besoin *m*, demande *f*.

requisite ['rekwizit] *n* condition *f; pl* articles *m pl*, accessoires *m pl; a* requis, voulu, indispensable.

requisition [‚rekwi'ziʃən] *n* requête *f*, réquisition(s) *f (pl)*, commande *f; vt* réquisitionner.

requital [ri'kwaitl] *n* revanche *f*, monnaie de sa pièce *f*, retour *m*.

requite [ri'kwait] *vt* recompenser, rendre, payer de retour.

rescind [ri'sind] *vt* annuler.

rescission [ri'siʒən] *n* annulation *f*, abrogation *f*.

rescue ['reskju:] *n* délivrance *f*, sauvetage *m; vt* délivrer, sauver.

rescuer ['reskjuə] *n* sauveteur *m*, libérateur, -trice.

research [ri'sə:tʃ] *n* recherche(s) *f (pl)*.

resemblance [ri'zembləns] *n* ressemblance *f*, image *f*.

resemble [ri'zembl] *vt* ressembler à.

resent [ri'zent] *vt* ressentir, s'offenser de.

resentful [ri'zentful] *a* plein de ressentiment, rancunier.

resentment [ri'zentmənt] *n* ressentiment *m*, dépit *m*.

reservation [rezə'veiʃən] *n* réservation *f*, réserve *f*, place retenue *f*.

reserve [ri'zə:v] *n* réserve *f; vt* réserver, retenir, louer.

reservoir ['rezəvwa:] *n* réservoir *m*.

reshuffle ['ri:'ʃʌfl] *n* refonte *f*, remaniement *m; vt* refondre, remanier, rebattre.

reside [ri'zaid] *vi* résider.

residence ['rezidəns] *n* résidence *f*, séjour *m*.

resident ['rezidənt] *a* résident; *n* habitant(e) *mf*.

residue ['rezidju:] *n* reste *m*, reliquat *m*, résidu *m*.

resign [ri'zain] *vt* résigner; *vi* démissionner.

resignation [‚rezig'neiʃən] *n* résignation *f*, démission *f*, abandon *m*.

resilience [ri'ziliəns] *n* élasticité *f*, ressort *m*.

resilient [ri'ziliənt] *a* élastique, rebondissant, qui a du ressort.

resin ['rezin] *n* résine *f*.

resist [ri'zist] *vt* résister à; *vi* résister.

resistance [ri'zistəns] *n* résistance *f*.

resolute ['rezəlu:t] *a* résolu.

resolutely ['rezəlu:tli] *ad* résolument, avec fermeté.

resolution [rezə'lu:ʃən] n résolution f.

resolve [ri'zɔlv] vt résoudre; vi se résoudre.

resort [ri'zɔːt] n recours m, ressort m, séjour m, station (balnéaire) f; vi recourir (à to), se rendre (à to).

resound [ri'zaund] vi retentir, résonner.

resource [ri'sɔːs] n ressource f.

resourceful [ri'sɔːsful] a débrouillard, ingénieux.

resourcefulness [ri'sɔːsfulnis] n ingéniosité f.

respect [ris'pekt] n respect m, égard m, rapport m; vt respecter.

respectability [ris,pektə'biliti] n respectabilité f.

respectable [ris'pektəbl] a respectable.

respectful [ris'pektful] a respectueux.

respecting [ris'pektiŋ] prep relativement à, quant à.

respective [ris'pektiv] a respectif.

respiration [,respə'reiʃən] n respiration f.

respiratory [ris'paiərətəri] a respiratoire.

respite ['respait] n répit m, sursis m; soulager, différer.

resplendent [ris'plendənt] a resplendissant.

respond [ris'pɔnd] vi répondre, obéir réagir.

response [ris'pɔns] n réponse f, réaction f.

responsibility [ris,pɔnsəbiliti] n responsabilité f.

responsible [ris'pɔnsəbl] a responsable (devant to); to be — for répondre de.

responsive [ris'pɔnsiv] a sympathique, sensible, souple.

rest [rest] n repos m, appui f, reste, m, réserves f pl; vt (faire) reposer, appuyer; vi se reposer, s'appuyer.

restaurant ['restərɔ̃:ŋ] n restaurant m.

restful ['restful] a reposant, paisible.

restitution ,resti'tju:ʃən] n restitution f.

restive ['restiv] a rétif, nerveux, impatient.

restless ['restlis] a agité.

restlessness ['restlisnis] n agitation f, impatience f.

restoration [,restə'reiʃən] n restitution f, restauration f, rétablissement m.

restorative [ris'tɔrətiv] an fortifiant m.

restore [ris'tɔː] vt restituer, restaurer, rétablir.

restrain [ris'trein] vt réprimer, retenir, contenir, empêcher.

restraint [ris'treint] n discrétion f, contrôle m, sobriété f, contrainte f.

restrict [ris'trikt] vt réduire, limiter, restreindre.

restriction [ris'trikʃən] n restriction f, réduction f.

result [ri'zʌlt] n résultat m; vi résulter, aboutir (à in).

resume [ri'zju:m] vt reprendre, résumer.

resumption [ri'zʌmpʃən] n reprise f.

resurrection [,rezə'rekʃən] n résurrection f.

resuscitate [ri'sʌsiteit] vt ressusciter.

retail ['riːteil] n vente au détail f.

retail [riː'teil] vt vendre au détail.

retailer [riː'teilə] n détaillant m.

retain [ri'tein] vt (con-, sou-, re-) tenir, conserver.

retainer [ri'teinə] n provision f, honoraires m pl, suivant m; pl suite f.

retaliate [ri'tælieit] vi rendre la pareille (à on), riposter.

retaliation [ri,tæli'eiʃən] n représailles f pl, revanche f.

retard [ri'tɑːd] vt retarder.

retch ['riːtʃ] n haut-le-cœur m; vi avoir des haut-le-cœur.

retentive [ri'tentiv] a fidèle.

retina ['retinə] n rétine f.

retinue ['retinju:] n suite f.

retire [ri'taiə] vt mettre à la retraite, retirer; vi se retirer, reculer, battre en retraite, prendre sa retraite.

retirement [ri'taiəmənt] n retraite f, retrait m.

retort [ri'tɔːt] n riposte f, cornue f; vi riposter, rétorquer.

retrace [ri'treis] vt reconstituer, revenir sur.

retract [ri'trækt] vt rétracter, rentrer, escamoter; vi se rétracter.

retreat [ri'triːt] n retraite f, abri m; vi battre en retraite.

retrench [riː'trentʃ] vt retrancher; vi faire des économies; —ment n retranchement m.

retribution [,retri'bju:ʃən] n juste récompense f.

retrieve [ri'triːv] vt rapporter, retrouver, réparer, rétablir.

retrograde ['retrougreid] vi rétrograder; a rétrograde.

retrospect ['retrouspekt] n regard m en arrière.

retrospective [,retrou'spektiv] a rétrospectif.

return [ri'təːn] n retour m, restitution f, rendement m, échange m, revanche f, rapport m; pl recettes f pl, profit m; — ticket (billet m d') aller et retour m; vi retourner, revenir, rentrer; vt rendre, renvoyer, répliquer, élire.

reunion ['riː'juːnjən] n réunion f.

reunite ['riːjuː'nait] vt réunir; vi se réunir.

reveal [ri'viːl] vt révéler, découvrir, faire voir.

reveille [ri'væli] n réveil m, diane f.

revel ['revl] n fête f, orgie f; pl réjouissances f pl; vi faire la fête, se délecter (à in).

revelation [ˌreviˈleiʃən] *n* révélation *f.*

reveller [ˈrevlə] *n* noceur, -euse, fêtard(e) *mf.*

revenge [riˈvendʒ] *n* revanche *f*, vengeance *f; vt* venger; **to — oneself** se venger.

revengeful [riˈvendʒful] *a* vindicatif, vengeur, -eresse.

revenue [ˈrevinjuː] *n* revenu *m.*

reverberate [riˈvəːbəreit] *vt* réfléchir, renvoyer; *vti* réverbérer; *vi* se réfléchir.

reverberation [riˌvəːbəˈreiʃən] *n* réverbération *f*, répercussion *f.*

revere [riˈviə] *vt* révérer.

reverence [ˈrevərəns] *n* révérence *f.*

reverend [ˈrevərənd] *a* révérend, vénérable.

reverent [ˈrevərənt] *a* respectueux.

reverse [riˈvəːs] *n* revers *m*, envers *m*, marche arrière *f*, contraire *m; a* contraire, opposé; *vt* renverser, faire reculer, annuler; *vi* faire machine arrière.

review [riˈvjuː] *n* revue *f.* révision *f*, compte-rendu *m; vt* revoir, passer en revue, admettre à révision, faire le compte-rendu de.

reviewer [riˈvjuːə] *n* critique *m.*

revile [riˈvail] *vt* vilipender, injurier.

revise [riˈvaiz] *vt* réviser, revoir, corriger.

revision [riˈviʒən] *n* révision *f.*

revival [riˈvaivəl] *n* renaissance *f*, renouv au *m* reprise *f.*

revive [riˈvaiv] *vt* ranimer, renouveler. remonter. *vi* revivre, renaître, reprendre connaissance, se ranimer.

revocation [ˌrevəˈkeiʃən] *n* révocation *f*, annulation *f.*

revoke [riˈvouk] *vt* annuler, révoquer.

revolt [riˈvoult] *n* révolte *f; vt* révolter; *vi* se révolter.

revolution [ˌrevəˈluːʃən] *n* révolution *f.*

revolutionary [ˌrevəˈluːʃnəri] *an* révolutionnaire *mf.*

revolutionize [ˌrevəˈluːʃnaiz] *vt* révolutionner.

revolve [riˈvɔlv] *vt* faire tourner, retourner; *vi* rouler, tourner.

reward [riˈwɔːd] *n* récompense *f; vt* récompenser, payer (de retour).

rhetoric [ˈretərik] *n* éloquence *f*, rhétorique *f.*

rheumatic [ruːˈmætik] *an* rhumatisai t(e) *mf.*

rheumatism [ˈruːmətizəm] *n* rhumatisme *m.*

rhubarb [ˈruːbɑːb] *n* rhubarbe *f.*

rhyme [raim] *n* rime *f; vi* rimer; *vt* faire rimer.

rhythm [ˈriðm] *n* rythme *m.*

rib [rib] *n* côte *f*, nervure *f*, baleine *f.*

ribald [ˈribəld] *a* paillard, graveleux.

ribaldry [ˈribəldri] *n* obscénité *f*, paillardises *f pl.*

ribbon [ˈribən] *n* ruban *m*, cordon *m.*

rice [rais] *n* riz *m.*

rich [ritʃ] *a* riche, somptueux, chaud, plein.

riches [ˈritʃiz] *n pl* richesses *f pl.*

rick [rik] *n* meule *f.*

rickets [ˈrikits] *n* rachitisme *m.*

rickety [ˈrikiti] *a* rachitique, branlant.

rid [rid] *inf pt pp of* **rid**; *vt* débarrasser; **to get —** of se débarrasser de.

riddance [ˈridəns] *n* débarras *m.*

ridden [ˈridn] *pp of* **ride**.

riddle [ˈridl] *n* crible *m*, énigme *f*, devinette *f; vt* cribler.

ride [raid] *n* promenade à cheval *f*, en auto, tour *m; vi* monter (aller) à cheval (à bicyclette), chevaucher, flotter, voguer. être mouillé; *vt* monter.

rider [ˈraidə] *n* cavalier, -ière, amazone *f*, écuyer, -ère, jockey *m*, annexe *f*, recommandation *f.*

ridge [ridʒ] *n* arête *f*, crête *f*, faîte *f*, ride *f.*

ridicule [ˈridikjuːl] *n* ridicule *m*, raillerie *f; vt* ridiculiser, se moquer de.

ridiculous [riˈdikjuləs] *a* ridicule, absurde.

riding-school [ˈraidiŋˌskuːl] *n* manège *m*, école *f* d'équi ation.

rife [raif] *a* commun, courant, fourmillant; **to be —** sévir.

rifle [ˈraifl] *n* carabine *f; vt* dévaliser, vider, fouiller, rayer.

rift [rift] *n* fente *f*, fêlure *f.*

rig [rig] *n* gréement *m*, accoutrement *m*, tenue *f; vt* gréer, accoutrer, truquer; **to — up** installer, monter.

rigging [ˈrigiŋ] *n* agrès *m pl*, équipemen *m.*

right [rait] *n* droite *f*, droit *m*, dû *m; a* juste, exact, droit; **to be —** avoir raison; *ad* droit juste très bien; *vt* redresser, réparer, corriger.

righteous [ˈraitʃəs] *a* pur, juste, sans faute vertueux.

righteousness [ˈraitʃəsnis] *n* impeccabilité *f*, rectitude *f*, vertu *f.*

rightful [ˈraitful] *a* légitime, équitable.

right-handed [ˈraitˈhændid] *a* droitier.

rightness [ˈraitnis] *n* justesse *f.*

rigid [ˈridʒid] *a* rigide, raide, strict, inflexible.

rigidity [riˈdʒiditi] *n* rigidité *f*, sévérité *f.*

rigmarole [ˈrigməroul] *n* calembredaine *f.*

rigorous [ˈrigərəs] *a* rigoureux.

rigour [ˈrigə] *n* rigueur *f*, sévérité *f.*

rim [rim] *n* bord *m*, cercle *m*, jante *f.*

rime [raim] *n* rime *f*, givre *m; vi* rimer.

rimmed [rimd] *a* cerclé, bordé, cerné, à bord.

rind [raind] *n* peau *f*, croûte *f*, écorce *f*, couenne *f.*

ring [riŋ] *n* anneau *m*, bague *f*, cercle *m*, cerne *f*, bande *f*, piste *f*,

sonnerie f, coup m de sonnette; vti
sonner; to — off couper; — finger
n annulaire m.
ringleader ['riŋ,li:də] n meneur m.
ringworm ['riŋ wə:m] n pelade f,
teigne f.
rink [riŋk] n patinoire f.
rinse [rins] vt rincer; n rinçage m.
riot ['raiət] n émeute f, orgie f; vi
s'ameuter.
rioter ['raiətə] n émeutier m.
riotous ['raiətəs] a turbulent, tapageur.
rip [rip] n déchirure f; vt déchirer,
fendre; vi se déchirer, se fendre.
ripe [raip] a mûr.
ripen ['raipən] vti mûrir.
ripping ['ripiŋ] a épatant.
ripple ['ripl] n ride f, murmure m;
vi se rider, onduler, perler; vt rider.
rise [raiz] n montée f, éminence f,
avancement m, augmentation f,
hausse f, source f, naissance f, essor
m; vi se lever, s'élever, se soulever,
monter, naître.
risen ['rizn] pp of **rise**.
rising ['raiziŋ] n lever m, crue f,
soulèvement m, résurrection f,
hausse f.
risk [risk] n risque m, péril m; vt
risquer.
risky ['riski] a risqué, hasardeux.
rite [rait] n rite m.
ritual ['ritjuəl] an rituel m.
rival ['raivəl] an rival(e) mf; vt
émule mf; vt rivaliser avec.
rivalry ['raivəlri] n rivalité f.
rive [raiv] vt fendre.
riven ['rivən] pp of **rive**.
river ['rivə] n rivière f, fleuve m.
rivet ['rivit] n rivet m; vt river.
rivulet ['rivjulit] n ruisselet m.
roach [routʃ] n gardon m.
road [roud] n route f, rue f, rade f.
roadside ['roud,said] n bas-côté m;
— repairs dépannage m.
roadway ['roudwei] n chaussée f.
roam [roum] vi rôder, errer.
roar [rɔ:] n mugissement m, rugissement m, grondement m, vrombissement m, gros éclat de rire m; vi
rugir, mugir, vrombir, hurler, s'esclaffer.
roast [roust] n rôti m, rosbif m; vt
rôtir, griller.
rob [rɔb] vt dérober, voler, piller,
détrousser.
robber ['rɔbə] n voleur, -euse.
robbery ['rɔbəri] n vol m, brigandage
m.
robe [roub] n robe f.
Robert ['rɔbət] Robert m.
robin ['rɔbin] n rouge-gorge m.
robot ['roubɔt] n automate m; a
automatique.
robust [rə'bʌst] a robuste, vigoureux.
rock [rɔk] n roc m, rocher m, roche
f; vt bercer, balancer, (é)branler,
basculer; vi osciller, (se) balancer.

rocket ['rɔkit] n fusée f; a à fusée.
rocking ['rɔkiŋ] a à bascule.
rocky ['rɔki] a rocheux, rocailleux,
instable.
rod [rɔd] n baguette f, tringle f,
perche f, gaule f, canne à pêche f,
verge(s) f (pl), piston m.
rode [roud] pt of **ride**.
rodent ['roudənt] an rongeur m.
roe [rou] n **hard** — œufs m pl; **soft** —
laitance f.
roe(buck) ['rou(bʌk)] n chevreuil m.
rogue [roug] n coquin(e) mf, fripon,
-onne, gredin m.
roguish ['rougiʃ] a fripon, coquin,
espiègle, malin, -igne.
roll [roul] n rouleau m, boudin m,
petit pain m, tableau m, roulis m,
roulement m; vt rouler, enrouler,
laminer; vi (se) rouler, s'enrouler.
roller ['roulə] n rouleau m, bande f,
laminoir m, grosse lame f; — skates
patins à roulettes m pl.
Roman ['roumən] a romain; n
Romain(e) mf.
romance [rə'mæns] an roman m; n
idylle f, romanesque m; vi romancer,
faire du roman, exagérer.
romantic [rə'mæntik] a romanesque,
romantique.
romanticism [rə'mæntisizəm] n romantisme m.
Romany ['rɔməni] n bohémien,
-ienne.
romp [rɔmp] n petit(e) diable(sse),
jeu de vilain m, gambades f pl; vi
jouer, s'ébattre, gambader.
rood [ru:d] n crucifix n, quart
d'arpent m.
roof [ru:f] n toit m, toiture f, (mouth)
palais m.
rook [ruk] n corneille f, bonneteur
m, escroc m.
room [rum] n chambre f, pièce f,
salle f, place f, lieu m.
roomy ['rumi] a spacieux, ample.
roost [ru:st] n perchoir m; vi se
percher, se jucher.
root [ru:t] n racine f, source f; vt
planter, enraciner, clouer; vi s'enraciner.
rope [roup] n corde f, cordage m,
câble m, glane f, collier m; vt corder,
lier, hâler.
rosary ['rouzəri] n rosaire m,
chapelet m.
rose [rouz] n rose f, rosace f, rosette
f, pomme d'arrosoir f; —bud n
bouton m de rose; —bush n rosier m.
rosemary ['rouzməri] n romarin m.
rosin ['rɔzin] n colophane f.
roster ['rɔstə] n tableau m, liste f,
roulement m.
rosy ['rouzi] a rose, rosé, attrayant.
rot [rɔt] n pourriture f, carie f,
démoralisation f, bêtises f pl; vti
pourrir; vi se carier, se décomposer.
rota ['routə] n liste f, roulement m.
rotate [rou'teit] vt faire tourner,
alterner; vi tourner, pivoter.

rote [rout] n routine f; **by — machinalement.**

rotten ['rɔtn] a pourri, carié, fichu, moche, patraque.

rotter ['rɔtə] n propre à rien m, sale type m, salaud m.

rotund [rou'tʌnd] a arrondi, sonore.

rouge [ruːʒ] n rouge m, fard m; vt farder.

rough [rʌf] a rugueux, grossier, brutal, rude, brut, approximatif; **to — it** vivre à la dure.

roughcast ['rʌfkɑːst] vt ébaucher, crépir; n crépi m.

rough copy ['rʌf'kɔpi] n brouillon m.

roughen ['rʌfn] vt rendre grossier, rude; vi grossir.

roughly ['rʌfli] ad en gros, brutalement, à peu près.

roughness ['rʌfnis] n rugosité f, rudesse f, grossièreté f.

roughshod ['rʌfʃɔd] a ferré à glace; **to ride — over s.o.** fouler qn aux pieds.

round [raund] n rond m, ronde f, tournée f, tour m, échelon m, (sport) circuit m, reprise f, série f, cartouche f, salve f; a rond; prep autour de; ad en rond, à la ronde; vt arrondir, contourner, doubler; **to — up** rassembler, rafler.

roundabout ['raundəbaut] n manège m (de chevaux de bois), rondpoint m.

roundly ['raundli] ad rondement, net.

roundworm ['raund.wəːm] n chique f.

rouse [rauz] vt réveiller, exciter, remuer.

rousing ['rauziŋ] a retentissant, vibrant.

rout [raut] n bande f. déroute f; vt. mettre en déroute.

route [ruːt] n itinéraire m, parcours m, route f.

routine [ruː'tiːn] n routine f.

rove [rouv] vi rôder; vt parcourir.

rover ['rouvə] n vagabond m, coureur m, pirate m.

row [rou] n rang m, rangée f, file f, partie de canotage f; vi ramer, faire du canotage; vt conduire à l'aviron.

row [rau] n dispute f, bagarre f, semonce f; vt attraper; vi se chamailler.

rowdy ['raudi] n voyou m; a violent, turbulent.

rowdyism ['raudiizəm] n désordre m, chahutage m.

rower ['rouə] n rameur, -euse, canotier m.

rowlock ['rɔlək] n tolet m

royal ['rɔiəl] a royal.

royalist ['rɔiəlist] n royaliste mf.

royalty ['rɔiəlti] n royauté f; pl droits d'auteur m pl.

rub [rʌb] n frottement m, friction f, hauts et bas m pl, hic m; vti frotter; vt frictionner, calquer, polir, masser; **to — out** effacer.

rubber ['rʌbə] n gomme f, caoutchouc m, frotteur, -euse; **— tree** n hévia m.

rubbish ['rʌbiʃ] n ordures f pl, détritus m, décombres m pl, niaiseries f pl; **— chute** vide-ordures m.

rubble ['rʌbl] n gravats m pl.

rubric ['ruːbrik] n rubrique f.

ruby ['ruːbi] n rubis m.

rudder ['rʌdə] n gouvernail m.

ruddy ['rʌdi] a coloré, rougeaud, rougeoyant.

rude [ruːd] a grossier, mal élevé, violent, brusque, brut.

rudeness ['ruːdnis] n rudesse f, grossièreté f.

rudiment ['ruːdimənt] n rudiment m.

rudimentary [.ruːdi'mentəri] a rudimentaire.

rue [ruː] vt regretter, se repentir de.

rueful ['ruːful] a triste.

ruefulness ['ruːfulnis] n tristesse f, regret m.

ruffian ['rʌfiən] n bandit m, brute f, polisson m.

ruffle ['rʌfl] n ride f, manchette f, jabot m; vt hérisser, rider, ébouriffer, émouvoir.

rug [rʌg] n couverture f, tapis m.

rugged ['rʌgid] a rugueux, inégal, sauvage, rude.

ruin ['ruin] n ruine f; vt ruiner.

ruinous ['ruinəs] a ruineux.

rule [ruːl] n règle f, règlement m, autorité f; vt régir, gouverner, régler, décider; **to — out** écarter.

ruler ['ruːlə] n souverain(e) mf, dirigeant(e) mf, règle f.

ruling ['ruːliŋ] n décision f.

rum [rʌm] n rhum m; a bizarre, louche.

rumble ['rʌmbl] n grondement m, roulement m; vi rouler, gronder.

ruminate ['ruːmineit] vi ruminer.

rummage ['rʌmidʒ] vti fouiller; vi fureter.

rumour ['ruːmə] n rumeur f, bruit m; **vt it is —ed** le bruit court.

rump [rʌmp] n croupe f, croupion m, culotte f.

rumple ['rʌmpl] vt froisser, friper.

run [rʌn] n course f, marche f, promenade f, direction f, série f, demande f, ruée f, moyenne f, enclos m, libre usage m; vti courir; vi marcher, fonctionner, couler, s'étendre, passer, déteindre, tenir l'affiche; vt diriger, exploiter, tenir, entretenir, promener.

runaway ['rʌnəwei] a fugitif, emballé.

rung [rʌŋ] pp of ring; n barreau m, échelon m.

runner ['rʌnə] n coureur, -euse, messager m, glissoir m, patin m.

running ['rʌniŋ] n course f, marche f, direction f; a courant, coulant, continu, de suite.

running-board ['rʌniŋ.bɔːd] n marche-pied m.

runway ['rʌnwei] n piste f.

rupee [ru:'pi:] roupie f.

rupture ['rʌptʃə] n rupture f, hernie f; vt rompre; vi se rompre.

rural ['ruərəl] a rural, agreste, des champs.

rush [rʌʃ] n jonc m, ruée f, hâte f, presse f, montée f; a de pointe, urgent; vt précipiter, brusquer, expédier, bousculer, envahir; vi s'élancer, se précipiter, se jeter, faire irruption.

rusk [rʌsk] n biscotte f.

russet ['rʌsit] n reinette grise f; a brun-roux.

Russia ['rʌʃə] n Russie f.

Russian ['rʌʃən] an russe m; n Russe mf.

rust [rʌst] n rouille f; vt rouiller; vi se rouiller.

rustic ['rʌstik] n paysan, -anne, campagnard(e) mf, rustre m; a rustique, paysan.

rustle ['rʌsl] n frou-frou m, bruissement m; vi bruire, faire frou-frou; vt froisser.

rustless ['rʌstlis] a inoxydable.

rusty ['rʌsti] a rouillé.

rut [rʌt] n ornière f, rut m.

ruthless ['ru:θlis] a implacable, impitoyable.

ruthlessness ['ru:θlisnis] n férocité f, implacabilité f.

rye [rai] n seigle m.

S

Sabbath ['sæbəθ] n sabbat m, dimanche m.

sable ['seibl] n zibeline f; a noir.

sabotage ['sæbəta:ʒ] n sabotage m; vt saboter.

sabre ['seibə] n sabre m.

saccharine ['sækərin] n saccharine f.

sack [sæk] n sac m, pillage; vt saccager, renvoyer, mettre en sac.

sacrament ['sækrəmənt] n sacrement m.

sacred ['seikrid] a sacré, saint, religieux, consacré.

sacrifice ['sækrifais] n sacrifice m, victime f; vt sacrifier, immoler.

sacrilege ['sækrilidʒ] n sacrilège m.

sad [sæd] a triste, cruel, lourd, déplorable.

sadden ['sædn] vt attrister.

saddle ['sædl] n selle f; vt seller, mettre sur le dos de.

saddler ['sædlə] n sellier m, bourrelier m.

sadness ['sædnis] n tristesse f.

safe [seif] n garde-manger m, coffre-fort m; a sauf, sûr, prudent, à l'abri, en sûreté.

safe-conduct ['seif'kɔndəkt] n sauf-conduit m.

safeguard ['seifga:d] n sauvegarde f, garantie f.

safely ['seifli] ad sain et sauf, bien.

safety ['seifti] n sûreté f, sécurité f; a de sûreté.

sag [sæg] vi céder, fléchir, se détendre, gondoler, baisser; n fléchissement m, ventre m.

sagacious [sə'geiʃəs] a sagace, perspicace, intelligent.

sagacity [sə'gæsiti] n sagacité f, intelligence f.

sage [seidʒ] n (bot) sauge f; an sage m.

sago ['seigou] n tapioca m.

said [sed] pt pp of **say**.

sail [seil] n voile f, voilure f, aile f, traversée f, promenade en bateau f; vi naviguer, mettre à la voile, planer, voguer; vt conduire, naviguer; —ing n mise à la voile f, départ m, navigation f; **to go sailing** faire du bateau.

sailor ['seilə] n matelot m, marin m; **to be a good —** avoir le pied marin.

saint [seint] an saint(e) mf.

sake [seik] **for the —** of par égard pour, pour l'amour de, pour les beaux yeux de, dans l'intérêt de.

salad ['sæləd] n salade f.

salaried ['sælərid] a rétribué, salarié.

salary ['sæləri] n traitement m, appointements m pl.

sale [seil] n vente f, solde(s) f.

saleable ['seiləbil] a vendable, de vente courante.

salesman ['seilzmən] n vendeur m, courtier m, commis m.

salient ['seiliənt] an saillant m.

saliva [sə'laivə] n salive f.

sallow ['sælou] a blafard, jaunâtre, olivâtre.

sally ['sæli] n sortie f, saillie f; vi faire une sortie, sortir.

salmon ['sæmən] n saumon m; —-trout n truite saumonée f.

saloon [sə'lu:n] n salon m, salle f, cabaret m; — **car** n (voiture f à) conduite intérieure f.

salt [sɔ:lt] n sel m, loup m de mer; a salé; vt saler; —**cellar** n salière f.

saltpetre ['sɔ:lt,pi:tə] n salpêtre m.

salubrious [sə'lu:briəs] a salubre, sain.

salubrity [sə'lu:briti] n salubrité f.

salutary ['sæljutəri] a salutaire.

salute [sə'lu:t] n salut m, salve f; vt saluer.

salvage ['sælvidʒ] n sauvetage m, matériel récupéré m; vt récupérer.

salvation [sæl'veiʃən] n salut m.

salve [sælv] vt calmer, apaiser; n pommade f, baume m.

salver ['sælvə] n plateau m.

salvo ['sælvou] n salve f.

same [seim] a même, monotone; **to do the —** faire de même.

sameness ['seimnis] n ressemblance f, monotonie f, uniformité f.

sample ['sa:mpl] n échantillon m; vt éprouver, tâter de, échantillonner, déguster.

sanctify ['sæŋktifai] vt sanctifier, consacrer.

sanctimonious [ˌsæŋkti'mouniəs] *a* bigot, papelard.

sanction ['sæŋkʃən] *n* sanction *f*, approbation *f*; *vt* sanctionner, approuver.

sanctity ['sæŋktiti] *n* sainteté *f*, inviolabilité *f*.

sanctuary ['sæŋktjuəri] *n* sanctuaire *m*, asile *m*, réfuge *m*.

sand [sænd] *n* sable *m*; *pl* plage *f*; — **dune** dune *f*; —**paper** papier de verre *m*; —**shoes** souliers *mpl* bains de mer, espadrilles *f pl*.

sandal ['sændl] *n* sandale *f*, samara *m*.

sandalwood ['sændlwud] *n* santal *m*.

sandbag ['sændbæg] *n* sac de terre *m*, assommoir *m*; *vt* protéger avec des sacs de terre, assommer.

sandy ['sændi] *a* sablonneux, blond-roux.

sandwich ['sænwidʒ] *n* sandwich *m*.

sane [sein] *a* sain, sensé.

sang [sæŋ] *pt of* **sing**.

sanguinary ['sæŋgwinəri] *a* sanglant, sanguinaire.

sanguine ['sæŋgwin] *a* sanguin, convaincu, optimiste.

sanitary ['sænitəri] *a* sanitaire, hygiénique.

sanity ['sæniti] *n* raison *f*, santé *f* mentale.

sank [sæŋk] *pt of* **sink**.

sap [sæp] *n* sève *f*, sape *f*; *vt* épuiser, saper, miner.

sapling ['sæpliŋ] *n* plant *m*, baliveau *m*, adolescent(e).

sapper ['sæpə] *n* sapeur *m*.

sapphire ['sæfaiə] *n* saphir *m*.

sarcasm ['saːkæzəm] *n* sarcasme *m*, ironie *f*.

sarcastic [saːˈkæstik] *a* sarcastique; —**ally** *ad* d'un ton sarcastique.

sardine [saːˈdiːn] *n* sardine *f*.

Sardinia [saːˈdiniə] *n* Sardaigne *f*.

sash [sæʃ] *n* châssis *m*, ceinture *f*, écharpe *f*; — **window** *n* fenêtre à guillotine *f*.

sat [sæt] *pt pp of* **sit**.

satchel ['sætʃəl] *n* sacoche *f*, cartable *m*.

sate [seit] *vt* assouvir, rassasier.

sated ['seitid] *a* repu.

sateen [sæˈtiːn] *n* satinette *f*.

satiate ['seiʃieit] *vt* apaiser, rassasier.

satiety [səˈtaiəti] *n* satiété *f*.

satin ['sætin] *n* satin *m*.

satire ['sætaiə] *n* satire *f*.

satirical [səˈtirikl] *a* satirique.

satirist ['sætərist] *n* satirique *m*.

satisfaction [ˌsætisˈfækʃən] *n* paiement *m*, rachat *m*, satisfaction *f*.

satisfactory [ˌsætisˈfæktəri] *a* satisfaisant.

satisfy ['sætisfai] *vt* satisfaire, convaincre, remplir.

saturate ['sætʃəreit] *vt* tremper, imprégner, saturer.

Saturday ['sætədi] *n* samedi *m*.

satyr ['sætə] *n* satyre *m*.

sauce [sɔːs] *n* sauce *f*, assaisonnement *m*, insolence *f*; —**boat** *n* saucière *f*; —**pan** *n* casserole *f*.

saucer ['sɔːsə] *n* soucoupe *f*.

sauciness ['sɔːsinis] *n* impertinence *f*.

saucy ['sɔːsi] *a* impertinent, effronté, fripon.

saunter ['sɔːntə] *n* flânerie *f*; *vt* flâner.

sausage ['sɔsidʒ] *n* saucisse *f*, saucisson *m*.

sausage-meat ['sɔsidʒmiːt] *n* chair à saucisse *f*.

savage ['sævidʒ] *n* sauvage *mf*; *a* féroce, brutal, barbare.

savagery ['sævidʒəri] *n* sauvagerie *f*, férocité *f*, barberie *f*.

savanna(h) [səˈvænə] *n* savane *f*.

save [seiv] *vt* sauver, préserver, économiser, épargner, ménager; *prep* sauf, excepté.

saving ['seiviŋ] *n* salut *m*, économie *f*; *a* économe, qui rachète.

saviour ['seivjə] *n* sauveur *m*.

savour ['seivə] *n* saveur *f*, goût *m*, pointe *f*; *vi* to — of sentir, tenir de.

savoury ['seivəri] *a* relevé, savoureux, succulent.

Savoy [səˈvɔi] *n* Savoie *f*.

savvy ['sævi] *n* jugeotte *f*; *vti* piger.

saw [sɔː] *n* scie *f*; adage *m*; maxime *f*, proverbe *m*; *vt* scier.

sawdust ['sɔːdʌst] *n* sciure *f*.

sawmill ['sɔːmil] *n* scierie *f*.

sawyer ['sɔːjə] *n* scieur *m*.

sawn [sɔːn] *pp of* **saw**.

say [sei] *n* mot *m*, voix *f*; *vti* dire.

saying ['seiiŋ] *n* dicton *m*, récitation *f*.

scab [skæb] *n* croûte, gourme *f*, gale *f*, jaune *m*, faux-frère *m*; *vi* se cicatriser.

scabbard ['skæbəd] *n* fourreau *m*, gaine *f*.

scabby ['skæbi] *a* galeux, croûteux, mesquin.

scabies ['skeibiiːz] *n* gale *f*.

scabrous ['skeibrəs] *a* scabreux, raboteux.

scaffold ['skæfəld] *n* échafaud *m*.

scaffolding ['skæfəldiŋ] *n* échafaudage *m*.

scald [skɔːld] *n* brûlure *f*; *vt* ébouillanter, échauder.

scale [skeil] *n* plateau *m*, balance *f*, bascule *f*, échelle *f*, gamme *f*, écaille *f*, dépôt *m*, tartre *m*; *vt* écailler, peler, écosser, râcler, décrasser, escalader, graduer; *vi* s'écailler, s'incruster.

scallop ['skɔləp] *n* coquille Saint-Jacques *f*, feston *m*.

scalp [skælp] *n* cuir chevelu *m*, scalpe *m*; *vt* scalper.

scalpel ['skælpəl] *n* scalpel *m*.

scamp [skæmp] *n* vaurien *m*; *vt* bâcler.

scamper ['skæmpə] *vi* détaler.

scan [skæn] *vt* scander, scruter, embrasser du regard, parcourir.

scandal ['skændl] n scandale m, honte f, cancans m pl.

scandalize ['skændəlaiz] vt scandaliser.

scandalous ['skændələs] a scandaleux, honteux.

scansion ['skænʃən] n scansion f.

scanty ['skænti] a mince, rare, insuffisant, étroit, peu de, juste, sommaire.

scapegoat ['skeipgout] n bouc émissaire m, souffre-douleur m.

scapegrace ['skeipgreis] n étourneau m, mauvais sujet m.

scar [ska:] n cicatrice f; vt balafrer; vi se cicatriser.

scarab ['skærəb] n scarabée m.

scarce [skɛəs] a rare.

scarcely ['skɛəsli] ad à peine, ne ... guère.

scarcity ['skɛəsiti] n rareté f, pénurie f.

scare [skɛə] n panique f, alarme f; vt terrifier, effrayer; —crow n épouvantail m; —monger n alarmiste m.

scarf [ska:f] n écharpe f, foulard m, cache-col m.

scarlet ['ska:lit] an écarlate f; — fever n (fièvre) scarlatine f.

scathing ['skeiðiŋ] a mordant, cinglant.

scatter ['skætə] vt disperser, éparpiller, semer; vi se disperser, s'égailler, se dissiper; —brain n écervelé(e).

scattered ['skætəd] a épars, éparpillé, semé.

scattering ['skætəriŋ] n dispersion f, éparpillement m, poignée f.

scavenger ['skævindʒə] n balayeur m, boueux m.

scene [si:n] n scène f, spectacle m, lieu m, théâtre m.

scenery ['si:nəri] n décor(s) m (pl), paysage m.

scenic ['si:nik] a scénique, théâtral.

scent [sent] n odeur f, parfum m, piste f, flair m; vt flairer, parfumer, embaumer.

sceptical ['skeptikəl] a sceptique.

scepticism ['skeptisizəm] n scepticisme m

sceptre ['septə] n sceptre m.

schedule ['ʃedjul] n horaire m, plan m, annexe f.

scheme [ski:m] n plan m, projet m, intrigue f, combinaison f; vi comploter, intriguer; vt combiner, projeter.

schemer ['ski:mə] n homme m à projets, intrigant(e) mf.

schism ['sizəm] n schisme m.

scholar ['skɔlə] n érudit m, savant(e) mf, boursier, -ière, écolier, -ière.

scholarship ['skɔləʃip] n science f, érudition f, bourse f.

school [sku:l] n école f, faculté f; vt instruire, dresser, former, entraîner.

schoolmaster ['sku:l mɑ:stə] n instituteur m, professeur m, directeur m.

schoolmate ['sku:lmeit] n camarade de classe mf.

schoolroom ['sku:lrum] n (salle de) classe f.

schooner ['sku:nə] n goélette f.

science ['saiəns] n science f.

scientist ['saiəntist] n savant(e) mf, homme de science m, scientifique m.

scion ['saiən] n rejeton m, bouture f.

scissors ['sizəz] n ciseaux m pl.

scoff [skɔf] n raillerie f; vt railler; vi se moquer (de at).

scold [skould] n mégère f; vti gronder; vt attraper.

scolding ['skouldiŋ] n semonce f, savon m.

sconce [skɔns] n applique f, bobèche.

scoop ['sku:p] n pelle f, louche f, écope f, cuiller f, reportage m en exclusivité; vt creuser, vider, écoper, rafler.

scope [skoup] n portée f, envergure f, champ m, carrière f, compétence f.

scorch [skɔːtʃ] vt brûler, roussir, rôtir; vi filer à toute vitesse, brûler le pavé.

score [skɔ:] n marque f, score m, point m, compte m, partition f, coche f, éraflure f, vingt; vt marquer, remporter, (en)cocher, érafler, orchestrer; vi marquer les points, avoir l'avantage; (US) réprimander, censurer.

scorn [skɔːn] n mépris m; vt mépriser.

scornful ['skɔːnful] a méprisant.

Scotch ['skɔtʃ] n Écossais(e) mf; an écossais m; n whisky m.

scotfree ['skɔt'fri:] a indemne, sans rien payer.

Scotland ['skɔtlənd] n Écosse f.

Scot(sman, -swoman) [skɔt(smən, wumən)] n Écossais, Écossaise.

Scots, Scottish [skɔts, 'skɔtiʃ] a écossais, d'Écosse.

scoundrel ['skaundrəl] n canaille f, gredin m, coquin m.

scour ['skauə] vt frotter, récurer, purger, battre, balayer, (par)courir.

scourge [skə:dʒ] n fléau m; vt châtier, flageller.

scout [skaut] n éclaireur m, scout m; vt reconnaître, rejeter; vi partir en reconnaissance.

scowl [skaul] n air renfrogné m; vi faire la tête, se renfrogner.

scrag [skræg] n squelette m, cou m, collet m.

scraggy ['skrægi] a décharné.

scramble ['skræmbl] n mêlée f, lutte f; vt (eggs) brouiller; vi se battre, se bousculer.

scrap [skræp] n morceau m, chiffon m, coupure f, bribe f, bagarre f; pl déchets m pl, restes m pl; vt mettre au rebut, réformer; vi se battre, se bagarrer.

scrape [skreip] n grincement m,

grattage *m*, embarras *m*; *vti* gratter, frotter; *vt* râcler, décrotter.

scraper ['skreipə] *n* grattoir *m*, décrottoir *m*.

scratch [skrætʃ] *n* égratignure *f*, trait (grincement *m*) de plume *mf*, coup de griffe *m*; — **pad** *n* (US) bloc-notes *m*; *vti* égratigner, gratter, griffonner.

scrawl [skrɔ:l] *n* gribouillage *m*; *vt* gribouiller.

scream [skri:m] *n* cri (perçant) *m*; *vi* pousser un cri, crier, se tordre (de rire).

screaming ['skri:miŋ] *a* désopilant, criard.

screen [skri:n] *n* écran *m*, paravent *m*, rideau *m*, crible *m*, jubé *m*; *vt* couvrir, cacher, protéger, projeter, cribler, mettre à l'écran.

screw [skru:] *n* vis *f*, hélice *f*, écrou *m*, pingre *m*; *vt* visser, (res)serrer, pressurer; **to — up one's courage** prendre son courage à deux mains.

screwdriver ['skru:ˌdraivə] *n* tournevis *m*.

scribble ['skribl] *see* **scrawl**.

scrimmage ['skrimidʒ] *n* bagarre *f*, mêlée *f*.

scrimp [skrimp] *vti* lésiner (sur), saboter.

scripture ['skriptʃə] *n* Écriture *f*.

scroll [skroul] *n* rouleau *m*, volute *f*, fioriture *f*.

scrounge [skraundʒ] *vt* chiper, écornifler.

scrounger ['skraundʒə] *n* chipeur *m*, pique-assiette *m*.

scrub [skrʌb] *n* broussailles *f pl*, coup de brosse *m*, frottée *f*; *vt* frotter, récurer.

scrubbing ['skrʌbiŋ] *n* frottage *m*, récurage *m*.

scrubby ['skrʌbi] *a* rabougri, chétif.

scruple ['skru:pl] *n* scrupule *m*; *vi* se faire scrupule (de about).

scrupulous ['skru:pjuləs] *a* scrupuleux, méticuleux.

scrutinize ['skru:tinaiz] *vt* scruter, examiner de près.

scrutiny ['skru:tini] *n* examen serré *m*, second compte *m*.

scuffle ['skʌfl] *n* bousculade *f*; *vi* bousculer.

scull [skʌl] *n* godille *f*; *vi* godiller, ramer.

sculptor ['skʌlptə] *n* sculpteur *m*.

sculpture ['skʌlptʃə] *n* sculpture *f*; *vt* sculpter.

scum [skʌm] *n* écume *f*, rebut *m*; *vti* écumer.

scurf [skə:f] *n* pellicule *f*.

scurrilous ['skʌriləs] *a* grossier, ordurier, obscène.

scurvy ['skə:vi] *n* scorbut *m*; *a* bas, méprisable.

scuttle ['skʌtl] *n* seau *m*, hublot *m*, fuite *f*; *vt* saborder; *vi* décamper.

scythe [saið] *n* faux *f*; *vt* faucher.

sea [si:] *n* mer *f*; *a* marin, maritime, de mer; **—-coast** *n* littoral *m*;

—gull *n* mouette *f*; **—-horse** *n* mouton *m*; **—-level** *n* niveau de la mer *m*; **—plane** *n* hydravion *m*; **—port** *n* port (maritime) *m*; **—-sickness** *n* mal de mer *m*; **—-wall** *n* digue *f*.

seal [si:l] *n* (zool) phoque *m*; cachet *m*, sceau *m*; *vt* sceller, cacheter.

sealing-wax ['si:liŋwæks] *n* cire à cacheter *f*.

seam [si:m] *n* couture *f*, suture *f*, cicatrice *f*, veine *f*, filon *m*.

seaman ['si:mən] *n* marin *m*, matelot *m*.

seamstress ['semstris] *n* couturière *f*.

seamy side ['si:misaid] *n* envers *m*, les dessous *m pl*.

sear [siə] *a* séché, flétri; *vt* brûler au fer rouge, flétrir.

search [sə:tʃ] *n* quête *f*, visite *f*, perquisition *f*, recherche(s) *f* (*pl*); *vt* fouiller, inspecter, scruter, sonder, examiner; *vti* chercher.

searching ['sə:tʃiŋ] *a* pénétrant, minutieux.

searchlight ['sə:tʃlait] *n* projecteur *m*, phare *m*.

season ['si:zn] *n* saison *f*, période *f*, bon moment *m*; *vt* endurcir, aguerrir, mûrir, assaisonner, tempérer.

seasonable ['si:znəbl] *a* de saison, saisonnier, opportun.

seasoning ['si:zniŋ] *n* assaisonnement *m*.

season-ticket ['si:zn'tikit] *n* abonnement *m*.

seat [si:t] *n* siège *m*, selle *f*, centre *m*, foyer *m*, propriété *f*, fond *m* (de culotte); *vt* contenir, faire asseoir, installer.

seaweed ['si:wi:d] *n* goémon *m*, algue *f*, varech *m*.

secede [si'si:d] *vi* se séparer.

secession [si'seʃən] *n* sécession *f*.

seclude [si'klu:d] *vt* écarter.

seclusion [si'klu:ʒən] *n* retraite *f*, solitude *f*.

second ['sekənd] *n* seconde *f*, second *m*; *a* second, deuxième; **— to none** sans égal; *vt* seconder, appuyer, (*mil*) détacher; **—hand** *a* d'occasion. **—-rate** *a* médiocre, inférieur.

secrecy ['si:krisi] *n* secret *m*, réserve *f*, dissimulation *f*.

secret ['si:krit] *a* secret, réservé, retiré; *n* secret *m*, confidence *f*.

secretariat [ˌsekrə'tɛəriət] *n* secrétariat *m*.

secretary ['sekrətri] *n* secrétaire *mf*.

secrete [si'kri:t] *vt* cacher, sécréter.

secretion [si'kri:ʃən] *n* sécrétion *f*.

secretive ['si:kritiv] *a* secret, réservé, cachottier, renfermé.

sect [sekt] *n* secte *f*.

sectarian [sek'tɛəriən] *n* sectaire *m*.

section ['sekʃən] *n* section *f*, coupe *f*, tranche *f*, profil *m*.

sector ['sektə] *n* secteur *m*.

secular ['sekjulə] *a* séculier, profane, séculaire.

secure [si'kjuə] *a* sûr, assuré, en sûreté, assujetti; *vt* mettre en lieu sûr, fixer, s'assurer, obtenir, assujettir.

security [si'kjuəriti] *n* sécurité *f*, sûreté(s) *f* (*pl*), sauvegarde *f*, garantie *f*, solidité *f*.

sedate [si'deit] *a* posé.

sedentary ['sedntəri] *a* sédentaire.

sedge [sedʒ] *n* jonc *m*, laîche *f*.

sediment ['sedimənt] *n* sédiment *m*, lie *f*, dépôt *m*.

sedition [si'diʃən] *n* sédition *f*.

seditious [si'diʃəs] *a* séditieux.

seduce [si'djuːs] *vt* séduire.

seducer [si'djuːsə] *n* séducteur *m*.

seduction [si'dʌkʃən] *n* séduction *f*.

seductive [si'dʌktiv] *a* séduisant.

seductiveness [si'dʌktivnis] *n* attrait *m*, séduction *f*.

sedulous ['sedjuləs] *a* assidu, empressé.

see [siː] *n* évêché *m*, siège *m*; *vti* voir, saisir, comprendre; — **here!** toi, écoute!

seed [siːd] *n* semence *f*, graine *f*, pépin *m*; *vi* monter en graine; *vt* ensemencer, semer.

seedling ['siːdliŋ] *n* plant *m*, sauvageon *m*.

seedy ['siːdi] *a* monté en graine, râpé, souffreteux, minable.

seek [siːk] *vt* (re)chercher.

seem [siːm] *vi* sembler, paraître.

seeming ['siːmiŋ] *a* apparent, soidisant.

seemingly ['siːmiŋli] *ad* apparemment.

seemly ['siːmli] *a* séant.

seemliness ['siːmlinis] *n* bienséance *f*.

seesaw ['siːsɔː] *n* bascule *f*, balançoire *f*.

seethe [siːð] *vi* bouillonner, grouiller, être en effervescence.

seize [siːz] *vt* saisir, s'emparer de; *vi* se caler, gripper.

seizure ['siːʒə] *n* saisie *f*, attaque *f*.

seldom ['seldəm] *ad* rarement.

select [si'lekt] *a* choisi, de choix, d'élite; *vt* choisir, trier, sélectionner.

selection [si'lekʃən] *n* choix *m*, sélection *f*.

self [self] *n* personnalité *f*, moi *m*, égoïsme *m*; *a* même, monotone, uniforme, auto-; **——conscious** emprunté gêné, conscient; **——contained** (ren)fermé, indépendant; **——control** maîtrise *f* de soi, sangfroid *m*; **——defence** légitime défense *f*; **——denial** sacrifice *m*, abnégation *f*; **——educated** autodidacte; **——government** autonomie *f*; **——indulgence** *n* complaisance *f* (pour soi-même), faiblesse; **——interest** égoïsme, intérêt personnel *m*; **——respect** amour-propre *m*; **——same** *a* identique.

self-determination ['selfdi,təːmi'neiʃən] *n* autodétermination *f*.

selfish ['selfiʃ] *a* égoïste.

selfishness ['selfiʃnis] *n* égoïsme *m*.

selfless ['selflis] *a* désintéressé.

selflessness ['selflisnis] *n* abnégation *f*.

self-possessed ['selfpə'zəst] *a* maître de soi, qui a de l'aplomb *m*.

self-starter ['self'staːtə] *n* démarreur *m*.

self-willed ['self'wild] *a* obstiné, volontaire.

sell [sel] *vt* vendre; *vi* se vendre, se placer, (US) populariser.

seller ['selə] *n* vendeur, -euse, marchand(e) *m*.

semblance ['sembləns] *n* air *m*, apparence *f*, semblant *m*.

semi-colon ['semi'koulən] *n* pointvirgule *m*.

seminary ['seminəri] *n* séminaire *m*, pépinière *f*.

semi-official ['semi'fiʃəl] *a* officieux.

semolina [semə'liːnə] *n* semoule *f*.

senate ['senit] *n* sénat *m*.

send [send] *vt* envoyer, expédier; **to —— down** renvoyer; **to —— for** faire venir; **to —— off** reconduire, expédier.

sender ['sendə] *n* envoyeur, -euse, expéditeur, -trice.

sending ['sendiŋ] *n* envoi *m*, expédition *f*.

senior ['siːnjə] *an* ancien, -ienne, aîné(e) *mf*.

seniority [siːni'ɔriti] *n* ancienneté *f*, aînesse *f*.

sensation [sen'seiʃən] *n* sentiment *m*, sensation *f*, impression *f*.

sensational [sen'seiʃənl] *a* sensationnel, à sensation.

sense [sens] *n* (bon) sens *m*, sentiment *m*; *vt* sentir, pressentir.

senseless ['senslis] *a* déraisonnable, sans connaissance.

sensibility [sensi'biliti] *n* sensibilité *f*.

sensible ['sensəbl] *a* raisonnable, sensé, perceptible, sensible.

sensitive ['sensitiv] *a* sensible, impressionable.

sensual ['sensjuəl] *a* sensuel.

sensuality [sensju'æliti] *n* sensualité *f*.

sent [sent] *pt pp of* **send.**

sentence ['sentəns] *n* phrase *f*, sentence *f*; *vt* condamner.

sententious [sen'tenʃəs] *a* sentencieux.

sentiment ['sentimənt] *n* sentiment *m*, opinion *f*.

sentimentality [sentimen'tæliti] *n* sentimentalité *f*.

sentry ['sentri] *n* sentinelle *f*, factionnaire *m*.

sentry-box ['sentribɔks] *n* guérite *f*.

separate ['seprit] *a* distinct, détaché, séparé.

separate ['sepəreit] *vt* séparer, détacher, dégager; *vi* se séparer, se détacher.

sepoy ['siːpɔi] *n* cipaye *m*.

September [səp'tembə] n septembre m.

septic ['septik] a septique.

sepulchre ['sepəlkə] n sépulcre m.

sequel ['siːkwəl] n suite f.

sequence ['siːkwəns] n série f, suite f, séquence f.

sequester [si'kwestə] vt séquestrer, enfermer.

seraglio [sə'rɑːliou] n sérail m.

serene [si'riːn] a serein, calme.

serenity [si'reniti] n sérénité f, calme m.

serf [səːf] n serf m.

serfdom ['səːfdəm] n servage m.

serge [səːdʒ] n serge f.

sergeant ['sɑːdʒənt] n sergent m, maréchal des logis m, (police) brigadier m.

serial ['siəriəl] n feuilleton m; a en série.

seriatim [,siəri'eitim] ad point par point.

series ['siəriːz] n série f, suite f.

serious ['siəriəs] a sérieux, grave.

seriousness ['siəriəsnis] n sérieux m, gravité f.

sermon ['səːmən] n sermon m.

sermonize ['səːmənaiz] vt sermonner.

serpent ['səːpənt] n serpent m.

serpentine ['səːpəntain] a serpentin, sinueux.

servant ['səːvənt] n domestique mf, serviteur m, servante f.

serve [səːv] vt servir, être utile à, subir, remettre, desservir, purger.

service ['səːvis] n service m, emploi m, entretien m, office m, culte m; a d'ordonnance, de service.

serviceable ['səːvisəbl] a serviable, de bon usage, pratique, utilisable.

servile ['səːvail] a servile.

servility [səː'viliti] n servilité f.

servitude ['səːvitjuːd] n servitude f, esclavage m.

session ['seʃən] n session f, séance f, (US) classe f, cours m pl.

set [set] n (tools etc) jeu m, collection f, (people) groupe m, cercle f, (tea etc) service m, (TV etc) poste m, appareil m, (theatre) décor(s) m (pl), (pearls) rangée f, (linen) parure f, (hair) mise-en-plis f, (idea) direction f; a fixe, pris, stéréotype; vt régler, mettre (à in), fixer, (print) composer, (jewels) sertir, (trap) tendre, (blade) aiguiser; vi se mettre (à), prendre, durcir, se fixer, (sun) se coucher; to — going commencer; to — aside mettre de côté, écarter; to — forth exposer, faire valoir; to — in vi avancer; — off vi partir, vt déclencher; to — out vi partir, vt arranger; to — up vti monter, s'établir, préparer; to — upon attaquer.

set-back ['setbæk] n recul m, échec m.

set-off ['set'ɔf] n contraste m, repoussoir m.

set-to ['set'tuː] n pugilat m, échauffourré m.

settee [se'tiː] n divan m.

setter ['setə] n chien d'arrêt m.

setting ['setiŋ] n monture f, pose f, cadre m, mise f (en scène, en marche etc), coucher m.

settle ['setl] vt établir, installer, fixer, ranger, poser, régler, placer; vi s'établir, s'installer, se poser, déposer, s'arranger; n banc m, canapé m.

settlement ['setlmənt] n établissement m, colonie f, contrat m, règlement m.

settler ['setlə] n colon m, immigrant m.

seven ['sevn] an sept m.

sevenfold ['sevnfould] a septuple; ad sept fois autant.

seventeen ['sevn'tiːn] an dix-sept m.

seventeenth ['sevn'tiːnθ] an dix-septième mf.

seventh ['sevnθ] an septième mf.

seventy ['sevnti] an soixante-dix m.

sever ['sevə] vt séparer, trancher, couper.

several ['sevrəl] a respectif, personnel; a pn plusieurs.

severe [si'viə] a sévère, rigoureux, vif.

severity [si'veriti] n sévérité f, rigueur f, violence f.

sew [sou] vt coudre, suturer.

sewage ['sjuidʒ] n vidanges f pl, eaux f pl d'égout.

sewer ['souə] n couturière, brocheuse f.

sewer ['sjuə] n égout m.

sewing-machine ['souiŋmə,ʃiːn] n machine à coudre f.

sewn [soun] pp of sew.

sex [seks] n sexe m; — -appeal n sex-appeal m.

sexton ['sekstən] n sacristain m, fossoyeur m.

sexual ['seksjuəl] a sexuel.

sexy ['seksi] a (fam) capiteuse, excitante; to be — avoir du sex-appeal.

shabby ['ʃæbi] a pingre, râpé, minable, délabré, mesquin, défraîchi.

shackle ['ʃækl] n chaîne f, maillon m; pl fers m pl, entraves f pl; vt enchaîner, entraver.

shade [ʃeid] n ombre f, retraite f, nuance f, (US) store m; pl lunettes de soleil f pl; vt abriter, ombrager, masquer, assombrir, ombrer; vi dégrader.

shadow ['ʃædou] n ombre f; vt filer.

shadowy ['ʃædoui] a ombrageux, vaseux.

shady ['ʃeidi] a ombragé, ombreux, furtif, louche.

shaft [ʃɑːft] n hampe f, trait m, tige f, fût m, manche m, brancard m, arbre m, puits m.

shaggy ['ʃægi] a hirsute, touffu, en broussailles.

shake [ʃeik] n secousse f, hochement m, tremblement m; vt secouer, agiter, hocher, ébranler, serrer; vi trembler, branler.

shaky ['ʃeiki] a branlant, tremblant, chancelant.

shallot [ʃə'lɔt] n échalote f.

shallow ['ʃælou] n bas-fond m, haut-fond m; a peu profond, creux, superficiel.

sham [ʃæm] n feinte f, trompe-l'œil m, faux semblant m; a faux, simulé, postiche, en toc; vt feindre, simuler, faire semblant de.

shamble ['ʃæmbl] vi trainer les pieds.

shambles ['ʃæmblz] n abattoir m, tuerie f.

shame [ʃeim] n honte f, pudeur f; vt faire honte à, couvrir de honte.

shameful ['ʃeimful] a honteux, scandaleux.

shameless ['ʃeimlis] a éhonté, effronté.

shampoo [ʃæm'pu:] n shampooing m; vt donner un shampooing à.

shamrock ['ʃæmrɔk] n trèfle m.

shandy ['ʃændi] n bière panachée f.

shank [ʃæŋk] n jambe f, tige f, fût m, manche m, tibia m.

shape [ʃeip] n forme f, tournure f, moule m; vt former, façonner; vi prendre forme, prendre tournure.

shapeless ['ʃeiplis] a informe.

shapely ['ʃeipli] a gracieux, bien fait.

share [ʃɛə] n part f, action f, contribution f, soc m; vti partager; vt prendre part à.

shareholder ['ʃɛə,houldə] n actionnaire mf.

shark [ʃɑ:k] n requin m, (US) n fort (en maths).

sharp [ʃɑ:p] a pointu, aigu, tranchant, aigre, vif, fin, malhonnête, (US) expert; ad juste, brusquement; tapant.

sharpen ['ʃɑ:pən] vt aiguiser, affiler, tailler.

sharper ['ʃɑ:pə] n tricheur m, escroc m.

sharply ['ʃɑ:pli] ad vertement, d'un ton tranchant.

sharpness ['ʃɑ:pnis] n acuité f, netteté f, finesse f.

sharpshooter ['ʃɑ:p,ʃu:tə] n bon tireur m, tirailleur m.

shatter ['ʃætə] vt mettre en pièces, fracasser.

shave [ʃeiv] vt raser, frôler; vi se raser; **to have a —** se (faire) raser; **to have a close —** l'échapper belle.

shaving ['ʃeiviŋ] n copeau m; **— brush** n blaireau m.

shawl [ʃɔ:l] n châle m.

she [ʃi:] pn elle, (ship) il; n femelle f.

sheaf [ʃi:f] n gerbe f, liasse f.

shear [ʃiə] vt tondre.

shearing ['ʃiəriŋ] n tonte f.

shears [ʃiəz] n cisailles f pl.

sheath [ʃi:θ] n fourreau m, gaine f, étui m.

sheathe [ʃi:ð] vt (r)engainer, encaisser, doubler.

shed [ʃed] n hangar m, remise f, étable f, appentis m; vt perdre, mettre au rencart, se dépouiller de, verser.

sheep [ʃi:p] n mouton m.

sheepdog ['ʃi:pdɔg] n chien de berger m.

sheepish ['ʃi:piʃ] a gauche, timide, penaud, honteux.

sheer [ʃiə] a pur, à pic, transparent.

sheet [ʃi:t] n drap m, feuille f, nappe f, tôle f.

shelf [ʃelf] n rayon m, corniche f.

shell [ʃel] n coquille f, coque f, cosse f, écaille f, carapace f, douille f, obus m; vt écosser, décortiquer, bombarder.

shellfish ['ʃelfiʃ] n coquillage m.

shelter ['ʃeltə] n abri m, couvert m, asile m; vt abriter, couvrir, recueillir; vi s'abriter, se mettre à l'abri.

shelve [ʃelv] vt mettre à l'écart, (en disponibilité, au panier), ajourner.

shepherd ['ʃepəd] n berger m; vt rassembler, garder, conduire.

sherry ['ʃeri] n Xérès m.

shield [ʃi:ld] n bouclier m, défense f; vt protéger, couvrir.

shift [ʃift] n changement m, équipe f, expédient m, faux-fuyant m; **to work in —s** se relayer; vti changer; vt déplacer; vi se déplacer; **to — for oneself** se débrouiller.

shifty ['ʃifti] a fuyant, retors, sournois.

shin(-bone) ['ʃin(boun)] n tibia m; vi grimper.

shine [ʃain] n brillant m, éclat m, beau-temps m; vi briller, reluire, rayonner.

shingle ['ʃingl] n galets m pl; vt couper court.

shingles ['ʃinglz] n pl zona m.

ship [ʃip] n vaisseau m, navire m, bâtiment m; vt embarquer, charger, expédier; **—broker** courtier m maritime; **—load** chargement m, cargaison f; **—building** construction f navale.

shipping ['ʃipiŋ] n marine f, tonnage m, expédition f, navires m pl.

shipwreck ['ʃiprek] n naufrage m; vi faire échouer, faire naufrager; **to be —ed** faire naufrage.

shipwright ['ʃiprait] n charpentier de navires m.

shipyard ['ʃipjɑ:d] n chantier maritime m.

shirk [ʃə:k] vt esquiver, renâcler à, se dérober à.

shirker ['ʃə:kə] n tire-au-flanc m, renâcleur m.

shirt [ʃə:t] n chemise f.

shirt-front ['ʃə:tfrʌnt] n plastron m.

shiver ['ʃivə] n frisson m; vi frissonner grelotter.

shoal [ʃoul] n banc m, masse f, haut-fond m.

shock [ʃɔk] n secousse f, heurt m, choc m, coup m; vt choquer, frapper, scandaliser.

shoddy ['ʃɔdi] n camelote f; a de pacotille.

shoe [ʃuː] n soulier m, chaussure f, fer à cheval m; vt chausser, ferrer, armer; —**black** cireur m; —**horn** chausse-pied m; —**lace** lacet m, cordon m; —**maker** cordonnier m.

shone [ʃɔn] pt pp of **shine**.

shoot [ʃuːt] n pousse f, sarment m, gourmand m, rapide m, partie de chasse f, chasse f; vi pousser, jaillir, tirer, filer; vt tirer, abattre, fusiller, lancer, décocher, darder.

shooting ['ʃuːtiŋ] n tir m, fusillade f, chasse (gardée) f; —**box** pavillon de chasse m; —**party** partie de chasse f; —**range** n champ de tir m; —**star** n étoile filante f.

shop [ʃɔp] n magasin m, boutique f, atelier m; vi faire ses achats; —**assistant** vendeur m, vendeuse f; —**boy** (-**girl**) garçon (demoiselle f) de magasin m; —**keeper** boutiquier m, marchand m; —**lifter** voleur m à l'étalage; — **window** vitrine f.

shore [ʃɔː] n côte f, rivage m, étai m; vt étayer.

shorn [ʃɔːn] pp of **shear**.

short [ʃɔːt] n brève f, court-métrage m, (drinks) alcool m; a bref, court(aud), concis, à court de, cassant; **in** — bref; —**ly** ad brièvement, de court, sous peu.

shortage ['ʃɔːtidʒ] n manque m, crise f, pénurie f.

shortbread ['ʃɔːtbred] n sablé m.

short-circuit ['ʃɔːt'səːkit] n court-circuit m.

shortcoming [ʃɔːt'kʌmiŋ] n défaut m, insuffisance f, imperfection f.

shorten ['ʃɔːtn] vti raccourcir, abréger.

shorthand ['ʃɔːthænd] n sténographie f.

shortness ['ʃɔːtnis] n brièveté f, manque m.

shorts [ʃɔːts] n culotte f, short m.

short-sighted ['ʃɔːt'saitid] a myope, imprévoyant, de myope.

short-sightedness ['ʃɔːt'saitidnis] n myopie f, imprévoyance f.

short-tempered ['ʃɔːt'tempəd] a irritable.

short-winded ['ʃɔːt'windid] a court d'haleine, poussif.

shot [ʃɔt] pt pp of **shoot**; n balle f, boulet m; plombs m pl, coup m (de feu), tireur m, tentative f, portée f, prise de vue f; —**gun** fusil m.

shoulder ['ʃouldə] n épaule f; vt mettre, charger, porter, sur l'épaule; —**blade** omoplate f; —**strap** bretelle f, patte d'épaule f; — **bag** sac m en bandoulière.

shout [ʃaut] n cri m; vti crier; to —

down huer; **to** — **for** (US) supporter.

shove [ʃʌv] n coup d'épaule m; vti pousser; vt fourrer.

shovel ['ʃʌvl] n pelle f.

shovelful ['ʃʌvlful] n pelletée f.

show [ʃou] n spectacle m, exposition f, montre f, étalage m, apparence f, simulacre m, affaire f, ostentation f; **motor** — salon m de l'automobile; vt montrer, exposer, exhiber, accuser, indiquer, faire preuve de; vi se montrer, paraître; to — **in** faire entrer, introduire; to — **out** reconduire; to — **off** vt faire étalage de, mettre en valeur; vi faire de l'épate, se faire valoir; to — **up** démasquer.

show-case ['ʃoukeis] n vitrine f.

shower ['ʃauə] n ondée f, averse f, pluie f, douche f, volée f; vt faire pleuvoir, arroser, accabler.

showiness ['ʃouinis] n ostentation f, épate f.

showman ['ʃoumən] n forain m, imprésario m.

shown [ʃoun] pp of **show**.

showroom ['ʃourum] n salon d'exposition m.

show-window ['ʃou'windou] n étalage m.

showy ['ʃoui] a voyant, criard, prétentieux.

shrank [ʃræŋk] pt of **shrink**.

shred [ʃred] n pièce f, lambeau m, brin m; vt mettre en pièces, effilocher.

shrew [ʃruː] n mégère f; (mouse) musaraigne f.

shrewd [ʃruːd] a perspicace, entendu, judicieux.

shrewdness ['ʃruːdnis] n sagacité f, perspicacité f, finesse f.

shriek [ʃriːk] n cri aigu m; vi crier, déchirer l'air, pousser un cri.

shrill [ʃril] a aigu, -uë, perçant.

shrimp [ʃrimp] n crevette (grise) f, gringalet m.

shrine [ʃrain] n châsse f, tombeau m, sanctuaire m.

shrink [ʃriŋk] vt rétrécir; vi se rétrécir, reculer.

shrinkage ['ʃriŋkidʒ] n rétrécissement m.

shrivel ['ʃrivl] vi se ratatiner, se recroqueviller; vt ratatiner, brûler.

shroud [ʃraud] n linceul m, suaire m, hauban m, voile m; vt envelopper, cacher, voiler.

Shrove Tuesday ['ʃrouv'tjuːzdi] n mardi gras m.

shrub [ʃrʌb] n arbrisseau m.

shrubbery ['ʃrʌbəri] n taillis m, bosquet m.

shrug [ʃrʌg] n haussement d'épaules m; vi to — **one's shoulders** hausser les épaules.

shudder ['ʃʌdə] n frisson m; vi frissonner.

shuffle ['ʃʌfl] vt brouiller, (cards) battre, mêler, traîner; vi traîner la jambe, louvoyer, tergiverser.

shun [ʃʌn] vt éviter, fuir.

shunt [ʃʌnt] *vt* garer, manœuvrer, écarter.

shunting ['ʃʌntiŋ] *n* garage *m*, manœuvre *f*.

shut [ʃʌt] *vtir* fermer, serrer; *vi* (se) fermer; **to — down** arrêter, fermer; **to — in** enfermer, confiner; **to — off** couper; **to — up** *vt* enfermer; *vi* fermer çà.

shut-out ['ʃʌtaut] *n* lock-out *m*.

shutter ['ʃʌtə] *n* volet *m*, obturateur *m*.

shuttle ['ʃʌtl] *n* navette *f*.

shuttlecock ['ʃʌtlkɔk] *n* volant *m*.

shy [ʃai] *n* sursaut *m*. écart *m*, essai *m*; *a* timide, ombrageux; (US) **to be — of** être à court de; *vi* sursauter, faire un écart; *vt* lancer.

sick [sik] *a* malade, écœuré, dégoûté; **—room** *n* chambre de malade.

sicken ['sikn] *vi* tomber malade; *vt* écœurer.

sickle ['sikl] *n* faucille *f*.

sickly ['sikli] *a* maladif, malsain, fade, pâle.

sickness ['siknis] *n* maladie *f*, mal de cœur *m*.

side ['said] *n* côté *m*, flanc *m*, côte *f*, parti *m*, équipe *f* chichi *m*; *a* de coté, latéral.

sideboard ['saidbɔ:d] *n* dressoir *m*, buffet *m*.

sidecar ['saidka:] *n* sidecar *m*.

sidelong ['saidlɔŋ] *a* oblique, de côté, en coulisse.

siding ['saidiŋ] *n* voie de garage *f*.

sidewalk ['saidwɔ:k] *n* (US) trottoir *m*.

sideways ['saidweiz] *ad* de côté.

siege [si:dʒ] *n* siège *m*.

sieve [siv] *n* tamis *m*, crible *m*, écumoire *f*.

sift [sift] *vt* cribler, tamiser.

sigh [sai] *n* soupir *m*; *vi* soupirer.

sight [sait] *n* vue *f*, hausse *f*, guidon *m*, spectacle *m*; *vt* apercevoir, aviser; (gun) pointer.

sightless ['saitlis] *a* aveugle.

sightly ['saitli] *a* bon à voir, avenant.

sightseeing ['sait si:iŋ] *n* tourisme *m*, visite *f*.

sign [sain] *n* signe *m*, marque *f*, indication *f*, enseigne *f*; *vt* signer; *vi* faire signe; **—board** enseigne *f*; **—post** poteau indicateur *m*.

signal ['signl] *n* signal *m*, indication *m*; *vti* signaler.

signatory ['signətəri] *n* signataire *mf*.

signature ['signitʃə] *n* signature *f*; **— tune** indicatif musical *m*.

significance [sig'nifikəns] *n* sens *m*, importance *f*.

significant [sig'nifikənt] *a* significatif, important.

signification [ˌsignifi'keiʃən] *n* signification *f*.

signify ['signifai] *vt* annoncer, signifier; *vi* importer.

silence ['sailəns] *n* silence *m*; *excl*

motus! chut!; *vt* réduire au silence, faire taire, étouffer.

silencer ['sailənsə] *n* silencieux *m*.

silent ['sailənt] *a* silencieux muet, taciturne.

silk [silk] *n* soie *f*; *a* de, en, soie; **—worm** ver à soie *m*.

silk cotton tree ['silkkɔtntri:] *n* kapokier *m*, fromager *m*.

silken ['silkən] *a* soyeux, suave, doucereux.

sill [sil] *n* seuil *m*, rebord *m*.

silliness ['silinis] *n* sottise *f*.

silly ['sili] *a* sot, sotte, bête.

silt [silt] *n* vase *f*; *vt* ensabler, envaser; *vi* s'ensabler.

silver ['silvə] *n* argent *m*, argenterie *f*; *a* d'argent, argenté; *vt* argenter, étamer; **— gilt** vermeil *m*; **— paper** papier d'étain *m*; **—side** gîte à la noix *m*; **—smith** orfèvre *m*.

silvery ['silvəri] *a* argenté, argentin.

similar ['similə] *a* semblable; **—ly** *ad* de même.

similarity [ˌsimi'læriti] *n* similarité *f*, ressemblance *f*.

simile ['simili] *n* comparaison *f*.

similitude [si'militju:d] *n* ressemblance *f*. apparence *f*, similitude *f*.

simmer ['simə] *vti* mijoter; *vi* frémir, fermenter.

simper ['simpə] *n* sourire *m* apprêté; *vi* minauder.

simple ['simpl] *a* simple.

simpleton ['simpltən] *n* niais(e) *mf*.

simplicity [sim'plisiti] *n* simplicité *f*, candeur *f*.

simplify ['simplifai] *vt* simplifier.

simplification [ˌsimplifi'keiʃən] *n* simplification *f*.

simulate ['simjuleit] *vt* simuler, feindre, imiter.

simulation [ˌsimju'leiʃən] *n* simulation *f*.

simulator ['simjuleitə] *n* simulateur, -trice.

simultaneous [ˌsiməl'teiniəs] *a* simultané.

simultaneousness [ˌsiməl'teiniəsnis] *n* simultanéité *f*.

sin [sin] *n* péché *m*; *vi* pécher.

since [sins] *prep* depuis; *ad* depuis; *cj* depuis que, puisque.

sincere [sin'siə] *a* sincère.

sincerely [sin'siəli] *ad* **yours —** recevez expression de mes sentiments distingués.

sincerity [sin'seriti] *n* sincérité *f*, bonne foi *f*.

sinecure ['sainikjuə] *n* sinécure *f*.

sinew ['sinju:] *n* tendon *m*, muscle *m*, force *f*; *pl* nerf(s) *m* (*pl*).

sinewy ['sinju:i] *a* musclé, musculeux, nerveux.

sinful ['sinful] *a* coupable.

sing [siŋ] *vti* chanter.

singe [sindʒ] *vt* roussir, flamber.

singer ['siŋə] *n* chanteur, -euse, chantre *m*; **praise —** griot *m*.

single ['siŋgl] *a* seul, singulier, pour

une personne, célibataire, droit, sincère; n (ticket) aller m. (tennis) simple m; vt to — ou distinguer, désigner; —handed sans aide d'une seule main.

singleness ['singlnis] n unité f, droiture f.

singular ['singjulə] a singulier.

singularity [‚singju'læriti] n singularité f.

sinister [‚sinistə] a sinistre, mauvais.

sink [sink] n évier m, cloaque m, trappe f; vt baisser, omber, s'abaisser, défaillir, sombrer, couler au fond, s'enfoncer; vi placer à fonds perdus, couler, baisser, forer, abandonner, sacrifier.

sinking ['sinkin] n coulage m, défaillance f, enfoncement m, abaissement m; —fund fonds d'amortissement m.

sinner ['sinə] n pécheur, pécheresse.

sinuous ['sinjuəs] a sinueux, souple.

sip [sip] gorgée f goutte f; vt siroter, déguster

siphon ['saifən] n siphon m.

sir [səɪ] n monsieur m.

sire ['saiə] n sire m père m.

siren ['saiərin] n sirène f.

sirloin ['səːlɔin] n aloyau m, faux-filet m.

sister ['sistə] n sœur f; —in-law belle sœur f.

sisterhood ['sistəhud] n état de sœur m, communauté f.

sisterly 'sistəli] a de sœur.

sit [sit] vi être assis, rester assis, se tenir, (s')asseoir, siéger, couver, poser, to — in occuper; vt asseoir.

site (sait) n terrain m, emplacement m.

sitter ['sitə] n couveuse f, modèle m.

sitting ['sitin] n séance f, couvaison f, siège m; a assis.

sitting room ['sitinrum] n petit salon m, salle de séjour.

situated ['sitjueitid] a situé.

situation [‚sitju'eiʃən] n situation f, place f.

six [siks] an six m.

sixteen ['siks'tiːn] an seize m.

sixteenth ['siks'tiːnθ] an seizième m.

sixth [siksθ] an sixième m f.

sixty ['siksti] an soixante m.

size [saiz] n taille, dimension f, grandeur f, pointure f format m, calibre m; to — up mesurer juger.

skate [skeit] n patin m (fish) raie f; vi patiner.

skating-rink ['skeitinrink] n patinoire f.

skein [skein] n écheveau m.

skeleton ['skelitn] n squelette m, charpente f, canevas m; — in the cupboard secret m tare f; —key passe-partout m, rossignol m.

sketch [sketʃ] n croquis m, sketch m; vt esquisser.

skew [skju:] a oblique, de biais.

skewer ['skjuə] n brochette f.

skid [skid] n dérapage m, sabot m, patin m; vi déraper, patiner.

skilful ['skilful] a habile, adroit.

skill [skil] n habileté f, adresse f, tact m.

skilled [skild] a qualifié, expert, habile, versé.

skim [skim] vti écumer, écrémer, effleurer; to — through parcourir, feuilleter.

skimmer ['skimə] n écumoire f.

skimp [skimp] vt lésiner sur, mesurer.

skin [skin] n peau f, outre f, robe f, pelure f; — deep à fleur de peau; vt écorcher, peler, éplucher, se cicatriser.

skinner ['skinə] n tourreur m.

skinny ['skini] a décharné.

skip [skip] n saut m; vi sauter, gambader.

skipper ['skipə] n patron m.

skirmish ['skəːmiʃ] n escarmouche f.

skirt [skəːt] n jupe f basque f, pan m, lisière f; vt longer, contourner.

skit [skit] n pièce satirique f, charge f.

skittle ['skitl] n quille f; pl jeu de quilles m.

skulk [skʌlk] vi se terrer, tirer au flanc rôder.

skull [skʌl] n crâne m, tête de mort f.

skull-cap ['skʌlkæp] n calotte f.

skunk [skʌŋk] n sconse m, mouffette f, salaud m.

sky [skai] n ciel m; —lark alouette f; —light lucarne f; —line horizon m; —scraper gratte-ciel m.

slab [slæb] n dall f, plaque f, tablette f, pave m

slack [slæk] n poussier m, mou m, jeu m; a mou, flasque, veule, desserré, creux; vi (fam) flemmarder, se relâcher.

slacken ['slækən] vt ralentir, (re) lâcher détendre desserrer; vi ralentir, se relâcher.

slacker ['slækə] n flemmard(e) mf.

slackness ['slæknis] n veulerie f, laisser-aller m, relâchement m marasme m, mollesse f, mou m.

slag [slæg] n scorie f, mâchefer m, crasses f pl.

slain slein, pp of slay.

slake [sleik] vt étancher, assouvir.

slam [slæm] n claquement m, schlem m; vt claquer.

slander [slɑːndə] n calomnie f, diffamation f; vt calomnier, diffamer.

slanderer ['slɑːndərə] n diffamateur, -trice c lomniateur -trice.

slanderous ['slɑːndərəs] a diffamatoire, calomnieux.

slang [slæŋ] n argot m.

slant [slɑːnt] n obliquité f, pente f, biais m (US) point m de vue; vi diverger obliquer, s'incliner être en pente; vt incliner, déverser.

slap [slæp] n gifle f, soufflet m, tape f; vt gifler; ad en plein.

slash [slæʃ] n estafilade f, balafre f, taillade f; vt balafrer, taillader, fouailler, éreinter, (price) réduire.

slashing ['slæʃiŋ] a cinglant, mordant.

slate [sleit] n ardoise f; vt ardoiser, tancer, éreinter.

slaughter ['slɔːtə] n abattage m, massacre m, boucherie f; vt massacrer, égorger, abattre; **—house** abattoir m.

slave [sleiv] n esclave mf; vi travailler comme un nègre, s'échiner.

slaver ['sleivə] n bave f, lèche f; vi baver, flagorner.

slave-trade ['sleivtreid] n traite des nègres f.

slavery ['sleivəri] n esclavage m, asservissement m.

slavish ['sleiviʃ] n servile.

slay [slei] vt égorger, tuer.

sledge [sledʒ] n traîneau m.

sledge(-hammer) ['sledʒ(ˌhæmə)] n masse f; (fig) massue f.

sleek [sliːk] a lisse, lustré, onctueux.

sleep [sliːp] n sommeil m; vi dormir, coucher; **to go to —** s'endormir, s'engourdir.

sleeper ['sliːpə] n dormeur, traverse f, wagon-lit m.

sleeping-car ['sliːpiŋkɑː] n wagon-lit m.

sleeping-draught ['sliːpiŋdrɑːft] n soporifique m.

sleeping-sickness ['sliːpiŋˈsiknis] n maladie du sommeil f.

sleeplessness ['sliːplisnis] n insomnie f.

sleepy ['sliːpi] a ensommeillé, endormi.

sleet [sliːt] n neige fondue f, grésil m, giboulée f; vi grésiller.

sleeve [sliːv] n manche f.

sleigh [slei] n traîneau m.

sleight [slait] n **— of hand** adresse f, tour de main m, prestidigitation f.

slender ['slendə] a mince, élancé, svelte, faible, ma gre.

slenderness ['slendənis] n sveltesse f, exiguïté f.

slept [slept] pt pp of **sleep**.

slew [sluː] pt of **slay**.

slice [slais] n tranche f, rond m, rondelle f, (fish) truelle f; vt couper (en tranches), trancher.

slid [slid] pt pp of **slide**.

slide [slaid] vti glisser; vi faire des glissades; n glissement m, glissement m, glissade f, glissoire f, coulisse f.

sliding ['slaidiŋ] a à coulisse, à glissières, gradué, mobile.

slight [slait] n affront m; vt manquer d'égards envers; a léger, frêle, peu de.

slightest ['slaitist] a le, la (les) moindre(s).

slim [slim] a mince, svelte, délié, rusé.

slime [slaim] n vase f, limon m, bave f.

slimy ['slaimi] a gluant, visqueux.

sling [sliŋ] n fronde f, bretelle f,

écharpe f; vt lancer, hisser, suspendre.

slink [sliŋk] vi marcher furtivement, raser les murs.

slip [slip] n faux-pas m, lapsus m, peccadille f, erreur f, bouture f, bande f, coulisse f, laisse f, enveloppe f, slip m; vt glisser, filer, échapper à; vi (se) glisser, se tromper; **to — away** se sauver, fuir; **to — off** enlever; **to — on** enfiler, passer.

slipper ['slipə] n pantoufle f, patin m.

slippery ['slipəri] a glissant, fuyant, souple, rusé.

slipshod ['slipʃɔd] a négligé, bâclé.

slit [slit] n incision f, fente f, entrebâillement m; vt déchirer, couper, fendre; vi se fendre, se déchirer.

slogan ['slougən] n slogan m, mot d'ordre m.

slogger ['slɔgə] n cogneur m, bûcheur m.

slope [sloup] n pente f, rampe f, talus m; vi incliner, pencher, être en pente.

slop [slɔp] vt répandre; vt **to — over** vt s'attendrir sur.

slop-pail ['slɔppeil] n seau m de toilette.

slops [slɔps] n eaux sales f pl, bouillie f.

sloppy ['slɔpi] a détrempé, inondé, sale, pleurard, larmoyant, bâclé.

slot [slɔt] n rainure f, fente f.

slot-machine ['slɔtməˌʃiːn] n distributeur automatique m.

sloth [slouθ] n paresse f.

slothful ['slouθful] a paresseux, indolent.

slouch [slautʃ] n démarche penchée f; a au bord rabattu; vi pencher, se tenir mal, traîner le pas; vt rabattre le bord de (son chapeau).

slough [slau] n fondrière f.

slough [slʌf] n dépouille f, tissu mort m; vi faire peau neuve, muer; vt jeter.

Slovak ['slouvæk] n Slovaque mf; a slovaque.

sloven ['slʌvn] n souillon f.

slovenly ['slʌvənli] a négligé, sale, désordonné.

slow [slou] a lent, en retard.

slowly ['slouli] ad lentement, au ralenti.

slowness ['slounis] n lenteur f.

slug [slʌg] n limace f, limaçon m, (US) lampée f (d'alcool); (tec) lingot m; vt terrasser.

sluggard ['slʌgəd] n paresseux m, flemmard m.

sluggish ['slʌgiʃ] a paresseux, inerte, endormi, lourd.

sluggishly ['slʌgiʃli] ad indolemment, lentement.

sluggishness ['slʌgiʃnis] n inertie f, paresse f.

sluice [sluːs] n écluse f; vt vanner, laver à grande eau; **—gate** vanne f.

slum [slʌm] n taudis m.
slumber ['slʌmbə] n somme m, sommeil m; vt somnoler, sommeiller.
slump [slʌmp] n crise f, dégringolade f; vi baisser, dégringoler, se laisser tomber.
slung [slʌŋ] pt pp of **sling**.
slunk [slʌŋk] pt pp of **slink**.
slur [slə:] n blâme m, tache f, bredouillement m, liaison f, macule f, griffonnage m; vt bredouiller, griffonner, couler, passer (sur **over**).
sly [slai] a retors, malin, madré, en dessous.
smack [smæk] n arrière-goût m, teinture f, bateau m de pêche, claquement m, gifle f, essai m, gros baiser m; vt gifler, faire claquer, taper; ad tout droit, en plein, paf; **to — of** sentir.
small [smɔ:l] a petit, faible, mesquin, modeste, peu important, peu de.
smallness ['smɔ:lnis] n petitesse f, mesquinerie f.
smallpox ['smɔ:lpɔks] n variole f, petite vérole f.
smart [sma:t] n douleur cuisante f; vi faire mal, picoter, en cuire à; a vif, débrouillard, fin, malin, chic.
smartness ['sma:tnis] n vivacité f, finesse f, élégance f.
smash [smæʃ] n collision f, coup de poing m, faillite f, sinistre m, effondrement m; vt mettre en pièces, écraser, heurter; vi faire faillite, se fracasser.
smattering ['smætəriŋ] n teinture f, notions f pl.
smear [smiə] n tache f, souillure f; vt graisser, barbouiller, enduire.
smell [smel] n odorat m, flair m, odeur f; vt flairer; vti sentir.
smelt [smelt] pt pp of **smell**; n éperlan m; vt fondre.
smile [smail] nm vi sourire.
smirch [smə:tʃ] vt salir, souiller.
smirk [smə:k] n sourire m affecté; vi minauder.
smite [smait] vt punir, frapper.
smitten ['smitn] pp atteint, épris.
smith [smiθ] n forgeron m.
smithereens ['smiðə'ri:nz] n miettes f pl, morceaux m pl.
smithy ['smiði] n forge f.
smock [smɔk] n blouse f, sarrau m.
smoke [smouk] n fumée f; vti fumer; vi sentir la fumée; vt enfumer.
smoker ['smoukə] n fumeur m.
smokeless ['smouklis] a sans fumée.
smoking-car ['smoukiŋ.ka:] n compartiment pour fumeurs m.
smoking-room ['smoukiŋ.rum] n fumoir m.
smoky ['smouki] a fumeux, enfumé, noirci par la fumée.
smooth [smu:ð] a lisse, uni, calme, doux, aisé, flatteur, apaisant, souple; vt aplanir, adoucir, lisser, apaiser, pallier.
smoothness ['smu:ðnis] n égalité

f, calme m, douceur f, souplesse f.
smote [smout] pt of **smite**.
smother ['smʌðə] vt étouffer, couvrir, suffoquer.
smoulder ['smouldə] vi couver, brûler et fumer.
smudge [smʌdʒ] n barbouillage m; vt barbouiller, salir.
smug [smʌg] a bête et solennel, content de soi, béat.
smuggle ['smʌgl] vt passer en fraude.
smuggler ['smʌglə] n contrebandier m.
smuggling ['smʌgliŋ] n contrebande f, fraude f.
smut [smʌt] n (grain m de) suie f, nielle f, obscénités f pl.
snack [snæk] n casse-croûte m.
snail [sneil] n escargot m, limace f.
snake [sneik] n serpent m.
snap [snæp] n claquement m, bruit sec m, déclic m, bouton-pression m, fermoir m, coup m (de froid), instantané m; a immédiat; vt happer, dire aigrement, casser, (faire) claquer, prendre un instantané de; vi claquer, se casser.
snappish ['snæpiʃ] n hargneux, irritable.
snapshot ['snæpʃɔt] n instantané m.
snare [snɛə] n piège m; vt prendre au piège.
snarl [sna:l] n grognement m; vi grogner, gronder.
snatch [snætʃ] n geste pour saisir m, fragment m, à-coup m, bribe f; vt saisir, arracher, enlever.
sneak [sni:k] n louche individu m, mouchard m; vi se glisser, cafarder, moucharder.
sneaking ['sni:kiŋ] a furtif, inavoué, servile.
sneer [sniə] n ricanement m; vt ricaner; **to — at** bafouer, dénigrer.
sneeze [sni:z] n éternuement m; vi éternuer.
sniff [snif] n reniflement m; vt humer; vti renifler.
snipe [snaip] n bécassine f; **to — at** canarder; (US) mégot m.
sniper ['snaipə] n tireur embusqué m, canardeur m.
snob [snɔb] n snob m, prétentieux m.
snobbery ['snɔbəri] n snobisme m, prétention f.
snooze [snu:z] n somme m; vi faire un somme.
snore [snɔ:] n ronflement m; vi ronfler.
snort [snɔ:t] vi renâcler, s'ébrouer, ronfler, dédaigner.
snout [snaut] n museau m, mufle m, groin m, boutoir m.
snow [snou] n neige f; vi neiger; **to — under** accabler; **—drop** perce-neige m or f; **—flake** flocon m; **—plough** chasse-neige m; **—shoes** raquettes f pl; **—storm** tempête f, rafale f de neige; **—field** champ m de neige; **—ball** boule f de neige.

snub [snʌb] *n* rebuffade *f*; *vt* rabrouer; *a* camus, retroussé.

snuff [snʌf] *n* tabac à priser *m*, prise *f*; *vi* priser; *vt* moucher, éteindre; **—-box** tabatière *f*.

snuffle ['snʌfl] *vi* renifler, nasiller.

snug [snʌg] *a* abrité, douillet, gentil, petit, bien.

so [sou] *ad* si, tellement, ainsi, comme ça, de même, à peu près, le; *cj* donc, si bien que; **—called** soi-disant; **— far** jusqu'ici (là); **—long** à bientôt; **—much** tant, autant de; **— much for** assez; **— on** ainsi de suite; **— and —** un(e) tel(le), machin; **in — far as** en tant que, dans la mesure où; **— that** de manière à (que), si bien que; **— as to** de façon à, afin de; **so** comme ci, comme ça.

soak [souk] *vt* tremper, imbiber, pénétrer, (US) abattre, donner un coup de bambou; *vi* s'imbiber, s'infiltrer, baigner.

soaking ['soukiŋ] *n* trempage *m*, douche *f*.

soap [soup] *n* savon *m*; *vt* savonner.

soapy ['soupi] *a* savonneux, onctueux.

soar [sɔː] *vi* prendre l'essor, monter, planer.

sob [sɔb] *n* sanglot *m*; *vi* sangloter.

sober ['soubə] *a* sobre, sérieux, impartial, non ivre.

soberness ['soubənis] *n* sobriété *f*, modération *f*.

sociable ['souʃəbl] *a* sociable, (US) *n* réunion *f*, réception *f*.

sociability [ˌsouʃə'biliti] *n* sociabilité *f*.

social ['souʃəl] *n* réunion *f*; *a* social.

socialism ['souʃəlizəm] *n* socialisme *m*.

socialist ['souʃəlist] *n* socialiste *mf*.

socialize ['souʃəlaiz] *vt* socialiser.

society [sə'saiəti] *n* société *f*, monde *m*.

sock [sɔk] *n* chaussette *f*.

socket ['sɔkit] *n* trou *m*, orbite *m*, godet *m*, douille *f*, alvéole *m*.

sod [sɔd] *n* motte de gazon *f*.

soda ['soudə] *n* soude *f*, cristaux *m pl*; **—-water** eau de Seltz *f*.

sodden ['sɔdn] *a* (dé)trempé, pâteux, hébété, abruti.

sofa ['soufə] *n* canapé *m*, sofa *m*.

soft [sɔft] *a* mou, tendre, doux, facile, ramolli.

soften ['sɔfn] *vt* amollir, adoucir, attendrir.

softness ['sɔftnis] *n* douceur *f*, mollesse *f*, tendresse *f*.

soil [sɔil] *n* terre *f*, sol *m*; *vt* salir, souiller; *vi* se salir.

sojourn ['sɔdʒəːn] *n* séjour *m*; *vi* séjourner.

solace ['sɔləs] *n* consolation *f*; *vt* consoler.

sold [sould] *pt pp of* **sell.**

solder ['sɔldə] *n* soudure *f*; *vt*

souder; **—ing iron** lampe *f* à souder.

soldier ['souldʒə] *n* soldat *m*.

soldiery ['souldʒəri] *n* troupe *f*, (*pej*) soldatesque *f*.

sole [soul] *n* plante du pied *f*, semelle *f*, sole *f*; *vt* ressemeler; *a* seul, unique.

solemn ['sɔləm] *a* solennel.

solemnity [sə'lemniti] *n* solennité *f*.

solemnize ['sɔləmnaiz] *vt* célébrer, solemniser.

solicit [sə'lisit] *vt* solliciter.

solicitation [sə.lisi'teiʃən] *n* sollicitation *f*.

solicitor [sə'lisitə] *n* avoué *m*.

solicitous [sə'lisitəs] *a* zélé, anxieux, préoccupé.

solicitude [sə'lisitjud] *n* sollicitude *f*, anxiété *f*.

solid ['sɔlid] *an* solide *m*; *a* massif.

solidify [sə'lidifai] *vt* solidifier; *vi* se solidifier, se fixer.

solidity [sə'liditi] *n* solidité *f*.

soliloquy [sə'liləkwi] *n* soliloque *m*, monologue *m*.

solitary ['sɔlitəri] *a* solitaire.

solitude ['sɔlitjuːd] *n* solitude *f*, isolement *m*.

soluble ['sɔljubl] *an* soluble *m*.

solution [sə'luːʃən] *n* solution *f*.

solvability [ˌsɔlvə'biliti] *n* solvabilité *f*.

solve [sɔlv] *vt* résoudre.

solvency ['sɔlvənsi] *n* solvabilité *f*.

solvent ['sɔlvənt] *an* dissolvant *m*; *a* solvable.

some [sʌm] *a* du, de la, des, un peu de, quelques, certains; *pn* quelques-un(e)s, certains, en; *ad* quelque, environ.

somebody ['sʌmbədi] *pn* quelqu'un(e).

somehow ['sʌmhau] *ad* de manière ou d'autre; **— or other** je ne sais comment.

someone ['sʌmwʌn] *pn* quelqu'un.

somersault ['sʌməsɔːlt] *n* saut périlleux *m*, culbute *f*; *vi* faire la culbute, culbuter, capoter.

something ['sʌmθiŋ] *pn* quelque chose.

sometime ['sʌmtaim] *ad* un de ces jours, autrefois.

sometimes ['sʌmtaimz] *ad* quelquefois.

somewhat ['sʌmwɔt] *ad* quelque peu.

somewhere ['sʌmwɛə] *ad* quelque part.

son [sʌn] *n* fils *m*; **—-in-law** gendre *m*, beau-fils *m*.

song [sɔŋ] *n* chant *m*, chanson *f*.

songster ['sɔŋstə] *n* chanteur *m*.

sonority [sə'nɔriti] *n* sonorité *f*.

sonorous ['sɔnərəs] *a* sonore.

soon [suːn] *ad* (bien)tôt; **as — as** aussitôt que, dès que.

sooner ['suːnə] *ad* plus tôt, plutôt.

soot [sut] *n* suie *f*.

soothe [suːð] *vt* calmer, apaiser, flatter.

sooty ['suti] *a* noir de (comme) suie, fuligineux.

sop [sɔp] *n* trempette *f*, gâteau *m*; *vt* tremper; *vi* être trempé.

sophisticated [sə'fistikeitid] *a* artificiel, blasé, sophistiqué, frelaté.

soporific [.sɔpə'rifik] *an* soporifique *m*.

sorcerer ['sɔːsərə] *n* sorcier *m*.

sorcery ['sɔːsəri] *n* sorcellerie *f*.

sordid ['sɔːdid] *a* sordide.

sordidness ['sɔːdidnis] *n* sordidité *f*.

sore [sɔː] *n* mal *m*, plaie *f*, blessure *f*; *a* douloureux, envenimé, sévère, malade.

sorely ['sɔːli] *ad* fâcheusement, cruellement, gravement.

sorrel ['sɔrəl] *n* oseille *f*.

sorrow ['sɔrou] *n* chagrin *m*; *vi* s'affliger.

sorrowful ['sɔrəful] *a* affligé, pénible.

sorry ['sɔri] *a* désolé, fâché, pauvre, pitoyable, triste, méchant; —! pardon! excusez-moi.

sort [sɔːt] *n* sorte *f*, espèce *f*; — of pour ainsi dire; out of —s hors de son assiette; *vt* trier, assortir, classifier.

sorting ['sɔːtiŋ] *n* triage *m*, assortiment *m*.

sot [sɔt] *n* ivrogne *m*.

sottish ['sɔtiʃ] *a* abruti par la boisson.

sough [sau] *vi* gémir, siffler, soupirer, susurrer.

sought [sɔːt] *pt pp* of **seek**; — after *a* demandé, recherché.

soul [soul] *n* âme *f*; **not a** — pas âme qui vive, pas un chat.

soulful ['soulful] *a* pensif, sentimental, expressif.

sound [saund] *n* son *m*, sonde *f*, détroit *m*, chenal *m*; *vt* sonner, prononcer, sonder, ausculter; *vi* (ré)sonner, retentir; *a* sain, solide.

sounding ['saundiŋ] *n* sondage *m*, auscultation *f*.

soundless ['saundlis] *a* silencieux.

soup [suːp] *n* potage *m*, soupe *f*.

sour ['sauə] *a* aigre, vert; *vti* aigrir; *vi* s'aigrir.

source [sɔːs] *n* source *f*, origine *f*, foyer *m*.

sourish ['sauriʃ] *a* aigrelet.

south [sauθ] *n* sud *m*, midi *m*; *a* du sud.

southern ['sʌðən] *a* méridional, du midi, du sud.

southwards ['sauθwədz] *ad* vers le sud, au sud.

sovereign ['sɔvrin] *an* souverain(e) *mf*.

sovereignty ['sɔvrənti] *n* souveraineté *f*.

sow [sau] *n* truie *f*.

sow [sou] *vt* semer, ensemencer.

sower ['souə] *n* semeur, -euse.

sowing ['souiŋ] *n* semailles *f pl*, semis *m*.

sown [soun] *pp* of **sow**.

spa [spɑː] *n* station thermale *f*.

space [speis] *n* espace *m*, place *f*, durée *f*, intervalle *m*, étendue *f*; *vt* espacer.

spacious ['speiʃəs] *a* spacieux, vaste, ample.

spade [speid] *n* bêche *f*, (*cards*) pique *m*.

Spain [spein] *n* Espagne *f*.

span [spæn] *pt* of **spin**; *n* durée *f*, longueur *f*, arche *f*, envergure *f*, écartement *m*; *vt* enjamber, embrasser, mesurer.

spangle ['spæŋgl] *n* paillette *f*.

Spaniard ['spænjəd] *n* Espagnol(e).

spaniel ['spænjəl] *n* épagneul *m*.

Spanish ['spæniʃ] *a* espagnol.

spank [spæŋk] *vt* fesser; **to — along** aller grand trot, filer.

spanking ['spæŋkiŋ] *n* fessée *f*; *a* épatant.

spanner ['spænə] *n* clef *f*; **screw —** clef anglaise *f*.

spar [spɑː] *n* épar *m*, mât *m*, perche *f*; *vi* boxer, se harceler, s'escrimer.

spare [spɛə] *a* frugal, frêle, libre, de reste, de réserve, de rechange, à perdre; *vt* ménager se passer de, épargner, accorder.

sparing ['spɛəriŋ] *a* économe, avare, chiche.

spark [spɑːk] *n* étincelle *f*; *vi* étinceler, pétiller, mousser; **—ing plug** *n* bougie *f* (d'allumage).

sparkle ['spɑːkl] *vi* étinceler, pétiller, chatoyer.

sparkling ['spɑːkliŋ] *a* mousseux, brillant.

sparrow ['spærou] *n* moineau *m*.

sparse [spɑːs] *a* clairsemé.

spasm ['spæzəm] *n* spasme *m*, accès *m*, quinte *f*, crampe *f*, à-coup *m*.

spat [spæt] *pt pp of* **spit**.

spat [spæt] *n* guêtre *f*; (US) querelle *f*.

spate [speit] *n* crue *f*, flot *m*.

spatter ['spætə] *n* éclaboussure *f*; *vt* éclabousser.

spawn [spɔːn] *n* frai *m*; *vi* frayer.

speak [spiːk] *vti* parler, dire.

speaker ['spiːkə] *n* parleur, -euse, orateur *m*, président des communes *m*; **loud —** haut-parleur *m*.

spear [spiə] *n* lance *f*, javelot *m*, épieu *m*, harpon *m*, sagaie *f*; **—head** extrême pointe *f*.

special ['speʃəl] *a* spécial, particulier; **— delivery** (US) express *m*, pneumatique *m*.

specialist ['speʃəlist] *n* spécialiste *mf*.

speciality [.speʃi'æliti] *n* spécialité *f*, particularité *f*.

specialize ['speʃəlaiz] *vt* spécialiser; *vi* se spécialiser.

species ['spiːʃiːz] *n* espèce *f*.

specific [spi'sifik] *a* spécifique, explicite, précis.

specify ['spesifai] *vt* spécifier, déterminer.

specimen ['spesimin] *n* spécimen *m*, échantillon *m*.

specious ['spi:ʃəs] *a* spécieux, captieux.

speck [spek] *n* grain *m*, point *m*, tache *f*.

speckled ['spekld] *a* taché, tacheté, grivelé.

spectacle ['spektəkl] *n* spectacle *m*; *pl* lunettes *f pl*.

spectacular [spek'tækjulə] *a* spectaculaire, à grand spectacle.

spectator [spek'teitə] *n* spectateur, -trice, assistant(e) *mf*.

spectral ['spektrəl] *a* spectral.

spectre ['spektə] *n* spectre *m*.

speculate ['spekjuleit] *vi* spéculer.

speculation [,spekju'leiʃən] *n* spéculation *f*.

speculative ['spekjulətiv] *a* spéculatif.

speculator ['spekjuleitə] *n* spéculateur *m*.

speech [spi:tʃ] *n* parole *f*, discours *m*.

speechless ['spi:tʃlis] *a* interdit, interloqué.

sped [sped] *pt pp of* **speed**.

speed [spi:d] *n* vitesse *f*; *vt* activer, hâter, régler; *vi* se presser, se hâter, faire de la vitesse, filer.

speediness ['spi:dinis] *n* promptitude *f*, rapidité *f*.

speedometer [spi'dɔmitə] *n* indicateur de vitesse *m*.

speedy ['spi:di] *a* rapide, prompt.

spell [spel] *n* charme *m*, sort *m*, maléfice *m*, tour *m*, moment *m*, période *f*; *vt* épeler, écrire, signifier.

spellbound ['spelbaund] *a* fasciné, sous le charme.

spelling ['speliŋ] *n* orthographe *f*.

spelt [spelt] *pt pp of* **spell**.

spend [spend] *vt* dépenser, passer, épuiser.

spendthrift ['spendθrift] *n* dépensier, -ière, panier percé *m*.

spent [spent] *pt pp of* **spend**; *a* fini, à bout, éteint, mort.

spew [spju:] *vti* vomir; *vt* cracher.

sphere [sfiə] *n* sphère *mf*, domaine *m*, zone *f*, ressort.

spherical ['sferikəl] *a* sphérique.

spice [spais] *n* épice *f*, pointe *f*; *vt* épicer, relever.

spick and span [,spikən'spæn] *a* flambant neuf, tiré à quatre épingles, propret.

spicy ['spaisi] *a* épicé, poivré, relevé, pimenté, criard.

spider ['spaidə] *n* araignée *f*.

spike [spaik] *n* épi *m*, clou *m*, crampon *m*, pointe *f*; *vt* (en)clouer.

spill [spil] *n* chute *f*, bûche *f*, allume-feu *m*; *vt* (ren)verser, jeter bas; *vi* se répandre.

spilt [spilt] *pt pp of* **spill**.

spin [spin] *n* tour *m*, effet *m*, vrille *f*; —**drier** *n* essoreuse *f*; *vt* filer; *vi* tourner, rouler, patiner.

spinach ['spinidʒ] *n* épinards *m pl*.

spindle ['spindl] *n* fuseau *m*, broche *f*, essieu *m*.

spindly ['spindli] *a* fluet, de fuseau.

spine [spain] *n* épine dorsale *f*.

spineless ['spainlis] *a* mou.

spinner ['spinə] *n* métier *m*, tisserand(e) *mf*, filateur *m*.

spinney ['spini] *n* petit bois *m*.

spinning-mill ['spiniŋmil] *n* filature *f*.

spinning-wheel ['spiniŋwi:l] *n* rouet *m*.

spinster ['spinstə] *n* vieille fille *f*, célibataire *f*.

spiny ['spaini] *a* épineux.

spiral ['spaiərəl] *n* spirale *f*; *a* en spirale, en colimaçon, spiral.

spire ['spaiə] *n* flèche *f*, aiguille *f*, pointe *f*.

spirit ['spirit] *n* esprit *m*, âme *f*, humeur *f*, cran *m*, ardeur *f*, feu *m*, alcool *m*; **to — away** escamoter.

spirited ['spiritid] *a* animé, fougueux, vif, hardi.

spiritless ['spiritlis] *a* déprimé, mou, terne.

spiritual ['spiritjuəl] *a* spirituel.

spiritualism ['spiritjuəlizəm] *n* spiritisme *m*, spiritualisme *m*.

spiritualist ['spiritjuəlist] *n* spirite *mf*.

spirituous ['spiritjuəs] *a* spiritueux, alcoolique.

spit [spit] *n* broche *f*, langue *f* (de terre), crachement *m*, crachat *m*; *vt* embrocher, mettre à la broche, cracher; *vi* cracher, bruiner, crachiner.

spite [spait] *n* dépit *m*, rancune *f*; *vt* mortifier, vexer.

spiteful ['spaitful] *a* rancunier, méchant.

spitfire ['spitfaiə] *n* boute-feu *m*, soupe-au-lait *m*.

spittle ['spitl] *n* crachat *m*.

spittoon [spi'tu:n] *n* crachoir *m*.

splash [splæʃ] *n* éclaboussement *m*, éclaboussure *f*, tache *f*, clapotis *m*, sensation *f*; *vt* éclabousser, asperger; *vi* piquer un plat ventre, clapoter, barboter; **to make a —** faire de l'épate.

splash-board ['splæʃbɔ:d] *n* garde-boue *m*.

splay [splei] *n* ébrasure *f*; *a* plat, large, évasé; *vt* ébraser.

spleen [spli:n] *n* rate *f*, spleen *m*, bile *f*.

splendid ['splendid] *a* splendide, magnifique.

splendour ['splendə] *n* splendeur *f*, éclat *m*.

splint [splint] *n* attelle *f*, éclisse *f*.

splinter ['splintə] *n* éclat *m*, esquille *f*, écharde *f*; *vt* faire voler en éclats; *vi* voler en éclats.

split [split] *n* fente *f*, fissure *f*, scission *f*; *pl* grand écart *m*; *vt* fendre, couper, diviser, partager; *vi* se fendre, se diviser, se briser.

spoil(s) [spɔil(z)] *n* butin *m*; *pl* dépouilles *f pl*, profits *m pl*.

spoil [spɔil] *vt* dépouiller, gâter, abîmer, avarier, déparer; *vi* s'abîmer, se gâter.

spoilsport ['spɔilspɔːt] *n* trouble-fête *m*, rabat-joie *m*.

spoke [spouk] *n* rayon *m*, échelon *m*, bâton *m* (dans les roues).

spoke, -ken [spouk, spoukən] *pt pp* of **speak**.

spokesman ['spouksmən] *n* porte-parole *m*.

spoliation [ˌspouli'eiʃən] *n* spoliation *f*, pillage *m*.

sponge [spʌndʒ] *n* éponge *f*; *vt* passer l'éponge sur, éponger, effacer; **to — on someone** vivre sur qn, vivre aux crochets de qn.

sponge-cake ['spʌndʒ'keik] *n* gâteau de Savoie *m*.

sponger ['spʌndʒə] *n* parasite *m*, pique-assiette *m*.

spongy ['spʌndʒi] *a* spongieux.

sponsor ['spɔnsə] *n* parrain *m*, marraine *f*, garant *m*.

spontaneity [ˌspɔntə'niːiti] *n* spontanéité *f*.

spontaneous [spɔn'teiniəs] *a* spontané.

spontaneously [spɔn'teiniəsli] *ad* spontanément.

spool [spuːl] *n* bobine *f*, tambour *m*, rouleau *m*.

spoon [spuːn] *n* cuiller *f*.

spoonful ['spuːnful] *n* cuillerée *f*.

sport ['spɔːt] *n* jeu *m*, jouet *m*, sport *m*, chic type *m*; *vi* s'amuser, se divertir; *vt* arborer.

sporting ['spɔːtiŋ] *a* loyal, de chasse, sport, sportif.

sportive ['spɔːtiv] *a* enjoué, folâtre.

sportsman ['spɔːtsmən] *n* sportif *m*, beau joueur *m*, chasseur *m*.

sportsmanship ['spɔːtsmənʃip] *n* franc jeu *m*, l'esprit sportif *m*.

spot [spɔt] *n* endroit *m*, tache *f*, bouton *m*, pois *m*, marque *f*, goutte *f*; *vt* tacher, marquer, dépister, repérer.

spotted ['spɔtid] *a* tacheté, marqueté, à pois.

spotless ['spɔtlis] *a* sans tache, immaculé.

spouse [spauz] *n* époux *m*, épouse *f*.

spout [spaut] *n* bec *m*, jet *m*, gouttière *f*, colonne *f*; *vt* lancer, déclamer; *vi* jaillir, pérorer.

sprain [sprein] *n* entorse *f*, foulure *f*; *vt* se fouler.

sprang [spræŋ] *pt* of **spring**.

sprawl [sprɔːl] *vi* s'étendre, se vautrer, tomber les quatre pattes en l'air, rouler.

spray [sprei] *n* branche *f*, embrun *m*, vaporisateur, *m*, bouquet *m*; *vt* asperger, vaporiser.

spread [spred] *n* envergure *f*, largeur *f*, diffusion *f*, propagation *f*; *vtir* répandre, (é)tendre, déployer;

vi se répandre, s'étendre, se disperser.

sprig [sprig] *n* branchette *f*, brin *m*, rejeton *m*.

sprightliness ['spraitlinis] *n* gaîté *f*, vivacité *f*.

sprightly ['spraitli] *a* vif, sémillant, allègre.

spring [spriŋ] *n* printemps *m*, source *f*, saut *m*, bond *m*, ressort *m*, élasticité *f*; *vi* bondir, s'élever, poindre, sortir, (*wood*) jouer, se fendre; *vt* lancer, (*trap*) tendre, suspendre.

spring-board ['spriŋbɔːd] *n* tremplin *m*.

springy ['spriŋi] *a* élastique, flexible.

sprinkle ['spriŋkl] *n* pincée *f*; *vt* asperger, éparpiller, saupoudrer.

sprinkler ['spriŋklə] *n* aspersoir *m*, goupillon *m*.

sprinkling ['spriŋkliŋ] *n* aspersion *f*, saupoudrage *m*.

sprite [sprait] *n* lutin *m*.

sprout [spraut] *n* pousse *f*; **Brussels — chou de Bruxelles** *m*; *vti* pousser.

spruce [spruːs] *n* sapin *m*; *a* net, pimpant, soigné.

sprung [sprʌŋ] *pp* of **spring**.

spun [spʌn] *pp* of **spin**.

spur [spəː] *n* éperon *m*, ergot *m*, coup de fouet *m*; *vt* éperonner, exciter, stimuler.

spurious ['spjuəriəs] *a* faux, controuvé, contrefait.

spurn [spəːn] *vt* rejeter, dédaigner, traiter avec dédain.

sputter ['spʌtə] *vti* bredouiller; *vi* grésiller, cracher.

spy [spai] *n* espion; *vt* espionner, épier; **—-glass** longue-vue *f*; **—-hole** judas *m*.

squabble ['skwɔbl] *n* bisbille *f*; *vi* se chamailler.

squad [skwɔd] *n* escouade *f*, peloton *m*, équipe *f*.

squadron ['skwɔdrən] *n* escadron *m*, escadre *f*.

squalid ['skwɔlid] *a* sordide.

squall [skwɔːl] *n* rafale *f*, grain *m*, cri *m*; *pl* grabuge *m*; *vi* piailler.

squander ['skwɔndə] *vt* gaspiller, dissiper, manger.

squanderer ['skwɔndərə] *n* prodigue *m*, gaspilleur, -euse.

square [skwɛə] *n* carré *m*, équerre *f*, square *m*, place *f*; *a* carré, régulier, loyal, tout net quitté; *vt* accorder, régler, payer, carrer, équarrir; *vi* s'accorder, cadrer.

squash [skwɔʃ] *n* foule *f*, presse *f*, (*drink*) jus de fruit *m*; bouillie *f*, bruit mou *m*; *vt* écraser, rembarrer; *vi* se serrer, s'écraser.

squat [skwɔt] *vi* s'accroupir; *a* trapu, ramassé.

squeak [skwiːk] *n* cri aigu *m*, grincement *m*, couic *m*; *vi* grincer, crier.

squeal [skwiːl] *n* cri aigu *m*; *vi* crier,

criailler, protester; **to — on** dénoncer, moucharder, vendre.

squeamish ['skwiːmiʃ] *a* dégoûté, scrupuleux, prude.

squeamishness ['skwiːmiʃnis] *n* bégueulerie *f*, délicatesse *f*.

squeeze [skwiːz] *n* pression *f*, presse *f*, écrasement *m*, (*pol*) l'austérité *f*; *vt* presser, serrer, écraser, faire pression sur, extorquer, faire entrer sur, extorquer, faire entrer de force; *vi* to — up se serrer.

squint [skwint] *n* strabisme *m*, coup d'œil oblique *m*; *vi* loucher.

squirrel ['skwirəl] *n* écureuil *m*, petit gris *m*.

squirt [skwəːt] *n* seringue *f*, jet *m*; *vt* lancer, injecter; *vi* jaillir, gicler.

stab [stæb] *n* coup *m* de couteau; *vt* poignarder, porter un coup de couteau à.

stability [stə'biliti] *n* stabilité *f*, constance *f*.

stabilize ['steibilaiz] *vt* stabiliser.

stable ['steibl] *n* écurie *f*; *a* stable, consistant, solide.

stack [stæk] *n* meule *f*, pile *f*, cheminée *f*, (*mil*) faisceau *m*; *vt* entasser, empiler.

staff [staːf] *n* bâton *m*, mât *m*, hampe *f*, crosse *f*, état-major *m*, personnel *m*.

stag [stæg] *n* cerf *m*.

stage [steidʒ] *n* scène *f*, estrade *f*, échafaudage *m*, étape *f*, phase *f*, relais *m*, débarcadère *m*; *vt* monter, mettre en scène.

stage-coach ['steidʒkoutʃ] *n* diligence *f*.

stage-fright ['steidʒfrait] *n* trac *m*.

stage-hand ['steidʒhænd] *n* machiniste *m*.

stagger ['stægə] *vt* faire chanceler, ébranler, renverser, échelonner; *vi* chanceler, tituber.

stagnant ['stægnənt] *a* stagnant.

stagnate ['stægneit] *vi* croupir, être stagnant, s'encroûter.

stagnation [stæg'neiʃən] *n* stagnation *f*, marasme *m*.

staid [steid] *a* posé, rangé.

stain [stein] *n* tache *f*, colorant *m*; *vti* tacher, colorer.

stainless ['steinlis] *n* inoxydable, immaculé.

stair [steə] *n* marche *f*; *pl* escalier *m*.

staircase ['steəkeis] *n* escalier *m*.

stake [steik] *n* poteau *m*, bûcher *m*, pieu *m*, (en)jeu *m*, risque *m*, pari *m*; *vt* parier, risquer, jouer, miser.

stale [steil] *a* rassis, éventé, vicié, rebattu.

stalemate ['steil'meit] *n* point mort *m*, pat *m*.

stalk [stɔːk] *n* tige *f*, pied *m*, trognon *m*, queue *f*.

stall [stɔːl] *n* stalle *f*, banc *m*, baraque *f*, étal *m*, étalage *m*; *vt* bloquer; *vi* se bloquer.

stallion ['stæljən] *n* étalon *m*.

stalwart ['stɔːlwət] *a* solide, résolu, robuste.

stamen ['steimən] *n* étamine *f*.

stamina ['stæminə] *n* vigueur *f*, fond *m*.

stammer ['stæmə] *n* bégaiement *m*; *vti* bégayer.

stammerer ['stæmərə] *n* bègue *mf*.

stamp [stæmp] *n* timbre *m*, cachet *m*, poinçon *m*, coin *m*, estampille *f*, marque *f*, trempe *f*; *vt* timbrer, imprimer, marquer, affranchir; *vi* frapper du pied.

stampede [stæm'piːd] *n* débandade *f*, panique *f*; *vi* se débander, se ruer.

stanch [staːntʃ] *vt* étancher.

stand [stænd] *n* halte *f*, position *f*, station *f*, socle *m*, guéridon *m*, étalage *m*, stand *m*, (US) barre *f*; *vi* se tenir (debout), se dresser, s'arrêter, rester, durer, tenir; *vt* supporter, offrir, payer; **to — for** représenter; **to — out** ressortir.

standard ['stændəd] *n* étendard *m*, étalon *m*, moyenne *f*, niveau *m*, qualité *f*; *a* classique, définitif, standard, courant.

standardize ['stændədaiz] *vt* standardiser, unifier.

standing ['stændiŋ] *n* réputation *f*, situation *f*, ancienneté *f*; *a* établi, permanent.

stand-offish ['stænd'ɔfiʃ] *a* distant.

stand-offishness ['stænd'ɔfiʃnis] *n* réserve *f*, hauteur *f*.

standpoint ['stændpɔint] *n* point de vue *m*.

stank [stæŋk] *pt of* **stink**.

stanza ['stænzə] *n* stance *f*, strophe *f*.

staple ['steipl] *n* gâche *f*, crampon *m*, agrafe *f*; *a* principal.

stapler ['steiplə] *n* agrafeuse *f*.

star [staː] *n* étoile *f*, astre *m*, astérisque *m*; *vi* tenir le premier rôle, être en vedette.

starboard ['staːbəd] *n* tribord *m*.

starch [staːtʃ] *n* amidon *m*, raideur *f*; *vt* empeser.

starched [staːtʃt] *a* empesé, gourmé, collet monté.

stare [steə] *n* regard fixe *m*; *vi* regarder fixement, s'écarquiller; **to — at** regarder fixement, fixer, dévisager; **it is staring you in the face** cela vous saute aux yeux.

staring ['steəriŋ] *a* éclatant, fixe.

stark [staːk] *a* raide, tout pur; *ad* complètement.

start [staːt] *n* sursaut *m*, départ *m*, début *m*, avance *f*; *vi* commencer; *vt* lancer, entamer, mettre en marche, provoquer.

starter ['staːtə] *n* démarreur *m*, starter *m*, partant *m*, auteur *m*.

startle ['staːtl] *vt* faire tressaillir, effarer, effrayer.

startling ['staːtliŋ] *a* saisissant, sensationnel.

starvation [staːˈveiʃən] *n* faim *f*, inanition *f*, famine *f*.

starve [stɑːv] *vi* mourir de faim, être transi; *vt* affamer, priver, faire mourir de faim.

state [steit] *n* état *m*, rang *m*, situation *f*, pompe *f*; *a* d'état, d'apparat; *vt* déclarer, prétendre, énoncer, fixer.

stately ['steitli] *a* noble, imposant, princier, majestueux.

statement ['steitmənt] *n* déclaration *f*, énoncé *m*, rapport *m*, expression *f*, relevé *m*.

statesman ['steitsmən] *n* homme d'état *m*.

station ['steiʃən] *n* poste *m*, gare *f*, station *f*, rang *m*; *vt* poster, placer; — **house** (US) poste *m* de police.

stationary ['steiʃnəri] *a* stationnaire, immobile.

stationer ['steiʃnə] *n* papetier *m*.

stationery ['steiʃnəri] *n* papeterie *f*.

stationmaster ['steiʃən,mɑːstə] *n* chef de gare *m*.

statistics [stə'tistiks] *n* statistique *f*.

statue ['stætjuː] *n* statue *f*.

stature ['stætjə] *n* stature *f*, taille *f*.

status ['steitəs] *n* rang *m*, titre *m*, position *f*, statu quo *m*.

statute ['stætjuːt] *n* statut *m*, ordonnance *f*.

statutory ['stætjutəri] *a* statutaire, réglementaire.

staunch [stɔːntʃ] *a* ferme, loyal, étanche; *vt* étancher.

stave [steiv] *n* douve *f*, barreau *m*, stance *f*, portée *f*; *vt* — **in** défoncer, enfoncer; **to** — **off** détourner, conjurer, écarter.

stay [stei] *n* séjour *m*, sursis *m*, frein *m*, soutien *m*; *vi* rester, séjourner, tenir; *vt* arrêter, ajourner, soutenir.

stay-at-home ['steiəthoum] *an* casanier, -ière.

stays [steiz] *n* corset *m*.

stead [sted] *n* lieu *m*, place *f*; **to stand s.o. in good** — être d'un grand secours à qn.

steadfast ['stedfəst] *a* ferme, constant.

steadfastness ['stedfəstnis] *n* constance *f*, fixité *f*.

steadiness ['stedinis] *n* fermeté *f*, régularité, stabilité *f*.

steady ['stedi] *a* ferme, régulier, constant, tranquille, rangé, continu, persistant; (US) *n* petit(e) ami(e); *vt* assurer, (r)affermir, caler.

steak [steik] *n* tranche *f*, bifteck *m*, entrecôte *f*.

steal [stiːl] *vti* voler; *vt* dérober; **to** — **in** entrer à pas de loup.

stealth [stelθ] *n* secret *m*.

stealthily ['stelθili] *ad* secrètement, à la dérobée.

stealthy ['stelθi] *a* furtif.

steam [stiːm] *n* vapeur *f*, buée *f*; *vt* cuire à l'étuvée, vaporiser; *vi* fumer, marcher à la vapeur.

steamboat, -ship ['stiːmbout, -ʃip] *n* vapeur *m*.

steamer ['stiːmə] *n* steamer *m*; marmite à vapeur *f*.

steaming ['stiːmiŋ] *a* fumant, sous vapeur, tout chaud.

steed [stiːd] *n* étalon *m*.

steel [stiːl] *n* acier *m*, baleine *f*; *vt* tremper, aciérer; **to** — **oneself** se raidir, s'armer de courage.

steep [stiːp] *a* raide, escarpé, fort.

steeple ['stiːpl] *n* clocher *m*, flèche *f*.

steeplechase ['stiːplˈtʃeis] *n* steeple *m*, course d'obstacles *f*.

steer [stiə] *vt* diriger, gouverner, piloter.

steering-wheel ['stiəriŋwiːl] *n* volant *m*.

steersman ['stiəzmən] *n* barreur *m*, timonier *m*.

stem [stem] *n* tige *f*, queue *f*, souche *f*, étrave *f*, branche *f*, pied *m*, tuyau *m*; *vt* arrêter, endiguer, remonter.

stench [stentʃ] *n* puanteur *f*.

stencil ['stensl] *n* pochoir *m*, poncif *m*; *vt* imprimer au pochoir, polycopier.

step [step] *n* pas *m*, marche *f*, marche-pied *m*, échelon *m*, promotion *f*, démarche *f*; *pl* échelle *f*, escalier *m*, mesures *f pl*; — **ladder** escabeau *m*; *vi* échelonner.

stepbrother ['step,brʌðə] *n* demi-frère *m*; —**daughter** belle-fille *f*; —**father** beau-père *m*; —**mother** belle-mère *f*; —**sister** demi-sœur *f*; —**son** beau-fils *m*.

Stephen ['stiːvn] Étienne *m*.

stepping-stone ['stepiŋstoun] *n* marche-pied *m*, tremplin *m*.

sterile ['sterail] *a* stérile.

sterility [ste'riliti] *n* stérilité *f*.

sterilize ['sterilaiz] *vt* stériliser.

sterling ['stəːliŋ] *a* pur, d'or, de bon aloi, massif.

stern [stəːn] *n* arrière *m*, poupe *f*; *a* sévère, austère.

sternness ['stəːnnis] *n* austérité *f*, sévérité *f*.

stevedore ['stiːvidɔː] *n* débardeur *m*.

stew [stjuː] *n* ragoût *m*, civet *m*; **in a** — sur des charbons ardents; *vt* cuire à la casserole, (faire) mijoter; *vi* mijoter, faire une compote.

steward ['stjuəd] *n* intendant *m*, gérant *m*, économe *m*, garçon *m*, commissaire *m*.

stewardess ['stjuədis] *n* femme de chambre *f*, stewardess *f*.

stick [stik] *n* bâton *m*, canne *f*, baguette *f*, manche *m*, crosse *f*; *pl* du petit bois, brindilles *f pl*; *vt* enfoncer, fourrer, piquer, percer, afficher, coller, supporter, tenir; *vi* s'enfoncer, se ficher, se piquer, s'attacher, (s'en) tenir, coller, happer, rester (en panne), persister; **to** — **it** tenir le coup, tenir bon; **to** — **at** répugner à, reculer devant, s'obstiner à; **to** — **out** *vt* passer, bomber, tirer; *vi* faire saillie, saillir; **to** — **to** s'en tenir à, persister à, adhérer à, rester fidèle à.

sticky ['stiki] *a* collant, visqueux, difficile.

stiff [stif] *a* raide, ardu, (*price*) salé, courbaturé, engourdi, gourmé.

stiffen ['stifn] *vt* raidir; *vi* se raidir.

stiff-necked ['stif'nekt] *a* têtu, intraitable.

stiffness ['stifnis] *n* raideur *f*, contrainte *f*, difficulté *f*, fermeté *f*, courbatures *f pl*.

stifle ['staifl] *vt* étouffer, asphyxier, suffoquer.

stigma ['stigmə] *n* marque *f*, stigmate *m*.

stigmatize ['stigmətaiz] *vt* stigmatiser, flétrir.

stile [stail] *n* échalier *m*.

still [stil] *n* alambic *m*; *a* immobile, tranquille, silencieux; *vt* apaiser, calmer; *ad* encore, toujours, cependant.

still-born ['stilbɔːn] *a* mort-né.

still-life ['stil'laif] *n* nature morte *f*.

stillness ['stilnis] *n* calme *m*, paix *f*.

stilt [stilt] *n* échasse *f*.

stilted ['stiltid] *a* guindé.

stimulate ['stimjuleit] *vt* stimuler, aiguillonner.

stimulant ['stimjulənt] *an* stimulant *m*.

stimulation [.stimju'leiʃən] *n* stimulation *f*.

stimulus ['stimjuləs] *n* stimulant *m*, coup de fouet *m*, aiguillon *m*.

sting [stiŋ] *n* dard *m*, aiguillon *m*, crochet *m*, piqûre *f*, pointe *f*; *vti* piquer, mordre.

stinginess ['stindʒinis] *n* ladrerie *f*, lésine *f*.

stingy ['stindʒi] *a* ladre, chiche, pingre, radin.

stink [stiŋk] *n* puanteur *f*; *vti* puer; *vt* empester.

stint [stint] *n* limite *f*, relâche *f*, tâche *f*; *vt* limiter, regarder à, mesurer.

stipend ['staipend] *n* traitement *m*, appointements *m pl*.

stipulate ['stipjuleit] *vt* stipuler.

stipulation [.stipju'leiʃən] *n* stipulation(s) *f* (*pl*).

stir [stəː] *n* remue-ménage *m*, sensation *f*, émoi *m*; *vt* remuer, secouer, agiter, émouvoir; *vi* remuer, bouger.

stirring ['stəːriŋ] *a* excitant, vibrant, mouvementé, empoignant.

stirrup ['stirəp] *n* étrier *m*.

stitch [stitʃ] *n* point *m*, maille *f*, suture *f*; *vt* coudre, raccommoder, brocher, suturer.

stoat [stout] *n* ermine *f* d'été.

stock [stɔk] *n* tronc *m*, souche *f*, provision *f*, stock *m*, fonds *m pl*, giroflée *f*, bouillon; — **cube** concentré *m*; *pl* rentes *f pl*; *vt* approvisionner, tenir, meubler, garnir, stocker; —**account** inventaire *m*; —**broker** agent de change *m*;

— **exchange** bourse *f*; — **jobber** agioteur *m*.

stocking ['stɔkiŋ] *n* bas *m*.

stock-phrase ['stɔk'freiz] *n* cliché *m*.

stocky ['stɔki] *a* épais, trapu.

stodgy ['stɔdʒi] *a* lourd, indigeste, bourré.

stoker ['stoukə] *n* chauffeur *m*.

stole [stoul] *pt of* **steal**; *n* étole *f*, écharpe *f*.

stolen ['stoulən] *pp of* **steal**.

stolid ['stɔlid] *a* stupide, obstiné, flegmatique.

stolidity [stɔ'liditi] *n* stupidité *f*, flegme *m*.

stomach ['stʌmək] *n* estomac *m*, ventre *m*, bedaine *f*, appétit *m*, courage *m*, patience *f*; *vt* manger, avaler, supporter.

stone [stoun] *n* pierre *f*, caillou *m*, noyau *m*, pépin *m*, calcul *m*, 14 livres; *vt* lapider, empierrer, énoyauter.

stony ['stouni] *a* pierreux, dur, glacial, glacé.

stool [stuːl] *n* tabouret *m*, escabeau *m*, selle *f*.

stoop [stuːp] *vi* se pencher, être voûté, daigner, s'abaisser.

stop [stɔp] *n* arrêt *m*, halte *f*, fin *f*; **full** — point *m*; *vt* arrêter, boucher, (*tooth*) plomber, barrer, mettre fin à, ponctuer, empêcher, bloquer, couper; *vi* s'arrêter, cesser.

stoppage ['stɔpidʒ] *n* arrêt *m*, encombrement *m*, occlusion *f*, obstruction. *f*.

stopper ['stɔpə] *n* bouchon *m*.

storage ['stɔːridʒ] *n* emmagasinage *m*, entrepôts *m pl*.

store [stɔː] *n* dépôt *m*, entrepôt *m*, magasin *m*, provision *f*, réserve *f*; *vt* garnir, rentrer, entreposer, tenir, emmagasiner, meubler.

stor(e)y ['stɔːri] *n* étage *m*.

stork [stɔːk] *n* cigogne *f*.

storm [stɔːm] *n* orage *m*, tempête *f*, assaut *m*; *vt* emporter d'assaut; *vi* faire rage, tempêter.

stormy ['stɔːmi] *a* orageux, houleux.

story ['stɔːri] *n* histoire *f*, version *f*, conte *m*, récit *m*, étage *m*; —**teller** raconteur *m*, narrateur *m*, griot *m*.

stout [staut] *a* brave, résolu, fort, gros, vigoureux.

stoutness ['stautnis] *n* courage *m*, grosseur *f*, embonpoint *m*, corpulence *f*.

stove [stouv] *pt pp of* **stave**; *n* poêle *m*.

stow [stou] *vt* bien empaqueter, arrimer.

stowaway ['stouəwei] *n* voyageur de fond de cale *m*.

straddle ['strædl] *vt* enfourcher, enjamber, s'installer sur, (*artillery*) encadrer, (US) s'abstenir.

strafe [strɑːf] *vt* (*fam*) punir.

straggle ['strægl] *vi* traîner en arrière, s'écarter.

straggler ['stræglə] n retardataire mf, attardé m, traînard m.

straight [streit] n ligne droite f; ad droit, juste, directement; a droit, rectiligne, loyal, juste.

straighten ['streitn] vt redresser, arranger, défausser.

straightforward [streit'fɔːwəd] a loyal, droit.

straightforwardness [streit'fɔːwədnis] n droiture f, franchise f.

strain [strein] n tension f, effort m, ton m, veine f, entorse f; pl accents m pl; vt (é)tendre, tirer (sur), forcer, filtrer, fatiguer, faire violence à, (se) fouler.

strainer ['streinə] n passoire f, filtre m.

strait [streit] n détroit m.

straits [streits] n détroit m, gêne f.

strait-jacket ['streit'dʒækit] n camisole de force f.

strand [strænd] n rive f; vt échouer.

stranded ['strændid] a perdu, en panne, sans ressources.

strange [streindʒ] a étrange, singulier, étranger, dépaysé.

strangeness ['streindʒnis] n étrangeté f, nouveauté f.

stranger ['streindʒə] n étranger, inconnu.

strangle ['stræŋgl] vt étrangler, étouffer.

strangulation [‚stræŋgju'leiʃən] n strangulation f, étranglement m.

strap [stræp] n courroie f, sangle f, bande f, étrivière f; vt sangler, attacher, aiguiser, bander, frapper.

strapping ['stræpiŋ] a robuste, solide.

stratagem ['strætidʒəm] n stratagème m, ruse f.

strategist ['strætidʒist] n stratège m.

strategy ['strætidʒi] n stratégie f.

straw [strɔː] n paille f, fétu m; it is the last — il ne manquait plus que cela.

strawberry ['strɔːbəri] n fraise f, fraisier m.

stray [strei] n bête perdue f; a égaré, espacé, épars, perdu; vi se perdre, s'égarer.

streak [striːk] n raie f, bande f, veine f; vt rayer, strier; to — past passer en trombe.

streaked ['striːkt] a rayé, zébré.

stream [striːm] n cours d'eau m, courant m, ruisseau m, flot m, (Africa) marigot m; down—, up— en aval, en amont; vi couler, ruisseler, flotter.

street [striːt] n rue f.

street-arab ['striːt‚ærəb] n gavroche m, voyou m.

strength [streŋθ] n force(s) f (pl), solidité f, complet m, effectifs m pl.

strengthen ['streŋθən] vt renforcer, fortifier, (r)affermir.

strenuous ['strenjuəs] a énergique, appliqué, ardu.

strenuousness ['strenjuəsnis] n vigueur f, ardeur f.

stress [stres] n accent m, force f, pression f, tension f; vt accentuer, insister sur, souligner, fatiguer.

stretch [stretʃ] n étendue f, extension f, envergure f, élasticité f; vt (é)tendre, étirer, exagérer, élargir, bander; vi s'étendre, s'étirer, s'élargir.

stretcher ['stretʃə] n civière f, brancard m.

strew [struː] vt semer, joncher.

strict [strikt] a strict, sévère, rigoureux, formel.

strictures ['striktʃəz] n critiques f pl.

stride [straid] n enjambée f; vi marcher à grands pas.

strife [straif] n conflit m.

strike [straik] n grève f; vt frapper, heurter contre, sonner, trouver, frotter, conclure, (flag) amener; vi faire grève, porter coup.

striker ['straikə] n gréviste mf, marteau m.

striking ['straikiŋ] a frappant, saisissant.

string [striŋ] n ficelle f, corde f, chapelet m, enfilade f, cordon m, fil m, lacet m, file f, (US) (journal) série f; pl instruments à cordes m; vt ficeler, enfiler.

stringent ['strindʒənt] a strict, rigoureux, étroit, serré.

strip [strip] n bande f, langue f; vt dépouiller, dégarnir, vider, écorcer; vi se déshabiller, se dévêtir.

stripe [straip] n bande f, barre f, raie f, (mil) galon m, chevron m; vt barrer, rayer.

strive [straiv] vi s'efforcer, lutter, rivaliser.

strode [stroud] pt of **stride**.

stroke [strouk] n coup m, attaque f, trait m, brassée f, caresse f; vt caresser, flatter.

stroll [stroul] vi flâner, faire un tour; n tour m, balade f.

strolling ['strouliŋ] a ambulant, forain, vagabond.

strong [strɔŋ] a fort, robuste, vigoureux, ferme, accusé, puissant, énergique.

strong-box ['strɔŋbɔks] n coffre fort m.

stronghold ['strɔŋhould] n forteresse f.

strong-minded ['strɔŋ'maindid] a volontaire, décidé.

strop [strɔp] n cuir m; vt affiler, repasser.

structure ['strʌktʃə] n structure f, construction f, édifice m, bâtiment m.

struck [strʌk] pt pp of **strike**.

struggle ['strʌgl] n lutte f; vi lutter, se démener.

strung [strʌŋ] pt pp of **string**.

strut [strʌt] n étai m, traverse f; vi

se pavaner; *vt* étayer, entretoiser.

stub [stʌb] *n* bout *m*, mégot *m*, chicot *m*, tronçon *m*, souche *f*, (US) talon *m* de chèque; *vt* déraciner, heurter; — out éteindre.

stubble ['stʌbl] *n* chaume *m*.

stubbly ['stʌbli] *a* hérissé, couvert de chaume.

stubborn ['stʌbən] *a* têtu, obstiné.

stubbornness ['stʌbənnis] *n* entêtement *m*, ténacité *f*.

stuck [stʌk] *pt pp of* **stick**.

stud [stʌd] *n* bouton *m*, clou *m*, rivet *m*, écurie *f*, haras *m*.

studded ['stʌdid] *a* semé, orné, clouté.

student ['stjuːdənt] *n* étudiant(e) *mf*, homme *m* qui étudie.

studied ['stʌdid] *a* étudié, délibéré, recherché.

studio ['stjuːdiou] *n* atelier *m*, studio *m*.

studious ['stjuːdiəs] *a* studieux, étudié.

study ['stʌdi] *n* étude *f*, cabinet de travail *m*; *vti* étudier; *vi* faire ses études, apprendre (à).

stuff [stʌf] *n* étoffe *f*, marchandise *f*, camelote *f*, substance *f*, sottise *f*; *vt* bourrer, empiler, empailler, farcir, fourrer, boucher.

stuffy ['stʌfi] *a* étouffant, mal aéré, guindé.

stultify ['stʌltifai] *vt* rendre ridicule, infirmer, ruiner.

stumble ['stʌmbl] *n* faux-pas *m*; *vi* trébucher, se fourvoyer.

stumbling-block ['stʌmbliŋblɔk] *n* pierre d'achoppement *f*.

stump [stʌmp] *n* souche *f*, tronçon *m*, chicot *m*, moignon *m*, bout *m*, (cricket) piquet *m*; *vt* estomper, coller; to — in entrer clopin-clopant.

stumpy ['stʌmpi] *a* trapu, ramassé.

stung [stʌŋ] *pt pp of* **sting**.

stun [stʌn] *vt* étourdir, assommer, assourdir, renverser.

stunk [stʌŋk] *pp of* **stink**.

stupefaction [ˌstjuːpiˈfækʃən] *n* stupéfaction *f*.

stupefy ['stjuːpifai] *vt* hébéter, stupéfier, engourdir.

stupefying ['stjuːpifaiiŋ] *a* stupéfiant.

stupendous [stjuːˈpendəs] *a* prodigieux, formidable.

stupid ['stjuːpid] *a* stupide, bête.

stupidity [stjuːˈpiditi] *n* stupidité *f*, bêtise *f*.

sturdy ['stəːdi] *a* robuste, vigoureux.

sturgeon ['stəːdʒən] *n* esturgeon *m*.

stutter ['stʌtə] *vti* bredouiller, bégayer.

sty [stai] *n* porcherie *f*, bouge *m*, orgelet *m*.

style [stail] *n* style *m*, genre *m*, titre *m*, espèce *f*; *vt* appeler.

stylish ['stailiʃ] *a* qui a du style, chic, élégant.

subaltern ['sʌbltən] *an* subalterne *m*.

subdue [səbˈdjuː] *vt* soumettre, maîtriser, dompter, adoucir, tamiser.

subdued [səbˈdjuːd] *a* vaincu, tamisé, étouffé.

subject ['sʌbdʒikt] *n* sujet *m*; matière *f*, objet *m*; *an* sujet, -ette; *a* soumis, assujetti, passible; *ad* sous réserve (de to).

subject [səbˈdʒekt] *vt* soumettre, subjuguer, exposer.

subjection [səbˈdʒekʃən] *n* sujétion *f*, assujettissement *m*, soumission *f*.

subjugation [ˌsʌbdʒuˈgeiʃən] *n* soumission *f*, assujettissement *m*.

subjugate ['sʌbdʒugeit] *vt* subjuguer.

sublime [səˈblaim] *a* sublime, suprême.

sublimity [səˈblimiti] *n* sublimité *f*.

submarine ['sʌbməriːn] *an* sous-marin *m*.

submerge [səbˈməːdʒ] *vt* submerger; *vi* plonger.

submersion [səbˈməːʃən] *n* submersion *f*.

submission [səbˈmiʃən] *n* soumission *f*.

submit [səbˈmit] *vt* soumettre; *vi* se soumettre.

subordinate [səˈbɔːdənit] *an* inférieur(e) *mf*, subordonné(e) *mf*; *vt* subordonner.

subordination [səˌbɔːdiˈneiʃən] *n* subordination *f*.

suborn [sʌˈbɔːn] *vt* suborner.

subpoena [səbˈpiːnə] *n* assignation *f*; *vt* citer.

subscribe [səbˈskraib] *vt* souscrire (pour); to — to s'abonner à, être abonné à.

subscriber [səbˈskraibə] *n* souscripteur *m*, abonné(e) *mf*.

subscription [səbˈskripʃən] *n* souscription *f*.

subsequent ['sʌbsikwənt] *a* subséquent, ultérieur.

subsequently ['sʌbsikwəntli] *ad* subséquemment, dans la suite.

subservience [səbˈsəːvjəns] *n* soumission *f*, obséquiosité *f*.

subservient [səbˈsəːvjənt] *a* utile, obséquieux.

subside [səbˈsaid] *vi* s'affaisser, déposer, s'apaiser.

subsidence [səbˈsaidəns] *n* affaissement *m*, baisse *f*.

subsidize ['sʌbsidaiz] *vt* subventionner, primer.

subsidy ['sʌbsidi] *n* subvention *f*, prime *f*.

subsist [səbˈsist] *vi* subsister, persister, vivre.

substance ['sʌbstəns] *n* substance *f*, matière *f*, fond *m*, fortune *f*.

substantial [səbˈstænʃəl] *a* matériel, substantiel, solide, riche, important, copieux.

substantiate [səbˈstænʃieit] *vt* fonder, justifier.

substitute ['sʌbstitjuːt] *n* substitut

m, équivalent *m*, doublure *f*, suppléant(e) *mf*, remplaçant(e) *mf*; *vt* substituer; to — for remplacer.

substitution [ˌsʌbsti'tjuːʃən] *n* substitution *f*, remplacement *m*.

subterfuge ['sʌbtəfjuːdʒ] *n* subterfuge *m*, faux-fuyant *m*.

subtle ['sʌtl] *a* subtil, fin, astucieux.

subtlety ['sʌtlti] *n* subtilité *f*, finesse *f*.

subtract [səb'trækt] *vt* retrancher, soustraire.

subtraction [səb'trækʃən] *n* soustraction *f*.

suburb ['sʌbəːb] *n* faubourg *m*, banlieue *f*; *a* suburbain, de banlieue.

subvention [səb'venʃən] *n* subvention *f*.

subversion [səb'vəːʃən] *n* subversion *f*.

subversive [səb'vəːsiv] *a* subversif.

subvert [sʌb'vəːt] *vt* renverser.

subway ['sʌbwei] *n* passage souterrain *m*; (*US*) métro *m*.

succeed [sək'siːd] *vti* succéder (à), réussir.

success [sək'ses] *n* succès *m*, réussite *f*, suite *f*.

successful [sək'sesful] *a* heureux, réussi, reçu, qui a du succès.

succession [sək'seʃən] *n* succession *f*, suite *f*, série *f*.

successive [sək'sesiv] *a* successif, consécutif, de suite.

successor [sək'sesə] *n* successeur *m*.

succinct [sək'siŋkt] *n* succinct, concis.

succour ['sʌkə] *n* secours *m*; *vt* secourir.

succumb [sə'kʌm] *vi* succomber.

such [sʌtʃ] *a* tel, pareil, le même; *pn* tel, celui (qui), en qualité de; —as tel que, comme.

suchlike ['sʌtʃlaik] *a* analogue, de la sorte.

suck [sʌk] *n* tétée *f*, succion *f*, sucée *f*; *vti* sucer; *vt* téter.

sucking ['sʌkiŋ] *a* à la mamelle, de lait, en herbe.

suckle ['sʌkl] *vt* allaiter.

suckling ['sʌkliŋ] *n* nourrisson *m*, allaitement *m*.

sudden ['sʌdn] *a* soudain, brusque, subit; —ly *adv* tout à coup.

suddenness ['sʌdnnis] *n* soudaineté *f*, brusquerie *f*.

sue [suː] *vt* poursuivre, demander.

suet [suit] *n* graisse de rognon *f*.

suffer ['sʌfə] *vti* souffrir; *vt* subir, éprouver, supporter.

sufferance ['sʌfərəns] *n* tolérance *f*.

sufferer ['sʌfərə] *n* patient(e) *mf*, victime *f*.

suffering ['sʌfəriŋ] *n* souffrance *f*.

suffice [sə'fais] *vt* suffire.

sufficiency [sə'fiʃənsi] *n* fortune suffisante *f*, suffisance *f*, aisance *f*.

sufficient [sə'fiʃənt] *a* suffisant, assez de.

sufficiently [sə'fiʃəntli] *ad* suffisamment, assez.

suffocate ['sʌfəkeit] *vti* étouffer, suffoquer.

suffocation [ˌsʌfə'keiʃən] *n* suffocation *f*, asphyxie *f*.

suffrage ['sʌfridʒ] *n* suffrage *m*, droit de vote *m*.

suffuse [sə'fjuːz] *vt* colorer, humecter, se répandre sur.

sugar ['ʃugə] *n* sucre *m*; **castor** — sucre en poudre; **loaf** — sucre en pain; *vt* sucrer; —**basin** sucrier *m*; —**beet** betterave à sucre *f*; —**cane** canne à sucre *f*; —**tongs** pince *f*.

sugary ['ʃugəri] *a* sucré, mielleux, doucereux, mièvre.

suggest [sə'dʒest] *vt* suggérer, inspirer, proposer.

suggestion [sə'dʒestʃən] *n* suggestion *f*, nuance *f*.

suggestive [sə'dʒestiv] *a* suggestif, équivoque.

suicide ['sjuisaid] *n* suicide *m*, suicidé(e) *mf*.

suit [sjuːt] *n* requête *f*, demande *f*, procès *m*, (*cards*) couleur *f*, complet *m*, tailleur *m*; *vt* adapter, accommoder, arranger, convenir à, aller à.

suitable ['sjuːtəbl] *a* approprié, convenable, assorti, qui convient.

suite [swiːt] *n* suite *f*, appartement *m*, mobilier *m*.

suitor ['sjuːtə] *n* plaignant *m*, solliciteur *m*, prétendant *m*, soupirant *m*.

sulk [sʌlk] *vi* bouder; —**s** *n* *pl* bouderie *f*.

sulky ['sʌlki] *a* boudeur.

sullen ['sʌlən] *a* rancunier, maussade, renfrogné.

sullenness ['sʌlənnis] *n* maussaderie *f*, air renfrogné *m*.

sully ['sʌli] *vt* salir, souiller.

sulphur ['sʌlfə] *n* soufre *m*.

sultan ['sʌltən] *n* sultan *m*.

sultana [səl'tɑːnə] *n* raisin de Smyrne *m*; sultane *f*.

sultriness ['sʌltrinis] *n* lourdeur *f*.

sultry ['sʌltri] *a* étouffant, lourd.

sum [sʌm] *n* somme *f*, calcul *m*; to — up calculer, récapituler, resumer.

summary ['sʌməri] *n* sommaire *m*, résumé *m*; *a* sommaire, récapitulatif.

summer ['sʌmə] *n* été *m*; *a* estival, d'été.

summing-up ['sʌmiŋ'ʌp] *n* résumé *m*.

summit ['sʌmit] *n* sommet *m*, cime *f*, comble *m*.

summon ['sʌmən] *vt* citer, convoquer.

summons ['sʌmənz] *n* citation *f*, convocation *f*, procès-verbal *m*.

sumptuous ['sʌmptjuəs] *a* somptueux, fastueux.

sumptuousness ['sʌmptjuəsnis] *n* somptuosité *f*.

sun [sʌn] *n* soleil *m*; *vt* exposer (chauffer) au soleil; —**burn** hâle *m*; —**burnt** *a* hâlé, basané, bronzé.

Sunday ['sʌndi] *n* dimanche *m*.

sundial ['sʌndaiəl] *n* cadran solaire *m*.

sunder ['sʌndə] *vt* séparer.

sundry ['sʌndri] *a* chacun à part, divers, différent; *n pl* faux frais *m pl*.

sung [sʌŋ] *pp of* **sing**.

sunk [sʌŋk] *pp of* **sink**.

sunny ['sʌni] *a* ensoleillé, de soleil.

sunrise ['sʌnraiz] *n* lever du soleil *m*.

sunset ['sʌnset] *n* coucher du soleil *m*.

sunshade ['sʌnʃeid] *n* ombrelle *f*, parasol *m*.

sunshine ['sʌnʃain] *n* (lumière *f* du) soleil, grand jour *m*.

sunstroke ['sʌnstrouk] *n* coup de soleil *m*, insolation *f*.

sup [sʌp] *n* gorgée *f*; *vt* boire à petites gorgées; *vi* souper.

superabundance [ˌsjuːpərə'bʌndəns] *n* surabondance *f*.

superabundant [ˌsjuːpərə'bʌndənt] *a* surabondant.

superannuated [ˌsjuːpə'rænjueitid] *a* en (à la) retraite, suranné.

superb [sjuː'pəːb] *a* superbe, magnifique, sensationnel.

supercilious [ˌsjuːpə'siliəs] *a* dédaigneux, pincé.

superficial [ˌsjuːpə'fiʃəl] *a* superficiel.

superficiality [ˌsjuːpəˌfiʃi'æliti] *n* superficialité *f*.

superfluous [sjuː'pəːfluəs] *a* superflu, de trop.

superfluity [ˌsjuːpə'fluːiti] *n* superfluité *f*, embarras *m*, excédent *m*.

superhuman [ˌsjuːpə'hjuːmən] *a* surhumain.

superintend [ˌsjuːprin'tend] *vt* contrôler, surveiller.

superintendence [ˌsjuːprin'tendəns] *n* surintendance *f*, surveillance *f*.

superintendent [ˌsjuːprin'tendənt] *n* surintendant *m*, surveillant(e) *mf*.

superior [sjuː'piəriə] *an* supérieur(e) *mf*.

superiority [sjuːˌpiəri'ɔriti] *n* supériorité *f*.

superlative [sjuː'pəːlətiv] *an* superlatif *m*; *a* suprême.

superman ['sjuːpəmæn] *n* surhomme *m*.

supernatural [ˌsjuːpə'nætʃrəl] *an* surnaturel *m*.

superpose [ˌsjuːpə'pouz] *vt* superposer.

supersede [ˌsjuːpə'siːd] *vt* supplanter, écarter, remplacer.

superstition [ˌsjuːpə'stiʃən] *n* superstition *f*.

superstitious [ˌsjuːpə'stiʃəs] *a* superstitieux.

superstructure ['sjuːpəˌstrʌktʃə] *n* superstructure *f*, tablier *m*.

supertax ['sjuːpətæks] *n* surtaxe *f*.

supervise ['sjuːpəvaiz] *vt* surveiller, contrôler.

supervision [ˌsjuːpə'viʒən] *n* surveillance *f*, contrôle *m*.

supervisor ['sjuːpəvaizə] *n* surveillant(e) *mf*.

supine ['sjuːpain] *a* couché sur le dos, indolent.

supper ['sʌpə] *n* souper *m*.

supplant [sə'plɑːnt] *vt* supplanter, évincer.

supple ['sʌpl] *a* souple, flexible.

supplement ['sʌplimənt] *n* supplément *m*.

supplement ['sʌpliment] *vt* ajouter à, augmenter.

suppleness ['sʌplnis] *n* souplesse *f*.

supplicate ['sʌplikeit] *vti* supplier.

supplication [ˌsʌpli'keiʃən] *n* supplication *f*.

supplier [sə'plaiə] *n* fournisseur, -euse.

supply [sə'plai] *n* offre *f*, fourniture *f*, provision *f*; *pl* vivres *m pl*; fournitures *f pl*, intendance *f*; *vt* fournir, munir.

support [sə'pɔːt] *n* support *m*, soutien *m*, appui *m*; *vt* supporter, appuyer, soutenir.

supporter [sə'pɔːtə] *n* soutien *m*, partisan *m*, supporter *m*.

suppose [sə'pouz] *vt* supposer, s'imaginer.

supposing [sə'pouziŋ] *cj* à supposer que.

supposition [ˌsʌpə'ziʃən] *n* supposition *f*.

suppress [sə'pres] *vt* supprimer, réprimer, étouffer, refouler.

suppression [sə'preʃən] *n* suppression *f*, répression *f*.

suppurate ['sʌpjuəreit] *vi* suppurer.

supremacy [sjuː'preməsi] *n* suprématie *f*.

supreme [sjuː'priːm] *a* suprême.

sura, surate ['suərə, su'ræt] *n* sourate *f*.

surcharge ['səːtʃɑːdʒ] *n* surcharge *f*, surtaxe *f*; *vt* surcharger, surtaxer.

sure [ʃuə] *a* sûr, assuré, certain; **to be — ** *ad* sûrement.

surety ['ʃuəti] *n* garant(e) *mf*, caution *f*.

surf [səːf] *n* ressac *m*, surf *m*, barre *f*.

surface ['səːfis] *n* surface *f*, apparence *f*.

surfboard ['səːfbɔːd] *n* aquaplane *m*.

surfboat ['səːfbout] *n* pirogue *f*.

surfing ['səːfiŋ] *n* planking *m*.

surfeit ['səːfit] *n* excès *m*, satiété *f*, indigestion *f*, écœurement *m*; *vt* gaver, rassasier.

surge [səːdʒ] *n* lame *f*, houle *f*, soulèvement *m*; *vi* se soulever, onduler, se répandre en flots.

surgeon ['səːdʒən] *n* chirurgien *m*.

surgery ['səːdʒəri] *n* chirurgie *f*, clinique *f*.

surgical ['səːdʒikəl] *a* chirurgical.

surliness ['səːlinis] *n* morosité *f*, air bourru *m*.

surly ['səːli] *a* revêche, bourru, morose.

surmise ['səːmaiz] *n* soupçon *m*,

conjecture *f*; [sə:'maiz] *vt* soupçonner, conjecturer.
surmount [sə:'maunt] *vt* surmonter,
triompher de.
surname ['sə:neim] *n* nom *m* de
famille; *vt* nommer.
surpass [sə:'pɑ:s] *vt* surpasser, dépasser, excéder.
surplice ['sə:pləs] *n* surplis *m*.
surplus ['sə:pləs] *n* surplus *m*,
excédent *m*, boni *m*, rabiot *m*.
surprise [sə'praiz] *n* surprise *f*; *vt*
surprendre; by —à l'improviste.
surprising [sə'praiziŋ] *a* surprenant,
étonnant.
surrender [sə'rendə] *n* reddition *f*,
capitulation *f*; *vt* rendre, renoncer à,
livrer; *vi* se rendre, se livrer.
surreptitious [ˌsʌrəp'tiʃəs] *a* subreptice, clandestin.
surround [sə'raund] *vt* entourer,
cerner.
surrounding [sə'raundiŋ] *a* environ-
nant.
surroundings [sə'raundiŋs] *n* *pl*
environs *m* *pl*, ambiance *f*, alentours
m *pl*.
surtax ['sə:tæks] *n* surtaxe *f*.
survey ['sə:vei] *n* coup d'œil *m*,
examen *m*, arpentage *m*, cadastre
m, aperçu *m*, expertise *f*, plan *m*.
survey [sə:'vei] *vt* examiner, relever,
arpenter, embrasser du regard,
contempler.
surveyor [sə:'veiə] *n* arpenteur *m*,
inspecteur *m*, ingénieur *m* du service
vicinal.
survival [sə'vaivəl] *n* survivance *f*.
survive [sə'vaiv] *vi* survivre; *vt*
survivre à.
Susan ['su:zn] Suzanne *f*.
susceptibility [səˌseptə'biliti] *n* susceptibilité *f*, sensibilité *f*.
susceptible [sə'septəbl] *a* susceptible,
sensible, impressionnable.
suspect [səs'pekt] *vt* soupçonner,
suspecter, se douter de.
suspect ['sʌspekt] *a* suspect.
suspend [səs'pend] *vt* (sus)pendre,
mettre à pied, surseoir à.
suspender-belt [səs'pendəbelt] *n*
porte-jarretelles *m*.
suspenders [səs'pendəz] *n* jarretelles
f *pl*, fixe-chaussettes *n* *pl*, (US)
bretelles *f* *pl*.
suspense [səs'pens] *n* attente *f*,
inquiétude *f*, suspens *m*.
suspension [səs'penʃən] *n* suspension
f, mise à pied *f*, retrait *m*.
suspicion [səs'piʃən] *n* suspicion *f*,
soupçon *m*.
suspicious [səs'piʃəs] *a* soupçonneux,
suspect, méfiant, louche.
sustain [səs'tein] *vt* soutenir, sustenter, souffrir, subir.
sustenance ['sʌstinəns] *n* moyens de
se soutenir *m* *pl*, nourriture *f*.
swab [swɔb] *n* faubert *m*, tampon *m*;
vt balayer, nettoyer, laver à grande
eau.

swaddle ['swɔdl] *vt* emmailloter.
swaddling-clothes ['swɔdliŋklouðz]
n langes *m* *pl*.
swagger ['swægə] *n* suffisance *f*,
rodomontades *f* *pl*; *vi* se gober, se
pavaner, crâner.
swain [swein] *n* berger *m*, amoureux
m, tourtereau *m*.
swallow ['swɔlou] *n* hirondelle *f*,
gosier *m*, gorgée *f*; *vt* avaler, engloutir.
swam [swæm] *pt* of **swim**.
swamp ['swɔmp] *n* marais *m*; *vt*
inonder, déborder.
swan [swɔn] *n* cygne *m*.
swank [swæŋk] *vi* faire de l'épate,
se donner des airs.
swap [swɔp] *vt* troquer, échanger.
sward [swɔ:d] *n* gazon *m*.
swarm [swɔ:m] *n* essaim *m*, nuée *f*;
vi essaimer, fourmiller, grimper.
swarthy ['swɔ:ði] *a* hâlé, boucané.
swash [swɔʃ] *n* clapotis *m*; *vi*
clapoter.
swastika ['swɔstikə] *n* croix gammée
f.
swath [swɔ:θ] *n* andain *m*.
swathe [sweið] *vt* emmailloter, emmitoufler.
sway [swei] *n* balancement *m*,
pouvoir *m*, gouvernement *m*; *vi* se
balancer, vaciller, incliner; *vt* balancer, courber, porter, faire pencher,
gouverner.
swear [swɛə] *n* juron *m*; *vti* jurer; *vt*
assermenter.
sweat [swet] *n* sueur *f*, transpiration
f; *vti* suer; *vi* transpirer, peiner; *vt*
exploiter.
sweater ['swetə] *n* sweater *m*, pull-
over *m*, chandail *m*, exploiteur *m*.
sweating ['swetiŋ] *n* suée *f*, transpiration *f*.
swede [swi:d] *n* rutabaga *m*.
Swede [swi:d] *n* Suédois(e) *mf*.
Sweden ['swi:dn] *n* Suède *f*.
Swedish ['swi:diʃ] *an* suédois *m*.
sweep [swi:p] *n* mouvement *m*,
large courbe *f*, allée *f*, portée *f*, coup
de balai *m*, godille *f*, ramoneur *m*;
vt balayer, emporter, ramoner,
draguer; *vi* s'élancer, fondre,
s'étendre; to — aside écarter; to —
down *vt* charrier, emporter; *vi*
dévaler.
sweeper ['swi:pə] *n* balayeur *m*,
balai *m* mécanique, balayeuse *f*;
mine— dragueur *m* de mines.
sweeping ['swi:piŋ] *n* balayage *m*,
dragage *m*, ramonage *m*; *a* excessif,
radical, impétueux, large.
swept [swept] *pt* *pp* of **sweep**.
sweet [swi:t] *a* doux, sucré, gentil; *n*
bonbon *m*; *pl* sucreries *f* *pl*, bonbons
m *pl*, douceurs *f* *pl*.
sweetbread ['swi:tbred] *n* ris de
veau *m*.
sweeten ['swi:tn] *vt* sucrer, adoucir.
sweetheart ['swi:thɑ:t] *n* ami(e) *mf*,
fiancé(e) *mf*, chéri(e) *mf*.

sweetish ['swi:tiʃ] a douceâtre.

sweetmeat ['swi:tmi:t] n bonbon m; pl sucreries f pl.

sweetness ['swi:tnis] n douceur f, charme m.

sweet-pea ['swi:t'pi:] n pois de senteur m.

swell [swel] n enflure f, houle f; pl (fam) élégants m pl, gens de la haute m pl; a (fam) chic, épatant; vt enfler, gonfler; vi se gonfler, (s')enfler, se soulever.

swelter ['sweltə] n fournaise f; vi étouffer de chaleur, être en nage.

swerve [swə:v] vi faire un écart, une embardée, donner un coup de volant.

swift [swift] n martinet m; a rapide, prompt.

swiftness ['swiftnis] n rapidité f, vitesse f, promptitude f.

swill [swil] n rinçage m, lavasse f, pâtée f; vt rincer, boire goulûment, lamper.

swim [swim] vi nager, flotter, tourner; vt traverser à la nage.

swimmer ['swimə] n nageur, -euse.

swimming ['swimiŋ] n natation f, nage f.

swindle ['swindl] n escroquerie f; vt escroquer.

swindler ['swindlə] n escroc m.

swine [swain] n cochon m, porc m, pourceau m, salaud m.

swing [swiŋ] n oscillation f, balancement m, balançoire f, cours m, courant m, entrain m, revirement m; vi se balancer, tourner, ballotter, danser; vt balancer, faire osciller, tourner.

swirl [swə:l] n tourbillon m, remous m; vi tourbillonner.

swish [swiʃ] n banco m; latérite f; vi bruire.

Swiss [swis] a suisse; n Suisse, -esse.

switch [switʃ] n baguette f, badine f, (rails) aiguille f, commutateur m, bouton m; vt cingler, remuer, aiguiller; to — on (off) donner (couper) le courant.

switchboard ['switʃbɔːd] n tableau m.

swivel ['swivl] n pivot m; vi pivoter, tourner.

swoon [swu:n] n syncope f, défaillance f; vi s'évanouir.

swoop [swu:p] n descente f, attaque foudroyante f, rafle f; vi fondre, s'abattre.

sword [sɔːd] n sabre m, épée f, glaive m.

swore [swɔ:] pt of swear.

sworn [swɔ:n] pp of swear; a assermenté, intimé, juré.

swot [swɔt] vti potasser, bûcher.

swum [swʌm] pp of swim.

swung [swʌŋ] pt pp of swing.

syllable ['siləbl] n syllabe f, mot m.

syllabus ['siləbəs] n programme m, ordre du jour m

symbol ['simbəl] n symbole m, emblème m.

symbolic(al) [sim'bɔlik(əl)] a symbolique.

symbolism ['simbəlizəm] n symbolisme f.

symbolize ['simbəlaiz] v symboliser.

symmetrical [si'metrikəl] a symétrique.

symmetry ['simitri] n symétrie f.

sympathetic [,simpə'θetic] a compatissant, de sympathie, sympathique.

sympathize ['simpəθaiz] vi compatir, partager la douleur (de), comprendre.

sympathy ['simpəθi] n compassion f, sympathie f.

symphony ['simfəni] n symphonie f.

symptom ['simptəm] n symptôme m.

synagogue ['sinəgɔg] n synagogue f.

syndicate ['sindikit] n syndicat m; ['sindikeit] vt syndiquer.

synod ['sinəd] n synode m.

synonym ['sinənim] n synonyme m.

synonymous [si'nɔniməs] a synonyme.

synopsis [si'nɔpsis] n vue d'ensemble f, résumé m, mémento m.

synoptic(al) [si'nɔptik(əl)] a synoptique.

syntax ['sintæks] n syntaxe f.

synthesis ['sinθisis] n synthèse f.

synthetic(al) [sin'θetik(əl)] a synthétique.

Syria ['siriə] n Syrie f.

Syrian ['siriən] a syrien; n Syrien, -ienne.

syringe ['sirindʒ] n seringue f.

syrup ['sirəp] n sirop m.

syrupy ['sirəpi] a sirupeux.

system ['sistim] n système m.

systematic [sisti'mætik] a systématique.

systematize ['sistimətaiz] vt systématiser.

T

tab [tæb] n étiquette f, oreille f, patte f, ferret m touche f.

table ['teibl] n table f, tablier m, plaque f, tabliée f.

tablecloth ['teiblklɔθ] n nappe f.

tableland ['teibilænd] n plateau m.

table-leaf ['teibli:f] n rallonge f.

tablespoon ['teiblspu:n] n cuiller à bouche f.

tablet ['tæblit] n tablette f, cachet m, comprimé m, plaque f, commémorative f.

tabloid ['tæblɔid] n journal m à sensation.

taboo [tə'bu:] n tabou m; vt interdire.

tabulate ['tæbjuleit] vt cataloguer, classifier.

tacit ['tæsit] a tacite.

taciturn ['tæsitə:n] a taciturne.

taciturnity [ˌtæsi'təːniti] n taciturnité f.

tack [tæk] n faufil m, (nail) semence f, bordée f, voie f; vt clouer, faufiler; vi louvoyer, tirer des bordées, virer.

tackle ['tækl] n poulie f, attirail m, palan m, engins m pl; vt empoigner, aborder, s'attaquer à, plaquer.

tact [tækt] n tact m, savoir-faire m, doigté m.

tactful ['tæktful] a de tact, délicat.

tactician [tæk'tiʃən] n tacticien m.

tactics ['tæktiks] n tactique f.

tactless ['tæktlis] a sans tact, indiscret.

tactlessness ['tæktlisnis] n manque de tact m.

tadpole ['tædpoul] n têtard m.

tag [tæg] n aiguillette f, bout m, appendice m, cliché m, refrain m; (US) fiche f.

tail [teil] n queue f, basque f, pan m, (tossing) pile m; to — off s'éteindre; (US) vt suivre, pister.

tail-light ['teil'lait] n feu arrière m.

tailor ['teilə] n tailleur m; — made a tailleur, fait sur mesure.

taint [teint] n grain m, touche f, trace f, corruption f, tare f; vt corrompre, vicier, gâter.

take [teik] vti prendre; vt gagner, captiver, tenir (pour), falloir, mettre, demander, vouloir; to — off décoller; to — out (faire) sortir, tirer, emmener; to — to prendre goût à, se prendre d'amitié pour; to — up monter, relever, ramasser, occuper.

take-in ['teik'in] n fraude f, attrape f.

take-off ['teikɔf] n départ m, décollage m.

taking ['teikiŋ] a attrayant; n prise f.

takings ['teikiŋz] n pl recette f.

taken ['teikən] pp of take.

tale [teil] n conte m, raconter m.

tale-teller ['teil telə] n conteur m, cancanier m, rapporteur, -euse, cafard(e) mf.

talent ['tælənt] n talent m.

talented ['tæləntid] a de talent, doué.

talk [tɔːk] n conversation f, parole f, causerie f, fable f; vi causer; vti parler.

talkative ['tɔːkətiv] a bavard, loquace.

talking of [tɔːkiŋəv] prep à propos de.

tall [tɔːl] a très grand, haut, raide, fort, extravagant.

tallow ['tælou] n suif m; — candle chandelle f.

tally ['tæli] n taille f, coche f, étiquette f; vt compter, concorder; vi s'accorder, cadrer.

talon ['tælən] n serre f.

tame [teim] a apprivoisé, domestique banal, plat; vt apprivoiser, aplatir.

tameness ['teimnis] n soumission f, banalité f, fadeur f.

tamper ['tæmpə] vi se mêler; to —

with se mêler de, toucher à, falsifier, altérer.

tan [tæn] n tan m, hâle m; vt tanner, hâler, bronzer; vi brunir, se basaner.

tandem ['tændəm] n tandem m.

tang [tæŋ] n saveur f, piquant m, goût m.

tangent ['tændʒənt] n tangente f; a tangent.

tangerine [ˌtændʒə'riːn] n mandarine f.

tangible ['tændʒəbl] a tangible, sensible, réel, palpable.

tangle ['tæŋgl] n confusion f, enchevêtrement m, fouillis m; vt embrouiller; vi s'embrouiller, s'emmêler.

tank [tæŋk] n réservoir m, citerne f, cuve f, tank m, char d'assaut m.

tankard ['tæŋkəd] n pot m, chope f.

tanner ['tænə] n tanneur m, pièce de sixpence f.

tannery ['tænəri] n tannerie f.

tantalize ['tæntəlaiz] vt tantaliser, tourmenter.

tantalizing ['tæntəlaiziŋ] a provoquant, décevant.

tantamount ['tæntəmaunt] a équivalent, qui revient à.

tantrum ['tæntrəm] n accès de colère m.

tap [tæp] n robinet m, tape f; vt mettre en perce, inciser, ponctionner, intercepter, taper, tapoter.

tape [teip] n ruban m, ganse f, bande f; vt attacher, border, brocher.

tape-measure ['teip meʒə] n mètre ruban m.

taper ['teipə] n cierge m, bougie f, rat de cave m; vt effiler; vi amincir, s'effiler.

tape-recorder ['teipri kɔːdə] n magnétophone m.

tapestry ['tæpistri] n tapisserie f.

tapeworm ['teipwəːm] n ver solitaire m, ténia m.

tapioca [ˌtæpi'oukə] n tapioca m.

tar [taː] n goudron m, (fam) loup m de mer; vt goudronner.

tardiness ['taːdinis] n lenteur f, tardivité f, retard m.

tardy ['taːdi] a lent, tardif.

tare [tɛə] n tare f, ivraie f.

target ['taːgit] n cible f, disque m, objectif m.

tariff ['tærif] n tarif m.

tarmac ['taːmæk] n macadam m, piste de décollage f.

tarnish ['taːniʃ] n ternissure f; vt ternir; vi se ternir.

tarpaulin [taː'pɔːlin] n bâche (goudronnée) f.

tarragon ['tærəgən] n estragon m.

tarry ['tæri] vi rester, attendre, s'attarder.

tart [taːt] n tarte f, fourte f; (fam) putain f; a acide, âpre, piquant, aigre.

tartness ['taːtnis] n aigreur f, verdeur f, acidité f.

task [tɑːsk] *n* tâche *f*, devoir *m*, besogne *f*; **to take to** — prendre à partie.

tassel ['tæsəl] *n* gland *m*, signet *m*.

taste [teist] *n* goût *m*, saveur *f*; *vt* goûter (à), sentir, toucher à, déguster.

tasteful ['teistful] *a* qui a du goût, de bon goût.

tasteless ['teistlis] *a* insipide, fade, sans goût.

taster ['teistə] *n* dégustateur *m*.

tasty ['teisti] *a* savoureux.

tatter ['tætə] *n* chiffon *m*; *pl* loques *f pl*, guenilles *f pl*.

tattle ['tætl] *n* bavardage *m*, commérages *m pl*; *vi* bavarder.

tattler ['tætlə] *n* bavard(e) *mf*, cancanier, -ière.

tattoo [tə'tuː] *n* (*mil*) retraite *f*, tatouage *m*; *vi* tambouriner; *vt* tatouer.

taught [tɔːt] *pt pp of* teach.

taunt [tɔːnt] *n* reproche *m*, quolibet *m*; *vt* reprocher (à), accabler de quolibets, se moquer de, se gausser de.

taut [tɔːt] *a* tendu, raide.

tavern ['tævən] *n* taverne *f*, cabaret *m*.

tawdriness ['tɔːdrinis] *n* clinquant *m*, faux luxe *m*.

tawdry ['tɔːdri] *a* criard.

tawny ['tɔːni] *a* fauve, basané.

tax [tæks] *n* impôt *m*, taxe *f*, contribution *f*; *vt* taxer, imposer, frapper d'un impôt.

taxation [tæk'seiʃən] *n* imposition *f*, taxation *f*.

tax-collector ['tækskə,lektə] *n* percepteur *m*.

taxi ['tæksi] *n* taxi *m*.

taxpayer ['tæks,peiə] *n* contribuable *mf*.

tea [tiː] *n* thé *m*; **—caddy** boîte *f* à thé; **—cloth** napperon *m*; **—pot** théière *f*; **—spoon** cuiller *f* à thé; **— chest** caisse *f* à thé.

teach [tiːtʃ] *vt* enseigner, apprendre (à), instruire.

teacher ['tiːtʃə] *n* professeur *m*, (*primary*) instituteur *m*, institutrice *f*, maître *m*, maîtresse *f*.

teaching ['tiːtʃiŋ] *n* enseignement *m*, doctrine *f*, leçons *f pl*.

teak [tiːk] *n* tek *m*.

team [tiːm] *n* équipe *f*, attelage *m*; *vt* atteler.

tear [tiə] *n* larme *f*, goutte *f*, bulle *f*.

tear [tɛə] *n* déchirure *f*, accroc *m*; *vt* déchirer, arracher.

tearful ['tiəful] *a* larmoyant, en larmes, éploré.

tease [tizz] *vt* taquiner, effilocher, démêler; *n* taquin(e) *mf*.

teasel ['tiːzl] *n* chardon *m*, carde *f*.

teaser ['tizzə] *n* problème *m*, colle *f*.

teasing ['tizziŋ] *n* taquinerie *f*, effilochage *m*; *a* taquin.

teat [tiːt] *n* tétin *m*, tétine *f*, tette *f*.

technical ['teknikəl] *a* technique.

technicality [,tekni'kæliti] *n* technicité *f*, détail *m* d'ordre technique.

technique [tek'niːk] *n* technique *f*.

tedious ['tiːdjəs] *a* ennuyeux, fastidieux.

teem [tiːm] *vi* pulluler, abonder, fourmiller, grouiller.

teeth [tiːθ] *n pl of* tooth.

teethe [tiːð] *vi* faire ses dents.

teething ['tiːðiŋ] *n* dentition *f*.

teetotal [tiː'toutl] *a* de tempérance, antialcoolique.

teetotaller [tiː'toutlə] *n* abstinent(e) *mf*.

telegram ['teligræm] *n* télégramme *m*, dépêche *f*.

telegraph ['teligrɑːf] *n* télégraphe *m*; *vt* télégraphier.

telegraphic [,teli'græfik] *a* télégraphique.

telegraphist [ti'legrəfist] *n* télégraphiste *mf*.

telepathy [ti'lepəθi] *n* télépathie *f*.

telephone ['telifoun] *n* téléphone *m*; *vt* téléphoner.

telescope ['teliskoup] *n* télescope *f*, longue-vue *f*; *vt* télescoper; *vi* se télescoper.

television ['teli,viʒən] *n* télévision *f*.

tell [tel] *vt* dire, conter, parler de, distinguer; *vi* porter, compter, militer; **all told** tout compris.

teller ['telə] *n* caissier *m*, conteur, -euse, recenseur *m*.

telltale ['telteil] *n* rapporteur, cafard (e) *mf*; *a* révélateur.

temerity [ti'meriti] *n* témérité *f*.

temper ['tempə] *n* humeur *f*, colère *f*, sang-froid *m*, mélange *m*, trempe *f*; *vt* mêler, tremper, tempérer.

temperament ['tempərəmənt] *n* tempérament *m*.

temperamental [,tempərə'mentl] *a* inégal, capricieux, nerveux, quinteux.

temperance ['tempərəns] *n* tempérance *f*, sobriété *f*, retenue *f*.

temperate ['tempərit] *a* tempéré, modéré, tempérant, sobre.

temperature ['tempritʃə] *n* température *f*, fièvre *f*.

tempest ['tempist] *n* tempête *f*.

tempestuous [tem'pestjuəs] *a* tempétueux, orageux, violent.

temple ['templ] *n* temple *m*, tempe *f*.

tempo ['tempou] *n* rythme *m*.

temporal ['tempərəl] *a* temporel.

temporary ['tempərəri] *a* temporaire, provisoire.

temporize ['tempəraiz] *vi* temporiser.

temporizer ['tempəraizə] *n* temporisateur *m*.

tempt [tempt] *vt* tenter.

temptation [temp'teiʃən] *n* tentation *f*.

tempter ['temptə] *n* tentateur *m*, séducteur *m*.

ten [ten] *ad* dix.

tenable ['tenəbl] *a* (sou)tenable, défendable.

tenacious [ti'neiʃəs] *a* tenace.

tenacity [ti'næsiti] *n* ténacité *f*.

tenancy ['tenənsi] *n* location *f*.

tenant ['tenənt] *n* locataire *mf*.

tench [tenʃ] *n* tanche *f*.

tend [tend] *vi* tendre (à), se diriger (vers); *vt* soigner, veiller sur, servir.

tendency ['tendənsi] *n* tendance *f*, disposition *f*.

tendentious [ten'denʃəs] *a* tendancieux.

tender ['tendə] *n* devis *m*, offre *f*, monnaie *f*, tender *m*; *vt* offrir; *vi* soumissionner; *a* tendre, délicat, sensible, fragile.

tenderness ['tendənis] *n* tendresse *f*, sensibilité *f*.

tendril ['tendril] *n* vrille *f*.

tenement ['tenimənt] *n* propriété *f*, appartement *m*, maison de rapport *f*.

tenet ['tenit] *n* doctrine *f*, opinion *f*, article de foi *m*.

tenfold ['tenfould] *a* décuple; *ad* dix fois.

tennis ['tenis] *n* tennis *m*; —**court** tennis *m*, court *m*.

tenor ['tenə] *n* teneur *f*, cours *m*, ténor *m*.

tense [tens] *n* temps *m*; *a* tendu, raide.

tension ['tenʃən] *n* tension *f*.

tent [tent] *n* tente *f*.

tentacle ['tentəkl] *n* tentacule *m*.

tentative ['tentətiv] *a* d'essai, expérimental.

tentatively ['tentətivli] *ad* à titre d'essai.

tenth [tenθ] *an* dixième *mf*, dix *m*.

tenuity [te'njuːiti] *n* rareté *f*, ténuité *f*.

tenuous ['tenjuəs] *a* délié, ténu, mince.

tenure ['tenjuə] *n* exercice de fonctions *m*, occupation *f*, tenure *f*.

tepid ['tepid] *a* tiède.

term [təːm] *n* durée *f*, fin *f*, trimestre *m*, terme *m*; *pl* conditions *f pl*; *vt* nommer, désigner.

terminate ['təːmineit] *vt* terminer; *vi* se terminer.

termination [ˌtəːmi'neiʃən] *n* terminaison *f*, conclusion *f*, fin *f*.

terminus ['təːminəs] *n* terminus *m*, tête de ligne *f*.

terrace ['terəs] *n* terrasse *f*.

terrestrial [ti'restriəl] *a* terrestre.

terrible ['terəbl] *a* terrible, atroce, affreux.

terrific [tə'rifik] *a* terrifiant, terrible, formidable.

terrify ['terifai] *vt* terrifier, effrayer.

territorial [ˌteri'tɔːriəl] *a* territorial, terrien.

territory ['teritəri] *n* territoire *m*.

terror ['terə] *n* terreur *f*.

terrorism ['terərizəm] *n* terrorisme *m*.

terrorize ['terəraiz] *vt* terroriser.

terse [təːs] *a* net, délié, sobre, concis.

terseness ['təːsnis] *n* netteté *f*, concision *f*.

test [test] *n* pierre de touche *f*, épreuve *f*, test *m*, réactif *m*; *vt* éprouver, essayer, mettre à l'épreuve, vérifier.

testament ['testəmənt] *n* testament *m*.

testamentary [ˌtestə'mentəri] *a* testamentaire.

testify ['testifai] *vt* attester, témoigner; *vi* déposer.

testily ['testili] *ad* en bougonnant, avec humeur.

testimonial [ˌtesti'mouniəl] *n* recommandation *f*, certificat *m*.

testimony ['testiməni] *n* déposition *f*, témoignage *m*.

testiness ['testinis] *n* irascibilité *f*, susceptibilité *f*.

testy ['testi] *a* chatouilleux, irascible.

tetanus ['tetənəs] *n* tétanos *m*.

tether ['teðə] *n* longe *f*, attache *f*, moyens *m pl*, rouleau *m*; *vt* attacher.

text [tekst] *n* texte *m*.

text-book ['tekstbuk] *n* manuel *m*.

textile ['tekstail] *an* textile *m*; *n* tissu *m*.

textual ['tekstjuəl] *a* textuel, de texte.

texture ['tekstʃə] *n* (con)texture *f*, structure *f*, grain *m*, trace *f*.

Thames [temz] *n* la Tamise *f*.

than [ðən] *cj* que, de.

thank [θæŋk] *vt* remercier, rendre grâce(s) à.

thanks [θæŋks] *n pl* remerciements *m pl*, grâces *f pl*; — **to** grâce à.

thankful ['θæŋkful] *a* reconnaissant.

thankfulness ['θæŋkfulnis] *n* reconnaissance *f*.

thankless ['θæŋklis] *a* ingrat.

thanklessness ['θæŋklisnis] *n* ingratitude *f*.

thanksgiving ['θæŋks'giviŋ] *n* action de grâces *f*; (US) fête *f* d'action de grâces.

that [ðæt] *a* ce, cet, cette; *pn* celui, celle (-là), cela, ça, qui, que, tant de; *cj* que, pour que, si seulement, plaise à Dieu que, dire que.

thatch [θætʃ] *n* chaume *m*; *vt* couvrir de chaume.

thatched [θætʃt] *a* (couvert) de chaume.

thaw [θɔː] *n* dégel *m*; *vi* dégeler.

the [ðə] *def art* le, la, l', les, ce, cet, cette, ces, quel(s), quelle(s); *ad* d'autant; — **more** plus.

theatre ['θiətə] *n* théâtre *m*.

theatrical [θi'ætrikəl] *a* théâtral, scénique.

thee [ðiː] *pn* te, toi.

theft [θeft] *n* vol *m*.

their [ðɛə] *a* leur(s).

theirs [ðɛəz] *pn* le (la) leur, les leurs, à eux (elles).

them [ðem] *pn* les, eux, elles, leur.

theme [θiːm] *n* thème *m*, motif *m*.

themselves [ðəm'selvz] *pn* se, eux-(elles)-mêmes.

then [ðen] *ad* alors, puis, ensuite, donc.

thence [ðens] *ad* de là, par conséquent.

thenceforth ['ðens'fɔːθ] *ad* dès (depuis) lors, désormais.

theologian [θiə'loudʒjən] *n* théologien *m*.

theological [θiə'lɔdʒikəl] *a* théologique.

theology [θi'ɔlədʒi] *n* théologie *f*.

theorem ['θiərəm] *n* théorème *m*.

theoretic(al) [θiə'retikəl] *a* théorique.

theory ['θiəri] *n* théorie *f*.

there [ðeə] *ad* là, y, il; *excl* voilà.

thereabout(s) ['ðeərəbauts] *ad* par là, environ.

thereby ['ðeə'bai] *ad* de ce fait, par là, par ce moyen.

therefore [ðeə'fɔː] *ad* donc.

thereupon ['ðeərə'pɔn] *ad* sur quoi, en conséquence, là-dessus.

thermometer [θə'mɔmitə] *n* thermomètre *m*.

these [ðiːz] *a* ces; *pn* ceux, celles(-ci).

thesis ['θiːsis] *n* thèse *f*.

they [ðei] *pn* ils, elles, on, eux, elles, ceux, celles.

thick [θik] *a* épais, touffu, dur, gros, fort, obtus; *ad* dur; *n* plus fort *m*.

thicken ['θikən] *vt* épaissir, lier; *vi* s'épaissir, se lier.

thicket ['θikit] *n* fourré *m*, bosquet *m*.

thickness ['θiknis] *n* épaisseur *f*.

thief [θiːf] *n* voleur, -euse.

thieve [θiːv] *vti* voler.

thigh [θai] *n* cuisse *f*; —**bone** fémur *m*.

thimble ['θimbl] *n* dé *m*.

thimbleful ['θimblful] *n* dé *m*, doigt *m*.

thin [θin] *a* mince, faible, fin, léger, grêle, clair(semé); *vt* éclaircir, amincir; *vi* s'éclaircir, maigrir, s'amincir.

thine [ðain] *pn* à toi, le (les) tien(s), la (les) tienne(s).

thing [θiŋ] *n* chose *f*, objet *m*, machin *m*, être *m*; *pl* affaires *f pl*, effets *m pl*.

thingummy ['θiŋəmi] *n* chose *m*, machin *m*, t.uc *m*.

think [θiŋk] *vti* penser, réfléchir; *vt* trouver, juger, s'imaginer; **to — about** penser à, songer à; **to — of** penser de, (à), avoir égard à.

thinker ['θiŋkə] *n* penseur *mf*.

thinness ['θinnis] *n* minceur *f*, maigreur *f*, fluidité *f*.

third [θəːd] *n* tiers *m*, tierce *f*; *a* troisième, tiers.

thirdly ['θəːdli] *ad* tertio, en troisième lieu, troisièmement.

thirst [θəːst] *n* soif *f*; *vi* avoir soif (de **for**).

thirsty ['θəːsti] *a* altéré, assoiffé.

thirteen ['θəː'tiːn] *an* treize *m*.

thirteenth ['θəː'tiːnθ] *an* treizième *mf*, treize *m*.

thirtieth ['θəːtiiθ] *an* trentième *mf*, trente *m*.

thirty ['θəːti] *an* trente *m*.

this [ðis] *a* ce, cet(te); *pn* ceci, ce, celui-ci, ceux-ci, celle(s)-ci.

thistle ['θisl] *n* chardon *m*.

thither ['ðiðə] *ad* y, là.

thong [θɔŋ] *n* courroie *f*, lanière *f*.

thorn [θɔːn] *n* épine *f*.

thorny ['θɔːni] *a* épineux.

thorough ['θʌrə] *a* soigné, minutieux, complet, achevé.

thoroughbred ['θʌrəbred] *an* pur-sang *m*.

thoroughfare ['θʌrefeə] *n* rue *f*, voie *f*, passage *m*; **no —** entrée interdite.

thoroughly ['θʌrəli] *ad* à fond, complètement, parfaitement.

thou [ðau] *pn* tu, toi.

though [ðou] *cj* bien que, quoique, même si; *ad* cependant, mais.

thought [θɔːt] *pt pp of* **think**; *n* pensée *f*, considération *f*, idée *f*, réflexion *f*.

thoughtful ['θɔːtful] *a* réfléchi, pensif, rêveur, attentionné, plein de prévenance.

thoughtfulness ['θɔːtfulnis] *n* réflexion *f*, méditation *f*, égards *m pl*, prévenance *f*.

thoughtless ['θɔːtlis] *a* étourdi, mal avisé.

thoughtlessness ['θɔːtlisnis] *n* étourderie *f*, manque d'égards *m*, imprévoyance *f*.

thousand ['θauzənd] *an* mille *m*.

thraldom ['θrɔːldəm] *n* esclavage *m*. servitude *f*.

thrash [θræʃ] *vt* battre, rosser.

thrashing ['θræʃiŋ] *n* battage *m*, correction *f*, raclée *f*.

thread [θred] *n* fil *m*, filet *m*, filon *m*; *vt* enfiler; **to — one's way** se faufiler.

threadbare ['θredbeə] *a* usé jusqu'à la corde, râpé.

threat [θret] *n* menace *f*.

threaten ['θretn] *vti* menacer.

threefold ['θriːfould] *a* triple; *ad* trois fois autant.

thresh [θreʃ] *vt* battre.

threshing ['θreʃiŋ] *n* battage *m*.

threshing-machine ['θreʃiŋmə.ʃin] *n* batteuse *f*.

threshold ['θreʃhould] *n* seuil *m*.

threw [θruː] *pt of* **throw**.

thrice [θrais] *ad* trois fois.

thrift [θrift] *n* frugalité *f*, économie *f*.

thriftless ['θriftlis] *a* dépensier, prodigue.

thriftlessness ['θriftlisnis] *n* prodigalité *f*.

thrifty ['θrifti] *a* frugal, économe, ménager.

thrill [θril] *n* frisson *m*, émotion *f*; *vt* émouvoir, électriser, faire frémir; *vi* frémir, frissonner; (*US*) **I am thrilled** ça m'intéresse.

thriller ['θrilə] n roman à sensation m; roman série noire.

thrilling ['θriliŋ] a émouvant, empoignant, palpitant, sensationnel.

thrive [θraiv] vi prospérer, pousser dru, bien marcher.

thriving ['θraiviŋ] a prospère, vigoureux.

throat [θrout] n gorge f.

throaty ['θrouti] a guttural, rauque.

throb [θrɔb] n battement m, pulsation f, palpitation f, vrombissement m; vi battre, vibrer, vrombir.

throes [θrouz] n pl douleurs f pl, affres f pl, agonie f.

throne [θroun] n trône m.

throng [θrɔŋ] n foule f, cohue f; vt encombrer, remplir; vi affluer, se presser.

throttle ['θrɔtl] n régulateur m, obturateur m; vt étrangler.

through [θru:] a direct; prep à travers, par, au travers de, pendant, dans, à cause de, faute de; ad à travers, en communication, jusqu'au bout, à bonne fin, hors d'affaire; I am — with you j'en ai fini avec toi.

throughout [θru:'aut] ad de fond en comble, d'un bout à l'autre; prep d'un bout à l'autre de, partout dans.

throw [θrou] n lancement m, jet m, distance f, portée f; vt (re)jeter (bas, dehors etc), lancer, projeter, désarçonner; piquer; to — away (re)jeter, gaspiller; to — back renvoyer, réverbérer; to — off secouer, abandonner, quitter, dégager; to — out chasser, mettre à la porte, rejeter, lancer; to — over abandonner, plaquer; to — up abandonner, rendre, jeter en l'air.

thrown [θroun] pp of throw.

thrush [θrʌʃ] n grive f.

thrust [θrʌst] n coup de pointe m, coup d'estoc m, attaque f, trait m, poussée f, botte f; vt pousser, imposer, enfoncer.

thug [θʌg] n assassin m, bandit m, voyou m.

thumb [θʌm] n pouce m, influence f; (US) —tack punaise f; vt feuilleter, manier; (fam) to — a lift faire de l'autostop.

thump [θʌmp] n coup de poing m, bruit sourd m; vt frapper à bras raccourcis, cogner sur.

thunder ['θʌndə] n tonnerre m; vti tonner, fulminer; —bolt foudre f; —clap coup de tonnerre m; —storm orage m; —struck foudroyé, renversé, sidéré.

Thursday ['θə:zdi] n jeudi m.

thus [ðʌs] ad ainsi, de cette façon, donc.

thwart [θwɔ:t] vt déjouer, contrecarrer.

thy [ðai] a ton, ta, tes.

thyme [taim] n thym m; wild — serpolet m.

thyself [ðai'self] pn te, toi-même.

tiara [ti'ɑ:rə] n tiare f.

tick [tik] n déclic m, tic-tac m, marque f, coche f, toile f, tique f, crédit m, instant m; vi faire tic-tac; to — off pointer, (fam) rembarrer.

ticket ['tikit] n billet m, ticket m, bulletin m, étiquette f, programme m; vt étiqueter; —collector contrôleur m; —punch poinçon m.

tickle ['tikl] n chatouillement m; vt chatouiller, amuser.

ticklish ['tikliʃ] a chatouilleux, délicat.

tidal wave ['taidl'weiv] n ras de marée m.

tide [taid] n marée f, courant m.

tidings ['taidiŋz] n nouvelles f pl.

tidy ['taidi] a bien rangé, ordonné, bien tenu, qui a de l'ordre, coquet; vt ranger, arranger, mettre de l'ordre dans.

tie [tai] n cravate f, lien m, match nul m; vt attacher, lier, nouer; vi faire match nul, être premier ex aequo.

tier [tiə] n gradin m, étage m.

tiff [tif] n pique f, petite querelle f bisbille f.

tiger ['taigə] n tigre m.

tight [tait] a compact, étroit, serré, tendu, étanche, ivre.

tighten ['taitn] vt (re)serrer, rétrécir, renforcer.

tight-fisted ['tait'fistid] a avare, pingre, radin.

tight-fitting ['tait'fitiŋ] a collant, bien ajusté.

tightly ['taitli] ad ferme, dur, bien, hermétiquement.

tightness ['taitnis] n compacité f, étanchéité f, étroitesse f, tension f.

tights [taits] n (maillot) collant m.

tigress ['taigris] n tigresse f.

tile [tail] n tuile f, carreau m; vt couvrir de tuiles, carreler.

till [til] n caisse f; vt labourer; prep jusqu'à; cj jusqu'à ce que.

tillage ['tilidʒ] n culture f, labourage m.

tiller ['tilə] n cultivateur m, laboureur m.

tiller ['tilə] n barre f.

tilt [tilt] n bâche f, pente f, joute f; vt bâcher, incliner, faire basculer; (faire) pencher; vi jouter, pencher, s'incliner, basculer.

timber ['timbə] n bois de charpente m, poutre f, (US) calibre m, envergure f.

timbrel ['timbrəl] n tambourin m.

time [taim] n temps m, fois f, époque f, moment m, cadence f, mesure f; vt choisir le temps de, fixer l'heure de, noter la durée de, chronométrer, régler, juger, mesurer; —server opportuniste mf; —table horaire m, emploi du temps m.

timeless ['taimlis] a éternel, sans fin.

timely ['taimli] a opportun.

timid ['timid] a timide.

timorous ['timərəs] *a* peureux, timore.

Timothy ['timəθi] Timothé *m*.

tin [tin] *n* étain *m*, fer-blanc *m*, boîte *f*; *vt* étamer.

tinfoil ['tinfɔil] *n* papier d'étain *m*, tain *m*.

tinned [tind] *a* en boîte, de conserve.

tin-hat ['tin'hæt] *n* casque *m*.

tin-opener ['tinoupənə] *n* ouvre-boîte *m*.

tinplate ['tinpleit] *vt* étamer; *n* ferblanterie *f*.

tinware ['tinwɛə] *n* vaisselle d'étain *f*.

tincture ['tiŋktʃə] *n* teinture *f*, saveur *f*, teinte *f*; *vt* colorer, relever, teinter.

tinder ['tində] *n* amadou *m*.

tinge [tindʒ] *n* teinte *f*, nuance *f*, saveur *f*, point *f*; *vt* colorer, teinter, nuancer.

tingle ['tiŋgl] *n* fourmillement *m*, picotement *m*, tintement *m*; fourmiller, cuire, picoter, tinter.

tinker ['tiŋkə] *n* rétameur *m*; *vt* rétamer, retaper; *vi* toucher, bricoler, tripoter.

tinkle ['tiŋkl] *n* tintement *m*, drelin *m*; *vi* tinter; *vt* faire tinter.

tinsel ['tinsəl] *n* paillette *f*, clinquant *m*; *vt* pailleter.

tint [tint] *n* teinte *f*, nuance *f*; *vt* teinter, colorer.

tiny ['taini] *a* tout petit, minuscule.

tip [tip] *n* bout *m*, pointe *f*, pourboire *m*, tuyau *m*; *vt* donner un pourboire à, graisser la patte à, donner un tuyau à, faire basculer, faire pencher, renverser, effleurer.

tippet ['tipit] *n* pèlerine *f*.

tipple ['tipl] *vt* boire sec.

tipsy ['tipsi] *a* ivre, gris.

tiptoe ['tiptou] *n* pointe des pieds *f*.

tiptop ['tip'tɔp] *n* le nec plus ultra; *a* de premier ordre.

tirade [tai'reid] *n* tirade *f*, diatribe *f*.

tire ['taiə] *vt* fatiguer; *vi* se fatiguer, se lasser; *n* (US) pneu *m*.

tired ['taiəd] *a* fatigué, las, dégoûté, contrarié.

tireless ['taiəlis] *a* infatigable.

tiresome ['taiəsəm] *a* fatigant, ennuyeux.

tissue ['tisju:] *n* tissu *m*, étoffe *f*.

tissue-paper ['tisju:'peipə] *n* papier de soie *m*.

tit [tit] *n* mésange *f*.

titbit ['titbit] *n* morceau de choix *m*, friandise *f*.

tithe [taið] *n* dîme *f*.

titillate ['titileit] *vt* chatouiller, émoustiller, titiller.

titillation [ˌtiti'leiʃən] *n* titillation *f*, chatouillement *m*, émoustillement *m*.

title ['taitl] *n* titre *m*, droit *m*.

titled ['taitld] *a* titré.

titter ['titə] *n* rire étouffé *m*; *vi* rire sous cape.

tittle ['titl] *n* fétu *m*.

tittle-tattle ['titl.tætl] *n* cancans *m pl*, potins *m pl*; *vi* cancaner.

titular ['titjulə] *a* titulaire.

to [tu:] *prep* à, de, pour, jusqu'à, (en)vers, contre, à côté de, à l'égard de.

toad [toud] *n* crapaud *m*.

toady ['toudi] *n* parasite *m*, flagorneur *m*; **to —** to faire du plat à, flagorner.

toast [toust] *n* rôtie *f*, pain grillé *m*, toast *m*, canapé *m*; *vti* griller, rôtir; *vt* boire à la santé de, porter un toast à.

tobacco [tə'bækou] *n* tabac *m*; **— pouch** blague à tabac *f*.

tobacconist [tə'bækənist] *n* marchand de tabac *m*.

tobacconist's [tə'bækənists] *n* bureau (débit *m*) de tabac *m*.

today [tə'dei] *n ad* aujourd'hui *m*; **— week** d'aujourd'hui en huit.

toddle ['tɔdl] *vt* trottiner, flâner.

to-do [tə'du:] *n* grabuge *m*, scène *f*.

toe [tou] *n* doigt de pied *m*, orteil *m*.

toffee ['tɔfi] *n* caramel *m*.

tog [tɔg] **to — oneself up** se faire beau.

together [tə'geðə] *ad* ensemble, à la fois.

toil [tɔil] *n* peine *f*, tâche *f*; *vi* peiner.

toilet ['tɔilit] *n* toilette *f*.

toilsome ['tɔilsəm] *a* pénible, fatigant.

token ['toukən] *n* signe *m*, gage *m*, jeton *m*, bou *m*.

told [tould] *pt pp of* **tell**.

tolerable ['tɔlərəbl] *a* tolérable, passable.

tolerance ['tɔlərəns] *n* tolérance *f*.

tolerant ['tɔlərənt] *a* tolérant.

tolerate ['tɔləreit] *vt* tolérer.

toll [toul] *n* droit *m*, péage *m*, octroi *m*; *vi* tinter, sonner le glas.

tolling ['touliŋ] *n* tintement *m*, glas *m*.

tomato [tə'mɑ:tou] *n* tomate *f*.

tomb [tu:m] *n* tombe *f*, tombeau *m*, fosse *f*.

tombstone ['tu:mstoun] *n* pierre tombale *f*.

tomboy ['tɔmbɔi] *n* garçon manqué *m*, luronne *f*.

tomcat ['tɔm'kæt] *n* matou *m*.

tome [toum] *n* tome *m*.

tomfool ['tɔm'fu:l] *n* nigaud *m*.

tomfoolery ['tɔm'fu:ləri] *n* pasquinade *f*, niaiseries *f pl*.

tomtit ['tɔm'tit] *n* mésange *f*.

tomorrow [tə'mɔrou] *n* demain *m*; **— week** demain en huit.

ton [tʌn] *n* tonne *f*, (*ship*) tonneau *m*.

tone [toun] *n* son *m*, bruit *m*, ton *m*, accent *m*; *vt* aviver, accorder; **to — down** dégrader, adoucir; **to — up** tonifier, ravigoter, remonter.

tongs [tɔŋz] *n* pincettes *f pl*, tenailles *f pl*.

tongue [tʌŋ] *n* langue *f*, languette *f*.

tonic ['tɔnik] *an* tonique *m*; *n* fortifiant *m*.

tonight [tə'nait] *ad* ce soir *m*, cette nuit *f*.

tonnage ['tʌnidʒ] *n* tonnage *m*.

tonsil ['tɔnsl] *n* amygdale *f*.

tonsilitis [‚tɔnsi'laitis] *n* amygdalite *f*, angine *f*.

tonsure ['tɔnʃə] *n* tonsure *f*; *vt* tonsurer.

too [tuː] *ad* trop (de), aussi, et de plus.

took [tuk] *pt of* **take.**

tool [tuːl] *n* outil *m*, instrument *m*.

tooth [tuːθ] *n* dent *f*; **milk** — dent de lait; **molar** — molaire *f*; **wisdom** — dent de sagesse; **false** — fausse dent; —**ache** mal de dents *m*; —**brush** brosse à dents *f*; —**paste** pâte dentifrice *f*; —**pick** cure-dents *m*.

toothless ['tuːθlis] *a* édenté, sans dents.

toothsome ['tuːθsəm] *a* succulent, friand.

top [tɔp] *n* haut *m*, sommet *m*, premier *m*, tête *f*, toupie *f*, impériale *f*, dessus *m*, haut bout *m*, prise directe *f*, hune *f*; *a* supérieur, plus haut, dernier, du (de) dessus, du haut, premier; *vt* couvrir, étêter, atteindre, dominer, couronner, dé(sur)passer, surmonter, être à la tête de.

top coat ['tɔp'kout] *n* pardessus *m*.

top hat ['tɔp'hæt] *n* chapeau haut de forme *m*.

top-heavy ['tɔp'hevi] *a* trop lourd par le haut.

topaz ['toupæz] *n* topaze *f*.

toper ['toupə] *n* ivrogne *m*.

topic ['tɔpik] *n* sujet *m*, thème *m*, question *f*.

topical ['tɔpikəl] *a* d'actualité, local, topique.

topmost ['tɔpmoust] *a* le plus haut.

topple ['tɔpl] *vi* culbuter, s'écrouler, trébucher; **to** — **over** *vt* faire tomber, *vi* tomber.

topsy-turvy ['tɔpsi'təːvi] *a* sens dessus dessous, en désordre.

torch [tɔːtʃ] *n* torche *f*, flambeau *m*, lampe électrique *f*.

tore [tɔː] *pt of* **tear.**

torment ['tɔːmənt] *n* souffrance atroce *f*, supplice *m*, tourment *m*.

torment [tɔː'ment] *vt* tourmenter, torturer.

torn [tɔːn] *pp of* **tear.**

tornado [tɔː'neidou] *n* tornade *f*, ouragan *m*.

torpedo [tɔː'piːdou] *n* torpille *f*; —**boat** torpilleur *m*; —**tube** lance-torpilles *m*.

torpid ['tɔːpid] *a* engourdi, paresseux, inerte.

torrent ['tɔrənt] *n* torrent *m*.

torrential [tə'renʃəl] *a* torrentiel.

torrid ['tɔrid] *a* torride.

torridity [tə'riditi] *n* chaleur torride *f*.

tortoise ['tɔːtəs] *n* tortue *f*; —**shell** écaille *f*.

tortuous ['tɔːtjuəs] *a* tortueux, sinueux, enchevêtré.

torture ['tɔːtʃə] *n* torture *f*, supplice *m*; *vt* torturer, mettre au supplice.

toss [tɔs] *vt* lancer (en l'air), jeter, ballotter, secouer; *vi* s'agiter, être ballotté, se tourner et se retourner, jouer à pile ou face.

tossing ['tɔsiŋ] *n* ballottement *m*.

total ['toutl] *an* total *m*; *n* montant *m*; *vt* totaliser, additionner; *vi* se monter à.

totalizator ['toutəlai‚zeitə] *n* totalisateur *m*, pari-mutuel *m*.

totter ['tɔtə] *vi* chanceler, tituber.

touch [tʌtʃ] *n* toucher *m*, touche *f*, attouchement *m*, brin *m*, soupçon *m*, contact *m*, communication *f*, courant *m*; *vt* toucher, effleurer, égaler; *vi* se toucher.

touchiness ['tʌtʃinis] *n* susceptibilité *f*, irascibilité *f*.

touchstone ['tʌtʃstoun] *n* pierre de touche *f*.

touchy ['tʌtʃi] *a* chatouilleux, susceptible.

tough [tʌf] *a* dur, coriace, tenace, ardu, solide; *n* apache *m*; — **guy** dur à cuire *m*.

toughness ['tʌfnis] *n* dureté *f*, ténacité *f*, coriacité *f*.

tour [tuə] *n* tour *m*, tournée *f*, voyage *m*, excursion *f*; *vt* faire le tour de, parcourir; *vi* être en voyage, être en tournée.

touring ['tuəriŋ] *n* tourisme *f*.

tourist ['tuərist] *n* touriste *mf*.

tournament ['tuənəmənt] *n* tournoi *m*, concours *m*.

tousle ['tauzl] *vt* tirer, emmêler, ébouriffer.

tout [taut] *n* démarcheur *m*, racoleur *m*, pisteur *m*, espion *m*; **to** — **for** relancer (les clients), pister, solliciter.

tow [tou] *n* filasse *f*, étoupe *f*, remorque *f*; *vt* haler, remorquer, prendre à la remorque; —**path** chemin *m* de halage.

toward(s) [tə'wɔːd(z)] *prep* vers, envers, en vue de, pour, à l'égard de.

towel ['tauəl] *n* essuie-mains *m*, serviette (de toilette) *f*; *vt* essuyer avec une serviette; —**rail** porte-serviettes *m* *inv*.

tower ['tauə] *n* tour *f*; *vi* planer, dominer; **church** — clocher *m*; **water** — château *m* d'eau.

towing ['touiŋ] *n* halage *m*, remorquage *m*, remorque *f*.

town [taun] *n* ville *f*.

town council ['taun'kaunsl] *n* conseil municipal *m*.

town councillor ['taun'kaunsilə] *n* conseiller (-ère) municipal(e) *mf*.

town hall ['taun'hɔːl] *n* hôtel de ville *m*, mairie *f*.

town-planning ['taun'plæniŋ] *n* urbanisme *m*.

townsman ['taunzmən] n citadin m, concitoyen m.

toy [tɔi] n jouet m, joujou m, jeu m; vi jouer, s'amuser.

trace [treis] n trace f, vestige m, trait m; vt tracer, calquer, suivre, trouver trace de, suivre la piste de; **to — back** to faire remonter à.

tracer ['treisə] n obus traceur m, balle traceuse f.

track [træk] n trace f; piste f, sillage m, sens m, sentier m, (rails) voie f, chenille f; vt suivre à la piste, traquer.

trackage ['trækidʒ] n (US rails) réseau m.

tracing paper ['treisiŋ peipə] n papier-calque m.

tract [trækt] n étendue f, tract m.

tractable ['træktəbl] a traitable, maniable, arrangeant.

traction ['trækʃən] n traction f; a moteur.

tractor ['træktə] n tracteur m.

trade [treid] n commerce m, métier m, échange m, affaires f pl; vi être dans le commerce, faire le commerce (de in); **to — on** abuser de, exploiter.

trader ['treidə] n négociant(e) mf, commerçant(e) mf, navire marchand m.

trade-mark ['treidmɑːk] n marque de fabrique f.

tradesman ['treidzmən] n commerçant m.

trade-union [.treid'juːnjən] n syndicat m (ouvrier).

trade-unionism [.treid'juːnjənizəm] n syndicalisme m.

trade-unionist [.treid'juːnjənist] n syndicaliste mf.

trade wind ['treidwind] n (vent) alizé m.

trading ['treidiŋ] n commerce m; **— in** reprise f (en compte); **— station** n factorerie f.

tradition [trə'diʃən] n tradition f.

traditional [trə'diʃənl] a traditionnel.

traditionalist [trə'diʃnəlist] n traditionaliste mf.

traduce [trə'djuːs] vt calomnier, diffamer.

traducer [trə'djuːsə] n calomniateur, -trice.

traffic ['træfik] n trafic m, circulation f, traite f.

traffic indicator ['træfik'indikeitə] n indicateur m (de direction), flèche f.

traffic jam ['træfikdʒæm] n embouteillage m.

trafficker ['træfikə] n trafiquant m, trafiqueur m.

traffic-light ['træfiklait] n feu m, signal m.

tragedian [trə'dʒiːdjən] n poète mf, (acteur, -trice) tragique.

tragedy ['trædʒidi] n tragédie f, drame m.

tragic ['trædʒik] a tragique.

trail [treil] n traînée f, trace f, piste f, sillon m; vti traîner; vt remorquer, traquer, filer; **to — off** s'éteindre, se perdre.

trailer ['treilə] n baladeuse f, remorque f.

train [trein] n traîne f, suite f, file f, série f, convoi m, train m; **express — rapide** m; **slow — omnibus** m; **through — train** direct m; **corridor — train** à couloirs m; vt former, dresser, entraîner, élever, exercer, préparer, braquer; vi s'entraîner.

trainer ['treinə] n entraîneur m, dresseur m.

training ['treiniŋ] n éducation f, instruction f, formation f, entraînement m; **— college** école normale f; **— ship** vaisseau école m.

traitor ['treitə] n traître m.

trajectory ['trædʒiktəri] n trajectoire f.

tramcar ['træmkɑː] n tramway m, tram m.

trammel ['træməl] n entrave f, crémaillère f.

tramp [træmp] n bruit de pas m, marche f, chemineau m; vi marcher (lourdement), trimarder; vt parcourir à pied, faire à pied.

trample ['træmpl] vt fouler aux pieds, piétiner.

trampoline ['træmpouliːn] n matelas m élastique.

trance [trɑːns] n transe f, hypnose f, catalepsie f, extase f.

tranquil ['træŋkwil] a tranquille.

tranquilliser ['træŋkwilaizə] n tranquillisant, calmant.

tranquillity [træŋ'kwiliti] n tranquillité f, calme m.

transact [træn'zækt] vt passer, traiter.

transaction [træn'zækʃən] n conduite f; pl transactions f pl, rapports m pl.

transcend [træn'send] vt dépasser, exceller, surpasser.

transcribe [træns'kraib] vt transcrire.

transcription [træns'kripʃən] n transcription f.

transept ['trænsept] n transept m.

transfer [træns'fəː] vt transférer, déplacer, calquer.

transfer ['trænsfə] n transfert m, déplacement m, transport m.

transfigure [træns'figə] vt transfigurer.

transfix [træns'fiks] vt transpercer, (fig) pétrifier.

transform [træns'fɔːm] vt transformer, convertir.

transformer [træns'fɔːmə] n transformateur m.

transfuse [træns'fjuːz] vt transfuser.

transfusion [træns'fjuːʒən] n transfusion f.

transgress [træns'gres] vt transgresser, violer.

transgressor [træns'gresə] n transgresseur m, pécheur m.

tranship [træn'ʃip] vt transborder; vi changer de vaisseau.

transient ['trænziənt] a passager, éphémère.

transistor [træn'sistə] n transistor m.

transit ['trænsit] n traversée f, passage m, transit m.

transition [træn'siʒən] n transition f, passage m.

transitory ['trænsitəri] a transitoire, fugitif.

translatable [træns'leitəbl] a traduisible.

translate [træns'leit] vt traduire, interpréter, transférer.

translation [træns'leiʃən] n traduction f.

translator [træns'leitə] n traducteur m.

transmission [trænz'miʃən] n transmission f.

transmit [træns'mit] vt transmettre; —ter n émmetteur m, transmetteur.

transmute [trænz'mju:t] vt transmuer.

transparency [træns'pɛərənsi] n transparence f.

transparent [træns'pɛərənt] a transparent.

transpire [træns'paiə] vi transpirer.

transplant [træns'plɑ:nt] vt transplanter, repiquer, greffer.

transport ['trænspɔ:t] n transport m.

transport [træns'pɔ:t] vt transporter.

transposable [træns'pouzəbl] a transposable.

transpose [træns'pouz] vt transposer.

trap [træp] n trappe f, piège m, traquenard m, cabriolet m; vt attraper, tendre un piège à, prendre; vi trapper.

trapdoor ['træp.dɔ:] n trappe f.

trapper ['træpə] n trappeur m.

trappings ['træpiŋz] n harnachement m, falbalas m, atours m pl, apparat m.

trash [træʃ] n camelote f, fatras m, niaiserie f, (US) racaille f.

trashy ['træʃi] a de camelote, sans valeur.

trauma ['trɔ:mə] n traumatisme m.

travel ['trævl] n voyage(s) m pl; vi voyager, être en voyage, marcher, aller; vt parcourir.

travel agency ['trævl'eidʒinsi] n agence f de voyages.

traveller ['trævlə] n voyageur, -euse; **commercial** — commis voyageur m.

travelling ['trævliŋ] a de voyage, ambulant; n voyages m pl.

traverse ['trævəs] n traverse f, bordée f, plaque tournante f; vt traverser.

travesty ['trævisti] n travestissement m; vt travestir, parodier.

trawl [trɔ:l] n chalut m; vi pêcher au chalut.

trawler ['trɔ:lə] n chalutier m.

tray ['trei] n plateau m, (trunk) compartiment m, éventaire m.

treacherous ['tretʃərəs] a traître, infidèle.

treachery ['tretʃəri] n traîtrise f, perfidie f.

treacle ['tri:kl] n mélasse f.

tread [tred] n pas m, allure f, (of tyre) chape f; vi marcher; vt fouler, écraser.

treadle ['tredl] n pédale f.

treason ['tri:zn] n trahison f; **high** — lèse-majesté f.

treasure ['treʒə] n trésor m; vt garder précieusement, priser.

treasurer ['treʒərə] n trésorier, -ière, économe mf.

treasury ['treʒəri] n trésor m, trésorerie f.

treat [tri:t] n plaisir m, fête f, régal m; vti traiter; vt régaler, payer.

treatise ['tri:tiz] n traité m.

treatment ['tri:tmənt] n traitement m, cure f.

treaty ['tri:ti] n traité m, accord m.

treble ['trebl] n triple m, soprano m; a triple, trois fois.

tree [tri:] n arbre m.

trefoil ['trefoil] n trèfle m.

trellis ['trelis] n treillis m, treillage m.

tremble ['trembl] n tremblement m; vi trembler.

tremendous [tri'mendəs] a énorme, formidable.

tremor ['tremə] n tremblement m, frisson m, secousse f.

tremulous ['tremjuləs] a tremblant, craintif, tremblotant.

trench [trentʃ] n tranchée f, fossé m; vt creuser.

trencher ['trentʃə] n trenchoir m.

trend [trend] n direction f, tendance f; vi se diriger, tendre.

trepan [tri'pæn] n trépan m; vt trépaner.

trepanning [tri'pæniŋ] n trépanation f.

trepidation [.trepi'deiʃən] n tremblement m, trépidation f.

trespass ['trespəs] n délit m, péché m, intrusion f, offense f; vi entrer sans permission; **to — upon** empiéter sur, abuser de, offenser.

trespasser ['trespəsə] n délinquant m, intrus m, transgresseur m.

tress [tres] n tresse f, natte f; vt natter, tresser.

trestle ['tresl] n tréteau m, chevalet m.

trial ['traiəl] n épreuve f, essai m, procès m, jugement m, ennui m.

triangle ['traiæŋgl] n triangle m.

triangular [trai'æŋgjulə] a triangulaire.

tribal ['traibəl] a de la tribu, tribal.

tribe [traib] n tribu f.

tribulation [.tribju'leiʃən] n tribulation f, affliction f.

tribunal [trai'bju:nl] n tribunal m, cour f.

tribune ['tribjuːn] *n* tribun *m*, tribune *f*.

tributary ['tribjutəri] *an* tributaire *m*; *n* affluent *m*.

tribute ['tribjuːt] *n* tribut *m*, hommage *m*.

trick [trik] *n* tour *m*, farce *f*, ruse *f*, truc *m*, levée *f*; *vt* tromper, (dé)jouer.

trickery ['trikəri] *n* tromperie *f*, fourberie *f*.

trickle ['trikl] *vi* couler goutte à goutte, dégouliner; *n* filet *m*.

trickster ['trikstə] *n* escroc *m*, fourbe *m*.

tricky ['triki] *a* rusé, épineux.

tricycle ['traisikl] *n* tricycle *m*.

trifle ['traifl] *n* bagatelle *f*, (*cook*) diplomate *m*; *vi* badiner, jouer.

trifling ['traifliŋ] *a* insignifiant, futile, minime.

trigger ['trigə] *n* détente *f*, gâchette *f*, manette *f*.

trill [tril] *n* trille *m*, chant perlé *m*; *vi* vibrer, trembler; *vt* rouler, triller.

trim [trim] *n* ordre *m*, état *m*; *a* net, soigné, propret, en ordre; *vt* arranger, tailler, rafraîchir, soigner, orner, arrimer.

trimming ['trimiŋ] *n* mise en état *f*, arrangement *m*, taille *f*; *pl* fournitures *f pl*, garniture *f*, passementerie *f*, rognures *f pl*.

trinity ['triniti] *n* trinité *f*.

trinket ['triŋkit] *n* babiole *f*, bibelot *m*.

trip [trip] *n* excursion *f*, faux-pas *m*, croc-en-jambe *m*; *vi* marcher légèrement, trébucher, déraper, se tromper; *vt* pincer, faire trébucher, faucher les jambes à.

tripe [traip] *n* tripes *f pl*, bêtises *f pl*.

triple ['tripl] *a* triple; *vti* tripler.

triplet ['triplit] *n* trio *m*, tercet *m*, l'un de trois jumeaux.

triplicate ['triplikit] *a* triple, triplé; **in —** en trois exemplaires; *vt* tripler.

tripod ['traipəd] *n* trépied *m*.

trite [trait] *a* banal, usé, rebattu.

triteness ['traitnis] *n* banalité *f*.

triumph ['traiəmf] *n* triomphe *m*, miracle *m*; *vi* triompher, exulter.

triumphal [trai'ʌmfəl] *a* triomphal, de triomphe.

triumphant [trai'ʌmfənt] *a* triomphant, de triomphe.

trivial ['triviəl] *a* trivial, banal, futile.

triviality [,trivi'æliti] *n* trivialité *f*, futilité *f*, insignifiance *f*.

trod, trodden [trɔd, 'trɔdn] *pp of* **tread**.

trolley ['trɔli] *n* chariot *m*, diable *m*, serveuse *f*, trolley *m*.

trombone [trɔm'boun] *n* trombone *m*.

troop [truːp] *n* troupe(s) *f* (*pl*), bande *f*; *vi* s'attrouper, marcher en troupe.

trooper ['truːpə] *n* cavalier *m*.

troop-ship ['truːpʃip] *n* transport *m*.

trophy ['troufi] *n* trophée *m*.

tropic ['trɔpik] *an* tropique *m*; *a* tropical.

tropical ['trɔpikəl] *a* tropical.

trot [trɔt] *n* trot *m*; *vi* trotter; *vt* faire trotter.

trotter ['trɔtə] *n* (bon) trotteur *m*.

trouble ['trʌbl] *n* difficulté *f*, trouble *m*, ennui *m*, peine *f*, affection *f*, panne *f*, conflits *m pl*, discorde *f*; *vt* inquiéter, affliger, soucier, déranger, embarrasser, troubler, prier; *vi* s'inquiéter, se déranger, se donner la peine (de **to**).

troublemaker ['trʌbl,meikə] *n* trublion *m*.

troublesome ['trʌblsəm] *a* ennuyeux, gênant, fatigant, énervant.

trough [trɔf] *n* auge *f*, cuve *f*, pétrin *m*, creux *m*.

trounce [trauns] *vt* rouer de coups, rosser, battre à plates coutures, écraser.

trousers ['trauzəz] *n* pantalon *m*.

trout [traut] *n* truite *f*.

trowel ['trauəl] *n* truelle *f*, déplantoir *m*.

truant ['truənt] *a* fainéant *m*, vagabond(e) *mf*; **to play —** faire l'école buissonnière.

truce [truːs] *n* trève *f*.

truck [trʌk] *n* benne *f*, (US) camion *m*, chariot *m*, troc *m*, camelote *f*.

trudge [trʌdʒ] *vi* traîner la jambe, clopiner.

true [truː] *a* vrai, loyal, sincère.

truffle ['trʌfl] *n* truffe *f*.

truly ['truːli] *ad* à vrai dire, sincèrement.

trump [trʌmp] *n* atout *m*, trompette *f*; *vt* couper; **to — up** inventer.

trumpet ['trʌmpit] *n* trompette *f*, cornet acoustique *m*; *vi* trompeter, barir; *vt* proclamer.

trumpeter ['trʌmpitə] *n* trompette *m*, trompettiste *m*.

truncate ['trʌŋkeit] *vt* tronquer.

truncheon ['trʌntʃən] *n* matraque *f*, bâton *m*.

trundle ['trʌndl] *n* roulette *f*; *vti* rouler; *vt* pousser, trimbaler.

trunk [trʌŋk] *n* tronc *m*, malle *f*, trompe *f*; **— call** appel interurbain *m*; **— line** grande ligne *f*; **— road** grand-route *f*, artère *f*.

truss [trʌs] *n* trousse *f*, botte *f*, cintre *m*, bandage *m*; *vt* botteler, renforcer, soutenir, trousser, ligoter.

trust [trʌst] *n* confiance *f*, espoir *m*, parole *f*, dépôt *m*, charge *f*, trust *m*; *vt* confier, en croire, se fier à, faire crédit à; *vi* espérer, mettre son espoir (en **in**).

trustee [trʌs'tiː] *n* administrateur *m*, curateur, -trice.

trusteeship [trʌs'tiːʃip] *n* administration *f*, curatelle *f*.

trustful ['trʌstful] *a* confiant.

trustworthiness ['trʌst,wəːðinis] *n* loyauté *f*, exactitude *f*.

trustworthy ['trʌst‚wəːði] *a* sûr, fidèle, digne de foi.

trusty ['trʌsti] *a* sûr, loyal.

truth [truːθ] *n* vérité *f*; **the — is, to tell the —** à vrai dire.

truthful ['truːθful] *a* véridique, fidèle.

truthfulness ['truːθfulnis] *n* véracité *f*, fidélité *f*.

try [trai] *vt* essayer, mettre à l'épreuve, juger; *n* tentative *f*, essai *m*, coup *m*.

trying ['traiiŋ] *a* fatigant, pénible.

try-on ['trai‚ɔn] *n* bluff *m*.

tsetse fly ['tsetsiflai] *n* tsé-tsé *f*.

tub [tʌb] *n* cuve *f*, baquet *m*, caisse *f*, tub *m*, bain *m*.

tube [tjuːb] *n* tube *m*, tuyau *m*, métro *m*, chambre à air *f*.

tubercle ['tjuːbəːkl] *n* tubercule *m*.

tuberculosis [tjuː‚bəːkju'lousis] *n* tuberculose *f*.

tuck [tʌk] *n* pli *m*, rempli *m*, pâtisserie *f*; *vt* (re)plier, remplier, plisser, border; **to — in** *vi* bouffer; *vt* border, retrousser.

Tuesday ['tjuːzdi] *n* mardi *m*.

tuft [tʌft] *n* touffe *f*, houpe *f*, huppe *f*, flocon *m*, mèche *f*.

tug [tʌg] *n* effort *m*, secousse *f*, remorqueur *m*; *vti* tirer fort; *vt* remorquer, tirer; **to — at** tirer sur.

tuition [tju'iʃən] *n* leçons *f pl*, instruction *f*.

tulip ['tjuːlip] *n* tulipe *f*.

tumble ['tʌmbl] *n* chute *f*, culbute *f*, désordre *m*; *vi* dégringoler, tomber, faire des culbutes; *vt* déranger, bouleverser, ébouriffer.

tumbledown ['tʌmbldaun] *a* délabré, croulant.

tumbler ['tʌmblə] *n* acrobate *mf*, gobelet *m*.

tumbrel ['tʌmbrəl] *n* caisson *m*, tombereau *m*.

tumour ['tjuːmə] *n* tumeur *f*.

tumult ['tjuːmʌlt] *n* tumulte *m*, agitation *f*, émoi *m*.

tun [tʌn] *n* tonneau *m*.

tune [tjuːn] *n* air *m*, ton *m*, note *f*, accord *m*; *vt* accorder, adapter; **to — in** régler.

tuneful ['tjuːnful] *a* harmonieux.

tuneless ['tjuːnlis] *a* discordant.

tuner ['tjuːnə] *n* accordeur *m*.

tuning-fork ['tjuːniŋfɔːk] *n* diapason *m*.

tunic ['tjuːnik] *n* tunique *f*.

tunnel ['tʌnl] *n* tunnel *m*.

tunny ['tʌni] *n* thon *m*.

turbid ['təːbid] *a* trouble.

turbine ['təːbin] *n* turbine *f*.

turbot ['təːbət] *n* turbot *m*.

turbulent ['təːbjulənt] *a* turbulent.

tureen [tə'riːn] *n* soupière *f*.

turf [təːf] *n* gazon *m*, motte *f*, turf *m*.

turgid ['təːdʒid] *a* boursouflé, enflé, ampoulé.

Turk [təːk] *n* Turc, Turque.

Turkey ['təːki] *n* Turquie *f*.

turkey ['təːki] *n* dinde *f*; **—cock** dindon *m*.

Turkish ['təːkiʃ] *an* turc *m*.

turmoil ['təːmɔil] *n* effervescence *f*, remous *m*.

turn [təːn] *n* tour *m*, tournant *m*, virage *m*, tournure *f*, numéro *m*, crise *f*, service *m*; **in —** à tour de rôle; **to a —** à point; *vti* tourner; *vt* retourner, changer, faire tourner, diriger; *vi* prendre, se tourner, se transformer, recourir (à **to**); **to — down** baisser, refuser, rabattre; **to — off** fermer, couper, renvoyer; **to — on** *vt* ouvrir, donner; *vi* dépendre de; **to — out** *vt* mettre dehors, à la porte, faire sortir, éteindre, retourner, produire; *vi* tourner, arriver, s'arranger; **to — up** *vt* relever, retrousser, déterrer, retourner, remonter; *vi* se présenter, se retrousser.

turncoat ['təːnkout] *n* renégat *m*, girouette *f*.

turner ['təːnə] *n* tourneur *m*.

turning ['təːniŋ] *n* tournant *m*.

turning-lathe ['təːniŋleið] *a* tour *m*.

turning point ['təːniŋpɔint] *n* tournant *m*.

turnip ['təːnip] *n* navet *m*.

turn-out ['təːn‚aut] *n* assistance *f*, grève *f*, équipage *m*, tenue *f*, production *f*.

turnover ['təːn‚ouvə] *n* chiffre d'affaires *m*, (cook) chausson *m*.

turnpike ['təːnpaik] *n* barrière *f*.

turnspit ['təːnspit] *n* tournebroche *m*.

turnstile ['təːnstail] *n* tourniquet *m*.

turntable ['təːn‚teibl] *n* plaque tournante *f*.

turpentine ['təːpəntain] *n* térébenthine *f*.

turret ['tʌrit] *n* tourelle *f*.

turtle ['təːtl] *n* tortue *f*.

turtle-dove ['təːtldʌv] *n* tourterelle *f*.

tusk [tʌsk] *n* défense *f*.

tussle ['tʌsl] *n* lutte *f*; *vi* se battre, s'escrimer.

tutelage ['tjuːtilidʒ] *n* tutelle *f*.

tutor ['tjuːtə] *n* précepteur *m*, directeur d'études *m*, méthode *f*.

twaddle ['twɔdl] *n* verbiage *m*, balivernes *f pl*; *vi* bavasser, radoter.

twain [twein] *an* (old) deux.

twang [twæŋ] *n* grincement *m*, nasillement *m*; *vi* grincer, nasiller, vibrer; *vt* pincer.

tweed [twiːd] *n* tweed *m*.

tweezers ['twiːzəz] *n* pince *f*.

twelfth [twelfθ] *an* douzième *mf*; *a* douze.

twelve [twelv] *an* douze *m*.

twentieth ['twentiiθ] *an* vingtième *mf*; *a* vingt.

twenty ['twenti] *an* vingt *m*.

twice [twais] *ad* deux fois.

twig [twig] *n* branchette *f*, brindille *f*.

twilight ['twailait] *n* crépuscule *m*, petit jour *m*.

twin [twin] n jumeau m, jumelle f; a accouplé, jumeau, jumelé.

twine [twain] n ficelle f; vt tordre, entrelacer, enrouler.

twinge [twind3] n élancement m, lancinement m.

twinkle ['twinkl] n clignement m, scintillement m, lueur f; vi cligner, scintiller.

twinkling ['twinklin] n clin d'œil m, scintillement m.

twirl [twə:l] n tournoiement m, fioriture f, pirouette f; vi tournoyer, tourbillonner pirouetter; vt (moustache) tortiller.

twist [twist] n cordonnet m, torsion f, papillote f, rouleau m, torsade f, tour m; vt tortiller, tordre, entrelacer, se fouler, fausser; vi se tordre, tourner, vriller.

twit [twit] vt reprocher, railler.

twitch [twitʃ] n secousse f, tic m, contraction f, crispation f; vt crisper, tirer, contracter; vi se crisper, se contracter.

twitter ['twitə] n gazouillement m; vi gazouiller.

two [tu:] an deux.

two-edged ['tu:'ed3d] a à double tranchant.

twofold ['tu:fould] a double; ad deux fois.

tympan ['timpæn] n tympan m.

type [taip] n type m, modèle m, caractère d'imprimerie m; vt taper à la machine, dactylographier.

typescript ['taipskript] n texte m dactylographié.

typewriter ''taip,raitə] n machine à écrire f.

typhoid ['taifɔid] n typhoïde f.

typhus ['taifəs] n typhus m.

typhoon [tai'fu:n] n typhon m.

typical ['tipikəl] a caractéristique, typique.

typify ['tipifai] vt incarner, représenter, être caractéristique de.

typist ['taipist] n dactylo(graphe) mf.

typographer [tai'pɔgrəfə] n typographe m.

typography [tai'pɔgrəfi] n typographie f.

tyrannical [ti'rænikəl] a tyrannique.

tyrannize ['tirənaiz] vt tyranniser.

tyranny ['tirəni] n tyrannie f.

tyrant ['taiərənt] n tyran m.

tyre ['taiə] n pneu(matique) m, bandage m; — lever n démonte-pneus m inv.

U

U-boat ['ju:bout] n sous-marin m allemand.

udder ['ʌdə] n pis m, mamelle f, tétine f.

ugliness ['ʌglinis] n laideur f.

ugly ['ʌgli] a laid.

ulcer ['ʌlsə] n ulcère m.

ulcerate ['ʌlsəreit] vt ulcérer; vi s'ulcérer.

ulterior [ʌl'tiəriə] a ultérieur, caché.

ultimate ['ʌltimit] a dernier, définitif, fondamental.

ultimately ['ʌltimitli] ad en fin de compte.

ultimatum [ˌʌlti'meitəm] n ultimatum m.

ultimo ['ʌltimou] a du mois dernier.

umbrage ['ʌmbridʒ] n ombrage m.

umbrella [ʌm'brelə] n parapluie m.

umbrella-stand [ʌm'brelastænd] n porte-parapluies m inv.

umpire ['ʌmpaiə] n arbitre m; vt arbitrer.

umpiring ['ʌmpaiəriŋ] n arbitrage m.

unabated ['ʌnə'beitid] a dans toute sa force, non diminué.

unable ['ʌn'eibl] a incapable, hors d'état (de to).

unabridged ['ʌnə'bridʒd] a intégral, non abrégé.

unaccomplished ['ʌnə'kʌmpliʃd] a inachevé, inaccompli.

unaccountable ['ʌnə'kauntəbl] a inexplicable.

unaccustomed ['ʌnə'kʌstəmd] a inaccoutumé.

unacknowledged ['ʌnək'nɔlidʒd] a sans réponse, non reconnu.

unacquainted ['ʌnə'kweintid] a to be — with ne pas connaître.

unadorned ['ʌnə'dɔ:nd] a simple, nu, pur.

unadulterated [ˌʌnə'dʌltəreitid] a non frelaté, pur.

unadvisable ['ʌnəd'vaizəbl] a malavisé, imprudent.

unaffected ['ʌnə'fektid] a naturel sincère, insensible.

unaffectedly [ˌʌnə'fektidli] ad sans affectation.

unalleviated [ˌʌnə'li:vieitid] a sans soulagement.

unalloyed ['ʌnə'lɔid] a pur, sans alliage (mélange).

unambiguous ['ʌnæm'bigjuəs] a catégorique, clair.

unambitious [ˌʌnæm'biʃəs] a sans ambition.

unanimous [ju'næniməs] n unanime.

unanimity [ˌju:nə'nimiti] n unanimité f.

unanswerable [ʌn'ɑ:nsərəbl] a sans réplique.

unanswered ['ʌn'ɑ:nsəd] a sans réponse, irréfuté.

unarmed ['ʌn'ɑ:md] a sans arme.

unassailable [ˌʌnə'seiləbl] a inattaquable, indiscutable.

unassisted ['ʌnə'sistid] a sans aide, tout seul.

unassuming ['ʌnə'sju:miŋ] a sans prétention(s), modeste.

unattainable ['ʌnə'teinəbl] a hors d'atteinte, inaccessible.

unattractive [ˌʌnə'træktiv] a peu attrayant.

unavailable [ˌʌnə'veiləbl] a inaccessible, impossible à obtenir, indisponible.

unavailing ['ʌnə'veiliŋ] *a* inutile, vain.

unavoidable [.ʌnə'vɔidəbl] *a* inévitable.

unaware ['ʌnə'wɛə] *a* to be — of ignorer, ne pas avoir conscience de.

unawares ['ʌnə'wɛəz] *ad* à l'improviste, au dépourvu.

unbalanced ['ʌn'bælənst] *a* déséquilibré, instable.

unbearable [ʌn'bɛərəbl] *a* intolérable.

unbecoming [.ʌnbi'kʌmiŋ] *a* malséant.

unbeknown ['ʌnbi'noun] *ad* — to à l'insu de.

unbelief ['ʌnbi'li:f] *n* incrédulité *f*.

unbelievable [.ʌnbi'li:vəbl] *a* incroyable.

unbeliever ['ʌnbi'li:və] *n* incrédule *mf*, incroyant(e) *mf*.

unbend ['ʌn'bend] *vt* détendre; *vi* se dérider, se détendre.

unbending ['ʌn'bendiŋ] *a* raide, inflexible.

unbiased ['ʌn'baiəst] *a* impartial, objectif, sans parti pris.

unbind ['ʌn'baind] *vt* délier, dénouer.

unbleached ['ʌn'bli:tʃt] *a* non blanchi, écru.

unblemished [ʌn'blemiʃt] *a* sans tache, immaculé.

unblended [ʌn'blendid] *a* pur.

unblushing [ʌn'blʌʃiŋ] *a* effronté, éhonté.

unbolt ['ʌn'boult] *vt* déverrouiller.

unborn ['ʌn'bɔːn] *a* encore à naître, futur.

unbosom [ʌn'buzəm] *vt* révéler; to — oneself ouvrir son cœur.

unbound ['ʌn'baund] *a* délié, broché.

unbounded [ʌn'baundid] *a* illimité, sans bornes.

unbreakable [ʌn'breikəbl] *n* incassable.

unbreathable ['ʌn'bri:ðəbl] *a* irrespirable.

unbroken ['ʌn'broukən] *a* intact, ininterrompu, continu.

unburden [ʌn'bəːdn] *vt* décharger, alléger, épancher.

unburied ['ʌn'berid] *a* sans sépulture.

unbusinesslike [ʌn'biznislaik] *a* peu pratique, sans méthode.

unbutton ['ʌn'bʌtn] *vt* déboutonner.

uncalled-for [ʌn'kɔːldfɔː] *a* non désiré, indiscret, déplacé, immérité.

uncanny [ʌn'kæni] *a* fantastique, inquiétant, mystérieux.

uncared-for ['ʌn'kɛədfɔː] *a* négligé.

uncaring [ʌn'kɛəriŋ] *a* insouciant.

unceasing [ʌn'si:siŋ] *a* incessant, soutenu.

unceasingly [ʌn'si:siŋli] *ad* sans cesse.

unceremoniously ['ʌn.seri'mouniəs-li] *ad* sans cérémonie, sans gêne, sans façons.

uncertain [ʌn'səːtn] *a* incertain, inégal, douteux.

unchallenged ['ʌn'tʃælindʒd] *a* sans provocation, indisputé.

unchangeable [ʌn'tʃeindʒəbl] *a* immuable.

uncharitable [ʌn'tʃæritəbl] *a* peu charitable.

unchaste ['ʌn'tʃeist] *a* impudique.

unchecked ['ʌn'tʃekt] *a* sans opposition, non maîtrisé.

uncivil ['ʌn'sivl] *a* impoli.

unclasp ['ʌn'klɑːsp] *vt* dégrafer, desserrer.

uncle ['ʌnkl] *n* oncle *m*; (*pawnbroker*) tante *f*.

unclean ['ʌn'kli:n] *a* malpropre, impur.

unclothe ['ʌn'klouð] *vt* dévêtir.

unclouded ['ʌn'klaudid] *a* sans nuage, limpide, pur.

uncomfortable [ʌn'kʌmfətəbl] *a* mal à l'aise, incommode, peu confortable.

uncommon [ʌn'kɔmən] *a* peu commun, rare, singulier.

uncommonly [ʌn'kɔmənli] *ad* singulièrement.

uncomplimentary ['ʌn.kɔmpli'mentəri] *a* peu flatteur.

uncompromising [ʌn'kɔmprəmaiziŋ] *a* intransigeant, intraitable.

unconcern ['ʌnkən'səːn] *n* indifférence *f*, détachement *m*.

unconcerned ['ʌnkən'səːnd] *a* comme étranger, indifférent, dégagé.

unconcernedly ['ʌnkən'səːnidli] *ad* d'un air détaché.

unconditional ['ʌnkən'diʃnəl] *a* sans conditions, absolu.

uncongenial ['ʌnkən'dʒiːnjəl] *a* antipathique, ingrat.

unconquerable [ʌn'kɔŋkərəbl] *a* invincible.

unconquered ['ʌn'kɔŋkəd] *a* invaincu.

unconscionable [ʌn'kɔnʃnəbl] *a* inconcevable, sans conscience.

unconscious [ʌn'kɔnʃəs] *a* inconscient, sans connaissance.

unconsciousness [ʌn'kɔnʃəsnis] *n* inconscience *f*, évanouissement *m*.

unconstitutional ['ʌn.kɔnsti'tjuːʃənl] *n* inconstitutionnel.

uncontrollable [.ʌnkən'trouləbl] *a* incontrôlable, irrésistible, ingouvernable.

unconventional ['ʌnkən'venʃənl] *a* original.

unconvinced ['ʌnkən'vinst] *a* sceptique.

uncooked ['ʌn'kukt] *a* mal cuit, cru.

uncork ['ʌn'kɔːk] *vt* déboucher.

uncouth [ʌn'kuːθ] *a* rude, grossier, gauche, négligé.

uncover [ʌn'kʌvə] *vt* découvrir, dévoiler.

uncrossed ['ʌn'krɔst] *a* non barré.

unction ['ʌŋkʃən] n onction f.
unctuous ['ʌŋktjuəs] a onctueux, huileux.
undaunted [ʌn'dɔ:ntid] a indompté, intrépide.
undeceive ['ʌndi'si:v] vt détromper.
undecided ['ʌndi'saidid] a indécis, irrésolu, mal défini.
undecipherable ['ʌndi'saifərəbl] a indéchiffrable.
undefiled ['ʌndi'faild] a sans tache, pur.
undeniable [,ʌndi'naiəbl] a indéniable, incontestable.
under ['ʌndə] prep sous, au-dessous de; a de dessous, inférieur, subalterne.
underclothes ['ʌndəklouðz] n pl sous-vêtements m pl, linge de corps m.
underdeveloped ['ʌndədi'veləpt] a sous-développé.
underdog ['ʌndədɔg] n (fam) lampiste m, faible m.
underdone ['ʌndə'dʌn] a saignant.
underfed ['ʌndə'fed] a sous-alimenté.
undergo [,ʌndə'gou] vt souffrir, subir.
undergraduate [,ʌndə'grædjuit] n étudiant(e) mf.
underground ['ʌndəgraund] n métro m; a souterrain, clandestin; ad sous terre.
undergrowth ['ʌndəgrouθ] n taillis m, fourré m.
underhand ['ʌndəhænd] a souterrain, sournois, clandestin; ad par dessous main, en dessous.
underline ['ʌndəlain] vt souligner.
underling ['ʌndəliŋ] n sous-ordre m, barbin m, subordonné(e) mf.
undermine [,ʌndə'main] vt miner, saper.
underneath [,ʌndə'ni:θ] prep au-dessous de, sous; ad dessous, par-dessous, au-dessous; a de dessous.
underrate [,ʌndə'reit] vt sous-estimer.
under-secretary ['ʌndə'sekrətəri] n sous-secrétaire mf.
undersell ['ʌndə'sel] vt vendre moins cher que.
undershirt ['ʌndəʃə:t] n (US) tricot m, gilet m (de corps).
undersigned [,ʌndə'saind] a soussigné.
understand [,ʌndə'stænd] vt comprendre, s'entendre à, sous-entendre.
understandable [,ʌndə'stændəbl] a intelligible, compréhensible.
understanding [,ʌndə'stændiŋ] n entendement m, intelligence f, compréhension f.
understatement ['ʌndə'steitmənt] n atténuation f, amoindrissement m.
understood [,ʌndə'stud] pp of **understand** compris.
understudy ['ʌndə'stʌdi] n doublure f; vt doubler.

undertake [,ʌndə'teik] vt entreprendre, s'engager à, se charger de.
undertaker ['ʌndə,teikə] n entrepreneur de pompes funèbres m.
undertaking [,ʌndə'teikiŋ] n entreprise f, engagement m.
undertook [,ʌndə'tuk] pp of **undertake**.
undertow ['ʌndətou] n ressac m, barre f.
underwear ['ʌndəweə] n sous-vêtements m pl, dessous m pl, lingerie f.
underwood ['ʌndəwud] n sous-bois m.
underworld ['ʌndəwə:ld] n pègre f, bas fonds m pl, enfers m pl.
underwrite ['ʌndərait] vt souscrire, assurer.
underwriter ['ʌndə,raitə] n assureur maritime m.
undeserved ['ʌndi'zə:vd] a immérité.
undeserving ['ʌndi'zə:viŋ] a indigne.
undesignedly ['ʌndi'zainidli] ad sans intention, innocemment.
undesirable ['ʌndi'zaiərəbl] a indésirable.
undigested ['ʌndi'dʒestid] a mal digéré, indigeste.
undignified [ʌn'dignifaid] a sans dignité.
undiluted ['ʌndai'lju:tid] a pur, non dilué.
undimmed [ʌn'dimd] a non voilé, brillant.
undiscernible ['ʌndi'sə:nəbl] a indiscernable, imperceptible.
undiscerning ['ʌndi'sə:niŋ] a sans discernement.
undischarged ['ʌndis'tʃɑ:dʒd] a non libéré, inacquitté, inaccompli.
undisguised ['ʌndis'gaizd] a sans déguisement, évident, franc.
undismayed ['ʌndis'meid] a imperturbable.
undisputed ['ʌndis'pju:tid] a incontesté.
undistinguished ['ʌndis'tiŋgwiʃt] a commun, médiocre, banal.
undisturbed ['ʌndis'tə:bd] a non dérangé, non troublé, paisible.
undivided ['ʌndi'vaidid] a entier, indivisé, unanime.
undo ['ʌn'du:] vt défaire, dénouer, dégrafer, ruiner, annuler.
undoing ['ʌn'duiŋ] n perte f, ruine f.
undone ['ʌn'dʌn] a défait, inachevé, perdu.
undoubted [ʌn'dautid] a certain, incontestable.
undoubtedly [ʌn'dautidli] ad sans aucun doute.
undreamt [ʌn'dremt] a dont on n'osait rêver, merveilleux.
undress ['ʌn'dres] n petite tenue f, négligé m; vt déshabiller; vi se déshabiller.
undrinkable ['ʌn'driŋkəbl] a imbuvable, non potable.
undue ['ʌn'dju:] a excessif, indu.
undulate ['ʌndjuleit] vti onduler.

undulating ['ʌndjuleitiŋ] *a* vallonné, ondoyant, onduleux.

unduly ['ʌn'djuːli] *ad* indûment, à l'excès.

undying [ʌn'daiiŋ] *a* immortel, impérissable.

unearned ['ʌn'əːnd] *a* — income plus-value *f*.

unearth ['ʌn'əːθ] *vt* déterrer, exhumer.

unearthly [ʌn'əːθli] *a* qui n'est pas de ce monde, surnaturel.

uneasiness [ʌn'iːzinis] *a* inquiétude *f*, gêne *f*.

uneasy [ʌn'iːzi] *a* mal à l'aise, inquiet, gêné.

uneatable ['ʌn'iːtəbl] *a* immangeable.

uneducated ['ʌn'edjukeitid] *a* inculte, sans éducation.

unemployable ['ʌnim'plɔiəbl] *a* bon à rien.

unemployed ['ʌnim'plɔid] *a* désœuvré, sans travail; the — les chômeurs *m pl*.

unemployment ['ʌnim'plɔimənt] *n* chômage *m*.

unending [ʌn'endiŋ] *a* interminable, sans fin.

unequal ['ʌn'iːkwəl] *a* inégal; to be — to ne pas être à la hauteur de, ne pas être de force à.

unequalled ['ʌn'iːkwəld] *a* sans égal, inégalé.

unessential ['ʌni'senʃəl] *a* secondaire.

uneven ['ʌn'iːvən] *a* inégal, irrégulier, rugueux.

uneventful ['ʌni'ventful] *a* sans incident, terne, monotone.

unexceptionable [‚ʌnik'sepʃnəbl] *a* irréprochable.

unexpected ['ʌniks'pektid] *a* inattendu, inespéré, imprévu.

unexpectedly [‚ʌniks'pektidli] *ad* à l'improviste.

unexpectedness ['ʌniks'pektidnis] *n* soudaineté *f*, caractère imprévu *m*.

unexplored ['ʌniks'plɔːd] *a* inexploré.

unfailing [ʌn'feiliŋ] *a* immanquable, impeccable, inaltérable.

unfair ['ʌn'fɛə] *a* injuste, déloyal.

unfairness ['ʌn'fɛənis] *n* injustice *f*, déloyauté *f*, mauvaise foi *f*.

unfaithful ['ʌn'feiθful] *a* infidèle; — ness *n* infidélité.

unfamiliar ['ʌnfə'miliə] *a* peu familier, étranger.

unfashionable ['ʌn'fæʃnəbl] *a* pas à la mode, démodé.

unfasten ['ʌn'faːsn] *vt* détacher, dégrafer, déverrouiller.

unfathomable [ʌn'fæðəməbl] *a* insondable, impénétrable.

unfavourable ['ʌn'feivərəbl] *a* défavorable, impropice, désavantageux.

unfeasible ['ʌn'fiːzəbl] *a* infaisable, irréalisable.

unfeeling [ʌn'fiːliŋ] *a* insensible, froid, sec.

unfettered ['ʌn'fetəd] *a* sans entraves, libre.

unfinished ['ʌn'finiʃt] *a* inachevé.

unfit ['ʌn'fit] *a* inapte, en mauvaise santé.

unflagging [ʌn'flægiŋ] *a* sans défaillance, soutenu.

unfledged ['ʌn'fledʒd] *a* sans plumes, novice.

unflinchingly [ʌn'flintʃiŋli] *ad* sans fléchir, de pied ferme.

unfold ['ʌn'fould] *vt* déplier, dérouler, révéler; *vi* se dérouler, se déployer.

unforeseeable ['ʌnfɔː'siːəbl] *a* imprévisible.

unforeseen ['ʌnfɔː'siːn] *a* imprévu.

unforgettable ['ʌnfə'getəbl] *a* inoubliable.

unforgivable ['ʌnfə'givəbl] *a* impardonnable.

unforgiving ['ʌnfə'giviŋ] *a* implacable.

unforgotten ['ʌnfə'gɔtn] *a* inoublié.

unfortunate [ʌn'fɔːtʃnit] *a* malheureux.

unfortunately [ʌn'fɔːtʃnitli] *ad* malheureusement.

unfounded ['ʌn'faundid] *a* sans fondement.

unfrequented ['ʌnfri'kwentid] *a* solitaire, écarté.

unfriendly ['ʌn'frendli] *a* inamical, hostile.

unfruitful ['ʌn'fruːtful] *a* infructueux, stérile.

unfulfilled ['ʌnful'fild] *a* irréalisé, inexaucé, inachevé.

unfurl [ʌn'fəːl] *vt* dérouler, déployer, déferler.

unfurnished ['ʌn'fəːniʃt] *a* non meublé.

ungainly [ʌn'geinli] *a* gauche, (*fam*) mastoc, dégingandé.

ungentlemanly [ʌn'dʒentlmənli] *a* indigné d'un galant homme, impoli.

ungovernable [ʌn'gʌvənəbl] *a* ingouvernable, irrésistible.

ungracious ['ʌn'greiʃəs] *a* sans grâce, désagréable.

ungrateful [ʌn'greitful] *a* ingrat.

ungratefulness [ʌn'greitfulnis] *n* ingratitude *f*.

ungrudgingly [ʌn'grʌdʒiŋli] *ad* sans grogner, de bon cœur, sans compter.

unguarded ['ʌn'gaːdid] *a* sans défense, non gardé, inconsidéré.

unhallowed [ʌn'hæloud] *a* profane, impie.

unhandy [ʌn'hændi] *a* difficile à manier, incommode, gauche.

unhappiness [ʌn'hæpinis] *n* malheur *m*.

unhappy [ʌn'hæpi] *a* malheureux, infortuné.

unharmed ['ʌn'haːmd] *a* indemne, sain et sauf.

unharness ['ʌn'haːnis] *vt* dételer.

unhealthiness [ʌn'helθinis] *n* état malsain *m*, insalubrité *f*.

unhealthy [ʌn'helθi] *a* malsain, insalubre, maladif.

unheard of [ʌn'hɜːdɔv] *a* inouï, inconnu.

unheeded ['ʌn'hiːdid] *a* inaperçu, négligé.

unhelpful ['ʌn'helpful] *a* peu serviable, de pauvre secours, inutile.

unhesitatingly [ʌn'heziteitiŋli] *ad* sans hésitation.

unhinge [ʌn'hindʒ] *vt* faire sortir des gonds, déranger.

unholy [ʌn'houli] *a* impie, impur, (*fam*) du diable, affreux.

unhonoured [ʌn'ɔnəd] *a* sans honneur, dédaigné.

unhook ['ʌn'huk] *vt* décrocher, dégrafer.

unhoped for [ʌn'houptfɔː] *n* inespéré.

unhurt ['ʌn'hɜːt] *a* sans mal, indemne.

unicorn ['juːnikɔːn] *n* licorne *f*.

unification [ˌjuːnifi'keiʃən] *n* unification *f*.

uniform ['juːnifɔːm] *an* uniforme *m*.

uniformly ['juːnifɔːmli] *ad* uniformément.

unify ['juːnifai] *vt* unifier.

unilateral ['juːni'lætərəl] *a* unilatéral.

unimaginable [ˌʌni'mædʒinəbl] *a* inimaginable.

unimaginative ['ʌni'mædʒinətiv] *a* sans imagination.

unimpaired ['ʌnim'peəd] *a* dans toute sa force, intact.

unimpeachable [ˌʌnim'piːtʃəbl] *a* irréprochable, irrécusable.

unimportant ['ʌnim'pɔːtənt] *a* sans importance.

unimpressed ['ʌnim'prest] *a* non impressionné, froid.

unimpressive [ʌn'impresiv] *a* peu impressionnant.

uninhabitable ['ʌnin'hæbitəbl] *a* inhabitable.

uninhabited ['ʌnin'hæbitid] *a* inhabité.

unintelligent ['ʌnin'telidʒənt] *a* inintelligent.

unintentional ['ʌnin'tenʃənl] *a* sans (mauvaise) intention, involontaire.

uninteresting ['ʌn'intristiŋ] *a* sans intérêt.

uninterrupted ['ʌnˌintə'rʌptid] *a* ininterrompu.

union ['juːnjən] *n* union *f*, accord *m*, syndicat ouvrier *m*.

unionist ['juːnjənist] *n* syndiqué(e) *mf*, syndicaliste *mf*, unioniste *mf*.

Union Jack ['juːnjən'jæk] *n* pavillon britannique *m*.

unique [juː'niːk] *a* unique.

unison ['juːnizn] *n* unisson *m*.

unit ['juːnit] *n* unité *f*.

unite [juː'nait] *vt* unir, unifier; *vi* s'unir.

unity ['juːniti] *n* unité *f*, union *f*.

universal [juːni'vəːsəl] *a* universel.

universe ['juːnivəːs] *n* univers *m*.

university [ˌjuːni'vəːsiti] *n* université *f*.

unjust ['ʌn'dʒʌst] *a* injuste.

unjustifiable ['ʌn'dʒʌstifaiəbl] *a* injustifiable.

unkempt ['ʌn'kempt] *a* mal peigné, dépeigné, mal tenu.

unkind [ʌn'kaind] *a* peu aimable, désobligeant, dur.

unkindness [ʌn'kaindnis] *n* méchanceté *f*, désobligeance *f*.

unknowingly ['ʌn'nouiŋli] *ad* sans le savoir (vouloir).

unknown to ['ʌn'nountuː] *ad* à l'insu de.

unlamented ['ʌnlə'mentid] *a* non pleuré.

unlatch ['ʌnlætʃ] *vt* ouvrir.

unlawful ['ʌn'lɔːful] *a* illégal, illicite.

unlawfulness ['ʌn'lɔːfulnis] *n* illégalité *f*.

unlearn ['ʌn'ləːn] *vt* désapprendre, oublier.

unleash [ʌn'liːʃ] *vt* détacher, déchaîner, lâcher.

unleavened ['ʌn'levnd] *a* sans levain, azyme.

unless [ən'les] *cj* à moins que (de), si . . . ne pas.

unlike ['ʌn'laik] *a* différent; *ad* à la différence de.

unlikely [ʌn'laikli] *a* improbable.

unlimited [ʌn'limitid] *a* illimité.

unload ['ʌn'ioud] *vt* décharger.

unlock ['ʌn'lɔk] *vt* ouvrir.

unlooked for [ʌn'luktfɔː] *a* inattendu, inespéré.

unlucky [ʌn'lʌki] *a* malchanceux, malheureux, maléfique.

unmanageable [ʌn'mænidʒəbl] *a* intraitable, impossible, difficile à manœuvrer.

unmanly ['ʌn'mænli] *a* peu viril, efféminé.

unmannerliness [ʌn'mænəlinis] *n* manque d'éducation *m*, impolitesse *f*.

unmannerly [ʌn'mænəli] *a* mal élevé, malappris.

unmarketable [ʌn'maːkitəbl] *a* sans marché (demande), invendable.

unmarried ['ʌn'mærid] *a* célibataire, non marié.

unmask ['ʌn'maːsk] *vt* démasquer, dévoiler.

unmentionable [ʌn'menʃnəbl] *a* innommable, dont on ne peut parler.

unmerciful [ʌn'məːsiful] *a* sans pitié, impitoyable.

unmerited ['ʌn'meritid] *a* immérité.

unmindful [ʌn'maindful] *a* oublieux, insouciant.

unmistakable ['ʌnmis'teikəbl] *a* impossible à méconnaître.

unmistakably ['ʌnmis'teikəbli] *ad* à n'en pas douter, à ne pas s'y méprendre.

unmitigated [ʌn'mitigeited] *a* pur, complet, fieffé, parfait.

unmoor ['ʌn'muə] *vt* démarrer.

unmoved ['ʌn'muːvd] *a* indifférent, impassible.

unnamed ['ʌn'neimd] *a* sans nom, innomé, anonyme.

unnatural [ʌn'nætʃrəl] *a* pas naturel, dénaturé, anormal.

unnecessary [ʌn'nesisəri] *a* pas nécessaire, inutile, gratuit.

unneighbourly ['ʌn'neibəli] *a* de mauvais voisin.

unnerve ['ʌn'nəːv] *vt* énerver, faire perdre son sang-froid à.

unnoticed ['ʌn'noutist] *a* inaperçu.

unnumbered ['ʌn'nʌmbəd] *a* innombrable, non-numéroté.

unobjectionable ['ʌnəb'dʒekʃnəbl] *a* qui défie toute objection.

unobliging ['ʌnə'blaidʒiŋ] *a* désobligeant, peu obligeant.

unobservant ['ʌnəb'zəːvənt] *a* peu observateur.

unobtainable ['ʌnəb'teinəbl] *a* introuvable.

unobtrusive ['ʌnəb'truːsiv] *a* effacé, discret, pas gênant.

unoccupied ['ʌn'ɔkjupaid] *a* inoccupé.

unoffending ['ʌnə'fendiŋ] *a* qui n'a rien de blessant, innocent.

unofficial ['ʌnə'fiʃl] *a* officieux, inofficiel.

unostentatious ['ʌn.ɔsten'teiʃəs] *a* sans ostentation, simple.

unpack ['ʌn'pæk] *vt* dépaqueter, déballer, défaire; *vi* défaire sa malle.

unpalatable [ʌn'pælətəbl] *a* dur à avaler, amer, désagréable.

unparalleled [ʌn'pærəleld] *a* incomparable, sans précédent.

unpardonable [ʌn'pɑːdnəbl] *a* impardonnable.

unperceived ['ʌnpə'siːvd] *a* inaperçu.

unperturbed ['ʌnpə'təːbd] *a* imperturbable, peu ému, impassible.

unpleasant [ʌn'pleznt] *a* déplaisant, désagréable.

unpleasantness [ʌn'plezntnis] *n* désagrément *m*, ennui *m*.

unpolished ['ʌn'pɔliʃt] *a* terne, brut, mat, fruste, grossier.

unpopular ['ʌn'pɔpjulə] *a* impopulaire.

unpopularity ['ʌn.pɔpju'læriti] *n* impopularité *f*.

unpractical ['ʌn'præktikəl] *a* peu pratique, chimérique.

unpractised [ʌn'præktist] *a* mal entraîné, novice inexpérimenté.

unprecedented [ʌn'presidəntid] *a* sans précédent.

unpredictable ['ʌnpri'diktəbl] *a* imprévisible.

unprejudiced [ʌn'predʒudist] *a* impartial.

unpremeditated ['ʌnpri'mediteitid] *a* sans préméditation, inopiné.

unprepared ['ʌnpri'pɛəd] *a* pas préparé, inapprêté, improvisé.

unprepossessing ['ʌn.priːpə'zesiŋ] *a* peu engageant, de mauvaise mine.

unprincipled [ʌn'prinsəpld] *a* sans principes.

unproductive ['ʌnprə'dʌktiv] *a* improductif, stérile.

unprofitable [ʌn'prɔfitəbl] *a* sans profit, ingrat, peu lucratif.

unprogressive ['ʌnprə'gresiv] *a* stagnant, rétrograde.

unprompted [ʌn'prɔmptid] *a* spontané.

unpropitious ['ʌnprə'piʃəs] *a* de mauvais augure, impropice.

unprotect d ['ʌnprə'tektid] *a* sans protection, exposé, inabrité.

unprovided ['ʌnprə'vaidid] *a* sans ressources, démuni.

unpublished ['ʌn'pʌbliʃt] *a* inédit, non publié.

unqualified ['ʌn'kwɔlifaid] *a* incompétent, sans titres sans réserve, absolu, catégorique.

unquestionable [ʌn'kwestʃənəbl] *a* indiscutable.

unravel [ʌn rævəl] *vt* démêler, affiler.

unr asonable [ʌn'riːznəbl] *a* déraisonnable, exorbitant, extravagant.

unreasonableness [ʌn'riːznəblnis] *n* déraison *f*, extravagance *f*.

unreciprocated ['ʌnri'siprəkeitid] *a* non payé de retour.

unrecognizable ['ʌn'rekəgnaizəbl] *a* méconnaissable.

unreconcilable ['ʌn'rekənsailəbl] *a* irréconciliable.

unredeemed ['ʌnri'diːmd] *a* non racheté, inaccompli, sans compensation.

unrelated ['ʌnri'leitid] *a* étranger, sans rapport.

unrelenting ['ʌnri'lentiŋ] *a* inexorable, acharné.

unreliable ['ʌnri'laiəbl] *a* peu sûr, incertain.

unremitting [.ʌnri'mitiŋ] *a* incessant, acharné; — **efforts** efforts soutenus.

unrepentant ['ʌnri'pentənt] *a* impénitent.

unreservedly [.ʌnri'zəːvidli] *ad* sans réserve.

unresponsive ['ʌnris'pɔnsiv] *a* renfermé, réservé, froid.

unrest ['ʌn'rest] *n* inquiétude *f*, agitation *f*, malaise *m*.

unrestrained ['ʌnris'treind] *a* déréglé déchaîné, immodéré.

unrestricted ['ʌnris'triktid] *a* sans restriction, absolu.

unripe ['ʌn'raip] *a* pas mûr, vert.

unrivalled [ʌn'raivəld] *a* inégalé, sans rival.

unroll ['ʌn'roul] *vt* dérouler; *vi* se dérouler.

unruffled ['ʌn'rʌfld] *a* imperturbable, serein, calme.

unruly [ʌn'ruːli] *a* indiscipliné, turbulent, déréglé.

unsafe ['ʌn'seif] *a* dangereux, hasardeux.

unsaleable ['ʌn'seiləbl] *a* invendable.

unsavoury ['ʌn'seivəri] *a* fade, nauséabond, répugnant, vilain.

unsay ['ʌn'sei] *vt* retirer, rétracter, se dédire de.

unscathed ['ʌn'skeiðd] *a* sans une égratignure, indemne.

unscrew ['ʌn'skruː] *vt* dévisser.

unscripted ['ʌn'skriptəd] *a* en direct.

unscrupulous [ʌn'skruːpjuləs] *a* sans scrupules, indélicat.

unseal ['ʌn'siːl] *vt* décacheter, desceller.

unseasonable [ʌn'siːznəbl] *a* hors de saison, inopportun, déplacé.

unseat ['ʌn'siːt] *vt* démonter, désarçonner, invalider, faire perdre son siège à.

unseemly [ʌn'siːmli] *ad* inconvenant.

unseen ['ʌn'siːn] *a* inaperçu, invisible.

unselfish ['ʌn'selfiʃ] *a* désintéressé, généreux.

unserviceable ['ʌn'səːvisəbl] *a* hors de service, usé, inutilisable.

unsettled ['ʌn'setld] *a* indécis, variable, impayé.

unshaken ['ʌn'ʃeikən] *a* inébranlable.

unsheathe ['ʌn'ʃiːð] *vt* dégainer.

unship ['ʌn'ʃip] *vt* décharger, débarquer.

unshrinkable ['ʌn'ʃrinkəbl] *a* irrétrécissable.

unsightly [ʌn'saitli] *a* laid, vilain.

unskilled ['ʌn'skild] *a* inexpert.

unsociable [ʌn'souʃəbl] *a* insociable, farouche.

unsoiled ['ʌn'sɔild] *a* sans tache.

unsold ['ʌn'sould] *a* invendu.

unsolicited ['ʌnsə'lisitid] *a* spontané.

unsophisticated ['ʌnsə'fistikeitid] *a* naturel, nature, ingénu.

unsound ['ʌn'saund] *a* malsain, dérangé, erroné.

unsparing [ʌn'spɛəriŋ] *a* prodigue, infatigable.

unspeakable [ʌn'spiːkəbl] *a* indicible, innommable.

unspoilt ['ʌn'spɔilt] *a* non gâté, vierge, bien élevé.

unstable ['ʌn'steibl] *a* instable.

unstamped ['ʌn'stæmpt] *a* non affranchi, non estampillé.

unsteadiness ['ʌn'stedinis] *n* instabilité *f*, indécision *f*, variabilité *f*, irrégularité *f*.

unsteady ['ʌn'stedi] *a* instable, mal assuré, irrésolu, irrégulier, chancelant, variable.

unstuck ['ʌn'stʌk] *a* **to come** — se décoller, se dégommer, (*fig*) s'effondrer.

unsuccessful ['ʌnsək'sesful] *a* malheureux, manqué, raté, vain.

unsuccessfully ['ʌnsək'sesfuli] *ad* sans succès.

unsuitable ['ʌn'sjuːtəbl] *a* inapproprié, impropre, inapte, inopportun.

unsuited ['ʌn'sjuːtid] *a* impropre (**à for**), mal fait (**pour for**).

unsullied ['ʌn'sʌlid] *a* sans tache.

unsurpassable ['ʌnsə'paːsəbl] *a* impossible à surpasser.

unsurpassed ['ʌnsə'paːst] *a* sans égal.

unsuspected ['ʌnsəs'pektid] *a* insoupçonné.

unsuspicious ['ʌnsəs'piʃəs] *a* confiant, qui ne se doute de rien.

untamable ['ʌn'teiməbl] *a* indomptable.

untaught ['ʌn'tɔːt] *a* ignorant, illettré.

untenanted ['ʌn'tenəntid] *a* vacant, inoccupé.

unthankful ['ʌn'θæŋkful] *a* ingrat.

unthankfulness ['ʌn'θæŋkfulnis] *n* ingratitude *f*.

unthinkable [ʌn'θiŋkəbl] *a* inconcevable.

unthoughtful ['ʌn'θɔːtful] *a* irréfléchi.

untidy [ʌn'taidi] *a* négligé, débraillé, en désordre, mal tenu, mal peigné.

untie ['ʌn'tai] *vt* délier, détacher, défaire.

until [ən'til] *prep* jusqu'à, avant, ne . . . que; *cj* jusqu'à ce que, avant que, ne . . que quand.

untimely [ʌn'taimli] *a* prématuré, intempestif, mal à propos.

untiring [ʌn'taiəriŋ] *a* infatigable.

untold ['ʌn'tould] *a* tu, passé sous silence, inouï, incalculable.

untoward [ʌn'touəd] *a* fâcheux, malencontreux.

untrammelled [ʌn'træməld] *a* sans entraves, libre.

untranslatable ['ʌntræns'leitəbl] *a* intraduisible.

untried ['ʌn'traid] *a* neuf, qui n'a pas été mis à l'épreuve.

untrodden ['ʌn'trɔdn] *a* vierge, inexploré.

untrue ['ʌn'truː] *a* faux, infidèle, déloyal.

untrustworthy ['ʌn'trʌst,wəːði] *a* indigne de confiance.

untruth ['ʌn'truːθ] *n* mensonge *m*.

untruthful ['ʌn'truːθful] *a* menteur, mensonger, faux.

unusual [ʌn'juːʒuəl] *a* insolite, rare.

unutterable [ʌn'ʌtərəbl] *a* inexprimable, parfait.

unveil [ʌn'veil] *vt* dévoiler, inaugurer.

unveiling [ʌn'veiliŋ] *n* inauguration *f*.

unwarranted ['ʌn'wɔrəntəd] *a* injustifié, déplacé, gratuit.

unwary [ʌn'wɛəri] *a* imprudent.

unwavering [ʌn'weivəriŋ] *a* constant, inaltérable, résolu.

unwaveringly [ʌn'weivəriŋli] *ad* de pied ferme, résolument.

unwearying [ʌn'wiəriiŋ] *a* infatigable.

unwelcome [ʌn'welkəm] *a* mal venu, importun, désagréable.

unwell ['ʌn'wel] *a* indisposé, mal en train, souffrant.

unwholesome ['ʌn'houlsəm] *a* malsain, insalubre.

unwieldy [ʌn'wi:ldi] *a* difficile à manier, encombrant.

unwilling ['ʌn'wiliŋ] *a* malgré soi, de mauvaise volonté.

unwillingly [ʌn'wiliŋli] *ad* à contre cœur.

unwind ['ʌn'waind] *vt* dérouler, dévider, débobiner.

unwise ['ʌn'waiz] *a* malavisé, imprudent.

unwittingly [ʌn'witiŋli] *ad* sans y penser, étourdiment, sans le savoir.

unwonted [ʌn'wountid] *a* rare, inaccoutumé.

unworkable ['ʌn'wə:kəbl] *a* impraticable, inexploitable.

unworthiness [ʌn'wə:ðinis] *a* indignité *f*, peu de mérite *m*.

unworthy [ʌn'wə:ði] *a* indigne.

unwrap ['ʌn'ræp] *vt* déballer, défaire.

unwritten ['ʌn'ritn] *a* tacite, oral, non écrit.

unyielding [ʌn'ji:ldiŋ] *a* inflexible, intransigeant.

up [ʌp] *a* debout, levé, droit, fini, expiré; *ad* en dessus, plus fort, en montant, en l'air, en avance; — **to** jusque, jusqu'à; **it is all — with him** il est fichu, perdu; — **there** là-haut; **to be — to sth.** mijoter qch, être à la hauteur de qch; **the —s and downs** les vicissitudes *f pl*, accidents *m pl*; **to walk — and down** marcher de long en large.

upbraid [ʌp'breid] *vt* morigéner, faire des reproches à.

upbraiding [ʌp'breidiŋ] *n* réprimande *f*.

upbringing ['ʌp,briŋiŋ] *n* éducation *f*.

upheaval [ʌp'hi:vəl] *n* soulèvement *m*, convulsion *f*.

uphill ['ʌp'hil] *a* ardu, montant; *ad* en montant.

uphold [ʌp'hould] *vt* soutenir.

upholder [ʌp'houldə] *n* partisan *m*, soutien *m*.

upholster [ʌp'houlstə] *vt* tapisser.

upholsterer [ʌp'houlstərə] *n* tapissier *m*.

upholstery [ʌp'houlstəri] *n* tapisserie *f*, garniture *f*, capitonnage *m*.

upkeep ['ʌpki:p] *n* entretien *m*.

uplift ['ʌplift] *n* inspiration *f*, prêchi-prêcha *m*; [ʌp'lift] *vt* élever, exalter.

upon [ə'pɔn] *prep* sur; *see* **on**.

upper ['ʌpə] *n* empeigne *f*; *a* supérieur, de dessus, haut.

uppermost ['ʌpəmoust] *a* le plus haut, premier, du premier rang; *ad* en dessus.

uppish ['ʌpiʃ] *a* hautain, présomptueux.

upright ['ʌprait] *a* vertical, droit, debout, juste, honnête.

uprightness ['ʌp,raitnis] *n* droiture *f*.

uprising [ʌp'raiziŋ] *n* soulèvement *m*, lever *m*.

uproar ['ʌp,rɔ:] *n* tumulte *m*, brouhaha *m*.

uproarious [ʌp'rɔ:riəs] *a* bruyant, tapageur.

uproot [ʌp'ru:t] *vt* déraciner, extirper, arracher.

upset [ʌp'set] *n* bouleversement *m*, renversement *m*, dérangement *m*; *vt* bouleverser, renverser, déranger, indisposer.

upshot ['ʌpʃɔt] *n* conclusion *f*, issue *f*, fin mot *m*.

upside-down ['ʌpsaid'daun] *ad* sens dessus dessous, à l'envers, la tête en bas.

upstairs [ʌp'stɛəz] *ad* en haut.

upstart ['ʌpsta:t] *n* parvenu(e) *mf*.

up-to-date ['ʌptu'deit] *a* à la page, au courant.

upturn [ʌp'tə:n] *vt* retourner, (re)lever.

upward ['ʌpwəd] *a* montant, ascendant; **—s** *ad* en montant, en-(au-)dessus, en haut, au-dessus, plus de.

urban ['ə:bən] *a* urbain.

urbane [ə:'bein] *a* affable, suave, courtois.

urbanity [ə:'bæniti] *n* urbanité *f*.

urchin ['ə:tʃin] *n* oursin *m*, gosse *mf*, gamin(e) *mf*.

urge [ə:dʒ] *n* impulsion *f*, besoin *m*; *vt* presser, talonner, alléguer, pousser, recommander.

urgency ['ə:dʒənsi] *n* urgence *f*.

urgent ['ə:dʒənt] *a* urgent, pressant, instant.

urgently ['ə:dʒəntli] *ad* instamment, avec urgence.

urn [ə:n] *n* urne *f*.

us [ʌs] *pn* nous.

usable ['ju:zəbl] *a* utilisable.

usage ['ju:zidʒ] *n* traitement *m*, usage *m*, emploi *m*.

use [ju:s] *n* usage *m*, emploi *m*; **it is no** — il ne sert à rien; **what is the** —? à quoi bon?

use [ju:z] *vt* employer, se servir de, traiter, avoir l'habitude de; **to — up** consommer, épuiser; **to get —d to** s'habituer, s'accoutumer à.

useful [ju:sful] *a* utile, pratique.

usefulness ['ju:sfulnis] *n* utilité *f*.

useless ['ju:slis] *a* inutile.

user ['ju:zə] *n* usager, -ère.

usher ['ʌʃə] *n* huissier *m*, répétiteur *m*, pion *m*; ouvreuse *f*; **to — in** inaugurer, annoncer, introduire, faire entrer; **to — out** reconduire.

usual ['ju:ʒuəl] *a* usuel, courant, d'usage.

usually ['ju:ʒuəli] *ad* d'habitude, d'ordinaire.

usufruct ['ju:sjufrʌkt] *n* usufruit *m*.

usurer ['ju:ʒərə] *n* usurier *m*.

usurp [juːˈzəːp] vt usurper, empiéter sur.

usurpation [ˌjuːzəːˈpeiʃən] n usurpation f.

usury [ˈjuːʒuri] n usure f.

utensil [juːˈtensl] n ustensile m, attirail m, outil m.

utilitarian [ˌjuːtiliˈtɛəriən] a utilitaire.

utilitarianism [ˌjuːtiliˈtɛəriənizəm] n utilitarisme m.

utility [juːˈtiliti] n utilité f.

utilization [ˌjuːtilaiˈzeiʃən] n utilisation f.

utilize [ˈjuːtilaiz] vt utiliser, tirer parti de.

utmost [ˈʌtmoust] n tout le possible; a extrême, dernier, le plus grand.

utopia [juːˈtoupiə] n utopie f.

utopian [juːˈtoupiən] a utopique.

utter [ˈʌtə] a extrême, absolu, achevé; vt émettre, exprimer, dire, pousser.

utterance [ˈʌtərəns] n voix f, parole f, expression f, articulation f.

utterly [ˈʌtəli] ad absolument.

V

vacancy [ˈveikənsi] n vacance f, vide m.

vacant [ˈveikənt] a vacant, vide, absent, hébété.

vacate [vəˈkeit] vt vider, évacuer, quitter, annuler.

vacation [vəˈkeiʃən] n vacances f pl.

vaccinate [ˈvæksineit] vt vacciner.

vaccination [ˌvæksiˈneiʃən] n vaccination f.

vaccine [ˈvæksiːn] n vaccin m.

vacillate [ˈvæsileit] vi vaciller, hésiter.

vacuous [ˈvækjuəs] a vide, hébété, niais.

vacuum [ˈvækjuəm] n vide m.

vagabond [ˈvægəbɔnd] n vagabond(e) mf, chemineau m.

vagabondage [ˈvægəbɔndidʒ] n vagabondage m.

vagary [ˈveigəri] n lubie f, chimère f, fantaisie f.

vagrancy [ˈveigrənsi] n vagabondage m.

vagrant [ˈveigrənt] n vagabond(e) mf, chemineau m; a errant, vagabond.

vague [veig] a vague, estompé, indécis.

vagueness [ˈveignis] n vague m, imprécision f.

vain [vein] a vain, inutile, vaniteux.

vainglorious [veinˈglɔːriəs] a fier, glorieux.

vainglory [veinˈglɔːri] n gloriole f.

vainly [ˈveinli] ad en vain, avec vanité.

vale [veil] n val m.

valiant [ˈvæljənt] a vaillant.

valiantly [ˈvæljəntli] ad vaillamment.

valid [ˈvælid] a valide, valable, solide.

validate [ˈvælideit] vt rendre valide, ratifier.

validity [vəˈliditi] n validité f.

valley [ˈvæli] n vallée f.

valorous [ˈvælərəs] a valeureux.

valour [ˈvælə] n valeur f.

valuable [ˈvæljuəbl] a de grande valeur, de prix, précieux; n objet de prix m.

valuation [ˌvæljuˈeiʃən] n évaluation f, prix m, expertise f.

value [ˈvæljuː] n valeur f, prix m; vt évaluer, apprécier, estimer.

valve [vælv] n soupape f, valve f, valvule f, lampe f.

vamp [væmp] n femme fatale f, vamp f, empeigne f; vt flirter avec, rapiécer, (fam) retaper, improviser.

vampire [ˈvæmpaiə] n vampire m.

van [væn] n camion m, fourgon m, avant-garde f.

vane [vein] n girouette f, aile f, pale(tte) f.

vanilla [vəˈnilə] n vanille f.

vanish [ˈvæniʃ] vi disparaître, s'évanouir.

vanity [ˈvæniti] n vanité f.

vanquish [ˈvæŋkwiʃ] vt vaincre, venir à bout de.

vantage [ˈvɑːntidʒ] n avantage m.

vapid [ˈvæpid] a fade, plat.

vaporization [ˌveipəraiˈzeiʃən] n vaporisation f.

vaporize [ˈveipəraiz] vt vaporiser; vi se vaporiser.

vaporizer [ˈveipəraizə] n vaporisateur m, atomiseur m.

vapour [ˈveipə] n vapeur f, buée f.

variable [ˈvɛəriəbl] a variable, inconstant.

variance [ˈvɛəriəns] n désaccord m, discorde f.

variant [ˈvɛəriənt] n variante f.

variation [ˌvɛəriˈeiʃən] n variation f, écart m.

varicose [ˈværikous] a variqueux; — vein varice f.

varied [ˈvɛərid] a varié.

variegated [ˈvɛərigeitid] a bigarré, panaché, diapré.

variety [vəˈraiəti] n variété f, diversité f.

various [ˈvɛəriəs] a varié, divers, plusieurs.

variously [ˈvɛəriəsli] ad diversement.

varnish [ˈvɑːniʃ] n vernis m; vt vernir.

varnishing [ˈvɑːniʃiŋ] n vernissage m.

vary [ˈvɛəri] vti varier; vi différer, ne pas être d'accord.

vase [vɑːz] n vase m.

vast [vɑːst] a vaste, énorme.

vat [væt] n cuve f.

vault [vɔːlt] n voûte f, cave f,

caveau *m*, saut *m*; *vt* voûter; *vti* sauter.

vaunt [vɔːnt] *n* vantardise *f*; *vt* se vanter de.

veal [viːl] *n* veau *m*.

veer [viə] *vi* tourner, virer, sauter.

vegetable ['vedʒitəbl] *n* légume *m*; *a* végétal.

vegetarian [,vedʒi'tɛəriən] *an* végétarien, -ienne.

vegetate ['vedʒiteit] *vi* végéter.

vegetation [,vedʒi'teiʃən] *n* végétation *f*.

vehemence ['viːimǝns] *n* véhémence *f*.

vehement ['viːimǝnt] *a* véhément.

vehicle ['viːikl] *n* véhicule *m*, voiture *f*.

veil [veil] *n* voile *m*, voilette *f*; *vt* voiler, masquer.

vein [vein] *n* veine *f*, humeur *f*.

veined ['veind] *a* veiné.

vellum ['veləm] *n* vélin *m*.

velocity [vi'lɔsiti] *n* vélocité *f*, rapidité *f*.

velvet ['velvit] *n* velours *m*; *a* de velours, velouté.

velveteen [,velvi'tiːn] *n* velours de coton *m*.

venal ['viːnl] *a* vénal.

venality [viː'næliti] *n* vénalité *f*.

vendor ['vendɔː] *n* vendeur, marchand(e) *mf*.

veneer [vǝ'niǝ] *n* placage *m*, glacis *m*, vernis *m*, mince couche *f*; *vt* plaquer.

venerable ['venǝrǝbl] *a* vénérable.

venerate ['venǝreit] *vt* vénérer.

veneration [,venǝ'reiʃǝn] *n* vénération *f*.

venereal [vi'niǝriǝl] *a* vénérien.

venetian blind [vi'niːʃǝn'blaind] *n* jalousie *f*.

vengeance ['vendʒǝns] *n* vengeance *f*.

vengeful ['vendʒiul] *a* vindicatif.

venial ['viːniǝl] *a* véniel.

venison ['venzn] *n* venaison *f*.

venom ['venǝm] *n* venin *m*.

venomous ['venǝmǝs] *a* venimeux, méchant.

vent [vent] *n* trou *m*, passage *m*, cours *m*, carrière *f*, fente *f*; *vt* décharger.

ventilate ['ventileit] *vt* aérer, produire en public.

ventilation [,venti'leiʃǝn] *n* ventilation *f*, aération *f*.

ventilator ['ventileitǝ] *n* ventilateur *m*, soupirail *m*.

ventriloquist [ven'trilǝkwist] *n* ventriloque *mf*.

venture ['ventʃǝ] *n* risque *m*, entreprise *f*; *vt* s'aventurer à, oser, hasarder.

venturesome ['ventʃǝsǝm] *a* aventureux, risqué.

veracious [vǝ'reiʃǝs] *a* véridique.

veracity [vǝ'ræsiti] *n* véracité *f*.

verb [vǝːb] *n* verbe *m*.

verbal ['vǝːbǝl] *a* verbal, oral.

verbally ['vǝːbǝli] *ad* de vive voix.

verbatim [vǝː'beitim] *ad* mot pour mot.

verbena [vǝ(ː)'biːnǝ] *n* verveine *f*.

verbose [vǝː'bous] *a* verbeux.

verbosity [vǝː'bɔsiti] *n* verbosité *f*.

verdant ['vǝːdǝnt] *a* verdoyant.

verdict ['vǝːdikt] *n* verdict *m*, jugement *m*.

verge [vǝːdʒ] *n* bord *m*, bordure *f*, point *m*, verge *f*, lisière *f*; **to — on** longer, côtoyer, triser.

verger ['vǝːdʒǝ] *n* bedeau *m*, huissier *m*.

verifiable ['verifaiǝbl] *a* vérifiable.

verification [,verifi'keiʃǝn] *n* vérification *f*, contrôle *m*.

verify ['verifai] *vt* vérifier, confirmer, justifier.

verisimilitude [,verisi'militjuːd] *n* vraisemblance *f*.

veritable ['veritǝbl] *a* véritable.

vermicelli [,vǝːmi'seli] *n* vermicelle *m*.

vermin ['vǝːmin] *n* vermine *f*.

versatile ['vǝːsǝtail] *a* aux talents variés, universel, souple, étendu.

versatility [,vǝːsǝ'tiliti] *n* diversité *f*, universalité *f*, souplesse *f*.

verse [vǝːs] *n* vers *m*, strophe *f*, verset *m*, poésie *f*.

versed [vǝːst] *a* instruit (de **in**), rompu (à **in**), fort (en **in**), versé (en **in**).

versification [,vǝːsifi'keiʃǝn] *n* versification *f*.

versify ['vǝːsifai] *vti* versifier, écrire en vers.

version ['vǝːʃǝn] *n* version *f*, interprétation *f*.

vertebra ['vǝːtibrǝ] *n* vertèbre *f*.

vertical ['vǝːtikǝl] *a* vertical.

very ['veri] *a* vrai, même, seul, propre; *ad* très, fort, bien, tout.

vespers ['vespǝz] *n* vêpres *f pl*.

vessel [vesl] *n* vaisseau *m*, vase *m*, récipient *m*.

vest [vest] *n* gilet *m*, maillot *m* (de corps), (US) chemise *f*; *vt* investir (de **with**), conférer (à **with**).

vested ['vestid] *a* acquis.

vestibule ['vestibjuːl] *n* vestibule *m*.

vestige ['vestidʒ] *n* vestige *m*, trace *f*, ombre *f*.

vestment ['vestmǝnt] *n* vêtement *m*.

vestry ['vestri] *n* sacristie *f*, conseil de fabrique *m*.

veteran ['vetǝrǝn] *n* vétéran *m*.

veterinary ['vetǝrinǝri] *an* vétérinaire *m*.

veto ['viːtou] *n* veto; *vt* mettre son veto (à, sur).

vex [veks] *vt* irriter, vexer.

vexation [vek'seiʃǝn] *n* dépit *m*, colère *f*, ennui *m*.

vexatious [vek'seiʃǝs] *a* vexant, fâcheux, vexatoire.

vexed [vekst] *a* très discuté, vexé.

via ['vaiǝ] *prep* par, via.

viaduct ['vaiǝdʌkt] *n* viaduc *m*.

vial ['vaiǝl] *n* fiole *f*.

viands ['vaiəndz] n pl victuailles f pl.
viaticum [vai'ætikəm] n viatique m.
vibrate [vai'breit] vi osciller, vibrer.
vibration [vai'breiʃən] n vibration f.
vicar ['vikə] n curé m, vicaire m.
vice [vais] n vice m, étau m; prep à la place de; prefix vice-.
vicinity [vi'siniti] n voisinage m, alentours m pl.
vicious ['viʃəs] a vicieux, pervers, méchant.
viciousness ['viʃəsnis] n perversité f, méchanceté f.
vicissitude [vi'sisitjuːd] n vicissitude f, péripétie f.
victim ['viktim] n victime f.
victimize ['viktimaiz] vt persécuter, tromper.
victor ['viktə] n vainqueur m.
victorious [vik'tɔːriəs] a victorieux.
victory ['viktəri] n victoire f.
victuals ['vitlz] n pl comestibles m pl, vivres m pl.
vie [vai] vi rivaliser, le disputer (à with).
view [vjuː] n (point m de) vue f, perspective f, panorama m, regard m, opinion f; vt. voir, regarder; **with a —** to dans l'intention de; **bird's eye —** vue f à vol d'oiseau.
viewer ['vjuːə] n téléspectateur, -trice, visionneuse f, viseur m, inspecteur, -trice.
view-finder ['vjuːˌfaində] n viseur m.
vigil ['vidʒil] n veille f, vigile f.
vigilance ['vidʒiləns] n vigilance f.
vigilant ['vidʒilənt] a vigilant, alerte.
vigorous ['vigərəs] a vigoureux, solide.
vigour ['vigə] n vigueur m, énergie f.
vile [vail] a vil, infâme, abominable.
vileness ['vailnis] n bassesse f.
vilify ['vilifai] vt vilipender.
village ['vilidʒ] n village m.
villager ['vilidʒə] n villageois(e) mf.
villain ['vilən] n scélérat m, coquin(e) mf.
villainous ['vilənəs] a vil, infâme.
villainy ['viləni] n scélératesse f, infamie f.
vindicate ['vindikeit] vt défendre, justifier.
vindication [ˌvindi'keiʃən] n défense f, justification f.
vindicator ['vindikeitə] n vengeur m, défenseur m.
vindictive [vin'diktiv] a vindicatif.
vindictiveness [vin'diktivnis] n esprit vindicatif m.
vine [vain] n vigne f.
vinegar ['vinigə] n vinaigre m.
vineyard ['vinjəd] n vignoble m.
vintage ['vintidʒ] n vendange f, cru m, année f.
vintner ['vintnə] n marchand de vins m.
viol ['vaiəl] n viole f.
violate ['vaiəleit] vt violer.
violation [ˌvaiə'leiʃən] n viol m, violation f, infraction f.

violator ['vaiəleitə] n violateur, -trice, ravisseur m.
violence ['vaiələns] n violence f.
violent ['vaiələnt] a violent.
violently ['vaiələntli] ad violemment.
violet ['vaiələt] n violette f; a violet.
violin [ˌvaiə'lin] n violon m.
violinist ['vaiəlinist] n violoniste mf.
violoncello [ˌvaiələn'tʃelou] n violoncelle m.
viper ['vaipə] n vipère f.
virago [vi'rɑːgou] n mégère f.
virgin ['vəːdʒin] n vierge f.
virginal ['vəːdʒinl] a virginal.
virginity [vəː'dʒiniti] n virginité f.
virile ['virail] a viril, mâle.
virility [vi'riliti] n virilité f.
virtual ['vəːtjuəl] a virtuel, de fait, vrai.
virtue ['vəːtjuː] n vertu f, qualité f.
virtuoso [ˌvəːtju'ouzou] n virtuose mf.
virtuous ['vəːtjuəs] a vertueux.
virulence ['virjuləns] n virulence f.
virulent ['virjulənt] a virulent.
virus ['vaiərəs] n virus m.
visa ['viːzə] n visa m.
viscount ['vaikaunt] n vicomte m.
viscountess ['vaikauntis] n vicomtesse f.
viscous ['viskəs] a visqueux.
visibility [ˌvizi'biliti] n visibilité f.
visible ['vizəbl] a visible.
vision ['viʒən] n vision f, vue f.
visionary ['viʒnəri] an visionnaire mf; a chimérique.
visit ['vizit] n visite f; vt rendre visite à, visiter.
visitation [ˌvizi'teiʃən] n tournée d'inspection f, épreuve f, calamité f, (fam) visite fâcheuse f, (eccl) visitation.
visiting ['vizitiŋ] a en (termes de) visite; **— card** carte de visite f.
visitor ['vizitə] n visiteur, -euse, visite f, voyageur, -euse, estivant, -ante.
visor ['vaizə] n visière f.
vista ['vistə] n perspective f, percée f, échappée f.
visual ['vizjuəl] a visuel.
visualize ['vizjuəlaiz] vt se représenter, envisager.
vital ['vaitl] a vital, mortel, capital, essentiel; **— statistics** statistiques démographiques f pl, (fam) mensurations f pl.
vitality [vai'tæliti] n vitalité f, vigueur f.
vitamin ['vitəmin] n vitamine f.
vitiate ['viʃieit] vt vicier, corrompre.
vituperate [vi'tjuːpəreit] vt injurier, vilipender.
vituperation [viˌtjuːpə'reiʃən] n injures f pl.
vivacious [vi'veiʃəs] a vif, vivace.
vivacity [vi'væsiti] n vivacité f, animation f.
viva voce ['vaivə'vousi] an. oral m; ad de vive voix.

Vivian ['viviən] Vivianne, Vivienne f.

vivid ['vivid] a vif, éclatant.

vividness ['vividnis] n éclat m.

vivify ['vivifai] vt vivifier, animer.

vivisect [,vivi'sekt] vt disséquer à vif.

vivisection [,vivi'sekʃən] n vivisection f.

vixen ['viksn] n renarde f, mégère f.

viz [viz] ad c'est à dire.

vocable ['voukəbl] n vocable m.

vocabulary [və'kæbjuləri] n vocabulaire m.

vocal ['voukəl] a vocal.

vocation [vou'keiʃən] n vocation f, carrière f.

vocational [vou'keiʃənl] a professionnel.

vociferate [vou'sifəreit] vti vociférer.

vociferation [vou sifə'reiʃən] n vocifération f, clameurs f pl.

vogue [voug] n vogue f.

voice [vɔis] n voix f; vt exprimer, énoncer.

voiceless ['vɔislis] a aphone, muet..

void [vɔid] n vide m; a vide, vacant, dénué, non avenu.

volatile ['vɔlətail] a volatil, vif, gai, volage.

volcanic [vɔl'kænik] a volcanique.

volcano [vɔl'keinou] n volcan m.

volley ['vɔli] n volée f, décharge f, salve f; vi tirer à toute volée; vt reprendre de volée, lâcher.

volt [voult] n volte f, volt m.

volubility [,vɔlju'biliti] n volubilité f.

voluble ['vɔljubl] a volubile, facile, coulant.

volume ['vɔljum] n volume m, tome m, livre m.

voluminous [və'lju:minəs] a volumineux, ample.

voluntary ['vɔləntəri] an volontaire mf; a spontané.

volunteer [,vɔlən'tiə] n volontaire m, homme de bonne volonté m; vt offrir spontanément; vi s'offrir, s'engager comme volontaire.

voluptuous [və'lʌptjuəs] a voluptueux.

voluptuousness [və'lʌptjuəsnis] n volupté f, sensualité f.

vomit ['vɔmit] vti vomir, rendre.

vomiting ['vɔmitiŋ] n vomissement m.

voracious [və'reiʃəs] a vorace.

voracity [vɔ'ræsiti] n voracité f.

vortex ['vɔːteks] n tourbillon m.

vote [vout] n vote m, voix f; vti voter; vt proposer.

voter ['voutə] n votant m, électeur, -trice.

voting ['voutiŋ] n scrutin m; — paper bulletin de vote m.

vouch [vautʃ] vt attester, garantir; to — for répondre de.

voucher ['vautʃə] n garantie f, attestation f, reçu m, bon m.

vouchsafe [vautʃ'seif] vt daigner, accorder.

vow [vau] n serment m, vœu m; vt vouer, jurer.

vowel ['vauəl] n voyelle f.

voyage [vɔiidʒ] n voyage m (par eau).

vulgar ['vʌlgə] a vulgaire.

vulgarity [vʌl'gæriti] n vulgarité f.

vulgarization [,vʌlgərai'zeiʃən] n vulgarisation f.

vulgarize ['vʌlgəraiz] vt vulgariser.

vulnerability [,vʌlnərə'biliti] n vulnérabilité f.

vulnerable ['vʌlnərəbl] a vulnérable.

vulture ['vʌltʃə] n vautour m, charognard m.

W

wad [wɔd] n bourre f, liasse f, tampon m; vt (rem)bourrer, ouater.

waddle ['wɔdl] n dandinement m; vi marcher comme un canard, se dandiner.

wade [weid] vi patauger; vti passer à gué.

wadi ['wɔdi] n oued m.

wafer ['weifə] n oublie f, gaufrette f, hostie f, pain à cacheter m.

waffle ['wɔfl] n gaufre f, (fam) radotages m pl; vi parloter, radoter.

waft [wɑːft] n bouffée f, souffle m, coup d'aile m; vt glisser, porter; vi flotter.

wag [wæg] n hochement m, branlement m, mouvement m, farceur m; vt remuer, hocher, lever; vi se remuer, aller.

wage(s) ['weidʒ(iz)] n salaire m, gages m pl; — freeze n blocage m des salaires.

wager ['weidʒə] n pari m, gageure f; vt parier.

waggish ['wægiʃ] a facétieux, blagueur, fumiste.

waggishness ['wægiʃnis] n espièglerie f.

waggle ['wægl] vti remuer.

wagon ['wægən] n camion m, chariot m, fourgon m, wagon m, (US) voiture f.

wagoner ['wægənə] n camionneur m, charretier m, roulier m.

wagtail ['wægteil] n bergeronnette f, hochequeue m.

waif [weif] n enfant abandonné m, épave f.

wail [weil] n lamentation f, plainte f; vi se lamenter, vagir.

wainscot ['weinskət] n boiserie f, lambris m; vt lambrisser.

waist [weist] n taille f, ceinture f.

waistband ['weistbænd] n ceinture f, ceinturon m.

waistcoat ['weiskout] n gilet m.

wait [weit] n attente f, embuscade f, battement m; pl chanteurs de Noël m pl; vti attendre; vi servir à table.

waiter ['weitə] n garçon m.

waiting-room ['weitiŋrum] n salle d'attente f.

waitress ['weitris] *n* serveuse *f*, (*US*) domestique *f*.

waive [weiv] *vt* écarter, renoncer à, lever.

wake [weik] *n* veillée *f*, sillage *m*; *vi* s'éveiller; *vt* réveiller.

wakeful ['weikful] *a* éveillé, vigilant.

wakefulness ['weikfulnis] *n* insomnie *f*, vigilance *f*.

waken ['weikən] *vi* s'éveiller, se réveiller; *vt* (r)éveiller.

Wales [weilz] *n* pays de Galles *m*.

walk [wɔːk] *n* (dé)marche *f*, promenade *f*, allée *f*, promenoir *m*; *vi* se promener, marcher, aller à pied; *vt* promener, faire à pied, faire marcher; **to — in** entrer; **to — off** *vi* s'en aller; *vt* emmener.

walker ['wɔːkə] *n* marcheur, -euse, piéton *m*, promeneur, -euse.

walking ['wɔːkiŋ] *a* ambulant; *n* marche *f*; **— stick** canne *f*.

walk-out ['wɔːk'aut] *n* (*US*) grève *f* (spontanée).

walk-over ['wɔːk'ouvə] *n* victoire *f* par forfait, jeu d'enfant *m*.

wall [wɔːl] *n* mur *m*, muraille *f*, paroi *f*.

wallet ['wɔlit] *n* porte-feuille *m*, besace *f*, sacoche *f*.

wallflower ['wɔːl,flauə] *n* giroflée *f*; **to be a —** faire tapisserie.

wallop ['wɔləp] *n* coup vigoureux *m*; *vt* rosser, fesser.

walloping ['wɔləpiŋ] *n* rossée *f*, fessée *f*, raclée *f*.

wallow [wɔlou] *vi* rouler, se vautrer, se baigner.

wallpaper ['wɔːl,peipə] *n* papier peint *m*, tenture *f*.

walnut ['wɔːlnət] *n* noix *f*; **— tree** noyer *m*.

walrus ['wɔːrəs] *n* morse *m*.

waltz [wɔːls] *n* valse *f*; *vi* valser.

wan [wɔn] *a* blafard pâle.

wand [wɔnd] *n* baguette *f*, bâton *m*.

wander ['wɔndə] *vi* errer, se perdre, divaguer; *vt* (par)courir.

wanderer ['wɔndərə] *n* voyageur, -euse, promeneur, -euse.

wandering ['wɔndəriŋ] *a* errant, vagabond, distrait, égaré; *n* vagabondage *m*; *pl* divagations *f pl*.

wane [wein] *n* déclin *m*; *vi* décliner, décroître.

wanness ['wɔnnis] *n* pâleur *f*, lividité *f*.

want [wɔnt] *n* manque *m*, défaut *m*, gêne *f*, besoin *m*; **for — of** faute de; *vt* manquer de, avoir besoin de, demander, réclamer.

wanted ['wɔntid] *a* on demande, recherché (par la police).

wanton ['wɔntən] *n* gourgandine *f*, femme impudique *f*; *a* joueur, capricieux, impudique, débauché, gratuit.

war [wɔː] *n* guerre *f*.

warble ['wɔːbl] *n* gazouillement *m*; *vi* gazouiller.

warbler ['wɔːblə] *n* fauvette *f*.

ward [wɔːd] *n* garde *f*, tutelle *f*, pupille *mf*, arrondissement *m*, division *f*, cellule *f*, salle *f* (d'hôpital); *vt* garder; **to — off** écarter parer.

warden ['wɔːdn] *n* directeur *m* (d'une institution, d'une prison) *f* recteur *m*; gardien *m*, conservateur *m*; **game — ** garde-chasse *m*.

warder ['wɔːdə] *n* gardien *m*.

wardrobe ['wɔːdroub] *n* armoire *f*, garde-robe *f*.

wardroom ['wɔːdrum] *n* carré des officiers *m*.

ware [wɛə] *n* vaisselle *f*; *pl* marchandises *f pl*.

warehouse ['wɛəhaus] *n* entrepôt *m*, magasin *m*; *vt* entreposer, emmagasiner.

warfare ['wɔːfɛə] *n* guerre *f*.

wariness ['wɛərinis] *n* prudence *f*, méfiance *f*.

warlike ['wɔːlaik] *a* belliqueux.

warm [wɔːm] *a* chaud, chaleureux, pimenté, vif, échauffé, au chaud; *vt* (ré)chauffer; *vi* se (ré)chauffer, s'animer, s'échauffer.

warming ['wɔːmiŋ] *n* chauffage *m*.

warming-pan ['wɔːmiŋpæn] *n* bassinoire *f*.

warmth [wɔːmθ] *n* chaleur *f*, ardeur *f*.

warn [wɔːn] *vt* avertir, mettre en garde, prévenir.

warning ['wɔːniŋ] *n* avertissement *m*, congé *m*.

warp [wɔːp] *n* chaîne *f*, corde *f*, (*wood*) jeu *m*, gauchissement *m*, dépôt *m*; *vt* ourdir, remorquer, jouer, gauchir, ausser; *vi* gauchir, se voiler, se déformer.

warrant ['wɔrənt] *n* autorité *f*, garantie *f*, bon *m*, brevet *m*, mandat *m* (d'amener), pouvoir *m*; *vt* autoriser, garantir, justifier.

warrantable ['wɔrəntəbl] *a* justifiable.

warrantor ['wɔrəntɔː] *n* garant *m*, répondant *m*.

warren ['wɔrin] *n* garenne *f*.

warrior ['wɔriə] *n* guerrier *m*, soldat *m*; *a* martial, guerrier.

wart [wɔːt] *n* verrue *f*.

wart-hog ['wɔːt'hɔg] *n* phacochère *m*.

wary ['wɛəri] *a* prudent, méfiant, avisé.

wash [wɔʃ] *n* lavage *m*, lessive *f*, lavasse *f*, lotion *f*, remous *m*, sillage *m*, couche *f*, lavis *m*; *vt* aver, blanchir, badigeonner; *vi* se laver; **to — away** emporter; **to — down** arroser, laver à grande eau; **to — out** rincer, passer l'éponge sur, supprimer; **to — up** faire la vaisselle.

washable ['wɔʃəbl] *a* lavable.

wash-basin ['wɔʃ,beisn] *n* cuvette *f*.

washed-out ['wɔʃt'aut] *a* (*fam*) lessivé; délavé, (*fam*) flapi.

washer ['wɔʃə] *n* laveur, -euse, rondelle *f*; **—up** plongeur *m*.

washerwoman ['wɔʃə‚wumən] *n* blanchisseuse *f*, lavandière *f*.

wash-house ['wɔʃhaus] *n* buanderie *f*, lavoir *m*.

washing ['wɔʃiŋ] *n* lavage *m*, linge *m*, vaisselle *f*, lessive *f*, blanchissage *m*.

wash-out ['wɔʃaut] *n* fiasco *m*, four *m*, débâcle *f*, raté(e).

washstand ['wɔʃstænd] *n* lavabo *m*.

washy ['wɔʃi] *a* insipide, fade.

wasp [wɔsp] *n* guêpe *f*; —'s nest guêpier *m*; **mason** — guêpe maçonne *f*.

waspish ['wɔspiʃ] *a* venimeux, méchant, de guêpe.

waste [weist] *n* désert *m*, usure *f*, déchets *m pl*, gaspillage *m*, perte *f*; *a* inculte, désert, de rebut; *v.* gaspiller, épuiser, perdre, rater, gâcher; *vi* s'user, se perdre, s'épuiser.

wasteful ['weistful] *a* ruineux, prodigue, gaspilleur.

waste-paper basket [weist'peipə‚baːskit] *n* corbeille à papier *f*.

waster ['weistə] *n* vaurien *m*, gaspilleur, -euse.

watch [wɔtʃ] *n* garde *f*, guet *m*, quart *m*, montre *f*; *vt* (sur)veiller, observer, regarder, guetter; *vi* prendre garde, veiller, faire attention.

watchdog ['wɔtʃdɔg] *n* chien *m* de garde; (US) — **committee** comité *f* de surveillance.

watchful ['wɔtʃful] *a* attentif, vigilant.

watchfulness ['wɔtʃfulnis] *n* vigilance *f*.

watchmaker ['wɔtʃ‚meikə] *n* horloger *m*.

watchman ['wɔtʃmən] *n* veilleur de nuit *m*, guetteur *m*.

watchword ['wɔtʃwəːd] *n* mot d'ordre *m*.

water ['wɔːtə] *n* eau *f*; *vt* arroser, abreuver; *vi* faire de l'eau, (eyes) se mouiller; **to** — **down** affaiblir, diluer, atténuer, frelater.

water bottle ['wɔːtə‚bɔtl] *n* bidon *m*, gourde *f*; **hot**— bouillotte *f*.

water-closet ['wɔːtə‚klɔzit] *n* cabinets *m pl*.

water-colour ['wɔːtə‚kʌlə] *n* aquarelle *f*.

watercress ['wɔːtəkres] *n* cresson *m*.

waterfall ['wɔːtəfɔːl] *n* cascade *f*.

watering ['wɔːtəriŋ] *n* arrosage *m*, dilution.

watering-can ['wɔːtəriŋkæn] *n* arrosoir *m*.

watering-place ['wɔːtəriŋpleis] *n* abreuvoir *m*, ville d'eau *f*, plage *f*.

water-lily ['wɔːtə‚lili] *n* nénuphar *m*.

waterline ['wɔːtəlain] *n* ligne de flottaison *f*.

waterlogged ['wɔːtəlɔgd] *a* plein d'eau, détrempé.

watermark ['wɔːtəmɑːk] *n* filigrane *m*.

water-melon ['wɔːtə'melən] *n* pastèque *f*.

water-pipe ['wɔːtəpaip] *n* conduite *f* d'eau.

water-power ['wɔːtə‚pauə] *n* force hydraulique *f*.

waterproof ['wɔːtəpruːf] *an* imperméable *m*.

watershed ['wɔːtəʃed] *n* ligne de partage des eaux *f*.

waterskiing ['wɔːtə'skiːiŋ] *n* ski nautique *m*.

waterspout ['wɔːtəspaut] *n* trombe *f*.

watertight ['wɔːtətait] *a* étanche.

waterway ['wɔːtəwei] *n* voie navigable *f*.

waterworks ['wɔːtəwəːks] *n pl* canalisations *f pl*, usine hydraulique *f*.

watery ['wɔːtəri] *a* aqueux, humide, dilué, déteint, chargé de pluie, insipide.

wattle ['wɔtl] *n* claie *f*, fanon *m*, barbe *f*.

wave [weiv] *n* vague *f*, ondulation *f*, (*radio*) onde *f*, signe *m*; *vt* brandir, agiter; *vti* onduler, ondoyer; *vi* s'agiter, flotter, faire signe (de la main).

wavelength ['weivleŋθ] *n* longueur *f* d'onde.

waver ['weivə] *vi* hésiter, défaillir, fléchir, vaciller, trembler.

wavy ['weivi] *a* ondulé, onduleux, tremblé.

wax [wæks] *n* cire *f*, (*cobbler's*) poix *f*; *vt* cirer, encaustiquer; *vi* croître, devenir.

waxwork ['wækswəːk] *n* figure de cire *f*, modelage en cire *m*; *pl* musée des figures de cire *m*.

waxy ['wæksi] *a* de cire, cireux, plastique.

way [wei] *n* chemin *m*, voie *f*, distance *f*, côté *m*, sens *m*, habitude *f*, manière *f*, point de vue *m*, état *m*; **by the** — à propos; **by** — **of** par manière de, en guise de; **this** — par ici; **under** — en train; **out of the** — insolite, écarté.

wayfarer ['wei‚fɛərə] *n* voyageur, -euse.

waylay [wei'lei] *vt* dresser un guet-apens à.

way-out ['wei'aut] *n* sortie *f*, échappatoire *f*.

wayside ['weisaid] *n* bord *m* de route, bas côté *m*; *a* du bord de la route.

way train ['wei‚trein] *n* (US) train *m* omnibus.

wayward ['weiwəd] *a* entêté, capricieux.

waywardness ['weiwədnis] *n* humeur fantasque *f*.

we [wiː] *pn* nous.

weak [wiːk] *a* faible, chétif, léger, doux.

weaken ['wiːkən] *vt* affaiblir; *vi* s'affaiblir, fléchir.

weakish ['wiːkiʃ] *a* faiblard.

weakness ['wiːknis] n faiblesse f,
faible m.

weal [wiːl] n bien m, zébrure f.

wealth [welθ] n richesse(s) f (pl),
profusion f.

wealthy ['welθi] a riche.

wean [wiːn] vt sevrer, guérir.

weaning ['wiːniŋ] n sevrage m.

weapon ['wepən] n arme f.

wear [weə] n usage m, usure f; vt
porter, mettre, user; vi s'user, tirer.

weariness ['wiərinis] n fatigue f,
lassitude f.

wearisome ['wiərisəm] a ennuyeux,
fastidieux.

weary ['wiəri] a fatigué, assommant;
vt ennuyer, fatiguer; vi s'ennuyer,
languir.

weasel ''wiːzl] n belette f.

weather ['weðə] n temps m; vt exposer aux intempéries, échapper à,
survivre à, (cape) doubler.

weather-beaten ['weðə,biːtn] a
battu par la tempête, hâlé.

weather-bound ['weðəbaund] a retenu par le mauvais temps.

weathercock ['weðəkɔk] n girouette
f.

weathered ['weðəd] a décoloré,
rongé, patiné.

weather forecast ['weðə'fɔːkaːst] n
bulletin météorologique m.

weather station ['weðə'steiʃən] n
station météorologique f.

weave [wiːv] vt tisser, tramer.

weaver ['wiːvə] n tisserand m.

weaving ['wiːviŋ] n tissage m.

web [web] n tissu m, toile f.

webbing ['webiŋ] n sangles f pl,
ceinture f.

web-footed ['web,futid] a palmé.

wed [wed] vt marier, se marier avec,
épouser.

wedded 'wedid] a conjugal, marié.

wedding ['wediŋ] n mariage m,
noce(s) f (pl).

wedding breakfast ['wediŋ'brekfəst]
n repas de noces m.

wedge [wedʒ] n coin m, cale f, part f;
vt coincer, presser, caler.

wedlock ['wedlɔk] n (état m de)
mariage m, vie conjugale f.

Wednesday ['wenzdi] n mercredi m.

wee [wiː] a tout petit; vi faire pipi.

weed [wiːd] n mauvaise herbe f,
tabac m; vt sarcler; to — out trier,
éliminer.

weeds [wiːdz] n pl deuil de veuve m.

week [wiːk] n semaine f; today —
d'aujourd'hui en huit.

weekday ['wiːkdei] n jour m de
semaine.

weekend ['wiːk'end] n weekend m.

weekly ['wiːkli] a hebdomadaire; ad
tous les huit jours.

weep [wiːp] vi pleurer, suinter.

weeping willow ['wiːpiŋ'wilou] n
saule pleureur m.

weft [weft] n trame f.

weigh [wei] vti peser; vt (anchor)

lever, calculer; to — down courber,
accabler.

weight [weit] n poids m, pesanteur f,
gravité f.

weighty ['weiti] a pesant, de poids,
puissant.

weir [wiə] n barrage m.

weird [wiəd] a fantastique, bizarre,
mystérieux.

welcome ['welkəm] n bienvenue f,
accueil m; a bienvenu, acceptable;
vt (bien) accueillir, souhaiter la
bienvenue à.

weld [weld] vt souder, unir.

welding ['weldiŋ] n soudure f,
soudage m.

welfare ['welfeə] n bien-être m,
bonheur m.

well [wel] n puits m, source f, fontaine f, cage d'escalier f, godet m;
vi jaillir, sourdre; a bien portant;
ad bien; — enough pas mal; all very
— bɔl et bien; excl eh bien!

wellbeing ['wel'biːiŋ] n bien-être m.

well-bred ['wel'bred] a bien élevé,
(horse) racé.

well-built ['wel'bilt] a bien bâti.

well-done ['wel'dʌn] a bien fait,
(cook) bien cuit; excl bravo!

well-meaning ['wel'miːniŋ] a bien
intentionné.

well-off ['wel'ɔt] a cossu, à l'aise.

Welsh [welʃ] an gallois m.

Welshman ['welʃmən] n Gallois(e)
mf.

welter ['weltə] n confusion f, fatras
m; vi baigner, se vautrer.

wen [wen] n loupe f, goître m.

wench [wentʃ] n fille f, gaillarde f.

went [went] pt of **go**.

wept [wept] pt pp of **weep**.

west [west] n ouest m, occident m;
a à (de, vers) l'ouest, ouest, occidental.

western ['westən] a see **west**.

westwards ['westwədz] ad vers
l'ouest.

wet [wet] n humidité f, pluie f; a
humide, mouillé, trempé; — blanket
rabat-joie m; vt mouiller, humecter.

wet-nurse ['wetnəːs] n nourrice f.

wetting ['wetiŋ] n douche f; to get a
— se faire tremper.

whack [wæk] n coup de bâton m,
essai m, part f; vt bâtonner, rosser,
écraser; excl vlan!

whacking ['wækiŋ] n rossée f,
raciée f.

whale [weil] n baleine f.

whaleboat ['weilbout] n baleinière f.

whalebone ['weilboun] n fanon m,
baleine f.

wharf [wɔːf] n quai m.

what [wɔt] rel pn ce qui, ce que, ce
dont; inter pn qu'est-ce qui?,
qu'est ce que?, que?, quoi?,
combien?; a inter excl quel(s)?
quelle(s); excl quoi! comment!

what(so)ever [,wɔt(sou)'evə] pn tout
ce qui, tout ce que, quoi qui quoi,

que, n'importe quoi; *a* quel que, quelque . . . qui (que), quelconque.

wheat [wi:t] *n* blé *m*, froment *m*.

wheatear ['wi:tiər] *n* traquet *m*.

wheedle ['wi:dl] *vt* cajoler, engager; **to — out of** soutirer par cajolerie.

wheedler ['wi:dlə] *n* enjôleur, -euse.

wheel [wi:l] *n* roue *f*, tour *m*, cercle *m*, (*US*) vélo *m*; *vt* rouler, tourner; *vi* tournoyer; **to — round** se retourner, faire volte-face, demi-tour.

wheelbarrow ['wi:l,bærou] *n* brouette *f*.

wheelwright ['wi:lrait] *n* charron *m*.

wheeze [wi:z] *n* respiration asthmatique *f*; *vi* respirer péniblement.

wheezing ['wi:ziŋ] *n* sifflement *m*, râle *m*.

wheezy ['wi:zi] *a* asthmatique, poussif.

whelp [welp] *n* jeune chien *etc*, petit *m*, drôle *m*; *vi* mettre bas.

when [wen] *cj* quand, lorsque, où, que; *inter ad* quand?

whence [wens] *ad* d'où.

whenever [wen'evə] *cj* toutes les fois que.

where [wɛə] *ad* où, là où, (à) l'endroit où.

whereabouts ['wɛərəbauts] *ad* où (donc); *n* lieu *m* où on est; **his —** où il est.

whereas [wɛər'æz] *cj* vu que, tandis que, alors que.

whereby [wɛə'bai] *ad* par quoi? par lequel.

wherefore ['wɛəfɔ:] *ad* en raison de quoi, donc, pourquoi.

wherein [wɛər'in] *ad* en quoi, où.

whereupon [,wɛərə'pɔn] *ad* sur quoi.

wherever [wɛər'evə] *ad* partout où, où que.

wherewithal ['wɛəwi'ðɔ:l] *n* moyen(s) de quoi *m* (*pl*).

whet [wet] *vt* aiguiser, repasser, affiler, exciter.

whether ['weðə] *cj* si; **— . . . or** soit (que) . . . soit (que).

whetstone ['wetstoun] *n* pierre à aiguiser *f*.

whey [wei] *n* petit lait *m*.

which [witʃ] *a* quel(s), quelle(s); *rel pn* qui, que, lequel, laquelle, lesquels, lesquelles, ce qui, ce que, ce dont; *inter pn* lequel *etc*.

whichever [witʃ'evə] *rel pn* celui qui, celui que, n'importe lequel; *a* que que, quelque . . . que, n'importe quel.

whiff [wif] *n* bouffée *f*.

while [wail] *n* temps *m*, instant *m*; *cj* pendant que, tandis que, tout en; **once in a —** à l'occasion; **to — away** passer, tuer, tromper.

whim [wim] *n* caprice *m*, toquade *f*, fantaisie *f*.

whimper ['wimpə] *n* geignement *m*, pleurnichement *m*; *vi* geindre, pleurnicher.

whimsical ['wimzikəl] *a* fantasque, bizarre.

whimsicality [,wimzi'kæliti] *n* bizarrerie *f*, humeur *f* fantasque.

whine [wain] *n* gémissement *m*, jérémiade *f*; *vi* gémir, pleurnicher, se plaindre.

whinny ['wini] *n* hennissement *m*; *vi* hennir.

whip [wip] *n* fouet *m*, cravache *f*, cocher *m*, piqueur *m*, chef de file *m*, convocation urgente *f*; *vti* fouetter; *vt* battre; **to — off** enlever vivement; **to — round** se retourner brusquement, faire un tête à queue; **to — up** fouetter, activer.

whipcord ['wipkɔ:d] *n* corde *f*.

whiphand ['wip'hænd] *n* haute main *f*, avantage *m*.

whiplash ['wip'læʃ] *n* mèche de fouet *f*.

whipping ['wipiŋ] *n* fouettée *f*; **to give a — to** donner le fouet à.

whir(r) [wə:] *n* bourdonnement *m*, battement d'ailes *m*, ronronnement *m*, ronflement *m*; *vi* bourdonner, ronfler, ronronner.

whirl [wə:l] *n* tourbillon *m*, tournoiement *m*; **to be in a —** avoir la tête à l'envers; *vi* tournoyer, tourbillonner, pirouetter, tourner, virevolter.

whirlpool ['wə:lpu:l] *n* tourbillon *m*, remous *m*.

whirlwind ['wə:lwind] *n* trombe *f*, tourbillon *m*.

whisk [wisk] *n* fouet *m* (à crème), frétillement *m*; plumeau *m*, épousette *f*; *vt* fouetter, battre, remuer; **to — away** enlever vivement, escamoter, chasser.

whisker(s) ['wiskə(z)] *n* (*of cat*) moustache(s) *f* (*pl*), favoris *m pl*.

whisper ['wispə] *n* murmure *m*, chuchotement *m*, bruissement *m*; *vti* murmurer, chuchoter.

whistle ['wisl] *n* sifflet *m*, sifflement *m*; *vt* siffler; **to — for** siffler.

whistler ['wislə] *n* siffleur, -euse.

white [wait] *a* blanc, à blanc; *n* blanc *m*; **— heat** incandescence *f*; **— horses** moutons *m pl*; **— hot** chauffé à blanc; **— lead** céruse *f*; **— paper** rapport ministériel *m*; **— slavery** traite des blanches *f*.

whiten ['waitn] *vt* blanchir; *vi* pâlir.

whiteness ['waitnis] *n* blancheur *f*, pâleur *f*.

whitening ['waitniŋ] *n* blanchiment *m*, blanchissement *m*.

whitewash ['waitwɔʃ] *n* lait de chaux *m*, badigeon *m*, poudre aux yeux *f*; *vt* blanchir, badigeonner en blanc.

whither ['wiðə] *ad* où, là où.

whiting ['waitiŋ] *n* merlan *m*.

whitish ['waitiʃ] *a* blanchâtre.

whitlow ['witlou] *n* panaris *m*, mal blanc *m*.

Whitsun ['witsn] *n* Pentecôte *f*.

whittle ['witl] *vt* (dé)couper, amenuiser, amincir, diminuer, rogner.

whizz [wiz] *n* sifflement *m*; *vi* siffler; **to — along** filer à toute vitesse.

who [hu:] *rel pn* qui, lequel *etc*; *inter pn* qui? qui est-ce qui? quel?

who(so)ever [ˌhu:(sou)'evə] *pn* quiconque, toute personne qui.

whole [houl] *n* tout *m*, ensemble *m*, totalité *f*; **on the —** en somme, à tout prendre, dans l'ensemble; *a* tout, entier, complet, intégral, intact.

wholeheartedly ['houl'hɑːtidli] *ad* de grand (tout) cœur.

wholeheartedness ['houl'hɑːtidnis] *n* cordialité *f*, ardeur *f*, ferveur *f*.

wholesale ['houlseil] *n* vente en gros *f*; *a* général, en masse; *ad* en gros.

wholesome ['houlsəm] *a* salubre, sain, salutaire.

wholesomeness ['houlsəmnis] *n* santé *f*, salubrité *f*.

wholly ['houlli] *ad* sans réserve, intégralement, entièrement, tout à fait.

whom [hu:m] *rel pn* que, lequel *etc*; *inter pn* qui? qui est-ce que?

whoop [hu:p] *vi* (US) augmenter.

whooping-cough ['hu:piŋkɔf] *n* coqueluche *f*.

whore [hɔː] *n* prostituée *f*.

whose [hu:z] *rel pn* dont, de qui, duquel *etc*; *poss pn* à qui? de qui?

why [wai] *nm ad* pourquoi; *excl* allons! mais! t'ens! voyons!

wick [wik] *n* mèche *f*.

wicked ['wikid] *a* méchant, vicieux, pervers, inique.

wickedly ['wikidli] *ad* méchamment.

wickedness ['wikidnis] *n* méchanceté *f*.

wicker ['wikə] *n* osier *m*.

wicket ['wikit] *n* guichet *m*, tourniquet *m*, barrière *f*, portillon *m*.

wide [waid] *a* large, vaste, (tout) grand; **— of** *prep* loin de, au large de.

wide awake ['waidə'weik] *a* bien éveillé, (*fam*) déluré.

widely ['waidli] *ad* grandement, très, largement.

widen ['waidn] *vt* élargir, étendre; *vi* s'élargir.

widening ['waidniŋ] *n* élargissement *m*, extension *f*.

widespread ['waidspred] *a* très répandu.

widow ['widou] *n* veuve *f*.

widowed ['widoud] *a* (devenu(e)) veuf, veuve.

widower ['widouə] *n* veuf *m*.

width [widθ] *n* largeur *f*.

wield [wiːld] *vt* (dé)manier, tenir, exercer.

wife [waif] *n* femme *f*, épouse *f*.

wig [w g] *n* perruque *f*.

wild [waild] *a* sauvage, fou, égaré, violent, farouche, déréglé.

wilderness ['wildənis] *n* déser *m*, pays inculte *m*.

wildfire ['waild faiə] *n* feu grégeois *m*, (*fig*) poudre *f*; **like —** comme une traînée de poudre.

wildly ['waildli] *ad* sauvagement, à l'aveugle, d'une façon extravagante.

wilds [waildz] *n pl* désert *m*, solitude *f*, sauvagerie *f*, pays sauvage *m*.

wile [wail] *n* astuce *f*, ruse *f*.

wilful ['wilful] *a* volontaire, obstiné, prémédité.

wilfulness ['wilfulnis] *n* opiniâtreté *f*, obstination *f*.

will [wil] *n* volonté *f*, vouloir *m*, (*free*) arbitre *m*, testament *m*; *vt* vouloir, ordonner, léguer.

William ['wiljəm] Guillaume *m*.

willing ['wiliŋ] *a* tout disposé, de bonne volonté.

willingly ['wiliŋli] *ad* volontiers.

willingness ['wiliŋnis] *n* empressement *m*, bonne volonté *f*.

will-o'-the-wisp ['wiləðə'wisp] *n* feu follet *m*, chimère *f*.

willow ['wilou] *n* saule *m*.

willy-nilly ['wili'nili] *ad* bon gré mal gré.

wilt [wilt] *vi* dépérir, se flétrir, se dégonfler.

wily ['waili] *a* retors, rusé.

win [win] *vt* gagner, remporter, vaincre; **to — over** gagner.

wince [wins] *n* haut-le-corps *m*, tressaillement *m*; *vi* tressaillir, broncher.

winch [wintʃ] *n* treuil *m*, manivelle *f*.

wind [wind] *n* vent *m*, instruments à vent *m pl*, souffle *m*, haleine *f*; **to have the — up** avoir la trouille; *vt* essouffler.

wind [waind] *vt* enrouler, remonter, sonner; *vi* serpenter, tourner, s'enrouler; **to — up** remonter, liquider, régler.

windbag ['windbæg] *n* moulin à paroles *m*.

winded ['windid] *a* essoufflé, hors d'haleine.

windfall ['windfɔːl] *n* aubaine *f*, fruit tombé *m*.

winding ['waindiŋ] *a* sinueux, tortueux, tournant; *n* enroulement *m*, cours sinueux *m*; *pl* méandres *m pl*, sinuosités *f pl*, lacets *m pl*.

winding-sheet ['waindiŋʃiːt] *n* linceul *m*.

winding-up ['waindiŋ'ʌp] *n* conclusion *f*, liquidation *f*, remontage *m*.

windlass ['windləs] *n* cabestan *m*, treuil *m*.

windmill ['winmil] *n* moulin à vent *m*.

window ['windou] *n* fenêtre *f*, croisée *f*, (*shop*) vitrine *f*; **stained-glass —** verrière *f*.

window-dressing ['windou dresiŋ] *n* art de l'étalage *m*, trompe-l'œil *m*.

window fastening ['windou'fɑːsniŋ] *n* espagnolette *f*.

window frame ['windou'freim] *n* châssis *m* de fenêtre.

window pane ['windoupein] n carreau m, vitre f, glace f.

window-shopping ['windou'ʃɔpiŋ] n lèche-vitrine m.

windscreen ['windskri:n] n paravent m, pare-brise m; — **wiper** n essuie-glace m.

windshield ['windʃi:ld] n (US) pare-brise m.

windswept ['windswept] a (hair style) en coup de vent, (place) venteux.

windy ['windi] a venteux, balayé par le vent, agité, creux, verbeux, vide, qui a la frousse.

wine [wain] n vin m.

wine-merchant ['wain'mə:tʃənt] n négociant en vins m.

wine-press ['wainpres] n pressoir m.

wing [wiŋ] n aile f, essor m, vol m; vt donner des ailes à, empenner, blesser à l'aile.

winged [wiŋd] a ailé.

winger ['wiŋə] n ailier m.

wink [wiŋk] n clin d'œil m; vi cligner, clignoter, faire de l'œil (à **at**); **to** — **at** fermer les yeux sur.

winker ['wiŋkə] n (aut) clignotant m.

winner ['winə] n gagnant(e) mf, vainqueur m, grand succès m.

winning ['winiŋ] a gagnant, engageant, décisif; —**post** n poteau d'arrivée m.

winnow ['winou] vt vanner, trier.

winnower ['winouə] n vanneur, -euse, (machine) vanneuse f.

winsome ['winsəm] a charmant, séduisant.

winter ['wintə] n hiver m; vi passer l'hiver, hiverner.

wintry ['wintri] a d'hiver, hivernal, glacial.

wipe [waip] n coup de balai m, de torchon, d'éponge; vt balayer, essuyer; **to** — **out** effacer, liquider, anéantir.

wire ['waiə] n fil de fer m, dépêche f, télégramme m; vt grill(ag)er, rattacher avec du fil de fer; vti télégraphier.

wire-cutter ['waiə,kʌtə] n cisailles f pl.

wire-haired ['waiəhɛəd] a à poil rêche.

wireless ['waiəlis] n radio f, télégraphie sans fil f; vt envoyer par la radio; vi envoyer un sans-fil; a sans-fil.

wire-netting ['waiə'netiŋ] n treillis (métallique) m.

wire-puller ['waiə,pulə] n combinard m, intrigant(e) mf.

wire-pulling ['waiə,puliŋ] n manipulation f, intrigues f pl, manigances f pl.

wiry ['waiəri] a tout nerfs, sec, nerveux, en fil de fer.

wisdom ['wizdəm] n sagesse f, prudence f.

wise [waiz] n manière f; a sage,

savant, prudent, informé, averti.

wiseacre ['waiz,eikə] n gros bêta m, faux sage m.

wisecrack ['waizkræk] n (US) bon mot m; vi faire de l'esprit.

wish [wiʃ] n souhait m, désir m, vœu m; vt souhaiter, désirer, vouloir.

wishful ['wiʃful] a désireux, d'envie; — **thinking** optimisme béat m.

wisp [wisp] n bouchon m (de paille), petit bout m, mèche folle f, traînée f (de fumée).

wistful ['wistful] a pensif, plein de regret, insatisfait, d'envie.

wistfully ['wistfuli] ad d'un air pensif, avec envie.

wit [wit] n esprit m, homme d'esprit m (de ressource); **to** — **à** savoir.

witch [witʃ] n sorcière f, ensorceleuse f; vt ensorceler.

witchcraft ['witʃkrɑːft] n sorcellerie f, magie noire f.

witch-doctor ['witʃ,dɔktə] n sorcier m.

with [wið] prep avec, à, au, à la, aux, chez, auprès de, envers, pour ce qui est de; **to be** — **it** être dans le vent.

withal [wi'ɔ:l] ad avec cela, d'ailleurs, en même temps.

withdraw [wið'drɔ:] vt (re)tirer, reprendre, annuler, soustraire; vi se retirer, se replier, se rétracter.

withdrawal [wið'drɔːəl] n retrait m, retraite f, rétraction f, repliement m, rappel m.

wither ['wiðə] vt dessécher, flétrir; vi se flétrir, se faner, dépérir.

withhold [wið'hould] vt retenir, refuser, cacher.

within [wi'ðin] prep dans, en dedans de, à l'intérieur de, en, entre, en moins de, à . . . près; ad au (en) dedans, à l'intérieur.

without [wi'ðaut] prep sans, hors de, en (au) dehors de; ad en (au) dehors, à l'extérieur.

withstand [wið'stænd] vt résister à, soutenir.

witness ['witnis] n témoin m, témoignage m; vi témoigner; vt attester, certifier, assister à, être témoin de.

witness-box ['witnis,bɔks] n banc m, barre des témoins f.

witticism ['witisizəm] n mot (trait m) d'esprit m, bon mot m.

wittingly ['witiŋli] ad à dessein, sciemment.

witty ['witi] a spirituel.

wizard ['wizəd] n magicien m, sorcier m, escamoteur m.

wizened ['wiznd] a ratatiné, desséché.

wobble ['wɔbl] n vacillation f, dandinement m; vi aller de travers, vaciller, trembler, branler, tituber, zigzaguer.

woe [wou] n malheur m.

woebegone ['woubi,gɔn] a lamentable, désolé.

woeful ['wouful] *a* triste, atroce, déplorable, affligé.

wold [would] *n* lande *f*.

wolf [wulf] *n* loup *m*; — **whistle** (*fam*) sifflement admiratif *m*.

wolf-cub ['wulfkʌb] *n* louveteau *m*.

woman ['wumən] *n* femme *f*.

womanhood ['wumənhud] *n* âge de femme *m*, féminité *f*.

womanish ['wuməniʃ] *a* efféminé.

womanly ['wumənli] *a* féminin, de femme.

womb [wuːm] *n* matrice *f*, sein *m*.

won [wʌn] *pt pp of* **win.**

wonder ['wʌndə] *n* merveille *f*, prodige *m*, émerveillement *m*; **no —** rien d'étonnant, (*fam*) bien entendu; *vi* s'étonner; *vt* se demander; **to — at** admirer, s'étonner de.

wonderful ['wʌndəful] *a* étonnant, merveilleux.

wonderingly ['wʌndəriŋli] *ad* d'un air étonné.

wonderment ['wʌndəmənt] *n* étonnement *m*, émerveillement *m*

wont [wount] *n* habitude *f*; **to be —** to avoid l'habitude de.

wonted ['wountid] *a* habituel, coutumier.

woo [wuː] *vt* courtiser, faire la cour à.

wood [wud] *n* bois *m*, forêt *f*.

woodcock ['wudkɔk] *n* bécasse *f*.

woodcut ['wudkʌt] *m* gravure sur bois *f*.

woodcutter ['wudkʌtə] *n* bûcheron *m*, graveur sur bois *m*.

wooden ['wudn] *a* de (en) bois.

woodland ['wudlənd] *n* pays boisé *m*.

woodman ['wudmən] *n* garde forestier *m*, bûcheron *m*.

woodpecker ['wud,pekə] *n* pic *m*, pivert *m*.

woodwork ['wudwəːk] *n* boisage *m*, boiserie *f*, menuiserie *f*, charpenterie *f*.

wool [wul] *n* laine *f*.

woollen ['wulin] *n* lainage *m*; *a* de laine, laineux.

woolly ['wuli] *a* de laine, laineux, ouaté, flou, cotonneux, (*fig*) confus, vaseux; *n* vêtement de laine *m*, pull-over *m*.

word [wəːd] *n* mot *m*, parole *f*; *vt* exprimer, rédiger, formuler, énoncer.

wordiness ['wəːdinis] *n* verbosité *f*.

wording ['wəːdiŋ] *n* expression *f*, rédaction *f*, énoncé *m*, libellé *m*.

wordy ['wəːdi] *a* verbeux, diffus, prolixe.

wore [wɔː] *pt of* **wear.**

work [wəːk] *n* travail *m* (*pl* travaux), ouvrage *m*, œuvre *f*; *pl* usine *f*, atelier *m*, chantier *m*, mécanisme *m*; *vti* travailler; *vi* marcher, fonctionner, agir; *vt* faire travailler, faire marcher, actionner, exploiter, diriger, opérer, façonner; **to — out** *vt* élaborer, calculer; *vi* se monter (à at); **to — up** *vt* perfectionner, développer, préparer, exciter; *vi* se développer, se préparer, remonter.

workable ['wəːkəbl] *a* faisable, réalisable, exploitable.

work-basket ['wəːk,baːskit] *n* corbeille à ouvrage *f*.

workday ['wəːkdei] *n* jour ouvrable *m*.

worker ['wəːkə] *n* ouvrier, -ière.

workhouse ['wəːkhaus] *n* asile *m*, hospice *m*.

working ['wəːkiŋ] *n* travail *m*, (*wine*) fermentation *f*, fonctionnement *m*; *a* — **class** classe ouvrière *f*, prolétariat *m*; — **majority** majorité suffisante *f*.

workmanlike ['wəːkmənlaik] *a* bien fait, pratique, en bon ouvrier.

workmanship ['wəːkmənʃip] *n* habileté manuelle *f*, fin travail *m*, façon *f*.

workshop ['wəːkʃɔp] *n* atelier *m*, usine *f*.

work-table ['wəːk,teibl] *n* table à ouvrage *f*.

world [wəːld] *n* monde *m*.

worldliness ['wəːldlinis] *n* mondanité *f*.

worldly ['wəːldli] *a* de ce monde, matériel, du siècle.

worldwide ['wəːldwaid] *a* mondial, universel.

worm [wəːm] *n* ver *m*; *vi* ramper, se glisser; **to — it out of s.o.** tirer les vers du nez à qn; **to — one's way into** se faufiler dans, s'insinuer dans.

worm-eaten ['wəːm,iːtn] *a* mangé des vers, vermoulu.

wormwood ['wəːmwud] *n* absinthe *f*.

worn [wɔːn] *pp of* **wear.**

worn-out ['wɔːn'aut] *a* épuisé, usé.

worried ['wʌrid] *a* soucieux.

worry ['wʌri] *n* souci *m*, tracas *m*, ennui *m*; *vt* tourmenter, inquiéter; *vi* se tourmenter, s'inquiéter.

worse [wəːs] *n* pis *m*; *an* pire *m*; *ad* pis, moins bien, plus mal.

worsen ['wəːsn] *vti* empirer; *vt* aggraver; (*fam*) avoir le dessus sur; *vi* s'aggraver.

worship ['wəːʃip] *n* culte *m*, adoration *f*, Honneur *m*; *vt* adorer, rendre un culte à.

worshipper ['wəːʃipə] *n* fidèle *mf*, adorateur, -trice.

worst [wəːst] *n* le pis *m*, le pire *m*, le dessous *m*, désavantage *m*; *a* le pire; *ad* au pis, le pis, le plus mal; *vt* battre.

worsted ['wustid] *n* laine *f*, peigné *m*.

worth [wəːθ] *n* valeur *f*, mérite *m*; *a* qui vaut (la peine de), de la valeur de; **to be — valoir.**

worthiness ['wəːðinis] *n* mérite *m*, justice *f*.

worthless ['wəːθlis] *a* sans valeur, bon à rien.

worthwhile ['wəːθ'wail] *a* de valeur, qui en vaut la peine.

worthy ['wəːði] *a* digne, respectable; *n* personnage (notable) *m*.

would [wud] *part. of* **will.**

would-be ['wudbi:] *a* soi-disant, prétendu.

wound [waund] *pt pp of* **wind.**

wound [wu:nd] *n* blessure *f*, plaie *f*; *vt* blesser, atteindre.

wove, woven [wouv, 'wouvən] *pt pp of* **weave.**

wrack [ræk] *n* varech *m*.

wraith [reiθ] *n* fantôme *m*, apparition *f*.

wrangle ['ræŋgl] *n* dispute *f*; *vi* se disputer.

wrap [ræp] *vt* envelopper.

wrapped [ræpt] *a* enveloppé, absorbé.

wrapper ['ræpə] *n* bande *f*, couverture *f*, écharpe *f*.

wrath [rɔθ] *n* courroux *m*.

wreak [ri:k] *vt* assouvir, décharger.

wreath [ri:θ] *n* couronne *f*, volute *f*.

wreathe [ri:ð] *vt* couronner de fleurs, tresser, entourer, enrouler.

wreathed [ri:ðd] *a* enveloppé, baigné; — in smiles épanoui, rayonnant.

wreck [rek] *n* ruine *f*, naufrage *m*, épave(s) *f* (*pl*); *vt* perdre, ruiner, saboter, démolir, faire dérailler.

wreckage ['rekidʒ] *n* débris *m pl*; piece of — épave *f*.

wrecked [rekt] *a* jeté à la côte, naufragé, ruiné; to be — faire naufrage.

wrecker ['rekə] *n* naufrageur *m*, pilleur d'épaves *m*, dérailleur *m*, (US) dépanneur *m* (*aut*), récupérateur *m* (d'épaves).

wrecking ['rekiŋ] *n* (US) sauvetage *m*, renflouage *m* (de navire); — train carvée *f* de secours; — lorry dépanneuse *f*.

wren [ren] *n* roitelet *m*.

wrench [rentʃ] *n* torsion *f*, tour *m*, secousse *f*, coup *m*, clé *f*, entorse *f*; *vt* tordre, arracher; to — open ouvrir violemment, forcer.

wrest [rest] *vt* tourner, forcer, arracher.

wrestle ['resl] *n* lutte *f*; *vi* lutter; to — with lutter contre, s'attaquer à.

wrestler ['reslə] *n* lutteur *m*.

wrestling ['resliŋ] *n* lutte *f*, catch *m*.

wretch [retʃ] *n* malheureux, -euse, scélérat *m*, pauvre diable *m*, triste sire *m*, fripon(ne).

wretched ['retʃid] *a* misérable, lamentable, minable.

wretchedness ['retʃidnis] *n* état *m* misérable, malheur *m*, misère *f*.

wriggle ['rigl] *n* tortillement; *vt* tortiller, agiter; *vi* se tortiller, s'insinuer, se faufiler, frétiller.

wring [riŋ] *n* torsion *f*, pression *f*; *vt* presser, tordre, détourner, extorquer.

wrinkle ['riŋkl] *n* ride *f*, tuyau *m*; *vt* rider, froncer; *vi* se rider, se plisser.

wrist [rist] *n* poignet *m*.

wrist-watch ['ristwɔtʃ] *n* montre-bracelet *f*.

writ [rit] *n* écriture *f*, assignation *f*, mandat d'arrêt *m*.

write [rait] *vti* écrire; to — down noter, coucher par écrit, estimer, décrier; to — off réduire, défalquer, déduire, annuler; to — up rédiger, faire un éloge exagéré de, faire de la réclame pour, décrire, mettre à jour.

writer ['raitə] *n* écrivain *m*, auteur *m*, commis aux écritures *m*.

writhe [raið] *vi* se tordre, se crisper.

writing ['raitiŋ] *n* écriture *f*, œuvre *f*, écrit *m*, métier d'écrivain *m*.

writing-case ['raitiŋkeis] *n* nécessaire à écrire *m*.

writing-desk ['raitiŋdesk] *n* bureau *m*.

writing-pad ['raitiŋpæd] *n* sous-main *m*, bloc *m* de papier à lettres.

writing-paper ['raitiŋ‚peipə] *n* papier à lettres *m*.

written ['ritn] *pp of* **write.**

wrong [rɔŋ] *n* tort *m*, mal *m*, injustice *f*, préjudice *m*; *a* dérangé, mauvais, faux, inexact; *ad* mal, à tort, de travers; *vt* léser, faire tort à; to be — se tromper, avoir tort.

wrongdoer ['rɔŋ‚duə] *n* malfaiteur, -trice, coupable *mf*.

wrongdoing ['rɔŋ‚du(:)iŋ] *n* méfaits *m pl*, mauvaises actions *f pl*.

wrongful ['rɔŋful] *a* injuste, faux.

wrongfully ['rɔŋfuli] *ad* à tort, de travers.

wrote [rout] *pt of* **write.**

wroth [rouθ] *a* en colère.

wrung [rʌŋ] *pt pp of* **wring.**

wrought [rɔ:t] *pt pp of* **work;** *a* travaillé, forgé, excité.

wry [rai] *a* tors, tordu, de travers.

X

X-ray ['eks'rei] *n pl* rayons X *m pl*; *vt* radiographier, passer aux rayons X; — treatment radiothérapie.

Y

yacht [jɔt] *n* yacht *m*.

yam [jæm] *n* igname *f*.

yank [jæŋk] *vt* tirer brusquement; *n* coup sec *m*.

yap [jæp] *n* jappement *m*; *vi* japper.

yard [jɑ:d] *n* mètre *m*, cour *f*, chantier *m*, vergue *f*; —stick mètre *m*, aune *f*.

yarn [jɑ:n] *n* fil *m*, conte *m*, histoire *f*.

yaw [jɔ:] *n* embardée *f*; *vi* embarder.

yawl [jɔ:l] *n* yole *f*.

yawn [jɔ:n] *n* bâillement *m*; *vi* bâiller, béer.

ye [ji:] *pn* vous.

yea [jei] *ad* oui, voire.

year [jə:] *n* an *m*, année *f*.

year-book ['jəːbuk] n annuaire m.
yearling ['jəːliŋ] a d'un an.
yearly ['jəːli] a annuel; ad annuellement.
yearn [jəːn] vi aspirer (à after), soupirer (après after).
yearning ['jəːniŋ] n aspiration f, désir passionné m; a ardent.
yeast [jiːst] n levure f, levain m.
yell [jel] n hurlement m; vti hurler.
yellow ['jelou] an jaune m; a lâche.
yellowish ['jelouiʃ] a jaunâtre.
yellowness ['jelounis] n couleur jaune f.
yelp [jelp] n jappement m, glapissement m; vi japper, gémir, glapir.
yes [jes] n oui m; ad oui, si.
yes-man ['jesmæn] n qui dit amen à tout, béni-oui-oui m.
yesterday ['jestədi] n ad hier m; the day before — avant-hier.
yet [jet] ad encore, de plus, jusqu'ici, déjà; cj pourtant, tout de même.
yew [juː] n if m.
yield [jiːld] n produit m, rendement m, rapport m, revenu m, production f; vt rendre, rapporter, donner; vti céder; vi se rendre, succomber, plier, fléchir.
yielding ['jiːldiŋ] a arrangeant, faible, mou.
yoke [jouk] n joug m, paire (de bœufs) f; vt atteler, lier, unir.
yolk [jouk] n jaune d'œuf m, suint m.
yonder ['jɔndə] ad là-bas.
yore [jɔː] n of — d'antan, du temps jadis.
you [juː] pn vous.
young [jʌŋ] n petit, jeune; a jeune.
younger ['jʌŋgə] a jeune, cadet, puîné.

youngish ['jʌŋiʃ] a jeunet.
youngster ['jʌŋstə] n enfant mf, gosse mf.
your [jɔː] a votre, vos, ton, ta, tes.
yours [jɔːz] pn vôtre(s), à vous; le, la, (les) vôtre(s); tien(s), tienne(s), à toi; le(s) tien(s), la tienne, les tiennes.
yourself, -selves [jɔː'self, selvz] pn vous-même(s).
youth [juːθ] n jeunesse f, jeune homme m.
youthful ['juːθful] a jeune, juvénile.

Z

zeal [ziːl] n zèle m, empressement m.
zealous ['zeləs] a zélé, empressé.
zealously ['zeləsli] ad avec empressement.
zebra ['ziːbrə] n zèbre m.
zebu ['ziːbu] n zébu m.
zenith ['zeniθ] n zénith m.
zero ['ziərou] n zéro m.
zest [zest] n piquant m, enthousiasme m, entrain m.
zigzag ['zigzæg] n zigzag m; vi zigzaguer.
zinc [ziŋk] n zinc m.
zip [zip] n sifflement m: — fastener fermeture éclair Ⓡ f.
zither ['ziðə] n cithare f.
zone [zoun] n zone f, ceinture f.
zoo [zuː] n jardin d'acclimatation m, (US) pénitencier m, prison f.
zoological [ˌzouə'lɔdʒikəl] a zoologique.
zoologist [zou'ɔlədʒist] n zoologiste m.
zoology [zou'ɔlədʒi] n zoologie f.

Mesures et monnaies françaises
French measures, weights and money

MESURES DE LONGUEUR—LENGTH

1 millimètre = ·001 mètre = ·0394 inch.
1 centimètre = ·01 mètre = ·394 inch.
1 mètre = 39·4 inches = *1 yard.
1 kilomètre = 1000 mètres = *1094 yards or ⅝ mile.
8 kilomètres = 5 miles.

MESURES DE SURFACE—AREA

1 are = *120 square yards.
1 hectare = 100 ares = *2½ acres.

MESURES DE CAPACITÉ—CAPACITY (FLUIDS AND GRAIN)

1 centilitre = ·01 litre = ·0176 pint.
1 litre = *1¾ pints = ·2201 gallon.
1 hectolitre = 100 litres = *22 gallons = 2¾ bushels.
1 kilolitre = 1000 litres = *220 gallons = 27½ bushels.

MESURES DE POIDS—WEIGHTS

1 milligramme = ·001 gramme = ·0154 grain.
1 centigramme = ·01 gramme = ·1543 grain.
1 gramme = 15·43 grains.
1 hectogramme = 100 grammes = *3½ oz.
1 livre = 500 grammes = 1 lb. 1½ oz.
1 kilogramme = 1000 grammes = *2 lbs. 3 oz.
1 quintal = 100 kilogrammes = *2 cwts.
1 tonne = 1000 kilogrammes = *1 ton.

MESURES THERMOMÉTRIQUES—THE THERMOMETER

Point de congélation⎫ —Centigrade 0°
Freezing point ⎬ —Fahrenheit 32°
Point d'ébullition ⎬ —Centigrade 100°
Boiling point ⎭ —Fahrenheit 212°

To convert Centigrade to Fahrenheit degrees, divide by 5, multiply by 9 and add 32.

MONNAIES—MONEY

100 centimes = 1 franc.
* roughly.

Notes on French Grammar

A. THE ARTICLE

(i) The *definite article* is **le** (*m*), **la** (*f*), and **les** (*mf pl*). **Le** and **la** are shortened to **l'** before a vowel or H-mute.

(ii) The *indefinite article* is **un** (*m*), **une** (*f*).

(iii) When the prepositions **à** or **de** are used before the definite article they combine with **le** to form **au** and **du** respectively. They combine with **les** to form **aux** and **des**. They make no change before **la** or **l'**.

(iv) The partitive article, **du** (*m*), **de la** (*f*), **des** (*mf pl*), corresponds to the English *some* or *any* when the latter denotes an indefinite quantity. e.g. Have you any milk? **Avez-vous du lait?**

B. THE NOUN

(i) The plural is usually formed in **s**. Nouns ending in **s**, **x**, **z** have the same form in the plural. Those ending in **au**, and **eu** (except **bleu**) and some in **ou** (**bijou, caillou, hibou, genou, chou, pou, joujou**) form their plural in **x**. Those ending in **al** and **ail** form their plural in **aux**. **Aieul, ciel, œil** become **aïeux, cieux** and **yeux**.

(ii) All French nouns are either masculine or feminine in gender. Most nouns ending in mute **e** are feminine, except those in **isme**, **age** (**image, rage, nage** are *f*) and **iste** (often either *m* or *f*). Most nouns ending in a consonant or a vowel other than mute **e** are masculine, but nouns ending in **tion** and **té** (**été, pâté** are *m*) are feminine.

(iii) The feminine is usually formed by adding **e** to the masculine. Nouns ending in **er** have a femine in **ère**, and those ending in **en**, **on** have a feminine in **enne**, **onne**. Nouns ending in **eur** have a feminine in **euse**, except those ending in **ateur** which give **atrice**. A few words ending in **e** have a feminine in **esse**.

C. THE ADJECTIVE

(i) The plural is usually formed by adding an **s**. Adjectives ending in **s**, **x** are the same in the plural. Those ending in **al** have a plural in **aux**, but the following take an **s**: **bancal, fatal, final, glacial, natal, naval**.

(ii) The feminine is usually formed by adding **e** to the masculine form. Adjectives ending in **f** change **f** into **ve**, and those ending in **x** change **x** into **se**. Adjectives ending in **er** have **ère** in the feminine form. To form the feminine of adjectives ending in **el**, **eil**, **en**, **et**, **on**, the final consonant must be doubled before adding an **e**.

(iii) Comparison of adjectives. The Comparative is formed
regularly by adding **plus** to the ordinary form, and the
Superlative by adding **le**, **la**, or **les**, as required, to the
Comparative form. **Moins** (= less) is employed in the
same way as **plus**, giving, for example, **moins long**—less
long, **les moins récentes**—the least recent. Irregular
forms are: **bon, meilleur**, **le meilleur**; **mauvais, pire**
or **plus mauvais, le pire** or **le plus mauvais**; **petit,
moindre** or **plus petit, le moindre** or **le plus petit**.
'Than' is always rendered by **que**. Other expressions of
comparison are: **aussi . . que**, as . . . as; **pas si . . . que**,
not so (as) . . . as; **autant (de) . . . que**, as much (or
many) . . . as; **pas tant (de) . . . que**, not so much (or
many) . . . as.

(iv) The demonstrative adjectives 'this' and 'that' and their
plural 'these' or 'those' are in French **ce**, **cet** (m), **cette** (f)
and **ces** (pl). **Ce** is used with all masculine words except
before those beginning with a vowel or an H-mute, in
which case **cet** is used. The opposition between 'this' and
'that' may be emphasized by adding the suffix **-ci** or **-là** to
the noun concerned. 'That of' is in French **celui** (f **celle**,
pl **ceux**, **celles**) **de**. Expressions such as 'he who', 'the one
which', 'those or they who' should be translated by **celui**
(**celle**, **ceux**, **celles**) **qui**.

(v) Possessive adjectives.

my	mon (m)	ma (f)	mes (pl)
your	ton	ta	tes
his	son	sa	ses
our	notre	notre	nos
your	votre	votre	vos
their	leur	leur	leurs

All of these agree in gender with the following noun.

D. THE PRONOUN

I. (i) Unstressed forms.

	Nom.	Acc.	Dat.	Gen.
1st sing.	je	me	me	
2nd sing.	tu	te	te	
3rd sing.	il, elle	le, la (se)	lui, y	en
	Nom.	Acc.	Dat.	Gen.
1st plur.	nous	nous	nous	
2nd plur.	vous	vous	vous	
3rd plur.	ils, elles	les (se)	leur, y (se)	en

(i) **Tu** and **te** are normally used when speaking to one
person who is a close relative or an intimate friend. They

481

are also used to any child or an animal. Otherwise the 2nd plural **vous** is normally used to address single persons. In this use it retains a plural verb, but its other agreements (with adjectives, participles etc.) are singular, provided it refers to a single person.

(ii) The forms **me, te, se, nous, vous,** se may be used in reflexive verbs, and also to denote mutual participation in an action. E.g. they looked at each other, **ils se regardaient.**

II. Stressed forms.

	Singular	Plural
1st Person	**moi**	**nous**
2nd Person	**toi**	**vous**
3rd Person m	**lui**	**eux**
f	**elle**	**elles**
Reflexive	**soi**	

(i) This form is used when the pronoun is governed by a preposition.

(ii) It is used where people are singled out or contrasted, i.e. for emphasis.

(iii) It is also used when a pronoun stands as the sole word in a sentence, stands as the antecedent of a relative, forms part of a double subject or object of a verb, is the complement of **être** or when it stands after **que** in comparative sentences.

III. When used together, personal pronouns are positioned according to the following scheme.

me	le	lui	y	en
te	la	leur		
nous	les			
vous				
se				

IV. Possessive pronouns.

	Singular	Plural
1st sing. m	**le mien**	**les miens**
f	**la mienne**	**les miennes**
2nd sing. m	**le tien**	**les tiens**
f	**la tienne**	**les tiennes**
3rd sing. m	**le sien**	**les siens**
f	**la sienne**	**les siennes**
1st plur.	**le (la) nôtre**	**les nôtres**
2nd plur.	**le (la) vôtre**	**les vôtres**
3rd plur.	**le (la) leur**	**les leurs**

482

E.g. I have lost my pen; lend me yours = **j'ai perdue ma plume, prêtez-moi la vôtre.**

V. Relative pronouns. 'Who' is translated by **qui**; 'whom' by **que** (or by **qui** after a preposition); 'whose' by **dont**; 'which' by **qui** (subject) or **que** (object). After a preposition 'which' is translated by **lequel** (*m*), **laquelle** (*f*), **lesquels** (*m pl*) and **lesquelles** (*f pl*). With the prepositions **à** and **de** the following contractions take place: **auquel** (but **à laquelle**), **auxquels, auxquelles; duquel** (but **de laquelle**), **desquels, desquelles.**

VI. Interrogative pronouns. 'Who' and 'whom' are both **qui**. 'What', when object, is **que** and when subject is **qu'est-ce qui.** When 'what' is used adjectivally it should be translated by **quel, quelle, quels, quelles.**

E. ADVERBS

Most French adverbs are formed by adding **ment** to the feminine form of the corresponding adjective. Adjectives ending in **ant** and **ent** have adverbial endings in **amment** and **emment** respectively.

Negative forms. 'Not' is **ne . . . pas**, 'nobody' **ne . . . personne**, 'nothing' **ne . . . rien** and 'never' is **ne . . . jamais.**

Examples. I do not know, **je ne sais pas.** I know nothing, **je ne sais rien.**

'Nobody and 'nothing' when subject are rendered by **personne ne . . ., rien ne . . .**

F. VERBS

I. Regular verbs.

There are three principal types of regular conjugation of French verbs, corresponding to the three infinitive endings: **-er, -ir, -re.** They provide patterns for conjugating large numbers of verbs which have one or other of these infinitive endings. As a convenient simplification, each part of a verb may be stated to consist of a basic stem and a characteristic ending. From the stem and ending of the present infinitive and of the present participle, all parts of a regular verb may be built up.

Examples. **parler, finir, vendre.**

Present infinitive	**parl/er**	**fin/ir**	**vend/re**
Present participle	**parl/ant**	**finiss/ant**	**vend/ant**
Past participle	stem+**-é**	stem+**-i**	stem+**-u**

Present indicative	stem+-e, stem+-is, stem+-s,
	-es, -e, -is, -it, -s, -,
	-ons, -ez, -issons, -ons, -ez,
	-ent -issez, -ent
	-issent
Imperative	2nd singular, 1st plural and 2nd plural of present indicative, without subject pronouns. First conjugation drops final **s** of 2nd singular, except before **y, en**.
Imperfect	stem of present participle+-**ais**, -ais, -ait, -ions, -iez, -aient.
Past historic	stem+-**ai**, -as, stem+-is, -is, -a, -âmes, -âtes, -it, -îmes, -îtes, -èrent -irent
Future	infinitive+-**ai**, -as, -a, -ons, -ez, -ont. Third conjugation drops final **e** of infinitive.
Conditional	infinitive+-**ais**, -ais, -ait, -ions, -iez, -aient. Third conjugation drops final **e** of infinitive.
Present subjunctive	stem of present participle+ -e, -es, -e, -ions, -iez, -ent.
Imperfect subjunctive	remove final **s** from 2nd singular of past historic and add -**sse**, -sses, ît, -ssions, -ssiez, -ssent.

Compound tenses are formed with the auxiliary **avoir** and the past participle, except reflexive verbs and some common intransitive verbs (like **aller, arriver, devenir, partir, rester, retourner, sortir, tomber, venir** etc.) which are conjugated with **être**. The following scheme is applicable to all three conjugations.

Perfect	present indicative of **avoir** (or **être**)+past participle.
Pluperfect	imperfect of **avoir** (or **être**)+ past participle.
Future perfect	future of **avoir** (or **être**)+past participle.
Conditional perfect	conditional of **avoir** (or **être**)+ past participle.
Perfect infinitive	infinitive of **avoir** (or **être**)+ past participle.

Note on agreement. The French past participle always agrees with the noun to which it is either an attribute or an adjective. It agrees with the object of a verb conjugated with **avoir** only when the object comes before it. E.g. I loved

484

that woman, **j'ai aimé cette femme**; the women I have
loved, **les femmes que j'ai aimées**.

For the conjugation of the auxiliaries **avoir** and **être**
consult the list of irregular verbs.

G. MISCELLANEOUS NOTES

(i) Verbs having a mute **e** or closed **é** in the last syllable but
one of the present infinitive, change the mute **e** or closed **é**
to open **è** before a mute syllable (except in the future and
conditional tenses). E.g. **espérer, j'espère, il espérera,
il espérerait.**

(ii) Verbs with infinitive endings in **-cer** have **ç** before
endings in **a, o**. E.g. **commencer, je commençais,
nous commençons.**

(iii) Verbs with infinitive endings in **-ger** have an additional
e before endings in **a, o**. E.g. **manger, je mangeais,
nous mangeons.**

(iv) Verbs ending in **-eler, -eter** double the **l** or **t** before a
mute **e**. E.g. **appeler, j'appelle; jeter, je jette**. The
following words do not obey this rule and take only **è**:
**acheter, agneler, bégueter, celer, ciseler, congeler,
corseter, crocheter, déceler, dégeler, démanteler,
écarteler, fureter, geler, harceler, marteler, modeler, peler, racheter, receler, regeler.**

(v) Verbs with infinitive endings in **-yer** change **y** into **i**
before a mute **e**. They require a **y** and an **i** in the first two
persons plural of the imperfect indicative and of the
present subjunctive. Verbs with infinitive endings in **-ayer**
may keep the **y** or change it to **i** before a mute **e**. Verbs
with infinitive endings in **-eyer** keep the **y** throughout the
conjugation.

IRREGULAR VERBS

Order of principal tenses and essential parts of the
French irregular verbs in most frequent use. (1) Present
Participle; (2) Past Participle; (3) Present Indicative;
(4) Imperfect Indicative; (5) Preterite; (6) Future; (7)
Present Subjunctive.

Prefixed verbs not included in this list follow the root
verb, e.g., sourire—rire: abattre—battre.

acquérir (1) acquérant; (2) acquis; (3) acquiers, acquiers,
acquiert, acquérons, acquérez, acquièrent; (4) acquérais;
(5) acquis; (6) acquerrai; (7) acquière.
aller (1) allant; (2) allé; (3) vais, vas, va, allons, allez, vont;
(4) allais; (5) allai; (6) irai; (7) aille.

asseoir (1) asseyant; (2) assis; (3) assieds, assieds, assied, asseyons, asseyez, asseyent; (4) asseyais; (5) assis; (6) assiérai or asseyerai; (7) asseye.

atteindre (1) atteignant; (2) atteint; (3) atteins, atteins, atteint, atteignons, atteignez, atteignent; (4) atteignais; (5) atteignis; (6) atteindrai; (7) atteigne.

avoir (1) ayant; (2) eu; (3) ai, as, a, avons, avez, ont; (4) avais; (5) eus; (6) aurai; (7) aie. *N.B.*—Imperative aie, ayons, ayez.

battre (1) battant; (2) battu; (3) bats, bats, bat, battons, battez, battent; (4) battais; (5) battis; (6) battrai; (7) batte.

boire (1) buvant; (2) bu; (3) bois, bois, boit, buvons, buvez, boivent; (4) buvais; (5) bus; (6) boirai; (7) boive.

bouillir (1) bouillant; (2) bouilli; (3) bous, bous, bout, bouillons, bouillez, bouillent; (4) bouillais; (5) bouillis; (6) bouillirai; (7) bouille.

conclure (1) concluant; (2) conclu; (3) conclus, conclus, conclut, concluons, concluez, concluent; (4) concluais; (5) conclus; (6) conclurai; (7) conclue.

conduire (1) conduisant; (2) conduit; (3) conduis, conduis, conduit, conduisons, conduisez, conduisent; (4) conduisais; (5) conduisis; (6) conduirai; (7) conduise.

connaître (1) connaissant; (2) connu; (3) connais, connais, connaît, connaissons, connaissez, connaissent; (4) connaissais; (5) connus; (6) connaîtrai; (7) connaisse.

coudre (1) cousant; (2) cousu; (3) couds, couds, coud, cousons, cousez, cousent; (4) cousais; (5) cousis; (6) coudrai; (7) couse.

courir (1) courant; (2) couru; (3) cours, cours, court, courons, courez, courent; (4) courais; (5) courus; (6) courrai; (7) coure.

couvrir (1) couvrant; (2) couvert; (3) couvre, couvres, couvre, couvrons, couvrez, couvrent; (4) couvrais; (5) couvris; (6) couvrirai; (7) couvre.

craindre (1) craignant; (2) craint; (3) crains, crains, craint, craignons, craignez, craignent; (4) craignais; (5) craignis; (6) craindrai; (7) craigne.

croire (1) croyant; (2) cru; (3) crois, crois, croit, croyons, croyez, croient; (4) croyais; (5) crus; (6) croirai; (7) croie.

croître (1) croissant; (2) crû, crue (*pl* crus, crues); (3) croîs, croîs, croît, croissons, croissez, croissent; (4) croissais; (5) crûs; (6) croîtrai; (7) croisse.

cueillir (1) cueillant; (2) cuelli; (3) cueille, cueilles, cueille, cueillons, cueillez, cueillent; (4) cueillais; (5) cueillis; (6) cueillerai; (7) cueille.

devoir (1) devant; (2) dû, due (*pl* dus, dues); (3) dois, dois, doit, devons, devez, doivent; (4) devais; (5) dus; (6) devrai; (7) doive.

dire (1) disant; (2) dit; (3) dis, dis, dit, disons, dites, disent; (4) disais; (5) dis; (6) dirai; (7) dise.

dormir (1) dormant; (2) dormi; (3) dors, dors, dort, dormons, dormez, dorment; (4) dormais; (5) dormis; (6) dormirai; (7) dorme.

écrire (1) écrivant; (2) écrit; (3) écris, écris, écrit, écrivons, écrivez, écrivent; (4) écrivais; (5) écrivis; (6) écrirai; (7) écrive.

être (1) étant; (2) été; (3) suis, es, est, sommes, êtes, sont; (4) étais; (5) fus; (6) serai; (7) sois. *N.B.*—Imperative sois, soyons, soyez.

faire (1) faisant; (2) fait; (3) fais, fais, fait, faisons, faites, font; (4) faisais; (5) fis; (6) ferai; (7) fasse.

falloir (2) fallu; (3) faut; (4) fallait; (5) fallut; (6) faudra; (7) faille.

fuir (1) fuyant; (2) fui; (3) fuis, fuis, fuit, fuyons, fuyez, fuient; (4) fuyais; (5) fuis; (6) fuirai; (7) fuie.

joindre (1) joignant; (2) joint; (3) joins, joins, joint, joignons, joignez, joignent; (4) joignais; (5) joignis; (6) joindrai; (7) joigne.

lire (1) lisant; (2) lu; (3) lis, lis, lit, lisons, lisez, lisent; (4) lisais; (5) lus; (6) lirai; (7) lise.

luire (1) luisant; (2) lui; (3) luis, luis, luit, luisons, luisez, luisent; (4) luisais; (5) luisis; (6) luirai; (7) luise.

maudire (1) maudissant; (2) maudit; (3) maudis, maudis, maudit, maudissons, maudissez, maudissent; (4) maudissait; (5) maudis; (6) maudirai; (7) maudisse.

mentir (1) mentant; (2) menti; (3) mens, mens, ment, mentons, mentez, mentent; (4) mentais; (5) mentis; (6) mentirai; (7) mente.

mettre (1) mettant; (2) mis; (3) mets, mets, met, mettons, mettez, mettent; (4) mettais; (5) mis; (6) mettrai; (7) mette.

mourir (1) mourant; (2) mort; (3) meurs, meurs, meurt, mourons, mourez, meurent; (4) mourais; (5) mourus; (6) mourrai; (7) meure.

naître (1) naissant; (2) né; (3) nais, nais, naît, naissons, naissez, naissent; (4) naissais; (5) naquis; (6) naîtrai; (7) naisse.

offrir (1) offrant; (2) offert; (3) offre, offres, offre, offrons, offrez, offrent; (4) offrais; (5) offris; (6) offrirai; (7) offre.

partir (1) partant; (2) parti; (3) pars, pars, part, partons, partez, partent; (4) partais; (5) partis; (6) partirai; (7) parte.

plaire (1) plaisant; (2) plu; (3) plais, plais, plaît, plaisons, plaisez, plaisent; (4) plaisais; (5) plus; (6) plairai; (7) plaise.

pleuvoir (1) pleuvant; (2) plu; (3) pleut, pleuvent; (4) pleuvait; (5) plut; (6) pleuvra; (7) pleuve.

pourvoir (1) pourvoyant; (2) pourvu; (3) pourvois, pourvois, pourvoit, pourvoyons, pourvoyez, pourvoient; (4) pourvoyais; (5) pourvus; (6) pourvoirai; (7) pourvoie.

pouvoir (1) pouvant; (2) pu; (3) puis *or* peux, peux, peut, pouvons, pouvez, peuvent; (4) pouvais; (5) pus; (6) pourrai; (7) puisse.

prendre (1) prenant; (2) pris; (3) prends, prends, prend, prenons, prenez, prennent; (4) prenais; (5) pris; (6) prendrai; (7) prenne.

prévoir like voir. *N.B.*—(7) prévoirai.

recevoir (1) recevant; (2) reçu; (3) reçois, reçois, reçoit, recevons, recevez, reçoivent; (4) recevais; (5) reçus; (6) recevrai; (7) reçoive.

résoudre (1) résolvant; (2) résolu; (3) résous, résous, résout, résolvons, résolvez, résolvent; (4) résolvais; (5) résolus; (6) résoudrai; (7) résolve.

rire (1) riant; (2) ri; (3) ris, ris, rit, rions, riez, rient; (4) riais; (5) ris; (6) rirai; (7) rie.

savoir (1) sachant; (2) su; (3) sais, sais, sait, savons, savez, savent; (4) savais; (5) sus; (6) saurai; (7) sache. *N.B.*— Imperative sache, sachons, sachez.

servir (1) servant; (2) servi; (3) sers, sers, sert, servons, servez, servent; (4) servais; (5) servis; (6) servirai; (7) serve.

sortir (1) sortant; (2) sorti; (3) sors, sors, sort, sortons, sortez, sortent; (4) sortais; (5) sortis; (6) sortirai; (7) sorte.

souffrir (1) souffrant; (2) souffert; (3) souffre, souffres, souffre, souffrons, souffrez, souffrent; (4) souffrais; (5) souffris; (6) souffrirai; (7) souffre.

suffire (1) suffisant; (2) suffi; (3) suffis, suffis, suffit, suffisons, suffisez, suffisent; (4) suffisais; (5) suffis; (6) suffirai; (7) suffise.

suivre (1) suivant; (2) suivi; (3) suis, suis, suit, suivons, suivez, suivent; (4) suivais; (5) suivis; (6) suivrai; (7) suive.

taire (1) taisant; (2) tu; (3) tais, tais, tait, taisons, taisez, taisent; (4) taisais; (5) tus; (6) tairai; (7) taise.

tenir (1) tenant; (2) tenu; (3) tiens, tiens, tient, tenons, tenez, tiennent; (4) tenais; (5) tins; (6) tiendrai; (7) tienne.

vaincre (1) vainquant; (2) vaincu; (3) vaincs, vaincs, vainc, vainquons, vainquez, vainquent; (4) vainquais; (5) vainquis; (6) vaincrai; (7) vainque.

valoir (1) valant; (2) valu; (3) vaux, vaux, vaut, valons, valez, valent; (4) valais; (5) valus; (6) vaudrai; (7) vaille.

venir (1) venant; (2) venu; (3) viens, viens, vient, venons, venez, viennent; (4) venais; (5) vins; (6) viendrai; (7) vienne.

vivre (1) vivant; (2) vécu; (3) vis, vis, vit, vivons, vivez, vivent; (4) vivais; (5) vécus; (6) vivrai; (7) vive.

voir (1) voyant; (2) vu; (3) vois, vois, voit, voyons, voyez, voient; (4) voyais; (5) vis; (6) verrai; (7) voie.

vouloir (1) voulant; (2) voulu; (3) veux, veux, veut, voulons, voulez, veulent; (4) voulais; (5) voulus; (6) voudrai; (7) veuille. *N.B.*—Imperative veuille. veuillons, veuillez.

English measures, weights and money
Mesures et monnaies anglaises

LENGTH—MESURES DE LONGUEUR
Inch (in.) = 25 millimètres.
Foot (ft.) (12 in.) = 304 mm.
Yard (yd.) (3 ft.) = 914 mm. (approximativement 1 mètre).
Fathom (fthm.) (2 yds.) = 1 mètre 828 mm.
Mile (8 furlongs, 1760 yds.) = 1609 mètres
  (approximativement 1 kilomètre et demi).
Nautical mile, knot = 1853 mètres.
5 miles = 8 kilomètres.

AREA—MESURES DE SURFACE
Square inch = 6 centimètres carrés.
Square foot = 929 centimètres carrés.
Square yard = 0·8360 mètre carré.
Acre   = 4047 mètres carrés.

CAPACITY (FLUIDS AND GRAIN)—MESURES DE CAPACITÉ
Pint = 0·567 litre (approximativement ½ litre).
Quart (2 pints) = 1·135 litre.
Gallon (4 quarts) = 4·543 litres.
Peck (2 gallons) = 9·086 litres.
Bushel (8 gallons) = 36·348 litres.
Quarter (8 bushels) = 290·781 litres.

WEIGHTS (AVOIRDUPOIS)—MESURES DE POIDS
Ounce (oz.) = 28·35 grammes.
Pound (lb.—16 oz.) = 453·59 grammes.
Stone (st.—14 lb.) = 6 kilos 350 grammes.
Quarter (qr.—28 lb.) = 12·7 kilos.
Hundredweight (cwt.—112 lb.) = 50·8 kilos.
Ton (T.—20 cwts.) = 1016 kilos.

THE THERMOMETER—MESURES THERMOMÉTRIQUES

Freezing point   ⎫ — Fahrenheit 32°
Point de congélation ⎭ — Centigrade 0°
Boiling point   ⎫ — Fahrenheit 212°
Point d'ébullition   ⎭ — Centigrade 100°

Pour convertir les mesures Fahrenheit en mesures Centigrade soustraire 32, multiplier par 5 et diviser par 9

MONEY—MONNAIES

20 shillings = 1 pound
12 pence   = 1 shilling
A partir de 1971:
100 pence   = 1 pound

Verbes forts et irréguliers anglais

PRÉSENT	PRÉTÉRIT	PARTICIPE PASSÉ
abide	abode	abode
arise	arose	arisen
(a)wake	(a)woke	(a)woken
be	was	been
bear	bore	born(e)
beat	beat	beaten
become	became	become
befall	befell	befallen
begin	began	begun
behold	beheld	beheld
bend	bent	bent
bereave	bereft	bereft
beseech	besought	besought
bespeak	bespoke	bespoke(n)
bet	bet	bet
bid	bade, bid	bidden
bid	bid	bid
bind	bound	bound
bite	bit	bitten
bleed	bled	bled
blow	blew	blown
break	broke	broken
breed	bred	bred
bring	brought	brought
build	built	built
burn	burnt	burnt
burst	burst	burst
buy	bought	bought
cast	cast	cast
catch	caught	caught
chide	chid	chid(den)
choose	chose	chosen
cling	clung	clung
come	came	come

490

cost	cost	cost
creep	crept	crept
cut	cut	cut
deal	dealt	dealt
dig	dug	dug
do	did	done
draw	drew	drawn
dream	dreamt	dreamt
drink	drank	drunk
drive	drove	driven
dwell	dwelt	dwelt
eat	ate	eaten
fall	fell	fallen
feed	fed	fed
feel	felt	felt
fight	fought	fought
find	found	found
flee, fly	fled	fled
fling	flung	flung
fly	flew	flown
forbid	forbade	forbidden
forget	forgot	forgotten
forgive	forgave	forgiven
forsake	forsook	forsaken
freeze	froze	frozen
get	got	got
give	gave	given
go	went	gone
grind	ground	ground
grow	grew	grown
hang	hung	hung
have	had	had
hear	heard	heard
hew	hewed	hewn
hide	hid	hid(den)
hit	hit	hit
hold	held	held
hurt	hurt	hurt
keep	kept	kept
kneel	knelt	knelt
know	knew	known
lay	laid	laid
lead	led	led
lean	leant	leant
leap	leapt	leapt
learn	learnt	learnt
leave	left	left
lend	lent	lent
let	let	let
lie	lay	lain
light	lit	lit
lose	lost	lost
make	made	made
mean	meant	meant
meet	met	met
mow	mowed	mown
pay	paid	paid
put	put	put
quit	quit	quit

PRÉSENT	PRÉTÉRIT	PARTICIPE PASSÉ
read	read	read
rend	rent	rent
rid	rid	rid
ride	rode	ridden
ring	rang	rung
rise	rose	risen
run	ran	run
saw	sawed	sawn
say	said	said
see	saw	seen
seek	sought	sought
sell	sold	sold
send	sent	sent
set	set	set
sew	sewed	sewn
shake	shook	shaken
shed	shed	shed
shine	shone	shone
shoe	shod	shod
shoot	shot	shot
show	showed	shown
shrink	shrank	shrunk
shrive	shrove	shriven
shut	shut	shut
sing	sang, sung	sung
sink	sank, sunk	sunk
sit	sat	sat
slay	slew	slain
sleep	slept	slept
slide	slid	slid
sling	slung	slung
slink	slunk	slunk
slit	slit	slit
smell	smelt	smelt
smite	smote, smit	smitten, smit
sow	sowed	sown
speak	spoke	spoken
speed	sped	sped
spell	spelt, spelled	spelt, spelled
spend	spent	spent
spill	spilt	spilt
spin	spun, span	spun
spit	spat, spit	spat, spit
split	split	split
spoil	spoilt	spoilt
spread	spread	spread
spring	sprang	sprung
stand	stood	stood
steal	stole	stolen
stick	stuck	stuck
sting	stung	stung
stink	stank, stunk	stunk
stride	strode	stridden, strid
strike	struck	struck
string	strung	strung
strive	strove	striven
swear	swore	sworn

sweep	swept	swept
swell	swelled	swollen
swim	swam	swum
swing	swung	swung
take	took	taken
teach	taught	taught
tear	tore	torn
tell	told	told
think	thought	thought
thrive	throve	thriven
throw	threw	thrown
thrust	thrust	thrust
tread	trod	trodden
wake	woke	woken
wear	wore	worn
weave	wove	woven, wove
weep	wept	wept
wet	wet	wet
win	won	won
wind	wound	wound
wring	wrung	wrung
write	wrung	wrung
write	wrote	written

English Abbreviations

ABRÉVIATIONS ANGLAISES

A	adults (*adultes*)
AA	Automobile Association (*association d'automobilistes*); Alcoholics Anonymous (*société antialcoolique*)
a/c	account (current) (*compte courant*)
am	before noon (L. *ante meridiem*) (*avant midi*)
approx.	approximately (*approximativement*)
assn	association (*association*)
asst	assistant (*auxiliaire ou aide*)
av	average (*moyen*)
b	born (*né*)
BA	Bachelor of Arts (*Licencié ès Lettres*); British Academy (*Académie Britannique*); British Association (for the advancement of Science) (*association britannique pour la promotion des recherches scientifiques*)
BBC	British Broadcasting Corporation (*organisation qui contrôle la radio et la télévision britanniques*=ORTF)
BC	Before Christ (*avant Christ*); British Columbia (*Colombie Britannique*)
BD	Bachelor of Divinity (*diplôme d'études théologiques*)
Bd	Board (*conseil d'administration*)
BDS	Bachelor of Dental Surgery (*diplôme sanctionnant les études dentaires*); bomb disposal squad (*une équipe spéciale pour le désamorcement des bombes*)
B/E	Bill of exchange (*lettre de change, bon*)
BEA	British European Airways (*compagnie aérienne qui dessert l'Europe*)
B. Litt.	Bachelor of Letters (*diplôme d'études littéraires, diplôme d'études supérieures*)
BM	British Museum (*grand musée d'art et d'antiquités à Londres avec une bibliothèque et une salle de lecture*; Bachelor of Medicine (*diplôme de médecine*)

BMA	British Medical Association (*conseil de l'ordre des médecins*)
B. Mus.	Bachelor of Music (*diplôme des études musicales*)
BOAC	British Overseas Airways Corporation (*compagnie aérienne qui dessert le monde entier*)
BR	British Rail (*chemins de fer britanniques = SNCF*)
Brit	Britain (*Bretagne*); British (*Britannique*)
Bros	Brothers (*Frères*)
B/S	Bill of Sale (*acte de vente, reçu*)
BSc	Bachelor of Science (*diplôme de sciences*)
C	Cape (*cap*); centigrade (*centigrade*); central (*central*)
c	cent (*cent*); centime (*centime*); century (*siècle*); chapter (*chapitre*); about (*L. circa*) (*vers*); (*in cricket*) caught (*mis hors jeu*)
Cantab	Cambridge (*L. Cantaburiensis*)
CIA	(*US*) Central Intelligence Agency (*agence américaine de contre-espionnage*)
CID	Criminal Investigation Department (*section de la police anglaise qui s'occupe de l'investigation des actes criminels*)
ci f	Cost, Insurance and Freight (*coût, assurance et fret*)
CND	Campaign for Nuclear Disarmament (*mouvement en faveur du désarmement*)
CO	Commanding Officer (*commandant*); conscientious objector (*objecteur de conscience*)
Co	Company (*Cie, compagnie*)
c/o	care of (*aux bons soins de, chez*)
COD	cash on delivery (*payable à la livraison, livraison contre remboursement*)
cwt	hundredweight (*quintal*)
d	died (*mort*); date (*date*); daughter (*fille*); penny
DC	District of Columbia (*district fédéral de Columbia*); direct current (*courant continu*)
DD	Doctor of Divinity (*docteur en théologie*)
doz	dozen (*douzaine*)
EEC	European Economic Community—Common Market (*Communauté économique européenne—Marché commun*)
EFTA	European Free Trade Association (*Association européenne pour le libre échange*)
eg	for example ((*L. exampli gratia*) *par exemple*)
EP	extended play (*un disque quarante-cinq tours*)
ER	Queen Elizabeth (*L. Elizabeth Regina*) (*reine d'Angleterre*)
esp	especially (*spécialement*)
est	established (*établi*)
FA	Football Association (*association qui contrôle le football*)
FAO	Food and Agriculture Organization (*organisation pour l'alimentation et l'agriculture*)
FBI	(*US*) Federal Bureau of Investigation (*police fédérale américaine*)
FO	Foreign Office (*Ministère des Affaires étrangères*)
fob	free on board (*franco à bord*)
FRS	Fellow of the Royal Society (*membre de la Société Royale*)
ft	foot (*pied*); feet (*pieds*); fort (*fort*)
gal	gallon(s) (*gallon(s)—5 litres=1.1 gallons*)
GATT	General Agreement on Tariffs and Trade (*convention générale sur les tarifs et la commerce*)
GB	Great Britain (*Grande Bretagne*)

494

GCE	General Certificate of Education (*brevet d'enseignement secondaire*)
GI	(*US*) Government issue (American private soldier) (*nom donné au simple soldat américain*)
GMT	Greenwich mean time (*l'heure de Greenwich*)
Govt	government (*gouvernement*)
GP	General practitioner (*médecin de médecine générale, omnipraticien*)
GPO	General Post Office (=*P et T*)
h & c	hot and cold (*chaud et froid*)
HE	His Excellency (*Son Excellence*); His Eminence (*Son Eminence*); high-explosive (*danger d'explosion*)
HM(S)	Her Majesty('s Service, Her Majesty's Ship) (*Le Service de Sa Majesté, Le Bateau de Sa Majesté*)
Hon.	Honorary (*Honoraire*); Honourable (*Honorable*)
hp	Horse-power (*cheval-vapeur*)
HQ	Headquarters (*quartier général*)
HRH	His (Her) Royal Highness (*Son Altesse Royale*)
I, Is	islands (*îles*)
ICBM	Inter-Continental Ballistic Missile (*missile intercontinental*)
ICI	Imperial Chemical Industries (*Industries Chimiques Impériales*)
i.e.	that is; namely (*L. id est*) (*c'est-à-dire*)
ILO	International Labour Organization (*Bureau international du travail*)
IMF	International Monetary Fund (*Fond monétaire international*)
in	inch(es) (*pouce(s)*)
Inc, Incorp	Incorporated (*incorporé*)
incl	included; including; inclusive (*ci-joint, ci-inclus*)
IOU	I owe you (*traite*)
IQ	Intelligence Quotient (*quotient intellectuel, coefficient de l'âge mental*)
ITA	Independent Television Authority (*la commission de contrôle du service de télévision indépendante*)
ITV	Independent Television (*le service de télévision indépendante*)
JP	Justice of the Peace (*juge de paix*)
jr	junior (*cadet, subalterne*)
Kt	Knight (*chevalier*)
L	Latin (*latin*); law (*le Droit*); Learner (*on motor car*) (*celui qui apprend à conduire une automobile*)
l	lake (*lac*); left (*gauche*); lira (*lire*)
lb	pound (*livre (poids)*)
LLB	Bachelor of Law (*licencié en droit*)
LP	Long-Playing (gramophone record) (*longue durée*); Labour Party (*le parti travailliste*)
LSD	lysergic acid diethylamide (*stupéfiant*); (also £sd) pounds, shillings and pence (*monnaie anglaise*)
Ltd	Limited (*Limité*)
m	male (*mâle*); married (*marié*); metre (*mètre*); mile (*mille*); minute (*minute*); month (*mois*)
MA	Master of Arts (*Licencié ès Lettres*)
MB, ChB	Bachelor of Medicine (*docteur en médecine*); Bachelor of Surgery (*docteur en chirurgie*)
MC	Master of Ceremonies (*maître de cérémonies*); Member of Congress (*US*) (*député*); Military Cross (*croix militaire*)

495

MCC	Marylebone Cricket Club (*les autorités qui contrôlent le cricket au Royaume Uni et dans le Commonwealth*)
MD	Doctor of Medicine (*docteur en médecine, médecin*); mentally deficient (*débile mental*)
Messrs	the plural of Mr. (*le pluriel de M. (MM), employé avec le nom d'une maison commerciale ou en tête d'une liste de plusieurs noms*)
MI5	Military Intelligence, Department 5 (*service du contre-espionnage*)
MOH	Medical Officer of Health (*directeur de la santé*)
MP	Member of Parliament (*membre de la chambre des communes, député*); Military Police (*police militaire*); Metropolitan Police (*police métropolitain*)
mph	miles per hour (*milles à l'heure*)
Mr.	Mister (*monsieur*)
Mrs.	Mistress (*madame*)
Mt	mount (*mont*); mountain (*montagne*)
n	name (*nom*); noun (*nom*); neuter (*neutre*); noon (*midi*); nephew (*neveu*); born (*L. natus*) (*né*)
Nat	National (*national*); Nationalist (*nationaliste*)
NATO	North Atlantic Treaty Organization (*l'Organisation du traité de l'Atlantique Nord*)
NCB	National Coal Board (*comité national pour l'exploitation du charbon*)
NCO	Non-commissioned officer (*sous-officier*)
NHS	National Health Service (*service de santé nationale—sécurité sociale*)
no(s)	number(s) (*L. numero*) (*numéro(s)*)
NW	nord-west (*nord-ouest*)
NY	New York
NZ	New Zealand (*Nouvelle Zélande*)
OAS	Organization of American States (*Organisation d'etats américains*); (*Organisation de l'armée secrète*)
OECD	Organisation for Economic Co-operation and Development (*Organisation pour la coopération et le développement économique*)
OHMS	On His (Her) Majesty's Service (*au service de Sa Majesté, service officiel*)
OK	all correct (*correct*); all right (*d'accord*)
OM	Order of Merit (*décoration civile accordée à certaines personnes en récompense de leur mérite particulier*)
OXFAM	Oxford Committee for Famine Relief (*Comité d'Oxford aidant les pays sous-développés*)
Oxon	Oxford(shire); of Oxford (*L. Oxoniensis*) (*d'Oxford*)
oz	ounce(s) (*once*)
pa	per annum; by the year (*par an*)'
P & O	Peninsular and Oriental (Steam Navigation Company) (*compagnie de navigation*)
PAYE	Pay as you Earn (income tax—*impôt sur le revenu*)
PC	police constable (*agent (officier) de police*); Privy Council (*conseil privé*); Privy Councillor (*membre du conseil privé*)
PhD	Doctor of Philosophy (*docteur en philosophie*)
PM	Prime Minister (*premier ministre*); Past Master (*ancien maître*)
pm	afternoon (*L. post meridiem*) (*après-midi*); after death (*L. post mortem*) (*après décès*)
PO	Post office (*bureau de poste*); postal order (*mandat-poste*)

POB	Post Office Box (*boîte postale*)
POW	Prisoner of War (*prisonnier de guerre*)
pp	on behalf of (*pour le compte de*); pages (*pages*)
Pres	President (*président*)
PRO	Public Relations Officer (*un agent de Public Relations*)
PTO	Please Turn Over (*tournez s'il vous plaît*)
QC	Queen's Counsel (*Conseiller de la Reine—poste juridique très important*); Queen's College (*collège faisant partie de l'université de Cambridge*)
qt	quart (*quart de gallon*)
qv	which see (*L. quod vide*)
RA	Royal Academy (*académie royale*)
RAC	Royal Automobile Club (*club royale d'automobilistes—association d'automobilistes comme l'AA*)
RAF	Royal Air Force (*forces aériennes royales*); Royal Air Factory (*camp de RAF*)
RC	Roman Catholic (*catholique romain*); Red Cross (*Croix-Rouge*)
regd	registered (*recommandé, enregistré, inscrit*)
Rep	Representative (*reps*); Republic (*république*); Republican (*républicain*); Repertory (*répertoire, compagnie en tournée ou compagnie provinciale*); Reporter (*journaliste, correspondant*)
Rev	Reverend (*révérend*); Revelations (*Apocalypse*)
RN	Royal Navy (*la marine royale*)
Rt. Hon.	Right Honourable (*très honorable—titre accordé à un ministre ou ancien ministre du gouvernement britannique*)
s	second (*deuxième*); shilling (*shilling*); son (*fils*); singular (*singulier*); substantive (*substantif*); solubility (*solubilité*)
Sch	School (*école*)
Sec, Secy	Secretary (*secrétaire*)
SHAPE	Supreme Headquarters Allied Powers Europe (*Quartier général des alliés en Europe*)
SRN	State Registered Nurse (*infirmière diplômée*)
St	Saint (*saint*); Strait (*détroit*); street (*rue*)
STD	Subscriber Trunk Dialling (*l'Automatique interurbain*)
SW	South-west (*sud-ouest*)
TB	Tuberculosis (*tuberculose*)
TNT	trinitrotoluene (explosive) (*explosif*)
TT	total abstainer (teetotal) (*abstinent, antialcoolique*)
TUC	Trades Union Congress (*confédération des syndicats (ouvriers)*)
TV	Television (*télévision, téléviseur*)
TWA	Trans World Airlines (*compagnie aérienne américaine*)
UDI	Unilateral Declaration of Independence (*déclaration unilatérale d'indépendence*)
UK	United Kingdom (*royaume uni*)
UN(O)	United Nations (Organization) (*Organisation des Nations Unies*)
UNESCO	United Nations Educational, Scientific and Cultural Organization (*Organisation des Nations Unies pour l'Education, la Science et la Culture*) qui s'occupe de l'éducation et de la vie scientifique et culturelle des pays sous-développés)
UNICEF	UN International Children's Emergency Fund (*fonds spécial pour l'assistance des enfants réfugiés*)
US(A)	United States (of America) (*États-Unis*)
USAF	United States Air Force (*forces aériennes des États-Unis*)

USN	United States Navy (*la marine américaine*)
VD	Veneral Disease (*maladie venérienne*)
VHF	very high frequency (*très haute fréquence*)
VIP	(*fam*) very important person (*fam—personnage très important*)
viz	namely (*L. videlicet*) (*nommément*)
W	West (*ouest*); Western (*de l'ouest*); Welsh (*gallois*)
wc	water closet (*W.C., cabinets*)
WHO	World Health Organization (*Organisation mondiale de la santé*)
wk	week (*semaine*)
wp	weather permitting (*si le temps le permet*)
yd	yard(s) (*yard=approx.* 1 *mètre*)
YHA	Youth Hostels Association (*les Auberges de jeunesse*)
YMCA	Young Men's Christian Association (*association de jeunes chrétiens*)
yr	year (*an*); younger (*cadet*); your (*ton, votre*)
YWCA	Young Women's Christian Association (*association de jeunes chrétiennes*)

Abréviations Françaises

FRENCH ABBREVIATIONS

AC	Avant Christ (*before Christ*)
a.c.	argent comptant (*ready money*)
ACF	Automobile Club de France (*French automobile club*)
AEF	Afrique Equatoriale Française (*French Equatorial Africa*)
AF	Air France (*French airline company*)
AFP	Agence France Presse (*French Press Agency*)
AM	Assurance mutuelle (*mutual assurance*)
Amal	Amiral (*Admiral*)
anme	Anonyme (*limited liability company*)
AOF	Afrique Occidentale Française (*French West Africa*)
AP	Assistance publique (*public assistance*)
AR	Arrière (*rear*)
arr.	arrondissement (*district*)
AS	Assurance sociale (*social security*)
ASLV	Assurance sur la vie (*life assurance*)
asse	Assurance (*insurance*)
AT	Ancien Testament (*Old Testament*)
à t.p.	à tout prix (*at any cost*)
auj.	aujourd'hui (*today*)
av.	avenue (*avenue*)
AV	avant (*front*)
Bac	Baccalauréat (*certificate of secondary education*)
b à p	billet à payer (*bill payable*)
b à r	billet à recevoir (*bill receivable*)
bd	boulevard (*boulevard*)
BF	Banque de France (*Bank of France*)
Bib	Bible (*Bible*), Bibliothèque (*library*)
BIT	Bureau international du travail (*International Labour Office*)
BN	Bibliothèque Nationale (*national library*)
BO	Bulletin officiel (*official bulletin*)
BNP	Banque Nationale de Paris (*large banking house*)
BP	Boîte postale (*Post Office Box*)

BSGDC	Breveté sans garantie du gouvernement (*patent without government guarantee of quality*)
bté	breveté (*patented*)
ca	courant alternatif (*alternating current*)
c-à-d	c'est-à-dire (*that is*)
CAF	Coût, assurance, fret (*cost, insurance, freight*)
CAP	Certificat d'aptitude professionelle (*certificate of general proficiency in industry*)
	Certificat d'aptitude pédagogique (*teaching certificate*)
Cap.	capitaine (*captain*)
CAPES	Certificat d'aptitude au professorat de l'enseignement secondaire (*certificate for teaching in secondary schools*)
cc	courant continu (*direct current*)
c/c	compte courant (*current account*)
CCP	Compte chèques postaux (*Post Office Account*)
CD	Corps diplomatique (*Diplomatic Corps*)
CEE	Communauté économique européenne—Marché commun (*European Economic Community—Common Market*)
CEG	Collège d'enseignement général (*Secondary Modern School*)
CEI	Commission Electro-technique international (*International electro-technical commission*)
CEP	Certificat d'études primaires (*certificate for primary studies*)
CES	College d'enseignement secondaire (*Secondary School*)
CFDT	Confédération française démocratique de travail (*Catholic trade union—branch of CFTC*)
CFTC	Confédération française de travailleurs chrétiens (*union of Catholic workers*)
cg	centigramme (*centigram*)
CGC	Confédération générale des cadres (*communist white collar union*)
CGE	Compagnie générale d'électricité (*large electronics company*)
CGT	Confédération générale du travail (*communist trade union*)
ch-l	chef-lieu (=*county town*)
CICR	Commission internationale de la Croix-Rouge (*International Commission of the Red Cross Organization*)
CM	Croix Militaire (*Military Cross*)
CNI	Centre National d'Information (*official government information department*)
CNRS	Centre national de la recherche scientifique (*national research board*)
CQFD	ce qu'il fallait démontré (*QED*)
CR	Croix-Rouge (*Red Cross*)
CRS	Compagnie républicaine de sécurité (*State Security Police*)
CT	Cabine téléphonique (*telephone box*)
c.v.	cheval-vapeur (*horse-power*)
cv	chevaux (*horses*); curriculum vitae
d	diamètre (*diameter*)
DCA	Défense contre avions (*anti-aircraft defence*)
déb	débit (*debit*)
déc	décédé (*deceased*); décembre (*December*)
dép	département (*administrative department*)
DM	Docteur Médecin (*Doctor of Medicine*)
DP	défense passive (*civil defence*)

499

EC	École centrale (*Central School of Engineering at Paris*)
éd(it)	édition (*edition*)
ÉLO	École des langues orientales (*School of Oriental Languages*)
É-M	État-major (*headquarters*)
ÉNA	École nationale d'administration (*national administrative school*)
env	environ (*about*)
et Cie	et Compagnie (*and Company, & Co.*)
Éts	Établissements (*establishments*)
EV	en ville (*Post. local*)
ex	exemple (*example*)
exempl.	exemplaire (*copy*)
F	Franc : NF Nouveau France (*new franc*) AF Ancien Franc (*old franc*)
fàb	franco à bord (*free on board, fob*)
fab	fabrication (*make*)
FEN	Fédération de l'éducation nationale (*University teachers' union*); Fédération des étudiants nationalistes (*extreme right union of student*)
FFI	Forces françaises de l'intérieur (*internal security forces*)
FFLT	Fédération française de Lawn-Tennis (*French Lawn Tennis Federation*)
FGDS	Fédération de la gauche démocratique et socialiste (*left-wing political grouping*)
FIFA	Fédération Internationale de Football Association (*body governing international football*)
FLN	Front de libération nationale (*nationalist movement in Algerian War*)
FMI	Fond monétaire international (*International Monetary Fund*)
FO	Fédération ouvrière (*left-wing trade union*)
fo(l)	folio (*folio*)
FS	faire suivre (*please forward*)
g	gramme (*gram*)
GC	Grand-Croix (*Grand cross of Legion of Honour*); (Route de) grande communication (*B road*)
GQG	Grand quartier général (*General Headquarters*)
h	heure (*hour*)
HC	hors concours (*not competing*); hors cadre (*not on the strength*)
HÉC	Hautes études commerciales (*business school*)
HLM	Habitations à loyer modéré (*accommodation at reasonable rents*)
hp	haute pression (*high pressure*)
HS	hors de service (*unfit for service*)
inéd	inédit (*unpublished*)
inf	infanterie (*infantry*); faites infuser (*infuse*)
in-f(o), infol	in-folio (*folio*)
IDHÉC	Institut des hautes études cinématographiques (*school for cinema-arts*)
in-pl	in plano (*broadsheet*)
JÉC	Jeunesse étudiante catholique (*catholic student association*)
JOC	Jeunesse ouvrière catholique (*young catholic workers*)
kil(o)	kilogramme (*kilogramme*)
km/h	kilomètres par heure (*kilomɛtres per hour*)
labo	laboratoire (*laboratory*)

500